No Laughing Matter

Rationale of the Dirty Joke:
Second Series

"The secret source of humor is not joy but sorrow; there is no humor in heaven."

— Mark TWAIN
Pudd'nhead Wilson's New Calendar

No Laughing Matter
Rationale of the Dirty Joke: Second Series
By G. Legman

HART-DAVIS, MACGIBBON
GRANADA PUBLISHING
London Toronto Sydney New York

Published by Granada Publishing in
Hart-Davis, MacGibbon Ltd 1978 .

Granada Publishing Limited
Frogmore, St Albans, Herts AL2 2NF
and
3 Upper James Street, London W1R 4BP
1221 Avenue of the Americas, New York, NY 10020 USA
117 York Street, Sydney, NSW 2000, Australia
100 Skyway Avenue, Toronto, Ontario, Canada M9W 3A6
Trio City, Coventry Street, Johannesburg 2001, South Africa

ISBN 0 246 11022 8

Printed in Great Britain by
Fletcher & Son Ltd, Norwich, and bound by
Richard Clay (The Chaucer Press) Ltd,
Bungay, Suffolk

CONTENTS

For a complete Analytic Table of Contents
see the Subjects & Motifs following the text.

NO LAUGHING MATTER

I

ONE of the most significant psychological documents of the twentieth century has passed by with almost nothing more than the usual once-over-lightly in the news magazines, scaling it down to the standard insignificance of the latest styles in women's fly-front pants and sewer-cleaner's boots (to 'bring out their femininity'). Probably it would not have rated any mention at all, except that it is very cruel. Yet as a key to the ruthless cruelty of our century – and of those past *and to come* – it is without peer.

This document, to which I hardly do justice in citing it here only in the context of the blinding light it brought to bear, by chance, on human laughter, is a brief article by a Yale socio-psychologist, Dr. Stanley Milgram, appearing first as *Dynamics of Obedience* (Washington, 1961, mimeographed), then enlarged in the *Journal of Abnormal and Social Psychology* in 1963 under the title, "A Behavioral Study of Obedience." It is wisely reprinted in a college freshman textbook, where one hopes it will become fixed in many young people's minds, *Controversy: Prose for Analysis*, edited by Robert S. Gold & Sanford Radner (New York: Holt, Rinehart, 1969) p. 136–56, followed by two briefer supporting pieces, including William L. Shirer's account of the ghoulish and sadistic "Medical Experiments" engaged in by the Nazis in their hospitals and extermination camps during the 1930's and '40's, from his book on *The Third German Reich* (1960), which is what the Milgram article is really destined to explain. It begins with the following sober *précis:*

> This article describes a procedure for the study of destructive obedience in the laboratory. It consists of ordering a naïve S [subject] to administer increasingly more severe punishment to a victim in the context of a learning experiment. Punishment is administered by means of a shock

generator with 30 graded switches ranging from Slight Shock
to Danger: Severe Shock. The victim is a confederate of the
E [experimenter]. The primary dependent variable is the
maximum shock the S is willing to administer before he refuses to continue further. 26 Ss obeyed the experimental
commands fully, and administered the highest shock on the
generator. 14 Ss broke off the experiment at some point after
the victim protested and refused to provide further answers.
The procedure created extreme levels of nervous tension in
some Ss. Profuse sweating, trembling, and stuttering were
typical expressions of this emotional disturbance. *One unexpected sign of tension – yet to be explained – was the
regular occurrence of nervous laughter, which in some
developed into uncontrollable seizures. . . .* [Italics supplied.]

Set up on the style of an elaborately sadistic fraternity-house
initiation or hoax, the Milgram experiment strikes level after
level of understanding of how atrocities can be *performed*, not
just permitted, by right-thinking people, obviously by the
millions, when the right kind of authoritarian pressure and
verbal suggestion is brought to bear on them. The brutal charm
of the experiment is that whereas all the subjects thought they
were torturing the presumed victim – and not one of them
copped out and refused to keep 'administering the shocks' until
the twentieth (of thirty) increasingly severe shocks they were to
inflict – the truth of the matter is that they themselves were
the only ones who were really suffering, and suffered very
much. Dr. Milgram tells us that one observer, watching the
'unwitting' subject through a one-way mirror, reported:

I observed a mature and initially poised businessman enter
the laboratory smiling and confident. Within 20 minutes he
was reduced to a twitching, stuttering wreck, who was
rapidly approaching a point of nervous collapse. He constantly pulled on his earlobe, and twisted his hands. At one
point he pushed his fist into his forehead and muttered: "Oh
God, let's stop it." And yet he continued to respond to every
word of the experimenter, and obeyed to the end.

[Milgram concludes, among other "Results":] SIGNS OF EX-
TREME TENSION. Many subjects showed signs of nervousness
in the experimental situation, and especially upon administering the more powerful shocks. In a large number of cases the

degree of tension reached extremes that are rarely seen in sociopsychological laboratory studies. Subjects were observed to sweat, tremble, stutter, bite their lips, groan, and dig their fingernails into their flesh. These were characteristic rather than exceptional responses to the experiment.

One sign of tension was the regular occurrence of nervous laughing fits. Fourteen of the 40 subjects showed definite signs of nervous laughing and smiling. The laughter seemed entirely out of place, even bizarre. Full-blown, uncontrollable seizures were observed for 3 subjects. On one occasion we observed a seizure so violently convulsive that it was necessary to call a halt to the experiment. The subject, a 46-year-old encyclopedia salesman, was seriously embarrassed by his untoward and uncontrollable behavior. In the post-experimental interviews subjects took pains to point out that they were not sadistic types, and that the laughter did not mean they enjoyed shocking the victim.

Agreed. Certainly not. But what *does* it mean? Obviously the first thing it means is that subjects, finding themselves suddenly tricked into becoming actual torturers, through the salestalk of a phoney 'scientific experiment' (purposely made as idiotic in its proposed results as the Nazi "Medical Experiments" it is intended to imitate and study), were horribly embarrassed and ashamed of what they were doing. But they did it anyhow. And, like Figaro, 'laughed so they would not cry.' This is the so-called polite Japanese laughter, or laughter of nervousness, the inane tittering and fishlike sucking-in of the breath of everyone in Japan from geisha girls on up to top-hatted diplomats at moments of social tension or conversational falsity and difficulty. Then too, Milgram's subjects also strongly identified with their victims: in fact, they were led to believe that it was only by the accident of drawing lots (faked) that they were not themselves sitting in the mock electric-chair, being brought close to death by the other fellow, pressing switches *when ordered to do so by the Experimenter*. Switches marked: "Intense Shock", "Extreme Intensity Shock", "Danger: Severe Shock," and finally a sinisterly undetailed "XXX," which more than half of them pressed *twice* anyhow.

Their convulsive laughter, under such circumstances, is the coefficient of their being torn between powerful identification with the human victim, and the willingness to continue tortur-

ing him, under the submissive format or excuse that it is someone else's responsibility: *"Ve vass only followink our Superiors'
orders!"* The only detail left unsolved here as to the secret
spring of the Nazi success with the whole German nation –
especially the ones that bullshit you now, about how they
were secretly against it, hid Jews in their attics, etc., and that
they would *never* do it again – is: *Did they laugh convulsively
while pushing the switches at Auschwitz?* Even the finest study
of the psychological substructure of the Nazi world and our
own, *The Authoritarian Personality*, by Drs. T. Adorno *et al.*
(New York: Harper, 1950), does not cover this point. Compare
the 'frequent obsessive symptom of laughter as a reaction to
the news of a death,' noted by Dr. Otto Fenichel in *Psychoanalytic Theory of Neurosis* (New York, 1945) p. 354–6, as to
sadism, torture, and hypnotism, concluding that the meaning of
all these is, obscurely, *"Better him than me."*

I don't think they did laugh. Specifically, one eye-witness
account by a surviving Kommando states that when the two
SS men drove up every morning in their official car – marked
with the *Red Cross* on top, to avoid danger from Allied aviators
– and dropped the blue poison-gas pellet in the slot, they stood
conversing with each other in calm tones while the naked
human sacrifices died by the hundreds behind the wall of the
'showers.' No, they might have kidded around a little: a few
good anti-Semitic gags out of the latest issue of the *Stürmer* –
but they didn't laugh. Perhaps they didn't identify strongly
enough with the subhuman Jews and Poles and Gypsies, of
whom they were thus 'cleansing' (read: defecating) the 'racial
blood.' In any case, whether with poison gas, phoney electric-
chair switches, or jokes, don't let the hysterical laughter fool
you. Under the mask of humor, *All men are enemies.*

II

As not all of us have the raw guts to set up a mock torture-
chamber in our home or office, here is a less nerve-wracking
psychometric 'test' anyone can make, without bad conscience.
This is a century-old but fascinating psychological game, played
with a photograph – preferably of oneself – and a mirror. The
photograph must be taken full-face, the subject looking straight
into the camera, and the mirror must be straight-edged and
without any frame. The mirror is stood up vertically on its

edge along the center-line of the face in the photograph, and one then *looks in at* (or rephotographs) the two completely different faces formed when the mirror is turned to the right side of the photograph, and to the left.

Each of the two new faces formed is obviously composed of half of itself, repeated and reversed. But with what a difference! One recognizes oneself in both, of course, but one also recognizes that one of the new faces is fatter and more gross than one really is, while the other is thinner and more 'intense.' The eyes, and eyebrows, and especially the mouth are also usually strikingly different in the two new faces, both from each other and from the face in the original photograph.

All this is an obvious enough result of the inevitable minor differences in weight and cast between the two sides of any face, as of the two sides of any animal body: any pair of shoulders, breasts, testicles, or feet never quite matching each other. But the effect of the two 'new faces' created by this mirror-game is almost always strangely disquieting to the person photographed, who feels uneasily that the two faces evolved or evoked in this way are somehow the unexpected unveiling or unmasking of his or her 'good' and 'bad' characters. Occasionally the subject will laugh the matter off by remarking: '*Oh yes, that's what I looked like when I was a lot younger,*' or, of the other face, '*That's what I'd look like if I put on about forty pounds, I guess.*' But most people are frankly disturbed by the game, and this even when the pictures used and produced – that of the real person, and of the two 'new faces' – are of someone entirely unknown to the person examining the photographs.

The reason for this disquiet is clear. Every human being, and most other animals as well, deeply believe in physiognomy and facial expressions as a sort of instantaneous character-reading, if not fortune-telling. That is why strangers smile nervously on being introduced – fang-baring or intimidation? – to weight the physiognomic 'reading' in their favor. "*Here kitty-kitty, good kitty-kitty!*" while the panther inside watches beadily for the opponent's baring of eye-teeth, and the snarl that will warn him to defend himself. In seeing a photograph of a human face – and thus the human being in essence – separated and dissolved in this way into two images only-too-easily identifiable as the 'good' and the 'bad' sides of the person photographed, one is

disquieted by the apparent and unexpected unveiling of unavowed depths.

This is also the crucial element in the animosity many people
feel even for the *idea* of psychoanalysis: at the thought that
their carefully adjusted masks can be suddenly and unwillingly,
almost hynotically, ripped away. Again, as with psychoanalysis,
the effect of the mirror-game is the same, is even increased,
when the facial expression in the original photograph is purposely posed to appear either 'saintly' or 'diabolical,' or wise,
foolish, disingenuous, or mysterious, or any other extreme or
purposely significant expression. The caricatured effect of the
resultant two *new faces* and their antipodal difference is then
even more striking, more 'revealing.' Again a cause of disquiet,
in the thought that *'Truth will out'*, *'There is no hiding-place'*,
or *'No escaping one's fate,'* subjects on which there are many
folktales, especially in the Orient, such as the well-known
Levantine story known in the West as "The Appointment in
Samarra." (And compare O. Henry's elegant story of the inevitability of one's fate, "Roads of Destiny," 1909.)

The standard and often the unconscious division of another
person into two antipodal components, to make more navigable
the necessity of responding to the same person with varying
responses of both love and hatred, has already been discussed in
the First Series of the present work, *Rationale of the Dirty Joke*
(New York, 1968) pages 524–5, in chapter 8.III.5, under "The
Taboo of Virginity," in connection with the puzzle-stories
known as "The Sleeve Job" (8.III.3) and "The Mysterious
Card." In all the world's folklore the Fairy Godmother and the
Evil Witch are similarly varying responses to the mother herself, divided up into two persons, for when she is loved and
when she is hated. Like Hamlet's murdered father whom he
loves but does not avenge, and his 'incestuous' uncle whom he
hates but with whom he identifies too strongly in his incest to
murder him.

These divisions into two diametrically opposed characters
have their dangers too, when they shift too rapidly or un-
manageably into one another in a hallucinating way. Or when
their underlying identity with each other is made suddenly
clear – as in reading a playbill by lightning flashes – to the unconscious participant or puppeteer. That is the deeper meaning
of both the "Sleeve Job" and the "Mysterious Card" stories, in
both of which: *The evil temptress, or female devil Lilith, leads*

*the newly-wed husband astray by flirting with him in the hotel-
bar on his wedding night, while his chaste bride is undressing in
the bedroom upstairs.* For in the final disclosure, in a terrible if
unconscious way, the evil temptress is suddenly discovered to
be the bride herself in a black mask, or rather, with the virginal
innocence that her husband fears will prove to be nothing *but*
a mask, stripped away. It is with such fearful and implied un-
veilings that the mirror-game plays, and from which it draws its
disturbing force.

All these effects are strengthened by their visual expression
(by means of the mirror) of the usual culturally determined
polar divisions of all or many things into two extremes or
opposites, with a tone of extreme moral judgment generally
immanent or explicit. Consider, for example, the many
irreversible word-combinations in English and many other languages, on the style of *'high & low'*, *'up & down'*, *'in & out'*,
'light & dark', *'black & white'* (and observe the reversal here of
the usual moral order, perhaps in response to the sensed inner
logic of *'something-before-nothing'*); not to mention *'right &
wrong'*, *'good & evil'*, *'profit & loss'*, *'ham & eggs'* – try reversing
that one! – *'God & the Devil'*, *'Dr. Jekyll & Mr. Hyde,'* and
many hundreds of others including some triads, from *'high,
wide & handsome'* to *'all that meat & no potatoes!'* A dualistic
Through-the-Looking-Glass world from which, once entered,
one can never altogether return. (For further details and examples on this curious subject, see my introduction, "On Sexual
Speech and Slang" in John S. Farmer & William Ernest Henley's
(*Dictionary of Slang & Its Analogues*, New Hyde Park, New
York: University Books, 1966, revised vol. 1: pages xxxii ff.;
and the important study of these 'irreversible binomials' in
English, by Dr. Yakov Malkiel, in *Lingua*, Amsterdam, 1959,
VIII. 113–60.)

These psychological and linguistic considerations are here
brought into focus to put before the reader, on their background, the difficult problem of organization involved in dividing the present study into two separate series of different
import. The First Series has already been published under the
title *Rationale of the Dirty Joke* (New York: Basic Books/
Grove Press, 1968, and translations into French, German, and
Italian), covering such relatively 'clean' dirty jokes as those on
the subjects of Children, Fools, Animals, The Male Approach,
Women, Marriage, and Adultery. That leaves for the present

Second Series all the more anxiety-creating 'dirty' dirty jokes, on the subjects of Homosexuality, Prostitution, Disease and Disgust, Castration, Dysphemism, Cursing, Insults, and Scatology. This has therefore been a very much harder book to write, though many readers have written to tell me that they 'missed the fag-jokes' or 'Where the hell are the shit jokes?' or were disappointed in the First Series because they did not find their favorite jokes there, and that 'The dirtiest jokes are the funniest.' I am not sure this is true, but it is certainly true that it is the dirtiest jokes that create the wildest laughter. And sometimes more laughter in those who tell them than in those who must listen.

As to the division of jokes into the 'clean' dirties and the 'dirty' dirties, I have noted in the original introduction that, as with the similar distinction between 'black humor' and 'good humor,' such divisions are purely relative and to a degree meaningless. The jokes that any specific reader or listener will consider 'clean' or 'dirty' are almost entirely so judged subjectively, on the basis of that reader's or listener's own life experiences and anxieties. There are just as many tellers-of and listeners-to jokes – I am one of them – in whom great anxiety is precipitated (or alleviated) as much by jokes about sexual sadism or marital humiliation as by jokes on such theoretically more 'nasty' or unsettling subjects as homosexuality, prostitution, venereal disease, castration, or scatology, which have been reserved for this second series. Along with the many dysphemistic or purposely crude jokes and recitations attempting to be disgusting, or turning crucially on irreverent and obscene attacks on whatever is culturally held sacred, such as religion or motherhood. In these there is often little further humorous element than the strictly taboo vocabulary, or insults, cursing, and unexpected ungallantry: for example toward cripples.

The appropriateness of the mirror-game described above to express this division of the present work into two halves or series should be obvious. The jokes fall neatly and frankly – though with certain necessary overlappings – into two main types: the 'good' or normally dirty jokes, and the 'evil' or specially dirty ones, as most people might divide them. This includes even those people who particularly relish the 'dirty-dirties,' but who would not like them at all if they did not think of them as outrageously dirty and marvellously vile. The subjects of the two series have also been grouped progressively, into jokes concerning the normal and usual experiences of the sexual life in the First Series: childhood sexuality, fools, animals, men and women and their premarital experiences, marriage, and adultery. And the less usual or less normal experiences in this Second Series: homosexuality, prostitution, venereal disease, castration, scatology, and the rest. But both groups interpenetrate each other on an unexpectedly broad front, overlapping and finally becoming identical in more ornate versions. That is the basic problem in any oversimplified division of jokes into the 'clean' and the 'dirty,' or even into a whole series or palette running from the 'mildly dirty' to the 'filthy dirty,' with endless divisions between. (To which should be compared the division of jokes by their effect on the listeners: from the polite 'titsa-de-bitsa' smile-creating witticism, to the bellylaugh-creating 'hupcha-de-bupcha' or 'hockcha-de-bopcha' knock-down-&-drag-out prize jokes – abbreviated to 'yocks' – of Yiddish-speaking professional comedians or bodchonim.)

For the paradox is that people, and therefore the games people play and the jokes they tell, are all of a piece. And what we admire is indivisibly mixed in them with what we deplore or detest: strength with cruelty, right with self-righteousness, humor with horror and hideousness. Blake's Marriage of Heaven and Hell (1790), with its bold title to set the tone of opposites interpenetrating, and its crucial observation that: 'Without Contraries is no progression. Attraction and Repulsion ... Love and Hate, are necessary to Human existence.' But – there is a but – people do have their favorites: their favorite foods, their favorite days, colors, books, remarks, games, parts of the female body ('tit-men' and 'leg-men,' which just goes to show you, because I happen to be a 'tit-man'), their favorite jokes and masks. If we are not to be left floating in a hopeless relativism, and without the possibility of making any distinctions or judgments at all, it is precisely in these favorites of every joke-teller's, in his or her special repertory, that we may discern the face hidden behind the mask.

The same is just as true of the listeners to jokes as it is of the tellers, since none of us are really as passive or as helpless in the face of compulsive and aggressive joke-tellers (also liars, anecdote-mumblers, etc.) as we usually pretend. There is almost always a pattern or similarity not only in the kind of jokes specific tellers tell, but also in the kinds and subjects of jokes to which specific listeners can and will listen with pleasure or at least with forbearance. Also a positive taboo as to the kinds of jokes – or even *words* – they will not listen to and cannot stand. Many people who do not mind, or even rather enjoy what are frankly called 'shit jokes,' cannot endure 'nasty-nasties' as to food-dirtying, and will turn pale or become visibly agitated if they must listen. Nevertheless, it is an important discovery, made during the more than thirty-five years involved in collecting the thousands of jokes for the present study, that far more people's truly favorite jokes will be found in this second series, of the 'dirty' dirty jokes, than in the First Series of *Rationale of the Dirty Joke.*

In any case, it is essential to bear in mind that the distinction between teller and listener is one of the least real or rigid, and most interpenetrating that exists. Few people ever actually make up or invent jokes, or would be capable of doing so. They are almost invariably repeating the jokes they have heard – usually quite recently – sometimes with minor changes, or the addition of the names of current celebrities in order to pass the jokes or stories off as 'true.' I myself have never made up a joke, nor have I ever met or heard of anyone who did. Many are called but few are chosen. Most people who believe and insist that they have made up jokes, or that they can do so ('by the dozens,' as they sometimes brag), operate strictly in the area of verbal puns, which are by no means the same thing as jokes, usually lacking any real situational humor and turning only on word-humor, laborious reversals, or the ringing of changes as in Spoonerisms. Many also specialize in revamping much older jokes to current situations or celebrities, and sometimes doggedly forget that they have done so. This is obviously not the same thing as inventing jokes.

Since the jokes that are told are really only being repeated from previous listening, in the deepest sense *teller and listener are indivisible and identical.* The favorite jokes of one are – by & large – the favorite jokes of the other. Otherwise these jokes would not survive, through centuries and civilizations hundreds of years and thousands of miles apart. The favorite jokes, this time of the large mass of teller-listeners, have therefore been chosen again and again by an almost always unconscious bent or selection from the larger float of jokes that any one person may have heard. Only the special favorites are retained, or are transmitted very often. The joke-repertory, and in the same way the repertory or vocabulary of slang, of proverbs and superstitions of any one person, is a sort of combination trap or lock which allows only one special sort of key or game to enter – or to leave. One laughs at many jokes, and listens to many songs, many superstitions, and much new slang and ephemeral lingo. But one retains only the superstitions that are somehow frightening, and sings only the songs ('dirty' or sentimental) and uses only the slang that speak for us as we ourselves could not have thought to speak. These are our true poetry, our true folklore. In the same way, one laughs at many jokes, and hears many more that one does not laugh at. But only those that touch us to the quick can make us laugh 'as though we thought we'd die.' It is those that we remember, and those we tend to repeat and to embellish. They are the 'best.'

I have tried to make the point repeatedly in this work, that in very many jokes on themes more taboo than simple sexuality, the person 'denuded' by the joke is really the teller himself, or herself. Most joke-tellers have their own personal styles, not only of treatment and vocabulary, airs & graces, but especially of preferred subjects. Most of their stories, or their favorite stories in particular, circle insistently about a single taboo theme, such as castration, homosexuality, or dirtying of food, or with feces. It is not difficult to see that, in telling such stories, they are allowing their own conscious or unconscious problems a socially acceptable signboard to the listener, or an avenue of expression and petcock of release. Listeners also have their styles: the 'dirty' stories over which they invariably break up in gales of laughter, where jokes of other types or on other subjects – sometimes dirtier and sometimes far less so – leave them untouched and often contemptuous. This does not prove that they are morally any better than the people who tell or enjoy jokes on the subjects that offend or even nauseate them. It merely means that their psychological problems, and therefore their personal cuticle as listeners, are somewhat different.

It may be stated as axiomatic that: *A person's favorite joke is the key to that person's character,* a rule-of-thumb all the more invariable in the case of highly neurotic people. The artless directness with which the joke-teller's deepest problem is sometimes expressed, under the transparent gauze of the 'favorite joke,' is like the acting out of a charade of self-unveiling, or like the sending of a psycho-telegraphic S.O.S. to the audience, whose sympathy and understanding are being unconsciously courted. For all the aggressiveness of most jokes, and the purposeful unpleasantness of many 'dirty' dirty jokes, which are strictly an assault on and exploitation of the listener as victim, the repetitive and compulsive nature of their telling marks them almost always with the unmistakable air of a bid for sympathy or *a cry for help.* Your favorite joke is your psychological signature. The 'only' joke you know how to tell, is you.

III

It has often been asked of me, on my developing the preceding axioms as to the meaning of individual choices in humor, whether I would go so far as to paraphrase the proverb about eating, and say *"Tell me what you laugh at, and I will tell you what you are."* That is to say, whether I would undertake to 'read someone's character' from his or her favorite joke, which is then usually delivered on the spot as a challenge (a bit nervously, every time). This does often make an amusing parlor-game, but is just as often horribly embarrassing – an embarrassment the favorite-joke-teller fortunately does not always share. In kindness, the best one can do sometimes is to say something like, "Well, I don't know about your favorite joke, Charlie, but why is it that ALL your jokes are always about shit?" (Or homosexuality, or castration, or food-dirtying, or anti-mother, or wife-humiliating, or whatever.) This puts the burden of the analysis, and of the first free associations – and rationalizations – on the teller himself, which is where it ultimately belongs.

Actually attempted, such blitz-analyses can be a great deal of fun for everyone involved, often more fun than the jokes themselves, so long as one realizes that pointblank jocography of this kind is somewhat closer to fortune-telling than to psychological or psychoanalytic certainty. I have had great fun with it for years; in fact it has been a principal relief to me (especially when done *without* discussing it with the joke-tellers) from the inevitable boredom of listening to and researching over sixty thousand variant versions of the some two thousand jokes given in the present work, all of which then had to be transcribed on index-cards for sorting. I have also seen blitz joke-analysis used very effectively to set back on their heels certain particularly obnoxious tellers of 'nasty-nasties,' where cries of horror, mock groans, and cat-calls from the listeners did nothing but encourage them. I do recommend it, therefore, and highly, but only as a parlor-game. Or perhaps I should say parlor, bedroom & bath. Don't marry a total stranger on the basis of your rapid analysis of his (or her) favorite joke, as I once nearly did. There might well be other or deeper analyses possible; in fact, there surely are. There might also be another, and more carefully hidden, favorite joke.

If, as is clear, the teller of a favorite joke betrays his prevailing anxieties by the choice of this joke, and often by the very manner and vocabulary of its treatment in the telling; what is to be said for the compulsive tellers-of and listeners-to nothing but the type of 'dirty-dirty' jokes that compose the present work? (That includes, does it not, both you and me, as Baudelaire says: *O lecteur hypocrite, mon semblable, mon frère!*) Or the tellers-of and listeners-to whole sessions of what they proudly refer to as "The Dirtiest Joke I Ever Heard," or "The Filthiest Story in the World," which is just as clearly the Through the Looking-Glass translation or transmogrification of the 'favorite joke.' Compare the very similar "My Most Embarrassing Moment" columns of letters from readers, in the kitsch-level digest magazines and tabloid newspapers, presumably reserved for the excruciating experiences of daily life, which one is trying to exteriorize and *get rid of*, by telling them – like King Midas whispering to a hole in the ground (for lack of any other safe audience) that he had the ears of a jackass: the real admission of many another favorite story as well.

It is the ambiguity of purpose of the 'dirty' dirty joke, as well as its tellers' openly compulsive need for it, that is disquieting. Far more so than its crude directness and purposely ugly images, lolloping up & down with screams of pretended pleasure and horror, as it so often does, in shit, snot, vomit, maggots, scabs, smegma, toe-punk, pus, dead and putrefying bodies, and cut-off parts of the body: all frequent motifs, as also in the identical but for some reason more respectable folktale format of the 'ghost' or horror-story. In the jokes certainly, the ambiguity or contradiction that is so difficult to endure, especially for the unwarned listener, is that the 'dirty' dirty joke apparently enjoys and offers as entertainment precisely those objects and images that both teller and listener really fear and are repelled by. Nor does the useful goal unconsciously pro-

posed, of the alleviation of anxiety, often come off very successfully. To the contrary, further anxiety is created, especially
in the listener, for all his hysterical laughter, as is proved by
many listeners' immediate reaction: to return the favor or
'pass on the blow.' And thus achieve temporarily the status of
the teller – he who has probably sloughed off some anxiety in
the process on his listener-victim.

Thus, both teller and listener are operating under masks – the
mask of humor – yet everyone flounders just as tackily as
though they were naked in shame and guilt, both in the listening and the telling. Everything is murky, mucky, and unpleasant. Nothing is clearcut or helpfully divided up into antipodes,
and one seldom knows quite how to react except with nervous
and over-loud or over-eager laughter. There is neither hero nor
villain: no St. George and no Dragon. Or, rather, the whole
dramatic recital seems to be taking place *inside* the Dragon's
guts, and everyone involved is bathed in the same fiery and disgusting dirtiness and wet, slipping and sliding together in the
same *humorous* blood, shit, piss, pus, puke, and slime. Worst of
all, as might be expected in the liqueous and nauseous stuffs so
often used as subject, there is no firm footing anywhere underneath. One is disgusted and yet one laughs, and one is disgusted
with oneself for laughing. Yet, as the whole mud-bath has been
entered into under the name of humor and under the mask of
jokes and good-fellowship, there can be no end until one does
laugh. The wild laughter overriding, that is one's only escape.

When men and sometimes women gather in mixed company,
as they not infrequently do, each to tell and listen to "The
Filthiest Joke I Ever Heard," in hour-long sessions sometimes at
midnight, punctuated only with the clink of drinks and the
screams and groans of mock-nausea and laughter, what disturbs
the squeamish listener is not altogether the purposeful awfulness of the images involved. Not even the standard ordeal of
frightening and repellent themes, generally involving such
matters as incest, homosexuality, castration, scatology, bestiality, sexually toned food-dirtying and scatologically toned
sexual smörgasbord, the stock-in-trade, for example, of the
cynically humorous bestseller, Philip Roth's *Portnoy's Complaint* (New York, 1968), as also the compulsive defiling of the
mother and of women generally; the gloating over venereal and
other loathsome diseases, aged and repulsive prostitutes (that is
to say, sexually available 'mothers'), intercourse with corpses,

and every sort of bodily disfigurement – which is also inevitably described as being used for sexual purposes.

What is so awful is, rather, the curious and blatant necessity that the participants feel to tell such stories and to listen to them; also to 'top' each other in vileness, in a sort of anal-sadistic mud-battle or duel in slime. Sometimes over the telephone, or in letters back & forth. And this on the very thin pretext, after all, of the 'filthiest joke' format, which the first teller at any such session has usually proposed himself, unsolicited and out of the blue, in order to excuse and allow his telling the first such 'joke': his own anti-favorite. The pretended or incipient nausea, the cries and gestures of fainting mock-repugnance by which the listeners respond in ritual fashion (while waiting for their turn to tell one) are of course the accolade or reward that the teller is visibly seeking. He has 'turned their stomach,' he has gloriously won! At a deeper level, however, in attempting to nauseate or frighten others – while he, presumably, is too strong, too 'manly,' or too blasé to respond in any such way – he is only attempting to reassure himself on the subject of his most desperate fears, whistling under his rictus-mask in the darkened parts of his own soul that nauseate and frighten him the most.

Certainly such jokes are not thought of by anyone as being 'funny ha-ha,' nor do they ever raise a really enjoyable laugh, though the laughers may collapse to the floor 'in stitches,' in their partly-simulated hysterical enjoyment. Most often the laughter really expresses relief that the story is at last *over*, as with horror-stories about ghosts and clanking chains, or theoretically non-sexual tortures (though sadism is by definition sexual, or homosexual). Or the story may be brought to an end by the welcome punctuation of the laughter itself, as by the pressing of a button, while the teller desperately tries to outshout the laughter with his best 'super-topper' punchline of degradation and filth. Sometimes the ambiguous backing & filling – or even stuttering – of an occasional teller of jokes on these themes also expresses his own fear and excitement in connection with his 'favorite' themes, a fear he is trying to share with or slough off on the essentially unwilling listener, who generally realizes just under the level of consciousness that he is being soiled and used. Dirty-talking professional entertainers in nightclubs and burlesque shows often visibly belong to this Nervous Nelly group. Their whole inner idea is to press as far as possible the limits of what they can 'get away with,' without receiving the punishment (from fathers, audience, police) that they almost consciously believe they deserve.

For jokes are essentially an unveiling of the joke-teller's own neuroses and compulsions, and his guilts about these, which he hopes to drive off and nullify by means of the magical release of exciting the listener's laughter. Thus forcing him to *forgive* the teller for having told the joke, and also to act as its butt and scapegoat. The laughter forgives and relieves the teller of his fears and guilt, through the listener's apparently agreeing and siding with him, and driving off the teller's fears by means of the format of 'humorous' presentation and the culminating laughter. If there is no laughter there is no forgiveness. That is why most tellers can be 'driven up the wall' in an almost visible anxiety crisis if the listeners refuse to laugh. And why members of the audience who – rejection of all rejections! – attempt to *get up and leave* are reserved the most violent and insulting Parthian shots of which tellers are capable.

Jokes are, not least, a disguised aggression or verbal assault directed against the listener, who is always really the butt, and whose natural response, in some matching aggression, it is attempted to evade or preëmpt by means of the humorous disguise. The unmasking of the jokester's insincere humor is expressed by Owen Wister in the character of *The Virginian* (1902), who, when asked to accept without reaching for a knife or gun the insulting term, 'son-of-a-bitch,' replies grimly: "*When you call me that*, SMILE!" Jokes originate as hostile impulses of free-floating aggression in the tellers of jokes, as a response to or an expression of social and sexual anxieties they are otherwise unable to absorb or express. The laughter created (which the teller generally does not share, though he may pretend to do so, and did laugh on hearing the same joke originally) depends on the listener's willingness to accept the hostility basic to the joke, in return for the satisfaction he feels in sloughing off, by means of laughter, the specific anxieties he shares with the teller – especially when struck suddenly in the face with them by the teller's *joke*. If there is no sharing of anxieties, and instead the listener feels the teller has 'gone too far,' there will be no laugh: the joke is 'stupid.' The social format of joke-telling, and the teller's accustomed art, are intended to prevent just such fiascos, but do not by any means always succeed. The listener's laughter, rising as it does from hidden springs, is therefore essentially uncontrollable, though the joke-teller's whole conscious effort is to create and control such laughter.

The tellers-who-laugh-at-their-own-jokes are not intended, here, to include those who simply laugh during the telling. This is usually the case with tellers in a power-position, gloating over their dominance. For example, the Boss, the General, or the Head-of-the-Department telling corny jokes to (or plainly insulting) underlings, paid stooges, and lowgrade yes-men who *have* to laugh or be fired. In most other cases, such laughter is just nervousness on the part of the teller, and is considered by all as a blunder or flaw in comic performance. Only the listener 'should,' according to the unspoken rules, be surprised or moved by the situation in the joke, its perhaps crude dialogue and dénouement, and express his astonishment or other emotion in explosive and appreciative laughter. This is, in fact, the crucial difference between *jokes* and all other forms of folk-tales, fables, parables, etc., in almost none of which the culminating laughter of the listener is desired or expected. It is seldom consciously realized that the laughter which greets the 'punchline' of jokes is really an expression of the anxiety of all concerned over the taboos that are being broken, both in the story and in its telling, and by both the teller and his listeners. Anxieties as to cruelty, hostility, 'dirt' or sexuality. If this were understood there would seldom be any laughter.

Laughing while oneself telling jokes is particularly common among amateur or infrequent tellers, especially when the joke is of extremely taboo content, or *when it alludes openly to something in the teller's own consciously remembered life or in that of one or more listeners present*. A good example is the telling of anti-Jewish, anti-Negro, or anti-homosexual jokes, when Jews, Negroes, or homosexuals of either sex are present, or when the teller himself is a member of such group (and wishes he weren't). In our society, autobiographical anecdotes, disguised or frank, concerning untimely farting or impotence, or other scatological or sexual lapses, are particularly likely to be recounted with an unearthly and unending *grin* on the face of the teller, still suffering from an embarrassment perhaps many years or decades in the past. This grin can sometimes escalate itself into perfectly hysterical laughter, with the teller falling on the wall or floor, and being completely unable to go on, if he senses that his audience is not accepting his autobiographical unveiling as an amusing peccadillo, but is really shocked or revolted. Freud has an important passage on such compulsive and almost hysterical tellers of anti-Semitic jokes (the tellers themselves being Jewish) during the dangerous anti-Semitic period of the Dreyfus Trial just preceding the First World War in Europe, in which the whole syndrome is classically described.

It is this necessary sharing of anxieties between all concerned that explains the modern rules or etiquette of joke-telling, seldom verbalized, that: 1) *None* of the people present when telling a joke should belong to the ethnic group – such as Jews, Negroes, Scots, or 'Polacks' – that the joke is about (*i.e.* against). Or else, 2) *Everyone* present should belong to the attacked ethnic group. (Anti-Negro jokes told by Negroes, anti-Texan jokes by Texans, or anti-Semitic jokes told by Jews.) Or, differently expressed, 3) *Not* to tell a story against any ethnic group you do not belong to, when your audience contains members of that group. Anyhow, not unless you know them very well – and probably not even then. Nothing is more sickening than the double-reverse chauvinism of cowardly squares who cannily restrict all ethnic insults in their jokes or anecdotes to presumably direct quotations, to be ascribed to the characters *in* the jokes. Or who pride themselves foppishly on being so 'in' with the 'outs' that they are able with impunity 'to call a nigger "a nigger" to his face.' To which the only possible answer is, of course, "Sure! And what do you call them behind their backs – *jungle-bunnies?*"

One essential rule or custom of the etiquette of jokes, usually overlooked though certainly ancient, is that the listener will often try to get rid of the blow to his self-pride, in having accepted the unadmitted hostility of the joke, by passing this along as soon as possible – *the blow:* the joke is merely secondary – to some further listener. The almost-conscious situation is not that of Wister's *Virginian,* which would be too frank for comfort, but rather that of the son of Sir Walter Raleigh (quoted from Aubrey's *Brief Lives,* in the First Series here, p. 743–4), *who does not strike his father back, after having received from him in company 'a damned blow over his face.' His son, rude as he was, would not strike his father, but strikes over the face the gentleman that sate next to him and sayd, "Box about: 'twill come to my father anon." 'Tis now a common-used proverb.'* (Aarne Tale Type 1557, and compare

Type 1372.) The tale is probably much older than either Aubrey or Sir Walter Raleigh, and seems to derive from the sacredness imputed to the person of kings – as ultimate fathers – seen in the use of whipping-boys in the education of princes of the blood. It is internationally known, with the 'topper' sometimes that: *The final person, who is to deliver the blow to the king (or father), returns it instead to the courtier from whom he received it.* Thus breaking the chain of evil response.

This is exactly the riposte of the person who responds to hearing a joke by insisting on telling one of his own – or a 'better' version of the same one! – or else simply refuses to laugh. Thus again breaking the chain. It was in this way that I myself got into the habit of collecting jokes, clipping them from the back pages of the *Literary Digest* and the "Short Turns and Encores" department of the *Saturday Evening Post* in my 'teens in the early 1930's, and memorizing them by the dozens in order to 'know a joke on any subject,' and be able to top my own father, a notable teller of tales.

In Mr. Richard Buehler's excellent manuscript work, *An Annotated Collection of Contemporary Obscene Humor* (M.A. thesis, Indiana University, 1964), the first informant tape-recorded is thus described by Mr. Buehler, a teacher of dramatics: 'This informant seems to have thought of himself as an accomplished joke teller. He told his jokes with an obvious relish, and no one laughed harder than he did at his own jokes and those told by others at this session.... I found his delivery a little painful because of the enthusiasm, almost hysteria, which was reflected in his voice. It was this informant's boast that he knew every Italian joke which exists. He told a number of dialect jokes, particularly Jewish and Negro, and displayed no particular talent for this kind of story.' There should be more people like Mr. Buehler criticizing comedians, and it is unfortunate that he does not state what this informant's own racial and religious background was. Anyone who has closely observed dirty-talking nightclub comedians, such as the late Lenny Bruce (and numerous others similar in both America and France), will have been struck by the 'painful enthusiasm, almost hysteria' in their delivery of their most outrageous lines, and it is very clear that they are continuously shuddering internally at the thought of their own presumed bravery and in fear of possible punishment or reprisals, by audience-rejection, police-action, or similar. Their brutal verbal treatment of members of the audience who try to walk out is particularly significant.

IV

I have tried throughout this work to avoid general theories of humor. Yet this is perhaps an appropriate moment to discuss one integral aspect of the whole subject of jokes and joking that is handled silently on every page, without ever treating the matter frankly in the round. It must never be overlooked that the tellers of jokes are also the principal audience for jokes. Jokes are told to the people from whom one hears jokes, as a sort of *exchange of hostilities disguised as an exchange of amenities*. That is the secret of jokes. Where a group of people gather and tell jokes, at a party, at the end of an evening, or at an informal meeting for just that purpose, each person goes away with more jokes than he or she came with. This – with the intended laughter during the listening to other tellers' jokes, for one is in the *mood* to laugh – is the expected profit from the group activity. Sometimes, of course, the profit is wholly social or peripheral, as when employees are required to listen to, and laugh at, the boss's lousy jokes; but they do not laugh very loud.

The search for sexual and aggressive pleasure in laughing at jokes that are unfamiliar to one, and which are then added to one's private repertory if they 'strike a chord' or suit one's inner needs, is the most prominent feature in the telling and exchanging of jokes among social equals, and even among the sexes. In the latter case, of course, an intention is unmistakably present in the jokes told, of expressing sexual desire for, or rejection of the listener(s) of the opposite sex, or one's own sexual availability to them; or of humiliating them publicly by the crude sexual display of their bodies or infirmities, or simply by attacking them or the sex to which they belong. This complicated situation, in which all persons present partake at different levels, has been beautifully analyzed by Freud, who is quoted on this point in the Introduction to the First Series here, section II, pages 12–13. This is just one more of the ambiguities of joke-telling. It must also not be overlooked that the principal subject of jokes really told at the folk level is and has probably always been *sex*. In a collection of 13,804 current jokes reported in New York City from 1956 through 1960 by ninety-two white 'rapporteurs,' 17% were about sex, and 11% about Negroes: these being the two main subjects. (Dr. Charles Winick, "A Content Analysis of Orally Communicated Jokes," in *American Imago*, 1963, xx. 271–91.)

Most modern men and women not too unutterably stuffy have, at one time or another, found themselves in such joke-telling groups, especially at drinking-parties. Many people create the joke-telling situation purposely, when none exists, by spontaneously beginning to tell dirty jokes, with some such line as, *"Have you heard this one? (or the latest one about ..."* naming some personage in the news). I have sat in on hundreds of such sessions over the last thirty-five years, with all kinds of people and in all kinds of places and conveyances, from ferris-wheels to airplanes, but I do not remember anyone ever starting off by saying something like, *"That reminds me of the one about ..."* and then telling a *clean* joke. Maybe some ministers and rabbis do this, but not the ones I have heard tell jokes. A letter which I receive from a theological seminary in Evanston, Illinois, on New Year's Eve, 1974, as I sit here typing this Introduction, makes the point unequivocally. The writer – a woman, offering to send some 'pretty seedy pieces of humour' for this Second Series – observes: 'Believe it or not, men studying to become ministers (Episcopalian) are the filthiest, raunchiest, horniest men on earth and also the least inhibited. Much more interesting than theatre people.' (I have also heard it claimed that Mormon bishops have the longest pricks of anybody; as is discussed further in section 13.II.1, "Negroes and Jews.")

Many people feel, and will state, that the telling of dirty jokes has an aphrodisiacal effect on persons of the desired sex, or at least on the tellers themselves. And that they tell dirty jokes as part of their 'approach.' This is implied in the description of parties at which dirty jokes, limericks, etc. are being told by both women and men in Christina Stead's *Letty Fox: Her Luck* (New York, 1946) p. 293–4, and a similar scene in the once scandalous *Bad Girl* by Viña Delmar (1928) p. 27–8. See also Prof. Richard Waterman's, curiously-titled "The Rôle of Obscenity in the Folk Tales of the 'Intellectual' Stratum of Our Society," in *Journal of American Folklore* (1949) LII. 162–5, of which one can only observe that the inner quotation-marks might just as rightly have set off obscenity and not 'intellectual.' One hardly expects brain-baiting of this kind in a learned journal.

Presumably, it is the search for laughter at the 'unexpected' element in unfamiliar jokes, and for additional and highly topical jokes to add to one's own repertory for retelling, that is the reason for the insistent emphasis on novelty – the absolute demand for 'new' jokes. Jokes already in circulation (in the particular listening-and-telling group) are poorly received, and are mocked as old 'chestnuts' dating from *Joe Miller's Jests* in the early 18th century, if not from King Rameses of ancient Egypt. Yet most jokes are, in fact, fairly old, as the tracings in the present volumes have surely proved, or are merely modern revampings, with new backgrounds and changed punchlines, of jokes far older than Joe Miller. King Rameses is closer to it. So we have this unassailable contradiction that jokes travel from mouth to mouth, over centuries and continents, but no one wants to hear the same joke *twice*. Every joke must be new. But they (almost) never are. There is also a further contradiction, less striking but very significant, that many people respond to hearing a joke by saying, *"That's not the way I heard it ... "* and then proceed to tell the SAME joke over again, often at full length. Also sometimes laughing heartily at their own punchline, when arrived at, which no one else can possibly laugh at since there is no surprise, and the 'punch has been telegraphed' by the announcement that this is simply a variant of the joke that has gone before. How now, *new jokes*?

One of the most astonishing features of the many reviews of the First Series of the present work, from the most serious and sympathetic reviewers such as Philip French in the *New Statesman* (London) and Mr. Richard Buehler in the *Journal of American Folklore*, to and including one London review done, as I recollect, by an American harmonica-virtuoso, was the whole-souled agreement of all the viewers, or almost all, that I had somehow cheated the readers – and had certainly cheated reviewers – by repeating about twenty jokes (more than once) in a work presenting nearly two thousand jokes! That there was an obvious and announced purpose to the repetitions – to point up varying aspects of these few and significant items, in different contexts or subjects – and that, in any case, the repetitions were usually of different versions from different tellers (*"That's not the way I heard it ... "*) made no nevermind at all. I had committed the unspeakable crime in telling jokes: I had told some twenty jokes TWICE, in among two thousand jokes told only once (by me). One repetition per each hundred 'new' jokes: that was the gravamen of my crime. As Mr. Buehler pitilessly put it: 'one roguish reader ruefully has said of the book, "To read it once is to read it twice".' (*Journal of American Folklore*, 1970, vol. 83: p. 87–9.)

One could almost see the mental process involved. After all, book-reviewers are just like everybody else – except in England, where they have harmonicas. A joke book is a joke book, and to *hell* with all that unfunny 'description' or 'weather' or 'scenery' and analysis – nay, even polemics! – in roman type, wasting the reader's time between the jokes. After all, who wants to bother with jokes one has already heard? And so recently too ... It's like wives: one does not want *old* wives; one wants *new* wives. *"Fresh cunt, fresh courage!"* Roll out the barrel, and bring on the dancing-jokes! No old and hated jokes can expect to be laughed at here!

It would be very nice, for the compiler of a work such as this, and would infuriate the reviewers somewhat less, if all jokes and folktales had only one theme, or one clear and pivotal *nexus*, and could thus neatly be placed in a subject-arrangement or other classification system in one place and one place only. That this is virtually never the case can most easily be seen in Prof. Stith Thompson's *Motif-Index of Folk-Literature* in five volumes, which is far & away the world's largest collection of jokes and folktales, reduced to their bare elements (except for the 'obscene' ones, which are in large part carefully omitted). This tremendous compilation, though set up on an intensely subdivided plan, nevertheless has thousands of cross-references to sub-themes or criss-crossing themes, each such cross-reference being tantamount to a repetition of a tale or element of a tale, and an admission that thousands of these motifs mutually interlock and interchange. Even so, the Thompson *Motif-Index* then requires a whole extra (and excellent) Index-volume, though it is itself intended to be, and correctly described as an index or *catalogue raisonné*. I believe this indicates the cold reality or logistics of handling any large body of folktales or jokes, and not only the unavoidableness of repetitions but also their clear necessity.

Of course, this is only logic, and will not affect anyone. And I am certain that the further two dozen jokes repeated in this Second Series – that's fifty in all – will also seem, to a certain type of reader or reviewer, an intolerable annoyance or an affront, if not a plain swindle amounting to nearly 20c on the published price of the book. What does this really mean? Why all this heat? Why does the repeating of a joke, or the telling of an 'oldie,' seem so very unforgiveable? When *nobody* ever tells jokes for the first time – anyhow, not anybody you or I have ever met – and is always repeating or revamping old jokes heard from someone else.

Why, after all, are the mutually contradictory stories of the first and second chapters of *Genesis* and the gospel stories of the *New Testament* acceptable two or four times over, or four thousand or four million times over; as with the world's franker folktales? Of these, the audience – especially of children – is likely to demand the repetition time after time, and *always exactly the same!* Why is the rule so different, nowadays, as to mere jokes, that one certainly hears less often? Perhaps they do not have the body of the longer folktales or the merit to bear any repetition. Perhaps. Yet repeated they are, and by every person who tells them and who is not their inventor. Or perhaps by their inventors more often than anyone else? Like all other folktales, fables, and conscious parables, jokes are in large proportion centuries old, and their changes from century to century and country to country are seldom of any essentials. Jokes have therefore long since – centuries, millennia since – proved their ability to take repetition thousands or hundreds of thousands of times, from mouth to mouth, and from continent to continent, without ever being written down (until recently), and certainly without ever being seen in print, so far as the tremendous majority of joke-tellers ever know. What then is the meaning of this purported resistance to hearing jokes repeated?

The truth seems to be that there is a bad conscience about jokes, not only about 'dirty jokes,' whether sexual or scatological, but about all jokes of the aggressive punchline type. What is so valuable psychologically about scatological jokes, in particular, is that they present in the most extreme and brutal form, and usually without any attempt to titillate or seduce the listener in the way that sex-jokes do, the one most important characteristic of all jokes since the development of the modern joke-form in the '*facezia*,' which has supplanted the longer and more leisurely folktale almost entirely, in urban societies, since the time of Poggio in the mid-15th century. This unique characteristic of the *facezia* or joke, as differentiated from the *novella* or folktale, and no matter how long-drawn-out the former may be, or how brief the latter, is the punchline – so very well named – in which the joke rushes headlong to some cruel climax, whether verbal or situational, and stops abruptly there, frozen in tableau. At this point all the actors, and particularly the 'butt' – again, so very well named – have presumably been destroyed by the explosive climax, which is also expected to create the matching explosion of the listener's laughter. And no further existence for any of the actors in the joke, except the protagonists (and then only if of *named* fool or trickster types, like Nasr'eddin, Goha, or Pat & Mike) can even be imagined.

This point has been discussed at greater length in *The Horn Book*, pp. 188 and 461–2, with historical materials showing the important formal change that had been achieved in the jest-books and popular novels between 1500 and 1600 (taking Béroalde de Verville's *Moyen de Parvenir*, about 1610, as the watershed-date). By that time the development of the plot-situation and of the tale-teller's leisurely art, which had once been the whole pleasure of the listeners to folktales, became the special province of the courtly novel. Simultaneously, there was evident a progressive shrinking back of the folktale, at the folk-level itself, but especially in the cities, to the punchline joke or *facezia*: originally a Levantine form of wit, brought to Europe through Italy during the centuries of the Arab domination.

A folktale tells a story, sometimes cruel and sometimes not. But the punchline joke must always end with a verbal climax, a surprise witticism or unexpected retort (the *punch*), in which the interlocutor or the butt is humiliated and sometimes annihilated. And the listener along with him, except that the listener bails out and joins the victorious joke-teller's side in a hurry, in the climactic laugh. This is not so much telling a story as it is setting up a backdrop – often freighted with anxiety for both teller and listener – against which the butt is scapegoated, sacrificed, and exploded in a cruel and explosive final spoken line, like the cutting of a throat. Or, even if there is no spoken line, or it is left aposiopoetically to be understood, the butt is just as certainly mocked, or harmed and destroyed nonetheless, and must die (be humiliated) and disappear from the stage. The only person who remains alive to tell the tale is the person who has *told* the tale, the tale-teller. Who rushes on now to find some new victim to tell it to – and never the same one twice! While the listener stays behind to absorb the blow. Or else sets out then on his own to find some new listener-butt, to whom he in turn transfers the 'punch.'

As to what are called dirty jokes, the bad conscience of the listeners and often of the tellers, as to this mutual comedy of *hostilities disguised as an exchange of amenities*, is massively evident. Just to begin with, that is surely why such jokes are called 'dirty.' Not only their subject is strictly and always the taboo – no other types of jokes are really popular – but both tellers and listeners always seem to sense, though they may not wish or even be able to put their finger on it, or bring it to utterance, that the telling of dirty jokes is always a hostile and aggressive act, no matter what the ostensible subject. As such, dirty jokes are always and inevitably a sort of anal-sadistic pétard or fire-cracker tied to the listener's tail, if they are not positively hammered up his arse and the fuse gleefully lit.

For, let me insist again, it is the listener who is generally the real butt of the joke, and that is precisely why he is so often anxious to pass on the blow, by telling the story at once to someone else. (New or old.) Most punchline jokes, and dirty jokes especially, are therefore told – and listened to with plea-surable identification in the teller's taboo-flouting boldness – only on a hit-&-run basis. One never wants to see the butt or victim again. *Or hear the joke.* Though telling it again, and sometimes again and again and again, is the essence of the activity to all people, without exception, who actually like telling jokes at all. Listeners do occasionally exist who do not insist on retelling the jokes they hear. Generally they are either those who do not identify strongly in the precise sexual or scatological anxieties hidden in the joke, or else are just the happy masochists or Willinghorses whom our civilization counts on to do its dirty work. He Who Gets Slapped.

Like the sexual 'oncing' of Don Juans of all sexes, the com-pulsive teller-of and even listener-to jokes must go on endlessly, to a new conquest or a new joke every day, or night. Good or bad, handsome or ugly, witty or flat, does not really matter, as long as the conquest – or joke – is *new*. Nor does it matter how many months (if I may continue the metaphor) the joke or con-quest has gone through already, so long as it is new to our Don Juan. Yesterday night's passionately desired woman or man is somehow hated by morning, and must be replaced, never to be seen again. In fact, to be fled from precipitately. That is 'oncing.' As to jokes, this operates strictly via the ear. Yesterday's joke is deliciously worth repeating today; yes, and tomorrow and another morrow too, because that is the way to other listeners who will take the blow and receive the 'punch.' But never twice to any one listener, if this can be remembered or avoided. And NEVER – oh never! – twice to the teller himself.

Here we have the real or proximal origin of the jokes we hear, and the secret mainspring of their geographical spread, and of the extraordinary speed of their transmission. I have known, in New York and Chicago, particularly in advertising, the theatre and the arts, men who would sit up until late at night, telephoning at fabulous expense to California all the 'new' jokes they had heard that day, and which would therefore arrive in California four hours ahead of the sun. I have also been informed by Mr. Joseph Fliesler, compiler of the original *Anecdota Americana* (1927) and former publicity director in America for UFA Films, that telegraph-operators 'in the old days' – meaning before the advent of the teletype machines, which would leave a guilty record in the morning – would keep the wires open all through the night by retailing jokes in this way over enormous distances. I have heard, too, of Army walkie-talkies being used in this same way, since World War II, to transmit the latest joke on the commanding officer and his wife to the front line of the battle during the silent, nerve-wracking waits of the night and early morning. This identical scene, elaborate bawdy jokes and all, but lacking only the walkie-talkies, is given in Shakespeare's *Henry V* (written about 1599), Act III, scene vii, where the French Dauphin and his officers wait out the night before the Battle of Agincourt. All this explains, at most, the method of the high-speed transmission of jokes. The motive, however, is another matter, and it is to this that the real effort of attempted interpretation in the present work has been turned. This motive can only be the shared anxieties and matching hostilities of the original creators and tellers of the jokes, and of the listeners who then pass the jokes along – with improvements. The rest must be sought in history.

V

As with all jokes, lies, parables, and other fiction, the teller visibly reveals himself in the choice of his subjects and in his special handling of them, though it is not always possible to put an exact psychological name-label to what one sees. In the specially 'dirty' or 'nasty' joke, the teller must often simultaneously try to hide or remain masked behind some such frantic pretense as that he is retailing a 'true anecdote' (it happened to a friend of his), or that he is simply trying to 'fool' the listener, or 'test his endurance.' The listener may even be warned in advance that he is being 'tested.' But this sword cuts two ways. The brutal and unpleasant story or joke, purportedly being told to 'test' the listener's emotional strength, is only too obviously intended in fact to prove and allay – for the thousandth time, perhaps – the teller's own hidden weakness. The unsatisfactoriness of the entire formula, for driving away anyone's terrors or testing anyone's real strength, is implicit in the teller's own compulsive repeating of the same or similar anti-favorite stories (generally always circulating about the same horrible few themes) again and again, and to as many new or 'virgin' listeners as he can find, who can be expected to react with the most satisfactory amount of horror and shock. Or the teller's desperately digging up even more horrible stories with which to regale his regular audience of 'unwilling' listeners, if no virgin listeners are to be found.

The idea that horror-stories of this kind have some sort of 'cathartic' value, for either the teller or the listener, is profoundly belied by the endless necessity expressed by both of them for this presumed psychic retching or fecal catharsis, which never actually takes place except verbally or in images, and must therefore be endlessly re-begun. It is a two-faced mirror this time, like that postulated in Lewis Carroll's *Through the Looking-Glass*, where all the real action takes place on the other side of the mirror. Every sort of excuse is proffered, one's hands are endlessly shown to be clean, however often one purposefully dirties them with mud, shit, and blood, and one's mouth as well. In fact, one's mouth especially, as in drinking blood – or eating shit. For after all one is only *saying*, not doing. This is the standard excuse and escape-valve of dreams or fantasies of the whole world of taboos, such as incest, murder, and other socially forbidden acts. Words, only words. The blood and shit and slime being flung about are not real, only verbal. *"No, no,"* says Hamlet (III. ii. 244), *"they do but jest, poison in jest; no offence i' the world."*

And yet . . . Were not the audience's reaction almost the same as might be expected to greet real blood, real tortures and horror, real shit and slime and the black froth of death, what *fun* would there be in such jokes and horror-tales for anyone concerned? In fact, what 'catharsis' could be hoped for? This whole aspect of the subject, as to the hoary fraud of the cathartic excuse or pretext – as old as Plato – for dealing in obviously undesirable and anti-social materials, need hardly be considered here. It has been exposed on an extremely broad social background, for several decades now, by all modern critics sincerely concerned with the massive doses of sadism and violence in all modern 'entertainment' media since the late 1920's, particularly those directed at children. The most trenchant and influential critic of all this, also the critic offering the most staggering array of examples taken from the presumably cathartic violence and horror itself – and not just in the usual sub-literary and pictorial 'media' forms, but also in violent modern life – has been the brain-specialist and psychiatrist, Dr. Fredric Wertham, especially in two books bridging the 1950's and '60's, the post-Atom Bomb decades when our world really went to pot: *Seduction of the Innocent* and *A Sign for Cain,* to which readers with strong stomachs and an honest conscience are directed.

These are the gruesome realities with which the shit- and horror-jokes and stories are only toying nervously, while waiting for a chance – as in prosecuting goldfish-in-rainbarrel wars against 'gooks' and 'chinks' – to happen in glorious fact. See also my own monograph, *Love & Death: A Study in Censorship* (1949), the two opening sections, "Institutionalized Lynch" and "Not for Children," specifically on murder-mysteries and horror comic-books, which latter have now again been bloated up enormously since the late 1960's, as a mock-revolutionary teenage kick, under the name of 'underground comics,' which specialize in the sexually repellent and fecally nauseating, under the guise of a hippie nobility or science-fiction elite.

In truth, below the level of so-called 'black humor,' the belly-laughs and yocks, and the audience's hysterical screams of mixed horror and delight (*"No, no! Stop! For god's sake!! Let me tell one now!"*) the teller or writer does not by any means love or enjoy the mucky materials with which he must construct his accustomed tower of verbal *merde*. He is not really at ease in the slime and blood and pus with which he often splatters his stories for cake-topping, in the disfigurements and castrations he habitually uses for décor, his face more often than not contorted into a fixed grin as he crashes on: a grin representing his nervous and guilty enjoyment of his listeners' unease. From any point of view, the whole scene is like the definition of a German joke: *'No laughing matter.'*

For the real activity of the teller or writer of horror-jokes and tales is not by any means the creation of 'catharsis' in his audience, as has been so often pretended since the time of Plato, but something much closer to proselytizing for his own brand of presumably attractive and amusing – but actually frightening and repellent – filth. Naturally he must peddle these under a disguise: it is amusing, it is humorous, it is 'all in fun,' or even historical. When the teller of the vomit-joke or horror-comic handles vomit and decaying cadavers (a frequent theme in the so-well-named 'underground' comics), he must offer this as ostensible wit or humor, and never frankly as his own sick and morbid fascination with unwholesome and antihuman physiological details: the glorification of sickness and death, under the name of retailing humor. Must hope that his audience's sick fantasies will match, or that they will accept his, to fill their imaginative deadness and void. He must present his pathological product as faraway fact or folklore – jokelore, smokelore; hearsay, fantasy, 'all a bad dream' – but never as the personal confession and private psychopathy it so evidently is. As the entertainment it obviously is not, rather than as the attempted seduction it must always be. Practically eviscerating both teller and listener, author-artist and audience, with all manner of excruciating details, while still trying to seduce and convince the listener that what he himself really wants and will truly enjoy is to bathe with the teller in the teller's own favorite vomit.

In truth, the teller – more than anyone else – is profoundly disturbed by his own materials and themes, like the noisome Augean sweepings of his own hidden emotional outhouses, and that is precisely why he must try so hard to disturb and scapegoat the listener, and send him off screaming into the desert with the nauseous weight of one more new 'funny' story or slime-dropping horror-tale to bear. Social activities of this kind, engaged in by perhaps tens of thousands of persons in all countries and over centuries of past time, have without any question a *function* they successfully perform, though this function may not be one covered in standard social-sadistic books of etiquette and the Boy Scout oath. Deep calls to deep. Though the listener is required by the rules to laugh (if only to make the teller stop), the teller seldom laughs at all. Why should he? It isn't funny to him. Or, which can be worse, sometimes it is *only* the teller who laughs, and in an awful and artificial or choking and screaming way, while the listeners not only do not laugh and are not amused, but seriously implore the teller to let up and stop ... Only to find that *he is unable to stop*, like any other addict or proselytizer, and must be allowed to void his crop of bile and blackness on everyone present, until he is either emptied and spent, or else is forcibly stopped, sat upon, gagged, slugged into unconsciousness, or kicked down the stairs : all excellent methods, though seldom used.

There is another possibility, of course. And that is, that as far as listening to nasty jokes and horror-stories is concerned, the audience may well be far more involved unconsciously than may appear, in the atmosphere created by such jokes and stories and in the profound feelings of guilt these generate, and therefore silently goes along with the tale-telling situation. That must certainly have been my own case during the many years over which the materials for this *Rationale of the Dirty Joke*, and in particular of the 'dirty' dirty jokes, were compiled.

At the milder levels of unpleasant joke-telling, the rôle of the listener or victim in such situations is particularly formalized and ambiguous. He must presumably loathe and detest the stories he is being 'forced' to listen to – the verbal version of the hazing to which he is forced to submit – yet he does not often either physically prevent the teller from continuing, nor himself leave and refuse to listen. This does occasionally happen, but only very infrequently (and then to the accompaniment of hoots and mocking laughter by the other listeners who have stayed), in the style recommended by the boys'-book hero of the 1900's, Frank Merriwell of Yale, who would silently leave any gathering where unseemly joking or conversation was engaged in. He also did not smoke or drink. The Catholic 'Holy Name' Society likewise proposes that the listener should respond in just this way, or by reprimanding the speaker, on hearing profanity used.

The listener to unpleasant jokes and tales is allowed and expected to groan over the repulsive details engaged in, and to
pretend to want the teller to stop. But in fact it is the essential
feature of the social ordeal or 'test of strength' involved that the
teller should *not* stop. And that the listener, after hearing him
out, should then 'top' him with an even more repulsive story if
possible, everyone thus bathing gloriously in shit together. As
stated, the listener's rationalization is offered to him ready-
made : he is only testing his emotional or 'manly' strength, or is
allowing it to be tested by the other persons present, to see if
he 'can take it.' He will certainly be laughed at and scorned as a
weakling, by both the teller and the other listeners, if he refuses
to listen or gets up to leave, thus demonstrating that he cannot
'take it.' The actual ideal 'failure response' which the teller and
circumambient listeners are trying or hoping to create, is to
make the impressionable listener turn pale at the gills, and to
send him reeling and retching from the room, leaving his drink
and sandwiches behind, untouched (among the cadavers, if in
the medical-school situation), for the tougher-minded listeners
then to share. Showing their own rock-like strength of character
and dizzying neurotic status by biting carnivorously into the
well-dirtied food (representing the cannibalistic feast on the
body of the weakling who has fled), and swallowing it with
gusto and a swig of his beer; while shit, pus, and vomit fly
verbally through the air.

In the more strictly sexual situation, of telling dirty jokes in
mixed company, the erotic rather than food equivalent of the
preceding scene is to follow up a string of such 'filthiest' jokes
known to everyone present, or most repulsive limericks, in
which one may also have partaken in the communal (com-
munional?) telling, by accompanying one of the ladies home at
the end of the session and attempting to have sexual intercourse with her. There is also the homosexual version of this, in
strictly monosexual or 'stag' joke-telling sessions. Homosexuals
seriously believe that telling dirty jokes, or 'sex talk' generally,
is an effective seductional situation with boys and young men.
Handsome is as handsome does. Or one man's aphrodisiac is
another man's bring-down – in every sense.

Whether, in heterosexual sessions, there are in fact women
who are sexually excited by dirty jokes – whether 'filthy' or
'mild' – or who are 'loosened up' and made sexually more
complaisant after being exposed to such jokes, I do not know.

I have never yet been able to bring myself to touch a woman, immediately after such a session, with a ten-foot pole, even assuming I had one. More than once, however, I have had hostile and reclamatory bitches of the classic penis-envy type tell me such stories privately – sometimes in avowed auto-biographical form, if only at the level of *"The girls used to tell this one when I was in high-school"* – with the obvious intention of turning off or parrying my expected sexual approach. In one such story that I remember only too well, *The beautiful young prostitute, upon whom the playboy flings himself in the darkened room, appears to be frothing at the mouth in an epileptic fit. She is dead.* (There is also a presumably hilarious punchline, given in section 12.IV.6, below.) I suppose it is just my own weakness, but I would like to meet the 'playboy' who could continue with an intended seduction after a conscious or unconscious statement by the girl of her view of the matter, quite so clear as that.

Aside from the obvious advantage in turning off a would-be 'wolf' or seducer, it seems clear that a woman's telling a man repulsive sex-jokes of this kind, whether privately or publicly, is intended further as a sort of turnabout rape, in which it is she who outrages and humiliates the man – her own secret assessment of what sexual intercourse amounts to, from the woman's position. She is also effectively denying her own sex as a woman. For in telling such stories, the woman openly telegraphs her demand to be accepted as a 'liberated woman' or imitation man, and not as a woman at all. As being just as 'strong' and capable of creating or enduring nausea as any man. In point of fact, it is men, not women, who are nausea-prone at the sight of even such natural matters as free-flowing or coagulated blood, and especially menstrual blood, or the bodily exudations of childbirth, and the vomit and feces of children. However, women who are anxious to compete with men and to achieve male status (pants, wage-slavery, sterilization, and all the glorious rest of it) cannot afford to, and never do take into account the real and natural differences between the sexes. They deny these differences angrily, insist on the presumed similarities between the sexes (horns? tail-feathers? breasts?) and compete solely on those grounds. That is also why they invariably lose, unless they have chosen obviously inferior, crippled or 'castrated' males to compete with and to dominate, as they generally do. Their own true superiorities, *as women,* are hateful to them.

Scatological jokes pose a particular problem to tellers and listeners, especially at presumably cultivated social levels, a problem that will be considered more in detail in the introduction to the entire chapter on scatological jokes, below. It is important to realize that persons at these social levels, who often express dislike or offense as to the riotous 'shit jokes' that hardly can be expected to shock a farm-hand or plumber in his off-hours, nevertheless have their own special scatology or *purposeful* dirtiness in jokes (or songs), though this does not necessarily involve actual feces or urine. For some people it is sex itself which is the 'dirt' they are smearing on the listeners to their jokes: this is one of the most important points about 'dirty' jokes of all kinds, and why it is so difficult to find two people whose ideas on the subject coincide. While most people will agree that mild jokes about children or animals (or birds) in quasi-sexual situations are jokes of the 'clean-dirty' variety, the argument starts when it is necessary to decide where the 'dirty-dirties' begin.

In general, the scatology of the cultivated person in our society is, precisely, the 'sick' joke involving food-dirtying, incest, anti-family situations, disease, and other purposely shocking or disgusting themes: the out-&-out 'nasty-nasties' of Chapters 12 and 14, and the castration horror-stories of Chapter 13, all of which are most frequently told nowadays by adolescent boys and sometimes by children.

Humor-as-ordeal is a subject that has never been handled. Yet what else is involved when medical students purposely tell gruesome jokes and macabre 'true' anecdotes to beginning students – also formerly, and still in France, singing matchingly gruesome songs – often at the beginning of or during meals in common? These students are conscious of at least the top-level purpose of their activity, and will explain that these are intentional food-dirtying ordeals supposed to accustom the neophyte to the horrors of the venereal ward, morgue, and dissecting-room. Actual cut-off parts of the body are even sometimes used in such hazing (rubber replicas of these, as also of great greasy turds, are available to the general public in 'magic' and 'novelty' shops, politely called in French *'farces et attrapes'*), for the creation of even greater verisimilitude and fright. The same care and fanatical exactness of horrible and bloody detail is, of course, a feature of all horror-films, whether under the euphemisms of 'fantastic,' or 'science-fiction,' or for that matter 'cowboy' or 'war.'

That the presumed testing of strength by means of repulsive jokes and horror-stories is only a rationalization of fear is conclusively proved by the alternating rôle of listener-into-teller in the usual sessions, or thereafter. In most cases, the listener to repulsive jokes (or tall-tales of horror, often told as true) becomes the teller of similar stories, turnabout, immediately after listening. Or else, if he realizes he cannot 'top' the first teller, he absorbs the stories he has heard and becomes the teller of the same stories in turn to other listeners later, in further sessions which he then engages in or even promotes. He thus sloughs off, in the style of the game of "Musical Chairs," the unspoken emotional blow he has received from the original teller, whose purpose has been precisely to deliver that blow.

The complete pattern, in the telling of repulsive stories, is for the listener to respond or riposte immediately, by refusing the blow intended for him by the teller, and, as it were, returning this blow to the original teller's face in the fashion of a verbal duel, by immediately telling another very similar and if possible even more repulsive story. A formal telling-session is thus set up, often proposed (by the *loser* of a preceding session, if not by a control-sadistic insistent *winner*) with the words: *"What's the dirtiest story you ever heard?"* Or, not taking any chances that the listener will refuse to play, *"Here's the dirtiest (or filthiest, or nastiest or most nauseating) story I ever heard."* Stories of this kind are therefore sometimes called "Nasty-Nasties," or, in the attempted further self-deprecation of mock-Cockney accent, "Narsty-Narsties." They are never, or almost never, the first stories told at a joke-telling session, though often they are the last, the session breaking up or turning to some other subject immediately thereafter. On the other hand, some sessions – going on for hours into the night and early morning – are solely concerned with horror-, ghost-, or merely nasty-nasty stories, usually told and listened to by special amateurs of these forms.

It is also sometimes the case that the teller of a specific nasty story or horror-tale is consciously though covertly *directing his story at some specific person* in the assembly of listeners. This is the standard technique of all fables and parables since those of the Bible and Aesop. Husbands and wives who no longer love each other, or never did, have a particular habit of sniping at each other in this way in public, as gruellingly represented in Edward Albee's sex-hate play, *Who's Afraid of Virginia Woolf?* In joke-telling sessions, as differentiated from tendentious books and disguised homosexual plays '*putting sand in the vaseline*' of the normally sexed, the person attacked has the opportunity of replying. This is usually done under a matchingly elaborate 'cover' – just like C.I.A. stooges who pretend to be minor literary critics, musical anthropologists, etc. – of telling another ghastly or hair-raising tale, but this one levelled at the first teller's soft bunions and hidden vulnerabilities. Note for example the two matchingly gruesome and mock-idiotic castration stories told by a husband and wife, in alternation – each story more horrible and insane than the other – quoted in full in the First Series, p. 695, in Chapter 9.I.4, as a fitting end to the section on "Sex Hate."

In practice, it is more common for the opponents to avoid the unmistakably direct crossing of verbal swords or humorous shit-bladders in this way, and to give their matching 'nasty-nasties' at some later turn, though in the same session, thus avoiding any overt appearance of a pointed retort. Why they wish to avoid this appearance, and keep their wrecked relationship going, is anybody's guess. Meanwhile, the impact of *both* stories passes in this way through the whole assembly – essentially innocent bystanders – reaching the intended victim at each end only anonymously and in turn. "*Box about, 'twill come to my father anon.*" The bystanders also carry off a good part of the freight of the unpleasantness, that being the only part 'in clear,' and which they can understand.

VI

Ultimately, it must be obvious to everyone that the real purpose of 'dirty' dirty jokes is something more intense and involute than the mere retailing of stories that the teller considers to be especially funny, for the purpose of entertaining other people and making oneself liked and admired by them – something it can never succeed in doing. No one really considers such stories as being *funny* (ha-ha) at all, as the terms for such humor of 'dirty-dirty' and 'nasty-nasty' make perfectly clear, showing nothing in their reduplicative alliteration (like the '*lustful, lewd, and lascivious*' of the obscenity laws of former years) but that they are afraid.

And yet, these repellent jokes evidently do some strange thing that somehow satisfies the tellers, and satisfies those listeners-turned-tellers who then repeat them, thousands upon thousands of times as the jokes travel through their decades and sometimes centuries, and in many countries ... the same jokes. The laugh they arouse, if any, is less often one of amusement than one of *relief*, when the ordeal of listening is over. And that is a clue to their mystery.

The horror-stories and the 'dirty' dirty jokes included in the present work can only be understood, finally, when considered as scapegoat ceremonials rather than as depraved folktales. Covered verbally or pictorially with all the filth and repellent things we hate and fear and execrate as sinful and wrong, they are driven into the wilderness as a sacrifice intended to leave all the rest of us shriven and (within the limits of what they have taught us) pure. But, as always, the proposed exorcism or catharsis somehow does not work. The next day or week the same or preferably a new scapegoat – that is to say, a new listener or *virgin victim* – must be found to debauch; must be spat upon, shat upon, and covered with all the same old horror and filth as last time, and be driven trembling and titubating into the ever-present desert, without either the teller or the listener being any the better for the sacrifice or one whit changed by it. That is what the telling of 'dirty' dirty jokes and other horror-stories really amounts to. And the cycle is endlessly repeated, only a little more democratic than the endlessly ghastly eviscerations of human victims with an obsidian knife by the Aztec priests in that in this case there is no privileged caste of priests who never pass finally under the knife, unless the dirty-talking nightclub comedians can be considered these highpriests. For in the standard cycle of dirty joke-telling, each listener-victim of the day before becomes the joke-teller or highpriest-*cum*-executioner the following day. Few ever refuse either rôle.

The emphasis on the teller's rôle is obviously the vital point. The listener can be anyone, and usually is. It is the teller's desperate neurotic need that spins the wheel and creates the format. Realistically and functionally considered in this way, even 'clean' jokes are never really intended to do anyone any good except the people who tell them: usually nervously grinning adolescent boys, such as you and I once were. For come-

dians (and horror-purveyors) did not originally come into existence because masochistic audiences, million-strong, wanted or
demanded them to arise from the dust. Instead, the tale-telling
format, unquestionably created originally in the nursery for
children by their mothers and by oldsters of both sexes tending them, and later employed for the transmission of the
heroic myths and traditions of the tribe, has been seized upon
by certain kinds of word-oriented neurotics, at least since the
time of ancient Egypt and Greece. The *weak-who-speak* who
can be the crippled, the blind, the aggressively handicapped
and the very old, and who often are.

These individuals, to the degree that they are neurotic, have
always felt an intense and hateful need to 'do their thing'
aggressively and publicly, in a way closely connected with the
ancient ritual sacrifices and combats, and the verbal symbolizations of these in the *flytings*, or contests in invective and abuse.
They have found a protective cover for their neuroses in ritual
forms such as hellfire preaching or professional humor and
entertainment in the circus or theatre. In fact, they create their
rituals themselves, as do all priests, and for their own purposes,
arrogating divine or other inspiration to them, depending only
on the gullibility of their primitive audience. Dance and the
mime-theatre were once considered religious acts, and still are
throughout the Orient and among the American Indians and
other hunter groups. These arts have not kept their sacerdotal
charter in our society, and have in fact been under centuries of
attack by the more verbally-oriented religions operated by
intellectual priests and physical and sexual cripples (such as
Moses and St. Paul), rather than by dancers and actors. The
same is certainly true of the merely comic theatre.

The audience necessarily responds to the ritual acts of both
sacrificial priests and comedians on an unconscious basis, composed of fear and identification-with-the-aggressor, and especially of mixed attraction and revulsion. *Many are called, but
few are chosen.* Some acts and some comedians succeed; some
are supported by the community, like the *bodchonim*, or
marriage-festival jesters of the Jewish communities of Central
Europe; and others find their way into the competitive theatre
world, of comic plays and 'moralities' since a relatively early
date, as also circus clowns and other mimes, coming down to
the nostrum-vendors' comedians and 'spielsters' from the 16th
through the 20th centuries in Europe and America, and the

burlesque theatre and vaudeville comics at least since the 17th century in Italy and France. These are indistinguishable from modern vaudeville (nightclub), theatre, and radio-television comedians sometimes using the same gags, such as onstage 'goosing.'

In all cases these men (rarely women) are self-chosen to the work, that is to say are driven to it by inner necessity. Most of them and most of their 'acts' fail, and their little hour on the stage is mercifully brief. The audience cannot and must not consciously express what it wants, and what it will respond to; and the comedian cannot consciously express why he does what he does and says what he says. But somehow a marriage of supply & demand takes place – or else it does not. Those are the failures. Since the marriage must be brought off in the dark, with one party unable to express its needs, and the other unable frankly to describe his offering, the failures are many. But there are notable successes too. Those comedians who succeed do so because they have unconsciously brought up to expression, and are able to express better than the others, the unconscious needs, anxieties, and identifications of the audience as well. Those acts, those comedians, that fail to do this fall at once through the audience-sieve and disappear – are sometimes hooted offstage. Sometimes they are too frank, often not frank enough, but in either case there is no appeal from the audience's decision: thumbs up, thumbs down. Mass adulation and a fortune, or "Off with his head!"

A format and a career have thus been created since very ancient times, indistinctly seen in the 'magicians' of Pharaoh's court during the XIXth Dynasty in Egypt (about 1210 B.C.) as described in *Exodus*, vii. 9 through viii. 19; the 'wise men and the sorcerers' with their tricks and mechanical miracles to amaze the king and his guests. Not quite priests, yet certainly connected with priestcraft, especially in those societies where the political or dynastic ruler is not himself considered the highpriest of the state religion, or is simply anointed (by the real highpriest, such as the Pope), and does not perform the magical and sacrificial rites of intercession with the god.

The dancers and mimes, who, as we have seen, were ousted by the more intellectual (philosophic, scientific) priests, have made numerous inroads into the priestly profession, but generally only in the lower echelons and not infrequently with a grossly sexual tone. For example the flagellating dancers or

fertility priests of the Saturnalia and Lupercalia (our Christmas
and Valentine's Day), who ran through the streets of Ancient
Rome disguised as 'madmen' – to whom everything is allowable
– striking all the spectators, and particularly the women, with
goatskin thongs, representing fertilization by the god, and
promising easy childbirth. Carnivals of this type are still massively performed and attended in predominantly Roman
Catholic countries, and even enclaved cities, such as New
Orleans and Nice. (See further my *The Horn Book*, 1964, p.
248–9.)

The late Lenny Bruce, whose nightclub specialty during the
1960's consisted of purposely shocking and obscene harangues
like those of the nostrum-vendors' comedians since the 16th
century, was a perfect example of the mock-madman of the
Saturnalia in the modern garb of the burlesque comedian. As a
matter of fact, at Bruce's one best-attended appearance, in a
large theatre on the lower East Side in New York, in November
1963, he actually affected the costume of a Protestant clergyman, minus only the reversed collar. There would be no point
in even mentioning here the frankly erotic and presumably
satirical 'underground' motion-pictures of the 1960's and '70's,
such as the hands-down prizewinner of the Wet Dream Film
Festival in Amsterdam, 1971, in which a young Swedish woman
performs oral intercourse on a pig (by which I do not mean a
policeman) – to the accompaniment of Beethoven's Pastoral
Symphony, as will be considered further, under "Orgies and
Exhibitions," in chapter 11.III.2. Spectacles of this kind are not
really intended as either humor or satire, and are not widely
popular. Too frank. Such more wilily expurgated public sex-
baths as the fake-hippie *Hair*, and Kenneth Tynan's naked
burlesque show, *O Calcutta!* (staged in New York, 1969, and
even more expurgated versions elsewhere), are the best modern
examples of the 'dirty dirties' that succeed, because they have
been laundered and faked to a fare-thee-well to suit the mass
audience.

In contrast to these, or rather, starting in where they leave
off, Stanley Kubrick's powerful satirical motion-picture, *Clockwork Orange* (1971) – the *Brave New World* of our decade,
politely transposing to England in an all-too-close 1984 the
American *lumpenproletar* thrill-murders of the Manson gang
(composed mainly of young girls), likewise attempts a sexual
shock-attack to match its lovingly detailed beatings, slashings,

rapes, and psychological prison-atrocities: a sort of kinder-garten course for the neo-Nazis of the *Totalitarian-musik* of rock-&-roll. But Mr. Kubrick's movie sex is, alas, all expurgated epoxy, from the clitoris tables in the breast-milk bar (for a tit-illating start), galloping through the Beethoven – the Ninth Symphony this time, not the Sixth – the high-speed Rossini, the ice-cream cone fellation and other musical kitsch and in-decipherable sex, to the final scene of simulated public inter-course with the redheaded Venus of everyone's dreams, who, astride the impenitent anti-hero, somehow never gets any lower than his *chest*. We are left with the now classic con-tradiction that the New Freedom is still only freedom for violence. Sex is only a come-on, a tittymilk-bar or half-nude waitress attraction, and a gag. Like the never-to-be-forgotten reviewer of Oscar Wilde's "De Profundis", *'Not so, we find our-selves saying, are souls laid bare.'*

VII

The first series of the present work, under the title *Rationale of the Dirty Joke* (1968), has shown how these socially-accepted formats operate over a large spectrum of more or less 'clean' dirty jokes – that is to say, those not openly intended to frighten or even to nauseate the listener. It should be evident then, that the jokes which *do* intentionally frighten or nauseate, and do little else, can only be intended to serve the conscious or unconscious purposes of the tellers alone. The audience on which these jokes are then 'sprung' is expected to respond on the unconscious swindle-basis of an ordeal suffered through for a promised reversal of rôles later, as already shown. Of course, it is really always a swindle, for even if there is some reversal of rôles later, the new victim who is verbally assaulted and nauseated in his turn is never the original comedian or joke-teller against whom this revenge is really desired.

The joke-teller or actor, the comedian or clown, is thus a sort of black-mass priest in the line of the ancient dancers and mimes even though he now speaks, and who expresses the courage – in openly breaking taboos, being cruel, sexual, etc. – that his audience by & large lacks. Of this function, too, the late Lenny Bruce was the perfect practitioner, as also the very similar recent comedians, Jackie Kannon in America, and – even more frank – "La Branlette" (The Jerk-off) in France. The

listeners or audience are, as it were, dragged into their rôle with
the unspoken bait not just of 'catharsis,' but of the belief that
they will be given the magical strength by the taboo-outraging
spectacle to turnabout tomorrow and, in their turn, perform the
opposite or 'top-banana' rôle. That of frightening or nauseating
some further victim, by retelling precisely the same jokes and
inflicting the identical cruelties and humiliations of their own
hazing upon others, right up to & including the balls of horseshit left behind by the ice-wagon horses in the street. (For using
the juice to write "Kosher" on the victim's forehead.) If they
are not artistically or courageously up to the cruel rôle of teller
and torturer, rather than listener – Mr. Big up there on the
stage, instead of He-Who-Gets-Slapped (and pays for the privilege) down in the audience – they will often compulsively insist
on touting or even buying tickets for further victims to see the
same 'tasteless' comedian or naked sex-show: *"You'll piss in
your pants. Be my guest!"*

One of the most extraordinary shows of this kind I have ever
seen – anyhow I saw the opening of this one – had nothing
sexual about it at all, except perhaps a few accidentally-bared
breasts as the female victims were manhandled onstage in the
style of the French *Grand Guignol* theatre-of-horror. This was a
purported "Tribute to the French Revolution" to which I was
taken in Paris in 1954, given by young French college-students
of the faculty of Decorative Arts, more famous for their yearly
naked sex carnival, which had apparently been prohibited that
year. This "Tribute to the French Revolution" consisted of nothing other than a two-hour *Grand Guignol* reënactment, in
costume, of the horrors of the guillotine and the 'Terror,' including an operating guillotine (with a rubber blade, I presume),
and imitation blood in the form of red paint being sloshed
wildly around in bucketfuls by the actors, on each other, on
the walls of the gymnasium in which the show was given,
and finally – a note on the program giving assurance that the
paint was washable – all over the audience, which had missed
the original French Revolution but was making up for it now.
As in the incredible slaughter, with axes and tire-irons, of the
opening scene of Jean Yanne's satirical film, *Les Chinois* [read:
Germans] *à Paris* (1974), in which nothing and no one is left
alive at last but the automatic windshield-wiper on one of the
abandoned automobiles, scraping off the ketchup-blood.

The similar ordeal-theatre, or theatre-of-cruelty and audience-

harassment since the 1960's in America, couldn't hold a candle
to it. Only the vaudeville act by an Austrian sado-masochist
troupe, at the above mentioned Wet Dream Film Festival in
Amsterdam, 1971, and elsewhere, of which the climax consists
of a man decapitating a "Sexy Goose" and then buggering one
of the actresses with the bleeding neck (enclosed in a plastic
condom so it will enter without a hitch), can even be compared. You have to feel the cold slosh of a bucket of gooey
blood hitting you in the face to understand the real *humor* of it
all, I was told. Ditto ditto ditto for the sexy goose's bloody
neck up your ass. Only then can you truly understand the
MESSAGE of the modern 'art-theatre.' (Be my guest!)

An error of emphasis and approach, similarly wrong-
headed, had pervaded most of the literature on the subject of
humor until Freud's *Wit and Its Relation to the Unconscious*
(1905), the model on which the present study is patterned –
longo intervallo! Freud liberated the discussion from the tram-
mels of the tiresome aesthetic approach of former critics of
humor, and of many since, based as these were on the crude
practical notion that the audience's laughter or entertainment
is the actual purpose of humor: the theory or paradox of the
comedian-as-*colporteur*, or humor-purveyor. Freud simply
dropped most of the aesthetics and insisted on a strictly functional approach, and one can imagine what he would have
thought of the recent revival of aesthetic criticism and mere
formalistic analysis in folklore and anthropological studies
under the transparent denomination of 'structuralism,' by purported Freudians. See also Freud's brief but deep "Humor," in
International Journal of Psychoanalysis (1928) vol. II; and
Ernst Kris on laughter and the comic, in *same* (1938–40) vols.
19–21.

Freud himself focussed powerfully, always, on the personal
intentions and functions of the jokester, author, clown, liar, or
tale-teller, and on his specific if often unconscious motivations
and satisfactions; and he showed precisely how these operate
behind what is only the screen of humor. For only when the
motives of the jester or jokester are recognized as paramount
can humor be understood at all, or can the actual meaning of
any joke be analysed, discovering then the secret springs by
means of which it excites the audience's response. The Psalmist
says it (42:7): *Deep calleth unto deep.*

It is to this hidden formula that Mark Twain also alludes, in his self-mocking character of 'Pudd'nhead Wilson' (most of the great humorists have taken the masochistic rather than the sadistic stance, vis-à-vis the audience, as very notably Charlie Chaplin and his imitators). I have used as motto to the present work this passage of Twain's, in which he tries to unveil the essential masochism and despair of every great or even success-ful humorist and comedian, like Twain himself, in the extra-ordinarily clear statement: *'The secret source of humor is not joy but sorrow; there is no humor in heaven.'* This is the next step down from Beaumarchais' Figaro, earlier, who *'laughs so that he may not cry.'* Farthest down, and darkest of all, is the earliest recorded statement on the subject of humor in human literature, that of *Proverbs*, xiv. 13: *'Even in laughter the heart is sorrowful; and the end of that mirth is heaviness.'* Only Nietzsche has plumbed that depth. And Victor Hugo, in the final chapter, "Residue," of his masterpiece of irony, *The Man Who Laughs* (1869), which inspired this book. "*When you think I'm laughin', I'm really cryin',*" says the Negro song. Perhaps laughter is just a less painful kind of tears?

Ultimately, all jokes, parables, lies, and in fact all fictions and fables of whatever sort, are simply the decorative showcases of their tellers' anxieties, their repressions, and generally of their neuroses – and these their most secret ones – being juggled with onstage to beg the audience's applause. Not just the audience's applause as a sign that it has been amused or entertained, but as witness that it has seen nothing in the comedian's juggling *but* humor, and has not understood and not rejected his neurotic and aggressive hidden message, which is often also rather poorly hidden. Thus, the true "Paradox of the Comedian" is not that famously sketched by Diderot in 1778. It is, rather, that the audience's laughter and applause are not really the signal that it has seen the joke, but *the signal that it has not seen the real joke at all*, and that the comedian is free to con-tinue without being lynched. For, by & large, the audience can never really be *allowed* to see the joke. This is also the secret mechanism of crude cultural hoaxes like modern fake-art or 'put-on' art – which is almost all of it – fake theatre and cinema, fake music ('of the Twentieth Century'), fake literature (and fake criticism of fake literature), fake psychiatry and fake politics – all of these being today particular plagues – and a great many other current fakeries and frauds, as discussed only too briefly in my pamphlet, *The Fake Revolt, or Gangsters of the New Freedom* (New York: Breaking Point, 1967).

By these artful means are allayed the jokester's, the hoax-ster's, the huckster's, the liar's the novelist's, or any other fictioneer's traumatic anxieties concerning his own deepest emotional wounds, by gaining through the very display of his wounds and scars the audience's noisy identification and ap-proval, whether this is expressed through laughter and applause or simply by laying down their entrance-money at the door. So understood, it becomes clear that all these habitual and profes-sional jokesters, pranksters, fakers and fictioneers (and many others who are presumably offering strict 'non-fiction') are really making use of their art or public activity, not just to earn the obvious money and acclaim, but to send out a desper-ate psychological S.O.S. – *Come in, Anyone! Calling C.Q.! C.Q.! Seek You!* – under the antick disguise of humor or entertain-ment, and often under the terrible disguise of truth. Nietzsche said it best and forever in his unfinished *The Will to Power* (1888), after which he went mad:

> Perhaps I know best why it is man alone who laughs: he alone suffers so deeply that he had to invent laughter ... A joke is the epitaph on an emotion. [*The secret meaning of 'sick' humor.*]

Few jokes or folktales can afford to be so frank as to the hid-den needs and identity of the teller. We identify or we do not identify in his secret problem and passion, his masked message and ritual, and that is the measure of his success or failure. In the same way, the audience's true and expected function is seldom demanded frankly by the teller, who does not con-sciously understand it himself, *or he could not go on.* Only in one form of humor is the swindling of the audience perfectly frank, and then only at the very end, when it is too late for the audience to draw back and refuse to 'bite,' and that is in those open assaults on the listener's patience or credulity called 'shaggy-dog stories,' which are entirely based on cheating him of his expected satisfaction at the end, and fobbing him off instead with presumable nonsense. (Though even there the Sense of Nonsense can often be discerned, if one will only take the trouble to try.)

Plainly stated, the listener or audience is not *ever* being amused or entertained, except accidentally, and is really being made the object, the confederate, the confidante, and often only the victim, the patsy, or butt, of the teller's expurgated and parabolic self-unveiling. Thus understood, the joke, and especially the dirty joke, unveils as little and is as far from the truth – even about the teller – as a striptease in a rain-barrel. Yet it is the truth nonetheless.

There is little more now to say by way of introduction, so let us be perfectly frank. The listener's true function is simply to stand patiently, and take it on the chin, in the gut, ear, eye, or up the arse, strictly at the jokester's whim and inner need – Andreyev's *He Who Gets Slapped*, but this one time entirely unexpurgated – in whatever type of 'humor' or other exhibitionistic activity the teller feels driven to perform and present himself. The audience has no more rights in the matter (except to refuse to laugh, or to pay), than Hamlet's father has as to what particular poisonous brew the murderer will pour into 'the porches of his ears.' Again, the similarity to the relation between teller and audience in ghost- and horror-stories (like *Hamlet*), whether in comic-books, plays, movies, television and the like, is very striking and highly significant.

Finally, to complete his rôle – and this the most important of all – the listener or audience must *shrive* the teller, at the end of his telling, by means of the ritual climactic acceptance of laughter or applause. The teller gains in this way from the audience, at that last dread instant when the laughter or the applause wells up – *or else does not!* – that reassurance which is the true motive of his whole masked and disguised 'comic' activity: the reassurance that his audience is still well-disposed toward him despite his muffled confession, and does not despise him. That the audience has, in fact, not really found him out at all in his hostile exhibitionism and breaking of taboo, whether sexual, scatological, or simply aggressive and 'clean.'

Translated functionally, the audience's laughter or applause means to the teller of the joke or tale that the merited moral judgment he so desperately fears, and to evade which he is so frantically jigging, juggling, and lying, has not been passed against him – not this time at least. Nay, further, that the audience has partaken guiltily with him, though perhaps against its will, in all the hostility, the sexuality, the scatology, or the plain horror of the joke or tale; has even perhaps acceded in being its victim or butt. The whole tragedy of the comedian or teller-of-jokes is this, that he can never really be shriven at all, since his true guilt is inevitably concealed from the audience by the very mechanism which excites the audience's laughter. Otherwise, they would not laugh. The cycle of telling and listening, listening and telling, must therefore be endlessly and compulsively repeated for a lifetime, the teller visibly taking the least pleasure of all in the humor at which he struggles so hard, and in which, at the end, he stands like the hungry child he is, darkly famished at their feasting while the audience laughs.

VIII

It is time now to go. Let me consider what has been attempted in the two Series of the present work, which have not been in any way either easy to compile or entertaining to write. Nor has the collecting of the jokes themselves, over more than thirty-five years of actually listening and reading *ad hoc*, and making out index-cards by the thousands, always been an un-alloyed pleasure. Far from it. As to myself, and aside from laughing when I heard the jokes (the first time ...) the greatest personal reward has been the research itself: the clambering backwards through history, and sideways like a crab, from country to country, and culture to culture, searching for the threads of historical continuity and human community that hold together all these modern jokes that are really ancient folktales refurbished.

If I have had any private motto at all, it is that prefixed by Isaac D'Israeli to the last volume of that paradise of serendipity, his *Curiosities of Literature*, in 1817. A passage which, having been 'lost in the republications' (meaning: expurgated by hands unknown), the 73-year-old researcher, only a few months away from the paralysis of the optic nerve which was to take away his eyesight at last, insisted on restoring in his final preface of 1839, where it was found and used again in just the same way, in the preface to H. Spencer Ashbee's great series of erotic bibliographies under the pseudonym 'Pisanus Fraxi.' It is a brief quotation that, as D'Israeli puts it, 'expresses the peculiar delight of all literary researches for those who love them': "*The struggling for knowledge (aptly observes the Marquis of Halifax) hath a pleasure in it like that of wrestling with a fine woman.*"

RATIONALE OF THE DIRTY JOKE attempts to do four things, none of which has ever been done before in a serious way. First: it attempts to give reasonably full and authentic texts of almost the entire basic float of bawdy jokes of sexual or scatological nature found in oral folk-transmission in the English language, in either America or Britain, over the last fifty to one hundred years – basically, the late-19th and 20th centuries. Jokes encountered only in other countries or languages, or only in print, have frequently been cited as parallels and perhaps sources, but they are not the main matter of this work. I leave them for other researchers.

From the standpoint of mere size, the two thousand jokes included here make this triple or quadruple the size of any collection of sex-jokes ever issued before, all of which have, until very recently, been issued privately if really unexpurgated in text, except for a brief period during the 18th century. The largest other collection of unexpurgated jokes and tales known to me, that of Volodymyr Hnatjuk and Pavlo Tarasevsky, *Das Geschlechtsleben des Ukrainischen Bauernvolkes* (Leipzig, 1909–12; forming *Anthropophytéia*, Beiwerke 3 & 5), in two heavy folio volumes, gives both the Ukrainian texts and German translations of over seven hundred tales, given at full length as transcribed during the collecting sessions. It has seemed desirable in the present work to strive rather for brevity and diversity in the jokes themselves – since stenographic transcripts of the jokes, as actually told, were not made and could not be given – and thus save space for other features of the research, as well as presenting an appreciable sample or 'universe' for comparative study.

Second: it has been attempted here to present the jokes rationally and meaningfully by subjects. Only Hnatjuk & Tarasevsky have done this before, as to erotic humor, and even there the arrangement is strictly and rather superficially by the *nationality* of the protagonist or butt of the joke, a subject I have hardly considered worth handling at all, except in the brief sections on "Foreigners" (2.VI), "Texans" (15.VI.1), and in chapter 14, "Dysphemism & Insults." I think it unnecessary to demonstrate that the various competing chapbooks of bawdy jokes which have mushroomed into existence since the publication of my First Series in 1968, are not actually intended to be taken seriously – which would doubtless be a contradiction in terms – though almost all now do attempt a rough arrangement

or index by subjects. One, in particular, proceeds (in its pro-
spectus) from "Humor of Infantile Sexuality" to end with
"Humor of Necrophilia and Other 'Perversions'," which hits a
level of scientific permissiveness – especially those quotation-
marks around 'Perversions' – to which the present work,
though admittedly proceeding through precisely the same
matters by the end of the 12th chapter, obviously cannot pretend. The most interesting new joke collection is Dr. Richard
Wunderer's interpretive *Jocus Pornographicus* (Stuttgart: F.
Decker, 1969) with a supplementary volume of illustrations.

Third: the effort has been made in the present work to trace
at least a sampling of important and often-told jokes historically, to earlier forms and other countries and cultures, thus indicating not only their hundreds of parenthetical 'Types' and
'Motifs' on the Aarne-Thompson Finnish folktale-study system,
but also their chronological as well as their geographical spread,
a matter hardly handled by Aarne and Thompson at all. In this
approach, if an answer is ever to be found, should be discovered
the solution to the 'mystery' of *where jokes come from*. To
which I have tried to answer, more at length, in *The Horn
Book* (1964) p. 462–8, in a bibliographical chapter intended to
supplement the present work, that: *Jokes are not invented;
they are evolved. And they arrive to us from other countries
and older civilizations, by way of oral and printed infiltrations
over a period of centuries, and along certain massive and rather
well delimited cultural highways.* I do not insist that this is the
only possible solution to the mystery. It is at least a useful
approximation, backlighted by the hypothesis of John Walsh,
in his *Songs of Roving and Raking* (1961) p. 96, that: 'Dirty
jokes probably originate in someone's chance remark which is
repeated as an anecdote with more and more embellishments
until it finally becomes a completed joke.' (*Roll Me Over*, ed.
Harry Babad, 1972, p. 105.) This must certainly often have
occurred, but will explain only the verbal 'punchline' type of
joke, originating in the Italian *facezia* popular since at least the
15th century – and in the Levant earlier – as seen in the collections of Poggio and Cornazano.

Many writers, most recently that lover-of-paradoxes, my
friend Martin Gardner, in a brief skit appearing in a British
magazine, have concerned themselves in humorous essays –
and, worse, in great hefty tomes like this one – with the question of the origin of folktales and jokes, generally admitting

themselves stumped, or fobbing us off with a clever paradox
at the end. Such as the paradox that *we are unconsciously inventing the jokes ourselves*, which I do not believe to be true.
The best theory on all counts is perhaps that suggested in passing, as has already been noted, in the publisher Charles Carrington's *Forbidden Books* (Paris, 1902), written by no-one-will-
ever-know what 'ghost' or hack – but I suspect by the slang-
lexicographer, John Stephen Farmer – who, in discussing Aleksandr N. Afanasyev's great seminal collection, *Russian Secret
Tales* (Geneva, 1872), asks: '*How do these quips and obscene
oddities travel from one language to another, through generations and generations? Does the Wandering Jew tell them in his
ceaseless peregrinations?*' Which is certainly not a bad guess.

Finally, and I believe most importantly, the present work has
made a beginning of analyzing obscene jokes both psychologically and socio-analytically. Discussing their meaning at both the
conscious and unconscious levels for both tellers and listeners,
and concentrating not on the formal aesthetics of humor but
on the intensely human question: *What do these jokes really
mean to the people who tell them, and the people who listen
and laugh?* To my best knowledge, bawdy humor has never
before been taken this seriously. I trust it has been shown here
that it is worth the trouble.

The model for his treatment has, of course, been Freud's *Wit
and Its Relation to the Unconscious* (1905), though it should be
observed that Freud never dealt with these materials from
the sociological or folkloristic point of view, but strictly
psychologically and as to their humorous *form*. Such a limitation of approach would, in the present case, much diminish
what can be learned from the folk-collected evidence, which
has here been organized so far as possible according to *subject*.
At the same time, in his great parallel and speculative works, in
particular *Totem and Taboo* (1913), Freud showed what can be
done in the way of drawing psychological and speculatively
historical, or proto-historical insights from anthropological and
even legendary folk-materials, without falling into the soft-
focus eccentricities and theorizings – obviously themselves a
sort of mystic occultism – of Freud's student, Carl G. Jung and
his school. The profound and sympathetic application of
Freudian principles to *Children's Humor* (1954), by Dr. Martha
Wolfenstein, has already been acknowledged. To avoid any
misunderstanding, it should also perhaps be mentioned here

that preliminary publication of the present work was begun as long ago as 1951, under the present title, in the final issue of my lay-analytic magazine, *Neurotica*, No. 9, with a very abbreviated first cast of Chapter 13 here, covering only jokes on castration.

It would obviously be too much to hope that, in combining and sometimes juggling all these attempts, all together, in a single treatment here, the jokes themselves have come through unscathed. I have certainly not attempted to spoil them (or improve them) in the telling. I have done my best with the sometimes terribly abbreviated notes I found myself left with, the morning after. In any case, no purpose would have been served by recasting the vocabulary of the jokes, as collected, into an elegant and expurgatory Latinity intended to forestall criticism, or by handling with pussyfooting tongs and linguistic horror the jokes we all have heard (and many of us have told), and the language we all understand.

I should add that it has been precisely this refusal to spoil the jokes by retelling them in uncolloquial form that has delayed publication for so many years after the issuing of the preliminary chapter in 1951. It has also resulted in what must be the publishing curiosity that the present work and series, after having been accepted enthusiastically for publication by five different American publishers, now finally sees print, and in the unabridged and unexpurgated form in which it was planned, only owing to the courage of a sixth publisher. A kind of courage still far from common, despite what one has been led to believe since the 1960's by loose talk about some 'New Freedom.' I believe I have had more experience than most writers with rejections, and once even printed (cover-ad in *Neurotica*, No. 5) the entire alphabet of rejecting publishers, from *A* to *Z*, that I had to run through TWICE with the manuscript of my best book, *Love & Death*, before I finally published it myself. But I did not know, until I undertook the present work, how much more damaging and deflating a certain kind of enthusiastic but uncourageous 'acceptance' can be.

It is clear, of course, that a book like this, retelling thousands of jokes, many or most of them hostile and aggressive, and some of them purposely repulsive, amounts to a hostile and aggressive act – thousandfold! – on the author's part. Quite aside from the digressions and polemics which I have allowed myself, on the great example of Victor Hugo in *Les Misérables*.

(Not to mention Sterne, Balzac, Wedekind, and Shaw.) Not only there has been no way of avoiding the built-in aggressiveness of the present text, but the reader may also find that he or she is in the identical position. For the essential hostility of all jokes is clearest in the fact that *most people who willingly listen to a joke wish to repeat it to someone else soon afterward, and do so.* The proverbial idea that 'the jest's felicity is in the listener's ear' (with which compare: 'Beauty is in the eye of the beholder,' and the *subjective nature of obscenity*, first pointed out by Pierre Bayle in the late 17th century), rather distracts attention from the *need* that the teller has for his listeners; particularly – and often repetitively – listeners for the joke that he himself has just heard.

Plainly put, what this means is that no one cares to accept without riposte or revenge the punch of the punchline, under no matter what excuse of humor, nor to absorb all to himself the blow he has unconsciously received in listening. The immediate response is to return the blow, by telling the teller himself another joke: a 'better' one, or even a better version of the same joke he himself has just told. (*"That's not the way I heard it!"*) People tend to treat jokes they have just been told like hot potatoes or a ticking bomb. Either they drop them immediately into the wastebaskets of their mind, or else toss them gingerly but expectantly from hand to hand, waiting until some new butt or victim can be found to throw them at, and thus divest themselves of the hostility they have been forced to absorb.

Nothing that has been said here is intended as an apology on the author's part, nor as a brag. That is simply the way it is. I am very conscious that this has been a difficult and aggressive book to read, all eleven hundred pages of it; as difficult, perhaps, as it has been to write. I wish to express my gratitude and commiseration to the reader who has come this far. And I would like to end here, not with some final joke supposed to be an ultimate crashing explosion or anal-erotic climax (see chapter 15.VI.3 for these), blowing the world orgastically and ecstatically to shit, as is the open intention of the disturbed politico-military and 'scientific' types toying humorlessly with the Atom Bomb; but rather with a very sober quotation from Dr. Otto Fenichel's *The Psychoanalytic Theory of Neurosis* (New York: W. W. Norton, 1945) pages 165 and 478–9, a work which has well been called the 'Bible of psychoanalysis.' I wish to parallel here two profound observations made by Fenichels, actually concerning the habitual proselytizing by neurotics, such as religious sectarians, and homosexuals and drug-addicts suffering from feelings of guilt. Observations of obvious relevance here to the *self-righting or gyroscopic function* sought by even the most normal individuals in the art of humor:

> Any guilt can be borne more easily if someone else has done the same thing. For the sake of the feeling of relief that can thus be attained, people who either have done something about which they feel guilty or wish to do such a thing are often searching for another person in the same situation; they feel greatly relieved if they succeed in finding anyone who does, or has done the same deed. They may even provoke other persons to do the things about which they feel guilty. The relieving function of sharing the guilt is one of the basic factors in the psychology of art. The artist relieves his guilt feelings by inducing the audience to participate in his deed in fantasy, and the spectator relieves his guilt feeling by becoming aware that the artist dares to express forbidden impulses. Similarly, the motive for telling a joke always consists of an attempt to get the approval of the audience for the underlying guilt in the offensive impulses concealed in the joke ...
>
> Many children feel compelled to play the jester to make other people laugh; they cannot stand seriousness. Similar disturbances occur in adults, too. Such behavior implies that the person fears being punished for his instinctual impulses. By pretending that he is merely jesting, he hopes to avoid punishment. Usually, however, the jesting is more than an avoidance of punishment; it has an exhibitionistic quality, and is an attempt to get confirmation from the spectators, and to seduce them to participate in the jesting sexual or aggressive acts. The idea of making others laugh is a substitute for the idea of exciting them. Without the jest, this excitement would be frightening.

G. LEGMAN

La Clé des Champs
Valbonne (Alpes-Maritimes)
FRANCE

10

HOMOSEXUALITY

I. ON THE CAUSE OF HOMOSEXUALITY

QUITE the contrary to what is generally believed and maintained, homosexuality is not a form of erotic attraction to persons of the same sex. Homosexuality is a form of neurotic sexual impotence, or *flight from normality*, in which the homosexual is to a degree impotent (and the lesbian frigid) only with members of the opposite sex. With members of the same sex, for reasons to be considered below, the homosexual or lesbian does not feel the same panic fright or 'disgust' and is capable of functioning sexually, up to and including achieving orgasm. That is to say, the homosexual or lesbian is incapable of pleasurably fulfilling his or her proper biological function, mainly owing to having been driven off or frightened off the biologically normal sexual goal. This essential and usually very early sexual intimidation is the hidden cause of the enormous aggressive content of most subsequent homosexual relations. The erotic activities engaged in with members of the same sex become largely a charade, not of love nor even of sexual attraction, but of repeated and organized expressions of hostility. This hostility is sometimes unconscious, though in many homosexuals it is flamboyantly the main part of their activity. In all cases it is to be considered the result of having been driven off the normal and original sexual goal, usually during childhood, by the domination and authoritarian power of the parent or parent-surrogate *of the same sex:* for the male homosexual by the father; for the lesbian by the mother.

Analytically considered, the sexual and parasexual activities of all homosexuals are usually therefore seething with aggression. This is sometimes self-directed masochistically as the easiest way out and as creating the least feelings of guilt. At best, homosexuality expresses itself compulsively, and very often on a wholesale and obviously unsatisfying basis, in erotic gestures unconsciously intended to placate the feared and hated parent or authority-figure of the same sex, and to triumph over him (or her) simultaneously in a secret genital way.

Persons of the same sex are therefore not really loved at all by the homosexual, but are hated, sometimes just below the level of consciousness, but often violently and visibly, as in the *macho* poses of prize-fighting and wrestling, hunting, spying, 'blood sports,' war, intense business and game competitions, and open sado-masochistic ('S. & M.') tortures and whippings. The physical sexual activities engaged in are essentially either dominations of the sexual partner – whether oral, genital, or anal – or efforts of submissive conciliation through the same organs. In many cases the sexual partner is commonly dropped at once, after only one single sexual or sado-masochistic interlude, owing to the homosexual's being overwhelmed by fear and guilt as to his hostility, whether hidden or overt. A new partner is sought immediately, and the whole cycle is repeated again, year after year. This type of Don Juanism or 'oncing' is also encountered, though it is far less common, in heterosexual relationships; and all Don Juans (of all sexes) are for that reason analytically assessed as unconscious homosexuals, who spend most of their time fleeing from their latest 'conquests' and looking for new ones – also soon to be fled from in panic self-hatred and disgust. Don Juans are great travellers, making available an endless supply of new victims. *Dropping people suddenly* is also very typical of neurotics. This 'professional infidelity' makes spying and cruelty easier.

It should be observed, and would save endless heartbreak if it were observed, that most lesbians and a large percentage of male homosexuals purposely avoid ostentation ('camping'), and disguise themselves instead as normals, to protect themselves from legal and social discrimination. The 'flaming queens' among the male homosexuals, and 'butch (or diesel) dykes' among the lesbians, are by far in the minority. It is therefore easy for the others to marry, and they do often marry – the feminine type of lesbians in particular – but they seldom warn the innocent parties to these marriages of what the real situation is. Nor do they let them understand beforehand that their marriage will be a social sham and a sexual tragedy, and that the hated normals are really being cynically used in these cases as the homosexual's or lesbian's public protection or 'cover,' or for the purpose of having children, qualifying for monetary legacies, and the like.

Even when homosexual mock-marriages or liaisons of long

duration are set up, instead, with individuals of the same sex (though this is probably the least common of all forms of homo-sexual 'marriage' or ménage), the sexual activity or 'inter-personal construct' created is rarely a frank expression of love. More often it is visibly and floridly a charade of hatred and domination of, or resistance to, the other partner of the same sex, representing again the revenge against the background parent or authority-figure. There are exceptions to this general rule – the homosexuals who wish to befriend a young boy, and identify with him (like Beethoven with his nephew, Karl), while treating him as they wish they themselves had been treated by their fathers, or mothers – but even in these cases the hostile undertones generally skew and destroy either the relationship or the weaker and more 'feminine' partner, who is crushed under the psychological weight and under the professional shadow of the dominant or 'masculine' partner.

A famous example was the long-standing ménage of the American lesbian and surréalist writer, Gertrude Stein, with Miss Alice B. Toklas, who did the cooking, authored the cook-books, etc., but whose whole personality and even identity were simply swamped and taken from her by Miss Stein, who went so far as to write a purported *Autobiography of Alice B. Toklas:* not ghost-written for Miss Toklas, but publicly under-stood to be by and about Miss Stein. Homosexual vampirizing of the presumably belovèd partner of the same sex in such a 'marriage' of many years' standing, who is actually being aggressed and destroyed, can hardly be taken farther.

More will be found on the subject of these hostile com-ponents of homosexuality, and in very full detail, in later sections of the present chapter, particularly "The Tough Fag-got" and "Sado-Masochism," and in the introductions to Sections IV and V, "Fellation" and "Pedication," to which the interested reader is directed. For the present it will be of more value, I believe, to document here briefly the whole matter of the psychodynamics of homosexuality, as stemming from the fear of and the 'withdrawing in favor of' the parent or parent-surrogate of the same sex. The homosexual or lesbian in this way abandons normality, and becomes sexually impotent (at least as to satisfactory orgasm) with almost every person of the opposite sex who would normally replace, after adolescence, the original sexual goal: for the male homosexual the mother; for the lesbian the father. A much fuller discussion of this whole problem will be found in my pamphlet, *On the Cause of Homosexuality* (New York: Breaking Point, 1950), of which a predated piracy with the imprint of a non-existent 'Oscar Wilde Guild' was slipped onto the market a few years back. Only the second half of the pamphlet is by myself, the first half being a reprint from *Encyclopaedia Sexualis* (1936) of Dr. G. V. Hamilton's valuable but very prejudiced article, "Homosexuality as a Defense Against Incest."

The most remarkable thing about Hamilton's article – and the reason why I thought it worth replying to – is that, after demonstrating with monkeys, to his own and everyone else's satisfaction, that *homosexuality in males is a defense against stronger males* (in the human situation, the father), Hamilton proceeds – by long detours concerning the mothers of alcoholics, &c. – to forget completely what he has demonstrated, and to try to use it to prove its exact opposite: namely that male homosexuality is somehow a defense against a stronger female (the mother). The evident bias with which he proposes this theory – homosexuality as 'prophylaxis' for his patients (page 12), 'victims' of incestuous mothers twice on a single page (10) and so forth – makes particularly glaring his omission of the father from the homosexual scene. For what, after all, makes incest with his mother so frightening to the son, if not his father's strength?

In his *Three Contributions to the Theory of Sex* (1915), Freud states the case sweepingly, on the basis of twenty years of homosexual case-observations, and almost all psychoanalysts since have endlessly observed this same classic formulation:

> In all the cases examined, we have ascertained that those who are later inverts go through in their childhood a phase of very intense but short-lived fixation on the woman (usually the mother), and, after overcoming it, they identify themselves with the woman and take themselves as the sexual object. That is, proceeding on a narcissistic basis, they look for young men resembling themselves in persons whom they wish to love as their mother loved them. (*Basic Works*, p.560 n.)

In this earliest formulation by Freud on the subject – later elaborated in his study of *Leonardo da Vinci* – the homosexual's repressed love for his mother is by no means presented as the cause of homosexuality, but simply as an observation regularly made in the analysis of homosexuals, and demonstrating basically that *homosexuality is a flight from incest with the parent of the opposite sex*. The temptation to such incest is, however, clearly a mere prerequisite, since it is always present yet does not always lead to homosexuality. It is in the necessity for flight that the deeper and essential cause of homosexuality must be sought.

Obvious as it may now seem, in the light of the much-ridiculed 'poetic' anthropologizing of Freud's *Totem and Taboo*, that this necessity for flight from sexual normality can only stem from the strength of the parent of the same sex, whose sexual prerogative or 'property' the incestuously-desired parent of the opposite sex is considered to be – or, often, from fear of the social surrogate of this strength embodied in the incest-taboo, without any actual hostile or threatening action or even presence of the parent of the same sex – it took years for Freud to get from the homosexual's repressed love for his mother to the father who makes necessary this repression :

'Retiring in favor of someone else' (says Freud), has not previously been mentioned among the causes of homosexuality. [In the homosexual male] the fear of the father is the most powerful psychic motive. In his imagination all women belong to the father, and he seeks refuge in men out of submission, so as to 'retire from' the conflict in favor of the father. Such a motivation of the homosexual object-choice must be by no means uncommon. ("Psychogenesis of a Case of Homosexuality," 1920; *Collected Papers*, II. 216, note 2.)

Finally, with the specification by Freud, in "On Certain Neurotic Mechanisms" (1922; *Collected Papers*, II. 241), of body-narcissism in the son, and fear of castration by his father, in punishment both for the incestuous wishes toward the mother and the resultant death-wishes or murder-attempts toward the father himself, as the effective threat by which the father clears his son from the field, the statement of the psychogenesis of homosexuality is complete. Dr. Otto Fenichel (in his *Outline of Clinical Psychoanalysis*, 1934, pages 244–64, as paraphrased by Hamilton) makes the statement direct and schematic: 'Homosexuality is a special outcome of the Oedipus-castration anxiety. In other words, the future invert so greatly fears castration as a punishment for his incestuous longings [for the mother] and his consequent death-wishes against the father, that he eschews heterosexual gratification as his consciously held erotic aim. If he copulates with women at all, it is usually for the sake of having children [sons!] or for his own reassurance. He typically speaks of heterosexual experience as unsatisfying.'

What makes hash of the violent accusations against their own mothers, and even more violent indictments of everyone else's mothers, commonly made (often in published books) by unavowed homosexuals, is the clinically observable fact that all homosexuals desperately love their mothers at first, and love them still under the homosexual veneer. It is the very extremity of this early love, in combination with the father's feared strength, that drives them ultimately, through guilt and fear, into homosexuality and the concomitant lunatic attacks on women. The original love for the mother, as observed by Freud, lies remarkably close to the surface, and plays a large part in the homosexual's subsequent life. Many homosexuals never do and never can leave their mother's side at all until she dies, maintaining, in all the impregnable innocence of filial love (sometimes at the age of sixty in the homosexual son) an intense closeness of which the erotic nature is at least partially demonstrated by the son's never marrying anyone else.

It is this lifelong clinging to the mother in unconsummated incest that observers like Dr. Hamilton see – or wish to see – as the mother clinging to her son. Though the mother is seldom entirely innocent of such clinging, or even of excessive seductiveness, in cases of this kind, the fallacy of a total reversal of responsibility is easily demonstrated by the regular displacement of the homosexual's repressed love for his mother upon his sister. (First observed in Lessing's Sinngedichte, Bk. II, "On Turan." Byron, Beardsley, and Melville in his novel Pierre, are also good examples of which the record still remains.) Or upon some older woman if the actual mother dies, remarries, or drives him away. The homosexual interior decorator (wife-manqué) or society photographer or clothing designer who spends his whole life adoringly at the feet of 'nice old ladies' to whom he is not related – generally rich ones – not hesitating, however, to exploit them ruthlessly for social advantages, and even to cheat them crudely, sucking out every dollar the traffic (*read:* titty) will bear, can hardly be said to be clung to by any evilly erotic mother. It is very obviously he who is doing most of the clinging.

As a very striking example, consider the case of the then 30-year-old Scottish zoölogist, later turned novelist, Norman Douglas, the most imperturbably self-advertising literary homosexual of this century outside of France, where homosexuality has been legal since the time of Napoleon, and the 60-year-old French woman novelist, 'Ouida' (Louise de la Ramée). Though this lady was twice his age, impoverished, and long past her prime, as Douglas records in *Alone* (1921) p. 112–13, he tried very hard, though unsuccessfully, to get her to live with him in Southern Italy. Since he was in any case married, she wisely evaded him, and despite a long correspondence they never actually met in person. Douglas' little literary revenge is the rather petty – in the homosexual jargon, 'bitchy' – conclusion: 'I dedicated to her a book of short stories; they were published, thank God, under a pseudonym, and eight copies were sold.' This was *Unprofessional Tales* (1901) by 'Normyx.' In fact, however, as Douglas later admitted to his bibliographers. McDonald and Woolf, this first work of fiction 'from his pen' was actually produced under the tutelage of another mother-figure, his wife Elsa FitzGibbon; only one of the stories, "Nerinda," being by himself.

There are some obvious exceptions to this very usual format of the homosexual's clinging to old ladies, especially when it is the mother-figure herself who is clearly the more clinging, but even then the willingness of the homosexual to remain in such a situation, or to insist upon it, sometimes at an advanced age, whether with his own mother or some other elderly woman, demonstrates clearly the repressed sexual nature of the attraction. A most extraordinary example of this kind of sexless affair was that of the English homosexual dilettante, Horace Walpole, in the late 18th century, with the aging Marquise du Deffand, already in her sixties and blind, who was formally forbidden by Walpole ever to mention the word 'love' in her letters to him – she was openly desirous of a sexual or at least a 'sentimental' affair – under threat of refusing to see or correspond with her any longer, if she ever again so much as hinted at such 'sentiment.'

The external aspects of this whole embarrassing story are briefly related by Jean Seznec in *The Listener* (London, 11 Dec.

1969, p. 825-6), but in the dishonest format still and quite unnecessarily common in British literary criticism, carefully avoiding the key word *homosexuality*, which would give the whole thing away, and which is therefore still thought of as too dangerous in the highly aggressive homosexual milieu of British literary criticism. (If I may be allowed one crashing understatement.) Instead, Walpole's perfectly classic 'old auntie' *cum* grandmother liaison is explained away in the *Listener* article by careful silence and sly misdirection, and we are told that Walpole's panic fright of the marquise's irrepressible sexual elbowings in the fourteen years he frequented her (from his 48th to his 62nd year, in 1780, when she died) was due simply to his being 'afraid of ridicule,' presumably for having so much older a mistress.

Similar unachieved epistolary love-affairs by famous but unavowed homosexuals, especially in the theatre – called 'closet-queens' in homosexual jargon – include those of Alexander Woollcott, and of George Bernard Shaw with Ellen Terry, in their *Letters* published in 1931. Shaw's resistance to physical sexuality, not only in this well-publicized fake love-affair (he comes off very poorly indeed in the *Letters*) but also in all his plays, is usually 'explained' on the even more delightful grounds that he was a vegetarian!

The 'nice old lady' who is pointedly *not* the homosexual's actual mother, is the commonest cliché of modern homosexual fiction, Gertrude Stein serving this purpose in the fiction of Ernest Hemingway, as in his life. All the young and sexually available women in such fiction tend to be described as either the guaranteed unfuckable 'fag-hags' and lesbians, who are the writers' drinking-pals and friends; or else as the worst kind of castratory bitches, in the social and sexual senses both. (Sometimes the two types telescope, as they do in real life, and it is the 'fag-hags' and lesbians who are the castratory bitches, but it is not often considered sporting to mention this.) Once the female characters hit the menopause, however, and are presumably 'safe' – that is to say, take on completely the unavailability of the mother as sexual partner – they need no longer be attacked sexually, and only an occasional irrepressibly erotic spoil-sport like the Marquise du Deffand must be slapped down and kicked out of bed. With this curious contradiction that while, to homosexual novelists and other deep thinkers, all *mothers* in the western world are nothing but frightful and evil 'Moms' (or 'Jewish Mothers,' the evillest and presumably therefore the most erotic of all), the 'nice old ladies' are the salt of the earth. See further my monograph, *Love & Death* (1949), the two final chapters. "Avatars of the Bitch-Heroine" and "Open Season on Women."

It would perhaps be unkind to list the various novels in English and French about overt or covert homosexuals and their mothers, virgin-sisters, grandmothers, theatrical 'crushes,' and such-like mother surrogates, from Proust and his confidantes to George Santayana's *The Last Puritan* and on. (As his title suggests, Santayana's explanation is old-fashioned 'puritanism.' What next?) One has only to leaf through the standard productions in recent years of the Truman Capote – Gore Vidal – Tennessee Williams axis, or, once smuggled in from France as the cream of the homosexual crop, Jean Genet's *Our Lady of the Flowers*, specializing in sacrilege, sadism (against women and little girls), and descriptions of 'the taste of spunk' &c. &c., all in Céline and Henry Miller's say-the-first-damn-thing-that-comes-into-your-head style, which in any case goes back to the early 16th century in Italy and Spain. There have been too many claptrap homosexual novels since to bear listing, and I leave the job to those who care.

The only such novels of real interest are those, like that of the actress known as Viva's *Superstar* (New York, 1970) – marvellously written, the female equivalent of Henry Miller's *Tropics* – and John Rechy's *City of [Dreadful] Night*, published at the beginning of the New Freedom in the 1960's, authentically describing the snakepit of big-city homosexual prostitution and the thousands of young men caught up in it every year in all Western countries. Most remarkable in this line is the bitterly titled *Gov't Inspected Meat* (New York: McKay, 1971) by Dotson Rader, the one & only really first-class naturalistic writer – except for 'Viva' – appearing in America during the fabulously overrated 1960's, whose cruel and total close-up of the life of a male whore makes Rechy's *City of Night*, as one reviewer put it, 'seem like *Bambi* in comparison.' See also my own unpublished study, with Thomas Painter, *Homosexuals and their Prostitutes* (MS. New York, 1940) repositoried in the Kinsey Institute for Sex Research, Indiana University, the first work written on this subject in English except for Stephen Crane's lost or perhaps apocryphal *Flowers in Asphalt* (ca. 1892). A well-researched but utterly immoral recent work also exists, under the title *Greek Love* (New York, 1964) by 'J. Z. Eglinton', which goes so far as to deplore the illegality of homosexual seduction of minors.

On the same subject, but at quite another end of the spectrum, is the posthumous homosexual confession, *My Father & Myself* (London, 1968) by J. R. Ackerley, which is probably the meanest and most sordid work of anti-family revenge ever published, and a total object-lesson in what has been said above as to homosexual hatred of the intimidating father. The author practically eviscerates himself in one of these long *Quest-for-Corvo* type of homosexual paranoid trackings-down of a man's secret life – in this case the author's own father – to demonstrate laboriously in two hundred pages what the reader has understood perfectly after the first twenty. Namely, that his father had been a homosexual prostitute when a young, steel-cuirassed Guardsman (photo in uniform at page 48), and owed his later fortune 'and the title of Banana King' [!] to the generosity of one of his early clients, who is also tracked down.

In passing, we are treated to the excruciating story (Chapter 7) of how the author, when an officer in World War I, left his older brother to die on the battlefield, in No Man's Land, and forbade his soldiers to go out and bring him in when they wanted to do so. No reason is given for this example of brotherly homosexual love, but at the end of the preceding chapter we are told, among the 'few physical details' of his brother that come to the author's jealous memory, of the brother's 'abnormally long dark cock, longer than my own or any other I had seen. I remember feeling rather ashamed of it when we went to the baths together . . .' (A likely story.) All in all, Ackerley's hate-legacy is the prose equivalent of the modern bawdy British ballad, "Piccadilly," but utterly lacking in the song's forthright *style:*

Oh, my little sister Lily is a whore in Piccadilly,
    And my mother is another in the Strand;
My father hawks his arsehole to the guards at Windsor Castle,
    We're a filthy fuckin' family – ain't it grand!!

Few terms less appropriate have ever been chosen than the euphemism *'gay'* to represent the world of female prostitution – an inappropriateness already ticked off in a famous cartoon in the London *Punch* a century ago – and more recently for male homosexuality. (As in the cruel jest, "*Gay is fag spelled backwards.*") This apparently does not strike the writers of books – as, for example, Donn Teal's *The Gay Militants* (1970) – on the subject of the American homosexuals' aggressive tactical blunder of confronting the police recently, in 'fire-queen' style, instead of quietly lobbying, as in England, for the repeal of the anti-homosexual laws. And even more strikingly, a homosexual guide-book, *The Gay Insider* (1971) by John Francis Hunter, thumbnail outlined in a remainder catalogue with perhaps thoughtless candor as an:

> Eclectic guide to where male homosexuals can find love, companionship, liberation, good gay food, a crash pad, new friends, a church that cares, *torture tools*, VD treatment, etc., anywhere in Gay America ... [italics added]

Homosexuality is, I believe, the only kind of love that advertises itself as being operated with '*torture tools.*' Between a 'church that cares' and 'VD treatment.' Let the buyer beware. In any case, 'Gay' here is obviously the equivalent of *sick*.

The almost total lack of folk-material or any type of humor concerning lesbians and lesbianism makes it necessary to deal with this psychological malady here from a literary or socio-logical viewpoint, if it is to be dealt with at all. Lesbianism has always been much more secretive than male homosexuality, both as to its sexual goals *vis-à-vis* other women, and its hatred of and castratory fantasies concerning men. The 'camp' tradition is almost entirely that of male homosexuals and their female aides, or 'fag-hags and culture-vulvas.' Overt lesbians will seldom descend to anything even approaching it, except as a very private joke. Only in the late 1960's, under cover of the various Women's Liberation agitations in America and else-where, has lesbianism thrown off its mask – and still not entirely – as in such astoundingly frank man-killing and man-castrating 'utopian' and 'revolutionary' fantasies as Valerie Solanas' *S.C.U.M. (Society for Cutting Up Men) Manifesto*, published in New York, 1968, which makes all the rest of the Lib literature up to that date sound like public-relations pap. Unquotable except by the page, I leave this fabulous highwater-mark of literary eccentricity and the poisoning of the relations between women & men to the cultural historians who had better not overlook it! But I am pretty sure they will.

As Miss Solanas felt, quite correctly, that so violent a program as hers should be accompanied by some at least token
action of matching violence, she followed up its publication
with a publicity-oriented murder attempt against certainly the
one most improbable and inappropriate male victim in America,
Mr. Andy Warhol, the well-known creator of homosexual
'camp' movies. For this murder-attempt, Miss Solanas curiously
dressed herself not in men's dirty slacks, as was her usual habit
– the standard phallic symbol of female protest in recent years
– but in her prettiest dress (for the death-wedding) with cosmetics to match. This should certainly suggest to any reasonable
observer that *all* lesbian statements as to hating men express
a top-level hostility only, and are to be taken with the same
grain of analytic salt as the similar homosexual statements as to
hating women and mothers, whether 'Jewish moms' or otherwise. It is from the lesbians of the world that we would really
like to hear some statements about the mother-hating which is
their hidden problem.

I have tried, in *Love & Death* (1949) p. 78 and following, to
show the logical infrequency, owing to the lack of status for
the dominated sex, of lesbianism under patriarchy. During the
dominant and ascendant period of *patria potestas*, a woman in
the situation that makes a man homosexual (fear of the parent
of the same sex, preventing competition for the parent of the
opposite sex), cannot really become a lesbian, since women
under patriarchy are presumably 'inferior' and unlovable, and
instead becomes *frigid*, at least with men. Frigidity should therefore be considered as halfway to lesbianism. Or, rather, lesbianism should be assessed just as male homosexuality is here
assessed, as a form of impotence (frigidity with men) taken to
its ultimate point. *It is very important to realize that, with the
end of patriarchal dominance, or under 'matriarchy,' with increased status for women, female frigidity would reach a cultural peak and be massively replaced by outright lesbianism.
Meanwhile, with the end of the father's dominance, male homosexuality would ultimately disappear, to be replaced by an
enormously widespread female-dominated masochism in men.*
To a degree this is actually happening already – which is what
writers like Gore Vidal (and Hemingway and Thurber and Philip
Wylie earlier) have been blindly driving at. But the self-congratulatory huzzahs of the new post-Kinseyan homosexual 'Gay
Liberation' have somewhat deafened observers to the actual

arriving echoes of pussy-whipped masochism.

Lesbianism in Europe had its heyday in France immediately after the breakdown of patriarchal authority in the Revolution of 1789, whose early goddess or firebrand was the lesbian and prostitute, Théroigne de Méricourt, who later went insane after being publicly whipped and rejected by the Revolutionary women of Paris. (This should make the first real Women's Liberation movie.) It reached its height, in literature at least, from the 1830's of 'George Sand' (Baroness Aurore Dudevant, who began the fad of men's clothes worn by women, a fad now in the 1970's reaching crisis proportions), to the lesbian-worshipping decades of the sado-masochist poets Baudelaire and Swinburne, and the homosexual Verlaine.

It may be observed in all periods of history where patriarchy collapses, that the predominantly male homosexual and female masochist characters – as well in the life of the culture, as in its literature and art – rapidly disappear, and are replaced by the similarly matching female homosexual and male masochistic characters. The signs are only too clear, socially as also clinically, that another such period is now at hand in both Europe and America, where homosexuals again, as just before and at the beginning of the Hitler era in Germany, are organizing feverishly and throwing off their earlier 'closet' disguises, in the frank hope of joining the fake-revolutionary (neo-fascist) 'Wave of the Future,' and somehow achieving social and political power. Meanwhile, the numbers of male homosexuals actually coming forward publicly – even in England, where this has now been legalized – are ludicrously small, by comparison with the previous claims of tens of millions of homosexuals ('One man in five!') made on the basis of Kinsey's faked and indefensible extrapolations of his sex-questionnaires of 5000 eastern U.S. white college-boys upon the whole U.S. population and even on that of the world. That the coming neurosis among men, both sexually and socially, is not homosexuality but *masochism* is not yet widely understood.

Oscar Wilde represents classically everything pitiful and flighty in the homosexual literary character at least. In particular the infantile inability to take oneself or anything else *seriously*, and the cynical substitution of back-door influence and 'pull' for real art or technique. This gives the clue to the profound sociological problem really posed by homosexuality, at the level of art and culture. Omitting from the discussion the heavily homosexual culture in the patriarchal Orient and Levant, for many centuries; in the 15th and 16th centuries in Italy and the rest of Europe, straight through to the mid-19th century of Whitman and Melville, many homosexual artists and writers were absolute titans, while the mere flibbertigibbets of the Oscar Wilde type hardly appear at all. Or else are mere footnotes, less literary than the unimportant froth of society life, for example the 'soft young Gentlemen' and 'Macaronis' of the late 18th century in England, and the matching French 'Incoyables' immediately after – so called because they affected the lisping inability to pronounce the letter r.

Meanwhile, as just stated, a striking percentage of the very greatest artists and literary men (possibly also musicians, but the data are lacking) were clearly homosexual during this whole tremendous sweep of five centuries, which was also the greatest period of Western literature, music, and art. During the century now just past, following the 1850's and '60's, the trend has drastically changed, and the literary or artistic homosexual has everywhere become typically the Wildean trifler or fake-artist. This type is still a principal plague on the literary and art scenes today, promoted into brief and precarious prominence and prosperity strictly through the influence of similar minuscule fakers and politicians in literary criticism, art propaganda, musical and theatrical balderdash and other 'camp,' and especially in the organization of foundation grants and subsidies – that sad mockery of the triumphs of art patronage in Renaissance Italy. The so-called 'Homosexual International.'

What was the cause of this disastrous cultural change? It seems to me that the preceding discussion of *the basic neurotic cause of male homosexuality in the fear of the strength of the father or father-surrogate as represented by the culture itself,* gives the answer. For five centuries in Europe, royal & noble patrons – even a few crass millionaires like Petronius' Trimalchio, toward the end, with the rise of monopoly capitalism – were in fact the rising world-powers, and the dominant cultural and family figures proper to intimidate and frighten a boy-child into giving up the mother-image, with resultant homosexuality. In those centuries, therefore, the homosexual artist could still be a titan – Michaelangelo is, forever, the greatest of examples – matching the titanic father-figures calling him forth, and to whom his sexual neurosis, and perhaps even his art, are a form of defiant social submission and sexual placating. (The case of Beethoven, gruellingly exposed in the Drs. Sterba's *Beethoven and his Nephew*, London, 1957, is too excruciating to do more than mention here.)

When, during this last century from the 1860's on, the accelerating collapse of the formerly triumphant system of monarchy and patriarchy made itself felt throughout Europe – when even countries like America and France, as they have only now realized, began their downward spiral into the morass of cynical materialism and money-grubbing, from the time of the American Civil War onward – the type of son who still felt intimidated, or even inspired, by that type of fake-patriarch or fake-patriarchy now current could obviously no longer compare with the titans of the true and ascendant patriarchy that had preceded. When fathers have become nothing, the sons who succumb to them become nothing indeed. The homosexual artist – in fact, every artist – linked to a world in its ascendant, rose. The homosexual artist, and any other artist, now so foolish and weak as to be linked in his neurosis to a world that is sinking and dying, must and will also sink and die with it. There is a warning here for those who will take warning. And who may yet escape. Homosexuality is the least part of the danger.

Homosexuality will last at least as long as the patriarchy which originally called it forth, and will necessarily become increasingly open and self-advertising as patriarchal capitalism writhes itself, with increasing terribleness, to death. The personified Machine is today the prime castrating and homosexualizing terror, since fathers personally have lost much of their status in the face of it. The intense need to dominate machinery physically, as in the crude homoerotic ritualism of the motorcycle-hoodlum cult; or to ingratiate oneself servilely with The Machine in its more terrifying and powerful forms – jet-planes, space-rockets, Atom Bombs, big technological know-how and the Big Money that controls it – is the resultant homosexual pattern today, whether in flattering *Fortune*-style sycophancy to millionaire 'aristocrats' (and *chichi* fashion-magazines and gossip-columns for their wives), or in the simple fascistic fantasies of science-fiction, the sickest literary phenomenon of our time.

The basis for the inevitable homosexual tie-up with spying, political Jesuitry, and fascism – as the ultimate patriarchy – is *fear*, whether in Germany, Washington, Hollywood, or elsewhere. The underhandedly 'feminine' or 'drag' and transvestist

arts of spying, terror-propaganda (*i.e.* machanized gossip), religious and occult faddery (not to mention literary), and similar
intellectual dirty-work necessary for softening up the population, are turned over to homosexuals, especially in the mass-
media, politics, the police, and the universities. Not so much
through any cellar-laid plots – though there are surely plenty of
those, even at the classical Oedipal level of assassinating presidents and other cynosure father-figures – as by the homosexuals' being fatally attracted to the work. Either as a placating
of the powerful father-figure, or as a roundabout and backdoor
way of triumphing over him and arriving, in ambush and disguise, at *strength through weakness,* light through darkness, and
similar surréalist and fake-révolté slogans. No longer needed
after the putsch, the homosexuals are then cleaned out – perhaps Roehmed out would be more reminiscent – in another
Night of the Long Knives.

In the early 1950's serious efforts were undertaken by influential British homosexuals, principally in politics, law, literature, religion and the like, to bring the British legal position
up-to-date with the *Code Napoléon,* by which, in France for a
century and a half, homosexual acts between consenting adults
had not been considered illegal. By the 1960's the groups backing this modernization of Anglo-Saxon sexual law had taken a
good deal of strength from the international publicizing of the
various permissive Kinsey Reports, and the general 'demythific-
ation' of sex in the public prints and public attitudes to which
this led: the rather precarious and possibly temporary 'New
Freedom.' (I have noted the relationship of this movement to
the pioneering pro-homosexual efforts, half a century earlier, of
Magnus Hirschfeld's Berlin 'Institute for Sexual Science,' in *The
Horn Book,* 1964, p. 112. See also *Rationale: First Series,* chapter
8.III.7, pages 536–7.)

By the end of the 1960's, the proposed liberalization of British
law had been achieved as to homosexual acts (only) between
consenting adults. The similar liberalization of American laws
has of course been proposed by homosexual groups, but seems
as yet very far from being achieved owing to the far greater
anti-homosexual prejudice in America, even at surprisingly
high governmental levels. The pro-homosexual propaganda has
therefore been intensely stepped up at the present time, in
America, and is in many ways its own worst enemy. It has also
attracted eager support from allied groups that can only be an

embarrassment, as for example transvestist entertainers (especially rank in recent England and Japan), self-castrated 'transsexuals,' homosexual clothing-designers, always anxious to promote transvestism and fetichistic wearing-apparel for all sexes on any or no excuse, and especially from the hateful lunatic fringe of Women's Liberation – a movement that has an exceptionally large lunatic fringe, now in its opening years, for a rather small rational cadre or fabric. A fringe whose avowed plan is to hate, castrate, and destroy all men, and who therefore gladly accept the male homosexuals who are their counterparts, as typifying just the kind of castrated men they would like to create. With friends like that, the homosexuals of the world do not need an enemy.

I have been accused – by ex-hustlers, authors of homosexual fiction, and similar unbiassed observers – of shouting in *Love & Death*, 'The homos are coming!' What I said, page 91, naming no persons, was 'The air is filled with shouting ... "The women are coming! Kill all the women!"' But let us let this particular projection of guilt pass. Homosexuality is making a great deal of noise in the world today, and even imagines itself to be gaining converts and numerical strength. This is a delusion based simply on the fact that many former covert homosexuals or 'closet queens' are dropping their public cover, owing to increased sexual permissiveness in the West. Homosexuality is not hereditary, cannot be created hormonally, and is not infectious, except at the level of the sexual intimidation and seduction of adolescents. Normal heterosexual adults cannot be transformed into homosexuals – no matter what homosexual acts they may briefly engage in, as in jail – and all serious attempts at homosexual proselytizing have proved and must prove ludicrous. Homosexuality is entirely environmental in cause, and is the direct result of a dominant and sexually repressive patriarchy, now on its way out, which male homosexuality cannot survive by more than one generation.

As I have tried to show more explicitly above, what is really happening is that a wave of social and sexual masochism in men, and frigidity and lesbianism in women, is now engulphing the Western world, as patriarchy grinds to its frightful end under the threat of the Machine. This is far from being the same thing as a resurgence of male homosexuality, even in the type of 'panic homosexuality' that I would postulate, in which the male masochist attempts to *escape into homosexuality* as a lesser evil than his masochism. Indeed, this is hardly an escape, since there are still only too many evilly grinning 'S. & M.' (sado-masochist) homosexuals waiting for him with 'torture tools,' at his ill-chosen Appointment in Samarra. In the long run, the homos are not coming. They are going. Kinsey and his imitators, and their faked figures and extrapolations and Hollerith-computer prophecies to the contrary, there is no future for homosexuality.

II. HOMOSEXUAL RECOGNITIONS

Despite the accusation by an embattled British critic, Brigid Brophy, in a review of the First Series of this work in *The Listener* (London), that I have villainously excluded homosexual jokes from that series of 'clean' dirty jokes, and am including them now among the 'dirty' dirty jokes out of nasty prejudice on my part, the fact of the matter is that it is the folk-approach to these materials which forces the inclusion of homosexual jokes among the 'dirty-dirties,' and not my own perfectly open prejudice. As differentiated from jokes and folklore, literary homosexual materials accord themselves any number of disguises, usually mock-heterosexual. In fact, until the last dozen years in the English speaking world (and only a bit longer for André Gide and Jean Cocteau in France), the well-disguised literary 'closet-queen' has been the prevailing kind. The important difference is therefore that most of the authentically folk-materials, and *all* of the homosexual jokes, are elaborated by people who hate and fear homosexuals, or by homosexuals who hate and are willing to dirty themselves. While the literary materials are written by either disguised or openly homosexual authors, or by fellow-travellers clearly intending to appeal to the homosexual and snob audience, and cut themselves in on the gravy, whether under the usual disguises or as out-&-out 'camp.'

It should also be evident that the First Series of the present work was concerned with subjects of more or less normal and usual occurrence in our culture: birth, childhood, identification with animals and birds, heterosexual love, marriage, and even adultery, which is 'a part of marriage.' Everything touched upon there is handled with humor, sometimes mocking and cynical, but always with a tone of *wishing it were not so*. In this Second Series, the stage is darkened, the atmosphere lowers, and flashes of fire and steel fill the ominous background. Also, except for the scatological insults and jokes in the final chapters, all the subjects handled are of *abnormal* occurrence. They are not to be expected in the average life, and are subjects of far greater emotional danger and psychological terror : homosexuality, contact with (hideous) prostitutes and the diseases contracted thereby; food-dirtying, castration, and various other gruesome forms of sex-hatred and mutilation. Folk-humor combines all of these significantly in an area of dangerousness, violence, and open hatred. That it then deals with all of these – and, of course, with scatology – in a '*dirty*-dirty' way, and with purposely dysphemistic vocabulary and the search for disgusting images and situations, is also of obvious significance.

As the sections of the present chapter progress, the more and more direct and unequivocally hateful and violent stories are given, and this is the plan of all the chapters in the present work. It is therefore only in the final sections, 'Pedicatory Rape' and 'The Ganymede Revenge,' that the true nature and real psychological cause of homosexuality come to the surface in the folk-materials themselves, and, for those who are willing to understand them, are made perfectly clear against the background of the open fantasy-fears expressed in the final jokes to be given. It is understood, of course, that all these jokes tell a great deal more about the homosexual fears (and tolerances) of the presumed normals who tell them, than they can possibly tell about the avowed homosexuals that the jokes are mocking.

A considerable number of the stories that might well begin a chapter on the humor connected with, and mostly directed against, homosexuals, will be found at the end of the First Series of the present work, preceding, in the chapter on Adultery, 9.III,3, the section entitled "Masking Homosexuality." These are mostly stories and jokes in which the *sharing of the wife*, or the relationship with the adulterer, presents very clear homosexual components, usually of an unconscious nature. Or, at any rate, of a nature which the tellers of such jokes do not admit to be intended for, or tantamount to homosexuality. Many of these jokes, however, are such obvious swindle-operations or statements-in-disguise, that the whole of section 9.III.3 should be considered a part of the present chapter – a sort of modulation into the subject of homosexuality as it is presented in folk-humor. For the essential element in the homosexuality of such stories and humor is not any physical homosexual act, since such seldom take place, but *the rejection of the woman,* both personally and sexually, and the renouncing of any interest in the question of her physical fidelity to the unvirile or homosexual male to whom she is stated to be married.

The homosexual husband is shown, in particular, as coming upon the adulterous couple *in flagrante delicto,* but either doing nothing whatever to revenge himself and 'vindicate his honor,' or else displacing his anger or even his interest, pettily and absurdly, upon some detail or some article of food or furniture. Here is a typical story, of great age, many times retold: *One fairy tells another that he has come home and found his wife making love with a man!* (The word 'man' delivered with exaggerated tone, and hand-gesture of revulsion.) *"But, Bunny,"* says the other, "what did you DO?" "Do? The way I thlammed the door when I went out, they knew I wathn't pleathed!" (Usually collected with all the *s*'s in the final line exaggeratedly lisped, in what passes for the homosexual manner of speech.) In less frank versions, the husband is not openly stated to be homosexual, but he displays his unvirility by simply destroying, or selling – or merely threatening or *planning* to sell – the couch on which he has found the 'guilty' lovers.

All such stories can be traced historically at least to Heinrich Bebel's *Facetiae* (MS. 1508) II. 17, *"De quodam pulcherrimo vindictae genere,"* still very much alive in a modern form given in the First Series, p. 737, section 9.II.6, "Conniving at Adultery," in which: *The husband of the wife raped by the Mexican bandits is meanwhile forced at gunpoint to hold the bandit's balls up out of the hot sand. When the wife complains later that the husband has not acted the part of a man, he replies, 'Is that so? Why twice, when he wasn't looking, I let his balls drop in the hot sand!"* (Bebel's wittol husband makes 'many a dagger thrust' in the highwayman's cloak or saddle, while holding merely his horse.) It will be observed how much closer the modern version comes to open homosexual domination of the husband by the bandit – that is to say, open homosexual identification in the 'innocent' situation of rape – by having the husband actually handle the 'other man's' genital anatomy meanwhile.

Another story, in which again the husband's whole resentment is shifted to the unclosed door of the room in which the adultery has taken place, is given by several of the old Italian *novellieri* (Rotunda, Motifs J2752.1 and K1569.2). In a British form, the homosexual accent or lisp – the use of 'w' to replace 'r,' as with the French 'Incoyables' discussed in the preceding section – is used to key or uncode the homosexual situation, not anywhere directly stated. This story has also been retailed as a true anecdote of a French nobleman of an earlier century, and may well have happened more than once in fact. Here it is transposed to England: *'Lord Augustus has just caught Lady Jane in gallant [i.e. 'criminal'] conversation with young Harry Short. "My dear," he grumbled, "I do wish you would be more careful. Now supposing the butler had entered in my place, you would have made me appear positively wediculous".'* (Kimbo, *Tropical Tales*, Nice, 1925, p. 69.)

This is the social reality of homosexuality, since, as already discussed in the introductory chapter preceding, a large percentage of male homosexuals and an even larger percentage of lesbians do marry, and have probably always married, for the usual reasons of social convenience and monetary inheritance and advantage, as well as the best possible disguise for their homosexuality. The wife (more often the 'date' or frigid girl-friend) of a homosexual, ostentatiously presented in public and made use of in synthetic publicity 'romances,' is known in modern homosexual jargon as a *'bitch's blind;'* the homosexual, not the girl, being the 'bitch.' Jokes of the kind just cited, and those others on sexual possession in common and conniving at adultery, in sections 9.II.6 and 9.III.3, in the First Series earlier, are a kind of un-blinding, or giving away the show, sometimes quite unconsciously on the part of the tellers, but often coming perilously close to candor underneath the humorous rationalizations.

When other pretenses fail, that of insanity or 'nonsense' is always available to fall back on, at least in humor. One of the stories of homosexual tone most frequently collected has long antecedents in European folktales and humor, in the crashing *non sequitur* or absurdity with which it attempts to milk humor out of its finale or punch-line. But the importation of an obviously homosexual dénouement (sometimes with accent to match) is new in the modern or American form, already told in the First Series: *A man who has lost his door-key is caught by a policeman climbing in through the window, and invites the policeman in to prove it is really his home. "This is my living-room," he says, switching on the lights boldly; "and this is my six-thousand-dollar Spanish living-room suite." And so*

*on continuing through the whole house, including the bedroom,
where a man and woman are discovered fucking frantically on
the bed. "And this is my carved French bedstead, and that's my
wife," finishes the man. "Now let's go downstairs and have a
cup of coffee." They go downstairs, and as they are drinking the
coffee the policeman can't prevent himself from bursting out,
"But what about that guy up in the bedroom on top of your
wife?" "Oh him?" says the man, "fuck him! Let him make his
own cup of coffee!"* (N.Y. 1939.)

Seldom presented as a homosexual story – though I have on
occasion collected it with the final 'giveaway' of an out-thrust
gesture of the wrist to accompany the final line, a gesture presumably homosexual – there can be little doubt that the real intention of the story is to rationalize *by its irrationality* the indifference as to his wife's fidelity that the man cannot rationally
explain, anymore than can the tellers of the story. The *flight
into nonsense* as the best defense. In the older and non-
American form of the story, the punchline is far more nonsensical, but also wittier, in the style of the 'Irish Bull,' and the
wise-fool's *bon mot* in much Levantine humor. This is given as
collected in Bulgaria, in Jean Nohain's interestingly illustrated
Histoire du rire à travers le monde (Paris: Hachette, 1965) p.
334, with end-line, in translation: *"Here's my bed, and that's
my wife in it." "But who's that young man in bed with her?"
"Oh, that's me when I'm not here."*

Truth to tell, the horror that the average Man-in-the-street
expresses of the equally average homosexual – unconnected
in any way with the media and subterranean machinations of
public opinion pro or con, camp fashions, 'fag-theatre,' religions
of 'brotherhood,' and the like – is really an expression of fear.
The sort of fear implied in the folk-phrase, *"There but for the
grace of God, go I."* Victorian and Edwardian humor on the
subject of homosexuality was elaborately arch, as this was supposed to be an even more unspeakable secret than the enormous
and perfectly open street-prostitution in almost all countries
of Europe at that period. When references to homosexuality
came to expression at all in England, at any time from the 18th
century on, the mockery and loathing expressed was nevertheless very extreme, even when intended simply as humor on the
comedy stage, as in Garrick's *Pretty, Soft Gentleman* (about
1775). There is, of course, a double irony here, since the theatre
is now and has always been one of the main areas of homo-

sexual activity, as is also true of such other proto-theatrical forms of activity as carnivals, circuses, frontier life, and the church.

Until the ultimate scandal of the Wilde case in the 1890's, ladies were still presumed to maintain a discreet verbal reserve – pretendedly ignorance – about the matter of homosexuality, as about prostitution, and their efforts to avoid saying the awful word *bugger* were a favorite theme. As, a century earlier, in the nasty-nice verbal archness concerning anything sexual ascribed in Sterne's writings to nuns and young ladies of protected life in England and France. '*Some elderly ladies lately discoursing about a gentleman who had been sent for trial at the Old Bailey on the charge of "Sodomy," were interrupted by a young lady present, who at length so insisted upon knowing what crime had been committed, that one of the matron's replied: "He had done those things which he ought not to have done, and left undone those things which he ought to have done".*' (*The Cremorne*, No. 3: p. 76, dated 'March 1851,' but actually published in 1882 by Lazenby as sequel to his *The Pearl.*) The same joke situation is turned charmingly to the problems of normality, 'up-dating' the matter to include an allusion to Wilde, as recorded in the mid-1920's in the Wilstach MS., of American theatrical provenance: *A young girl of the period, who had just been married to an elderly roué at the time of the Wilde trial, asked her new husband exactly what it was that Wilde was guilty of. "He did it twice in one night."* It is worth recollecting that Wilde was married – and to a famous beauty – and that no small part of the tragedy of his over-publicized trial was its effect on their young children, whose names were suddenly changed, their real initials cut off their clothing traumatically, etc., as described in the memoirs of Wilde's son, 'Vyvyan Holland.'

A much more florid example, again playing up the presumed mystery (to women) of what homosexuality is really all about, dates at least from the Boer War, about 1900, when, as we are told, *The family of Queen Victoria used to read the German newspapers aloud, and came upon a reference, in an eye-witness account of an attack on the Boers, to the British soldiers advancing with shouts of "Kill the buggers!" The ladies of the royal family are perplexed as to the meaning of the word* bugger, *and finally decide that it must be a misprint for* burgher: *"Kill the burghers!" Queen Victoria is not entirely satisfied with this, and turns to the chamberlain. "James," she says imperiously, "What is a bugger?" "A bugger, Your Majesty," replies the courtier imperturbably, "is a man who does another man an injury behind his back."* (England, about 1927. An 1880's version is given in the rather superficial chapter on Victorian sexual humor in Ronald Pearsall's *The Worm in the Bud*, N.Y. 1969, p. 399.) In a grosser version, the butler (not chamberlain) replies: *"A bugger is an individual who enlarges the circle of his acquaintances."* This is obviously only a crude gag, and would not answer the stated question at all. Both also assume, incorrectly, that the principal or only homosexual act is pedication or anal intercourse.

The same is true of the never-to-be-forgotten punchline of an anonymous and continuously punning book-review slipped into the *Times Literary Supplement* at about the same period (London, 24 Feb. 1905, page 64, col. 3), concerning the expurgated edition of Oscar Wilde's *De Profundis*, then just published and making a certain stir:

> This is an unfailingly and now and then poignantly interesting work; it contains some beautiful prose, some confessions that cannot leave the reader unmoved and may even touch him a little with shame at his own fortunate rectitude ... and yet ... possessed by every wish to understand the author and feel with him in the utter wreck of his career, it is impossible, except very occasionally, to look upon his testament as more than a literary feat. Not so, we find ourselves saying, are souls laid bare.

This is noted by Robert Graves in his *The Future of Swearing and Improper Language* (revised ed. 1936) p. 91, apparently crediting the review to Christopher Millard ('Stuart Mason'), the bibliographer of Wilde. Aside from the final pun on *arseholes*, carefully announced by the parenthetical 'we find ourselves saying,' a further word-play may have been intended in 'every wish to ... feel with him in the utter wreck of his career.' Despite all allusions to the anus and anal intercourse in connection with Wilde, it seems far more likely, from everything about his character and his avowed tastes in boys, that he was not a pedicator at all, but a fellator. The characteristic differences are made very clear in an American manual of homosexual technique, *The Gay Girl's Guide*, a very rare mimeographed pamphlet privately issued, probably in Boston or Cambridge, Mass., in 1949, with imprint: 'A Phallus Press Publication,' and presumed author 'Swarsant Nerf' (copy: Kinsey Institute), which I have quoted at much greater length in *Oragenitalism* (New York, 1969) p. 232–5. The author observes: '... generally speaking, the orally minded [homosexuals] are the most concerned with the factors of youth, looks, and genital dimensions. Conversely, the ones who show no great interest in the genital dimensions, age or looks of their potential partners are very likely to be anally-minded, assuming they are not commercial [*i.e.* male prostitutes].' It is rather evident where Wilde stood in this hegemony.

The excessive innocence of the jokes on women who understand nothing about homosexuality, not even its name, is hardly more than a special form of the mock-innocent sexual 'mistakes' and misunderstandings of women, treated at length in the First Series, chapters 2.III–IV, and 4.I.3, "Purposeful Perversion." Hidden beneath is the unspoken realization that women are the rejected sex, so far as male homosexuality goes. And women respond in jokes, though seldom so responding in fact, by purporting to be as upset and angered by homosexuals as are many men. In actual fact, women are tempted to take a more moderate view as to homosexuals, whom they do not find either frightening or threatening in the way that men do. ("*There but for the grace of God, go I.*") Women also find it possible to discuss, with the overt and less hostile types of homosexuals, certain minor matters of presumed 'feminine interest,' such as hairdressing, cosmetics, lavish clothing, cooking, and interior decorating, in which normal men are seldom interested under patriarchy, and in which the homosexuals' arch and over-accentuated interest is seldom recognized by women as the anti-woman mockery and caricature that it is intended to be.

The real objection that normal women express to homosexuality is usually simply that it is such a 'waste of the available men,' as I have heard it phrased. Meaning that they are wasted, as far as most women are concerned, for the purely social activities of dates, dancing, escorting, and even marriage! Beyond that, women do not often demonstrate any anti-homosexual bias, except in connection with the homosexuals' *competition for all the other men.* Essentially, women seem to feel even a sort of flattery in the homosexuals' imitation of them, however caricatured this may be, since normal men – even

those who do not explicitly share the culturally proposed contempt for women – never express the desire to *be* women, in
the sense that women under patriarchy very often and quite
consciously wish that they had been born men. Which is why
they now disguise themselves in men's clothes.

At the even less normal level, it is a common neurotic symptom in women who are not at peace with their own sexuality,
to enjoy the company of male homosexuals, and the freedom
from sexual demands that they can generally count on in such
sub-erotic relationships. Another explanation of the inner
motivation of these so-called 'fag-hags' – given to me *jestingly*
by one of them – is that *"It's nice to think that there's something lower than a woman!"* (Compare with this the philan-
thropic attempts of Jewish liberals to ameliorate the position
of the Negro, matched by the attempts of at least one Negro
sociologist in recent years to improve the position of the Jews.)
Women of this type occasionally avoid homosexuals entirely,
even express an avowed hatred of them; but such women
consort pleasurably only with weak or masochistic men, or
'cured homosexuals,' whose 'oil they have changed,' as they
brag, and who are no real challenge in fighting it out with the
women for social and emotional domination.

As noted at the end of the preliminary section to the present
chapter, this is precisely the relationship between the lesbian
and man-hating fringe of the Women's Liberation movement,
and the homosexual males or other socially-castrated males
who are the only ones with whom such women feel at ease
and can drop their aggressive posture. Women of this type are
often conscious of the contradictions to which they are prey,
but the desperate thrusts toward normality that they sometimes
make, attaching themselves transiently to powerful and active
men with whom they over-identify at first, almost invariably
end in violence or divorce, when both parties find that the
woman can master neither the powerful man she has chosen
nor her desire to *be* a man.

A wartime joke, actually a reversal of a well-known story
given in the First Series : *'Rosie the Riveter gets married to a
fairy. So she comes home at 6 o'clock and he's got a lovely
supper cooked for her, and the table set with doilies and
flowers in the middle and everything. "Oh," she says, looking at
him in his organdie apron, "If you could only fuck!"'* (N.Y.
1945, supplied in manuscript by a girl working in a shipyard.)

This reverses a line usually said joculary of beautiful-but-dumb women: *"If you could only cook!"* but it has not been traced earlier than *Anecdota Americana* (1927) 1:29, in which it is put into the mouth of a Negro having intercourse with a she-mule. Is that clear enough?

Another jocular expression of the same problem: *The wedding night of the girl who has married a homosexual, as she describes it later to her mother. "Well, he laid me on the bed and undressed me completely. Then he undressed too. Then he put on all my clothes, and I haven't seen the son-of-a-bitch since!"* (N.Y. 1942.) This is a well-intrenched popular error, it being completely unknown at the folk level (and to many highly educated people) that the largest though not the most self-advertising percentage of male transvestites are *not* homosexuals but masochists. Just as the wave of female transvestites – in pants – now inundating the world is not actually composed of lesbians, though it often seems that way, but of girls and women struggling for equality with, or aggressive-sadistic domination over men.

In the end, the plight of the woman who has knowingly married a homosexual is that she must stand for being treated like a homosexual herself, which is usually the unconsciously-desired emotional position of such a woman in real life: if she cannot be a man, she is at least willing to be the equal or superior of a homosexual. In jokes such a wife is always presented as unwilling, with additional allusions to the probability that her husband will want to have anal, rather than vaginal relations with her. The Greeks being theoretically (after all these centuries of population expansion!) still given to homosexuality and specifically to anal intercourse, according to American folklore at least – and the Evzone soldier-dancers in their skirts and petticoats and pompomed shoes being thought of as proving this, though the Scottish soldiers' kilts are, contrariwise, thought of as offering easy optical proof of *their* virility – such jokes or gags usually make humorously insulting reference to Greeks. *The Greek bride who was so confused she didn't know which way to turn.* (Nightclub comedian, Florida, 1945, who, when he got a laugh with this line, topped it with: *Her husband was in-different.* Which got a tremendous laugh.) Almost any reference to 'Greeks' in a humorous context, in English, is nowadays likely to be understood as an allusion to homosexuality, in the same way that any allusion to 'Italian' or the 'Italian fashion' was so understood during the late Renaissance, in England and France, as seen in many satirists of the period.

Among the many jokes and puns on the presumed homosexual and pedicational, er, tastes of the modern Greeks: *The Greek wife who had a baby by accident. – The Greek wife who put her teats under her armpits so her husband could suck them.* (N.Y. 1965, the latter was given to me with the statement, 'That one was made up by somebody who knew how to milk a goat!') And so forth. Other examples, less mild, will be given in the later section V, "Pedication." It should be underlined that the whole thrust of these mock-Greek jokes is to imply that the husband is actually homosexual, and is having intercourse with a woman at all only as his marital duty. Compare the explanation given at the folk-level, as to how Oscar Wilde, though married to a famous beauty, could have fathered any children at all: " '*E just shut 'is eyes an' thought of Alfred!*" (Compare also *The Limerick*, No. 499.) The use of adulterous imaginings – homosexual or otherwise – during intercourse is discussed further in my *The Horn Book*, p. 110–11. This is precisely in the vein of a joke already noted in the First Series: *The high-society bride whose mother advises her to submit to her marital duty by covering her face with an American flag and* "*fucking for Old Glory.*" (Or with the Union Jack and "*doing it for England!*")

Several homosexual toppers or variants exist to the well-known story about 'tact' commonly told by children. See 2.V.1, page 154, in Series One. In the original: *A plumber (or bellboy) who opens a bathroom door unexpectedly and finds a lady in the tub, says "Excuse me, SIR!" He explains to his helper (or to the listener): "The 'excuse me' was politeness, but that 'Sir' was tact."* (Scranton, Pa. 1930.) Grammatical stories like this, which are of course only pretexts for the sexual situation, are more popular among children than is realized. No adult is all that interested in the exact difference between politeness and tact, or similar. As to the toppers, my favorite version (not really relevant here) is British: *'Lord Peter is defining "faux-pas" to his flunkey. "Well, now I come to think of it, you yourself provided a good example this morning." "I, m'lud?" "Yes. You will recall that her Ladyship and our distinguished visitor were out early picking blooms in the rose-garden? As they entered, her Ladyship, alluding to a thorn he'd had in his*

*hand, asked, 'Is your prick still throbbing?'" "Yes, m'lud."
"Well, on hearing this you dropped the tray of coffee you were
serving. That was a faux-pas!"'* (Chelmsford, Essex, 1953.)
This is all set up as a framework for her Ladyship's impossible
line. The joke is also notable in having no punch-line (except
that), the actual final line merely serving as a throwback or
delayed unveiling: the usual technique in bawdy-'innocent'
riddles. Observe also, of course, that the hidden element in the
joke, and that which actually gives it its humorous pleasure for
the listener, is the unconscious or implied wittoldry of the complaisant husband, winking at his wife's obvious adultery with
the 'distinguished visitor.' The humor is thus available at two
levels.

As already observed, the homosexual is often thought of as
'unfair competition' to women, *vis-à-vis* the available men.
People who perfectly seriously take this unscientific view are
unaware that the essential sexual choice of every individual is
usually made during puberty at the latest, and that grown men
cannot really be *seduced* into homosexuality, nor are they
homosexualized by temporary such contacts, for lack of 'anything better,' as in prison. Homosexuals profoundly believe
that they can homosexualize other men, and though this is
often quite true of seducing young boys it seldom has any
meaning at all as to grown men, for all the proud boasting of
homosexuals as to how many unconscious homosexuals or
'closet queens' they have 'brought out' or have taught to
'switch.' (*"I'd rather switch than fight!"* a gag motto, parodying
a 1960's cigarette advertising slogan in America, usually accompanied by a picture of theoretically super-tough males, often
tattooed, and covertly intended as the sado-masochist type of
homosexual or the similar masked homosexual type called
'rough trade,' who would 'rather fight than switch' – cigarette
brands, of course.) The same error or pretense is often made by
'fag-hags,' especially middle-aged ones, who explain that they
are really only weaning the poor homosexual boys they sleep
with back to normality, and that such boys are really all right
once they 'get their oil changed.'

*A minister with a chronic tic in his eyelid arrives in a strange
town, and asks a policeman where he can find a hotel. (Stage-
business of winking.) He is directed of course to a whorehouse,
where he innocently asks for a room with a bath. (Wink.)
"What kind of a girl you want?" asks the madam; "white?" "I*

don't want a girl," says the shocked minister. (Wink.) The madam leans over the desk and calls up the stairs. "Oh, Clarence! This one's for you." (D.C. 1947.) Often collected with the abbreviated punch-line: *"Oh, Percy!"* Like the great old English family-names of Milton and Seymour, now thought of in America as 'typically Jewish' forenames for boys, the great Germanic name, Percival (Parsifal), is considered typically homosexual, possibly owing to the legend of the extreme sexual purity of this hero in both the German and English forms of the chivalric romances.

The earliest version I have found of this story omits the elaborate rationalization and pantomime as to winking, but makes the competition of the homosexual with women even more explicit. It is given in Robert Graves' *Lars Porsena: The Future of Swearing* (London, 1927, ed. 1936, p. 22): '*A worried old country clergyman arrived [at a lounge frequented by Edwardian prostitutes] ... in search of a son of his who had run away from home with money from the Parish Organ Fund. A woman swooped down on him at once: "Are you looking for a naughty little girl?" The old clergyman beamed gratefully at her. "No, Madam, I thank you kindly all the same: I am looking for a naughty little boy." The woman threw up her hands. "I don't know what's to become of us poor women these days!"* '

As in many of the stories in the earlier chapters on "Fools" and "Women," the technique used here is that of artful misunderstanding, used to imply an attempted seduction, or sexual overture made to a woman, where none is intended. Here it is used in reverse, to imply a homosexual *rejection* of the woman, again where none is really intended. The most complex version, given in the second series of *Anecdota Americana* (1934) 2:408, fathers the tale on Oscar Wilde, as the legendary or prototypical homosexual of modern folklore, crossing him with the equally stereotypical character of the *bored* boulevardier or worn-out old roué. *Oscar Wilde is in a Paris whorehouse. Madam: "A lovely French girl, Monsieur? From Marseilles. Very salacious. True Latin tempérament ..." "No, thank you. I'm tired of French girls." "A lovely Swedish girl. Only fifteen years old. Very blonde. Wonderful spécialités." "No, I'm tired of Swedish girls. Do you happen to have a nice, fat-bottomed boy?" "Monsieur! I shall call a gendarme!" "Don't bother. Really, I'm tired of gendarmes too."* In another version the madam is not shocked and keeps trotting out every possible and impossible sexual partner including finally a *"Black Nubian goat – washed twice a day, Monsieur, drenched in finest perfume!"* *"Er, no,"* says the blasé boulevardier, *"but tell me, Madame, what have you got in the way of fish?"* (Brooklyn, N.Y. 1951, with hand-gestures of a fish swimming.)

The simplistic view of the situation, as to the competition between homosexuals and women, specifically prostitutes, is summed up completely and succinctly in two words in a joke given in *The Limerick*, p. 445, note 1284, dated to the song-collection *Unexpurgated*, published in Los Angeles in 1943: *Homosexual (passing whore in street): "Prostitute!" Whore (to homosexual): "Substitute!"* In a British version, rather arch, *Two nancy-boys walking down Regent Street see two whores lounging in front of a shop-window on the other side. One says to the other, "Algernon, look! Piwats!"* (Chelmsford, Essex, 1952.) This reverses the nature of the accusation, and makes women rather than homosexuals into the hated competition.

I. THE TOUGH FAGGOT

Conrad Aiken's *Blue Voyage* (1927), a product of the Harvard poets' group to which the late T. S. Eliot belonged, includes a number of passages in imitation of Joyce's *Ulysses*, but which, sadly lacking in the true Irish madness of Joyce, must try to make up for this by stringing flatly together vaudeville comedy materials and punch-line allusions to current jokes. Here is the one such most interesting passage from *Blue Voyage*, page 201:

> ... at the Orpheum [*vaudeville theatre*], in Boston, two weeks ago, dressed as a woman with a great big brass padlock hanging down behind, and biting a little Japanese fan – saying he'd been followed right to the stage-door by two sailors and a fireman – "Have you a little fairy in your home? [Parodying the slogan of the Fairy Soap company.] Well, we had, but he joined the navy!" "– and this guy went into a saloon in Chicago, leading a tiger on a leash! A big rattle-snake put his head out of his breast pocket, and he slapped it in again. When the tiger wouldn't lie down, he kicked it in the snout. 'Say!' says the bartender. 'The town you come from must be pretty tough!' ... 'Tough! You said a mouthful,

bo. That town is so tough it kicked us fairies out' " ... "You know that one about the lonely fairy in Burlington, Vermont, and the alarm clock? ... smothered it with kisses! I like that story." [*No more given.*]

Of particular interest here is the touch as to the *tough* homosexual pose or contradiction, since, to the folk-mind, the homosexual is the opposite of tough and is weak and unvirile indeed. Yet this joke neatly unveils what is perhaps the commonest of all homosexual disguises: that of super-toughness – the cowboy, the truck-driver, the athlete, the prize-fighter and bull-fighter, the explorer and animal-killer, and the professional soldier; all of these professions which turn out, on actual study, to be the rendezvous largely of homosexual sadistic types in flight from any public recognition of their essential sexual neurosis. I have discussed this further in "On the Cause of Homosexuality," at the opening of the present chapter. Of other interesting touches in Aiken's transcript of homosexual humor at the Orpheum in Boston in the middle 1920's, note the 'little Japanese fan' being bitten – probably straight out of Gilbert & Sullivan – and especially the chastity-belt padlock 'hanging down behind,' *i.e.* rectally, to protect the comedy homosexual from anal rape. The same sort of item is worn, but in front, as a rivetted boiler-plate chastity padlock, by the whip-handling Miss Raquel Welch – presumably 'the most beautiful woman in the world,' but here in her anti-sexual phase, no doubt, to all except ravening masochists – in Terry Southern's black-humor movie, *The Magic Christian* (1969). This might also be compared with a production of Alfred Jarry's deathless farce, *Ubu Roi* (a play-cycle which I have translated completely into English, New York, 1953), given in London in 1966, in which Mama Ubu was played in drag by a male actor with bare imitation-breasts which *lighted up* at various times, for comedy effect.

The joke included by Aiken, as to the *tough* fairy, is printed from folk sources in *Anecdota Americana*, 2:117, a few years later, and is still commonly encountered. In Newbern & Rodebaugh's *The World's Dirtiest Jokes* (Los Angeles, 1969) p. 197, a quite different form is given, leaving out the tiger and rattlesnake: '*A cowpuncher rode in off the range, on a charcoal grey horse, with a pink dotted-swiss saddle, and tied its satin reins to the hitching rail at the saloon. Then he pranced inside,* *adjusted his lavender chaps, and said in a high mincing voice,* "Where'th the fellowth?" *The bartender said,* "They're out at Boot Hill, hanging a queer." *So the cowboy boomed in a deep voice,* "NO SHIT?" ' Observe the artificial character of *both* the 'camp' and 'butch' acts here, and the pointed observation of their ease of reversal. In what is obviously a variant of this joke, all the emphasis is placed not on the fake virility of the homosexual's voice, but on his dog: *An obvious fairy goes into a bar leading an enormous, ferocious-looking dog. When he orders a drink the bartender says,* "Get outa here, you fag. We don't serve no fags here." "You'd better serve me," *says the homosexual,* "or I'll sic my dog on you." "Come on! Eighty-six! eighty-six!* [restaurant code-number, meaning "No service; undesirable person."] *Get outa here and take your husband with you, before I call a cop." "Alright," says the fairy ominously,* "I warned you – SIC HIM, MARCO!!" *The dog leaps instantly up on the bar, bares his fangs and snarls,* "Bowthie-wowthie!" (L.A. 1965; Newbern & Rodebaugh, p. 190.)

In Aiken's original "All us fairies" form, this is one of the essential and crucial American jokes, and should be recognized as such. It represents a clear resistance to the impossible pose of pretending to be ultra-tough – *"or else stand to be called a fag!"* It also correctly observes that the pose of toughness is not really virile at all, and implies that tough-guys are certainly to be suspected not only of blustering and over-reacting to their hidden cowardice, but also of simply being homosexuals putting on a tough-guy act. The same point was first frankly made, in connection with the mock-virile American hero, the bad-ass cowboy, in "The Myth of the Western Hero," in *Neurotica* (1950) No. 7: p. 3–7, by a group of writers signing themselves somewhat timidly 'Alfred Towne,' specifically noting that the moving-picture cowboy heroes 'are fantastic in their blatant homosexuality, and it takes no psychiatrically oriented audience to understand it.'

The morbid homosexual orality of Bret Harte's "What the Bullet Sang," glorifying its lethal kiss that kills the man it loves, is the perfect 'S. & M.' (sado-masochistic) example. Compare the Mafia 'Kiss of Death,' or Judas-kiss given by one man to another on the lips, to designate the victim. The death of the 'belovèd' male is not only what Bret Harte's bullet sang, but is also the not-very-secret message of a large proportion of homosexual literature, when it is not insanely attacking women: for example, Wilde's *Ballad of Reading Goal* in 1898, and the even more unpleasant gloating on the death of fine young men in A. E. Housman's *A Shropshire Lad* (1896), which inspired Wilde.

As to the pose of 'toughness,' whether leather-chap clad or not, I have noted in *Love & Death*, p. 18–19, the inherent homosexuality of the Superman theme, both Nazi and comic-book, as the real meaning of all this mock-toughness. Most professional fighters, paid killers, big-game hunters, stock-market operators, detectives, 'secret agents' and plain spies are *disturbed characters* in the psychiatric sense (no one else is attracted to the work), and the percentage of homosexuals in such professions is exceptionally high. These trends and personalia culminate in the psychopathic western killer on the American frontier in the 1870's, 'Wild Bill Hickok, our own homosexual hero out thar where men were men – with his long silk stockings and his Lesbian side-kick, Calamity Jane – who are too unvirile to throw off fear, and kill as criminals. Instead, unseen and unsuspected in some corner, they put on a black mask, a sheriff's badge and a Superman suit, and do all their killing on the side of the law.' One much prefers the outlaw types, dangerous as they may be, as approaching somewhat more honestly their fantasy ideal of rebellious Oedipal strength.

2. SADO-MASOCHISM

Other than in the crucial joke quoted above from Aiken, the recognition is almost never made in folk humor that the tough-guy is really homosexual, and that the homosexual commonly disguises himself as 'tough.' Instead, the homosexual appears in humor as utterly weak and ingratiating, and especially in sado-masochistic situations where he invariably is the beaten and humiliated party. *The secret of homosexuality* is that it is almost always a deeply hostile relationship, masked as eroticism or love, in which the homosexual acts out his hatred of the powerful father-figure, societal or real, who has driven him out of the competition for the mother and all other women. As such, the homosexual does fit more logically into the pattern of the defeated victim than of the brutal victor. Homosexuals, however, may play either of these parts and sometimes both: alternating rôles with different partners. The masochistic homosexual, which includes the passive pedicant, allows to be acted

out upon his body the humiliations and punishments he himself would like to inflict upon more powerful males representing the father, but which he is too intimidated to wreak on
anyone but himself. Sudden reversals of this pattern, as are
always likely in sado-masochism, are made possible by the
underground achievement of power, as in such professions as
spying and police-work, where the homosexual spy and inquisitor has been a standard figure since the time of the
Inquisitorial torturers of the Middle Ages to their more recent
recrudescence in the Nazi Gestapo and similar secret-police
organizations. More on this matter will appear in the main
section following, "The Short-Arm Inspection."

In *The Guilt of the Templars* (1966) pp. 104 and 116–34, in
discussing homosexual ordeals and initiations, and in various
passages of my books *Love & Death* (1949) especially in the
section "Open Season on Women," and in *Oragenitalism* (1969)
p. 227–31, I have tried to show that homosexuality is of no
danger or even importance socially when it is a *love* phenomenon, being then merely an unfortunate and accidental perversion or misdirection of the biologically proper aim. Homosexuality takes on social importance, usually of very sinister
dimensions, only when it is overwhelmed by the frustration of
normal sexuality that lies at its base, and becomes instead a
hate phenomenon.

The hatred against the presumed sexual object or belovèd
male, as in Bret Harte's "What the Bullet Sang," will be considered again in section 10, IV.2, "Fellation as Rape." From the
social point of view, what is more important is the homosexual's hatred of the 'normals' of both sexes. Here homosexuality attempts to wreak its revenge, and express its
anti-sexual rejections, by means of stealth, spying, indirection,
propaganda tricks, and all the palette of subterfuges of those
considering themselves weak or overpowered or socially out-
cast: the sort of thing now coming into public attention under
the homosexual jargon term 'camp' (from the French *camper*,
to strike challenging poses or otherwise make oneself conspicuous). This conversion of normal love into abnormal hate
is true both of male homosexuals and of lesbians, and is particularly prominent when homosexuality is the main line or
secret spring of any social or religious movement, as for
example in the Nazi party in recent 20th-century Germany, of
which the homosexual orientation and leadership was openly

admitted at the time of its presumed extermination in the "Night of the Long Knives." Compare our own new fake-*révolté* motorcycle gangs.

The necessity for the Homosexual International, or Sexual Fifth Column, to operate in disguise where it is socially destructive, as differentiated from its perfectly open seductory activity where it is merely a sexual inversion, is made obvious by the open hatred and detestation expressed toward homosexuals by normal men (and women occasionally), at the conscious level of almost all folklore and of most recorded history. The earliest date in this social abhorrence of the homosexual is that of the wholesale destruction of the religious cult of 'sodomites,' briefly mentioned in *1 Kings*, xiv. 23–4, xv. 12–13, and xxii. 46, as having occurred in the tenth century B.C., during the reign of King Asa of Judah and his son Jehoshaphat. This is without doubt the same event as that given divine authority in the legend of the volcanic destruction by Jehovah of Sodom and Gomorrah, in *Genesis*, xix. 4–24. On the later recurrence of this homosexual cult as 'the Essene or Nazirite sect to which the founder of Christianity is presumed to have belonged,' on the evidence of the newly-discovered Dead Sea Scrolls, see further *2 Kings*, xxiii. 7 (in the 18th year of King Josiah: 622 B.C.); also *The Guilt of the Templars*, p. 130–131.

A recent anti-homosexual and pro-prostitution propagandist in the United States, Mr. Fred "Buster" Cherry, becomes particularly distraught over the fact that 'the Reverend Robert W. Wood, pastor of the Zion United Church of Christ, Newark, New Jersey ... has written a book in which he insinuates that Jesus Christ was a homosexual,' but here the weight of the evidence seems to be on the side of the Reverend Wood, if one accepts the actual historicity of the man Jesus. It should be observed, however, that whether or not Jesus Christ, Shakespeare (*and* Bacon), George Washington, and even a few presidents and politicians more recent, were or were not homosexual, it is not by the promulgation of great examples of this kind that proselytes to homosexuality are really obtained. If, in fact, it is actually possible, which is highly unlikely, that any person can really be changed from heterosexual to homosexual after adult age has been achieved. (Reversals in the opposite direction, of adult homosexuals into heterosexuals, are just as difficult and infrequent, and few reputable psychiatrists or psychoanalysts will actually undertake to 'cure' an adult homo-

sexual.) As to the great examples, see the lists of famous homosexuals, generally not recognized as such, in Albert Moll's
Berühmte Homosexuelle, about 1900, and 'Angelo Arcangelo's'
Homosexual Handbook (New York: Girodias, 1969), which
misses almost all the great 'closet queens,' or covert homosexuals of the past. H. Spencer Ashbee gives a brief 19th-
century list, in his *Index Librorum Prohibitorum* (1877, and
modern reprints) p. 340, in an article on *The Phoenix of Sodom,
or the Vere Street Coterie*, a work concerning the suppression
of a 'Sodomitical Club' in London in 1810, on which Ashbee
gives, p. 328–42, many interesting details.

The frankest admission of the animosity of the homosexual,
not toward society but toward the presumably belovèd other
male, is the sado-masochistic barroom ('S. & M.' or 'Sadie-
Maisie' bar), and in the private whipping-orgies and actual
torture and whipping-clubs connected with these, 'strictly for
men.' This is fairly new in America but has long existed in other
markedly homosexual countries, especially Germany and Holland, and strikingly demonstrates the inherent hostility of
homosexual relationships in actually organizing a semi-public
situation or framework in which men who have never met
each other before can move on from the first casual '*hello*' to
actual murder in a matter of a few hours.

The homosexual, in such situations, is presumably the
masochistic partner who takes the passive rôle as beat-up
victim, whippee, or corpse. Yet in fact, the homo-killer is just
another kind of latent homosexual, usually unconscious but
sometimes perfectly aware, who punishes the more blatant
types for the homosexuality he dares not admit to or identify
with, but which he achieves just as completely in lethal or sub-
lethal acts, often without any other physical (sexual) acts. A
particularly common form of this, in which none of the parties
need ever admit to being homosexual, is the ordinary barroom
brawl, especially in countries such as Ireland and America,
where this is a socially-accepted type of combat. The usual
pretext for such brawls is admittedly meaningless or insufficient, considering the violent bodily harm it then allows the
participants to do to each other. In fact, none of the men
involved are actually angry at the others, but simply suffer
from the unconscious homosexual need, as I have heard it
phrased, "*to smash somebody in the face once in a while.*"
(San Diego, Calif. 1964.) When I insisted on knowing how often

this meant, I was told, *"Oh, I don't know; at least once or twice a year or I go crazy!"* All this can be admitted to frankly, as can the fact that the would-be face-smasher sometimes ends as the smashed-up victim himself, without any loss of feelings of virility. Whereas a similar admission that one would like to engage in oral or anal intercourse with another man "at least once or twice a year" (or twice a week?) would be suffocatingly impossible to the usual barroom brawler types.

It should be observed that one is not referring here to encounters between male prostitutes and homosexuals, but between men who are presumably as homosexual or as normal as each other, and who express their homoerotic attraction by violence (sometimes non-sexual) rather than in connection with genitally directed eroticism. As to the violent relations between homosexuals and admitted male prostitutes, and their mutual preying on each other, this has long – possibly always – been a pesthouse of cold exploitation on the one hand, and robbery and murder on the other. Homosexual men – of whom a very large percentage are lifelong compulsive fellators, searching for 'fresh meat' at all times – are particularly exposed to a dangerous kind of panicky fear and resentment on the part of the men they fellate, who correctly feel they have been used or 'vampirized.' There even exists a special type of male prostitute or self-constituted *agent provocateur*, known in homosexual slang as *'dirt,'* whose whole activity is to lead homosexuals on to perform fellation, after which the male prostitute or 'dirt' beats and often robs the homosexual, on the self-righteous pretext of hating and despising him for being a 'cocksucker.' I was once rather surprised to hear an American college professor of political science – one of those strange, new, hurry-up professors created by mysterious government agency influence to stock the spy-center 'colleges' for Americans abroad – remark to me, as humor, before leaving for a sudden, 10-day vacation in Prague: *"Hey, let's go out and beat up a coupla queers! Har-har-har!!"* (Nice, France, 1968.) What this rather obvious government agent was before he became a 'college professor' is not difficult to guess.

With or without the 'Sadie-Maisie' bars of snobbish upper Third Avenue in New York, and the similar areas in Los Angeles, London, and other great cities, this is the background of typical humorous stories in which homosexuality is seen as a sort of psychological stain, or social insult, and is played for cruel comedy on the sado-masochistic pattern. A particular feature is the insistence on special homosexual *areas* for such encounters, similar to the Muntplein in Amsterdam, in which homosexual encounters consist not of friendly gestures and offers of drinks etc., but of men cursing at and insulting strangers in bars or even in the street, hoping for the proto-homosexual activity of a fight. All the homosexual need be in such situations is provocative, in any sense, to achieve or administer the physical thrashing he identifies as 'love.'

Quoted exactly as collected (written down) from an Army corporal, D.C. 1943: *'A little Hollywood fruit was following a husky, goodlooking man down the street, murmuring, "My, what a pretty man." Unable to resist temptation, he went up and felt his ass. The man swung round. "What the hell is coming off here? Beat it, will you?" Sadly the queer retired, but kept following, and unable to control himself, felt his ass again. "I thought I told you to beat it," the man snarled. A third time, however, the queer couldn't resist, and lovingly felt the attractive can. The man swung round and knocked him to the ground. The injured fruit looked up at the big brute and said sarcastically, "Tourist!"'*

Accentuating the *area* element: *A man in a public park is accosted by several homosexuals while he is out trying to take a walk. Irritated he complains to a policeman, who replies: "If you don't like our park, you can jutht leave, you know!"* (N.Y. 1939; earlier in *Anecdota*, 2:325.) This is usually collected with reference to Central Park, Manhattan, but sometimes also as of Fire Island, near New York, the main homosexual bathing-beach rendezvous on the American east coast, to which humorous allusions are legion. Mock advertising-slogan: *'Fire Island, where the élite meet to eat. And a man of moderate means can live like a* queen!' (N.Y. 1953, the inner rhymes being accentuated when delivered in singsong.)

Since the 1950's Fire Island has become almost equally well-known as a summer resort for high-speed homosexual rendezvous as well, similar to the springtime 'make-out' festival for heterosexual college students at Fort Lauderdale, Florida, at the other end of the eastern seaboard. A peculiar male-motherhood story is published, for example, in *Avant Garde* magazine (New York, May 1970) by Gary Youree, capitalizing strictly on the name of the island, under the title "Laid on Fire Island," the allusion being actually a cop-out since it refers to

an *egg* that the male-motherhood hero lays. (The same author
has a long fantasy-biography of a 'friendly rapist' in New
Orleans, in the same magazine, same issue, entitled "Jack the
Raper," which has almost as much truth in it as the story of the
man who laid an egg.)

A very famous publishing joke spoils its effect for many
listeners who do not appreciate 'camp' humor of this kind, by
insisting on just such an allusion in its final line: *A young
author, just back from a dangerous trip to Africa, calls on a
publisher with the manuscript account of his adventures, entitled* "I FUCKED A GORILLA." *"The book is marvellous," the
publisher assures him, "but that title, you know ..." "Too
hot?" says the author. "No, no, it isn't that," says the publisher.
"It's just that everything nowadays has to have that self-help,
do-it-yourself-kit angle." "Alright," agrees the helpful young
author, "let's call it:* HOW I FUCKED A GORILLA." *"That's good,"
says the publisher, "that's very good; but it still lacks something. There's no patriotism in it." "Got it!" says the author.
"We'll call it:* HOW I FUCKED A GORILLA FOR THE F.B.I." *Wonderful, wonderful!" says the publisher, "but you still haven't got
anything about religion." "I see," says the author. "Well, let's
call it:* HOW I FUCKED A GORILLA FOR THE F.B.I. AND FOUND GOD!"
*"You know," says the publisher enthusiastically, "I really like
dealing with a coöperative young chap like you. So many of
our authors act like prima-donnas when you want the least
little change. Our trends-editor would really appreciate it if you
could, just possibly you know, get in something about – well,
about homosexuality." "Of course," says the young author. "I
understand perfectly. But this is the last change I'll make:* HOW
I FUCKED A GORILLA FOR THE F.B.I. AND FOUND GOD – ON FIRE
ISLAND!" (N.Y. 1952.) They jest at scars, that never felt a wound.
Compare John Collier's satirical novel, *His Monkey Wife*, 1930.

This joke was told me by the publisher who originally com-
missioned this book, the late Henry Schuman, who requested
no changes whatever in either my title or manuscript – anyhow, not seriously – a unique experience! The joke is apparently built up on the pattern of a rather mild writing-course
or school joke concerning: *The professor who tells his class in
composition that a well-written magazine story should combine a reference to religion, an appeal to snobbery (or royalty),
and something about sex, all as close to the beginning as
possible. One student turns in, as opening line: "My God!" said*

the duchess, "take your hand off my leg!" (Ann Arbor, Michigan, 1935.) A French version adds a fourth element: *mystery*, with the resultant opening: *"My God!" said the duchess, "who can be the father of my child?"* (Paris, 1954.)

In a story related in theme to that of the gorilla on Fire Island, the element of homosexuality is very prominent, not as the final turn of the screw but as a plain insult. *A man tells his psychiatrist that he is perfectly normal in every way, except for one thing: he likes to have intercourse with horses. "I see," says the psychiatrist, stroking his beard soberly. "Do you prefer male horses or female horses?" "Female, of course!" replies the patient indignantly. "What do you think I am – queer?!"* (N.Y. 1940.) 'Queer' has long been the commonest 'outsider's' slang term for homosexual, both as noun and adjective, when no gross insult is intended. People will therefore sometimes specify that someone is *'queer – peculiar,'* to avoid or disclaim any homosexual implication, when the individual is merely eccentric. In the same way, verbally-oriented people will specify that a thing is either *'funny – ha-ha'* or *'funny – peculiar,'* which does essentially bring us back to *'funny – queer.'* A British form of the joke ends: *"You think I'm kinky?!"* This is a Briticism for sexually-perverted, on which see the glorification of sexual and sadistic perversion in print and fact, in Britain, in Mrs. Gillian Freeman's *The Undergrowth of Literature* (London: Nelson, 1967), a photographically-illustrated item making everything only too clear. For rubber-goods perverts (also sado-masochistic), the similarly titled *Outer Fringe of Sex* was also published in London, 1970, by the Odyssey Press, a bookclub subsidiary of the main British men's magazine, *Penthouse*, which is presumably for the mere inner fringe: the amateurs simply of 'normal perv.' Accentuating the sado-masochistic element, in which the aggressiveness is in many cases expressed purely at the verbal level, sometimes sadistic and sometimes masochistic:

Two homosexuals are arguing, and one screams at the other, "Well, you can kiss my ass!" "This is a fight, dearie. Let's keep romance out of it." (2:98.) Also with end-line: *"Well, I won't. I'm not ready to make up yet."* (N.Y. 1950, the two homosexuals being named Hugh FitzMorris and Morris FitzHugh.) This is further improved upon, how authentically I do not know, in a section of bawdy jokes curiously intruded into another book-length glorification of kinky sexual perversions and mechanical masturbation, under the title *The Humor and Technology of Sex* (New York, 1969) by Dr. Paul Tabori, in which some of the jokes contained in the First Series of the present work are revamped. (This is also the case with a British pocket-item, *Rugby Jokes* and *Son of Rugby Jokes*, London: Sphere Books, 1968–70, anonymously compiled by the late John A. Yates.) In Dr. Tabori's built-up dysphemistic version of the joke, p. 254: *A truck smashes into the rear end of a 'new pink sports car' piloted by two homosexuals, one of whom leaps out 'and starts screaming at the driver ... The driver, who looks somewhat nastier than an enraged gorilla, spits at him, "Kiss my hairy ass, cocksucker!" Shocked beyond belief, the gay boy runs back to his companion in the sports car. "I think everything's going to be all right. He wants to settle out of court!"'* Some people say I am ruining all the jokes in the present work by telling them too briefly. I submit that it is, rather, the would-be artistic tellers who overload their jokes with bric-à-brac details and new & improved punch-lines who are really destroying the humor.

Another example: '*The lampshade queen* [effeminate homosexual] *meets his butch boyfriend* [supra-masculine homosexual] *in a lovely "Black Leather Jackets and Motorcycle Boots" bar. They immediately start fighting, with insults, slaps, kicks, and plain slugging. The butch kicks the lampshade queen in the balls, knocking 'her' to the floor, then jumps up and down on her head, dislocating her jaw, and snarls, "Whaddya got to say about* THAT?' *The poor queen get groggily to her feet, tries to replace her jaw, and says flutily, "Oh, darling, you always were such a tomboy!"'* (Supplied in manuscript, Boston, Mass. 1966.) This joke not only leaves the presumed beat-up victim far ahead, verbally at least, but is an excellent example of homosexual recognitions, here specifically under the supermasculine butch pose of the 'S. & M.' homosexual. An even more obviously masochistic example: *One fairy is telling the other how he was beaten up by a great big truck-driver, and thrown out the second-story window. "Right up there," he says, pointing with his bandaged arm – "Oh! there he is now! Hel-lo!" he calls, waving frantically; "I'm not ma-ad!"* (N.Y. 1950.) This is worth a whole lecture on homosexuality as a sado-masochistic charade.

3. HOMOSEXUAL RECOGNITIONS

Parallel with the homosexual art of self-disguise as 'normals' (the so-called 'closet queens'), and for the purpose of avoiding, or at least theoretically for avoiding sado-masochistic encounters of the sub-lethal kind just described, either with 'S. & M.' homosexuals of the unconscious kind, and those other out-&-out homo-killers known in homosexual slang simply as *dirt*, the real homosexual world has created in all countries a whole system of high-signs and signals, intonations and exclamations, and in particular a complete slang vocabulary intended in part to conceal and in part to advertise, as may be desired, the homosexuality or homosexual awareness of the speaker. Spies of various kinds (of whom a large percentage have probably always been homosexual) also use secret language of this kind, as that concerning the 'witting' and 'unwitting' agents of the C.I.A. infiltration of American and European college-student organizations during the 1960's. (See further, my glossary "The Slang of Homosexuality," in Dr. George W. Henry's *Sex Variants*, New York: Hoeber-Harper, 1941, end of vol. II; omitted from the one-volume reprint.)

The recognition of homosexuality by homosexuals is seldom a problem, either in folklore or in fact, but its recognition by non-homosexuals is construed as very difficult and important. The heterosexual is very afraid of being called or thought homosexual, and is quick to make this accusation of others, as the ultimate insult. *The field-boss in a steel mill calls the office and demands three men to be sent out at once as blowers on a hot job. The phone-clerk is new and does not understand. He calls the main office and says, "Where can we get three men in a hurry out here for a hot blow job?" "Take it easy, will you?" says the voice at the other end. "The boss's special assistant is out of the office right now, but there's a stock-room clerk here we're not so sure of."* (L.A. 1965.) Occasionally a less insulting approach is taken, as in the following sentimental item, more usually told of a young waitress. *A man sits down in a restaurant and orders ham & eggs. The waiter begins writing on his pad and keeps on writing. "Just ham & eggs," the man repeats, but the waiter replies, "Just a moment, sir," and keeps writing. Finally he tears off the sheet of paper, sets it down, and goes out to the kitchen. The man picks up the paper and reads: "Sir — This is a high-class place and we cater only to the best clientele.*

When you sat down I noticed that your fly is open and your prick is hanging out. I will convey your order to the chef, and serve you well. When I return, I trust you will have corrected your personal appearance. Sincerely yours, Harold. – P.S. I love you." (N.Y. 1964, printed in *World's Dirtiest Jokes*, 1969, p. 20, as of a waitress.)

Scene, an army induction center. The new recruits are lined up by the tough sergeant and told to count off into groups of four. They count off briskly, "One – Two – Three – Four! – One – Two – Three – Four! – A-wahann! ..." The sergeant looks up angrily. *"Count off again,"* he orders. *"One – Two – Three – Four! Ooo-wahn ... yoohoo! ..."* The sergeant strides up to the yodelling Number One, and looks him up and down in revulsion. *"Are you One?" "Of courthe I'm one. Are you one too?"* (N.J. 1942. Many languages have similar code-phrases for homosexuality, such as the German '*to be one of the brotherhood,*' or, in Dutch, '*on the other side.*') This joke is probably all the scientific basis that exists for the post-Kinseyan propaganda line that '*one man in five*' is homosexual, and similar bull.

The following is a British story, or one intended to mock the British, '*all*' of whom are considered practically homosexual at a certain level in American folklore. (This is not altogether folklore.) *Two camels slowly approach each other in the desert, their riders identically dressed in excessively long Bermuda shorts and topee helmets. They pause, and the riders speak (in exaggerated British accent): "English?" – "Of cawss." – "Foreign office?" – "Cinema photawgraphy." – "Oxford?" – "Cambridge." –"Hormosexsh'l?" – "Certainly nawt!" – "Pit-y!" – And the two camels continue their separate ways across the desert.* (London, 1954, told by an American, and getting a great laugh from his British audience.) Again, this is worth a whole lecture as to the problem of homosexual accosting and recognitions, the first camel-rider trying desperately to set up some area of mutuality, while the second man just as desperately takes his anti-homosexual or sub-homosexual pleasure in the typically upper-clahss (British 'U') fashion of snubbing, evading and frustrating him.

There is furthermore a great complicated mess created by the existence of two different homosexual acts of principal choice: fellation and pedication. In both of these there must be an active or dominant party and a passive or accepting party, though *these rôles do not necessarily correspond* to the social characters of the individuals involved. Fellators in particular – as also masochists, who are often the same individuals – are usually the active or *dominant* party, though their preferred sexual act and/or demanded masochistic humiliations are erroneously thought of as passive. (The secret is given away by the word 'demanded.') This confusion has led to the classic joke concerning homosexual recognitions and rôles: *Oscar Wilde has picked up a street boy in Hyde Park, and suggests going to a hotel together. "Orl right, guv'nor," says the boy, "but 'oo does wot to 'oo – an' 'oo PYES?"* (1 : 440. Compare the authentic scenes almost exactly like this in Joe Mancini's "Body Painting: The Youngest Profession," in Philip Nobile's *The New Eroticism*, New York, 1970, p. 108–19.) The joke has also been recast in limerick form concerning a homosexual and a lesbian '*Who argued all night, Over who had the right, To do what and with which and to whom.*'

On occasion, the homosexual recognition is, as it were, flung into the audience's face for its shock value, this being the essence of 'camp,' as is implied in the origin of this term in the French *camper:* to strike blustering attitudes or brag noisily, as warriors before battle. *One man on a street-car nudges another. "Some beautiful pair of legs on that dame there, eh buddy?" The other man, dubiously, "Yeh-h ..." Even more chummy: "And what a set of tits, huh?" "Er, that's right ..." "I'd sure like to screw the living bejesus out of her, wouldn't you?" "Oh, I don't know. Just look at the ass on that motorman!"* (2 : 8.) To be compared with the two-camel joke above, for the format of continuous and sub-hostile evasion and frustration, here of the crude 'normal' by the homosexual.

There is a level in the homosexual material deeper than the jokes can even imply, and I should like to consider this now, entering the subject through the superb unveiling or unmasking implicit in a famous joke. A most extraordinary example of the disgraceful or insulting quality of any homosexual allusion or accusation is to be seen in the would-be 'clean-up' – from homosexual to merely scatological! – of this hilarious Yiddish story, known in English since the early 1930's when the Einstein theory began to filter down to the popular level, and immediately became the caricature of itself that all great ideas invariably become when popularized. In any case, the caricature of the Einsteinian theorems as meaning that "*Everything is rela-*

tive" is not half so bad as the dangerous extrapolation of the same idea to ethics, with the resultant axiom or postulate that "*There is no such thing as right or wrong*," and that value judgments are somehow the new sin against the Holy Ghost and should never be made: a pitiful cop-out now most particularly infecting the university world.

Two schnorrers [Jewish hobo-beggars] *are discussing Einstein's theory. One explains to the other patiently that, "All it means is that everything is relative. It's like this, but it's also like that. It's entirely different, but it's the same thing. You understand?" "No," says the other schnorrer; "could you give me an example?" "Of course. Let's say I fuck you in the ass. I have a prick in the ass, and you have a prick in the ass. It's entirely different, but it's the same thing. Now do you understand?" "Ah-hah!" agrees the other; "but I got one question: This way Einstein makes a living?"* (N.Y. 1952.) The clean-up is given in Immanuel Olsvanger's *Röyte Pomerantsen* (The Red-haired Pomeranian Woman; New York: Shocken Books, 1947), a collection of Yiddish jokes printed in English transliteration with the result that neither Jews nor Goyim can really understand it. In Olsvanger's CLEANED-UP version the '*prick in the ass*' becomes, instead, '*a noz in hinten*' (a nose in the behinder), which is apparently considered a more respectable object to insert in another man's rectum than the penis. That is to say – to underline what is now made obvious – that a merely scatological act, even one involving the 'nose' (*i.e.* the face and mouth: thus 'arse-kissing') can be accepted as humor at certain levels, despite its humiliating nature; but that an overtly erotic act involving the rectum of another man would be obscene and a disgrace.

Thus, the usual comedy concern with homosexuals is seldom direct and unequivocal, but involves instead all sorts of arch and fey allusions or partialisms connected with the homosexual's mock effeminacy of manners and speech (the lisp), drooping wrists, etc., with lace handkerchief tucked into the cuff, tight clothes moulding the waist and buttocks (this style has been put across recently for normals as well), the use of cosmetics, perfume, and long artificial eyelashes, and especially any excessive concern with *clothes*, and the overall carrying-agent of the campy or *la-de-dah* language ('Harvard' or 'British' accent) of the comedy homosexual. These last have a long genealogy, certainly as old as the attack on the homosexual poet, Spenser, and his school of Euphuistic floridity of speech in Shakespeare's time, as in the character of Laërtes' second, Osric (traditionally played in overwhelmingly florid costume and with extravagantly homosexual airs & graces), who challenges Hamlet to a duel in language so ornate that recourse must finally be made to the marginal commentary to understand what he is saying. (*Hamlet*, V.ii.80–192.)

Alexandre Dumas similarly goes to extraordinary trouble, in the concluding volume of his "Three Musketeers" series, *Le Vicomte de Bragelonne* (1850) to indicate, almost solely by means of incessant references to his concern with *clothes*, the homosexuality of Philippe, Duc d'Orléans, the brother of King Louis XIV, and of Philippe's 'favorite,' the Chevalier de Lorraine. Duelling, as a homosexual activity, was brought to its most extreme level by the cowboy killers of the Old West in America, and in the face-slashing duels of German students before World War I (*'displacement of lower to upper'*). We still have homosexual duellists today: mock-cowboys and other 'S. & M.' queens, gangster motorcyclists, chicken-runs, drag-racers, etc. etc. Nowadays the linguistic and sartorial disguise of all these groups is rather that of being ultra-tough than of being effeminate. (*"It's entirely different, but it's the same thing."*)

A case in point: Mention has been made, in the First Series, 9.I.2, pages 680–81, of the ravening verbal sadism of Edward Albee's characters in the play *Who's Afraid of Virginia Woolf?* (1963), in which actors representing a husband-&-wife team rip each other verbally to shreds before the audience, with sexual- and status-insults, for several hours. An ordeal for any normal person to sit through. The movie version of this verbal slaughter, played by the British actor, Richard Burton, and his wife, also packed the suckers in solid, for its presumable verbal freedom, theoretically allowing the motion-picture screen the same verbal liberty as the stage for the first time in the English-speaking world. Actually, the violent dialogue is carefully expurgated even in the original play, which was produced just before the New Freedom really hit, and such unusual slang terms as 'hump' continuously replace the usual colloquial terms for fucking, etc. throughout the dialogue. However its dialogue may be phrased, the Albee play is flatly presented as a ruthless and bitter exposé of just what marriage really amounts to (and at the most intellectual levels – that of college-professors: hoo-hah!) in the twentieth century. The fact of the matter is, however, entirely different. Here is the truth, which was of course never any secret from the 'in' characters squirting this particular bit of dirty anti-human propaganda upon the hated 'normals' of the world, possibly to assist in making normality just that much harder for them. I quote, in translation, from the French news-magazine, *Candide* (29 August 1966), No. 279: p. 20/5:

AMSTERDAM DARES
WHAT LONDON DID NOT DARE

EVEN in London, where people nowadays are very broadminded, no one would dare present *Who's Afraid of Virginia Woolf?* in its original version. Hot nights ahead for Amsterdam: the Dutch have thrown themselves into this dangerous venture.

The play by Edward Albee (interpreted on the stage in Paris by Madeleine Robinson and Raymond Gérôme, and in the cinema by Liz Taylor and Richard Burton) was not originally intended to be played by male and female actors, but by male-male couples. It was not for a man and wife that Edward Albee wrote the terrific domestic squabble – which will no doubt remain forever the model of a modern marital fight – but for two men, united but torn to bits by the passion that you can imagine. It is his exclusively male version that will be presented, this fall, at an involved (*engagé*) theater in Amsterdam.

In other words, Albee's homosexual hate-play is, at the last, presented without its specious mask of heterosexual normality, and as what it really is and always was, only in a small and very special theater in Amsterdam, for homosexual audiences, 'in'-snobs, and other hipsters and far-outniks. But, as presented to the world-audience in America, England, and France, on both stage and screen, in its (shall we say) inverted-drag version – *as though* it were the truth, not about homosexual 'love,' but about normal men and women – it is, in fact, nothing other than the Homosexual International's propaganda equivalent of writing a ruthless exposé of the crimes of the Nazis, and putting this on all over the world (except in some narrow whore-alley in Amsterdam) *with all the Nazi characters disguised as Jews.* Or staging an exposé of white-supremacy tactics and the torturing of Negroes in South Africa and the American South, with only the *minor editorial change* of having actors in Blackface do all the torturing, of whites. 'It's entirely different, but it's the same thing." Or is it? Consider the total reversal of historical truth, as to who-massacred-who, in the standard cowboys-&-Indians movies and the matching novels.

In case any innocent reader, or member of the normal and non-'In' chump audience, imagines that there is something new or peculiar about such propaganda reversals and cross-maskings in the world of books, the theatre, and motion pictures – as also in the larger world of political propaganda, god knows – reference might be made to the long career of the late Somerset Maugham, the king-pin or queen-bee of the homosexual propaganda world, a career almost entirely composed of profitably attacking and denigrating, in fictional disguise, the normal relations of women and men, beginning with his most famous attack, *Of Human Bondage* (1915), and continuing right on through to the end, likewise including a number of his imitators, as I have analyzed at some length in *Love & Death* (1949) p. 83–6, in the chapter "Open Season on Women." Many more examples will be found in the neo-feminist study of anti-womanism in literature, *Sex and Politics* (1970), by Prof. Kate Millett, which either purposely overlooks or is not able to recognize the homosexual slant or disguise in many of its cases, and which ends crashingly for some reason with a long paean to the principal avowed homosexual writer of our time, Jean Genet.

The homosexuals of the world are being very noisy at the present time, particularly in America and Europe, about not wanting to be treated prejudicially, harassed by cops, etc. Wouldn't it be fitting, then, if the same homosexual propagandists would take an equally fair and honorable view of how things ought to be done in the public arts, where mere 'normals' are concerned? And undertake not to treat prejudicially, and from ambush, with all the advantages of normal disguise, in the theatre, literature, arts, and the mass media, the difficult relationship between normal women and men: a relationship at which homosexuals, lesbians, and similar have avowedly failed, and concerning which all that is wanted or needed of them is *silence*. Or let them admit, frankly and at last, to themselves at least, what is the obvious psychological truth: that homosexuality is by no means a form of unfortunate or misplaced *love*, neither for persons of the same sex nor anyone else, but is almost invariably and inevitably a dangerous neurotic avatar of sado-masochism and hatred. The 'fire-queens,' or sado-masochistic would-be killers and shit-bombardiers of the new and aggressive 'Gay Liberation' movement in the United States, have now made glaringly obvious this substructure of uncontrollable hostility in the homosexual neurosis.

4. THE 'NORMAL' AS HOMOSEXUAL

Hidden behind the question of homosexual recognitions, for the 'normal,' is an entirely different problem than that facing the homosexual who wishes to be sure that the man he is accosting in barroom or public-toilet will not (or will) beat him up for unveiling his homosexuality, or 'letting down his back hair,' as the slang phrase has it. As has already been shown, the normal person or heterosexual is worried very much by the *secrecy and mystery* of the homosexual world, and by the fact that he has really no way of being sure that his super-virile best friend will not turn out to be homosexual on the hunting- or fishing-trip they may go on together, and perhaps 'rape' him homosexually when one or both of them are under the inhibition-releasing power of sleep or alcohol. This is, of course, connected with the fears of castration more clearly expressed in the materials to be given below under the heading of "Pedicatory Rape." For the homosexual is thought of – quite correctly, in the psychodynamic sense – as an individual who has somehow been desexed or castrated ... *'but it doesn't show!'* At a further and more nervously private level down, is the even greater fear : that one oneself will turn out to be homosexual! Or at least, not able to resist a homosexual seduction.

'A man is visiting in France. Does a little wandering the first night. Fucks the host's wife, his daughter, the cook, the second maid, etc. The host berates him in the morning. "What's the big idea? Here you're my guest. I receive you as a friend. And what do you do? You fuck my wife, my daughter, and half the servants – and for me, nothing?"' (N.Y. 1939, as supplied in manuscript by a magazine-writer of articles on humor.) Note the laying of the story – as well as all the women in the family – in France, where an easy sexual latitudinarianism about homosexuality is believed to exist, and where it is easier for the Anglo-Saxon joke-teller to conceive of the normal host, or father-figure, with all the standard patriarchal impedimenta of

wife, daughter, and female servants, who really turns out to be homosexual in the end, and passively homosexual at that. This also comes very close to the idea of 'raping' the father-figure sexually: "The Ganymede Revenge."

As it happens, the preceding joke actually is French in origin, so far as I have been able to determine. It first appears in the excessively rare little three-volume set of erotic tales-in-verse, *La Légende Joyeuse, ou Les Cent-une leçons de Lampsaque* ('A Londres, chez Pynne' [in France], 1749–51), of which only two complete copies are now known: that in the British Museum Private Case, and my own. The entire text of this work is engraved, and it was obviously done for some rich patron or backer in a very limited edition, explaining its rarity. Fortunately the entire text was later reissued in printed form, both under the same title and as *Le Cabinet de Lampsaque* ('A Paphos,' 1784) 2 vols., with curiously naïve engraved illustrations to each tale, also as *Le Bijou de la Société*, 2 vols. It is, under all its titles, a most important collection of 18th-century erotic humor in the *conte-en-vers* form. The present tale or joke is No. 15 of *La Légende Joyeuse*, and goes even farther homosexually than the modern form, the final line being even more direct a demand or invitation, in crudely money-oriented fashion, and in this case to a servant, not a guest: *"Come, Sir Jacko, finish off your work on me. I might as well have my share too; I'm the one that pays your wages."*

The most recent French form combines this with No. 14 of *La Légende Joyeuse*, concerning a priest in confession – a particularly frequent subject in this series of *contes-en-vers* – in which the excuse or subterfuge of the final homosexual invitation is: *The priest's supposed indignation over what he has just heard in confession: "What?! You fucked my cook, my sister, and my mother too?!" The priest leaps out of the confession-box and pulls down his drawers, shouting, "Then fuck me too! You might as well have the whole family on your conscience!"* (Paris, 1954.) Even in its ecclesiastical disguise, of concern for conscience and damnation, this is obviously a pretty paltry pretext. Note the implication in all forms of the joke that what really excites the father-figure's final homosexual submission to the 'son' is the latter's powerful and wholesale virility. This is a tenet of folklore belief, even concerning that presumed appanage of great virility: a long penis. Compare, for example, the line in the American mock-virile recitation, "The Grooving of Dan McGrew," entirely concerned with pedication among Gold Rush miners in the Klondike, that when the pedicator pulls out his enormous penis in the barroom full of men, *'everyone's asshole squirmed!"*

Many of the jokes concerning the 'normal' as homosexual involve the act of fellation, which is considered particularly disgraceful in Western society when engaged in (orally) by a man. One such joke of particular significance will be considered again at the opening of section 10.IV.1, "The Fellatory Accusation." *A stranger is being shown about a southern town in the United States. This is the Josiah Whiffle football stadium, he is told; this is the Josiah Whiffle maternity hospital, etc. "Say, this guy Whiffle must be quite a big-shot around here," marvels the tourist. "Yes," says his guide, "and if it wasn't for one little mistake he made, when he walks down the street people would say, 'There goes Whiffle the philanthropist,' instead of 'There goes Whiffle the cock-sucker!'"* (1:126, a version using the name Cohen.)

An even more dangerous form of homosexual recognition is that in which it is oneself that one recognizes as homosexual, as is brought out with particular clarity in various jokes in section 10.IV.2, "Fellation as Rape," especially that about the Jewish travelling salesman in the southern town who seeks the advice of his rabbi as to a case of conscience. The present section is unusually brief, since many of the stories that might well figure here are grouped under "Fellation," "Urinary Disguises," and similar headings later, by the physical act involved. It has nevertheless seemed worthwhile creating the present section, if only to point out the existence of this social or psychological theme, "The 'Normal' as Homosexual," and its specific but unexpected unveiling or homosexual recognition.

One recognition story which clearly belongs here, and nowhere else, has been collected in English only by courtesy. It is probably Argentine or Spanish originally, and was told to me in translation, in Paris, 1965, by Sr. Ismael Adolfo Cerceda-Corda, a stage-entertainer and *origami*-artist who has honored me with his friendship, and who – though his repertory of stories is quite remarkable, and his telling of them (with fluent gestures) absolutely magnificent – does not feel at home in the English language, and specializes only in sensational stage-acts in which he never speaks. *A Christian martyr is being tortured in the arena, where he is tied naked to four stakes, on his back, and is left to be eaten by lions. The cage door slides up and an enormous lion slinks into the arena. He approaches the spread-eagled Christian and sniffs him hungrily. The poor fellow remembers that he has heard that a lion will not eat a dead body, and determines that no matter what the lion does he will pretend to be dead. The lion begins by licking the soles of his feet, and though it tickles terribly the martyr keeps himself from laughing by an intense effort of will. Proceeding further, the lion begins licking his balls, and though now he has no desire to laugh, the martyr realizes with horror that he is getting an erection and the lion will know he is really alive. He looks down apprehensively at the lion drooling there between his legs, and tries to strangle his feelings and keep the erection from progressing. But it is too late. The lion is now licking his penis, which stands up perfectly straight. The lion stops, lifts one paw and smoothes back his mane, and says flutily, "Oh, my dear boy!" (It was a fairy lion, the teller concludes.)*

The identification-coefficient of this story, if such a thing could be measured, and the reassurance available from it, in jesting disguise, must be very great indeed. The Christian martyr is perfectly the listener's own idea of himself, whoever the listener may be, and he cannot but sympathize with the martyr's last-gasp attempt at *passive defense* by holding his breath, strangling his emotions, and playing dead. This is the whole meaning of the modern pose of being 'cool,' with which compare also the opposite response: the Say-It-Isn't-So popularity in Europe and America of *judo* and similar bare-handed fighting techniques from Japan, immediately following the massive recognition, in the explosion of the Atom Bomb (over Japan) at the end of World War II, that *no* defense is now possible, the bare-handed defense most ludicrously least of all. In the joke, the martyr is clearly in the position of being dead already – spread-eagled and helpless, and waiting to be eaten alive – yet his penis still erects, and against his will! This is precisely the *Resurrection of the Flesh* punned upon in exactly the same context, of phallic erection, in Boccaccio's *Decameron*, in its most famous story, "Putting the Devil in Hell" (Day III, novel 10).

In *The Horn Book*, p. 248, I have mentioned the phallic toys offering the same reassurance of resurrection-after-death (that is to say, despite death) hawked as souvenirs in Mexico on All-Souls Day, November 2nd, 'in the form of a little dead Pharaoh in his coffin [also a toy skeleton], who, by means of a hidden rubber-band, still represents the Resurrection of the Flesh.' This is in particular thrust upon young ladies, both natives and tourists, as is also the case with the similar phallic toys and processional figures at Herculaneum and Pompeii, and in Japan. The same toy, and the same idea, has also been encountered in the United States in the form of a little naked man in a barrel – also operated, as to his hidden erection, by a rubber-band – with the inscription around the barrel in dog-Latin: '*Nil Illegitimi Carborundum!*' (Don't let the bastards wear you down!)

Finally, as to the joke about the lion and the martyr, the *lion* is of course the most famous and powerful of all father-symbols in folklore, along with eagles, the mountain, and the sun. If, as we see in the present joke, even the kingly lion turns out to be homosexual, yet not only does not castrate his son (by biting off his penis) but actually caresses and revives the son's genital apparatus in the standard oral-homosexual way; then clearly it is the father who has been spread-eagled, humiliated, castrated and homosexualized, and just as clearly the martyred son who triumphs. This is also, of course, the deeper meaning of the Christian myth of the Crucifixion, in which Jesus, whose torture and death are 'demanded' by Jehovah, triumphs in that very death over the father-god, whose worship (Judaism) is thereafter to be driven out and superseded by Christianity. 'Triumph' through suicide and failure.

5. URINARY AND OTHER DISGUISES

The one unfailing symptom of homosexual recognition, other than an actual verbal overture, is naturally any attempt to touch or handle the body of another man, in particular his genitals (or buttocks), or even to stare at these, as on beaches or in public toilets where this sort of 'optical rape' by homosexuals is standard fare. The extreme over-evaluation of the penis by the homosexual is the result of his own overwhelming castration fears, and in turn causes his total or partial impotence with women: the true definition of homosexuality. So much anxiety is militated by the sight, or sometimes the mere presence of the female genital organ – considered by the-child-that-the-homosexual-once-was as 'proof' that persons without the penis, or who have 'lost' the penis, can actually exist – that the homosexual is generally unable to have an erection in the presence of this frightening female organ, though he may be highly potent genitally with men, especially when the man's genitals can be stared at, touched, sucked, or otherwise handled in such a way as to give continuous reassurance of their un-castrated presence. Homosexuality is thus best defined as an uncontrollable though sometimes only partial impotence with women, combined with a sexual withdrawal toward, and an attempted sexual conciliation of men. The specifically homo-sexual acts engaged in are the principal gestures of this con-ciliation.

For the rest, homosexuals seldom make good friends, either to each other or to normal men, and most homosexual activity is plagued with extreme infidelity and Don Juanism, as the reassurance of any one particular penis rapidly loses its effect on the neurotic sensibility of the homosexual, and another penis must rapidly be sought: the bigger the better, *i.e.* the more positively uncastrated. Such activities actually disguise a violent fear of men and a powerful *hatred* of them, for having driven the homosexual off the natural sexual goal of the woman, particularly the mother, and for the feared and puni-tive castration threatened if the normal sexual goal is ap-proached. It is the hidden train of hatred and aggression ('S. & M.') in homosexuality which defines its specific neurosis, and makes all pretenses that it is 'another kind of normality,' or a 'Third Sex' and the like, ludicrous.

The extreme amount of homosexual activity taking place in and around toilets is not sufficiently explained by the necessity of haunting such unsavoury places in order to see penises un-furled. Normal men in our culture seldom or never wave their penises about wildly, when urinating where any other man can see them, but make obvious efforts to hide the penis, by special covering 'holds' with the fingers of the hand supporting the penis while urinating, by pressing the body in close against the ceramic urinal, etc. The real explanation of the homosexual attraction to toilet-rooms is that it is a specific attraction, owing to the idea of urination and evacuation as 'dirty,' and the further identification of dirt – also workmen's blue-jeans, or leather pants – with virility and strength. Thus it comes about, as I have heard it sadly observed in France, that: *"Homo-sexuals prove that they are more refined than anybody else, by dressing up in their best clothes* (or: *in kid gloves) to make love in toilets."*

Disguises are of course necessary, as much in the humorous expression of these neurotic attractions as in actual life. The best and most obvious disguise in a public toilet is that one has come there to urinate. Thus one duly sees homosexuals endlessly taking up urinal space (while people who have to pee wait helplessly in line ...) and waggling their pricks hopefully about; but more particularly *looking* with an intense eagerness at the other men's penises when these are accidentally to be seen. In a typology of *"Kinds of Men at the Urinal"* printed up as a novelty obscoenum in America during the 1930's and since (various versions, including one of "Girls in the Powder Room"), the ever-present homosexual is not specifically mentioned, but a prominent place is given to the *'NOSEY guy: Always wants to see how the guy in the next cubicle is fixed. Pisses on his leg to get attention.' And to the 'SHOWOFF: Waves it around to show how well he's hung.'*

There are also numerous jokes which are essentially only comebacks or retorts intended to be said, or presumably said, to ward off obtrusive attention by other men in this way. Almost always the retort is in the anti-modest or bragging form of insisting that one's penis is even longer than the admiring stranger observes it to be. *The Texan at the urinal is holding his penis with his whole arm instead of with two fingers. The man next to him asks why. "Got to," says the Texan laconically; "otherwise it'd hang down in the water."* (N.Y. 1963. A paranoid version is given in the First Series, 5.V.1, "Phallic Brag," p. 292–3.) – *A man at a urinal says to the man next to him, "Say, that's the biggest prick I ever saw. How big is it when it gets stiff?" "Damned if I know," says the other, "it draws all my blood and I pass out every time."* (L.A. 1968, version printed in *World's Dirtiest Jokes*, p. 34.) It should be unnecessary to point out that a man asking a stranger how big his penis is when stiff – or commenting upon it in any way – is obviously making a homosexual overture to him.

Occasionally this type of joke is perfectly frank as to its unvoiced homosexuality, but then the stared-at normal is not sure of coming off as winner. In a favorite 1920's joke: *An American in a Paris street pissoir is annoyed by a Frenchman ogling his penis. Finally he turns to him angrily and begins, "Say, bo!" "C'est beau?" agrees the Frenchman, "mais c'est* MAGNIFIQUE!!*"* The demand simply to *look* at the penis is the usual, and obvious enough expurgation of the desired *touch*. The jokes are in no doubt about this psychological substitution: *A young man in a public toilet expresses admiration for the very large*

*penis of another man in the urinal-booth next to him late at
night. "Would you let me touch it?" asks the young man.
"Sure," says the other, "go ahead." The young man then progressively touches it, strokes it, gets hold of the other man's
penis with his fist, and finally slips the man's testicles under his
armpit. "All right, schmuck!" he suddenly snarls, "now hand
over your wallet!"* (Bronx, N.Y. 1953, from a young science-
fiction writer.) Observe that the robbery is intended to *explain*
the homosexual overture.

The following joke must certainly be a favorite, as it has been
endlessly collected in both America and England over the last
thirty years, in as many as five different versions, all of which
circulate about the idea of one man somehow getting another
man to touch or otherwise concern himself with the first man's
penis, usually under the pretext of needing help in urinating.
This harks back, certainly, to childish recollections of being
helped in urinating, especially by the mother. *A drunken (or
wounded) American soldier on a train needs help in unbuttoning his fly and holding his penis while he urinates, then in putting it back in again and buttoning him up, all of which is
done for him by a gallant British army officer out of esprit de
corps. At the end the American soldier says boozily, "Hey, bud!
Did you shake off the last drop?" "Why no," say the British
officer, "I didn't." "A hell of a lot you fucken Limeys know
about pissing!"* (N.J. 1942. Told by a soldier on a troop-train, with
a variant by one of the listeners concerning a girl helping a
spastic cripple to his hotel-room.)

A pantomimed allusion to this joke or situation is made, a
dozen years earlier, in one of Charlie Chaplin's best movie-
comedies of the early 1930's, *City Lights*, with Chaplin shown in
boxing-gloves helplessly gesturing toward something he needs
at the other end of the room, and with which the powerful
father-figure actor (the standard 'menace' in all Chaplin's early
comedies) is to help him. Naturally, as cleaned-up for the movies
here, it turns out to be *a glass of water* that he cannot get himself from the water-cooler, owing to the gloves. It might be
added that the preceding joke is told in America as anti-British,
with gloating accent on the insulting final line; while it is told
in England as anti-American, owing to the fine unconsciousness
of the American type described as to his boorishness and ingratitude, thought of by the English as so typically American,
since English ingratitude is lethally polite. The insulting traits

here again bring back the joke to childhood reminiscences and the defiant childish character.

The drunk or cripple in the public toilet seems to be the favorite humoristic device for arranging somehow for one man to concern himself excessively with another man's penis, or even touch it, for a man to draw his penis (in its function of urination) to the attention of other men, without anyone admitting to the homosexuality, hidden under the drunkenness, etc., of either the situation or the joke. The Larson manuscript, collected in Idaho, 1932, gives a sort of catch-question or nonsense form of this, at No. 22: *Drunk, to stranger in lavatory: "Say, is my cock out?" "No, it isn't." "Well, it* ought *to be. I'm pisshin' as fasht as I can."* This is modified or expurgated still further of its homosexual tone, until it involves hardly more than a riddling allusion of which the real meaning becomes apparent only at the otherwise worthless punch-line: *'There was a drunk standing at a bar one day. He turned, to the man on his right, and said, "Did you pour beer in my pocket?" The man said, "I certainly did not." Then the drunk turned to the man on his left and said, "Did you pour beer in my pocket?" The man said, "I most certainly did not pour beer in your pocket." The drunk said, "Just like I thought. An inside job".'* (Guam mimeograph: *Smile and the world smiles with you,* 1948–1952, p. 13.)

Completely frank, however, is a version given as a long narrative *poem,* not heard by myself but so described in a note by another collector, who heard it in Monterey, California, in 1942. The poem involved: *'A man with no hands visiting a bar, and represented the obliging bartender as pouring his beer for him, helping him drink it, etc. Finally, when the drunk had to pee, the bartender, at his request, even went into the can with him, unbuttoned his pants and took his peter out. As the bartender held it for him, it erected, and the drunk whispered to him, "Kiss me." Disgusted, the bartender kicked him out instead.'* (The same punch-line or unveiling occurs in various stories in the section "The Short-Arm Inspection," below, addressed to the examining physician.) Here is the roccoco British version of the same story, as collected the following year, 1943, in the prison at Chelmsford, Essex. Here it is a joke, not a poem, and turns presumably on the superiority of Players Virginia cigarettes to the cheap Woodbines. *'Armless ex-soldier in public house urinal offers pack of Woodbines to another, who's a bad case of shell-shock palsy, if he'll help him to piss. After a minute or two of the latter's trying to help, the former says: "Keep on, and I'll make it 20 Players".'*

Wounded soldiers and cripples seem to be considered fair game for the gruesome aggressiveness of this type of macabre 'black humor,' which has of course led to the more recent 'sick jokes.' With the partial castrations of the British joke preceding – armlessness, shell-shock, and palsy – compare the total statement in the following, which was told TO A SPASTIC YOUNG MAN IN A WHEELCHAIR by an American college-girl who practically collapsed laughing at her own joke at the end. Her exact text is given in the First Series, 4.I.2, page 230: *A war-veteran afflicted with a nervous quivering* (acted out throughout the joke) *goes into a drugstore and orders a chocolate sundae at the soda-fountain. The waitress keeps offering him various extras, all of which he accepts: hot fudge, marshmallow dip, maraschino cherry, etc. Finally the waitress asks, "Crushed nuts?" "No," says the war-veteran, quivering uncontrollably, "shell-shock."* (Los Angeles, Calif. 1940.) This leads back to an even more hateful form of the proto-homosexual jokes being considered here, again in a sort of obviously aggressive catch-question form: *'A man was standing hunched over in a men's room, with his arms drawn up in his sleeves as if he were armless. Several men came in and urinated without paying much attention, until finally one asked, "Need any help?" "All right," the man answered, while his Good Samaritan undid his fly and held it [sic] for him while he pissed. As he put it back, he asked, "Korea?" "No, gonorrhea," the man said. "I didn't want to touch it."'* (N.Y. 1952, from a hillbilly singer. The reference to the Korean War shows that the man is supposed to be an armless war-veteran; this was not stated.)

It has not often seemed worthwhile, in the present work, to take the space necessary for developing all the variants of a single joke, and all the less so since there is not even room to give all the jokes collected on the various themes. In the present case, however, it is felt that the progression has been worth tracing which is here visible in the variants: from the quasi-homosexual seduction of one man trying to touch another man's penis, under some urinary pretext and with the permissive 'sacred person' status of being dead-drunk or a wounded soldier (whose idea the whole thing is said to be, anyhow, in extrojection of the homosexual guilt), to the final sadistic forms. The ultimate variant also exists, in which the seduced or victimized male retorts with a 'practical joke' of his own, which casts both guilt and punishment gruesomely on the hitherto 'sacred' drunk : *A man in a barroom is drunk and has to urinate, but cannot remember whether he has buttons or a zipper on his fly, and asks a friend to help him to the toilet. The friends pretends to unzip him, but shoves a banana into his his hand from the free-lunch counter and pushes him into the toilet cubicle. The drunk urinates, lifts his hand, looks wildly at the banana, feeling the wetness down his legs. He lurches back into the bar screaming, 'My god! I tore my pecker out at the roots and I'm bleeding to death!'* (N.Y. 1952.)

This should be compared with sadistic homosexual hazings of a pretended castratory kind, in which for example, *The blindfolded victim is made to tie a string with a heavy weight on it to his penis and testicles, and is then ordered to throw the weight out the window. (The string has silently been cut meanwhile.) He is then handed an icicle and two freshly-shelled hardboiled eggs!* Other initiations of this kind similarly involve being forced to eat objects – such as wet doughnuts, or frankfurters with the skin peeled off – shown floating in a chamber-pot and presumed to be turds. (See the later section "Scatology.") Homosexual materials of this kind more correctly belong in the later chapter on "Castration." Their significant relevance here is their ultra-hostile concern with the genital apparatus of another male person : a form of sadistic homosexual intimacy very similar to duelling, and very prominent in 'modest' initiations ordeals and flagellations between young men, in which latter, for instance, the victims are made to *'grab a pooch,'* that is to say hold the pouch or scrotum containing the testicles forward between the legs to prevent damage to the testicles during the flagellation of the buttocks. (Texas Agricultural & Mechanical College – actually a quasi-military school – 1949.)

Milder approaches to the genitals of the other man again pass by way of *looking* to *touching*, and similarly betray their masked homosexual intent. *Tense moment in the final baseball game of the world [U.S.A.] series. The pitcher trots in to homeplate to speak to the catcher. While thousands of spectators hold their breath, the supersensitive microphone picks up the pitcher's hurried remark: "For Christ's sake, button your fly! I'm getting your signals all mixed up."* (N.Y. 1950. *Footnote for history:* Baseball catchers crouch behind the batter at home-plate,

signalling to the pitcher from between their legs with their un-
gloved hand.) Very elaborate is the mechanism involved in
bringing the two men's genitals into symbolic contact or parallel in the following, in a sort of symbolized mutual masturbation. *Two men have to make speeches at a banquet, and one
of them has the nervous habit of fiddling with his fly in public.*
[Why say any more?] *The other bets that he cannot prevent
himself from touching his fly while making his speech. They
then each secretly put itching-powder in the other's underwear
while changing to their lodge-uniforms in the locker-room. The
man with the nervous habit makes the first speech, and begins
describing a parade he saw, indicating with gestures everything
he describes, and scratching frantically meanwhile under cover
of the gestures. The soldiers he saw parading had medals down
to here (scratch-scratch), and Sam Browne belts there (scratch-
scratch), and they had epaulets (scratch), and fur shakos on
their heads (scratch-scratch-scratch). The other man leaps up at
this point and shouts: "What he forgot to say is that they were
Highland Scots – with kilts!" (Scratch-scratch-scratch-scratch!)*
(N.Y. 1949, from a musician. Aarne Tale Types 1463 and 1565,
Motif K263, listing an enormous geographical spread of texts.)

The urination pretext appears, probably earliest of all, in
explaining why one man touches another man's penis, in a
story told at a stag-smoker and intended to explain: *Why a
famous resort in the Pocono Mountains is known as Ginniger's,
though two partners own it, the second being named Schmulkowitz. You might think it's anti-Semitism, but it isn't. The reason
is this. Here were these two partners with this big, expensive
resort, which they kept full all summer, but all winter long
nobody came. Absolutely nobody. So Ginniger says to Schmulkowitz, "You know the old saying: 'A man's got to know how
to piss his name in the snow.' Let's go out and advertise." They
go out on a high, snow-covered slope in full sight of the highway, and begin pissing in large letters. Ginniger writes his name
with a flourish, but Schmulkowitz hardly gets started when he
stops, puts his prick in Ginniger's hand, and says, "Here, you
take it. You know I can't spell!"* (N.Y. 1942, given at a magician's
special 'blue' show, with off-color tricks such as a wand which
stiffened when stroked by the magician's young assistant, at the
magician's command, etc.)

An excuse to cover homosexual approaches, rather similar to
that of drunkenness or the overpowering need to urinate, is

that of *being asleep* and 'not knowing what one is doing.' (I believe the Kinsey Report on the *Human* [U.S.A.] *Male* cites an amusing offer of this 'explanation' by an army-officer interrogated.) *A travelling salesman is put up for the night by an old farmer who has only one bed. In the middle of the night the old farmer wakes up and begins shouting excitedly, "Bring me a woman! I've got to have a woman! Look at that hardon! I haven't had a hardon in twenty years!" The salesman tried to quiet him down. "Now look, you don't want a woman. That's some hardon, all right, but it isn't on you – it's on me."* (Earliest American text, recollected in Larson MS. 1952, No. 61. Also collected as of Nazi soldiers, from an American corporal, Washington, D.C. 1943. This joke is also known in France.) *Anecdota Americana*, in 1927, 1:235, gives a more frankly homosexual version, in which: *A travelling salesman in Chicago is all keyed up with tales of the wild women there, but cannot even get a hotel room for the night, and has to sleep on a billiard table with the hotel porter. During the night the porter is wakened by the salesman's screaming in his sleep, "Hurray fer Chicago! Hurray fer Chicago!"* 'The porter shook the sleeper till he woke. *"Listen," he said, "holler 'Hurray fer Chicago!' all you like, but leave my cock alone".*'

But the most elaborate disguise, certainly, and one of the most frequently collected stories in recent years, is that of a pretendedly true anecdote which began circulating during World War II in English, and has been fitted to every American war (or whatever the hell they are) since. *The Nazi leader, Goering, is seated next to a fine blonde Aryan fräulein at a state dinner, and begins feeling her leg under the table. As his hand moves up her thigh he hears a hoarse masculine whisper: "Don't be surprised when you get to my balls – I'm Secret Agent X-7."* (D.C. 1943, from a soldier.) In the British version, which is much milder and thus appeared several times in magazine humor-columns: *An English officer left behind at the retreat from Dunkerque is disguised as a nun in a convent, and after eight months cannot stand the enforced chastity any longer. He begins making overtures to another nun, followed up with unmistakable gestures. "All right, mate," comes a masculine voice from under the nun's veil, "knock it off. I've been 'ere since Dunkerque too."* Revived during the American 'police-action' in Korea: *The draft-evader hides out in a nunnery, and whispers to one of the nuns, "You know, Sister, you've got two of the prettiest legs I've ever seen." "Yes?" says the nun, "well get your hand out of there, because I've got two of the prettiest balls you ever saw too. I don't want to go to Korea either!"* (N.Y. 1953. British version on 'knickers' and 'knackers,' 1954.)

Hidden behind this archly accidental discovery of the maleness of the person whose genitals one is trying to explore, is the homosexual or fetichistic neurotic problem already noted: *the fear of the female genitals*, and the attempt to furnish even presumed women with male genitals. From the historical point of view also, the story is not quite what it seems. (There is even a doggerel poetry version reported.) In actual fact this story appears first, as a true incident occurring in a diligence or stage-coach during the Franco-Prussian War of 1870/71, and it is attested to by the greatest name in modern French literature (and politics), Victor Hugo, in his indictment of the Emperor Napoléon III, *Histoire d'un Crime* (1877) Day IV, end of chap. xii, "The Banished." (English translation, London: Ward ed., page 405–7.) Hugo gives this as a 'grimly comic' but authentic anecdote of the *French parliamentary representative, Barthélemy Terrier; smuggling out of France his brother-in-law, Préveraud, dressed as Terrier's wife and under a thick veil. A gendarme, travelling in the coach with them on a part of the trip, takes advantage of Terrier's falling asleep to start playing footie, then handie, etc., with the presumed wife. 'Préveraud, full of anger and disgust, repulsed the hand of the gendarme gently. The danger was very great. A too demonstrative* [i.e. exploratory] *evidence of affection on the part of the gendarme might ... change the eclogue into a criminal trial.' However, the coach arrives at the Belgian frontier before the gendarme's hand gets too high, and as he gets down from the coach on French soil, 'he heard behind him a voice which shouted through a thick veil, "Get out of this, or I'll smash your face!" '* There is a sick British movie version of this transvestist situation, called in France *Triple Echo* (1973), heavily exploiting the various homosexual overtones.

The only real difference between Hugo's original and the more modern joke form is that in the latter it is the gendarme (spy) who is disguised, and who is given the taunting punch-line intended to vindicate his physical virility despite the female disguise, and to express it in aggressive terms. On the subject of spies as homosexuals – owing to their fatal attraction to transvestist drag, and to the achieving of 'strength through weakness,' as in *jiu-jitsu* – and the similar homosexual and political accusations classically made against the entire Jesuit order, too much material exists for abbreviation here. Even in so unlikely a source as Alexandre Dumas' *Three Musketeers*, the third musketeer, Aramis, is finally unmasked as the worst villain of them all (in the final sequel, *Le Vicomte de Brage-lonne*), as spy, conniver – and as the secret Commander General of the Jesuits! There is no mention of homosexuality. All spies are or soon become disturbed persons, under whatever patriotic rationale they operate; and their whole activity consists of betraying *some*one, often both sides. The sexually-toned nature of spying has also been made very clear by the real and fictional careers of Kim Philby, Mata Mari, and the spate of suspiciously super-virile secret agents in recent novels and excessively violent movies, particularly (to be sure) those of Mickey Spillane, and Ian Fleming's fake-phallic 'James Bond, Secret Agent 007,' and his imitators, whose homosexual substructure is meticulously anatomized and its mask ripped off by the late Cyril Connolly in the brutal parody, "Bond Strikes Camp."

III. THE SHORT-ARM INSPECTION

Although ostensibly a routine part of the physical examination intended to check on the state of physical health and eligibility of soldiers and others, the 'short-arm inspection' or public examination of the soldier's or prisoner's or secret-society initiate's penis by another male person, is essentially nothing other than a homosexual ordeal, or a not-very-symbolized rape of the soldier, prisoner, or initiate, by the physician or other person doing the inspection, representing a homosexual rape or intimidation by the organization itself: army, navy, jail, secret society, or similar. The forced showing and handling of the individual's penis is a very obvious devirilizing and an open humiliation, breaking him to the will of the accepting group. I have described at length, in *The Guilt of the Templars* (1966) p. 102–34, the homosexual initiation and rape of new members of the Knights Templars in the 13th century. Even more specifically, Most Ancient and Puissant Order of the Beggar's Benison and Merryland, a Scottish secret society in Anstruther, in the East Nook of Fife, active from the early-18th century till the late-19th, when its *Records* were privately published on the dissolution of the order in 1892, required its members to show their penises and to masturbate publicly, ejaculating on the so-called 'Test Platter,' at a signal given by the sounding of a trumpet. The proceedings of the Society, at its half-yearly meetings note, for example: '1734. *Lammas* [August 1st]: 18 assembled, and Frigged upon the Test Platter. The origin and performance were discussed. The Platter was filled with Semen, each Knight at an average did not *"benevolent"* quite a horn spoonful.' (*Supplement to the* ... *Records*, Anstruther, 1892, p. 14. Note that the resultant platterful of semen was measured with a spoon, and 'averaged.')

No adult society in Western cultures now demands masturbation and ejaculation as an initiatory rite, though there is folklore to this effect concerning certain Greek-letter fraternities in American colleges. Such rites are, however, still very common among young and adolescent boys, under the name of 'circlejerks,' 'chain-jerks' or 'pulling-parties,' in which all the boys masturbate together – sometimes betting as to who will ejaculate first – exactly as in the Beggar's Benison, which doubtless developed from just such children's games. The boy's penis is also sometimes struck with a knotted handkerchief, or smeared with paint, or is urinated upon by one or all of the other boys, under the name of 'cockalizing' or 'making a freeman' of him, under pretense of 'catching a bird' in his hat. The humiliating intention of such forms of 'cockalizing' is perfectly evident, as is the similar purpose of all initiations, 'hazing,' and the like. Symbolic homosexual acts of a public kind, such as taking part in a 'gang-bang' or multiple rape of a single girl – sometimes chosen as being specially unattractive (or a Negro girl) – now replace overtly homosexual rites of initiation and continuation in such ultra-virile groups as the California motorcycle gang, the Hell's Angels. In the 'short-arm inspections' in the army, etc., the demanded urination into a little bottle (for albumin tests) apparently has the same homosexualizing tone as the franker ejaculation into a platter of the Beggar's Benison. At least, all jokes and folklore mentioning the required urination show open resistance to it, and mocking of it by the soldier or prisoner; implying that he recognizes in it a humiliation and devirilization, with or without overt homosexual tones.

As to the Scottish society, the ostensible purpose of their masturbatory initiation and half-yearly rite was in some way or other to conform to the secret motto or prayer – the Beggar's *Benison* referred to in the title of the order – "May your prick and your purse never fail you!" This secret motto was divulged by Capt. Francis Grose in his *Classical Dictionary of the Vulgar Tongue* (1785). The requirement of virility is in any case of Biblical authority, from *Deuteronomy*, xxiii.1, 'He that is wounded in the stones, or hath his privy member cut off, shall not enter into the congregation of the Lord.' Curious as this rule may seem in a Semitic religion which requires also that a *portion* of the penis be removed (the foreskin, in circumcision) precisely in order to allow of, or symbolize, entry 'into the congregation of the Lord,' both together are certainly indicative of the ambivalent and neurotic concern with the male genitals on the part of those originally formulating the rules of the religion. On the one hand they are anxious for the symbolic maleness and strength implied by the integral male genitals. On the other hand they demand the right to snip off part of the same genitals from helpless boy-babies of eight days (Jewish rite) or adolescents of thirteen years (Mohammedan rite), the action symbolized and recollected in both the Jewish and Christian rites of confirmation at thirteen years (i.e. at puberty) as *Bar-Mitzva*, 'the Son of the Commandment.'

Stemming from these rules are the further rules by which a priest can no longer officiate at Catholic rites if he lacks or has lost *any* member of his body; while the investiture of the Pope involves a very sober examination – on a special open-bottomed chair set on a dais – to determine whether or not '*Testiculos habet*,' and his foreskin as well. This means simply that even the Pope is required to submit to a short-arm inspection by the other members of the College of Cardinals from whose number he is elevated to the Papacy.

In discussing jokes on the 'short-arm inspection,' we are of course not concerned with private or spontaneous displaying of the male genitals, or the urge to see them in other male persons. The unexpected sight of the adult male genitals by the immature boy, as during the urination of father, scout-leader, workman, etc., can be very traumatic, and often determines a life-long need to reduplicate this optical discovery of the superior genitals of other males. This is the case often with 'tearoom queens,' or homosexuals who frequent public-toilets, peeping at the penises of other men, sometimes even through special holes ('glory-holes') bored in the toilet-compartment walls. The informal contest or wager as to the size of the penises of the men at a dinner party, settled 'upon some clean plates,' noted by Frederick J. Furnivall, in *Jyl of Breyntford's Testament* (Ballad Society, privately issued supplement-volume 7a, 1871, pp. 6 and 29–33), in connection with the "Talk of Ten Wives on their Husbands' Ware" – which I have paralleled to the modern song, "Three Old Whores from Canada," in *The Horn Book*, p. 414–5 – appears at first sight to be wholly spontaneous. Yet it is possible that this too involved some remnant of an initiatory rite or 'forfeit,' as those of the mock *tenures* of earlier centuries, in which the yearly tribute of the property-holder to the lord of the district was reduced to the humorous but humiliating 'a leap, a cough, and a fart.' Such contests in penis size or copulatory performance are also reported at princely hunting-parties in India, in K. Gauba's *H.H., The Pathology of Princes* (1930).

Even the verbal exposure of the penis, so to phrase it, has a powerful magical and frightening effect, as in solemn oaths taken upon the testicles either of oneself or of another man, as where the patriarch Abraham (*Genesis*, xxiv 2–9) requires the eldest servant of his household: "Put, I pray thee, thy hand under my thigh [*the euphemism used*]; And I will make thee swear by the Lord, the God of heaven, and the God of the earth, *etc.*" And the similar oath which the patriarch Jacob makes his son Joseph swear, in *Genesis*, xlvii. 29, not to bury him in Egypt, but to carry his body up out of Egypt to be buried in his homeland, the probable origin (and legendary contents) of the Ark of the Covenant the Jews are said to have carried with them solemnly on their flight from Egypt many years later. (*Exodus*, xxv. 10, *et seq.*) The *Supplement to the ... Records of the Beggar's Benison Society*, p. 9–10, quotes an amusing passage from the anti-clerical *Scotch Presbyterian Eloquence Display'd*, in the 18th century, concerning 'One Mr. Strange, in Berwick, preaching on *Acts*, II. 37, before several ladies of the best quality, [who] said: "*Well now, I doubt not but that several of you who have come in late have been too long this holy morning kicking against the pricks ... I fear few of you as yet have gotten a prick – but some of you may get a prick within a short time.*"' He is referring, as he hastens to assure his tittering audience, to "the sweet prick of conscience."

Vance Randolph records a survival of this sort of libel against the ranting preachers, or a chance re-occurrence of the same thing, in *Pissing in the Snow* (MS.) No. 89, "How Many Peters?"

recollected from Lawrence county, Missouri, about 1905, of a
'buckbrush circuit-rider' preacher who, referring to the denying
of Christ by the Apostle Peter, 'all of a sudden . . . hollered out:
"How many Peters is in this room?"' with a resultant uproar
of laughter among the young girls and boys present. Randolph
notes that 'A related story was long remembered in Pineville,
Mo. (Dialect Notes, 1928, VI. 61.)' The Randolph manuscript
also gives, No. 60, as "Twelve-Dollar Jack," a most interesting
account of a contest in penis-size and display, 'related as a true
story' in Galena, Missouri, in 1939, having first been heard about
1899. (He notes that whickerbill, which plays a prominent part
in the story, is the Ozark word for the foreskin or prepuce.)

One time there was some fellows hanging around the store,
and they got to talking about which one had the longest tool.
So finally Jim Henson laid eight silver dollars in a row on the
counter. Then he out with his old jemson, and it sure was a
dandy. He brushed seven of them silver dollars off onto the
floor. The eighth dollar moved a little bit, but Jim's pecker
wasn't quite long enough to knock it off'n the table.

Then old Harmon Kenny stepped forward and done the
same thing, only he brushed ten silver dollars off onto the
floor. "I don't never do no bragging about things like that,"
says Harmon, "but I will bet twenty-five dollars. If there is
any man in this town can do better, let him put up or shut
up."

Pretty soon there was a big fellow spoke up, and his name
was John E. Brown, but everybody called him Jack. "Does
whickerbills count?" says he. The boys argued awhile, but
there ain't no denying that a whickerbill is part of a man's
prick, so finally Harmon Kenny says yes. Well sir, Jack pulled
out the God-awfullest tool you ever seen, only on a jackass.
And when he drawed his whickerbill forward it made the
thing about three inches longer. "Line up your money," says
Jack Brown, and then he swung around and raked twelve
silver dollars off'n the table.

Harmon Kenny handed over the money without no argument, and John E. Brown was knowed as Twelve-Dollar Jack
from that day forward. There was some foreigners [non-
Ozarkers] tried to get him to travel with a side-show, but
Twelve-Dollar Jack just laughed in their face. "It is kind of
vulgar for a man to go around showing his pecker to

strangers," says he, "and therefore I don't want no part of it."

This anecdote is clearly connected, by methods unknown, to the joke already given in the First Series, concerning: *The women bragging about the size of their husbands' penises, one of whom says it is so long that twelve birds can stand on it when erect. Later she admits that it's only eleven birds, and that last one has to "go like this" (flapping motion of wings)*. Observe that this brings the matter back to the "Talk of Ten Wives on their Husbands' Ware" in the Porkington Manuscript dating from about 1460.

One other sort of formalized exposure of the penis is alluded to in the joke about *The actor who is prevented from reciting by a drunk in the balcony repeatedly shouting "Sing something!" When the actor advances to the footlights and expostulates with dignity, "But I cawn't sing!" the drunk replies "Then show us your prick!"* (N.Y. 1952.) This is almost ununderstandable except that it certainly suggests a rather low conception of what may be considered entertaining. The real meaning will be found in an article on "Rural Traditions of the Snake River Valley [Idaho/Oregon]," by Louie Attebery, in *Northwest Folklore* (1965) vol. I, no. 2: p. 28–9, explaining the catchphrase *"Whistle or sing, Or show your thing."* During the harvesting of grain, 'when there was a breakdown in some machine or when it was raining, the crew would get together and entertain themselves while awaiting repairs or sunny skies. (During a *breakdown* or whenever there was occasion to lay the *hoe down*, we are led to think that there was occasion also for dancing and merrymaking.) The idle crew usually assembled in a barn or bunkhouse, and each man in turn was challenged to "Whistle or sing, Or show your thing." Each man then did what he could to provide some kind of entertainment, which was not nearly so limited as the trio of suggested activities. Some men would recite verse, "Mona's Waters," for instance, an old sentimental piece. Another might sing. A third might perform a feat of strength and challenge the rest to try to duplicate it. The bull wheel off a header [wagon] was heavy, and provided a challenge to all local strong men. Wrestling was quite common, both grappling and "side-holt" [*compare wrist-wrestling as a test of strength*]. Almost all the men responded to the challenge in some way, lest he have to pay the penalty.'

(The modern hippie phrase, 'Do your thing,' is perhaps an ex-purgation of 'show your thing,' as meaning to follow one's own bent.)

What is involved here is a historical decay of the original *honorable and solemn* display of the genitals, as in the Biblical oaths described earlier, through a substitution of symbolic virilities such as wrestling, to prove a man's 'mettle' or 'spunk' (both of which referred originally and specifically to the semen). The last step down is then the notion of being irretrievably disgraced if even the symbolic virilities or strengths cannot be displayed (*"Sing something!"*) and the virile organ itself must be shown. Certain modern rock & roll singers display their penis to the male-female audience, or outline it through their pants, as an act of super-virile daring. (The phallic posing with the electric guitar, or obvious fellatory gestures with the bulb-tipped microphone, often replace this.) Whether or not this means they admit *they can't sing* is an open question. In allu-sion to this, one rock & roll phonograph recording of British origin was merchandised internationally in 1972 in a paper dust-jacket featuring a photograph of the lower half of a man in blue-jeans, with an operating zipper fly by means of which the envelope was to be opened. The voice-as-phallus, rather the phallus-as-voice, could hardly be more openly expressed.

Compare also the stories given earlier as to village *idiots* being incited to display the penis, and then to masturbate to the point of ejaculation, for small sums of money. Also the tell-tale courageously printed by Prof. Richard Dorson, in *Journal of American Folklore* (1951) vol. 64: p. 234, concerning: 'Horse-cock Charlie, who would exhibit his oversized organ for twenty-five cents, and who met his death when, asleep in an upper bunk, his outsized member fell over the side and the weight pulled poor Charlie crashing to the floor.' The reference to *money* as somehow respectabilizing the display, from Twelve-Dollar Jack to Horsecock Charlie, whether in the form of a bet or a cash-payment, as to village idiots, is a noticeable American trait.

The 'forfeit'-challenge, *"Whistle or sing, Or show your thing,"* must have had a wide tradition among the harvesting gangs before World War I, and the American hoboes or migrant-workers ('hoe-boys' presumably) who lived a vagrant life of drunkenness and homosexuality while looking for this seasonal stoop-labor. One may parallel the standard barroom recitation, by means of which the dead-broke hobo or bum, desperate for a drink (but not so desperate as to "Show his thing") would earn a shot of whiskey from the bartender, falling dead at the end over the girl's face he has sketched on the floor in chalk while reciting! *"Gimme a drink bartender,"* other offered recitations begin, as for example the bawdy "Down in the Lehigh Valley," a hobo favorite. It is also clear that the obscene recitation in doggerel verse *is* a sort of sexual, though not an anatomical, display, and only as such can be understood the long series of these in the Victorian bawdy songsters (see *The Horn Book*, pp. 201, 488), in the curious and very rare American erotic miscellany, *The Stag Party* [Boston? *ca.* 1888], and particularly in the similar *Bibliotheque Erotique* ('London' [Detroit] 1929) in two volumes, reissued in twenty parts as *Library L'Amour* (sic) about 1930.

The most popular of all surviving bawdy recitations of this kind, "Our Lil" or "Lady Lil," of which I discuss the possible origins in *The Horn Book*, p. 417–20, specifically describes a public contest in sexual intercourse. This is very much like the masturbation displays and contests of the Beggar's Benison in Scotland, which latter were incidentally complete with an encouraging song composed mostly of grunts and shouts, beginning: *"Ram it in. Jam it in. Still there's more to follow."* (*Records*, p. 20). The halfbreed hero of "Our Lil," named Mexican Pete, is also invariably described as displaying his penis to the men in the barroom, and it is this display that leads to the fatal contest in sexual intercourse with Our Lil:

> And when he laid it on the bar,
> The damn thing stretched from thar – to thar!
> (*measuring gesture with both hands*)

The 'forfeit' display of the penis is only a step from similar acts required plainly as an ordeal – also presumably a 'proof of manhood' – as in ritual initiations since at least the time of the Knights Templars, if not of the proto-Christian Essene or Nazirite male sect, whose naked communal bathing establishments have recently been discovered near the Dead Sea. (See further, *The Guilt of the Templars*, pages 116ff. and 130.) In my own lightly-fictionalized autobiography, *Portrait of the Artist as Flowing Teat* (Tangiers, 1966, edition limited to ten copies of which a number were destroyed by interested parties: repository copy in Library of Congress) p. 10, I describe such an ordeal of which I myself was more than eyewitness in Scranton, Pennsylvania, in 1928, at the age of ten. These ordeals always involve some hostile act against the penis of which the display has been demanded, such as urination on it by all the other boys (or into the victim's mouth), or painting it red or blue and sprinkling it with feathers, etc. Often pretended castrations are engaged in, the victim being blindfolded and made to *assist* in his own presumed castration. In Dotson Rader's savage novel of homosexual prostitution, *Gov't Inspected Meat* (New York, 1971) p. 163, a group of West Point cadets – the government-inspected meat – make an underclassman, played with a Southern accent to indicate his White Nigger status, shine the shoes of one of them, kneeling before him in his underwear, as an act of symbolic fellation. Unsatisfied, one of them then verbalizes the matter: ' "He'd suck an officer if it'd mean a stripe [promotion], wouldn't you Masters?" The kid ... glanced at Peter, looking directly at him, the muscles at the back of the boy's jaw twitching. He hated us both. "Yes, Suh!" he said, very loudly. "Anytime you want, Suh!" ' This is verbal castration.

But no private atrocity of this kind, however formalized, can even begin to compare with the authentic routine ordeal of the short-arm inspection at the hands of jail officials and guards. This is played for its bitter humor in Stanley Kubrick's motion-picture, *Clockwork Orange* (1971), including the symbolic touch of the prison guard holding his flashlight phallically *in his mouth* to free both hands to pull the new prisoner's buttocks apart. The reality behind the satire here is coldly described in Michael Agnello's "Ssecorp" ("Process' spelled backwards), published in the *Los Angeles Free Press*, August 26, 1966, page 9, as part of a purposely dead-pan description of the routine matriculation of prisoners in the Los Angeles City Jail, and possibly in hundreds of others:

> PLACE: Los Angeles City Jail, located in downtown Los Angeles, near the City Hall. FUNCTION: To limit the mobility of certain individuals who have either been sentenced by a court for short terms, or do not have sufficient money for bail and are awaiting trial ... PROCESS ... involves the following: prisoners strip naked, sit, check clothes; they then take showers (the shower room is not very well maintained) and finally are lined up against a wall, their genitals closely

checked by someone (maybe another sheriff) and when checked superficially, the checker asks them to raise them up for closer examination underneath, then bend over for an anal inspection. After one line of prisoners are checked, they must stand up straight and another sheriff comes with a special dispenser that emits creamy white fluid on each prisoner's genitals and again bending over (together) on each prisoner's anus. After this phase the prisoners are issued special uniforms (navy blue pants and shorts).

I have caused inquiries to be made into the objective truth and ostensible purpose of this final ritual, the 'creamy white fluid,' and have been assured – not by the author, Mr. Agnello – that it is correctly described and perfectly routine, and not only in California. The official purpose is to protect the blue dungaree pants, which are prison property, from infestation by crab-lice or 'crotch-pheasants' (*Pediculus pubis*), which vagrants and 'winos' (alcoholic bums) might otherwise bring into the prison. The 'creamy white fluid,' about which I asked in particular, turns out to be a special foaming salve – once known colloquially as '*mercury salve*' or '*blue ointment*': but it was blue then – which kills the bugs. Unfortunately, my informant then rather destroyed my faith in the whole thing, as anything but a vulgar charade of '*creaming up the prisoners' asses*' (which is what the prisoners call it) in obvious homosexual pantomime, by assuring me that, though the police would really rather not have to do it, so important is this process that on one occasion, when there was no foaming salve left in the dispenser, owing to a very large haul of vagrants at Christmas, the similar white fluid in a fire-fighting device was substituted, hoping it might be of some use! This is therefore clearly nothing but an unconsciously homosexual initiatory humiliation or joke, in which everyone but the prisoners purports to see only an unfortunate hygienic necessity.

Very similarly to the American police-station 'frisk,' in Nazi Germany, the penis of persons suspected of being Jewish would be examined publicly. I have been told by a man who was studying in the Vienna Institute for Sexual Research during the 1930's that, at the time of the German *Anschluss* in 1938, he was in a motion-picture theatre near the Prater or main amusement park. Suddenly the projection of the film was stopped, the house-lights came up, and a jackbooted s.a. man strutted out on the proscenium and snarled: *"It stinks here of Jew!"* The men in the audience thought to look Jewish, including my informant, were lined up at the front of the theatre and made to take their pants down and show their penises, after which they were put out. *"How do you like it, ladies?"* said the S.A. man prophetically, as the Jews were herded out. *"That's our kind of show."*

As a similar humiliation, displaced upward from the penis (until Der Tag), American Negroes are nowadays sometimes required by Southern sheriffs to open their mouths and show their *teeth*, presumably to demonstrate their age as shown on their proffered 'I.D.,' with the contemptuous explanation that *"Everybody knows you can tell a horse's and a nigger's age by their teeth."* This was told to me by a Negro novelist as having happened to 'a friend,' at gun-point, while driving through the South in an expensive automobile, in explanation of his having gone into 'writer's block' for years afterward, and finally taking a job as an F.B.I. informer. Just one human atrocity-story among thousands.

By comparison to the *realities* of the subject, as above, the jokes and other folklore connected with the 'short-arm inspection' seem rather mild. The term itself is military in origin, parodying 'side-arms' for pistol, with a bow to the folk-idea of the penis as a fifth member: one actual slang synonym for the penis is 'third leg' or 'middle leg,' as here it is an *arm* shorter than the other two. The utter absurdity and irrelevancy of the inspection of a soldier-recruit's genitals is perfectly clear to all soldiers, but they presumably forget this when they become officers and command the same process for other men. It can also, of course, be considered 'revenge,' as with most initiations, which this year's upperclassmen inflict cruelly on recruits (called '*piss-heads*' and '*turds*') for no other real reason than that they suffered the same tortures and humiliations when they were '*piss-heads*' themselves. In the homosexual sense, hidden in all of this, there is the 'gay' (homosexual) proverb: '*This year's wolf is last year's punk – out for revenge!*' which I first heard during the 1930's.

A soldier is refused for having undescended testicles. His father is outraged and asks the draft-board doctor, "What do you want him for, doc, fighting or fucking?" (N.Y. 1941.) In variants in which the mother speaks, her line is modified to 'fighting or *breeding*.' The alliterative form is of folk origin, as in the comedy toast: *"Here's to the Three F's: Fame, Fortune (Fighting) – and a Foot-race!"* (N.Y. 1936.) A non-military version, very obviously derived, sets the scene in: *A New Orleans whorehouse. A customer demands a virgin and one is procured for him, a Negro girl of fourteen. He refuses her on seeing her naked, saying curtly "No wool!" "Listen," says the madam, "what do you want to do: fuck or knit?"* (N.Y. 1953.) The artificial Southern set-up here, involving New Orleans and the Negro girl, is only to justify the use of the term 'wool,' necessary for the joke, since the term is really only used as to the Negro head-hair.

As the original of the alternatives, "fighting or fucking," in the principal joke, the rather similar Polish riddle might be offered, given in German translation by B. Blinkiewicz, "Polnische Rätselfragen and Rätsel," in *Anthropophtéia* (1911) VIII. 395, no. 3: *"Wo zu hat Gott den Menschen erschaffen: zur Arbeit oder zum Genuss? – Zur Arbeit, denn er hat zehn Finger, doch nur einen Zumpt."* (For what purpose did God create man: for work or for pleasure? – For work, because he has ten fingers, but only one prick.) To be compared with: *The fat woman who describes in detail her day of incredible overeating to the doctor. "I'm sorry, madam," he says, "I can't help you. You've got to die. You only have one ass-hole."* (Scranton, Pa. 1936, probably of Hungarian-Jewish origin.)

The homosexual tone of the short-arm inspection is actually its principal feature and the main one seized upon in jokes. The homosexuality is almost always projected upon the inspecting officer or doctor, as is obviously the underlying truth. The only exceptions to this format that I have encountered concern men pretending to be homosexuals, or homosexuals flaunting their peculiarity by way of 'camp.' In Tuli Kupferberg's manual of *1001 Ways To Beat the Draft* (New York, 1968), among hundreds of excessively clever hippie-style suggestions, a few old folk-remedies for the problem are included, such as: *When the doctor gives you the old finger up the ass and says, "Cough," just reach back and kiss him.* Kupferberg makes a number of far wilder suggestions, adding up to just about the same thing but more aggressively. In a joke we have: *A homosexual volunteer who wants to join the army. Tough recruiting sergeant: "Do you think you could kill a man?" "Oh thertainly, thir, but it might take dayth and dayth."* (2:373, version without the lisp. The text form was delivered with the recruit's answer very crisp and military at first, despite the lisp, but lilting off flutily on the closing words in the standard mock-homosexual exaggerated drawl. – N.Y. 1942.)

The actual purpose of refusing known homosexuals in military service is obscure, especially when the men in service are refused sufficient access to women at the same time. (Now you see it; now you don't!) It is probably a survival of the overvaluation of virility in warriors – thus again pointing to ancient phallic examination rituals – though in fact the greatest warrior cultures, such as the Levantine Moslems, the Japanese samurai, and the Germans of recent centuries have been outstandingly homosexual, especially in the armies. The turn-of-the century scandals set off in Germany by the exposés of the journalist Maxmilian Harden-Witkowski brought this for the first time to very public attention, and made it the subject of much cartoon humor. Some striking examples are collected in John Grand-Carteret's scarce volume of caricature reproductions, with the obvious punning title, Derrière "Lui" (1908). The "Lui" referred to was the German Kaiser, who was not homosexual.

An army doctor is examining a recruit at Fort Custer, and on finally requiring him to strip naked says, "You don't seem to have much there." "Just wink at it, doc," says the boy, "and see what happens." (N.J. 1944, from an army private.) Possibly the least humorous of the jokes on this theme, but it significantly recognizes the doctor-as-castrator, though here only verbally, in his denigration of the size of the recruit's penis. Recruits are being examined for a Scottish regiment, and the officers are discussing one particular Highland giant. "I'm not sure," says the captain; "I don't like the tilt of his kilt." The sergeant salutes: "Well, the fact is, sir, he's taken a liking to you." (London, 1953.) The hidden meaning here is that the soldier-giant is going to bugger the officer. See further the section on "Pedicatory Rape," below.

Possibly the most common joke on this theme has been collected in both France and America, and seems to have originated with the French short-arm inspection of soldiers, which is even more rigorous than that elsewhere. The army doctor is examining the recruit's penis for venereal disease. He pushes the foreskin back and lets it slip forward. Then, not certain of his diagnosis, he pushes the foreskin back again. Soldier: "If that's for the government, sir, you go right ahead

and do it your way. But if it's for me, a little faster, please!"
(1:72.) Also collected – again in both France and America –
with variant punch-line: *Soldier: "Kiss me, Captain, I'm coming!"* (N.J. 1942.)

Replacing the Kaiser of World War I as the hated Heinie of
World War II, Adolf Hitler was also the object of much sexual
vilification in humor, generally turning on the imputation of
homosexuality, which was apparently untrue. (A movie, on
The Sexual Life of Adolf Hitler was announced in preparation
in 1965, twenty years after Hitler's suicide.) *Hitler is reviewing
the short-arm inspection of the German troops, which Goering
has set up in precise Teutonic order, by the numbers. He
explains his system to Hitler, the troops obeying in unison.
"One – pull out cock. Two – draw back foreskin. Three – piss.
Four – push back foreskin." Hitler is very pleased. "Fine, fine!
The true German orderliness. Now let me try it. Two! Four! –
Two! four! – Two! four!"* (2:309, published in 1934.)

Finally, of course, the hostile element in the homosexual
syndrome appears, and the short-arm inspection is used as the
pretext for phallically-directed torture of the soldiers. *Rasputin
is reviewing the cossack troops on the eve of the Revolution.
He stamps on a cossack's toe, and asks, "Does that hurt?" "No,
your worship!" "And why doesn't it hurt?" "Because a cossack
feels no pain, your worship!" Rasputin pulls open the greatcoat
of the next soldier and burns his chest-hair with his amber
cigarette-holder. "Does that hurt?" "No, your worship!" "Why
doesn't it hurt?" "A cossack feels no pain, your worship! God
bless the Czar!!" He pulls open the trousers of the next soldier,
rumples through his underwear and pulls out his penis which
he strikes violently with his riding-crop. "And does that hurt?"
"No, your worship!" "And why doesn't it hurt?" "Because it
belongs to the man in back of me, your worship!"* (N.Y. 1948.)
Every element is combined here: the absurd overcompensatory
mammoth length of the penis, the turning of the punishment to
a third party, even the implied buggery of one soldier by the
other – to refuse and to evade the intended homosexual torture
of the penis, which is, of course, nothing other than a hardly-
symbolized or partialized castration. The 'social castration' is
also very prominent here, of forcing the slave-soldiers to accede
patriotico-verbally in their torturing and humiliation, as is
stunningly satirized in Cyril Connolly's "Year Nine" (in Dwight
Macdonald's *Parodies: An Anthology*, 1960, p. 386–91), and, less

well, in Aldous Huxley's *Brave New World* (1932) and George Orwell's *1984*, imitated from it. This 'joke' on Rasputin is not a bad satire either.

An excellent American novel of life on the frontier in the pioneer days of the Conestoga wagons, Merle Colby's *All Ye People* (1931) p. 136–8, brings into the action the historical truth travestied above. This is the castratory 'bollocking' that was considered fair-fighting among men at that period, and in all periods of war. (See *The Guilt of the Templars*, p. 128–9; and compare *Deuteronomy*, xxv. 11–12.) Colby is describing a 'towelling match' or whip-fight: 'This time his whip's long length flashed down, up, perpendicularly ... "A draw for the cullions. Aimed at the groin. If it had landed, the young feller'd be done for, and dead after half an hour of agony" ... Dag just avoided another deadly cut at the groin.'

The homosexual cowboy movies in which Hollywood has specialized over the last twenty-five years, replacing the earlier 'clean' Indian-killing type of cowboy films – as is briefly discussed in *Neurotica* (1950) No. 7: p. 3–7 – have entirely given away the show as to the essential and apparently inevitable sado-masochism of homosexuality, in their insistence upon cruel scenes (in ketchupy color photography) of body-smashing, whip-lashing, etc., the latter being particularly featured in a 1960's item, *One-Eyed Jacks*. The sexual censorship of the films, fortunately, does not (as yet!) allow them to show scenes of genitally-aimed sadism such as that just quoted, even in a recent and most brutal cowboy-killer orgy on film, directed by Sam Peckinpah, and advertised – in France, at least – with a gloating plug quoted from a perturbed reviewer who observed that '*It contains scenes of a cruelty difficult to endure.*' (Every knock a boost!) But is this really the homosexually advertised '*love* of David and Jonathan' and all the rest of the noble sentimental eyewash of which we once heard so much from the propagandists of the 'Gay Liberation' movement in America? Strictly from a propaganda viewpoint, it might really be wiser, if anyone still wants to convince anybody that homosexuality is a form of *love*, and not just the neurotic charade of sado-masochistic hatred that its every public appearance proves it to be, to soft-pedal at least for a while the 'S. & M.' western-killer orgies, the drag motorcyclist sagas, the out-&-out whipping stuff, and the quite comparable though merely verbal-sadistic spectacles, in both theatre and films.

The mystic notion of somehow achieving virility through homosexual murder, torture, and cruelty – or, failing that, through violent anal intercourse with the enemy, woman – has best been analyzed in Prof. Kate Millett's elegantly bitter *Sexual Politics* (New York, 1970), especially in her final chapters anatomizing the literary message of those stalwarts of sexism, Henry Miller, Norman Mailer and Jean Genet. I have attempted to do the same, of the earlier wave of insane *machismo* and woman-hating of Ernest Hemingway & Company, in *Love & Death* (1949), the final chapter, "Open Season on Women." Of Dr. Millett's targets, only Mailer was stung into a reply, the hopelessly drivelling defense of Miller and himself as "The Prisoner of Sex" – she had called him a 'prisoner of the virility cult,' which would of course have made a less jazzy title – to which an entire issue of *Harper's Magazine* was for some reason devoted.

IV. FELLATION

As it is not very well known, and is essential to the understanding of the present and following sections, it should be emphasized here that the homosexual *acts* of choice are not entirely determined by personal psychological preferences, but are culturally stabilized over long periods of time, and differ in various cultures. Until the French Revolution, oragenital acts of all kinds, whether between heterosexual or homosexual couples, were taken for granted in Europe, as erotic foreplay, and were seldom even considered worthy of mention, though they were of course very well known to cultured persons if only through the inordinate attention paid to them by the Latin satirists, especially Martial's *Epigrams*, which every educated young man studied. (There was even a specially expurgated edition prepared in the 17th century for the education of the French dauphin, the son of Louis XIV, all the highly-flavored passages being grouped at the end, possibly for greater convenience in finding them – whence the sardonic phrase '*ad usum Delphini*.') The *Facetiae* or joke-collection of Heinrich Bebel, about 1510, is one of the few non-classic texts to make frequent reference to oragenital acts, but Bebel wrote in Latin, in classic tradition.

Simultaneous oragenital acts – the now world-famous *soixante-neuf* or 'sixty-nine' (so-called from the appearance of the two bodies joined in that way) – are doubtless prehistoric in origin, since animals such as kittens can often be observed licking each other's genitals mutually, while twins in the womb usually lie in precisely the 'sixty-nine' position. Nevertheless, except for a brief appearance on certain Greek vases, and in very florid form (such as the twisted or 'crossback' *soixante-neuf*) in East Indian temple sculptures, no reference to this has been found in pictorial or literary form before certain manuals for courtesans published during the French Revolution, and probably the work of the extraordinary lesbian woman-revolutionary, Théroigne de Méricourt, whose tempestuous life and pitiful death would make a marvellous biographical play-and-movie for the new Women's Liberation movement audience.

With the exception, of course, of lesbians such as Mlle. Théroigne, homosexuals in the European and Levantine traditions appear to have been almost exclusively given to anal intercourse, as their act of choice, or to have condescended to oragenitalism only as foreplay. In America, at the present time, the popular notion of homosexuality seldom involves the conception of anal intercourse, as it does in England, except among prisoners, soldiers, miners, and other basically normal men deprived of women and desperate for sexual relief; and this is the precise truth. The popular idea in America concerning 'real' homosexuals is instead (whatever the truth, this time, may be) that they engage principally in the act of fellation, or the 'sucking' of the penis, which is considered deeply disgraceful, as would be taking the passive position in anal intercourse, or pedication. Certain foreign nations, particularly Greece, are nevertheless still considered to be given to pedication, but more particularly to the pedication of women. This was also once a classic thrust against Italy and the Italians in European satire, as Diderot's *Bijoux Indiscrets* (1748) vol. II, chap. 8, "Fricamone & Callipiga."

Words referring to pedication, such as 'bugger,' can therefore be accepted in popular American and even British speech as more or less occult, good-humored or affectionate (*e.g.* 'little bugger' or 'booger,' or 'lucky bugger!' though obviously 'dirty bugger' is an insult, as would be 'dirty' anything). But words referring to fellation, in particular '*cock-sucker*,' are almost invariably deathly insults, and I have even heard a homosexual, whose act of choice this was, refusing the term owing (he said) to the word 'cock,' which, to him as a Southerner, referred instead to the female genitals (from the French coquille). It is also not altogether irrelevant to observe that the effective action in fellation is never actually sucking, but any form of continuous oral friction imitating vaginal intercourse, and therefore capable of bringing the 'passive' male to orgasm. The slang term 'blow' is even farther from the physiological truth, as is noted in a rough folk-proverb or catch-phrase : 'Suck, you son-of-a-bitch! "Blow" is just a figure of speech.'

Many or most of the jokes on these subjects have no real situational humor, and turn simply on the insulting quality of the accusation of homosexuality, specifically of fellation. Some of the horror-emotion involved, as far as the non-homosexual public is concerned, has been diminished by the overuse of the word 'cock-sucker' as an expletive, as discussed in Edward Sagarin's excellently-researched The Anatomy of Dirty Words (New York, 1962) p. 109–12. But this has not changed the great difficulty that practising homosexuals have in finding male prostitutes who will allow the homosexuals to kiss them on the mouth. This has apparently been the case for nearly two thousand years, as the Roman satirist Martial specifically mentions it, rationalizing the matter by a presumed 'evil odor' about the mouth of the fellator. The same subject was brought pointedly into the evidence at the crucial moment of the Oscar Wilde trial, as has already been noted, turning on the question of whether or not Wilde had kissed a certain boy. This matter seems in fact to have obsessed Wilde, as it is also made the gruesome climax of his play Salomé (imitated from Flaubert's Hérodias and Salammbô), with the heroine grovelling about on the stage with the decapitated head of John the Baptist, whom she has had killed because he refused to kiss her, gloating and screaming – and all the more shrilly in Richard Strauss' operatic version, the greatest success of the 1900's – "I have kissed thy mouth, Iokaanan!" The kiss on the mouth is also made climatic as to the 'bringing out' of a repressed homosexual Don Juan (as a revenge by a drag-queen) in Rona Jaffe's mordant freak-show of sexual decadence in show business, The Fame Game (New York, 1969) chap. 14.

I. THE FELLATORY ACCUSATION

The joke has already been given, in section 10.II.4 above, "The 'Normal' as Homosexual," as to the southern philanthropist who would have been referred to by everyone in town as 'Whiffle the philanthropist,' had he not made *one little mistake*, as a result of which he is known instead as 'Whiffle the cock-sucker.' (1:126, using the name Cohen.) Reduced to a proverb or catch-phrase: *"There ain't no justice. You lay one brick and you're not a bricklayer, but you suck one cock and you're a cock-sucker."* (N.Y. 1940.) The philosophical point here is neatly made. More often the catch-phrase is one of mere insult or provocation: *"Did you ever take it into your head to make a living?"* (Scranton, Pa. 1932: young boys.) Or: *"Say, you could make a good living – if you don't bite."* To someone smoking a cigar: *"EVERYbody's sucking mickeys!"* And, said also to women 'as a joke': *"Get your ass off the table, Mabel* (or: *Put back your false teeth, Dracula) – that dime is to pay for the beer."* (Cleveland, Ohio, 1963.)

As an example of the purely disgraceful quality of the accusation, here backed up by the purely linguistic humor of the story: 'The Dinktown band was doing its best, when someone called the piccolo player a cock-sucker. The leader's baton beat a tattoo on his music stand, and the players became silent. He turned to his audience. "Who called my piccolo player a cock-sucker?" he demanded. A voice in the rear of the theatre yelled back: "Who called that cock-sucker a piccolo player?" ' (1:11, misspelling 'piccolo' consistently.) The humor here, such as it is, is a good example of one of the ancient Graeco-Roman rhetorical figures – *chiasmus* or crossing-over, as the letter X, *chi* – fallen away to a joke. This is a quite common occurrence in folklore, though seldom observed; as also the similar falling away of older ballads and traditions to nursery rhymes and games. The 'voice in the rear of the theatre,' or more usually *'voice from the balcony'* is a standard device in jokes, similar to the *'Man in the Upper Berth,'* discussed in the First Series, 8.II.3; and a rather good case could be made for identifying both of these as none other than the anonymous or masked Greek *chorus*, who speaks the editorial truth or the true hidden thought of the audience.

The fellatory accusation, so often made as a mere general insult – or even used absolutely, as an expletive, as one might say 'God damn!' – can also be taken with a good deal of aplomb. *On the movie-set the producer is thundering for the imported director: "Where the hell is that Russian cock-sucker, Borislavski?" The imported director: "Please ... Polish cock-*

sucker." (Hollywood, Calif. 1939, told as a true anecdote and the name therefore changed.) This is of a piece with one of the crudest of the many and very venomous jokes attacking Franklin Delano Roosevelt, the American president whose enormous efforts to save the capitalistic system during the 1930's 'Depression' and the Second World War did not save him from this type of vilification, almost entirely originated by the radical Right composed of millionaires like himself. *A man petitions the court for the right to change his name. "What's your name now?" asks the judge. "Franklin Delano Shit." "Well, certainly you can change it. What do you want to change it to?" "Joe Shit."* (N.Y. 1942.) By 1952 this was collected several times simply as a nonsense joke, with the reference to Roosevelt omitted – more probably out of lack of timeliness than as expurgation. Again, purely as an insult: *Open confession hour at the Oxford Group. A tall, cadaverous man gets up to give testimony, ending, "And I can truly say that in my forty years in the movement I have never once had sexual relations with a woman." Voice from the back row: "Sit down you dirty cock-sucker!"* (N.Y. 1940.) The anonymous 'voice' here comes closer to the sort of mentality that writes anonymous poison-pen letters, and outhouse *graffiti*, or the 'unknown hand' in the Mediterranean area that puts the *vendetta* dagger into a man's back in a crowded street.

The most famous and complex fellation story turns solely on the use, or rather the non-use, of a word here being considered. It seems to have begun as a simple pun: *An Irishman and a Swede share a cabin together while working their way across the ocean on a steamship, though they work in different parts of the ship. The Irishman is a deck-hand; the Swede works in the stoke-hold wetting down the fuel coke to prevent dangerous fumes. When the ship docks and they are saying goodbye, the Irishman asks, "Say, phwat the hell was it you were doin' to work your way over, Oley?" "Ay bane coke-soaker," says the Swede. "Ye dirrty divil," says the Irishman, spitting, "and I nivir suspicted ye!"* (1:39.) The more recent form has developed this into a complete linguistic production, working every possible spoonerism on the theme, for all the simple fun of tantalizing the audience waiting for the expected word. *Four fairies are brought before the night-court judge for soliciting in a public park. "What do you do for a living?" the first one is asked. "Your Honor," he says, "I'm a coke-sacker. I work in a coal-*

*yard putting the coke in sacks." "Thirty days!" shouts the
judge. (To the next:) "What do you do?" "I'm a sock-tucker,
your Honor. I work in a sock factory turning down the tucks."
"Thirty days! (To the next:) And you?" "I'm a teak-soaker. I
work in a lumber yard soaking the wood." "Thirty days! (To
the next:) What about you?" "I'm guilty, your Honor." "Well,
go and sin no more."* (N.Y. 1938. Many variants, and extremely
common, but seldom collected with the judge's final retort or
topper.) The format here is appropriated exactly from an older
joke on prostitution, which will appear in a later chapter, the
situation of the prostitute taken before her judge being standard
in literature at least since the time of the Woman taken in
Adultery, told with superb pathos in the *Gospel according to
Saint John*, viii. 3–11, from which, of course, the punch-line or
topper here is taken: 'And Jesus said unto her, *Neither do I
condemn thee: go, and sin no more.*'

2. FELLATION AS RAPE

The betrayal of one's own homosexuality, by the irrefutable
evidence of engaging in fellation upon another man, is the
point toward which almost all fellatory jokes are leading, when
they do not turn on the mere linguistic humor of insults and
shibboleth terms, as above. The milder self-accusation of allowing oneself to be fellated (by a man) or expressing any willingness in this direction, is considered halfway to the final self-
betrayal, and is encountered generally in the form of some
elaborate or accidental misunderstanding. *A young priest, who
is not very sure yet of the proper penances to mete out in
confession, asks an older priest what he should give a fellator.
"Oh," says the older priest, "give him a dollar or so, if you feel
like it. Personally, I never give them more than fifty cents."*
(2 : 24. This is perhaps connected with Rotunda's Motif T463.1,
"Sodomist forces confessor to absolve him," and compare Motif
V29.4, "Sodomist makes sport of confession," from Bandello,
I. 6.) A Jewish joke, since it involves a knowledge of the *shofar*,
or ram's horn, blown ceremonially before the congregation at
the Jewish New Year: *The butler is explaining to the new
maid, "Yes, working for a Jewish family is very interesting.
They have all sorts of curious customs. For instance, during
their holidays, before they sit down to dinner, the head of the
family blows the shofar." Maid: "Say, they sure know how to
treat the help wonderful!"* (N.J. 1962, told by an ultra-modern

rabbi, who apparently did not know what 'hillul ha-Shem' or religious sacrilege is, nor whether it mattered.)

Endlessly repeated, often published in cartoon form in the semi-expurgated humor magazines throughout the two decades or more (1930's to 1950's) preceding the New Freedom, the following joke involves an extraordinary implication of the infectious or weakening and 'tainting' power of homosexuality, specifically of fellation, though this is not actually specified in the joke: *A powerful sailor is cast away on a desert island with six women after the sinking of their ocean liner. The harem of six women, getting food for him and making love to him, is like paradise for a while, but finally he realizes it is getting to be too much for him. One day he sights a life-raft offshore with a man wildly gesticulating, and he swims out to help the new-comer in, congratulating himself that now his work satisfying the women will be cut in half. As he approaches the life-raft he sees the man on it combing his hair with the back of his hand, and calling, "Yoo-hoo! Help me ashore, will you?" "Oh, shit!" says the sailor, "there goes my Sundays."* (N.Y. 1948, and often since.)

Since fellation is the same, for the passive male, whether en-acted by a woman or by a man (homosexuals of course state that it is *better* when done by a man!) the only problem in-volved in accepting this caress from a man is, as the jokes see it, avoiding the feeling of guilt or abnormality, and this is done by refusing to admit precisely what is happening. That is to say, some *situational disguise*, comparable to the verbal disguises just preceding, must be evolved, such as the standard evasions used by women, of being drunk, asleep, not knowing what one is doing, etc., and finally raw necessity. *Two salesmen are in bed together in a hotel room, as they could not get single beds. "Don't answer now," says one of the salesmen, "but are you by any chance sucking me off?"* (2:308. This is to be compared with the strange and even spooky Negro story, in the final chapter on "Scatology," with end-line, *'Is you by any chance peein' on me?"*) – *Three hoboes beat their way across country by having one of them bet the bartender that the other two are engaging in fellation in the toilet. The two others arrange them-selves in compromising positions in the toilet, after having gorged on the free lunch, one of them with a wooden rake-handle painted red sticking out of his fly, and the other sucking it. The bartender throws them out, and pays the third man the*

*bet, and on the proceeds they all manage to live till they get to
the next town. One evening in Denver, the 'low man on the
totem-pole' says to the other, "We'll have to get that rake-
handle repainted. All the shellac came off in my mouth tonight." "Shellac, hell!" says the other. "I lost the rake-handle a
week ago in Detroit."* (2:90, a variant with a sausage and the
punchline excuse of fooling a Jewish bartender, who is "far
too clever" for anything but the real thing.)

The oral concentration of this story is much over-determined:
the free lunch, the presumably starving men, etc., and might
perhaps just as correctly be given in the later section, "The
Relationship with the Semen.' It is also connected in situation
with the materials given earlier under "The Short-Arm Inspection," as to the showing of the penis, or other homosexual
ordeals, specifically in barrooms or other wholly male situations, as a forfeit or 'dare.' This orality is a crucial element in
the latent homosexuality of almost all male alcoholics (and
other drug addicts), who are of course the 'bums' and 'winos'
of the barroom stories and dares – bringing the matter back
again to the crucial oral concentration. Also, the hostile element
in the preceding joke is visibly its most prominent feature: the
'low man on the totem pole' being made a fool of (cheated,
'fucked') in a fellatory rape.

Hostility is seldom lacking in oragenital relationships, of
whatever kind, and between whatever sexes, though usually
much covered over by the romantic idea, or glozing pretense,
that they are being engaged in for the benefit of the passive or
genital partner. It may be stated as axiomatic that *all oragenital
acts are really for the psychological benefit of the active or oral
participant, and not for the physical pleasure of the passive or
genital participant.* I have made this the underlying theme of
my practical manual, *Oragenitalism: Oral Techniques in Genital
Excitation* (New York: Julian Press, 1969), especially in the
chapters on "Fellation" and the related "Irrumation," p. 227 ff.,
to which the interested reader is referred. The classified advertisements for genital partners – always genital – in the
'underground press' of the late 1960's and since, by fellators and
cunnilinguists, also make this matter perfectly clear.

During oragenitalism, the unconscious hostility or resistance
of either partner can easily cause physical danger. The hostility
of the so-called passive participant is particularly easy to express, by means of violent gestures – disguised as caresses –

choking or otherwise harming the active participant. *A homosexual is fellating a man he has picked up, in a dark alley, when a policeman appears. The homosexual disappears in a flash and the man is left looking stupid. "What are you doing there with your prick out?" says the policeman. "I'm, uh, taking a leak officer." "Taking a leak, eh? Well what are them ears doin' in your hands?"* (N.Y. 1941.) Much more realistic, and practically a photograph of the amenities of the American Sadie-Maisie (sado-masochist) bars : *A tough faggot is puffing on a slender cigar in a beer-joint. He follows another man into the toilet and snarls at him, "Ya ever get your cock sucked?" "No," says the man. "Ya ever get your goddam face pushed in?" "No." "Ya wanna get your face pushed in?" "No." "Then keep this cigar goin' while I suck you off.'* (N.Y. 1953.) After which, one can really draw the curtain.

In various forms, the idea of fellatory rape is promulgated as the best excuse for homosexual acts, until the final and unexpected admission that it was not rape at all. *A travelling salesman complains that his best customer has a peculiar habit: when they have to sleep together in hotels on the road, the customer takes the salesman's head and pushes it to the middle of the bed. "What do you do?" asks the listener. "What can I do? He's my best customer."* (Anecdota, 2 : 176, given in Yiddish dialect, on the stereotypical idea that *"Jews will do anything for money."*) The more powerful pretext of raw necessity or desperate danger is more commonly met. *A man is describing a terrible experience he had in one of the criminal quarters of Paris. An Apache dragged him into an alley and held a knife to his throat, snarling, "Go down on me, or I'll cut your heart out!" "What did you do?" asks his listener, appalled. "Well, I'm here, ain't I?"* (1 : 412.) What is really the same story, retold with only one significant difference, gives the whole differential diagnosis between homosexual practices by normal men, for any reason, and actual homosexuality. *A man goes to the rabbi for advice. "Rabbi," he says, "I'm ruined. I'm a drummer, a respectable married man, and I make all the southern towns. I was in Atlanta, Georgia, coming home from eating dinner in a restaurant, and this big baytzimmer* [Cossack or Irishman] *dragged me into an alley and grabbed me by the neck, and said to me, 'You're going to suck my prick, you mocky son-of-a-bitch, or I'm going to break your head!' Rabbi, I'm ruined!" "No, no," says the rabbi placatingly. "The Talmud rules that a man can do anything but spit on the Bible to save his life." "No, rabbi," the man insists, "I'm ruined. I* LIKED *it!" (N.Y. 1940.)*

The frequency of French and Jewish actors and backgrounds in these stories of homosexual self-discovery – which are more frequent than the texts chosen to present here would imply – is part of the attempted *distance* the presumably Anglo-Saxon joke tellers and listeners wish to place between themselves, at the obvious identification level, and these distressing possibilities of perversion which clearly both fascinate and perturb them very much. In actual fact, male homosexuality is not particularly evident nor of much public concern in France, as compared to its excessive visibility in the Anglo-Saxon cultures of Germany, Holland, Britain, and America, where it has become a public plague over the last century or more, in particular owing to its anti-woman propaganda tricks, as for instance the women's fashion industry (operating out of Paris).

Though there are, of course, certain well-known Jewish homosexuals, homosexuality is even less common among Jews than in France, owing to the cultural weakness of the father-figure in the Jewish family during the centuries of external domination in ghettos, making of the standard Jewish father an essentially weak or clownish figure – for all his patriarchal puffing – beaten and humiliated in full view of his family by every minor 'goy' official or Cossack. ('*Baytzimmer*' actually means a person with large testicles and – therefore – a small brain, in Jewish folklore and folk-speech.) A comedy father like this is ultimately quite incapable of frightening his sons off any incestuous attachment to the mother. It is therefore the mother – the all-too-famous *Yiddishe momma* or 'Jewish mother' of the comedy stage, and now of self-hating Jewish fiction like Philip Roth's *Portnoy's Complaint* – who is the real center of the Jewish family, as with the Negro family everywhere but in Africa, and for the same reason. (See the important grouping of materials on this point in Dr. Roger Abrahams' *Deep Down in the Jungle*, 1964, p. 21–30, as to the 'matrifocal' Negro family in the white world.) The real cultural neurosis of both the Jewish and Negro males is therefore not homosexuality, but masochism and oral dependency – with the usual flights into oral sadism – both *vis-à-vis* the culture, and in their relation with the dominant woman whom they search out and succumb to, as representing and reduplicating the mother-figure to whom they are masochistically drawn.

There are also further levels down, as will be seen in chapter 12.IV.6 below, "The Defiling of the Mother." As another and different escape, there is also a type of bogus or pretended homosexuality intended as a *flight from masochism* and oral dependency, in which homosexuality and submission to men is seen as a lesser psychological danger, and in which the dominant or 'matriarchal' sexual figure being fled from is violently rejected – along with all other women. This is discussed further in the introduction to the present chapter. Though this feint or ploy has sharply and visibly increased among all classes and religions in America since World War II, it is statistically and psychologically as unimportant as the matching flight *into* masochism (*vis-à-vis* women) of homosexuals looking for a way out, but eternally chained to the mother-figure they dare not adore and must therefore pretend to hate.

3. THE RELATIONSHIP WITH THE SEMEN

In Western society, the semen is considered 'messy' and disgusting. Women who dislike sexual relations express a particular resentment of the 'messiness' of the semen left in and on their pelvic anatomy during intercourse, and this resentment was even more marked in centuries preceding, when withdrawal-at-ejaculation (the 'sin of Onan,' according to *Genesis*, xxxviii. 9–10, for which Jehovah slew him) was the commonest method of birth-control in all classes. Freud gives, for example, in his *Collected Papers*, the case of an 'engineer' who practised withdrawal for all the opening years of his marriage *until his father's death*, with the usual harmful neurological results; and it seems rather clear that this was Freud's own autobiographical admission, that it was he who was the 'engineer,' and that this was the real genesis of his discovery of the Oedipus complex and of psychoanalysis, though no reference whatever is made to this case in any of his biographies.

In other cultures, such as Japan, where the sexuality of the human being is accepted with the same calm with which we, in the West, accept that of household animals, such as cats and dogs, and formerly chickens, horses, and cows; the semen is considered a signal mark of virility, as indeed it is, comparable to the fantasied and yearned for large size of the penis. (Among men, that is. Women are usually afraid of the large penises men talk so much about.) The Japanese 'pillow-books' or *shun-gwa*, artistically showing various positions of intercourse for the edification of newlywed husbands and wives – an ancient artistic genre revived in the West during the 1960's in Denmark and elsewhere in photographic form – not only invariably show the penis as excessively large and heavily-veined, in what is really a sort of conventionalized 'close-up' rather than mere exaggeration, but also clearly delineate the puddle or backwash of semen between the woman's buttocks, pouring onto the mattress-pad after intercourse. This is never shown in Western erotic art, and would be considered 'disgusting,' as the emission of blood is not. At the same time, pornographic literature in both cultures equally exaggerates the amount of the ejaculated semen, which seldom really averages even so much as a 'horn spoonful,' as noted by the Beggar's Benison men's club at their public trials in 1734, quoted above.

A particular sexual pride is also expressed by boys and men in the number of *times* they are able to have sexual intercourse (*i.e.* to ejaculate) in a brief period or during a single night. As this seldom really means, or attempts to imply, that the woman has been brought to orgasm the same number of times (or more!) its real import is clearly the implication that the boy or man is able to produce a great amount of semen. 'Big' or 'much' as equalling 'best.' No such pride would be felt, but rather shame, in male orgasm without ejaculation, and several old folktales turn on this matter : *The woman expresses her disappointment in elaborate symbols (submitted to her husband as a pretended argument between herself and her secret lover) concerning a wagered number of nuts knocked from a tree, several of which have proved to be hollow or blanks.* (Thus, by implication, old or rotten.) This story is best known as rewritten in Balzac's *Contes Drolatiques*.

The homosexual over-evaluation of the penis naturally includes a similar over-evaluation of the semen, and it is possible that the ancient physiological error or misapprehension, still occasionally found in pornographic novels – that women also ejaculate a fluid at their orgasm – is based on neurotic fear of the 'castrated' female who has no penis and cannot emit semen, and who is therefore supplied with both in neurotic male fantasies. Aside from male fellators, other kinds of homosexuals also place great emphasis on the semen, in particular the minor group known to themselves as 'body-lovers,' whose usual sexual act is a sort of mutual masturbation against each other's torsos (if not simply with the hand), and who revel in the ejaculated semen deposited on their bodies just as much as the 19th-century wives of Onanistic husbands seem to have detested it as 'messy' (*i.e.* dirty or fecal). What is, to the woman, a *rejection* of the femaleness of her vagina, and therefore repugnant, is, to the homsexual, an *acceptance* of some part of his body as female, and therefore utterly welcome.

The swallowing of the semen in fellation is considered an ultimate act of sexual complaisance, and the purposeful rejecting of it in any way, as by choking or spitting, is correctly considered vulgar and an act of hate. This is both visible and superficial, as is the charade of animosity of women who engage in fellation as birth-control, but then spit the ejaculated semen on the front of the man's trousers, with some such remark as *"Now explain* THAT *to your wife!"* (La Jolla, California, 1964.) As with punch-line jokes, the relationship is obviously over at that point, as no man in his right mind can be expected to continue an affair with such a woman after so brutal an expression of her animosity. (But some do!) However, the acceptance and ingestion of the semen has itself a hostile layer, particularly when it is unconsciously thought of by the fellator or fellatrice as 'draining' the man, or somehow triumphing sexually over him. As for instance when – as is extremely common at the present time in America – fellation is offered instead of sexual intercourse by adolescent girls who in this way 'protect their virginity.' Masturbating the man would give the same 'protection,' but this is nowadays seldom offered, on the grounds that it is 'messy.' The oral-incorporative partner's satisfaction does not always require that the semen be swallowed: often the mouthing of the penis is enough.

Scene: A parked car in Lover's Lane on Saturday night. A young man is trying to seduce his girl-friend but she, as a good Catholic, refuses him. He persuades her to suck him off instead, and at the moment of his orgasm she confronts him with her mouth bulging, looking for somewhere to spit. (Acted out.) "For God's sake, don't spit it on the upholstery!" he cautions her. "Why don't you just swallow it?" he adds angrily, as she continues her pantomimed agony. "I can't," she says out of the corner of her mouth; "I've got to take communion in the morning." (N.Y. 1963, told by a young Catholic woman as having been learned from other girls in high-school, and turning on the ritual requirement that Communion be taken on an empty stomach.) Other jokes of this type are grouped in a later chapter, 12.IV.2, etc., under the section "Food-Dirtying," where the curious tendency of many such stories toward religious sacrilege will be noted. One that can only follow here: *'A girl goes to confession and tells the priest that she handled a man's penis; priest tells her to deposit coin in charity box and rinse her hands in holy water. Second girl tells him she had intercourse with a man, and priest tells her to wash her vagina. While both are at the basin [sic] of holy water, third girl approaches, and says: "Before you shove your cunt in there, move over and let me gargle".'* (N.Y. 1953.) The striking concern with *forgiveness* for sexual sin in many 'girls' stories' matches the concern with venereal disease and castration as *punishment* in men's stories, as will be seen.

One final and essential relationship of the homosexual to the male semen must not be overlooked: the function of impregnation. Various jokes on this have been given in the First Series, 8.VI.3, p. 599–602, under the headings "Male Motherhood" and "Rectal Motherhood." These cannot all be repeated here, though all are homosexual. The child-bearing by the raped male is generally achieved rectally, whether the semen has been intruded into his body by pedication or by fellation. Actually, the method of entry is not always specified, but the rectal birth is standard. Stories of this kind are very ancient. In the surviving Arab form of the "Fortunate Fart" story, treated in Chapter 2.VII.2, the Kazi gives birth to a child as a result of a 'fecund fart.' (*Histoires Arabes*, 1927, p. 256–8.) This is Thompson's Motif J2321.2, noting that it entered Europe in Basile's *Pentamerone* (1634) Day II, Tale 3, of a foolish ogre.

The most ancient such story is that of "The Monster Made of Stone," a Hittite tale written down about 1250 B.C., and translated and 'retold' in Dr. Theodor Gaster's *The Oldest Stories in the World* (1952) No. 7, p. 110–33. In this, Kumarbi becomes pregnant from having bitten his adversary's penis and swallowed some of his semen. (Motif T531.1. Castratory fighting of a manual kind is mentioned in *Deuteronomy*, xxv. 11; was notorious on the American frontier, and is still the stock-in-trade of the 'killer-tactics' and *judo* handbooks issued for soldier commandos in wartime, and for aggressive women worried about rape in peacetime. None of these works ever mention the *biting* of the opponent's penis or testicles, though the attack on both is constant, with the hand, foot, knee, and other weapons.)

Kumarbi is helplessly pregnant for a long while with two monstrous children in his entrails, and Dr. Gaster comments, p. 127, on the obvious humorous intent with which the problem of how they are to be brought to birth is treated in this jocular tale thousands of years old: *'The gods are at sixes and sevens trying to persuade them to emerge from the various orifices of Kumarbi's body. Each time the embryos protest ironically that this would be "unnatural" and might impair them. Finally he is forced to submit to what can best be described as a primitive Caesarean section; Ea, the god of wisdom and science, cuts a "window" in his side, but only one of the monsters comes forth.'* This is Motif T541, usually referred to the birth of Dionysus through Zeus' 'thigh,' *i.e.* anus, in Greek mythology. Obviously this is also the identical motif to that of the birth of Eve from Adam's rib, during an operation on Adam by Jehovah, in *Genesis*, ii. 21. No reference is made in the Bible to the preceding impregnation of Adam by Jehovah, as is made central in the present Hittite burlesque theogony. At the last, Kumarbi's second monster is born rectally: it is the 'infant spirit of the wind ...' Compare the Arab tale of the Kazi's 'fecund fart' referred to above, and that of *the homosexual who 'gives birth' to a monkey by means of an explosive enema,* in the First Series, 8.VI.3, p. 601.

Without exception, all modern jokes that have been encountered on the homosexual relationship with the semen have been blatantly anti-homosexual mocks. Many of them are not jokes at all, but are puns or impossible situations connected with fellation and presented in various ways, such as 'one-liners' (derived from the cartoon-caption format), or as riddles disguised as jokes by means of standard openings like 'Have you heard (the one) about ...?' or 'Then there was this fairy who ...' *Did you hear about the shortage of cundrums? – No, what's the trouble? – The fairies are using all the new ones for chewing gum.* (N.Y. 1946.) *– One homosexual congratulates the other on his pearl tie-pin. The other brushes it away, remarking, "Oh that? Just carelessness!"* (2:6) Occasionally the humor is achieved by means of gestures thought of as specially homosexual, such as fluffing or smoothing one's back hair with the hand (used in the Argentine-Spanish joke concerning the homosexual lion, earlier). *Homosexual, enthusiastically: "What a man! Oh, what a man! He had balls down to* HERE *(pointing to his Adam's apple)."* (N.Y. 1970.)

The weakest kind of verbal humor is considered quite funny when it involves an allusion to homosexuality, and especially to fellation as a homosexual act, or uses as key word some slang synonym for this, such as *to blow* or *to french.* – *Homosexual, in restaurant: "I'd like some potatoes too." Waiter: "You want them frenched [i.e. french-fried]?" Homosexual: "No, I'll french them myself."* (N.Y. 1946. Tending toward the theme of food-dirtying, Chapter 12.IV.2, below.) – *The confused cop who got off his whistle and blew his horse.* (N.Y. 1946. A spoonerism: 'got off' alludes to orgasm.) Homosexual accusations against policemen, whether or not founded in fact, are common in jokes, as a standard denigration or diminution of authority-figures. There are also plenty of homosexual cops. The horse as the ultimate sexual partner for any Messalina, male or female, is also a standard jest, topped in antiquity by Europa and her ultra-male *bull.*

Purely verbal: *A homosexual clarinetist continually blows the wrong note at the orchestra rehearsal of a sensuously beautiful passage by Debussy, excusing himself to the conductor: "I'm sorry. That passage moves me so much, instead of blowing I suck."* (N.Y. 1963.) Another purely verbal joke has already been cited, in a presumably non-homosexual version concerning: *The Boston aristocrat meeting his chorus-girl mistress at the boat on her return from her vacation. "Have you been blue while I was gone, darling?" she calls. "Blown, dear, blown," he corrects her coldly.* (N.Y. 1938.)

4. SEMEN AS FOOD

The ingestion of semen is seldom thought of in folk-humor as part of the essential pleasure of the fellator or fellatrice, though of course it is; owing to the prejudice which insists that the semen is 'disgusting,' though of course it is not. Various rationalized reasons and purposes for swallowing the semen are therefore imagined. *The homosexual is on trial for having 'gone down' on a policeman, who has arrested him afterward. The policeman is asked to produce the evidence in court. "But, your Honor, he swallowed it!"* (2:7.) The principal rationalization is the presumed food-value of the semen, based on its similarity in appearance to the white of an egg, as in the American children's and adolescents' song, "Christopher Columbo": *'She sprang aloft, her pants fell off, The villain still pursued her. The white of an egg ran down her leg; The son-of-*

a-bitch had screwed her!' (Scranton, Pa 1929.) – *One homosexual sees another escorting a midget into his apartment.
"Whoops, dearie! Are they rationing men?" "Doctor's orders,
you swishy thing! I'm on a diet."* (N.Y. 1942.) Jokes like this are
told with the exaggerated homosexual accent and gestures
implied in their vocabulary, and it is extremely curious to
observe men who think of themselves as very virile indeed
descending to such verbal pantomimes *under the impression*
that they are thus showing their superiority to, and detestation
of, overt homosexuals.

*A man asks directions of a handsome stranger in an unknown
part of town. The stranger does not answer, but reaches into
his pocket for a pad and pencil, and carefully writes out the
needed information, with a little map. "Say, thanks!" says the
man, "you're a pal!" And he slaps the stranger gratefully on the
back. The stranger splutters, coughs, and retorts: "Oh, you
nasty man! You shouldn't have done that. I was taking home a
hot lunch for a sick friend."* (2:4, a much less detailed version.)
Though *Anecdota Americana, Series II*, in 1934, gives quite a
string of the homosexual jokes, which reached their present
popularity first at that time, during the Depression – see, for instance the endless series of anti-homosexual cartoons and gags
in *Broadway Brevities* (incomplete run in Kinsey Library, Institute for Sex Research, Indiana University) and in the minor
bawdy joke-magazines of the period, such as *Whiz Bang* and
the *Calgary Eye-Opener* – the following is given only as a
colloquy between two female prostitutes, though it is equally
well-known as between homosexuals. *A New York whore
complains of price of a 'trick'* [French *truc*, a single act of inter-
course] *falling to $1 during the Depression. Second whore: "I
call that pretty good. Why in Philadelphia we're sucking pricks
for food."* (2:10.)

The unusual and somewhat acrobatic form of oral masturbation scientifically known as *auto-fellation*, or self-fellation, is
described first in the literature by Dr. Louis J. Bragman, "A Case
of autofellation," in *Medical Journal and Record* (New York,
1927) vol. 126: p. 488, the man achieving this by bending forward in a sitting position. The alternative form, which is also
physically possible, in which the man lies on his back and
throws his legs over his head, is shown in an Egyptian papyrus
in the British Museum, No. 10018, and has been reproduced in
a work on homosexual art, as well as in Giupseppe Lo Duca's

Érotique de l'Art (Paris, 1966) p. 21, an important work on the style of Fuchs', Karwath's, and Brusendorff & Henningsen's illustrated histories of erotic art. The auto-fellator is shown under the arched body of a much larger female figure, as in other Egyptian illustrations given on the same page by Lo Duca, and it is evident that the conventional presentation of the matriarch in this way, as though she were an animal mother (compare Romulus and Remus being nursed by the she-wolf, a pre-Roman legend or relic used by the Romans as a sacred totem), as well as the act or fantasy of auto-fellation itself, is an expression of the intense *oral* needs of the male persons here shown as children overshadowed by the mother, also of the artist drawing the papyrus illustrations, and of the Egyptian culture supporting and applauding this art.

In a later medico-psychiatric article on the same subject of autofellation, by Drs. Eugen Kahn & Lion, the case described leaves very clearly to be understood that the auto-fellator is not attempting, by means of this act, to achieve special penile sensations – which are obviously available by simpler methods of masturbation – but yearns for the mouth and throat sensations involved, and for the semen as imagined nourishment. In other words, the act is a charade of oral strivings to regain the mother-figure, always so prominent in the repressed or strangulated normal sexuality of homosexuals of the fellator type, if not of all types. *Auto-cunnilinctus* seems to be physically impossible, owing to the deeper positioning of the vulva between the thighs, but I have myself encountered at least two fantasy references to it in conversations with young women, one of whom *expurgated* the matter by saying *it was something she thought she might try if she had to urinate out in the woods without any toilet paper.* (N.Y. 1942.) A 'set' of erotic photographs which I was offered in London, in one of the little shops off Leicester Square, in 1959, showed a young girl with rather long and pointed full breasts (and her fingers heavily cigarette-stained) nursing herself alternately at both breasts with a very placid expression on her face. This is clearly the real ideal. Compare also an anti-war rationalization of similar auto-oragenital attempts, in an *obscœnum* or 'novelty card' described by Jerry Hopkins, in *Los Angeles Free Press* (19 August 1966) p. 10, as being shown to 'people' by a young woman: *'a card ... neatly printed with the words: "In the event of* NUCLEAR ATTACK *follow these instructions: 1. Place both hands behind*

head. 2. Place head between legs. 3. Kiss your ass good-bye".'
Turning on the metonymic use of *'ass'* as meaning oneself or
one's body.

The ultimate rationalization of oragenital acts, specifically of
fellation, as a search for nourishment, involves the fantasy of
the *soixante-neuf* or sixty-nine as a sort of incestuous orgy with
the mother-figure, out of hunger! *'Did you hear how they
found* [a woman aviator] *and her companion alive on a desert
island? All this time they kept alive by him sucking her tit and
her sucking his cock. A vicious circle, you know. They just
kept the food in circulation.'* (D.C. 1943, from a soldier.) This is
a folk-reminiscence or re-creation of the legend of the Greek
father, Cimon of Athens, kept alive at his daughter's breast in
prison, discussed in the First Series. The apparent pun on
'vicious circle' seems to have been unconscious. Obviously a
European story but collected in English (from a Dutch girl in
Paris), the following appears in various French joke collections
openly published in the 1920's and '30's, and is apparently an
old army favorite mocking the superior officer. *A group of
mountaineer troops are lost during a snowstorm for three days
and are starving. They stagger blindly through the snow, and
just at nightfall they find a sheepfold below the timber-line,
and pile into it for shelter. Each man grabs a sheep and sucks it
all night for milk. In the morning light they find that the captain has grabbed the ram.* (Paris, 1955.)

The rejection of food by the child, or food-dirtying, is considered in a later chapter, 12.IV.2, in various forms. A homosexual story, frequently collected, attempts to reduce the desired semen specifically to the milk or cream with which it is
consciously identified (though never as *mother's milk*, except
in the story preceding), and then rejects it with a violent spilling
gesture, after having another homosexual (storekeeper) act out
the genital part. *Two homosexuals are to go to a masquerade
party and can't think what to wear.* [Standard joke situation.]
*One finally breaks their piggy-bank and takes all the money to a
supermarket where he buys twenty cans of condensed sweetened milk, opens them all and then says to his friend: "Now
throw it all over me – I'm going to the ball as a wet dream!"*
(N.Y. 1942.) Exceptionally, this joke *is* told by homosexuals,
and it will be observed that there is no specific mockery of the
homosexual, as such, and the whole situation is handled as *the
flight into nonsense*. Homosexuals also consider it an amusing

'camp' to inquire soberly as to "the calorie-content of a mouth-ful of semen" in connection with their narcissistic-feminine dieting and other excessive concern with their own bodies, rising from ideas of castration.

A reduction of the preceding joke, also as 'nonsense', and on the standard situation of the masquerade: *A man buying condoms asks for one big enough to wear over his head: he wants to go to a masquerade as a prick.* (D.C. 1943.) Compare Melville's masterpiece, *Moby Dick* (1851) chapter 95 following the incredible homosexual chapter on sperm-squeezing – concerning the apparently authentic ritual use of the skin of the dead whale's penis as a hooded cape in which the victorious whale-killer clothes himself. The modern condom is of course intended – other than its use to prevent venereal disease – as a method of contraception, by restraining the semen from entering the womb. Few jokes consider it in this form. (*A man is told that the condoms he is buying are the best quality and are guaranteed. "But what if they break anyhow?" he objects. "In that case," replies the clerk, "the guarantee, uh, runs out."* – N.Y. 1938.) Instead, the condom is considered principally as a slip-case for the penis, and most of the concern with it is in connection with its reduction of the man's feeling during inter-course, and the question of penis-size here reflected. In a war-book, *Daybreak for our Carrier*, by Max Miller (1944) p. 133, the use of condoms of various sizes by the Japanese enemy as water-tight cases for various equipment is humorously discussed. '*We once found a dead Jap flyer who had his automatic in a special bag like that. We took the rubber – it must have been more'n a foot and a half long – and sent it back to a friend of ours in the States. We wrote him: "This will give you an idea of the men we are fighting." I don't know what the friend thought. We haven't heard from him yet.*' This is either derived from a joke or was immediately turned into one: *Russian government orders one million condoms, each a foot long, from a rubber goods company in Ohio. The manufacturer does not know whether to fill the order or not, and calls in the F.B.I. After consultation with Washington he is told: "Go ahead and fill the order. But put a label on every box marked 'Medium'."* (N.Y. 1949.)

V. PEDICATION

The excessive strength of the parent, combined with a domineering approach to the child, is understood by the child (of either sex) as representing a danger of physical castration at the hand of the jealous parent, for the 'sin' of loving too much, or too sexually, the parent of the opposite sex, who is the 'property' of the parent feared. Girls suffer just as much as boys from castration anxiety, and from the notion that their penises will be (or have been!) removed. To the intimidated and neurotic girl-child, that is why nothing larger than the clitoris ever grows in the genital area; and the clitoris and its orgasm-possibilities are therefore very much over-accentuated by such a girl in later life, as representing all that she has been able to retain or to grow of her expected penis. There is also a matching and generally unconscious fear that the vulvar lips will be sewn or locked together (whence the historical fantasy of the 'chastity belt'), or that the vagina will be plugged up and made useless. Semi-barbaric practices still used in the public schooling of children, such as sealing shut with court-plaster tape the lips of children who are caught *talking to each other* (a heinous crime) during school class periods, make the child to whom this happens – and many of the others watching – traumatically certain that the other mouth-like organ, the female genital, could also be so attacked or sealed up.

The threats made against little boys, that their penises will be cut off if played with – or will 'shrivel and drop off,' which is thought of as less cruel a threat! – are still much more common than is believed by writers and talkers on those subjects, most of whom come from or adhere to the upper or middle economic classes, and do not have any real knowledge of what actually happens at the folk-level of the working classes and the poor, which represent more than half of the population.

The boy who is convinced that his father will castrate him for loving his mother too intensely, and who therefore withdraws or 'retires from the competition,' as Freud puts it, is actually engaging in a sort of psychological self-castration of a partial kind, intended to ward off the physical operation he fears. This is identical with the Jewish institution of circumcision as a *partial* or symbolic sacrifice (castration) of the child by the father, as authorized by the intended blood-sacrifice of

Isaac by his father, the patriarch Abraham, in *Genesis* xxii. (And compare *Genesis*, xvii. 9–14, actually requiring circumcision, a passage unquestionably part of a later redaction, probably by the prophet Ezra, who is believed to be the real editor of the existing text of the Old Testament.) In highly neurotic homosexuals, these fantasies and fears do not end here, but proceed to the further belief that the boy who has now been castrated and effeminized will be *raped rectally* by the father-figure in the act of pedication, or anal intercourse (often erroneously called 'pederasty,' which actually refers to boy-love), and furthermore – though few persons other than pre-psychotics go so far as this final fantasy – that the son who has been thus used as a female will then have a rectal baby, known as a 'jelly-baby,' *i.e.* one composed of feces.

Thus, in seeking rectal intercourse, to be engaged upon their bodies by other men, homosexuals of the passive-pedicant type are attempting to embrace what they fear most, and thus, as it were, to control its occurrence. Homosexuals of the active-pedicator or 'wolf' type are taking the simpler and more direct escape of 'identification with the aggressor,' which in action comes to the reverse of the Golden Rule, *i.e.* "Do unto others what you *do not* want them to do unto you." This reversal is of course the real and operative human principle that the Golden Rule of *Matthew*, vii. 12 and *Luke*, vi. 31, is intended to combat, as earlier the Old Testament's "Thou shalt love thy neighbor as thyself" (*Leviticus*, xix. 18, and compare *Mark*, xii. 31), a precept finally examined psychologically in Freud's *Civilization and Its Discontents*, and found absurd and humanly impossible.

Jokes on these homosexual themes are intentionally cruel and mocking, as is any merely verbal attack on the rectal area, or involving it, such as the international catchphrase of contempt or vilification, '*Kiss my arse!*' which very possibly takes much of its force from the now-forgotten accusation against heretics over the last two thousand years that this is their special way of worshipping the Devil: namely, by kissing him under the tail. (The phrase is very common also in German: '*Leck mir im Arsch!*' expurgatorily abbreviated to L.M.I.A., which has also been used as a book-title. Compare Joyce's '*Kiss My Royal Irish Arse*' or K.M.R.I.A. in the newspaper-office, or hall-of-winds [n.b.] chapter of *Ulysses*.) The verbal assault is more usually on the other person's rectal area, nowadays, in the American and

British 'shove (or stick) it up your arse!' often abbreviated and varied as a verbal folk-art of insult, in the British 'shove it up and give it a left-hand turn!' and the American 'up yer gigi!', 'up your poopadoop!' or even the ornate and dysphemistic 'up your fur-lined shit-chute!' (All dating from the 1930's.)

Where recourse is to action, rather than mere words, the act of *goosing* or prodding another person's, usually a man's, buttocks or anus, or actually reaching through his legs from behind and seizing his testicles and penis (which is the ultimate but very uncommon form), is an obvious pantomime of pedicatory rape. It is at least as old as the slap-sticks and goosing-sticks of circuses and the comedy stage, which, as noted in my *The Horn Book* (1964) p. 248–9, 'are an evident survival, descended now to the nursery forms of humor, of the ancient phallophoric street-processions of the Saturnalia, with the envoys of the gods, in the form of erotic "madmen," sexually handling and presumably impregnating the barren women standing on the sidelines for that purpose. In the intermediate development, one sees the same phallically posturing street-clowns of the Italian *commedia dell'arte,* as in Callot's *Balli di Sfessania (ca.* 1623) concentrating very much on "goosing" with wooden swords, manipulated by the comedy *braggadocio* or bully. The 20th century form – the electrified goosing-stick of American Legion paraders [actually a slaughterhouse device for stunning animals before killing them, and particularly used against pretty young girls on the sidelines of the parades] – naturally seem to the bystander more crude, and openly sadistic; yet it is an even closer return to the older form of the street-running "madmen" of the Saturnalia, or the priestly "wolves" of the Lupercalia (February 15th), striking women in the street with goatskin thongs to insure fertility and an easy delivery in childbirth!

I. BEND OVER

The popular belief concerning the pedicational activities of homosexuals is that these take place in a standing position, with the passive person bending far forward. This is of course untrue, as at the very least the further comfort of the kneeling position, on knees and elbows, is sought when pedication takes place from behind. Many homosexuals also prefer to lie upon their backs, raising the legs as does a woman in intercourse, and thus to feel as much as possible *like* a woman. Homosexual prostitutes (to normal men), who dress in women's clothes and often actually pass themselves off on their clients as women, engage in intercourse by means of a *'rubber pussy,'* sometimes also nowadays called a *'merkin'* or *'mugget'* (which is actually a female pubic wig) lubricated with cold-cream or the non-fatty K-Y jelly. They naturally must lie upon their backs to maintain the illusion – on the part of both persons – that they are women. When the client is more or less drunk, the 'rubber pussy' is dispensed with, and anal intercourse is substituted in the same position, with heavy lubrication, apparently without the client's being any the wiser. What is really involved is, usually, a polite pretense on the part of both, by means of which anal intercourse is engaged in by 'normal' men who cannot admit to their homosexuality, and therefore can only achieve this under cover of being terribly drunk or dumb.

Folk-humor invariably insists, however, on the bending-over position, between two standing men, and this for the reason that the action is thus easier to construe as a pedicatory *rape*. The passive pedicant is always presumably unwilling, and is taken by force or by subterfuge, sometimes simply by accident or misunderstanding. This notion fits easily into the situation of the "Short-Arm Inspection" already discussed above. *A young man is being examined for the navy. "Bend over," says the navy doctor, "and pull your buttocks open." "What, so soon, Admiral?" asks the boy plaintively.* (1 : 140.) How very close this 'joke' is to the reality of the short-arm inspection is seen in the bitterly matter-of-fact quotation given earlier, from Mr. Michael Agnello, as to the actual process of genital-anal examination on admission in the Los Angeles city jail at the present time. *A sailor is sitting on the toilet in the 'head,' wiping himself and examining the paper which is all bloody. "What's the matter," says his buddy; "you got piles?" "No, I was in the shower with this big nigger, and I asked him what his name was. He said 'Ben Drover,' and I guess I misunderstood."* (D.C. 1964.)

In both of these jokes the passive party is clearly predisposed to the 'mistake' he has made, and *wants* to be 'raped.' Women are understood to be predisposed to such sexual misunderstandings, and even to fantasies of being raped, thus allowing them to engage in sexual intercourse without feelings of guilt. *("It wasn't my fault!"* – Spoonerism: *Man: "So help me, I'll rape you!" Woman: "So rape me; I'll help you!"* – N.Y. 1963.) However, passive male urges for rectal sensations, either during intercourse – the French *'postillioning,'* by means of an inserted finger – or instead of heterosexual intercourse, are almost impossible to be admitted to by men in panic fear of homosexual tendencies in themselves. The jokes express these sinlessly for them, as 'mistakes.'

The mere taking of the bending forward position is considered a dangerous invitation to pedicatory rape. *The sailor who got his head caught in a porthole (or who bent over to pick up the soap in the shower), "and when he turned around he found his ass-hole bleeding and two dollars and forty cents in change on his locker."* (N.Y. 1939.) Abbreviated further, to a riddle – note that the preceding form is not actually presented as a joke – *"Did you hear about the sailor who got his head stuck in the port-hole?"* (*"No, what about it?"* the listener is elliptically supposed to have answered.) *"He couldn't get it loose to save his ass."* (D.C. 1944, from an army private. This is again the use of *'ass'* as referring to the individual himself or to his entire body.) As a 'catch' or hazing-trick : *A sailor is told that the ship he is on is not a real ship but a dummy in drydock, with forty wheels under it on each side, and is invited to put his head out through the porthole to see. "What are you talking about?" he says, with his head out the porthole, "I don't see any* WHEEEELS!!" (Los Angeles, 1969.) – A burlesque comedian, on being called stupid, excused himself by saying that his father was "stupider" than he was, taking a stooped, bent-forward position when his interlocutor pretended to be hard of hearing. The interlocutor retorts : *"Hell, I don't care what he did for a living."* (Washington, D.C. burlesque theatre, 1945.) As with the Italian *commedia dell'arte* from which the burlesque theatre evolved, the gestures here are the essential dialogue, and its real key.

'Saint Peter gave wings to a soldier and a sailor entering Paradise, with the proviso that they would drop off if the wearer had a dirty thought. Proud of their wings, the two young men started walking smartly down the golden streets, naked. A naked female angel passed coyly by, glancing at them, and the soldier's wings fell off. He looked and saw the sailor's still secure, so he shamefacedly bent over to pick up his wings. As he stooped, the sailor's wings fell off.' (Berkeley, Calif. 1942, told at a meeting of the American [Bawdy] Limerick Society by the late Dr. C. F. MacIntyre, one of the two principal American limerick poets.)

This version makes use of the hoary accusation against sailors, as to buggery, which is unquestionably true, as witness the very extreme punishments meted out for it (if engaged in on shipboard) in most Anglo-Saxon navies. Another version uses the even hoarier similar accusation, against monks, also probably true. *The Archangel Gabriel gives each new angel of a company of martyred monks a pair of golden wings, but also affixes a golden bell to their penises. If the bell tinkles the wings fall off.* [Proceeds as text above.] *When the one young monk whose bell has tinkled, and who has lost his wings when the female angel passes by, stoops over to pick up his wings, there is a chorus of "Tinkle – Crash! Tinkle – Crash!" from the other monks' bells and wings.* (Nice, France, 1965, from an American tourist.) Note the 'bell,' or male chastity-belt, similar to certain seriously promulgated anti-masturbation devices.

Aside from *bending over*, the idea of *turning one's back* also is used as keying the allusion to pedication; the phrase '*to back up to* (another person)' being an outright synonym. "*Why were the Romans such great warriors?*" ("*I dunno – why?*" the listener presumably asks.) "*They were afraid to retreat. They couldn't turn their back on the Greeks.*" (Cannes, France, 1966, also from a tourist.) It has already been observed that almost any humorous allusion to the Greeks, in modern English, will be understood as an allusion to homosexuality, or specifically to pedication, of either men *or women*, an accusation once also made similarly against the Italians, as is recorded in Benevenuto Cellini's *Autobiography* (before 1570), he being the Italian involved. *Three Greeks were showering; one dropped the soap and no one dared to pick it up.* (Berkeley, Calif. 1939, from a married woman.) – *The Greek maiden on her wedding night who was so embarrassed: she didn't know which way to turn.* (Berkeley, 1942, given at a meeting of the American Limerick Society.) – *Did you hear about the absent-minded Greek whose wife had a baby?* (Berkeley, 1940.) – *Did you hear about the young bride who married a Greek? On her wedding night she complained, "You're indifferent."* (St. Louis, Mo. 1943.) Observe that not one of these is a joke.

The standard homosexual accusation against sailors is balanced by the matching libel that they (nevertheless) '*have a girl in every port.*' Soldiers, who have neither this tradition of easy acceptance of the homosexual and pedicational accusation, and the equally traditional recourse to brothels and prostitutes in every port-of-call, find it more difficult to accept such allusions calmly. Here is a joke monitored on a national American radio comedy program, with a soldier audience present (1941) and laughing uproariously at all the jokes BUT this one. *An army colonel was technical adviser on a motion picture, and had to drill the Hollywood extras pretending to be soldiers. At his command, "Right face!" the extras faced right; at his command, "Left face!" the extras faced left. But when he cried "About face!" nobody moved, and one extra objected plaintively, "That ain't in my contract!"* (Almost no laughter from the audience.) An even worse frost, also personally observed, was that of a comedian entertaining a nightclub audience largely composed of soldiers, on offering the patter: *'I used to be a song-plugger. I plugged "Margie," I plugged "Ida," I plugged "Jeanie with the Light-Brown Hair." I even plugged "The Old Gray Mare."* (Laughter.) – *All good pieces!* (Loud laughter.) – *But I gave up the job when they asked me to plug "My Buddy!"'* (Not a laugh in the house.) (D.C. 1946.) Aside from the offensive fake-patriotism here, the word 'buddy' or 'buddies' refers, in American army slang of World War II and since, to an extremely close friendship among soldiers, so close to *non*-physical homosexuality, out of the need for love, that the term itself was not lightly used. The jocular reduplication 'buddy-buddy' could be considered an affront, while the open homosexual accusation of the derivative 'asshole-buddy' was fighting words, though it could also be used (with care) as an in-group term of affection, as with 'son-of-a-bitch' or 'nigger' among whites and Negroes ('blacks') respectively.

The key-word 'bottom' is not commonly used in America in allusions to homosexuality, though it is as well understood as in Britain. Robert Graves gives in *Lars Porsena, or The Future of Swearing,* a British children's rhyme of the 1920's or probably earlier:

> Ma's out and pa's out, let's talk dirt:
> *Pee, poh, belly, bottom, drawers!*

The last two words would certainly not be used in such an American rhyme, where 'ass' and 'pants' would perhaps be substituted, as in skip-rope rhymes. (The second word, 'poh,' is also not the American children's 'poo,' meaning feces, but the British 'pot,' i.e. chamber-pot, pronounced as though it were a French word, 'poe,' by way of expurgation.)

The Pearl, No. 15, for September 1880, *ad fin.*, gives a story of: *A male servant who 'had been frequently reprimanded ... for his free behaviour with the female servants ... He promised amendment, and matters went on very well for a time. One evening, he was not to be found when wanted, and on search being made was discovered in the beer-cellar, buggering the page-boy. "How now," he was asked, "is this your amendment? You promised to turn over a new leaf." "So I have," said he, "only I have begun at the bottom of the page!" History does not give us the conclusion of the matter.'* Note the editorial afterword or tag, indicating dissatisfaction with the punch-line ending, however witty, as somehow 'destroying' all the participants, without the possibility of any future for them. This story was naturally assimilated to Oscar Wilde, with Frank Harris as interlocutor, in *Anecdota Americana* (1927) 1:129. It has often been collected since, its purely verbal humor – overlaid on the homosexual situation, to be sure – being attractive to the educated group that favors puns in general. Reduced to: *'A king and his jester were cast off alone on a desert island. It was no time at all until the king was at his wit's end.'* (D.C. 1940, given by the same informant as a version of the preceding pun.)

The purely verbal approach gingerly applied, in all the jokes preceding, to the homosexual act of pedication, is a sort of linguistic tongs, used by the joke-tellers to deal antiseptically with a subject obviously of great interest to them, yet from which they must pointedly withdraw insofar as any 'personal' interest is concerned. It is for the same reason that many persons will only tell homosexual jokes with exaggerated homosexual intonation and gestures, though the same persons will often not bother to attempt dialect effects in telling, for example, comedy Jewish, Negro, or Italian stories.

Lesbian jokes are of great scarcity, since jokes are a male art. Though women do often tell jokes – especially women of openly virilistic competitiveness with men – such women are seldom out-and-out lesbians and pointedly avoid the subject. Real lesbians are proud of a tradition of 'gentlemanly' reserve about the physical details of their sexual acts. This is perhaps really a cover for their shame that, in the end, their sexual actions must remain purely female, since they cannot engage in penile acts except by the use of prosthetic organs (the *dildo*, or artificial

penis), which is in any case rarely used, and more often proposed *by men* than by women. Most lesbian jokes are, therefore
'outsider' jokes, and are also almost always purely verbal in
approach, without physical details. One striking exception is
given in a later chapter, in the section on dysphemistic "Water-
wit," or public insults.

First lesbian: *"Now I want to be frank ..." Second lesbian:
"No, I want to be Frank. You can be Ernest."* (N.Y. 1943.) –
Matinée fan, to his idol, an actress who happens to be lesbian
[always specifically named], *though he does not know this:
"You're the most wonderful person in the world! I want you for
my wife." Actress: "All right, bring her around. Maybe I can
use her."* (2:159.) Not just a play on words but a cruel cut-down
of the man offering marriage. Very arch, however, in its allusiveness, as is the following: *A lesbian actress* [always named]
*dies and is kept waiting a very long time at the gates of Heaven.
She begins rattling on the gate and demanding to enter. "In a
minute,"* says Saint Peter, *"when we've got the Virgin Mary
safely hidden."* (2:177.) The closest to actual physical detail in
the usual sort of anti-lesbian joke: *"Did you hear about the
lesbian who came home drunk and ate up half the mattress
before she found her lover wasn't home?"* (N.Y. 1938.) Note the
implication that the usual lesbian act is cunnilinctus, which is
not true though this is the popular belief. The principal lesbian
act seems to be mutual masturbation, usually by means of the
hand, though sometimes with the nipples or other substitute.
(*The breast as phallus.*) Oral acts, single and mutual, are of
course common, but they do not appear to be the lesbian act
of choice.

2. PEDICATION AS INSULT

The joke has already been cited in an earlier chapter as to:
*The husband and wife on their wedding night in a Pullman car
berth, arguing as to where the child resulting from their first
act of intercourse is to go to college. The husband insists on
Yale, the wife on Harvard. Finally a Voice from the Upper
Berth is heard disgustedly: "Aw, turn her over and shove it up
her ass, and send the result to Princeton!"* (San Francisco, 1942,
one of the listeners insisting that the final college named 'ought'
correctly to be Stanford, the traditional opponent of the University of California.) This seems to be a decayed version of the
well-known "Who Is the Greatest Fool?" story, Aarne Tale

Types 1332, 1384, and 1685(A), in which: *The bridegroom is disgusted by the in-laws weeping over the possible death by drowning of the first child he and the bride will have.* But it also involves the idea of the *rectal-child* or 'jelly-baby,' usually appearing only in the fantasies of children or of highly neurotic adult homosexuals, owing to ignorance of, or refusal to admit the mechanics of impregnation and the rôle of the vagina. Told as a Bulgarian story, the key phrase being considered merely a good-humored imprecation among the South Slavs: *A postman wants to leave a registered letter, and calls to a little boy at the top of the staircase of the house to come and get it. "I fuck you in the ass!" cries the child, "can't you see I'm not old enough to walk?"* (N.Y. 1937, from a young Bulgarian woman.)

Standard situation: picking a costume for the masquerade ball, but with one special comedy difference. *A man with a wooden leg* [the comedy difference] *wants to rent a costume for a masquerade ball. The costumer naturally suggests a pirate costume to go with the wooden leg, but the customer objects to the price: $5. "Well," says the costumer, "I'll rent you the three-cornered hat and the cutlass for only $2, and you can use an old raincoat for the cape." "Yes-s-s," says the customer dubiously, "but can't you think of anything cheaper?" "Sure I can," cries the costumer, at the end of his patience. "How about a costume for only 35c? All you need is a can of molasses and some red paint. You undress naked and pour the molasses all over you, and then the red paint. Then you stick your wooden leg up your ass, and go as a jelly apple!"* (N.Y. 1942.) This is the ultimate pedicatory insult, of auto-pedication, on which see *The Limerick* (Paris, 1953) Note 459, concerning the run-on limerick of the 'Young man of Calcutta,' in *The Pearl* (1879), who goes through a complicated procedure similar to the present joke, but '*not for greed after gold* [nor] *thirst after pelf; 'Twas simply because he'd been told, To bloody well bugger himself.'* The fantasy of auto-sodomy is of great psychological interest, as both an acceptance of passive homosexuality and a simultaneous defiance of it. The conclusion here, one of the commonest of folk-taunts in English, but considered less insulting than the similar advice to fuck one's own mother, is also used in Don Marquis' privately printed *Ode to Hollywood* (1929), ending: "Go fuck thy suffering self!"

A publicly-issued joke book, Bennett Cerf's *Pocket Book of War Humor* (1943) p. 124, includes an item doubtless rather daring for open publication at that period, despite its carefully covert allusiveness: '*An infantry private beseeched his lieutenant for three days' leave. Asked for a reason, he explained that his wife had just been made a sergeant in the* WAAC'*s. "That's fine," commented the lieutenant, "but why should that get you a three day leave?" "Lieutenant," the doughboy* [!] *answered earnestly, "I want to do something that every private has dreamed of doing for the past hundred years".*' A rhymed reduction almost immediately appeared, in *B.M.A. Blitz* (Oct. 1944) vol. 3, no. 10: p. 18, a staff publication of the Officers' Training Centre, Brockville:

> *Here lies the body of Corporal Stark,*
> *He mistook the sarge for a girl in the dark.*

The examples that precede are the type of insult in which it is the fact of *being buggered* that insults or degrades the passive participant, and this is the principal sort of homosexual 'taint' or danger feared at the folk-level. Curiously, it is the orally active 'cock-sucker' who is disgraced by fellation, and not the passive male, who is generally considered, and considers himself to be, non-homosexual. As to pedication, even the mere concern with one's own anus or rectum, at the hygienic level, is thought of as somehow homosexualizing, though it is always allowable – since the pleasure felt is simply an unspecified 'relief' – to admit that one "*really enjoys taking a good, healthy shit.*" Also, of course, the fecal column is extruded from the body, whereas the pedicating penis must be accepted inside: two opposite directions of motion. The insertor is male, the inserte*e* homosexual. This also holds for the oragenital acts, where the oral rape of another man is thought to disgrace and homosexualize the oral partner, while expressing the brutal virility of the phallic partner.

Enemas and rectal suppositories, even the taking of the temperature rectally, are always disgraceful for a man, as witness in particular the 'true anecdote' with which the present chapter ends. Observe the total homosexualization of such interests in the following: '*Two nancy-boys side by side in hospital beds, one complaining that he hates the nurse fiddling and farting about the way she does, and always grumbling. The other: "I know, Cedric, and the Matron's a perfect* bitch. *I wouldn't stay in the place another minute if it weren't for my morning* enema".' (Chelmsford Prison, Essex, 1953.) – *A homosexual is squatting before the mirror in the bathroom, inserting a rectal suppository for constipation. Suddenly he realizes he is getting an erection. He stares at his penis in the mirror, then smiles, and says, "You silly thing, it's only* ME!*"* (L.A. 1968.) This joke seems to have been developed from a 1930's cartoon, often reprinted, in which: *A dachshund, curved around a fire-hydrant, is smelling its own bottom,* with the same end-line. In any case, a marvellous illustration of narcissistic self-directed sexuality, mirror and all.

There is also the type of pedicatory insult in which it is the act itself that is the presumed disgrace, even for the active or phallic party, and in fact even when the pedication involved is with a woman, as in all the jokes about 'Greeks' and their wives. This element of insult is nowadays crumbling, as far as pedication of women is concerned, which is getting to be considered terribly 'in' among the *machismo* and other unconscious homosexual males, as for example some of the heroes of Norman Mailer's novels (who also, in fairness to them, dream of buggering men too, as a way of dominating or 'topping' them virilely), and as the presumed shock-climax of the movie *The Last Tango In Paris,* 1972.

Sometimes the urge to denounce other men is openly an unconscious self-denunciation: *'Cabin-boy, to the captain: "Sir, there's been buggery aboard!" Captain: "That's a foul statement. How do you know?" Cabin-boy: "This morning the mate's foreskin tasted distinctly of shit!"'* (MS. Chelmsford Prison, Essex, 1954, captioned "Jealous?") Hardly necessary to observe that this 'foul statement' is a non-homosexual 'outsider's' mock, and not an 'insider's' admission. The real meaning of the joke is to make *mere* buggery seem mild by comparison. Note the prison provenance of this text. This is apparently an old sea joke, and is alluded to, in a form purposely so studded with asterisks as to be ununderstandable, in Gene Fowler's *The Great Mouthpiece,* the biography of a famous lawyer of the 1920's, in a chapter on a homosexual scandal concerning Thomas Mott Osborne, the crusading warden of an American prison, Sing Sing, entitled "An Allegation in Lavender," this being the classic color of homosexual insult. *Two sailors are talking aboard ship. "You know," says one, "the best tail I've ever had was right here on this ship." "No shit?" "Well, not enough to really matter."* (L.A. 1965.) This touches, lightly but certainly, on the one most inacceptable element in pedication: the dirtying of the active male's penis with feces. This does not always happen, but once is enough. This is also why cultivated men will not perform pedication with women. Men in jails or in the army, where homosexual practice can seldom be avoided, try to brazen out the matter, as in the baroque homosexual threat or 'invitation,' made at knife-point, reported from more than one American prison: *"Your shit on my prick, or your blood on my blade!"* (U.S. 1964.)

An elegant insult, which really writes off the subject of homosexuality with high philosophy, is traditionally ascribed to Voltaire, with story to match. *Voltaire is invited to one of the homosexual Saturday-night orgies at the palace of his German protector, Frederick the Great, but refuses to attend. Frederick makes him understand that he must take part in the orgies or leave Prussia, so Voltaire appears on Saturday night, and acquits himself honorably on the backside of a white-uniformed hussar. Frederick the Great is delighted, and invites Voltaire to come to Sans-Souci again the next Saturday night. "No, Your Majesty," says Voltaire. "Once, a philosopher. Twice, a degenerate."* (N.Y. 1953.) This really says everything, quite aside from the imperturbable putdown of the Prussian king as just the kind of 'degenerate' Voltaire (and the listener) does not plan to be. It is not of course to be construed as the true explanation of why Voltaire quarrelled with his protector in 1753, left Prussia, and spent the last twenty years of his life in exile near Geneva.

As can be expected, in a status-oriented society where position is everything, and everything must be *signed* (even public toilets, with the names of the mayor and architect engraved in marble!), the *position* taken in rectal intercourse is of great importance, insofar as it indicates the status or, shall I say, pecking-order of the participants. The 'topman' or 'top-banana' (prison and theatre terms, respectively) is the victor over the 'low man on the totem pole,' of course, and only being the low man carries any real disgrace. *Lady Chichester finds her husband in bed with the butler. "My Lord," she expostulates, "the least you could be is on top!"* (2:400, illustrated with a line-drawing in the style of one of the best *New Yorker* artists of the 1930's. Note that all the illustrations have been omitted from the photographic pocket-reprint of *Anecdota-II*, under the title *The Unexpurgated Anecdota Americana*, North Hollywood: Brandon House, 1968.)

The joke has already been given in the First Series here, concerning: *The young married couple in Paris who see three bell-boys in a daisy-chain across the area-way. The husband calls up the manager and points to the scene. "What do you say to that!?" he asks angrily. "What do I say?" says the manager, "Lucky Julius! Always in the middle!"* (1:95.) This joke is in fact originally French, and appears as collected in Picardy, in *Kryptádia* (1907) XI. 154, *"Les trois moines,"* with a similar but less laconic punch-line put into the mouth of a bishop. As "Lucky Pierre," the name has become a well-known American catchphrase, even among people who do not know the joke, and is slily given in Al Capp's popular *Li'l Abner* comic-strip as the name of a Paris guide. Having once myself guided Mr. Capp around Paris in taxicabs half the night (looking for *milk of magnesia* ...) I can testify that he really believes that scenes like that are as common in Paris as French-fried potatoes, if you could only get the right address. This joke, and the others connected with it (given in the First Series, 9.II.5, page 725) involve almost the only admissions in English-language humor of passive-anal urges, or of the possibility of such 'feminine' or passive activities being pleasurable to a man, or anything but painful and a 'rape.' The great popularity of the story – if only as a knowing allusion – suggests its value in 'speaking for those who dare not speak.' See further, on anal digitation, my *Oragenitalism* (New York, 1969) p. 88–94.

The most insulting story concerning pedication is tricked out with nasty-nasty elements intended to make it even more disgraceful to its anti-hero: *There is a suspicious spot on the head of Hitler's penis, and none of the venereal disease specialists called in can diagnose it. The first suggests clap, and is thrown out. The second diagnoses chancre, and is shot. The third carefully asks for permission to taste the Führer's organ, and says, "I would suggest, your Excellency, that the spot may be a bit of shit." "It's possible, very possible," muses Hitler.* (2:27.) This joke really antedates the Hitler régime in Germany by decades at least. It appears as a recitation, with *"Il Re Umberto"* of Italy as its butt, in a manner of speaking, in the first and largest collection of the French medical and art students' bawdy songs, or *'chansons de salles de garde,"* entitled *Anthologie Hospitalière & Latinesque* (1911–13) I. 200, edited under the pseudonym 'Courtepaille' by Edmond D. Bernard, a text noting that the present story is also 'attributed by some to Dr. Ricord being consulted by the Emperor Napoleon III.'

3. PEDICATORY RAPE

The essential fantasy in homosexual fears has been formalized since ancient times in the Greek myth of Jupiter and Ganymede, the handsome boy whom Jupiter carries off to Mount Olympus *by the back of his neck*, in the guise of an eagle, there to rape the boy rectally and keep him as his pathic, or homosexual 'mistress.' Every part of this over-determines the homosexual fears involved, even the paranoid 'back of the neck' element, which may be considered a *displacement upward* of the pedicatory rape for which it is in any case a preparatory maneuver. The father-god as eagle is still a common symbol or totem, and appears for instance on the American coat-of-arms (or 'seal' as it is politely called in a democratic government), surmounting the flag on flagpoles – a survival of the Roman eagle – and on the largest coin, the silver dollar; also in France, as the government hall-mark intrusively stamped twice on the outside (!) of every wedding-ring. The 'vulture' of Leonardo da Vinci's childhood dream, analyzed in Freud's psychosexual study of that artist, is also of course a substitute-eagle, and Leonardo's dream is frankly one of homosexual rape, in this case oral – probably indicating the actual form of the artist's own homosexual activities – which Freud notes is 'elaborated into a homosexual situation. The mother whom the child suckled was transformed into a vulture which stuck its tail into the child's mouth. We maintain that the "coda" (tail) of the vulture, following the common substituting usages of language, cannot signify anything else but a male genital or penis.' (Brill translation, opening of Chapters 3 and 4.)

Pedicatory rape, in humor, is generally achieved by misunderstanding or subterfuge, and seldom by direct homosexual assault, which would generally not be considered humorous. Even when, in the earlier joke on the travelling salesman who is raped orally in a Southern town, a homosexual rape takes place, the real rape is not the physical action but the victim's psychologically overwhelming realization that he *'liked it!'* The people who tell, or appreciate, such jokes are of course not homosexual, and the jokes represent only their homosexual fears, sometimes panic-stricken. So also their response to physical 'goosing' of the anal area, to which they may respond by leaping into the air and whinnying like a horse. 'Goosing' is the lowest-common-denominator form of playful or pretended homosexual rape. The almost invariable violent response to it by the male victim shows how close to the surface the panic dread of homosexual rape remains in men under patriarchy.

In a curious story apparently first printed in John Newbern's *Homo Sweet Homo* (Dallas, Texas, 1968) signed 'Tom Wade III,' p. 137, the mother figure appears as an accessory in pederastic rape: *'Nick the Greek had a restaurant and hired a new waiter, a nice fellow in the prime of youth. Nick liked him very much and invited him to his home for dinner. Nick left the room, and the restaurant owner's beautiful, luscious wife started making passes at the new waiter. Being a normal, healthy man, the waiter seized on the opportunity, and in no time at all, the wife had the waiter in the bedroom, their clothes off, and her arms around his neck and her legs wrapped around his waist. Then she screamed, "OKAY, Nick, come and get it! ..."'* More than one man who answers classified ads for 'swingers' in the current underground press, finds that something like this is what is really involved. The same compiler's *World's Dirtiest Jokes* (1969) pp. 40 and 46, gives two versions of a long-penis joke also given in *The Limerick*, Note 1722, fifteen years earlier. In the homosexual version, *A young man is being buggered behind a bush in the park by a stranger with whom he has flirted. "How's that, buddy boy," says the stranger; "is that all right?" "I guess so." The stranger drives deeper. "Is that all right too?" "I guess so." The stranger gives a tremendous lunge. "And is that all right?" "I ghecc gho," comes the strangled reply.* (2:163. Text, N.Y. 1953.) Who is this Mysterious Stranger who simultaneously pedicates and irrumates the boy? Is it perhaps his father? We shall see.

The homosexual fantasy has already been discussed in which the pedicated homosexual boy becomes pregnant and gives birth to a 'jelly-baby' composed of feces. Not many homosexuals take their fantasy lives this far, in their jealous yearning for female prerogatives, though many are of course good housekeepers, decorators, sew or even knit clothes (dress-designing as a homosexual profession), and shine particularly as cooks. Thus the foregoing legend of 'Nick the Greek,' the cook at the Greasy Spoon lunch-room around the corner. My own introduction to homosexuality, as a young boy, was an attempted seduction by a plump, friendly gentleman who bragged to me that he was a professional cook for hunting safaris in Africa. Perhaps he was just trying to put a bit of glamour into his sales-spiel – I don't know. *Men who write cook-books* are certainly a peculiar lot. As to the fantasy of male motherhood, a series of jokes on this theme will be found in the First Series, Chapter 8.VI.3, p. 599–602, the section "Rectal Motherhood," owing to the development of this subject in connection with animosity toward the wife and jealousy of her functions, in the chapter on "Marriage." See also Section 10.IV.3 above. All these jokes on rectal motherhood are self-evidently homosexual in tone, and should be consulted at this point, as forming an integral part of the present chapter.

The importance of homosexual scandals in England, during the early 20th century, beginning with the case of Oscar Wilde, has already been alluded to in the introduction to this chapter. These cases, and in particular those occuring during the 1950's, polarized the resistance of English-speaking homosexuals to the prehistoric English law under which they had been harassed for centuries, and began the background machinations which led finally, in very recent years, to the legalization in England of homosexual acts 'between consenting adults,' as had been legal in France under the *Code Napoléon* for over a century and a half, with the result of diminishing homosexual publicity to a minimum in France. The American "Gay Liberation," beginning in the later 1960's, on the inspiration of the English victory, must also look, as its patron saint or martyr, to Oscar Wilde and certain other martyrs since. At the folklore and folk-humor level, these cases precipitated a cloudburst of jokes and puns in England, making fun of homosexuals and homosexuality under the stalking-horse figures of Oscar Wilde, etc. Needless to say, not a single one of these puns or jokes had the slightest specific truth in it, as to the unfortunate persons involved. A large such group of semi-jokes was collected in England in 1954, concerning the latest such scandal, but most of them have not been heard since, though the Oscar Wilde jokes remain hardy perennials.

These field-days of anti-homosexual mockery also involved resistance to and mocking of aristocracy and hereditary nobility also in some cases splashing the prime minister and the Royal Family. Folk humor seldom resists the Oedipal authority of the father-figure in just this way, by calling him homosexual, but either turn the tables wholly upon him, as will be seen in the later section, "The Ganymede Revenge," or else completely submits to pedicatory rape by him. The linguistic and situational subterfuges of misunderstanding and accident are also used, apparently with yoicks of wild humor, to lubricate the rape of the son by the father, and this time without any symbolization, and accede to it. *A young man, who has been treated by the doctor by means of prostatic massage, decides to ask his wife to do it for him to save the costs of treatment. He explains to her how it is done. "It's very simple," he says. "I just bent over with my pants down, and he put one hand on my shoulder, and then with the other hand – wait a minute, come to think of it that son-of-a-bitch had* BOTH *hands on my shoulders!"* (2 : 135.) In a heterosexual version, first encountered eight years later than the preceding, and almost certainly redeveloped and 'expurgated' from it: *A woman is being palpated rectally by a physician for a colonic obstruction. Suddenly she says very suspiciously, "Doctor, are you sure that's your finger?" "Well if it isn't, I'm sure as hell in the wrong hole!"* (N.Y. 1942.)

The sexual guilt of the Knights Templars, the principal mercenary soldiers of the Crusades, whose order was extinguished in the early 14th century, was used as the excuse for seizing their wealth. The pretext, at least, was their sacrilegious and homosexual initiation ceremony, and I have therefore treated at some length in *The Guilt of the Templars* (1966) p. 116–29, the whole subject of homosexual ordeals and initiations. This material need not be repeated here. One odd substitution of folklore for historical truth, there detailed, is that of Sir Richard Burton, himself homosexual, discussing the homosexual abuse of European soldiers taken prisoner by the Mohammedans during the wars in the Levant as late as the 19th (and 20th) century, 'in the much-overrated "Terminal Essay" to his translation, or rather adaptation from Payne's of the *Arabian Nights*.' Burton tells of a Levantine governor, "famed for facetious blackguardism," who would use his prisoners as a "man-cannon" or *Adami-top*, with peppercorns inserted into the victim's anus; "the match was applied by a pinch of Cayenne in the nostrils; the sneeze started the grapeshot and the number of hits on the butt [target] decided the bets." ("Terminal Essay" to Burton's *Arabian Nights*, 1888, x. 235–6; Burton Club edition, x 203–4; reprint of Burton's "Terminal Essay" in *The Book of Exposition*, Paris: Carrington, 1900, p. 213.) As with much of what Burton retails, this is basically improbable and anatomically incredible

– he also tells, on the same page and of the same governor, as a fact, the well-known joke about champagne *"making the rectum sore"* the morning after – but the "facetious blackguardism" involved is by no means beyond likelihood as a Levantine homosexual humiliation.

The champagne joke is still current, and it is again not impossible, though highly improbable, that it really began with the facetious Levantine 'blackguard' to whom Burton ascribes it as a true incident: *An innocent bellboy is invited by a homosexual guest in a hotel to have a glass of champagne. Then another, and so forth, until he is drunk. The boy passes out completely and the homosexual takes the opportunity to bugger him. In the morning the bellboy is discussing champagne, which he had never tasted before, with another bellboy. "It was real good,' he says, "but it sure does make your asshole sore the next day!"* (2:70.) 'Going even farther in the direction of a joke ... the wholly jesting Aleister Crowley works up Burton's above note, in his homosexual leg-pull, *The Scented Garden* – NOT the well-known work by Nafzawi – "translated by Major Alain Lutiy" (1910) p. 71, as follows: "Thou mayest doubtless ask why ... I did not cause thee to be violently enlarged by the eunuch with divers fruit": This is a common practical joke among friends ...' (See further, *The Guilt of the Templars*, p. 118–19, for the full quotation.)

Crowley is perhaps alluding here to a famous joke concerning: *Three shipwrecked sailors who must each make a present to the cannibal king. The first presents him with bananas, which the king finds an unworthy gift and orders that they be shoved up the sailor's ass. The second sailor brings mangoes, and laughs uproariously the whole time he is being given the same treatment with the mangoes. When asked why he is laughing he says, "I'm just thinking about my other pal: he's bringing pineapples!"* (N.Y. 1940.) This also exists in a musical version in which the cruelty is modified by driving it to the impossibility of utter 'nonsense' concerning *The three shipwrecked musicians who must play before the king, and whose instruments are shoved up their ass when they play badly. The piccolo-player laughs the whole time, thinking of his two friends whose turn is next, and whose instruments are the trombone and the tuba.* (N.Y. 1952.) Also collected simultaneously, an an improvement, in a florid variant in which: *The king rewards the musicians when they play well, by having their instruments stuffed with gold. The piccolo player (who is telling of the incident) curses his instrument. When they play badly, their instruments are stuffed up their asses, and the piccolo player then blesses his instrument.* (Tale Type 1689; Rotunda, Motif J2563, "Grateful Fools.")

A minor note in the preceding texts is the rapprochement of food and feces: 'food-dirtying,' to which an entire section is devoted in a later chapter, 12.IV.2. This is the hidden or under-lying meaning of such phrases of rejection and contempt as *'Stick it up your ass!'* of which the contemptuous or homo-sexual tone is the open meaning. *A salesman refuses the* soupe-du-jour *in a New Orleans hotel, in spite of the waiter's insist-ence. Later that night, by a mistake in room numbers, he is given a high-colonic enema intended for a sick person in the next room. Back in New York he tells the next salesman cover-ing the same route: "Listen, if you stop at the Wardour House, in New Orleans, and the waiter offers you soup, take it! Because you're going to get it one way or the other."* (N.Y. 1938.) This probably dates from the heyday of the clyster or enema, in the 18th or early-19th centuries, but no earlier version has been traced. In my burlesque autobiography, *Portrait of the Artist as Flowing Teat* (1966), rectal feeding and the narcotic enema – ultimately *the poisoned enema* – are made use of systematic-ally as a running-gag, to indicate the virile domination, and finally the murder, of 'inferior' males by the magazine-publisher overlord suffering from homosexual paranoia and delusions of grandeur. This is consciously modelled on the notorious Over-bury case in Shakespeare's time, in which Sir Thomas Over-bury – a minor writer and court hanger-on – was killed in the Tower of London by means of a poisoned enema, administered probably by the royal physician, Mayerne, by order of the homosexual King James I.

The most commonly collected joke about pedicatory rape significantly makes use of a national 'inferior,' in this case the Chinese cook, laundryman or railroad-worker, once the most important cheap-labor element in the Western United States, as were the similar Irish and Italian immigrants in the Eastern United States, and the Scandinavians, 'Bohunks' (Hungarians and South Slavs) and 'Polacks' in the Midwest. All these 'in-ferior' immigrant groups are still the butts of much popular American humor, justifying – as is imagined – and gloating over their economic exploitation. *A western miner, desperate* for a woman, is told by the bartender that there is no woman in the mining-town, but that he can "use the Chinese laundry-man." He thinks this over, and asks nervously, "Well, will any-one know?" "Of course not," the bartender reassures him; "only the five of us." "Five of us?! Why five?" expostulates the miner. "Well, you'll know, won't you? And I'll know. And the Chinaman will know." "Yes, but that's only three; who're the other two?" "Oh, they hold the Chinaman." (2:227.) In a variant, collected D.C. 1942, and since, much is made of the verbal humor of the miner rejecting the offer at first because he doesn't "go for that shit," the final explanation being that "The Chinaman don't go for that shit, either."

A minor reduction, curiously touching on the theme of the poisoned enema, as humor: "What do you do about rats in the cellar?" "I know a wonderful way to get rid of them. You simply smash up a whiskey bottle and stuff it in the rat's hole." "It sounds good, but who holds the rat?" (N.Y. 1942. Alluded to in Anecdota, 1927, 1:487, as 'put wax in rats' holes.') The prototype of both these jokes is clearly visible in a standard bit of American humor noted in Leopold Wagner's Names and their Meanings: A Book for the Curious (revised ed. 1892) p. 129: 'A very bad wine of whatever kind usually bears the name of Three Men Wine, owing to the idea that it requires one man to hold the drinker, and another to pour it down his throat, while the third is the unfortunate individual himself.' Mr. Wag-ner spoils what is obviously a joke by recounting it backwards: the intended punch-line certainly being, 'and another to pour it down his throat.' (Food-dirtying.) Dr. Roger Abrahams, in his brief article, "Trickster, the Outrageous Hero," in Our Living Traditions, edited by Tristram P. Coffin (New York, 1968) p. 177, notes a recent 'Polack' joke or blason populaire concern-ing stupidity, also belonging to this type of plural-responsibility situation: How does a Polack screw in a light-bulb? – One man holds it and three turn him around. It is probably connected as well to the anti-proletarian stories accusing working-men (particularly those on public relief or government dole) of being extravagantly lazy, as in a story given later, under "Scatalogy," concerning: 'two men going, two coming, two shitting, and two working!'

A most extraordinary recitation or popular ballad has been current in Mexico for perhaps a century under the title "El Ánima de Sayula" (The Ghost of Sayula), which concerns fears

of pedicatory rape of panic proportions, the rape being achieved
by a ghost representing powerful but unnameable male beings
or father-surrogates. This recitation is discussed by Prof.
Américo Paredes in an important article on the Hispano-
Mexican pose of *machismo*, or super-maleness, and the Mexican
erotic and anti-Gringo folklore in which this is expressed, "The
Anglo-American in Mexican Folklore," in *New Voices in
American Studies* (Purdue University Studies, 1966) p. 113–28,
at p. 121–4, where the parallel is drawn to the profound
Mexican fear of effeminization, even by *albur*, the verbal rape
or insult. The exactly similar 'cult of the male' in Portugal and
Brazil, is called *marialva*, and has been studied in an essay,
"*Cartilha do Marialva*," by José Cardoso Pires. (See further,
Yves de Saint-Agnès, "Votre passeport pour Lisbonne," in
Plexus, Paris, Novembre 1969, No. 29: p. 94–100.) This generali-
zation of the *machismo*, or super-male pose, and the matching
albur, or effeminizing insult, throughout the Hispanic world
makes rather strained, as Prof. Paredes observes, any attempt
to trace these 'with uncompromising Freudian logic ... to
oedipal conflicts arising at the moment when the first Spaniard
threw the first Indian woman to the ground and raped her,
thus laying the foundations of modern Mexico.' More specifically, he continues:

> The American ... may refer to someone who nags or pesters
> him as "being on his ass" [or "riding his ass"], without fear
> of being the target of ridicule or humiliation. On the con-
> trary, many would take this as a manly way of speaking.
> Such an expression would be unthinkable to the Mexican,
> who will say that someone is "irritating his penis," [In French,
> "*casser les couilles*," exactly the American "breaking his
> balls."] He must avoid all reference to his own buttocks or
> rectum, since this will put him in a vulnerable position,
> open to insult and ridicule. The most popular obscene poem
> in Mexican tradition, corresponding to the "Diary of a
> French Stenographer" in the United States, is "*El Ánima de
> Sayula*," about a poor man who is raped by a ghost and
> passes the rest of his life with a protective hand on his back-
> side and his back to the wall, his other hand holding a knife
> threateningly before him. This attitude of truculent de-
> fensiveness – the Mexican's well-known mistrust (*des-
> confianza* – is the basis of his *machismo* and the dominant

feeling behind the veiled hostility ... more to the ever-present image of the Anglo-American than to the racial memory of the conquistador.'

Since, however, precisely the conquistador countries of Spain and Portugal also show the same *machismo* or *marialva* – probably derived in any case from Levantine attitudes picked up during the Moslem conquest of the Spanish peninsula (till the Expulsion in 1492), Levantine attitudes which themselves doubtless developed, in turn, under even more distant conquerors and much farther back in history – there can be no question of anything specifically Mexican or even Hispanic about these fears of pedicatory rape, even by insult, and the overcompensatory 'cult of maleness.' These can only be derived strictly from the historic and personal Oedipal conflicts in an intensely patriarchal culture: what might be called an unconscious memory of periods, perhaps not very far back in time, when actual pedicatory rape (and possibly castration as well) could be expected from the dominant Moslem conquerors, as they were earlier from their fathers and older brothers. Arabs today still castrate or pedicate their captives in war.

As to the folkloristic, rather than the emotional, "*Ánima de Sayula*," a full text is given in *Picardía Mexicana*, a best-selling once-over-lightly of Mexican erotic folklore edited by 'A. Jiménez' (Sr. Armando Jiménez Farias), first published in Mexico City by Libro Mex, in 1960, with a list of earlier articles on this recitation, by the author, p. 242. The recitation is given in facsimile of an 1897 folk broadside, but in a revision signed by Sr. Jiménez and dated 1947, and is printed on special colored paper imitating a *corrido* or Mexican broadside ballad, p. 153–60, the form in which it apparently circulates. There is a final illustration of the unfortunate anti-hero posed just as Prof. Paredes describes him, defending himself from being raped by the ghost while defecating in a graveyard – his foolhardy offense against the spirit of the dead, which is the ostensible cause of his pedicatory punishment. The title-page of the entire volume is also illuminated with a drawing on the same nationally-known theme, doubtless intended to represent the whole soul or spirit of Mexico, showing the anti-hero of this pederastic ballad as a snarling wildcat wearing a large sombrero, and squatting with his brocade trousers down, relieving himself in a symbolic cactus patch, his curved dagger in hand. (*Nueva Picardía Mexicana*, 1971.)

Prof. Paredes sees in the "Sayula" recitation more than the mere folk-humor, and uses an allusion to it in the extraordinarily frank and oversized national *albur* of his summing-up as to the hostile situation between Mexicans and Anglo-Americans, and the recent Hollywoodization of Mexican culture by pop-singers, women's styles, and so forth: 'Basic Mexican symbols have become Hollywoodized. If [the Mexican] takes a walk along any busy city street, he may enjoy the spectacle of Indian girls with their hair bleached a strawy blond, so sadly reminiscent of the American Negro's attempt to straighten out his hair. Thus the Mexican, on guard against the United States, finds that while he has been facing north in a posture of defense, he has been outflanked and taken from behind.'

These fears and accusations of pedicatory rape are international, of course, and exist in all powerfully patriarchal cultures. Prof. Paredes also cites (p. 128) a particularly relevant quotation from the Scandinavian *Volsunga Saga*, many centuries before, in which, during the 'flyting' in insults between Sinfjotli and Granmar, the first tells the second that he was once 'a witch-wife on Varinsey' and later became a Valkyrie in Asgarth, but that the speaker, Sinfjotli, then had to do with him 'as a man does with a woman, and nine wolf-whelps I begat on thy body in Lowness, and was the father to them all.' (*Volsunga Saga*, translated by William Morris, New York, 1962, p. 113.) Though clearly alluding to rape, and to the impregnation of the male as the ultimate domination by another male, this evades the pedicatory insult by having Granmar *become a woman* beforehand! (*You can't fire me – I quit!*) Consider Siegfried in the *Nibelungenlied* being speared by the evil father-figure, Hagen, in a specially vulnerable spot in his back. In the Homeric legends, this 'spot' – evidently the anus, as in the hunting of unicorns – is displaced 'upper-to-lower' to Achilles' heel.

An Alaskan version of these fears of being mysteriously pedicated while at stool, exactly as in the Mexican "*Ánima de Sayula*," is noted in a letter by Jim O'Neil to the editor of a mimeographed New York poetry magazine, *Kauri* (named for the vulviform cowry-shell, depicted on the outer page of various issues), January 1967, page 32. This is given in the form of a patriotic catch or brag, but the similarity to the mysterious danger in the *"Ánima de Sayula"* is obvious:

[The editor] wants to know if there's anything alive up in this here Alaskan mud. Should tell him about the most dangerous beast in Alaska, the *ice worm*, sometimes called the ice snake or the holy terror of the north. Can't see it against the background of ice and snow. Can't hear it. Damn thing just sneaks up on you. Isn't poisonous but its body tem[perature] is 50 below. Likes to crawl into warm holes, so,

Man, don't shit on Alaska!

(The final line is a nationalistic brag, very similar to that on the early American rattlesnake flag, with motto: "DON'T TREAD ON ME.") Mr. O'Neil does not indicate whether this jocular superstition, or *imaginary critter*, obviously of the white settlers, is of Alaskan Indian origin, but does express his admiration for the autochthons: 'Thought NYC [New York City] was hip, but these Mongolian cats have been making the scene for centuries.' This is presumably a reference to the use of the poisonous fly-agaric mushroom (*Amanita muscaria*) by the Eskimos as an hallucinogenic drug. He also does not state how the non-poisonous *ice worm* does its harm: presumably it crawls up the anus of anyone so unwise as to 'shit on Alaska' and freezes him to death internally. Snake superstitions have of course also been part of the scene for centuries, everywhere in the world, with the specific idea that the snake will slip sexually into some body-aperture. This is the blatantly apparent meaning of the Devil-Snake's sexual initiation of Eve in the Garden of Eden (*Genesis*, iii. 1–7), and compare the eccentric Hadriaan Beverland's first public identification of the 'Original Sin' of Adam & Eve as sexual intercourse, not ventured until the early 18th century. Paranoid fears of pedication by snakes are transformed by South American Indians into the superstition of the *caïnero*, described by Henri Michaux in *Ecuador*, and Jean Hallier in *Chagrin d'Amour* (1974): *The caïnero is 'a small red fish in the Amazon river ... that penetrates the imprudent bather through the fundament, and slowly devours his heart!'* (Motif G328, 'rectum-snake;' and compare Freud's 'Rat-man' case.)

To come down to the present, and close this section on a less strictly historical note. The horror-sensation of the year 1969 in America, at the time when Indo-Chinese were being uninterestingly killed daily by the hundreds in Vietnam, by means of high explosives and burning gasoline-jelly ('napalm') dropped by American aviators, was the mysterious killing and mutilation of five Hollywood 'swingers,' including a beautiful movie-actress, Sharon Tate, and a group of her house-guests. Miss Tate, the wife of a horror-film director, Roman Polanski, was then seven months' pregnant, her unborn baby being also stabbed and apparently ripped from her womb. The murderers were soon discovered to be a group of drugged hippies, mostly girls, presumably acting under orders from a sort of Old Man of the Mountain, an undersized but 'hypnotic' pop-musician, Charles Manson, later put on trial for this crime. I have discussed the social context of these *lumpenproletar* murders in my anti-drug pamphlet, *Models of Madness*, and wish to draw attention here not to anything authentically connected with them, but to a presumed 'solution' of the crime, put into print during the journalistic no-man's-land period before the capture of the murderers was announced by the police. This astonishing document, of which the relevance to the present chapter will be immediately evident, was printed in one of the two main hippie or 'underground' newspapers, the *East Village Other* ("*EVO*," New York, August 27, 1969) p. 5, in the column of the editor, Allen Katzman, a column doubtless significantly called "Poor Paranoid's Almanac":

The murders and mutilations of Sharon Tate, hair stylist Jay Sebring, coffee heiress Abigail Folger, Voityck Frokowsky, and Steven Parent in the home of Miss Tate's husband, director Roman Polanski, on August 8th, had brought the whole community of moviedom to a point of psychotic silence. The applause was deafening because no one's hands were moving as well as no one's lips ... in an hysteria of unprecedented fright as well-known music and movie figures had become afraid of compromise in a case which could expose them as confidants in a covenant which included hard drugs [*i.e.* stronger than marijuana], orgiastic rituals of lust and buggering as well as weird sadistic rites ...

It seemed that Polanski's own words in the June 25, 1968 issue of *Look* magazine had come all too true: "It excites [!] me to shock bourgeois audiences who cannot accept that other people may be different from them."

And different these people were. Of the four suspects that police are seeking, only one, as friends of Sharon Tate are telling it, had reason to murder all four; and his name is E—.

E— was disgraced and humiliated by the four victims in front of twenty-five prominent movie and music figures at the home of Mama Cass of the Mamas and Papas fame. He was taken there by Sebring and Frokowsky, stripped, whipped by Miss Tate and Miss Folger, and then buggered by Sebring and Frokowsky because he had dared to "burn" [cheat] them on a cocaine deal. Friends of the four victims claimed E— swore that he would get revenge for what they had done to him.

After the apprehending of the Manson Family or gang, by the police, and their confession to the Tate murders (and others similar), I asked the Hollywood writer who had brought Katzman's detailed story to my attention, what to think of it now? He sternly refused to let go of the bait, told me I was very naïve indeed, that the case was positively as just described, and that E— had simply been *revenged* by the Manson Family. (See their further activities in Ed Sanders' *The Family*, 1970.) I admit that there is perhaps nothing very unusual in scenes of pedicatory rape, such as that presumably enacted on the possibly-mythical Mr. E—, and I have been present myself at such scenes both in hobo-encampments and in jail, though without any of the Black Mass accoutrements implied in the alleged Hollywood 'covenant' and 'weird sadistic rites.' However, even my credulity balks at the picture of a seven-months' pregnant woman wielding a whip on a naked man in an orgiastic flagellation ceremony. I submitted the question to a woman who is anything but naïve, and after thinking about it very seriously she answered: 'A woman who would whip a man at all, in front of an audience, would do it whether she was pregnant or not.' Observe finally that the alleged whipping scene was presumably the sadistic aphrodisiac necessary for the two pedicatory rapists – who were neither sexually starved hoboes nor prisoners – to *do their thing*.

A heterosexual version of the following joke has already been given in the First Series, 5.I, page 265, tracing it to *La Légende Joyeuse* (1749) I, No. 51, where it appears as concerning the pedicatory rape of an artist's male model by the artist, with a verbally sadistic punchline. The situation is illustrated with a crude etching in the later edition, under the title *Le Cabinet de Lampsaque* ('Paphos,' 1784), where it is No. 51; and also in a French publicly-published joke collection of the 1930's, where the rapist is shown as a gendarme! *A man is driving along the highway when robbers overtake him, seize his wallet, his clothes, and his automobile, and tie him to a tree. They then all take turns raping him pederastically, and drive off in his car. A truck-driver sees the man tied to the tree, stops, and comes over to ask what has happened. The man tells him the story, ending, "So please untie me now, will you?" The truck-driver looks at him thoughtfully, and instead begins to undress. "You known, friend," he says, "I guess this just isn't your lucky day."* (L.A. 1967.)

4. PEDICATION THROUGH MISUNDERSTANDING

My wife tells me that the *title* of this section is the funniest joke in the whole book. And yet ... What is to be thought of a joke like this : *A fourteen-year-old boy tells his mother, "I just got laid today."* He is sent to his room to wait till his father gets home. The father tells him, *"Son, women don't understand things like that, but I do. I was young once myself. How did you like it?" "Great, dad. I can hardly wait till the next time!" "Fine. When do you expect that to be?" "I don't know for sure. As soon as my ass isn't sore any more."* (Jersey City, N.J. 1969, winner in the joke contest of the main New York sex-newspaper or 'pornzine,' *Screw*, and published under the heading "Buckley's [the editor's] Ball Busters," 27 June 1969, No. 18: p. 17.) This is apparently a *new joke*, and has not been collected at any earlier date. Another version, much cruder and more homosexualized, appears in *World's Dirtiest Jokes* (1969) p. 123: *'The kid who just got out of high school and went to work at the glass factory said, "Pop, I am now a man. I got my first blow job last night at the factory." Pop asked, "How'd ya like it, son?" And the kid spat at the closest fly and said, "Terrible!"'* Note the hedged and equivocal presentation, probably that of the editors.

The subject of pedication through misunderstanding has been alluded to already in section v.1, "Bend Over," in the title-joke there, which might even better be placed here. Runner-up in popularity, in pedicatory stories over the years, is another which – like the "Ben Dover" story – combines the motifs of elaborate and unlikely misunderstanding and the inferior 'native.' *A western cowboy, hard-up for a woman, asks the bartender's advice and is told just to go out on the Indian reservation and jump on the ass of the first squaw he sees. He does so; puzzled by the squaw shouting "Wahoo! Wahoo!" the whole time. Later, in the pool-parlor, he hears Indian bucks giving the same cry over the pool-table. He asks, and is told that "Wahoo" is an Indian word meaning "Wrong hole."* (Larson MS., No. 48, collected in Idaho, 1919.) Larson follows this with a variant in which: *The hard-up cowboy rapes an Indian, who keeps shouting, "Me buck! Me buck!"* But he omits the punch-line, possibly added later, where: *The cowboy replies, "You can buck all you like, you red-assed bitch. I'm in the saddle, and here I stay!"* (N.Y. 1940; earlier in *Anecdota*, 2:301.) Here, a story which has begun as the *accidental* pedicatory rape of a woman is insistently brought around to the equally accidental pedicatory rape of a man – with rodeo horse-talk 'in the saddle,' to overdetermine the *riding* metaphors (compare Shakespeare's *Henry V*, III.vii.45–70) – which effectively makes the man into the equivalent of a female. The African hunter story, later to be given in the final chapter, "Scatology," also turns on this motif of the *misunderstood native phrase:* "Mgumbo mgumbo, bwana!" Thus, whether the error is that of the subject or the pedicant, one is indeed pedicated through misunderstanding.

'*A sodomist is given a room in a hotel with another man who, the room-clerk assures him, is "not averse to a bout, but that for form's sake he might put up a struggle. But don't you pay any attention to him. You go ahead; he likes it." Next morning the sodomist came down, and the clerk asked him how he had fared. "It was quite easy," he answered. "He put up no struggle at all." "My God," said the clerk, "I put you in the wrong room. That was the archbishop".'* (1:458.) One observes the not-very-well hidden disappointment here, that there was no sado-masochistic homosexual struggle, implying again that the essence of homosexual relationships is not sexual love or even the urge toward sexual pleasure, but the desire for some charade of sexual domination or intimidation of or by another man.

Standard situation: *The hard-up miner or western cowboy who is told by the bartender that there are no women in town, but that (in this case) he can "use the barrel." He is shown a large barrel in the stable, with a fur-lined bunghole at one end, and is left alone with it. After some hesitation, worrying about possible disease, he fucks the barrel and finds it wonderfully lifelike in feeling. He rushes back to the bartender and asks, "Say, can I use that anytime I want?" "Sure," says the bartender, flipping over the pages of a well-thumbed ledger; "any day except Wednesday. Wednesday is your day in the barrel."* (N.Y. 1938.) Here, finally, the situation to which all the pedicational stories seem to be tending is brought into the open: the pedication of the teller of the story, or identification-character, himself.

At least two other stories, much milder in *dénouement* than that preceding, also trick the listener into accepting identification with the butt of the story, who will end up pedicated 'through misunderstanding.' Both of these are in animal disguise. *The bird from Texas, who is so tough it kills rattlesnakes for fun, decides one day to get laid. It leaps on a lark who goes off trilling, "I'm a lark and I've been sparked." Then on a dove: "I'm a dove and I've been loved." Then a duck comes by, and, after a good deal of commotion and feathers torn out, the duck waddles away muttering, "I'm a drake and there's been a mistake."* (L.A. 1968. This is of the 'tease-song' type of humor, in which the expected *rhyme*, in this case on 'duck,' does not arrive.) The other story is a great favorite, endlessly collected, a popularity hardly to be explained by the foolish alliteration of its continuing punch-line: *Two buck-rabbits agree to line up all the female rabbits, and to start at opposite ends fucking them as fast as they can. The first rabbit starts out: "Wham, bam! Thank you, ma'm! – Wham, bam! Thank you, ma'm! – Wham, bam! Oh, pardon me, Sam."* (Pittston, Penna. 1943.) In another version the homosexual element becomes auto-castratory instead, by means of an obviously contrived situation: *The male rabbit is making love to female rabbits lined up in a graveyard. In his erotic frenzy he does not notice that there is one less female than he thinks, and leaps on a marble urn on one of the graves: "... Wham, bam! Oh, god* DAMN!!" (N.Y. 1945.)

The idea of the 'rectal virginity' of the pedicated male – meaning in this case the son *vis-à-vis* the more powerful father-figure – is made very explicit in another favorite story, very frequently collected, in which again we are made to share in the pedicatory rape of the listener's identification-character: *At a crude meal in a logging-camp out in the wilds, the newly-hired logger notices how freely and noisily the men fart after their heavy evening meal of beans and cabbage. All around him*

he hears the noisy explosions, "Ptooh!" "Ftrooff!" "Trooomp!!"
He decides to be uninhibited himself and ventures a discreet
"thbbb!" The head logger leaps to his feet, whirls his double-
bitted axe over his head and slams it quivering into the plank
table. "All right, men!" he snarls, "the virgin is mine!" (2:219,
as of two homosexuals watching a Marines' parade.) A very
similar story appears two centuries earlier in the graffiti collection, *The Merry Thought, or Bog-House Miscellany* (London,
1731) IV. 23, entitled "The Italian *Goût.*"

Another period-piece on pedicatory rape is given in *The Pearl*,
No. 3 (Sept. 1879), the rape here being of the Levantine pederastic ordeal variety, and here of the father-figure. It is reduced,
however, to mere masturbation, on the pretended misunderstanding of the phrase *'frig them,'* actually intended to mean
'damn them!'

> In the wars in India, in the year 1800, Major [Henry]
> Torrens's party was pursuing some of the enemy. One day,
> while they were dining and very merry, a sergeant came and
> reported to the Major that two prisoners were brought in,
> one old and one young. The Sergeant requested orders re-
> garding them. The Major merrily answered: "Oh, take them
> away and frig them." The Sergeant retired. In an hour he
> returned, and respectfully made this report: "Please, your
> honour, we have frigged the young one, but we can't make
> the old man's cock stand."
>
> This story was related to me in 1818, by Torrens, who was
> then an old General at Madras.

The humiliation of the father-figure here, through a 'misunderstanding,' is all the more complete in that he proves to be too
impotent even for the intended rape or Ganymede Revenge.
That is to say, he is desexed by the mere attempt: precisely the
castratory fear paramount in the son's unconscious, as to the
result – upon his own body – of the homosexual and homosexualizing rape by the father.

As opposed to the idea involved here, that the masturbation
of the old man in the anecdote was all a misunderstanding,
the extraordinary young writer and researcher signing himself
'Allen Edwardes' shows in his *Erotica Judaica: A Sexual History
of the Jews* (New York: Julian Press, 1967) pp. 67 and 98, that
the ultimate humiliation of the Biblical hero Samson, and of

the last King of Judah before the Captivity, Zedekiah in 597 B.C., was not or not only the standard Levantine pedicational rape, but the requirement that the vanquished male *masturbate publicly;* in this case Samson, before 3,000 spectators of both sexes, all of whom he kills in revenge (*Judges,* xvi. 25–7); and Zedekiah 'in the presence of Queen Amyitis and her body-wenches, a mockery and disgrace reserved for only the noblest [n.b.]' (Edwardes, p. 98, note 8, citing the *Tarikh el-Yahud* of the Arab chronicler, Abdullah et-Trablusi, who also reports the legend of the similar humiliation of the prophet Ezekiel along with the king.)

One of the most famous and widely circulated Oriental folk-tales is that of "The Silence Wager" (Type 1351, Motif J2511), best known in English in the comic ballad version, "The Barrin' o' the Door" (Child Ballads, No. 275), which is importantly traced by Reinhold Köhler in Child's headnote, in W. N. Brown's "The Silence Wager Stories: their origin and their diffusion," in *American Journal of Philology* (1922) XLIII. 289–317; most completely by W. A. Clouston in his *Popular Tales and Fictions* (1887) II, 15 ff., and in *The Athenaeum* (18 March 1893) p. 346–7; and in further European and Levantine sources listed by Aarne and by Thompson. The story is apparently known everywhere in the world, but most of the recorded texts are much softened and expurgated in the transmission. The story is: *Of a husband and wife who agree that whichever speaks first will have to close the street door which has accidentally been left open. Robbers find the open door, enter, and seeing the silent couple making no move, eat the food on the table, take all the valuables, and finally 'kiss' the wife, and propose to shave off the husband's beard. "All right," the husband cries at that point, "I'll close the god damn door!"* One assumes that the *shaving off of the beard* is the same sort of euphemism or partialism for pederastic rape, as the 'kissing' of the wife is an obvious euphemism for ordinary rape. (See further, Paul G. Brewster, "The Silence Wager in Ballad and Tale," in *East and West,* Rome, 1971, N.S. 21: p. 363–76, giving all Oriental versions.)

Meanwhile, the unexpurgated and even more Oedipal version continues to exist, underground, in the following very well-known joke form: *A dinner guest is told that it is a family custom that the first person to speak after dinner has to wash the dishes. Emboldened by the parents' absolute silence, the*

guest begins kissing the daughter, then has intercourse with
her, and with the mother as well, since the father continues to
make loud grunts of protest but does nothing else. The guest
then lights a cigar, burning his finger while doing so, and goes
upstairs to the bathroom to find something to put on it. "Say,
where do you keep the vaseline?" he shouts down. "All right,
all right!" cries the father, "I'll wash the fucken dishes!"
(2 : 129.) Some versions attempt to smooth out the presumed
error of the guest's speaking, but it seems clear that the guest –
who probably doesn't *care* whether he has to wash the dishes
later – is not held to the family rule, being in fact nothing other
than one of the robbers of the original Levantine version, who
verbally propose to 'shave off the husband's (father's) beard.'

A similar joke exists, or the same joke in another form, in
which the framework of the silence-wager has been lost, and is
replaced only by an almost meaningless or 'nonsensical' punch-
line, which is, however, an interesting reversal of the usual
mentula loquens or 'speaking penis' motif, in which (as in
Portnoy's Complaint, quoted at 11.III.4, "Impossibilities") the
penis speaks to its possessor, as a sort of *advocatus Diaboli,*
urging him on to sexual acts : an interesting verbal typification
or personalization of the physiological fact of erection. Here,
instead, the man addresses his own penis, as though (again) it
were a creature apart from himself, with its own will and
senses. In almost all jokes in English in which the penis is
addressed in this way, the person speaking is stated to be a
Negro. *A Negro is on trial for having raped an entire family, and*
the father testifies against him: "First he fucked my daughter,
then he fucked my wife, the dog, and the cat, and the keyhole.
Then he got out a big pair of spectacles and put them on his
prick and said, "Look aroun', friend, an' see if you done forgot
anything!" That's when I figured I better call the police." (N.Y.
1942.)

What is so striking in all these stories is, of course, precisely
the trait of the stubborn *silence* and immobility of the presumably outraged head and members of the family. I have
suggested, in *The Horn Book,* p. 471–2, that this is a survival of
a magical bewitching or ensorcellment in an earlier or other
related tales, here rationalized as the result of a family wager.
In the same way, in a story given earlier, traced to Bebel in the
early 16th century, a man watches his wife being raped, while
he holds up the rapist's testicles *'out of the hot sand'* (or simply

holds his horse) under the rationalization that he is petrified by fear of the rapist's threat to kill him if he moves. One of the Levantine versions of the silence-wager story itself uses the rationalization or modernization, at that date, of being concerned with hashish-eaters. This whole story-group has, therefore, important similarities, not noted by Aarne or Thompson, to the ensorcellment tale-type of the *Arabian Nights'* "City of Brass," also to Barbarossa and his frozen army, sleeping for centuries under the mountain while waiting for the Götterdämmerung or Ragnarok (the ultimate destruction of the world in a final conflict, or "Twilight of the Gods" – any day now!), and likewise to "The Sleeping Beauty," who can be awakened only by a 'kiss' in polite versions, exactly as in the polite versions of "The Silence Wager." Compare, however, the full-blooded and farcical original version of "The Sleeping Beauty" in Basile's *Pentamerone* (1636), in which everyone and everything in the house, including the furniture, the dishes, and the chamberpot (*i.e.* "the dog, and the cat, and the keyhole"?) are magically impregnated by this 'kiss,' and give birth to little furniture, little dishes, and little chamberpots.

Vance Randolph gives a further American trickster version, also rationalized as a *bet*, to explain the parents' ensorcelled immobility. This is given in Randolph's manuscript collection, *Pissing in the Snow*, No. 16, as "It Didn't Cost Him Nothing," collected in 1953 from an informant who first 'heard it near Green Forest, Ark., about 1900.' In this case the homosexual element has completely disappeared, except in the implied orgiastic scene of the whole family being piled up by the young man trickster in a sort of 'daisy-chain' or erotic spintry, with the two men *insulated* away from each other by the two women's bodies. Afanasyev's *Russian Secret Tales* (about 1895) has a similar tale of implied homosexual intercourse given as an orgy or spintry, No. 60, "The Soldier and the Priest," in which: *The soldier fucks the wife who is lying on top of her husband, the priest, who has been tricked into lying down in a cart to evade an imperial ukase stating that all priests must be fucked by the soldiers. The priest's prick erects sympathetically and sticks out through the bottom of the cart. The daughter, entering, marvels: "Oh, what a terrible prick that soldier has! It's gone through my mother and my father, and the tip of it is still wagging."* (Meaning, of course, that she is wondering if there is still room for her.)

In a limerick version, *"En brochette* in Tibet," in *The Limerick*, No. 351, the penis goes through 'six Greeks' in this way; while in Limerick No. 242 the tip also goes through the bedding *'And shattered the chamber utensil.'* In a less frankly homosexualized form, *Two farm-hands needing a woman decide that they will fuck a sheep.* 'First chap gets up sheep, in course of which his exertions make it put its tongue out. Second, a bit short-sighted, calls out, "Cripes mate, you're coming through the front!" "All right, stick on another sheep!"' (London, 1954.) Newbern & Rodebaugh, *World's Dirtiest Jokes* (1969) p. 131, give this as of two men who 'accidentally' rape a homosexual dressed in women's clothes.

5. RAPE BY ANIMALS

This subject has already been considered in another sense, in the First Series, final section of Chapter 3, "Animals." Although sexual relations of humans with animals are not uncommon, it is invariably understood that the human being, in such miscegenational acts – if that is the correct term – is the dominant partner, and is calling the turn. It is difficult to distinguish here between fact and fiction, folklore and jokelore. In the picaresque novel, *The Sot-Weed Factor* (New York: Doubleday, 1960), Prof. John Barth's pastiche of the style of Rabelais' 17th-century translators, Urquhart and Le Motteux, in among a good deal of very insistent scatology, much is made of a scene in which the hero fucks a pig. So also in a late-1960's American *avant garde* movie, *Futz*. The Japanese-Swedish film, *A Summer's Day – 1970*, in which essentially a woman rapes a pig, both orally and genitally, is described further under "Orgies and Exhibitions," 11.III.2. A popular and intentionally sensationalist sexological work, built up from case-histories and letters from readers, R. E. L. Masters' *Sex-Driven People* (Los Angeles: Sherbourne Press, 1966), gives, according to its blurbs, 'The Red-Hot Truth about Human-Animal Sex Acts.' This with a picture of the snout and trotters of a pig on the advertising brochure, and the following sample quotation from the work: *'One letter-writer confides to Masters: "The jackpot is when animals rut or come into heat ... you haven't lived until you'd had what they* [who? the animals?] *call a 'heat ride'"* ... *This is the same man who enjoys homosexual affairs, but once turned down the offer because: "I was planning to have inter-*

course with a sow when I returned home, and wanted to save it for her!" '

The writer of the brochure continues: 'Obviously, this book is one of the most vitally important documents ever published about what is really going on among a frighteningly large segment of the American population!' Which is perhaps not actually as obvious as is claimed. Anyhow, who's frightened? Even the 'heat ride,' and other such entertainments, invariably involve the idea, and ideal, of the human partner as dominant. The case is otherwise in jokes, which give possibly a truer picture of the fantasy life of a 'large segment' of the population, than the letters (truth or fantasy) of proudly perverted correspondents. In jokes the most significant theme is, instead, that of *rape by animals*, almost always of homosexual nature. In the most striking of these, the overpowering animal clearly represents the god or father-figure, as in similar folk-myths of antiquity in which human beings (generally stated to be female) have intercourse with divine beings disguised as powerful animals or birds – the *horse* as rapist is curiously lacking in these myths – and have monstrous or heroic offspring from such intercourse: Leda, Europa, and the rest.

In the mildest form collected, the dominant animal is smuggled into the story in a sort of mock-innocent 'catch' or swindle of the listener-interlocutor. *A little girl playing with her pet dog is asked by a passer-by* [the listener], *"What's your name, little girl?" "My name is Candy. They call me that because I like candy so much. And this is my dog, Porky." "I suppose they call him that because he likes pork so much?" "No," says the little girl, "they call him Porky because he fucks pigs."* (Los Angeles, 1967. This seems to be one Dr. Masters overlooked.) Many of the jokes on the dominant animal have already been given in the earlier chapter on "Animals," in the First Series, but two or three of the main such jokes are briefly given again here, in variant collected forms: *Pat and Mike are out hunting, disguised in the skin of a cow. Suddenly Pat, who is the head-end, begins to run, while Mike, who is the tail-end, follows blindly as fast as he can. Pat runs faster and faster, and finally Mike shouts to him: "Slow down, bejabers! I can't run any faster!" "All right, then," shouts Pat, "brace yourself. Here comes the bull!"* (N.Y. 1936.) Printed in various French jokebooks of the 1930's, as of 'Marius & Olive.'

A very ornate revision of this was given to me by a young

woman in France, in 1966, who had heard it the same year in Reno, Nevada, with extravagant sound-effects. *A promising but distraught young business executive is advised to take a two-week vacation in the north woods. The company plane flies him to Canada, where the travel agent has been alerted to prepare him the de luxe hunting trip. The agent explains to him that the key to the whole trip is the French-Canadian guide, Pierre, who paddles the canoe, baits the fishhooks, builds the fire, cooks the food, and arranges the eiderdown sleeping-bag for the executive. Then, when they reach the hunting-grounds, the executive is to load his gun while Pierre makes the sound of the female moose in heat: "Be-ee-eep! Bre-e-e-eep!" And from far away will come the reply of the male moose: "Bo-o-oop! Br-o-o-oooop!" coming closer and closer, until finally the bull-moose is right there, and all the executive must do is shoot him. "But what if I miss?" he asks nervously. "Oh well," says the agent, "in that case, Pierre gets fucked."* That Pierre is the temporary wife is very clear. That he also represents the female terrors of the 'distraught young business executive,' overlorded by his bull-moose executive superiors, does not take much consideration of the matter to understand as well. Except that only in the north woods is faithful Pierre there, as a sort of female whipping-boy, to 'get fucked' for him.

An actor must take off forty pounds in a hurry to play Hamlet. At the luxurious gymnasium he is offered a 12-hour crash course for $1000 or a 24-hour course for $500. He chooses the 24-hour course, and is ushered naked into a large empty room with a padded table in the center. The door opens and a beautiful, naked girl enters wearing only a sign over her breasts: "YOU CATCH ME, YOU FUCK ME." Wondering what he must have missed in refusing to pay the extra $500, he tells the girl to go back and send him the director, to whom he explains that he has reconsidered and would prefer the $1000 course. He is taken to another identical room and locked in. A door opens at the far end, and a gigantic ape (or Negro) with an enormous erection enters, wearing only a sign: "I CATCH YOU, I FUCK YOU." (N.Y. 1952. French version as *"Au hammam"* [At the Turkish bath], without the two signs or any reference to money, in Louis Perceau's *Histoires raides,* 'Marseille,' ca. 1929.) In Charlie Chaplin's 1910's movie comedy, *The Cure,* something close to this joke is implied when Chaplin mimes explicit homosexual flirtations with the enormous bearded villain – a father-image appearing in most of his early comedies – and a brawny Turkish bath-house attendant and masseur, whom he also unsuccessfully attempts to wrestle.

A journalist in the Southern mountains is told of a raccoon hunter who is the local champion. "No one can touch him for hunting raccoons," the journalist is told; "he has his own style." The champion hunter offers to take the journalist out with him on a hunt and show him how he does it. No guns are taken by the champion, who assures the journalist he will not need one either, but the journalist takes a gun along anyhow. The secret of the hunter's art is his marvellously trained dog, Blue (or Beau), who sniffs out the raccoons and chases them up a tree. The hunter shakes the tree till the raccoon falls out, and Blue then seizes the raccoon and fucks it to death. At the third try, a particularly big raccoon is treed, and the hunter cannot get it down by shaking the tree. He climbs the tree himself to poke it down, but the raccoon fights back and bites the hunter savagely, causing him to fall out of the tree. As he falls, he screams to the journalist, "Shoot Blue! Shoot Blue!" (Great Neck, N.Y. 1964, told by an automobile salesman as the *friendly* part of his sales-spiel.) A version of this story was first printed in *World's Dirtiest Jokes* (1969) p. 151, with the addition of a pigmy gun-bearer – to shoot the dog – and the additional castratory touch that the dog's method consists of grabbing the treed animals (apes) by the testicles, which causes them to faint. In both versions the rape by the animal is overdetermined, in that it really takes the combined efforts of both the animal and the dog to achieve the hunter's rape: a sort of animal gang-shag of the father-figure or master hunter. The listener's identi-fication-*persona*, the gun-bearing journalist or Hamlet (representing the son), has no real function to perform except to save the father from this rape, but we are not actually told whether he does so. One presumes he does not.

A theoretically innocent little joke, often publicly printed, directly expresses the homosexual threat of pedication by the dominant male or master-of-the-herd: *A zebra arrives from Africa but the zoo is crowded so they put him up on a stock-farm. He wanders about asking the animals how they like the place, and what they do. The chickens say they lay eggs, the pigs admit they're being fattened for bacon and pork, etc. The zebra sees a big red bull and asks, "And what do you do here, sir?" "Take off those silly striped pyjamas, and I'll bloody-*

soon show *you what I do!"* (Chelmsford Prison, Essex, 1954.) There is also the outsider's, or wholly innocent point of view, here put into the mouth of a boy who is trying to say (for the joke-teller) that he is not being taken in by his father's lies, and well understands the presumable danger he himself runs : *A boy sees two dogs locked in intercourse, and is watching them interestedly when his father comes along. "You know, son," says the embarrassed father, "that's the real lesson of the Good Samaritan. The dog on top is sick, and the dog on bottom is helping carry him home." The son just looks at him. "I guess you're right, dad. But isn't it funny, any time you try to help somebody else you always end up getting fucked in the ass."* (Arlington, Texas, 1966, told me by a Texas millionaire-publisher to, as it were, explain the ground rules of our future business relations.)

A minor form of animal rape, obviously a 'pure' joke without too important an unconscious level, is oral rape by the animal, as in : *The man who is left tied naked to a tree by robbers, or in a haunted barn on a bet, and is driven to frenzy by a motherless calf licking his penis.* (Scranton, Pa. 1934, told simply as anecdote.) The more paranoid form, in which the oral rape becomes even more fearsomely uncontrollable, involves the displacement of the animal by a machine, as with the mechanical man for female masturbation, (*'Wound up for forty-eight hours to fuck the Queen of Spain'*), with the song-variant over-accentuating all the cruel and violent element possible on such a theme, "The Great Fucking Wheel." Note that the machine in the following oral-rape joke is, essentially, an animal-machine: *A farmer becomes intrigued by the new patent Sucking-and-Blowing Cow-Milker device which is clipped onto the cow's teats, and finally puts his penis into it. At first the sensation is wonderful but soon he becomes fatigued, and finds he cannot shut off the machine. He calls for help, and his wife comes running, but she too cannot shut off the machine. She phones the factory to ask what to do, and the old trouble-shooter whom she finally gets on the wire says, "Well, lady, all I can tell you is keep feeding him and fanning him. That machine is set for twenty-four quarts!"* (N.J. 1942.)

6. THE GANYMEDE REVENGE

In terror of the overwhelming rape by the father-figure or Jovian god, the pedicated boy, Ganymede, is still able to imagine a revenge or a triumph over his aggressor. By the inevitable *lex talionis* of almost all folklore and the underlying unconscious processes, the pedicator is to be punished precisely in the organ by means of which he has harmed or dominated the boy, namely his penis. Ganymede's revenge is achieved by means of his rectum, which bites or lacerates or otherwise harms the penis of Jove. This still involves a continuing assimilation of the boy to the female rôle into which he has been thrust, as the fantasy of the Ganymede revenge is clearly nothing other than the *vagina dentata* transposed into a sort of toothed rectum. The clearest expression of this is not in joke form but in folk-poem or song, "The Good Ship *Venus*," of which a text is given in *The Limerick* (1953) p. 107–8, No. 523–9, and note, p. 403–4, dating from collection in New York in 1946, and describing the various sexual adventures and misadventures of the crew, with the two-couplet stanza, just before the end:

> *The cabin-boy was the captain's joy,*
> *A cunning little nipper;*
> *They filled his ass with broken glass,*
> *And circumcized the skipper.*

First publicly published in Harry Morgan's *Why Was He Born So Beautiful*, and *More Rugby Songs* (London: Sphere Books, 1967–8) 1. 70. In an equally famous British bawdy song or parody, "Cathusalem, the Harlot of Jerusalem" (*Why Was He Born So Beautiful*, 1. 78), the final Ganymede revenge is enacted by a woman, outraged at having been pedicated by a giant, whereupon: 'She closed her arse and blew a fart, That sent him flying like a dart, Right over old Jerusalem.' The obvious implication of this old army song is that the whole thing is really in code, and is to be understood homosexually, with the giant and woman representing father & son.

A further and self-evidently weakly vengeful step toward harming, or imagining that one is harming the pedicator, by way of revenge, is the concentration on the dirtying of his penis, "the best part of a man," by the feces in the pedicated boy's or man's rectum. A curious satirical work of the mid-18th century, imitating the *Gulliver's Travels* of Swift, especially as to Swift's insistent scatology, is entitled *A Voyage to Lethe*, by 'Capt. Samuel Cock' (London, 1741), and all the names on the list of subscribers – lacking in the reprint of *ca.* 1875 – also involve punning references to the word '-cock.' The following description is given (ed. 1875, p. 26–7) of one of the 'religious' ceremonies of Lethe by this Swiftian traveller:

> ... another temple on the opposite shore, parallel to that of Dildona [*the Lesbian goddess, identified with the worship of the Bona Dea by the Roman women*], dedicated to an idol called *Paederarstia*, worshipped by the Sodomanians, a very infamous people, of a mean sallow complexion, and with an odious squeak in their voices ... The idol, or rather monster, is in a most unseemly attitude, representing a young boy crouching down, with his head pendent, and his posterior projecting to his votaries. The offering they make to it appeared to me like human ordure. I saw several of the great conquerors of the world prostrate before it, all besmeared with excrement – Alexander, Caesar, Pompey, with diverse others among the ancients.... The Italians made the most considerable figure among the Europeans – the French were not far behind them – their slavish imitators the Dutch were, as Sawney says in the play, hard at their arse –

Curiously popular is the purely verbal misunderstanding of the following joke, which is actually nothing more than a pun in which the real situation is suddenly revealed. *Three Irishmen are treated by a doctor (or haled before the night-court) for bruised and bleeding genitals as a result of some sort of disorderly behavior. The first two explain that the accident happened to them "Up Hogan's Alley." When the third man comes before him, the doctor (or judge) says, "I suppose you were up Hogan's Alley too?" "No, judge, I'm Hogan!"* (2:53.) Sometimes collected in the form of an even more impossible pun in which: *The two men explain that the accident happened to them while they were "blowing Bubbles." The third man: "I'm Bubbles."* (N.Y. 1940.) An expurgated version attempts to turn this to 'mere' cruelty: *Two men are up before the judge for misbehavior and explain that all they were doing was "Throwing peanuts in the lake." Third man: "I'm Peanuts."* (N.Y. 1953.)

By far the most ornate and complete of the Ganymede revenge jokes is of European origin: it is known in France as "L'Hercule Suisse," and as such it is apparently directly translated, from the French, in *Anecdota Americana* (1927) 1:457, credited to the repertoire of a 'distinguished critic.' It is, however, far more commonly encountered in English in a naturalized form, in mock Cockney accent. *Scotland Yard is perturbed by the number of homosexuals haunting London Bridge at night, and several handsome young plainclothes detectives are stationed on the bridge to try to apprehend the homosexuals. One young detective brings in a record number, and when asked by the commissioner about his method, he answers: "Very simple, sir. I just puts me 'ands in me pockets and leans over the bridge, like this. And when one of these 'ere now degenerates shoves 'is prick up me bum, I ups with me butticks and* ORF *we go to Scotland Yard!"* (N.Y. 1940, acted out with the triumphant capturing motion of the 'butticks,' followed by waltzing off with tiny steps like two dogs locked in copulation.)

Absurd and overdone as this joke may seem, I have myself observed a homosexual prostitute or 'hustler,' thought to be nothing lower than 'dirt' – a person who beats up and robs homosexuals – but who later turned out to be an *agent provocateur* detective (exactly as in the joke), winding a handkerchief around his penis perfectly openly in a public toilet in a New York subway station, beneath the intersection of Eighth Avenue and 42nd Street, the principal area of homosexual encounter at that time (1938) and possibly still. As I came in unexpectedly late in the evening – searching for toilet graffiti, I should perhaps mention – he made no attempt to disguise what he was doing, and said to me jokingly: *"It's my decoy!"* The explanation, if any is necessary, is that in fact (as differentiated from the joke, preceding), homosexuals of the predominantly fellator group are particularly attracted to large and bulging genitals, as seen through the cloth of the trousers – and thus called 'the basket' – and particularly 'cruise' (accost) young men making such a display.

The ultimate response to the fear of pedication by the father-figure, and what is essentially the normal or non-homosexual response, is to *'get there fustest with the mostest'* and rape the father-figure oneself. When done early enough, in imagination at least, this reverses the homosexualizing situation and the dominated boy-child does not become homosexual (and the girl dominated and repressed by her mother does not become frigid or lesbian). When, however, the break for freedom is made too late, which appears to mean, in psychological fact, at any time after early puberty or the mid-teens, homosexuality is not evaded. Instead, the homosexual neurotic develops cruelly as the kind of violent and aggressive 'wolf' whose sexual act of choice is the endless domination and pedication of other males, representing the father who was never attacked at all. Thus we have a second form of the Ganymede revenge, which is phallic rather than rectal – active rather than passive – a true revenge rather than a poisoned succumbing.

Obviously, the most innocent form of the rape of the father-figure is when it is done by accident. In a singular and very rare erotic animated-cartoon motion picture, made in the United States about 1930, under the title *"Buried Treasure"* or *"Abie's Buried Treasure"* (presented by 'Fuckaduck Films'), the little title-hero is modelled after Harry Hershfield's comic-strip character, Abie Kabibble, the comedy-Jewish travelling sales-man. In this animated fantasy he finds himself on a desert island on which all the animals, birds, snakes, etc. are engaging in rapid sexual intercourse. He is similarly invited by a naked woman's genital organ, which forms itself into a clutching mouth or hand, and beckons to him. (Compare the similar but very arty transformation of a hand into a fellatory mouth in Jean Cocteau's homosexual movie, *Blood of a Poet*, a few years later.) The woman then hides herself coyly in the sand, and the hero leaps upon her and 'rapes' her. Only to find, when the sand is shaken off, that he is actually pedicating *a gray-haired man*, who gallops off dragging the hero with him, like two dogs locked in intercourse. (*Shaggy-dog story: Two young men are cycling madly on a tandem bike while a dog is chasing them, trying to throw a bucket of water on them.* – London, 1952.) It needs no demonstrating that the eroticized desert island is intended for the Garden of Eden, that the diminutive hero is a child grown up, and that the beckoning woman is the mother and the pedicated gray-haired man the father.

A careful study of Hieronymus Bosch's masterpiece, *The Garden of Delights* (in the Prado Museum, Madrid, and repro-duced in all its deliciously sensual pinks in Jacques Combe's monograph on this artist, Paris : Tisné, 1946, English-language editions, plates 81–99, especially detail-plates 88–92), will show that it is filled with very similar fantasies, painted before 1516. Note especially the sub-erotic groups called "The Teeming Earth," in that part of the triptych specifically showing the Garden of Eden, and in the central panel of the Garden of Delights itself. The bold and direct symbolism of the strange

glass rods plunging into and through the fleshy pink excresc-
ences surging up out of the marshy water (Combe, pl. 92) is the
most extraordinary element in the entire work, though the
same sort of art-critics who somehow manage to understand
purposely meaningless non-objective modern art purport to find
Bosch's glass rods and pink flesh 'ununderstandable.'

In its most polite form, the rape of the father-figure or father-
surrogate is purely verbal, though a sufficiently direct symbolism is necessary to make clear just what is being done to whom
– and by what aperture. *An old ship's carpenter is giving a
lecture on technical details to army officers preparing the invasion of France during World War II. He is continually interrupted when he pronounces words like "helm" and "hash," as
the names of trees, by a very la-di-dah voice from one of the
officers, correcting him: "You mean elm, of course, and ash,
don't you?" Finally, exasperated, the old carpenter says: "Now
'ere we 'ave the hoak." – "You mean oak, of course!" – "Of coss.
It is the very finest wood to use for pounding piles into piers.
And for the benefit of our young friend 'ere, I* don't *mean
pushin' 'emmeroids hup the harses or hanuses of the Haristocracy!"* (London, 1952.) Under the surface reversals in age, of the
'old carpenter' and his 'young friend', *i.e.* enemy, of the aristo-
cratic persuasion, it is clear that the rebellious rape or verbal
pedication involved is nobly achieved by the socially 'inferior'
figure, being corrected like a child (the listener's presumed
identification-image), and that it is the dominant father-figure or
class of the 'Haristocracy' that is getting it in the end.

The defiance of the father-figure, culminating in pederastic
rape enacted symbolically upon him, appears most clearly in
a joke of which a non-homosexual version (concerning *a
schoolboy betting with his lady-teacher that she is menstruating*) has been given earlier in the First Series. *A young officer is
sent to his new regiment with the highest recommendation but
with the plea that his new colonel should cure him of his habit
of betting, which has made him a nuisance. In his first conversation with the new colonel, the young officer mentions
having heard of that "terrible affair in Gulwa Pass (in India)
when you got that awful wound in the backside." The colonel
expostulates that he never heard of Gulwa Pass or was wounded
in the backside, and, when the subaltern offers to bet £10 that
he still has the scar, the colonel sees an opportunity to cure
him of betting and takes down his pants. The young officer*

admits there is no scar, apologizes, and pays over the money. The colonel later receives the following letter from the commanding officer of the young man's former regiment: "I suppose you feel very bucked about winning ten pounds off young L. Unfortunately it is our money, for, before leaving us, he bet the mess over one hundred and fifty, that he would have your trousers down the first evening he met you." (Kimbo, *Tropical Tales*, Nice, 1925, p. 56-7. Also well-known in French.) In certain other forms collected since 1925, the quasi-pedication or humiliation of the father-figure is made even more specifically physical, and the young officer insists upon and succeeds in putting his *finger* up the colonel's anus, to 'assure himself' of the absence of piles or a scar, the size of the bet being made enormously higher (ten thousands pounds, or dollars) to excuse the enormity of the actual physical palpation of the father-figure's arse. Even so, observe that he is not actually penilely pedicated. A castratory form, by a woman, also exists.

Even when the whole line of the story or joke clearly points to the physical pedication of the father, some evasion or dislocation of the intended attack is almost certain to take place. This is what makes the unequivocal buggery of the *gray-haired man* in the animated cartoon described above so unusual. An old *cante fable* entitled "Fill, Bowl, Fill" shows this mechanism of evasion with great clarity. This is given in expurgated form in Vance Randolph's *Who Blowed Up the Church House* (1952) p. 17–19, with folklore annotations by Dr. Herbert Halpert, p. 185–6; and in unexpurgated form – from the same tale-teller! both texts being collected from him in Lamar, Missouri, in 1927 – in Randolph's MS. supplement, *Pissing in the Snow* (1954) No. 29. This *cante fable*, which is too long to quote here in full, is a form, possibly the original, of Aarne Tale Type 570, "The Rabbit-herd" (and compare Type 850).

Briefly: *The king's daughter is promised to the hired man, Jimmy, in marriage, if he can keep the king's pet rabbit for a week. The king sends the servant girl to bribe the rabbit away from Jimmy, but he refuses the money telling her, "If you will lay down and let me hone you off, you can have the rabbit." After she leaves with the rabbit, he rings a bell and the rabbit breaks loose and runs back to him. The king's daughter is then sent to get the rabbit, with a quit-cash dowry of two hundred pounds, but the hired man scorns the money and tells her she can have the rabbit free if she will let him "hone her off." She does so, but again the rabbit is brought back to Jimmy by the ringing of the (magic, or neo-Pavlovian) bell. Finally, 'Late in the night here comes the king himself, and says he will give five hundred pounds for the rabbit. "Hell no," says Jimmy. "But there stands my old jenny[-ass]. I will back her up to the fence, and if you hone her off you can have the rabbit." So he un-hitched the old jenny from the cart, and the king honed her off. He picked up the rabbit and told Jimmy to come home with him. When they got to the king's house there was a big bowl setting in the middle of the floor. The king says, "Jimmy, are you a good singer?" and Jimmy allowed he was pretty good. "Well," says the king, "if you can sing that bowl full, you can marry my daughter. But if you don't sing it full, I am going to cut your pecker off".' Jimmy's song:*

> *The first to come was the king's hired servant,*
> *To steal away my skill.*
> *I layed her down and honed her off –*
> *Fill, bowl, fill!*

Further stanzas follow, about the king's daughter, and wife (who is not mentioned in the prose text), ending:

> *The last to come was the king himself,*
> *To steal away my skill.*
> *I backed old Jinny up to the fence*
> *And —*

' *"Hold on, Jimmy," says the king. "Don't sing another word. The bowl's plumb full, and you can have my daughter!"* '

Again, one observes that not only the king is not "honed off," thus bringing him to the level of the women who precede him in the hired man's rabbit-hutch (compare the similar anti-aristocratic 'levelling' of Lawrence's *Lady Chatterley*, who finds orgasm only in the game-keeper's cabin, likewise in Lawrence's *The Virgin and the Gypsy*, and *Sun*), but he is allowed to retain his male prerogative and himself "hones off" the jenny-ass, itself sufficiently disgraceful as the audience un-questionably agrees. Another response to being caught in a dis-graceful sexual act is indicated in a story given by Newbern & Rodebaugh, p. 145: '*One morning, a big she-bear raided Joe's cabin, scattered everything, ate everything, tore up everything, and ambled away. Joe trailed her, shot her, and then noticing how much she resembled a woman, he satisfied his passion with her carcass. Just then he noticed another hunter cowering in the branches of a nearby tree. Realizing his deed had been observed, Joe pointed his gun at the man, made him climb down, and said, "Have you ever fucked a bear?" And the hunter said, "No, but I'm getting ready to try."'* Essentially, this is the whole mechanism involved in the offensive proselytizing for new converts by drug-addicts, homosexuals, and other socially-reprobated groups.

In another story connected in form with the *cante fable* "Fill, Bowl, Fill," given just above, but without any song involved, the pedication of the king or father-figure is again evaded, though the spectators are *made to believe* that it has occurred. *The hired boy gets the youngest girl in the farmer's family to go out into the hayloft with him. She comes back and tells her sister, "Say, the hired boy sure knows some good tricks!" The sister goes out to the hayloft too, and comes back saying the same, followed by the mother, and finally the farmer himself who has heard his wife's remark that "The hired boy certainly does know some tricks." When the boy sees the farmer coming, he thinks fast and begins doing cartwheels and acrobatic tricks all over the walls of the barn. The farmer watches him, and then goes back and tells his assembled wife and daughters, "Guess you're right. That boy sure knows some fancy tricks." "God almighty!" cry the wife and daughters, "did he fuck you too?"* (L.A. 1968.) This story is Russian in origin, appearing in Afanasyev's *Russian Secret Tales,* almost exactly a century earlier, as No. 45, "The Priest's Family and the Servant," and turning identically on the twist that the manservant has not really buggered the priest at all. The American story may, in fact, be a direct translation.

About the closest that the triumph of the intimidated son ever comes to the actual turning of the erotic tables on the father-figure, and plainly pedicating him, involves the rectal taking of the temperature of hospitalized patients as tantamount to pedicatory rape. This is used as the main running-gag in the French play (1930), Jules Romains' *Dr. Knock, or The Triumph of Medicine,* in which the new physician in the astoundingly healthy little town systematically intimidates everyone into the hospital with imaginary diseases, including finally the doctor who is his principal competitor, all being required to submit to the initiatory rectal-temperature rape. (Shown in the movie in a close-up of the competitor doctor's buttocks, with the thermometer being jabbed in). If any confusion existed as to this identification or symbolism, it is certainly clarified by a fool-joke already given in the First Series: *Doctor caught in bed with the farmer's wife explains that he is only taking her temperature. The farmer takes a shotgun down off the wall, cocks the hammers, and says grimly, "I guess you know what you're doin', doc, but that thing better have numbers on it when you take it out!"* (Somerville, N.J. 1943.)

The following, credited by a woman informant to one G.J.G. – possibly meaning 'Junior Grade' officer – appeared in *The Reader's Digest* for April, 1958, p. 134, under the rubric "Humor in Uniform," at a time when America was presumably not at war. It is reproduced here by special permission. Observe the opening disclaimer of the incident's confirmable truth:

The first part of this I know is true; perhaps the rest could never be properly checked. But when I was a Red Cross hospital worker on Guadalcanal during World War II, Navy doctors and nurses gloated over the case of a certain admiral who, bedded snugly in a Navy hospital with nothing worse than athlete's foot and non-critical complications, spent his time chasing nurses, "pulling rank" on enlisted patients, and harassing the overworked medical staff. This went on until the day an enterprising young seaman inmate borrowed a surgical gown, cap and face mask, swept into the admiral's room with a brisk "Good morning," glanced at the chart, ordered the patient over on his stomach and proceeded to take his temperature. Before he could finish the job, however, the man in white explained that he had another urgent case to attend to and left, gravely warning the grumbling seadog not to move until his return.

One hour later the nurse, making her rounds, froze in consternation on the officer's doorstep. "Admiral!" she gasped. "What – what happened?"

"Taking my temperature," the admiral growled. "Anything unusual about taking an admiral's temperature?"

"N-no, sir," the startled nurse managed to reply, "but, Admiral – with a daffodil?"

Though all the terminal accent is on the daffodil, it is obvious that this is simply planted like a flag on a conquered mountain-top, to indicate in graffiti fashion: "KILROY WAS HERE." The real humiliation of the obnoxious admiral – the very model of a model father-figure, or king to be killed by the regicide Killroy – actually consists of the intrusion of *any* thing into his anus by the son-surrogate: the 'enterprising young seaman' in a physician's gown ... and mask. Another such story, also presumably concerned with a flower, leaves little doubt as to the obvious phallic symbolism intended: *'Two nancy-boys out walking; taken short. Nip smartly over a hedge. One returns, waits, hears groans. Pops back over. Says, "What's the matter, Cuthbert?" "Lord Cecil, I cahn't get up; I've closed my arsehole over a daisy!"'* (Chelmsford, Essex, 1954).

D. H. Lawrence has his game-keeper twine flowers in Lady Chatterley's pubic hair, but this is intended as playful adoration, not humiliation. In various pictorial examples of European erotic art, and in the acted-out fantasies of masochists, the victim of humiliation – male or female – is made to prance about on all-fours, or be ridden on like a horse by the dominant partner. Often a mock bridle is fitted into his or her mouth, and a *peacock feather* or even a feather-duster (the horse's 'tail') is thrust up the rectum to symbolize the ultimate humiliation of pedication, especially when done by a woman. Sado-masochist scenes of this kind in erotic art and folktales are usually assimilated to the rationalizing legend of the wise Aristotle, ridden like a horse by the vengeful queen Phyllis. (Tale Type 1501, Motif K1215; and compare Virgil the magician trapped in the basket, Motifs K1211 and D1711.2.) I believe there is also a similar story in the *Arabian Nights*.

Let me close this chapter with a silly enough joke, one that expresses however – and only too well – the final sort of Ganymede revenge, in which it is not only the father-figure who is to be pedicated, 'reamed', 'screwed', 'fucked', 'buggered,' or what-have-you, but all the hated normals of the world. *Two homosexuals are talking. First Homosexual: "Have you heard of the latest scientific discovery? Normal intercourse causes* CANCER!" *Second Homosexual: "Is that so?" First Homosexual: "No, of course not. But* SPREAD THE RUMOR!!" (Los Angeles, Calif. 1968.) Absurd as it may seem, precisely this 'latest scientific discovery' has actually been announced in recent years, by the usual 20th-century scientists, no doubt operating under water – as the television advertisements for detergents would have it. Specifying, in this case, that it is only the *un-circumcised penis* which can thus 'cause cancer' of the womb in the unfortunate wife. Believe it if you will. On this and even more marvellous anti-sexual discoveries of modern science, see the later chapter on "Castration," 13.III and V, the sections on "Circumcision" and "Self-Castration." Meanwhile ... spread the rumor.

11

PROSTITUTION

I. THE OLDEST PROFESSION

WHETHER one likes it or not, the prostitution of women to men – under one disguise or another – is almost inevitable so long as men earn and control the principal amounts of money, social position and credit, and other advantages, under the patriarchal system. A brutal demonstration of the underlying problem, which is MONEY, and which cuts through any amount of emotional and aggressively dishonest talk about the 'rights of women' (to be wage-slaves instead of wives), is offered by the cold statistics of the United States Bureau of the Census, *Characteristics of the Population* (1960) vol. 1.I.D, pages 1–590, Table 223, "Income in 1959 of Persons 25 Years old and over, by Years of School completed." I came across this chart while preparing a lecture I was to give at the University of California at Berkeley, on "The New Freedom" in 1964, to try to determine what the plain cash-value of a modern college education might be.

It is not for their manifest unfairness that these figures are cited here, demonstrating as they do, to the naked eye, that in contemporary America, and despite all the bullshit about equality, men receive an average of $2,750 per year more than women if both are equally public-school graduates; $3,250 more per year than women if both are equally high-school graduates; and $3,900 more per year than women if both are equally college graduates or beyond. The situation is, of course, the same or worse in other countries – usually worse. The figure which it is the real purpose of these calculations to cite is, instead, one that is almost invisible owing to its being too glaringly obvious to notice: that of the number of women announcing themselves as *'Persons without income'* at the time of the 1960 census. As opposed to the 1,800,000 American men recorded in this category, in a population of 47,900,000 men – these presumably invalids and the aged, prisoners, bums, etc. – only 28,900,000 of the 51,500,000 women reporting had any incomes at all. An almost equal number: 22,600,000 – i.e. *nearly half the women in the United States of America* above the age of twenty-five – announced themselves as 'Persons without income.'

Who are these twenty-two million or more adult American women 'without income'? Are they prisoners, prostitutes, female hippies, invalids and the aged – and twelve times as many of these as of men of the same kind? Certainly not. At least, they are certainly not prostitutes, since prostitutes *do* have incomes. *They are the wives.* (More than half of the women working for their income are also wives.) And that is why there are prostitutes. Ruthlessly considered, the only real difference between the two groups – since both wives and prostitutes cook, keep house, have children, and make love to men – is that the *prostitutes are paid*, at least for making love. That, under the circumstances, what they make is a great deal closer to hate, is only to be expected.

A good deal of emphasis has been placed recently, by writers and speakers rushing to get into the leadership positions of the new neo-feminist Women's Liberation movement in America, on the presumed 'prostitutory' status of wives – young wives, especially – who have no jobs outside the home. This is basic-ally a fraud, since emotionally-toned words like *prostitute* would never be applied to a black slave kept to do housework (who would be called a *slave*), or even to a horse, dog, or auto-mobile kept by a man as a pet, or for a show of status, as many men do in fact keep their idle and childless wives. Actually, the sexual complaisance of wives of this type, which might justify the term 'prostitute,' is often the least part of their marital func-tion: a dark secret! Is it then really prostitution at all, or is it just economic feather-bedding, like the grotesquely overstuffed employment rolls of government 'cost-plus' contract firms, or the supernumeraries and stand-around girls in nude theatrical productions, really just there, as the French say, *'pour faire beau.'* Perhaps it is prostitution of a kind, at least in the woman's guilty subjective assessment of herself, on dark days when she is menstruating and feels ugly; assessments often re-inforced by hard words said to her by her husband on the subject of *money*, during marital spats.

The status of wife, with or without children, is really pro-stitution when the wife sets out to sell her specific sexual com-plaisance to her husband, which sometimes includes the having of children that the husband desires, perhaps to found a dynasty or make him feel he is immortalizing his family-name (not hers ...). In its most common form, married prostitution consists of the woman's allowing her husband sexual intercourse when he wants it, in return for special monetary gifts, jewels, fur coats, cars, new homes, vacation trips – even mere household appliances – and for various types of social succumbing on the husband's part to the woman's ideals of social and monetary status and social climbing. Unless and until they are paid off (beforehand) in these ways, such wives show themselves cold, emotionally withdrawn or frankly hostile, and sexually uninterested; and sometimes when they *are* paid. The husbands are being 'pussy-whipped,' or 'trained with cunt,' as other men phrase it, the way a puppy is traditionally trained by shoving its nose in shit. (The owners then being shocked when he learns to eat it.) Such marriages are, of course, essentially sado-masochistic. More will be said as to these true 'married whores' in section 11.I.3, "Status of the Prostitute." But it is morally wrong and false, and tactically very stupid, to try to assimilate to such classes of perverts and prostitutes, or otherwise to smear, all women who are not totally throwing their lives down the sinkhole of meaningless and repetitive factory work and office jobs, but are instead making homes for themselves and for the husbands and children whom they love.

The Women's Liberation movement, as at present newly rebegun in America and Europe, principally by reclamatory manhaters, lesbians, and upper-middle-class young women who have personally seldom suffered from actual male domination, is both economically and politically totally naïve. As opposed to Negro activists, who rapidly formed a single, powerful voting bloc, women have for three-quarters of a century now thrown away their crucial voting power by splitting it – as brainwashed into doing – between the wornout totems of the Republican and Democratic (Conservative and Liberal) male politicos. Instead of either joining up to a revolutionary party, or creating immediately a monolithic and *instantly politically dominant Women's Party*, composed of 52% of the voters (or more, since many men are too cynical now to bother to vote). One reason – perhaps the basic reason for this failure, has been the self-cannibalizing destroying of its own leaders by the various Women's Liberation movements, under mock-egalitarian excuses. This is a very striking example of the classically self-destructive operation of the castration complex ("No one's gonna boss *me* around!") in the group of women most massively suffering from it ... and who deny that it exists at all.

On the economic front, Women's Liberation and its briefly reigning leaders seem entirely unaware that, if they do succeed in their only announced goals, they will be performing an enormously desirable function for decadent capitalistic money-based structures, and will assist in keeping these going well into the next century, when even capitalism itself assumes it must die. The Establishment has already seen the highly important function Women's Liberation can be made to serve – and the danger of its monolithic vote – and may soon be expected to offer Women's Lib militants and competing boss-persons enthusiastic amounts of publicity, moral support, media-time, and finally plain co-opting cash. Doubtless in the usual tax-exempt 'business expense,' 'foundation grant,' or 'charity' swindle format.

Even the most advanced economic thinker of the radical feminist movement, Shulamith Firestone, who in her *The Dialectic of Sex* (New York, 1970) writes brilliantly of the poisoning of women's self-esteem by the males-&-sales directed "Culture of Romance" (chapter 7), and even more incisively, p. 207–13, of the decay of classical art in the face of undigestible technology, plumps down finally in a crashing conclusion for the 'Freedom of women from the tyranny of reproduction,' meaning the rejection of childbirth (because it hurts ... 'like shitting a pumpkin'), and the total abdication of women's fertility – if not their sexuality – to laboratory parthenogenesis, *i.e.* male motherhood, combined with 'oral contraceptives for males.' Along with the essential destruction of marriage & the family, of course; in place of which she proposes, in a pathetic footnote, p. 239, 'good' orphan-asylums for *all* the children of the world (instead of the current bad ones for only some), which will then be nobly administered by the 'spread [of] family emotions over the whole society.' Sure. How many childless people spend their time & money on orphans today?

What will monopoly capitalism, now at its most over-expanded stage, actually buy of this program? Certainly not Firestone's proposed communal 'households' composed of 'ten or so consenting [!] adults,' to whom the parthenogenetic children would be farmed out as pets, and doubtless as 'non-incestuous' sexual objects as well. No, what counts now for capitalism is the feminist-inspired creation of *more and smaller family units*.

Even better would be unmarried unit-groups composed of a single individual, thus doubling the number of consumer sales and resultant billions. Each such extra 'home,' each man and woman who can be brainwashed by eager feminists and 'over-population' scare-stuff (no problem, really, with the Atom Bomb . . .) into 'single living,' means simply and specifically one more bed, one more refrigerator, t.v. machine, battery-driven automobile and air-conditioner – *one more than would normally otherwise be sold.*

This is the whole thing, the secret hocus-pocus or trick, the nimble-go-thimble that will inevitably make Women's so-called Liberation the manna in the desert for famishing billionaires down to their last yacht or moon-rocket. And who will tell their treasurers : "Throw those noisy bitches a bone. We ought to be able to make them – useful." The essential thing, if the American and world-economy is to get this new and unnecessary blood transfusion of tens of millions more reduplicative sales, representing hundreds of millions or billions more dollars expended pointlessly and needlessly (also marks, pounds, francs, yen, kroner, etc.), is that *marriage must be destroyed.* Women and men must be convinced that they will all be marvellously happier alone and apart – lonely young women and men (and old ones) in tiny, self-contained bird-box apartments – endlessly and desperately consuming *double* the former amount of everything in $-based consumer goods. It is for this Operation Overload that Women's Liberation is unconsciously setting itself up as patsy and as front.

Owing to highly dubious ego-boost leadership or self-cannibalistic *anti*-leadership, and total economic naïveté, the Women's Liberation movement begun only recently in America is already becoming a sell-out and a travesty before it has even thrown away its last humiliating 'maidencup' brassiere. It is already the opposite of the hard-headed original suffragette, feminist, and women's union organizations of the past century, who allowed themselves only the one man-hating and husband-hounding luxury of Prohibition, and CUTTING OFF THE WORKING-MAN'S BEER ! His prostitutes he could have – and never more cheaply and more humiliating than in the anti-alcohol Victorian nineteenth century. Not even in the Las Vegas of I'll-suck-off-a-party-of-six-for-my-airplane-ticket-home callgirls in the epoxy slick hotel rooms, while the pink-and-purple neon lights over the gambling palaces makes the night hideous. This is our way of dirtying women. The nineteenth century had its way too, as witness the revolting paid child-seductions of *My Secret Life* (1888). Children are consumer-goods too. Ask any advertiser of breakfast food, or manufacturer of drugs, plastic guns, or rock-&-roll Totalitarian-musik recordings. Or your local draft-board. They know best what to do with kids.

The man-hating and pointless sneering and parading of the callow beginnings of Women's Liberation, while waiting for THE LEADERESS who will eventually tell them which way to jump – and where to send the dough – is not the phoney struggle that was intended or that was fought by the pioneer women militants and propagandists of past centuries, vindicating women's rights but seldom by frankly attacking the men who then owned and controlled everything, as they no longer do. Yes, there were exceptional attacks on men : Rachel Speght's forgotten *Muzzle for Melastomus* (1617), and Jane Collier's anonymous and annihilating irony in *The Art of Ingeniously Tormenting* (1753), but the true struggle was recognized to be-gin with Mary Wollstonecraft in 1792, vindicating the right of women to be educated. They have this now. (See further the other writers, on both sides of the struggle, cited in my own old-line pro-feminist, pamphlet, *Love & Death*, 1949, the chap-ters "Avatars of the Bitch-Heroine" and "Open Season on Women.") The new struggle should not limit itself to bogus man-hating, and, even more self-destructively now, strictly to the stupidity of vindicating women's right to become wage-slaves like the men. While giving their children – if they have any – to be brought up in state orphan asylums, and fed off a pushcart chow-wagon from the age of two, as in 'forward-looking Sweden,' on plastic-stamped IBM programmers, while Big Brother watches through closed-circuit television. *Brave No World!*

The freedom of women, their liberation from slavery either to nature, to men, to custom, or to fashion, does not and can-not ever consist of forcing them to become neuters and sex-toys whose only social function is the earning and consuming of manufactured products, either directly or via the men who can be made to pay. While denying women their natural and bio-logical function as *mothers* – the only function out of which their personal liberation and psychological completion can ever really come, and which is now on the point of doing so, the control of pregnancy and fertility having at last been put firmly into women's own hands by the sophisticated biochemical techniques of Dr. Gregory Pincus' birth-control 'Pill.' Women's real liberation does not consist of being brain-washed by snotty wisecracks emanating from the left-behind female uglies on the shelf, telling them they are 'prostitutes' and 'soft-core hookers' if they love or marry men, and want to look pretty to please and excite them; or that they are chumps and 'kitchen-niggers' if they yearn to feel a baby's mouth – rather than always a man's bristly chin – nuzzling for once at their breasts. But, above all, women's liberation does not consist of female Judases delivering them over, with slogan-filled mouths and crossed knees, as wage-slaves and *separate-domicile consumers* to overstuffed monopoly capitalism by the end of this century, while the babies of Africa and India starve, and bloat, and die.

I. PRIESTESS, PROSTITUTE, NURSE, AND NUN

The French have a very useful phrase, known in English but seldom used in the same sense in this language: to be *intéressé*, which translates best as 'having an interest,' in the special sense of being an 'interested party' to some personal or business matter. The real meaning of the phrase is to describe the situation or pre-disposition of someone looking for his or her *advantage* – generally mercenary – and thus unfailingly egoistical or self-interested. Perhaps the best translation in one word is 'selfish.' In this sense, the *intéressé*-ness or selfishness of men, in regard to women, is SEX. The selfishness of women, in regard to men, is MONEY, or some equivalent social advantage or 'motility upward' on the social scale, a type of payment to the woman which is considered less coarse than spot cash, and is therefore enormously more often accepted.

In almost every relationship of a man with a woman, there is the not-very-well hidden tone of a seduction, generally not achieved and often almost unconscious: *"For what I give you, give me sex."* In almost every relationship of a woman with a man (except the relationship of a mother with her child, and sometimes not even then), there is the hidden tone of a business transaction: *"For the sex I give you, give me something."* (If only an orgasm.) This is not always charming to think about, but it is true. The normal social operation of the 'selfishness' in women under patriarchy is to trade one's sexual company, and a lifetime of housework and loyalty, for the man's physical protection and monetary and moral support, during pregnancy and after, of the mother and of the resultant children. All this is usually termed in a word: *marriage*. The abnormal operation of such 'selfishness' in women is to batten on the matching sexual selfishness of men, in the crude transactional or monetary exchange of *sex for money*, which is prostitution. When Adam delved and Eve span, their relationship was an honest and basically non-commercial exchange. But when Adam delved and Eve refused to spin, but wanted the advantage of eating the produce of Adam's delving anyhow, for nothing more than the apple of sexual intercourse, prostitution had come into being as a profession. At any rate, that is the folk-idea. In fact, prostitution probably did not really begin that way at all. The "Oldest Profession" was a quite different matter.

The true social origin of prostitution was, in all likelihood, a development or degeneration of the temple duties of the priestesses of the matriarchal religions which long preceded those of patriarchy. The Jewish Bible is the essentially legendary record of this historic changeover from matriarchy to patriarchy, actually a seizing of social power by the men owing to more rapid accumulation of social wealth possible to the male shepherds and animal-husbands (formerly hunters) than was possible to the immemorially agricultural women. As the essence of the matriarchal cult is the glorification of the fertility of nature and of human beings from which the matriarchal power and status take their rise, the matriarchal religions involved and required the act of sexual intercourse as an act of worship, 'dedicating' each such act to the Magna Mater, Ishtar, Aphrodite, or some other female goddess. For precisely the same reason, when patriarchy and patriarchal religion came to power, these attempted to reprobate and condemn sexuality, or at least to control it in everyone other than the patriarchs themselves, since logically sexual intercourse is as essential for fatherhood as for motherhood. The Jewish Bible is filled with hardly-hidden allusions to this struggle on the part of the evolving pastoral patriarchy (whose Sacred Book the Bible is) against the earlier sexual and matriarchal religions of the Near-East.

In its social or '-archic' aspect of family domination, the most visible record of this struggle is that of the *Book of Esther* made canonic probably just for this reason, though the name of the Jewish god Jehovah does not occur in it. See its opening record of how Queen Vashti was humiliated by her husband King Artaxerxes (for refusing, according to the legend, to appear naked before his feasting guests), and was then repudiated by the king, who sent royal letters to all his provinces, according to *Esther*, i. 15–22, commanding that the spirit of all other wives must be equally chastened, and 'that every man should bear rule in his own house.' Even so the new queen, Esther, dominates the whole story (she is doubtless a Jewish version of the Near-Eastern mother-goddess, Ishtar), and her sexual prostitution to the king saves her people. In its religious aspect, the same struggle for domination was engaged in by the nascent patriarchy of the Middle East by making a duty of destroying the mother-worship altars, and cutting down the sacred *groves* (as required by Jehovah in *Exodus*, xxxiv. 13–17), in which the earlier sexual worship was enacted, often under a male statue of the demi-god, Priapus, furnished with the one visible attribute of ultimate male sexuality – an erect penis. Just as, under the later Christian patriarchy, the act of worship is placed under the protection of a female demi-goddess, the Virgin Mary, shown in the act of expressing her ultimate sexuality – motherhood – but only in the modified or partial form of nursing her sacred male child. Each sex thus idealizes, and finally idolatrizes, the sexual function of the other, taking care, however, to limit the dominated sex to this merely sexual rôle, while keeping all the social power and position for itself.

Further discussion of these matters, and of the history of prostitution since the time of its degeneration from matriarchal cult worship, will be found briefly sketched in my *The Guilt of the Templars* (1966) p. 98–107. Also, much more importantly, in the very full compilation of the historical and documentary evidence in the two standard works on the subject: Iwan Bloch's masterfully-researched *Die Prostitution* (Berlin, 1912–25, 2 vols.), completed by Dr. G. Loewenstein after Bloch's death, and never yet translated into English; and the much more popularized *Histoire de la Prostitution* (Bruxelles, 1861) by 'P. Dufour,' the pseudonym of the bibliographical hack, Paul Lacroix, of which latter an excellent modern English translation by Samuel Putnam has been published.

The essential element in the prostitutory act, as seen in our recent centuries, is in its forthright monetary exchange ('the hire of a whore,' already reprobated in the 6th century B.C., in *Deuteronomy*, xxiii. 18), intruded into what was originally conceived of as an act of worship or of love – or even an act of rape. A further very significant element is the relative impersonalness of the act, the de-personalization of what is certainly a very personal relationship. Neither the man nor the woman involved in prostitutory sexual intercourse feels any significant emotion as to the other – except perhaps unconscious hatred or simple dislike, mixed with a temporary sexual pleasure – and both are willing, within limits, to engage in the same type or any type of sexual relationship with almost any presentable individual (client or prostitute) who offers the required money or the required sexual or fetichistic complaisance. It is this shotgun impersonalness that makes prostitution possible, and that correctly defines it.

The folk-mind does not enjoy this state of things, and makes every effort to bring the prostitute back, mentally at least, to the splendid position and lost glory of the juicy and maternal Earth-Mother. But finally the attempt is given up and the plain truth is admitted in every folk statement concerning prostitution: that the real relationship between the prostitute and her (or his) client is, and can only be, *hatred* and exploitation, expressed in sexual form. This is the wishful origin of the legend of the whore-with-the-heart-of-gold, in song and story, as for example Maupassant's most famous bit of writing, *Boule-de-suif*, and the American movie-version of this (not crediting Maupassant's inspiration) as *Stagecoach*. Not to mention the more recent cinematic soufflés and heart-of-gold whore-epics such as Jules Dassin's charming *Never on Sunday*, and *Irma la Douce*, an ugly sado-sexual comedy by the Viennese director, Wilhelm "Billy" Wilder.

The prostitute is identified importantly at the folk-level with various professions open mainly to unmarried women, since the time of and including temple-priestesses, such as old maids, nuns, nurses, schoolteachers and sometimes lady-librarians, grass-widows (positively identified as prostitutes in American folklore), and most recently airline-stewardesses. Some of the airline advertisements nowadays, in national and international magazines, so pose the girls in the photographs – for instance at the top of a staircase, while the camera is at the foot, peeking up the stewardess' mini-skirt – as to imply that their prostitution, presumably in the toilet-cubicle during the late hours of the night (!) or at stopover hotels, is practically guaranteed. The first French erotic comic-book, *Les Travaux d'Hercule* [Paris: Losfeld, *ca.* 1960] uses this dreamed-of aerial orgy as its plot background. A more recent American cartoon, in the Texas sex-humor magazine, *Sex to Sexty*, brings this back to the American orally-oriented level, with: *The big-breasted airline hostess on the "executive flight," stripping down in the aisle, while balancing her food tray, and saying to the executive she is serving, "When we say 'Milk, tea – or me!' on these flights, that's what we mean!"* The original catch-phrase, "Coffee, Tea, or Me?" was built up into two popular mock-autobiographies by the pseudonymous air-stewardesses, 'Trudy Baker & Rachel Jones;' the first volume under precisely that title, and the second, *The Coffee-Tea-or-Me Girls Round-the-World Diary* (New York, 1970), simply teeming with phoney tales of sub-erotic adventure, in which precisely nothing erotic whatsoever happens to *these* two air-hostesses: they act in a Danish porno-graphic movie – but only as English-speaking stand-ins – and so forth. Cock-tease stuff.

All such classes of women are the focus of much folklore, both jesting and serious, as to their prostitutory activities or simple 'immoral' availability. The entire section 6.IV.2, "Old Maids and Nuns," in the First Series, p. 360–63, is relevant here, and should be consulted at this point. It would take us much too far afield to attempt even to indicate here all the post-Renaissance folklore and folktales as to the secret erotic life of Christian nuns, so similar to the earlier libels, by pagans, as to the 'sexual communism' of the early Christian converts. Nuns are, after all, only the pale survivors of the priestesses of earlier matriarchies, and the formal descendants of the Vestal Virgins – allowed almost priestly status, even under the Roman *patria potestas* – who were presumed to engage, once a year, in almost precisely the same formal sexual license, lesbian or normal, in their deepest 'Mysteries,' as those sins (with monks) of which nuns are more modernly accused.

A joke has already been given in the First Series on: *A man who excuses himself, when caught masturbating in a public toilet, by saying "I'm a Christian Scientist, and I'm screwing my girl-friend in Boston."* Hopelessly contrived, this should be compared with the perfect simplicity with which the same sacred prostitution is indicated in the following joke – with a stinger in its tail: '*A hiker at a youth hostel hears they do things very well there, and that you even get a woman at the end of every evening. He has a good meal and goes to his room, and hasn't been there long when a girl comes in without knock-ing and begins to undress. "Do you need a piece?" she asks.*

"Oh, do I ever!" he replies enthusiastically. "Long time since you had a piece?" "I've lost count!" "By the way," she adds, "are you married or unmarried?" He (off his guard): "Married." She begins to dress again. "No go," she says; "I'm here to serve the needy, not the greedy".' (London, 1954.) The cold prostitution of 'hippie' girls nowadays, for no further payment than the sharing of one's bed, even if on the floor, and one's hallucinatory drugs, often has this same odd tone of 'sacred hospitality,' and the same unexpected hostility.

Jokes on the immorality of schoolteachers are given in the earlier chapter on "Children" in the First Series, and it is perfectly obvious in all of these, almost without exception, that intercourse with the schoolteacher (or baby-sitter) is construed as a sort of surrogate incest with the mother, the schoolteacher being in all cases the sexual leader and aggressor of the schoolboy child, as in Eugene Field's "Only a Boy." Lady librarians are assimilated to schoolteachers by folklore, especially in the belief that they are all extremely sexy – under their horn-rimmed spectacles – which is perhaps not altogether folklore. What is practically the locus classicus on the American 'widder woman' as town prostitute – whether a real widow or simply a 'grass' widow, abandoned by her wandering husband during the Gold Rush of the middle 19th century and since – is the magnificent but little-appreciated novel by John Sanford, Seventy Times Seven (New York: Knopf, 1939, originally entitled I Let Him Die in its earlier partial appearance in Contact magazine), perfectly hitting off the heartless exploitation and friendless death of such a small town 'widder'-whore, in rural upstate New York, as discussed in my review of this splendid work in Fact magazine (July 1965).

The nurse is a particular focus of such folk material, though she more often appears in her forbidding aspect, owing to her relationship with the feared and hated doctor, as in chapter 13 below, on "Castration." (Many nurses are also sadists.) In this sense, the nurse is the true surviving matriarch of real folklore, as opposed to the presumed bitch-mom or bogus family 'matriarch' of modern popular thinkers and alarm-criers. A number of late-starters and intellectual fad-pluggers, on the 'bitch-mom' or 'matriarch' canard, have been tooling along industriously in recent years in continuation of the anti-mother attack begun by the late Philip Wylie and Ernest Hemingway, as I have discussed at some length in "Open Season on Women," in Love &

Death (1949). Some of the newer batch are listed in Dr. Kate Millett's *Sexual Politics* (1970) p. 330, note 107, as part of her anatomization of the latter-day or poor-man's Hemingway in the woman-hating line, Norman Mailer. (She dismisses in five lines, p. 325, as 'monumental infantilism,' the even more virulent attack – on 'Jewish mothers' only: the wuss kind – in Philip Roth's *Portnoy's Complaint*, 1968.) And yet no one can mistake the urge to return to the mother, under all the screaming and stamping and beating at her breasts, if only in the fantasy of the erotic mother-nurse, as only too clearly in Hemingway's *A Farewell to Arms* (1929) and endlessly since.

In the spring of 1966, a German-American businessman travelling in Europe had a nervous attack while in Czechoslavakia, leading to his temporary hospitalization there. Later he assured another American businessman travelling with him – who retailed it to me as absolute fact – that the hospital staff were very sympathetic to him, as he had formerly been in a German concentration camp, and when his trouble was diagnosed as excessive shyness with women, and resulting sexual repression, *a nurse was assigned by the head doctor to "give him a blowjob" and calm him down*. The hero of the story himself told me later that he did a gross business of a quarter of a million dollars a year; but the thought that he might – with such an income – afford the services of a more formal prostitute, even in Communist Czechoslovakia, never seemed to occur to his companion, or, presumably, to the head doctor. This identical fantasy is acted out in the American medical-satire film, *M.A.S.H.* (1969), in this case to 'straighten out' or 'change the oil' of a presumed male homosexual – identified as Jesus at a parody of the Last Supper!

What really seems to be involved here is the fantasy of the *nurse as mother*, in this case as the seductive mother performing acts of sexual complaisance for her passive-erotic son. From the psychoanalytic point of view, this involves a drawing together (by the grown-up son) of the urinary and sexual functions: the mother's action in assisting the infant or small boy to urinate is recollected and reconstrued as a sexual approach, and the exciting of the flow of semen in ejaculation is identified with the passive flow of urine. The *male passivity* in the hands of the mother-or-nurse is very central here. This is taken to its extreme limit in a work of fiction, Dalton Trumbo's anti-conscription novel, *Johnny Got His Gun*, published on the eve of

World War II, in which the hero is a 'basket-case' (armless and legless war-victim, also blind and unable to speak) as a result of a shell-explosion, who tells his own story by tapping it out in Morse code on the head of his bed with his skull! Until this possibility of communication with the outside world is arrived at, his anguished tossings & turnings are misunderstood by the nurse as sexual need, and she masturbates the 'basket-case' war-victim, he giving himself of course, helplessly and gratefully to her ministrations. I have myself heard similar stories concerning Canadian nuns, acting as nurses, who are also stated – by folk-informants – to wash male patients completely, including the penis and testicles, as part of the hospital routine, *striking the penis* with a practised snap of the fingers if the patient has an erection, to reduce him to flaccidity. Here again, the nurse (nun) is seen as both seductive-mother and castrator combined, which is certainly the real description of the legendary Mother Goddess or Magna Mater, of both the Near East and India.

In my childhood in Scranton, Pennsylvania (middle 1920's) a favorite anecdote among schoolboys, not precisely a joke, concerned: *The sailors on a whaling ship who masturbate into a barrel during the whole voyage. On docking, this barrel is mixed with the other barrels of sperm oil, and candles are made from it. A whole establishment of nuns gets pregnant.* The fantasy of the child's impregnating the forbidden older women (mother-surrogates) by means of his masturbation is naïvely apparent here. The complete lack of heterosexual contact is also very significant: all the whaler-sailors and nuns, masturbating separately in their own sex groups. This story must be fairly old. I have traced it only as far back as the French medical and art students' song, or 'Chanson de Salle de Garde,' entitled *"Histoire d'un paquet de bougies,"* in which the vessel is a French warship coming back from New Caledonia, as printed in Edmond Bernard's rare and important *Anthologie Hospitalière & Latinesque* (1911–13) I. 310–11, noting that it was sung to the nursery tune of *"Il était un P'tit navire,"* in the Latin Quarter of Paris since 1846. Other jokes and 'true stories' as to groups of girls masturbating with a candle or banana will be found in the chapter on "Castration."

The idea of plural *impregnation* – aside from just erotic pleasure – occurs curiously often in stories concerning nuns, or other imprisoned and captured women, and it may be suspected again of being (if the term is allowable) a folk-recollection of earlier sexual rituals or 'orgies.' *All the nuns but one, in a Belgian nunnery, are found to be pregnant just after the war. The cardinal makes personal inquiry, and learns that the nuns have all been raped by German soldiers. "But why didn't they rape you?" he asks of the one thin little nun who is not pregnant. "Who, me?" she says; "I resisted."* (N.Y. 1945.) With this should certainly be compared the milder story of: *The new doctor making his morning round of the maternity ward. All the women are unmarried and all expect their babies the first week in January. One of the women has gone to the toilet. "I suppose Miss Jones expects her baby in January too?" asks the doctor. "It's Mrs. Jones, not Miss," he is told, "and we don't know when she's expecting her baby. She didn't go to the picnic."* (Amsterdam, 1955, from a young unmarried woman.) There is no disguise here of the quasi-public orgy or 'picnic,' the preceding spring, which has made all the women pregnant. The connection with the 'raped nuns' is perhaps still present in the curious insistence that all the pregnant women are 'Miss' rather than 'Mrs.,' which adds very little, otherwise, to the joke.

The minor quasi-nursing or body-service professions open to women, such as waitress, chambermaid, bathhouse attendant, manicurist, and masseuse, are all popularly and often correctly considered to be tantamount to, if not mere 'fronts' for, prostitution, and most of the jokes on these themes concentrate on the *hostile* relations between these subtypes of prostitute-nurse and the men who approach and exploit them. In the opposite form, here showing the prostitute-nurse as revivifying mother-goddess, my own favorite story has been given in full in the First Series, 8.V.4, pages 581–2, concerning: *The dying man whose nurse is told to give him anything he wants during the night. He wants to perform cunnilinctus on her, even though she turns out to be menstruating. In the morning not only he is not dead, but announces: "One more transfusion like that, and I'll live forever!"* (N.Y. 1943.)

Frankly presented as a prostitute, the woman-for-hire nevertheless is supposed to have a special warm spot in her heart for young boys: this is the direct identification of her as the mother, or, rather, as a sort of sexually available mother-surrogate, never dropping her dominant and protective position vis-à-vis the boy client. *A man wants to give money or some valuable present to a girl whom he has seduced without any trouble and who he is sure is a prostitute. She refuses everything, but when he insists, asks if he will give her his pocket-knife. He is amazed, but gives it to her, and she puts it in a drawer full of other pocket-knives. "I'm young and pretty now," she explains, "but one day I'll be old and grey – and you know what a boy will do for a jack-knife!"* (1 : 433. A great favorite once in both America and England. An early 'sick' variant, in which *the girl refuses to take anything but a dime*, is given in the section "Cash on Delivery." 4.V, First Series, p. 251.)

The folklore of the *knife* as virility symbol – also, ambivalently, as the instrument of castration – deserves a whole monograph to itself. Very much on the basic theory of the preceding joke were the 'hi-cuts,' or laced leather snow-boots, made specially appealing to young boys during the 1920's (and since?) in America, by the mock wild-west or frontier touch of having a many-bladed scout-knife *given free* with these virile boots, in a special snap-pocket on the side of the right-footed boot, presumably for quick drawing. The current fantasy-knife of adolescent boys in America is the secretly-sold 'switch-blade,' a ganster version of the Italian *vendetta* dagger, opening mechanically by touching a button. The exotica of the many-bladed knife, so dear to the men's magazine advertisements appealing to would-be virilists, has never been taken farther than in the satirical poem, signed M.R.G., *"Description du nouveau couteau réglementaire de l'armée Suisse,"* of which the unconscious mechano-sexual tone, as representing the (impotent) owner's penis, is strikingly evidenced by its being the one and only *non-erotic* poem or song in the entire two volumes of the otherwise highly erotic *Anthologie Hospitalière & Latinesque* (1911–13) II. 116–17. A British version of the joke specifies that the girl asks, not just for a pocket-knife, but for *"A knife with two blades, a corkscrew and a spike for getting stones out of horses' hooves, &c."* (Chelmsford, Essex, 1953.) The scout-knife or Swiss knife that *does everything* obviously over-determines the unconscious identification of knife with the owner's penis, that *does nothing.*

The late Alexander Woollcott made his greatest success – other than with the "Vanishing Hotel Room" or "Mysterious Mother" story (concerning the bubonic plague, already noted in section 8.III.3, "The Sleeve-Job") – with a well-known joke, apparently of French origin, on the prostitute and her boy-client, which he enlarged to short-story length, under the title

"Entrance Fee," in his *While Rome Burns*, on the style of Balzac's *Contes Drolatiques* (1834) a century earlier. *All the students at a military school put up fifty cents apiece, out of their meagre allowances, and draw lots for which of the students is to take the resulting 'pot' of three-hundred dollars and spend one night in the arms of a famous prostitute who demands that sum for her fee. The prostitute is intrigued by a young military student being able to afford her expensive charms, and asks him in the morning where he got so much money. Touched by his tale, she assures him she is terribly flattered by such devotion and that she cannot accept his money. She gives him back his fifty cents.* Though pegged to the usual "Money and Sex" theme, the approach to the un-attainable mother-figure is here very evident, through the combined strength of the imprisoned and impoverished sons. The type-similarity to the combined seminal strength of the sailors masturbating into a barrel and impregnating a whole establishment of nuns, is also rather clear.

Similar in pattern though entirely different as to theme, which is here an attempted making of one's peace with the inferior sort of prostitutes available to soldiers, by debunking the offering of the prostitutes of the highest class: *All the soldiers of an American regiment in Korea put up a dollar apiece, and draw lots for which of them will take the resultant money and spend one night in the finest brothel in the Orient. Hymie Kaplowitz, the terror of Brooklyn, naturally wins, and on his return from the legendary brothel describes to his assembled bunk-mates what happened: the hanging gold curtains, the sensuous oriental music, the exotic aphrodisiacal meal served by little naked twelve-year-old girls beforehand, etc. etc., ending every passage with "– nothing like Brooklyn!" Finally he describes how the most beautiful woman he had ever seen comes slowly down the ornate staircase, wearing only a pagoda-head-dress with trailing veils of white lace, and leads him up the stairs by the hand to her perfumed bed. "– Nothing like Brooklyn!" "And then?" all the other soldiers ask feverishly. "And then?" answers Hymie; "oh, then it was just like Brooklyn."* (N.Y. 1953.) Women appreciate this joke.

One of the most significant situations found in jokes is that of the adolescent male (or the husband) who is given money and is encouraged to have sexual intercourse 'for his health,' and who – through one subterfuge or another – uses this permission and this money to have intercourse with some forbidden female such as the grandmother, culminating in the almost classical Oedipal *tu quoque,* when the father cries *"My god, you didn't fuck my mother, did you?" And the son answers imperturbably, "Sure, why not? You fucked mine."* In what is certainly a modification of the same sort of stage-machinery, the prostitute-grandmother is projected into a sort of universal prostitute-nurse, or 'Mother Carey' (*Mater Cara: Magna Mater*), whom all women are presumed to be ready to play under the proper circumstances. *A woman who has just had a baby, and is still in bed, gives her husband two dollars from under her pillow to go to a whorehouse and not bother her, as she does not feel well yet. On the way he meets the Lady Who Lives Downstairs* ["from Philadelphia"?] *who says, "Why go to strangers? I'll do the same thing for you even better." He returns home unexpectedly soon, explaining to his wife what has happened. "Then give me back the two dollars," she demands. "Oh, I gave that to the lady downstairs: she asked for it." "Can you imagine!" the wife cries, turning up her eyes to heaven, "when she had her second baby didn't I give her husband the finest shtup* [Yiddish: *fuck*] *he ever had in his life, and I didn't ask him for a dime!"* (N.Y. 1942.)

The folk identification of the prostitute as priestess or nun now exists only in the form of humor, a 'descent' common to much earlier lore. This seems to be the step just before the relegation of any particular bit of historic folklore to its last surviving position: in the songs, rhymes, and catches or riddles of children. In the same way, the fairy-godmother of so many earlier folktales now exists in America and England (bereft of her balancing 'bad-mother' image: the witch) only as Mary Poppins, the floating marvel, or "The Lady with the Alligator Purse," of rope-skipping rhymes, who is herself only the last avatar of "The Lady from Philadelphia," who sets all things right in the hare-brained family of Lucretia P. Hale's *Peterkin Papers* (1880) and *The Last of the Peterkins* (1886). Two jokes in particular quite candidly show the prostitute in the process of becoming the priestess or nun, and though this is the opposite of the historical truth, it is quite close enough to be astonishingly apt. *A reformed prostitute has joined the Salvation Army and is giving testimony on a street-corner. "I used to lay in the arms of men,"* she confesses: *"white men, black men, Chinamen! But now I lay in the arms of Jesus!"* "That's right, sister," cries *a drunk in the back row, "fuck 'em all!"* (1 : 266, a version not making any racial references. – Text: N.Y. 1942.)

The other story has perhaps developed from the first. The situation is identical, but has been outfitted with sound-effects. *The reformed prostitute is giving testimony with the Salvation Army on a street-corner, on a Saturday night, punctuating her discourse by beating on a big bass drum. "I used to be a sinner!" she shouts.* (Boom!) *"Used to be a bad woman.* (Boom!) *I used to drink!* (Boom!) *Gamble!* (Boom!) *Whoor!* (Boom! Boom!) *Used to go out Saturday nights and raise hell!* (Boom! Boom! Boom!) *Now what do I do Saturday nights? I stand on this street-corner, beating on this mother-fucking drum!"* (N.Y. 1948.) The voice from the crowd (or voice from the gallery, upper-berth, etc.) is now unnecessary. In the irrepressible 'return of the repressed,' and with the violent punctuation of the drum, the reformed prostitute herself expresses the listener's presumed reaction of mockery, or dissatisfaction with her change to sacred from profane, without the use of any external 'chorus' or ventriloquial mouthpiece for the audience.

2. THE SATISFIED CLIENT

Certain earlier sections of the First Series have already discussed prostitution in various aspects, and have given important groups of jokes which cannot all be repeated here, as to prostitutes, their clients, and some of the amenities and asperities of their relationships. For example, chapters 4.V, "Cash on Delivery;" 8.VII.1, "Payment for Intercourse;" and especially 8. VIII3, "Prostitutes Preferred," pages 621–3, to all which the reader is referred. Their one most significant theme is that a man cannot really get a 'good sex-job' from a mere wife or sweetheart, and that – as a young prostitute once told me with a mysterious smile – *"There's nothing like professional work."* Really meaning that one can do specially 'dirty' things with prostitutes that one would not dare to try with 'decent women,' as is discussed more at length at the end of the present chapter, under "Impossibilities."

Generalized satisfaction with the prostitute, on the part of the male client, is not the usual situation in jokes on prostitution, and, where it is expressed, the prostitute is usually described as particularly helpful, patient, etc. – in a word, maternal. *An elderly client in a whore-house insists on having a special girl, who happens to be occupied. "But what's she got that all my other girls haven't got?" asks the madam. "Pati-ence," says the old man.* (1:157. Also collected, London, 1953, as of a "granddad.") The reference here is to the additional length of time it takes the older man to arrive at orgasm, which presumably makes the ordinary prostitute impatient, as she wishes to get the act over with and go on to the next client. The non-prostitute would, contrariwise, find the extra-long act of intercourse with the older man specially satisfactory. The *patient* girl here is, therefore, by that token hardly a prostitute at all.

The specific comparison of the prostitute's sexual complai-sance with the inferior sexual offering of the wife is made classically in a story already given: *A boy meets his father coming out of a whorehouse, and expresses shocked surprise. "Son," says his father, "say nothing. I prefer the simulated enthusiasm of a paid prostitute to the dignified acquiescence of your mother."* (2:416. Possible earlier sources have been dis-cussed in the First Series, 8.VIII. 3, page 622.) In collecting this story again more recently (1966), the Hollywood writer repeat-ing it added the observation: 'This is just like the plot of Arthur Miller's *Death of a Salesman*, only there isn't a line of dialogue that good in the play.' The present writer is not able to see the similarity to the Miller play, but the implied com-parison could certainly be made to Eugene O'Neill's last, very worst, and talkiest stage-elephant, *The Iceman Cometh*, con-cerning a travelling salesman who kills his wife because she was so '*good*,' meaning, of course, frigid.

Feedback stories show the wife as attempting to compete with the prostitute, but never in sexual abandon – which is pre-sumably impossible for the wife (with that all-too-familiar husband!) – and simply by some special complaisance and warmness: *i.e.* again by maternalism. *A wife tries to win back her husband's love, on the advice of a woman friend, by bring-ing him his slippers and pipe when he comes home late one night, giving him a tall drink, cuddling up in his lap dressed only in a silk dressing gown, and ending with the murmured offer, "Let's go upstairs, darling!" "I might as well," says her bemused husband; "I'll get hell when I get home anyway."* (Minneapolis, Minn. 1937.) The same idea of fake-adultery is used consciously, as a sort of marital spice, in a French joke: *A man takes his wife to dinner for their silver wedding anniver-sary at a notorious restaurant, taking a private room upstairs,* and ostentatiously locking the door after the waiter has served the dessert. "Oh, dearest," trills his wife, "isn't it exciting!? I feel just as though I were being unfaithful to you!" (Histoires Italiennes, Paris, 1956, p. 12.) Observe that the wife is winning the tournée hands-down, the husband's notion of imaginary adulterous spice backfiring on him.

G. K. Chesterton's curious novel, Manalive (1912) which involves an autobiographical fantasy at the least, is similarly based on the theme of a man continuously refurbishing the excitement and 'newness' of his otherwise too-sedate marriage by means of fake-adultery or fake-seduction: The wife is to move to various parts of town; he pretends to meet her by accident, and 'seduces' her; she then moves to another part of town, and the comedy begins all over. This is the identical notion of the marriage-manuals and sex-technique handbooks such as Weckerle's fantastic Golden Book of Love (1907, in German; English translation, New York, 1970) that "It is just as exciting to make love to one woman (one's legitimate wife) in five hundred positions – [Weckerle gives 531!] – as to make love to five hundred women in one position." It's a gallant try, perhaps, but not necessarily true. Compare: The duke and duchess are on a train which stops to take water out in the country. In a nearby field a bull is mounting cows, one after the other, in fine fashion. The duchess becomes a bit overwrought watching this. "Why aren't you men able to do things that way?" she asks the duke. "Oh, but we are, my dear," he answers urbanely. "Just let us change cows each time." (Paris, 1954. Known in both French and English, the same insulting pun on woman-as-cow existing in both languages.)

Anecdota Americana (1927) No. 287, gives the most perfect 'satisfied-client' story, which has often been collected since and is also used – with a Texas millionaire as client – as a trail-in sequence to the "Billy" Wilder whore-with-heart-of-gold movie in the early 1960's, Irma la Douce, a title inevitably punned upon by the public as Irma la Douche: 'Young Burton was away from home, visiting relatives. A woman accosted him on the streets and took him to her flat. It was the first time young Burton had ever yielded to the flesh. For several hours the woman gave him of her best. Finally, inert, he asked her how much he owed her. "Oh, give me what you think it was worth," said she, carelessly. The youth took out a swollen pocketbook and deposited its entire contents on the dresser. "Here's eighty-

seven dollars," he said. "That's all the money I have with me now. I'll send you the rest later!"' This is a standard folk-humor trait, as in the 'giant-penis' story in which: *The man whose penis has been magnificently enlarged by magic (or by a mysterious medicine) comes home wheeling his penis before him in a wheelbarrow, and tells his astonished wife, "That's nothing! My balls will be here tomorrow in the dray-wagon."* (Scranton, Pa., about 1930.) Money-as-virility!

3. THE STATUS OF THE PROSTITUTE

The folk-mind is not certain whether being a prostitute is really the disgrace pretended. Taken from the economic point-of-view of the working classes and the poor, prostitution often represents the easiest and best step *upward* on the social scale that a girl can really hope for, whether in the crude 'fucking-for-hire' forms, or in the more polite disguise of 'making a good marriage.' The anonymous *My Secret Life* (1888–94?) which, in the introduction to its recent integral reprint (New York: Grove Press, 1966), I have argued is probably the work of the erotic bibliographer, H. Spencer Ashbee, is particularly and unconsciously eloquent on the simple temporary buying for cash of underpaid working-girls engaged in by rich young Victorian gentlemen, and this has certainly not changed in the century that has passed. *'Rolls Royce, chauffeur driven, pulls in to kerb in East End* [poor quarter of London] *and girl in furs gets out and, after speaking to an urchin gives him £1. When the car has gone, the boy's awestruck companion says, "Cor lummie, ain't she beautiful! Was that an angel from heaven guv you that pound?" "Gorn, that's my sister wot's been ruint!"'* (London, 1953.) This has been set in verse – not as well told as in the folk-version above – by Thomas Hardy. No one needs to be reminded of the superb folk-satire of the British music-hall song, "Ayn't it all a bloody shyme?!" bemoaning in broad cockney accent the seduction of poor girls by rich squires. With the family *'Drinkin' champyne as she sends 'em, But they never speaks 'er nyme!'*

The pride of the 'lower-class' child, at least, in the sister who has *made good in life* as a prostitute, is neither jokelore nor folklore. It is calmly recounted, as a standard aspect of the life of underprivileged families in England (and of course elsewhere) in the 19th century, in the remarkable "Letter from a London Prostitute," signing herself 'Another Unfortunate' and describing without sentimentality the realities of a prostitute's career, published in *The Times*, London, 24 February 1858. (Reprinted as an appendix to Martin Seymour-Smith's *Fallen Women*, London, 1969, a valuable and level-headed literary study.)

The ultimate statement of the advantages of prostitution is presented as a fool-joke, and is very frequently encountered. An American version has already been given; the British version is stated (probably apocryphally) to have been given over the B.B.C. decades ago, by the comedian, Max Miller: *'Two chaps discussing working conditions. The first says they've improved out of all recognition. "Why, you get to work at 9 a.m., and the boss arrives at 10. At 11 there's coffee, and he invites you out to lunch and tea, maybe late dinner, drinks and a show. If you miss the last train you spend the night at his flat." "It's happened to you?" "No, to my sister – but it just shows the way things are going."'* (London, 1953.) The most recent form collected is of the knock-down-&-drag-out variety: *A man in a bar notices that all the bar-stools have numbers on the seats, and asks the man next to him what it's for. "They have drawings every night," the man explains, "and whoever has the lucky number gets taken in the back room for a free piece of ass." "Have you ever won?" asks the new man. "No, but my wife won three nights in a row last week."* (L.A. 1968.)

Well on its way to becoming a modern classic is an under-played scene whose popularity among women is obviously a bitter commentary on the relative uselessness of education for women, as demonstrated with the actual census figures at the opening of the present chapters. *A man picked up by a prostitute in a bar is amazed by the college pennants and diplomas ornamenting the walls of her room. "Are these your diplomas?" he asks. "Sure," she says airily; "I have my Master of Arts from Columbia, and took my Ph.D. in Shakespeare at Oxford." The man is incredulous. "But how did a girl like you ever get into a profession like this?" "I don't know," she says; "just lucky, I guess."* (Berkeley, Calif. 1942, from a college woman, and very often since.)

This joke, or something very close to it, is played out every day of the year as a true event nowadays, certainly in America. I have lived it, and so, very possibly, have you. In fact, the situation is now becoming trite, as amateur prostitution, part-time prostitution and the politely so-called 'party-girl' kind of prostitution become just one more career for educated young

women, thrown on the labor market in their presumed liberation, only to find every field they might turn to overcrowded
with girls like themselves. Also, they are desperate in their
inability to meet rising costs for the clothes, cosmetic treatments etc. they are certain they must have, if they are even to
approximate the luxurious dream simultaneously being squirted
all over them by the advertising media, both as the natural
habitat of the human female, and as the *sine qua non* for
catching a rich husband. The whole rationale of the elegant
female bar-fly, or cocktail party butterfly, has also been
splendidly put down on paper in highly-aware psychological
prose by a showgirl, Carol St. Julian ('better known in show-biz
as Beavy LeNora, The Nevermore Girl'), as "Through the Cocktail Glass," in a short-lived jazz review, *Climax*, No. 1, published
in New Orleans, 1955, an article that makes the magazine well
worth rooting out.

To see the distance that has been traversed in the automatic
self-recruiting of girls in this way for prostitution, one has only
to compare the gruelling details of sordid wartime whoredom in
the authentic French autobiography, *Marie-Thérèse* (English
translation by Robert Nurenberg as *I'm for Hire*, Paris, 1955),
with the unaccented but unequivocal details of the apparently
equally authentic, *Lily: The Diary of a French Girl in New
York*, in the form of a novel, signed 'Sandrine Forge' (New
York: Grove Press, 1969), but this time with what a difference
in the evident level of culture of the young woman involved!
These books are a very far cry from the polite 'realism' of
earlier generations, in the then-scandalous novels of the prostitute's life: W. L. George's *A Bed of Roses* (London, 1911) and
David Graham Phillips' *Susan Lenox: Her Fall and Rise* (1917) –
not to mention John Cleland's *Fanny Hill, or Memoirs of a
Woman of Pleasure* (1749), written entirely in romanticized
rose-water, in the pretended character of a woman. Of all such
works, the only one that is still a meaningful document is
Aleksandr Kuprin's *Yama: The Pit* (1909–15), a novel of pre-
Revolutionary Russian prostitution, superlatively translated into
English by B. G. Guerney. Finally, as far beyond *Marie-Thérèse*,
Lily, and even *Yama* as these are beyond Cleland, W. L. George
and Phillips, is what must now surely be the ultimate such
work, *Troia: or Memoirs of a Curious Courtesan*, by Bonnie
Bremser (New York: Tompkins Square Press, 1969, the opening
chapter having first been printed in a little-mag, *Down Here*,

No. 2), a book beyond citations, written in the vitriol of hideously calm understatement. One brief fragment is quoted below, in section 11.III.3, under "Oragenital Acts."

Folk-humor makes no bones about the semi-prostitutory situation, or at least the almost total availability to the *seigneur* or the 'boss,' of girls working in fields and factories since the earliest centuries of pot and rug production and tobacco-growing in the Middle East. As, more recently in the West, since the invention of the sewing machines of Thimonnier and Elias Howe (in 1830 and 1843) and the typewriters of Xavier Progin and Christopher Latham Sholes (1833 and 1867), the machines which presumably 'liberated women' by throwing them on the work-market in tremendous numbers, eventually in competition with men. The situation of the sales-girl and office-girl, as earlier the housemaid (see *Genesis*, xxx. 1–13), is thought particularly to depend on her sexual complaisance to the boss, and at least two recent volumes by women writers have blatantly purported to demonstrate the proper way for girls in offices to work their way to the top – *on their backs*. The even less-well-paid professions of waitress, nurse, manicurist, etc. have immemorially been considered close to prostitution, while the bare-breasted 'topless' waitresses of San Francisco nightclubs since the early 1960's have made this crudely obvious.

An article on the slightly more refined 'Bunnies' in the so-called Playboy Clubs in America, printed in *Candide* (Paris, 29 Aug. 1966), "Sex Made In USA: *Le Mystère Playboy*," shows these indoor drum-majorettes wearing only low-cut strapless satin bathing-suits, cut as high as the hipbones to show the maximum of sexy silk-mesh opera-hose, but insists on their unapproachable sexual purity *vis-à-vis* the customers at least. (Unless the reader happens to know better . . .) All this is now 'old stuff' in America, and the author, François Corre, also notes that similar nightclubs demand an even more humiliating peekaboo exploitation of the female bodies of the waitresses: 'There are in the United States,' says Corre (in translation), 'hundreds of establishments in which the waitresses wear a uniform similar to that of the Bunnies. There are many in which the girls are far more denuded: in *monokini* [French for topless bathing suit; a back-formation from *bikini*], in a sarong, or in a blouse closed by means of a zipper ornamented with a tag reading: "I'm not wearing a bra[ssière]. Pull the zipper: One dollar".'

The end-point can of course only be that already in operation in Japanese strip-tease theaters, where the girls come crawling out with their asses to the faces of the clients, to whom they present large *magnifying glasses* with which to stare at, and in fact up, their cunts. When this will hit America, can't you just see the ads? *"World & Interplanetary Enterprises' motion-picture and vibrating-trampolin drive-in family theaters are serviced by our brisk new Bare-Ass Naked Bendover Bottomless carhops or 'Wunkies' – you gotta see 'em to believe it!"* In any case, this too is old stuff, as the entire situation – omitting only the magnifying glasses – is exploited in an apparently true anecdote retold in Béroalde de Verville's *Moyen de Parvenir* (about 1610), chap. 8, "Cérémonie," in which a naked woman is required to bend down and pick up a basketful of cherries, scattered about the floor, as a spectacle for a party of men. The similar ritual spectacles of the men's club, the Beggar's Benison, in Scotland, over the last two centuries, have already been noted.

The professional prostitute theoretically objects to the inroads of *amateur prostitution* – as she typifies the activity of sexually-liberated girls – into her professional income, and much humor is made of this. *The decayed Shakespearean actor who is rejected by the prostitute to whom he offers an evening of love, without pay. "Madam," he says, "let us avoid all unseemly controversy. Both of us belong to great and ancient professions, ruined by the competition of amateurs."* (N.Y. 1935.) This has become a folk-phrase. In the notes (unpublished) to Dr. C. F. MacIntyre's collection of original limericks, *That Immoral Garland* (1942) p. 20, it is observed of a prostitute: 'It's lucky the little quiff didn't try making her living in an age when amateurs have reduced the ancient profession almost to a state of having no takers.' *Anecdota Americana* (1927) 1:44, gives the prostitute's point of view: *'Two girls met on Broadway and exchanged greetings. "What are you doing now?" asked one. "Oh, I've got a swell job," was the answer. "I get in at noon, do very little work, the boss takes me for lunch, and then for a drive in the afternoon. In the evening, mostly, we take dinner at a road house. What are you doing?" "Oh, I'm a whore too," the other answered.'* (Reprinted, almost verbatim, in Joe "Miller" Murray's *Smoker Stories*, Hollywood, 1942, p. 4, captioned "Is that nice, girls?" Note the relationship to the Max Miller story above.

From grudging admission to prideful arrogation is only a simple protective step. A Jewish story, told me by a young girl working in a tie-manufactory sweatshop on the New York East Side, in 1942, is based on the ritual bathhouse, or *mikveh*, to which religious Jewish women must go after menstruation, before they are ritually 'clean' for intercourse with their husbands. *The rabbi's wife at the* mikveh *on Friday afternoon asks the last lady in line: "Can I go ahead of you? The rabbi is waiting for me." And so along the whole line to the first woman waiting. "Can I go ahead of you? I'm the rabbi's wife* (rebbitzin), *and he's waiting for me." "No, you can* not *go ahead of me. I'm the town whore* (nafkeh), *and for me the whole town is waiting!"* The intended humor, for the Jewish audience, is – aside from the chastening of the *rebbitzin's* pretentiousness – the mixing of religion and prostitution in the idea of the town whore who must take her ritual bath too.

In the end, as everyone knows but seldom says, the most common kind of prostitution is not the kind in which the lives and emotions of a few hundred thousand women (per country) are bartered for cash to the crude sexual needs of horny men, in even the lowest type of crib-house brothels, and in street-accosting by drunken, draggle-tailed whores. (They still exist.) There is a level which does not think of itself, ever, as prostitution, which not only is nothing else, and of a particularly repellent kind, but is also emotionally the most debilitating of all. This is, needless to say, the prostitution of young women and wives for their material advantage in loveless marriages or in *affaires-de-convenance*. In all the books on prostitution I have ever read, I have never read anything more humiliating than a passage at the opening of a presumably light-hearted soufflé called *How to Make Love in Five Languages* (London, 1965?) by an American, Doris Lilly, presented as a novelized guide for kept-women abroad. On page 18 of this item, the rich man who is sending the heroine to Europe (to lay a lot of other men, and see if this will make him forget her; or learn, instead, that It Is She He Loves), cannot for some reason appear publicly with her to see her off. So she waits for him in front of the local drugstore, before which he then slides along surreptitiously, 'crouched' in the back of his 'long red Bentley' (note for history: a fashionable British motor-car), and *throws her a large manila envelope* containing her expense money, which she catches 'with both hands.' Thus subsidized, her adventures abroad then begin. Nothing in any of the jokes I must chronicle can touch that for excruciating realism, and I won't even try. Life in the U. S. A.

Men are not always particularly conscious of the prostitutory status, rationally considered, of such women and girls. It is more salving to the man's ego to find any possible pretext for avoiding the admission that a cash payment is being made. We are not all of heroic enough stuff to *throw a woman a manila envelope full of money* from a hidden position 'crouched' in a fake-phallic sports-car. We are not all that kind of sports. Also, if the woman will (as most do) accept anything other than plain cash, it is a great deal easier to avoid thinking of her activity in terms of prostitution. I can well remember being present at a conversation between a hard-driving American businessman and a sentimental middle-aged artist, not long ago, in which the businessman gave the artist some news of the artist's divorced wife. (I wrote this down immediately afterward, to make sure of getting it letter-perfect.) *"You heard about Pascale?" asked the businessman. "Pascale who?" asked the artist, who must have been thinking of something else. "You know! Pascale. She's gone up in the world terrifically since she left you. You had a wonderful effect on her."* The artist *waved a modest hand. "Yep, after she left you she took up with Old Joe Grubnitz, the movie-producer. She has that thing about older men, you know."* (No answer from the middle-aged artist.) *"Now she's living with Harold Farkas. They've got a beautiful thing going." "I thought Farkas was a fairy,"* said the artist; *"you mean the dress-designer, don't you?" "Oh,"* said the businessman, *"he makes it with girls too."*

One of the best-selling 'women's books' in America, in the early 1960's and since, is a sort of Bible for achieving this kind of success. Careful explanations are given of how to get a man to take the success-oriented girl to expensive restaurants, where he may introduce her to another and richer man (her only 'investment' in the new man, on their first date, then being a newer and tighter brassière, as the author plainly states), and so on from hand to hand and bed to bed until presumably the girl emulates Nell Gwyn, former orange-girl and theatre prostitute, finally mistress to the King of England. Entitled *Sex and the Single Girl* (1962), by Helen Gurley Brown, editor of the middle-class women's magazine, Hearst's *Cosmopolitan*, the message of this book is, without the slightest blush but in politer words: *How to fuck your way to the top*, Mademoiselle! (Also of its supplement, on advanced tactics for girls in the business world.) Or, rather, how to do as little fucking as possible, and yet get men to pay and pave your way to the top anyhow.

Millions of American girls and women must read and be influenced by sinister drivel like this, given them as serious advice from a ranking female 'personality.' It is, in any case, identical with the blatant message of all the women's movies, t.v. serials, advertisements, and doubtless many of their mothers' repeated advice. But in book form, nothing quite so revoltingly coarse has ever hit American publishing in the way of self-satisfied and unconsciously immoral adviseering, since that all-star best-seller of all time in the self-help field, Dale Carnegie's *How to Win Friends and Influence People*, the gutter-guide to success, and publishing miracle of the 1930's. Also a runaway best-seller was the technical supplement of sex-techniques, continuing on after Mrs. Brown and couched in even more vulgar style, *The Sensuous Woman* (New York, 1969) by "J," stated in Dr. Albert Ellis' we-wuz-robbed reply, *The Sensuous Person* (Secaucus, N.J., 1972) p. 11, to have been written by Miss John "Terry" Garrity. Intended to introduce repressed American career-girls and housewives to the dubious joys of anal intercourse and similar, to 'hold their man,' *The Sensuous Woman* lacks the sociological importance of its original.

Helen Gurley Brown's *Sex and the Single Girl* has also certain overtones of Stephen Potter's cynically humorous *Gamesmanship*, but transposes and revises all the proposed shabby tricks, dishonesties and cheapnesses, for the use of the gameswoman or up-&-coming business girl, ready-willing-&-able to fuck her way to the top. The delicate distinction between this and straight prostitution is that the men are not to be wangled into paying the girl directly for her sexual garbage-can activity: they are to be angled into paying for any and everything *else* she needs or wants, including of course a wedding-ring. Miss Doris Lilly's message in *How to Make Love in Five Languages* is essentially the same, but far more disarmingly frank, as also in her earlier *How to Marry a Millionaire*. Helen Gurley Brown, for all her snide tough-talking, is never that candid.

One also appreciates Miss Lilly's candor about the higher stakes involved. A 'good marriage' – *i.e.* a lucrative one, offering leisure and luxury to the gameswoman – is on every amateur prostitute's, party-girl's, and kept-woman's ultimate agenda, whatever the sucker's age may be, and whether or not he also 'makes it with boys.' After which the *real* Waltz of the Hundred-Dollar-Bills begins. There are, certainly, sweet and loving women who also wish to marry, millions of them, and in all countries, who want nothing more than a chance to love and be devoted to their husbands and children, and to be a little bit protected from the violence of the life-struggle so that they can have the children they biologically yearn for. But these are not the women who have been decisively influenced by the amateur whore-ethic of women's movies, t.v., bitch-heroine novels, and *Sex and the Single Girl*. Or who are meant when men trade bitter wisecracks and proverbs like: *"Next after dogs, women are the worst free-loaders."* (La Jolla, Calif. 1965, said to me by a stranger waiting with me to pay for goods chosen by womenfolk in a dress-shop.)

The new Women's Liberation movement now recognizes, in the message of Brown, Lilly, and Co., and the women's magazines they sparkplug, the simple career of 'soft-core hooker.' But the same Liberation movement leaves little else open in the way of careers for women, by propagandizing with even more, and more voluble contempt against the career of wife-&-mother, which is now somehow discovered to be the most humiliating and enslaving of all! It is right and fitting to boycott the producers of offensively advertised (or any) vaginal deodorants, which shame and humiliate women in the attempt to frighten them into buying consumer goods. It is also certainly right to fight the exploitation of women's bodies, both for touching, for emotionless fucking, and even just for staring at unhealthily in men's magazine centerfolds and in striptease and 'topless' bars. But the real prostitution, on the broadest scale, which saps and destroys the self-respect of hundreds of millions of women, is by no means the mere prostitution of women's bodies by exploitative men, not even in the ultimately humiliating magnifying-glass stripteases of Japan, and the 'split-beaver' and 'spread-shot' photos of women pulling open their vaginas before the camera, in Los Angeles and Copenhagen, which are the Western equivalent nowadays. The real prostitution of women is that engaged in *by themselves*, on the marriage market, and in the brutal competitions of 'upward motility,' for the available sports-cars and suburban villas, in the world of business-girl and professional success, which is precisely the world that is the only present ideal of the wholly misled and man-hating 'Women's Liberation.'

Jokes on these subjects are becoming increasingly popular as the activity involved becomes increasingly evident. Men are not trying in such jokes to 'keep women in their place.' They are simply expressing, mostly to other men, in the stable-cleaning catharsis of laughter, their disgust at female cynicism disguised as available sex. These jokes begin far back, in the stage-settings of jokes on children and animals, and many of these have already been given in the earlier chapters on these subjects in the First Series here. In a not-very-shaggy shaggy-dog story: *A man has a dog that takes a dime in its mouth every Sunday morning to the store and brings back the Sunday paper. One day the man has no change and gives the dog a five-dollar bill instead. The dog does not return, and is found later by his owner in a back-alley, violently fucking a female dog who is holding the five-dollar bill in her mouth.* (Note this line.) *"Rover!" says the owner sadly, "you never did anything like this before." "'Course not," says the dog; "I never had the money!"* (Cleveland, Ohio, 1948.) The touch as to the five-dollar bill being in the bitch's mouth – insisting on the prostitutory situation – does not appear in the earlier version of this joke given in the First Series, 4.V, "Cash on Delivery," p. 248. Not essential, but hateful. A long version, without the talking-dog punchline, is in *The Stag Party* (1888) p. 185 unnumb., with the then-standard $2 bill in the bitch's mouth.

A standard cute-kid story, often collected in shorter form and with various end-lines: *A little boy who has hidden in the back seat of his big brother's roadster, to learn how to act with girls, pedals down the sidewalk the next day in his toy auto picking up little girls. "Hello, li'l girl," he says, "you wanna go for a ride?" "Yes." "Det in." "Ya wanna take down your panties?" "No." "Det out." And on he pedals after another little girl. At the third or fourth encounter one little girl agrees, and they go down in the cellar together. "Gee," says the little boy, "now what do I do?" Little girl: "You give me a nickel to pull up my dress and pull down my pants, or I won't do it." Little boy: "Yeah. Pull up your dress and pull down your pants." Little girl: "Where's the nickel?" He gives her the nickel and she pulls down her pants and shows him her cunt, which he examines curiously. "Is that all?" "Waddya mean, all?" "I mean you ain't got no hair like the big girls." "What do you want for a nickel*

– TURLS ? !" (N.Y. 1953.) The punch-line here always gets a laugh, but 'turls' are hardly the real point of the story. The point of the story is MONEY. The projection of the story backwards into childhood is strictly intended to soften the crude encounter; and other stories of the same kind, even including the concern with the girl's pubic hair, will be found later in this chapter as between adult men and professional prostitutes. It should be evident (apparently it is not, and to millions of girls) that the little girl's activity it just as prostitutory if she gets only the luxurious ride in the sports-car, as payment for showing her genitals, as it is if she demands and gets the cash payment of so little as five cents.

An ancient story, earlier even than *Joe Miller's Jests* in 1739, has : *A woman whose husband has just bought her new shoes, and who finds her with her feet in the air over the back of a man making love to her. "A truly good wife," the husband muses sarcastically. "You'll never wear out your new shoes that way!"* This is modernized as of : *A man who is told that if he needs a woman he should just go to the Indian reservation with a pair of beaded moccasins, and offer them to the first squaw-girl that attracts him. During intercourse with the squaw-girl she waves her feet wildly in the air over the man's back. "Oh honey," he says, "I thought you Indian girls didn't like sex, but this is great!" "Ugh," she says, "squaw tryum on moccasins."* (N.Y. 1941.) This is given in *World's Dirtiest Jokes* (1969) p. 37, modernized further as concerning intercourse in the inevitable automobile, and with 'pretty red shoes' which the girl will do 'anything' to get. Actually, in all forms the story has evident foot-fetichistic elements, and should be compared with Rétif de La Bretonne's staggering autobiographical fantasy eroticum, *L'Anti-Justine* (1798), in which he describes himself as buying specially tiny shoes for his daughter, with whom he has incestuous relations – also pimping her to other men – so that she will *click her tiny heels over his head* to bring on his orgasm during intercourse.

Tradesmen of all kinds are presumed to be easy marks for offers of sex-instead-of-money, and a special group of such jokes will be found below, in section 11.II.4, "Male Prostitution," though it is a toss-up whether they do not just as well concern female prostitution. *A girl gets a pair of panties tattooed on her hips. When the tattooer asks $25 for the job, she complains, "But you tattooed a pair of panties just like this for my girl-*

friend for only $5." "Yes," says the tattooer, "but I went into the hole on that job." (N.Y. 1958. A version from Los Angeles, ten years later, adds a topper given to the girl: "Well then, how about taking a licking on this one?") See the fabulous photographs of actual erotic tattooing almost all involving fetichistic chains and padlocks infibulating the penis, by means of a hole bored through the foreskin, with an artless letter from the British tattooer, noting that he "don't have much at all in the way of tattooed cunt," in the main British sex-newspaper or pornzine, Suck (Amsterdam, 1970) No. 3: p. 19, which makes the earlier and similar American productions, Intercourse, Screw, Kiss, Pleasure, X, and the New York Review of Sex, look 'like boy-scout manuals.'

The briefest story of housewife casual prostitution is also the most recent and the most crude: A woman goes into a hardware store to buy a hinge for her kitchen-closet. She picks a hinge off a stand, and the salesman approaches her with a big smile. "Can I give you a screw for that hinge?" he asks. "No," she says, "but I'll give you a blow-job for that electric toaster." (L.A. 1968.) See the whole section on such "Propositions in Error,' First Series, 4.I.2–3.

Actually, and by that I mean today, young women and men are seldom able to draw the fine line between giving or accepting a love-gift, and being or making someone else into a whore. It is a collapse of standards, as much or more than a collapse of traditional morality, and it is precisely the insanely repetitive advertisements of materialistic objects and goals, in both openly-admitted advertising, and in the hidden 'kiss of Capitalism' that movie- and t.v.-writers are required, if they wish to succeed, to slip into their scenarios in the form of opulent and seductive backgrounds, furnishings, fancy liquor, fast cars, foreign travel, etc. (even turquoise-studded marijuana pipes for the theoretically 'anti-materialistic' hippies, whose underground newspapers also advertise expensive imported leather-&-macramé stash-bags for their drugs) that have really destroyed moral standards for young people. People propagandized up to this trigger-level will do anything – not just sexually, but anything – to get hold of satisfactory slices of the materialistic bait held out before their dazed and dead eyes as the social cynosures of status and success. One pathetic little joke, still struggling with the moral problem, nevertheless phrases it in terms of the principal modern status-object, the automobile:

Question on an Economics quiz: "Why is the automotive in-dustry the greatest in America?" The girl-student replies: "Be-cause if you do it in a car, it's just a mistake, but if you go to a motel you're a dirty whore." (Berkeley, Calif. 1965.) Note that the immemorially older distinction, that *it's not a sin if it's really love,* has disappeared under the wheels of the Juggernaut. One could mention some very 'big' names.

That the quasi-prostitute in the following story is taking her payment in food is perfectly obvious even to the actors in the story itself, as is also the peculiar tone of a food-oriented *revenge* against the man, out of whom the excessive and ex-pensive food is being forced or mulcted, in return for any anti-cipated sexual act. Evidently the girl expects and gets more physical pleasure from the food she puts into her mouth-end, and is therefore sure she has *got,* than she can ever expect at the other end from the orgasm she is just as sure not to achieve. *A man picks up a beautiful girl in a bar, and spends twenty dollars or so on drinks for the two of them, then suggests that they go over to his duplex apartment in his supercharged foreign sports-car, and listen to Tibetan folk-music on his stereophonic, hi-fidelity, super-duper phonograph. The girl is very impressed, and agrees. On the way she suggests stopping somewhere for a snack, as all the drinks have made her hungry. They go to a little French restaurant where she orders* paté de foie gras, *lobster cocktail, boneless shad, and vichyssoise soup; lamb-chops and a sirloin steak right after, with Chinese chicken egg-rolls to hold things down while she is picking out two or three desserts. As she is looking over the wine-list for the right liqueur to order with her coffee, the man asks mildly, "Say, do you always eat like this?" "No," she replies with a smile, "only when I'm having my period."* (L.A. 1968.) First published by Newbern & Rodebaugh, p. 42, who note that the girl eats *'like there was no tomorrow.'* Exactly. Cookbooks are the porno-graphy of women.

4. PROSTITUTION AS INSULT

The word 'prostitute,' and any of its more vulgar synonyms such as 'whore' (popularly always pronounced *whoor,* as in the Dutch *'hoer,'* from which it comes), or, in the Latin languages such as French and Italian, *'putain'* (the American 'poontang') and *'puta,'* are necessarily considered insults. They are applied generally only to women, but are even more insulting when applied to a man, as in the self-applied and would-be humorous "*I'm a whoor*," offered as excuse by many journalists and other pop-culch prostitutes, such as advertising men and commercial artists. This may be considered a dysphemistic, or purposely dirty, abbreviation of the more elevated phrases of shock concerning the 'prostituting of one's art,' of the romantic and aesthetic period of the middle-19th century, when the nature of the struggle finally became clear. The earliest reference I have found in which a man actually calls himself an intellectual prostitute, is in the *Life and Letters* of Sir Edmund Gosse, librarian to the House of Lords, edited by Evan Charteris (London, 1931) p. 303, in a letter to Maurice Baring, 21 March 1907, dated from 'House of Lords, S.W.' :

> I have not been at all well, and the labour of bringing out "Books" [*a newspaper column*] every week has been a very trying one, largely because I am an old dog to be set at a new trick ... The dilemma is one which I heard put by a perfectly awful old woman, years ago, who was describing with horror the exposure of her person which some maiden had to make at a music-hall. "What an awful position for a chaste young girl! Of course – she is generously paid to do it." That is exactly my prostituted case.

This is also the first reference I have been able to find to the curious reversal of morals, now so well-known in the moving-picture and publishing world, not to mention politics, that doing something immoral for money is the *extenuating circumstance*. It used to be considered the worst part of the disgrace! Note that Gosse is accepting all this, even yearning to whore – and sorry he cannot do it more easily – just for the money, of course. The idea that people who do immoral things are *not* doing it strictly for money (as proved by the many other people who would also like the money, but who can't bring themselves to do these things) is carefully lost sight of.

This is not the place to discuss the various non-verbal signs of infamy which prostitutes have been required to wear at various periods of history, such as yellow arm-bands similar to those for lepers and Jews. (See the study by Ulysse Robert, *Les Signes d'infamie au moyen âge: Juifs, sarrasins, hérétiques, lépreux, cagots, et filles publiques*, Paris, 1891, copy in my Anti-Semitica collection, now in Ohio State University Library.)

As one particular such sign, the *shaving off of the head-hair* of women known to have consorted with the enemy was much practiced in France at the end of the World War II, especially on prostitutes. This is the basis for the ugly style of short and boyish hair for women (much shorter and more ragged than the 'boyish bob' of the male-protest 1920's), beginning about that time. It recollects in part the folk-belief that prostitutes shave their pubic hair to reduce the danger of venereal infection, or infestation by crab-lice, or that their hair has fallen out as a result of such infection. In joke form : *Ladies' night at the Turkish bath. One girl has no pubic hair, and explains, "Did you ever see grass grow on a busy street?"* (1:434.) The same punchline is also used to 'explain' why men go bald and women usually don't.

Curzio Malaparte's *The Skin* (London, 1952), chap. 3, one of the best-written but most repellent books that came out of the aftermath of World War II, takes its title from the ultimate symbol of the humiliation of the Italian people by their American conquerors : the presumed wearing by the dark-haired Neapolitan prostitutes (offering themselves with ostentatiously spread knees on the staircases of the hilly 'old town') of *blonde cunt-wigs* or 'merkins,' in order to make themselves attractive to American Negro soldiers desirous of blondes! (Only Malaparte could be there to record one like this ...) The trait of blonde head-hair – especially if made artificially blonde by bleaching – as a sign of a prostitute is at least as old as ancient Rome, according to the satirists of the period such as Martial. All this concern with the *hair* of prostitutes both pro and con, is based on an avowed recognition of the head-hair as a principle female secondary sexual characteristic (along with the breasts), and on a semi-conscious identification of its attractiveness to men with that of the pubic hair. The liking for armpit hair – in the Anglo-Saxon cultures the intimidated shaving off of this hair by women – is based on a similar and quite conscious identification of it with the pubic tressoria. *"Man, those Italian girls all have three pussies!"* (Overheard in a conversation between two American sailors, in the old market, Verona, Italy, 1959.)

Even the euphemistic words connected with prostitution fall under a ban, as is classic with all euphemisms eventually. (This is equally true of euphemisms in subjects other than sex : for example, undertaker, originally an elegant euphemism for

grave-digger, which must now be avoided as too crude, and is
itself further euphemized to 'mortician', 'funeral director,' and
other exotica.) *An ex-prostitute out shopping asks to have her
packages delivered, and gives an address. Salesgirl: "Is that a
house, Madam?" "No! It's* not *a house, and* don't *call me
Madam!!"* (2:328.) Where, on the one hand, the term '*son of a
bitch*' (earlier '*son of a whore*') has lost much of its bite, partly
owing to the newer connotation of 'bitch' as meaning a woman
of evil emotional character, rather than one sexually immoral;
the term '*prostitute*,' which, as used in English, is only a
Latinistic euphemism for '*whore*,' has remained a deadly insult
over the centuries. In "The Green-Room Scuffle, or Drury-Lane
in an Uproar," in *The Foundling Hospital for Wit* (1748) V. 19,
one of a company of '*brims*' (short for '*brimstones*'), swapping
insults with her compeers, finds that she has been called a '*Red-
Fac'd* Bitch,' and casts her deadliest insult in answer:

> Now bristles bonny Kate;
>   All ready, fierce and fiery,
> "Such BRIMS (cries she) I hate
>   Cou'd Davey e'er admire Ye? –
> PROSTITUTE!"

Compare with this a joke given in *The Limerick* (1953) Note
1284: *Homosexual* (to whore): *"Prostitute!" Whore* (to homosexual): *"Substitute!"* Two limerick versions, both less succinct
than the joke, and one abysmally worse, are also noted as dating from about 1942, though one would imagine that even the
over-educated limerick poets would realize that this colloquy is
perfect and cannot be improved.

In my extended Introduction to John S. Farmer & William
E. Henley's *Dictionary of Slang & Its Analogues* (New Hyde
Park: University Books, 1966) revised vol. I: p. lxv-lxvi, I have
given a long and remarkable passage of Billingsgate insult between two women, one presumably French and one English, in
Prof. John Barth's picaresque novel of colonial life and scatology in 17th-century America, *The Sot-Weed Factor* (New York:
Doubleday, 1960), the first best-selling American novel in which
the hero fucks a pig. In Book III, chapter 38, the two women
just referred to fling at each other's heads several score of
synonyms for *prostitute* or *whore*, alternately in French and in
English, and in a fine frenzy well worth looking up. The English

synonyms are apparently mostly of Prof. Barth's own invention, and do honor to his linguistic flair. Compare also – a passage also reprinted as above – the Spanish work which created the picaresque genre (*pícaro*, Spanish for rogue, the whore's companion or match), the *Retrato de la Lozana Andaluza* by Francisco Delicado, first published in Venice, 1528, and unquestionably the model for Aretino's more famous but in no way more remarkable *Ragionamenti*, or Dialogues of Whores (Venice, 1532–4). Delicado's is a lava-like eruption of language, which only Rabelais has ever matched, before James Joyce, and which no one has matched since, except one other writer in Spanish, Carlos Fuentes, in his remarkable *La Muerte de Artemio Cruz* (México, 1962) p. 143 ff., in an inordinately long passage glorifying and orchestrating every possible form and useage of the Spanish word, *chingar*, to fuck. (See the quotation from this work in section 14.I.3, below.)

Various elements in the prostitute's profession, considered insulting, range from the mere name or statement of this profession to allusions to the physical details or positions of the prostitute's activity. *A London taxi-driver is tired of hearing American tourists running down England. The next American who gets into his cab says, "Drive me to Soho; I want to see where the real Swinging London is! I hear there are at least three whores working on every street corner." "Yurss," says the driver bitterly, "but there used to be twice as many until you Yankees started marrying them and tyking them home!"* (L.A. 1967.) Compare another British complaint left over since World War II, that: *"The Yanks are overpaid, overfed, oversexed, and over here."* (Coventry, Warwickshire, 1969.) – *"What do they call a pross's children? – Brothel's sprouts."* (Chelmsford, Essex, 1954. The insult in this one is quite lost in its verbal charm.) – *A businessman is lunching with a new client, and becomes expansive over the cocktails as to his college experiences and prejudices. He is particularly down on the University of Alabama, and states flatly, "Nobody goes to Alabama except football players and whores." The client flares up. "I'll have you know that MY WIFE is a graduate of Alabama." "That's very interesting," gulps the first speaker; "what position did she play?"* (L.A. 1968.)

Of the types concerned with physical details: *A group of enthusiasts for occultism are having a table-rapping séance. They realize they are in contact with the spirit world, as the raps and taps and wild slides of the ouija board on the table prove. The medium goes into a trance and tells them they are in contact with the departed spirit of Millicent Kettle, actress extraordinary, the toast of all the Green Rooms of the last century, and mistress to three kings and two emperors. "But how do we know it's really her?" mumbles the Doubting Thomas sent by the Rationalist Society as an observer. As if in answer, the table leaps angrily out of their hands, turns upside down, and lands with its legs in the air and drawers wide open!* (Cf. Randolph, no. 63.)

' *"Jack, my boy, what a devil of an appetite you have this morning," said one friend to another as they were breakfasting at their hotel. "And so would you," replied Jack, "if you had only had a whore's tongue and a toothbrush in your mouth since yesterday!"* ' (The Pearl, No. 3, Sept. 1879.) The dysphemistic intention here – of crushing the interlocutor by the unexpected reference to the sexual details of prostitution – is made even clearer in the American version, set on an anticlerical and anti-Catholic background, actually entirely irrelevant as the original just cited shows: *A man in the confessional, challenged as to whether or not he has broken his fast before coming to communion Sunday morning, says, "Father, as God is my witness, I swear to you I've had nothing in my mouth but a whore's tongue and a toothbrush since eight last night!"* (N.Y. 1952. To be compared with the fellation story on the same religious background, given earlier in 10.IV.3.)

The relationship between prostitution and the sacred women of earlier religions (Vestal Virgins, nuns, now nurses, etc.) has already been discussed in a preceding section. It is still considered particularly insulting to suggest any relationship between the priests or parsons of patriarchal religion and the female prostitutes representing the last vestiges of the matriarchal religion preceding. Witness the hoary libel against the Church of England – possibly once true, for all I know – that a part of its revenue consists, or once consisted of rents on the buildings in the prostitutes' quarters of London in Tudor times, such as Southwark, Turnbull Street, Smock Alley, and Futter Lane (*causâ modestiæ* 'Fetter' Lane). This would appear to be a leftover from Catholic usages, preceding Henry VIII. One of the worst of the popes of Rome, Fransesco della Rovere (Sixtus IV), to whom nevertheless the building of the Sistine Chapel is due, published at Rome immediately after his election to the pontificate in 1471 the *Taxa Penitentiarie*, 'one of the mose odious and most detestable books ever written,' says Guillaume Ranchin, advocate of Montpellier somewhat later, who adds: 'Every sin, every crime, no matter how enormous, here has its price; so that one need only be very rich to have licence and impunity to do evil, and yet have a sure passport to Paradise for oneself and one's malefactors.' According to Prosper Marchand, *Dictionnaire historique* (1759) p. 270, this tax-scale for sins was added by the following pope, Innocent VIII, in 1486, to the *Regule ordinationes et constitutiones cancellarie* of 1471. The complete text has been republished by Dupin de Saint-André with an important introduction and bibliography of the subject, as *Les Taxes de la Pénitencerie apostolique* (Paris, 1879), based on the edition of 1520, when most of these taxes still existed — four popes later.

Among other taxes of this kind originally levied by Sixtus IV was one on prostitution, in which each Roman whore ('*puttana*' in the text, to avoid any mistake) was taxed one *julius* per week. According to Agrippa von Nettesheim in his *De Vanitate et incertitudine scientiarum* (before 1535), this tax brought in more than twenty thousand ducats yearly to the papal treasury. (Quoted in *Le Mal français à l'époque de l'expédition de Charles VIII en Italie*, by Dr. Louis Thuasne, under the pseudonym 'Hesnaut,' Paris, 1886, an important source-work on the European history of venereal disease.) High dignitaries of the Roman church became the renters-out of brothels, and this was repressed by Sixtus' successor, Innocent VIII, reiterating a bull of Pius II (Aeneas Silvio Piccolomini, the most cultivated *littérateur* in the history of the papacy) which, about 1460, had prohibited priests from owning 'butcher-shops, cabarets, gambling-dens, and brothels, and from making of themselves, for money, the pimps of prostitutes.' Meaning that the Roman Catholic priests had been doing all this since at least the time of Pius II, and that Sixtus IV had merely legalized the matter with a cynical penitentiary 'tax'. The papal bull in question is "*Romanum decet pontificem*," printed in Rinaldi's *Annales Ecclesiastici* (1877) xxx 157. See further Burckhardt's *History of Civilization in Italy*, Appendix 4.

It would have been impossible for a scandal such as this not to have had its repercussions during the centuries of religious controversy and polemic immediately following the Protestant schism under Luther and Calvin, within fifty years of that date.

Aside from the question of the church ownership of real estate or buildings in the prostitutes' quarters by various bishopricks of England, at or since the time of Henry VIII, the same shaft has been traditionally used against the American Protestant clergy, especially in the eastern seaboard states that were the first settled from England. It is used very tellingly in the final courthouse scene in John Sanford's novel of mock morality in backwoods New York State, *Seventy Times Seven* (1939) – a great American novel if ever there was one – as to the ownership by the local church-elder of the house in which the town 'widow' or 'widder-woman' has been living. More than one vestige of this truth or libel exists in jokes. *The Negro minister who preaches his yearly charity sermon on the subject of "The Widow's Mite." One of his parishioners approaches him later and complains about the sermon: " 'Might,' hell, parson! You knows as well as Ah do dat dere's only two widows in town, an' bof DOES!"* (N.Y. 1946.)

The ultimate anti-clerical insult is, of course, to accuse the priest or minister, less often the rabbi, of being himself a client of prostitutes. *A whorehouse madam pays off her bank loan several months before due, explaining to the banker, "I plumb forgot about the Eucharistic Congress being in town this month."* (U.S., 1920's; seldom collected since.) – *The elders of the church plan to run a notorious prostitute out of town. The deacon is elected to tell her she must leave, while the others wait outside for him. After half an hour he comes out and tells the others, "There must be some mistake. This young lady is a highly cultured piano teacher, and not a prostitute at all. We have no right to make her leave town." "All right, deacon,"* says the minister, *"if that's your final opinion, button up your pants and let's go."* (1:349.) This is very similar to the plot of Somerset Maugham's *Rain* (1932), especially in the theatre version by John Colton, and were the date of the joke not earlier than the play, it might be considered a simple travesty. The play (combined with the similar *White Cargo*, and *Pagan Lady*, 1930) was certainly travestied in a favorite burlesque skit during the last decade of the American burlesque and strip-tease theatres, 1935–45, usually with the white trader 'gone native,' and shown crawling on the floor in delirium tremens, shouting for the 'Mammy-palaver' the native girl has promised him.

The actual age of this joke is much greater than might be imagined: it is one of the oldest traced in the present research.

The original form – intended perfectly seriously and even didactically – appears in the commentary by Rabbi Nathan on the Talmudic *Pirké Avoth*, about the 5th century A.D., to gloss the rabbinical recommendation: 'Judge everyone with the scale weighted in his favor.' As given in Dr. Judah Goldin's translation as *The Living Talmud* (Yale Univ. Press, 1955, ed. 1957) p. 57–8: '*There was once a young girl who had been taken captive, and two saintly folk went after her to ransom her. One of them entered the harlot's apartment. When he came out he asked his companion: "What didst thou suspect me of?"* ... (The verbal ending given here is of course noble and homiletic.) Compare also Shakespeare's *Pericles*, IV. v–vi, the scene in which the innocent Marina 'preaches divinity' to the clients of a brothel. This is repeated, almost burlesqued, yet perfectly authentically as it appears, in Kuprin's *Yama: the Pit*, on pre-Revolutionary Russian prostitution, in which: *The idealistic young girl dedicated to the liberation of women* (in 1900) *takes a job in a whore-house, and gives little speeches and even pamphlets to her clients, begging them not to defile and exploit their 'little sisters' in this way.* How now, Women's Lib? The preceding story, on the 'Eucharistic Congress,' is by comparison quite recent. It has been traced only to the Roman Catholic Council of Constance in the year 1418. As then recorded by Gebhard Dacher, the amount the prostitute earns at the Council (and then retires on) is stated to be 800 florins. See further, Charles Franklin's *They Walked a Crooked Mile* (New York: Hart, 1972) p. 45–90, "Scandals of the Medieval Church."

Folk-jokes on these subjects are, to be sure, much more explicitly sexual-cum-clerical, in the tradition of the anti-clerical folk-tales and novellas of Italy and the rest of Europe, which reach some sort of highpoint in the many bawdy tales mocking the local 'popes' or priests collected in Afanasyev's *Russian Secret Tales* (posthumously published about 1872 in Geneva). *Some Catholic women living across the street from a whoreshop peep through the window-curtains to see who it is, everytime a man comes out. They comment dismally on clerical corruption when a protestant minister is seen coming out, casting his eyes piously to heaven. A rabbi is then seen emerging, buttoning up his pants, and the women comment, "Isn't that just like a dirty Jew!" When a Catholic priests comes out, the woman look silently at one another. Finally one whispers, "There must be somebody sick in there."* (D.C. 1945.) Rabbi

Nathan couldn't have said it better.

A folk-obscœnum, in the form of a printed satirical 'novelty' card, sent me by an American folklorist in North Carolina, 1952, is pretendedly an appeal for advice to a popular radio program:

Dear Mr. Anthony,

I am a sailor in the U.S. Navy, and I also have a cousin, who is a Democrat. My father has epilepsy, and my mother has syphilis, so neither of them can work. They are totally dependent on two of my sisters who are prostitutes in Louisville, because my only brother is serving a life term in prison for rape and murder. I am in love with a streetwalker who operates near our base. She knows nothing about my background, but says she loves me. We intend to get married as soon as she settles her bigamy case, which is now in court. When I get out of the Navy we intend to move to Detroit and open a small "house."

My problem, Mr. Anthony, is this: in view of the fact that I intend to make this girl my wife and bring her into the family, should I tell her about my cousin, who is a Democrat?

This really belongs to the dysphemistic anti-family and anti-gallant type of humor, treated in Chapter 14.I.14, under 'Dysphemism." The heavy-handed political bathos is keyed, however, to the implied idea that nothing (but a Democrat!) is lower than a prostitute and her intended pimp. The hidden importation of the same idea, that one's own family is really a tribe of whores and whoremongers, is the real point of another joke, usually presented (as by a night-club comedian in Florida, 1952) as turning harmlessly on the discomfiture of the husband, with whom both teller and listener are to identify. A briefer text is given in the First Series, 3.II, page 203, with some discussion of "Parrots and Other Fowl." *A woman buys a parrot at an auction of the furnishings of a fancy whorehouse, and keeps the parrot's cage covered for two weeks to make it forget its profane vocabulary. When the cage is finally uncovered, the parrot looks around and remarks, "Awrrk! New house. New madam." When the woman's daughters come in, he adds, "Awrrk! New girls." When her husband comes home that night, the parrot says, "Awrrk, awrrk! Same old customers. Hello,*

Joe!" (From a traveling-salesman, on the "The Argonaut," Southern Pacific railroad, between San Antonio and Houston, Texas, March 1945 – proving that travelling-salesmen *do* tell dirty jokes in smoking-car trains.)

While I do not suppose that the authors would agree that they were being particularly cruel, no more brutal and unvarnished a display of the ugly reality, not of prostitution but *of prostitutes*, has ever been made than the luxurious photo-illustrated volume, *Izas, Rabizas y Colipoterras* (Barcelona: Lumen, 1964) by the academician, Dr. Camilo José Cela, of Palma de Mallorca, a work truly subtitled *'Drama con acompañamiento de cachondeo y dolor de corazón.'* The text by Dr. Cela is of great interest, lexicographically and otherwise, as can be expected of the compiler of the great Spanish *Diccionario Secreto*, in progress (Madrid: Alfaguara, 1968–71) vols. I–II, covering the testicles and penis only. But it is the street photographs by Juan Colom which must surely break any heart, in their total concentration on supremely fat and ugly whores, who must be seen to be believed. And even then, they are photographed at their best possible, as they display themselves – corseted and cosmeticked – in the streets, and have been doing for centuries. A document worth a million words.

II. SEX AND MONEY

Enough has been said, at the beginning of the present chapter, as to the plain economic basis of prostitution, to which it should perhaps be added only that the figures there given represent the *highest* level of earnings ever available to non-prostitute women in the history of the world, both absolutely and by comparison with men. If for no other reason, prostitution has long been diminishing, at least in the crude form of street prostitution and window-accosting, which latter once was the rule in all the great European ports and capitals, but which survives today (I believe) only in Hamburg and Amsterdam in a perfectly legal and permitted fashion. The modern visitor to Amsterdam who has the slightest bowels of compassion can only be shocked, not by the middle-aged prostitutes, sitting at their plate-glass windows waiting for clients in the 'reserved quarter', but by the tasteless cold-heartedness of the Dutch burghers, who take tourists through this part of town as a sort of spectacle, occasionally (I am an eye-witness of this) pushing baby-carriages while pointing out the 'sights.' This may explain, to Europeans and Americans who otherwise could not understand it, the curious spectacle which Holland made of itself to the world, during the riots of the Dutch hippies or '*provos*' (provocateurs) in 1966 and again in 1970, when the pimps of the reserved quarter rushed thousand-strong to aid the Amsterdam police in their stand against the revolutionary threat the 'provos' presumably represent. Prostitution in Hamburg and Amsterdam is still what it once was everywhere: an accepted (if not respectable) profession, with vested interests and monetary prerogatives clearly worth protecting by those profiting from it. And advertised in a government tourist-industry magazine, *Holland Herald* (1974) vol 8, no. 10: p. 9–11, with a posed 'window-girl' photo right up to the panty-crotch. Explaining that the girl students doing the posing '*did it for their country.*' (*Heil!*) How about Queen Juliana doing a little posing *for her country*?

The principal amounts of money actually changing hands, in connection with prostitution, are seldom received by the prostitutes themselves, nor even by the whorehouse 'madams' who bulk so large in the folklore of the institution. The main profits accrue to male speculators, either at the low level of simple pimps and procurers (such as taxi-drivers and other 'steerers,' including small boys and young men on street-corners in countries of depressed economy like Mexico and Spain, offering their presumed sisters' sexual complaisance to passers-by), or in the important quasi-organized fashion of the offering of both liquor and women – and rooms in which to enjoy both – by the operators of drinking establishments.

This is a very ancient combination of appetites and professions, and was already very highly developed in Shakespeare's day, and earlier, as the satirists of the period indicate. Its customary modern forms include the western 'dance-halls' used in cowboy movies to disguise the real situation being depicted, and the night-clubs with 'cigarette girls' and other waitresses in tights, usually combined with a good deal of loud and pious insistence (originally for the benefit of the police) that these uniformed waitresses are not really prostitutes at all. Simultaneously, it has been quite frankly understood by the public, at least since the time of the American attempt at Prohibition (of alcohol as a beverage, during the 1920's and early '30s), that organized gangsters control both 'vice and crime' – 'vice' meaning prostitution – and absorb most of the profits from these professions and the other rackets connected with them, such as gambling, drugs, shake-downs and blackmail.

Nothing of this reality appears in folk humor. All the jokes about prostitution are still geared to the period either of old-time street-accosting, the barman or hotel bellboy who can supply girls, or the local brothel or whorehouse which was once nothing other than the 'upstairs rooms' of the same drinking establishments or hostelries. The whorehouse 'Madam' bulks very large in the folk-humor of prostitution, and it seems clear that she is the real focus of what remains of the sacerdotal or mother-priestess side of the profession, while the sexual functions are agreed to reside wholly in the 'girls.' French neurotic writers of the 19th century, such as Baudelaire and Maupassant, have made traditional the figure of the nervous or impotent client in the brothel, who prefers to sit talking or playing cards[!] with the Madam, than to take a turn 'upstairs' with one of the girls. This rather artificial tradition at least shows the strength of the idea of the Madam as mother-figure : as being somehow less dangerous – less of a sexual challenge than the prostitutes – and certainly not as diseased. It is also assumed, however, that the Madam is herself only a prostitute grown too old to serve, though many prostitutes continue professionally until their sixties!

A perfectly astonishing attempt to milk this sort of tradition for laughs are two cartoon-pamphlets, possibly edited by the nightclub humorist Jackie Kannon, taking off from the permitted open publication of Cleland's erotic novel of a prostitute's life, *Fanny Hill* (1749), after two centuries, in America and England, under the title *Fanny Hillman: Memoirs of a Jewish Madam* (New York: Kanrom, Inc. 1965), with sequel, *Fanny Hillman in Washington*. It is hard to know which is in worse taste in these pamphlets: the gloating over the details of prostitution and political corruption, or the persistent dietary-Yiddish humor of the borscht-and-bagel type, with the orally rather than genitally satisfying Mrs. Hillman shown passing out free kosher chicken-soup (p. 23) to her satisfied clients in the kitchen. The endemic and stereotypical anti-Semitism of these pamphlets – after all, there must be some Irish Catholic and German Protestant whore-madams too – is also intended brashly to underline the Madam's function of being the person actually to demand and receive the *money* or hand out the ancient, specially-stamped *brass checks*. These checks or tokens – also the *towels* used – were a common method of bookkeeping in the oldtime whorehouse, thus reducing somewhat the anti-aphrodisiacal tone of a commercial transaction between the client and the prostitute 'turning the trick.' (Not from the 'trick' in card-games, as sometimes believed, but from the French slang, *truc*, thing.) Or the 'all-night' client could tuck the money under the clock on the mantlepiece in the morning.

I. UPSTAIRS MONEY

Certain forms of quasi-prostitution should be recollected here, particularly those of wives who demand some type of material or monetary payment from their husbands for their sexual complaisance or 'use.' See the jokes and other materials on this in the First Series, chapters 4.V, "Cash on Delivery," and 8.VII.1, "Payment for Intercourse." So crude an approach to marital prostitution is perhaps not as common in fact as in folklore, but men identify it clearly with the more disguised or refined use of 'sexual leverage' upon them by their wives. This is perfectly described by Dr. Hugo Beigel in *Sex from A to Z* (New York: Stephen Daye Press, 1961), an altogether fine psychological handbook, at "Superiority," p. 398–9: 'Women often try to prove their moral superiority. They may do so by displaying aloofness toward sexual matters and, at best, contemptuous tolerance of the male's animal needs. Other women use their own restraint or frigidity, as the case may be, to make the man feel his dependence. The concession that they make becomes a reward for good behavior, a means to "educate" the husband toward certain goals [usually monetary or status] they have set for him, which is withdrawn whenever he gives signs of doubting their superior position.'

Faced by this type of dog-whip training, or sexual conditioning, which is enormously common in modern marriage, and may well have been even more common in the arranged or 'dowry' marriages of the past, many men counter by offering valuable gifts of clothing or jewelry, new automobiles, trips abroad, etc., or the mere promise of these, as a counter-move, in order to have the sexual company of their wives without having to beg for it. A humiliation which will often destroy the man's potency *with that woman*, except in obviously sado-masochistic marriages. A striking example of this is given in an earlier chapter, in the First Series, in the case of the jeweler whose 'guaranteed European virgin' wife got his whole business away from him in this way. When the wife is caught emptying the funds from a joint bank-account, or when valuable gifts are actually demanded by her – whether verbally or by her mute pressure – the husband recognizes of course that he is married to a prostitute, and often counters by frequenting professional prostitutes. Or by seducing younger women whom he encounters in his business or professional life, by means of similar presents, usually much less costly than those the wife requires. The joke has already been cited earlier as to *The man who, after ten years of marriage, wants to have intercourse with his wife from behind, "the way the dogs do it." She refuses persistently, despite his promise to love her specially for this, that it will renew his potency, etc. When she still refuses, he offers her gifts: a new dress, a fur coat, trip to Europe, etc., and she finally succumbs when he offers to send the children to a college he has formerly said he could not afford. "All right, then," the wife agrees, "I'll do it for the children, but for god's sake don't drag me down the street backwards where the neighbors can see."* (N.Y. 1950, told with comedy-Jewish accent, as explaining the concentration on money.)

The prostitution of the daughter, similarly, was once hidden under the excuse of the dowry that the father cannot afford. See in Grose's *Classical Dictionary of the Vulgar Tongue* (1785) references under "Rochester portion", "Tetbury," etc., to various mock-dowries for poor girls, all of which add up finally to something like 'two torn smocks and what Nature gave,' or, even more crudely, 'a cunt and a clap.' *A retired businessman is nearly ruined by his sons' demands for money to pay off the girls whom they have seduced and made pregnant. But he pays in order to keep from seeing the family name disgraced. 'A few days later his daughter came to him and confessed, "Papa, I'm pregnant." "Thank God, business is picking up," said the old man.'* (*Anecdota America,* 1:27b.) The same source combines this with an even more cynical reversal, of which a variant has been given earlier. Only the father's attitude remains the same: *The father pleads with his daughter's seducer, "If it's a miscarriage, will you give her another chance?"*

Sums of this large type are involved only in the quasiprostitutions connected with marriage. A record amount of unfunny puns and allusions still exists as to *two dollars*, as the price of a whore in the United States, though this minimum or standard price actually rose to five dollars in the late 1930's, when preparations for the war-boom ended the economic Depression. The 'hire of a whore' (*Deuteronomy*, xxiii. 18) is still considered an 'abomination' at the folk-level, more than two-thousand years after its Biblical rejection. The American two-dollar bill, necessitated by the decimal monetary system, is popularly believed to cause bad luck, and many men will refuse it when given as change for a larger bill, or feel uncomfortable about having it in their possession. Bolder souls *collect* two-dollar bills, thus daring or challenging Fate or luck. This, or any payment made to a whore, is *'upstairs money.'* It can never 'bring anyone happiness.' It carries a curse. Negro prostitutes, who charge less than white, often accost white men with the offer, *"Change your luck?"* This is strictly connected with the idea of intercourse with a person of different skin color as somehow 'unhexing' or 'uncrossing' an unlucky person or a 'streak of bad luck,' as at gambling; and also as being a sure method of getting rid of a venereal disease [!]. I have, however, during the years in which I lived in Harlem, in New York, in the late 1930's, more than once heard a Negro prostitute add to the usual *"Change your luck, white boy?"* invitation, the additional promise: *"You don't have to touch no two-dollar bill with me."* Meaning, of course, that the price would be only one dollar.

Among the allusions to the two-dollar price: *Two male deers see two females by the edge of the forest. One of the male deers says to the other, "Wanna pick up a little doe?" One of the female deers asks the other, "Howja like to make a coupla bucks?"* (N.Y. 1936. This has been used in various humorous cartoons, as two jokes, the second part sometimes showing two Indian squaws talking about two male Indians walking by.) – 'From a soldier's letter to his young bride: "Come down next Sunday, if you possibly can – and I am short of cash, so please bring me $10." P.S. "If you can't come, send me $12." ' (Bennett Cerf, ed. *Pocket Book of War Humor*, 1943, p. 79.) This is of an unexpectedly vulgar directness, especially in the hostility expressed against the war-bride. Real soldier humor would more likely focus directly on the prostitute. *'I sez to her, "Penny for your thoughts," and she sez to me, "Penny, hell. It's two*

bucks".' (D.C. 1945, from a soldier, overheard.) – *A beggar asks
for two dollars and ten cents for a cup of coffee. "What's the
two dollars for? Coffee is only a dime!" "Can I help it if it
always makes me passionate?"* (N.Y. 1942.) There are a number
of non-erotic cleanups and buildups of this, going as high as
$200, *e.g.* to buy a suit as well as the coffee, with explanation:
"I can't go into Longchamps in a suit like this." (N.Y. 1952.) Not
presented as 'really funny,' but as unexpected or droll, without
consciousness of its being a cleanup. The flight into nonsense.

The specific resistance to the price the prostitute demands
will be the subject of the following section. There are also
generalized references to beating down the price: *'What did
the Scotchman do with his first 50-cent piece? – He married it.'*
(*Smile and the World Smiles With You*, 1948.) Or: *"No,"* she
*said indignantly, "I'm not that kind of a girl. Besides, a quarter
is not enough!"* (Roth's *Anecdota*, 1933, No. 456.) At the actual
folk-level the girl's explanatory line is usually: *"And besides, a
big red apple isn't enough!"* or *"And besides, the grass is wet!"*
(N.Y. 1936.) This harks back to the old 16th-century idea of
"giving a girl a green gown," by making love to her on the
damp grass, a hidden allusion to female immorality being
present in any reference at that period to the color *green* in
connection with a woman's clothing, as in the song "My Lady
Greensleeves."

The following has been collected concerning various American presidents beginning with Franklin D. Roosevelt. It is also
reported to exist on a printed 'novelty' card, but I have not
seen this: *The president, 'trying to get into his new secretary's
pants, explained that he usually paid $25 a crack* [!] *and asked
if it was all right with her. "Mr. President," she said, "if you
can raise my dress as high as you've raised taxes, and pull my
pants down as low as wages, and screw me as good as you've
screwed the public, you can have it free!"'* (Washington, D.C.
1951, told by a man at a bar.) Somehow connected, if only by
the theme of wilful or accidental misunderstandings, and the
crucial use of sexual terms in the sadistic sense of meaning 'to
cheat': *A Negro woman tells a bucket-shop operator that she
wants to invest fifty dollars in a stock where she is sure to get
"proper intercourse." "Oh, you mean interest," said the clerk.
"No, ah means intercourse," she insisted. "Ah's bin fucked
before."* (1:302) This female-fool theme appears again in: *A
woman who hands a twenty-dollar gold piece to a bank-teller*

*for deposit. "Been hoarding, eh?' he chaffs her. "Never mind
how I got it. Is it any good?'* (2:355, told of a buxom actress of
the 1930's, Mae West, the butt of innumerable jokes.) Also:
*Salesgirl, to a woman buying an expensive fur coat: "I'll bet
you've been hoarding for this." "Only half."* (N.Y. 1948.)

In a story under the heading of "Cash on Delivery" in the
First Series 4.V, page 253, the real point is expressed strictly by
reversal: *The secretary whose boss has given her $100 to parade
through the room in her underwear, and then $300 to undress
stark naked, is finally asked by him, "And now, how much do
you want for the monkey business?" When she says, "Just the
usual two dollars," he jumps out the window.* (N.Y. 1938.)
An even more direct expression of the theme of the secretary
or stenographer who is really an amateur prostitute: *A girl
taking a job in a office is asked by her intended employer how
much she hopes to earn. "Twenty dollars a week," she answers.
"Twenty dollars?" he says: "I'll give you that with pleasure."
"Making thirty dollars in all," she replies.* (N.Y. 1940, told by a
young woman researcher at a *Time* news-magazine Christmas
party, and collected often from other women since, sometimes
giving the punchline heavily spelled out: *'With pleasure, that
will be thirty dollars,"* or *"ten dollars more."*)

When the girl who told this story at *Time* saw me noting it
down, she asked me what I was doing and I told her I was
collecting jokes for a book – this book (and that it would
probably go in the chapter on Prostitution. She argued vehe-
mently that this was the wrong classification, and stated that
she had received offers more or less of the same kind on every
job she ever had, but did not for that reason consider herself
a prostitute. "Of course," she added, "the girl in the story *does*
give in." Other officegirls and girls working in sweat-shops or as
store-clerks have assured me that there is no girl who will not
give in "if the price is right," *i.e.* high enough. This is also the
implication of the ghastly and perverted prostitution of very
young shopgirls and actual children in the Victorian sexual
autobiography, *My Secret Life* (1888–94), but here the prices
offered are pitifully low.

The absolute and absurd minimum price of a whore, in
American humor, is ten cents (a dime) as in the dreadful story,
already given, of *the beautiful but insane girl who carries
dimes in her mouth,* doubtless symbolically. (First Series, 4.V,
page 251.) In stories about children this may be scaled down to

half: five cents (a nickel) as in the perennial favorite ending, '*What do you want for a nickel* – TURLS?' Also very much from the woman's viewpoint, with the implication of prostitution left to be understood: *The big white hen brags to the poultry-yard that her eggs sell for thirty-five cents a dozen at the market. "And how much do your eggs make, dearie?" she asks patronizingly of the little red hen. "Twenty-five cents," snaps the little red hen. "Only twenty-five cents, my dear?" "Sure. You don't catch me stretching my ass for a dime!"* (N.Y. 1948.) Consider also the very old witticism discussed under "Anti-Breast Fetichism" in chapter 12.IV.3, opposing marriage as unnecessary: *"Why buy a cow when the milk is only ten cents a quart?"* The allusion to prostitution is obvious, though many people miss it. Freud cites a Viennese witticism of the same import, also lightly disguised: *"Marriage is like an umbrella. It it rains you can always take a cab."*

Unmistakably hostile, but here as between the presumed client (the male teller of the story: the Invisible Man) and the whore: *An ignorant Polish chambermaid increases her earnings by amateur prostitution in the hotel where she works, asking twenty-five cents as her price. A big-city drummer generously gives her a dollar. Washing herself afterwards, she finds inside the condom that he has used and which has come off. "Wouldn't you just know it!" she soliloquizes, "the minute I get in the big money, I bust a gut."* (N.Y. 1953.) Again on the theme of ignorant foreign girls asking absurd prices for prostitution, but always with the implication that that is really all it is worth: '*Jones, while on a drunk, picked up a Swedish girl, and, taking her into a hallway, gave her a standing screw. When he had finished he searched in his pockets to pay the girl, and discovered to his horror that he had only a thin dime. He was very sorry, for he was really not the sort of chap to bilk a girl. So he apologized. "Sorry, girlie," he said, "all I got is a dime." The girl hesitated a moment, then said, "Ay bane sorry too. (Or: Do it couple more times.) Ay bane got no change".*' (1:453.)

This is connected with various stories of: *The man who forgets himself on his wedding morning and leaves two silver dollars behind the clock on the mantlepiece, tiptoeing away while his bride is asleep. Realizing his error, he rushes back only to find her sitting up in bed, biting shrewdly, 'with a distressing air of experience,' at one of the coins.* (After a poem by Thomas Burke.) In a closer form: *The bridegroom is telling a friend of the terrible mistake he has made, giving his bride a five-dollar bill on their wedding morning. "Oh, don't think anything of it," says the friend. "Tell her it was for groceries. It could happen to anybody." "I suppose so. But what really bothers me is, she gave me three dollars change."* (N.Y. 1939.) In another form, far more aggressive on both sides, the pose of error is suddenly dropped: *When the husband, a returning soldier, accidentally leaves a dollar for his wife, he attempts to brazen it out by telling her it's a habit he picked up with the whores in France. She gives him back fifty cents, saying contemptuously: "I only charge half-price to members of the family!"* (L.A. 1968. In some versions she takes a whole roll of half-dollars out of a drawer.)

Less hateful, but equally exploitative: *A Negro girl has just prostituted herself for the first time, for which she has received a shiny new dime. Stepping off a curb she sees the reflection of her cunt in a puddle, and says happily, "There you is, you l'il ol' money-maker!"* (*Anecdota Americana*, 1934, 2:48, with frontispiece illustration.) One wouldn't perhaps call the joke that follows the British version of the one just told, but that is how it was given to me: *Three girls are "trading" on Piccadilly. One earned £5 the first day. The second earned fifty shillings, but she also stole the man's pocket-watch and got £1.10 for it at the sheeney's* [Jewish pawnshop]. *When the third and youngest met the others and they asked what her takings were, she said: "How much are forty-eight tuppences?"* (London, 1954, from an American tourist, who also told the one before.) An English painter present at the same session said he had heard the joke about the tuppences, and suggested there might be a pun involved on 'tup,' the British dialectal word for the intercourse of rams and he-goats. This seems a bit strained. A final "dime" joke, which I am going to break down and admit I told at the same session, though it is hardly more than a riddling pun: *"Why didn't the Yank buy the little doggie in the pet-shop window, the one with the waggley tail? – Because he'd spent his last dime on the pussy in the doorway."* The young lady I was with said later that she was furious with me about this, and considered it a reflection on herself. Which shows that you can't be too careful about the unconscious elements in telling jokes. Especially other people's unconscious elements.

Finally, there are Rousseau's noble savages, who do not

understand money and will presumably not allow their sexual lives to be sullied by its touch. That is the message, purposely denied by the action of the joke already given, of: *The Indian girl who will not accept money, but who asks for a pair of red beaded moccasins. During their lovemaking the white man feels her waving her legs wildly in the air. "You like it, huh?" grins the white man. "Ugh," she agrees, "squaw tryum on moccasins."* (Minneapolis, 1935, and very often collected since, almost identically.) Though this is now obviously naturalized in America – in fact almost native – the fact is that a Near-Eastern version will be found given in French in Jean Nicolaïdès' *Contes licencieux de Constantinople* (Kleinbronn, 1906) p. 169, "Les Chaussures," giving the man the final line: *That she will not use up many shoes that way.* This also appears in various older English jestbooks.

In a cruder approach, the tellers of jokes admit that even the noble savages will, on occasion, accept money. *A tenderfoot out west, hard-up for a woman, is told to go out to the Indian camp and lay his penis on a tree-stump with a silver dollar beside it, and that a squaw will eventually come along and "fix him up." He sits two hours with his penis and silver dollar on the stump, without any squaw coming along. Finally, a tall old Indian brave comes along, wrapped in a blanket. (In other versions this is a Paris gendarme, whores in Montmartre, etc.) He stops, examines the situation very carefully, sits down next to the white man, puts another dollar on the stump, takes out his own penis – which is a good deal longer than the white man's – and walks off with both dollars.* (D.C. 1945.)

This interesting story, which will come up again in another context, and which listeners of both sexes seem to find hilarious, involves an important mechanism in humor, seldom seen in so easily graspable form. It is the *shifting of identification* in the course of the joke – something that does not happen in listening to folktales without these sudden reversals, 'switches,' and punchlines – while the joke-listener strives always for the morally or emotionally best position available, as in a game of "Musical Chairs." At the opening of this particular story, the listener *is* the poor tenderfoot suffering from sexual privation. That he is, for all his pitifulness, socially much the superior of the Indians he intends to exploit sexually, in the crudest possible gesture-language, is accepted by the listener merely as a matter of course: the social scene or background.

Suddenly, however, with the irruption of the 'tall old Indian brave' upon the ludicrous and vaguely castratory situation in which the white man has got himself, with his penis on the stump, it becomes clear that some other interpretation of the scene is possible than the sexual exploitation of the red-skinned woman (or the Paris whore) by the white-skinned American. Before the joke is ended, the 'successful' listener must manage to *become* the Indian brave, and now triumphs over the exploitative white, who is also (as it were) castrated as well, by turning out to have a shorter penis – *i.e.* less sexual strength – than his intended racial cuckold. The 'unsuccessful' or non-competitive listener would be one who does not drop his original identification and native loyalty fast enough, and take up the new one by 'identification with the enemy;' and who thus finds himself suddenly and unexpectedly the real butt of the joke. (This is probably the type of masochistic listener who laughs the hardest, because it is at himself.) Here, in perfectly exposed form, is seen the duel between the wily teller and the unwary listener.

2. RESISTANCE TO PAYING (BILKING)

The largest number of jokes on prostitution turn on the male client's resistance to paying the prostitute's fee, often by trickster subterfuges. This is also implicit in the concern, in the jokes already given, as to just how low a price the prostitute can be had for. Where possible, the prostitute's clients are also often shown, in the older tales, running off without paying, and thus *bilking* the whore: a word now seldom used in any other connection. The whore also is said to bilk the client if she runs off after having been paid beforehand, without giving him satisfaction. This was once a common theme of comedy, but is now almost unknown at the level of prostitution, though it is the whole and basic activity of the 'cock-teaser' (French: *allumeuse*), or '*demi-vierge*,' so well known and so much complained of in Western society – this is now actually fading – among girls who do not consider themselves prostitutes at all. Almost the only surviving joke on the 'bilking whore,' presents the situation as a drunken accident, or the humor-of-nonsense. '*An American airman is standing on a street-corner eating fish & chips, with his cock hanging out. Up comes a policeman who takes him to task for indecent exposure. Yank: "Whaddayer mean –?" Looks down at himself: "Well, whaddayer know!*

Shucks goddammer, she's gone!"' (London, 1953, with the ludicrous American dialect in the British informant's spelling.) In an American variant, seen from the opposite point of view : *A prostitute is being arrested for indecent exposure, having been found lying on the ground in the park with her legs spread and her dress up. She looks up at the policeman bleary-eyed and confused. "Is the gentleman gone?" she asks.* (N.Y. 1955.)

The unbusinesslikeness of the profession of prostitution is considered very amusing by men. *At a fire in the whorehouse, the Madam screams: "Where's that wench with the towels? If she's gone, my accounting system is shot to hell!"* (N.Y. 1948. 'Wench' is a U.S. southernism, originally British, but no longer surviving in Britain, for a Negro serving- or cleaning-woman of any age. I have heard it used as far north as Somerville, New Jersey, 1943, for a Negro woman over sixty years old.) This joke is bloated up almost to book length, in William Bradford Huie's *The Revolt of Mamie Stover*, on wartime prostitution in the Pacific, reprinted in part from the *American Mercury* (Jan. 1951).

A roomful of Jews are discussing what business is best. Finally one bearded old man says, "Let's stop lying to each other. The nafkeh-byiss [whore-house] *business is the best: They got it – they sell it – they still got it." "What are you saying?!" cries another horrified old man. "What am I saying? I'm saying: no overhead, no upkeep, no inventory. Who can beat it?"* (N.Y. 1952, told in heavy dialect but with only the single Yiddish word given. Another version adds the merely verbal topper, " – *Yes, and it's all* wholesale*!"*) Collected the following year, sadly reduced to a poor pun: *An Italian gangster building a fancy whore-house in Chicago tells the architect he wants it all built on the ground floor, "so there'll be no fucking overhead."* (Chicago, 1953.) Compare a story known equally in England and America, in which, again, a sexualized interest in money is attributed to the comedy Jew, complete with gestures: '*A Jewish textile merchant instructing his growing son in the uses of the fingers of the hand in the business. The thumb and first finger (gesture of rubbing these together) are used for feeling the quality of the cloth. The baby finger is for cocking for tea-drinking. (Gesture.) The third finger is to scratch the head with. (Gesture.) But the middle and longest finger is the most important, and that gives the greatest pleasure of all: it's the one used for pressing the till-key.*'

(London, 1953.) In the American version the direction of the final gesture is reversed: '*The middle finger is the best of all: that's for your competitors. (Gesture of the finger rising in the air with a reaming motion.)*' (From a tourist arriving from New York, 1974.)

The implication is always present in jokes that the prostitute knows very well how to make love, even at the beginning of her professional career, but that learning how to make the profession unemotional and lucrative is her main problem. (As Dr. Beigel elegantly remarks, in *Sex from A to Z*, 1961, p. 307: 'Prostitution is not a profession that one chooses for an occupation. Most girls slip into it gradually.') *An experienced prostitute tells a younger beginner that the moment to ask men for money is "when their eyes go glassy." The next day she asks the beginner how she made out. "Rotten," says the beginner; "when their eyes go glassy, I go stone-blind!"* (1 : 183.) This girl is too *engagée*. Compare the British story, turning on a verbal play of the same kind: '*Chap who died "on the job." His widow-wife reports to the enquiring doctor: "It was like this – he had me gasping – I thought he was coming – he was grunting – I was coming – then up went his eyes and he was going!"*' (London, 1953.) The same word-play often appears spontaneously on the phrase, "not to know whether one is coming or going."

In another form, the problem is stated as simply one of stupidity, on the pattern of the female fool, or of foolish literalism. *A Swedish girl, who is trying to become an amateur prostitute, tells another girl her troubles. In the morning when she has said to the man, ' "Giff me fife dollars, or ten maybe," he bane say, "go take a good shit for yourself." Und when aye coom back, he bane gone".*' (1 : 169.)

Not actually about prostitutes but unmistakably intended to assimilate the kept-women present to that group, through the continuous cheapening of price: *In a first-class railroad compartment two beautifully dressed ladies are discussing clothes while a gentleman in the corner pretends to be asleep. When one lady says she finds the cost of clothes impossible nowadays, the other suggests she should follow her example and take a boy-friend on the side: 'He'll give you five hundred a month for a little present – your husband would never do that." "But what if I can't get a friend with five hundred dollars?" "Then take two with two hundred and fifty each." The gentleman speaks up: "Listen, ladies, I'm going to sleep now. Wake me up when you get down to twenty bucks."* (Cannes, France, 1969. Probably of continental origin.)

The variety of approaches to the client's objection to the prostitute's price, no matter how low this price may be, leaves only one conclusion possible: he wants it to be *free, i.e.* 'for love, not money.' In the impossibility of having the whore fall in love with him on a moment's notice, he responds with immediate hatred (matching her evident hatred), and tries to bilk her, or at least to beat her down or denigrate her charms, or otherwise resist and evade the essential question of payment. '*A pimp was trying to interest a Scotchman in some whores, naming their various prices. At last he said, "Now, with this one here, you get a bottle of bourbon thrown in – all for $2." The Scotchman looked the girl over carefully, and asked: "Pint or quart?"* (Los Angeles, 1941.) The Scotchman as comedy cheapskate is obviously dragged in here bodily: bourbon (corn whisky) is typically an American alcoholic drink. The British version has: *The pimp chalking up a mysterious sign composed of four capital B's. He explains to the prospect that this stands for what he peddles: Blondes, Brunettes, Beer, and Bed. "Bottle or draft?" the prospect inquires.* (London 1946, from a stage-entertainer.)

Resistance to paying turns rapidly to direct complaints that the prostitute's activity is not worth the money, as in the examples above, or to even more insulting complaints that her vagina is too large and 'fucked out.' This is a standard complaint also made against wives, but in this case on the explanation that they have been made 'too roomy' by bearing children. This is equally open to the riposte that it is not the bore of the vagina that is at fault, but the calibre of the penis, *i.e.* that the man is 'too small' or plainly impotent: Mistress Kate's final twit against all men before she knuckles under to her husband in Shakespeare's *Taming of the Shrew,* V.ii.169: "Come, come, you froward and unable worms!" – *A street-whore accosts a passerby late at night, asking two dollars and trying to excite him by showing him her genitals under a lonely street light. "It's very nice," he says politely, "but haven't you something smaller for about a dollar?"* (N.Y. 1939.) – *A man tries to beat down a chorus-girl's price from the five dollars she demands, but she snarls, "I'd rather sew it up than do it for less!" "Go ahead, says the man, "it could use a couple of stitches."* (1:292.) For the whole subject of female circumcision and infibulation, both anthropological and in the folklore avatar of the mythical 'chastity belts' and of the female Struwwelpeter whose *mouth* is sewed up for lying, or the lips held shut with a padlock (Pinocchio, the little wooden boy whose *nose* grows phallically long for lying), see the extended notes in the First Series, 6.VI, pages 382–9.

Occasionally the prostitute's genitals are actually assaulted, as by the man who, at the high prices demanded, is *"going to make his own hole."* Hardly more than a curleycue allusion or code-reference to the ghastly reality of lust-murders like those of 'Jack the Ripper' (Dr. Alexander Pedachenko, a Ukrainian physician in London, during the late 19th century, who used a woman accomplice as decoy and was never caught until he returned to Russia). Mere bilking is also an excuse : *'Two prosses have two blokes, and compare notes next morning. – "Mine must've been a gardener: an earwig fell out of his foreskin." Second: "Mine was a barstard. Had it in, as I thought, all night. Told me he'd pay me when we woke up. In the morning I wake up alone with a soda-bottle up me arse, with two marbles rattling in it".'* (Chelmsford, Essex, 1954.)

Nothing is more obvious than that what every man wants from any prostitute is to offer to give it to him *free.* 'For love.' I once heard an undersized American movie-agent in Paris, working for various American firms and married to a superbly beautiful American woman who had been a secretary in one of the firms, confide to a handsome young Lothario, when all three of us were driving to a studio conference on the Champs-Elysées, *"Yeah, I got three dames on Pigalle absolutely nuts about me. Met 'em when we were doing a location thing on* Moulin Rouge. *They give me anything I want – free – tongue-up-the-ass, anything! Free! They wanna give me money, work for me. It happens to me like that all the time." "What do you say to them?" said the Lothario, who had nearly wrecked the car trying to keep from laughing, while he looked over the little guy's head at me in stupefaction. "I just laugh at 'em," said the agent calmly. "After all, I got my pick of the stars."* (Paris, 1955.) This man, later the same day, furiously walked out of a restaurant where a party of six of us were eating dinner, when I bought roses from an itinerant old woman vendor, and insisted on pinning one myself on his lovely wife's blouse, hoking it up that I was going to smell the rose after it was pinned on.

*A wizened little client in a fancy whorehouse is heard shout-
ing from the upper floor, "No! Not that why! I want it MY way.
The way we do it in Brooklyn. So quit it! Do it MY way, or
forget it!" The madam climbs the stairs and erupts into the girl's
room. "What's the matter with you, Zelda?" she says. "Give it
to him his way."* She leaves, the girl lies down, and the man
makes love to her in perfectly routine fashion. *She sits up, puts
on her dressing gown, lights a cigarette, and says, "That's your
way, Hymie, huh?" "That's it," he says proudly from the bed.
"That's how you do it in Brooklyn?" "Right you are!" "So
what's so different about it?" "In Brooklyn I get it for nothing!"*
(N.Y. 1938, told in Yiddish accent by the main erotica publisher
of the period.) In *World's Dirtiest Jokes* (1969), this is given in
three different versions, the only joke so honored, pp. 89, 95,
and 98; the last being the above original version, as "the *Lower
East Side Way*," which is working awfully hard to say the
word 'Jewish' without coming out and pronouncing it. In one
of these variants, *The madam says to the girl, ' "Tell me, Sherry,
how does he want it? Against the wall? In the bathtub? On the
carpet? Bottoms up?" Sherry replied, "No, he runs the popcorn
stand on the corner, and he wants it for PEANUTS!"'*

3. FRAME-SITUATION: 'NO MONEY'

Supplied with the sardonic notation, "Short and sweet," the
following joke poses the classic situation, and the even more
classic sort of moral or sentimental excuse used to cover it,
since money is seldom really all that short and scarce as pretended: *'Tough Old Bag [whore]: "You want to come up and
see me? It's five bucks." Very Moral Young Man: "I'm sorry,
Madam, there are three reasons why I can't. First, I don't have
the five dollars –" Tough Old Bag: "Stick the other two reasons
up your ass!"'* (Cleveland, Ohio, 1939.) Perhaps what she does
not want to hear, under the pretexts of morals, aesthetics,
religion, being married, fear of disease, and the like, is the *real*
reason she is being rejected: namely, that she is Tough, Old
and a Bag. Often, rather than bargain, the man states simply
that he does not have the price the prostitute demands, but does
not reject her, and asks what she will agree to give him for less.
A famously mocking example: *A workingman accosted by a
streetwalker tells her that he has no money at all on him, but
asks if she will take him on for nearly two dollars' credit left
on a half-used meal-ticket on a restaurant nearby. She agrees*

to give him a blow-job for the meal-ticket, and kneels down on the ground before him. Suddenly, just as she is clamping her mouth down on his penis, she stops, looks up, and says out of one corner of her mouth: "Say, is that a CLEAN *place?"* (N.Y. 1940, told by a six-foot Irishman with a great reputation among the women, who enthusiastically pantomimed the final line and the woman's mouth on the man's penis.)

Both this joke and that following are essentially "Food-Dirtying" (12.IV.2, below under "Narsty-Narsties"). *A man is accosted by a woman late at night, but has only fifty cents which she says is not enough. He asks her if she will go down a dark alley with him and piss in an old tin can for the fifty cents, and she agrees. He then swishes his penis around in the tin can, saying, "Take soup, you son-of-a-bitch; meat is too expensive!"* (2 : 126.) The address to one's own genitals, which has already been seen in the ignorant girl who calls her vulva her 'little ol' money-maker,' is connected by reversal with the theme of the speaking genitals or '*pudenda loquens*,' than which it is thought somewhat less magical or incredible. Both equally endow the sexual organs with independent life and senses, especially with the ability to speak. This is made much of in Philip Roth's *Portnoy's Complaint* (1968), in which the speaking penis, inciting the young boy to sexual adventures including religious 'miscegenation,' is assimilated to the traditional Jewish *yetzer ha-rá*, or Evil Spirit, presumably the voice of the Devil, as with the serpent-penis tempting Eve in the Garden of Eden.

The *locus classicus* on speaking sexual organs is certainly the great conference and battle preparation of the assembled sexual organs and anuses, about to declare war on each other in Vignali's *La Cazzaria* (1530), a most remarkable work of folk-humor of which an English translation has been issued in rather crude form as *Dialogue on Diddling* by 'Sir Hotspur Dunder-pate' (City of Industry, California : Collectors Publications, 1968). In a less graphic version of the preceding situation : '*Eager to "change his luck" a white man approached a negress. "Ah charges two dollars," said the black whore,' but the white man refuses at that price, and also at a dollar. ' "Well, then," said the negress, "yo' can have it fo' fifty cents, but at fifty cents ah'm losin' money".'* (Provenance unknown, before 1940.) Verbally this is of course wittier than the other, but just as clearly lacks the real vitality of the essentially hateful situation. When I lived for many years at the edge of Harlem in

New York, during the 1930's, one would overhear much more brutal offers and exploitations of Negro prostitutes by white customers at any hour – particularly late at night – than the mere 'chiselling' on price suggested in these jokes. The girls would sometimes have to agree to accept some second-hand article of the men's clothing, such as a necktie or belt, "*if it'll fit my man.*"

When the man is not actually hard-up for money, what is involved in the recourse of white men to Negro prostitutes is the form of impotence called by Freud "The Most Prevalent Form of Degradation in Erotic Life," the title of one of his most important essays. In this he shows that where the Oedipus complex overwhelms the man with fear of approaching or marrying women reminding him too much of the mother he loves, he is likely to be impotent with such women, and potent only with women as far as possible removed from his real mother-ideal. That is to say, with women who are ugly or dirty or of a completely different racial or national group: Negro women or Jewesses for white Protestant men; Christian women (especially 'dirty blondes') for Jews, and so forth. This has been taken the whole distance, with horrendous examples showing how it works, in Philip Roth's best-selling *Portnoy's Complaint* (1968), which is cast in the form of the patient's self-related confession or anamnesis, presumably at the beginning of the psychoanalysis of a man suffering massively from this type of impotence, and responding in the fashion just described. This naturally wowed the chumps, who see themselves only-too-well mirrored, but conveniently disguised, in the ugly confession put by Philip Roth in the mouth of his doubtless imaginary Jewish square, or NJB ('Nice Jewish Boy'), matching the WASP or 'White Anglo-Saxon Protestant' who is the reader.

The obvious source of Roth's inspiration is Saul Bellow's similar but less gruesome epic of Jewish self-hatred, *Herzog* (1964), whose malady is nothing more shocking than writing long, complaining letters which he never mails. (Mr. Bellow pointedly disclaims any credit for the parentage of Roth's *Portnoy* in "Are the Miracles Ended?" in the *Jerusalem Post Weekly*, 13 July 1970, p. 14.) In any case, the prize item in the Jewish self-dirtying sweepstakes is Prof. Karl Shapiro's gruellingly masochistic novel *Edsel* (New York, 1971), in which, however, the hilarious send-up of the India-inspired 'modern'

Jewish poet – obviously intended as Allen Ginsberg – in chapter 15, is worth the price of admission. All the rest is a nightmare.

In the miscegenational department, Robert Gover's *The Hundred-Dollar Misunderstanding* (1964) and its sequels are solidly based on supplying to the white reader the *frisson* of the square hero (in this case a Christian) who shacks up with a Negro prostitute. Further on this subject, see the far more sincere and more bitter 'black humor' of Chester Himes' *Pink-toes*, originally published in Paris in 1961 in the Olympia porno-graphica series, though it is simply a plain-talking satirical indictment of Negro-White sexual relations. (This gives some idea of what the literary repression still repressed in the early 1960's, when the New Freedom for publishing in America was only beginning to get under weigh.) A brief selection from Himes' book, giving something of the bitter tone of the original, is reprinted in the Paris publisher's, Maurice Girodias' *Olympia Reader* (New York: Grove Press, 1965) p. 598–623, with a biographical note on this remarkable writer.

In at least one joke the standard anti-Negro situation is varied, and the sexual attractiveness of the Negro woman to white men is vindicated. This is, of course, not secret, when the woman is 'not too dark,' but it is seldom mentioned in American folklore. *An American in Paris visits the famous House of All Nations, where he is particularly captivated by a fine Negro woman, but as she is the belle of the establishment he cannot afford her fee, and has to settle for a Chinese girl for two dollars less. Years later he meets his son by this encounter, who asks him, after the mutual introductions are over: "Say, Dad, why is your skin so white and mine so yellow?" "You little bastard, if I'd had two dollars more you'd have been black."* (2:216.) This is certainly a Negro revindication, the situation being absurd, of the Chinese prostitute's son not know-ing that his mother was Chinese. In the hegemony of skin-color relationships, the Negro in America consistently considers him-self or herself superior to the 'Chinee laundryman.'

A whole sociological study remains to be made (of which Jan Harold Brunvand has made a beginning in his study of con-temporary jokes, in *Fabula*, 1972, vol. XIII: p. 7–9) of the Negroes' own self-hating concern with the whiteness or black-ness of skin-color, and with the gradation of tone between. as seen in the perfectly improbable range of color-adjectives de-scribing the various skin-tones of Negro society women in the

Negro picture-magazines, ranging from 'honey-brown' to 'peach-lavender,' and beyond. The implication is always, of course, that the lightest tones (and least Negroid features) are the best. At these levels, the new motto of the Negro militants, *"Black is beautiful!"* has not yet worked its leaven. Even at the militant level, too, what still often seems to be meant is really: *"Whitey is shit!"* Meanwhile, the hair-straightening 'de-kinking' preparations still sell by the millions of bottles yearly to American Negroes.

Lower than the wrong or 'bad' race, there can only be the wrong or bad aperture, or even animal. *'A white man bargained with an Indian squaw for a piece of ass, offering only a bag of corn as the price. He found her in her tent lying on her stomach, and when he asked her to turn over she said, "Front hole, money hole. Back hole, corn hole!"'* (D.C. 1944, from a soldier; also from another soldier within a year, but with no reference to Indians, the girl being simply 'a country girl' in a barn.) This joke is in part a jocular attempt to folk-etymologize the mysterious American term *'corn-hole'* or *'corn-haul,'* a verb meaning to pedicate, especially as homosexual rape; still understood but not much heard since the 1940's. The joke is also not specially American, except for its vocabulary when told as above. British form: *'Woman pays for coal on bed. One day the coal man brings nutty slack* [U.S., slag], *so she turns her back to him with the comment: "Large coal: front hole. Nutty slack: arsehole".'* (*Union Jack*, MS. Chelmsford, Essex, 1953.)

The anus is naturally a lower or subsidiary *gentillesse* on the part of the whore. *The Limerick* (1953) Note 1035, quotes a curious passage touching upon this, a: 'Chinatown price-list from Herbert Asbury's *The Barbary Coast* (1933) p. 177: *"Two bittee lookee, flo bittee feelee, six bittee dooee!"* (a bit being an imaginary American coin worth $12\frac{1}{2}$ cents), *preceded by "China girl nice! You come inside, please?" to which is invariably added ... this extraordinary information, seldom, if ever, correct: "Your father, he just go out!"'* To this Asbury adds the pre-analytic note: 'Some of the Chinese considered it an honor to possess a woman whom their fathers had also possessed.' (See the opposite position in Anglo-Saxon folk-attitudes, in the story told as true of Sir Walter Raleigh and his son in Aubrey's *Brief Lives*, MS. 1680, quoted in full in the First Series, 9.III, pages 743–4, under "Possession in Common.") *The Limerick* adds: 'Apocryphal Shanghai brothel-sign: *"Sholt-time piecee –*

1 buck Mex. Longtime piecee – 1 buck 'Melican. Ass-hole flee if stay all night".' (From the American erotic artist, Mahlon Blaine.) There is a lower possibility too: *A man in a cheap whorehouse refuses all the whores offered by the madam, in descending order of price, and finally admits he only has fifty cents. "Mac," she calls to the bouncer, "grease up the cat's ass!"* (N.Y. 1958.) Also with the punch-line: *"Albert, see if anybody's using the skunk."* Anti-woman in every possible implied comparison.

The cheapening of price taints everyone connected with prostitution. A World War I joke: *The scene is Hyde Park in London, at 9 P.M. A young man gets into a taxicab with a girl, saying to the chauffeur, "Just drive us a couple of times around the Park, very slowly!" Chauffeur: "I ain't got much petrol, Guv'nor, so if it's all the same to you, supposin' we stays 'ere? I'd make a reduction."* (Kimbo, *Tropical Tales*, Nice, 1925, p. 68.) The joke has earlier been given about: *The child who steps on a man's back in the dark, and a woman's voice cries, "Thank you!"* Applied to the present subject this turns into: *'Sambo was jes' teasin' Mandy, pushing it up a little at a time; but she was charging him $1.00 an inch. Then along comes a fool niggah, gooses him and runs his bill up to $9.00.'* (Fredericksburg, Virginia, 1952.) Supplied by an American folklorist, the late Josiah Combs, who explained that this is actually only the end of a joke explaining: *Why one Negro has cut up another Negro with a straight razor.* These combined stereotypes, of the Negro's very long penis – and the razor – will be returned to in Chapter 13 below.

Explanations are sometimes demanded, or seem in order, as to precisely why one prostitute should be 'worth' more than another, when *"the work is always pretty much the same."* In ornate form: *'Visiting the negro [sic] quarter of Chicago, a travelling man accosted a neat looking wench [colored girl] and asked her what she charged. "My charges," said the girl, "is one dollar, two, and five dollars." "Why the different prices?" the horny stranger asked. "Well," said the negress, "for one dollar you gets a straight fuck. For two dollars ah also fucks. But for five dollars, ah makes a perfect fool of mahself".'* (1:258.) Also collected without any mention of race: *"I got three prices,"* says the prostitute: *"twenty-five cents, fifty cents, and a dollar. For twenty-five cents you do all the work. For fifty cents I cooperates a little. But for a dollar, all you got to do is* HANG ON!*"* (N.Y. 1942.)

What is meant here is to allude humorously to what is, for the proud male, the sorest point of all about prostitution: that the paid prostitute's 'simulated enthusiasm,' and even her pre-tended orgasm, are strictly conformable to the amount of money she is paid. In recent years the tough or 'beatnik' and 'hippie' types of amateur or semi-prostitutes do not engage in this pretense, but their sour, hostile pose is acceptable only to the unvirile and masochistic or semi-homosexual type of chump who is their perfect psychological and sociological match, as I have tried to show in *Love & Death* (1949) p. 79, in "Avatars of the Bitch-Heroine." In an article on modern American street-prostitution, published in a men's magazine, this kind of beatnik prostitute has been depicted as a mere 'street cocksucker' by Miss Valerie Solanas, never-to-be-forgotten authoress of the one sincerest modern cry of man-hating, in the *SCUM Manifesto* (New York: Olympia Press, 1967) of her own private *Society for Cutting Up Men*. This was the most embarrassingly candid of the modern Women's Liberation statements of the 1960's, after which, in fact, there was nothing left to say. Actually, Miss Solanas should have all our gratitude for her ballsy honesty – infinitely more than that of many men.

As to the tough young prostitute, amateur or hobo, it is now perfectly well understood at many levels that this type of Angry Young Woman in pants has now become a social plague and a personal disaster to herself and everyone whose life she touches. The Western world will soon have to deal on a very large scale with the problem of what to do with this type of wasted human life, in what could be its finest women. The girl or young woman of this kind is typified by an extreme form of what Wilhelm Reich brilliantly called 'character armor': in this case her sullen, bitchy look, oral twitching and demand-ing (usually badly repressed), her swaggering or slouching walk and stance, posing as though ready to shoot from the groin, often with her arms defensively crossed over her breasts, and her icebound orgastic impotence or almost-total frigidity. Also by the string of unvirile males who dance attendance on her – she sees to that by abbreviating her relationship with any one, out of fear that love or tenderness might develop, and to insure that the relationship is always one of competition and domina-tion – these usually dressed in almost the identical dirty pants and disorderly haircut. Most of these young women prefer fellation to vaginal coitus, which latter they identify unconsciously as a domination or rape-assault upon them by the man. This represents a very large part of the sexual aspect of the current hippie scene in many countries. And the end is not yet ... !

Numerous jokes on prostitution show an attempt at modern de-personalization of the situation, by having everything and everyone done in figures, numbers, graded levels and other forms of 'socially sadistic' control, organization, and subdivision to infinity. Finally even in little printed *signs*, which all somehow have the power of so many machine-guns trained on the helpless social victims. This is *'technosis,'* the disease of the IBM-Hollerith punched-hole system of *dealing with human beings as though they were things.* It is also the most dangerous of all modern infectious social diseases, similar to the mere gonorrheic and endemic pose of *'cool,'* and developing parallel to it, since these too are a perfect and inevitable match. (See further, *"Cool* as the New Venereal Disease," in my *The Fake Revolt,* 1967, p. 22–32.) *A man enters a modern Chicago whorehouse-nightclub run by the gangland "Syndicate," which is now planning to "streamline its image." The whorehouse takes up various floors of a skyscraper hotel, and he is received by a lovely young receptionist in a sexy uniform, who sits him at a teakwood interview desk and asks how much money he wants to spend. She explains that prices range from $5 up to $1000, depending on the quality and number of girls wanted. Everything is shown on the television intercom. The higher prices are for the lower floors, which have higher ceilings, mirrors over the beds, three and four girls in bed with you at one time, etc. Lower prices are for lesser delights, ending with $5 for "A coal-black nigger mammy with big nostrils," as the lovely young receptionist explains, with a significant wriggle of her eyebrows. The client thinks it over. "Haven't you anything cheaper than five dollars?" he asks at last. "Of course," says the receptionist, "seventh floor – roof-garden. One dollar a shot. Self-service."* (N.Y. 1963.) Told by a young woman even more beautiful than the receptionist described. In some versions there is no receptionist-madam: only marked elevator buttons.

A British version at the same period comes closer to the format of the ubiquitous intrusive government 'questionnaire': *'Chap goes to a brothel. Opens doors into passage, at end of which are two doors, on one of which is marked* MARRIED, *and on the other* SINGLE. *Chap chooses* SINGLE, *and finds himself in another passage with two doors, marked* EXPERIENCED *and* IN-EXPERIENCED. *Entering by the door marked* INEXPERIENCED *he finds himself in yet another corridor with two doors marked* UNDER 5 INCHES *and* OVER 5 INCHES. *Opening the former, he finds himself in the street.'* (Chelmsford, Essex, 1953.) The usual form of this now collected in America generally concerns: *A man going to a Mayo Clinic type of assembly-line psychoanalytic institute. The last two doors are marked* INCOMES UNDER $10,000 A YEAR *and* INCOMES OVER $10,000 A YEAR. (N.Y. 1965.)

In only one story is the question of price, and the situation of no-money or not-enough-money – or, "Goddamit, I've *got* the money, but I just hate to have to give it for sex" – apparently solved to the man's satisfaction. *A man in a whorehouse craftily asks for an hourly rate. "Alright, a dollar an hour," says the madam. Later the girl complains, "Some cheap shit! He fucked me four times in fifteen minutes, and then gave me a quarter!"* (N.Y. 1943.) Compare William Bradford Huie's *The Revolt of Mamie Stover* (1951), already mentioned, on wartime prostitution to American soldiers, touching on situations of this type but very glozingly presented. In a merely verbal British joke, the client finally refuses even the rock-bottom price, by means of the standard humor techniques of "Literalism" and "Propositions in Error," covered in the First Series in the sections "Bloody Englishmen," and following, 2.VI.2–4, and 4.I.2. *A chap rushes into a grocer's and asks for some rock salt. Girl behind the counter: "We haven't any loose salt right now, sir, but you can have a block for 4d." He: "Don't fuck about – my chimney's on fire!"* (London, 1954.)

The hostility of the client against the prostitute is always greater in jokes than that which the prostitute is allowed, and this will be seen even more strikingly in the section "Oragenital Acts," below. This is the opposite of the real situation, in unspoken fact, where the prostitute is generally seething with carefully hidden hatred of her clients, who damn her to a mockery of her sex life and to the thousand-time-repeated defeat of frigid coitus, without orgasm for her, in which she has the added humiliation of having to *fake it!* The jokes thus, as it were, allow the clients the last hateful word. *A farmer visits an expensive brothel in the big city, and is surprised at the price of twenty dollars. "Gosh," he says, "down on the farm it's only fifty cents, and they put a towel across the bottom of the bed so you don't have to take off your boots." "Get out of here, you cheap appleknocker!" screams the madam, "before I have the bouncer put a dent in your head!" "Now look here, lady," replies the farmer with dignity; "don't you start gettin' so uppity about a job than kin be done just as well by a caow."* (Auribeau, France, 1956, told by an American tourist before his own party of two other middle-aged men and their three wives.)

A story popular among soldiers during World War II, but much more restrained in its expression of money-oriented hostility: *A soldier (or Scotchman) picks up a fancy whore in a bar, and takes her to a hotel room. When she insists that her price is $100, he goes into a corner and begins masturbating. The whore is amazed. "At these prices," says her client cannily, "you don't think I'm going to give you the EASY one, do you?"* (N.Y. 1940.) Appears actually to be a rationalization of the panic or temporary impotence many young men feel when faced with their first real sexual experience with a prostitute, an experience common in wartime among men who would never otherwise even consider accepting the blow to their self-esteem of *"having to pay for it."* A young white student who was taken to a reglementary 'gang-bang' of an old and distressingly ugly Negro prostitute (as discussed just above), forming the final ordeal – or reward? – of his sadistic and flagellational hazing at the quasi-military Texas "Aggie" college (Texas Agricultural and Mechanical) during the 1940's, noted that both he and several other men present had to masturbate in order 'to raise a hardon' and successfully perform. This is the opposite of the situation implied in the joke here.

All these hostilities reach their end-point where either the client or the prostitute simply bilks or otherwise cheats the other out of the intended conclusion – monetary or erotic as the case may be. *Several college professors are discussing the frigidity of prostitutes, and whether some 'auto-erotic' way might not be found to help them feel the passion they must simulate with each customer. 'The college janitor, who was standing nearby, interrupted: "You means you wants to know how to get a whore hot?" "Yes," said the professor. "To get a whore hot, real hot," said the janitor, "fuck her and don't pay her!"'* (1:56, not noting that the janitor is a Negro, as his accent would indicate.) This sort of meeting of the two presumed extremes of the intellectual scale, as represented by the college professor and (Negro) janitor, specifically at the men-among-men level of the 'bull-session' or sexual discussion and sharing of erotic lore, is also made central to an apparently serious short story by Prof. Leslie Fiedler, "The Girl in the Black Rain-coat," in *Partisan Review* (Winter, 1964/65) XXXII. 35–42, a sort of professorial kissing-&-telling also suggested in a recent fictional volume by Kingsley Amis, sometime British exchange-professor in America. At the level of obvious fiction, the same sort of bull-session is made the plot-gimmick or framework of a series of American erotic novels concerning *"The Oxford Professor"* all written about 1940, the first entitled *An Oxford Thesis on Love.*

No other story concerning prostitution and money has been so frequently collected as that which follows, and it seems clear that this particular way of cheating or exploiting the client is not altogether distasteful *to him,* and that, in fact, the story represents his wishful dream. *An American in Paris goes to an expensive bordel, where he is given his choice of ten lovely girls by the madame, who asks, "Which one would you like, or would you like them all?" He chooses six girls, and is royally entertained by them in an enormous bed all night long. When he staggers happily out the next morning and asks for his bill he is told it is all free. He hurries back the next night, and goes through the same entertainment, but this time when he makes the gesture of paying the next morning he is given a bill for seven hundred dollars, including towels. "What!?" he shouts, "yesterday it was free!" "But of course," says the madam; "yesterday was for the movies."* (N.Y. 1952, also with punch-line: *"Tuesdays we're on t.v."*) A more hostile variant, given by a young college woman in San Diego, 1964, has: *A young man who has invited a girl to his apartment and makes love to her, tells her afterward, "You have just starred on 'Meet the Public'."* [A television program.]

Too much material exists on this sort of exhibitionistic fantasy, as attemptedly translated in fact and in life, to do more than cite one or two examples, centuries apart: The French 'farmer-general,' or court-financier A. Le Riche de La Popeli-nière, in the mid-18th century, an ugly little gnome of a man who had prepared for him a unique printed copy of Crébillon's *Tableaux des Mœurs du temps* illustrated with miniatures showing himself in the process of making love to the wives of various nobles of the realm and other persons, to whom he had lent money to pay their gambling debts and so on, with interest being demanded and paid in the form of sexual services of their wives. The 'farmer-general' La Popelinière, being only a *nouveau-riche* vulgarian, he had either the bad taste or the grotesque sense of humor – or let's just call it the braggadocio, or plain perversion – to hide his staff portrait-artist, Marolles, behind a screen in the bedchamber (if he had to hide), there to sketch recognizably the ladies blackmailed into bed in a variety of extravagant positions. (See further my *The Horn Book*, 1964, p. 107–8, on the fortunes of this unique copy, sold at auction for over $30,000, in Paris, 30 November 1973, by the Librairie Giraud-Badin, no. 128 of the printed catalogue, reproducing in color one of the milder illustrations.) This is rather close to the fantasy of the present joke.

By far the most successful spy-fantasy movie of the 1960's, *From Russia with Love*, in the enormously popular cold-killer 'James Bond' series, was a sensational piece in technicolor with unpleasantly obvious concentration on scenes of pyromania and fire-fetichism. In this the redoubtable spy is invariably played as a male sex-job who gets the women he seduces to do most of the real spying and hard work. (In the later *Goldfinger* they are also killed in his stead.) At one point he is to be blackmailed by having erotic movies made of him in bed with the beautiful lady-stooge or inside agent at the Russian embassy, the films actually being shown as taken through a two-way mirror by a corps of specialists hidden behind the headboard of the huge bed. Contemptuous of such attempted blackmail, he merely tosses the 'incriminating' films into the lagoon at Venice. This is the only elegant touch in any of the 'James Bond' movies which are, otherwise, essentially only photographic comic-books, as is particularly obvious in *Goldfinger*.

This series is the best example of the current and dangerous sexual perversion of the media, exactly in the way that Aldous Huxley in his prophetic *Brave New World* (1932) foretold: the combination of the old sadism of the Roman circuses with the 'New Freedom' for sexuality, in an irreversibly perverted form. Audiences in Western society are just as repressed and excitable about their hostilities as they are about sex, perhaps more so. Any kind of public cruelty and horror – especially as now tittivated up with full-color sex, and broadcast to hundreds of millions of people in the lightning-flash of t.v. – can easily be made their favorite dish. The exploitation of war-horrors and assassinations for public consumption has already shown how far the public is willing to be led in this direction. And would finally watch with delight, on closed-circuit television, their own world and themselves go up in flames. With or without nude orgies for background.

As it used to be my own foolish whim to tell nosey people, who would ask how I managed to make a living in Europe, that I lived by taking infra-red erotic movies of visiting dignitaries at the motion-picture festival at Cannes, nearby, later black-mailing them with the resultant films; the following joke – which shows how the wind is really blowing in these matters – was sent to me by a friend in San Francisco, in 1958, inquiring whether or not I was perhaps its anti-hero. *An American businessman at an 'industrial fair' in a foreign city, picks up a cheap prostitute and spends three days in bed with her at his hotel, sending out for food from time to time. On his return to his respectable position in the United States, he is surprised one morning to receive the visit of a shady-looking character who brushes past the corps of secretaries, and spreads out on the desk in the businessman's office a series of erotic photos showing him in all known varieties of sexual intercourse with the cheap foreign prostitute. "Well, what about it?" says the shady-looking character menacingly. "What about it?" says the businessman; "well, I'll take a dozen of these and a dozen of those, and can I have this one printed up in color? It'll give my grandchildren a hell of a laugh."*

Compare, with this avowed fantasy, the extraordinary statements made as absolute fact, in an interview with Mr. Hugh Hefner, promoter of a successful American bosom-and-leg-art magazine, *Playboy*, and associated nightclubs, in the French imitative sex-magazine, *Plexus* (Paris, Oct. 1966) No. 4: p. 92–105, under the rubric "Sociologie." To wit, that Mr. Hefner lives in a forty-room house in Chicago, from which he had not emerged, at the time of the interview, for some two-and-a-half years, surrounded by young women in tights, but of high morality, actually hired as waitresses or 'Bunnies' for his nightclubs, in which they appear in abbreviated *rabbit* costumes, complete with artificial ears and fluffy tail. They are discharged (it says here) if they accept any social dates with customers, off the premises, and 'several squadrons of private detectives are charged to keep [them] under surveillance.' Despite this perhaps unexpected jealous primness about the morality of the young ladies of this so-explicitly non-sexual harem; one *also* learns, p. 94, that Mr. Hefner's master-bedroom is outfitted with a motor-driven circular bed (apparently of the womb-return variety, on the style of the sarcophagus-home or bomb-shelter from which the owner does not emerge for years at a time, onto the radiation-polluted earth), and – in translation – 'a wall with an automatic camera which nothing prevents from recording whatever happens on the bed. I don't know if you're following me,' the interviewer adds. *Zut! mon vieux*, we're way ahead of you! In fact, the subject was made into a novel, *The Voyeur* (New York, 1969) by 'Henry Sutton,' pseudonym of David Slavitt, omitting only the cocaine parties, more recently divulged.

4. MALE PROSTITUTION

Male prostitution really only exists on a large scale in homosexual form, for the reason that it is not physiologically possible for a male prostitute to 'serve' women in the repetitive and disinterested way in which female prostitutes can deal with as many as fifty men in one night. In homosexual prostitution the male prostitute is generally allowed to be equally passive, as to fellatory or pedicatory acts performed upon him, or fetichisms to which he must lend himself. See further Dotson Rader's brutal novel of homosexual male prostitution, *Gov't Inspected Meat* (New York, 1971). One of the first, and certainly the scarcest novel of the Swiss mystery-writer Georges Simenon is *Mémoires d'un Prostitué* (Paris, 1929, under the pseudonym 'Georges Sim': copy Ohio State University. He has also used the pseudonym 'Gom Gut,' on a similar item now in the British Museum, Private Case). This gives the life-story, possibly in part authentic, of a male prostitute to rich women; the type of man formerly called in English a *gigolo*, and generally referred to politely as the mere 'dancing partner' of the female client or keeper. This is the usual symbolism, as in Franz Lehar's *Merry Widow* operetta (1905), and all sensuous dances, where 'dancing' is intended to be understood as meaning sexual intercourse.

Numerous jokes have been given in earlier chapters, in the First Series, which ought to be recollected here, though there is not the space to give them all again in full, where one comes close to the idea of male prostitution, without actually admitting it. From the point of view of Anglo-Saxon jokes and other folk-humor, such prostitution does not exist at all, either in heterosexual or even in the very-much existing but unavowable homosexual form, since either idea would be too humiliating for men to endure. Instead, any approach to male prostitution is presented in some complicated roundabout way, or under some flabbergasting pretext, intended to make it look like something else: generally something aggressive and thus honorably male, such as cheating some other man, or a woman, or simply bilking a whore. It can also be offered as mere ignorance or stupidity, or concentrating on this in order to deny the inherent prostitutory situation, as in an old favorite among children in America: *'A man applying for a post as footman in a country house is asked by her ladyship to raise his trouser leg so that she may ascertain whether his legs will be sufficiently shapely in plush knee-breeches. Does so. She then appears satisfied but asks to see his testimonials. "And that," he says, recounting the event, "was where I made my big mistake (or: spoiled everything)!"'* (Chelmsford, Essex, 1951). The purposeful similarity of the scene to the raising of skirts by young women trying for theatrical jobs, 'to show their legs,' cannot be missed.

Far more interesting, and infinitely funnier since they are situational rather than merely verbal in humor, are a number of jokes in which the man's prostitution either does not exist at all, or is hardly touched upon in the contrasting emphasis on the exploitative amateur prostitution of the woman, trying to get 'something for nothing.' *A poor farmer is selling a load of peaches from his wagon, going from house to house early in the morning. One housewife has him bring a peck basket of peaches into her kitchen, where she keeps offering him less and less money for the peaches, meanwhile letting her dressing-gown fall farther and farther open. "Oh, you'd give me those peaches for seventy-five cents if you really liked me," she says: adding suggestively, "you don't know how nice I can be. Anyhow, I'll bet those peaches aren't as soft as I am, right here – (pulling open her gown)." The farmer begins to cry. "Please, lady," he says, "I'm only a poor farmer. The mortgage is coming due, my wife ran away with a big nigger, my kids ain't got nothing to eat but turnips, yesterday I had two crates of cherries that went bad on me in the rain, and now I am going to get fucked out of my peaches!"* (N.Y. 1946.)

This should be compared with the classic: *Young housewife in her dressing-gown in the morning, to the elderly painter who*

has just come to work: "Oh, good morning. Please come into
the bedroom. I'd like to show you where my husband put his
hand last night." Painter: "If you don't mind, lady, I'm an old
man and I got a hard day's work to do on the ladder. How
about I settle for one of your husband's cigars?" (N.Y. 1944, the
painter sometimes answering in a comedy Russian-Yiddish accent, ending: "I'd just as soon hev a gless tea!") This is essentially a burlesque-theatre skit or 'black-out,' as developed from
the Elizabethan 'jigs' and interludes of bawdy songs and dialogue. Note that what is common to both jokes is *the rejection
of the woman's offer.*

The peddler situation appears again in what is more a folktale than a joke, reminiscent of the adventures of the Levantine
folk-hero, *Goha the Fool,* who achieves his trickster victories
by pretending stupidity like the Czech anti-hero, Jaroslav
Hasek's *Schweik the Good Soldier.* (See in particular the last
chapter of the superb fictional re-creation of the legend of *Goha
the Fool,* by Adès & Josipovici, 1917, of which an excellent
English translation exists – well worth reprinting.) *A pushcart
peddler with a load of peaches is shouting, "Peaches! Peaches!
Good peaches!" He is called up to the third floor by a woman,
who gets him to make love to her and then refuses to pay for
the peaches. He goes back down to the street and continues
pushing his cart, shouting (much more loudly): "Peaches, Fucking! Peaches!"* The pretended offer of sexual sale here – but of
course it is only pretended – is the closest approach so far to
unequivocal male prostitution to women. Note the use of the
lay-figure of the idiot or 'sacred fool.'

It has already been emphasized at the opening of this section
that men's jokes never really concern male prostitution, if its
recognition can be avoided; and such jokes, like all those of the
"Peach" family preceding, actually involve more often a woman
who is prostituting herself in them, though on an amateur, occasional, or "impulse" basis, in the style more particularly discussed in section 2.I.3, "Status of the Prostitute." For example:
*The hardware-store clerk who asks a woman customer holding
a hinge in her hand, "Can I give you a screw for that hinge?"
"No, but I'll give you a blow-job for that electric toaster."* The
pimp is also extremely rare in jokes, being even lower than the
male prostitute – who at least is very much a man! One gets
the impression, from the total concentration on *money* in the
following item (London, 1952), that the money is somehow be-

ing offered as the pimping husband's justification, or at least as the 'extenuating circumstance' of the puzzle-joke. Also, of course, the action takes place far away in notoriously immoral and *intéressé* France. *A French couple are short of funds, so the wife takes in male "paying guests" with her husband's approval, and accepts as payment "whatever they want to give her." Being French she keeps a methodic little account book, as follows:*

No. 1 (very poor) ... paid	*55fr.*
No. 2 (better off)	*350*
No. 3 (generous)	*660*
No. 4 (wealthy)	*15,600*

Total receipts ... 16,665 fr. However, being French, she decides she will cheat, and keeps out the 665 francs about which she will say nothing to her husband; and she shows him her accounts as coming to 16,000 francs for the four men. "No, no, chérie," he says, "that can't be right. You'll admit that all four came to you like this:

6 6 6 6 and they left
like this: 9 9 9 9

The figure should be 1 6 6 6 5 : so hand it over!"

The concern with the 6's and 9's in the final *addition* is also, of course, presumably very French, aside from the further phallic-symbolic meaning given them. (Actually, this may very well be originally French.)

One of the few jokes specifically on male prostitution turns the whole thing to mockery by the impotence of the men who propose to become prostitutes. This is, in fact, the whole problem of male prostitution (to women), and why the oft-reported supposed existence of luxurious male brothels for rich women is really mostly a hostile dream on the part of male-protest women who would like to imitate men's prerogatives. *Two old playboys down on their luck are considering methods of making a living. "How about going to Paris?" says one. "I hear there are places where the women will give us twenty-five dollars apiece for a good screw." "Maybe so," says the other dubiously, "but who can live on fifty dollars a month?"* (N.Y. 1940, also collected with lesser sums.)

In another rare out-&-out joke on male prostitution, the whole situation is again attempted to be denied – and the woman bilked – by the man falling short. The heroine of this joke, and in numerous others on 'tough' or obvious Lesbian females, is almost always stated to have been the late Tallulah Bankhead. *An actress picks up an out-of-work tramp and takes him to her apartment because he has very large shoes on, and she has been told that men with big feet have big pricks. She gives him a steak dinner with plenty of pepper and beer, and then drags him off to bed. In the morning the man wakes up alone and finds a ten-dollar bill on the mantlepiece, with a brief note: "Buy yourself a pair of shoes that fit you."* (N.Y. 1948.) The total reversal of the prostitutory situation, to the detriment of the man, is here very marked, with even the classic payment left behind on the mantlepiece – though the man has not earned it! – not to mention the insulting cut-down or 'killer line' at the end. A British version (London, 1954) has the end-line reverse the meaning: *"By Christ, I bet your boots nip you!"* Elvis ("the Pelvis") Presley, the original American rock-&-roll singer, since 1954, apparently made use of an illusion to this superstition in the excessively long circus-clown shoes he wore onstage, overdetermining the open meaning of the pelvic gyrations with which his songs are delivered.

An amusing but almost unclassifiable item, probably closer to male pimping than to prostitution, is given as a fool-joke, and possibly expurgated-down *racially* from an anti-Negro joke (the new censorship, to suit the times) in *World's Dirtiest Jokes* in 1969, p. 63: *'Old Snake Hollow Sam, who farmed on shares, told the land-owner, "Boss, I'll just have to have more money. Groceries are mighty high." Said the boss, "Don't tell me you and your wife eat up all you make." Sam replied, "It ain't so much us ... it's that big relative of ours that's such a powerful eater." The boss asked, "Relative? Who's that?" And Sam said, "He's my brother-in-law, or half-brother, or something. I don't rightly know what relation you'd say ... anyway, he's my wife's first husband!"'* (See further, in the First Series, section 9.III, "Possession in Common.") Many jokes of this kind exist on non-sexual backgrounds, dealing with bold beggars of the Jewish 'schnorrer' type, or with unwelcome relatives.

My own favorite 'clean' joke is of this kind: *The husband and wife are being driven crazy by the continued presence of the wife's brother, who came to spend the weekend but is still there six months later. They decide that the wife will cook a chicken, and the husband will pretend it is overdone. They will put the matter to the brother-in-law. If he says the chicken is good, the husband will throw him out. If he says the chicken is bad, the wife will throw him out. It can't fail! The scene is set up as planned, with much pretended shouting and recrimination, while the brother-in-law silently stows away his food. Suddenly the husband and wife stop shouting and turn to him. "Harry," says the husband, "what do you think?" "Me?" says Harry, biting into the chicken-leg, "I think I'm staying another three months."* (Scranton, Penna. 1946.) I often get the impression, when I observe how colleges, politics, research 'institutes,' and charity organizations set up their idealistic high-paid staff – and not just in America – that this is not so much a joke as a *cultural blueprint.* This too is male prostitution.

If jokes are scarce describing the prostitution of men and women, those directly stating the existence of homosexual prostitution – that is to say, of 'normal' men to homosexuals – are rare indeed, though the reality is massively common and visible in all large cities. Many jokes on homosexuality describe every aspect of the homosexual prostitutory situation: the accosting in public toilets, bars and parks, the fencing for position and code-recognition before 'letting down his hair' by the homosexual making an unequivocal overture or offer (usually by touching the other man's penis through his clothes); even all the physical sexual acts. But when the fact that this is prostitution is admitted at all, the saving grace is added, or pretext inserted, that it is the homosexual who prostitutes himself to the 'normal,' and not the far more usual reverse. The reader may pick in the following joke on homosexual prostitution, who is supposed to be normal and who homosexual. *One doctor is telling another about his latest operation, which consisted of "grafting tits on a sailor's back." "Was it a success?" the other doctor asks. "A success?! I did it on a percentage basis, and if his asshole holds out, we'll both be millionaires pretty soon."* (N.Y. 1950.)

Another method of admitting to male prostitution is to fob it off on animals. The breeding of cows to bulls, though paid for, is seldom thought of in quite this way. In one case: *A young farm-girl, who is usually given the job of taking the cow to the stud-bull at the neighboring farm, is made pregnant herself by one of the sons there. When he learns the details, her father rushes to the stud-farm, but no one is home except the younger son, whose brother Elmer has made the girl pregnant. He listens to the farmer storming for a while, and when the farmer shouts, "What do you figure your father's going to do about this?" he replies: "I don't know, Mr. Brown. We usually charge three dollars for the bull, but I don't know what my father charges for Elmer."* (Cleveland, Ohio, 1940.) I knew a young married woman about the same period, in Binghamton, New York, who got such a satisfactory fee for the stud-services of her pedigree black Chow-Chow dog that she began faking the dog's documents or somehow arranging to give far more services than were presumed to give good results. She usually fed the dog on canned food, but would give him fresh chopped hamburgers or fish-cakes after every service, saying *"Here's your share, honey-boy!"* Later she told me : *"I guess I ran it too fine. Just when things were going perfect, the damn dog fucked himself to death."* Of course, this is not conscious male prostitution, but female pimping or proxenetism. Actually, the woman was a respectable housewife and told me in all sincerity that she had *"married the first man that ever laid her, and never laid but one man in her life."* The dog did all the rest.

A beautiful story on this theme is usually told in America in such a way as to concern 'excessive' female sexual appetite. The following British form places most of the emphasis, instead, on money. Quoted exactly as supplied in manuscript: *'Spivs not doing so well on barrow. Buy a sow expecting big litters and bigger money by breeding from fucks, but on going to nearest farm for service learn it's £5, 10, 15, or 20, according to pedigree of the boar. Doesn't matter about all that class, they'll have the cheapest. The sow is bred to the cheapest boar. Weeks go by – nothing happens, so they put the sow in the wheelbarrow and take her back and have her bred to the £10 boar. Again nothing. Try with £15 boar. Nothing, Spivs very cheesed off, but a champion prizewinner will now do the trick, and recoup all they've laid out already. Have her served to best boar on the stud-farm, at £20. Next day, spiv calls down to his wife on waking up: " Well, any piglets yet?" "No, but the sow is sitting in the wheelbarrow".'* (Chelmsford Prison, Essex, 1952.)

From the same source comes the following full-blown example of the male prostitution joke, in which as usual all the emphasis is on the man's stalwart refusal. This was supplied in manuscript, with the statement that it is merely the *plot* of a poem or song which the informant could not remember exactly. I should be sorry to think that this poem or song is lost, and would appeal here to any reader who knows it to send me a complete copy: *'Lady millionaire in Daimler is passing Buckingham Palace and is struck by the fine fig of the guardsman: a strapping specimen of manhood. Gets her chauffeur to stop nearby and to ask if he'd care to spend the weekend with the lady in the car. Guardsman stays stiffly at attention and pays not the slightest attention. So she gets the chauffeur to drive alongside, and says to him herself: "Come to my place in the country, and the car's yours." No reply. So she thinks, "I'll get him somehow," and comes back next day in her Rolls Royce. Says to the guardsman who today is marking time, "One night with me and the Rolls is yours, and almost anything else you'd like to go with it." Guardsman, still marking time: "Madam! I'd have you know that I am a Viscount, of noble lineage of the greatest antiquity. I've money, castle, three country estates, two town houses, and properties in Portugal and Brazil. I've 2 Rolls Royces, a sports car, a hunter, and a yacht. I don't know what you want, but if anyone wants fucking it's* ME, *for getting drunk one afternoon and signing up for this bloody guardsman business!"'* (Chelmsford Prison, Essex, 1954.) If this is really a song the end-line is doubtless, *"If anyone wants fucking, it's* ME!*"* Symbolically, the man's panto-mimed marking time up & down represents the intercourse that does *not* take place.

Observe that the offer here is still being made in terms of objects of value, such as swank automobiles. Offering the man *money* for sex presumably disgraces him everywhere except in France, where, for example, most of the title-heroes in Dumas' *Three Musketeers* (1844) and its sequels cheerfully accept every type of material assistance and cash from women. The *'bayt-zimmer'* character (*"Strong back, weak mind, and a big prick"*)' Porthos, is particularly shown to have run up his physical prowess into several estates, châteaux, etc., very much in the style of the preceding story, all from the *largesse* of an ugly wife.

One of the closest direct approaches in jokes to the subject of male prostitution to women, in this Continental style, artfully evades and reverses this in the finale into mere bilking. *A Hungarian army officer picks up a beautiful young prostitute at a band-concert in the park in Vienna, and goes to her little apartment with her. She makes love to him in every possible position, and in the morning gives him a "nourishing breakfast" ending with coffee topped with whipped cream.* [Magic seminal refill.] *He then puts on his cape, adjusts his cap in the mirror, and is about to leave, when the girl says diffidently, "Aren't you forgetting something?" "Forget?" he says, looking around, "what?" "Well, you know – money?" "Never!" he replies proudly. "A Hungarian officer* never *accepts money from women!"* (N.Y. 1937.) A weaker form is given in the First Series, 4.V, page 252, where the man relents far enough to agree to accept "*a couple of ties.*" Compare also the riddle, stated to be Hungarian : "*When are the four times in her life that a woman blushes? – Well, there's the first time. Then the first time with somebody else besides her husband. And then the first time she does it for money. (The fourth time is the first time she has to pay for it herself.)*"

A lightly expurgated rendition of the "Hungarian officer" joke is made one of the turning-points of the plot in Norman Krasna's New Freedom farce, *Sunday in New York*, beautifully played in the movie-version (1963) by Miss Jane Fonda as the smalltown virgin in the big city, whose pinned-on rose gets symbolically tangled with the lapel of a young man on the bus. (In the burlesque theatre this is done with the man's necktie – which is later chopped off with a large pair of scissors – being caught in the zipper of a woman's dress-placket.) They then have to climb off the bus together, like two dogs 'stuck' in intercourse. Again no doubt symbolically. After which one would imagine that the ice is broken.

III. TRICKS OF THE TRADE

One of the most common locales in folk-belief, for what is thought of correctly as the enforced quasi-prostitution of female employees, is that traditional target, the theatre (now motion-pictures), and any similar form of irregular life such as circuses, carnivals, and most recently the entourage of rock-&-roll bands 'on the road,' with unpaid *groupie-girls* begging for that status-making fuck. All this is perfectly true, of course, though actually no more so than in business-offices, department-stores (and small stores even worse), sweat-shops, factories, farms, etc., as these have evolved and operated over the centuries. But these larger areas are overlooked by the folk-mind in the face of the ancient connection between the theatre and prostitution since the time of Greece and Rome. Then, the women who might have become the sacred prostitutes of earlier matriarchal religions had no profession open to them under patriarchy but to work their way back up from flute-player (all senses), at private parties and in the theatre, to the exalted status of high-paid *hetaera* or companion, who might not make love as she chose, similar to the modern Japanese *geisha*.

Exposés of prostitution and the call-girl's life have become so hackneyed, and at so low a level of journalism and paperback trash, that serious observers and competent writers will now seldom touch the subject. One is lucky therefore to have an authentic portrait of theatrical prostitution at every level in contemporary Hollywood, the New Babylon of a thousand moralistic attacks since the Fatty Arbuckle case and similar in the early 1920's, but this time written strictly as satire, and by a master hand, Ray Russell's *The Colony* (Los Angeles: Sherbourne Press, 1969). This is a work that can be cited only in whole pages-full of detail, in among the author's string of elaborate revenges and bitterly sarcastic portraits of current notables in the movie business, under disguised names not too hard to penetrate – now. Later it will all seem impossible and unbelievable, though really stingingly true. *The Colony* takes up where Nathanael West's *Day of the Locust* left off.

One is struck, on occasion, by the persistence of folklore themes, and their reappearance over the centuries in real life. For example, Béroalde de Verville's well-known anecdote, in *Le Moyen de Parvenir* (about 1610) chapter 8, "Cérémonie," of the young woman required by the lord of the manor to crawl about the banqueting room nude, picking up a basketful of cherries, to entertain his male guests, and so earn her dowry; a story which Béroalde tells as true. Thus also Mr. Russell, who shows us for example, p. 259, 'the casually decadent party' that his hero fondly recalls, where: 'There had been a girl, bent forward with ass poised high, at which vulnerability some of the men took turns tossing a rubber dart. She had been wearing nothing except shoes and the # 4560 *Bull's-Eye* ("Fun for his holidays! Sheer bikini pantie that's open at the sides with an embroidered satin bull's-eye on the derrière. The pantie comes packed with its own suction dart. Wild! ...")' the quotation being presumably from the *Fredericks of Hollywood* catalogue of fetichistic and 'whorehouse' underwear, mildly comparable to the

openly degenerate *Diana-Slip* catalogue, a bibliographical rarity
of Paris in the 1930's.

Mr. Russell also has a whole chapter, p. 97 ff. on the call-girls
and other naked dainties at the L'Amour Toujours L'Amour
Motel in Malibu, ending with cunnilinctus with a can of Reddi-
Whip cream (supplied by the bell-hop); and reaches an excruciating level of perfect moronic dialogue in the anatomizing
of the 'casting-couch' technique of the grubby little 'best agent
in Hollywood, Avery Bletch,' pp. 35–9 and 219–32 (full treatment, with monologue *à la* Molly Bloom), which ends with
Bletch symbolically buggering his up-&-coming actress client
while she is signing her contract. As no brief quotation could
do justice to this hilarious satirical monologue, let me extract
just one reply the actress makes, which says everything about
the *real* prostitution in the movies. *The agent forbids her,
now that she is moving up, to make 'exploitation' movies,
' "Which is a word we use meaning bikini pictures." "Well, is
nudity the same thing? Because Ira is using me in his new picture,* The 120 Days of Sodom, *you know, from the Marquis de
Sade's book – And there's this scene not for domestic release,
just for Europe, and* Playboy, *where I'm raped by a zebra and
then tortured. And I just wear a blond wig in that." "Not that
it matters ... " '*

As it is often hard to make people understand that satire, no
matter how broad, is generally far less humorous or unbelievable than the material it is presumably travestying, Russell's
tongue-in-wig humor as to the movie-rape by a zebra should
perhaps be followed by this only-too-authentic criticism of a
big-budget Hollywood film, *Myra Breckinridge,* issued in 1970
and based on the best-selling novel of the year before, by Gore
Vidal, about a man who undergoes a 'sex change' or vice versa,
and is transformed – in the movie – into no less than Raquel
Welch, 'the most beautiful woman in America,' according to
the ads. (Changes this advantageous cannot be guaranteed.) Mr.
Al Goldstein, the no-shit movie reviewer of the main New York
pornzine, *Screw* (July 20th, 1970) No. 72: p. 21, gives *Myra
Breckinridge* 70% on the Peter-Meter register in his column,
"Dirty Diversions," noting that it is:

a modern day rags to riches story, posing the question: "If
one gives up his balls and cock to gain worldly fortune, is he
still a man for all seasons?" ... The film has a certain muti-

lated vitality that is as fascinating as watching someone picking nose in public and being unable to take your eyes off him in spite of a rising tide of nausea ... But the great perverse joy in this big-budgeted film was the famous, not too explicit, dildo scene, when Raquel shoves that ersatz cock up Rusty's tight but unwilling rectum.

Any questions? ... I can only add that any sick sexual Hollywogs accidentally omitted by either Ray Russell or Al Goldstein are wrapped up (in spades) in Terry Southern's black-humor evisceration of the subject, *Blue Movie* (New York, 1970), in which the studio-head has a special affinity for 'paying his last respects' to corpses; and take it from there. The question remains however: is the secret sexual life of Hollywood – no longer very secret – *really* so different from the private sexual life and letches of patrician statesmen, WASP air-force officers, millionaire stock-brokers, and other of nature's noblemen? Prostitutes do not think so.

I. SPECIALITIES

Unless one is 'kinky' (sexually perverted) oneself, one cannot have the slightest notion of how horrible the profession of prostitute really is, and of the abnormal and repellent fetiches to which the prostitute must lend herself, or himself, often with great physical pain, not to mention the continual pyschic outrage and humiliation. Some obvious extreme cases are noted here in the final chapter, 15.III.4, under *'Pet-en-Gueule'* and Scatophagy; and a complete conspectus of the overrich slang vocabulary of prostitution and perversion in German will be found in Ernest Borneman's recent thesaurus, *Sex im Volksmund* (Hamburg, 1971).

At the oldest fully recorded period of prostitution, in ancient Greece, all that seems to have been asked in this line was that the prostitute give herself in special *positions*, principally those from behind, and with the woman on top. Greek art of the ordinary kind shows that the now-common position for intercourse, with the woman supine on her back and the man prone above her, had already been standardized by at least the 6th century B.C., and probably much earlier in Egypt. This is made naïvely clear on a decorated Etrurian vase of that period, now in the Kunsthistorisches Museum in Vienna, No. 3577, showing the legend of Dionysus and the club-footed mechanic Hephaestus. Accompanying Dionysus are two satyrs, busily raping two unresisting maenads – in the classic position – while a third girl resists a bit by pulling the hair and beard of one of the satyrs. (Reproduced in Martin Robertson's *La Peinture Grecque*, Geneva: Skira, 1959, p. 74.) Félicien Rops in his powerful 19th-century drawing, "Prehistoric Rape," makes the same error or concession to habit, overlooking that an actual such rape would almost certainly, and surely originally, have been engaged in from behind, when the fleeing female is overtaken, as is the case with all other animals. However, when one has to do frankly with prostitutes, in Greek and Roman erotic art, and on actual Roman brothel tokens (the 'brass check' is at least that ancient), as in the final plates 98–113 of Dr. Gaston Vorberg's magistral *Die Erotik der Antike in Kleinkunst und Keramik* (1921, and reprinted), much emphasis is placed on satisfying the client by means of intercourse with the woman from behind, and in the position of "Pendula Venus," or the girl astride.

With the development of prostitution as a career, at least by Biblical times (Tamar in *Genesis*, xxxviii. 15; Rahab in *Joshua*, ii.1; the legend of Mary Magdalene in the New Testament; and the rather full details of the sisters Aholah and Aholibah in *Ezekiel*, xvi and xxiii), it is clear that other 'specialities,' such as oragenital acts, were regularly offered. Just what these 'specialities' might be – these fabulously erotic and expensive *tricks of the trade* – is a matter of much folklore and humor in all languages. I have translated some of the more exotic (but authentic) specialties of fellation from various French sources of the 1910's, in *Oragenitalism* (New York, 1969) p. 216–21, and also cite there at p. 239 a humorous broadside or printed novelty-slip of about the same period entitled: "*Catalogue des Prix d'Amour de Mademoiselle Marcelle* LaPompe, *69 Rue du Chat-Noir, 69*," which gives a long tabulation of mock forms and specialities of exotic intercourse, all with absurdly low prices carefully indicated, and ending – in translation – "*Suçage à la Menthe:* before having your asparagus gargled (*glouglouter le poireau*), have the operatress suck a mint candy. Delicious little burning sensation!" They have not caught up with that one yet, in among the 'Raspberry Douches' now advertised in the Hollywood-& hippie underground press. Similarly, Villiers de l'Isle-Adam in his *Contes Cruels* (1883), "The Bienfilâtre Sisters," has two prostitutes whose personal calling-card, after their name, recites modestly but alliteratively the advantages of dealing with them, in the three words: "SECURITY – CELERITY – SPECIALITY." (From the late Keene Wallis, translator extraordinary.) Intended of course to parody the French national revolutionary motto: *"Liberty, Equality, Fraternity."*

On the legend and lore of the 'knowledgeful whore,' see – if you can find them! – the lost love-books of the Greek and Roman matriarch- or priestess-prostitutes (the hetaerae), as listed in Iwan Bloch's magistrally researched *Die Prostitution* (1912) I. 510–15, and in the German *Index* to Martial, edited by Gilbert (Leipzig, 1896) p. 388, at "Didymae puellae." One magnificent, but alas only pretended restoration of a 'lost love-book' of this sort is *Die Weisheiten der Aspasia* by 'Fritz Thurn' [Fritz Foregger von Greiffenthurn], privately and beautifully printed in Vienna, 1923, and reprinted since. Here all the very advanced erotic lore is given in simple and direct phrasing, cleverly avoiding the cumbersomeness of having to carry any documentation in or under the text, by pretending to be the oldest such book of all: a newly 'rediscovered manuscript' of the 5th century B.C. by the Greek hetaera Aspasia, consort and later wife of Pericles, the greatest ruler of Ancient Greece.

In the practical sense, the prostitute's specialties are intended to explain how she justifies her price, which is inevitably complained of as too high, too immoral, or otherwise objectionable. (Even the Bible complains about this in *Deuteronomy*, xxiii. 18: 'Thou shalt not bring the hire of a whore, or the price of a dog [male prostitute], into the house of the Lord thy God for any vow.') Actually, price and *specialty* respond to the clients' special or fetichistic demands, which make the prostitute's life a real and endless hell, meaning that the price is really always absurdly low. Prostitutes are the repository of all the neurotic and vicious demands which are possible to make when paying flat cash for the use of a human body, but which are a bit difficult to maneuver in a hypothetical 'love' situation. Also, since many of these demanded fetiches are sado-masochistic in nature they destroy or otherwise 'use up' their victims, and so cannot be allowed full freedom within the clients' marriages. Most sadists nowadays save their whips for whores, and satisfy themselves at home and at the office or factory with the *merely* social forms of verbal and intimidatory sadism. (Certain orchestra conductors are very good examples of this.)

Few jokes actually describe the horrid little tragi-comedy scenes required of prostitutes by their masochistic clients in particular, as detailed in such specialized works as Krafft-Ebing's *Psychopathia sexualis* (1886) – still selling well after nearly a century to the midnight-bookstore bibliophiles. Instead they allude only to such minor matters as the difficulty which elderly men experience in arriving at orgasm. This is perhaps what is alluded to by the *'Celerity'* on the prostitute's visiting-card just cited. *The elderly client in a whorehouse will not take any girl but Mary, who happens just then to be 'occupied.' "What has Mary got that the rest of my girls don't have?" asks the madam. "Mary has patience."* (1:157.) This is as mild as specialties come.

The principal prostitutory specialties noted in the wish-fufillments as jokes are almost all connected with fellation or related oragenital acts, and these will be grouped in the section following. All the others are so excessively absurd and ornate that one may suspect that their real meaning is to disguise, facetiously, the *real* specialties required of prostitutes, most of which are (when not simply oragenital) either sado-masochistic or repellently scatological. These range from flagellation by or of the client – recommended in a famous line by Nietzsche – to urinary and fecal 'games,' intercourse while wearing fetichistic clothing (by both parties), or in mock coffins, etc. There is also the burning or killing of small animals or other living creatures allowed to move on the prostitute's body during intercourse, which thus openly represent the torturing or killing of the prostitute. This is also common in homosexual prostitution, which is almost always very hostile in nature. The French novelist, Proust, for example, is reported to have habitually taken live mice with him to male-brothels, which he would kill with needles on the boys' bodies during homosexual intercourse. (Mice cost less than boys ...) It is demands of this kind that are really implied by the absurdities in the jokes following.

Here is how things are disguised in folk humor; or, perhaps, are 'turned into a joke' and heavily rationalized, to relieve them of some of their horror: *A young man tells a streetwalker who accosts him that he has only 25c. For this sum she allows him to look at her genitals, down a dark alley. He strikes his cigarette-lighter in order to see better in the dark, complimenting her on her magnificent pubic hair. "Would you mind if I ask a personal question?"* he says. *"Is it really possible for you to piss through all that hair?"* "Oh yes," says the girl. *"Then you better begin now. You're on fire!"* (2 : 169, illustrated.) This joke is very popular, and I have even collected it among children (San Diego, Calif., 1965), less elegantly phrased. The elaborate politeness of the man's speech is of course in counter-point to the obvious hostility of his act. The fact is that there is no accident at all about his lighting the prostitute's pubic hair: that is his perversion, for which he is paying. Though not often discussed, this perversion takes its place in the stupefying catalogue of German slang terms as to prostitution and sexual perversion in Ernest Borneman's remarkable thesaurus of slang, *Sex im Volksmund* (Hamburg: Rowohlt, 1971) Part II, § 48 and especially 80.23, where it is specifically listed by the Latin name of the medieval torture, *'Tormentum ignis ... Brandmarkung und Flagellation ... das Absengen* [singeing] *des Schamhaars,'* continuing with a slang synonymy of the types of burns and instruments used. You really have to be a German to appreciate this.

In ostensibly less perverted situations one has also at least the pretense of the continuing worry about money. *A cowboy offers to pay a prostitute double her demanded fee if she will keep both hands on his buttocks (or on his head) during intercourse. Afterwards she asks him what special thrill he got out of this. "No thrill,"* he says, *taking a large roll of bills out of his pocket; "but for two bucks extra I know your hands are on my ass and not in my pockets."* (1 : 160.) There appears actually to be an allusion here to the need many men have for the manipulation or striking of their loins by the woman's hands (or, preferably, her heels) just before and at orgasm, to increase the intensity of the man's orgasm; or to anal digitation – the French *'postillon'* or postillioning – for the same purpose.

Though the biologically-linked need many women feel for handling and kneading of their buttocks as an excitant to, and during, intercourse, is widely known and accepted as natural and justifiable, any such anally-oriented needs on the part of men are considered disgraceful (*i.e.* homosexual). Most men will not admit to such impulses or needs to their wives or to the women they love, and can only achieve the much more violent orgasm of simultaneous anal digitation with prostitutes or other women for whom they have no respect and with whom they do not intend any future or emotional relationships. The whole subject is entirely omitted – along with that of oragenital acts, hardly more than alluded to – in most popular English-language manuals of sex technique. It appears only as the mysterious "Cleopatra's Secret" (in folk-transmission, the "Secret of Marseilles," the most famous prostitution-center of France before World War II, on the style of the even more mysterious "sleeve job": Henry Monnier's *"Diligence de Lyon,"* earlier), in a little-known work, *The Naked Truth About Sex,* published for the author, J. V. Wynn, in the American south, during the 1930's. For technical details see my *Oragenitalism* (1969) Section X, pages 88–96.

The subject is specifically mentioned in what is the most hostile of all anti-prostitute jokes, again pegged to the subject of money, though here it is the client who postillions the prostitute, and not the reverse. *A man objects to the high fee of fifty dollars that a prostitute demands from him in advance, but finally gives it to her. After having intercourse with her, he puts his thumb into her vagina and his middle finger in her anus. "What do you call that?" she asks, amused by his manipulations. "I call it the bowling-hold, you old bitch!" he snarls. "Now give me back my fifty bucks, or I'll tear out your god-dam partition!"* (N.Y. 1938.) Observe that postillioning is here shown as the ultimate hostile act or threat, equivalent to pedicatory rape.

A joke that should possibly have been grouped with those in the prostitute-as-nurse (or nun) also involves the fantasy of the overlong penis that only a prostitute can accept, and even she unwillingly. *A man gets into a foot-doctor's office by accident, after having asked directions to a whore-house, and he thinks the nurses and receptionists are whores and that the whole office is just a high-class front they are putting up. When it comes his turn, the nurse asks whether his limb bothers him very much and he replies that it is stiff a lot. She tells him to show it to her, whereupon 'he whipped out his tool and slung it across the desk.' "My god," says the nurse, "that's not a foot!" "Oh, c'mon," he says, "let's not quibble about a few inches."* (D.C. 1945, from an 18-year-old sailor on a train.) This 'specialty,' of being able to accept the client's overlong penis, apparently exists in fact, as well as in folklore.

Rectal intercourse with a woman is not habitually considered desirable by any men other than unconscious homosexuals. The archi-famous *Lustful Sonnets* of Aretino, written in the

1520's, betray by their concentration on this penchant the real psychosexual organization of their author. The rough-&-ready feeling of the normal man on the subject is presumably that shown in the following joke, but the mutual hostility of both parties – hardly hidden beneath the surface – is the real point. *A sailor in New Orleans has only a dollar left for a good time. He spends half on a pack of cigarettes and a bottle of beer, and offers the remaining 50c to a tough whore, who accepts. She takes him to her untidy cubicle, and immediately bends over and throws up her dress, presenting her anus to him. "Come on, turn around," he says gruffly, "who the hell wants it up the brown?" "Don't you want to get the cap off that bottle?" she asks.* (N.Y. 1951.) Less roughly, and simply as an adjunct: *Two whores standing on a street corner. "How's business, Sadie?" one asks. "It's been so damned good lately, I'm thinking of putting a little wig around my ass-hole and opening up a second front."* (D.C. 1944, from an Army sergeant, obviously on the World War II 'second front' rumors.)

Homosexual prostitutes – those who are actually homosexual, disguised in women's clothes – often brag that they wear a hidden rubber 'gimmick' or 'grummet' or 'mugget' (meaning respectively and literally: any nameless object; a circle of rope; and a 'merkin' or 'cunt-wig') by means of which their clients, accosted in the street or in beer-joints, are made to believe they are having intercourse with a woman vaginally, but who, if they are drunk enough, are "slipped the real thing," *i.e.* are fobbed off with rectal intercourse, presumably without knowing. The idea that the clients are also consciously seeking homosexual intercourse, under the polite pretense of drunkenness, apparently never occurs to the homosexual prostitute.

Rectal intercourse is always considered inferior to the *real* 'real thing' (vaginal intercourse) as in the jokes already given on "corn-hole *vs.* money-hole" and "greasing up the cat's ass." *Anecdota Americana* gives two jokes, apparently variants, making this quite clear. In 1:450, *A Civil War soldier in Mississippi accosts a Negro prostitute and asks her 'to accommodate him. "Is you from the 6th Ohio?" she asked. "No," said the soldier. "Or the 12th Massachusetts?" "No." "Or the 69th New York?" "No." "Then ah's sorry," said the wench, "but ah kain't do nothing' fo' you. Ah's kept private fer them regiments".'* (In another form, *A beautifully groomed female donkey is kept "for the regiment," according to the man tend-*

ing her, or *she is "the town gambler's mistress."* Prof. Krauss, in *Anthropophytéia,* retails an anecdote like this as true, concerning jenny-asses and the soldiers of the Czarist army, before World War I.)

In the variant in *Anecdota,* 1 : 363 : *'Observing a negress bending over a tub of wash, a soldier approached her, and, with a practiced flip of the hand, raised her dresses from behind. He was just about to backscuttle her* [sic] *when, without looking up from her wash, the dinge asked, "Officer or private?" "Private," the soldier answered. "Upper hole, upper hole," said the negress.'* The erroneous use here of the term 'back-scuttle,' which specifically refers in American slang (as also 'back-scull') to rectal intercourse, as meaning its intended opposite, is perhaps only the Return of the Repressed. Another form of the same joke has already been noted, in the earlier chapter on "Children," in which *The Negro cook lets the young master have intercourse with her from behind while she bends over the table rolling dough. Finally she says, "Come to bed, boy. You got talent!"* (I was once made temporarily impotent, at the age of twenty, by the traditional 'passionate young red-headed woman' tossing this punchline at me, as a joke.)

Other announced specialties in jokes are elaborately overdone to show that they are intended as impossibilities. All nevertheless express the not-at-all hidden idea that the male has become *blasé,* and that something very extraordinary is necessary to 'excite his languid spleen' (as Gilbert & Sullivan remark, in *Patience,* alluding to Oscar Wilde's 'attachment *à la* Plato for a bashful young potato, or a not-too-French French bean'). *Shanghai madam, to British civil-servant: "Ah! ze nize yong man from Hinglish consul. I have jost ze thing: tan-year-old Javanese dancing-girl – no hair on body, positively wirgin." "No thank you, Madame Wishnigradsky, not today." "Lahvely, plomp Chinese boy, dobble-clutch ektion esshole –" "Not today, thank you." "Hmm! Spacialty of the house: black Nubian goat, drannnnnched in jasmine perfume!" "Er, no. But tell me, Madame, what have you got in, er –* (hand motion) *fish?"* (N.Y. 1951, told by a master-raconteur, and not done justice to her.) In an earlier form, already given, *The client, Oscar Wilde, states that he is bored with every type of girl offered, and finally asks for a boy. The French madam is indignant. "Monsieur, I will call a gendarme." "Don't bother, madame, I'm tired of gendarmes too."*

Also a pantomime joke, delivered, as heard, with the eyes half-closed, and vague hand-motions as though told by a completely worn-out *roué*, speaking in exaggerated French accent. *A patriotic Frenchman abroad comes to a whorehouse with three colored ribbons in his pocket, which he gives to the girl explaining: "Ze red rib-bon you put around ze fore-head. Ze white rib-bon around ze tit-tees, and ze blue around ze hips. When I say, 'Ze red!' you press ze mouth for-ward, like zis. When I say, 'Ze white!' you press ze tit-tees, and 'Ze blue!' ze hips.* (Motion of a long, slow, tired bump). *The girl says she understands, and they begin intercourse. The Frenchman starts giving his patriotic orders: "Ze red! Ze white! Ze blue! – Ze red! Ze white! Ze blue! – Ze red, ze white, ze blue! – Ze red ze white ze blue!! Ze blue! Ze blue!! Ze blue!!!"* (N.Y. 1942, the teller screaming at the end.) Purely a humiliation story, gloating over the idea of total 'sadistic control' of the woman by means of the paid fee, under the mask of humor. This is told as a true story happening in Italy (with punchline: *"Dentro, fuero; Dentro, fuero; Dentro, dentro, dentro! – In, out; In, out; In, in, in!"*) in that treasury of erotic anecdotes, *Les Vies des Dames Galantes* of Brantôme, who died in 1614, end of Discourse VI, chap. 5, "How we should never speak ill of Ladies."

2. ORGIES AND EXHIBITIONS

Although jokes often bring on-scene exhibitions of sexual intercourse before an audience – these will be given at the end of the present section – real orgies are seldom described in any recognizable way. The partialisms or symbolisms of this type in little girls' competitive 'clothespin clubs' (the winner is the little girl who can insert the clothespin the farthest), and young boys' 'chain-jerks' or 'circle-jerks' (the winner is the boy who ejaculates first, as with the Beggar's Benison club in Scotland, where the winner was the one who ejaculated *most*), have already been discussed. Though these are of course orgies in the strict sense, they are essentially plural or consecutive exhibitions, and do not actually involve – as any real orgy should – more than two people having sexual intercourse together at the same time.

For some consideration of the topographical and permutational problems created by orgies, and particularly by the '69' and the 'spintries' or 'daisy-chains' known since ancient Greece, at least, (dogs engage in the same; they are perhaps ageless), see my *Oragenitalism: Oral Techniques in Genital Excitation* (1969) p. 304–10. A brief list of foursome combinations and beyond is given in the appendix of postures to the well-known *Manual of Classical Erotology* (1824) originally written in Latin by the Fichtean philosopher, Friedrich Karl Forberg. A recent Swedish work, *Ju fler vi är tillsammans* ("The More the Merrier"), by a schoolteacher, Mr. Ragnar Aaslund, published in 1966, is intended frankly as a manual of group-sex. This has not been translated.

In a story concerning prostitution on the face of it, the client's revenge for the high price he must pay is presented in the purest form: by getting his money back against the prostitute's will, thus, as I have heard it phrased by one of the tellers of this story, *'double-whoring'* her (on the analogy of 'double-crossing,' or betraying). *A fashionable prostitute refuses a Jewish client on the grounds that she hates Jews. He finally prevails upon her to accept him for a hundred dollars for one night, but she insists that she will only allow him to make love to her in silence and in the pitch-dark, "So she won't see his damned hook-nose." He agrees urbanely, and, on the agreed night, amazes her by making love to her fifteen times in a row, stopping only to go to the bathroom between each bout. "My god, Julius," she says finally, "I never imagined you were so virile!" "Ah ain't Julius, ma'm," says a Negro voice; "Julius is downstairs takin' tickets."* (*Anecdota Americana*, 1927, 1:150, the present text collected ten years later.) Among other touches, note that the substitution of the Negro for the Jew is intended as a further humiliation of the prostitute, of course. This trait also appears in various stories of accidental adultery, sometimes only in 'imaginary' form, as in the First Series, 9.II.1, page 706, but always somehow with the husband's connivance as here by "Julius."

The original story is given in extended storiette form in Kimbo's *Tropical Tales* (Nice, 1925) p. 124–7, with the hero named Methusaleh, to imply that the story is very old. It is indeed very old, being given in the first European jestbook, Poggio's *Facetiæ* (MS. 1451) No. 238, as a true incident that happened to an English fuller during Poggio's stay in England in the early 15th century. However, this rather falls to the ground when he gives almost the identical story *again* at No. 270, as having happened to an Italian miller named Cornicolo (*i.e.* "Horn-bearer") and as being 'well-known in Mantua.'

D. P. Rotunda's *Motif-Index of the Italian Novella in Prose* (Bloomington, Ind. 1942) lists over twenty such versions in Italian literature at K1544, with others in Stith Thompson's *Motif-Index of Folk Literature* at the same numbers; and compare K1844.1, Type 519, the legend of Brünhilde. The identical story also appears in Afanasyev's *Russian Secret Tales* in the mid-19th century, and a version extremely close to the "Julius" form is given in Andréa de Nerciat's famous eroticum, *Le Diable au Corps* (MS. 1788, published in 1803). This story has found its way around the world.

An ornate French version (not collected in English) omits the presumably crucial element of darkness altogether, as in Rotunda's K1843.2, in which the wife takes the servant's place in her husband's bed, and concentrates simply on the ruse of the trickster or swindler. This lacks the orgy element, and is therefore not strictly relevant, but it seems likely that the second story or situation has been developed from the first. *During the Dreyfus Trial in the 1890's in France a fashionable actress refuses a young man who begs for her favors, on the grounds that he is Jewish (or that she does not love him), and laughs at his offer of one hundred thousand francs. She tells him that to show how little she cares for his money, he can make love to her for as long as it takes the hundred thousand francs to burn. He comes back the next day with the money, lays ten (or one hundred) bills out in a line with the ends just overlapping, lights the first one, and leaps into bed with her. As the last bill burns away she pushes him off her. "Well, I've had you!" he says triumphantly. "Yes," she smiles, "and your hundred thousand francs are burnt to ashes." "What does it matter?" he says, lighting a cigarette; "they were counterfeit."* This is practically a movie scenario.

Compare the novelty item in America since the late 1960's, of toilet-paper printed to look like money (fifty-thousand dollar bills, etc., stated to be 'legal tender and for all deposits'). What the people who buy this, and who really admire the subterfuge of the mad lover in the preceding story, do not understand is that *"If it isn't for real, you don't feel anything,"* as a woman once told me frankly when turning me down for the same parenthetical reason given by the actress in the preceding joke. If you want the thrill of wiping your ass on money, you have to wipe your ass on money. Otherwise there is no thrill.

Italian and Spanish literature of the early 16th century were at their raciest and most fascinating period from almost any point of view, and it was largely from this source that most of the French and English poetry and drama of their greatest period, at the time of Shakespeare, drew inspiration. The materials in folklore and erotology of the same period in Italy were also by far the richest and most significant since Greece and Rome. Several extraordinary examples are offered by this Italian literature of the orgy or 'gang-shag,' and it cannot be doubted that these descriptions on paper reflect a fairly commonplace event in the real erotic (and especially the military) life of the time, though not perhaps in the lives of the literary men writing about them. Both types of orgy appear: the residual erotic ritual or permitted quasi-religious license of the carnival period – the kind appearing in the jokes and folktales concerning 'accidental' wife-sharing – and the decadent and aggressive form where the orgy appears as a rape or revenge.

It is not now possible to determine whether these orgies had simply survived in Italy – as I believe – since the time of its Roman pre-Christian and anti-Christian religious origins, as far back as the Etruscans, whose language has still never been deciphered. Perhaps the aggressive orgy, at least, was a Levantine reimportation, drawing directly from the masturbatory and pederastic rituals and initiations of earlier Levantine religions, a subject on which much will be found in Allen Edwardes' *Erotica Judaica: A Sexual History of the Jews* (New York: Julian Press, 1967). This could easily have been picked up at any time from the martial manners and sexual atrocities of the Moslem conquerors, in Italy and especially her islands, during the thousand years of the Arab and Turkish conquests in Europe (700 A.D. to 1605).

What is apparently the earliest reference to this matter in Italian literature is also its *locus classicus:* the poem *La Zaffetta* by Lorenzo Veniero, published anonymously and without place or date, but probably in Venice about 1540, and venomously attacking Angela or Angiola, called "La Zaffetta," the most beautiful and most talented courtesan of Venice. At any rate, so she was if we are to believe the most famous literary whore-monger of that period and of all time, Pietro Aretino, who has written pages of extravagant praise, in letters dated from 1537 to 1552, for her superlative art and charm as a prostitute, similar to the paeans in the Hindu love-books such as the *Kama Sutra* of Vatsyayana – which is mostly about prostitutes and their wiles – or in *Proverbs*, chapter xxxi. 10–31, on the Ideal Wife. (See First Series, 8.VII.2, pages 610–13.)

La Zaffetta is a very rare book, only four copies being known, but the Italian text was reprinted in Paris in 1861, and fuller details concerning it will be found in M. Hubaud's *Notice bibliographique sur ... P. Arétin* (Marseille, 1857), reproduced in part in the Gay-Lemonnyer *Bibliographie des ouvrages relatifs à l'amour* (4th ed. 1899, III. 1393–7), and in a valuable study on the Italian *novellieri* by 'Philomneste Junior' (Gustave Brunet) prefixed to a translation of *Sept petites nouvelles sur le jeu et les joueurs*, by Aretino (Paris: Gay, 1861), doubtless a companion-item to the reprint of *La Zaffetta*. Burnet thus abridges the action of this virulent poem, which is also filled with insulting descriptions of its victim:

> In this very free opuscule will be found the account of a vengeance wreaked by a lover, irritated by the disdain of this beauty. He conducted her to the Chioggia, under the pretext of a party of pleasure, and there delivered her over to the brutality of a gang of ruffians. This is called *dare il trent'uno* ["to give the thirty-one"], a number which, in this case, if the poet is to be believed, was more than doubled. In one of the *Historiettes* of Tallemant des Réaux we find the expression *passer par les piques* ["to pass under the pike-staves"], an expression which was then the equivalent in France, it would appear, of the *trent'uno* of Italy. In one of the *Proverbie in facetie* of Cornazano, there is also some question of a damsel who was *trent'unata* all over the country.

I have not been able to turn up this passage in Cornazano's *Proverbs in Jests* (English translation, Paris: Liseux, 1888). As the original edition of this important jest-collection following Poggio's, dates from Venice, 1518, and the manuscript from well before Cornazano's death in 1500 – probably about 1480, the date of the death of its dedicatee – this would doubtless be the oldest allusion to the *trent'uno*, if found. A reference should also certainly be made to the sadistic and flagellational version of the same thing in Bandello's *Novelle* (1573) IV: No. 16, in which *A prostitute who has refused to pay a debt is publicly spanked* [!] *with canes:* the more modern 'running the gauntlet,' but here obviously erotically. See also *Ezekiel*, xvi. 37.

In a descripion of a modern erotic 'gang-bang' quoted in full in the First Series, 9.III.3, page 780, from Hunter S. Thompson's *Hell's Angels* (New York, 1966) end of chapter 17, the author, who lived for some time among the 'Angels' motorcycle gang, makes the highly significant remark, in view of the fact that the girl being 'gang-banged' (*trent'unata*) in this case was entirely willing and cooperative: 'It was not a particularly sexual scene. The impression I had at the time was one of *vengeance*. The atmosphere in the room was harsh and brittle, almost hysterical.' (Italics supplied.) If this is the atmosphere of the consenting type of rape-orgy, one wonders about the consciously vengeful type, either in Italy or in the presumed case detailed above at the end of section 10.V.3, "Pedicatory Rape," from a source offering it as the secret story behind the gruesome Sharon Tate murders in Hollywood in 1969. In Fellini's motion-picture, *Amarcord* (1973), a sardonic valentine of folk-life and adolescent sexuality in Mussolini's Italy in the 1920's, the little local *trent'unata* at the springtime festival is played as a twitching underaged nymphomaniac. We had one of those in Scranton, Pa., too, in the 1920's: 'Jeanie with the Dark Brown Hole,' we called her: twelve years old, and took on all the boys in a packing case (the Dark Brown Hole ...) under her family's front porch. Also the local painted homosexual: presumably just one of each!

Two streams obviously have separated from the ritual male orgies of the distant religions of Babylonia and Egypt, and those more natural and heterosexual in mystery-religions preceding and combatting early Christianity. On the one hand the European orgy-type, from whose traditional naked dances ("Buff-Balls" and "The Ball o' Kirriemuir") the modern wife-swappers and 'swingers' take their inspiration, almost forgotten except in the still-surviving subterranean term for intercourse, '*to ball*.' And on the other hand, the Levantine orgy-type of the initiatory and pederastic rape of men, and the vengeful 'thirty-one' of women. The crux or essence of the original joke, at the beginning of the present section, concerning "Julius" the Jewish trickster, and the prostitute for whose overpriced charms he is secretly '*downstairs takin' tickets*,' is now seen to be the aggressiveness of all such orgiastic situations, whether or not covered by the cloak of the demanded darkness, or the even more common cloak of the demanded money. The real essence here is that of the 'biter-bit,' of aggressively cheating the cheater; of 'reaming', 'fucking', 'scrounging', screwing' and generally out-hostiling (thirty-oneing, gang-shagging, horse-fucking) the hostile, in the fashion implied by the nonce-word the teller coined to describe it: 'double-whoring,' or betraying.

An authentic specialty of houses of prostitution, always and everywhere, is the staging of those lesser orgies, the consenting erotic exhibitions in which no one is actually raped, and of which the clients are presumably only the spectators, though they are often encouraged – seldom very successfully – to engage with the actors in the heap. This has already been alluded to in the joke in section 11.II.3 above, as to the client who finds that when he was being entertained for nothing in the brothel, it was "for the movies" or television. I note, in *The Guilt of the Templars*, p. 127–8, the point often overlooked that the erotic motion-picture, now becoming an important social industry, is not just a mechanized sex-exhibition, but is also the scaling down of the orgy to a spectator-sport, the coward's orgy, in which the surrogate activity of *watching* erotic movies replaces any real engagement in erotic acts. (Some people do, nowadays, watch erotic movies while they 'ball.' I am sorry for their partners.) Persons who have been physically present at an orgy realize that they have been involved in a sexual act, even if they have not actually engaged genitally with the other people present or on-scene. No such involvement need be admitted as to merely *watching* a movie, even by the censor who is hypocritically watching it only in order to censor it – for others. In the same way, horror-movies and sadistic movies, of a type still far more common in our public theatres than sex-movies, wallow happily in scenes of horrifying executions and deaths, whippings, and ghastly tortures (the Japanese movies are the most sickening, and modern American 'westerns' next), which many or most members of the same middle-class audiences would be profoundly disturbed by, were they to witness them in fact.

Perfectly taking-off this urge toward polite *non*-involvement (here, with purposeful ludicrousness, even on the part of the performer), *Anecdota Americana*, 1:62, gives the following burlesque:

At a stag party on upper Broadway, a negress was giving a "circus." She lay stripped on a matting and went through all the eye-rolling, bosom-heaving contortions of a woman with a lusty man screwing her. She wriggled her buttocks, locked and unlocked her thighs, squirmed and tremored.

Overcome with emotion one of the stags shouted: "Fuck her hot!" The negress stopped and turned towards the offender: "If you-all cain't be gentlemen," she said, with grave dignity, "this performance cain't go on!"

The implicit idea of sex as a religious ritual almost comes to open expression here: in fact it *is* expressed, but only to mock it. The 'performance' is, in any case, like all Levantine belly-dances, far removed from the reality of intercourse, of which it is only a sort of ghost or gloat or masturbatory simulacrum: the solitary 'bumps and grinds' of a burlesque dancer miming intercourse, or a nightclub singer pretending to suck-off the microphone, or a swinging- or stag-party girl masturbating with a vibrating dildo (for the camera), while every one of the males watching her presumably identifies himself as the virile lover for whom her body 'passionately' but emptily yearns and squirms. The end-point in many ways is the scene at the notorious "Blue Fox" nightclub (real name "The Green Note") in Tijuana, Mexico, across the border from San Diego, California, described in the First Series, 9.III.4, page 785. Here the drawing-card is public cunnilinctus with the strip-teasers on the stage by members of the audience, who are restricted however to this one act – to the exclusion of intercourse – and are also not allowed to touch the woman with their hands. (For fear that they might rape her ...)

Robert Briffault, in his tremendously-researched *The Mothers* (1927) vol. III, pp. 199–205 and 260–61, gives an important sampling of the available evidence as to public or ritual sexual intercourse among primitive and early civilized peoples. These include ceremonials which still survive and figure today as the stars of whispering touts' advertisements by word-of-mouth as to the 'spectacles' to be seen at erotic exhibitions, in such countries as Mexico or France, in particular that of a woman having intercourse with a burro or horse. Says Briffault, III. 205: 'The Godiva procession in Coventry [alluding to the legend of Lady Godiva, the legendary English Queen Esther, riding on a horse naked in full view of her subjects – all of whom refrain from looking, except one, like Doubting Thomas at the Resurrection: *John*, XX. 25–9 – and whom she saves from harm by these means] refers, no doubt, to an ancient ritual which has many parallels. In India the great Pongol festival is character-

ised by the indecency of the officiating women. At the Vedic
sacrifice of the horse, not only did the queen go through the
ritual of symbolic [n.b.] union with the animal, but obscene
jests were exchanged between the priests and the attendant
women.'

Two popular paintings, from Jaipur, showing a woman in
intercourse with a pony or donkey, are reproduced in Friedrich
S. Krauss' yearbook of sexual folklore, *Anthropophytéia* (1906)
III. plate ii, as being at that time in the Museum für Völker-
kunde at Leipzig. Other paintings of the same kind are reproduced in the volumes of Levantine erotic art in the important
series published by Nagel in Switzerland in the 1960's. I have
myself been sent – by an American woman tourist – a very
similar printed 'novelty' card of Mexican origin, about 1955,
with a few lines of humorous doggerel printed in Spanish commenting on the illustration, which shows a woman gripped
under a donkey's belly in intercourse.

The original meaning of such orgy-exhibitions has now, of
course, been lost sight of; but orgiastic exhibitions do survive
with human performers and even occasionally with animals,
generally in sadistic rather than sexual form. When seeing the
lion-tamer at the three-ring circus, or the *matador* at a bullfight,
or a bulldog 'mascot' on a football field, or even in hearing
"Hold that Tiger" played by a jazz-band (sometimes with a
stuffed toy animal held up and made to growl and menace at
the trombone *chaloupés*), few people remember back to animal
totemism, to ancient hunting rites and sacrifices. Yet that is
what lies solidly behind all these: the sacred drawings of
hunted bison in the prehistoric caves at Altamira, the animal
dancers and acrobats of Greece, the murderous Roman circuses,
the benediction of the dying Jewish patriarch, Jacob, in which
his sons and the tribes they are to father are typified in terms
of animal totems (*Genesis*, xlix. 9–27). Animals doubtless
shown on the banners, later the coins, of all such peoples, just
as today on the mock-Indian 'beaver' and 'elk' banners of Boy
Scout troops.

As observed above, the orgiastic references of which polite
survivals are still allowed in public are all of the sadistic or
warlike type, which are considered more proper than the
sexual. The Boy Scouts, or at least the Indians they are imitating, might not fuck the beavers and elks (if they could catch
them), but they would certainly *kill* them if these were the

totems of opposing tribes. Sometimes even if they were not. Olaf Stapledon's neo-Fascistic science fiction novel, *Odd John*, makes much of just such a naked manhood ceremony of animal-killing. And there are few big-game hunters who do not realize that their 'virility' is involved, or imagine it is, while native beaters in jeeps herd the animals to be slaughtered before their luxurious shooting-divans or helicopters. What Price Manhood? Further details *in extremis*, in Roger Caras' *Death as a Way of Life* (Boston, 1970). Worth thinking about when you thrill to the human sacrifice of a stage 'magician' sawing a semi-nude woman in half (or electrocuting her horribly), while a hidden assistant throws ten pounds of liverwurst sausage into the first row of the audience just when the buzz-saw hits her guts!

Ancient peoples were just as frankly interested in erotic animal-human exhibitions as in the similar sadistic exhibitions. It is even highly probable that they thought of ritual erotic acts with animals as having a fructifying magic, or a magic connected with and propitious to hunting, which, in their case, was their livelihood and what they ate. Much pictorial material of this kind exists, principally from the Levant, and the literary references have been gathered in a history of bestiality by G. Dubois-Desaulle. The fascination with the un-biological notion of mythical and monstrous births as the result of intercourse of women with animals, or of animals with other animals of dissimilar biological form, is also of ancient lineage. Such notions are deified in the Greek myths of the loves of the father-god Zeus (Jupiter), in which he takes various animal and bird forms for his intercourse with women. These myths clearly descend from those of Egypt, in one of which the woman is impregnated by a crocodile! As shown in the ads for the French shocker-movie, François Jouffa's *La Bonzesse*, reproduced unexpurgated in *Le Canard Enchaîné* (Paris, 29 Mai 1974) page 7.

The ludicrous and irreverent legend of the impregnation of the Virgin Mary through her ear, by the action of Jehovah or his messenger in the form of a Pigeon (picked up from *Matthew*, iii. 16), is the exact parallel of the pagan legend of Leda and the Swan, except that swans have an intromittent male organ. According to Charles Guignebert's great critical study, *Jesus* (English translation, 1956) chapter IV.iii, page 126–7, the Virgin's conception by the ear 'is not met with until the fourth century ... but its ingenuous simplicity places its date of origin much earlier.' Guignebert adds that it 'may also have been of Egyptian origin, since Plutarch [*Of Isis and Osiris*] tells us that the idea was prevalent amongst the people of Egypt that cats conceived by the ear and were born from the mouth.' Which brings us back to animal-identifications. Obviously, the Egyptians knew very well how kittens are born, just as we know how Israeli babies are born, but the animal or bird myth has superior mystic power.

The line of development is thus quite clear between such a legend as that of Europa, raped and impregnated by Zeus-Jupiter in the form of a bull, and the matching human legend of Pasiphaë, wife of the Cretan king Minos (the grandson of Europa by her intercourse with Zeus), who attempts to repeat her grandmother-in-law's exploit by offering herself to the white bull *sacred to* – note well! – the god Poseidon, hidden inside a brazen cow. This is constructed for her by the inventor and engineer Daedalus, the Leonardo da Vinci of antiquity, and congener of Hephaestus, the crippled half-human mechanic who rises to heaven and there marries the Goddess of Love strictly owing to his mechanical gifts. Pasiphaë is punished for her pretention by giving birth to a monster, the Minotaur, half human and half bull (the bull-half is the head, making possible ritual dance-impersonation by a masked or horned priest), which had then to be confined in a labyrinth constructed for her husband, the king, by the same Daedalus. Somewhat like modern merchants of death who sell guns to both sides. The later ritual human sacrifice to the Minotaur, enacted in combat form, touches on a tremendous ancient theme and reality. (Compare the sacrifice of Isaac, also that of Jesus, and of Jephthah's daughter in *Judges*, xi. 30–40, to the demanding father-god.) It is reduced to a mere sadistic spectacle – for both the audience on the screen and the audience in fact – in Fellini's sado-homosexual motion picture version of the *Satyricon* of Petronius (1968), an anti-epic which concentrates on all the repellent horrors of antiquity.

These legends of the human brides of gods-as-animals, later the brides of the sacred animals of the gods, may be considered the female form or Ladies' Auxiliary of the more ancient Babylonian and Egyptian all-male masturbatory and orgiastic ceremonies of ritual character, such as the worship before the Golden Calf of Egypt in *Exodus*, xxxii (Hathor, identical with the Minotaur, but female), and all the other sexual worships excoriated by the Jewish Bible. The line of development is at least equally clear between all these various orgiastic legends and rituals involving animals, and the modern orgy-exhibitions of intercourse between a woman and a large dog or donkey. Other than the depictions of such intercourse in India, as cited above from Robert Briffault, the first popular European reference is in Alfred de Musset's erotic novel, *Gamiani*, in the 1830's. Similar exhibitions between a woman and a bull (!) are reported currently in Tijuana, Mexico; and earlier of a woman and a male pig in the Barbary Coast prostitution and gambling quarter of San Francisco in the 1900's. These exhibitions authentically take place, and have in recent years been photographed frequently for 'stag' motion-pictures, the stag-party itself being a form of ritual orgy. In the films *Futz* (1968) and *The Butcher and the Star* (1975), a man and woman have sexual intercourse with pigs for audience laughs.

The end-point has now been reached – anyhow one hopes so – with an 'art' motion picture of a woman sucking-off a male pig, over a soundtrack of Beethoven's "Pastoral" Symphony. Entitled *A Summer's Day* – *1970*, this film was made in Denmark by Shinkichi Tajiri, Ole Ege, and Peter Fleming. The starring female part was taken by a young Danish woman (born in 1944) who apparently had 'got into' animal intercourse quite young, in part owing to her routine duties in masturbating bulls for artificial insemination. The culminating photograph of her heavily made-up face combined with the pig's ejaculating corkscrew member is featured as cover-photo of one of the last issues of the principal European 'underground' sex-newspaper, *Suck*, published in English in Amsterdam. (Only nine issues appeared altogether, between 1969 and 1974, each one more incredibly ugly and 'liberated' – read, perverted – than the one before.)

A Summer's Day – *1970* was awarded first prize at *Suck's* "First Wet Dream Film Festival" at Amsterdam in 1970. The only member of the jury who voted against the film, stating that 'pig, horse and dog-fucking was ANTI-EROTIC,' was Al Goldstein, film-critic of New York's sex-newspaper, *Screw*, who has been quoted above as to *Myra Breckinridge*. However, he was outvoted seven-to-one by the other judges. These included the principal British Women's Liberation activist, Germaine Greer, author of the excellent *The Female Eunuch*, who was one of the editors of *Suck*, and who objected that the pig did not really

seem interested in the woman, but who voted for the film anyway, apparently considering it not a gruesome exploitation of a
neurotic woman's body, but an exploitation of the pig! She
drew the line, nevertheless – as did a number of other people
also – at a later "Wet Dream Festival," at a live animal-sadism
'avant-garde happening' by the Austrian group of Otto Muehl.
This spectacle, entitled "Sexy Goose," which won the special
Dirty Old Man Award, is described as follows by Michael
Zwerin, as the climax of Muehl's naked group act:

> Muehl produces a live goose. He brandishes a knife. Those
> who remain tremble with the expectation of horror. People
> back up from the front rows. Should we leave? Stay and not
> look? Stay and stop the slaughter? Muehl will behead the
> goose. Blood will fly. He has been doing it all over Europe for
> years [nota bene]. He will drape himself with entrails, wrap
> the headless, twitching goose neck in plastic, and penetrate
> one of his girls with it.
>
> Not tonight. Heathcote Williams, avant garde playwrite
> ... interferes ... Williams freaks [panics]. His electric hair
> bobbing, he grabs for the goose. Journalist Anthony Haden-
> Guest charges over red-faced to help. Muehl loses. Tonight's
> Event is the saving of the goose.
>
> Winding it up, Muehl is obviously furious at the loss of an
> orgasm. He whips and pushes his band even more brutally
> than usual. They become raw and bruised. Muehl takes a
> healthy crap on the stage and that's it.

This is quoted from *Suck's* final publication, *Wet Dreams*, the
festival yearbook, edited by William Levy & Willem de Ridder
(Amsterdam: Joy Publications, 1973) p. 178. This heavily
illustrated folio volume also gives, between pages 155 and 229
inclusive all the details and photos of *A Summer's Day – 1970*,
from the autobiography of the star, "My Men, My Pigs, My
Orgasms," by Miss Bodil Joensen; through Otto Muehl's im-
provised fecal finale to his aborted 'theatre of cruelty' happening, "Sexy Goose." (Compare "The Aristocrats," in 15.VI.3,
below.) A document for history. The pig photos also appear
among the truly repulsive color-plates in Mr. Earl Kemp's
pornographically illustrated edition of the American government *Report of the Commission on Obscenity and Pornography*
(San Diego: Greenleaf Classics, 1970; repr. Darmstadt: Melzer

Verlag) vol. II, pls. xx – xxiv, for which Mr Kemp was indicted for literary 'pandering.'

Folk-humor approaches these themes very gingerly, usually confining itself to wholly human exhibitions, and these often by 'error.' As in the *"Last night was for the movies"* joke, the essential danger being flirted with emotionally is the thought that the protagonist, or identification-image of the listener – let us be frank : the listener himself or herself – might 'accident-ally' and unwittingly, and therefore heavens-knows unwillingly, be cast in the starring rôle of just such a secretly-desired orgy or exhibition. Not all of us are as frank as Queen Pasiphaë, or have the neurotic courage of her nameless Mexican or Danish granddaughters who can stand up to, or lay down to, the monstrous stiffle of a bull or donkey, or the corkscrew pizzle of a pig.

Like the orgy or erotic exhibition as a *spectator-sport,* the orgy joke thus becomes a modern equivalent of eating your moral cake and having it too. The censor's trick. Or the standard double-shuffle excuse of "I-didn't-know-what-I-wuz-doin'-I-wuz-drunk." Substitute today 'high' or 'spaced-out' for *'drunk,'* depending on whether the now snobbish hashish or LSD have been taken, or 'hard drugs,' which have to be sniffed or injected, to replace the more old-fashioned alcohol (which gets there just the same). I have already remarked in *The Fake Revolt* (1967) p. 8, on the cheap new Dutch courage that has been found socially, by means of such drugs, actually to *do* everything that was once only a titillatingly dirty dream or joke. Now under such names as 'the underground' (long after Dostoy-evsky!) or 'the family,' the 'theatre of cruelty,' 'joy,' and other *dernier cri* masks set up by the Gangsters of the New Freedom. 'The real point, if not the conscious and intended purpose, is simply to make sure that the New Freedom is turned safely [from any economic or social revolt] into something indistin-guishable from the old *non*-freedom; or into just a new and not very convincingly soundtracked arty-farty version of the same old freedom for screwing and turning-on, but this time with and to perverted chicks, orgies, whippings, sick "happenings," marijuana, heroin, and LSD, instead of the now *déclassé* prosti-tutes and booze that were good enough for grandpa.'

A man is accosted by a beautiful woman in Paris and taken to her room, where they have intercourse in a variety of posi-tions, soixante-neuf, *etc. Out in the street again, a few hours later, a pimp accosts him, but the man refuses to go along, saying that he's tired. "Ah, you are tired? You weesh to relax? Come wiz me to Pig-Alley* [Pigalle, the nightclub area of Paris]. *Marvellouse peepshow – only one hundred francs." The man accepts, and is ushered into a dark room where fifteen other men are already gathered at peepholes in the wall, and warn him to be quiet as he stumbles about finding a place. He looks through one of the holes and sees the same woman, the same furniture, the same positions and* soixante-neuf – *but a different man.* (Los Angeles, Calif. 1952.) *Anecdota Americana II*, in 1934, gives an elaborate if unconsummated version of this as its final or punch-line joke, at No. 502: *A man picks up a young woman in a hotel lobby and goes to her apartment with her. They both undress, but then she says, "First chase me! I want to be inflamed – excited!" He chases her for two hours but cannot catch her, and leaves in disgust. The next night he sees her pick up another victim in the same lobby, and he sneaks up on the fire-escape to watch the new sucker's discomfiture through the window. As he watches the bare legs flashing by, under the partly-drawn window-shade, he says to himself out loud, "Oh, brother, get a load of that!" "You said it!" breathes a man's voice in his ear, "but you should have seen the son-of-a-bitch that was here* last *night!"*

Although it has been my effort in the present work to avoid reduplicative versions of the same jokes – thus, many thousands of collected texts have been omitted as too close to the some two thousand jokes here printed – I would like to give even a third version of the joke just above. This is the most recent form printed in *World's Dirtiest Jokes* (1969) p. 97, and brings the matter significantly back, though in a burlesque way, of course, to the matter of orgies and exhibitions with animals just discussed. *'A man went to a whore house and asked the madam if she had anything unusual for him to try. She told him she had a Rhode Island Red hen that was trained to do blow jobs. He could hardly believe this, but paid the fee and took the hen to his room. After several hours, he figured out that it was just a plain old chicken, but he had so much fun trying that he came back the next day and asked what else was new.' This time he is taken to a room full of people watching through a one-way mirror, while numerous couples engage in an orgy on the other side. When he says to the man next to him, "Boy! this is great!"*

the man answers: "This is nothing! You should have been here
yesterday and seen the guy with the chicken!"

This is in the style of American practical jokes, where: *A*
man sees signs on the highway saying "ONE MILE TO GRANDMA'S
CAT-HOUSE" *and finally* "STOP HERE FOR GRANDMA'S CAT-HOUSE."
Overcome by curiosity and surprise that anyone should have
the nerve to advertise so plainly, he goes in. An old lady admits
him, and snaps "Two dollars, please, and you can go right
through the door ahead of you at the end of the hall." He pays,
goes through the door, which slams shut behind him, and finds
himself out in the yard, which is full of wooden boxes with
wire fronts, inside of which are some mangy cats. Overhead is
a small, hand-lettered sign: "YOU HAVE NOW BEEN SCREWED BY
GRANDMA. PLEASE DO NOT TELL THE SECRET. I AM JUST AN OLD
LADY TRYING TO MAKE ENDS MEET." (New Orleans, La. 1967.
Inferior and hostile version, headed "Fucking Shame," in
World's Dirtiest Jokes, 1969, p. 106, with only the first line of
the sign, and no cats!) Observe again the attempted de-
personalization of the whole prostitutory situation, with the
slammed door, prepared signs (of two kinds) etc., as earlier
under "No Money," 11.I.3. Vance Randolph gives a non-sexual
form of the joke, from the Ozarks. *The signs on the highway*
read: "SEE THE WHITE BATS – I MILE." *What one sees in the*
eventual wooden cages with wire fronts are a couple of base-
ball bats, painted white. A sign asks the victim not to give the
show away. Actually, the show is given away quite clearly by
all the stories of the preceding type, where the victim or
listener-identification hero outdoes all other victims by the very
intensity of his efforts. The point can only be that – even in
being made a fool and an erotic spectacle of – 'our' man, who is
us, has proved the most spectacular and erotic fool of all.

3. ORAGENITAL ACTS

In the real situation of prostitution, the hatred of the client
for the prostitute is very noticeable, more noticeable even than
the matching hatred of the prostitute for the client, since it is to
her advantage to conceal this. Their mutual hostility becomes
massively evident in the purposely 'nasty' jokes on prostitution,
which are grouped in the later chapter on Venereal Disease &
Disgust, 12.IV. The particular erotic specialty in which – even
without any open 'nastiness' – this hostile element is most
particularly visible, is the oragenital act of fellation. Men do not

in general perform cunnilinctus upon prostitutes, though some remarkable exceptions do exist, as in the "Blue Fox" exhibition in Tijuana, already described. The intensely masochistic Pierre Louÿs, who particularly frequented young Levantine whores, and eventually lost both his eyesight and his sanity from venereal disease contracted in this way, makes the careful point in one of his erotic writings that he had made it an absolute rule never to engage in cunnilinctus on a woman 'who had other lovers.' The underlying homosexual fear, of as it were, *meeting another man in the woman's vagina*, is frankly expressed here. A jazz-enthusiast speaking to me recently (jazz people – especially the musicians – almost all pride themselves on being a highly erotic group, with sophisticated oragenital tastes, etc.) was probably alluding to the same thing, under hygienic disguise, when he said concerning cunnilinctus, "Sure, I'll give it to any girl the *first* time. But if they want it after that, they have to *clean up*." The hostility here, against the presumed 'dirty girls,' is open.

Jokes seem to vacillate in their estimation of oragenital acts, sometimes considering fellation as the ultimate humiliation of the woman, and cunnilinctus as the ultimate humiliation of the man; but at other times admitting to a tremendous urge to cunnilinctus for the man's own satisfaction, and envying the prostitute her presumed oral pleasure in fellation or even the 'nourishment' she is thought to derive from it. That such oral jealousy implies an infantile fixation in the adult male client (on the breast, nursing-bottle, food, candy, ice-cream, liquor or other drugs) is evident. One may be certain that the urge to humiliate others, by means of or because of oragenital acts, is really only an attempted warding off of one's own unavowable attraction to the same acts, and to their profound – but even more unavowable – infantile satisfactions. More will be found on this aggressive aspect of the subject in my practical manual, *Oragenitalism: Oral Techniques in Genital Excitation* (New York, 1969) especially at pages 223–32, and 258, materials not appearing in the original edition of 1940.

The joke has already been cited in which: *One whore complains to the other that times are bad. "You call this bad? Why I hear that in Philadelphia they're sucking cocks for food!"* (Heard often as a sort of catch-phrase during the American economic depression of the 1930's.) Other examples of the idea of the swallowed semen as food are given above, in the chapter on Homosexuality, 10.IV.3–4, but none is as striking as the following, very often collected over the last thirty years and still quite popular. Its first appearance is in *Anecdota Americana* (1927) 1:359. *A man is recounting to a friend his experiences in a de luxe brothel: "A beautiful blonde came in, wearing a trailing negligée, and carrying a mysterious box. Out of the box she took a sugar-doughnut and put it around my prick. On top of that she put whipped cream and maraschino cherries, and then ate it all off. It was sensational!" The friend to whom he has told this goes to the same brothel, but the blonde is "occupied," and he is too excited to wait, so he asks madam for another girl and gets a voluptuous Jewish brunette. She puts a bagel-roll around his penis, and smothers it in cream-cheese and lox [smoked salmon]. "How did it feel?" asks the first friend later. "I don't know. It looked so good, I ate it my-self."* (N.Y. 1952, given by the informant – a Jewish publisher in his fifties, who died shortly thereafter of cancer – as his *favorite story*. This has been collected as the favorite story of at least two other men as well, both Christians.) The substitution of food-taboos for sex-taboos in many cultures and religions, such as both Judaism and Christianity – 'kash-ruth,' Passover and Lent – necessarily involves this intense physical or humorous pleasure in the matching abrogation of the taboos. See further the whole section on "Food-Dirtying" in chapter 12.IV.11, below.

One of the rare references to cunnilinctus by the prostitute's clients: '*In Leicester Square a covey of partridges* [whores] *were discussing the merits of various toilet preparations. Milton, Gyraldose, Sanitas, and even Scrubbs had all been mentioned, when one lady then confessed, "Personally, I prefer salt water; it makes clients thirsty".*' (Kimbo, *Tropical Tales*, 1925, p. 7.) Other jokes under "Cunnilinctus" (First Series, 8.V.3–4) have already shown how this can end dangerously for the man, not always stated to be the client of a prostitute: *The girl douches with champagne, and the man has a terrific hangover the next morning. Or: The movie-starlet who uses Paris green for pubic crab-lice – three movie-directors die of poisoning.* The same theme returns in the idea of sex-as-food (here indignantly rejected) in a British joke concerning: *The prostitute who takes a client to her room, but finds that she is menstruating. "I say," she remarks, "I see I've come off poorly. Would you like a drink?" " 'Oo d'you think I am?" cries the outraged client angrily, "Dracular?"* (Referring to the Hungarian vampire, Count Dracula.)

References to oragenitalism in connection with prostitution are seldom either charming or erotic *("Heard about the little mouses? They felt each other's mouse-organs!"* – Chelmsford, Essex, 1954). Usually such references are anti-erotic and grim, with the open implication that these are really humiliations being forced or heaped upon the prostitute or other woman. Again and always as food: *An old lady sees a group of whores lining up to get their yellow-ticket permits at the police station, and asks what the line is for. As a joke, one of the whores tells her that it is for sugar (or oranges), and she lines up too. The priest comes by and is horrified to see the old lady in line. "What are you doing in this line, Grandma?" he says severely. "You shouldn't be here." "Why not?" she replies defensively; "I can still munch it around with my gums and suck it as well as anybody else!"* (*Histoires de Curés*, Paris, 1925. Often collected in English, and most recently printed in *World's Dirtiest Jokes*, 1969, p. 91.)

Occasionally the humor is made a bit lighter by avoiding any real oragenital situation and sticking to mere verbal play with the idea: *The male whore whose silent advertisement to ladies is* LICKING HIS EYEBROWS! (L.A. 1968) – *"Have you heard about the girl who was so modest she always ate bananas sideways?"* (London, 1952). This is a last survival of various French pictorial 'typologies' of the late-19th century, showing "How Women of Various Types Eat Bananas (or Asparagus)." A similar typology exists in English as to men (and girls) in the toilet; and an even closer imitation could easily be made nowadays of college-girls and underage 'townies' purposely posing suggestively with their mouths and tongues, in the fabulous 24-flavor ice-cream palaces in America. Presumable girls' humor: *Two girls are talking. "How did you make out on your date last night?" "Lousy. I had a chance to ball [fuck] him, but I blew it."* (L.A. 1968.)

A not-very-funny favorite has already been given in which the oragenital act humiliates and disgraces the uneducated kept-woman because she cannot *pronounce* it correctly. Typical, as a notion of humor, of over-educated snobs. In a newer form, possibly a sequel: *A man looking for a fishfood restaurant in Boston asks a policeman finally in desperation: "Say, officer, do you know where I can get scrod?" The policeman looks surprised: "Shure, an' I've bin on the p'lice farce in Bahston fer farty years now, an' this is the firrrst time I ever heard the past participle o' that!"* (San Diego, Calif. 1965, collected with the statement that it was a Massachusetts Institute of Technology joke.) Newbern & Rodebaugh, p. 111, give up on the grammatical problem this poses, and end: *"I never knew the plural of it before!"*

The idea of oragenital acts, especially fellation, as an exotic specialty is nowadays disappearing, but it was at one time considered one of the very special attractions of prostitution and 'lore of the knowledgeful whore,' when prostitutes tapping at their windows in 'whore-alleys' or slouching under street-lights would offer prospective clients *'the French way: something your wife'll never give you!'* This has changed greatly since World War II in America, not only in fact but in public attitudes. Young people now correctly consider oragenitalism normal. While the best-selling sex-technique manual for old-style female squares, *The Sensuous Woman* by "J" [Joan Garrity], published in 1969, fits it all juicily under the chapter-heading of "How to Drive a Man to Ecstasy ... Nibbling, Nipping, Eating, Licking and Sucking," which wraps up the subject for any wife. The high-point in normal erotic movies in America, so far, and the one drawing the largest crowds, has been the recent fellation-training film, *Deep Throat*, directed by Gerard Damiano and starring the actress known as Linda Lovelace. She stated in an interview in the New York sex-newspaper, *Screw*, that she learned through her psychiatrist how to relax the usual gag-reflex of the muscles of the throat. This should be showing on the educational television circuit within a few years. For details of technique, see her autobiography (1973): *Inside Linda Lovelace.*

Three whores are discussing their 'Johns.' One says, "I can't stand these guys with little peckers like Chinamen, and you got to roll up into a ball to take it." "Yeah," says the second, "but it's not good when they're too long either. What I like is when they're really stubby and thick, like a baby's fist." "The third whore says nothing, and finally the other two ask her, "Well, what kind of pricks do you like best?" "What the hell does it matter?" she replies sourly; "they all taste alike, don't they?" (Santa Monica, Calif. 1964.) Jokes and songs on this pattern have a long genealogy, reaching back to "A Talk of Ten Wives on their Husbands' Ware" in the Porkington MS. (about 1460), printed by Furnivall in *Jyl of Breyntford's Testament* (1871, Ballad Society, vol. 7a, pp. 6, and 29–33), which I discuss further in *The Horn Book*, pp. 222, and 414–15, in connection with the Scottish song "Our John's Brak Yestreen," in Burns' *Merry Muses of Caledonia.*

Roth's expurgated *Anecdota Americana* (1933) No. 391, still operating under the old rules, attempts to flirt with the subject, as the *ne plus ultra* of the prostitute's art, in a contrived example concerning: *A sailor who picks up a whore on the Commons, as he has observed that she is carrying a copy of the* Kama Sutra *under her arm* [!] '*As they sat on a bench discussing the ancient sexual lore in these rare books, he became aware of strangely pungent odors which he soon realized came from her mouth. "Hum," he breathed ecstatically, "like a breath from the Orient!" "Well, it ought to be," she replied casually. "I just had a* [fellatio] *session with a Chinaman".'* The collapse intended in the final line here is the combination of both the disgrace of fellation – for all the 'ancient sexual lore in these rare books,' etc. – and that of the invidious nationality of the 'Chinaman.' Compare the folk-taunt, of the *"Ya fodder's moustache!"* type: *"Ya mudder takes Chinamans on the roof!"* (Harlem, New York, 1937), heard as part of a brief game of 'the Dozens' or contest-in-insult between two small Negro boys. Actually, Roth's "Kama Sutra" joke is enormously expurgated from an elaborate food-dirtying item one could never suspect behind the façade he erects. The real situation is entirely gone, and the punchline 'refined' down to the *blason populaire* of an invidious racial taunt. The dysphemistic original finds its correct place among the "Narsty-Narsties" of the later chapter 12.IV.4, under "Sexual Smörgåsbord."

Lilywhite liberals nowadays are very sensitive to such invidious or insulting racial terms, and I was recently gently corrected by a rich but Socialistic Hollywood writer abroad when I told a joke in which it was necessary to use the word 'Chinaman.' He explained to me carefully before the assembled company, including his 12-year-old son, that nowadays we say, 'a Chinese.' *Never* 'a Chinaman.' To show he was no prig, however, he then immediately followed up with a bilingual joke of his own in French, of which the punchline involved calling somebody a *'con'* (cunt), meaning fool, as its total humor. When I asked him about the contradiction here, he said, "You better join Women's Liberation." No 'Chinks' and no 'Chinee's' (the 's' being misplaced), and god knows no 'Niggers.' But 'cunts' – why not? As my friend observed, "It doesn't mean a thing. It's just a phrase." For that matter, 'prick' is an insult in English and Yiddish too. (Catch-phrase: "Don't call him a prick. Call him a pussy-hair! A prick is a part of a man!" – Baltimore, Md. 1951, probably on the Spanish, pendejo, pubic hair, as a term of insult.)

The word 'cocksucker' is now the ultimate pejorative term in English (see section 10.IV.1, The Fellatory Accusation), a function in which it has replaced the more ancient 'son of a bitch': earlier 'son of a whore' – the 'bitch' referred to – or 'whoreson.' In America, by the middle 1930's, 'son of a bitch' had already become almost an endearment, if correctly intoned and preceded affectionately with 'you old ...' as remarked upon in H. L. Mencken's The American Language. This descent from insult to humor was already noted by the end of the 19th century, in the one most famous line, "When you call me that – smile!" in Owen Wister's The Virginian (1902). – A man picks up a lovely girl at a concert, opening the conversation with the large "V" on her sweater, as he has gone to the University of Virginia. "I suppose it stands for 'Victory,' not 'Virginia'," he says. "It doesn't stand for either," she admits shyly; "it stands for ... well, it stands for 'Virgin,' if you really want to know." They end up in her apartment for a cup of coffee and to listen to more music on the phonograph, but she refuses to let him have intercourse with her when he tries, offering to fellate him instead. When he leaves, the man says he will phone the next day. "Well, if you do," she cautions him, "my roommate is named Virginia too, so be sure to ask for 'Ginny the cock-sucker'." (N.Y. 1953.) Obviously not the girl's own assessment of her cock-teasing tactics, but the man's.

Aside from the evident oral hostility in women of the habitual fellatress type – bilking the man's genital anticipation – there are also dangerous unconscious overtones of oral incorporation (biting and eating) of the male victim, as I have discussed at some length in Oragenitalism (1969) pp. 226–32, and 262–8, material which cannot all be repeated here. It is really these hostilities which, along with the cultural animus against male homosexuality, have given all the sting and hatred to the insulting term 'cocksucker.' Only the fool or foreigner can accept the word without flinching. Two sailors in the Orient go to a brothel, where they are invited in smil-

*ingly by two very small girls. "They can't be whores," says one
sailor to the other indignantly; "why they ain't even old
enough to have tits!" "No no," say the girls, tee-heeing politely,
"we no whores. We cocksuckers. We working our way up to
be whores."* (N.Y. 1953, told at the same session as the preceding, and in reply to it.)

Fellation has obviously to be learned, and not all women care
to learn to do it well (which is why I thought it worthwhile to
write a dignified technical manual of the art). The late John
Newbern, who was very fond of erotically insulting all his
friends and employees, in the ultra-square American tradition,
told me he was 'dedicating' the following joke to me in his
World's Dirtiest Jokes (1969) p. 92: *Business in a small hotel is
very bad, so the manager sets up a call-girl in one of the empty
rooms. The second day a guest phones him angrily to complain
about the girl, and the manager hurries up to find out what she
has done wrong. "I paid this little bitch twenty-five dollars for
a blow job," says the man, "and you know what she did – she
took it in both hands and blew on it!" The manager turns
wearily to the call-girl and says, "All right, Mabel, now watch
closely. This is the* last *time I'm going to show you how this is
done!"* Many jokes on oragenitalism show not only this fear of
homosexuality but, even better hidden, the fear of oral incorporation. (*The Chinese client who wants to 'eat' the blonde
prostitute – with chopsticks.*) But nothing in the oral incorporation line can top this total statement (same source, p. 93): *'He
was bedded down with a call girl, who seemed to be rushing
him, so he complained. She then said, "I'm sorry. I didn't mean
to be in such a hurry, but it's gotten to be second nature with
me. My last John was a racing car driver, and I had to suck out
his vapor lock during pit stops".'*

The hostile freight of jokes on fellation by prostitutes is also
evident in certain contrived puns, presented as jokes, in which
the whole message is only too evidently this hostility. *A man
in a whorehouse is being fellated by a prostitute. The place being understaffed, the madam keeps knocking at the door and
hurrying the girl, who keeps answering in a muffled voice, "I'll
be wight ououout!"* At the third interruption the man shouts,
"You heard her! She'll be right out! And as for you, quit using
my prick for a telephone!" (L.A. 1952.) Also in a more elegant
form in which: *A man picks up a young war-widow, who
keeps lamenting as she prepares, with many a pause, to give*

*him a five-dollar blow-job. "Oh," she moans, "I know I ought
not to be doing this, but I need the money. Oh, if only my husband Joe were still alive!" "Say," the man finally interrupts, "is
this a blow-job or a phone-call?"* (N.Y. 1953.) He means, a
prayer. Observe in this variant that no verbal pantomime of
the actual fellation appears.

The humiliation of the oral participant in oragenital acts, engaged in as prostitution, is still covered lightly in the preceding
examples, as humor. But all pretense of anything but purposeful degrading, hatred, and insult is eventually dropped. *Two
movie starlets are talking about the producer. "Did he give you
a good part?" asks one. "No he did not! Why, he made me such
a ridiculous offer that I laughed right in his balls."* (N.Y. 1953.)
Even more disgraceful, presumably, than fellation is anilinctus,
better known under a variety of slang names than in actual
practice, as *'rimming'* or a *'rim-job,'* or *'eating pound-cake,'* or
as part of a *'trip around the world (to the moon).'* Phrases all
common since the 1930's at least. The presumable terrible
humiliation involved here has a very long line of descent, in
part from the kissing of the Devil's posterior during the 'Black
Mass.' It has become formalized in the Anglo-Germanic world
for centuries now in the classic insulting invitation, *"Kiss my
arse!"* about which more will be said in chapters 14 and 15,
under Insults and Buttock-humor.

Though most of the hostility in the following citation is self-
directed, or burnt away in the woman's drugged daze, Bonnie
Bremser tells it like it is – but really is – in her novel *Troia* (as
printed first in *Down Here*, New York, 1967, No. 2: p. 7–8):

Have I told you about Gayou – the coach at Mexcity U.,
fat plump with falstaffian belly – best therefore, always good
for a blow job – in fact I could otherwise not make it with
him – he always asking to turn on to pot also ... I usually
receive him into the room unclothed, in drawers, I play pin-
up that way – we smoke and he sits next to me, totally undesirable he – the old time revolutionary, he relates episodes
to me of his times with Pancho Villa – about the time they
all held up the train, full of gringos to rob them and raise
money for supplies for the revolution and fuck all the American women, who secretly loved it – I can well imagine ... I
lay back and he does not hesitate, taking off his clothes carefully – the overflow of his slack and dead flesh not at all

make him modest, he being so rightfully proud of days gone by and not given up yet at all, I can not help but admire him ... the old cocksucker – he straddles my head and shoulders and plants one on me, dangling his eensy cock imperiously for me to fondle ... he teases me with his mouth pleasantly so that the pleasure and the pot go to my head simultaneously and every once in awhile I am nudged by his drooping thigh to get busy on him also – his ass is so awful fat with old flesh drooping that I can feel the bones with flesh sacks hanging – I gag on his cock, but I am not repelled knowing it is good old Gayou ...

How can one compare, with the slow-burning carbon steel of this *reality*, the hopeless contriving of the following proudly male-chauvinist example, supplied in manuscript by a night-club master-of-ceremonies with the statement that was one of the 'ten best blue-jokes' he knew, and 'guaranteed to get yocks.' *'Guy tells a whore that he's hard to excite, and she has to give him a tongue-bath and a rim-job and a trip around the world. She's tickling his ass with her tongue when she sees he's reached over to the table and is making a telephone call. "No wonder I can't get your cock up!" she yipes. "What the hell is the big idea? And me working like a slob to give you some kicks!" "My dear young woman," he says – very elegant – "I'll thank you to keep a civil tongue in my ass!"'* (N.Y. 1943.) The stage-direction 'very elegant,' tells everything.

In jokes of this kind, the ostensible humor is self-evident, purely linguistic. The situations have been creakingly set up so as to allow the hateful application of some conversational cliché, in which the whole point is not amusement over the cliché, as pretended, but a fierce delight in the expressed hatred and contempt. This is very similar to the 'educated' folk-humor of "Polluted Proverbs" (*A fool and her legs are soon parted*, etc.), or of disrespectful or scatological parodies of the words or titles of popular, patriotic, or even hymn tunes ("*Onward Christian Foreskins*," and the like). Linguistic jokes like these are not really jokes at all, but puns.

The disposition of the man's ejaculated semen in fellation is very important to him, both physically and emotionally. He not only wants the physical pleasure of the woman's mouth at the moment of his orgasm, but he also does not want her to reject him symbolically in the vulgar spitting or hawking out of his semen. In jokes he nevertheless is not above bilking her, at that very moment (so as to have it for 'love, not money'). *A Scotchman is having a street-whore suck him off under a bridge in Edinburgh. As he is about to come, he seizes her wildly by the ears and cries, "Swallow it all an' I'll gie ye an extra shilling!" The whore: "(Gulp!) What did you say?" Scotchman: "Oh, nothing ..."* (Paris, 1954, from an English pornographer. Rhymed version in *The Limerick*, no. 379, ending: '*She said "(swallow hard) – I beg pardon?"* ') The same point as that of the joke, that for an extra payment the prostitute will 'swallow it all,' is made the humorous climax of a French students' bawdy recitation, "Madame Furina," appearing in various editions of the students' *chansons de salles de garde* (first in the edition entitled *Trois Orfèvres à la Saint-Eloi* [edited by Edmond Bernard], Paris, 1930). This is cast entirely in the form of the over-polite and over-detailed salestalk or spiel of Madame Furina's husband-*cum*-pimp, who also offers to 'prepare' the client for his wife by homosexual manipulations. This recitation is considered absolutely hilarious in France.

The most famous musical bawdy joke is very often collected in either fellatory or cunnilinguistic forms. It is really an 'impossibility' joke, of the sort discussed in the following and concluding section of this chapter, but the emphasis on oragenitalism is of course central: *A woodwind player overwhelmingly excites a woman in the audience at a performance of Wagner's "Tristan & Isolde" with his slow solo introduction to the Third Act. She goes backstage to meet him after the performance and says to him frankly, "You know, the whole time you were playing that shepherd's-pipe solo, I had the fantasy that you were kissing my pussy." "What do you think I'm thinking about the whole time?" he replies, and they repair to a hotelroom where he goes through the entire Wagnerian score on her, lingually, while his hands finger her breasts and vagina. Just as she is about to have her orgasm, the man stops. "My god!" the woman screams, "don't stop now or I'll kill you!" "I've got to stop," says the musician; "there's an eight-bar rest here." "Well, ad-lib, you son-of-a-bitch!" she screams; "ad-lib!!"* (Hollywood, Calif. 1949.)

The fellational version is extremely different in tone, and combines the original joke with the classic problem of the oral participant's *silence* during fellation, making this the key 'impossibility' of the action. This idea appears first in the rhymed farce-recitation, "*La Ventriloque*," printed in the rare original collection of French students' erotic songs, *Anthologie Hospitalière & Latinesque* (Paris, 1911–13) anonymously compiled by 'Dr.' Edmond Dardenne Bernard, 1. 423, in which the poet laments the impossibility of finding a fellatress who will *also* be a ventriloquist, so that she may intone the "Marseillaise" and other national anthems while fellating him. The joke takes up from there: *A sybaritic millionaire or Indian prince, educated at Oxford, etc., and completely blasé sexually, offers a thousand pounds to the madam of the best brothel in London for a girl who must be beautiful, blonde, with large breasts, be no more than five feet, two inches tall – he being five feet three – and able to fellate him while standing on her head and whistling (or humming) the coloratura air, "Listen to the Mocking-Bird," at the same time. After weeks of search, a beautiful blonde 5 ft. 1 in. high is found, and is given a quick course in music, and sent by limousine to the millionaire's country estate at Creeping-on-Thames. Rather nervously, the girl begins her specialty standing on her head, but becomes confused by the multiplicity of the demands on her, stops completely just at the man's orgasm, and explains that she has forgotten the next few notes. "Fake it!" the man screams; "Improvise!"* (As "Vive le Hangleterre!' in *Kryptádia*, 1888, IV. 334. Also: *"Try 'The Rose of Tralee' in D!"* – Chicago, 1975.)

Note here that it is the girl's silence itself that is her hostile riposte. There is an even franker recitation, in the character of: *A French pimp who is complaining of what he has to go through in order to keep his best 'chick' (poule) on his string. He must kiss her here, tongue her there, lick her from head-to-toe every Saturday night, listen to her bullshit-crying when she is menstruating, and most of all half-kill himself trying to make her come, the way none of her clients can: " 'O Jacques, twiddle my nipple! Plink my clit! Now the other nipple! Now my clit again! O Jacques!' – God almighty!" he finishes, "a guy has to be a* one-man band *to satisfy these crazy dames!"* (Paris, 1959.) This is Cyril Connolly's "the tyranny of the orgasm."

I have observed, in the Introduction to the First Series, beginning of section VII, page 36, the lesson that the two preceding versions of the "*Ad-lib!*" joke offer, as to the changing of jokes by means of minor variations over a period of time, or from mouth to mouth, because of conscious refashioning by the tellers to suit their own psychological bent. In the "Ad-lib!" joke, in the two versions of what is visibly the same story, the entire meaning is shifted. One version presents the ultimate humiliation of a blonde prostitute by a blasé Indian prince – with the silent punchline as her suitable revenge. The other is merely an amusing misadventure in a perfectly mutual love-passage between a musician and a woman in the audience who has sought him out after being excited by his playing of the lovers' pastoral during a performance of *Tristan & Isolde*. These two versions do not appeal to the same sort of person – or even to the same sexes! – and certainly were not evolved by the same sort of persons, though both may very well have been musicians.

Nevertheless, it can hardly be overlooked that whether the crucial action is given to a man or a woman – the musician or the blonde prostitute – the whole sexual edifice is brought down by the same hostile *stopping* or silence, on one pretext or another, surely representing the let-down and disappointment of both sexes in the hated birth-control technique of *coitus interruptus*, now many thousands of years old. (Onan's actual 'sin,' in *Genesis*, xxxviii. 9.) The last word on the hostile response of silence: *American tourist in Mexico, to a prostitute in a short skirt slouching up against a wall: "Soixante-neuf? Sexaginta-novem? Sesenta-nueva?" "Talk Eengleesh. I can't count."* (Los Angeles, 1968.)

In an elegantly underplayed jest, in Freud's *Introductory Lectures on Psychoanalysis* (London, 1922) 21st Lecture, p. 270–71, the important point is made, concerning sexual perversions in general, that:

> Abominated as they are, sharply distinguished from normal sexual activity as they may be, simple observation will show that very rarely is one feature or another of them absent from the sexual life of a normal person. The kiss, to begin with, has some claim to be called a perverse act, for it consists of the union of the two erotogenic mouth zones instead of the two genital organs. But no one condemns it as perverse; on the contrary, in the theatre it is permitted as a refined indication of the sexual act.

The essence of Freud's rather ponderous joke – and there are many of them in his writings, especially in his lectures – is that, to pollute a proverb, '*Perversion is as perversion does.*' These things are strictly matters of contention and definition, and it is easy indeed to cover with confusion and shame the poor herd-mentalities we are all being turned into, whose only real sin has been appearing in public in the wrong kind of sports-car, décolletage, stingy-brim hat, or intellectual pose. If, as Freud is pointing out, the union of the two top ends of the digestive tract in kissing ought to be called a 'perversion,' strictly defined, then obviously the union of any *other* two ends – two bottoms, or tops-&-bottoms, or any other permutation, as in coitus, oragenitalism, or even anilinctus! – comes closer to genital normality than does the non-biological perversion called kissing, in which no other mammal engages. I have tried to show some of the strictly practical applications of this principle, as to erotic 'daisy-chains' or spintries, and various forms of the sixty-nine, in *Oragenitalism* (1969) p. 303–11, though I do not really recommend most such plural entertainments. As to the philosophical implications of Freud's little paradox, these would lead us rather far afield here, and the subject may best be left where it is left by Freud.

4. IMPOSSIBILITIES

Implicit in all the lore concerning marvellously apt prostitutes, and the orgies and exhibitions they put on for paying customers, there is the not-very-well hidden reversal of the usual male-female rôles, in that here it is the female who is courting and attempting to excite the male, instead of the biologically determined reverse. Throughout the mammalian order to which we belong – and up to and including whales – the male is uncontrollably attracted to the female largely through the action of his sense-organs: smell, touch, taste, and sight. The sexual activity of the sense of hearing is almost entirely restricted to the female, as the appreciative and seduced audience of the male's rutting cries and calls: in its modern form, the passionate lectures of crusading young political reformers (once ministers), and the musical activities of operatic tenors and rock-&-roll singers, with their push-over audience of thousands of creaming & screaming girls.

In the situation of prostitution, all this is reversed, and the male is passive, and presumably unexcited, difficult to excite, or even sexually burnt-out. The whole activity must be initiated and brought to a successful conclusion by the special knowledge and extravagant erotic complaisances of the whore. To the contrary of our whole mammalian pre-history of the search for, and capture of the female, by the nervously violent male, tracking her by means of her spoor in her period of heat, then chasing her at full speed when she breaks into the open, and raping her then & there; we have instead the picture of the flabby, rich client in the over-decorated and over-priced Paris or New Orleans brothel (and far fancier in the Orient), sitting playing cards or darts in a slumped position, with an iced drink in front of him, while gossiping with the madam, and casting a tired eye at ravishing beauties of All Nations parading in front of him in their open-crotch scanties, with red lace frills & furbelows in the worst possible taste, while trying to liven him up with the artificial sexual smell of commercial perfumes called "*Screw Moi*," sprayed on their bellies and breasts.

Thus, in all the jokes of the present section, the male is shown as progressively blasé and burnt-out sexually, to the precise degree that he becomes progressively civilized and rich, and thus financially able to satisfy the most brutal or outlandish sexual letches and fetiches, by means of which he hopes to excite himself one more time, or one last time, to the sexual intercourse that has long since been drained of emotional meaning for him – and for the whore. The simple or unspoiled male position as to the overwhelming excitements of these unbiological displays of the female, in strip-teases and evening gowns down to *here*, and short skirts and bikinis up to *there* (now finally 'topless' monokinis, as the girls begin to get desperate), is that he would really rather see up a girl's dress by accident, walking up a stairway behind her, or be excited by an unexpected view of her bosom as she bends over to serve him food: another natural female rôle, god knows. As to the prostitutory and de luxe foofaraw, the unspoiled male knows very well that it is only for rich old men, and that only they have need of it. As in the polite food-expurgation of the problem: "*Rockefeller would give a million dollars to have your . . . digestion.*"

That is why so many of the preceding jokes have brought the subject of prostitution insistently back to the crude question of *money*, which is not a real problem to most men telling such jokes. The real nagging problem is how much all this fancy fucking and fake fetichistic femininity is going to cost the man, when he truly wants and feels he ought to be getting it free, 'for love.' That is to say, for the love he himself is not offering, but wants nevertheless to get. As though he were really in the emotional and economic position of the Negro blues singer who refuses to look at the naked belly-dancer, '*Cuz every time she wibble, The pore man dollar's gone.*'

Parallel with the reality of endlessly rich, impotent, and perverted clients, runs the legend of the infinitely clever and seductive courtesan : the 'knowledgeful whore' already discussed at the beginning of the preceding section on "Specialties." With all her electrifying hair-dress and cosmetics, her sumptuous costumes and sensuous stockings, her exotic backgrounds and aphrodisiacal perfumes and potions, and of course her infinite variety of bedroom 'specialties' and athletics, and her totally self-degrading submissions and obeisances; all guaranteed to turn the trick, to do the job, to fan the customer's dying phallic flame back to temporary life, at any price and even if only this one last time. "*I'll pay anything! Do anything! Just make it stand up stiff again once more!*" The miracle of the Resurrection of the Flesh, for which Faust pays the Devil with his soul, so that he may be young and rejuvenated again – and *damn* being wise and old! – and frolic in the fabled arms of Helen of Troy.

Actually, there is fire behind this hyperexcited smoke, and always has been, as in the strange and authentic story of the weaning of the Persian king Artaxerxes II from homosexuality to heterosexuality by the courtesan Milto, called Aspasia the Younger, about 400 B.C., who dressed herself at first in boy's clothes to approach the bereaved king in the character of his favorite page who had just died. Unfortunately, mere transvestist subterfuges like these – today being employed by millions of women in the West – simply do not do the job; in fact, they generally frighten off the men even worse. So then, *what* was Aspasia's erotic secret that could perform these miracles? We will never know.

Perhaps the truth is that in searching to excite one's dying flame once more by means of perfectly impossible forms of sexual intercourse and more and more horrendous perversions to demand of the prostitute, or to be offered by her in the fantasies of jokes and folktales – pretending, but only pretending, to laugh at the very idea – both the male client in the stories and the listener who laughs are searching for an entirely different woman than the prostitute, or than whatever woman he must bed down with in the end. An entirely different woman whom he hopes somehow *to encounter in her body.*

That is the real meaning of Dr. Johnson's famous remark to Boswell: *'Sir, were it not for Imagination, a man might be as happy in the arms of a chambermaid as of a duchess.'* The impossibility of finding the woman he is really seeking, in the person of the prostitute, is displaced by the ever-hopeful man to impossible parts of her body, to impossible women she can never be. (The real meaning of Faust-Goethe's *'ewig Weibliche,'* or Eternal Woman.) To impossible apertures, specialties, possibilities and impossibilities he wishes to force or to fantasy into existence in this degraded female flesh, so totally and yet so unsatisfyingly available to him – because it is he who is degrading it.

Under the significant title of "The Most Prevalent Form of Degradation in the Erotic Life," Freud has strikingly analyzed, in his *Collected Papers*, that form of partial male impotence which is experienced by men as the need to have intercourse with women of low social class, and specifically prostitutes, for whom they do and can have no respect but with whom they are powerfully potent; while with women of their own social class, race, or religion, or for whom they feel tenderness and respect, they find themselves unaccountably impotent. I have already mentioned the two most striking fictional examples of this, played desperately as 'black humor' comedy and published under the guise of novels in the 1960's with enormous success: Robert Gover's *The Hundred Dollar Misunderstanding* (1964) ringing the changes on the theme of white-man-and-black-whore; and Philip Roth's *Potnoy's Complaint* (1968) which actually cites Freud's article, above-mentioned, as title to its crucial scene.

Roth allows the reader the delight of wallowing in Jewish self-hatred, and in his anti-hero's impotence with all but the *non*-Jewish 'dirty girls' whom he identifies brashly as the carefully unrecognizable opposite or counterpart of his mother-ideal: the blonde Christian *'shikse'* or white-trash, with whom sexual relations are gloriously possible because they are really a sort of pubic revenge, dirtying the woman by complex and repeated sexual demands, often of an anal-sadistic or oral-sadistic nature. This is Portnoy's presumable complaint – long after Molly Bloom's monologue in Joyce's *Ulysses* – with special emphasis on the anti-hero's fantasies of sexually dirtying the women, carefully signboarded by the author as Freud's "Most Prevalent Form of Degradation in the Erotic Life." Yes,

and in current fiction too, I betcha ... Here y'are folks! Why
go elsewhere to be screwed, reamed, and cheated? Stop here!
Here it is, the new American, best-selling, food-filthying,
mother-fucking "Epistle to the Philippians," *Portnoy's Complaint*, middle of chapter entitled "Cunt Crazy," on the dream
of the dirty-fucking blonde. And all in less than the legal limit
of three hundred fucking words. How can you beat it? Whose
Erotic Life can get any more Fucking Degraded than that?
Going, going, gone!!

Schmuck, this is the real McCoy. A *shikse!* And asleep! Or
maybe she's just faking it, but saying under her breath,
"C'mon, Big Boy, do all the different dirty things to me you
ever wanted to do." "Could that be *so?*" "Darling," croons
my cock, "let me just begin to list the many different dirty
things she would like you to start off with : she wants you to
take her hard little *shikse* titties in your hands, for one."
"She does?" "She wants you to finger-fuck her *shikse* cunt
till she faints." "Oh God. Till she faints!" ... In sixty seconds
I have imagined a full and wonderful life of utter degradation
that we lead together on a chenille spread in a shabby hotel
room, me and ... the sluttiest-looking slut in the chorus line.
And what a life it is, too, under the bare bulb (HOTEL flashing
just outside our window). She pushes Drake's Daredevil Cup-
cakes (chocolate with a white creamy center) down over my
cock and then eats them off of me, flake by flake. She pours
maple syrup out of the Log Cabin can and then licks it from
my tender balls until they're clean again as a little baby
boy's. Her favorite line of English prose is a masterpiece:
"Fuck my pussy, Fuckface, till I faint." When I fart in the
bathtub, she kneels naked on the tile floor, leans all the way
over, and kisses the bubbles. She sits on my cock while I take
a shit, plunging into my mouth a nipple the size of a toll-
house cookie, and all the while whispering every filthy word
she knows viciously in my ear. She puts ice cubes in her
mouth until her tongue and lips are freezing, then sucks me
off – then switches to hot tea! Everything, everything I have
ever thought of, she has thought of too, *and will do.*

Men of this kind always find it necessary to insist on the
presumable 'lowness' or 'badness' or even the ugliness of the
preferred prostitute, or woman of foreign ethnic group. ('The

sluttiest looking slut in the chorus line.') This is the letch for cheap whores expressed by artistic dandies like Baudelaire and Toulouse-Lautrec, who made sure – just as sure as *Portnoy* – that they left a careful verbal or pictorial record of the dirty bitches and raddled harridans they frequented. Often such men must also whip up their own potency by expressing themselves in verbal or physical sadisms directed against the woman herself, and intended to debase and degrade her even further, by the fact of her putting up with it, even if 'only for money.' Other than the standard confusion of sadism with sex, now at its apogee in the Western world in the 'sadistic concept of coitus' of popular literature, movies, snob poses, etc.; these sadisms – whether verbal or physical – are intended to show contempt for the woman, and to maintain her firmly in the 'low' or non-respectable status which is the essential precondition of the neurotic male's sexual potency with her. For the short course in the perverted enjoyments offered to this type of male by modern urban prostitutes – female and male – see Ernest Borneman's erotic slang dictionary, *Sex im Volksmund* (Hamburg: Rowohlt, 1971) thesaurus sections 65–81; and the even more graphic and detailed whorehouse address-book, with suggested prices for each sadistic specialty, etc., *Das Strich-Buch* [The Stroke-Book] ed. Alexander Niss (Frankfurt: Zero Press, 1971) pp. 19–30, and 65–9, art. "Freier;" with a hundred-page slang dictionary supplementing Borneman's. Krafft-Ebing brought up-to-date.

At the lowest and crudest level, dirtyings of this kind are fantasied, or actually achieved, by the use of excrement, as throughout the writings of De Sade. (This indicates the precise neurotic and sexual problem of the literary bell-wethers or Judas-sheep now whooping it up for Sade.) I myself have met an adult male – a theatre-actor: classically an infantile group – whose name I obviously cannot give here owing to the libel laws, though it is very well known, who told me perfectly frankly that, under the self-created psychological name of "De-filation," he would pay women to eat his feces and to allow him to rub it over their bodies. Infantile anal-sadism can hardly be taken farther than that. He was not bragging or swanking: the girls in the show had already told me about him. Scenes like these are the subject of certain folk-rationalizations in jokes, in some of which, however, it is the man who eats the feces, and not the prostitute. (See, specifically, chapter 12.IV.1, "Cloacal

Intercourse;" and also chapter 15.III.4, *"Pet-en-Gueule,"* and 15.V, "Scatophagy.") Urination on other persons in this way is actually rather common, and is known among perverts and prostitutes as the "Golden Stream" – long after Danaë! Again, it is not always the prostitute (female or male) but often the client who is the passive participant or He-Who-Gets-Pissed-Upon. This too has been made the subject of a best-selling 'New Freedom' novel in the 1960's in America, *The Exhibitionist* by 'Henry Sutton' [David Slavitt], in which – if I understand it correctly – a movie-magnate has six girls urinate on him in a bathtub ... Sometimes I wonder what the New Slavery will be like. Will it be worse, when it comes? As come it must, if this be Freedom.

These are the hidden specialties and impossibilities of prostitution that the jokes never mention at all, or, if they do mention them, do so in such a way as to make clear that the essential subject is not really prostitution but "Defilation," or some folk-effort to *rationalize* such materials into mock reasonableness or humor. These extreme jokes are therefore not included here, but must be sought – by them as likes 'em – in the following chapter, on Disease & Disgust, 12.IV, under "Narsty-Narsties," where a further effort is also made to identify the purposely defiled and degraded woman generally presented as an 'old and unappetizing' whore. An example of the whole ugly thing, in which the status of prostitute is essential to the turning of the creaky wheel of the story, is given by Mr. Newbern and Miss Rodebaugh in *The World's Dirtiest Jokes* (1969) p. 142, a source which, as its title promises, contains a record number of items of the 'defilation' type. *A man with a large St. Bernard dog smuggles it into a hotel and puts it in a closet, and then tells the bellhop to get him "a beautiful blonde woman, as close to six feet tall as possible." When the woman arrives, he has her undress naked and get down on all fours (with her ass facing the closet). He then opens the closet door, lets out the big dog, and says to it: "Now, see what you're going to look like if you don't eat your Red Heart dog food!"* Probably a decayed survival of the ancient superstition, Tales Types 1091–95: *Man sends his wife backwards on all-fours, naked and tarred-&-feathered, to frighten away the Devil (ogre, bear, thunder).*

This is obviously not the scene intended by whoever originally set up the woman-and-dog situation in his mind, nor does the effort to turn it into the anti-woman 'nonsense' humor of *mere humiliation* at the end fool anyone. (Imagine the same pretext in a story elaborately setting up an ass-to-front confrontation of a woman with a donkey in a Mexican hotel ...) The most extraordinary example I have ever seen of trying to present open sexual perversion as humor or 'nonsense' was a motion picture of the mid-1960's in America, entitled *Good Neighbor Sam*, a friendly little around-the-corner movie-house domestic comedy, concerning a dairy-farm millionaire and his efforts to get good, clean advertising slogans to promote his brand of milk – and nothing smutty, see! (Ho-ho-ho.) By some magical transmogrification this all ends up with the appointed advertising executive in a sleazy hotel-bedroom with a can of red paint and a large brush (he's going to paint out some offending billboard outside the window, you see), who then chases down the stairs a harmless *prostitute* who has been sent to his room by accident, sloshing and streaking her wildly with brushloads of paint, while she is locked in an open-cage elevator. I italicize *prostitute*. This prize-item in the Defilation Sweepstakes was naturally very popular when released later in shit-oriented Germany, where I'll bet they understood very well what the 'red paint' was supposed to be, and why it had to be a *prostitute* who gets sloshed with it, under the sex-come-on translated title of *Lend Me Your Husband*, with Jack Lemmon at the sloshing-brush.

Lest it be thought that women are the inevitable victims in this type of defiling, whether as fantasy, 'humor,' or reality, it should be emphasized again that at the present time, and owing to the advancing degradation of the sexual relations between men & women generally, a new and unbiological type of woman (usually young) is now becoming common who is *not* searching for the finest man she can find, with whom to marry and mate and thus improve the genetic and biological line. (In kennel parlance, "to get the best sire for her pups.") Instead, girls or women of this type express an open neurotic preference – exactly similar to that just discussed as to impotent men, frightened of approaching the mother-image – for men whom they cannot and do not respect, and who are no competition with them, and are expected to be no competition, in fighting it out for position as top-banana around the house.

The men preferred are weak men, 'Organization' cogs, homosexuals, or men of some racial group considered inferior to the woman's own, as for example Orientals or Negroes. Only with men of this kind is such a woman able to break through her otherwise total orgastic frigidity. With men of her own social class, or for whom she otherwise does or must feel respect – or identifies them in any way with the forbidden father-image – she is attacked by intractable impotence, and cannot arrive at orgasm except by means of mechanical assists such as prolonged clitoral excitation with a vibrating massage-motor, preferably with her back turned to the man. Here, precisely matching that of the impotent male neurotic described by Freud, the woman's frigidity is the inevitable result of the matching identification of all desirable peer-group men with the forbidden father – forbidden to her by the dominant position in her own family of a mother just like herself. With whom can the lioness mate? The rule, or Legman's Law is: *When Oedipus fucks the pig, Elektra mates with the mutt.* Such women also have the matching need to harm or vilify or psychologically to castrate all men with whom they have sexual relations, as a pre-condition of their own sexual excitement and potency. I have discussed this important 20th-century malady, which is an obvious and crucial problem in the now-developing 'Women's Liberation' movement, in *Love & Death* (1949), the article "Avatars of the Bitch-Heroine." Some further curiosa of the subject are grouped in the later chapter on Castration, in sections 13.I, "Vagina Dentata," and 13.III.2, "Circumcision and Women," to which the reader is referred.

The castration theme is curiously echoed or adumbrated in various jokes in which some type of physical harm comes to either the prostitute or the client during their sex intercourse with each other. The physical harm – sometimes only a modification of the body – is naturally in a sexual area, or is of such form that it can be made use of sexually. The hostile tone is of course unmistakable in such an 'impossibility' joke as that in which: *A man objects to the price a prostitute has charged him, and attempts to have intercourse with her violently in and around her navel, shouting, "At these prices, I'm going to make my own goddam hole!"* The same hostility, merely rationalized as being the result of a beneficial surgical operation appears in: *The prostitute who had her appendix out, and made quite a bit of money on the side.* (N.Y. 1953: not presented as a joke, but frankly as a non-dialogue pun, gag, or 'wisecrack.' Probably derived from the anti-homosexual taunt:

"Did you ever take it into your head to make a living?")

The gag-form just given represses all explanation, which would immediately lead to anatomical gruesomeness, concerning a 'wound healing open,' or similar: the presumed *ne plus ultra* or banko-bingo-premium of prostitution, as will be seen. The usual explanation of the man's urge for unusual apertures and thrills is that he is bored, *blasé*, has tried everything, and is no longer excited by anything. The obvious cure for such a state of sexual exhaustion would be sexual REST, possibly for a protracted period, as in Mark Twain's burlesque "Hunger Cure" story, which sets the matter symbolically on its head, under the aspect of a cure of the jaded appetite for food. As with much that Twain wrote, this has to be read with the mathematical symbols correctly cancelled out, and the expurgations filled in. In jokes, as in neurotic life, the impossible cures of further, newer, more expensive and more exotic sexual thrills, taste thrills, drug thrills, speed thrills, aphrodisiacs for every sense-organ and biological function – *"One for a man and two for a beast!"* as with the old snake-oil vendors' pills – become the erroneous panacea sought instead. In quest of the impossible and nonexistent super-orgasm that no one ever had before, and no one ever will.

Consider Baudelaire's repugnant punchline 'specialty' in *"A Celle qui est trop gaie"* in his *Fleurs du Mal* (1857), written for the celebrity-fucker, Mme. Sabatier, and threatening: *'One night, when the voluptuous hour tolls ... to make, in your astonished flank, a large and hollow wound; and – vertiginous delight! – through these new lips infuse my venom into you, my sister!'* Baudelaire denied that by 'venom' he had meant syphilis, but the hateful degradation of the woman in the search for some *dernier frisson* between her 'new lips' is unambiguous. This later became the specialty – in fact, not fantasy – of Dr. Alexander Pedachenko, a Ukranian physician in London, better known as 'Jack the Ripper.'

Probably the mildest cure of all is: *big tits*. This is even normal if one is young enough. (In diapers.) The apotheosis of the American tit-dream is alluded to in William Bradford Huie's *The Revolt of Mamie Stover* (1951), concerning the fortunate G.I. customer in Mamie Stover's whorehouse in Honolulu for American soldiers, who *'could revel in the biggest, most luscious tits in the world. He could enjoy to the limit our whole tit-culture; he could have tits in his hands, tits in his ears, tits in his mouth. He could walk away from Mamie's sur-feited, for the moment, with tits.'* (A pity this couldn't have been written by Henry Miller instead. He could have done it justice.) Any matching description of more normal or more adult clients' satisfactions in Mamie's place is significantly ab-sent. In the choice, however, of this partial exposition of the whorehouse paradise or philosophy, the infantile client's not-altogether unconscious approach to the mother-image is made certain and clear. The greatest exposition of the American tit-dream and underwear fetich is the superb Balaamic anathema by Seymour Krim, "The Magical Underwear Panty," in his *Views of a Nearsighted Cannoneer* (New York, 1961) p. 98–104, six brief pages that are the high-point of modern dithyrambic prose since Céline.

The layers of the onion peel off, and one descends rapidly into one's own internal hell – foolish or frantic, one does what one can. The glory of *big tits* is only temporary. Kid stuff. The new baby comes, and one day you are weaned. Your true play-boy then moves on to higher things and rougher stuff. He is bored; he is *blasé*. He has taken the trip all the way from Kan-kakee to Kalamazoo without losing his didies, and he is a Man of Distinction. Bring on the girls! So he can wipe his feet on them. Or, at the very least, rip and dirty the *big tits* that have rejected him at last. *'A man who visited a whorehouse was complaining to the madam: "I've had every kind of treatment here. I've been screwed, sucked, jerked, everything. I've tried every way. Haven't you got a new thrill for me?" The madam thought hard for a while, then said, "Have you tried our radio girl?" "No, what's that? Who's that?" the man asked in surprise. "Why, it's that girl over there," the madam pointed. "You take her tits, put one in each ear, and hear her coming".'* Anecdota Americana, 1927, 1:353. Also made into rather contrived limerick sequence, "Dr. Zuck," dated 1941, in *The Limerick*, Nos. 365–6, with narcissistic improvements: notably that the man hears *himself* coming, not the woman. It would be too easy to make fun of this as the high-flying humor it so evidently is, of the yokcha-de-bopcha 1920's of cat's-whisker radios and Amos 'n' Andy. More importantly, and for all its callowness, it is one of the first folk expressions of *the erotization of the machine*, on which see the later section, under Castration, 13.VI.3, "The Mechanical Man" – the dangerous miscegenational marriage we are now all being 'integrated' and brainwashed to accept: *Machine Fucks Man.*

Meanwhile, another dangerous current pulls the sand out from under the feet of the shipwrecked client or human dere-lict, searching for his ultimate passion on the distant Calvary of a whorehouse hill. This is the possibility of *revenge* by the whore, for the dirtyings and perversions he heaps upon her in his pretended search for the ultimate, the search in which she accompanies him as 'female-nigger' or butt. Much has been said already, in the First Series, section 8.III.3–6, pages 501–34, as to stories of this type, in which the ultimate erotic thrill searched for, under the names of "The Sleeve Job," "The Mysterious Card," or similar, always ends in killing, ruining, or disgracing the man, *without his ever learning what the ultimate thrill may be.* (It is death.) All 'shaggy dog' stories of this kind, and in particular the original "Sleeve Job," can be traced to a recitation by the French Mark Twain, Henry Monnier, called *"La Diligence de Lyon"* (The Lyons Stagecoach), and some-times *"Le Chemin-de-fer japonais,"* first published in Jules Gay's bibliographical magazine, *Le Fantaisiste* (San Remo, 1873) I. 176–85. Beyond that, however, lies an East Indian "Tunic of Nessus" story published by Prof. Thompson (Motif K1227.4.1): *A girl tells her seducer that she cannot give herself to him until he bathes. She prepares the bath herself, and poisons it with caustic acid.* The modern versions have simply transformed this into a puzzle or mystery by omitting – or pantomiming – the final line.

Obvious burlesques of the title, "The Sleeve Job," or "The Little Japanese Train" are sometimes used as meaningless running-gags or insiders' allusions. There is also the "Wax Job," retailed at length by the compilers of *The World's Dirtiest Jokes* (1969) p. 97. Reducing this to its essentials: *An American tourist visiting Japan is told he must go to a whorehouse and get a geisha girl to give him a "Wax Job." After a long build-up in which he undresses and waits for the girl, who leads him wordlessly into a bath with her* [compare the original Indian "Sleeve Job," above], *she rubs and massages him while 'hum-ming soft Japanese love songs.' She then takes his penis 'and laid it on a small red velvet cushion, and before he knew what was coming, gave it a mighty karate chop right on the head. Quick as a wink, he jumped up, his ears popped, and boy! you should have seen the ear wax shoot out!* (Meaning semen, no doubt.) This is a frank enough castratory statement to end all "Sleeve Job" stories, but their mystery to a certain kind of eager chump will of course keep them going forever.

In Ray Russell's satirical novel of up-to-the-minute Hollywood perversion, *The Colony* (Los Angeles, 1969), the author wrings a bit of humor out of a presumed reference by Henry Miller – under the name of 'Blaise Mullen,' p. 169–71 – to a mysterious "Persian Perversion' (an alliterative title taken from a well-known rhyme: *The Limerick*, no. 337). This ultimate specialty the author-hero actually has performed upon him, at the studio's expense, at the hands [???] of a silent Armenian prostitute – he says she's a Persian, but I have my doubts – named Lulu Hormuzijan. And he ends by warning the reader solemnly: *'Never ask what The Persian Perversion is. The knowledge of it, gained at first hand, will darken your soul yet lighten your hair with silver. After she left, I made out an expense slip* (for the studio) *which I later handed in: L. Hormuzijan, Research: $25.'*

The ultimate specialty or impossibility is presumably intercourse in the *eye:* 'In the cavity of the extracted eye,' as the sexologists Rohleder and Hirschfeld humorlessly specify, in Latin, just before World War I. *A prostitute asks her client what he wants. "What's your specialty?" he asks. "Well," she says, "my prices are one dollar, two dollars, five dollars, and twenty dollars, and you can take your pick. I'll jerk you off, suck you off, fuck you off, or take out my glass eye and wink you off!"* (Allentown, Pa. 1936, the man telling the story pantomiming a terrific final *wink*.) Even here, however, the menacing note of danger in all these marvellous specialties is to be heard, in a 'topper' or improved version, carrying the preceding joke on past its punchline to a new ending: *The client being 'winked off' feels a sudden intense pain. "It's nothing to worry about," says the prostitute airily; "just a stye."* (N.Y. 1953.).

In *Anecdota Americana*, 1:298, the original idea is built up practically to novelette length, concerning: *'A Russian nobleman, who had become a refugee in Paris, after the successful establishment of the Bolshevik regime,' and who is reputed to be 'the most blasé man in Paris.' He bets with a prostitute that she cannot 'offer him a refinement he had never known before.' He refuses the offer of her mouth or arm-pit, her 'close and bountiful' breasts, and her vagina. 'There was not even any abnormality visible, no wound that had healed open, no natural growth or unnatural excrescence that offered the possibility of anything new to him. He flicked the ash from his cigarette and rose to claim his bet. But, as he raised his eyes, he lost for a fraction of a second his air of utter boredom. She was unscrewing a false eye. "Put it back," he said with consummate indifference* [posing to the end]. *"Put it back, and put on your clothes. You win".'* In the presence, finally, of the presumed heart's desire of the new and unknown thrill – the still-virgin aperture even in a whore! – the hidden unease or buck-fever of the nervous bridegroom, worried if perhaps what he is really going to get is the dangerous, castratory "Sleeve Job" reasserts itself, and the *blasé* client cops out.

12

DISEASE & DISGUST

GRATUITOUS unpleasantness, and a purposeful concentration on repulsive details, are the common characteristics of most of the jokes to be presented from this point onward, and anyone who does not care for these might be well advised to do a bit of judicious skipping here & there. This refers not only to the present chapter, sufficiently warned against in its title, but also those following on Castration and Scatology. The materials in the intervening chapter, on Dysphemism & Insults, are largely of an anti-gallant and anti-godlin nature, and their empty vaporing and would-be 'obscene' abuse do not really have – or no longer have – the aggressive and even magical power that persons telling such jokes or attempting such verbal abuse generally believe. Like all magic, it has its effect only on those who believe in it.

The scatological jokes are of an ultimately hostile nature, at least in intent, and do not consciously express any distaste for, or disgust with the fecal and urinary materials flung insultingly in all directions – particularly on the listener. Rather, they gloat and glory in infantile pleasure at their own bold abrogation of the cultural taboos against both hostility and scatology: here combined in classic anal-sadistic form. This is typical of children of about the age of two-and-one-half to five years, which is thus the mental or developmental age of the tellers. But the jokes on the subjects of Disease & Disgust and of Castration, though just as insistent as the scatological jokes on taboo details intended to be nauseating and harrowing to the listener, show no real pleasure, even for the tellers, in either the subject or its details. Rather is the prevailing emotion one of evident *fear*. Fear being driven away, 'laughed off,' and denied.

Historically and logically, the jokes on the venereal diseases take much of their special format from the connection between venereal disease and prostitution. Certain overlapping themes between the two subjects must therefore be presented here, especially in the final section 12.IV.6, "The Defiling of the Mother." It is not intended to discuss here such large subjects as the origin of venereal disease in Europe, an epidemiological event still partly under controversy, as 'medical folklore.' The prevailing opinion is that syphilis became epidemic throughout Europe after the campaign of the army of Charles VIII, King of France, in Naples, in 1495, through sailors returning from America with Columbus, probably from Haiti. There is nothing specially 'venereal' or sexual about syphilis, gonorrhea, etc., except the usual mode of their transmission, but this has been sufficient, over the last five centuries, to create an inevitable connection in the folk mind not only between venereal disease and Venus, but also between such disease and the female prostitutes who have unquestionably been a main link in its transmission. That all prostitutes who are diseased have themselves received the disease from 'innocent' male clients is, of course, purposely overlooked.

Since the development of Sir Alexander Fleming's penicillin during World War II, as a rapid and fairly certain antibiotic cure for syphilis in its early stages, the overwhelming fear and dread of venereal disease has notably diminished everywhere in the civilized world. Similarly, the development of "the Pill," by Dr. Gregory Pincus, publicly launched in the 1950's as a foolproof and reliable chemical preventive of conception – though it has not yet resulted in statues being raised in Dr. Pincus' honor in every great city in the world, as once foretold by Freud for such a benefactor of humanity – has already shown signs of diminishing the unreasonable sexual panic of girls and young women, on the score of unwanted pregnancy, a panic which once served the same anti-sexual social purpose for women as the fear of venereal disease was expected to serve for boys and men.

The jokes on these subjects are therefore already and visibly a bit out of date, and modern readers may even have difficulty believing that these jokes concern subjects once matters of panic dread, which the jokes were intended to make light of and to allay. They will nevertheless serve to complete the historical record of what the basic social purpose of sexual humor really is, in the face of great social forces and perils such as the fear of pregnancy and disease. Both these fears have always been consciously fostered by anti-sexual Western religion and society, particularly in Calvinist Protestant cultures with their morbid concentration on unforgivable 'sin' and unavoidable punishment. Such repressive fears are still attempted to be inculcated in the horrendous 'sex lectures' to freshman students of both sexes, separately, entering college even today (as mocked in the jokes given in the First Series, 8.I.1, page 446). Folk humor has, *per contra*, done its damndest to make light of these fears by jesting precisely with their ugliest and most frightening details, as the jokes that follow will only-too-clearly show. As the whole present study is intended to document and demonstrate – and as, in any case, everyone well knows and admits in the folk-phrase, 'to laugh something off' – such *casting off of fear* by rollicking in its details is the one classic function of jokes and humor generally.

I. THE FEAR OF TOUCH

It is certain that we are not yet, by any means, free of sexual fears, for all the recent medico-chemical triumph over venereal disease and undesired pregnancy. These fears have merely displaced themselves from a specific fear of certain specific results of sexual contact, to a generalized fear of and withdrawal from any sexual or human contact at all. Thus, *impotence* in men, and female impotence or *'frigidity'* in women, have become the new symptoms of the new venereal disease, and are increasingly common under various disguised forms such as homosexuality and lesbianism – in which one is impotent 'only' with members of the biologically attractive opposite sex – and in various fetishisms and sado-masochistic perversions, in which the hatred and fear of the opposite sex are spelled or acted out in evil and aggressive charades and tortures.

The new venereal disease of the 20th century, and doubtless of the future (as the world becomes more frighteningly overcrowded), is therefore not actually genital but emotional, though still just as 'venereal' as when transmitted for centuries at the genital level. It is the emotional plague of what is already self-congratulatingly known among young people and adults in America as *'cool,'* the up-to-the-minute pose of purposeful, quasi-British emotionlessness, covering the reality of *being unable to experience human emotions*, and especially the inability to feel the emotion of love. In the sexual sphere, which remains the main theatre of this new plague, as it has been of those that preceded, this expresses itself further as *the dehumanization of sex*, even its mechanization, as has already been noted briefly in the First Series, 6.IV.4, "The Sex Machine," and will be returned to more fully below, at 13.VI.3, "The Mechanical Man." *Cool* is the new venereal disease. Total affectlessness, the inability to feel, and the fear of touch, especially in sex.

I have devoted chapters to this new plague in my propaganda pamphlets *Love & Death* (1949) p. 74–80, in the section "Avatars of the Bitch," and in *The Fake Revolt* (1967) p. 22–32, in which I try to show that it is the worst and most dangerous aspect of the new and fake 'revolt of youth,' and at least as dangerous as hallucinating drugs, if not more so. I am far from being the first critic to have assailed this. In his splendid critical essay in modern stoicism, on the overwhelming *angoisse* and 'quiet desperation' of 20th century men and women, *The Modern Temper* (New York, 1929) by Joseph Wood Krutch, the author records in the chapter, "Love – or the Life and Death of a Value," p. 98–9, the passing in our own day of the belief in love as a literary theme, and in the value of attempting to base a human relationship upon it. The passing of this belief not for everyone, but for many. Krutch is here speaking of the wooden and disillusioned characters in the wooden and disillusioned novels of Aldous Huxley and Ernest Hemingway, taken as typical of the crucial moment of the beginning of the 20th century.

To Huxley and Hemingway – I take them as the most conspicuous exemplars of a whole school – love is at times only a sort of obscene joke. The former in particular has delighted to mock sentiment with physiology, to place the emotions of the lover in comic juxtaposition with quaint biological lore, and to picture a romantic pair "quietly sweating palm to palm." But the joke is one which turns quickly bitter upon the tongue, for a great and gratifying illusion has passed away, leaving the need for it still there. His characters still feel the physiological urge, and, since they have no sense of sin in connection with it, they yield easily and continually to that urge. But they have also the human need to respect their chief preoccupation, and it is the capacity to do this that they have lost. Absorbed in the pursuit of sexual satisfaction, they never find love and they are scarcely aware that they are seeking it, but they are far from content with themselves. In a generally devaluated world they are eagerly endeavoring to get what they can in the pursuit of satisfactions which are sufficiently instinctive to retain inevitably a modicum of animal pleasure, but they cannot transmute that simple animal pleasure into anything else. They themselves not infrequently share the contempt with which their creator regards them, and nothing could be less seductive, because nothing could be less glamorous, than the description of the debaucheries born of nothing except a sense of the emptiness of life.

What is most significant about the novels that Krutch is anatomizing so perfectly here – what is significant about his own book too – is the total inability, the impotence in every sense, of either the writers or their anti-heroes to *do* anything about what is troubling them; and, all the more obviously, their inability to trace, isolate, or even imagine the causes of their humanly isolated situation. Something is shutting up their tongues, making these just as impotent to open the lock of their prisons as are their penises. How, then, is one to be freed from the plague, and be made able to love? Certainly not by these depressing and disillusioned intellectual ballets, of which many others could be cited.

Even so splendid a book about the mystery of *the emotion of love*, its genesis in the individual, and the source of its overwhelming power in those who really feel it, as Dr. Theodor Reik's *Psychology of Sex Relations* (New York, 1945, and pocket-reprinted) cannot really aid in creating love in those incapable of feeling it, because it has been burned out of them, or rather, never grained in. Another book of extraordinary value as to the terrible physical blunder in Western parenthood and pedagogics, of attempting to bring up children *without ever touching them* – meaning everything from closeness to caressing – is Ashley Montagu's *Touching: The Human Significance of the Skin* (Columbia University Press, 1971), probably the best work of this fecund polygraph. People who have been brought up without closeness and touching, even physically, will certainly have difficulty achieving this emotionally. They will be unable to touch, and will fear it. But there is more to the problem than just that.

This human alienation and the inability to feel – in particular the inability to feel love – which was seen as a problem in intellectual novels since the 1920's in England and America, had already been the underlying message of Dostoyevsky (who died in 1881) and the rest of the Russian introspectionist school, reaching its culmination in Mikhail Artzybasheff's *The Breaking Point* (1915) with its glorification of suicide – not to mention Schopenhauer's similar *Essays in Pessimism* (by 1850), arriving at the same 'solution.' Today this has broadened out to all levels, under the impact of repressive machine-society and anti-human 20th-century life, which leaves the enormous majority of individuals with no viable rôle but that of consumer and chump. No real function but to *pay* for everything, and to transform – per person, per life – one mountain of shoddy plastic merchandise into another mountain of broken trash. And the same at the intellectual and emotional levels of con-sumership: of attitudes, poses, required feelings, and fads. A magnificent and total anatomization and indictment of the entire machine age swindle and the technological holocaust which must be its end, is the final work of the great American culture-critic, Lewis Mumford, *The Myth of the Machine: The Pentagon of Power* (New York, 1970), a book beyond super-latives.

Thus, the new impotence and human alienation are not by any means the result of mysterious genital disease or subjective bodily malformation, but are directly the result of the re-pressive and warping action of society on the individual. In particular should be observed the unvirile *succumbing* de-manded ('joining 'em because you can't lick 'em') by an economic status-structure, whether this operates by means of plain punishments or through little gadgety rewards. (*'Octophonic-stereo for that ALL AROUND Sound!'*) Make no mistake about it: the existence of any one billionaire (Arab or white), any one movie-star, requires and mathematically in-volves that one million *other* men and women will be damned to meaningless work, to loveless lives, lives without meaning or future, and almost total emotional frustration. Lives slimed over slickly in the West by the media-proposed idol-worship of false emotions, of overpaid actors, singers, racing-car drivers, crooked presidents, and other will-o'-the-wisp men and women 'of Distinction.' Behind whom, pulling the strings, stand the creepy old billionaires for whom the ever-changing idols are merely the mask. These are the social seeds and forcing-grounds of the new emotional plague and cynical and ego-centric 'cool,' which is in the end only a desperate and pathetic I-don't-care attempt by the individual to pretend that he or she never really wanted the human reality, the happiness and close-ness, that are mutely realized to be beyond reach.

It is evident that merely the fear of a disease was never a sufficient explanation of the alienated human condition, even during the centuries when venereal disease was thought of with panic dread as an almost inevitable punishment for sexual 'sin.' D. H. Lawrence, for example, begins the Introduction to his *Paintings* (1929) – worthless would-be modern daubs in the style of Gauguin – with a long and remarkable discussion of English anti-sexuality from Shakespeare on, in terms of an irrational fear of syphilis, by which he admits being himself oppressed, though he does not go any deeper into its cause: 'I have never had syphilis ... Yet I know and confess how pro-found is my fear of the disease, and more than fear, my horror.' (*Phoenix*, 1936, p. 551 ff.) In many pages of the un-paralleled Victorian erotic autobiography, *My Secret Life* (1888–94?), the continuous bogey of venereal disease, under such devil-may-care slang synonyms as 'ladies' fever,' similarly lurks behind every sexual contact – especially with prostitutes, of course. The great Belgian engraver of the same period, Félicien Rops, specialized in drawings of the horror of venereal disease, the rotted skull behind the beckoning mask of prosti-tutes and pornocracy. In those days an explanation of the Fear of Touch was still possible, without rocking the boat or crack-ing the social veneer. Not today.

At an utterly different level of expression, our unrepressed contemporary, the purposely tasteless and dirty-talking sex newspaper, *Screw*, in New York, purports to speak to and for the generation of rudderless adolescents and young adults who are its audience. Here is a sample of *Screw's* humor and social reportage, at its actual best (July 20, 1970, No. 72: p. 26), in a cartoon-strip imitating Jules Feiffer's "Sick Sick Sick," and signed 'John Thomas.' *A naked girl is standing, speaking end-lessly to a naked man kneeling and embracing her belly, later lying supine at her feet. She says: "My life is empty ... it's a mockery ... I'm nothing – just a façade – a shell ... a dead and useless thing! I'm 26 years old ... and I've never had a mean-ingful relationship ... never had a truly meaningful relationship ... I shouldn't even admit that, I suppose ... It's very humiliat-ing! I've passed from one shallow sexual episode to another. That's the story of my entire life ... one tawdry, shallow, clutching incident after another. My relationships have had no deep, lasting significance. – If I could just* once *lie down and have something meaningful happen!"* The man replies, from the floor: *"Have you ever tried talking less ... and lying down SOONER?"* Note that neither of them uses either the word 'orgasm' or the word 'love,' though the girl is certainly talking about one of these – or both – under the hip *interpersonal* jargon of 'meaningful relationships.' It would not be COOL to use a word like 'love.'

The first publicly-published unexpurgated jokebook in English in the present century, John Newbern & Peggy Rodebaugh's *World's Dirtiest Jokes* ('by Victor Dodson,' Los Angeles, 1969) gives the complete course in current, purposely nasty and alienated jokes, as the title promises. In this department it is a bit in advance of such imitative items as *The World's Greatest Dirty Jokes* (attributed to the nightclub entertainer, Jackie Kannon, and published in New York: Kanrom, Inc. 1969), Paul Tabori's *The Humor and Technology of Sex* (New York: Julian Press, 1969) – of which the title is perhaps the most interesting thing in the book – and the British contender, the late John A. Yates' anonymous *Rugby Jokes* and *Son of Rugby Jokes* (London: Sphere Books, 1968–9), for some or all of which the First Series of the present work is perhaps to blame. Newbern & Rodebaugh give one touching little item perfectly expressing the Fear of Touch, and pointedly mocking the fake 'Togetherness' of the phoney endearments, under the title, p. 68, "The Little Old Woman and the Little Old Man": SHE: *"Honey, let's screw."* HE: *"I can't, sugar, I don't have a rubber."* SHE: *"Oh, lambsie pie, we don't need a rubber at our age. I'm too old to get pregnant."* HE: *"I know, baby doll, but if it gets wet, I'll get arthritis"*. The arthritis-attack expresses here, of course, the 'venereal' disease of impotence in old age, when sexual appetite presumably fails in the man, and he must seek every excuse to avoid the continuing sexual demands of his old wife, who is eagerly caressing him with a foreplay of endearments. These old people, however, are like the synthetic little kitschy grandmothers and grandfathers on saccharin greeting cards: they are *children* with preternaturally white hair. For the same fears and impotencies attack the young even worse, and without the convenient excuse of arthritis.

Seldom is the specific statement made in the milder kinds of jokes that venereal disease is even in any way frightening. To the contrary, the purpose of the jokes is to make light of it.

The admission begins to be formed when the disease is thought of as the *revenge* of the woman or prostitute against the man's rape or exploitation of her. This is also the case with the violent itching and irritation of infestations with pubic vermin or 'crab-lice.' But finally, the terrifying seriousness of the disease is admitted to in panic, when it appears that the ultimate 'cure,' at the hands of the terrible Doctor, is invariably nothing less than castration. Every effort is made at first to deny everything, and laugh off even the denial. In the end, everything is admitted, and even more violent laughter accompanies the admission. The following sections of this chapter, and of the later chapter 13, "Castration," make this curious development and ambivalence clear.

A joke already given in the chapter on Fools is all the more interesting in that it specifically combines both the 'anti-venereal' and contraceptive functions of the condom, of which the latter function has always been required legally in the United States to be denied, in the openly mendacious labels on both condom packages and their vending machines in public toilets: "SOLD FOR PREVENTION OF DISEASE ONLY." – *A travelling sales-woman stopped overnight at a farm, and was attracted by two of the big gangling farm-boys, 'all elbows and prick.' After supper she took them out in the barn and incited them to have intercourse with her. 'At the crucial moment she took out two rubbers. "What are them things?" one of the lads asked. She said, "If you wear these, you won't be worried about pregnancy or venereal diseases." Three days later one of the young fellows asked the other, "You pregnant?" "No," he replied. "Got any venereal disease?" "No." "Well, then, let's take these damn things off. I got to piss or bust!"'* (Berkeley, Calif. 1941.) In a more charming recent version: *She tells the two farm-boys that if they wear the condoms she won't have to worry about becoming a mother. Three days later one says to the other, "I sure hope that lady'll be a good mommy, because I got to take this thing off and piss, or I'll explode!"* (Arlington, Texas, 1967.) Earlier versions are given in the First Series, 2.I, under "Nincumpoops," p. 120.

The opposite position as to the condom is taken in what is presented as a true anecdote of the army-induction of a Negro soldier, 'Reported by E.W.A. from the neuropsychiatric exam of a Wisconsin board,' during World War II: *'Doctor – "Have you ever had syphilis?" Ans. – "No suh, I ain't never had no venereal diseases. I always wears a muzzle".'* (*Journal of the American Medical Association*, June 26, 1943, vol. 122, adv.-p. 26.) This is the proud priggishness now known as the 'Uncle Tom' pose, of Negroes trying to curry favor with whites. Similarly insincere is the descent to mere verbal 'nonsense' or excessive literalism, also of army provenance, in: *The girl who 'warned two corporals that she had "syphilis." The word was new to them*[!] *and they looked it up in the dictionary, finding it defined as a "disease of the privates." Being corporals, they felt safe, and fucked her anyway.'* (D.C. 1952.) That anything so weak, as humor, can really be retailed at all, even in the linguistic 'dictionary joke' format, is indicative of the real meaning of such pretended misunderstandings. They are not misunderstandings, they are refusals to understand, as with the children in Henry James' "The Turn of the Screw" who refuse to admit that they have seen the ghost. The ignorance involved is merely cast upon stock comedy-figures such as the dumb soldier or farm-boy, or the dumber stereotype Negro. *The Negro woman in the maternity hospital who names her baby "Wasserman Positive Jones" because she has found this written on her hospital card, and "it sounds so fine!"* (N.Y. 1937.)

It would be untrue to pretend that the idea or fear of venereal danger is never expressed at all. Kimbo's *Tropical Tales* (1925) p. 5, gives a politely allusive clerical joke, mildly perverting Scripture to its purpose: *The Archdeacon has got back from London, and confides to his friend the doctor, "Like Saint Peter, I toiled all night. Let us hope that like Saint Peter I caught nothing."* (The allusion is to *Luke*, v. 5, 'And Simon [called Peter] answering said unto him, Master, we have toiled all the night, and have taken nothing.') The traditional incubation period of nine days, or three weeks, for the development of gonorrhea is also used as an allusion to the venereal danger. *'Two married men met on the street. One, a timorous fellow, said to the other, "Do you cheat* [i.e. *on your wife*]?" *"Sure," was the reply. The shy one looked at his friend with envy. "Don't your conscience bother you?" he asked. "Yes, for nine days. After that if everything is all right ..."* (1:262.) A clear statement of the idea of venereal disease as *punishment* for sexual sin. This will appear more clearly in the following chapter, where the medical 'cure' of the disease invariably is or adds up to castration by the terrible Doctor.

The contempt for possible disease is also conveniently expressed as contempt for the doctor himself, for his diagnosis, or by stating that his diagnosis is wrong. Vance Randolph's *Pissing in the Snow* (MS. 1954) No. 18, gives a florid verbal example:

One time there was a young fellow named Collins, that didn't have much sense. Collins was always a-laying up with them girls on South Mountain, so pretty soon he got the clap. We all seen him go tearing into Doc Holton's office that morning, and there was several people a-waiting, but Collins didn't pay them no mind. "Oh, Doc," says he, "there's something wrong with my prick – " but just then Doc pulled the damn fool into the office, and told him not to talk like that no more. "If you've got to holler," says Doc, "call it your arm." He give Collins some clap medicine, and told him to come back Saturday morning.

Well, the office was plumb full of folks on Saturday, and there was lots of woman amongst them. Doc seen Collins a-coming this time, so he sung out, "How's your arm this morning?" Collins drawed a deep breath. "Swole plumb to a strut, Doc," says he. "So goddam sore I can't hardly piss through it...." (*Pineville, Mo.* 1921, 'experience of a physician at Anderson, Mo., about 1910.')

The challenged diagnosis is equally bald. *Doctor: "You either have a very bad cold, or syphilis." Patient: "Now where the hell would I catch a cold?"* (2:100.) Usually the 'cold' is the patient's own feeble pretext. *The doctor is looking judiciously at the man's dripping penis on the examination desk. "Whaddy think, doc?" mumbles the patient, "Maybe I just caught a cold in it, huh?" "Maybe," says the doctor, "but just to be on the safe side, I'll treat it for the clap until it sneezes."* (L.A. 1968.) This pretended identification is most common in the folk-phrase concerning gonorrhea, that it is "no worse than a bad cold," because both involve a continuous mucous 'running.' The penis and nose are also symbolically identified here, as often. (This phrase has reportedly been used in the American theatre as a telegram of congratulations on the thousandth performance of the kitsch items *Abie's Irish Rose* in the 1920's, and/or *Tobacco Road* a decade later.) Another classic excuse: *A man goes to the doctor with a bad case of gonorrhea. "Where did you get it?" asks the doctor, pulling out a notebook obviously full of 'bad girls' names. "Er, ah, I dunno, doc," says the man gallantly, "maybe I picked it up off a toilet-seat?" The doctor looks at him disgustedly. "That's a hell of a place to take a nice girl!"* (N.Y. 1937.)

Gonorrhea is unmistakable, but as the mystery of the venereal infection deepens, the tone of fear and panic becomes more marked. *A man goes to the doctor with a suspicious red ring around his penis. The doctor merely hands him an alcohol-soaked piece of cotton and says, "Wipe off the lipstick, you fool!"* (N.Y. 1939.) Also exists in a rhymed version, in *The Limerick,* No. 431. The entire 13th chapter in this work is devoted to various limerick examples on "Diseases;" the theme bulks very much larger in limericks than in jokes. See particularly the long medical poem in the limerick metre, "Luetic Lament," No. 1075–81, printed in variant form as "Venereal Ode," in the *Journal of the American Medical Association* (Jan. 31, 1942) vol. 118: No. 5, p. 24. This was co-authored by Dr. William G. Barrett and another medical student at Harvard in 1928. It is also known in a more elaborate pantomime form, here as told by a young married woman: *A man goes to the doctor because he is worried about a purple ring around his penis. The doctor examines him carefully, and finally says, "I think it will be alright. But next time you have huckleberries for supper, tell your wife to wipe her ass this way (motion of hand wiping in back), and not* THIS *way (reaching through the legs with a long wiping motion from back to front)!"* (Scranton, Pa. 1940, the young woman telling the story mentioning that the effect is 'most beautifully vulgar' if told in a sitting position, hoisting up the buttocks to demonstrate the various strokes, 'the way a lady reading a book *tilts* to let a little wind.')

Newbern & Rodebaugh tell, as usual, the crudest version in *The World's Dirtiest Jokes* (1969) p. 10, entitled "Seat of the Problem," in which the hero is named Merdely, and there is no situation in the doctor's office. Instead: *Merdely noticed that his scrotum was beginning to turn brown. He dashed home from the office to tell his wife the alarming news, but before he could utter a word, his wife started screaming at him, "Am I glad you're home ... I've had one helluva time".' Follows a long account of her household troubles, ending, ' "And then the cat had kittens. In fact, I've been so damned busy I haven't had time to wipe my ass!" Merdely, finally getting a word in edgewise remarked, "Yeah, THAT is what I wanted to speak to you about!"'* No direct reference to disease; just marital 'defil-ing.' (*Kryptádia*, IV. 314.)

Other expressions of the braggadocio I-Don't-Care! or Say-It-Isn't-So response to the fear of venereal disease, or of having already caught it, include straight bragging. Both examples of this collected are ascribed to comedy-Negroes, as presumably very braggartly and 'stupid.' *Two Negroes are bragging. One says that he has invented electricity, gas refrigeration and the pants-zipper. The other says, "You ever heard of syphilis?" "Now don't tell me you's de inventor o' dat!" "Maybe not, but ah'm de Southern distributor."* (L.A. 1968, told by a Texas businessman.) – *One Negro complains to the other that the doctor has filled him with mercury (for syphilis). The other Negro brags, ' "Ah's got what you might call mercury in me. Ah's got so much, in fack, that ah'm nine foot two inches tall in the summertime".'* (1 : 139.) Hard to miss the overcompensa-tion here. The specific brag, or tall-story 'gimmick' being used is traditional American, and is probably adapted from the 19th-century anecdote of : *A drunken man into whose mouth the bystanders pour half a pint of brewer's yeast, which 'raised him instantly, and he went on his way, growing taller every minute.'* (Robert Kempt, *American Joe Miller*, London, 1865, No. 265.) – *One soldier asks another, "Say, what did you get all those medals for?" "Gunnery." "Gonorrhee? How do you like that!? I've had it for years and they never even gave me a furlough!"* (N.Y. 1941.)

In a long story, of which many of the details were lost owing to noise in the barroom in which it was told, the victim of venereal disease finally expresses himself as – or, rather, is ob-served to be – completely happy with his lot: *A travelling salesman strikes up a conversation on a train with a heavily-bandaged invalid, who apologizes for not shaking hands, owing to his bandages, and confides that his life has been saved by a miraculous operation for 'multiple V.D.' He now has no penis and no digestive tract, but he is perfectly healthy, and is look-ing forward to a happy life. The salesman looks at him sourly. "You know, Jack," he says, "for a guy that can't shit, fuck, or shake hands, you're the happiest guy I know!"* (N.Y. 1953.) Here the mocking punch-line is visibly intended to express the listener's own position.

The results of venereal disease must nevertheless be faced, and these range in jokes from mere inconvenience to total castration. As in the joke preceding, the whole intention is to imply that none of these results, however total or horrible, are terrifying in the least, and that all of them can be 'laughed off.' In a way, this is the response at the folk level comparable to that taken in literary form by such famous victims of venereal disease as Guy de Maupassant and Pierre Louÿs, both of whom died insane – and the latter blind as well – as a result. Maupassant left the terrifying record of his increasing madness in *Le Horla* (1887) which out-Poe's Edgar Allan Poe to a fare-thee-well; but he also allowed his paean to cunnilinctus to circulate, as *"Ma Source"* (first published without permission in the *Parnasse Satyrique du XIXe. siècle*, Kistemaeckers' enlarged edition, Bruxelles, 1881, III. 134–8), the title itself making clear that Maupassant nevertheless was willing to celebrate the genitals of women as the fountainhead of his inspiration.

At the mildest level there are the verbal euphemisms for venereal disease, such as the archaic *'ladies' fever,'* used by the author of *My Secret Life*. The McAtee MS. (1914) envelope 5, item entitled "Pterrible Ptomaines," tells of : *A man with gonorrhea who refers to it politely as "ptomaine," which he got from "some tainted chicken."* When President Warren G. Harding died suddenly during a speaking tour in 1923, popular rumor did not fail to attribute his death – officially announced as 'ptomaine poisoning' – to a mysterious and discreditable disease. In the same way, when President Roosevelt later died suddenly while having his portrait painted by a woman, I was 'reliably informed' that the same thing had happened to him as was reported of the French president, Félix Faure, fifty years earlier. (See *Oragenitalism*, p. 249. Sanche de Gramont tells the same story, probably more correctly, in *The French: Portrait of a People*, New York, 1969, p. 390–91.) That both died of heart-attacks during fellation. The woman involved in France was later also accused of murdering her husband.

In an old favorite story : *A travelling salesman whose expense-sheet is sent to his firm, periodically includes the cryptic notation (to avoid shocking the bookkeeper, who is an old lady), "One isn't made of wood: $20." Having on one occasion been rolled by the prostitute and her pimp; the pimp, who is hidden under the bed, taking the salesman's wallet out of his jacket which he has hung over the bedside chair, the salesman includes this item on his next expense-sheet as: "One isn't made of wood: $250." He immediately receives a telegram* *from the home-office:* "ONE ISN'T MADE OF STEEL EITHER. YOU'RE FIRED." (N.Y. 1938, possibly with a play on words intended on 'steel' and 'steal.') The same code-format is earlier made to do for contracting a venereal disease. Only the code-word changes. *'A salesman frankly puts on his expense account: "Woman, 2 guineas. Durex* [condom]*, 2 sh. 6d." He is told that such candour shocks the lady bookkeepers, and that he should mark such expenses instead as "Day's shooting, 2 guineas." He does this several times, and finally sends in the closing item, "For repair of gun, 20 guineas".'* (London, 1953. French version in Léon Treich's *Histoires de Chasse,* 1925.)

Code stories of this kind are of great psychological interest, as indicating the semi-conscious understanding of sexual and other symbolisms by the people who make use of them. In joking form, and *about someone else,* recourse to such codes and symbols can be admitted, though never about oneself of course. *'A soldier writes home, saying that he mustn't divulge where he is, but that he has just shot a polar bear. In his next letter he says that he mustn't divulge where he is, but he has just fucked a hula-hula girl. A fortnight later he writes from the hospital to say that he mustn't divulge what's wrong, but he wishes he had shot the hula-hula girl and fucked the bear.'* (Chelmsford, Essex, 1953.)

The hostility against the prostitute from whom the disease has been contracted is both reasonable and frank. It would take a philosopher of the type of Dr. Pangloss – who reasons his venereal disease and lost nose away, as mere details in "The best of all possible worlds" – to prefer to be angry at the earlier client from whom the prostitute unquestionably got the disease herself. *'A sailor in Atlantic City, asked by a streetwalker if he didn't want his watch fixed* [n.b.]*, naively refused. Told by a buddy she had intended an invitation up to her room, he eagerly accepted the next such offer. A year later, however, when another whore asked him if he wanted his watch fixed, he replied, "I had it fixed a year ago, and it's been running ever since".'* (D.C. 1945, from an Army sergeant. 'Running' or 'dripping' always refers to gonorrhea.) The melancholy truth behind this story is that few clients are so conscientious, and many take a hideous revenge in immediately *reinfecting* prostitutes, when they know they are diseased themselves – thus, of course, infecting a whole line of other men as well. Prostitutes do what they can to examine their clients for disease, before intercourse, as in the French prostitutes' polite disguising of this as mere preparatory washing in the *bidet:* "*On se lave, chéri?*" Even more dangerous is the folk-superstition that gonorrhea can be 'cured' in a man by 'giving' it to a virgin, by rape if necessary!

The most hostile story collected shows the interesting folk-identification of (female) cancer as a venereal disease. *An American businessman in Puerto Rico at a 'business convention' is hailed seductively by a beautiful prostitute in front of the biggest hotel, saying, "Hallo, Americano. You wanna buy what I'm selling?" The man goes with her and, on his return home, finds that he has caught gonorrhea. The next year, in front of the same hotel, he is hailed by the same girl again. "Hallo, Americano. You wanna buy what I'm selling? – " "Sure," he says. "What is it this time, cancer?"* (N.Y. 1952.) Also collected, N.Y. 1963, ending: *"Now what are you selling, leprosy?"* Clearly, any disease thought of as specially *loathsome*, such as cancer or leprosy, can be mentioned in the punch-line here, but the implication is perhaps that syphilis – now known to be curable – is losing its terrifying punch.

As it would not be fair to end on so strictly a male point of view, the matching female story should also be given. Again, it concerns a southern beach resort, and the easy amours for which these are notorious – thus sinfully punished? – in both America and Europe. *A girl and her mother go for a vacation at a Florida resort and rent a beach cabaña. One morning the mother says, "Honey, I don't think I'll go out to the beach today. I got the clip." "Mother! You mean the clap?" "Clip-clap – I got it!"* (N.Y. 1939, the reduplicative in the final line, and the singsong in which it was delivered, being intended for the Jewish accent.) The identical story, minus only the cabaña, was told of an American college-girl and her mother visiting Venice during the daughter's 'Junior year abroad,' with a gondola serving as local color. (Paris, 1966.) Told by an American college-girl, with the added 'morality': "Well, you know, the main thing is *not to bring your mother* on your year abroad!" The girl telling the story also added the gratuitous misinformation: "Italy is just *full* of disease, and all the gondola-pushers have got it." The whole sub-structure is still the unconscious certainty that sexual happiness is sinful (and the prerogative only of the 'lower' or dark-skinned Latin races), and that it will be punished by venereal disease – or worse.

II. THE BITER BIT

Castration as the punishment for venereal disease, if enacted specifically by the fearsome Doctor, will be considered in the following chapter. The examples of its occurrence given here are those in which it is presented as a spontaneous result of the disease. One joke, given as a mere gag or pun, again makes the folk identification of venereal disease and leprosy: *"Did you hear about the whore in the leper colony at Molokai?"* (*Victim is supposed to answer in formula fashion: No, what about her?*) *"She did all right till her business dropped off."* (N.Y. 1942.) Given as 'the most popular castration joke current' in New York at that time, in the preliminary form of the following chapter appearing in *Neurotica* (1951) No. 9: p. 53: *A young man in China (or Africa) goes to the doctor and is told he has the Chinese crut, or leprosy from intercourse with a native girl [the punishment element and mention of the girl are sometimes omitted], and that his penis must be cut off. In desperation he goes to the native doctor who assures him that this is not true, and that amputation will not be necessary. "No cut off. Two three weeks – fall off by itself."* See other versions and 'toppers' in chapter 13.II.6, "The Doctor as Castrator."

Another almost 'automatic' form is curiously presented as a satire on the alphabet-soup of initials and acronyms, now widely accepted though early recognized as a plague when relatively new during World War II in military and governmental agencies. (Mr. James R. Masterson has published some incredible examples of U.S. government gobbledygook of the 1940's, and see further Prof. Etiemble's *Le Jargon des Sciences*, Paris, 1966, a marvellous compilation from the newest and worst focus of infection.) From the whole *verbal* form of the humor here, and its translation of all the action into the drivelling collegiate stupidity of honorary degrees, it is very evident that this juggernaut story was developed among the over-educated and over-intimidated, possibly officer-trainees. As punishment, the alphabetical or acronymic castration would hardly appeal to non-college people as being very terrible. (Text collected, N.Y. 1953; also in forms with the name 'John.')

Mr. Peter Dingle – went to Princeton and got a B.A.
Mr. Peter Dingle, B.A., went to war and got a D.S.C.

Mr. Peter Dingle, B.A., D.S.C., went to a whore-house and got V.D.

When the Army heard that Mr. Peter Dingle, B.A., D.S.C., had got V.D., they took away his D.S.C.

When Princeton heard that the Army had taken away the D.S.C. from Mr. Peter Dingle, B.A., D.S.C., V.D., they took away his B.A. too.

Mr. Peter Dingle, V.D., then got cured of his V.D., but that took away his dingle, and that's how Mr. Peter got into business.

It is perhaps unnecessary to mention that 'D.S.C.' is the abbreviation for the military decoration, the Distinguished Service Cross. The similar 'D.S.O.' (Distinguished Service Order) also appears in a story of World War I – purely castrational, and not mentioning venereal disease – from which the present form was probably developed: *An ignorant woman who is informed by telegram that her husband in the army has got his* D.S.O., *is terrified, believing that this is the abbreviation for* 'Dick Shot Off.' (2:217. See the 'topper' in chapter 13.I.3, below.) Telegrams are still generally believed to carry only bad news. Newspapers, in fact, seldom carry anything else – not on their front pages, nohow. Sadism and anxiety-peddling purely. *"All the news that's fit to print ... "* If it's bad enough. Good news is no news.

The response to the ultimate fear and punishment of venereal disease is dealt with rather drastically in jokes, once the existence of the disease is admitted at all. Other than fatalistic acceptance – rather rare, in humor at least – there is immediately *the flight into nonsense:* the whole thing is absurd, therefore unbelievable, therefore it does not exist, and one need not be afraid of it. Both under-reaction and over-reaction, if sufficiently absurd, will serve this purpose. *"Do you know a good cure for the clap?" "Sure, suicide."* (N.Y. 1942.) – *Two men side by side at a urinal. "Say, what's the first symptoms of syphilis?" "I don't know. Why?" "My cock just came off in my hands."* (2:104.) Already given in another context: *"Does your penis burn after intercourse?" "I don't know. I never tried lighting it."* (N.Y. 1954.)

All these are visibly the flight into nonsense, by way of excessive under- or over-reaction. This is also the formula of the 'shaggy-dog' story, in which, as Dr. Wolfenstein observes in

Children's Humor (1954) p. 151, 'something very far-fetched happens and ... someone grossly underreacts to it.' The nonsense begins to break down, however, from mere excess, and the repressed returns in full force. *A drunk in a bar-room asks someone to help him go to the toilet. As a prank, another man pushes him to the urinal bank and thrusts an unlit cigar in his hand, saying, "Here's your prick. Now piss." The drunk pisses in his pants, feels the wetness, and lifts the cigar to eye-level, looking at it in amazement. "My god!" he says, "I must've smoked my prick!"* (N.Y. 1953.) The logical process is obviously a bit fuzzy here. All that is certain is that under the standard excuse of drunkenness the man is made to believe that he has lost his penis, and through his own fault.

Little by little it becomes clear that the only real solution for venereal disease, as the jokes envisage it, is the same as that of folk-superstition: *it must be given to someone else.* This is of course identical with what the joke-tellers (and many listeners) do with the jokes they hear and suffer through: *they pass them on to other people, and only thus are free of them.* Any excuse will do. Open revenge is the best, though the rarest. '*A romantically inclined sailor was leaving a hard-bellied whore* [Roth's expurgation, No. 342: '*a hard-boiled woman*'!] *he had fallen in with "down the line" in San Francisco. "If anything happens to you in nine months," he said to her in leaving, "you'll call it Fatima, won't you. I like that name."* She: '*And if anything happens to you in three weeks you kin call it eczema if you likes that better".'* (1:384.) This is patriotically fitted to wartime, in classic fashion, in the *Journal of the American Medical Association* (20 Sept. 1941) voy. 117: adv.-p. 28, entitled "Variation on a Theme by De Maupassant," obviously referring to Maupassant's *"Boule de Suif,"* and stated to be an 'Anecdote going the rounds in some of our better hospitals at the moment': '*A young woman in occupied France had just made the Supreme Sacrifice to a German officer. At the conclusion* [!] *he said,* "Heil Hitler, Fräulein. *In nine months you will have a handsome son, and if you wish you may call him Adolf."* The young woman responded, "Vive la France, Leutenant. *In three weeks you will have a rash, and if you wish you may call it German measles".'* One strongly doubts that this anecdote was 'going the rounds' of any hospitals.

Most diabolic and fitting of all is the venereal revenge in which the disease is given to a person who believes that he is

doing the same thing: the ancient folklore motif of 'the biter
bit' or the swapper out-swapped. This may be presented as
accidental: 'Chap just cured of V.D. goes with a prostitute,
after which he tells her he has just come out of the lock-
hospital. She: "What's the food like? I'm going in tomorrow".'
(London, 1953.) No one is actually innocent here: the prostitute's very conscious and irresponsible viciousness merely
matches that of the client, layered over as this is with the polite
eyewash about having 'just' been cured. Nevertheless, is it just
an accident that he gets his comeuppance? (See another in
The Horn Book, p. 50.)

Even when the client of the prostitute over-determines his
solicitousness about disease, the inevitable result is always the
same. A man enters a whore-house and demands a girl who has
the clap. The madam is indignant and wants to put him out,
but one of the girls offers to take this obviously harmless nut.
'So the madam called the man back, pointed out the girl to him,
and they went upstairs. When he had finished screwing her,
the girl looked up at him and simpered, "I fooled you, mister, I
ain't got any clap." "Oh, yes you have," said the man.' (1:332.)
We will see in a moment why the client really wanted the
disease in the first place. The same situation, with the sexes
reversed, has already been noted in the First Series, in a chapter
on "The Male Approach." A man who is fed up with his girl-
friend's cockteasing him, takes her out in his car ten miles from
town and tells her she can "Fuck or walk." She walks. The
next week he takes her twenty miles out of town, but she still
walks. The third week, despite her entreaties, he drives seventy-
five miles out of town into the wilderness and gives her the
same alternative. This time she submits. Afterwards, as they
are smoking cigarettes together, he says, "Now weren't you a
little fool, walking all those miles those other two times?" "I
don't know," she says; "I figure I'd walk ten miles, or even
twenty miles, but damned if I'd walk seventy-five miles just to
keep a friend of mine from catching the clap." (N.Y. 1936. –
Waggish Tales, p. 302.)

This is very clearly a modern revamping, in all forms, of a
much older story of which the history has already been traced
to France in the 18th century in the Introduction to the First
Series here. The oldest form is given in Giraldi-Cinthio's Gli
Hecatommithi (1565) Introduction, No. 10, a source much used
by Elizabethan playwrights such as Shakespeare, and Beaumont

& Fletcher. Here the story is simply that of: *A prostitute who knows she has venereal disease and refuses herself to the man she really loves, in order not to infect him.* (Rotunda, Motif W22, as "The Loyal Prostitute.") This is expurgatorily omitted from Smith Thompson's *Motif-Index of Folk-Literature*, which simply jumps from W21 to W23, though it presumably includes the totality of Rotunda's motifs from the Italian *novelle*. Actually it omits all those – quite a few! – which Prof. Thompson disapproved of as too erotic, or even too bibulous, thus excluding half a dozen motifs on "repartees concerning wine" at Rotunda's J1319.

The 18th-century form is traced further in the Introduction to the First Series, part VII, p. 36–7, beginning with the *conte-envers*, "Le Placet", attributed to Alexis Piron, in which: *A nobleman, to whom a petition is submitted by a pretty young girl, will not stay to read it but seduces her forthwith, only to find – on finally reading her 'placet' – that it is a complaint against the doctor who was not able to cure her of venereal disease.* A milder French version is also given, as "La Consultation épineuse," with the nobleman changed to a mere lawyer or doctor, and the crashing venereal climax changed to the girl's sobbing that the man had done "that and more, and more, and more," namely that he had *begun all over again*, which the lawyer-doctor finds himself unable to do. This modified form does not seem to have survived, and the venereal disease original is still often collected in English, but now always of a priest in confession rather than a nobleman.

All these 'biter-bit' stories clearly culminate in the so-called "Happy Family" story, which is the venereal-disease joke most commonly collected, and one of the jokes most frequently encountered in this research. It has already been discussed at some length in the First Series, the chapter on Adultery, 9.III.1, "Possession in Common," drawing from the analysis of its prototype (the genealogy of Dr. Pangloss' syphilis in Voltaire's *Candide*, 1759) by Dr. Theodor Reik. This brings into focus its pattern similarity to Schnitzler's play *Reigen* (Hands Around) and other fantasies of sexual chain-relationships of a consecutive kind, as differentiated from the quite openly orgiastic simultaneous 'daisy-chains' or spintries. The whole form of the story also connects it obviously with the extremely common joke on incest-scenes: *Sister, to brother: "Your prick is longer than dad's." Brother: "That's what mother always says."*

(London, 1954: often collected, as the 'dirtiest story' the teller knows.) Randolph, No. 10, notes that his informant told a much longer and circumstantial version of this, 'deadpan and earnestly, without the least trace of merriment.'

The principal element in the equally incestuous "Happy Family" story is also the sexual 'dirtying' of all members of the family – particularly the father – but here with the addition of venereal disease, as it were to poison the barb. The story is often stated to be very old, but the earliest recorded sources found have been: a 'kissing' version on an unidentified clipping dated December 20, 1935 (possibly from the *Journal of the American Medical Association*), a text in *Anecdota Americana* (1927) 1:182, and the McAtee MS. (1912) envelope 7, entitled "Bill's Revenge," noting that it is 'Based on a popular tale.' Randolph's text No. 39 is almost identical with the text already given in 9.III.1, collected on a transcontinental train in 1938 from a Cleveland physician. *A man in a brothel asks for a girl with gonorrhea. He is thrown out angrily. Finally he finds a brothel where the madam admits that one of her girls is sick, but asks why he wants her. "I'll get the clap," he explains, "and give it to the cook. She'll give it to dad, and he'll give it to mother. She'll give it to that cock-eyed new minister we've got, and* that's *the son-of-a-bitch I'm after!"* (Sometimes adding: *"He kicked my dog!"*)

The whole thing is obviously in disguise. The person the revenge is really intended for is the *father*, who has cut the son out not only with the mother but with the surrogate-mother the cook, as well. Even so, he is too strong to be attacked directly, and is given the disease only in passing, as it were, while pretendedly aiming for the father-figure of the 'cock-eyed new minister,' who is *also* sharing the mother. She too receives her part of the disease-revenge, or 'poisoned kiss,' on the style of Hamlet attempting to kill his mother, first in her bedroom – where the ghost restrains him, to 'speak daggers' but not use them – and finally in the closing duel, where she is in fact killed with the poisoned cup. The son has thus had intercourse with the whole family, and diseased his whole family, though physically he has touched only a sick prostitute and the cook. Far from denying or disguising his guilt, however, he glories in it: strong in his bearing and transmitting of disease, where he is too cowardly simply to kill his father and fuck his mother, as he would doubtless like. Where love cannot be expressed physically, hatred and death are allowable. That is our ethic.

III. VERMIN

The tiny *Pediculus pubis* or crab-louse (colloquially 'crabs'), which can be transmitted externally in large numbers during sexual intercourse, is not commonly encountered except at very low social levels, as among vagrants, hippies, tramps and the low prostitutes who consort with them. The appearance of the crab-louse at any higher level of the social scale is considered violently dismaying and horrifying, in a way making it clear that such an infestation is thought of as a minor venereal disease and – as always with such diseases – a punishment for sexual 'sin.' The ordinary or body-louse, encountered suddenly by the American soldiers during World War I, was made the subject of much wry humor concerning 'counting cooties,' and numerous war movies of the 1930's considered it funny to show the soldiers 'reading their underwear,' and dropping the caught lice into the candle flame. The crab-louse is not considered 'funny-haha' in this way. Fleas (and mosquitos), which are much more painful and dangerous, and which can carry fatal disease, are nevertheless not considered anything but a minor annoyance, particularly fleas, which are assimilated to the humor concerning dogs and other pets, and which are even displayed doing tricks, pulling little golden chariots etc., at carnivals and circus side-shows. The disgracefulness of the crab-louse clearly stems from its concentration in the hairy genital area (and armpits).

In the older folktales and joke-lore, small insects of this type also appeared occasionally as identifications of the child. This is also a standard symbol in dreams and other unconscious fantasies, where *a multitude of small animals* (such as mice) or crawling insects (such as ants, Lilliputians, etc.) regularly represent children: desired or feared. These are conceived of as eating the parent-figure whose fantasy it is, or as burrowing into the parent's body. Where great oral guilts – for oral-incorporative needs – are being repressed, as with alcoholics, such fantasies of crawling ants, bugs, maggots, etc., appear in the anxiety-dreams or hallucinations: 'seeing snakes,' leading to 'the screaming meemies,' or resultant hysterical fits. In non-neurotic persons, the small animal or insect is considered charming and amusing, and the direct identification with it, as the child, is made. *A flea sneaks into the grand Imperial ball at Budapest, and leaps up to the chandelier where he watches the dancers. When a particularly beautiful lady in décolleté whirls by, he drops down into her bosom, slips through her corset, and falls asleep in the warmth and perfume of her pubic hair. He wakes up suddenly next morning in an army barracks, where an officer of the hussars is combing him out of his moustache.* (Scranton, Pa. 1936, from a Hungarian married woman.) *Anecdota Americana*, 1:468, of which the editor was also Hungarian, gives a brief one-line version: ' *"What a life," said one flee* [sic] *to another the other day. "I fell asleep on a cunt and I wake up on a moustache".'* (Printed version with lady harpist and bearded orchestra conductor, in Kannon's *The World's Greatest Dirty Jokes*, 1969, p. 57.)

The *Russian Secret Tales* of Afanasyev, collected before 1865, gives a simple and childlike story of this kind as No. 7, "The Louse and the Flea," in both the complete French translation published as the 1st volume of the yearbook of erotic folklore, *Kryptádia* (1883), and the anonymous English translation of Paris, 1897, which has been reprinted in 1967 with my own introduction to the whole subject, and important folktale tracings by Prof. Giuseppe Pitrè. (His tracings and parallels of the present story will be found in the First Series here, 8.VI.1, page 585, with Afanasyev's text.) Possibly via folk-transmission, but just as possibly translated directly from *Russian Secret Tales* (of which various other reprints have also appeared in recent years, under such titles as *Ribald Russian Classics*, Los Angeles, 1966, and *The Bawdy Peasant*, London, 1970), Newbern & Rodebaugh give an item very similar to the Russian story, in *World's Dirtiest Jokes*, p. 25: *Two fleas have spent the night in a woman's body, one in front and the other in the rear. In the morning they compare notes. The rear flea complains that '"The south wind blew foul all night long, and almost blew me out of bed. How about you?" The front flea said, "Oh, fine at first, but then some bald-headed son of a bitch stuck his head in the window and puked all over me".'*

But to return to our crab-lice. Every aspect of such an infestation is made the occasion of would-be humor, naturally to attempt to make light of either the disgusting reality or the mere possibility. *"How much are crabs today?" Fishmonger: "Forty cents for a dozen (or: apiece)." "Shake hands with a millionaire.*" (2 : 148.) Not even a catch-question this, though the final handshake is perhaps intended to transfer the disease! Just a whistling-in-the-dark attempt to turn an obvious disaster to a pretended profit. Again concerning money, this time on the classic or frame situation, 'No Money in the Whorehouse' : *A man who has only one dollar is given the dirtiest girl in the whorehouse, and discovers a few days later that his crotch is covered with crabs. He rushes back to the whorehouse and complains to the madam, who retorts, "What do you expect for a dollar, LOBSTERS?"* (*World's Dirtiest Jokes,* 1969, p. 97.) The humorous device involved here, the pretended mistaking, or answering of the wrong question, is patterned after another angry female reply, not specifically involving money, first noted in the manuscript *Treasury of Facetious Memorabilia* (U.S. about 1910): *A girl is climbing to the top of a London bus, when the wind blows her skirt up. The conductor looks up briefly and says, "Hairy hup there today, hain't it?" "Wot d'ye hexpect," she snaps back, "hostrich feathers?!"* Compare also the childhood item, already cited several times. with the little girl's retort, "*What do you expect for a nickel, TURLS?*" All old favorites.

Various riddles or catches also concern themselves with crab-lice, principally with the problem of how to get rid of them. Given in *World's Dirtiest Jokes,* p. 35, entitled, "*Granny's Old Sure-Fire Home Crab Cure": Lather up your hair. Shave a strip down the middle for a fire trail. Add lighter fluid and light. Grab an ice pick, and when they run out to the fire trail, STAB THEM!!* Other, less self-castratory versions involve *hanging ice-cubes from the testicles* and similar absurdities, the meaning of which is, of course, that there is *NO* way of getting rid of these vermin. In the Gulliver-in-Lilliput format of "Life on Man" : "*What's the bravest thing in the world? – A crippled crab crossing a bloody cunt* (or: *moldy jockstrap) on a broken cunt-hair.*" Possibly a reminiscence of Charles Blondin's crossing Niagara Falls on a tightrope in 1859: the bravest man, but a meaningless feat.

Other 'heights' of this kind include: "*What's the cleanest place in the world (or: the Height of Cleanliness)? – The strip between a woman's cunt and her asshole. When she piddles she washes it, and when she poops she dries it.*" (N.Y. 1940.) The same area, anatomically the perinaeum, is vulgarly denominated '*the crabwalk,*' as purposely crude humor; with which compare the answer to the question above as to the *"bravest thing in the world."* Similar formats of humor, in catch-questions and 'heights,' are well-known in both French and German, and are apparently very old, though nothing exactly like them has been traced in print before the 19th century. See, however, the account of the anthropomorphized "War Between the Big and Little Pricks," in Vignali's *La Cazzaria* (1530), which says it all more completely than anyone ever since.

One curious form of folk humor attempts to explain strange place-names by obviously absurd stories, similar to the folktale explanations of popular proverbs in Cornazano's *Proverbs in Jests* (MS. before 1500). Randolph's *Pissing in the Snow* (MS. 1954) ends with such a tale, about a prostitute demanding of a miner, *"It's ore, or no go!"* to explain the Spanish place-name, Oronogo. More recently, an anti-Negro story explains: *The origin of the place-name, Yuma, in Arizona, as the broken-off last words of a lynched Negro who wants to call the cowboys who have killed him, "YOU MAtherfuckers!" as he dies.* (Bloomington, Indiana, 1963. It may be anti-Negro, but I kind of like that story.) Another presumed wild-west item was: *An old prospector buries his donkey with a sign,* "HERE LIES MY ASS." *The sandstorms wear away all but the last two words, which later inhabitants believe to be the name of the place, Myass. A travelling-salesman in the local café asks for oyster stew, but the waitress answers, "We don't have any oysters. My husband looked all over Myass for some this morning, but all he found was two red-snappers and some crabs."* (L.A. 1968.)

The mid-Victorian author of *My Secret Life* (ca. 1890), whom I believe to have been the erotica-bibliographer, H. Spencer Ashbee, galumphs into a vein of pachydermatous verbalizing – if not of actual humor, which is beyond him – on this subject, at the opening of volume X, chapted 2 (Grove Press edition, 1966, II. page 1973):

I found to my annoyance one hot morning that crabs had assailed me, had lodged in motte [pubic hair], bum furrow, anus, and the wrinkles of my scrotum. It's impossible to say where I got these irritators of the genitals, having varied recently my amours, and a night or two before had revelled in three cunts yet warm and lubricated by other pricks. I keep mine in the ladies till it will remain no longer, luxuriating in their lubricious baths, giving great chance to these parasites of changing their abode, and I have escaped them well I think. The annihilation of the crustacea took quite ten days, and caused me much inconvenience.

He is struggling very hard here to reap some advantage for his ego from the danger to his pego, if his own terminology may be employed. He has 'escaped them well' in the past, but he has bloodywell caught them now; and though the 'annihilation of the crustacea' (a folk-joke?) has cost him time and inconvenience, he proudly admits that the whole thing has simply been caused by his *connoisseur* sexual habits, his luxuriating in the vaginal 'lubricious baths, giving great chance to these parasites of changing their abode.' Sometimes I think that if 'two great horse-fucking volumes' of this kind of impossible prose are acceptable in this day & age, just for the raw sex in them, I ought to forget about folklore altogether and get to work on my own memoirs, *Wives & Concubines* (or *Legman's Complaint*). Though I admit I never had crabs. The opening chapter, already privately issued, *Portrait of the Artist as Flowing Teat* (Tangiers, 1966), hardly more than scratches the cervix. John Clellon Holmes' sentimental knife-job on me, as an old pal, "The Last Cause," in *Evergreen Review* (Dec. 1966, No. 44), reprinted in his *Nothing More to Declare* (1967) without the full-page photograph, does not even scratch that.

The main thing, of course, about back-biting – I mean ball-biting – insects like crab-lice, is their itching. Since they are so small as to be unnoticeable, it is genital irritation and itching that finally make their presence evident. The 'trick' or 'novelty' itching-powder (also in the armamentarium of the French 'farces & attrapes,' on which see the fantastic *Encyclopédie ... des mystifications*, by François Caradec & Noël Arnaud, Paris: Pauvert, 1964) is intended to cause the victim, into whose clothing or down the back of whose neck this powder is introduced, to act as though he – or even she – is infected with fleas, lice, or unknown vermin. Note the violent form of this, in Rabelais' *Gargantua & Pantagruel* (1532) Book II, chap. 22, in Panurge's revenge against the lady who has rejected him: *A powder is made from the vulva of a female dog in heat, thus causing all the dogs of Paris to piss on the proud lady.*

A modification also exists in which no physical contact is sought with the victim, who is simply made to sneeze and cry by means of sneezing-powder. The police have an even cruder form of this sort of anal-sadism: tear gas, and "Mace," a paralyzing spray operating on the principle of a primitive blow-gun and its poisoned darts. The army form is even cruder still: mustard gas, poison gas, napalm (burning gasoline jelly), lethal nerve gas, and purposeful infestations with disease bacteria, or sterilizing or mutational sprays. All these, which are nothing but patriotic itching-powder raised to the nth, were first suggested in a 'humorous' work of science-fiction, even more humorously illustrated and showing them in exact operation – the Germans took the idea of poison gas in World War I from this – the very rare *Le Vingtième Siècle* by Albert Robida (Paris, 1883–90, 2 vols., the second and even more stupefying volume entitled *La Vie Electrique*), on which further details will be found in *The Horn Book*, p. 313–35, in my discussion of the psychology and pre-history of science-fiction.

Folklore, through Greek mythology, is the actual source of these sinister realities. Jokes revert on occasion to such tricks, generally in the mild form of itching-powder, contests being set up in the jokes on itching & scratching – or, rather, itching and *not* scratching. Stories of this kind are of wide geographical dispersion, as is always the case when the idea is ancient. See the broad area of report at Aarne Tale Type 1565, "Agreement Not to Scratch," to which should be added the further references at Types 1047* and 1095, from other literatures and folk-populations, "The Scratching Contest," Thompson Motif K83.1. In its sinister form this is the myth of Hercules and the poisoned Tunic of Nessus, the centaur, by which the hero is at last killed (actually driven to suicide); and, in philosophical form, in the question: *"Why is it harder to endure itching or tickling without moving, than to endure pain?"* which obviously leads into the present group of tales.

Another version of the following joke has already been given, concentrating on its element of proto-homosexual strip-teasing, or bodily intercourse by *mimicry*. Here the hostile contest is the point, obviously with no holds barred. *A Jewish tailor-trickster bets with a Russian cossack who has called him "lousy Jew," as to which of them can go the longest without scratching, at the parade ball at which they are both in service on the sidelines. The Jew secretly sprinkles black-pepper inside the collar of the cossack's coat, but the cossack meanwhile puts lice into the Jew's pants. In the heat of the ball the cossack begins to scratch, trying to disguise this by telling a story about*

*his uncle who was given medals "Here!" and "Here!" and
"Here!!" by the Czar, with prods and pokes at his itching parts
with every indicated medal. "Hoo-hah!" says the tailor. "You
call that an uncle?! I had an uncle from Pinsk who had so many
medals he couldn't wear them all on his chest. He had to keep
then in his pants pockets, and shake them up and down – like
this!! – all the time!"* (N.Y. 1953, told with every sort of pantomime scratching.)

This is self-evidently a Jewish joke, though Americanized versions are also in circulation. The same is perhaps true of the
following, collected at the height of the Nazi period before
World War II. *'Everybody had been fucking Goebbels' wife, so
he got a boxful of crabs and sprinkled them on her snatch. The
next day all the officers were waltzing around and scratching
their pants. So he goes to Hitler to complain. "Fucking your
wife, hah?" says Hitler, scratching his moustache. "How do you
know??"'* (N.Y. 1939, supplied in manuscript.) Hitler's toothbrush moustache was the subject of much 1930's humor, as in
Charlie Chaplin's *The Great Dictator*, with the presumed similarity to a woman's pubic hair more than once exploited in
private cartoons. This in part explains the allusion here, with
the obvious reference to cunnilinctus being intended also as the
accusation of unvirility or homosexuality against Hitler, as
against most hated persons : a form of imaginary castration of
them. Actually, Hitler kept his mistress, Eva Braun, with him to
the end.

Though itching crab-lice may be disgraceful, one can at least
scratch. When scratching is prevented somehow, this is thought
of as a kind of further torture, increasing the harmfulness of
the 'disease' infestation, as part of its sexual punishment. *A
man is being taken to the insane asylum handcuffed (or in a
strait-jacket). A 'Hebrew tailor' sitting in the opposite seat on
the train asks the keeper why the man is handcuffed. "Bugs,"
said the keeper briefly. "What?" asked the Hebrew. "Nuts," said
the other. The Jew raised his hands in horror. "He's got bugs on
his nuts and you keep his hands tied opp like dat?"* (1 : 406.)

Any kind of constriction, or reduction of bodily freedom in
this way – as by tight collars or clothing – is considered unconsciously as a sort of castration, which is the explanation of
the twitching and tics of very many young people, and of the
affectation of 'soft' or loose clothing by male homosexuals. This
is underlined in another joke on the same theme, which adds

the explicit 'castration' of nail-cutting, always the focus of neurotic rituals, as with the pulling of teeth (especially as to the disposition of the removed nails or teeth) and the cutting of hair, which, as is well known, many neurotic young men today are no longer able to endure. *An American in Berlin after World War I, 'struck by the cheap prices, treated himself to many luxuries. Among these was a manicure.' Later he takes the manicure-girl out for the evening, and to his hotel room. Two days later he meets her again in the street, and is not nearly as cordial as he should have been. "What is it?" she asked. "Are you angry with me?" "Why shouldn't I be?" demanded the American. "Not that I mind so much that you gave me crabs the other night. But why did you have to cut my nails so short?"* (1 : 386.) This comes strangely close to the "Contest in Scratching" in Rabelais' "Diable de Papefiguière" story, Book IV, Chap. 47. (Tale Types 1095 and 1047*.)

Obviously, the thing to do about body-lice of any kind is to destroy them when discovered. As crab-lice cannot be caught physically in the way that 'cooties' can, recourse is necessarily to chemical means : powders and salves, the famous 'blue ointment' of the rough songs and recitations of the cowboy and hobo period. (Parody of "Blue Bonnet" : *'Put on the old blue ointment, For the crabs' disappointment, And go out and hustle up some dough ...'* A pimp's or a prostitute's version.) Jokes about lice and flea-powder are rarely encountered except in jokes of European provenance, particularly Russian Jewish. *A peddler is being examined by a doctor, who asks, "How is it the hair on your head is black, and on your chest it's gray?" "That's not gray hair, doctor. That's louse-powder. You don't use it?"* (N.Y. 1939.) Compare: *A bum goes into a drugstore and asks for a nickel's worth of blue ointment (or flea-powder). The clerk tells him they do not sell it except in sealed tubes. "Oh, come on, be a sport," says the bum, pulling open his fly (or shirt). "That's all the money I've got. Shoot it right in here!"* (Chicago, 1949, pantomimed hilariously.) Probably an allusion to drug-taking.

The 'blue ointment' lends itself easily to the creation of *vagina dentata* stories, the poisonous (mercurial) salve becoming combined with the idea of the vagina as a trap for the male, as in the Earl of Rochester's rhyme on Nell Gwyn and King Charles II: *"However weak and slender be the string, Bait it with Cunt and it will hold a King,"* (See further, N. M. Penzer's

Poison-Damsels, and Other Essays in Folklore, London, 1952, a
rather superficial work.) – *One young movie-actress complains
to another of having crab-lice. "Just rub in some Paris green,"
says the other; "that'll kill them." A week later they meet
again. "Did you rub in the Paris green I told you?" "Yes." "Did
it kill the crabs?" "Yep, and a couple of directors too."* (1 : 17.)
The reference to 'Paris' is intended to clue-in the allusion to
cunnilinctus which makes the punch-line. Hollywood, as the
American sexual paradise on the style of Paris, is presumably
the home of all erotic refinements; and various 'true tales' are
current in American folklore as to this or that movie-director
*'getting drunk in [a famous Hollywood restaurant], and going
down on [a named movie actress],'* with the result that nightclub comedians thereafter bring down the house, as long as the
story is current, with throwaway lines to the effect that *the
famous restaurant named is now 'cutting out the box-lunches.'*
(Is it all right this way, Counsellor?)

In a florid version of the *vagina dentata* story, told by an
elderly woman supporting herself after her divorce by occasional prostitution : *A woman visiting Paris catches crabs.
She goes to a drugstore and says to the druggist in pidgin-
French, "Got bugs in the bush." He gives her an ointment and
tells her to come back in a week. "Did it kill ze bugs in ze
bush?" he asks, when she comes back. "Yes," she says; "killed
the bugs, killed the bush, killed the pekinese, killed two
Brazilians."* (N.Y. 1947.) A related story making much more
graphic the allusions to cunnilinctus essential here, is given in
the following section, "Narsty-Narsties." Also *The Limerick,*
no. 1118. Then too, the escape or retreat to nonsense can be
made use of. *'A guy says to a friend, "Hey, I was in the subway
toilet and got the crabs. What's good for them?" "Blue ointment." "Hell, that ain't good for them. That'll kill 'em!"'* (N.Y.
1952.) This is one of the few allusions in jokes to the standard
excuse for having contracted venereal disease, that one has
caught it 'in a public toilet,' the implication being, of course,
that these are used only by the 'lower classes,' who are presumably more likely to be dirty and diseased.

The cynical doctor appears in at least one other venereal
disease story. His cynicism, which is represented always as
hard-headedness and no-nonsense, is really a part of the doctor's
folk-character as a castrator, and leads into his unemotional
castratory 'cures' of the disease, as in Chapter 13 following.

Also, verbal toughness is itself a kind of conversational castration or 'bring-down' (note the colloquial term) of the other person, and is thus very common among male-protest women and out-&-out lesbians. *A man tells a doctor that he has a friend who has a venereal disease, and who wants to know if it is difficult to cure. The doctor assures him that it can be done. "Well, my friend would like to know if it's very expensive." The doctor assures him that the fee can be suited to the client's ability to pay, that it only takes several months, that no one else will know, etc. The man is finally leaving, but hangs back at the door. "There's just one more thing," he says. "My friend would like to know if the treatment hurts." "Well, I don't know," says the doctor; "take out your friend's penis and let's see."* (San Diego, Calif. 1965, from a college-student.) There may also be an unconscious fossilization or survival here – conscious, perhaps, when the story was new – of the older British and American slang term, 'that friend of mine' or 'my best friend,' referring to the penis.

IV. NARSTY-NARSTIES

It is certainly significant of the great anxiety created by the fear of venereal disease, that the jokes in the present section, which are presumably the most unpleasant and disgusting that exist, are also among those most frequently collected. These are specifically the jokes that are intended to allay anxiety by revelling in the most fearful details of what is feared. As though *challenging* the disease to frighten the teller of the joke, or the listener who must then later get rid of the freight of anxiety that the joke itself has created – through its purposely unpleasant images – by telling it to someone else. An endless chain. This is very similar to the activity of mountain-climbers and wild-animal hunters, who, though obviously searching suicidally for the sudden death they often find, *never feel secure except in the violent moment when they have safely navigated the danger of which they are most afraid*, and which they must therefore endlessly court and confront. An important secret motivation in many other social overcompensations as well: the 'heroism of cowards,' the achievements of undersized Napoleons (positive that their penises are also too short), and the like.

It is also very similar to the whole theory of ordeals and

initiations, which are supposed to 'prove' the worth or manli-
ness of the initiate coming through the ordeal, but which admit
the cruel and unbearable nature of the whole thing by allowing him later to force the same ordeal that he has suffered upon
next year's initiates, when he is himself a member of the
hierarchy of insiders. The gruesome hazings of medical students, involving real or pretended corpses and parts of bodies,
and the homosexual and flagellational initiations of so-called
military colleges, are very much to the point here. Few of the
initiates are, of course, satisfied with the feminine-passive
acolyte position they have had to take, whether sexually or
simply cruelly (or both, sadistically combined), *vis-à-vis* the
active-virile received members. And they wreak their revenge
later, when they are themselves in the active position, often all
the more cruelly in proportion to what they have themselves
suffered. The rationalization of 'proving their worth', 'making
a man of them,' or some other *rite de passage* sound-track,
which has sufficed to intimidate them is later used to intimidate others.

It should be observed that all this takes its archaic form in
the cruel or scatological 'training' of children by their parents,
as animals are trained, by means of beatings, or other cruel
intimidations. And it is precisely the children who have themselves been beaten, who beat their children later. This is a very
ancient chain-phenomenon, as witness the incredible chapter of
perverted gloating on the subject in *Ecclesiasticus*, XXX, two
thousand years ago, beginning, '*He that loveth his son causeth
him oft to feel the rod.*' It is not by any means a thing of the
past. Many lower-class fathers in America, and other countries
such as Poland and Italy, still beat their pubescent daughters
(on the buttocks and back) with a trouser-strap, a combination
which sufficiently indicates the real sado-erotic nature of such
scenes. Cat-o'-nine-tails whips for small children (under the
name of '*martinets*') are still openly displayed and sold in
French housewares stores, with gaily, multi-coloured plastic
thongs. "*Madame, beat your children in beauty!*"

The preceding details, though extreme, are very common
examples. But all hazings and pranks, even at the mildest level
of mere persiflage or teasing, such as sending new employees or
apprentices, recruits, and students for non-existent objects such
as 'waybill-clippers' or a 'left-handed monkey wrench,' or the
'sky-hook' (for holding up tents) and 'rubber chevrons for rain-

coats,' or for the absolutely necessary signature of some non-existent person (such as the Assistant Dean of Student Registrations) who 'was here just a minute ago' but must now be sought elsewhere, all similarly involve the unspoken permission that the person who has once been fooled – or terrified – is then allowed to fool or terrify others in the same way. That is his bribe for keeping the system going. And that is the reason for the great and continuing popularity of horror-jokes. Another example, in which the anal-sadistic hostility involved comes frankly to verbal expression at the end, will be seen in the scatological prank of *'selling bargains,'* in the closing paragraphs of chapter 15.I.1.

At any rate, no one is being hazed or 'sold' *here*, for the present section is very carefully titled as what it is. These are the stories of Dickens' fat-boy (really Dickens himself), who *"likes to make their blood run cold,"* in this case with un-expurgated sex-horror stories, as – in Dickens' case and that of his endless theatrical and movie Grand-Guignol imitators since, and the Gothic novelists who preceded him – with non-[?]-sexual horror stories of ghosts, nightmares, monsters, mad doctors, clanking chains, cowboy-killers, death, torture, cannibalism, ray-guns, Martian invaders, and other sado-masochist cuisine. Those who listen to these tales are the scapegoats of *Leviticus*, xvi. 10, for those who tell: sent into the wilderness with the freight of the tellers' guilt and terror. Abandon all laughter, ye who enter here.

I. CLOACAL INTERCOURSE

In his *Three Contributions to the Theory of Sex*, in the study of "Infantile Sexuality," Freud drew attention to the birth-theories of young children, whose proposed anatomical solutions interestingly parallel the myths of the youth of the human race: that babies are born out of the head, breast, or navel (compare the birth of Minerva-Athena from the brow of Jupiter); 'finally' that they are born from the rectum. Freud makes the statement even more broadly, in *The Interpretation of Dreams*, chap. 6.E: 'An interesting relation to the sexual investigations of childhood emerges when the dreamer dreams of two rooms which were previously one, or finds that a familiar room in a house of which he dreams has been divided into two, or the reverse. In childhood the female genitals and anus (the "behind") are conceived of as a single opening, according to the infantile cloaca theory, and only later is it discovered that this region of the body contains two separate cavities and openings.'

This makes rather clear the frightened infantilism of such supreme statements of early Christian anti-sexuality as St. Odon of Cluny's '*Inter faeces et urinam nascimur* (We are born between shit and piss).' This is very typical too, of the infantile approach, in that it attempts mentally to combine the sexual and scatological strictly for the purpose of *dirtying* or making undesirable the sexual. The child attempts to dirty that which it hates or resents, by rejecting upon it either food or feces, though actually the child does not at first consider either of these substances as being dirty themselves. Later sex and 'dirt' become inextricably combined for many neurotics.

Stories evidently intended by their tellers to mix in a purposely disgusting fashion the sexual and oral (or oro-nasal) components, will be dealt with in the following sections, "Food-Dirtying," and "Sexual Smörgåsbord." Such stories are much more primitive and much more common than those here treated, in which the attempt is made to mix the sexual and fecal, or, in the sense in which Freud expresses it, which seem to labor under the childish misconception of the 'cloacal theory': that the vagina and the rectum are the same organ and have the same aperature, through which the child is not only born but is also 'planted' during intercourse.

It is symptomatic of the infantile strength of this theory that many city-bred adults respond with utter incredulity or even irritation and anxiety upon learning, in later life, that chickens and other birds do, in fact, have only a cloaca; that the cock or male bird has no intromittent organ (with the exception of Leda's swan!), that no genital intercourse takes place, and that the impregnating fluid of the cock 'dribbles' down its tail feathers – which is why they curve downward – into the female's cloaca. This realization seems, in some cases, to reactivate the whole anxiety process of the early cloacal theory, by making it suddenly seem *as though it really might be true after all*. Jokes of the present kind may in the same way be considered to draw their panic strength – and thus the extremes of laughter or of disgust which they elicit – from their almost intentional reactivation of the same cloacal theory.

Here is a typical, and in fact a perfectly frank statement of this retrograde or regressive confusion: '*A man at a hotel calls room service for fifteen martinis, a violin, a bedpan and a blonde. When asked what for, he replied: "The fifteen martinis are to get drunk, and when I get drunk, I don't know whether I want to fiddle, diddle, or piddle".'* (Rockford, Illinois, 1951.) Note the excuse of drunkenness, to explain the confusion. The slang phrase, 'to be so dumb (or so drunk) that one doesn't know one's ass from a hole in the ground' also very possibly involves the idea of similar cloacal or vagino-anal confusion. I can remember my surprise many years ago, at a midnight bookstore in New York's Times Square, on one of the clerk's entering the washroom where I was, and pushing me aside to urinate in the same toilet-bowl with me. "It's all right," he said, "we're good friends." And added, "You know the old Yiddish saying, *'They're such good friends they pissed together in one hole':* I guess that means their mother, doesn't it?" (N.Y. 1938.) The *blitz*-analytis connection he was making seems to be with other similar ideas, such as that of the 'blood'-brotherhood of persons who have nursed at the same mother's breast.

The Guam mimeograph, *Smile and the World Smiles With You* (1948) p. 9, gives a version of the joke above, expurgating out the scatological element, and replacing it with the 'nonsense' of whittling. *'A man called down to room service in a hotel one day and said, "Send me up a piece of board, a violin, and a blonde." They questioned him about this unusual order. The man said. "I can't make up my mind – whether I want to whiddle [sic], fiddle, or diddle".'* That the original version did contain the scatological element, and that this is in fact an expurgation-toward-normality, as it were, is demonstrated by the form collected, where it appears simply as a purely scatological riddle: *'If Nero fiddled while Rome burned, what did he do to put it out? – He piddled.'* (Los Angeles, Calif. 1941.) With this should be compared Freud's remarks, in *Civilization and its Discontents*, as to civilization resulting from man's primitive giving up of the childish pleasure of urinating into fires to put them out (or on hot stove doors, to make a stink, one might add), and that women are traditionally the guardians of the hearth & home because they anatomically cannot do this. (This is not a challenge.)

The preceding jokes can be accepted, certainly, as harmless humor, if of a rather childish punning and alliterative kind. But this is no longer possible when the same sexo-scatological confusions are expressed in terms of pure hate, as in the item later to be given: *"Are you going to pluck it, fuck it, suck it, or muck it?"* And the following, supplied in manuscript, from the telling of a military officer: '*A prostitute had a trained dog that used to lick a man's nuts while he fucked her, until one customer objected that he was getting nowhere. He couldn't tell which he wanted to do most: come as a result of his fucking, or shit as a result of the dog's manipulations.*' (D.C. 1945.) This is very close to St. Odon of Cluny's approach to the matter.

Less verbally crude, but identical in its hatred of the woman and the identification of her with shit (or the sexual enjoyment of her with shitting: the partial statement which the joke actually makes), is what appears to be a newly-created joke – at any rate, one fitted out with modern appliances such as airplanes and intercommunication systems: '*The pilot turned on the loudspeaker system and intoned the usual, "We are landing at LaGuardia [New York airport] in two minutes ... fasten your seat belts ... hope you had a pleasant trip, etc."* THEN, *forgetting to turn if off, he remarked to the co-pilot, "The first thing I'm gonna do when we land is to take a dump, and the second thing I'm going to do is to throw the harpoon into that blonde stewardess in the back cabin." Embarrassed to death, the blonde stewardess dashed toward the front to tell him to shut up or shut off. She tripped, fell all over herself, and a catty middle-aged lady passenger* [i.e. the teller of the joke?] *said, with a cutting smile, "Don't hurry, dearie ... he has something else more important he has to do first!"* ' (Sex to Sexty, 1966, 9:4.)

This derives at least its form from a long obscoenum circulated toward the end of World War II in which: *Lt. Col. Rutter, the air-hero, meets the press, to tell how he feels now that he is back in the States. "What's the first thing you're going to do, Colonel?" asks a reporter, holding out the microphone. "Get fucked!" Rutter replies. The Air Force Public Relations Officer interposes suavely: "Lt. Col. Rutter means that he's rushing back to his home town to say a prayer for his departed comrades, in the First Presbyterian Church, and taste his mother's home-baked apple pie!"* It is a pity this hilarious 'send-up' has not been published in full. A contemporary private phonograph recording exists, and the full text is given to end the thermofax "Addenda" (1959) in William J. Starr's *Fighter Pilot's Hymn Book* [Cannon, New Mexico, 1958]. A high-point.

Another identification of the genital and cloacal turns on the slang term, 'to dump' or 'take a dump,' referring to defecation. *Sex to Sexty* (1966) 8:61, gives this under the caption ' "The Four Roman Generals": Caesar, Squeezar, Humper and Dumper ...' the play on words here turning, at the ostensible or conscious level, on the parallel meaning of 'to dump,' to discard or get rid of an unwanted person or thing. The form here survives from the 19th century, at least, when naughty riddles would circulate such as, *What three authors' names would a person mention who accidentally sat on a hot stove? – Dickens, Howitt, Burns!* The seat of the humor here is openly analsadistic, though such a riddle would pass in any company. Closer to the surviving form in *Sex to Sexty* is that given on the title-page of a rare collection of bawdy tales and poems (only one copy is known), issued in Scotland about 1890 under the title: *'Forbidden Fruit: A Collection of popular tales by popular authors, including Meitor, Walker, Caesar, Cowper, Turnor, Ryder, Wyper, Lover, Howitt, Burns.* (See further my type-facsimile edition of Burns' *Merry Muses of Caledonia*, New Hyde Park, 1966, p. 288.)

Few jokes are so frank as to the cloacal identification of women as the bit of Army advice, dating from World War II in Italy, given in full in another context in 12.IV.5 below, in which: Soldiers are told to treat the local women the way a dog treats an unknown object. *"If you can't eat it or fuck it – piss on it!"* (D.C. 1945.) At the opposite end of the scale, compare the charmingly gallant male approach, going in the other direction – from scatological to erotic: *A young woman at a garden party in the late evening goes out under the trees to piss. Just as she squats and starts, she realizes a man is standing behind the same tree doing the same thing. "Well," she falters, "here's to you!" "And here's to you!" he replies, giving a fillip to his penis; "but what do you say we clink glasses?"* (Printed in several French 1920's collections, and later appearing almost identically in America.) Compare also *The Limerick*, No. 1, on the young girl and miller of Aberystwyth – usually attributed to Swinburne – who move on similarly from the anal to the genital stages, in obvious rhymes.

More recently, the same French joke comes back to the scatological with a crash, the man and woman actually being shown putting their heads into the privy – where they meet! – while the sexual is reduced to the pop-culch symbolization of 'dancing.' (See *The Horn Book*, 1964, p. 294 for other examples, as in Franz Léhar's *The Merry Widow*, and Oscar Wilde's and Richard Strauss' eroto-sadistic *Salomé*.) '*A lady boarder on the farm goes to the ladies' outhouse that is attached to the men's. A new male boarder follows her in a few minutes. He goes into the men's side of the outhouse and sticks his head down in the hole, hoping to see something, but finds the lady boarder is doing the same thing! With rare aplomb, he smiles and says, "May I have the next dance?"*' (*Sex to Sexty*, 1966, 9:27.) The 'Escape into Nonsense' perfectly portrayed.

Again insisting on the primacy of the fecal over the sexual: '*The sexy celebrity chaser had the famous explorer cornered at a cocktail party. "And what," she asked, twisting herself provocatively, "did you miss the most when you were deep in the jungle?" The explorer smiled a little and replied, "Contrary to what you think, what I missed the most was* toilet tissue!"' (*Sex to Sexty*, 1966, 8:39.) This girl is really better off without a schmoe that says '*toilet tissue*' for '*toilet paper*' anyhow. Curiously enough, and without meaning to back up the intended sexual rejection of such a joke, the authentic experience of people in jails and concentration camps is that sexual urgencies are much blunted, unless excited by the demands of the guards and newly-arrived prisoners, and that the real lack, most seriously felt – if there is sufficient food, of course – is for TOE-NAIL CLIPPERS! Remember that the next time your favorite nephew goes to jail in Tunisia or Mexico for offering an *agent provocateur* of the police force, disguised as a friendly hippie, a marijuana joint.

Also pure hatred, unmistakably, is the identification of copulation and defecation in a story so popular that it's punch-line (the beginning only!) has been used as a 'throwaway gag' in a Three Stooges motion-picture comedy during the 1940's: '*A Jew, out walking with a girl, tried to talk her into having intercourse with him. He lured her into an alley, continued his persuasive tactics, and finally thought he had convinced her. He took his pants down, and made as if to get ready, but then she changed her mind and walked away. Hopelessly, he shrugged his shoulders, and muttered, "Vell, so it von't be a total loss, I'll shit"*.' (D.C. 1944.) As first recorded, in *Anecdota Americana* (1927) 1:295, there is no scatological tone: *A Jewish drummer is bilked by a prostitute who takes his money but leaves him in a dark alley with his erect penis out. 'Pursuit being useless, in his condition, Cohen seized his eager tool, and beginning to rub it up and down, said with a shrug of his shoulders, "Nu, so long as I'm here ..."'* The Jew, the shrug of the shoulders, even the *mise-en-scène* of the dark alley, have all stayed the same. But the I-don't care rejection of the woman is no longer the self-sufficiency of masturbation, and has become instead the purposeful dirtying of her by identifying the function she has refused to fulfill with that of defecation. *Portnoy's Complaint* is quoted to this same ugly effect in chapter 11.III.4, above.

The only joke which has been observed of a purposely 'nasty' kind in the rare American collection, *The Stag Party* (published by a men's club [The Papyrus Club?] apparently in Boston, 1888) p. 251 – unnumbered – is really a period piece in the style of anti-Negro, or 'nigger minstrel' and Currier & Ives print humor ... this one time unexpurgated!

Uncle Moses and Dinah sneaked up into the haymow and were soon going it under a full head of steam. It was just at this time that an old hen roosting on a pole overhead took occasion to void about a ladlefull of soft paste. The gob fell spat upon Dinah's lip, ran into her nose and mouth and smeared all over her face. For just one instant the old wench held her wind, then she heaved the old man about six feet away and jumped up spitting and sputtering.

"G'way from heah, you ole fool. You is vomicked all ovah me. For [before] he lawd, you is rotten. 'Pears lak you done got only one gut and you'se frowed up dat chicken you eaten las' week. By de tas'e and smell you oughter been buried mo'n [more than] a month. Don' you nebber come a-nigh dis ole woman any mo'. Tw! tw! tw!!!"

This final ejaculation represents an African Negro sound of disapprobation (something like the white 'tsk-tsk,' done by clicking the tongue), still common in the West Indies in adjective-form as 'twa-twa.' The food-dirtying so prominent in the dialogue here, and the anal-sadistic attack against the mouth, cannot disguise the cloacal identification of intercourse, the chicken's dropping representing the semen. This whole skit is similar to the insanely anti-Negro 'humorous' newspaper story by George Washington Harris, *Sut Lovingood's Yarns* (1867, repr. New Haven, 1966) "Sut at a Negro Night-Meeting," p. 128–37. Edmund Wilson has, in particular, given this sadistic lunatic the benefit of a cold, critical look.

Various jokes already given under other headings in Series One, 2.I, and 4.II, should be recollected here, particularly those regressing to childhood positions of ignorance of intercourse, or confusion of the anal and sexual areas and functions. *A little boy is telling his mother what he has seen his older sister and her music teacher doing. "First she took off her pants and he took off his pants. Then they began climbing around on the piano bench." "And then what did they do, Johnny?" asks the horrified mother. "I don't know. I figured they were going to shit in the piano, so I left."* (N.Y. 1953.) This is the child's nescience. That of the grown fool or 'nincumpoop' is not satisfied with mock ignorance or confusion, but turns this immediately to the uses of hatred against the woman, rejecting her, dirtying her fecally, or making the almost editorial statement that intercourse is the same thing as urination into the woman, or 'not as big a relief as taking a healthy crap,' as I have heard it expressed. *An ignorant lad is advised by a friend to go ahead boldly and "put the boots" to his bride. "But where?" he asks. "You know: where she pisses." He watches his bride guardedly until she goes into the bathroom. Then he rushes in after her, throws his shoes into the toilet and flushes it.* (D.C. 1945, from a naval officer.) In some versions: *The fool is told to "put the biggest thing he's got where she makes water." He ends up phoning home: "Hello, ma, here I am at the Palmer House in Chicago. I've got my head (or: ass) caught in the toilet-bowl. What do I do next?"* (Arlington, Texas, 1967.) See further, "Pure Fools" in First Series, 2.II.

In the style of plain fecal dirtying, to which allusions to such things as shoes, 'dirty socks,' old underwear, and so forth are simply halfway approximations, when not to plain shit and toilets: *'A hired farm boy used to wake up every morning just as hard as a rock (arm-gesture: clenched fist). One day he told the farmer about his trouble. The farmer advised him to go in the barn, get two shovels of cow manure and stick it in that. As the boy did so, the farmer's wife came in, learned what was up, and asked him up to her room. She stripped, lay down in bed, and spread her legs. "Now, put it in," she said. "You mean the whole two shovelfuls?" the boy asked.'* (D.C. 1951.)

Earlier in the present chapter, under "the Fear of Touch," a joke is given concerning: *A woman whose unsanitary toilet habits lead her husband to believe he has a venereal disease, as he finds that his penis is all purple after intercourse.* In Samual Roth's magazine, *American Aphrodite* (New York, 1953) No. 9, a quite eccentric discussion is engaged in concerning *marital purpling of the penis,* not as a joke but as a purported reality: evidently the same sick fantasy. Compare also: *The medical students' prank, usually against young girl students, of impregnating a chocolate bar with harmless methyl-blue coloring, then refolding it carefully into its wrapper and presenting it to the victim to eat. This causes* bright green urination *within a few hours, and great anxiety to the victim, who is assured that she has caught some terrible venereal disease from a toilet-seat.* (Ann Arbor, Mich. 1935.)

The favorite joke of a middle-aged married woman leading a terrible life with her husband has already been quoted in the First Series, Introduction, end of section II, concerning: *A man who wants to divorce his wife because she has such filthy habits: every time he goes to piss in the sink, it's always full of dirty dishes.* Another European version is brought into the notes to the very rare *A Collection of Limericks* ([Berne?] Switzerland, 1944) signed by the pseudonymous 'Nosti,' p. 18, in connection with Norman Douglas' autobiographical limerick on the Old Man of the Terminus: *The Limerick,* No. 1124. I have already suggested that the husband's 'pissing in the sink' is perhaps to be understood symbolically, here as an infantile reference to marital intercourse. Also, though the wife's sink-full of dirty dishes (food) is sardonically pretended here to be defiling the husband's penis, the real meaning of course is that the husband is urinating on the wife. Observe the total transposition of this ultimate ungallantry into its 'gallant' opposite in the little theatrical riddle: *"How can you tell a vaudeville actor from an actor on the legitimate stage? – The legitimate actor, always closes the dressing-room door when he pisses in the sink."* (N.Y. 1953, from a nightclub entertainer.) *Noblesse oblige.*

Closer to the food-dirtying theme is a related spoonerism, in which the alternative of sex is construed cloacally as 'muck': *"What's the difference between fucking a woman who is 'riding the rag,' and fucking a woman in the ass?" – One way you muck up her fuck-hole, and the other way fuck up her muck-hole."* (N.Y. 1950, also spun out into a joke on a marital squabble.) A British joke, never collected in quite so insistently alliterative form in America, makes the identification of sex and shit only-too positive: *A man in a chemist's shop* [drug-store] *finds there is only a young lady clerk to serve him. He is too shy to ask her for condoms, so he asks for an eyebrow-tweezer instead. Goes out, comes back ten minutes later, but gets the same lady clerk. Asks her if they carry rubber-goods, is told yes, but loses his nerve again and asks for a nipple for a baby's bottle. Tries again in half an hour, but it's still the same lady clerk. "Still want rubber-goods, sir?" she asks with a smile. "Er, yes, I'll have some – ah, well, do you have an enema tube?" This time he waits about until he sees the manager, dashes over to him and breathlessly blurts out, "Quick, I want some French Letters, please!" "Ah yes," says the manager, "French letters. I daresay you mean contraceptives, sir? Miss Twigget, forward please. Serve this gentleman a contraceptive sheath." And he disappears into his office. The martyred client accepts the merchandise from the young woman, who eyes him scornfully as though he were some kind of worm. He pays, and is about to leave, when she says to him, "Pardon me, sir, do you mind if I ask a question? What are you planning to do with it, pluck it, suck it, fuck it, or muck it?"* (London, 1951.)

Equally obvious is the intended identification of the woman as one of the 'lower animals,' and of the sexual enjoyment of both as being on a par, by means of fecal dirtying, which really wraps up the whole subject in one package. *The Australian sheepherder who rolls his clothes up into a neat bundle and puts it on the table, saying: "I've never had a woman before, but if it's anything like with a sheep, this place is going to be full of shit up to* HERE *in about five minutes."* (N.Y. 1950.) More oblique, but of identical meaning: '*A couple of sheepherders were talking about an excursion they had made to town, and how embarrassed they had been during a visit to a house of prostitution. One said, "When that girl opened my pants up and took mine out to look at it* [for disease], *I was as red as a beet." The other said. "And was I embarrassed! When she unbuttoned my pants and took mine out, she skinned it back and two sheep turds fell out".*' (Told by a St. Louis attorney in the smoking compartment of an American transcontinental train, 1943.)

Some British form of this joke is apparently alluded to earlier in the purported erotic autobiography of a woman, *The Confessions of Nemesis Hunt* (1902) I. 41, a rare work larded in the 'Pink 'Un' style with bawdy jokes curiously much milder than

the quasi-pornographic text. This is also told as an embarrassment joke, by the autobiographer's lady-typist, who explains
that it happened to her: *While dining one evening in a large
restaurant in Piccadilly Circus.* 'Suddenly *a particularly tempestuous piece of music came to a particularly sudden end, and
in the quiet that followed a man's voice rang out distinct and
clear through the room: these were his words, words that I
have never been able to forget:* – *"And when I pulled my
foreskin back I saw* – *".'* No more of the joke or punch-line is
given, and it therefore cannot be identified positively with the
one preceding.

In at least one joke, however, the almost open identification
of scatology with sex is put into the mouth of the woman,
again at a symbolic level (using an animal as intermediary), and
for the matching purpose of denigrating the man, in this case
the crude or too-timid lover. *A young man is courting with a
girl in her parlor, but he keeps farting all the time. Each time
he farts, he (or the girl) attempts to cover the embarrassment
by looking under the sofa they are sitting on, and saying
severely, "Fido! Come out from under there!" Finally the man
'fires off a hell-rouser,' and the girl says, "Fido! Come on out
from under there before the man shits all over you!"* (N.Y.
1942.) Actually, of course, it is the man who is doing all the
scatological rejecting of the amorous situation here, by his
farting, but the joke is so laid out as to give him a not-very-
severe verbal comeuppance.

More florid, and far more frank, but reversing the situation
completely: *A girl is waiting for her beau, meanwhile bent
over the kitchen sink doing the laundry. Without her knowledge, the man arrives and stays quietly watching her from the
doorway behind her. She farts noisily as she works, fanning it
away with the tail of her apron and saying, "Well, that's the
first relief!" This continues on, up to the "eighth relief." Suddenly she hears the man sniggering behind her and whirls to
face him, blushing scarlet. "How long have you been here?" she
demands. "Oh," he replies airily, "since about the second
relief."* (Idaho, 1920. Text version: Rutland, Vermont, 1938.)
This is a very old joke in France, and elsewhere in Europe,
often in a polite form in which: *Robbers are accidentally
frightened away by a sleepy woman counting her 'yawns.'*
(Types 1641.II and 1653F; Motifs N611.2 and N612: the Levan-

tine original. Type 1453****, chastely in Latin only, as *"Peulla pedens."*)

One observes in the two contrasted jokes just preceding that, where the man farts virilely in the sexual situation, he carries no real blame or shame, which is pretendedly put on the scape-dog instead. When the woman farts, however, she has presumably made herself impossible and ludicrous as a sexual object. Male-supremacist as this point of view certainly is, it is just as certainly that of the average sexually-normal man. This is true not only in the West but also in the Orient. Howard S. Levy notes in his translation of Cho Yong-Am's *Korean Sex Jokes in Traditional Times* (Washington D.C.: The Warm-Soft Village Press, 1972; Sino-Japanese Sexology Classics Series, III) p. 4, that in Korea several centuries ago, '*the village bride must have had drilled into her two commandments: Thou shalt not fart. Thou shalt not wear heavy make-up.*' With jokes to demonstrate the rule. The abnormal point of view, of fetichistic attraction to the woman's farting, is discussed in chapter 15.III.4 below, under *"Pet-en-Gueule."*

As will be seen plentifully in the final chapter, "Scatology," the act of farting is now and has for centuries been considered an expression of contempt for any other person present, and is further considered halfway to defecation on the other person as well. A correspondent in Berkeley, Calif. 1943, noted in passing that: '*Traditionally, the honeymoon is over when the husband begins to fart in his wife's presence.*' This appears also in Prof. Leslie Fielder's autobiography of his life in pedagogics, *Getting Busted* (1970), p. 33, a work singularly reticent on sexual subjects, where it is cited as an older man's advice on Fielder's marriage, that: *A man should be intimate with his wife, but not unfamiliar. "When you have to fart in bed, lean your ass over the edge."* The wife is never supposed to fart at all. Much humor is intended in the Elizabethan *Shoemaker's Holiday* by Thomas Dekker (1600), from the line: *"She has a secret fault: she farts in bed."* At an American revival of this comedy in the late 1930's, the line 'froze' the audience so badly on the opening night that it was omitted from later performances. In the later chapter 15.III.4, a sadistic couple is described as being 'very fond of each other,' whose public lovemaking is done in the form of violent verbal insults bandied back & forth. The woman is known as "La Trombona" because her final sally is always that she would 'look over her shoulder and wink affectionately, as she let him have a blast so terrific that it fanned her skirt into a complete circle.' Many people would not think of this as expressing love. A woman once told me (Chicago, 1963) that she had been a prostitute for several years, as a call-girl, but had 'gotten out of the life' when a client, on ushering her out of his hotel room, let a loud fart and said to her over his shoulder: *"There's a nice juicy kiss for you, sweetheart!"* At that instant she realized she had had enough.

Dr. Ernest Jones has courageously drawn attention, in his psychoanalytic article on "Salt," to certain implications of the special form of the child's cloacal theory in which it is quite seriously believed by the child that intercourse is performed by the father's farting into the mother's vagina. He points out that the Christian myth of the Annunciation, in which the angel (or bird) impregnates the Virgin Mary by breathing or whispering into her ear, is nothing other than a fossilized survival of this childish cloacal theory, 'displaced upward' as is usual when expurgation is necessary, from the vagina to the ear. In this case to support the legendary virginity of the mother-goddess which is of course shared with many other Near Eastern goddesses and mothers-of-heroes, such as the mother of Gautama Buddha five centuries earlier. In this highly rarefied or symbolized religious form, the cloacal theory is thus nevertheless made to serve the purposes of anti-sexuality, by substituting for vaginal intercourse.

In making presumably higher moral and aesthetic demands on women than on men, during the era of the patriarchial 'double standard,' now drawing rapidly to its end in the West, the patriarchal tacticians of male supremacy were quick to realize that such demands made it simultaneously very easy to vilify and attack women – for not being able to live up to them. For example, the virginity of the Virgin Mary is doubtless a very beautiful concept, to a certain kind of religious mind, but from any human point of view it would be and has been a disastrous ideal, as damning women to the frustration of their deepest instinct of fertility. Most misogynistic literature in all centuries is visibly the work of highly neurotic, impotent, or homosexual men. As Joseph Wood Krutch has observed, in *The Modern Temper* (1929), of the writings of Aldous Huxley and Ernest Hemingway, in a passage already quoted in full, such men are pleased to *'mock love with biology,'* and at the very least to have a bit of quiet fun – shared always with the reader – at the voyeuristic scene of the two lovers absorbed in each other but, as seen by an outsider, simply 'sweating together palm to palm.' This means, of course, *belly to belly*, as is made more than clear in the legend of "The Lovers of Toledo" retold in his *Contes Cruels* (1883) by Villiers de l'Isle-Adam: *The wife of the head Inquisitor (or Duke) of Toledo is unfaithful to him. He has her seized 'in the act' with her lover, and mockingly tells them that since they love each other they must be given what they want. He then orders his servants to strip them completely naked and bind them together 'face to face' with leather straps. They are left that way for three days, after which they are untied, given a 'badly needed bath' and set free. Both enter convents, and never wish to hear of love again for the rest of their lives.* This is an anal-sadistic version of the legend of the "The Eaten Heart," 8.VIII.10, well smeared with the implied feces of the helpless lovers who are thus *forced* to shit upon themselves and each other by the jealous husband. *Waggish Tales* ([by Roy McCardell], 1947) p. 181, simplifies this to: *A man secluded with his bride on a week-long honeymoon, who* vomits *when another man mentions wanting a woman!*

D. H. Lawrence has noted how the fecal denigration of the woman is an absolute mania in the writings of Dean Swift, much even being made of the harmless urination of the tea-drinking girl in "Strephon and Chloë" (compare the similar scene, presented instead as a charming undinist interlude in Gourmont's *A Night in the Luxembourg*), though clearly if Swift really hated such scenes he was not required either to watch them, nor to imagine them, nor even to write about them. His avowed love for horses (what! no snakes?) in Gulliver's ultimate *Voyage to the Country of the Houyhnhnms* is naturally only a feint whereby the author's hatred of humanity – but particularly female humanity – is expressed by describing them all as a race of filthy brutes or *Yahoos*, by comparison with the wise and fine horses, whose smell, Swift-Gulliver ends his book by stating, is the only effluvium that can drive from his nostrils the 'intolerable' odor of his children and of his wife, whose kiss, upon his return from his voyage, so disgusted him that he 'fell into a Swoon for almost an Hour.' He adds: 'And when I began to consider, that, by copulating with one of the *Yahoo* Species, I had become a Parent of more; it struck me with the utmost Shame, Confusion, and Horror.'

D. H. Lawrence draws particular attention to the insane anti-love incantation, or 'cure of love' chorus – really a sort of amulet or exorcism, rather than mere gloating – in another of Swift's poems, in which his ideal of the woman is destroyed because, though she is lovely indeed, '*But Celia, Celia, Celia, shits!*' As Lawrence says, of *course* she shits. If she didn't, she would have to go to the doctor. (Swift shat too.) But, to Swift, this makes her taboo as a sexual object. One may suspect that this absurd over-niceness was simply a way of rationalizing or excusing his own impotence, and that the fecality of *Gulliver* represents Swift's hatred of the women (including of course the mother) with whom, and thus 'because' of whom, he found himself impotent.

Riddle-stories in courtship, as a test of the lover, are of a kind that can be traced back three thousand years to the contest in riddles between Balkis, Queen of Sheba, and King Solomon (Type 851A, Motif H540.2.1), reported in 1 *Kings*, x. 1–13; with further details and traditions in the *Koran*, sura 27, and Arab commentators. This is discussed further in chapter 15.V.2, under "The *Escoumerda*," the most hostile such contest. A modern riddle, given in *The World's Dirtiest Jokes*, p. 13, is also on an ancient Biblical 'numerical' pattern (see the riddling 'triads' of *Proverbs*, XXX. 15–33): *A woman challenges a man in a hotel lobby, for a five-dollar bet, with the rhyming rigmarole, "Three, four, six, nine; I can measure the length of yours, but you can't measure the depth of mine." She wins in this way over all the men present, 'except one little shrivelled old man with an ear trumpet.' When she goes up to him and hollers her riddle into his trumpet, he hollers back: "Six, five, four, three; I can piss in you, but you can't piss in me!"*

The so-called 'riddle' here is really a direct challenge, cast in the form of a numerical spell or incantation, which the old man nullifies by reciting the witch's numbers backwards or 'withershins.' Only the impotent old man (or wizard) can win, because only he can match the witch in substituting his urinary-cloacal hostility for the seminal-sexual genitality of more potent men. Mark Twain's *1601* (written in 1876), ends with a reversal of this, in which a young girl tricks an old man into substituting the cloacal for the sexual: *When the old man tries to rape the girl, she asks him to take out his tool and piss before her. 'Which doing, lo his member fell, and would not rise again.'*

'Cures of love' invariably involve a denigration of the woman, since love is, after all, a superb over-valuation of and identification with the woman (or man) loved. The *Remedy of Love* written about A.D. 8 by Ovid – the first great folklorist, as in his *Fasti* and *Metamorphoses* – is worth consulting on this matter. It was probably not thought of strictly as an exercise in paradox, but as a practical manual for 'unhexing' the lover: love being considered a form of madness or ecstasy, if not of plain ensorcellment. His parallelling of this work to his *Art of Love* suggests that similar problems were discussed in the Greek and Egyptian love-books which preceded his, all of which are lost except for the coital posture drawings of the so-called "Obscene Papyrus" of Turin: one for each month of the zodiacal year. The curious posture drawings of this papyrus are published for the first time, from tracings in Dr. Frederick Hollick's *Phallic Album* (MS., Columbia Univ. Libr.) made during the last century when it was still legible, in *Studies in Erotic Art*, ed. Theodore Bowie & Cornelia V. Christensen (New York, 1970) pl. 30, p. 94–5.

Mental anti-aphrodisiacs are still believed in by all men (without exception), many of whom use forms of counting or mathematics, or other intellectual exercises, to ward off their own orgasm, in order to insure the woman's orgasm in *coitus prolongatus*. (See John Davenport's *Aphrodisiacs and Anti-Aphrodisiacs*, London, 1869.) Long walks, or 'a stiff workout in the gym' are the anti-aphrodisiacs of the narcissistic-homo-sexual athlete, or cretin. Persons of even the lowest intellectual pretentions will use something a bit more 'mental,' such as crossword-puzzles or the midnight reading of murder-mysteries, which latter also replace the sexuality being evaded with the more sinister thrills of vicarious murder and manhunt. *The college-professor's wedding-night: he kisses his bride chastely on the forehead and sits up reading a book. She falls asleep in disgust, but wakes up when she feels his finger in her vagina. "Do you want me, darling?" she says tenderly. "Don't disturb yourself," he replies, without looking up; "I'm only wetting my finger to turn this page."* (Amsterdam, 1955.) As already observed, in discussing this same story in another context in the First Series, this is essentially Rabelais' story of "Hans Carvel's Ring" reworked to the uses of sex-hatred and the rejection of the woman. Compare: *"A French enema. – You put one thumb in your mouth and the other thumb up your ass, and just keep alternating them till you either shit or puke."* (N.Y. 1953, from a Bronx druggist. Variant ending: *"shit or go blind."*)

The usual folk-cures of love, still believed in two millennia after Ovid's *Remedy of Love*, are more in the style of St. Odon's and that failed saint, Dean Swift's religio-scatological imaginings. They also occasionally combine (or substitute) the defiling of food. When I was a boy in Scranton, Pa. in the early 1930's, I was quite seriously told by a highschool-mate that: *The way to 'fall out of love' was to conjure up the image of the girl one loves 'sitting on the toilet with her ass-hole wide open, and the lumps of shit just dropping out.'* This was guaranteed never to fail. I have not seen this in print before an allusion made to it in the Texas sex-humor magazine, *Sex to Sexty* (1970) No. 28: p. 19, in an unsigned cartoon by George Ludway in which: *Two country boys, with noses in the air and pained looks, are passing rapidly by a girl sitting on an outdoor toilet, her bare buttocks (seen full-face) draped over a horizontal branch propped over a hole in the ground, roll of paper festooning a branch of a nearby tree, etc. One boy is saying to the other: "That always sets back my sex urge a couple of days."*

Also about 1932 in Eastern Pennsylvania, I heard the same sick imagining expurgated to the food level, for public presentation before a group of young teen-agers, including girls. In fact, it was a girl who told it, explaining that the disillusionment is to come from imagining the beloved *"with her mouth stretched wide open chewing the corn off a cob."* The 'cob' was also perhaps intended as a hidden scatological allusion to the real superstition, since farmers and country-people are supposed, in folk-humor, still to use dried corn-cobs for toilet paper, as will be seen in chapter 15.I.5. A more recent formula of the same type was stated to be useful in avoiding 'nervousness' with a pretty girl – it isn't 'cool' to fall old-fashionedly *in love* nowadays: *"Just think, when you look at her, that inside she's only a tube of palpitating shit, thirty yards long!"* (Bloomington, Indiana, 1963, from a Ph.D. candidate.) Although it is an important rule in folklore collecting not to interrupt or argue with the informants about the lore they offer, I could not in this case resist asking, "But, what if, when she looks at you, she's thinking that you're a palpitating tube of shit too?" "Well then," he grinned, "I guess that's the beginning of a *pretty shitty* relationship." Which is also typically 'cool.' *He:*

"You wanna fuck?" She: "Your place or mine?" He: "If it's gonna be a hassle, forget it!" (N.Y. 1963. Told at the end of a long session of dirty-joke telling among theatre people, as his only contribution, by a quiet art historian, who got the biggest laugh of the evening with it.)

Mr. Newbern & Miss Rodebaugh, in their *World's Dirtiest Jokes* (Los Angeles, 1969), p. 43, head this sentimental item "Let Go and It'll Snap Back," but I wonder: *'He'd been dating this girl for a month or so. This night he had made up his mind, he was going to hug and kiss her more than ever, and maybe get up nerve enough to ask her for some tail. He did, and she said, "Okay with me," so he started pumping. After a few pumps, he said, "Oh, it's wonderful. I'm coming! Are you coming too?" She said, "No honey, I'm shitting. You've stretched my ass wide open with both hands".'* Beyond this type of misadventure lie the castratory accidents attacking the man during intercourse, owing to various other arrangements of the tightness or looseness of the woman's genitals, her artifically-renewed virginity, and so forth, as will be seen in chapter 13, on Castration.

In Dr. Roger Abrahams' *Deep Down in the Jungle* (1964) p. 203–5, two long American Negro texts are given of the following joke, combining with a type of tale common in the Italian *novellieri* of the Renaissance, in which an old woman is substituted (here substitutes herself) for the young girl waiting for a man in bed: Motif K1317.2.1. *A man in a whorehouse finds that his wallet has been stolen in the barroom he has stopped in on the way, and he has no money but 50¢ in silver in his pants pocket. After some bargaining, the madam agrees to "fix him up" for this sum with the old cleaning-woman, "who used to be a famous actress," the madam assures him, "and will give you a great ride." He goes upstairs to a dark room where the old woman is waiting on the bed with her legs spread. As he is plunging away at her he suddenly notices a terrible odor. "Did you fart, Grandma?" he asks; "there's a terrible smell." "No," she cackles, "I'm too old to come, so I just shit!"* (N.Y. 1938.)

The tone of mere dirtying or attempted cloacal defiling of the sexual situation can also deepen, on the same background, into what is conceived of by men as the far greater danger of accidental homosexualization, *i.e.* castration. *A man picks up a woman in the London fog (wartime blackout) and starts feeling*

her in a nearby hallway. He flips up her dress and slides his
hand exploringly up between her legs, where suddenly he en-
counters what seems to be an enormous penis. "Get away!" he
cries, pushing her violently against the wall, "you're a man!"
" 'Oo's a man?!" she asks indignantly; " 'ere, Guv'nor, feel of me
tits." "I don't want to feel your tits. Look at that great big
bulge in your underwear!" "Well," she says regally, "since
when can't a lydy shit in 'er own drawers?" (London, 1959,
told by an American as a criticism of English pretentiousness.)
The sex-comedian, the late Lenny Bruce, who tells in his autobiography, *How to Talk Dirty and Influence People* (Chicago,
1965) chap. 5, how he wangled a discharge from the U.S. Navy
at the end of World War II by appearing mysteriously on deck
at midnight in a specially fabricated Wave's (female) uniform,
also mentions his panic when he is picked up after a show by
what he suspects is a tall male homosexual posing as a woman,
whom he begs to tell him the truth before they go to bed
together, because he will not be able to endure it if the presumed woman comes out of the bathroom in the morning
needing a shave! Bruce had a lot of faults, and certainly took
all the drugs that his drug-taking partisans denied he took. But
he always told it like it was. And never did succeed in escaping
from his blatant oral sado-masochism.

The homosexual occultist, Aleister Crowley, was a bird of
another color, and flying in the opposite direction. His pretended
Arabian love-book, *The Scented Garden, or "Bagh-i-Muatter* of
Abdullah the Satirist of Shiraz" (Paris, 1910) ends with a poetic
glorification of the pleasures of passive pederasty, signed with
the upside-down acrostic of his real name. Ten years later,
Crowley set up with a few disciples an occult *ashram* in a
house in Cefalu, Sicily, under the name of the "Abbey of
Thelema," with motto, also taken from Rabelais (Bk. I, last
chapter); *"Do what thou wilt shall be the whole of the Law."*
The doings in the Abbey largely consisted of sex-circuses
gravitating around Crowley, who was by this time combining
his homosexuality with sado-masochistic activities involving
women. The ridiculously detailed and exacting occult ceremonial apparently ended, in its 'full' form, with a Black Mass
in which a skinny and unattractive American Jewess, presumably named Leah (in occultism "Alostrael" : her name reversed),
would have intercourse with a goat, representing the Devil,
which was then killed in accordance with the Biblical cere-

mony of tribal purification, in *Leviticus*, xvi, 3–28, as to the scapegoat Azazel; its blood being thereafter drunk.

Some account of Crowley's Abbey of Thelema, and its sex-rituals, is given in all the various adulating and horrified biographies of this not-very-amusing occult quack. The most authentic details will be found only in the privately printed – and largely pentagrammatic or occult-mathematical *Znuz is Znees: Memoirs of a Magician* (Los Angeles, 1969–70) I. 29–30, and II. 174–92, by C. F. Russell, who was an acolyte at the Abbey under the name of "Genesthai," and who here attempts to clear himself of the accusation of impotence in Crowley's erotic *Diaries* (see Symonds' edition) at the entries for 10 May 1921 and others, as reprinted by Russell, p. 176, with parenthetical annotations and emendations. Mr. Russell also appears to be one of the few people to possess a manuscript copy of Crowley's most extraordinary poem, entitled "Léa Sublime," which he had written in Tunis in 1920 and later painted on the "Hell" wall of the *Chambre des Cauchemars* (Chamber of Nightmares: his bedroom) at Cefalu. Another copy is in the hands of Crowley's literary executor in England, Gerald Yorke. In one of his high-handed letters of occult bluster, Crowley refers to this poem – which is really just the world's longest outhouse *graffito* – as 'part of my apparatus for cleansing the human mind;' adding that its 'extreme value is to show that this [sexual] instinct is not connected with the will to live but with the will to die,' which goes even Freud one better on the so-called 'Death Instinct.'

"Léa Sublime" has never been published and probably never will be. It is in imitation of the style of Swinburne at his worst, and in the vein of Crowley's own howlingly dysphemistic parodies of Hamlet's "soliloquy," etc., in his *Snowdrops from a Curate's Garden* (Paris, 1904). It gets progressively muckier as it goes along, ending in stanza 26 with an avowal sworn to on Satan: *'Léa, I love you, I'm going insane. Do it again!'* It is entirely composed, however, of sexual and scatological insults and filthyings of the woman, Léa, whose name is also rhymed with 'gonorrhea' and 'diarrhea,' and who is described as engaging in standard acts of fecal and cloacal 'defilation,' with Crowley as the oral-submissive partner. This is not in accordance with Crowley's record in his *Diaries* of what really went on at the Abbey of Thelema, where, in the entry for 13 May 1921, for example, the perfectly plain statement is made in

absurd Latin code: 'Opus V Fra G in ano meo. Op[eratio]n very
lengthy. Alostrael had to masturbate G to effect erection, and
he hand-introduced his penis into my anus. Orgasm very strong
and savage. El. nearly all absorbed; Alostrael to whom I offered
it, could only get a few drops. Obj[ect]: To establish the Law of
Thelema.' Note the reference to 'offering' the rectally-injected
semen to the woman afterwards, apparently orally; this being
accepted vaginally in Pierre Louÿs' equally or even more masochistic novel, Trois filles de leur mère. All this is the opposite of
the story Crowley's poem tells, in standard sado-masochistic
alternation of rôles. See further the discussion of Freud's "Most
Prevalent Form of Degradation in the Erotic Life," at the end of
the chapter on Prostitution above, 11.III.4, under "Impossibilities," concerning men who cannot be potent at all unless the
woman is made to seem degraded. The three central stanzas of
Léa Sublime are quoted here, which should be enough for all
normal purposes and any others:

> Spend again, lash me! Léa, one spasm
> Screaming to splash me, Slime of the chasm.
> > Choke me with spilth
> > Of your sow-belly's filth.

> Stab your demoniac smile to my brain!
> Soak me in cognac, cunt and cocaine;
> > Sprawl on me! sit
> > On my mouth, Léa, shit!

> Shit on me, slut, creaming the curds
> That drip from your gut, greasy with turds!
> > Dribble your dung
> > On the tip of my tongue!

I don't know very much about occultism, nor want to. But I
don't think anyone can be taken seriously as a poet who, in
what is supposed to be his one wildest barbaric yawp to his
master, Satan, forces the pronunciation of cognac as 'coney-
ack' (in his Triune Credo: "cognac, cunt, and cocaine"), for an
inner rhyme with 'demoniac." I don't think any self-respecting
demon would take him seriously either.

Nasty imaginings of the type Crowley is parading here – and,
as I say, I have preferred not to give the ending – are by no

means limited to literary men taking cocaine, on the style of Sherlock Holmes. Here is what is supposed to be just a good joke or prank, well-known in both England and America: *The wife sleeps with cocked knees taking up all the room in bed, and the husband, in desperation, tells her that this will cause the "collywobbles," and all her guts will fall out. When she goes back to sleep again and immediately pokes him in the back with her cocked knees, also snoring and keeping him awake to brood over the matter, he goes down to the kitchen, kills (or cleans out) a chicken which he finds in the ice-box, creeps silently back to the bedroom and spreads the chicken-guts around under her. In the morning she hobbles down to breakfast looking very haggard. "I guess you were right about those collywobbles," she tells her husband. "My guts all fell out in the night." "How do you feel now?" he asks, with mock concern. "I'm all right," she says. "With a little pushing and some vaseline I got them all back in again, except for about two feet of green stuff at the end." (Turns and pulls up her dressing-gown in back to show him. This is pantomimed by the teller.)*

This form, with the final pantomime, was collected from a tourist arriving from New York, 1970. He told it to me behind the back of his wife, who was tending their two children, of whom the smaller, a baby girl, was not allowed to wear panties because the mother was too much of a cleanliness-neurotic to wipe her child's bottom, with the result that the poor kid wandered around looking like an ambulating toilet-seat, and dirtying everything she sat on. This is perhaps the background of the man's finding the joke, as he put it, 'terrific.' This farce or 'practical joke' is very old, and appears in the *Giornate de' Novizi* of Pietro Fortini in the 16th century, Day VII. 40, concerning: *A sick peasant who thinks he has to take an enema with a rooster's head.* (Rotunda, Motif J1742.4, replaced by a different and more anodyne jest by Thompson at the same rubric.) Actually, and in all forms, the joke is nothing more or less than an attempted 'folk rationalization' of some of the horrors of animal sadism, particularly the paddling around in the dead animal's or bird's guts. Note the re-creation precisely of Fortini's joke-form, as a sadistic spectacle for far-out audiences, under the title "Sexy Goose," by the Austrian theatre-of-cruelty group of Otto Muehl, during the 1960's, as described under "Orgies and Exhibitions," in chapter 11.III.2, above. No pretense here about being a joke. The Return of the Repressed.

The following joke on the identical cloacal or coprophilous subject as Crowley's poem, "*Léa Sublime*," is placed here rather than in chapter 15.V, under "Scatophagy" where it would logically go, as the total example in current folk-humor of intercourse as a cloacal way of dirtying the woman. This joke is considered perfectly awful by its tellers – who nevertheless adore telling it. Despite the attempted sexualization of the situation, with the 'impotent old man' and 'destitute whore' (anybody's prey), nothing can be more clear than that it is a mock or neurotic recollection of the ordinary nursery scene of the infant's daily defecation at the mother's urging, with the child being rewarded with love for its copious 'bowel movement.' Quoted from manuscript, as collected in Los Angeles, Calif. 1941 : *A destitute whore who allowed an impotent old man, who paid well, to shit on her face, got to enjoy this a great deal with time, and to wait eagerly for his daily visit. One day when his efforts failed to produce more than a fart, she bitterly accused him of having another lover!'* This was collected again, also in Los Angeles, twenty-five years later, from a college professor, who told it without any mincing of words *while cuddling in a reclining armchair with his wife*, while his teen-aged daughter promenaded about in her underwear preparing for bed. In this version : *The woman shit upon was stated to be the most beautiful woman imaginable; she had been revolted when the ritual began, but had grown to like it, and at the end she asks petulantly, "What's the matter, honey – Don't you love me any more?"* (Compare : *'Pee for Mama!'*) The teller stated, over his wife's shoulder, that this was 'the most disgusting story' he knew.

2. FOOD-DIRTYING

Overeating and a generally regressive oral orientation are a classic response in groups that are prohibited from having proper sexual release, for example priests, nuns, and elderly people generally – when their health allows this – all of whom also transfer much of their status-search and personality-expression to their mouths, generally in the aggressive forms of *demanding love* by excessive talking, complaining, arguing, verbal showing-off, and plain insults. (That is why many religious communities enforce the rule of silence, making the hostility and despair even worse.) It is this shading off into the externalized oral sadism of spitting anger and biting insult, instead of the more in-turned if equally sadistic oral greediness, grasping, and bodily incorporation *via* the mouth, that is the real danger, and on a very large social scale. The moment of fear and desperation that changes the food-ostentation and food-status sought by the overstuffed adolescent, or adolescent society – with its Diners' Cards, fractured-French menus, and imported fake Bordeaux, million-strong – into the much more unpleasant and sinister *food-dirtying* of the resistful child.

Thus, in the days of the American frontier, and the Conestoga wagons joyously invading the Indian territory and killing off the redskins as they went; when pioneer teams who thought to make it over the Continental Divide or through the Donner Pass to the promised heaven of California, found they were going to die instead, of thirst or starvation in the desert or mountains, or ambushed by the inexplicably 'hostile' Indians' attacks; their strange, their unimaginable reaction was ... what? Their reaction to the realization of their impending death was an ugly parody of the blind Samson's bringing down the Philistines, palace and all, with him in his death. The dying pioneers would burn their own Conestoga wagons, rip up their pillows and scatter the stuffings in a fury, and pour kerosene or piss into their supplies of sugar, so that other, more fortunate teamsters coming on after them *"should not get the good of it!"* Many a survivor told this tale.

Nothing of this has changed in America (also in England), except that now the government spends millions of dollars yearly, pissing into the sugar, in the form of subsidies paid to millionaire farm-owners not to plant, or if they plant not to harvest, or if they harvest then simply to stock or destroy, thousands of tons of grain, fruit, and other foodstuffs in order to keep the price up, by creating artificial scarcities. This at a time when the question of world-overpopulation and the already-failing food supply and beginning famines must be faced. Not to mention the simultaneous spraying of defoliant chemicals over hundreds of thousands of acres in those parts of the Chinese sub-continent already attacked by the United States, in order to starve the population into submission. Why all this revolting barbarity? Why dirty and destroy these thousands of tons of foodstuffs and miles of arable land yearly? Why not distribute the food to the poor and starving instead? Well, distribution would cost something too – which would

mean a further government subsidy, but this time to the trans-
porters. And besides, the poor (except in Africa and India) have
a *little* bit of money. So let the bastards buy a little bit of
whatever kind of food they can get, at the artificially-supported
price level which will show the farm-owners and distributors
a hefty profit. In other words, poison and destroy the food if
necessary, but just make sure that nobody *gets the good of it!*
That is food-dirtying on the global scale.

This is no doubt intended to solve, in a sense, the humorless
impasse in which we now find ourselves as to the world's food
supply, that: *'Half the people in the world are starving, while
the rest are dieting.'* (Karl-Erik Fichtelius, *Smarter Than Man?*
1971, chap. 7.) Meanwhile, here's the latest. – Are you ready
for this? – 'Surgical dieting:' not just the subcutaneous removal
of slabs of unsightly fat, but a major operation cutting out most
of the smaller intestine, so that 'the *ingesta* quickly become
excreta' without ever being digested, and the gourmand patient
can keep on eating like a pig without getting unfashionably fat.
(Dr. Norbert Bensaid, in *Le Nouvel Observateur*, 7 Oct. 1974,
p. 62–3, with mortality figures.) Actually, how is this an improvement over the old Roman method of vomiting beside the
banqueting table? An operation without a future; but what a
commentary on the present!

Food-dirtying, even when it is done with shit, is not quite the
same thing as simple scatology, which does not much care
where its exploding paper-sack full of shit hits, but would prefer for it to hit the victim (the listener) in the face; or to 'hit the
fan,' and thus defile the largest audience possible. The dirtying
specifically of food, or the mother's breast, is not the exclusive
target of that kind of scatology. In the same way, it should be
observed that the jokes in the preceding section, on "Cloacal
Intercourse," are not so much concerned with merely scatological materials – on which see the final chapter 15 – but with
the intentional *combination of the sexual and scatological:* the
essence of the cloacal theory of the child. The obvious purpose
is to shock and disgust the listener, and presumably to 'prove'
one's own superiority by being able to recount such material,
or even to create it (as, for instance, in the limerick form) with
visible expressions only of high good humor.

Thus, there are men of affairs who pitifully spell out their
anal aggressiveness, morning after morning of the business
week, sitting in toilet-cubicles side by side, and shouting their

business discussions, or witticisms, over the tops of the intervening partitions (or through the open doors) to or at each
other. Gene Fowler so describes the daily newspaper editorial
conference in *Timberline:* apparently a true biography of a
famous western journalist, and I have been present at similar
'conferences' in both book-publishing, advertising, and the
theatre and moving-picture industry, which is the sickest of
them all. Just so, at the level of *humor,* other men rush to
telephone each other in the morning the scatological limericks
and other doggerel they have made up during the night, or
jokes they have heard the preceding day, especially the 'rich,
meaty fecal ones,' as the main American limerick poet, the late
John Coulthard once put it, concerning his own activity with
friends. This does not necessarily have anything to do with the
specific dirtying of food, though the casual audience or regular
listener may even be formally warned that this is 'the most
disgusting story' that the teller knows, etc. Almost all the jokes
and materials in the present section do not simply involve oral
rejections or food-dirtying of a merely infantile kind, but *combinations of orality and sexuality* in ways expected to be unpleasant or nauseating. It is the food that is being dirtied by
the sex.

This is quite a different matter from the anal-sadistic flaunting of taboo by exposing the forbidden feces and urine, either
in fact or in 'jocular' form. It is the *combination of the abrogated oral taboo with sex* that is expected to be particularly
distressing and shocking to the audience, and it is evident that
the tellers of such stories do themselves feel a particularly close
and distressing, even dangerous, connection between orality
and sexuality. The danger can only be this same combination of
food and sex, with supreme attractiveness, in the mother. In
rejecting food by vomiting, especially if sexually 'tainted,' the
emotional and incestuous attraction to the mother is supremely
denied.

The nexus or nugget of difference which both links and sep-
arates the food-dirtying joke from the scatological or frankly
coprophagous joke, in which feces are actually eaten or wildly
flung about, is that in the food-dirtying joke it is the food which
is being 'dirtied' by the touch of sex, while in the scatological
or coprophagous joke it is the victim or butt of the joke who is
being dirtied by the touch of shit. Jokes of this second type will
be found in the final chapter, "Scatology." It will also be noted

that they often have a certain rough humor about them which does not cause digust, despite the subject matter, whereas the whole point and purpose of the 'narsty-narsty' or food-dirtying jokes, especially in their extreme form, of defiling the mother (see the section following this one), is to disgust the listener and make him feel queasy.

If the listener shrugs off such jokes without reacting visibly, or *says that he knows much more disgusting ones* – and then politely but firmly refuses to tell them – he will usually precipitate a good deal of anxiety in the teller, by having thus refused to dirty himself in the same fecal bath. This is the identical reaction, and for more or less the identical reason, when any person present at a drug-taking session, religious 'revival' ceremony, or homosexual party appears not to have been proselytized, and refuses to partake. In the case of 'nasty-nasty' jokes, such refusal will generally force the teller on to more and more awful specimens intended to blast the recalcitrant listener out of his calm, as though by a boiling enema (misplaced), and force the expression of his unwilling disgust. The open anxiety that the tellers of such jokes feel, that the listener *must* be brought to express dislike and distaste for jokes being told him (that is to say he *must vomit*), is not only the most openly hostile element ever encountered in the presentation of jokes, but is also strikingly opposed to the theoretical situation or pretext of joke-telling: namely, that the teller is trying to amuse the listener and make him laugh. The genre is openly very much closer to the telling of ghost-stories, or to the descriptions of horrible scenes of tortures and war (as, for example, in *Beowulf*, the *Iliad*, and many Scandinavian and Scottish folk-ballads), or other unflinching sado-masochistic folktales. Much more is said on this subject at the end of the Introduction to the present Second Series, "No Laughing Matter."

There is clearly a significant difference between a sexually toned food-dirtying 'gag' – a term of which the origins in the theatre are obscure, though it is certainly relevant here! – intended to be passed off as sardonic wit, such as: *"The three most over-rated things in the world: home-cooking, home-fucking, and Los Angeles!"* (N.Y. 1964: a joke that perhaps sums up America), and the queasy and abnormal interest shown by whole family-audiences in the carnival or circus side-show 'geeks.' These are subnormal masochistic or pre-psychotic types hired to stand as targets and be hit on the head or face by thrown baseballs, or to bite the heads off chickens and drink their blood, or swallow mice (and bring them up again alive, dazed with cigarette smoke); or for similarly heavily sexually-toned 'acts' such as sword-swallowing and snake-charming, the latter by a half-naked woman who usually ends à la Mother Eve by putting the snake's head in her mouth. (Any questions?) This whole subject, of *how one becomes a carnival 'geek,'* has been made the plot-framework of a powerful novel of carnival life, *Nightmare Alley* (1943) by William Lindsay Gresham, which has been stated to be a secret parable showing how ordinary people can finally be led to become political spies, or 'fingermen and squealers.' It certainly does show that; but so clear a parabolic intent would seem unlikely, or unconscious at most.

It is the unmistakable sensation of nervous dread and anti-humorous insistence that both tellers and listeners betray in connection with these 'nasty' themes, that leads to their classification here with Venereal Disease, quite aside from the fact that the most extreme examples of this type generally involve the accidental contracting of such disease. There is no such *dread* experienced in connection with ordinary scatological or even coprophagous stories, which are expected to cause the listener to laugh, willy-nilly. That the dread involved in the 'nasty-nasty' story or carnival act is *the sexual tainting of food* – whether swallowed or regurgitated – and of all the bodily secretions themselves (such as milk!) *by the incestuous attraction to the mother*, will become increasingly clear in the study of the actual stories following. From a hidden false note, it becomes the entire cacophony, as the stories change and intensify, passing from the sexual dirtying merely of food to the sexual dirtying of the mother herself, or of the 'old woman' or prostitute- with-hidden-face who is her surrogate.

One of the clearest expressions of this strange dread of the contamination of food by sex, and the reverse, is found in the elaborate structure of the ancient Jewish religious laws of *kashruth* or permissible and taboo foods. These laws not only ordain the prohibition of the wholly unpermitted totem foods of the earlier matriarchies, such as the jig and shell-fish which still represent the female genitals in the folklore of these cultures (now patriarchal also); but involve even further prohibitions concerning the permissible foods themselves, such as the cloven-hooved and cud-chewing animals (*Leviticus*, xi. 3–12), which are divided into the strictly separated milk and meat taken from the bodies of these animals. This separation is based on the uninflected and arbitrary statement, repeated three times in the Old Testament: '*Thou shalt not seethe a kid in his mother's milk.*' (*Exodus*, xxiii. 19, and xxxiv. 26; also *Deuteronomy*, xiv. 21.) This rather brusque prohibition clearly refers to some repudiated sacrifice of a former matriarchal (Demeter) worship at the 'feast of the harvest' or first-fruits, and is certainly not sentimental in nature: "The poor little kid; oh, think of it! using its own mother's milk!" etc. Nevertheless, upon it a whole dietary structure was created in the first thousand years of Jewish history ending with the Talmudic period, resulting in the still-surviving division among all religious Jews of meat and dairy dishes ('*milchigs*' and '*fleischigs*,' in Judaeo-German Yiddish), meaning that not only the foods, but even the dishes and cooking utensils in which they may be placed or cooked, and silverware with which they may be eaten, are rigidly controlled.

These and the many other food-taboos of Judaism give rise to one of the main neurotic traits of the Jewish people: an oral-masochistic fixation on food, especially on rejecting it, combined with an open sexualization of food as *something connected with the mother*, leading to an even more intense rejection as part of the incest-taboo. The cynical bestseller of the late 1960's in America, Philip Roth's *Portnoy's Complaint*, attempts the high-point of its 'Jewish self-hatred' humor and its mother-defiling, by means of food-dirtying – actually food-sexualizing – here in the anti-hero's ultimate confession to his psychoanalyst (*i.e.* rabbi-confessor):

Surely, Doctor, we can figure this thing out, two smart Jewish boys like ourselves ... A terrible act has been committed, and it has been committed by either my father or me ... Now: did he fuck between those luscious legs the gentile cashier from the office, or have I eaten my sister's chocolate pudding? ... Who looks into the fine points when he's hungry? I'm eight years old and chocolate pudding happens to get me hot. All I have to do is see that deep chocolatey surface gleaming out at me from the refrigerator, and my life isn't my own ... Well, where is this right mind on that afternoon I came home from school to find my mother out of the house, and our refrigerator stocked with a big purplish piece of raw liver? I believe that I have already confessed to the piece of liver that I bought in a butcher shop and banged behind a billboard on the way to a *bar mitzvah* [confirmation] lesson. Well, I wish to make a clean breast of it, Your Holiness. That – she – it – wasn't my first piece. My first piece I had in the privacy of my own home, rolled round my cock in the bathroom at three-thirty – and then had again on the end of a fork at five-thirty, along with the other members of that poor innocent family of mine.

So. Now you know the worst thing I have ever done. I fucked my own family's dinner.

Note that the presumed defiling of the family's dinner with semen, or by the simple sexual touch of the boy's penis, is only part of his 'sin.' There is also the implied cannibalism, in thus giving an element (the semen) of the non-kosher human body to eat, as in the folk-joke about *The boy who gives his family slices of his buttocks to eat, when he has gambled away the shopping-money*, in chapter 13.III.3, below. One gets the impression that Portnoy's *real* complaint or problem is that he identifies the refrigerator – so cold, so white, so blonde and *goyishe* – with the non-Jewish mother he wishes he had, and is not in love with his mother at all, but with the refrigerator. I do not mean this as humor. A well-known Jewish joke similarly concerns a boy who is frightened of *kreplach* (meat-pastries), because he identifies the warm, food-producing oven with his mother's pregnant body. (Given in full in Isaac Rosenfeld's "Adam and Eve on Delancy Street," in *Commentary*, New York, Oct. 1949, VIII. 385–7, a brief article which created an outcry and an epoch in Jewish cultural criticism in America.)

A joke which almost approximates this type of heavily structured neurotic taboo, has the observer in the joke immediately point out its irrational and inconsistent character: '*When a man at a restaurant indignantly refused the waitress's suggestion that he have some lamb tongue, alleging he never ate anything that came out of an animal's mouth, she suggested, "How about an egg?"* ' (D.C. 1943, from manuscript.) The concern among neurotics with food is generally organized in this way on a pretended systematic basis, similar to the Jewish laws of *kashruth* discussed above, often with the parallel authority appealed to, of some food-fad or diet being followed. Often, there is a matching regression from normal sexual life – either to no sex life, or to oragenital and oral-masochistic acts replacing this, of which the privations of the diet are one. The oral regressions in sexually-deprived situations are famous : for example the army, jail, or religious convent life.

It is axiomatic that all food-neurotics show such disturbances of the sexual life, though a more correct statement would be that all neurotics show disturbances of *both* their food and sex lives, usually in combination. The use of food-objects or drinks in connection with fellation and cunnilinctus – always offered as a luxurious exoticism, never as the food-neurosis it is – is the most unmistakable such combination, as discussed (with recipes and menus, so to speak) in my manual of oral techniques, *Oragenitalism*, enlarged edition of 1969, p. 108–18. Food-neurotic and sex-neurotic patterns are the substructure of the current disoriented 'hippie' interest not only in drugs but also in food-fads, particularly those of a dietetically dull and basically food-rejecting kind, which are all the hippie drop-outs can afford (after paying for their drugs), and which simultaneously serve as a masochistic self-punishment for the nursery 'sin' of rejecting food.

Prostitutes, whose sex-lives are by definition a horrible mess and mockery, are also in large numbers food-faddists; also believers in every other type of religion, occultism, kooky-cosmetics of the sexually-toned "Queen Bee Jelly" variety, fortune-telling, astrology, good- and bad-luck, hexes, jinxes, Tarot cards, medical (and psychological!) miracle cures, and other mental trash. The same is also true of Negroes, of both the 'urban peasant' and rural population. The most pathetic form of this that has come to my attention – other than the wasting of money on mail-order "High-John-the-Conqueror Mandrake Roots" by consumptive Negroes who cannot afford to pay a doctor – is that of the topless waitresses or 'Bunnies' and 'Pussycats' in various American night-clubs and glorified beer-joints exploiting young women's partly unclothed bodies. Many of these wretched girls, who do not even make the wages a prostitute could hope for, spend much of their free time and cash in the snobbish hot-steam 'Sauna' baths, trying hopelessly and not always unconsciously, as one of them said to me, "to clean off the cruddy *touch* of the men's eyes!" (N.Y. 1965.)

Anti-gallant army and wartime humor allows a large palette of possibilities for food-dirtying, combined with the rejection of women, who are of course actually deeply desired. (*You Can't Fire Me, I Quit!*) – *A hospital nurse in Vietnam complains to the army doctor that one of the soldier-patients has insulted her by saying, "Stick the dessert up your ass, nurse!" "I'm not going to stand for being talked to like that," the nurse almost weeps. "And you shouldn't, either," agrees the army doctor. "If that's the way he's going to talk to you, fuck him! Don't give him no fuckin' dessert!"* (Bloomington, Ind. 1963.) This is the dysphemistic trick of "heaping Mount Ossa on Mount Pelion" (*Hamlet*, V.i.274), generally made to operate in just this way by means of a pretended misunderstanding. *The whore is complaining to a sympathetic customer about how hard the life is. "I thought Harry was a right guy," she laments, "but it turns out he's just a dirty pimp. The other day you know what he says to me? He says to me, 'You better bring me in a yard [$100] today, or you're gonna get a kick in the cunt!'" Customer, shrivelling: "I don't like language like that." Whore: "You don't like it?! What about me? The next time that cocksucker talks to me like that, I'm gonna shit in his mother-fucking EAR!"* (N.Y. 1970. Motif S112.3, poison in ear; as in *Hamlet*, ca. 1600, the Play-within-the-play, III.ii.145.)

Many war-phrases and other slang attempt to achieve rough humor, and to show the toughness of the users, by means of food-dirtying images, such as calling chipped chicken on toast '*shit on a shingle*,' or calling tomato *Ketchup* (a Malay word for soy-sauce) '*sorority sauce*' or '*Bloody Mary.*' These terms are taken over in part for peacetime or civilian uses as well, with expurgatory omission of any reference which would show their real etymological origins. For example, '*Bloody Mary*' (or '*Dracula*') now refers in civilian life in America to a spiced alcoholic drink including a dash of red tabasco sauce, without any recollection of the actual reference to menstruation. When I once asked about this name in a folksong and marijuana night-club on MacDougal Street in New York, I was told absolutely straight-faced by a young girl, "*You know, that was the name of a queen in England. She killed a lot of people.*" (N.Y. 1964.) I have not heard that '*douche-water highball*,' meaning bourbon-&-soda, has yet been washed quite so clean in the Blood of the Lambs. (L.A. 1942.)

The rejected breast, which is the original food-dirtying image, has long been a favorite and in many cultures. In some of these, such as Imperial China (until 1908, under a woman empress, when this atrocity was actually photographed in public), the breasts of women might be cut off as a routine torture. This was shown in a recent American Civil War movie. The ablation of women's breasts in the presence of cancer, in our own culture, is probably the identical torture (though done under anaesthetic, of course), since it rarely saves the sick woman's life nor even extends it very long, while destroying her image of herself. At the mere verbal level, the war phrase, *'tough shit!'* meaning that something was just too bad (the French *'tant pis!'* which involves no verbal joke, would be modified politely, when necessary, to *'tough titty.'* This was then again dysphemized into such phrases as that something was *'a case of tough tit,'* while someone who had bad luck or was called for fatigue-duty was *'sucking the hind tit.'* (Actually it is the hind-tit that is the fullest of milk.) Compare *'eating high on the hawg,'* meaning the exact opposite, but here the touch of the hog does not dirty the food.

Much of this type of humor is common among children, both at the primary level of word- and slang-coinage, and in simple riddles and jokes. *"Who was the first soda jerk?"* – *"Adam: he made Eve's cherry pop!"* (D.C. 1943, from a soldier.) – *"Who was the first carpenter? – Eve: she made Adam's banana stand."* (Printed novelty card, U.S. 1940, in which Eve is actually shown, with Adam standing close to her, as though she is sawing off his penis.) Other food-sexualia, or sexual smörgåsbord, include the *'Honeymoon Sundae'* offered by ice-cream-vending Good Humor men on bicycles to unwary young girls, who would be told, if they 'bit' and asked what it was: *"Banana ice cream with cherry sauce!"* (Bronx, N.Y. 1950.) All the many folk references in the West to the banana, as a simple and direct phallic symbol, are an interesting return to the lost (red) tropical banana of Levantine folklore, which is there understood to have been the fruit with which Eve tempted Adam. The *apple* appearing in Christian art representations of this scene is, if not an obvious expurgation, an assimilation of the symbol to the female breast instead. The Bible does not specify what fruit, stating only that the food-taboo concerned *p'ri ha-eytz,* 'the fruit of the tree.' (*Genesis,* iii. 3.)

The more recent stories on this subject, since that of Adam & Eve, ring only the significant change of dirtying food with sex instead of dirtying sex with food, as does their great prototype, the Bible. Sometimes the jokes are satisfied with the mere 'spooneristic' jingling statement of the connection. *'At an isolated lumber camp, the cook ran out of meat, and served up for dinner a sheep he found tethered behind one of the buildings. In the midst of the meal, he mentioned his predicament and how he had solved it. The lumberjacks, one and all, stopped eating. "What's the matter, boys," he inquired, "did I fuck up the cooking?" "No," they replied, "you cooked up the fucking".'* (D.C. 1952.) A briefer version, more commonly collected: *A French chef is brought to America by a* nouveau-riche *Texas millionaire at his wife's insistence. One day the Texan finds the chef performing cunnilinctus on his wife. "How do you like that!" he cries. "First he fucks up my eating, and now he's eating up my fucking!"* (N.Y. 1946.) This has also been worked into a nightclub burlesque 'routine' in which: *The two comedians assist the magician, who prepares to saw a beautiful girl in half. They bet (in the Italian gesture-game of "La Moré") for the two halves of the girl which will result. The comedian who gets the top half says, "Wouldn't you just know I'd get the half that* eats?!" *Then he looks at the other comedian gloating over his sexual victory and ostentatiously licking his lips, and adds: "Well, some guys eat the half I don't get!"* (Miami Beach, Florida, 1946.) In all of these, the insistence on the little spoonerism that makes the joke operate at the verbal level (*hipallage* or *chiasmus*, the Latin *submutation* or 'hidden changes'), indicates very clearly that the simple statement of this 'hidden change,' or secret connection between sex and food is itself considered a fine joke. One observes that it is here *rationalized* as merely referring to cunnilinctus – not cannibalism.

In Vance Randolph's *Pissing in the Snow*, No. 38, "The Better End," an old Arkansas item, heard by the teller about 1890, comes to the same verbal conclusion, when: *The town boy who has been visiting the 'widow,' is peeking through a knot-hole at the two lovers in the bedroom, and his 'head was a-spinning like a top, and he didn't know if he was afoot or horseback. The widow-woman giggled just then, and she says, "Don't squeeze me so hard." But her steady fellow let out a whoop. "I got a notion to squeeze you plumb in two," he says. The town boy couldn't keep still no longer. "Throw me the end with the pussy in it!" says he.'* This fits the ending, as to dividing the woman in half, to an ancient folktale or format concerning peeping on lovers from a tree or hayloft, appearing five centuries earlier in La Sale's *Cent Nouvelles Nouvelles* (1460) No. 12, as "Le Veau," of which the original will be found in the First Series, 6.V.4, page 381, with further variants. (Aarne Type 1355B.) As in many of his Ozark tales, Randolph's text goes on after the verbal conclusion to express its unease that everything has come to an end then in tableau, as though exploded : '*The story don't say what happened after that. But it stands to reason there was the devil to pay and no pitch hot, as any fool can plainly see.*' On the idea of the woman-cut-in-half, meaning the woman of two profoundly different characters, see chapter 8, III.2–4 in the First Series, p. 500–25, centering about the "Sleeve Job" story of wedding-night fears and deceptions of the groom. Also, the legend of the snake-bride, *Mélusine* (Motifs B656.2, and A642.1), which, as encountered by Freud in the now-forgotten American novel, *Elsie Venner* (1861) by Oliver Wendell Holmes, led him to the discovery of psychoanalysis.

Vance Randolph's *Pissing in the Snow*, No. 91, gives another Ozark item, essentially intended as food-dirtying, as are of course all versions of the 'pissing in the sink' joke already given under "Cloacal Intercourse." '*One time there was a young farmer had some folks come over to his place for supper. The fellow's wife didn't know how to cook much, and the house looked kind of dirty, but everybody was eating the best they could. The people that live on Horse Creek are all hell for politeness, because they don't want to hurt nobody's feelings. Just then the baby come a-crawling out on the floor, and you could see where he has shit all over himself. The kid's mother didn't pay no attention, but the man spoke right up. "Marthy," says he, "fetch the dishrag, and wipe that young-un's ass. If there's one thing I can't stand it's nastiness!" . . .*' (Verona, Missouri, 1951, heard by the informant 'near Horse Creek, in Stone county, Mo., about 1935,' and going on to say that the phrase had become proverbial.) Randolph also gives another story, No. 36, "The Boy Needs Pants," of almost the same kind, without any scatological element, in which the food is dirtied simply by the touch of the boy-child's 'tally-whacker,' which he drags across the table. This will be discussed in the following chapter, 13.III, under "Circumcision."

The fear expressed in Randolph's 'nastiness' story, of hurting the host's feelings, actually seems to allude to the almost universal fear of complaining about or otherwise (verbally) soiling offered food, which is one of the underlying problems in the grotesque social sadism of the rules for eating – proper fork to use, etc. – codified rigorously in the Jewish laws, and in modern works of 'etiquette' as those of Emily Post, and more recent items (trying to gild the pill), *The I Try to Behave Myself Book* and *What Do You Say, Dear?* These are a type of folklore and an ethnological source grossly overlooked by social historians, as are the matching mail-order catalogues of *kitsch* gifts and furnishings for the thus 'standardized' homes. Many primitives (and more than a few civilized people) do not like to be watched while eating, and will immediately stop if they are conscious that another person is watching them, whether envy of the food ('hexing') is expressed or not. That animals growl over their food jealously, and fight off any other animal coming near, is a well-known and primordial form of the same fear.

Even the minced and modified *sidewise peeping* at what another person is eating is understood as an expression of dangerous jealousy, and the French term *guigne,* for bad luck (the English '*jinx*'), actually refers to just such a sidewise look : the 'evil eye.' English working-class joke : '*When a bloke overlooked* [n.b.] *a fellow opening his lunch sandwich and remarked, "Beetroot, mate?"* – *he got the reply, "No, arse out of the missus' drawers".*'. (Chelmsford, Essex, 1953.) The mocking food-dirtying is here evidently intended as an *apotropaion,* to drive off the mystic danger or 'bad luck' of the other man's intrusive peeping or verbal 'nosiness.' Randolph's *Bawdy Ozark Speech* (MS. 1954) p. 65, has: *An ugly old woman serving bad food in a dirty boarding-house, but 'all the bachelors in town ate there* ... *"Betsy puts a granny-rag* [menstrual cloth] *in the soup, and them old stags can smell it a mile off".*' Cf. First Series, 8.V.4, p. 575–9.

The comic anti-Irish song of about the 1910's, "Who Threw the Overhauls in Mrs. Murphy's Chowder?" seems to involve a modification of the theme, but with the mystic 'dirt' of male sweat or shit replacing that of female menstrual-secretion. There are also children's joking allusions, as in the English joke just quoted, but not quite rising to joke form, as to *soup made of the mother's bloomers boiled up.* Dr. Martha Wolfenstein's *Children's Humor* (1954) p. 121, gives such a joke where: *Children are hidden in their mother's pants, and have "lemonade and chocolate ice-cream."*

To dirty sex with food is obviously not easy, and is anti-natural, no matter what the Bible may say. To the contrary, the mere touch of food often suffices instead to 'clean up' the sexual element. The following joke was broadcast over the American radio, during an amateur contest. At the punch-line, the master-of-ceremonies groaned, and made the sound of being struck on the chin, doubling up as though at a 'foul blow' (a boxing euphemism meaning a blow at the testicles, or 'below the belt'), and promised the audience, "Next time I'll look at their scripts!" But that was all. The program was not cut off the air, as was (and still is) usual when anything presumably 'obscene' is said. The slurring pronunciation of the punch-line also of course helped: *Three moles were working their way along underground when one said, "Hmmm, I think I smell pancakes." The second sniffed and said, "Waffles!" The third took a long sniff and said, "Mmmm, mole-asses!"'* (D.C. 1951.)

A similar radio 'boner' – probably not authentic – was reported from England in the days before the New Freedom, which is still so inelegantly and uncharmingly being exploited by British intellectual mags and monthly rags. This particular item plays on the British transitive verb, 'to do,' referring to sexual intercourse. *'Wilfred Pickles interviewing a young lady: "If you weren't yourself, Miss, who or what would you like to be?" She: "A Christmas Pudding." W.P.: "A Christmas Pudding?!"'* [The British are terribly slow-witted, exactly as folklore states, and usually temporize when faced by anything they don't understand, by *repeating* the statement or question that confuses them, but with a querulous, rising inflection?] *She: "Yes, a Christmas Pudding. I'd like to be done slowly for six hours".'*

A fairly ancient form in folk-humor involves the playing on proper names with a view to erotizing or scatologizing them. This is not only considered insulting by all concerned, but both primitive and cultivated peoples secretly believe that a person's name is a sort of occult 'handle' that controls him, and that he can be hexed or harmed if his name is mis-pronounced or mocked. (See further chapter 14.I.1, on "Spelling Out Names.") I have noted in *The Horn Book,* p. 207–9, the earliest humorous item involving name-perversions that I have been able to find: the *Processus contra ser Catium Vinculum,* printed about 1530, which I believe was a work of revenge by the original 'macaronic' humorist, Teofilo Folengo ('Merlin Cocciae'), against the head of the religious order from which he had been expelled, who is named therein. In modern name-obscoena – usually on the names of food, drink, songs, plays, etc. – it is not so much the dirtying of the food-names that is involved, as an attempt to make these more interesting by sexualization:

DO YOU KNOW YOUR WHISKEY?

Old Oscar Pepper told Mr. Boston, who was an Old Quaker, that he saw Paul Jones take Virginia Dare down to Cobb's Creek, through Crab Orchard, back of the Log Cabin. For a Silver Dollar, she lay her Bottoms Up in a bed of Four Roses. He tickled her Vat 69 with Three Feathers, stuck his Canadian Club into her Old Drum, gave her a shot of Cream of Kentucky, and so began the Wilkins Family.

Newbern & Rodebaugh precede this, p. 184–7, with a shorter sexualization – a style of humor on which see further *The Horn Book*, p. 189–91 – in this case of the Great Overstuffed American Indoor-sport of dieting: 'RECIPE: *The latest diet: ½ ounce Metrecal, ½ ounce castor oil, ½ ounce Spanish Fly, and 1 Pint of Whiskey. Take it five times daily, and at the end of a month you'll be the skinniest, shittiest, sexiest alcoholic in town.*' (Please do not cut this recipe out of the book to send to People You Know. I will be glad to make you all the photocopies you may need.)

Another standard source for dirtying or sexualizing anything is the humor of drunkards, the foolish things they say and do, and especially the wicked tricks that can be played on them, which are, in fact, often of an orasexual or castratory nature, exactly as the jokes indicate and probably help to perpetuate. *A drunk in an all-night lunchroom orders two scrambled eggs, but the cook only has one egg. Seeing that the client is stenching drunk, he mixes up a gob of Limburger cheese with the egg and serves the whole thing well scrambled. 'Shay,' says the drunk boozily, after eating the mess, "where do you get your eggs?" "Got our own hen-house out in back." "Do you have a rooster too?" the drunk asks. "No, we don't." "Well, you sure as hell better get one, because a skunk is fucking your chickens!"* (Pittsburgh, Pa. 1967.) Note: The bad taste of modern 'chicken-factory' eggs is really the result of feeding the chickens a pulverized mash made of fish-heads. Or of their own droppings, under the tasty euphemism of 'fientes'!

Monkeys and parrots are also useful surrogates for expressing all sorts of disorderly or improper human aspirations, as can be seen in the entire chapter 3, devoted to them in the First Series. Here is the perfect and almost total gesture of food-dirtying – the total gesture would be simply shitting on it, as above – and the perfectly absurd monkey-business excuse accompanying: *A woman at the zoo tosses the monkey a handful of peanuts. He carefully sticks each one up his ass, pulls it out, and eats it. When the woman asks the attendant why the monkey does this, he tells her: "Zozo doesn't trust anybody anymore, lady. Ever since he swallowed a whole peach, and the pit gave him the bleeding shits, he's been trying out everything first for size."* (N.Y. 1965.)

The World's Dirtiest Jokes, p. 130, gives a long version of what may be a derivative of the preceding animal-favorite. In brief: *A man is advised by a hospital chaplain that he can help his brother to give up smoking cigars, which are killing him, by this simple method: "All you have to do is buy a box of cigars, unwrap them, stick each one up your rear end and roll it around a little, then carefully rewrap each one and give them to him. I assure you he will not smoke very many more cigars." The brother rapidly stops smoking after this treatment, saying, "I've decided to quit smoking cigars. They've started to taste shitty." But the man now has a new problem for the chaplain: "How do I cure myself of this awful urge I have to stick cigars up my ass?"*

When I made the mistake of remarking, a few years ago, in *The Fake Revolt* (1967), that marijuana and most other drugs can be taken rectally, as well as by smoking or drinking – they are also usually faster-acting that way, and a little bit goes a much longer way – I was not altogether surprised when a young Anglo-German fashion-model picked *this one line* out of the pamphlet to comment on, asking if it were really true, and underlining her inquiry with the perfectly unnecessary gesture known in America as 'the Finger.' However, as other complaints came in, in particular from one man who had tried using up in this way heel-taps of mixed liquors after a party, which he administered to himself through a woman's douche-bag tube, with the result, as he wrote, that he "nearly burned (his) ass-hole off," I should perhaps add here the caution that this is not a good way of administering any beverage containing a high degree of alcohol. The same is true when used in oragenital acts: never to be combined with anything more alcoholic than champagne, or strong sweet wines (20% alcohol), and even these the genital partner sometimes finds a bit more tangy than desired. (See fuller details in *Oragenitalism*, 1969, p. 108–15 – with caution.)

Though the joke about the chaplain and the cigars is of course pure food-dirtying, here combined with the anti-clerical mocking of good Samaritans and good advice, it is nevertheless perfectly true, as the joke implies, that habit-forming drugs are just as habit-forming rectally as any other way. Perhaps more so. Compare the jokes in the chapter on Scatology on such themes as: *The bandaged-up accident victim in the hospital who is being fed rectally through a tube. As a special treat the nurse is giving him coffee this way, when the man begins to shout muffledly through his bandages* (pantomimed), *and attempts to shove the tube away with his buttocks. "What's the matter?" asks the solicitous nurse, "too hot?" "Mmmno-no-no!" comes the muffled response: "too much sugar!!"* This is an old-time classic burlesque 'routine,' which I first saw in one of the last of the strip-tease and bawdy humor burlesque theaters on the Bowery in New York, in 1937. It is topped by another favorite, almost implying the addiction problem as above: *The faithful butler is describing to the cook how the old millionaire, who has to be fed rectally, has responded to the delicacies the cook has prepared for him that morning. "Did he like the fried brains?" "Only so-so." "What about the toasted cheese-crumpets?" asks the distraught chef; "I was sure he'd like those." "Oh, he was crazy about them! It certainly did my old heart good to see the way his asshole* SNAPPED *at them."* (N.Y. 1940). Query: Does the whole process eventually reverse itself, as implied in feeding the man brains rectally, and so forth? Does he end up shitting through his mouth? This is not asked as a joke. What do the joke-smiths really mean?

An unclassifiable item on food-dirtying, which might just as well be referred to "Sexual Smörgåsbord" later, where all these themes pick up again after a necessary excursus as to the attack on the (mother's) breast: *A stranger in a small town is enjoying a musical session in the local country grocery-store, at which a field-worker in torn overalls is sitting on a board across the pickle-barrel and singing to his own guitar accompaniment. The stranger notices that the singer's balls are hanging through a hole in his overalls into the opening of the barrel. He slips up beside the singer and whispers in his ear, "Do you know your balls are hanging in the pickles?" "No," says the singer cheer-fully, "but you hum it and I'll strum it!"* (Bloomington, Ind. 1963.) For lists of the oddly bawdy titles of many country fiddle-tunes and the matching dance calls – presumably of 'dia-bolic' origin, in Scotland – see Vance Randolph's *Ribaldry at Ozark Dances* (MS. 1954).

3. ANTI-BREAST FETICHISM

A very significant note, barely touched upon in jokes and then gratingly, eventually proves to be a real and key intent of the whole food-dirtying genre. This is the *dirtying of the mother's breast* (or her milk) by means of feces, representing vomit in the infant-situation; or by the statement that the breast itself is dirty. *'Lawyer heckling an 80-year-old witness on the stand: "You say you have worked all your life? What did you do the first year of your life?" Old Man: "Milked and spread manure".'* (Fredericksburg, Va. 1952. The "milked the first year" line appears alone in *The Stag Party*, Boston, 1888, p. 259–unnumbered.) This makes its point so fast and then gets away from it, that one almost does not observe – in identifying admiringly with the smart old geezer getting the better of that snippety Lawyer – that he has, in effect, identified his mother with a cow, and has put nursing at her breast on a par with "spreading manure." Why mince words? He has shit on his mother's breast and in her milk.

No one who has been bouncing around in the literary and cultural hipster activities of the last few decades in America can be ignorant of the fact that the late Ernest Hemingway (*olav ha'shalom* – that means 'peace on his memory') chose as running gag or pudibund profanity of his mock-revolutionary *For Whom the Bell Tolls*, in 1940, the Spanish food-dirtying oath, *"I shit in the milk of your mother!"* This appears, how-ever, in his work, as: "I *obscenity* in the milk of your mother," the explanation being circulated – folklore, of course – that as he was being paid $1 a word, each *obscenity* netted him one buck, where he would have been paid nothing for dashes. There are a lot of other Spanish profanities too, some of them mar-vellously sacrilegious and obscene (for a few samples see *The Limerick*, p. 388, note 266), but this is the one that Mr. Heming-way preferred. As food-dirtying it has at least the merit of being clear, total, and succinct: it includes the mother, the milk – and the *obscenity*.

The ambivalent attraction to the mother's breast, which makes such extremes of pretended rejection necessary, is never lost sight of. The breast of the wife is substituted, whether for being kissed or slapped, as in the work of 'James Hadley Chase' (René Raymond) an imitator of Hemingway and Faulkner, as I have indicated in Love & Death, p. 67–8. This originated with Dashiell Hammett, as to the tough private-detective and even tougher (but alas, so homosexual) secret-agent or spy stories of recent popularity. In Chase's Twelve Chinks and a Woman – crudely adapting its background of violence and sex from Hemingway's To Have and Have Not – no bones are made about the slapping of a woman's bare breasts by the 'gangsters' who represent and enact the readers' wish-fulfillment of toughness. In other works of even lower imitators and continuators in this group, such as Mickey Spillane and Ian Fleming, I am told the women's breasts are pistol-whipped. Please do not send me the page-references, or (as did two helpful readers) Ian Fleming's or Mickey Spillane's complete works, marginally marked in red and blue crayon to indicate the nastier sadistic passages. I've read enough to know what these characters are peddling. Have you? In one degenerate movie, Hell for Breakfast, a lighted cigarette is ground out against a woman's bare breast, the scar later being displayed. In another, Soldier Blue, a woman's breasts are cut off. We have come a long way from Baudelaire, bragging in "Le Léthé" that he sucks poison from the sado-masochist nipples of his 'adored tigress.'

Endless anti-breast fetichism and violence is retailed at levels other than and below that of joking, usually pictorially and almost without words. The humorously-illustrated 'novelty' cards once given away as advertisements for saloons, as late as the 1930's, with a few still lingering on even now in Florida 'night-clubs,' have become almost extinct now owing to the competition of the more and more free magazine cartoons. The last two really successful 'novelty' cards were both of the anti-breast kind: one showed a cow stepping on its own udder, and screaming "So you think YOU got troubles!" (N.Y. 1950), while another gruesomely illustrated the situation implied in the folk-phrase, "Ain't seen so much excitement around here since Maw got her tits caught in the clothes-wringer" (also printed with the same caption as the card showing the cow).

A less popular – because over-frankly yearning – card showed: A man practically swallowing a beautiful young

woman's breast, with wide-open mouth, captioned: "OUT TO
LUNCH" (N.Y. 1951.) The latest in this line is an extraordinarily
cruel cartoon, signed Ted Trogdon, and printed in *Sex to Sexty*
(1966) 8:38, showing: *a man lifting off a platter-cover in a
restaurant with the result that a live lobster seizes the fat and
screaming woman opposite him (the mother, to be sure) by the
nipples with its claws.* This is nothing other than the ancient
folksong of "The Crab-Fish," appearing in *Bishop Percy's Folio
Manuscript* about 1640, reduced to a cartoon, and displaced upward from the original seizing by the crab-fish of the woman's
vulva (and her husband's nose) to the uses of anti-breast violence. Omitted here is an example of breast-attacking or defiling
so violent that it has been placed, instead, in section 14.II.3,
under "Water-Wit" (the aggressive folk-form in which it is
cast), in the chapter on Dysphemism & Insults.

The great male interest in female décolletage – as on the T.V.
screen – also turns sour under the influence of this anti-
fetichism, and what is wanted is no longer the exciting sight of
the (mother's) breasts, or at least of the generous cleft between
them, but that some harm should come to the thus freely displayed breasts. The minimum harm is that they should fall out
when the woman does not want them to. In at least one joke
this is curiously considered *dangerous* to the male viewer: *A
boy comes home from school and tells his mother he will no
longer wear his v-neck sweater, explaining, "Teacher had on a
sweater just like it, and when she bent over one of her lungs
fell out!"* (N.Y. 1940.) Clearly expressing castration anxiety,
with the breasts identified with the male genitals – note well –
as is also very commonly done by neurotic women compulsively displaying their breasts in tight or pointed brassières, or
naked on the beach.

*A girl in a bar keeps ordering 'Martinis' and drinking them
until she is very drunk. When the bartender asks her if she
wants another she says, "Ah g'wan, I don't like your fuckin'
Martunis, they give me heartburn!" The bartender freezes and
replies, "For your information, Miss, they're not Martunis,
they're Martinis. And you haven't got heartburn: your left
knocker's in the ashtray!"* (*Sex to Sexty*, 1966, 7:23, opening
by calling the girl "well-endowed,' *i.e.* with large breasts.) The
joke already given, about *helping the woman put back her
breast, which has slipped out, 'with two warm spoons,'* is really
only an over-reacted expression of hostility to the breast, not

gallantry, in handling the breast with tongs as though it may not be touched.

Dr. Martha Wolfenstein, in her important study *Children's Humor* (1954) p. 159–60, analyzes the permissive element in the following story in which I would rather prefer to observe the hostility: *A British anthropologist visiting an African tribe is told by its Oxford-educated chief that they do everything just as in jolly-old England. He is invited to observe the court trial at which the chief is presiding, with the lawyers all wearing tasseled wigs, and so forth. He is puzzled, however, by a black boy in white gloves running through the audience and feeling the women's breasts, without anyone taking any notice of him, and asks why the boy is not put out for disturbing the trial. "Why, we're doing it the way it's done in England, old chap," the chief tells him. "He's the Court Titter. You know, you're always reading in the accounts of trials, 'A titter ran through the crowd'."* It is certainly true, as Dr. Wolfenstein notes, that the mythical African tribesmen have found a permissible way for one 'black boy in white gloves' to do what is surely not permitted to us, yet I wonder if any man would be flattered to learn – in accounts of a newly-discovered Amazon tribe, joking or not – that a woman known as a 'ballocker' would run through the crowd and give all the men's balls a tweak.

Dr. René Guyon, the French proponent of what he calls in several books, *Sexual Freedom*, has similarly been observed, in a review by Dr. Frederic Wertham, to define freedom as a state of affairs where men have the right to pinch women's buttocks in the subway, but women don't have the right to call the police. Compare also, for undisguised hostility, the similar profession of: *Chief Spitter (or Pisser) in the harem: His job is to spit (or piss) on all the harem-beauties, and when he finds one that SIZZLES he takes her to the sultan.* (N.Y. 1940.) I suspect the 'titter' story is only a polite modification of this. Is it really an enjoying of the idea of 'sizzling' female passion, or is it a spitting (or pissing) on all the *other* women in the world by the harem-eunuch?

Squeezing or even sucking the woman's breasts, for the man's own pleasure, is not always an acceptance of their erotic function. It is more often a replacement of the intended baby's mouth by the father's or some other man's – while the baby gets cow's milk. So that, in our culture, many or most young women have been brainwashed into construing their breasts

mainly as organs of excitement for (and control over) men, and
not of nourishment for children. The now popular operations
of mammoplasty on older women have simply followed this
change or sexualization of rôle, as also the similar injections
with paraffin or silicones to make the sagging breasts look firm
– but making them *feel* cancerous! *A girl takes an ailing infant
to the doctor's. The doctor looks the weakling over, then suddenly turns and starts squeezing the girl's breasts, finally pulling open her shirtwaist and sucki:;g powerfully at each nipple
in turn. "But my dear girl," he says at last, "it's no wonder the
baby's sickly. You haven't any milk." "Oh yes," the girl gasps,
"it's not my child. It's my sister's."* (London, 1954.)

Though the sucking of the woman's breast by the man is
usually considered, as here, an attempt to excite her to intercourse, its real purpose – like that of all oragenital acts – is to
excite the *oral* partner, in this case the man, and to satisfy his
orasexual needs. As such, this desire must be denied and dirtied
by oral-neurotics suffering from feelings of guilt for their semi-
conscious cannibalistic fantasies. Only in a highly eccentric
work, *The Marriage of Happiness*, by one Carl Buttenstedt,
published (in the English language) in Germany about 1910, is
the plain recommendation made that the breasts of the woman
are to be sucked by the adult man for his own emotional or
physical needs. The alleged "Marriage of Happiness" consists of
the man sucking the woman's breasts, during *coitus prolongatus*, until eventually they begin to secrete milk, though the
woman has not recently had a child! The unstated idea is, as
with many pre-psychotic and occult sex lunacies of this kind,
that the woman's milk will replace the 'penis-milk' that the
man fears he is losing, and which is also sometimes identified
by such lunatics as 'the marrow of the brain.' The next step is,
of course, the 'poisonous penis-milk' with which the late Dr.
Edmund Bergler attempted to embroil the question of the
psychodynamics of homosexuality, in his rather peculiar
maunderings on the subject, fortunately not relevant here.

In the style of simultaneously searching for, yet denying, the
mother's breast and milk, with the great freight of incestuous
(and cannibalistic) danger these seem to carry for the adult
neurotic, one can hardly top the following anecdote, in which
the alleged search for 'the dirtiest woman' possible to find
hardly disguises the violently-denied search for the mother,
whose *clean* and beautiful breast is to be sucked all night:

'Nat Goodwin used to tell the story of the chap who got drunk and went to a whorehouse. He picked for his partner the dirtiest woman in the place. In fact, said this chap [Mr. Goodwin?], relating his experience afterwards, when he woke up the next morning the only clean part of her was the teat next to him!' – (1 : 199.)

Another statement, not quite so frank, projects upon the long-suffering Ozarkers the situation of the 'dirty' or neglectful mother – who obviously cannot give the growing boy enough milk to satisfy him for the rest of his life. *A social-worker in the Ozarks sees a hill-woman feeding her baby on sops of bread and pan-drippings, and remonstrates that the child should be nourished at the mother's breast if there is no other milk available.* "Well, m'am," says the hill-woman, "I guess you know, seein' as how you're book-learn'd. But you see my oldest boy there? – " *(pointing to a gangling youngster of seventeen).* "He's purty healthy-lookin', ain't he? Well, he never had a tit in his mouth till the night he got engaged!" (N.Y. 1953. Also a very similar item, London, same year, on a British background.) The real meaning is probably that the woman *has* no breast-milk owing to her poverty.

The same hillbilly background is always used in an all-too-perennial favorite, referring to the nursing of children well past the usual weaning-time on the superstition that this will 'prevent' pregnancy. (Confusion of cause & effect, since pregnancy makes the breast-milk dry up.) *The Ozark boy of fourteen who asks his father for a chaw of tobacco. "You're too young for that, son. Whaddya want it for?" "Want to get the taste of milk out of my mouth, paw. Maw's been eatin' wild onions again!"* (N.Y. 1939.) Thomas Hardy, who knew all the rural British jokes and superstitions but did not often put them in his novels, alludes to the underlying belief here – if not to some form of the story itself – in *Tess of the D'Urbervilles* (1891), where the milkmaids are all sent out to clear the meadow of this wild plant because one of the clients complains that the butter tastes of garlic! How now, Mother Cow? The identification of woman with the cow has already been observed several times as an obvious and ancient mock, dating not only from the time of Leonardo da Vinci's little mathematical proof or paradox that a woman's vagina is proportionately *larger* than that of a cow, but from millennia earlier, in the various Biblical regulations in which woman (and her children) are placed at the level of various other cattle as in the legend of the Patriarch Jacob's animal-husbandry experiments, with the Divine help, in *Genesis* xxx–xxxi.

The actual *giving of milk* by the woman (*mirabile dictu!*) during the lactation of her child is of course the crucial connection pretended between woman and cow, though all other mammals – such as lionesses and tigresses – also nurse their young, without for all that being considered cows. The mere statement of fact of human lactation is somehow funny or embarrassing to the same people who, for public consumption, ooze gooey sentimentality over advertising pictures in the magazines showing radiant young mothers holding their babies to breasts which have been scientifically dried out immediately after childbirth with injections of Stilbestrol (to keep them sexually attractive to the husband, and to hell with the child), and who are stated in the advertising plug adjacent to be feeding the poor kids instead on Dr. Gubble's Patented Triple-Enriched Condensed Sweetened Machine-Mashed Homogenized Canned Milk – "The Milk from Laughing Cows" (see the funny cow laughing on the label: who is the funny cow laughing *at?*) – which has somehow been prevented chemically from going rotten in the can, in which it has lain for several years in the gentleman-wholesaler's stockroom.

Many people sincerely believe that the following story about an advertising contest is true. In fact, *all* stories about advertising contests and slogans (such as the tiresome tale of the 'million-dollar' slogan: "Be Happy, Go Lucky!" for Lucky Strike cigarettes) are generally believed to be true. Which shows how pitifully easy it is to soften up the population by means of 'white propaganda' whether in peacetime or in war. *A prize is offered for the best advertising jingle for canned milk. The prize is given to the usual sentimental slop, but the judges all admit privately that the best slogan was really:*

> *No tits to twitch,*
> *No shit to pitch,*
> *Just punch a hole in the son-of-a-bitch!*
> *– Carnation!*

The food-dirtying of the breast-milk – only of a cow of course, but 'Things equal to the same thing equal each other,' do they not? – with the 'shit to pitch' in the barnyard, is not the 'best slogan' because it will sell the most canned milk, but because it most boldly expresses the infantile attack on the mother's breast. It should be emphasized again that this attack is not in anger, though the pretense is always immanent that the breast-food the mother offers is somehow bad, and that *she* is bad. To the contrary, the child would like to eat the mother alive, by sucking sustenance out of her breast, or would do so without feelings of guilt were it not for the deeply resented food-training and eventual weaning. It is precisely the child's guilt over the hostility against the mother thus created, and the ambivalent incestuous attraction to her, which is being projected upon the mother herself in these images of food-dirtying. Thus, the vomit or feces in jokes like this, told by adults, are the verbal equivalent of the identical use made of real vomit or feces in the nursery by the child.

Another few examples, which leave nothing for the psychoanalytic critic to add: *'While their mothers are in a clinic, three babies waiting outside in their prams get into conversation. Discussing things of mutual concern, the subject of nutrition soon occupies their little minds. One complaining he's had nothing but Benger's* [canned baby-food] *from birth; his neighbour, reared entirely on "Cow & Gate" adds that he's sick to death of the stuff. But the third objects, "I don't see you chaps have anything to grumble about. How would you relish the prospect of tackling a pair of old, cold tits reeking of stale 'Digger Plug' tobacco every time you were hungry? (Union Jack*, MS. compiled in Chelmsford Prison, Essex, 1953, with caption "Baby's Bane.") Note that here the breast is hated and rejected for the same tobacco flavor that – in the American hillbilly story in which "Maw's been eatin' wild onions again" – is specially sought for, to clean the mouth of the hated taste of milk. *Heads, I win; tails, you lose.*

From the same source: *'Two Englishman in a café in a small French town early one morning. One asks the waitress for some hot milk for his coffee, whereupon she unbuttons her bodice and proceeds to milk herself by hand, squirting the milk copiously into his cup. Afterwards the two men sit silently for a while, and the second man says: "Bloody good thing I didn't ask for hot water for my tea!"'* In the American form: *A man at a lunch-counter asks for two hamburgers. The waitress, who is also the cook, takes the hamburger patties out of the refrigerator and slaps one under each of her arms, where she holds them as she works. "What's that for?" the man asks. "I've got to thaw them out," she explains; "the fridge is freezing everything solid." "Gosh," he says, "I'm glad I didn't order a hot dog!"* (L.A. 1967.) A similar joke on the shaping of dough-nuts, etc., is told elsewhere. Other forms stick more strictly to verbal dirtying. *A party of four in a busy nightclub. The men order Budweiser beer, and the waiter shouts, "Two Buds, comin' up! – Whad'll ya have ladies?" "Well," says one of the women, 'we were going to order Country Club, but change that to Miller's High-Life."* (San Diego, Calif. 1965.) Anyone who does not now fully understand the mechanism and technique of food-dirtying in folklore will be drawn a map.

On a very much larger scale, the attack on the mother-figure as 'bad,' in much propaganda, and especially in tendentious homosexual literature in recent decades, as for example in tirades against 'momism', 'matriarchy,' and so forth, is hardly more than food-dirtying or the Defiling of the Mother on a pre-tended sociological or fictional backdrop. The accusation as to 'matriarchy' is particularly absurd, for in an operating matri-archy women would certainly not disguise themselves by the tens of millions in men's pants, to impersonate the kudos-bearing men. The clothes situation, at least, would be the re-verse. I have tried to take this matter further in my pamphlet *Love & Death* (1949) p. 83–92, "Open Season on Women," and in the introductory section to chapter 10 here, "On the Cause of Homosexuality," to which the reader is referred.

It is worth adding that the recent exploitation of women's bare breasts by the manufacturers of bathing-suits and other *chic* clothing, and in American 'topless' (and 'bottomless') nightclubs and restaurants, beginning in the neo-Barbary Coast of San Francisco's night-entertainment area in the 1960's, is not by any means to be construed as an example of the presumed 'New Freedom,' or any other sort of advancing sexual freedom. To the contrary, it is the most cynical and ruthless *gangsteriz-ing of the New Freedom* that could possibly be imagined. The absolute bottom is certainly that hit in the "Topless Shoeshine," publicly offered (at $2 per shine) by a bare-breasted blonde shoeshine girl in leotard lace stretch pants, at The Harry's Shoeshine Palace, as incredibly photographed in the *San Fran-cisco Chronicle,* July 26th, 1966, page 4, for history to wonder at and remember. As with all slave-revolts, Women's Liberation *had* to develop after that. There was nowhere to go but up.

Even *Sex to Sexty* turns thumbs-down on that one: '*Whoever thought up topless shoeshines didn't know* TIT *from Shinola*' [a shoe-polish].

In a private communication, my friend Capt. Gregory Gulliver, R.N., attempts to put in its larger social background the whole matter of anti-breast fetichism in current literature and motion-pictures, especially those emanating from Italy, France and Japan, where the New Freedom has been gangsterized even worse. He remarks, in his salty naval style: 'These money-grubbing shit-asses, sucking Hemingway's festered teat from beyond the grave, simply do not know how to get across frankly what they're dying to say, and ought to be shown.' In a brief passage from the autobiographical *Portrait of the Artist as Flowing Teat* (Tangiers, 1966), Capt. Gulliver is introducing his new business-associate, Mr. Yamashita "Kooky" Shitakuku, formerly known as Harold Blowjob:

Listen, you lousy slobs, line up and buy your tickets NOW! Mr. Shitakuku is one of the world's greatest geniuses in the making of nauseating little horror films on dirt-cheap million-dollar budgets. All our new and exciting GG World & Interplanetary Enterprises T.V.-Feelie broadcasts (Hello, out there, Aldous!) and vibrating-trampolin drive-in family theaters, serviced by our brisk new Bendover Bottomless car-hops or "Wunkies" – you gotta see 'em to believe it! – are specially outfitted with air-sickness vomit-bags in chlorophyll-treated, ocean-fresh plastic, since we started showing Mr. Shitakuku's masterpieces. Next year we are bringing back public floggings for curtain-raisers, and Sunday guillotinings on the Mall in Central Park, with topless lady sexecutioners in black masks and black S.S. jackboots right up to their cunts. Sign up, *now*, girls, and get in on the ground floor on these Trail-Blazing careers!

We are also publishing five new beeyootiful art-books about "Kooky" Shitakuku and his camera Art, with four thousand nude lust-murder victim illustrations in *full color*, from his most recent Art movie, *THE TIT-STRANGLER*. The first book we are going to have out on Mr. Shitakuku is by our own staff fag-hag and camp critic, Beatrice Blowjob (his wife), and is called *Karaté: Philosophy of Peace*. It shows how to break bricks with your pecker, slap women's tits till the blood spurts out the nipples, and strangle an average-sized policeman in fourteen seconds, or your money back. With built-in anti-Freudian interpretations ...

I also strongly urge every reader not to miss GG World & Interplanetary Enterprises' new and artistic family film, done in the Imperial Leprosarium at Hiroshima by Mr. Shitakuku, BREAST CANCER FOR PEACE. This is the first film issued through my tax-evasion schematic, Climax-Interstellar Unlimited : T.V.-Satellite Entertainment for the Up-And-Coming Family. BREAST CANCER FOR PEACE ends with an unprecedented scene, unknown hitherto in the history of the cinema, if not of the world, and that makes *Soldier Blue* and the baby-eating scene in Pastrone's *Cabiria* look like peanuts. In this scene – don't miss it, folks : take the kiddies, buy plenty of popcorn and cundrums, and have yourself a ball – seven thousand dead little chinky Vietnamese women with their tits torn off by chlorophyll-treated ocean-fresh plastic hand-grenades, are lovingly pushed off the screen in great fucking piles by our Reitermeister Bulldozers, the Bulldozer That Makes Corpse-Pushing a Pleasure. This scene is a deep and passionate appeal for World Peace Under God, like the book by our staff fag-hag explains, see! ? It was already plagiarized from our Mr. Shitakuku, seven years before he made his first film, in a French collaborationist movie called *Night, Shit, and Fug – Mon Amour*, by the dynamic old French movie-maker, Maréchal Putain, and an American item entitled *Fud, or Hoof-and-Mouth Disease for Beginners*. Terrifying, scarifying, you'll piss in your pants watching it, and it's All For Peace!

4. SEXUAL SMÖRGÅSBORD

Essentially, the anti-breast fetich or attack is too frank a statement for jokes, since it leads directly to the mother figure, whereas the whole point of this type of humor is to reject and evade the attraction to the mother. Various disguises are employed, the two main ones being those already indicated : fecal dirtying of sex, and food-dirtying sexually toned. These increase their sexual tone until the intention of being disgusting or nauseating is perfectly apparent, and effect is piled on effect to try to make them more nauseating still. Curiously enough, many persons who can accept, or shrug off, obvious 'nasty-nasty' stories that restrict themselves to food and fecal themes, finally succumb to the expressions of disgust and irritation that

are what the tellers are obviously trying to elicit, when exposed
to similar stories in which the food and fecal themes are combined as vomiting, or where the semen or other sexual secretions are in a sense *expurgated* for presentation as nasal mucus
or snot. 'Displacement upward' has been made use of in both
cases, yet instead of decreasing the emotional effect on the
listener, in these cases it seems to increase it. This will be
observed as the present section, and that following, progress;
and the reader is reminded again that there is no law against
skipping or omitting what is found distressing.

A prefatory note: The wives of American presidents are
national mother-figures in the same sense that the presidents
are father-figures. The same is naturally true of kings and
queens. When the king or president is hated, the queen or First
Lady becomes a hate-figure also. The most outstanding case
was that of Louis XVI and Marie-Antoinette at the time of the
French Revolution, neither of whom was sufficiently bad or
immoral to support the weight of necessary hatred, and about
whom most of the sexual scandal retailed had therefore to be
invented. As to American presidents' wives, the best example is
the motion-picture version, in 1964, of the Tennessee Williams
play, *The Night of the Iguana* – a gloating crock of assorted de-
generacies, such as a man tied upside-down in a hammock by
women in some ugly sado-masochistic game, ludicrously sentimentalized, and (as god is my witness) with poetry recited to
the audience by a white-haired old Poet, chugging up looking
for that final rhyme like The Little Locomotive That Could.
This movie went to the trouble of having one of the minor
female characters chosen for her exact dental resemblance to
the wife of the late President Franklin D. Roosevelt, with this
resemblance underlined by the playing, as leitmotif, of what
appears to have been her favorite song. She is similarly brought
onstage, and named, for the same purposes of mockery, in a
number of stories of the type here under discussion:

*Mrs. Roosevelt is inspecting South Pacific army installations,
and she enjoys the rolls so much at lunch that she goes to the
kitchen to find out how they were made. The cook demonstrates by pulling out his greasy sweat-shirt and slapping himself with the raw dough on the belly-button, then tearing off
the formed roll and flinging it into the baking-tin. "Why on
earth do you make them that way?" asks the First Lady,
shocked. "I've got to, m'am," he explains earnestly; "it's the*

quickest way I've found, with all these thousands of men to feed all at once." "Now look here!" the press-relations officer interjects, "you know better than that. You have a tool for that job. Why don't you use it?" "But I do use my tool!" cries the cook. "You should have been here yesterday: I was making doughnuts." (D.C. 1951.) This obviously can give cards & spades to the lesser version of the same story given in the preceding section, under "Anti-Breast Fetichism." Not the least interesting aspect of this particular food-dirtying joke is its open identification of navel and penis, as in the Greek *phallos* and *omphallos* (though you will find the usual paradox-pushing phudnicks to assure you that these words are not connected). Its classification in the present section is owing to the representation of the 'dirtied' food – being eaten by thousands of men – as a supreme sexual insult to the self-evident mother-figure that is the President's wife.

Other jokes of this kind insist on the food-dirtying element, with such standard coefficients of low pantomime humor as: *The waiter who puts his thumb in the soup while carrying it.* This is built up into a whole edifice of revenge in a classic of this type: *The boys on the ranch decide for New Year's resolutions that they will not tease the Chinee cook any more, and troop in to the kitchen to apologize to him for the tricks they have played on him all year. "No pull China-boy's pigtail anymore?" he asks incredulously, "No, John, we're going to treat you right, from now on," they assure him. "No put rattlesnake in pants?" "No more rattlesnakes, John." "No mo' dead frog in shoe?" "No, John, we're really going to treat you right, from now on." "Velly good. China-boy no piss in coffee anymore."* (N.Y. 1940.)

The effort is often made to sexualize food, in jokes, by bringing it directly into contact with the genitals, rather than go the long way about Robin Hood's barn, of identifying sex cloacally with defecation and then rejecting it *via* feces, urine, and so forth. Cunnilinctus and masturbation are the two usual and logical pretexts for such combinations of food with sex, in what is invariably an insulting or defiling combination, as the jokes see it. The entire section on "Oragenitalism" in the First Series, in particular the subsection on "Cunnilinctus and Masochism," 8.V.4, pages 576–84, presents joke after joke of this kind, and these cannot all be repeated here. One of the briefest, turning on the reputation of the French as cunnilinguists: *French husband: "What's for supper tonight?" Wife: "Guess!" Husband: "I thought you were sick!"* (Paris, 1954, told in English by an American comic-strip artist who said he had heard it at a French nightclub.) – *A man in a hotel dining-room complains to the manager about the dinner, and says he will not pay for it because he has found a hair in his spaghetti. Later the manager accidentally observes the man performing cunnilinctus on the hotel call-girl. He lets himself into the room with his pass-key and says, "Well, I see you don't mind having hair in your mouth now!" "No, I don't," says the man, "but if I find any spaghetti down here, I'm not paying for this either!"* (*World's Dirtiest Jokes*, 1969, p. 209.) The original of this, given later, on *the lunatic who will not eat shit "because it has a hair on it – right there!"* makes even more clear the intended food-dirtying.

In the erotic magazine, *The Pearl* (July 1879) No. 1, a very popular story of this kind, internationally circulated, is given in versified form, as a song, entitled "The Wanton Lass." *A woman masturbates with a carrot, which sticks inside her vagina. The doctor is called. He thumps the woman on the back, and the carrot flies out the window into the street. A chimney-sweep* [the standard child-identification image] *passing by, sees it fly out the window, and picks it up and eats it; saying for the rhyming conclusion: "By God! it's not right, it's a damned shame I say, That people should throw buttered carrots away."* As still current in America, this is no longer a song but a story: '*One morning when the mother was making her teen-age daughter's bed, she came upon a large carrot under the pillow. When Ellie May came home from school, her mama tore into her about finding the carrot in such an unusual place. "I must confess, mother," said Ellie May, "that for the past four months, that carrot has been my husband." The mother replied, "Well consider yourelf divorced; it went into your old man's* [father's] *beef stew for lunch!"* ' (*Sex to Sexty*, 1966, 7:19.) The same compiler repeats in *World's Dirtiest Jokes*, another version with a liverwurst, p. 123, in which: *The butcher refuses to sell a customer the sausage with which he has seen his daughter masturbating, claiming that he has none. "What's that hanging on the hook?" asks the customer. "That's my son-in-law."*

In Europe, the original version in which the carrot is eaten – clearly the essential touch – has remained common as a students' song, and has appeared continuously since about 1910 in all published collections of the French medical and art students' bawdy *Chansons de Salles de Garde*, usually under the title "Charlotte" or "Le Cordonnier Pamphile," as in the *Anthologie Hospitalière & Latinesque* (1911) 1. 170–71. Here the carrot is caught and eaten not by a chimney-sweep, as in the English song, representing the hungry child, but by the old shoemaker representing the orally-cuckolded father. (On this identification see Sándor Ferenczi's "The Sons of the Tailor," in his *Further Contributions to Psychoanalysis*, 1926.) Some French texts also have a chorus, in which the audience joins, encouraging the woman in her masturbation, with the repeated line or burden, *"Branle, Charlot-te, jusqu'à demain!"*

In the oldest American form collected, the joke has already turned sour, and the defiling of food by the touch of sex is not considered sufficient: the sex must be defiled somehow by the food, as well. It is usually told concerning bums or tramps who, being *hungry* all the time and altogether orally-oriented – which is why so many of them are drug-addicts (now under the politer name of 'hippies') – are presumably ready to eat anything. *Two tramps are offered a corn-on-the-cob dinner by the unattractive woman of the house, it they will have intercourse with her. The first tramp uses one of the ears of corn to masturbate the woman with, and eats the remaining ear. Second tramp, later: "The corn was fine, but the butter was rancid."* (2:279.) In other versions, even closer to the British and French songs preceding: *He throws the ears of corn out the window to other tramps, after using them on the woman, who is syphilitic. The other tramps shout up to him, "Just keep throwing out more of that good, hot buttered corn!"* (St. Augustine, Florida, 1949, from a 19-year-old sailor.) In final version: *A sausage is used, and the woman is menstruating. The other tramp shouts, "Keep it coming with those hot-dogs and ketchup!"* (N.Y. 1952.) In all versions, the insistence that the woman is *unattractive* – even syphilitic – is a feint which will become one of the most prominent features of the jokes in the following section, "The Defiling of the Mother." Its purpose is to distract attention from the fact that, in the present jokes visibly, as 'the woman of the house,' she *is* the mother. In the most famous passage by the decadent American novelist, William Faulkner, a girl is similarly raped with a corncob.

A formalization of the intentionally nauseating and food-dirtying sexual smörgåsbord images are the parody "Menus" circulated as printed novelties or obscœna. Not being jokes, these cannot be dealt with at length here. They give long lists of travestied dishes such as '*Red Snapper, with Clam-Piss Chowder*' ('snapper': foreskin), and '*Roast split Pussyfish with Dingleberry Sauce*' ('dingleberry': clotted feces on the pubic hair), and others of which this should be a sufficient sample. The form is very old in France, as in the "*Plaisant Contract de Mariage ... Grand-Jean-Ventru*" (ca. 1627), especially the fourth course, 'Quatriesme Service: Issues,' at the wedding-feast, including such items as: 'XII *tartes de morpions et cirons*' (crab-lice and maggot tarts), along with '*vesses de loup*', '*macarons de gland*', '*semence de Naples*', '*crottes de Paris,*' and '*cresme venerienne.*' (Reprinted in full in J. Gay's bibliographical magazine, *Le Fantaisiste*, San Remo, 1873, I. 59–75, at p. 67; following up a less graphic mock marriage-contract of the same type in his *Le Bibliophile Fantaisiste*, 1869, p. 456–62.)

These merely take up where Rabelais' descriptions of the eating (and especially the pissing & shitting) of his hero in *Gargantua* (1535) Bk. I, chaps 7–21, left off a century earlier. Modern menus of this type, in both French and English, are more particularly sexualized, with nasty and diseased forms of the sexual organs, especially of women – Negroes and Chinese being the dainties of choice – and with much equivocal humor as to the identification of the female genitals with seafood and shellfish (as in the Jewish dietary code of *Leviticus*, xi. 9–12) ... '*Cunt-hair optional,*' this being the equivalent of the grated cheese. A particularly nasty such menu was printed in the New York 'pornzine' (sex-newspaper) *Pleasure* or *Kiss* in 1969, the author later proudly circulating it in mimeographed form at $1 a shot, apparently as part of a vest-pocket religious cult of which he was the leader. French and English price-lists for whorehouses also exist, of a very similar kind, dating from about World War I, and filled with absurd sexual 'specialties' at ridiculous prices. See also a long such narsty-narsty menu bloated up into a would-be humorous dinner-party in Thomas Pynchon's *Gravity's Rainbow* (1973, Bantam ed. p. 834–6).

The menu-idea seems to have been brought to America from Germany, as with many other erotic and scatological 'novelties' in ephemeral printed form. A particularly gruelling German example is given in the special supplement – lacking from most copies – of Dr. Magnus Hirschfeld's 'moral history' of the First

World War, *Sittengeschichte des Weltkrieges* (Leipzig, 1930). This one is as strong on the scatological as the American example quoted above, with the inevitable '*Klapusterbeeren*,' of which the American 'dingleberries' are simply a nonsense translation. It lacks the curious concentration on fish-foods, which is the main touch of normality in the American 'menus,' since sea-foods and especially shell-fish of vulviform shape have immemorially been representations of the female genitals, and as such the totems of early matriarchal cultures, surviving even into patriarchy as in the American Indian '*wampum*,' or sea-shell money. Compare the chorus-line of an American jazz-song of the 1930's, referring to cunnilinctus: "*I get my favorite dish – FISH!*" Traditional in America as the ultimate dietary luxury of the rich are "*quails' fingernails and peacocks' pukings.*" In Alan Sillitoe's British working-class novel, *Key To the Door* (1961) p. 347, a soldier jestingly suggests for the cookhouse menu "*hummingbirds' foreskins on toast.*" Compare 1 *Samuel*, xviii. 25–7, on David and the foreskins of the Philistines.

The joke has already been given, in the First Series, the chapter on "Premarital Sexual Acts," concerning: *The musician in a theater orchestra on whose bald head a 'gob' of semen is thrown by a young man petting with a girl, and who 'takes it big' with great expostulation.* (In a British 'topper' he is told: "*That's wot you get for playing like a cunt*" – London, 1953. On the French and British use of *con/cunt* as meaning 'fool.') Another version of the same joke insists elaborately on somehow having him taste the semen as well: '*A fellow took his girl to the Follies and sat in the first row of the balcony. During the first act he put her hand in his lap and had her feel his stiff prick. During the second act he took it out, and by the middle of the third act she had jerked him off. The come flew over the railing and landed below on a man's bald head. He put his finger in it, smelled it and tasted it, saying, "It's not spit." Tasted it again, "It's not piss." Tasted it again, "It's not shit." And finally cried, "Someone threw a fuck at me!"*' (D.C. 1944, manuscript transcription from the telling of an army sergeant.) The bald-headed father figure, who is thus 'defiled' by the son's furtive sexuality, is noticeably, at least in imagination, made to eat every other kind of bodily excrement as well. This same theme will appear again in the final chapter on "Scatology," with certain significant reversals.

Nothing is left to the imagination in the '*Joke about a boy fucking a girl. When the girl's father came in the room later he found a glob [sic] of fuck on the floor. Thinking it an oyster, he ate it with relish.'* (D.C. 1943, from a soldier.) As people cannot really be expected to eat oysters off the floor (or even off the sofa, in another version), this has been improved as follows, with the sexes of the parents reversed: *'A traveling salesman who had spent the night at a farmhouse found the farmer's daughter downstairs in the kitchen next morning preparing him the breakfast which the farmer had generously promised him. After he had laid her on the table, and left, her mother came down, noticed something on the table, and tasted it, saying, "He left the best part of his eggs on the table".'* (D.C. 1952.) The daughter, with whom the traveling salesman (teller's and listener's identification) has had intercourse, does not even speak. She is a lay-figure – if the phrase may be excused – representing the mother with whom the 'oral intercourse' is really achieved. It is understood, of course, that the mother is disgraced by the error, owing to which she has ingested semen, just as the bald-headed father would be. Such incestuous intercourse is achieved only by negation, and with implied mockery and disgrace, all of which is projected on the parent.

We are in a position now to understand somewhat better, or to take at a much deeper level of interpretation, a joke which has already been given in an earlier chapter, and which involves complicated food-dirtyings of obviously sexual tone. *'A traveling salesman, approaching a farm house, noticed the farmer's daughter leaning forward slicing bread on the kitchen table. Sneaking up behind her, he slipped it in and quickly finished the performance. She became pregnant, and sued. He got a good lawyer, who got him off with the argument that things could have been much worse: "He could have pulled out, shot on the bread, and knocked up the whole goddam family".'* (D.C. 1952.) Far beyond this, in the same direction, is the more-than-total statement of sex and food-dirtying in the schoolroom story given in full in the First Series, 1.II.1, page 69, concerning: *The good and bad little boys in school who have each been given a penny by the teacher, to spend wisely. The bad little boy reports: "I bought a sossidge. I ate out the sossidge-meat and gave the skin to my father. He fucked my mother wiv it. I poured out the juice to grease a wagon-wheel, and used it for a catapult [slingshot] all afternoon. Then I shit*

434 DISEASE & DISGUST

in it, took it back to the butcher, told him it was rotten, and got my penny back." Hands the penny to the teacher. (London, 1954, from a music-hall entertainer, who had been specially asked if he knew this story, and who ended by handing the listener a large English penny with a defiant gesture. – Tale Type 1339A.)

Where, as in the preceding examples, the touch of sex does not sufficiently dirty the food to prevent it from being eaten, the scatological touch is obviously stronger and more success-ful. Various bodily elements that are considered scatological, or tantamount to feces, are the ear-wax, nasal mucus (which is often a semen-substitute in jokes and limericks), 'toe-punk,' vomit, and any sexual secretion in health or disease, such as semen, the vaginal liquor, menstrual blood, 'clap-juice,' and the preputial smegma of both sexes, which is visibly present only when the genitals are not sufficiently clean (as with the similar anal adhesions or 'dingleberries'), and which is known col-loquially as 'cheese' or 'head-cheese,' these last being food-dirtyings in name as well.

It is the smegma that is alluded to, or assimilated homo-sexually to chewing-gum, in : *The miners who are being given a physical examination. The doctor finds a wad of chewing-gum under each miner's foreskin, and they explain that it is so dirty down in the mine, with coal-dust, that this is the only clean place to 'park' their chewing gum. The next man he examines has two wads of chewing gum inside his foreskin, and explains, "I'm keeping the other one for a friend of mine who's still down in the mine."* (Arlington, Texas, 1966.) Compare the 'two sheep turds' that fall out of the foreskin of the sheepherder be-ing examined by a prostitute before intercourse, given earlier under "Cloacal Intercourse."

A personal testimony. In connection with some advance publicity presumably being done for the present work, I agreed to allow an American journalist to examine the unpublished manuscript. He hunched over a small table, flipping the pages and feverishly writing down jokes (only), while I tried to indicate to him some of the subjects of the accompanying text; mentioning, as to the present chapter, that some people even like – or at least tell – jokes on such subjects as vomit, nasal mucus, 'toe-punk,' and preputial smegma. He looked up at me with an air of intense expectation, the way Balboa must have looked when he first sighted the Pacific. "Mr. Legman," he pleaded, gripping both legs of the table, "tell me a *smegna* joke! Tell me a joke about SMEGNA!" As I observed he couldn't even pronounce it, I figured he probably couldn't spell it, and was mean enough to refuse. He revenged himself in a hilariously offensive smear-piece, "Gershon Legman Doesn't Tell Dirty Jokes," in *Oui,* the glossy magazine of 'hip' sexual perversion (Chicago, March 1975) p. 94–131, noting severely that I look 'like an exhausted wart-hog' and am hung-up on the subject of homosexuality in jokes – which nobody can deny.

Homosexual self-unveiling is actually a favorite theme, in jokes as well as in the anxiety-ridden theatre of the 20th century; as an early instance, in J. B. Priestley's *Dangerous Corner* (1932) where the whole play is dominated by a character who never appears, and whose progressive unveiling – ending with the divulging of his homosexuality – destroys the life-illusions of all the other characters, each of whom has been imagining that the one little failing of which each knew had been the only stain on the escutcheon of their hero. Jokes make the same sort of point often, and much more simply, as in the preceding chapter, 10.II.3 and 4, "Homosexual Recognitions" and "The 'Normal' as Homosexual." The preceding joke might well have been indexed in either of those sections, were not the *intention to be disgusting* clear and paramount, putting it here with the rest of the "Narsty-Narsties." The same is evident in the following : '*A man at a restaurant ordered a second service of tapioca, which fascinated him by its delicious taste. The waitress called into the back room, "Come again on the tapioca." "Oh, that's what it is," the man said; "I thought it had a familiar taste".'* (D.C. 1953.) Compare the "billiard-drinker" story in the final chapter, Scatology, and *The Limerick,* No. 788. In another version of the present joke, the homosexual implication is just as pointedly rejected : *Waitress (to short-order cook): "Come again on the rice pudding." Customer: "You do, and I won't eat it!"* (N.Y. 1945.) Clearly, whether the customer says 'yes' or 'no,' the joke remains identical. This is a good example of the ambivalence of powerful emotions, and the irrelevance of punchlines.

Also on the theme of accidental self-unveiling, whether with or without any tone of mocking at hypocrisy, are two further jokes generally collected (like that on chewing-gum, preceding) with some mock-apologetic preliminary statement, or with the proud announcement that it is 'the dirtiest joke' that the teller knows. As with the similar announcement that a joke is the 'funniest' one knows, or one's favorite, this always indicates that the joke carries a powerful clue to the teller's *own* psychological bent, and leading neurotic problem, which he or she is struggling to unveil without admitting it. Here hypocrisy and food-dirtying are combined, to their ultimate degree: *A patient in a lunatic asylum will not eat anything but a bowl of shit at every meal. One day he refuses his accustomed bowl. The head-doctor rushes to his cell, thinking the man is cured, but the patient explains that he is simply on a hunger-strike. "I don't like the way I'm being treated here," he says. "Can you imagine serving a man shit to eat, with a cunt-hair on it? Look – right there!"* (2:369. Text version, Boston, Mass. 1951, from a physician.) Mark Twain's heavily masochistic food-rejecting story of the "Appetite Cure," in *The Man That Corrupted Hadleyburg* (1900), seems to turn on a polite version of this joke, or something close to it, if not on a 'parallel inspiration.' In Twain's story the jaded *bon vivant* is brought back to normal appetites by an upside-down menu ranging from his accustomed exotic and acceptable dishes of the "quails' fingernails and peacocks' pukings" variety – this is a folk-phrase, not Twain's – down to the terrible, frightening plain brown bread & butter, which he is only able to eat when cured.

Supplied in manuscript, and very often heard: '*A man was showing his collection of petrified cunts to another collector. Very proud. He took them out of the ice-box and laid them out on the table, and said, "Well, what do you think of them?" The other collector wetted his finger-tip and took a lick of each one of them. "It's pretty hard to know," he said, "what with them just coming out of the ice-box like that. But I can tell you this much: somebody slipped over two ass-holes on you – one nigger's and one Chinaman's!"* ' (Baltimore, Md. 1941.) Difficult as this may be to believe, what many listeners find most objectionable in the preceding story is not any part of its plot or anatomical *mise-en-scène*, but the two final anti-racial terms, and the white-supremacist implication that the "ass-holes" of any foreign races are somehow more undesirable than our own! The same kind of unease is experienced with the purposely ugly "Chinaman-and-rice" joke given later.

Meanwhile, few of the racially-conscious listeners of such delicate digestion (and of no matter what race) would find anything except humor and even wit in the following food-dirtying, sex-dirtying, and woman-dirtying example – unless, of course, they happened to be women : *A woman in a butcher-shop is examining an old chicken very suspiciously. She prods it, pokes at its breast, and finally spreads its legs wide apart and sniffs its rump very carefully. Then she turns to the butcher and says elaborately, "Do you have any liver today?" The butcher is seething. "Listen, lady," he says, "I'll bet you couldn't pass that test either, and you're alive!"* (N.Y. 1963.) Observe the care with which one is made to understand that the woman *is* the "old chicken" being rejected. The Defiling of the Mother.

5. SPUTUM AND VOMIT

The sexual smörgåsbord (or 'indelicatessen'), by means of which jokes attempt to combine the themes of food and sex, are almost never for the purpose of accepting either, but in order physically to reject them. The soiling of food or food-images is like a wordless statement or charade to the effect that the food the mother offers, and therefore the mother her-self, is worthless, dirty and to be refused and rejected. The actual rejection takes its most primitive form in spitting or vomiting, which are the real food-rejections of the child. Various partial rejections, such as *throwing* the food away after it has been sexually or scatologically soiled, have already been noted several times in the preceding section. These clearly lack the emotional effect which is being sought in stories of purposely 'nasty' content, and only vomiting is the desired total statement. The point need hardly be made again that the stories are purposely so laid out, and delivered (often with obviously excessive details of a repulsive nature insisted upon, and re-peated several times), as to bring the listener also as close as possible to vomiting. This is a very different thing from telling jokes in order to 'amuse' one's audience, and the massive and underlying hostility of the teller's real intention is nowhere else so clear.

Intimidated listeners to stories of this type will often mis-takenly 'go along with the gag,' and *reward* the teller with the desired vomiting-reflex in mock or formalized scapegoat ex-pression, by pronouncing certain conventional or onomato-poetic choking syllables, such as *"Blaghh!"* (of the kind com-mon in horror comicbooks), with hand-gestures of mock re-jection to match; also covering the eyes and lolling out the tongue as though they are authentically about to vomit or faint. Short of giving him the Victoria Cross, it is hard to see how they could reward the teller more. Actually, it is the teller himself who is doing the mock-vomiting by proxy, by identification with the listener-victim, who in this case also represents the parents upon whom the symbolic vomiting of the joke is really being done. As the Introduction here has tried to show, under the title No Laughing Matter, *in all jokes it is really the teller who is laughing when the listener laughs.* And vomiting when the listener vomits.

An American army proverb of World War II is embodied in a joke didactically showing all the various stages of the intended rejection of women, at the oral, anal, and genital level, all in one package. The sadistically codified school-lesson setup here is notable. *A tough army officer is briefing a group of paratroopers, about to parachute into France at the Liberation in 1944. "Men!" he shouts, "remember one thing now. You're gonna see a lotta good-looking Frog women down there. Stay away from them! The women, the rabbits, and the cows are all diseased! Before you shack up with one of them women, put her under a pump for ten minutes and wash off some of the paint. They're all old enough to be your mother! You wanna have at least the sense a dog has got, don't you? Well, watch what a dog does. If you can't eat it, and you can't fuck it –* piss on it!" [That is the proverb.] *One of the paratroopers throws up at this point. The sergeant looks at him disgustedly, and adds, "Well, that's good too."* (Los Angeles, Calif. 1965.) This little speech or allocution is very similar to those actually given to American soldiers, the parts about women, rabbits and cows, and putting the 'native' women under a pump, being real army catch-phrases dating from World War I. The whole thing sounds like a parody of the famous and authentic speech by General George S. Patton to his troops, during World War II, first courageously printed by Dwight Macdonald in his magazine, *Politics*, and reprinted in his volume of essays, *The Responsibility of Peoples* (London, 1965). Patton's speech is, however, purely aggressive, scatological and profane, without any discernible sexual tone or anti-sexual advice.

The Limerick (Paris, 1953; enlarged edition, New York, 1970) includes an entire chapter, entitled "Gourmands," and pointedly following the chapter on "Excrement" as being considered somewhat more disgusting. It is entirely devoted to imaginings in verse of eating the sort of inedibles included in the preceding section here, "Sexual Smörgåsbord." Jokes similar to these particular limericks are very common among children, and represent one of their most powerful taboo-breakings. One of the first jokes I myself ever heard, or can remember, is the following, quoted from memory: *Two bums find a bologna and get into a fight about dividing it. They decide that the one who can hawk up the most snot will get the bologna. They bring up slime etc. into an old tin can. Seeing that the other is winning, one of the bums drinks down the entire contents of the can and brings it up again. He wins the bologna.* (Scranton, Pa. 1927.) I heard this joke when I was ten years old, told by another boy of my own age, of German origin. I can still remember the tremendous impression it made on me: not of disgust but of actual fright. I could not get it out of my mind for weeks, and can, as seen above, still remember it over forty years later. It has been collected again many times, but has long since ceased to affect me emotionally. In a more recent version a verbal punch-line is added: *The bum who wins the bologna says, "I think I'll eat it later. I'm not hungry now."* (San Diego, Calif. 1965.) Not so much a rationalization as whistling in the dark.

The sexual implications of jokes of this type do not always appear, where everything is left at the purely oral-dirtying level. These become more evident when the sputum or vomit jokes take on the nature of an ordeal even more visibly than in the "bums-and-bologna" joke above, which is of course also set up as an ordeal. Such ordeals classically take place in the all-male environment of bar-rooms or saloons of the Wild West type, as has already been discussed in connection with the folk challenge, "*Whistle or sing, or show your thing.*" The bum or tramp is always the fall-guy or loser in these ordeals because he is dead-broke and always hungry – like a child – and will do anything for food or for a drink of the whiskey to which he is hopelessly addicted. *A bum pesters a saloon-keeper for a free drink. The saloon-keeper finally tells him he can have the drink if he will swallow the contents of the cuspidor. The bum lifts it in both hands and begins swallowing greedily. All the men present are nauseated and turn livid watching this. The saloon-keeper himself cannot stand it and shouts, "All right, you win, stop, STOP!!" The bum lowers the cuspidor and wipes his mouth on his sleeve. He gulps several times and says in a croak-*

ing voice, "I wanted to stop, but it was all in one piece!" (Los Angeles, Calif. 1952.)

The *mise-en-scène* here is curiously like that of the real drinking-ordeals of the Germanic and Scandinavian peoples, which survive today, with their large-size flagons, double-length beer 'yards,' and 'boots,' all of which are supposed to be *drunk dry* (as in the joke above). These ordeals and 'loving cups,' still used in Anglo-Saxon countries as sport trophies, are alluded to in scenes like that in *Hamlet* where "The King drinks!" (*"Le Roi boit!"* followed by cannonfire: an ancient usage.) See further, on the drinking of toasts, and other sexual ordeals connected with drinking, *The Horn Book*, p. 441–5. A brief joke or gag, turning on the same lighthearted and 'necessary' sadism of doctors and surgeons, especially in wartime, as was made the subject of all the 'black' humor in the prize-winning American movie, *M.A.S.H.* (1969), gives the final meaning of all the sexualized jokes of this kind: *'Orderly: "Doctor, there's a case of syphilis outside." Doctor: "Bring it in – I could drink anything!"'* (Chelmsford, Essex, 1954.)

The drinking-ordeal in jokes is sometimes modified to a mere drinking situation, but it quickly becomes clear that some other person in the joke – really the listener – is being exposed to the ordeal. The vomiting of drunkenness is an easy 'out' for ordeal-humor. From *The World's Dirtiest Jokes* (1969) p. 87, captioned "UGH!" – but printed nonetheless: *'The call girl dropped her miscarriage into a trash can, to eliminate all the red tape. That night, a drunk staggered up, puked into the can, backed off, looked in, and said, "I'll never suck another snatch as long as I live!"'* The implication here of infant cannibalism or foetophagy is considered by all tellers the ultimate taboo, even when there is no sexual allusion, as in the baby-eating "Ritual Murder" accusations.

Mysterious bottles are a standard scatological 'prop' or bait. *Three Scotchmen on a train, who are passing a bottle from one to the other, allow another Scotchman who gets on at a small station to have a swig at the bottle when he asks for it. He is surprised at their generosity but says nothing until getting off the train, when he thanks them saying, "You gentlemen have been verra kind to me. And your liquor is verra good too, though I never tasted anything like it before." "It's nothing to drink, lad," says one of the others. "We're three consumptives, and have been spittin' our blood into that bottle since we left*

Edinburgh." (2 : 103.) An American children's joke revises this
with the standard tramps as actors : *Two hoboes, walking along
a railroad track, fight over a bottle of consumptive sputum
thrown from a train, and drink its contents without knowing
what it is.* (Scranton, Pa. 1930.)

The sexualization of this sort of story in many more examples
than those simply of the sputum variety, shows that even these
draw their horrid attractiveness, to persons who tell them,
from the underlying identification of the sputum with semen,
and of the lung disease unwittingly contracted orally with
venereal disease. *A man 'getting a blowjob in a whorehouse'
notices that the girl spits his semen into a jug under the bed.
"What's the matter?" he asks. "I thought you girls liked
swallowing it." "We do," she admits. "The fact is, another
girl and I have a contest on. The one that has the most at the
end of the week gets to drink it all."* (N.Y. 1942.) A rather similar
scene, as a serious part of an orgy in a brothel, occurs in a very
rare or unique New Orleans eroticum of about 1850, published
openly during the pre-Comstock era. Here the semen is served
up in wineglasses.

In an eroticum published in Paris a century later during the
1950's, entitled *Chariot of Flesh*, this sort of fantasy is taken to
the ultimate degree of having a woman take a bath in semen
which is supplied by the masturbation of old men in a rest-
home (*i.e.* the usual tramps, somewhat dolled up), and which is
kept *warm* by means of electrodes in the bath! Both the joke
and the pornographic novels bring in the element of contest or
ordeal; in the novels the usual masturbation contest or 'ring
jerk' of very young boys : here disguised as clean old men. A
similar scene of connoisseur spermatophagy is made one of
the climaxes of Aubrey Beardsley's *Venus and Tannhäuser* (MS.
1896) chap. 8, with the additional exotic touch that it is the
semen of a unicorn being 'lapped' as an apéritif by the virgin
Venus who has tamed the beast.

Both the expurgated *Anecdota Americana* and the original
(1 : 489) give more or less modified versions of an ordeal joke on
this style, turning on attempts to make the idea of fellation
gruesome or disgusting for the listener. Even the second series
of *Anecdota Americana* (1934), which seldom hesitates to be
dysphemistic and crude, gives only a modification, possibly
connected with the tapioca or rice-pudding item already given :
A sailor is complimented by a homosexual who has just fellated

him, who says his semen tastes "just like rice-pudding." "Well, it ought to," says the sailor; "I just cornholed a Chinaman." (2:143. Text N.Y. 1940.) As actually collected 'in the field,' many times, the real story works much harder than this at its attempt to be nasty. An interesting element is the mention of a neurotic oral or facial tic (not present in the expurgated version already quoted in 11.III.3, under "Oragenital Acts"), with which compare the 'shaggy dog' or riddle-story, given earlier, on the insane girl who carries dimes in her mouth while she makes love. *A girl is winking at a man, and goes "tsk-tsk" at him out of the side of her mouth. He picks her up, and they end having intercourse, standing up, in a dark hallway. As she keeps going "tsk-tsk" while he tries to kiss her (sometimes pantomimed as the girl continuously spitting, or picking between her teeth), he asks her to stop, saying that it disgusts him. "Believe me," she says earnestly, "I don't like it either. I just sucked off a nigger that was buggering a Chink, and I must have some rice caught in my swivel-tooth."* (N.Y. 1939.) The dysphemistic Ossa-on-Pelion style, or "calling a spade a bloody shovel," here in the service of dirtying even an attempted kiss. A Louisiana campus song or mock-cheer, reported 1969, on traditional football rivalries: *"What comes out of a Chinaman's ass? – Rice! Rice! Rice!"*

Very much in the same line, and again complicating the intended unpleasantness with racial slurs: '*At a Nevada ranch town, miles from civilization, a cowboy came into the bar and asked if there was a whore-house in the town. "I'd like to tear me off a piece," he said. The bartender replied, "There ain't one for miles around, but out in back we got an old nigger with great big nostrils." The cowboy agreed to give him a try. When he returned to the barroom later buttoning up his pants, the barkeep asked: "How was it?" "Pretty good," he said. "I'll try it again sometimes." Then he left. Soon the nigger came in. "Did a nice clean white boy go thru here jess' now, boss?" "Yes, he looked like a nice clean boy." "Thanks. Tha'ss all I want to know," said the nigger, and vigorously drew into his throat his slushing nasal contents.*' (Los Angeles, Calif. 1941, from manuscript, as told to one member of the Sigma Nu fraternity, U.C.L.A., by another. The closing words are intended to represent a culminating pantomime.) Collected again, in manuscript, in Washington, D.C. 1952, with no anti-Negro stereotypes such as the 'great big nostrils,' though this element is left to be divined, from the reference to the girl being 'in the back': '*A man desperately in need of a piece of ass resorted to a whore-house, but his prick was so small that none of the whores knew how to take it. [One girl] in the back did the best she could, and as he left, gratified, she called after him, "You don't have a venereal disease, do you?" When he replied in the negative she inhaled deeply. (Pantomimed.)*' The man with the too-small penis always, of course, represents the child. The presumably Negro woman here is therefore his 'mammy,' or wet-nurse. (Not an abbreviation of 'mama,' as is usually believed, but the French '*m'amie,*' my darling.) A nursery reminiscence or fantasy?

Connoisseurs of the matter have assured me that the three following stories are '*the most awful*' that exist, and it seems clear that their special awfulness is being sought in references to such matters as vomiting and pus, and especially the idea of swallowing these. (Under the name of 'antibodies,' pus cures infections when swallowed by animals as a form of self-treatment, and such animals also swallow the afterbirth.) The first story is authentically told by children, and I myself heard it first at the age of ten, though it did not frighten me, as did the other story told with it – already given – concerning the 'bums-and-bologna.' It is, of course, a story in which the child finds an easy and very satisfying identification. *Two big Irish-men and a little Jew bet on who can satisfy the insatiable town-widow. The two Irishmen work at her by turns for several hours, and come out all green around the gills, while the widow keeps calling, "More! More!" The little Jew then goes in, while the others laugh at him. There is a long, mysterious silence. Finally he comes swaggering out, while behind him the widow can be heard calling, "Oh, thank you! Thank you!" "What did you do?" the Irishmen ask him, amazed. "It was easy," says the Jew. "I just stuck my head in, wiggled my ears, and puked."* (Scranton, Pa. 1927.)

The two essential elements here are seldom quite so frankly stated: the fantasy of '*the return to the womb*' (head-first), and that of '*the body as phallus.*' A version of this story is printed in *Anecdota Americana* (1934) 2:289, and it has been collected many times. It is developed into folktale form, as delivered by an army sergeant, D.C. 1944, with no mention of Irishmen or Jew, but turning on an even more evident mother-figure: *The 'Insatiable Queen,' who has messengers searching continually*

for 'a john that could fill her enormous box,' and who is finally
satisfied by 'the village dwarf, "Peewee",' whom no one had
taken seriously, and who was not even given the usual 'short-
arm inspection' by the Insatiable Queen's messengers, along with
all the other men. (With the identical punch-line, including 'wig-
gling his ears.') This is an open assimilation of the standard trait
of the 'Little Tailor' or the 'seventh son' variety (Joseph in
Egypt), where the strength or valor of the 'despisèd and rejected' youngest son is finally vindicated – usually by his
trickster tactics or miraculous means. It is also clearly patterned on the Cinderella folktale, especially the touch concerning the messengers. In the older form of these tales, such
as that of the messengers of Pharaoh searching for the infant
Moses-Oedipus, the messengers frankly intend to kill the
wonder-child, once he has been identified by his undisguisable
superiority, in intelligence, strength, etc.

Compare the following, supplied in manuscript from England,
with the collector's note or caption, "Nasty work!" 'Some
blokes in a pub were competing to see who could tell the
filthiest tale. After a while a little man said from a corner: 'My
trade's a peculiar one. I'm a professional Boil Sucker. I was
once called to attend a fat, elderly lady [n.b.], who'd a boil in
such an awkward place that I hardly knew whether to stick
my nose into her cunt or her arsehold. Deciding on the latter
as the lesser evil [n.b.], I'd sucked out all the yellow pus, and
had begun on the green, when the lady farted. Instead of spitting it out, as I'd intended, I gulped and swallowed the lot. Can
anyone best that?" – "Well, gentlemen," said the landlord, "as
far back as I can remember, up to the night I got married I
fucked my father's old sows, but this is the first time I've been
in fit company to mention it".' (Chelmsford, Essex, 1953.)

As noted in an earlier chapter, intercourse with a pig is likewise made the surpreme image of dirtying of, or contempt for,
the woman, in Prof. John Barth's The Sot-Weed Factor (1960).
I have not attempted to read his more recent Giles Goat-Boy: I
am told it indeed involves intercourse with goats. An extremely
mild form of this British joke, or one related, was given as a
skit by the great dialect-actor, Peter Sellers, in a Bob Hope
comedy motion-picture in which Sellers plays: A Hindu dentist,
the sound of whose drill brings a cobra up out of its basket.
When the patient expresses fear of the cobra, the dentist
assures him that it is not dangerous at all. If it bites, one merely

makes two cross-cuts in the bite and sucks out the poison. "But what if it bites you in a place you can't ... er, get to?" objects the patient. "That's when you find out who your real friends are."

The American vomit-story supposed to be unmatchably terrible, and reserved as the ultimate horror-tale or Parthian shot by numerous tellers, piles detail upon detail in the effort to be horripilating, though this really only demonstrates that the stated situation – a visit to the 'clap-doctor,' Dr. Krankheit – would probably not seem quite so terrifying without the wealth of roccoco detail, always present as told. The version given here is much abridged: *A man (sometimes a minister) has a mysterious sickness that none of the doctors can diagnose or cure. After they have all given him up, and have told him he has only a few weeks left to live, he hears of the famous Dr. Krankheit in Vienna who can unquestionably cure him. He rushes to Vienna, and finds that Dr. Krankheit lives in a very sinister quarter of the city, where the sick man passes under windows out of which chamberpots are emptied on him. He finds the address but cannot find the right apartment, and is searching through the dark hallway, ankle deep in turds, and placing each step carefully. A little boy comes along the hall, sliding at full speed through the slippery mess, and calls out at him, "Sissy!"* [The joke sometimes ends here.] *The little boy offers to show him the right apartment if the man will fellate him, which, in desperation, he does, kneeling in the mess. He finally gets to Dr. Krankheit's apartment, which is evil and dank, the doctor himself having no nose, and the hole in his face being partly covered by a dirty bandage held in place with greasy strings. He demands that the patient give him a urine specimen, meanwhile coughing and hawking in the patient's face, for which he apologizes, stating that he has "Just a touch of consumption." As there is no urine bottle, the patient must urinate into the doctor's cupped hands. He swills the urine about in his mouth, spits it on the floor, and then asks for a specimen of the patient's feces. Same treatment. At this point the patient vomits. Dr. Krankheit rushes forward with cupped hands to receive the vomit, swills it about in his mouth, and shouts, "Aha! Just as I thought! All that's the matter with you is a weak stomach!"* (Anecdota Americana, 1934, 2:447, with a further feces-flinging postscript at No. 449.)

This is strictly a shaggy-dog story of the "Mysterious Card" type (8.III.4), with the punch-line being openly directed at the listener. A much briefer form, or connected 'nonsense' story, which will be discussed further in the final chapter, "Scatology," has: *Two men starving in the desert. Just as they are about to die of hunger they find some camel-dung. One man suggests that they should eat it, but the other recoils in horror saying, "What do you think I am?!" The first man breaks up the camel-dung, moistens it with his own urine, and begins eating it. He can only get down about half, and then throws up. The other man rushes forward with cupped hand to catch the vomit, saying, "Just what I wanted – a nice hot meal!"* (N.Y. 1942.) A similar story, with the same ending and punch-line, was collected in French from a cabinet-maker, this time concerning: *Two 'clochards'* (tramps) *who are starving to death, who find a 'macchabé'* (human corpse) *floating in the Seine with the putrefying belly burst open, from which exudes the dead man's last meal of macaroni, which is the first clochard's favorite dish. He has no sooner got it all down when he throws up,* etc., etc. as above. (Plascassier, A.-M., France, 1971.)

These are of course supposed to be jokes. Anyhow, they were told as such. Compare, however, the perfectly serious 'vomit therapy' proposed by Mr. I. F. Regardie (formerly a follower of the occultist, Aleister Crowley), in the amateur psychological magazine, *Complex* (New York, 1952) No. 8. A full quotation of Mr. Regardie's vomit therapy or 'gag-reflex' – just the essentials will be sufficient here – is given in Martin Gardner's *In the Name of Science* (1952) p. 290–91. The relevant matter of this wonderful new 'Active Psychotherapy' is as follows:

The second of these somatic procedures is to ask the patient to regurgitate by using a tongue depressor and a kidney pan. Usually, the patient is puzzled and resists with some vigor. If a brief and simplified explanation is given, or if the therapist states unequivocally that this is no time for intellectual discussion [!] which must wait for a later occasion, the patient as a rule will comply. My procedure is to let him gag anywhere up to a dozen times, depending on the type of response. In itself, the *style* of gagging is an admirable index to the magnitude of the inhibitory apparatus. Some gag with finesse, with delicacy, without noise. These are categorically, the most difficult patients to handle. Their character armor is almost impenetrable, and their personalities rigid almost to the point of petrifaction. They require to be encouraged to regurgitate with noise, without concealment of their discomfort and disgust, and with some fullness. Others will cough and spit, yet still remain unproductive. Still others sneer and find the whole procedure a source of cynical amusement. Yet another group will retch with hideous completeness.

What is crucial about the "Dr. Krankheit" story is that it identifies this whole complex of vomit and sputum humor with *the fear of venereal disease,* to the degree that this has not already been done by the minor stories of the same type all circling around this clear identification but in euphemized forms concerning 'mere' tuberculosis, etc., and the matching muco-purulent discharges of those diseases. The extreme emphasis given to scatological elements here cannot be taken seriously : they are unmistakably intended as comedy relief! This is made even more clear in the British story from which that of "Dr. Krankheit" seems to have developed, in which none of the gratuitous vomiting scene takes place, though it is implied in the disgust of the principal interlocutor, stated to be the Prince of Wales. This is printed in the very rare supplement to the erotic magazine, *The Pearl,* "*Christmas Annual 1881.*" (Few copies of this 64-page item seem to have survived, but there is a 1960's reprint made in Atlanta, Georgia.)

The joke is given as a playlet, and appears in the opening story, "New Year's Day; the Sequel to *Swivia,*" end of chap. 1, p. 13, as told by the host, the Hon. Priapus Bigcock, who asks the company, waiting for supper, '*if they had heard the new anecdote about the Prince of Wales' visit to the East London Hospital?*' Here is the dialogue with the final patient in the 'paradise for the sick poor,' who has a mouth-ulcer : '*H.R.H.: Have you got any complaint to make? – PATIENT: Yes, your Royal Highness, I want to go into No. 1 bed; I want to see the doctor first. – H.R.H.: What's that for; don't you have proper attention? – PATIENT: Well, your Royal Highness, the doctor goes to that fellow in No. 1 bed and pulls his cock about, then he goes to No. 2, and shoves his finger up his arse, and then he comes and puts his finger in my mouth: I want to see the doctor first. – H.R.H.: Very reasonable, shouldn't like that myself; I'll make a note of it, (and then sotto voce), filthy places these hospitals after all, I pity the poor beggars who get into them, they have to eat shit or pox juice, or what not; I don't think I'll go much further round, I've a most pressing engagement.'*

That says everything that the heroic Ignaz Semmelweis, the discoverer with O. W. Holmes of puerperal fever (and thus of the germ theory improperly credited to Pasteur and Lister), went through martyrdom to prove hardly thirty years before, and then went insane when no one would listen to him, and women continued to die in obstetrical wards of the 1860's for precisely the reason described by *'the man in No. 3 bed ... in a very sepulchral voice.'* Also, as observed in the closing remark of his Royal Highness, it is not really Dr. Krankheit at all, but the patient – that is to say, the listener! – who has to 'eat shit or pox juice or what not.' This British original is still current, in a very abbreviated army joke concerning the 'short-arm inspection': *A recruit, waiting to be examined by the army doctor, sees him examine the preceding man by pulling open his mouth to examine his teeth, then pounding his back and chest, handling his penis and testicles, and ending by putting a finger up his rectum to check on possible piles. "All right, you can go," says the doctor. Then, to the recruit, "Now what about you? Open your mouth." "I'm o.k., doc," says the recruit hurriedly. "Gimme a gun!"* (D.C. 1944.)

6. THE DEFILING OF THE MOTHER

The Defiling of the Mother is a theme so common and so popular in the humor of our culture that most people do not notice that it exists at all. Instead, it is generally believed that 'Mother' is the principal cultural fetich, especially in America, and even more especially among Jews, comparable to the cult of the Virgin Mary among Catholics. (The position of mothers in England, where, in the boys' private schools that are the national forcing-beds of homosexuality and snobbery, 'it was a disgrace to have a mother,' is sardonically described by E. M. Forster in *Two Cheers for Democracy*, New York, 1951, p. 12, in a passage quoted in full in the First Series here, 3.III.2, page 215.) Meanwhile, all the really popular comedians of the American theatre, radio, and t.v. consider the dragging of mocking references to their own mothers onstage – carefully avoiding the offense of mentioning anyone *else's* mother – as the *ne plus ultra* of the comedian's art. See, for a good example,

Mark Twain's "My First Lie" (in his *Autobiography*, ed. 1959, chap. 11), which is sexually perverted to boot.

Since Jewish comedians and joke-tellers are, and have been for centuries, a very important contingent of the humorous profession or community in all countries where Jews have been allowed to live, the 'Jewish mother' (formerly the frankly dialectal '*Yiddishe mama*') has borne a good deal of the brunt of this type of humor, and is still doing so. Among the principal stage & screen providers of this sort of mother-dirtying – or, at the least, mother-exploiting – have been Milton Berle, Lenny Bruce, and the four Marx Brothers: all Jews. The Marx Brothers in particular never made a motion-picture comedy after their first, *On the Mezzanine*, in the early 1930's and for twenty years following, but what the principal butt of the humor was a portly dowager or mother-figure, with her pearl necklaces cascading over her balcony-style bosom (usually played by Margaret Dumont), whom the orally-sadistic character in the comedies, the virilely moustachioed brother, Groucho, would alternately make up to sexually – but only for her money – and then defile, in both verbal and real pratt-falls. This anti-mother format or formula was apparently also created for the Marx Brothers by a Jewish script-writer, the *New Yorker* humorist, S. J. Perelman, who wrote their early movies. I am not aware that anyone ever objected to it from that day to this, or even ever drew attention to it for what it so blatantly is. It is all just terribly terribly funny, so "*Why spoil a good joke by analyzing it?*" as I have been told myself at story-conferences.

In case anyone were ever in any doubt as to what this par-ticular joke really amounts to, but just under the level of achieving consciousness where one might have to object to it or miss out on all the jolly fun, the formula of the *horribly* (but horribly) funny 'Jewish mother' was made the central theme of Philip Roth's *Portnoy's Complaint* (New York: Ran-dom House, 1968), of which both author and publisher were Jews, and which is just one long paean of mother-defiling – with side-forays into food-dirtying and cloacal sexuality – all directed to holding up to laughter and disgust the fabulously evil and over-protective 'Jewish mother.' (It then proceeds to *shikse*-defiling, as already quoted in section 11.III.4, "Impos-sibilities," above.) Far from there being any objection – except for some private mutterings among a few sore-head Jews,

inquiring "How much did Nasser pay for this?" and suggesting that the author *be given back his foreskin and be kicked
out of the Jewish race* – Mr. Roth's book was the object of an
unprecedented barrage of critical acclaim and public acceptance. It became and remained the No. 1 Bestseller in America
for over a year, with foreign editions and translations of course.
What could I possibly add here to Mr. Roth's 'humorous' once-
over-lightly of family-filthying and mother-defiling at the
literary level? It is the total statement. Or so we are led to believe.

Actually, it is less than zero. The *real* Defiling of the Mother
is her proposed replacement now by mad neo-Nazi geneticists,
tinkering with human foetuses in laboratory test-tubes in order
to be father & mother both. Male motherhood for a self-elected
fascistic élite of men. And for women – *Brave No World!*

Before proceeding to the various levels, from minor to wholly
repellent, taken by the theme of the Defiling of the Mother in
folk-humor, as well as in the professional cliché-milking of
movies, bestsellers and other commercial entertainment arts, it
will be of interest to pose, as a point of departure, the absolute
ultimate in the defiling of the mother-figure *in fact* (not in
literary or other fantasy), and this time not of a single family
or 'self-hating' racial group, but of a whole and proud nation.
Here nothing is left to the imagination. Everything is perfectly
underplayed, and in subdued light indeed. Then suddenly – as
by a flash of lightning – illuminated forever, for those who have
eyes to see. In Jean-Louis Chardans' excellent research, *Dictionnaire des Trucs: Les faux, les fraudes, les truquages* (Paris:
Pauvert, 1961) p. 407, at the article "Spirite et Spiritisme," the
following anecdote is related of the homosexual British spirit-
medium, Daniel Douglas Home. (*In translation:*)

Napoléon III and the Empress Eugénie had as their favorite
medium a certain Home. One evening at Biarritz, at the request of the Empress, Home gave a séance in the presence of
four persons. Sitting before the traditional little guéridon
table, he was preparing to conjure up the spirits of Charlemagne and Louis XVI. The Empress Eugénie held his right
hand; Napoléon III, placed at his left, held his other hand.
Facing him was placed the major-domo of the palace. Standing at the chimneyplace, a certain Morio, Officer of the
Imperial Guards, was charged with the lights; at the orders

of the Empress he was to turn up or turn down a large kerosene lamp. The spirit-séance began, and the light was turned
down. The medium, Home, twisted and turned in the dark,
and entered into a trance. The Empress Eugénie stifled a cry;
in the darkness, a hand was caressing her face.... a soft and
perfumed hand ... Very troubled, she clutched the hand of
the spirit in both her own. Officer Morio, at the ready,
thinking he had heard an order, rapidly turned up the large
lamp. Horrors! ... the invisible hand was still there ... the
soft and perfumed hand, caressing the face of the beautiful
Empress, was only the medium's foot. Napoléon iii had him
thrown out of France.

Not everyone who would like to wipe his feet on the face of an
Empress in the dark, by way of defiling the mother-image – or
just of wiping his feet on somebody's face – has all that luck.

One obviously cannot overlook today the 'media' of mass
electrical audience in any discussion of folklore themes. Though
these 'media' motion-pictures, t.v. programs, advertisements,
and the like are seldom themselves folklore in the classic sense,
they nowadays massively replace and reconstruct to a disastrous degree the area in folk-life that earlier would have been
teeming with real and satisfying folk-transmitted materials:
songs, jokes, witticisms, proverbs, tall-tales, superstitions, etc.,
of precisely as long-lived and satisfying nature as the vapid and
evil garbage of the 'media' is short-lived and vowed to forget-
fulness. I have written long pages on precisely this subject in
The Horn Book – in fact, the whole book, and especially its
closing pages, are a set of variations on this theme. I would
nevertheless like to mention some few striking examples of the
present theme, of the Defiling of the Mother, in the morass of
fake popular-culture of the 'media,' especially in motion-
pictures, some of which (despite their fragile celluloid support)
may still be preserved for a few brief decades as materials of
social history.

The first clear breakaway from the usual saccharine handling
of the theme of the Mother in the movies was Charlie Chaplin's
brief, sadistic anti-breast gag, in *Modern Times* in the 1930's, in
which the factory-worker (Chaplin) gone berserk on the speed-
up chain with two monkey-wrenches in his hands, suddenly
confronts in the street into which he has fled a portly, middle-
aged woman with two large nipple-buttons on the bosom of her

dress, just the size and shape that the two monkey-wrenches fit. He stares at her, advances; she panics and flees. That is all: a touch. I recollect my own mother (who was a dressmaker and had nursed all her children) saying that it was one of the funniest things she had ever seen.

The themes of the Defiling of the Mother and the concomitant rejection and dirtying of food are insistently expressed in movies at the present time far more at the presumed art-level than at the folk-level, in work appealing not to the large public but to a sick insider group that of course attempts to enlarge its audience. These are above all the numerous *avant-garde* motion pictures, seldom exposed to any type of criticism but the usual drivel by other insiders, in which hand washes hand and back scratches back, in technical twaddle concerning strictly & only their cinematic technique, plus wild yoicks of approval for their swaggering moral degeneracy, as being 'modern', 'with-it,' or 'free.' This is obviously a begging of the question, an enforcing by embarrassed or implicated movie critics of an art-for-art's-sake or rather an immorality-for-immorality's sake position upon films that are, in blatant fact, *all* 'message': all emotional and intellectual content, and begging to be understood, in their purposeful ugliness and daemonism. Witness the cannibalistic and scatological *La Grande Bouffe*, Marco Ferreri's scandal-shocker of the 1973 cinema season. And that of 1974: the totally fake-revolt and scatologically anti-woman *Sweet Movie* of Dusan Makavejev, in which a fat female Bluebeard on a barge (representing Marxism!) seduces and then murders young boys.

The *Jeux de Nuit* (1966) of the Swedish directress, Mai Zetterling, for example, is almost entirely concerned – as was her preceding and much better film, *Loving Couples* – with homosexual and impotent men, evil mothers, child-seducers and assorted degenerates and their parasites and pimps, in what is clearly intended, as Holbrook Jackson has remarked of Beardsley's *Venus and Tannhäuser*, in *The Eighteen-Nineties* (1913), as a set of 'romanticised excerpts,' in this case a careful cinematic homework or abridgement, of Krafft-Ebing's *Psychopathia Sexualis*, with more than a little tendentious or propagandistic misstatement of Freud, all directed at and for the purpose of vilifying and defiling the mother.

Miss Zetterling is a considerable artist, actually the first great woman artist in the history of cinema-directing. She began as a conscious imitator of the cinematic syle of the current Scandinavian cynosure, Ingmar Bergman, of whose *Brink of Life* and *Smiles of a Summer Night* her *Loving Couples* is essentially a very superior remake. As is also visible, she draws a good part of her inspiration from the matching Spanish glorifier of sick cinema and celluloid degeneracy, Luis Buñuel, whose *Chien Andalou* in the 1920's was and remains – with its faked scene of the razor-blading of a woman's eye to watch the vitreous humour spurt – the nausea thriller of the Surréalist goon-show. To make sure that nothing shall be missing, in the defiling of the mother, Miss Zetterling's *Jeux de Nuit* begins with a mock or travesty of the scene with which her preceding film (and Bergman's *Brink of Life* – itself heavily death-oriented) had ended: the act of childbirth. The beautiful and seductive mother is shown with her swollen belly naked and straining, while she gives birth to a *stillborn* child before the tortured eyes of an audience of guests and other parasites. The doctor explains that it is all her own fault. The audience in the movie-house is cannily left out, by turning the camera around and shooting over the parturient woman's shoulder. She also wants her little boy to watch, and *"See what your mother can do!"* – which is not an unreasonable brag – but the aunt-witch takes him around to pray at the head of the bed (along with the well-bilked audience) so that neither he nor we shall see the tremendous mystery of childbirth, which is the central act of human life.

Much in the same way, Luis Buñuel in *The Forgotten Ones*, had presented a once-over-lightly exposé of the sad condition of Mexican juvenile delinquents (the true Mexican slang name for whom would be *"Los Deabajos"* – Those from the Depths – and not the polite *"Los Olvidados"*), carefully showing under the shallow pretext of a 'dream' how the bad boy's even badder mother throws bloody chunks of raw meat on his bed, over which she dances in her nightdress, while bitchily refusing him love when they are awake. Cannibalism as coitus. There are apparently just as many bad mothers in Mexico as in Sweden. In Sweden they are bad because they are rich; in Mexico they are bad because they are poor. What does it matter, as long as they're *bad*?

Buñuel's masterpiece, *Viridiana*, rises to the ultimate food-dirtying of all, in a parody scene showing the paschal Last Supper of Christ and the disciples, played by drunken bums and hideous cripples, of whom the 'photograph is taken' (*i.e.* the movie made) in an exact parody pose of Leonardo da Vinci's masterpiece, also of course being mocked, by a prostitute, with *"the camera her daddy gave her."* That is to say, by throwing up her skirt at the mock-Christ and his disciples – with her back to the camera – and showing them her cunt. As Buñuel's unmistakable purpose in all his films is to drag down and shit upon everything his audience may be expected to hold holy, it would surely not be straining the interpretation to assume that this curious scene, of the 'cunt-camera,' is also intended to allude to the superstition known in all Latin countries (Rabelais' *"Diable de Papefiguière,"* Bk. IV, chap. 47), that the Devil can be put to flight by the display of a woman's genitals. Meaning here that Christ and the Devil are one.

This all has no doubt a terrific sacrilegious voltage in priest-ridden Spain, Italy, and other Latin countries. In the atheistic Protestant West, no one gives a damn about Buñuel's sacrilege except professional clerics; and his intended food-dirtying scene to end all food-dirtying scenes, of the shat-upon Last Supper of the Christian god, can only be gravely considered as a bit of decadent genre-painting in the tradition of the cripples and *gueux* of Breughel and Callot, the mock-*Laocoön* parodied with monkeys and snakes, and the blood-dripping, bug-eaten crucified Christ of Grünewald, and of Mexican religious baroque, which is even sicker. Buñuel's Last Supper parody is itself light-heartedly parodied – at third remove from Leonardo – in the American film satire, *M.A.S.H.* (1969).

Though I would rather not discuss a mere neo-Buñuel like Alexandro Jodorowsky, it would be unfair to seem to be selling short the enormous artistic power of Mai Zetterling and Luis Buñuel, both of whom (surely the latter, in his sex-maniacal *Criminal Life of Archibald de la Cruz*) make such other competitors for the title of cinematic decadents as Ingmar Bergman (his *omnia opera*), Fellini's *La Dolce Vita*, and various recent British and American homo-pukeo efforts seem like adolescents playing at circle-jerks in a barn. In a desperate fruitcake-technicolor effort to regain the title for Italy, Fellini's homo-sado *Satyricon* (1968), long after Petronius, vomits the whole sewer of ancient Rome in the audience's face. It is a deeply uneconomic waste of genius – and in the only *new art* of our century – for such splendid technical appanage to be so narrowly limited and crippled in the mazes of these sexually-toned and purposely defiling themes. One is reminded somehow of the French traitor and collaborator with the Nazis, Louis-Ferdinand Céline, who nevertheless has proved to be – through his imitators, such as Henry Miller – the most influential writer and, with Joyce, the most considerable literary stylist of the 20th century. One is also reminded of the deathless assessment, by John Randolph of Virginia, of his political enemy Henry Clay, that he was *"so brilliant, yet so corrupt; like rotten mackerel by moonlight, he shines and stinks."* (Cited by Joseph Rosner, in his *The Hater's Handbook*, New York, 1965, p. 182, with several other of Randolph's gems.)

The literary and sub-literary versions of modern anti-womanism are mainly the products of the 'bad mother' or 'evil matriarch' school of cutrate cultural analysis and homosexual fiction, as scheduled already a quarter of a century ago in my monographs, *Love & Death* (1949) and *On the Cause of Homosexuality* (1950). Except for the new anti-motherhood pamphlets of Women's Liberation, few real mother-defiling items of this kind exist written by women, with the rock-bottom exception of the brief horror-thriller, *"A la Tartare"* (the title is a macabre pun, as will be seen), by Mrs. E. M. Winch, published in *A Century of Horror Stories*, edited by Dennis Wheatley (London, *ca.* 1938), in which a poor Russian woman feeds the body of her dead nursling-child, mixed with rat-poison, to Bolshevik soldiers who demand food. This is obviously intended as the ultimate horror, or last turn of the screw, in the style of the legend of "The Eaten Heart" (see the First Series, chapter 8.VIII.10, pages 650–63), but it is entirely incredible and does not come off. It is more particularly in the lineage of the 'poisoned vagina' (Tunic of Nessus) or *vagina dentata* stories, and would have made both better fiction and better food-dirtying if the poor Russian woman had poisoned her own breast-milk directly, and fed it to the Bolsheviks straight from the teat. The movie-rights to that one practically sell themselves.

Mrs. Winch's *"A la Tartare"* attempts to find its ultimate tabasco or *dernier frisson* simply in the attribution to a woman – thus the defiling of the mother – of the standard sacrifice of the child, which, contrariwise, we are expected to fall down and worship as glorious, beautiful, sacred and divine, when it is the father-god Jehovah playing at Moloch – the anti-god or devil – and demanding the identical sacrifice of Abraham, as to

Abraham's son Isaac, and allegedly that of his own son, Jesus, as well. Seen in this context and comparison, "*A la Tartare*" is not really the last turn of the screw at all, but only the last pinch of the winch – or twitch of the bitch – while waiting for the patriarchal gods and generals (like Milton's Moloch, in *Paradise Lost*) to show what baby-killing REALLY is.

Sometimes one finds oneself in very strange company. Working through my files on these subjects, I find simultaneously San Francisco newspaper clippings of late 1966, and *Time* magazine tear-sheets for the first week of 1967, in both of which figure the well-known child movie-star of the 1930's Shirley Temple, by then a California matron, who felt it necessary to express her objection to Mai Zetterling's film, *Jeux de Nuit*, by storming out of the San Francisco Film Festival when this film was first shown, under the title *Night Games*. I feel very sympathetic with her indignation, but am no longer positive that I understand it, in view of the following brief note in *Time*, concerning other activities of the same lady and at the same time, here quoted complete. (Compare: Fenichel, page 348.)

> There are bird watchers and bee watchers, satellite watchers and girl watchers – in fact, watchers for just about everything. But *Mrs. Charles Black*, 38, once known as Shirley Temple, belongs in a category all her own. "I'm an operation watcher," she explained to the *New York Times*. It started when Shirley was 14, visiting an army hospital in Oregon. "A boy asked me to be with him while his leg was amputated. I held his hand the entire time, and since then have watched many operations. Gall bladders are the best – the colors are gorgeous!"

The simplest approach to the mother-figure is the natural act of nursing at her breast, leading in the neurotic and often in the normal child to the eventual fantasy – seldom the fact – of sexual intercourse with her. This also naturally leads to jealous conflict with the father or father-figure, and often to the withdrawal of the son from this conflict, thus entering homosexuality in the attempt to conciliate the more powerful male sexually. In white Western culture, the idea of the taboo son-mother incest as a form of *mother-defiling* is generally projected on the Negro, in part owing to the Negro vocabulary of insult on this subject, and in part on a simple scapegoat basis for the unconscious urges and guilts shared equally by both black and white. There is also a further projection of guilt – here on the mother, as well as on the Negro – in the tacit assumption by whites that such incest is the result of the mother's seduction of the son, rather than the reverse. There is thus very little guilt left to bear. Many homosexuals similarly insist on the contradictory but simultaneous memories, that they both 'hated' their mothers and found them purposely seductive sexually. That, presumably, is why they hated them: *"Walking around in her underwear all the time, and things like that!"*

Most jokes expressing the idea of sexual closeness between mother and son, or even approaching it, such as the anti-Negro jokes in the extraordinary Bohannon MS. collection (Indiana Univ. Folklore Archives), present this in a format intended to mock the Negro's stereotypical willingness to use the insulting term 'mother-fucker' on any occasion. *The white social-worker is complimenting the Negro mother on her fine little boy. "My, my,"* he says, *"only a year old and he can walk already." "He can talk too,"* says the mother proudly. *"Sam, say* mother-fucker *for the gen'leman!"* (Bloomington, Indiana, 1963.)

Jokes directly defiling childbirth, as the essential function of motherhood, are not common. Even in folk-life, the principal attack is that disguised by the *couvade* of primitive peoples, in which the father is immobilized in bed, instead of the mother, to prevent him from killing or harming (eating?) the child. See further, in the First Series, 8.VI.3, "Rectal Motherhood," p. 603–5, and particularly Theodor Reik's brilliant psycho-analytic interpretation of this, in his *Ritual* (1931) p. 27–89; as also Wayland Hand's "American Analogues of the Couvade," in *Studies in Folklore, in honor of Stith Thompson* (Indiana Univ. 1957) p. 213–29.

Nothing in any joke on this subject even approaches the glee-ful ghastliness of an unpublished medical poem or recitation, entitled "The Ballad of Chambers Street," written by Dr. Frederick Irving of the Harvard Medical School, about 1910, which is quoted as to its unexpected castratory conclusion or punishment in chapter 13.II.6, below, "The Doctor as Castra-tor." The defiling of the mother cannot be taken further: *Two bumbling obstetricians, one of them being named "Jojo" Pratt to set the tone, are at a loss how to bring to birth the baby of the local Jewish prostitute, Big Rosie. After she has been in*

*labor for several days, they simply fill her vagina with dyna-
mite and explode it, killing both the mother and baby in what
is described poetically as a volcanic explosion like that of
'Proud Aetna in her salad days, on that Sicilian shore.'* Only
some thirty years later, during the invasion of Ethiopia by
Italy in 1935/6, did that greatest of all modern aesthetic critics
– he only said one line, but it was enough – Vittorio Mussolini,
son of the Italian dictator, make the deathless observation,
similar to that concerning Mount Aetna above, that when he
dropped bombs from his airplane on the fleeing Ethiopians on
the roads, their bodies and blood exploded into the air *'like a
beautiful rose unfolding.'*

The mild anti-motherhood jokes are sometimes given as puns,
for example two of the current 'Elephant' jokes or riddles, a
format that very often gravitates about sexual or anti-family
subjects (*'Big* Willies'?) under its cumbersome camouflage-
cover of nonsense: *"How do you know when you've been
raped by an elephant? – When you've been pregnant for thirty-
six months."* (La Jolla, Calif. 1965, from an 18-year-old girl
student, who stated that she had just lost her virginity the
night before.) Drs. Roger D. Abrahams & Alan Dundes give an
important collection and interpretation of elephant-jokes in
"On Elephantasy and Elephanticide," in *Psychoanalytic Review*
(1969) vol. 56: p. 225–41. They do not seem to include one very
relevant here: *"What's a womb? – The noise an elephant makes
when it farts in a cave."* (L.A. 1968.) This obvious mother-
defiling item is built up into a long schoolroom story in *World's
Dirtiest Jokes,* p. 169, sexualized further with the heading, "Big
Blow Job."

How are these for direct defilings of childbirth? *The bride
asks her mother what having a baby really feels like – the
pains. The mother says, "Take hold of your lower lip, dear, and
pinch it as tight as you possibly can." The daughter does so, and
says, "I believe I can stand that." "Now," says the mother,
"grasping it firmly between your thumb and forefinger, stretch
your lower lip, skin it over your skull, and staple it to the back
of your neck!"* – *World's Dirtiest Jokes,* 1969, p. 210, titled
"That's It!" In her Women's Liberation polemic, *The Dialectic
of Sex* (1970) page 227, Shulamith Firestone gets quite a bit of
mileage out of a variation of this, in which the sensations of
childbirth are described as being *'like shitting a pumpkin.'* – *A
drunk lurches against a pregnant woman carrying a shopping-*

bag containing some eggs and a bottle of ketchup, which over-turns and everything breaks in a mess on the ground. The woman bursts into tears. "Aw, don't cry, honey," says the drunk. "With its eyes that far apart, it never could have lived anyhow." (Cleveland, Ohio, 1939, sometimes also *a live rabbit: "From the length of its ears, and its eyes that far apart ..."* See Tale Type 1319.) Joke given elsewhere in which: *The drunk, vomiting into a garbage-can in which a woman has deposited her miscarriage, thinks he has sucked it out during cunnilinctus.* A similar fantasy is expressed, as having actually happened during a Hell's Angels' initiation ceremony, quoted in full in the First Series, 8.V.4, page 577, under "Cunnilinctus and Masochism."

British item similar: *'Stormy midnight. A humpbacked boy searches along a dark street, finally knocks at an old maid's door. – "Yes?" – "Mrs. Smith?" – "No, it's Miss Smith." – "Well, may I ask you a very personal question?" – "What is it?" – "Fifteen years ago, Miss Smith, didn't you have a miscarriage?" – "I don't see why I should stand here to be insulted like this!" – "But didn't you?" – "Well, what if I did?" – "And you put it in the dustbin* [British: *ashcan*], *didn't you?" – "Yes I did. How did you know that?" – "Mother!!!"* ' (Chelmsford Prison, Essex, 1954.) Compare the legend of the lost-&-found-again King Oedipus and his mother; also Straparola's *Piacevoli Notti* (1550) III.1: *Parents accidentally meet daughter who has survived their attempts to drown her.* Rotunda, Motif N732.3. An important touch in the British joke, not to be overlooked, is that the boy is 'humpbacked,' *i.e.* has been improperly brought to birth, or perhaps harmed at birth, by the mother who has also rejected and abandoned him.

As differentiated from the proto-incestuous candor projected upon the theoretically 'animal-like' and unrepressed Negro in jokes, three elements of disguise are particularly used in humor to *evade* recognizing the mother-figure – when she is the mother of a white man – and yet to arrive, somehow and never-theless, at fantasy intercourse with her. These disguises all represent the mother as a prostitute, but as a prostitute no reasonable person would ever want. Specifically, that she is *old, dirty, and diseased.* That is to say, the exact opposite of the real mother desired and remembered, who was ideally young, clean, and sweet-smelling of milk: the mother in her ultimate expression.

Stories of old and diseased prostitutes with whom intercourse is possible only by means of some disgusting use of their venereal lesions are, analytically viewed, not merely real warnings against venereal diseases. They are also pretendedly humorous expressions of Oedipal terror, in which the venereal disease is construed as a deserved punishment, *lex talionis,* for intercourse with the old prostitute (always old and hideous) representing the mother. Or, rather, disguising the mother, whom no one would presumably recognize as the raddled old crone pushed into service unfittingly as a disgusting sexual aperture. This is the hag or witch theme (and disguise) of all cultural folktales in the West, and perhaps elsewhere. The mother is split into the young and good, but sexless, fairy-godmother on the one hand; and on the other into the evil, castratory, orally-dangerous (sexual) crone, full of appetites: Hänsel & Gretel's witch, demanding that the boy put out his penis-finger, to see if he, or it, is plump enough yet to eat. The gruesome and nauseating joke or story is thus the erotic 'cautionary tale' of the nursery or *Struwwelpeter* type (see *Neurotica,* 1951, No. 9), but here specifically directed against the breaking of the incest taboo.

Here is a *real* children's joke on such themes, and quite artlessly makes apparent the true identity of the actors in these over-decorated tales of vomit and sputum, as being simply the human trinity of: the pregnant mother, the father – and the observant child. *Little Boy: "Let's play house." Little Girl: "All right. You shave and I'll vomit."* (N.Y. 1952.) Mild as this may seem, I have seen it put an untidy young career-girl into sullen shock for a whole afternoon, when told as an oblique explanation of why a man would rather take her to the movies than accept the offer of a homemade supper in her cockroach-infested kitchen plus a night in her dirty bed.

In the same way that the mother-figure, no matter how *old* and tough she may be, is only seen as dangerous in the fear-joke, or joke of nastiness and disease; even being *dirty* is not necessarily repugnant in the prostitute, if she is not 'otherwise' identifiable with the mother. Dirtiness is a good disguise, and another is excessive *youth.* They can also be combined: *Client, to a very young prostitute whom he has picked up on the street: "How old are you, kid?" "Sixteen." "Don't try to fool me, you never could have got those drawers that filthy in only sixteen years!"* (2:307.) The client is here rejecting her dirtiness, though he has accepted her youth. This is not the same as the sexual fetich of dirtiness, in which refined gentlemen in cream-colored spats and gloves, writing old-style sonnets and artistic love-poesy in their spare time, on the style of Pierre Louÿs, turn out absolutely to require some filthy or bedraggled street-waif, 'native girl,' or 'colored wench,' who must be paid to engage in urinary or scatological rituals to arouse the same gentleman's badly decayed virility. Again on the style of Pierre Louÿs in his unpublished private erotic poetry and fictions, which have made strong men – and stronger women – blench.

Compare too the *Hundred-Dollar Misunderstanding* (1964) by Robert Gover, a much-touted American comedy novel turning on the supposed humor of a white college-boy 'of good family' being made a monkey of in his intercourse with a fourteen-year-old money-minded Negro whore, presented as deliciously light-skinned and attractive (especially for the proposed movie version) to avoid shocking the white audience harder than will titillate them. Very much more charming – and true – was the splendidly done American animated-cartoon movie, Ralph Bakshi's *Fritz the Cat* (1971), of which the highpoint was the mating-dance and chase between the white boy, played in feline disguise by Fritz, and the magnificently big and fat Negro prostitute, who leads him a merry chase along the edge of Harlem, before spread-eagling in more-than-total surrender. Bakshi's later, much greater *Heavy Traffic* (1973, issued as *Flipper City* in Europe, on the pinball-machine dream of America) goes several leagues even deeper into the morbid private hell of the slums and ghettos of poverty-ridden America, and is, aside from its obvious retort to Disney's empty sadistic kitsch, the 20th-century version of Callot's *Beggars* and Piranesi's vertiginous *Prisons*.

The psychological point in sub-literary material of wide or 'best seller' folk-acceptance must not be lost sight of. In this case it is that the black, or excessively young girl, even more than the excessively old prostitute, *cannot possibly be identified with the mother*. Were a normal man to want intercourse with a fresh young girl, he would doubtless choose one – or a dozen, if possible, in the standard harem-dream peddled by the nudie pictures of the men's magazines, etc. – at her sexually freshest and most youthfully ripe, in her late 'teens or early twenties. But he would *not* pick a barely pubescent girl of twelve, without even any hair on her genitals and her breasts hardly formed. This is the real neurotic point behind the recent spate of delighted public gloating over the idea of intercourse with excessively young girls, since an expatriate Russian professor at a sedate American coëducational college, Vladimir Nabokov, published his novel, *Lolita* (1955) in a Paris pornography series, "The Traveller's Library."

The final disguise of the mother-figure is that she is not only too old (or too young) and too *dirty*, but that she is also diseased, which is essentially what is meant by 'dirty.' Now obviously no one in his right mind would want to have intercourse with a woman he believes has venereal disease, not even on any of the incestuous pretexts made use of in the preceding section, "The Biter Bit." In setting up such a situation, the tellers of jokes are trying to make it purposely ludicrous and unbelievable that such a woman would ever be chosen, and thus to deny the guilt for having chosen her, and to make light of and 'laugh off' the disease that is the classic punishment for the sexual sin of incest, and tantamount to castration. It is always necessary, however, even in jokes, somehow to reject the idea of incest with the mother-figure, and it is precisely the 'old prostitute' mustered into service who is therefore made the target of the most violent anal- and oral-sadism ever appearing in jokes or folklore of any kind. The cloacal identification first serves to defile, and therefore to reject and deny the mother. Then food-dirtying by means of vomiting, disease, death, and even the eating of the dead woman's body, if the primitive anal-sadism proves an insufficient disguise.

But it is her *oldness* that is most unforgivable in the mother, because it is that which really makes her – unavailable. '*An American soldier in London, one dark evening in a blackout, found a rather accommodating wench beside him, and began to talk. He whispered sweet nothings, felt her up, and soon found she could be had for money, so he fucked her. As they talked afterwards, she said she didn't have much trade any more; in fact, he was her first man in some years. "How do you live?" he asked. "Oh, I gets by with me old age pension," she explained.* (Los Angeles, 1942.) This is no more than an Oedipal idyll. The tone sours rapidly, however. *An American soldier in London picks up a woman during a blackout and makes love to her in a hallway. She makes no effort to help him, but rests limply up against the wall where he is embracing her. He strikes a match to see what the trouble is, and is horrified to see that she has white hair. "My god!" he cries, "your hair is white!" "It may be winter on the mountain," she replies with dignity, "but there's summer in my heart." "O.k., grandma," he says, "then you better get some spring in your ass, or we'll be here till fall!"* (Chicago, 1953.) Playing on words to cover the unease he feels. The original erotic proverb or retort on which this is based is simply: *"There may be snow on the roof, but there's a fire in the furnace (or cellar)."* Compare the obviously equivocal advertising slogan for gasoline in the 1960's: *"Put a tiger in your tank."*

The reality of male impotence, and the difficulty of arriving at ejaculation with advancing age, is reversed and projected upon the 'old woman,' with the cloacal identification – or accusation – very preponderant: *The customer in the whorehouse does have enough money, but all the girls are 'occupied,' as it is Saturday night and the place is very busy. He insists he is in a great hurry and must catch a train, and he is directed to a dark room on the top floor, where he is told there are no lights. After having intercourse rapidly with the woman he finds there, he notices a disagreeable odor. "For Christ's sake, what stinks?" he cries. A feeble old voice answers: "Sir, they pressed me into service tonight. I'm too old to come, so I shit."* (2:290. Text form: D.C. 1945.) This is very often collected, and many tellers consider it extraordinarily funny. In some versions there is no attempted surprise element, the woman being stated at the very beginning to be old: *'A guy was fucking an old woman to beat hell, and all of a sudden he smelt something terrible . . . etc.'* (D.C. 1943.) We will see further along that this mysterious and terrible 'smell' is really the smell not of feces, but of death.

The standard accusation against the woman that her vagina is too large has already been handled in the chapter on Women, 6.V.4. It appears again in the present connection as a special attribute of the *old* woman, whose vagina is presumably larger, and thus less attractive or more 'disgusting' than that of any other woman. It will also not be overlooked that in making the vagina of the old woman *large*, the guilt has been projected upon her for the thus-only comparatively *small* size of the man's penis. Again, this identifies him as the son of this mother, any illusion to or implication of small penis size regularly representing the identification with a child, as with 'the village dwarf "Peewee",' in the preceding section. Set up here as a

'typology' of women according to their relative virtue, the following anecdote (it is not actually a joke) is really on the
"Seven Ages of Man" or "Three Ages of Women" pattern,
which is at least as old as Shakespeare's *As You Like It* (1600)
II.vii.140–66, the "All the world's a stage" speech. *A doctor,*
after examining a young lady brought to him by her parents
who feared she had been having intercourse, explained to them
that with a girl who diddles only a little, the urine flows in a
thin little stream. (Illustrated by the narrator filling his mouth
and purling out a little water.) If she diddles reasonably, the
stream comes fuller (he lets out quite a stream); but if she's a
whore, it comes out like this (and he opens his mouth and lets
a mouthful of water fall all over everything).' (Los Angeles,
Calif. 1942.) The action here is merely artfully built up to a
charade of vomiting, 'disguised' as urination.

Specifically connecting the too-large vagina with the old
woman, here with the implication that it is the continuous
intercourse of the prostitute (and not the mother's child-bearing, as is the truth) which enlarges the vagina. *The old whore,*
rolling home drunk, cannot walk straight. She sits down
heavily on a fire-hydrant, and sinks slowly to the ground. (N.Y.
1953.) Again, this is not a joke; hardly even an anecdote. It is
simply a statement, cast in attempted humorous form, of the
phallic appearance of fire hydrants, here stated to be of the
exact calibre of the 'old whore's' vagina. The hostility is not
disguised, since the action is obviously that of impalement, a
subject gloated upon, to a degree not believable, in the modern
'historical' novel, *The Burnished Blade* by Lawrence Schoonover.

The most florid joke, and concerning the largest vagina –
other than those in folksongs, in which birds and sailing-ships
go in and out, such as that of "The Captain's Wife," in T. E.
Lawrence's *The Mint* (1936) – is again a sort of hostile impalement, punishing the woman for, and specifically by means of,
her overlarge vagina. *A lady circus-acrobat, of advancing age, is*
giving her farewell performance in the biggest music-hall
theatre in London. For her final and greatest trick, she skids
halfway along the tight-wire, turns three back somersaults in
the air, and lands in the exact center of the stage in a spread-
legged 'split.' The applause is tremendous, and she bows in both
directions from the floor. Several curtain-calls, more applause,
while she remains sitting on the floor, with her arms spread,

smilingly accepting the audience's plaudits. Finally the stage-manager slides out behind the swirling curtain and whispers, "For Christ's sake, get up! The applause is stopping." Without relinquishing her smile or poise, she hisses to him between her teeth, "Rock me back and forth, and break the suction!" (London, 1956. First printed in *Grim Hairy Tales*, 1966, p. 42.) This is the *vagina dentata* story to end them all.

No holds seem to be barred in this type of story. Probably the most popular of the erotic shaggy-dog stories, which circulated simultaneously with the noisy public fad for the merely 'non-sensical' types during the 1930's and since, brings again into prominence the idea of the 'specialty' prostitute (Chapter 11.III.3), whose impossibly marvellous and exciting form of intercourse somehow manages always to harm or kill the man, as in the most famous and mysterious 'speciality' of all, "The Sleeve Job" (First Series, 8.III.3–4). Here rationalizing the fetich for crippled women:

A salesman in a strange city (or a sailor on shore-leave) is looking for a woman, and asks a bellboy in the hotel (or a passing stranger) for directions to the nearest whorehouse. The bell-boy or stranger has a hare-lip, and speaks throughout with an extreme stammer and impediment (not imitated here), telling him mysteriously: "You go down the hall, turn left, take the service elevator to the basement, and go out the back door. That lets you out in the alley. Go to the corner and walk three blocks left, and then two blocks right. There's a big hole in the street there with a plank over it. You cross the plank, and there's a big pile of bricks." "Bricks?! You don't understand!" cries the salesman. "I'm looking for a woman." "Wa-wa-wa-wait a minute," says the bellboy; "I'm coming to that. You take one of the big bricks – don't take the little ones – and then you come back two blocks left and three blocks right. Big number on the door: 334 Juniper Street. Don't go in there – that's the police station. But across the street is the best gosh-darned whorehouse in town. The girls there are beauts! Real honeys! But don't take any of them, see? You ask for Cross-Eyed Nellie. You'll know her because one of her legs is shorter than the other. She'll give you what you want, and darn cheap too." "But what about that damn brick that I'm carrying around?" asks the puzzled salesman. "Oh, that's the main thing! I was just coming to that. You don't lay Nellie on the bed, see? You give it to her up against the wall, so you have to prop her short leg up on the brick." "But why?" "You haf' to! Otherwise she'd fall on her duff." "But why can't I lay her on the bed?!" "Because – " (very mysteriously now) "*– because, just when you're gonna shoot your load, see, you* KICK OUT *the brick! And then when she starts wobbling back and forth, and fee – eel – ing around for it with her short leg (acted out) – oh, boy!* what *a sensation!!"* (N.Y. 1942. Also in a version 'telegraphing' the punch-line by calling the girl "Skip-Step Annie," told by a San Francisco literary critic, 1944.) This is the sadism of total control and of 'disappointing.' Control, not over the non-existent salesman and crippled prostitute, of course, but over the listener. It is also an elaborately ungallant *rationalization* of the perverted sexual fetich for crippled and amputated women, as is shown further in chapter 15.IV, "Symbolic Castrations."

When, finally, the sought-for 'specialty' is plainly recognized as venereal disease or castration – which is perhaps not what the man is looking for, but is what he gets – the most violent and slashing jokes in existence bring to bear all the armamentarium of their oral sadism to deny the disease, or make light of it, by gloating over its most nauseating imaginary details. There is a superlative example of this psychological mechanism in Shakespeare's *Henry V*, Act II, *ad fin.*, where the cowardly Dauphin of France insists that he longs for the morning of the battle to come, 'plays at dice' for his English enemies' loot with his officers, and blusters, *"I will trot tomorrow a mile, and my way shall be paved with English faces."* (This image was also a favorite of hellfire Calvinist preachers, Hell being said to be paved with the skulls of unbaptized children, and each skull impaled on a red-hot iron stake – which didn't really make the torture any worse for anyone but the listeners.)

In the style of "Food-Dirtying," already covered in section 12.IV.2, above, but here with further trills. '*A traveling salesman, in a small town, thinking to stay several days, bought a meal ticket for five meals, a dollar apiece. On the third day his home office called him back, leaving him with two tickets left. On his last night in town he decided to visit a whorehouse, and he had the madame persuade a girl there to take the $2 food ticket for Myrtle's Café as payment for a piece of ass. In the room with the girl, he stripped, and thought he would have her french him a little. The picture is of this girl with his huge dong in her mouth. Busily at work on it, speaking out of the side of her mouth, she asks, "This Myrtle's Café – is that a* clean *place* to eat?"' (L.A. 1942.) Here, visibly, it is the sex that dirties the food, or is dirtier than the food no matter how dirty it may be!

Another form of this joke has already been given, and still another – it is a great favorite – was collected in Scranton, Pa. in 1940, increasing the presumed ludicrousness, but actually the dirtying, by having the client 'a miner covered with coal-dust, "going down the line" on a Saturday night.' This reference is nowadays becoming obsolete. Scranton, Pa., and (I believe) Allentown nearby, were among the last towns in the Eastern United States to have an open 'red-light' district or 'whoor-alley' of tolerated houses of prostitution until World War II, similar to those of New Orleans' "Storeyville." Boys and men would slowly saunter down such streets or alleys (the 'line'), sizing up and joking with the whores sitting at the windows trying to angle them in, exactly as in travellers' accounts of Venice in the 16th century, and Amsterdam and Hamburg to-day. Further interesting notes on old-time American prostitu-tion preceding World War I are given in Herbert Asbury's series of books on American towns, and in the interestingly illustrated pamphlet, Brass Checks and Red Lights (Denver, Colorado, 1967), by Mr. & Mrs. Fred Mazzulla. The idea of the preceding joke is also sometimes reduced to a puzzle: A drunk comes out of the men's room and says with amazement to the bartender, "There's a nigger in there with a white pecker!" "Nah," says the bartender, "he's just a coal-miner that goes home for lunch." (World's Dirtiest Jokes, 1969, p. 189, a version adding 'and one white finger!' intended to imply some leprous disease.)

The insistence on the horrible details of the 'old whore's' venereal disease, which is supposed to make the identification with the mother utterly impossible at any conscious level, is not what in the end proves to be the most distressing about such jokes, but rather the insistence upon having intercourse with her, anyhow. It is this which shows most clearly that these bravely awful jokes are not by any means what they appear to be, and must certainly not be construed as real wal-lowings in the idea of intercourse with the diseased woman, whether mother, whore, or both. To the contrary, they are pitiful expressions of the desire for the one remembered woman who, most of all women, is thought of as supremely beautiful, lovely, and pure, by the very persons telling these ghastly jokes, but who have been petrified by the incest-taboo into this necessity of expressing their deepest dream in the terrible rictus of a repellent ordeal or mocking travesty. Thus also the ludicrous and perhaps only accidentally scatological subterfuge suggested to Moses by his god, Jehovah, in *Exodus*, xxxiii. 23: "*And thou shalt see my back parts:* BUT MY FACE SHALL NOT BE SEEN."

From the telling of an army private, all direct quotation having been expurgated in the transcription, as can be seen from the opening adverb 'viciously.' From manuscript: '*When a man complained viciously to a prostitute about the huge size of her vagina, she took time out a minute and had him try again. This fit was better but still not perfect, so she made another adjustment. The result was a perfect fit. After coming, he asked her how she managed to vary the size of her vagina this way, and she explained that the first hole was her real cunt, the next a syphilis hole, and the third a gonorrhea hole.*' (D.C. 1945.) Note the punishment for the wishful-dream of the 'adjustable vagina,' now often encountered in expurgated form as the humorous suggestion that a woman 'should have a zipper put in' – but only into her abdomen – when she has had a Caesarean section during childbirth.

Many minds have worked on this particular joke, which is encountered in a large number of variants. *A man complains that a prostitute is "too loose." She fiddles around and fixes it. "It's wonderful now. What did you do?" "I just buttoned the carbuncle holes over the chancres."* (N.Y. 1939.) Also, same place and date of collection, but from a different teller not present at the first joke-telling session. One observes the tone here of some mysterious 'specialty' of the "Sleeve Job" kind: *A sailor in Singapore complains that the prostitute's vagina is dry and is hurting him. "Wait, I'll fix that," she offers. "Wonderful! Wonderful!" he says. "What did you do? Use vaseline?" "No," she says, "I got my own ways." "K.Y. jelly, I suppose?" he insists. "Well, if you really want to know, I scraped off the scabs and spread the scum around."* (N.Y. 1939.) This is the most usual form of the joke, and it is usually stated to be the 'worst (or rottenest)' that the teller knows. Taking such a statement as a challenge, another person present at a session where this joke was once again told, thousands of miles away and fourteen years later, stated: '*I've got a nausea-topper* [sic] *for that one. She says: "I just scratched off the scabs, and slid you in on the puss".*' (Los Angeles, 1953.)

These purposely gross images are not new. In the old English folksong of "Tom-a-Lin" (who is stated to be a Welshman), the final stanza as given in the rogue-biography and jestbook, *The Pinder of Wakefield* (1632; ed. Horsman, Liverpool Univ., 1956) p. 73–5, takes this even further, into sexual smörgåsbord or food-dirtying:

> *Tom a Lin hee danc't up the Hall,*
> *Ginny came after, ragges and all.*
> *Shee scrapt the scabs all from her skin:*
> *Wee'l have them fry'd in butter,*
> > *quoth Tom a Lin.*

The full text is given in Prof. Douglas Short's monograph (in progress) on "Tom-a-Lin" and the related Scottish song, "Duncan Macleerie." Irish versions, where the song is called "Brinzi O'Flynn," also concentrate on ugly and shocking images, of scatology, incest, etc.

The least gruesome, perhaps, but certainly the most illuminating of jokes of this type turns on the standard pretext or situation of 'not having enough money,' here insisted upon as the *sine qua non* of the whole action: *A boy goes to a whorehouse to lose his virginity, but knowing nothing of such things he has only 25¢ with him. For this the madam agrees to let him have the oldest "girl" in the house, whom he will find upstairs in Room 8, lying on the bed, "because she hasn't been feeling so good lately." However, she will "fix him up" for the small sum of a quarter, which is all he has. The boy goes up and finds the woman lying on the bed in the dark. "Don't turn on the lights," she says; "my eyes hurt." He feels his way to the bed, then: 'He starts hugging her and screwing her and kissing her. Being of a romantic turn of mind, he presses a grateful kiss on her mouth when he's finished fucking her, and says, "What lovely lips you have!" "Them ain't my lips, sonny," she says. "That's where my nose used to be!"'* (N.Y. 1946.)

The British form: *A man dying of venereal disease in a hospital surprises the doctors by asking for "just one more grind" as his dying wish. 'So they procured him an advanced case from the Women's Ward and left them together in a darkened cubicle.' The two human derelicts lurch together into the bed, and, without knowing it, the man has intercourse in 'the hole where her nose used to be.'* (Chelmsford Prison, Essex, 1953, with the notation "Narsty Bit of Business.") The oldest form collected dates from World War I: *'During the war, when lights were dim, a warrior met a "bird"* [immoral woman] *near Victoria Station. He escorted her to her room on the fourth floor. There she lit a lamp. "Good god," he shrieked, "you haven't got a nose!" "Mighty fastidious, ain't yer, fer two bob?" sneered the lady. "I suppose yer expects ther Belle Otero!"'* (Kimbo, *Tropical Tales*, 1925, p. 80. "La Belle Otero": a fashionable actress-prostitute of the turn of the century.) Observe that no intercourse is achieved here, all the horror being supposed to arise from the mention of the missing nose in the face ravaged by syphilis.

Among numerous other remarkably clear touches in the original American version, showing that the Oedipal situation of the joke was just under the threshold of the teller's consciousness, if not actually conscious, is the candid identification of the hero as a virgin boy. The woman lying upstairs sick in bed – who calls the boy 'Sonny' – is practically the standard mother of glozed Victorian fiction. Note that she appears in the same way, sick and dying (though still young and beautiful), in Henry Monnier's *"Diligence de Lyon,"* the prototype of the famous "Sleeve Job" or "Little Japanese Railroad Train" story, where the searcher after the ultimate thrill or speciality – as here the boy's first thrill – actually gets into bed with the dying woman, who, *alone of all the women in the world*, is able to afford him this thrill. But, of course, she dies before he learns what it is! The full text of this recitation is given in English (except for the punch-line) in the First Series, 8.III.3, page 509–12, as "The Sleeve Job," and should be looked up. It is one of the high-points of the whole repertory of dirty jokes in our society. As to the essence of the story, and all such 'mystery' stories, or riddles in folktale form, it should be obvious that there is only one woman, *alone of all the women in the world*, who can do something for a man that no other woman can. That woman is the mother who gave him birth.

Finally, the mother must die. Not only in the stories, but in reality. Perhaps that is why these stories exist, still searching, under the mask of hideousness, for the unachieved incest. And, as foretold in Monnier's *"Diligence de Lyon,"* the son climbs into bed with the dying mother – brave in the face of her hideous disease and old age, as he was cowardly in the years of her youth and freshness. Nothing more clearly demonstrates who the woman really is and remains, for all the whorishness and hideousness and disease insisted upon, than this matching insistence upon having intercourse with her at the hour of death ... and after. Even the odor of death has already been encountered in stories of this kind, assimilated to that merely of feces, in the joke on – as always – *The old woman who has been 'pressed into service' in the brothel, and, when the client objects to her horrible smell, she must finally confess: "I'm too old to come, so I shit."* No detail of the standard gruesomeness of death is spared in these stories, in the defiling of the mother. We *fear* the dead human being, whereas a dead cow's carcass in a butcher-shop, or a plucked, trussed, dead chicken is delicious because we are going to eat it.

The oral-incorporative contradictions here are played for all they are worth in a satirical science-fiction novel, *The Space Merchants* (1953) by Frederik Pohl and C. M. Kornbluth, a terrific parable of consumer capitalism, exploring the problems of the population-explosion a hundred years from now. The most luxurious flat is the size of a cupboard. All mass-produced food is synthetic, except water, and even that is laboratory-synthesized by atomic desalination of sea-water. Only the richest gourmets can hope to taste real meat or 'natural proteins.' (The obvious solution, of cannibalism – "*Eat the Old People!*" – does not seem to have been arrived at yet in this utopia.) The major source of protein is *'Chicken Little ... a grey-brown, rubbery hemisphere some fifteen yards in diameter that started as a lump of heart tissue. Dozens of pipes ran into her pulsating flesh.'* This cancerous tumor has a *'master slicer'* called Herrera: *'He swung a sort of two-handed sword that carved off great slabs of the tissue ... Chicken Little grew and grew, as she had been growing for decades. She didn't know any better than to grow and fill her concrete vault and keep growing, compressing her cells and rupturing them. As long as she got nutrient, she grew. Herrera saw to it that she grew round and plump, that no tissue got old and tough before it was sliced, that one side was not neglected for the other.'* Chicken Little, *'multiplying cancerously in the basement,'* is then retailed to the public by means of the usual scientifically religious advertisements: "*From the sun-drenched plantations of Costa Rica, tended by the deft hands of independent farmers with pride in their work, comes the juicyripe goodness of Chlorella Proteins ...*"

But the absolute and complete limit in the way of defiling the mother-image, whether by oral incorporation or after death, is hardly sexual at all. This last outpost is reached, forever, in a brief short-story appearing in the final issue of the 'underground' mimeographed poetry magazine, *Entrails* (New York, February 1967) No. 3: p. 87–90: a story entitled "Butterballs" by Fred Dawson. This is marked as having been given a special cash award by the magazine's editor, Gene Bloom, who was at the time awaiting jail sentence for having been 'busted [arrested] in Grand Central Station passing 32 pounds of pot for literary purposes.' (New York newsletter by Eric Oatman, in *Small Press Review*, El Cerrito, Calif. 1967, No. 1: p. 17. 'Pot' is the current euphemism for marijuana or hashish.) Dawson's "Butterballs" was evidently intended to go one better, or worse, over the literary horror-success of the decade, Hubert Selby's *Last Exit to Brooklyn* (New York: Grove Press, 1964). I have been present at the reading aloud of the main murder-rape scene from this novel before a large audience of university professors and their wives, in La Jolla, California, 1965, by a visiting professor (who had just published an article attacking obscenity, in *Harper's* magazine: this was read aloud as his sample of *what he was opposed to* ...) without anyone apparently being shocked except myself. It seems likely, therefore, that no one will be shocked by Mr. Dawson's *tour de force* either.

"Butterballs" concerns a boy about to give an injection of morphine to his mother, who is dying horribly of breast cancer, in order to reduce her suffocating pain. The mother's sores and lesions are as carefully described as in the depictions of those of the crucified Jesus in Grünewald's notorious altarpiece at Isenheim; and her pain in the terminal stage of the disease that is killing her is compared by the author to 'lying on a bed of white hot coals and having molten lead flow through one's veins.' This is again in the style of the descriptions of hellfire from the pulpit over the last several centuries – the Protestant verbal version of the physical tortures allowed to the Catholic torturers of the Inquisition. As will be seen, incest with the mother on her death-bed is not enough for Fred Dawson's hero, but hardly more than an appetizer:

He pulled down the sheets and ripped away her night-gown, stained by the fluids that drained from her body in ceaseless flow. He bent and turned her over, for the only place she could now receive an injection was in the buttocks.

He was nauseated by the decay smell her body gave off. He paused. She certainly was a revolting sight to behold, with all her tumors and her sallow hue. One of her breasts had been removed by surgery a year ago, the other was puffed up, lumpy with tumors, and covered with ugly holes from which a puss-like fluid ran.

He took up the syringe and flask, and was about to load up with morphine, when he again paused. She was writhing in agony now, squirming in the sheets like a beheaded chicken, flapping like a fish, smearing the sheets with her discoloring fluids. Then both her bladder and her bowels, with noise and stench. The bed was filled with a pool of her thin, watery excrement.

Bill put down the syringe. Quickly he went to the door to make certain the others hadn't returned. Then he hurried back to the bed, slipping out of his trousers and shorts. His penis stood out its full length. He mounted his mother and started working his penis between her bony legs. A purplish fluid was excreted from her vagina, evidence of the cancer's attacking that part of her.

He forced his cock into her all the way, shoving it in and out rapidly, while his mother screamed and writhed in hideous torment. His lips found her breast, where he had sucked milk as an infant, and from which he now drew only the deadly fluids of her ailment. He came, spurting his semen into her cancerous womb.

But this wasn't enough. His hunger wasn't appeased. He started biting into her breast, chewing at the tumors, sucking the vile, bitter juices of decay. Then he succeeded in breaking the skin, and with his teeth he ripped the flesh. His mouth closed on a tumor the size of an egg. Twisting his head violently he wrenched it free, chewing the tough, unpleasant substance and swallowing it. Then he went after more. They were of all sizes; her flesh abounded in them.

With his fingers he ripped away her skin, tore open her stomach, smashed into her thorax, stretched into her womb [n.b.] And everywhere he probed he found more malignant tumors – the supply seemed inexhaustible. No sooner could he gulp one down than his profane, probing, ripping fingers would find another. He could not make his jaws work fast enough.

Then, filled up to the gills, he called it quits. "I just hope the fuck I don't get sick," he said. Then he took up the syringe and administered to himself the shot of morphine.

This is the end of the story. By not getting 'sick,' the boy is referring not to disease, but to the nausea that would deprive him of his Last Supper. The final gag – it is intended as a joke, or a humorous punchline to the story – is derived from a well-known vaudeville stage 'bit of business' in which: *A person who has fainted is to be given a drink of whiskey or brandy. After several false starts, the person administering the liquor ends by drinking it himself.* This always gets a laugh. Note that the oral incorporation of the mother's diseased body is intended here as presumably the next or final thrill after incest and necrophily, which are plainly stated not to have 'appeased' the son's hunger. Yet one may doubt whether the real meaning is not, instead, the taking of an oral-sadistic revenge against the mother for the unforgivable sin of *dying*, and leaving the son without her. This kind of unconscious revenge is certainly the implication of a much more sentimental account of a woman's death by cancer, published as a memorial to his recently dead wife by a millionaire author at his own expense (offset from typewriting, in *The Independent*, New York, Sept. 1969, No. 191: p. 21), and giving all her childhood pictures, the story of their life together, etc. The woman, who suffered massive agony for months, was refused all narcotics until the very last day on crackpot medical grounds. Her deathbed scene is for some reason described in exact anatomical and rectal detail: *'We kissed again. It was about* 11:30. *At* 12:30, *she called to the nurse, "Would you wipe me, please?" She had begun to hemorrhage from the rectum ... By the time [the doctor] hurried into the bedroom, she was sitting in a pool of blood and there was a gurgling sound in her throat. "She's dying," the nurse said ... I was hugging her to me and kissing her cheek. "I love you! I love you! Don't leave me!"'*

When the mother-figure has died, no indignity is too great for the son to heap upon her in anger. Whatever the reticences of fiction and autobiography (as above), jokes recoil at nothing. Flies, worms, and maggots are present at the wake. *'A chap about to enjoy a prostitute first enquired how much she would charge, and on being informed "half-a-crown," wondered what sort of a crib it would be for so inconsiderable an outlay. Having persuaded her to let him look before he leapt, he was so taken aback by what he saw that he could only gasp, "Maggots!" "What the blazes do you expect for half-a-crown," she sneered, "silkworms?"'* (Chelmsford, Essex, 1953.) This type of punchline has already been seen more than once – always turning on money – and all the sexual forms are probably connected, since all involve an optical examination of the female pubic hair or genitals, as in the children's story ending *"Turls?!"*

The straight sex-hate versions add another of the attributes of death circulating about the frightening female genitals. *A beautiful but obviously bleached blonde is sitting watching a ball game. Enthralled, she forgets to keep her knees crossed. In the bleachers below, two men are looking up her skirt. One asks, "How come that blonde has such dark pussy-hair, do you suppose?" "Pussy-hair, nothing!" snorts the other. "That's flies!"* (Paris, 1954.) This was told by the American Negro novelist, Richard Wright, in the presence of numerous young white women including his wife. It should be added that it 'came up in the conversation,' as it were, by my being engaged in taking down from the singing of one of the other people present the French students' and soldiers' song on this theme or problem, a song touching it only with wry amusement, and no flies : *'Je ne suis pas curieux, mais je voudrais bien savoir, Pourquoi les femmes blondes ont les poils du cul noirs!'*

All these are obviously unreasonable, as admitted by the format of juvenile 'ignorance' or adult 'nonsense.' The ignorance or nonsense on the part of the actors *in* any joke is equal to and expresses the fear and unease on the same subjects on the part of the tellers *outside* the joke. This is the secret spring or nexus of all nonsense jokes. The story of the flies looks very modern, but is not. Thompson-Balys list it among the folktales of India, in a form continuing on to something more sinister than the mere verbal conclusion of the modern joke : *'Step-sisters scatter sugar in girl's litter so that flies congregate. Would-be bridegroom disgusted, and tells bearers to abandon her in jungle.'* (Motif K2129.3.) There is even an Estonian folktale about : *"The Flies on the Crucified Christ,"* which look like nailheads and thus prevent more nails from being driven in. But here what is nauseating is not the story itself but the mock-pious miracle intended to cover such evident morbidity, as with the *flies* on the dead body of Jesus in Grünewald's altarpiece.

Here, without any pretense of 'nonsense,' religion, etc., is the theme of the hairy flies applied or developed into the style of the ultimate defilement jokes: *'A Scotchman visiting a house of prostitution objected to the high prices, and was finally sent up to the eighth floor, where he could have it for fifty cents. He returned and, when asked, said it was all right except for the flies. "Flies?" said the madam. "Hell, those weren't flies; those were maggots. That gal's been dead two days!"'* (Transcontinental train, U.S. 1943, told by a travelling salesman, just the way that folklore insists.) Note the relationship between this and the *"Shit in the corner and bunch the flies"* scatologic catch-phrase, of which this is perhaps a further dysphemistic variant. On my asking why the number eight – Room 8, the eighth floor, etc. – so often appears in these jokes, I was given the interesting folk-symbolic explanation that *"Eight is the most female number: two holes!"* Compare its use, lying on its side, as the mathematical symbol for eternity, *i.e.* endless procreation: ∞

The same story appears in what is expected to be an even more repulsive or disgusting form, in which it is combined with cunnilinctus. *A man in a whorehouse has only half a dollar, and is told that he cannot be accommodated at that price. On pleading, he is allowed by the madam to "use the nigger girl up in the attic." Later the madam asks him with an enigmatic smile, "Well, how was it?" "It was o.k., except for the rice in her snatch." "Rice, my ass! You shouldn't have gone down on her. That was maggots. She's been dead a week, and we're waiting for the city to bury her."* (N.Y. 1939.) This was told with the self-congratulatory remark that the joke is a 'package deal,' meaning that nothing had been omitted from the attempt to make it purposely vile. Note the 'enigmatic' (*i.e.* cruel and fanged) oral-incorporative smile of the female sadist, coupled here with her blatant verbal sadism, as discussed more in detail in Cav. Mario Praz' *The Romantic Agony*, chap 4, "La Belle Dame sans Merci," and in my own *Love & Death*, "Avatars of the Bitch," p. 58–9. (For "maggot surprise" see *The Limerick*, No. 1736.)

Also presented as a riddle, and more often as a pretended 'true' anecdote: *"Did you hear about the fellow who went down on a girl he found asleep on the beach at [a local place is named], and got a mouthful of worms?"* The teller then explains – if there is anyone left to listen – *"She'd been dead for three days."* (N.Y. 1940; and heard again in La Jolla, Calif. 1965, from a male surfboard enthusiast – or 'beach-bum' – who insisted that it had happened behind one of the large rocks, right on the beach where we were standing. When I told him that I didn't believe him because I had heard it before, he 'topped' it with: *"did you ever hear about the two maggots that were fucking in dead Earnest?"*) 'Surfers' need to have a whole study made of their peculiar habits. For a beginning, see Ed Sanders' *The Family* (1970), on the Manson torture-&-murder gang, and occult adjuncts. Also, on the normal sexual aspects of surfing, and 'beach-boys' as male prostitutes, James Michener's broad historical novel, *Hawaii* (N.Y. 1959) p. 818–41. As the ultimate thrill, in the fictional presentations of Krafft-Ebing – Aleister Crowley's *White Stains* was already stated to be such an attempt, in Swinburnian verse, in 1898 – there is David Gurney's *The Necrophiles* (New York: Bernard Geis, 1969), a vile concoction inspired by the British Moors Murders, where the victims were children.

Necrophily and cannibalism are the end-points to which all the jokes on these themes (and related 'occult' practices) are tending. As with all such stories, they concentrate excessively on the *old age* of the diseased or otherwise undesirable woman or prostitute made use of sexually. Obviously, being *dead* is the oldest age anyone gets to. The following is frequently presented as the 'most disgusting' story the teller knows. *'Three men and a woman were cast away on a desert island. After three days the woman felt so guilty she committed suicide. After three more days the men felt so guilty they buried her. After another three days they felt so guilty they dug her up again!'* (N.Y. 1952, from manuscript.) Note the insistence on the 'male' number three, overdetermining the guilts and uncertainties clearly felt to be somehow less than male, and as inevitably leading to homosexuality – which is rather close to the truth. This is even more clear in versions where there are three women as well as three men, but the women feel guilty anyhow about their Paradisiacal idyll and all commit suicide, leaving the men to be homosexuals together. Also, it is obvious that the necrophily is being rationalized or excused as, after all, less 'guilty' than the homosexual intercourse to which the men (who have buried the woman) find themselves driven at the third turn of the screw. All the horrid details of the necrophily

– both before, and after, burying the woman – are carefully omitted, and are left only to the imagination of any listener who cares to pursue the matter that far, or who is forced to do so by the continuing intrusion of these gruesome images upon his mind *after* listening to the joke. (Oral rape, with the 'voice as phallus.') The whole concern of the joke itself is very singularly with *increasing levels of guilt.*

'Ghoul' stories of this kind are not common in joke-form in the West, though several such tales appear in the *Arabian Nights* and other Levantine sources. (A mere 'quickie' : *Two ghouls in a graveyard: "Let's dig up a coupla girls." – Grim Hairy Tales*, 1966, p. 30.) However, it is of extreme significance that the greatest success achieved over the last half-century in the emotionally diseased genre of the 'horror movies,' in both America and Europe, has been the "Dracula" story originally made into a novel, on an authentic historical original, by Bram Stoker at the turn of the 20th century. The obvious sexual tonality is always much hoked-up in these films of vampirism (and their endless sequels and imitations), beginning with the first European version, Murnau's *Nosferatu*. The American versions, as *Dracula*, concentrate on eroticized close-ups of the evil Hungarian count (or no-account) rape-biting his fainting female victims in the neck with his protruding canine teeth – which is hardly the way the actual vampire-bat operates. More recently, in the usual cheap imitation by presumably *révolté* Negroes of everything evil and aggressive in white culture (Negro "Tarzan" comicbooks, Chester Himes' Negro strong-arm detective stories, etc. etc.), there is now even a Negro Dracula film, the vampire hero being called, of course, *Blackula*.

No other jokes have been encountered in which necrophily is actually engaged in, of set purpose, by the actors in the joke. But it will not escape the reader's observation that *all* these jokes, with their purposely awful images of horror-coitus and necrophily, are certainly being 'engaged in' on purpose by the people who tell them, and by those who repeat them after having been exposed to them. (This includes the present writer, evidently.) The necrophily or horror-coitus is presented in the jokes as, at most, an accident; as something the actor has been completely unconscious of while engaging in it, and of which he expresses himself as vociferously horrified. The teller, however, is neither. *A prostitute dies during intercourse. The man runs out screaming, "My god! She's dead! What am I gonna do?!" "Now, just keep cool," says the madam, "and I'll call the coroner." "The coroner? What for? I can't fuck him!"* (N.Y. 1942.) Again the maniacal persistence about engaging in or completing such intercourse, even after the woman's death, as with the *"Diligence de Lyon,"* but with the attempted ludicrous 'turn-off' here into nonsense, of the actor's pious rejection of imagined homosexuality. Essentially the identical excuse or rationalization as in the joke preceding.

The same joke is also told, combining almost all the elements that have already been dissected out, including the final attempted descent into 'pure nonsense', here of a strikingly oral-sadistic kind, but with the exceptional touch of its concerning a beautiful young prostitute, rather than a diseased and hideous old one. This is perhaps due to its provenance, and may have represented the teller's own self-image, as will be seen. *A man goes to a whorehouse, but has only fifty cents. He is led (nevertheless) into a magnificent room, lined with satin, with a gorgeous naked blonde lying on the bed. He pounces on her, and begins making love to her. She starts foaming at the mouth, and he runs out of the room screaming. He finds the madam in the parlor, and shouts, "Do something! The girl in 721 is foaming at the mouth!" "Calm yourself," she says, "calm yourself." She turns to the telephone, and dials. "Hello, City Morgue? Send over another girl – this one is full up."*

This story was told by a young career-girl in 1963, who told it in a rapid and compulsive way and with a fixed smile. She stated that she had heard it ten years before, at a girls' high-school in one of the tougher sections of New York City, in her early 'teens. The story cannot really mean that the girl had been filled with semen, from the bottom up, and more likely refers symbolically either to dislike for the semen, in fellation, or to the frothing at the mouth of epileptic seizures. (These can usually be controlled by taking magnesium and vitamin B-6 daily.) Owing to the line stating that the man 'pounces' on the girl, I interrupted the teller to ask if that was how she personally felt about these things, or if that was just the way the story had to be told. *"It has to be told that way,"* she said, and hurried on with her terrible story.

It has seemed worthwhile to give so intensive a treatment, perhaps disproportionately, to this segment of the subject of dirty jokes, because it is just this segment which is hardest for the usual audience to accept, and which is intended by the tellers to be impossible to accept. Once understood, not as the venereal-disease jokes they pretend to be, but as food-dirtyings and fecal dirtyings in *the attempt to defile the image of the hidden mother*, these jokes do not really seem very frightening, or even disgusting, but somehow pitiful. They are the folk equivalent of the modern decadent art (Surréalist) attempts to milk 'black humor' and bile out of the classics, by painting graffiti moustaches on such accepted neo-Virgins as Leonardo da Vinci's "Mona Lisa" and "Whistler's Mother," or by setting travesty dialogue-captions under classics like these.

One must want to get back to the mother very much, to be willing to get back to her disguised as a sort of mad Jack-the-Ripper with an erection, while disguising her, in turn, as a rotting corpse. *Camera:* – The scene that Buñuel and Fellini and Mai Zetterling forgot – a small child (boy or girl, or somewhere between) beating at the mother's breasts out of spite, with violently clenched little fists, and teetering up shakily on tiptoes; vomiting on her belly in the agony of rejected love and fear, and shrieking convulsively, *"See how bad I am? See how bad I am? Well then,* HATE *me, if you can't love me! Hate me!!"*

13

CASTRATION

THE FREQUENT occurrence of ghastly images, horrible accidents, genital injuries and mutilations – in a word, the castration theme – in 'dirty' jokes and poems known to men and women in our culture, and particularly transmitted among adolescents, requires a word of explanation as to the function of sexual humor. This subject is studied in greater detail in the Introduction to the First Series here, which might well be consulted now.

The ordinary dirty joke (or limerick, or ballad) engages directly, and apparently therefore pleasurably with taboo themes: sex, scatology, incest, and the sexual mocking of authority figures, such as parents, teachers, policemen, royalty, nobility (Englishmen), clergymen, and gods. The telling of dirty jokes, like the whispering of bawdy words to strange women or the chalking of genital monosyllables on walls, can also serve – as Freud has shown in *Wit and the Unconscious* – as a sort of vocal and inescapable sexual relationship with other persons of the desired sex: verbal rape or verbal seduction, depending on the gross clarity of subtle indirection in the telling of the joke.

There is, however, an entirely different function that the retailing of obscenities performs. For this function, the grosser the vocabulary and the more horrible and excruciating the actual content of the joke or poem, the better it seems to serve. The purpose here is to absorb and control, even to slough off, by means of jocular presentation and laughter, the great anxiety that both teller and listener feel in connection with certain culturally determined themes. A non-sexual example of this technique would be the "My Most Embarrassing Moment" columns vying for popularity with the "Clever (*i.e.* unrepressed) Sayings of Children" in newspapers, where the anxiety allayed is concerned with socially rather than sexually taboo behavior.

In our society, the Judaeo-Christian middle-class society of the last five hundred years, the really fearful themes are, above all, venereal disease, homosexuality, and castration. Since homosexuality is, basically, an escape from sexual (incestuous) situations felt to involve danger of castration by the jealous parent *of the same sex*, while venereal disease is conceived of as a punishment for similarly taboo sexual acts, the current themes of really fearful nature narrow down identically to one : castration.

Scatological themes, which will be treated in the chapters following, clearly fall into the anxiety-laden group too, if only from the dysphemistic grossness of their vocabulary and the graphic images employed. The significant difference between the verbal sadism of the 'nasty' or scatological joke, and that of the castration joke, is in the effect sought to be produced. The purpose of the 'nasty' or scatological joke is to shock. The purpose of the castration joke is to reassure, though its images may be just as nasty and shocking as those of any other. When medical students spread their lunches among the partly cut-up cadavers – as folklore has it that they do – and try to drive out retching the newest members of the class, by means of a long and detailed appetizer-story about, for instance, two hungry bums fighting for the possession of a bottle of snot (or tuberculosis sputum, thrown from a train, as in chapter 12.IV.5, preceding), the purpose – like the purpose of most surgical humor – is clearly sadistic, and not at all, as rationalized, to inure the new student to the horrors of his profession. But when crop-headed young fraternity brothers in engineering or the arts sit down to a late evening bull-session – with the homosexual sub-stratum of 'just among us boys,' *bien entendu* – to swap castration and vagina-dentata stories (told and sworn to as actual occurrences, with a wealth of verisimilitudinous details), the purpose, just as clearly, is to reassure both teller and listener that these horrible things, though they may happen, happen only to somebody else.

Charles Doughty records, in his *Travels in Arabia Deserta* (1888) that he often heard tell of a 'fanatical, wild, cruel, malicious tribe,' *El-Kahtan*, among whom 'atrocious circumcision' was 'fabled to be used.' They were also reputed to be cannibals, drank blood, and killed tobacco-smokers – this last evidently a thrust at himself. But however far he progressed into the desert, he never could find them. (The name *Kahtan* – ed. 1936, pp. 170 and 633 – appears to be simply a corruption of the Arabic *khitan*, circumcision.) In the same way, Bronislaw Malinowski tells the tale, in *The Sexual Life of Savages* (1929) pp. 273–9 and 422–6, of the wild Amazons of the Trobriand

Islands, of whom he kept hearing from every quarter of the compass: the *yausa* weeding-women of Okayaulo in the south, and the 'rabid' nymphomaniacs of Kaytalugi in the north, who grow 'a new kind of banana,' the *usikela* (Pat O'Brien's joke about the nymphomaniac on the pulsating-banana ranch?) and who copulate with men's noses and toes – after using them up in the ordinary way – until they die. Halfway between jest & earnest, Malinowski spends several pages explaining that he could not, or was not sure he dared (p. 276) find out at first hand about these terrible, dominant women, 'the anthropologist's bugbear.'

One explanation for both Doughty's wild men and Malinowski's wild women – both castratory, it will be observed, and both with a strong flavor of practical joke in the native telling – would perhaps be that they are just over the chronological hill, not the geographical: that their legends are really to be projected into the past, as history. Of the prehistory of the nymphomaniacal Trobriand Amazons we know nothing, though it should be observed that their reported eroticism is really only a sort of *vagina dentata* attack on the dominated men, who are destroyed in this way. Of the 'fanatical, wild, cruel, malicious tribe,' *el-Kahtan*, of the Sinaitic peninsula, there may actually be an historical prototype, in the terrible Khorasmians, or Kharzimians, a semi-barbaric Asiatic people, who had invaded the Levant after they were driven from their territory east of the Caspian Sea during the 13th century by the advancing Mongol hordes of Genghis Khan.

According to G. A. Campbell's *The Knights Templars, Their Rise and Fall* (London, 1937) p. 165: 'The Khorasmians under Barbacan consisted of some twenty thousand horsemen, but so great was the fear inspired by these savages that garrisons fled at their approach, and town after town fell to them without any attempt at defence being made. The Khorasmians were believed to drink the blood of prisoners, inflict terrible tortures on the wounded and mutilate the dead [*n.b.*], and whole areas were depopulated by the terror-stricken people when the savages were reported to be in the vicinity.'

An entirely different explanation is, however, possible for both Doughty's wild men and Malinowski's wild women, suggested here for the form rather than the content of these legends. It is that castration anxieties (in patriarchal Arabia stemming from the father; in matrilocal Melanesia from the mother) often tend to be presented as *distant fact* rather than as *local humor*, thus driving off into the desert with the living scapegoat a greater freight of anxiety than a mere joke can carry. It is essentially to this that Freud refers in his great speculative essay, *Totem and Taboo* (1918), chapter IV, parts 4–7, in developing the 'totem-feast' studied in *The Religion of the Semites* by William Robertson Smith (who was dismissed from his professorship in Scotland for the 'advanced Character' of his articles on Bible criticism in the *Encyclopaedia Britannica*), into a presumed folk-memory or legend of the assassination of the 'primal father' or patriarch in the night by his assembled sons, who then *eat* the father's entire body to do away with the evidence of their crime. The Greek legends of the consecutive killing (and eating) of the father-gods Kronos and Saturn, each by his son – or vice versa! – also point to similar and very ancient guilt-ideas, for fantasies of reversing the usual attack on, or domination of the child by the father.

Only recently has the fact been discovered, which strikingly corroborates Freud's thesis, that, as noted in *The Guilt of the Templars*, p. 124, French gypsies of modern times are reported similarly to cannibalize the head, heart, *and genitals* of every seventh gypsy 'king' at a great ritual gathering after his death. These represent of course the principal elements of the life and virility of the king, and may be taken as tantamount to a total eating. There is a similar totem-feast – entirely without human elements or recollections – still celebrated among Germanic immigrants in the American Midwest, in which only products taken from the body of a pig are eaten for several days until the pig is gone. This is almost identical with the modified Semitic *camel*-eating feast described by Robertson Smith.

It is unfortunate that Freud was not aware of the even more remarkable corroboration of his thesis, documented in Jewish Talmudic legend for some two thousand years (Babylonian Talmud, tractate *Sanhedrin*, folio 70a), that the sin of Ham, the son of Noah, was not that he *saw* or even laughed at his father's drunken nakedness, as reported in *Genesis*, ix. 22, but that he castrated his father then, in order that there might be no further heirs than himself and his two brothers after the Flood to share the earth. This identifies Freud's *Ur-Vater* as Noah, to the degree that any of these human and divine individuals of so early a period, such as Noah, Ham, Kronos, Saturn, and Jehovah, can be considered to have had any historical existence at all. The legend of the castration of Noah by his son Ham, the presumed progenitor of the Negro race, is also intended to 'explain' the dark skin-pigmentation and even the protruding lips of Negroes, as well as to excuse their enslavement by the Semitic and Gentile descendants of the two good brothers, Shem and Japhet, who refused to share in their brother's crime (*Genesis*, ix. 23–27). The Biblical text insists twice that Ham – and thus all Negroes – 'shall be a servant unto his brethren.' The Arab peoples (who are Semites) have used this Biblical authority for over a thousand years to justify their slave-trading in Africa. They are still engaged in slave-trading there today.

The legend of the castration of Noah by his son is also still in oral transmission. My father, who was a butcher (of Transylvanian origin), confided it to me as a footnote on Rashi's commentary to the Bible, the same week that he broke my Daisy air-rifle in half on some pretext or other. In the very similar story of Lot and his daughters (in *Genesis*, xix. 31 ff.), there is the same theme of a father's sexual drunkenness among his children, this time incestuously, with his daughters – again the sole survivors of a presumed world-holocaust: the volcanic destruction of the cities of the plain, Sodom and Gomorrah. It would appear thus that Noah-Lot is the Ur-Vater of Freud's *Totem and Taboo*, which would make an interesting historical novel for Hollywood, on the new religious kick, possibly under the title *Lot and his Daughters*, or *Ol' Man Noah and his Sons*.

In what is essentially the encyclopedia of psychoanalysis, Dr. Otto Fenichel's *The Psychoanalytic Theory of Neurosis* (1945) p. 77–9, a very concise statement is made as to the psychogenesis and forms of the castration complex, which is among the most unassailable discoveries of psychoanalysis. The passage also interestingly brings into the question the matter of castration jokes and threats again children:

> Castration anxiety in the boy in the phallic period can be compared to the fear of being eaten in the oral period, or the fear of being robbed of the body's contents in the anal period; it is the retaliatory fear of the phallic period; it represents the climax of the fantastic fears of bodily damage ... it is based upon the archaic retaliatory idea of talion; the very organ that has sinned has to be punished.

However, children's surroundings meet their disposition

toward such fantastic ideas of punishment more than half-way. Many adults, upon seeing a boy masturbate, still threaten him with "cutting it off." Usually the threat is less direct, but other punishments are suggested, either seriously or jokingly, which the child interprets as threats of castration ...

In many primitive (and civilized) societies, the adult generation places restrictions on the sexual freedom of the younger generation. The initiation rites that associate sexuality with painful experience are an example of such conditions imposed upon the younger generation. It may be that in certain cultures genital injury was actually perpetrated against those who rebelled.

That adults so easily and eagerly threaten or joke about castration is, of course, an expression of their own castration complexes. *Frightening others is an excellent method of quieting one's own fears.* In this way castration complexes are passed on from generation to generation. We do not know how they came into being originally, but certainly they have a long history of development.

The extremes to which this 'easy and eager' threatening or joking about castration is taken by adults are perfectly astonishing. I was not long ago the witness to such a scene, in which a charming little boy hardly two years old was playing on the doorstep of the kitchen of a French outdoor restaurant in the Midi, whereupon the *chef* appeared, in balloon hat, white apron and all, and – by way of expressing his sincere pleasure in this unexpected visit to his kitchen – banged violently on a cutting-table three or four times with the flat of an enormous chopping-knife, about half as long as his leg, shouting ominously at the little boy (with a good-humored wink at myself): *"Allez! Allez! Je vais te couper le zizi!"* (Come on! Come on! I'm going to cut off your weewee!) The little boy fortunately did not understand that much French, but began to cry anyhow at the threatening gestures and noise. These are the real humorous and not-so-humorous threats to be understood, behind the apparent over-statement of the tailor cutting off the little boy's head with an enormous shears, for mocking him, in Wilhelm Busch's children's book, *Naturgeschichtliches Alphabet* (about 1880), reproduced in the final "Castration Complex" issue of *Neurotica* (New York, 1951) No. 9: p. 22–3, in which a first draft of this chapter also appeared.

The most extraordinary example of such jocular threatening that I have ever encountered is all the more extraordinary in its appearance under the letterhead of the New York Institute for Advanced Study in Rational Psychotherapy, signed by the head of that Institute. It is the opening of a letter (here printed by permission) which I received from Dr. Albert Ellis, of New York, on the publication of the First Series of the present work, in connection with my contention in the Introduction there, p. 16, that: 'It may be stated axiomatically that *a person's favorite joke is the key to that person's character*, a rule-of-thumb all the more invariable in the case of highly neurotic persons.' Dr. Ellis writes, in high good humor, dated January 13, 1969, complaining of not having received the book published two months earlier:

> Many thanks for sending me along some of the printed sheets on the *Rationale of the Dirty Joke*. You might not believe it, but our ordered copy, now demanded for the second time around, STILL has not arrived!!! We get a great discount on all new books from one of the booksellers here, and send him lots of orders. Within a few weeks, about 80% of the books arrive ... Yours has twice been in the missing 20%, but we'll get it yet, if we have to slice off his cock s-l-o-w-l-y. Anyway ... *My* favorite joke, incidentally, is the one about *the girl who says to her girlfriend about a goodlooking male: "Don't you think he has a beautiful profile?" "Don't be silly,"* *the girlfriend replies, "that's only his keys."* I must admit that it says something about my basic character in at least *one* respect: I delight in remarks, ideas, statements, and jokes that are short and sweet. But if you and the goddamned Freudians think that my preference for this joke indicates my concern about the size of my pecker, think again! It's not exactly a twelve-incher, but few of my girlfriends have found that it fell short of their hopes and expectations.

I don't know about Dr. Ellis' favorite joke, but this is surely my favorite fan-letter, goddamned Freudian as I may be. My only question is: what would *Irrational* Psychotherapy be like?

Though the present work is in principle limited to the folklore of jokes, the examples cited here will begin with castrations told of as absolute fact, proceeding to those admitted to be jokes. More 'true' anecdotes which are demonstrably false (on the evidence of their being continuously collected in various localities, with entirely changed local names and places) are told on the subject of castratory accidents, to both men and women – usually together – than on any other sexual theme except the attribution of homosexuality to famous artistic and political figures on no evidence. I am myself accused of just this type of fake-folklore retailing, or sexual gossip, in the sentimental-*cum*-snide presumed biographical sketch of me, "The Last Cause," by John Clellon Holmes, in *Evergreen Review* (New York, Dec. 1966) No. 44: p. 98–9, reprinted in his *Nothing More to Declare* (1967), which states for example that I am a 'walking dossier of scandalous info about the sex habits of politicians, actors, and Roman Catholic Cardinals' – what! no Popes? – and that I once described Shakespeare in conversation 'as hardly more than "a talented fruit".' (But then who would believe me if I said he was untalented?)

As in the 'true' tales, an obvious gradation can be seen in the jokes too, from those accepting the castration, to those evading or denying it. The usual evasion is to mingle the castration with nonsense, or to have it happen only to persons of 'inferior' but sexually-envied races, such as Jews and Negroes. Finally the jokes grossly overcompensate, with tales involving the same protagonists – man and doctor, usually – but all the humor centering about the excessive and inconvenient length, rather than the incontrovertible absence, of the penis. Whether or not the same relief from castration anxiety is available in jokes about having no penis and about having too big a penis, I do not know. That both are castration jokes seems clear. Limericks, ballads and folksongs (such as "The Bastard King of England"), toilet epigraphs, and folk customs and survivals concerned with castration have almost entirely been omitted here, and could easily form a study by themselves. The typical jokes and 'true tales' given, from the several hundred available in *Anecdota Americana* (both series, 1:1928 and 2:1934) and other printed and oral sources, are presented in the simplest possible form, with no attempt to make the material funny. The motto here could be the superb line attributed to a British 'officer & gentleman,' during the wars against the African Negroes in the 19th century (or the Boer War), when his troops found laughable the contortions of enemy soldiers struck with the then-new expanding *dumdum* bullet: *"Don't laugh, boys, the poor fellows are dying."*

I. VAGINA DENTATA

1. PENIS CAPTIVUS

Although extremely uncommon in medical literature, and even
there half the reports are pre-scientific (see George Gould &
Walter Pyle, *Anomalies and Curiosities of Medicine*, 1896,
p. 512), anecdotes are continuously told as true among American boys and men of cases of *penis captivus*. In its commonest
form: *A girl's vagina tightens in spasm at the backfire of an
automobile in Lovers' Lane, or in the sudden glare of the captain's searchlight on the top deck of an ocean liner* [*i.e.:* "God
sees all hidden sins"], *imprisoning the man inside her until a
veterinary can be summoned to separate them, usually with
calmative injections in the small of the back, of either the girl
or man.* This was reduced to print in an American erotic novel,
The Oxford Professor [New York, 1950?] p. 103–7, chapter entitled 'Tenacious Theresa,' with the father-image a backfiring
truck: the form of this equally tenacious legend suddenly appearing as a wildfire rumor among the students at the University of Michigan at Ann Arbor, in the Winter of 1935/6, with
exact details in the telling as to the very place where the lovers
'were found' in the university Arboretum.

The presence of the *veterinary* in such stories suggests that
one element in the transmission of this fantasy is simply the
observation of dogs locking in coitus. Accordingly, cold water is
sometimes thrown on the unfortunate pair, or cold compresses
applied, instead of the more scientific and 'castratory' lumbar
injection. This is a particular terror to men (as often observed
in the army) with pronounced castration anxieties, who
identify such injections as a combined form of the feared
castration and subsequent pedicatory rape (when they have
been 'made into a woman') by the father-doctor.

Two classic forms of the preceding castratory 'true tale' are
given in Vance Randolph's great Ozark manuscript collection,
Pissing in the Snow, Nos. 8 and 79. Randolph observes of both
of these that they are 'always related as the truth, usually a
recent occurrence, with names and dates,' though he had
heard both tales 'a dozen times' and 'in a dozen other villages
in Missouri, Arkansas, and Oklahoma.' The male form, No. 8,
"Billy Fraser Got Stuck," is the standard form, similar to the
text just given above, but it is notable for the intrusion into it
of the actual castratory threat against the boy, here made by

the girl's father. The female version of the Ozark legend is given by Randolph as No. 79, "Cora and the Bottle," p. 223-5, noting that: 'It is always given as a true story, with the name of some local girl.' I have also collected it numerous times in cities of the Eastern United States, though never in quite so highly ornamented a version:

One time there was a wealthy family named Wilson that lived in this county, and they had a pretty daughter about sixteen years old. Lots of boys wanted to go with her, but Cora wouldn't have nothing to do with them. She says they ain't good enough for her, and the whole Wilson family acted like they thought Cora's shit didn't stink.

It was a Saturday morning when old man Wilson come a-riding into town, and he looked plumb worried. Pretty soon Doc Holton got into his buggy, and followed the old man home. Everybody seen Doc's rig a-standing in front of the Wilson place pretty near all day. The word got around that Cora had took sick, but nobody knowed what was the matter with her.

After while the folks found out that Cora has been screwing herself with a beer bottle, and all of a sudden she couldn't get the bottle out. It was the suction that done it. Cora got scared, and begun to holler so loud she roused the whole neighborhood. The womenfolks all pulled hard as they could, but the bottle never budged. They was afraid to bust it for fear the glass would cut Cora's cunt, and maybe she'd be jill-flirted [*everted uterus*] for life. So finally they had to send for the doctor.

When Doc got there he says for them to drill a hole in the glass, because soon as you let in a little air the bottle will slip out easy. But the Wilsons didn't have no tools to bore a hole in glass. They tried files, and emery-dust, and the blacksmith's drill, and glass-cutters, and strings soaked in kerosene [*to be set alight, n.b.*] and God knows what-all. Finally the glass cracked on one side just a little bit, and then Doc pulled the bottle out slick as a whistle.

Soon as Cora got to feeling better, Doc Holton give her some good advice. Nobody ever did find out what Doc said, but pretty soon she married one of them long-peckered Bradley boys. Him and her never did get along very good. But it is better than sticking a beer-bottle up your cunt, anyhow. (*Siloam Spring, Arkansas*, 1930.)

2. 'TOOTH-BREAKER'

All the sexual blame is projected here on the bottle, the girl being ostensibly the victim. Yet there is no real attempt to disguise the revenge nature of the story, punishing Cora for thinking herself too good for the local boys, and because her family 'thought Cora's shit didn't stink.' Actually, tales of this type are *the reply to the vagina dentata,* as with the 'Tooth-Breaker' stories collected in folktale form – among the American Indians and elsewhere. 'Tooth-Breaker' appears in cultures where *vagina dentata* stories are still told in their primitive simplicity as of a race of Amazonian women (sometimes the original 'mothers of men,' showing the deepest historical meaning of the legend), who have actual teeth in their vagina, which must be broken by the culture-hero 'so that women will be harmless to men.' These vaginal teeth are displaced upward as the *spears* of the Amazons, or female warriors, the last form of the legend, whose removed breast – presumably self-removed, to make their shooting of the bow more exact! – is perhaps a reminiscence of the activity of 'Tooth-breaker.' (Motifs A1313.3.1 and F547.1.1, with references.)

Randolph gives a further story, No. 21, "The Half-Wit and the Eel," collected in Berryville, Arkansas, in 1953, from a man who said he had heard it in the same vicinity in the 1890's. Here 'Tooth-Breaker' openly appears, in the character of the local half-wit, or sacred fool, who is noted to be 'long-peckered' – a standard attribute of the fool *or priest* in many cultures, as will be indicated in the following section "Negroes and Jews." (Note also the similar slur against the evidently low-class Bradley boys in "Cora and the Bottle.") *'One time a rich man's* [sc. king's] *daughter got to playing with a live eel, and she lost it in her.' The scapegoat or half-wit is then persuaded by the rich man* [or king], *for a payment of ten dollars* [purse of gold], *to draw the eel out of his daughter's vagina by allowing it to bite hold of his penis during unsuspecting intercourse with her.* Perceau's *Histoires Raides* (1929) p. 37, has a French version, also with an eel, attempting weakly to turn this into a joke with a verbal punch-line. This is Thompson's Motif K1222, in which a woman puts another toothed fish, the pike, into her vagina to intimidate her 'importunate lover.' (*Russian Secret Tales,* No. 13; rationalized in *Kryptádia,* IV. 193, 315.)

In Howard S. Levy's extremely valuable annotated translation of *Korean Sex Jokes in Traditional Times* ("*Kogum soch'ong,*" by Cho Yong-am, orig. published in Seoul, 1962; transl. Washington, 1972) p. 14–15, a similar story is given of : *A widow into whose vagina a mouse accidentally runs, later biting the penis of her lover.* A folksong on the same rationalized 'mouse' theme exists in English (in late editions of Burns' *Merry Muses*), but here there is no mention of the harming of the man's penis with the displaced vaginal teeth. In Levy's earlier *Sex, Love and the Japanese* (Washington, 1971) p. 65, he notes both Taiwanese and Norwegian versions in which the woman's vaginal teeth – either her own or those of a *herring* – are finally worn down or 'fall out,' after killing or frightening various suitors. Even more displaced and rationalized are the vaginal teeth in two Korean stories (1972) p. 113–16, in which, as in Boccaccio's *Decameron*, Day VII, Tale 9 (Motif J2324): *A prostitute gets her client to pull out a tooth [!] to give her as a memento. When he tries to get it back he finds that she has a whole bag filled with clients' teeth, and she tells him contemptuously: "I don't know which one is yours, so you'll have to pick it out yourself."* Here we see very clearly the naïve folktale anti-heroine of the *vagina dentata* (her own, or a set of false fish-teeth) changing into the modern bitch-heroine, who is the identical castrator but by different means – not yet *very* different in the toothpulling Korean whore.

The intermediate form is the standard figure of the bitch-Queen of Sheba, the shrew, whose 'taming' is the subject of grisly folk-humor in Italian and English, as in "The Curst Wife Lapp'd in Morel's Skin" (Child Ballads Nos. 277–278, with inadequate headnotes; see Tale Type 901), a matter much softened in Shakespeare's *Taming of the Shrew* by 1594. A contemporary stall-ballad of the same title does not mince matters, but shows the shrew's husband boldly as 'Tooth-Breaker,' who has his male friends bind his wife to a post while he cuts her 'under the tongue,' and pulls out one of her teeth 'with a payre of pinsers strong,' threatening to do the same to 'hir toung and all.' This is sung without self-consciousness by Ewan MacColl on his gramophone recording with Peggy Seeger, *The Paper Stage* (London : Argo, 1968, ZDA-98. The text is printed in Joseph Ritson's *Ancient Songs and Ballads*, 1820, II. 242, noting a similar Scottish "Ballat of Matrimonie.") This actual barbaric practice still exists among young Italian gangsters in America : see my *The Fake Revolt* (1967) p. 15. Without bothering with any excuse of curing shrewishness, the French 'black-humor' magazine *Hara-Kiri* goes the whole distance on this in its issue of October 1974, with a cover-illustration in color stating that it plans to "Demystify Sex." It shows 'Tooth-Breaker' in his final disguise as *a fierce-eyed surgeon holding up and thrusting bloodily at the reader a woman's complete, torn-out genital anatomy: vagina, uterus, ovaries and dripping adnexa, with caption: "That's all there is to it!"* Jack the Ripper's specialty: the total Pornography of Violence.

While waiting for 'Tooth-Breaker' to appear in his anti-feminist avatars (Henry Miller, Hemingway, Mailer, etc.) in literature, he appears again in what must be his last frankly genital reincarnation in Randolph's Ozark folktale, *Pissing in the Snow*, No. 6, "Betsey and the Mole Skin," curing 'a pretty schoolmarm named Betsey' of cock-teasing. Her sexual refusal is all that is left of the primordial *vagina dentata* of the Amazonian matriarchs – or, rather, their frigid bitch grand-daughters. *'The trouble was that Betsey liked to play with his pecker, but she wouldn't let him get it in her very often ... A girl like that will run a man crazy,'* and Betsey's young man goes to the old witch-woman ('Gram French,' not stated to be a witch), who *'told him what to do; so then they killed a mole and skinned it. The fellow put the mole skin on his pecker, and it fit like a glove, with the sharp teeth sticking out in front.'* The mere touch of this makes Betsey begin to cry as soon as she *'got her hand in his britches,'* and when he lights a match and shows it to her, saying that he is ' *"going to the doctor to-morrow and have an operation,"* the schoolmarm figured he *was ruined forever, and she knowed it was all her fault.'*

This most remarkable story is stated by Randolph to have been told him in Eureka Springs, Arkansas in 1951, by an in-formant who 'heard it near Green Forest, Ark., about 1910.' It includes what are probably the most ancient survivals of any folktale ever collected from a white informant in America, in our times. The *'sharp teeth sticking out in front'* of the penis are to be seen in some of the oldest known depictions of the Devil, such as that of the Tarot cards in the Leber collection at Rouen (*Catalogue*, 1839–52, 4 vols.), and, as humor, in the illustrated *Songes drolatiques de Pantagruel* (1545), most easily available in the 1823 variorum edition of Rabelais' works, and in the complete translation of Rabelais into English by Samuel Putnam (New York: Covici-Friede, 1929, vol. III). Compare the modern 'French tickler,' or head-decorated condom of

European cultures and Japan, very similar in form and ostensible purpose – to satisfy the 'unsatisfiable' female (*i.e.* break
her vaginal teeth?) as discussed in the First Series, 7.V, page
429 – and the *ampallang* of primitive Dyaks of Borneo, which
is attached to the penis by a transverse hole cut through the
glans. The cure here of female sexual demandingness seems a
good deal worse than the disease! Or, rather, it is simply the
return of the repressed: rather than let the *vagina dentata* bite
off his penis, the man bores a hole in it himself. Self-castration
to avoid castration.

A very valuable article on the various mythic personifica-
tions of the *vagina dentata* has been published by Dr. Jacques
Schnier as "Dragon Lady," in *American Imago* (July 1947,
reprinted in *Yearbook of Psychoanalysis*, IV). These range from
the Gorgon Medusa, with fanged snakes instead of proper teeth
– as with the more primitive eels, herring, and pike-fish fought
by 'Tooth-Breaker' – but which nevertheless kill the victim by
turning him to stone [*n.b.*], to the 'Lena the Hyena' of Al
Capp's comic-strip "Li'l Abner," representing the most modern
version of the same frightening, prehistoric anti-beauty, with
the witch's inevitable castratory and protruding facial teeth.
(Repulsively illustrated in a series of drawings submitted to
Capp's contest for the 'best picture of Lena the Hyena,' in *Life*
magazine, 28 Oct. 1946, p. 14–15, which are probably the two
most disgusting pages of pictures ever printed: Fun for all the
Family!) *Vagina dentatas* – plainly drawn – which cannibalize
the entire male victim, not just his penis, are a specialty of the
new underground horror-comics or 'squinkies' of the 1970's. As
in the repellent maso-sadistic 'science porno' novels of Philip
José Farmer, anatomized by J.-F. Held in *Nouvel Observateur*
(Paris, 10 Feb. 1975) p. 40–41, with squinkie illustrations.

What may be a modified form of Randolph's sacred-fool
story, but now told simply as a joke, again presents 'Tooth-
Breaker' as a male sexual fool or 'nincumpoop' who does not
understand the mechanism of intercourse nor the anatomy of
the female genitals. *An ignorant farm-boy has been making love
to a hole in a tree.* [Apollo and Daphne, already in comedy
form in the Pyramus & Thisbe skit, after Ovid, in Shakespeare's
Midsummer Night's Dream.] *Unfortunately there is a hornets'
nest in the tree-trunk, and the hornets sting his penis. On his
wedding-night, later, he outfits himself with a heavy stick
which he thrusts into his bride's vagina, grinding it in all direc-*

tions like a pestle. She screams, and demands to know what he is doing. "Don't you worry," he says craftily, "if there's any hornets' nests in that hole, this is one time I ain't getting caught!" (N.Y. 1939.) Compare the folk-superstition, reported among children in the Bronx, New York, about 1925–30, that A boy should take a stick with him in making love to a virgin for the first time – i.e. in taking her virginity – "so she won't close up on you." (Hornet story: Tale Type 1159.)

The man who retailed this (N.Y. 1952) from his own child-hood, still suffered so powerfully from castration anxieties that, when receiving male guests in his home – I don't know about female – he would sit in a special armchair on a large pillow laid cater-cornered in the seat, continuously pulling up the front corner of the pillow to cover and protect his genital region, like the 'tail' of a baseball catcher's chest-protector up-side down. Reported sex-lecture authentically given by a British army medical officer during the World War, holding himself rigidly erect meanwhile (strangulated body-phallic type) and slashing about with a swagger-stick as he spoke, his voice tense and high with hardly-repressed hysteria (the voice of Hitler): "I don't want to mention any names," he began, almost in a scream, "but some of you men will put your pricks where I wouldn't put this stick!"

A final expression of the fantasied vagina dentata danger is perhaps the curious fish-lure, illustrated as the laugh climax in A. E. Brown & H. A. Jeffcott's Beware of Imitations! (1932), a fascinating collection of eccentric patented devices, p. 124–5, showing a naked-breasted mermaid with a three-pronged hook emanating from her pubis. (Design patented in 1928, No. 74,759.) This has since been manufactured and sold as a novelty or conversation-piece, in a catalogue of kitsch items for home 'playrooms' and cellar-bars. The World's Dirtiest Jokes (1969) p. 82 gives an interesting folktale version of the 'Tooth-Breaker' joke, with the preliminary danger posed thus: A boy attempts to have intercourse with his fiancée through a hole in the kitchen door, but the girl's father is waiting with a catfish head, 'and when he saw the thing coming in, he took the fish head and clamped it down hard. This really shook the young man, and he ran home.' The pair then marry, but the husband does not consummate the wedding for six months. When his wife finally seduces him to his marital duty, one rainy day, 'he put the end of his umbrella right on [in] her fuss box. This

startled her so much, she let a big fart. He jumped back and
said, "Bark, you son of a bitch, but you're not going to bite me
again!" ' (Motif K1222.)

This is very similar to the Russian form, "The Pike's Head,"
collected before 1865 and published in Afanasyev's *Russian
Secret Tales* (1872) No. 13, but here there is no stick or umbrella-
ferule to disarm the fish-head, this primitive weapon having
been dropped. *When the marriage is still unconsummated after
three weeks, the bride with the pike's head in her vagina asks
her husband to try again. He says, "No, you won't catch me
again. Your cunt bites!" And he ties up her legs first, so that he
can escape if necessary.* All the modern forms are in any case
but a weak echo of the earliest *vagina dentata* story in the form
of a joke or anecdote. This appears in Poggio's *Facetiae* (MS.
1451) No. 170, and is outfitted in Liseux' English translation
(Paris, 1879) II. 77-9, with a record number of words *not* translated from the Latin, as though the translator were himself a
bit disturbed by the story:

> Friar Lupo (the Wolf) seduces a young maiden, who agrees
> to accept his embraces if he will put a board between them
> with a hole in it, to make sure his penis does not enter too
> far. However, the touch of the girl's genitals so excites him
> that his penis swells immoderately, 'and was like strangled. It
> was held so tight that it could neither go in nor out without
> acute suffering. The expected pleasure was converted into
> harrowing pain, and the Friar, writhing under the infliction,
> began to groan and scream. The lass, thoroughly scared,
> endeavoured to comfort him with her kisses, and to achieve
> the desired end. But the alleviation she tried to apply only
> increased his anguish, for, the greater the swelling, the more
> excruciating the compression. The luckless Friar was on the
> rack, and begged for cold water wherewith to bathe and
> reduce the tumor which tortured him.' Finally, 'the Friar,
> hearing somebody stirring about already [*in the morning*],
> felt anxious to get away, and pulled his member out of the
> board, galled to the quick.'

Though the woman hardly appears here at all, but remains
hidden behind the 'love-board' like a helpful and seductive
angel, it is obviously she who has caused and is even increasing
the man's anguish, as Poggio underlines. From this recognition
to recognizing that the hole in the board is really only her own

vagina, in its dentate aspect, is not a difficult step. Thus, whether the woman is modest and virginal, demanding the interposed bundling-board to prevent the penis from going in too far, or whether she is shown as erotically excited herself – thus causing the penis to swell further and be hurt worse – the hapless hero has been caught again by the 'cunt that bites.' Clearly it bites even against the will of the woman herself. In *The Real Gone Girls*, the third volume of Ted Mark's *The Man from O.R.G.Y.* series, an almost identical scene is played as a farce-travesty of D. H. Lawrence's *Lady Chatterley's Lover* – with a bow to Edmund Wilson's *Memoirs of Hecate County* – the hero making love to a heavy-set Greta, with passionate arse-cheeks 'like some Germanic Jell-o,' who is in a plaster cast owing to an accident. Naturally, he gets his penis caught in the hole he scrapes in the plaster, in order to get into her vagina, and cannot get out again. (The passage is quoted complete in the Introduction to Dr. Paul Tabori's *The Humor and Technology of Sex*, 1969.) Only 'Tooth-Breaker' can help here.

3. CASTRATION BY WOMEN

It is certainly more than interesting, after all these centuries or millennia of attacks on women, as dangerous to men, to be able to record the reply or *Revenge of the Vagina Dentata*. The same highly-educated and very articulate young woman, whose joke concerning the epileptic prostitute 'foaming at the mouth' concludes the preceding chapter, and who prided herself visibly on her gruelling – but, alas, her wholly verbal – sexual bravura, in which she saw herself as the equal of any man, also expressed herself with unusual candor on this subject as well.

This was the result of observing, in a seafood restaurant, the saw-toothed nasal bone or weapon of a sawfish displayed on the wall (starring in a panoply of yonijic *cypraea* shells), to which she referred, in some irritation, as a *'penis dentata.'* I refrained very carefully from making any reference to the legends of Tooth-Breaker and Dragon-Slayer, as discussed above, and to the implement they are said to have used: obviously no swagger-stick or umbrella-ferule, but just such a sawfish-sword! I think I did murmur, "*A bon chat, bon rat!*" which I felt was one-up for my sex. She then returned to the subject, after musing sullenly a while, and added with an oddly sinister pursing of her mouth intended to be passed off as a smile: "*Be reasonable. After all, what's the matter with the vagina dentata? It would be nice to get one and keep one* [referring, with a look, to the penis]. *When you eat a good meal, you don't expect to have to throw it up again right away."* Men usually refer to women's unstructured way of thinking as 'bitch-logic.' (Politely: 'women's logic' or 'feminine intuition.') Bitch-logic as it may be, this conscious reply of the *vagina dentata* is logical indeed, and worth a whole bookful of theorizing by men on oral-incorporative fantasies and the female castration complex.

The same idea is expressed, also on the framework of intended reasoning, in a joke which I have never collected in the field in just this form, and have found printed only by Mr. Newbern & Miss Rodebaugh, in *World's Dirtiest Jokes* (1969) p. 87: *Two men are arguing as to whether a man or a woman can stand more pain. The first woman they ask is a prostitute, and she replies without any hesitation, "A woman." When asked to explain she says, ' "Could you stand to have your peter pulled out of you?" Both men agreed that they couldn't. "You see," laughed the prossy; "I've had seven of them pulled out of me since suppertime!" '* Unfortunately, as this story suggests, not all men are searching for, or arguing about simple sexual pleasure. In the main 'underground' newspaper, the *Los Angeles Free Press*, issue of July 19th, 1968, all wraps are off as to male fantasies of masochistic pleasure in being castrated by a woman – a subject generally overlooked. This is a dithyrambic piece, pp. 32 and 43, on a woman pop-singer, and curiously entitled "Big Brother's Boobs," by R. E. Maxson. It is a high-point in the new and aggressive style of rock-music criticism:

Fists of erotic fury smashed at eyes and ears last weekend ... that means Janis Joplin in all her white Blackness, socking her violent sensuality toward the believers and witnesses ... it's the best kind of hype I know of, the kind I feel in my deepest height, 'cause she makes it for me, like holy mojo lips caressing the dick of my soul. Like ecstasy tongue's magic hand squeezing my thought waves ... She may look innocent, but her sound is not. It causes all her many camp followers to turn up at all her concerts, wherever they may be, to get right next to the [loud-]speakers, to dance and wiggle in total release, to dream of guitar necks ramming into their little foxey boxes, frying and curling pubic hair in everlasting orgasm ... Yea. Evil black violent sex: the most beautiful girl in the world is jacking you off – just before lovemaking's liquid treasure geysers upward and outward, she pulls out a butcher knife, grins menacingly, and ... [*Mr. Maxson's three trailing-off dots.*] Her demonic gyrations and wild-beast freneticism rip into me like the steel claws of a feline nightmare. I gladly bleed to death pleading for my utter destruction. And her voice, her booming passion-filled voice, which rolls and flows with tumultuous majesty up and down in howls, shrieks and screams, conjuring up images of evil satanic blackness, violence and sensuous sadism/masochism.

The similar male Negro singer, Jimi Hendrix, would finish his act by spraying gasoline on his guitar and burning it, while his apocalyptic *lumpen*-audience screamed with delight. Both singers died of overdoses of drugs, within a few days of each other, in September 1970. The real meaning of all these wild yoicks of low-grovelling masculinity seems to be that Janis Joplin's violent singing represented to certain Western male listeners the same fantasy identification of sex and violence, under a woman's or evil goddess' domination, as is the racial and religious dream of the Hindu male. In addition, Miss Joplin, being white, offered her white listeners the sinless fantasy-receptacle of making love to a sizzling 'nigger wench' (but actually to a big-breasted, overwhelming black mammy), Southern style, who would be simultaneously 'sweet-angel faced,' demure, and WHITE. As to the butcher knife, 'just before love-making's liquid treasure geysers upward and outward,' well ... keep your eye on the balls. An almost identical fantasy is published in another underground newspaper, the *Nola Express* (New Orleans, 25 Aug. 1973) # 138: Charles Bukowski's "Notes of a Dirty Old Man," in which *An ex-stripteaser bites a man's glans penis off and leaves him to bleed to death*, as I have complained of in the same paper (2 Nov. 1973) # 142: page 10, suggesting to the editors that they ought to be 'getting the arty-farty libertarian feces out of their blood, and cutting off [Bukowski's] free speech.' In the internationally exploited Swedish sex-movie, Vilgot Sjöman's *I Am Curious (Yellow)*, in 1967, the final scene shows the heroine gunning down her lover – her 24th, she states – then unbuttoning his pants, and castrating him with a knife. This is a 'dream sequence': take that in any sense you please. Resisting a little, Ernest Hemingway is quoted in *Fact* (Jan. 1965) II. 47, as saying of his twenty cats: '*My former wife killed some of them when she tried to castrate some of them. I kicked the living shit out of her for that one.'*

Willing victims aside, there is also castration by women when the male victims don't even know they have been elected to the chopping block. The first of the Women's Liberation organizations in America in the 1960's was announced briefly by its founder, Miss Valerie Solanas, some time before Miss Betty Friedan's NOW, in a letter in the New York *Village Voice*, stating that 'S.C.U.M., the Society for Cutting Up Men,' would shortly be getting into operation. The immediately-ensuing run on aluminum jock-straps at the local sporting-goods stores was also not diminished by the publication a year or more later of Miss Solanas' *S.C.U.M. Manifesto* (New York: Olympia Press, 1968) with an introduction interestingly assessing the author, by her publisher, M. Maurice Girodias. I have several times compared Miss Solanas with Théroigne de Méricourt, the inflammatory woman-leader and dark angel of the French Revolution, but nothing in the two paltry manuals for prostitutes attributed to Mlle. Théroigne will compare with Valerie Solanas' frankly neo-Hitlerian programme, all minutely detailed, and more in the style of Fritz Lang's motion-picture of the mad *Dr. Mabuse* than of Hitler's *Mein Kampf* that both are parodying – in this case perfectly seriously. Note that S.C.U.M. had at the time apparently only one member: Miss Solanas herself.

A small handful of SCUM can take over the country within a year by systematically fucking up the system, selectively destroying property, and murder ... SCUM will destroy all useless and harmful objects – cars, store windows, "Great Art," etc ... SCUM will couple-bust – barge into mixed (male-female) couples, wherever they are, and bust them up. SCUM will kill all men who are not in the Men's Auxiliary of SCUM. Men in the Men's Auxiliary are those men who are working diligently to eliminate themselves ... men who kill men; biological scientists ... journalists, writers, editors, publishers and producers who disseminate and promote ideas that will lead to the achievement of SCUM's goals; faggots, who by their shimmering, flaming example encourage other men to de-man themselves, and thereby make themselves relatively inoffensive ...

Simultaneously with the fucking-up, looting, couple-busting, destroying and killing, SCUM will recruit. SCUM, then, will consist of recruiters; the elite corps – the hard core activists (the fuck-ups, looters and destroyers) and the elite of the elite: the killers.

Actually, Miss Solanas had a better pitch when she was talking about castrating men, than when she threatens *merely* to kill them, if what she wanted was to scare them. To most men, the fear of castration far transcends that of death. *A man is killed in an automobile accident while joy-riding with a girl, who is also killed. He is found, at the morgue, to have no penis. After a good deal of puzzled searching, they pry open the dead girl's jaw, and find the man's penis there. The accident is then reconstructed: the girl has been fellating the man while he drove. He has driven the car faster and faster as he became more and more excited, finally losing control as his orgasm approached. The girl has bitten off his penis at the moment of his orgasm, and the resultant wrecking of the car, in which her neck has snapped and broken.* (N.Y. 1950.)

This story has been consistently collected over the years, and is always told as authentically true. In joke-forms approaching it, the man is not killed (though the woman is), and the concentration is again on 'God's punishment' for sex, by means of the accident, exactly as in hellfire works of the 17th century. *A man is berated by the state-troopers for not having strapped on his girl friend's seat belt before the accident in which she was thrown through the windshield and killed, while he is still alive behind the steering-wheel. "So what?" he says bitterly, "go take a look at what she's got in her hand!"* (L.A. 1968.) Again castration is clearly defined as the equivalent of death, or worse than death, a point that will be returned to again.

Or, the definite last word in *vagina dentatas*, told by a heart-breakingly beautiful young harpy, who stated that this obvious wish-fulfillment folktale or fantasy was positively true: *A girl's revenge against the detective who has sent her gangster-brother to jail: She has a protracted affair with him, ending one Sunday afternoon, after fellating the detective in his apartment, by stabbing into his glans penis the tip of a burning cigarette she has purposely left in an ashtray nearby; his foreskin then being drawn up over the glans and cigarette tip together by her long and evil fingers [sic], and the girl rising to her feet and leaving the apartment before the man is even able to scream!*

(N.Y. 1951.) Practically an opera libretto (I was shown, in the street, the window of the apartment house on the West Side where it positively happened), this one led immediately into the joke about the man at the urinal with the holes in his penis and the piccolo teacher (see below, under "Circumcision"), but is offered as it stands, free of charge, as the plot for Mickey Spillane's or Ian Fleming's next homo-sado-pukeo pocketbook murder-*cum*-spy job, or those of whoever will replace them – and there are plenty trying. Though obviously folklore and not fact, note well that these are the fantasies some people have, and the games they would play if they dared. YOU HAVE BEEN WARNED.

These are the castratory folktales told as true stories, or 'almost true.' Those told frankly as jokes have the embarrassment already noted, in the French and Ozark tales of 'Tooth-Breaker,' of needing to make the stated situation credible. The attempt generally fails, and recourse must be taken to the descent or escape into 'nonsense.' This is not only a technical device but tactical as well. For it has the further reassurance value of implying that the whole idea of any human or castratory danger really existing is perfectly absurd, and that it only takes place, if at all, in far-off and nonsensical places. *"Have you heard about the new game, African Roulette?"* – *"No, how do you play it?"* – *"You put your prick through a hole in the fence. Behind it are five cock-suckers and a cannibal."* (N.Y. 1953.) This is of course on the analogy of the suicidal 'game,' *Russian Roulette*, supposed to have been played by dead-end revolutionaries and blasé students at the close of the Czarist period, in which one bullet is placed in a six-shooter, the two players then passing the revolver back & forth, and firing at their own foreheads. Two other mock 'roulettes' apply the same idea to problems of birth-control: *"Vatican Roulette," the rhythm method of birth-control* (owing to the complicated calculation, other than with the basal thermometer, and general chanciness anyway); and *"Birth-Control Roulette": You shake up five aspirins and a Pill, and let your girlfriend pick one.* (Berkeley, Calif. 1966.)

In the rare stories in which castration by women is specifically described, there is generally some excuse or rationalization; 'stupidity' or sexual ignorance on the woman's part being the favorite. In Vance Randolph's erotic collection, *Pissing in the Snow, and other Ozark Folktales* (MS. 1954) No. 22, there is a story he calls "Cut Their Knockers Off!" – a line which appears nowhere in it, and which may be a clue to some of the original dialogue. This story was collected in Berryville, Arkansas in 1953, from a man who heard it 'along the Arkansas-Oklahoma border in the 1890's':

One time a fellow had a wife that was a lot younger than him, and she got to fooling with other men. So he sold the farm and moved a long way off, to get a new start where the people was all strangers. He told his wife that the folks in this part of the country didn't do no fucking, because every man was cut like a steer. And he told the neighbors that his wife had been in the lunatic asylum because she carried a little sharp knife, and would whack a man's knockers off every time she got a chance.

So that was why the menfolks kept away from the new-comer's wife, but the woman didn't care because she thought they was all geldings anyhow. But finally she got to thinking that maybe some of the young fellows has not been dehorned yet. They had a hired man that was only fifteen years old, but big and stout for his age. One night the woman went down to the shed-room where the hired man slept, and she slipped into bed with him.

The boy kind of waked up and grabbed her, before he rightly knew who it was. But the moonlight come in the window, and he seen her face. And just then the woman put her hand under the blanket, to feel whether he was cut like a steer. Soon as she done that, the young fellow was scared pretty near to death, and he jumped out of the bed. "I've heard about you!" he says. "Nobody is going to whack *my* balls off!"

The woman says for God's sake shut up, but the boy wouldn't stay in the house another minute. He run right down the road in his shirt-tail, and told it all over the neighborhood how the crazy woman tried to cut his knockers off. She had a hard time after that, because no man in the whole country would let her come within ten foot of him. So finally the poor woman just kind of give up, and got along with her old husband the best she could.

In this, which is almost the closest to actual castration by a woman in any English-language story that I have encountered – except for the equally 'true' stories about the automobile accident, and the cigarette and foreskin, told earlier – it will be observed that the woman is really the opposite of castratory. She is shrivelling on the vine of life, yearning to make love. This entire Arkansas-Oklahoma terror tale or fantasy of castration by an innocent woman is wholly concocted, is repeated by someone who swears to it as true from his personal experience (the hired boy, a misleading witness if ever there was one), then snowballing to every man 'in the whole country,' all of whom repeat it thereafter as an absolute fact. Yet it is hardly more – when the historical evidence is considered – than the trickster's device in an ancient story reported from India by Thompson, Motif K1569.6: 'Husband persuades wife to light wicks and carry knife in hand [n.b.] before committing adultery; lovers frightened away.' How this story got from India to the Ozarks in the 1890's, I do not know, but there it is.

A story has already been discussed, in the Introduction to the First Series, section III, page 21, which is of the family of the "Literal Fools" (various tale-types indexed in Aarne-Thompson, p. 568) who do exactly what they are told, with disastrous results of course. This is invariably a mock or defiance of the person giving the orders, and never more clearly than in the story here referred to, of which a very florid text is given by Dr. Alan Dundes in Southern Folklore Quarterly (1964) XXVIII. 259–61. As usually found it is the answer or pendant to the stories of another great tale-family, Type 1406: "The Merry Wives' Wager," as to which can best fool her husband. In the fool story: Three men are explaining how they have defied their wives. One was wiping the dishes and dropped one, and his wife said, "Why don't you break them all!?" He does so. The second was lighting his pipe and dropped a match. "Go ahead, set fire to the house!" his wife screamed. So he does. The third says, "Last night I said to my wife when we went to bed, 'How about a little, honey?' and she said, 'Oh, cut it out!' And say, fellows," he finishes, with an insane grin, holding out his cupped hands, "have you ever seen one of these up REAL CLOSE?" (Bloomington, Indiana, 1963.) The story does not actually specify that it is the wife's genital organ that has been castrated, but the use of 'cut it out' instead of 'cut it off' makes this rather clear, as also the husband's final display, under the catch-all excuse of mere insanity.

Dr. Dundes gives the contrasting story too, in his 1964 article, in which the husband is castrated by the wife, and notes that these two stories were collected by him at a single séance from a husband and wife, each of whom told the story about castrating the opposite spouse! In my forty years of collecting folklore, I have never had so openly significant an experience as that. The wife's story is also the main exception to the statement made just above, that actual castration by women seldom appears in stories told frankly as jokes and not as 'true'.

Such stories are the opposite of rare in limericks. Several of the most castratory examples in *The Limerick* (1953) chap. 13, "Losses," are ascribed to the actions of women – by the men who write the limericks – in particular Nos. 1136 through 1196. The first of these, ending: *"The size of my phallus, Was just right for Alice, Till the night that she bit off the knob!"* happens to have been written by a masochistic friend of mine. When I asked him why he wrote it, he said: "For the *rhyme*." The most total statement of castration by a woman is limerick No. 1371, a tremendous favorite among limerick fanciers, and endlessly collected:

> There was a young Queen of Baroda
> Who built a new kind of pagoda.
>   The walls of its halls
>   Were festooned with the balls
> And the tools of the fools that bestrode her.

Though I do not know who wrote that limerick, I am sure that if I met him and asked him why, he too would tell me: "For the *rhyme*," of which, obviously, a great deal is being made. It was when I had a bellyful of rationalizations and 'aesthetic criticism' like that, that I decided to write a book like this.

Whatever may be the cause in limericks, in jokes women are almost always put into the castratory situation simply by accident, as above, or sheer 'dumbness.' *The Indian brave goes to the big city and learns how things are done in the high-class brothels there. His voice is heard coming out of his wigwam the night he gets back: "Ugh! squaw no chewum cigar – smoke um!"* (N.Y. 1948.) A 'party-record' on sale in New York, 1942, called "The Old Rake," gives the practically classic female-fool situation in skit form: *A girl goes into a department-store to buy a rake for her lawn, but accidentally gets into the wrong department. The clerk does not understand what she wants, as she has forgotten the word 'rake,' and he pretends to misunderstand sexually everything she says, answering all her questions as though she is referring to wanting his penis. "Oh, you know what I mean," she flounders; "it has teeth on it." "Teeth?" he replies cautiously, but continuing to leer; "well, you could* put *teeth on it."*

In both of these, the reference to fellation plainly involves the fear of danger to the penis from the woman's teeth. This may be considered a rationalization of the fantasy of the *vagina dentata:* the dangerous teeth are not found in the vagina but in the woman's mouth, when using that as a vagina. Compare the case (this time authentic, though there is no way of knowing whether the accusation was true or not) of Theora Hix, the victim in a famous American murder trial of the 1920's. The defense of the murderer, Dr. Snook, was that Theora Hix had *bitten his penis* during fellation in an automobile, and that he killed her unintentionally and almost by reflex with a hammer that was lying on the floor of the car. Dr. Snook was briefly something of a folk-hero.

Other examples of 'dumb' castration, or implications or imaginings of castration, by women, are often without any actual *dentate* elements: *The boss has been out all afternoon and returns with two small balls which he puts on the desk. When the new stenographer looks at these quizzically, he says briefly, "Been out shooting golf." The next week he brings back two more golf balls. Stenographer: "I see you shot another golf."* (1:348.) Similarly: *A wife misinterprets her soldier-husband's cablegram from the war-zone,* "GOT MY D.S.O." (Dis*tinguished Service Order), as meaning "Dick Shot Off." She feels positive when she writes asking for money, and he answers:* "Go fuck yourself." (2:217.) Another wartime story, on abbreviations for army decorations – and other things – will be found at the beginning of section 12.II above, "The Biter Bit."

In all Western countries, largely inauthentic and openly travestied 'funny letters' exist, usually making fun of the illiterate spelling and syntax of the uneducated, or overeducated, as the "Babu" English of 'Wogs' (Westernized Oriental Gentlemen), once considered terribly funny by the British residents in India, Japan, etc. Compare the American Civil War 'humor of misspelling' of 'Artemus Ward' (Charles F. Browne), 'Sut Lovingood' (Geo. W. Harris: a real maniac, frothing with sadism and hatred when the South lost the war), and 'Petroleum Vaseline Nasby' (David R. Locke). Also, a century earlier, *La Pipe cassée* and the *Lettres de La Grenouillère* of

Jean-Joseph Vadé, in imitation of French fishwives' slang. In collections of letters of this kind circulated in America since the 1930's, and collected (as 'true') under the name of 'Miss Juliet Lowell' in several booklets, on the style of the World War I, *Dere Mable* by Ed Streeter (1918), one never omitted is this: *"Dere Mr. President: I ain't had no relief since my husband's project was cut off."* (Footnote for history: this is punning on 1930's political jargon in the U.S.: 'relief,' for doles for the poor; 'project,' short for Works Progress Administration Project, a governmental make-work or boondoggling activity for men receiving the dole.)

A complicated and very popular story, usually told with sound-effects of the "Rap-a-Tap-Tap" variety: *George Washington and his troops at Valley Forge have nowhere to sleep. Washington rides along with a dozen of his men, billeting them in the local citizens' houses. He knocks at the first door and is offered one bed. "All right, Peters," he says to the first soldier; "you take that one." When he knocks at the second door, an old lady sticks her head out the upper-story window in a mobcap. He explains what is wanted. "Well, how many of you are there?" she asks. "There are twelve of us," says Washington; "no, eleven – without Peters." "How about that!?" cackles the old lady.* (N.Y. 1964.) Heard much earlier as of: *Sailors asking for rooms: There are nine of us, without Peters." Landlady: "Those damn Nazis!"* (N.Y. 1950. Peters had a room somewhere else.) The wholesale reassurance-value of the woman's error is particularly clear.

A woman leaves explosive cleaning fluid in the toilet bowl. Her husband tosses in a cigarette butt while urinating. There is a tremendous explosion, and his wife rushes in to find him bleeding in the bathtub. "My God!" she screams, "where's your ear?" "To hell with my ear! Find my right arm. It's got my prick in it." (N.Y. 1951.) The same story is generally published, as very naughty, in an expurgated scatological form in which: *The grandfather is blown sky-high by an explosion of kerosene poured into the outhouse to drive away flies, when he goes in smoking his corncob pipe. He is found in the meadow by his daughter, who cries, "Grandpa! are you all right?" "Wal," he says, feeling himself all over [n.b.], "can't say I'm as good as I was."* (Minneapolis, 1940.) The punch-line still seems to allude to castration by the explosion, but is accepted as pure down-on-the-farm dialect humor or 'nonsense.' In another version he

answers: "*Well I can't say it done me real* good." In both forms
the woman has caused the castratory accident by her foolish
use of explosives in the genitally-toned toilet or outhouse. (Representing her *own* genitals, as with 'pissing in the sink'?)

A briefer automobile-accident joke has the woman carry a
similar freight of castratory guilt simply by *pointing out* the
castration: *After the automobile accident, the man and the
woman who have been joy-riding find themselves sprawled on
the ground under the wrecked car. She: "You all right?" He:
"Sure." She: "Then whose balls are those up on that hook?"* (N.Y.
1936.) The punishment element here, for petting while driving,
is identical with that in the 'true anecdote' given earlier in this
chapter. In another form, *Two Irishmen are thrown out of a
honky-tonk when they try to enter. "Wasn't I after tellin' ye
it's a tough joint?" says one. "Shure an' a tough joint it is. But
– whose balls are these I have in me hand?"* (2:105.) Observe
that they are not stated to be his own. Similar jokes in which a
wrestler bites his opponent's unguarded testicles – which always
turn out to be his own – will be seen in section 13.V, under
"Self-Castration."

British forms exist of both the preceding jokes, clearly
related: '*Chap and girl courting behind the gas works. Gas
works blow up. Girl: "George, where are my knickers?"*
[British for panties] *"Bugger your knickers! Where's your cunt?
– my cock's in it!"* ' (Chelmsford, Essex, 1953.) Note the 'Hand
of God' explosion, on the 17th-century hellfire style of "God's
Revenge against the Sins of Fornication and Adultery," in which
both actors are here castrated. The other British variant rejects
and reverses the whole castratory situation, and vindicates the
man gloriously as lover and swain: '*Just after the 1939–45 war,
'Arry and 'Arriet courting strong. Walking in the dark, arms
about one another, he with "the horn" up to his neck, she with
cunt all a-lather. He gets her up against a fence bordering some
derelict property and begins to fuck her, when the fence
collapses and she falls arse over tip into a huge bomb crater.
He calls down, "Are yer oright, 'Arriet!" "Yep, gor blimey!"
"Well, keep it goin' wiv yer fingers while I run fer a ladder!"* '
(London, 1954, supplied in manuscript on my expressing my
appreciation of the joke on hearing it told.)

A whole series of jokes exists in which the man who has
been the victim of a castratory accident mocks the woman who
dares to ask him about it by implying that she, as a woman, is

'castrated' too – and even worse! The straight version of this type of joke, without the *tu quoque* to the woman, is the latest form collected and may simply be a clean-up: '*She: "So you were hurt in the war? Where were you wounded?" He: "Lady, I was hit in the Dardanelles." She: "Oh-h-h, how dreadful!"*' (Joe "Miller" Murray, *America's Spiciest Stories*, Hollywood, 1942.) As usually collected this has the earmarks of being set up as an 'Irish bull' or improbability story, again with the intention of resolutely denying the castration at all. *Woman visitor (sometimes: The Queen) in veterans' hospital: "And where did the bullet hit you, my good man?" "Madam (Your Majesty), if it had been you, it would have missed you completely!"* (N.Y. 1939.) This is unmistakably a taunt, but Mr. Robert Graves manages nevertheless to mistake it for gallantry, owing to its verbal evasiveness, in his *Lars Porsena, or The Future of Swearing* (1927, ed. 1936) p. 20: '*The wounded soldier situation is one that has given rise to a whole anthology of prettily turned jokes, an education in perfect gentlemanliness. One popular version is: "If you had been shot where I was shot, lady, you wouldn't have been shot at all".*' (Also told as of Lincoln: "Madam, the bullet that hit him would have missed you." – D.C. 1952.)

The same situation tends toward a denial of the castration and revindication of the woman, as somehow saving the man – as will be seen. '*Early in the war* [World War II], *a Cameronian, MacPherson, stationed in France, was swimming in a stream near the Maginot Line. He stepped out on the bank, and stood there naked, then suddenly fell forward unconscious. He revived in a base hospital, where the doctor said a sniper had shot at him and hit both testicles, blowing them off so cleanly there was nothing for him to do but sew up the wound. The Scotsman scratched his head and said, "It was sure lucky for me, Doc. If I had'na been thinkin' of me wife's maiden sister at the time, I'd ha' lost me gun".*' (Berkeley, Calif. 1943, from an army sergeant, supplied in manuscript, which may explain the defective rendition of the Scottish dialect.) Randolph, *Pissing in the Snow*, No. 97, gives a much milder Ozark version, without the testicular castration or sharpshooter, collected in 1940, and 'heard near Walnut Shade, Mo., about 1916.' Very early in my own field-collecting, I spoke to a former German sniper in World War I, at that time (1934) running a small ice-cream parlor and bakery in Scranton, Pa. This man, who was actually

of Czechoslovak origin, told me with great shame and difficulty
– and without any leading questions having been asked – that
it had been the habit of his sniping group, when standing on the
firing-step with telescopic sights on their rifles, to try particularly to 'shoot off the balls' of Allied soldiers squatting on the
battlefield to shit.

In the preceding joke, the primacy of the penis is very clearly
represented, the loss of the testicles being considered hardly
any sort of castration at all, as long as the penis has been
'saved,' though actually of course it is the testicles which are
the seat of the virile character, in the endocrinological sense.
Another joke in which the man is saved by thinking of the
woman, and thus getting an erection, has already been given in
section 5.V.1, "Phallic Brag," in the First Series, p. 298–9: *The
sailor who is shipwrecked, floats on his back, thinks of his
sweetheart, ties his handkerchief to his resulting erection for a
sail, puts his thumb up his ass with his palm for a rudder, and
sails safely home to port.* (N.Y. 1940.) The earliest collected
version of this is French, being printed in *L'Intermédiaire des
Chercheurs et Curieux* (Paris, 25 April 1886) vol. XIX, col. 251,
in reply to an inquiry (XIX. 197) calling the story *"Le pieu à
tout faire de Caraguez,"* mentioned in Gérard de Nerval's
Voyage en Orient. This specifically implies a Levantine original,
in the Turkish puppet-plays of the ithyphallic Karaghuez, and
the writer giving the story – which he calls Gascon or Mar-
seillais in origin – adds that in Cairo he saw a *similar* Arab
guignol-play during the religious festivals of *'la Dosseh, d'une
pornographie inimaginable.'* I have already noted the similarity
to the American Negro recitation, "Shine," or "The *Titanic*"
(not identical with the folksong!) in Dr. Roger Abrahams'
Deep Down in the Jungle (1964) p. 111, where several texts of
"Shine" are given, p. 111–23, in all of which the sexual hero,
Shine – possibly the original of Eugene O'Neill's *The Hairy Ape*
(1922) – swims home safely and at lightning speed from the
sinking of the *Titanic*, though not by the method described in
the joke.

One other well-known overcompensatory joke is also perhaps relevant here. Thompson gives this as North American
Indian, as well. K1391 : *The giant who sees the Indian maid on
the opposite side of the Grand Canyon and lays his erect penis
across the gorge for her to walk over. At the last moment she
refuses, saying, "But how will I get back?"* (N.Y. 1937.) In the

woman's castratory 'topper' (not in the Indian version), she appears as the vaginal 'castrator' of all penises, however large and strong, rather than as having saved either the man or his organ. Thus: *The little boy whom the housewife [i.e. mother] sees snapping beans over the wall with his erect penis. She calls him into the house and shows him how to perform sexual intercourse. The next time she calls him to come in, he refuses, saying, "G'wan, you busted my beanshooter!"* (Illustrated in *Anecdota Americana*, 1934, vol. II.) Also versions with: *Castaways on a desert island; the Robinson Crusoe boy ending by saying, "Go away, I hate you. You ruined my clam-digger!"* And: *The idiot in the insane asylum, to the nurse who has seduced him, after which he refuses to stop crying, but doesn't want a dime, a candy-bar, etc., "I just want my play-toy back."* (L.A. 1968.) The sexual ignorance here, of the 'nincumpoop' or innocent boy, is only a pretext for the rejection of the 'castratory' normality of the woman representing the mother.

4. POISON-DAMSELS AND VAGINISMUS

In attenuated form, the castrating element is made (by courtesy) not the vagina but some medication rubbed into it – which somehow never hurts the woman. This has already been seen, in the preceding chapter on Venereal Disease, 12.III, end of the section on "Vermin," where a woman uses 'blue ointment' or some other medication to kill pubic crab-lice, with the immediate creation of jocular *vagina dentata* stories in which the poisonous (mercurial) salve becomes combined with the idea of the vagina as a trap for the male. In the usual form: *Various men perform cunnilinctus on the woman who has put Paris-green on her vulva to cure crabs, and are killed by the poison.* (Compare Dr. Norman Penzer's *Poison-Damsels*, 1952, not taken at this analytic level. Motif F582.) – *A man complains to a girl whom he has taken to a hotel that she was 'too tight for him. "I haven't been stayed with in a long time," she answered. "But if you'll look in the bag on the dresser you'll find a tube of vaseline. Rub it on the head and it'll slip in easy." Her partner reached out in the dark, got the tube, and followed instructions, with satisfactory results. Next morning, however, he was startled to observe that the head had fallen off his penis. "What the hell is this? Did you bite this off?" he roared. The lady gazed a moment at him in perplexity. Then she burst out, "My Gawd, you must of used my corn cure!"'*

(1:244. In *World's Dirtiest Jokes*, 1969, p. 104, 'black-head remover' is used.)

Two elements to observe here are first, the idea that venereal disease announces itself as just stated. *Two men in the toilet at the urinal bank. One asks the other, "Say, what's the first symptoms of syphilis?" "I dunno – why?" "My cock just came off in my hands."* (N.Y. 1939.) The other element, more significant, is the widespread idea that there is something about the vagina and its secretions that is essentially poisonous or disgusting if not actually castratory, as in the joke already given under "Narsty-Narsties," in section 12.IV.6, "The Defiling of the Mother," in which: *The old prostitute tells the man that she has made intercourse less scratchy and painful by "scraping off the scabs and spreading the scum around."* Here the attack is clearly not by poison, nor even the announced disease, but by the attempted awfulness of the verbal image. As to the actual 'corn cure' story: in the *Novelle* of Bandello (1554; ed. Bari, 1912) II. No. 48, *A prostitute watches a priest use rose-water and determines to do likewise. In the dark she mistakes the ink bottle for the rose-water.* (Rotunda, Motif X524, not included in Thompson later.)

This is all much modified in the direction of humor and innocuousness in a British joke on 'modern times,' in which, however, the actual masticatory or dentate activity of the *vagina dentata* is described – the only such survival of the primeval legend encountered in any self-evident joke: *'Newly-wed wife retires first and prepares herself. When hubby goes up she is already on her back with her cunt exposed, but he notices too that her cunt would appear to be making the movements and sounds of mastication. He tells her so and she says, "Pass me the hand-mirror and let me see. – Good lord, yes, I must have slipped in a Wrigley's instead of a Rendell's".'* (I.e. a chewing-gum tablet instead of a birth-control pastille. – Chelmsford, Essex, 1953, from manuscript.) *The Limerick*, No. 1186, gives a minced version of the *vagina dentata* threat in a very well known folk-item:

> *There was a young couple named Kelly*
> *Who had to live belly to belly,*
> > *Because once, in their haste,*
> > *They used library paste*
> *Instead of petroleum jelly.*

This is simply a jocular form of the various *penis captivus* stories told as true, detailed in the section preceding.

No pretense is any longer made in a form of the 'Paris-green' joke where the nonsense element is much bloated up to make the idea of the *vagina dentata* – here rationalized as a swallowed razor-blade (!) – endurable. *A woman swallows a razor-blade. The doctor takes an X-ray photo and tells her to come back the next week, but she does not come back. He meets her in the street, and tells her severely that she must come to his office, they must find the razor-blade, it is very dangerous, etc.* "Oh," *she says,* "I located the razor-blade myself. It's already circumcised three of my boy-friends, and cut the fingers of five casual acquaintances." (Fort Lauderdale, Florida, 1953.) The doctor as 'Tooth-Breaker' fails here. He has appeared again, perfectly seriously, in modern life as the 'marriage counsellor,' burlesqued in *The Limerick*, No. 825, concerning *a young girl* 'With a hymen in need of relief,' owing, apparently to its being impossible for a man to penetrate with his penis: but the doctor solves all when he 'prodded and shocked her, And stretched it with fingers and teeth.'

Freud, in one of his great speculative papers, "The Taboo of Virginity" (1918), *Collected Papers*, IV. 217–35, discusses the peculiar psychological depths of ritual defloration, which still survives in the 'marriage counsellor's' premarital stretching, here burlesqued. Vaginismus as an expression of the bride's hostility against her husband is importantly discussed by Karl Abraham, "The Female Castration Complex," in his *Selected Papers* (1927) p. 355. Vaginismus is unquestionably the psychological and physical problem at the root of the legend of the *vagina dentata*, to which ritual defloration is simply a patriarchal reply, in recollection perhaps of the matching legend of 'Tooth-Breaker.'

Only in the Biblical legend of the hero, Samson, blinded and fettered by the Philistines in Gaza, does any reminiscence of 'Tooth-Breaker' remain (other than in folktales and jokes). The Midrashic tradition, on the passage in *Judges*, xvi. 21, stating that Samson was forced to *'grind in the prison house,'* relates that this refers to the remnants of his great physical strength being pressed into the service of satisfying the Philistine women sexually: on the pattern of the bitch-prototype, Delilah, who had endlessly betrayed him. As the Philistines cannot be considered to have been matriarchal at the period referred to, and thus the sexual satisfaction of women important, Samson's activity in 'grinding' can only be considered some form of vaginal tooth-breaking for the frightened patriarchal Philistines.

All 'hard-men' and heroes of the Samson type are invariably great tamers of women: this is one of their most important functions and identification-activities for the men who tell the tall tales concerning them. See the list of famous folk-heroic 'hard-men,' from Hercules, Achilles, and Samson, to Rasputin, Tarzan, John Henry, and Li'l Abner, in *The Horn Book*, p. 227, with an important and little-known gloss on the secret of the power of such heroes in John Aubrey's 17th-century *Remaines of Gentilisme and Judaisme* (ed. Britten, 1881) pp. 75–6, 152–4, and 237–8: they are 'double-j'inted'! Extensive folktale materials are cited under 'Strong John,' in Aarne–Thompson, Types 650A and 301B. The most interesting literary treatment of the sexual part of the legend of the super-strong hero, or hard-man, is "Olivier's Brag," by Anatole France, on an old French *chanson de geste*, detailed as the head-note to Child Ballad No. 30, "King Arthur and King Cornwall," I. 277, in which Olivier's 'gab' or brag is that he will 'testify to his love' of the king's blonde daughter one hundred times in a single night. (She says in the morning that she lost count.)

5. THE OVERLARGE VAGINA

There is also the matching or contrasting theme, of course, that of the 'Strong Woman': Brünnhilde, the Valkyrie who is tamed by the invulnerable, dragon's-blood-dipped Siegfried in the *Nibelungenlied*, especially as rewritten by Wagner in the opera-cycle that has become or expresses the real German religion of modern times. One of her principal legends is that: *The woman is far too big and strong for her husband, and either purposely or accidentally stifles him in bed (simply by putting her hands and feet on him ... so you can imagine!) He asks permission to 'go outside,' and in the darkness the 'strong man' substitutes for him and overcomes the woman sexually.* (Tale Type 519, "Günther and Brunhild" – Siegfried being the 'strong man,' of course. Motifs T173.1, and K1844.1, from the Icelandic.) This ancient legend is still very much alive at the joke level, and has been fully handled above in chapter 11.III.2, under "Orgies," in the burlesque story of *'Julius,'* who, *when he goes outside in the darkness, has a whole line-up of 'strong men,' to whom he is selling tickets, including the final Negro.* (Motif

K1544.) Negroes are the most famous of modern white folk-lore's sexual 'strong men.' They substitute for the anti-hero this time, not to take an impenetrable bride's virginity, but as a revenge.

See further, on literary handlings of the theme of the admit-tedly evil Delilah or erotic 'vamp,' the Hispanic 'Devoradora' or devourer-of-men who has become a heroine in neurotic and sado-masochistic popular literature of the 19th and 20th cen-turies, my Love & Death (1949), the article "Avatars of the Bitch-Heroine," beginning with a list of examples, p. 57–80. In jokes, no social or psychological superiority is admitted, as re-gards any woman except the wife, who, having been lifted to power by her husband's name, now has a 'whim of iron' – and a cunt of steel. Her power or fearfulness derives strictly from the presumed danger of the symbolic teeth in her overlarge (i.e. Strong Woman's) vagina dentata. Briefly but completely: "When I got married thirty years ago, it looked good enough to eat – now it looks like it's going to eat me ..." (World's Dirtiest Jokes, 1969, p. 71, captioned "The Thing Has Changed," trailing-off dots in the original.) Consider: 'Powerful Katrinka', 'Maggie & Jiggs', 'Blondie.'

Displacements are always possible of the fear of the woman's vagina to fear of her mouth itself, the two being naturally inter-changeable at both the unconscious and practical levels. Two of the World's Dirtiest Jokes, pp. 95 and 191, go even further in displacement of the explicit fear, found especially in limericks, that the woman has bitten or will bite off the man's penis (or just the 'head' of his penis: Say It Isn't So!!). Instead, the fear expressed is burlesqued as a concern that the woman will either 'suck or blow' the penis, in either case with the same castratory result: 'A little bitty short man' in a whorehouse charms the prostitute when he undresses, by his small size. "My, what a cute little organ," she says. "Can I kiss it?" He: "Oh, all right, kiss it – but don't suck it! I used to be ten feet tall." It would be hard to miss the identification here of the man's phallic and bodily insufficiency as those of a child, being treated maternally in the orasexual situation. Men of this type often identify cloac-ally the flow of semen with that of urine, in distant recollection of the nursery demand, "Pee for mama!" when the penis was also held or caressed by the attentive mother. The man's castra-tion by a woman's or women's mouths, from 'ten feet tall' down to 'a little bitty short man,' is, however, the crucial point here:

meaning that it is women's oral sexuality (*vagina dentata*) that is responsible for his inferiority. Adam began this story circulating: *"The woman, she gave me of the tree, and I did eat."* (*Genesis*, iii. 12.)

The other story is the precise opposite. *A woman is intrigued by a hunchback in a barroom, and, encouraged by the bartender, she asks him, ' "Is it true that hunchbacks have a real big unit?" "Yea, baby, wanna see?" She said yes, so they went to his car, and he showed her. She said, "It's so beautiful – may I kiss it?" He said, "You can kiss it, but don't blow it! That's the way I got my hunchback!" '* (*World's Dirtiest Jokes*, p. 191.) A brief riddle or gag-line, popular about 1950 in both England and America, says it all: *"Did you hear what the hurricane said to the palm-trees? – 'Hold onto your nuts, boys; this is no ordinary blow-job'."* (British form: 'blow-through.') Based, perhaps, on the meteorological anti-feminism of referring to all approaching hurricanes, in coded radio storm-warnings, by women's names.

The theme of the overlarge vagina, in which one swims and finally is lost, rather than the more evidently 'oral' danger of the too-small vagina, also is fodder for *vagina dentata* jokes and fantasies. A number of these have already been discussed earlier, in the First Series, in the chapter on Women, 6.V.4, "Vaginal Size." The all-time classic in this line in unquestionably: *'They were in bed and he begged her to spread her thighs wider apart. She obliged, but still he begged her: "Spread them a little wider ..." Exasperated, she said to him: "What the hell are you trying to do, get your balls in?" "No," he answered, "I'm trying to get them out."* (1:48, endlessly collected, often with the girl asking, *"Are you trying to get your balls in TOO?"*) This or something like it, has been considered a very good joke for several centuries. It is the frame-question or pretended theme of Antonio Vignali's *La Cazzaria* (1530), on which the author explains at the end of the introductory dialogue that this *Book of the Prick* is intended to enlighten the ignorance of his auditor, Underslung, *who had disgraced himself when, 'dining at Salavo's house in a pleasing company of young men, when asked why it is that the testicles never get tangled up in the cunt or arse-hole, had to reply that he did not know.'* The work that then follows, on this opening, is one of the greatest collections of erotic folk-beliefs and just-so stories in the literature of the world. An English translation has been published in

California, 1968, in rather crude pocketbook style, as *A Dialogue on Diddling.*

A few variations on the theme: the first in the comedy anti-Negro dialect that was considered particularly funny in the 1920's and '30's of Octavus Roy Cohen's "Florian Slappey" stories in the *Saturday Evening Post*, and the blackface white comedians, Amos 'n' Andy, who put radio across. '*"Ah say, Mary, would you jes' 's soon – ?" "Looke yer, Jim Jackson, don' you git fresh wif me. Mah name's Miss Smif, not Mary. Ah don't 'low only mah bes' and mos' intimate friends to call me Mary." "Ah begs yo' pahdon, Miss Smif. But say, Miss Smif, would you mind moving yo' ass a little to de lef'. One ob mah balls is cotched".'* (1:400.) This has sub-varieties, not openly of the *vagina dentata* or *penis captivus (cum testiculos)* type, in which: *The girl berates her soldier-boyfriend angrily for saying to her, "Honey, I'm leaving for France in the morning. Won't you be good to me tonight, and let me screw you?" (Or simply for running into her apartment with his penis sticking out.) After listening to her reprimand him for a while, he says, "Allright, I'm sorry. Leggo my cock and I'll leave."* (1:390.) Also in an ornate comedy-Jewish form, in which: *The man keeps begging to be allowed to say "Two words! Two words!" while the shocked young woman berates him. The two words, when he finally is allowed to say them, are: "Let go!"* (N.Y. 1937.)

No reference here to the vagina at all, dentate or otherwise, the whole implication being piled into the accusation of excessive female sexual appetite, coupled with mock-modesty (*i.e.* cockteasing). Essentially, *all* jokes and superstitions about nymphomania are references to the fear of the clutching *vagina dentata*, which is really what is meant in such phrases as "*A woman like that will drain (or suck) a man dry*," or "*will melt the fat off your bones*" (a Trinidadian Negro expression), or "*will break your back and spit you out the window*," again apparently a reference to the (broken) phallic 'bone.' The matching belief in the existence of aphrodisiacs is a yearning for some magical means of matching or taming the equally mythical nymphomaniac and her dangerous vagina, or for the 'unhexing' of impotence.

Pitiful grotesqueries are engaged in conversationally, by men, alluding to the fear of the too-large vagina, and the measures that must be taken to keep from falling in, such as: '*The under-endowed man who married the village whore, and when asked about precautions, said he'd tied his feet to the bottom of the bed.'* (Nottingham, 1970, told at a political dinner-party with six men and three ladies present: from one of the ladies.) *'A man complaining about the loose fit of a certain woman's vagina said he "had to tie a railroad tie across his ass so he wouldn't get sucked in".'* (D.C. 1951.) Or an 'oar.'

Strictly as jokes: *A fat lady is stuck in the bathtub, and the plumber must be called. Her husband is embarrassed at the idea of the plumber seeing his wife naked, and gives her his derby hat to hold over her pubis. The plumber studies the scene with some puzzlement. "What do you think we ought to do first?" the husband asks frantically. "First," says the plumber, "we got to get the man out."* (N.Y. 1939.) Also set up even more elaborately as a humiliation-story with the woman as butt: *A girl who has been cock-teasing her boyfriend in his hotel-room is thrown out into the hallway naked by him, when she refuses at the last moment to 'come across.' She bangs on the door but he refuses to let her back in. She pleads with him at least to throw out her clothes and purse, so she can get home, but he will not answer. Suddenly she hears someone getting off the elevator and coming down the hall, and she cowers against the door, covering her breasts with one arm, and snatching up a pair of men's shoes – set outside the door to be shined – and holding them against her pubis. A drunk comes lurching noisily by. He stops and examines the blushing girl thoroughly, especially the shoes clutched against her. "Wow!" he says finally; "is that guy IN!!"* (N.Y. 1940.) The standard 'drunk,' who is always the little boy who dares to say that the King has no clothes on, here expresses the ambivalent and positive half of the fear of the too-large vagina: the unabashed desire *to return to the womb of the mother.*

Ultimate variants no longer show any fear, but are evident charades of life in the womb, as with the stories given in Chapter 6.V.4, under "Vaginal Size," where, for instance, *A man falls into his wife's vagina, and wanders around for three days, looking for the way out, and finally meeting another man with a lantern who is looking for a horse and wagon.* This is an older Russian tale; in America he has lost a motorcycle! *A girl tells her mother about the marvellous new position for making love that her husband has taught her: she is to lie on the bed with her legs spread, while he charges across the room and swan-dives into her embrace. The next day the girl has a hurry-call from the hospital where her parents have been taken. "How are they?" she asks fearfully. "Your mother is all right," she is told, "but they're still probing for your father." (2:313.)* Louis Perceau gives an earlier French version of this, with an unexpurgated illustration, as the opening joke in his anonymous *Histoires Raides* ("Stiff Stories," ca. 1929), entitled *"A la hussarde!"* In this: *At the last moment, the father slips on the polished floor, and strikes the mother head-first, crippling her.*

The harming of the woman, here combined with the head-first womb return, takes over completely in another form of the same scene which has lost all other similarity to the original. *A man and woman are trying out a new position in a hotel-room: the woman stands against the door, and the man dashes across the room to penetrate her standing. She becomes terrified as she sees him charging at her, shrieks and falls backwards, thus unnerving him and causing him to miss his footing and fall out the window into the alley. After being unconscious for some time, he picks himself up and sneaks into the hotel by the service entrance, asking the porter to loan him a raincoat so he can get back upstairs unnoticed. "You can go right through the lobby," the porter assures him, "There's nobody there. They're all up on the third floor watching the doctor trying to get that woman off the doorknob."* (N.Y. 1952. Randolph, No. 67, "Let's Play Whammy," gives an Ozark version dating from the 1940's.) In a sense this is a revenge story: a revenge for the danger of the overlarge *vagina dentata*. Though the man hardly avoids harm – falling through the window – it is here largely reversed upon the woman, who is publicly humiliated in her pedication with the 'toothbreaking' implement of the doorknob.

Penis captivus, which is frequent in 'true' tales, seldom appears frankly in jokes. *A Scotchman begs his wife to let him have intercourse with her 'dog-fashion' but she refuses. Later they become stuck together in having intercourse in the ordinary or 'missionary' position. They are taken to the hospital on a stretcher, covered with a blanket, and are there separated by injections by the doctors. On receiving the hospital and ambulance bill later, the Scotchman hands it to his wife, saying, "This is for you, Annie." "Why for me, mon? Did you no go to the hospital too?" "Oh, as far as thot's concerned, lass, I'd just as soon ha' walked."* (N.Y. 1953.) Various subterfuges are also used to hide the *penis captivus* idea. *'Chap with cinema cramp.*

Can't straighten up after coming out of the movies with his girl. Doctor: "Ah yes, just as I thought. Quite a lot of cases like this. She's buttoned your waistcoat to your flies".' (London, 1954: 'flies,' British plural for the American singular 'fly,' the front opening or 'ballap' of a man's trousers.) A reversal of this has already been given, in which it is the woman – or sometimes a mare or bitch! – that is so treated : *'Peabody Buildings: couple on one of the flights of stairs having-a-go for all they're worth. He: "Now, don't keep noddin' yer 'ead like that, Dearie!" She: "Oi can't 'elp it, 'Arry; yer tuckin' me vest in!"* (Chelmsford, Essex, 1953. The British names for women's underwear are not identical with the American; 'vest,' is undershirt or chemise; 'knickers,' panties or bloomers.) Note that the American version given earlier also is taking place in England during World War II, as between *'An American soldier ... and a British broad, who insisted on performing coitus standing,'* with endline: *"You've got a bit of me scarf tucked in."* (D.C. 1951.)

Such stories have probably developed from the anecdote of the 18th-century erotic French poet Piron, *tucking in the lady's handkerchief which has fallen into his lap in public.* A modern French version is much more frank than the English, in its direct expression of the castratory danger. The *vagina dentata* – which, in the English versions, merely chews cloth! – is here made by courtesy something other than the woman, but it acts directly against the man's testicles. *A man is making love to the cook hurriedly on the kitchen table, and keeps screaming louder and louder at every stroke. "Are you coming, that makes you scream like that?" she asks, wriggling her bottom even harder. "No," he says, rolling his eyes up in torture, "No! I've got my balls caught in the drawer!"* (Louis Perceau, *Histoires Raides,* 1929, p. 113, reprinted in *Histoires Aérodynamiques: Petites Histoires de rire,* 1935, 1.77.) The snapping drawer does the biting, but it is the man's own 'fault.'

The most direct statement is that in which the *vagina dentata* is stated actually to exist, but is rationalized as some device which the woman has inserted into or attached to her vagina to counterfeit virginity. Jokes of this kind in which the false maidenhead merely slips off during intercourse (sausage-skin, etc.) and must be fished for with a straw, matchstick, etc., are not relevant here, except perhaps in the *protection* of the penis from the vaginal danger sensed in such a situation – in which, after all, the man is being betrayed and befooled – by means of the false maidenhead which ends up as a protective penis sheath. (Compare Randolph's "Betsey and the Mole Skin," given earlier.)

One joke of this type plainly rejects the castratory danger upon the woman herself, stating that she has herself been castrated by this type of subterfuge. *'A bride, to counterfeit virginity, inserted a piece of liver in her vagina; her young groom, after ejaculating, went to the bathroom to wipe the semen off his penis, and found to his surprise this piece of meat wrapped around his organ. He shouted to his wife, "Hey, honey, look. Your cunt came off".'* (Los Angeles, Calif. 1939.) A female-fool modification of this has already been given, under Venereal Disease: *The farm-girl who becomes a prostitute in the big city. A client gives her ten dollars, but the condom he has used has slipped off inside her, where she finds it later. She has never seen one before, and bemoans: "Wouldn't you just know that the minute I got in the big money, I'd bust a gut?!"* (Chicago, 1952.) Other than the obvious castration of the woman in both of these, there is also the *lex talionis* mentioned by Fenichel in these fantasies: the castratory punishment is directed against the very organ that has 'sinned.'

An American realistic novel by Robert Mende, a decade before the 'New Freedom,' its title absurdly expurgated as *Spit* [!] *and the Stars* (New York, 1949) p. 125, attempts the working-class genre touch of the most direct of these wedding-night fraud stories. The danger to the husband here, from the bride's counterfeiting of virginity, should be compared with the elaborate hoax-story, concentrating on such wedding-night dread and danger, "The Sleeve Job," in the First Series chapter 8.III.3. Note the authentic telling, *all in dialogue* so far as possible:

You want to hear a dirty joke the big guys told? ... Well, this girl is a whore see, but she married a respectable guy. But she's worried see that this guy is going to find out that she's a whore. So she calls up her girl friend.

"Margie," she says, "I'm so terrible worried. Because to-night is the wedding night. And when Bill plows into me. And he don't hear my cherry snap. He'll know I ain't no virgin. Then he'll divorce me."

"Why don't worry," her girl friend says, "just use the old cigar box and rubber band trick. And when he plows into you, just snap the rubber band. And he'll think it's your cherry." "Oh, thanks! thanks! Margie," she says. "I'll do it."

Well. It's the wedding night. And her husband comes in. He says, "Hello, Honey." And she says, "Hello, Dearie." "Are you ready, Honey?" And she says, "Ready, Dearie." So her husband takes off all his clothes, gets under the covers, piles on top of her, and starts pumping.

Then! She *snaps* the rubber band. And her husband asks, "What was that, dearie?" And she says, "My cherry just snapped, Honey." Then he says, "Well, snap it again, you son-of-a-bitch. You got my balls caught!"

The Larson manuscript, No. 43, gives the identical story, collected in Idaho in 1919. *World's Dirtiest Jokes* (1969) p. 43, also of *a 'hot-tail gal' who doesn't want her new boyfriend to think she's 'TOO bad, so she popped her garter and said, "That must have been my maidenhead." He screamed, "Well, pop it again – you've got me caught by the goolies!"'* (American Southwest and New Orleans pronunciation of the French *couilles*, testicles.) Of European provenance, this appears as *"Le Pucelage et la tabatière"* (The Maidenhead and the Snuff-box), in a group of Flemish stories collected in Belgium, in *Kryptádia* (1901) VII. 4–5, and there given in French: *When the bride snaps the concealed snuff-box, by clipping her legs together and 'wriggling like an eel,' she begins to cry, "Oh, John, my maidenhead! Oh, John, my maidenhead!" "That's nothing at all, Godverdomme!" says John; "my balls are caught in it!"* 'And if she hasn't opened the snuff-box (the story-teller ends), they may still be there.' Rotunda, at Motif K1912, cites half a dozen Italian Renaissance stories on various deceptions practiced to mask the bride as a virgin, also including the Spanish *La Tia Fingida*, attributed to Cervantes. One of the closest to the present story is that in Pietro Fortini's 'most licentious' *Le Giornate de' Novizi*, 1562, Part II, No. 9. (Type 1159.)

As usual, Vance Randolph gives the best and oldest American version, in *Pissing in the Snow*, No. 3, "Fireworks Under the Bed," told by a married woman in Pineville, Missouri, 1930, who heard it from another married woman in the same place, 'who heard the story about 1885.' Here, *'The contraption might have been all right, only there was another girl found out about the snapper, and she put one of these giant-powder caps inside of it, just to make trouble. When the fresh-married couple got in the bed, the bride give a yell just like the granny-woman told* her. *But when she pushed the top of the snapper it went off loud as a gun, and like to have blowed both of 'em clear out of the bed. The whole place was full of smoke, with everybody a-yelling at the top of their voice, and hell to pay generally.'* Here the *vagina dentata* element is combined or confused with the *charivari* or 'horning,' a survival of marriage-by-capture and exogamy, in which the friends or relatives of the bride attempt to prevent the consummation of the marriage (see further, the First Series, 8.II.2) through rough pranks or cacophonous music, or 'practical jokes' by means of which the marriage-bed is made impossible to use.

6. NURSES AND THE MACHINE

For jokes on male castration to qualify, among those who tell them, as rough humor, the displacement of the danger must be effected upon the foreskin or the testicles (always considered secondary to the penis, no matter how vulnerable), or upon the woman herself – if a woman appears in the joke, as is usual. Where the penis itself is endangered, either the joke must be so extravagant as to allow the necessary reassurance that it is merely 'nonsense,' or the tendency toward telling as a 'true' horror-anecdote appears, thus driving off the danger with the unknown male scapegoat who *has* been caught and castrated, as neither the teller nor listener has been – yet! Told as true, or 'almost true,' are tales of masturbation devices of an unpleasant (can of worms), repulsive (slice of liver), or dangerous nature, upon which to displace the fear of the vagina. In particular cow-milking devices, as will be seen below. The essential note here is that of *helpless inevitability* before the God of the Machine, on the style of a mechanical eagle tearing at the new Prometheus' unexpurgated groin.

In Rotunda's *Motif-Index of the Italian Novella*, at Motif T67.3 (repeated at H1196), a 16th-century story is cited from Straparola and Sansovino, rather similar to that of the male sex-doll in the First Series, 6.IV.4, page 369, but elegantly concerning *a king who marries the girl who frees him from the clutches of a magic doll.* This appears later in Basile's *Pentamerone*, v, No. 1 (Tale Type 571C) in greater detail: *'A girl is kind to an old lady and receives a magic doll that produces a quantity of money. An envious neighbor borrows the doll and it soils her bed. She throws it out of the house. It bites the king when he passes by. Only the girl is able to make it stop biting . . .'* (As the story is noted to be still alive in Turkey, one assumes that is its source.) Translated from the elegant peri-phrases of Prof. Thompson's précis, *the doll shits money for the girl, but shits shit for the neighbor, and then starts biting the king:* the part of interest here. A doll with all these attain- ments is hardly more than a projection of the girlish fantasies of certain aggressive female listeners, and what the 'biting' of the king means, at that level, is not hard to understand. (Com- pare the gold-dropping donkey and Magic Cudgel of Grimm's No. 36 : Type 563, with enormous references.)

In mechanical and not magical form, this ill-fated doll ap- pears again in the early 19th century in the *Tales* of E. T. A. Hoffmann, specifically "Undine" (1816), made into an opéra- bouffe as the masterpiece of Jacques Offenbach, *The Tales of Hoffman*, but not produced until 1881, the year after Offen- bach's death. Here the two scenes no one ever forgets are the leg-lifting of the French Cancan (to the music of a wild *chahut* which has become a sort of secondary French national anthem, for export purposes), and the arm-dropping glissando of the Mechanical Doll, whose voice and 'dancing' – the usual polite symbol – run down in the middle of her song, and she has to be wound up again with a key in her backside ('waist') like the Mechanical Horse of the *Arabian Nights*. This touches the theme only farcically, as does the title of Prof. Marshall McLuhan's first book, on advertisement themes, *The Mechani- cal Bride* (1951 : preprinted in part in *Neurotica*, No. 8), and numerous gag-cartoons of the 1960's, showing, for example, *A corner-prostitute with a large key in her back, who is saying to another: "Of course it's not real, but it takes a good gimmick to bring in business."* Frankly bawdy is Aleister Crowley's humorous poem, "The Automatic Girl," in his anonymous *Snowdrops from a Curate's Garden* ('Cosmopoli, 1881' [Paris, *ca.* 1904] copy : B.N. *Enfer* 1355) p. 154–6.

Simultaneously with Hoffmann's 'doll' story, something very close to this theme was being played for horror, as it merits, in Prosper Mérimée's novelette, *La Vénus d'Ille* (1846), a sort of female-dominant version of the legend of Don Juan and the statue of the Commander which comes alive and drags him off to Hell. In *"La Vénus d'Ille": A man who accidentally puts his ring on the hand of the statue of Venus is claimed in the night by his statue-bride, and is found 'mutilated' in the morning.* (See further, on Mérimée, masochism, and this story, the First

Series, 8.III.5, "The Taboo of Virginity," p. 522–3.) Somewhere between Hoffmann and Mérimée, the themes of the mechanical *vs.* the magical doll or statue are seen to combine and become modernized.

A refined version of Mérimée's story, and his obvious source, appears in the older French *exempla* (Motif T376, with references), in which the statue is of course not Venus but the Virgin Mary. Here the castratory punishment or conclusion is made specific, if politely phrased: '*She afterwards forbids him the embraces of an earthly bride.*' (Compare the legend of Thomas the Rhymer of Erceldoune – best told in the headnotes to Child Ballad No. 37 – who is identical with Tannhäuser in his visit to Venus or the 'Queen of the Fairies:' Motif F302. When these Rip van Winkles return they are all *old* – and impotent.) When I was a little boy, my mother told me in much the same way that: *If she ever hit me with a broom when I was bad, I would "never be able to get married."* (From Rumania, 1890's.) This appears in the Frank C. Brown *Collection of North Carolina Folklore*, IV. "Popular Beliefs and Superstitions," ed. Wayland D. Hand (Duke Univ. 1961) No. 2927: '*It is bad luck to get a lick on the foot with a broom, unless the one struck spits on the broom;*' noting a German form as well. Our family version did not include the remedy or un-hexing with spit, but was very specific about the un-manning with which one was endangered.

Merkins (vulgarly called 'muggets') were originally in the 17th century, at the Restoration in England, small triangular wigs for women's genitals when the pubic hair had fallen out owing to venereal disease. In modern times, the terms 'merkin' or 'mugget' refer usually to artificial vulvas for masturbation by men. Such succedanea are also strapped to their crotches, to cover and replace the penis, by highly neurotic homosexuals who prowl the streets at night dressed in women's clothes and pretending to be female prostitutes. More than one homosexual transvestist has shown me such a device, one of them home-made of a folded piece of rubber greased up with K-Y jelly; and in one case with the statement that it is only used 'at first,' and that as soon as the client, who is usually drunk enough to think his street pickup is really a woman, is convinced that he is *in*, the homosexual raises his legs somewhat higher, to the man's shoulders, simulating great passion, and slips the man's penis past the 'mugget' and up his rectum.

Such objects have long been called *'Dames de voyage'* in France, and, similarly, 'Sailors' Brides' in Germany. They have been manufactured commercially in Japan for at least a century, and old examples are illustrated in Krauss & Satow's *Japanisches Geschlechtsleben* (*Anthropophytéia*: "Beiwerke," Leipzig, 1931) II. 185–91, under the name of *"Azumagata,"* the cleverest being in the form of a small hot-water bottle; following a long similar chapter on dildos for women, one being activated by a small archery bow. Items of this kind were commonly advertised in the famous, and now quite rare printed catalogue of the Kobé "Sex Store" since the period of World War I. They are now much more widespread, the sex stores having now come to the West, first in Frau Beate Uhse's world-famous mail-order enterprise in Flensburg, Germany. A current merkin-model is illustrated in Dr. Roger Blake's highly detailed pocket-book, *Sex Gadgets* (cover-title: *The Stimulators*, Cleveland, Ohio: Century – K.D.S., 1968) p. 144, broadening out into a chapter on "The Fornicatory Doll," p. 157–65. A joke on the subject has already been given in the First Series, 9.III.1, pages 745–6, to illustrate "Possession in Common": *Two prospectors are outfitted at the Last-Chance General Store & Saloon with 'love-boards,' consisting of a piece of pine board with a knothole in it, and a small fur pocket tacked to the back. Some months later one of the prospectors struggles back to civilization alone. "Where's your partner?" he is asked. "Had to shoot him," he answers; "I caught the son-of-a-bitch using my love-board!"*

The modern note that has been injected into these ancient entertainments is strictly the touch of the *Machine*. Such authentic masturbatory dolls are strictly female, and the "Rubber Man" of the earlier jokes remains still only a joke. One assumes that every man who has ever seen a cow-milking device has considered – unconsciously, to be sure – whether or not it might have sexual possibilities. But the moment the Machine meddles with these intimate human matters, there is hell to pay. The catastrophic cow-milking device joke is very well known, ending with: *The farmer's penis caught in the cow-milker, with which he has been experimenting. His wife phones the factory and is told, "We're sorry, madam, there's nothing that we can do. Just keep feeding him and fanning him – that machine is set for four quarts!"* (N.Y. 1948.) This is nothing but the Queen of Spain's Sex-doll, the Rubber Man, turned inside-out.

For women, nowadays, there is quite an industry in vibrating massage machines (including entire vibrating and water-filled mattresses), which are not likely to be replaced by the excessively frank vibrating or rotating dildo – of which I happen to have been co-inventor in 1938, on the inspiration of the Japanese bow-strung model mentioned just above – built by the late Dr. Vladimir Fortunato, the world's greatest anatomical model-maker. (It is not patented: our gift to the world. Details of construction are given in *Oragenitalism*, 1969, p. 99–101.) Under the title, "Think Tank ... Thanks," an anonymous exchange of letters is printed by Prof. Victor J. Papanek in *Designcourse* (Lafayette, Indiana: Purdue University, 1969) No. 1: p. 14–19, satirizing an imaginary "Volita Project" for merchandising inflatable fornicatory female dolls to the American playboy public on a mass scale, with built-in actresses' faces – your choice – fetichistic spiked heels, etc. Though intended as satire, this was already outstripped by reality and existed in fact before the end of the year, as is often the case, at the Danish 'Sex Fair' of 1969. (On which see the end of the section on "Impotence," 8.VIII.2, First Series, p. 619–20.)

Obviously, the ultimate in Anti-Gallantry (chapter 14.I.3, below) is to kick the living woman into the garbage-can, as requiring too much real, 'uncool' human emotion and involvement, and to replace her with an epoxy fucking-doll. No longer a minor Japanese novelty for horny sailormen at sea, these dolls have now become a major sex-shop industry and the one sickest triumph of the modern male's impotence quadrophoney gadgetry. (Illustrated details in Roger Blake's *Sex Gadgets*, 1968, chap. 9.) But, of course, the mechanical mistress turns out to be the most dangerous and castratory of all. In Luis Berlanga's softcore porno film, *Life Size* (1974) – softcore differs from hardcore in that '*Softcore gives you a soft-on*' – the gadget-surrounded playboy is finally destroyed by his passion for the 'life size' fucking-doll. This is the entire plot: she devours him, body & soul. We are close here to the Empusae or Succubae of ancient Greek mythology, who destroy men by 'sucking their strength' during intercourse in their sleep. (Queen Mab in *Romeo & Juliet*, I.iv.53–95.) Originally these were the *Lilim* or daughters of Lilith, the Devil-snake's consort, and enemy of the sons of Eve, in the legends of *Genesis*. Under "Decapitation," in the following section, we will consider the paranoid machine-penises that 'Tooth-Breaker' now uses to triumph sadistically over these fantasied dangers of the mechanized *vagina dentata*.

These same fantasies, but with the Machine not as masturbator but as castrator, are considered from the opposite viewpoint, that of the Mechanical Man *who has already been castrated* and is therefore 'out of danger,' at the end of the present chapter, 13.VI.3, which somewhat broadens the whole question of its serious and factual, rather than folkloristic, aspects. Here is pretty much the total statement, from the collection of cruel and sadistic jokes, *Grim Hairy Tales* (1966) p. 8 – also reprinted in *Sex to Sexty*, 9:29 – facing a fantastic cartoon of an overcrowded machine-shop filled with naked buzz-saws whirling, menacing the enormous breasts of a young lady mechanic, hardly contained in her overall-bib, to whom the undersized machine-tender is saying significantly, *"Welcome, girlie ... we need new blood around here!"*

A forward type of girl saw a most attractive man in a bar. Although he made no advances, she did all the advancing. She introduced herself, invited herself to sit down for a drink, and finally asked him if he'd like to go home with her. So they went home, he turned on the television and she retired to her boudoir, where she donned a flimsy negligee, paraded herself out and announced, "Paris, 1966." He smiled and went on watching the late show. Flustered, she went back, put on a topless bathing suit, came out, paraded again and said, "San Francisco, 1967," Again he looked, smiled appreciatively and went back to the teevee. Really obfuscated, the girl went back in, then paraded out in nothing but her shoes and said, "Here and now, 1968," with still no results. Then she screamed, "What's the matter with you, anyway?" The attractive man jumped up, jerked his pants down and said, "Mowing Machine, 1963!"

Nurses are not liked. The sexual approaches made to them, in recognition of their quasi-prostitutory status, as in chapter 11.I.1 above, are intended to reassure the patient of his virility in spite of operations and sickness. Hemingway's *A Farewell to Arms* (1929) makes a very clear statement of this, though the girl is really only a hospital slavey. When she dies in childbirth, of the hero's child, he tries to have intercourse with her body before it gets cold, by way of 'leavetaking,' but finds this unsatisfactory. All the usual results of the hero's sickness have thus been transferred to the nurse, including death: the attempt to violate the corpse – the final revenge, or reassurance that the victim *really is dead* – being undertaken under the shallow pretense of sentimentality, as an ultimate form of sick 'Togetherness.' (On this see the remarkable chapter, "Causes and Consequences of Clinging Between Mates," in Dr. Edrita Fried's *The Ego in Love and Sexuality*, 1960, p. 184–205.)

In approaching the nurse sexually, there is also, in jokes as in fact, an attempted conciliation of nurses as assistants to these dangerous persons, doctors. Many nurses are sadists and/or lesbians, especially surgical nurses. The nurse herself is often shown as dangerous and castratory, but again the accusation is usually made as merely the result of 'dumbness' or ineptness. *The nurse who is unpopular because of the way she gives bed-pans. The head doctor agrees to look into the complaints against her, and has her give a male patient a bedpan while he watches. Later he explains (with gestures): "Miss Crutwasser, we usually give the men bedpans like this (gesture of lifting with the palm upward, and sliding the pan beneath), and not like* THIS! *(gesture of yanking the man upward by the penis with one fist, and shoving the bedpan underneath with the heel of the other)."* (N.Y. 1952.) This is a very good example of the displacement of the castratory threat from doctor to nurse. Likewise: *A nurse is chasing a male patient with scissors, the doctor bringing up the rear shouting, "Nurse! Nurse! I said 'Slip off his spectacles!'"* (Transcontinental train, 1943.) Actually a nonsense-cartoon or 'one-liner,' possibly derived from those 1930's 'novelty'-cards showing a Jewish baby being circumcised with scissors. Note also the insistence on the spooneristic verbal *reversal* of the apparent image of castration; the doctor here offering protection and reassurance instead.

Compare also the hidden castration, and key use of the signal-words 'cut off,' in a curious story in which the doctor teaches the wife how to act against her husband's objectionable activities genitally, in his sleep, *à la* Delilah. '*A young bride whose marriage was threatened by her husband's terrific snor-ing consulted her physician, who advised, "When he falls asleep, pull his legs apart." To her surprise, this simple method worked wonderfully and on a subsequent visit she pressed the doctor for the physiological basis for this efficacious measure. He was reluctant to explain, but when she insisted, he said, "When you pulled his legs apart, his balls dropped down over his ass-hole and cut off the draft".'* (Berkeley, Calif. 1947: from manuscript.)

As often collected, generally from older men, the end-line is more frankly: *"... and cut off his draft,"* which leaves very little doubt about the actual meaning. Key- or signal-words like this are common folk-evasions of the censorship, both at the conscious and symbolic levels. For example, the open allusion to castration in the American World War I jingoistic song, "Oh, How I Hate To Get Up In the Morning!" in which the soldier complains that he hates the army bugler worst of all, and threatens: *'I'll amputate* (sometimes sung: *cut off all) his reveille, And step upon it heavily, And* SPEND *the rest of my life in bed!'* Even this being considered too frank for singing before mixed publics of men & women, the phonograph-recording of the song made in the 1920's gives instead: *'One day I'll take his reveille,' etc.* The fake-letter has already been cited in which: *A woman writes to the Works Progress Administration (or to the President): "I ain't had any relief since my husband's project was cut off."* (U.S. mid-1930's.) Very common, almost a folk code-remark symbolizing the impotence millions of American men felt during the widespread economic Depression.

Violent attacks on the man's genital organization, especially the testicles, are seldom ascribed to any other type of women except nurses. Stupidity and ignorance are the excuses for all others, as has already been seen. *'The vicar taking tea after his afternoon on the links, takes hankie out of his pocket and spills a couple of T's [tees] on the floor before his lady host. She: "Why, whatever on earth are those?" Vicar, stooping to pick them up: "They're what I use to put my balls on when I hit them with the golf club." She, giggling: "Well! I suppose one must expect silly answers to silly questions, mustn't one?"'* (Chelmsford, Essex, 1952. This is nearly the British version of the equally 'dumb female' joke, already given: *"I see you shot another golf."*) There is a well-known cartoon strip dating from the 1890's, by 'Caran d'Ache,' which shows: *A dog is sent for a forgotten pair of gentleman's gloves after smelling his guest's hand, and he comes back with the housemaid's drawers in his mouth.* This is modernized as follows in *World's Dirtiest Jokes* (1969) p. 189, titled "Chiller-Diller": *A 'gorgeous blonde' who has spent the evening in a barroom 'nursing a drink,' forgets her handbag there, and sends her enormous St. Bernard dog to fetch it, after giving him her hand to smell. 'The dog bounded out of the room and down the stairs, and a few minutes later he bounded back. Clenched in his teeth, instead of her purse, were the bartender's balls!'*

Cannibalistic implications are also not lacking. As in ritual cannibalism, the real intention and essential act is the eating of the enemy's penis and testicles, to arrogate to oneself all his virile strength. It is the nurse that is seen so acting against the male patient, without any disguise, and finally with the result – though not with the stated desire – that in some jokes she becomes a man herself, at least as to some visible secondary sexual trait. *The nurse is to give the patient a Sitz-bath, and puts his testicles into water that is almost boiling. After a moment of shock and near-strangulation, trying not to scream, he says in a controlled voice, "Nurse!" "Yes?" "Bring a fork, will you? I think the smaller one is almost done."* (Chicago, 1953.) Compare the more recent 'sick' joke or quickie, given in riddle form: *"Do you know what one cannibal said to the other? – No, what? – I'm havin' a ball!"* (La Jolla, Calif. 1964, from an 18-year-old college girl.)

No question about the following: *A man with an unusually deep and husky voice appeals to a doctor to castrate him, as his voice is a social nuisance. Later the man returns to complain of his new falsetto voice, and the doctor offers to graft the testicles back, and starts searching through his medical cabinets for them. "Oh nurse," he calls, "did you see a little bottle standing on this shelf the other day?" The nurse replies (in a deep, booming voice), "You mean the one with those two olives in it?"* (2:430.) This has also been encountered in an obvious modification in which: *The doctor speaks in falsetto at the first meeting with the patient, who speaks basso profundo. Meeting him again afterwards, the patient (in falsetto) asks the doctor, "Say, what do you do with the things you cut out in operations like that?" Doctor (in a deep, husky whisper): "Don't worry, we know what to do with them."* (D.C. 1951.) Or: *In a deep voice: "I'm sorry, that's a medical secret."* (N.Y. 1953.) Or, even more obviously: *The patient asks (falsetto): "Doctor, may I have my balls grafted back on?" Doctor (basso profundo): "Impossible!"* (London, 1953, told in a group of the then-popular "Christine" jokes on sex-changes.) This falsetto doctor is simply a disguised nurse. *Kryptádia*, IV. 305, substitutes housekeeper for nurse: *"Isn't it enough you suck my prick, without eating my bollock too?!"* Motif J2182, on eating eye.

In their excellent study of the elephant jokes popular in the 1960's, "On Elephantasy and Elephanticide," in *Psychoanalytic Review* (1969) vol. 56: pp. 233 and 240, Roger D. Abrahams & Alan Dundes observe that: 'The use of voice qualifiers in castration humor is common. For example, the use of a high-pitched falsetto occurs in the emphasized portions of the following punch lines: "Operator, I've been *cut off!*" – "Hey, there's sharks in *these waters!*" – "Watch out for the barbed wire fence!" "What barbed wire *fence?*"' The joke to which this note is added shows a rather different 'voice qualifier' following castration, which in this case is openly symbolic: *"What did the elephant say when the alligator bit off his trunk? – Very funny* (nasalized)." I heard this joke told for the first time in New York in 1964 by a young woman, in the presence of her husband and myself. She was perfectly conscious of its symbolic level, and knew that we were too, and had the good grace to honk out the final (nasalized) *"Very funny"* with a shamefaced grin.

In folklore, the effeminizing results of castration are immediate – instantaneous – especially on the voice, indicating clearly that the psychological effect is all that is cared about or considered, since this traumatic shock is instantaneous indeed. *A man swimming calls out in a bass voice, "Help! Sharks! For God's sake, help!!" Then, in falsetto: "Too late! Too late!"* (Lake Winola, Penna. 1927, told by children about ten years old.) An elderly employee in an army accounting office, at Orangeburg, N.Y. 1942, insisted on telling this joke several times, to all comers (it was the only one he knew, or else his favorite), carefully accentuating a pun he had discovered in the last line: *"Too late – tool ate."* This corroborates again Freud's observation that the infantile castration fear – as here the elderly fear connected with impotence ("too late") – concerns the penis only, while the testicles, which first develop dramatically at puberty, are hardly involved.

Concern over the sexual effects of castration is carefully displaced in the preceding jokes to concern over its secondary effect, principally on the voice, in an elegant metonymy accentuating the lesser rather than the greater loss. As to castration and the male voice, this was a subject long before public attention in the male *castrati* singers – an accidental cultural survival in Europe of relics of the Arab Conquest – who vied with coloratura sopranos for popularity in the concert life of the 18th century (Mozart's great aria, "Exsultate Jubilate," was written for a *castrato*), and continuing a century longer in the choir of *castrati* of the Sistine Chapel in the Vatican, in contravention of God's unequivocal command in *Deuteronomy,* xxiii, 1: *'He that is wounded in the stones, or hath his privy member cut off, shall not enter into the congregation of the Lord.'* See, of great meaningfulness on the subject of the voice and sex, Henry Alden Bunker's "The Voice as (Female) Phallus," in *Psychoanalytic Quarterly* (July 1934).

Aside from those by nurses, many quasi-castrations by women are suggested in jokes. Those involving actual decapitation will be made the subject of a brief concluding section, following. Other than these, there are also the overcompensatory types. *Vagina dentata* as hero: *An old Negro on public charity is castrated for getting his wife pregnant. She gets pregnant again anyhow. The man explains: "It's all de fault ob that old woman of mine, what's got a cunt dat would suck up a tack."* (1:418.) The extraordinary erotic animated movie-cartoon, *Abie's Buried Treasure* (U.S. about 1930), actually shows a vacuum-cleaner vagina like this in action, reaching out like a mouth to caress labially and then engulph the penis of the midget-son. In the privately issued collection of verses to the main World War I army song in English, *Mademoiselle from Armentières*, by Melbert B. Cary, Jr. (New York: Press of the Woolly Whale, 1930–35) II. 24, something of the same kind is shown under the usual polite veil of a *kiss*, the Mademoiselle being shown drawing the very life out of her A.E.F. lovers in a kiss like a suction-pump, similar to that used for emptying shithouses in the night, which leaves them totally emptied (through the mouth). All references to men being weakened by intercourse, even symbolically, like Samson, and to *women being strengthened by it*, or – politely – made 'happy' or 'skimming through the housework next morning,' are undisguised expressions of fear of the woman and her vagina as '*La Devoradora,*' the vampire-that-eats-men.

The following joke has been told me only by women, including one of middle age and very unhappy with her husband, who told it in the presence of her grown-up daughters. *A woman (or princess) tries to get rid of an insistent suitor by demanding that he have ten million dollars, hair on his chest like a bear-skin rug, and a penis twelve inches long. He says he can easily satisfy the first two requirements, but will be damned if he'll cut off two inches for any woman.* (2:423.) I have been told that there is a similar Midrashic legend on the meeting between King Solomon and Balkis, Queen of Sheba, at their contest in riddles (*1 Kings*, x. 1–13), on which see further section 15.V.2 below; but have not been able to trace any such joke – unless it is the present one – with the Queen of Sheba as the captious princess.

Of over-compensatory stories on castration of men by women, whether symbolically (as with Delilah commanding the cutting off of Samson's hair, in *Judges*, xvi. 4–20, and thus destroying the God-given strength of the Nazirite), or directly phrased as the attack against the penis with cutting instruments, none is more glorifying than a folktale traced to Scotland in the 1880's, given in the First Series, 8.1.6, under "Incest with the Mother-in-Law," p. 472–3. (The Scottish form in *Kryptádia*, 1884, II.261, contains no reference to castration.) Self-evidently a story of genital hexing and unhexing, the American version, given earlier in full along with the Scottish, has the man's penis become enormously long and his sexual appetite insatiable, not frankly by magic, as in older form, but by an overdose of an aphrodisiac – as though aphrodisiacs were *not* magic! In the end-situation: *'Three hours later, the wife went up and found granny pinned to the ceiling, yelling, "Get an axe, get an axe!" She did, and was about to cut her down, when the old woman cried, "No, not that! Not that, you stupid bastard! Chop a hole in the ceiling, and kiss your Granny good-bye!"'* (D.C. 1952.) In the Scottish version she says it far better, in a little *cante-fable* rhyme: *"Farewell freens, farewell foes, For I'm awa' to heaven on a pintel's nose!"* Magical elements aside, this involves a charming allusion to the woman's gratitude to the penis for her 'heavenly' orgasm.

7. DECAPITATION

No more obvious a symbolic equivalence could be imagined than that of decapitation as representing castration. In both, an essential part or 'end' of the body is chopped off, either ending the individual's life or, as castration (and even impotence) are often described, leaving the man 'as good as dead' – meaning, as *bad* – or with 'life not worth living' afterward. Almost at the punning level, yet perfectly seriously, the penis also has a 'head,' and it is specifically this which is sometimes thought of as the part castrated, especially where the fantasy accusation is made that the woman has 'bitten it off.' (*The Limerick*, No. 1136. See also the opening joke, on the 'corn cure,' in the section, "Poison-Damsels and Vaginismus," 13.I.4, above.)

Fenichel's *Psychoanalytic Theory of Neurosis*, p. 78, notes briefly the fear of decapitation, among displacements of castration fear in boys and men:

> After an operation the castration fear may be displaced to the operated area – for example, after a tonsillectomy [or the pulling of teeth]. A child who has had to witness the decapitation of a fowl, or has been impressed by stories about decapitation, may substitute the idea of decapitation for that of castration. Conscious or unconscious fears of blindness or of injury to the eye, and also of being *petrified* [Lot's wife, and the Gorgon Medusa] point to conflicts around scoptophilia.

Where the castratory punishment is expected for scoptophilia, or sexual peeping, the punishment is being 'displaced upward' away from the genital area, to the offending eye. Compare the statement twice ascribed to Jesus in *Matthew*, v. 29, xviii. 9: '*And if thine eye offend thee, pluck it out, and cast it from thee.*' With a further series of auto-castratory recommendations for cutting off one's hands and feet, to avoid hellfire. (The penis is not mentioned.) These absurd passages have led to, and are to blame for, the permitting by the Christian church for centuries of the worst excesses of sadistic hellfire predication – to children as well as to adults – by both the Redemptorist brothers among Catholics, and Calvinist ministers among Protestants.

A curious and almost unclassifiable story must be assimilated to the present section; though no reference is made directly to castration, the decapitation is quite clear. It was presented as a stage 'routine' by a comedian in a burlesque theatre in Washington, D.C. 1943: *He complained that the ceiling had fallen in his bedroom that morning, and a large piece of plaster had struck his wife in bed, on the stomach. "If it had fallen five minutes earlier, it would have broken my back," he said. When the audience's laughter subsided, he* explained: "*I always sleep on my stomach. It's the* snake *in me, I guess." (More laughter at the word 'snake,' suggestively pronounced.)* This story was collected again, twenty years later, from a man in New York who had been divorced from a woman far gone in neurotic degeneration, and who had just remarried very happily. It was now outfitted with great emphasis on the miraculous '*luckiness*' of the man presumably (and in fact) telling the story, the climactic luckiness being: "*And you think* that's *something? Well, you better not call me Lucky-Lucky. You better call me*

Lucky-Lucky-Lucky! This morning after my wife and I got up, the chandelier in the bedroom crashed right through the middle of the bed and busted it to bits. And am I lucky?! If it had fallen five minutes before, it would have hit me right on the back of the neck!" (N.Y. 1963.) Quite unmeaningful here is the insistent reference to the 'Lucky-Lucky' character of the man (Motifs J2564–72, "Thankful Fools") from which the second teller imagined he was milking all the humor in his tale. On the other hand, consider his biography.

In another joke, actually on overcompensatory reactions to ideas of impotence and castration (see section 13.VI, below), the presumed emphasis is again on the 'luckiness,' but here it is the open irrelevance of this that is the point of the joke: *Three American soldiers are captured during the border action against Pancho Villa. When he learns they are from Texas, Pancho Villa says, "You Texans are always bragging that you are so* big. *You are only big because you stole two-thirds of our country from us!" ("You tell 'em, Pancho!" cries one of his lieutenants; "the dirty Gringos stole the part with all the paved roads, too!") "Well," says Villa, "I'm gonna show you* big *men up. You can go free if your pricks measure seventeen inches between the three of you – and that's less than six inches each. If not, we're gonna line you up and shoot 'em off!" The soldiers' penises are measured. The first has nine inches, the second has seven inches, and the third – who is the commanding officer – has only one inch. This makes seventeen inches, so they are set free. As they trudge back through the dust toward the American border, one of the big men says to the little man, "Say, Major Asshole, you were sure lucky you had us along, weren't you?" "What do you mean, lucky?" says the officer querulously. "Talk about lucky! You big dog-faces are just lucky I was so scared I had a hard-on!"* (San Diego, Calif. 1965, told by an ex-marine. First printed in *World's Dirtiest Jokes*, 1969, p. 174.)

Many non-erotic 'puzzle' stories are connected with beheading and guillotining. *The man who falls asleep in church while dreaming of being guillotined, who is struck on the back of the neck by his wife, to wake him, and who dies instantly. Puzzle: How did the teller of the story know what the man was dreaming about?* This is the riddle of Odin and Balder in Norse mythology (F. J. Child, *The English and Scottish Popular Ballads*, 1888, 1.404–5.) The famous magical hoax of the Hindu or "Indian Rope Trick," which no one has ever seen performed, and no one ever will, is a not-very-subtle allusion to the erection of the penis, similar to the purposely suggestive manipulations of the Indian snake-charmers – and, even more suggestively, those of women snake-handlers in side-shows – in which the autonomous rising and dancing the cobra's head up from the basket is magically intended as a form of sexual allusion and dangerous sexual worship. The castratory elements in the "Indian Rope Trick" are very prominent, particularly as to the boy-hero (of the Aladdin type) who is stabbed and sliced repeatedly through the basket to make sure he is dead, before his marvellous reappearance – it says here – alive and smiling at the top of the rope, again an allusion to the Reincarnation that the erection of the penis openly represents in the East, as in Egyptian religious art.

In one puzzle-story form of the Indian Rope Trick, to which I have unfortunately lost the reference, it is a modern sex-hate story of the John Collier kind, published in English: *The man in the basket wakes mysteriously at the top of the rope in an Eastern harem-paradise, only to find – when he is then endangered – that his wife is at the foot of the rope, jealously cutting it down with an axe.* This is simply the fairy-tale of "Jack and the Beanstalk" crossed with the Indian Rope Trick (on which see further the First Series, 1.III.1, page 80), and with more than a bow to Aladdin and his lamp. And as to castration, well ...

In folklore the woman herself is often frankly considered the direct cause of the man's decapitation or other castration. As in the stories of Jael and Sisera, in *Judges*, iv–v; of Judith and Holofernes (in the *Apocrypha*), or Salomé in *Matthew*, xiv. 3–11, and in the morbid play and opera based on this last by Oscar Wilde and Richard Strauss. Despite the number of times Delilah has been shown in art and the theatre shaving off Samson's seven locks, the Biblical story in *Judges*, xvi. 19, specifically says that 'she called for a man' to do it from among the Philistines, though afterward '*she began to afflict him* [?] *and his strength went from him.*' My essay, "Avatars of the Bitch-Heroine," in *Love & Death* (1949) contains a good deal on this theme in modern literature and life, especially on the false or rotted sexuality of this type of *heroine*, made use of to harm or castrate the male.

Finally, a purposely 'sick' cartoon of the 1960's shows the woman as the actual decapitator: bare-breasted and hooded (the phallic female: Penis-Woman!) she is shown about to decapitate her husband, who nevertheless recognizes her as he kneels, his hands bound behind his back, his head on the block. (*Sex to Sexty*, 1964, 2:61.) This is then redrawn as the title-illustration to the same editor's *Grim Hairy Tales* (1966) with the caption significantly changing the relationship of the man to the headswoman who is about to decapitate him: "MOTHER! *You wouldn't!*" The cover also shows the beheading of Anne Boleyn by Henry VIII (drawn as the actor Charles Laughton) before an audience composed entirely of gloating men.

The very famous limerick on the "Queen of Baroda" (*The Limerick*, no. 1371), already discussed in section 13.I.3, makes no bones whatsoever about the woman as the wholesale castrator of the male, in a fantasy very similar to the more cautiously expurgated scenarios of H. Rider Haggard's *She* (1887), Pierre Benoît's *L'Atlantide* (1919, attacked at the time as a plagiarism of *She*), and similar male-masochist fictions. In the movie-version in English of *L'Atlantide*, as *Siren of Atlantis* – a Grade Q thriller – the dominant queen keeps the male captives in a cage, and has them blinded if they beat her playing chess! It is important to insist on the sexual or sex-substituted nature of these sado-masochist fantasies, which are obviously not mere cruelty. See – or, rather, do not see – the horrible fantasy illustrations of this kind, mostly of anti-woman sadism and taken from Italian-French comic-books 'for adults' in the 1960's, printed in William McLean's *Iconographie populaire de l'érotisme* (Paris, 1970) p. 102 ff., a work otherwise concerned mainly with outhouse epigraphs and wall graffiti.

One of the most remarkable illustrations published during the German *Jugend* period in art, centering about World War I, and reproduced in the staggering *Bilder-Lexikon der Erotik* (1928–31) vol. II: at p. 353, is a pictorial summing-up of Berlioz' *Symphonie Fantastique*. Entitled "*Das gemeinsame Ziel*" (Everyman's End) by Willy Geiger, and dated 1915, it is a most striking sketch in red and black, showing a man being executed at the top of a high scaffold, reached by a long staircase. The guillotine is in fact an enormous and beautiful naked woman standing over him with her legs spread, enclosing the scaffold in her lace panties and 'cutting off his head' – actually stabbing him to the heart! – with her chain-mail vulva, spread wide open and dripping blood.

A less romantic approach to this sort of theme depicts the woman as somehow more *mechanical* than a mere guillotine:

rather as a 'machine for swallowing pricks,' as I have heard it phrased. The modern cartoon-artist, Art Hurric, who draws the loveliest, juiciest, fine-breastedest fantasy women in the *Sex to Sexty* series – his drawings an oasis, usually of Viennese-style woman-loving, in among the purposely ugly and grotesque female *beef* of most of the illustrators in these cartoon books – somehow drops everything with a castratory-masochistic thud in a cartoon in *Sex to Sexty* (1970) No. 31 : p. 57. Hurric here shows us a man, tied by an executioner to a lift-truck and being trundled, penis-first, to an enormous PENCIL-SHARPENER, of which the crank is waiting to be turned by another executioner, while over the symbolic sharpening-hole a stark naked woman with outstretched arms smilingly agitates her hips to make sure the victim will have an erection worth grinding off. The idea is identical with that of Geiger's "Everyman's End," but what a drop in tone, even in *vagina dentata*, between the woman-as-guillotine and woman-as-pencil-sharpener! Muddy waters at the bottom of the Beautiful Blue Danube.

For that matter, in admiring the superb draughtsmanship of Willy Geiger, it would be an error to lose sight of his own perfectly sick identification of sex with death – and worse. Another of his drawings, here much derived in style from that *fin-de-siècle* sickie, Aubrey Beardsley, shows a dead woman in her coffin while a man – the artist – is displaying her bloated underbelly and sex. (Reproduced in Dr. Richard Wunderer's *Jocus Pornographicus*, Stuttgart, 1969, supplementary volume of illustrations, No. 167.) Hardly '*jocus*,' this must be the '*pornographicus*.'

More symbolically, but not so differently, the frontispiece of the very rarest, the most terrible, the most prophetic, the funniest, and the best-illustrated of all science-fiction and 'anticipation' works, Albert Robida's *Le Vingtième Siècle* (volume II : *La Vie Electrique*, 1890), shows "*L'Electricité, la grande esclave*," chained to a machine marked "FORCE" by one leg and one arm, while she turns the crank with the other hand, and little grinning devils help her on a subsidiary squirrel-wheel. This is hardly more than a polite rendition. (See further, on Robida's masterpiece, the First Series, 9.III.5, page 786.) The French satirical artist, P. Veber, at almost the same period, gives the unexpurgated fantasy : an enormous, eager female with her naked legs embracing a machine pistoning madly in and out at her cunt.

The last turn of the mechanical screw, however, is reserved

for an overpriced art-album entitled *Fornicon* (New York: Rhinoceros Press, 1969) by Tomi Ungerer, an artist better-known as an illustrator of children's books ... which says a good deal about modern children's books. *Fornicon* is a series of 64 plates, mostly showing masturbatory torture-machines for women, who are attached to the machines and being enjoyed by them, either actually tied to the machines or through masochistic need. Though entirely on sexually perverted subjects, these illustrations are far from erotic, being almost entirely in the style of the sick sado-masochistic "Nutrix" cartoon books, of a type prohibited by the U.S. Supreme Court in the same historic first-day-of-Spring decisions in 1966 which liberated *Fanny Hill* after two centuries underground, and thus began the new flood of American pornographic publication. One drawing from *Fornicon*, for those who cannot afford the set, is reproduced as an advertisement in *Avant Garde* (New York, March 1970) No. 11: p. 2, showing a woman tied hand-&-foot inside a masturbation wheel composed of spiked penises and spurs. Any questions?

Rather than describe or assess Mr. Ungerer's album further myself (it was immediately offered for sale much more cheaply by Grove Press, in their popular erotic art series), I quote from two American critics who seem to have considered it worthy of their best every-knock-a-boost prose: Howard Smith in the New York *Village Voice* observes that Ungerer 'has gone beyond sex of the flesh, to sex of nuts and bolts. The people in his ink drawings are a race of energetic masochists, wearing Spiderman masks and boots, who have created elaborate and impossible machines for total gratification.' While Richard Lingeman, in the *New York Times* (where copies of *Spiderman* and *Nutrix* comics obviously never filter in) wholly erroneously calls Ungerer 'a caricaturist in the George Grosz tradition,' adding that his drawings in *Fornicon* are 'savagely satirical [?] portrayals of a bizarre world of totally mechanized sex, involving machines and strange, hooded Beardsleyesque figures in various states of joyless self-gratification.' (Note also the similarly-drawn *sadistic automobile designs* by François Dallegret, in *Avant Garde*, May 1968, No. 3: p. 46–51.) The word 'joyless,' above, is the key. Dr. Otto Fenichel sums up clearly the whole essence of these sadistic and schizophrenic 'influencing machines' (see further Viktor Tausk in *Neurotica*, 8:35–42), all of which represent their inventors' genitalia or buttocks whether in fantasy-inventions or actually constructed; in

Psychoanalytic Theory of Neurosis (New York, 1945) p. 430:

> The most remarkable fact about all these machines is that these replicas of the patient's body are not used in pleasurable fantasies, but appear instead as cruel objects in the hands of imagined persecutors ... The [paranoid] defense has turned the intended erogenous pleasure into a threatening horrible pain.

Decades earlier, the bawdy hate-song, "The Great Fucking Wheel," had already turned on a machine-fantasy exactly similar to Veber's pistoning masturbation-machine, which was certainly intended as a satire on the machine-century glorified – underneath the rictus laughter – by Robida, and now upon us full blast. In the song, a point is made very clear that is wholly omitted or concealed in Ungerer's and Dallegret's cold and cruel blueprints for sadistic onanists: that *all such machines represent the genitalia of impotent men*, who thus achieve a fantasy revenge on the woman who has shamed them, by torturing or destroying her in a sadistic simulacrum of coitus.

The song begins frankly with the husband of the woman *'who never could ever be satisfied,'* and he sets out to build a gigantic mechanical succedaneum or Influencing Machine for her, mostly composed of a large piston and a "Great Fucking Wheel," as promised in the title. There is no disguising here that the machine is the man's penis. This sexual substitute or erotic *Golem* draws some of its formal inspiration from the novelty cartoons commonly circulated in the 1920's and since, of "The New Fuckmobile" and similar, being female masturbation devices combined and crossed with the new and thus erotized automobile. Numerous examples of this are in the files of the Institute for Sex Research (Kinsey Library) at Indiana University, with all manner of Detroit-style flivver attachments, such as a "Grease Injector", "Suction Pump", "Tit-Kisser," and "Pussy-Wiper," as illustrated ultra-mechanically in one manuscript copy seen. (Full texts of "The Great Wheel" are in Harry Morgan's *More Rugby Songs*, London, 1968, II. 136, as "The Blacksmith told me before he died;" and in Ed Cray's *The Erotic Muse*, New York, 1969, p. 136, as "The Fucking Machine.") I might mention that the last two gynecologists I met professionally each had several thousand dollars' worth of *toy trains*, tunnels, electrical switches, and so forth, and spent hours each evening playing with them. This is not hearsay. I have seen and handled these toy installations.

As to the Fucking Machine or "Great Fucking Wheel," it all most certainly does satisfy the woman as the man cannot. But, as the song goes on to explain: *'This was the case of the biter bit, There wasn't no method of stopping it – The whole damn contraption went up in shit!'* And this whole sorcerer's-apprentice tale ends dreadfully in a fecal explosion, which can most conveniently be described in psychoanalytic terms as an anal-sadistic substitute orgasm (very similar to that planned for all the rest of us, by means of the Atom Bomb), in which the machine avenges its impotent creator by tearing the woman – *read:* humanity – to bits. This is nothing other than a minor, modernized or mechanical form of the legend of the *vagina dentata*, of the insatiable and nymphomaniacal primeval earth-mothers or Amazons of the Trobriand Islands and elsewhere, with their vaginal 'teeth' broken and the women finally reamed out, tamed or slain by the culture-hero, 'Tooth-Breaker' or 'Dragon-Slayer.' Here seen in his last and flimsiest avatar, as boy-sized Captain Nemo with his monkey-wrench and engineer's cap – the sexually impotent little push-button 'scientist' or machine-tender, operating the "Great Wheel" or "Fucking Machine" destined to replace him.

II. CASTRATION

1. NEGROES AND JEWS

Actual castration in jokes is most commonly enacted on animals, or men of 'inferior' races – Negroes and Jews in particular – or on both animal and combined 'inferior,' as in certain of the following examples. The element of revenge-punishment is always made very clear, and central, in the insistence on the extreme *length* of the castrated penis, or on the excessive sexual potency 'requiring' the castration. As stated earlier, real castration of the type engaged in on animals, involving the testicles only, is not that with which folklore concerns itself often, though there do exist several favorite limericks on this theme, and one horrible and very long and detailed cowboy ballad of this kind, "The Castration of Strawberry Roan." Castration in jokes is usually of the 'harem' type: the ablation of the penis to prevent coitus. (The "Attack on the Testicles" will be considered in section II.4.)

The black penis is given a disproportionate amount of atten-

tion in white folklore. More, certainly, than the white penis –
in these discussions by whites – as to its size, shape, color, stiffness, and other characteristics. Negroes never discuss the white
penis at all. They just smile. The concern of the white with the
Negro's penis begins practically in the cradle: the folk-simile,
'as cute as the pecker on a baby jig' (short for *jigboo*, a variant
of *bugaboo*, a black demon or *'booger,'* itself used as an insulting term for a Negro, shortened to *'boog'*). Most white males in
the United States are agreed that the Negro penis – of which
they personally may never have seen an example in their lives
– is appreciably longer than that of white men of the same
physical height or build, *"the same way that a jackass has a
longer prick than a horse."* If asked about actual dimensions in
inches (and often when not asked), helpful informants will state
that penises from twelve to fifteen inches long, 'when erect,'
are common among Negroes, or are the rule, and that lengths
from twenty inches to two feet are sometimes encountered!
(*"That's why they used to call a prick a 'yard',"* I was once
told.)

Would-be serious discussions are then engaged in as to
whether the Negro's penis ever really does become stiff and
erect, or just 'waggles around like a donkey's prick' during
erection. This is the first of many castrations to come. I have
even heard it seriously held that the Negro's penis is longer than
the white man's *only* when it is flaccid, and that, when erect,
the afflux of blood somehow shrivels it down or *"firms it up
till it's no longer than mine or your'n."* Occasionally the statement is also made that the Negro's penis takes peculiar shapes
when erect. Spirals, 'like a porcupine's prick,' and 'lurchy kind
of twists' have been reported to me (with gestures) but the main
peculiarity stated is the pronounced *downward* curve, the opposite of the moderate upward curve usually observed in the
heaven-seeking white penis when erect. This is, of course, again
tantamount to saying that the Negro is castrated 'by nature,'
and cannot get an erection at all. Like *Genesis*, ix. 25, making
him a slave by 'God's curse.'

The frank statement is also often made that the Negro is
only a kind of 'physical beast' or 'lower animal' (than the
white), and that one therefore need not be vexed by his sexual
equipment and powers beyond those of white men. In the
matchingly heroic sexual feats ascribed to Negroes, the imputation of animal-like powers is a great deal more common than

any real assimilation of the Negro sex-hero to other 'hard men' of white legend, such as Samson, Siegfried, or Li'l Abner. In jokes, the Negro's admitted sexual advantage is often offset by his 'dumbness,' in which the comparison to a monkey, ape, gorilla, or orang-utan seldom is omitted to be made. *A Southern planter has a 'big nigger' who is borrowed from him by another planter up the river, to impregnate his fifty black 'wenches.' The Negro comes back very dissatisfied, saying, "Boss, ah cain't see why Ah had to bother wid all that travelin' jes fo' two hours wuk."* (N.Y. 1938. This is "Olivier's Brag," a survival of the legend of Siegfried in the *Niebelungenlied*.) Or the Negro may spoil everything by his 'dumbness,' as in another version where: *He arrives at the second plantation, serves thirty-four of the girls, keels over in a dead faint, and is shipped home in disgrace on the next riverboat. When his owner asks him how it happened, he says, "Ah cain't rightly tell yo', Mistuh Boss. Ever'thing went jes' fine when Ah tried it out in the mawnin' befo' Ah tuk de boat."* (Paris, 1954, told by the Negro novelist Richard Wright, the final line being delivered in an exaggerated plantation-darky whine.)

My father once managed an overall factory for a brief time, in Scranton, Pa., during the early 1930's, and 'just for fun' one day had the women workers cut out and stitch a pair of overalls in which all the dimensions were twice as large as the largest size they ordinarily made. The resultant pair of overalls, which were naturally four times as large (and not twice as large, as had been expected) as the largest size stocked, were then hung out the window of the second floor as an advertisement, reaching almost to the ground. My father is a great *pince-sans-rire*, and when asked about the overalls denied that they were being displayed, and stated they had been ordered specially by a Southern tobacco planter for a 'big nigger' who couldn't be fitted in the local stores, or even by Sears-Roebuck. The overalls had just been finished, he said, and were hanging out the window to air, and would soon be packed and sent south. Within a few hours, a photographer arrived from the local newspaper to take a photo of the object, and get the story. It did not occur to anyone to question whether a human being could actually exist of such dinosaur size. When it comes to Negroes and *bigness* – especially in the trouser department – the valves of white intelligence seem to freeze solid.

Insulting comparisons of the Negro's penis to a roll of linoleum or tar-paper seem to be considered a high-point of wit. *'Coloured chap at the door delivering a roll of linoleum. "Will you take this in front, Mum, or do you want me to shove it up your back passage?"'* (Chelmsford Prison, Essex, 1954.) – *The great new building of the Unesco is being constructed in World Peace Park, and one of the delegates from East Africa, leaving an important conference in the existing building, stops behind a stanchion to take a leak. A building guard high up in the steel structure shouts down, "Hey, you! Put down that roll of tar-paper and get off this property!"* (San Francisco, Calif. 1965.) This was also told of Dr. Martin Luther King, and still is, of any other Negro leader in the news, with the idea of reducing him to the dimensions of 'nothing but a big black prick.' The sexual accusation of raping white women is naturally involved. *'How did they discover that a black man has a big prick? – Some cunt split!'* (Chelmsford Prison, Essex, 1954. *'Split'* is criminal slang for tattle or 'squeal.' The anti-woman use of 'cunt' as meaning a stupid fool, or disprized person of either sex, seems to have been taken over in Britain, since the time of the First World War at least, from the French *'con.'*)

The interest in the size and performance of the Negro penis is not limited to men, and white women have been reported by more than one Negro celebrity to inquire about the matter in drawing-room conversations at a certain 'cultural level,' sometimes with other people present. The late Richard Wright once told me that whenever a white woman asked him about the size of his penis, he would reply *"How big is your cunt, honey? We can work something out."* He said this usually stopped the conversation there – but not always. A young Australian woman, completely unknown to me, wrote me as follows from London, 1970: *'When I once mentioned a coarse Australian expression – Whip it in, whip it out, and wipe it – to a Negro opera singer, he hid his head under the pillow and later remarked that he'd never seen a country in which there was so much missionary work to be done.'* Observe that this woman is, *en passant,* bragging to a perfect stranger about her Negro lover, than whom she feels she has proved herself, at least conversationally, to be 'tougher' and more male, even though his penis may have been longer than hers.

Compulsive swanking in this way of 'dirty talk' by women, and flaunting of the details of their sex lives, sometimes as an opening gambit to other men, is an unconscious (?) expression of *jealousy and animosity against men, whom such women think they are imitating,* just as homosexuals parody certain feminine gestures of women. Consider: a young woman, mistress of a New York psychiatrist in 1965, is receiving visitors at dinner in a magnificent open-work white pajama suit. I have never met her before, and when I ask her – thinking about my own life – why a girl like herself has thrown in her lot with a middle-aged man, she answers, in a loud grating voice, like an ash-can dragged over a cement floor: *"What I like about Al is his* GROOVY COCK!" (Note: Al talks the same way.) – Another: I am showing a group of young Englishwomen the sights in Paris in 1954. I have never met any of them before. Afterwards, all but one board a bus to go sight-seeing elsewhere. The one left behind had been as polite and superficial as all the others the whole while, but the moment we were alone she said with a daredevil grin: *"Let's have a drink. My mouth tastes like the inside of a Greek wrestler's jockstrap!"* – An American college-girl, on her 'junior-year-abroad' at the same period, sitting quietly in a restaurant with myself and two other men in Paris, decided suddenly she did not like the cut of the jib or last remark of the man sitting next to me, and leaned across the table to say to him in an artificially hard voice, *"Well, fuck you, half-ass!"* When I asked her if that's what she had learned at Vassar or Smith, or wherever it was, she smiled very sweetly and said, *"Exactly. It's an acrostic in a sonnet by John Peale Bishop."* (Which is true. Bishop was swanking just the way she did.)

The castratory attack on the Negro in fantasy is in at least one case reversed, and this exceptional joke is therefore given first and separately. In this it is the Negro who is doing the castrating, or something close, under circumstances that will be seen. *A Negro moves to a small western town from New Orleans. He cannot find any black women in town, and is not allowed into the local whorehouse. Finally, in desperation, he rapes a white prostitute who accidentally accosts him in the dark late one night. She screams, he is caught, and, as hanging is considered too good for him, he is buried by the townsmen up to his neck in sand, in a rodeo enclosure, the next morning, and a wild bull is turned loose on him. The bull makes a wild dash for the Negro's head, but he ducks. When the bull turns and tries again, the Negro ducks in the opposite direction. The bull paws the ground frantically, sights head-on at the Negro and plows down the field straight at him. The Negro twists his head up desperately to meet the bull's attack, and bites him violently by the balls. All the spectators leap to their feet shouting, "Fight fair, nigger,* FIGHT FAIR!!" (L.A. 1965. Printed in *World's Dirtiest Jokes,* 1969, p. 129, *expurgating* the word 'nigger' to 'Slobb.') Observe that in this, as it turns out, *pro*-Negro joke, the Negro has been humiliated, half-lynched, and practically buried, and his future chances do not look too good either. Friends of the Negro, who show their solidarity with the 'black soul-brothers' by telling jokes like this, are like the proverb about Hungarians: *"When you have a Hungarian for a friend – you don't need an enemy!"* (Scranton, Pa. 1940, from a Polish girl discussing my violent temper.) Actually, the joke is simply a long gloat.

The present chapter will attempt to parallel the sexual folklore about Negroes and Jews only in part, since there is a great deal more such material about Jews than about Negroes, and for many centuries. But the similarities are very striking, particularly in the ambivalent uneasiness, on the part of the people believing and retailing such folklore, as to whether Negroes and Jews are in fact sexual inferiors or admitted superiors. The absurd intensity with which it is attempted to denigrate the Negro, and to judaize the Jew, shows how uncertain their detractors really are. I have heard it stated by young boys, when I was a boy myself, that *Negro blood is darker in color than white blood.* As is well known, one 'drop' of Negro (or Jewish) blood 'changes' white blood irretrievably if mixed together by parents of differing races. The same boys were also of the opinion that *Negro semen is black.* (Scranton, Pa. 1932.) The semi-conscious idea here, nowadays, is the sexual 'defiling' of any woman with whom such semen comes into contact. This is a superstition that has hung on a long time. The Greek historian, Herodotus, in the 5th century B.C., tells it as true of the Ethiopians: having never visited Ethiopia, he could speak freely. This is something like Gore Vidal's rather nervous remark in a review (more recent than his *Reflections Upon a Sinking Ship,* 1969) that Negroes don't *really* have longer penises than whites. You can almost hear the tremor in his voice. That *'nigger mammies give chocolate milk'* (Pa. 1932) is understood to be a joke. Also, too many white babies have drunk that milk to be fooled.

For most people, Negroes may not have the fabled tails of

Russian Jewish peddlers, but whatever they do have is very *long*, very *strong*, very *black* (except for their teeth, which are preternaturally white), and far far deeper than just skin-deep. *"When you cut a nigger, the meat is black right down to the bone!"* (San Diego, Calif. 1965.) This bit of fabulous physiology was told me by a man selling books in an 'America First' bookshop, in connection with a story about lynching and castrating ('cutting') a Negro. This implied that the *bone* referred to is in the Negro's penis, though I could not wangle my informant into saying this right out. He was also an absolute mine of information on local Negroes 'jumping out of their big white second-hand Cadillacs' late at night and raping white women – orally especially, because they are 'built too big' for vaginal intercourse with any kind of women but 'their own,' who therefore have to 'shake it like jello' during intercourse, to make the men feel anything at all. The white women were 'too scared' to go to the police. But he knew.

Jews are not popularly believed to have longer penises than anyone else (though of course they *do*), but it is generally agreed that their brains, ability to make money, and family and racial loyalties are abnormally enlarged. These being practically human characteristics, there is no Western folklore assimilating the Jews, owing to these overdevelopments, to any other animal or simian, as with Negroes and Irishmen (chimpanzees). The phallic or sexual accusation is made instead in various 'mental' or monetary forms, particularly that Jews unfairly use money or their abnormal intellects to make 'fancy kinds of love' to Christian women, after which these women will no longer bother with men of their own religion. (I have had my own books cited to me as proof of this.) Consider the claim absurdly made, as will be detailed in the following section, 13.III, that the circumcision of Jews in infancy makes them *'almost if not completely immune for cancer of the penis,'* and that women who have intercourse only with men so circumcised are *'immune from cancer of the neck of the womb.'* This is an extravagant example of a sexual or genital libel against the Jews, here posing as medical folklore and politely reversed into a mock-medical 'superiority.' In fact, cancer is not infectious, and circumcision does not prevent it in men. (Except in the foreskin.)

In this line, everyone knows or should know the superb reply made by Alexandre Dumas, author of *The Three Musketeers* and over ninety other best-sellers, when: *Someone who had insulted him then refused to fight a duel with him, on the grounds that Dumas "had Negro blood." "Yes," said Dumas. "I am an octoroon. My father was a quadroon, my grandfather was a mulatto, and my great-grandfather was a pure-blooded Negro. And his father was an ape! My family began where your family has ended."* For a spur-of-the-moment reply to an insult, that is the world's greatest. (Dumas was also exaggerating artistically, or gallantly avoiding any mention of the maternal side of his family from which, in fact, his 'Negro blood' came. His father, the heroic Napoleonic General Alexandre Davy de La Pailleterie, called Dumas – the model for 'Athos' in *The Three Musketeers* – was the natural son of a Negro woman and a French colonist in Santo Domingo; exactly the case also of the great American ornithologist and painter, Audubon, born in Haiti.)

Many sociologists have observed in recent years the curious 'emotional thinking' whereby one-eighth Negro or Jewish descent – 'one drop of blood,' as it is usually phrased – is thought to 'defile' or contaminate the other racial seven-eighths, or four quarts of arterial blood, making the individual a Negro or a Jew. Whereas the other seven-eighths white or Christian descent never suffice to make the individual 'white' or 'Christian,' as these racial purists see things. It is surprising that it took so long to observe this peculiarity: it was always *intended* to be unfair. But what is still not often observed is the imputation of tremendously superior strength or 'staining power' to the theoretically inferior race's sexual genes, when one drop of its blood – really meaning one spermatozoön or ovum – can outweigh an ocean of *sangre azul*.

The logical problem is very obtrusive here, that if Negroes and Jews really have longer or thicker penises than other races or religions, and are really more potent genetically and sexually (or 'know how to use it better'), they are not 'inferiors' at all but superiors. Everyone senses this. The Negro's presumed sexual and physical superiority is explained away as a mere function of his being 'closer to the ape' – the official Nazi line in the 1930's, when Hitler's pet boxer and bodyguard, Max Schmeling, was practically slaughtered by the American Negro boxer, Joe Louis, whom Schmeling had innocently called a *'Neger'* (the polite German term) to newspaper reporters before the fight. This will not serve for the Jews, however, and their presumed intellectual and sexual superiorities – *Every knock is a boost, fellas!* – are somehow to be considered just a mean, low, sneaky trick. The proper response in either case is the same: fantasy castration, becoming *real* castration, as in Nazi Germany, when the moment was ripe.

These fantasies exist at levels much more dangerous than just joking, though a half-humorous approach is usually evinced, sometimes with the de-balling knife in hand. In a small manuscript collection of jokes and bum gags, received from Arlington, Texas, at Christmas 1966, under the title (supplied by the collector), *Cream of the Crap*, several such anti-Negro items appear, directed particularly at the prominent Negro libertarian leader, Dr. Martin Luther King, who was later assassinated. The suggestion was made, for instance that he was *'called Doctor, because everywhere he goes, he carries his little black bag* [prostitute] *with him,'* and that *'Maybe they ought to castrate him, so he can win the No-Ball Prize.'* (Punning on the Nobel Prize, the distinction that was responsible for his being killed from ambush.)

In D. J. Bennett's "The Psychological Meaning of Anti-Negro Jokes," in *Fact* (March, 1964) No. 2: p. 53–9, no reference is made to these recurrent castration fantasies and threats against the Negroes, though the article ends with an expurgated version of a story about pulling out a Negro's teeth in such a way that the castratory intent or symbolism is perfectly transparent: *The Negro chauffeur of a California movie magnate driving through Alabama to Florida complains of a toothache, and the local dentist asks $500 to pull the infected tooth, though admitting it would cost only $20 to pull a white man's tooth. He explains to the outraged movie magnate, "Well, it's a major operation. Here in Alabama a nigger doesn't dare open his mouth to a white man, so we have to pull it out his ass."* (This is presumably a *pro*-Negro joke: please keep your eye on the ball.) It is alluded to in a group of mythical magazine-article titles, or bumper-stickers, on the back cover of Jackie Kannon's humorous magazine, *Ratfink* (New York, Feb. 1965) No. 2: "MEDICAL REPORT: *Rectal Tonsillectomy – Is It Safe?*"

The vacillation between ideas of the Negro's sexual *superiority*, and frank fantasies of castrating him in revenge for this, is made clear in a castration-story just as often collected of obviously superior father-figures such as bishops and ministers, as of Negroes. Vardis Fisher, in *Children of God*

(1939) p. 652, seems to be telling the following story of the Mormon leader, Brigham Young, though this somehow gets side-tracked between the first and last sentences. *'When the railroad first came through, a lot of persons back East wanted to see Brigham Young and his wives – because Brigham before he died was the most discussed man in the world. One time a society woman was riding through Nebraska when the train ran into a herd of buffalo. She ran to a window and looked out; and though she did not know it, what she saw was an old buffalo bull that had been cut to pieces and scattered up and down the track. She looked at a certain part of him and then threw up her hands and yelled, "Great God, we've run over a Mormon bishop!"'*

This story does not make any sense at all, after such a beginning, unless it is supposed to end, *"Great God, we've run over Brigham Young!"* Like Mark Twain's death, the report of the number of Brigham Young's wives was grossly exaggerated. *The Limerick*, Note 328, reports: 'Actually Young had only 21 wives. His reputation as a man of parts may not, however, have been entirely without foundation. At his birthplace in Whitingham, Vermont, a simple marker records: *"Brigham Young, born on this spot 1801, a man of much courage and superb equipment".'* In the simplest form of the anti-Mormon joke: *A man on a train going through Utah tells a woman passenger that the Mormon bishop has sixty wives. "Why he ought to be hung!" she cries. "Ma'm, he IS – like a bull!"* (D.C. 1940.)

The identification of superior individuals, particularly the priest, by the sexual attribute of phallic length, has already been noted in a joke first recorded in "Some Erotic Folk-lore from Scotland," in *Kryptádia* (1884) II. 261–2, of: *A man whose wife complains of his penis being too small, and who persuades the minister to substitute for him behind the screen with a hole in it, through which his penis is to be passed for examination by a jury of women.* 'He put his virility through the hole, when one of the matrons cried out, "That's the minister's: I ken't by the wart o' the point o't".' (This story will be found in an Italian version in Giraldi-Cinthio's *Gli Hecatommithi*, 1565, IX. 4.) Observe the castration imported into the American anti-Negro version: *Two 'negro wenches' find the amputated penis and testicles of a horse, shaken out of a veterinarian's buggy* [doctor as castrator] *on a country road.* 'They stopped to examine the objects in the road, and then one said in awe-

stricken tones: "See what the Ku Klux done to our pastor!" '
(1 : 136.)

Identical in form, though the element of the priestly phallic
attribute has been lost: *Two spinsters in their chauffeur-driven
limousine hit a cow on the road. 'The old girls were considerable
shake up. When they came to, one found a long cylindrical
hunk of the cow's udder in her lap. Taking it up affectionately,
she cried piteously, "Great heavens, Zebbie, the chauffeur's
been killed!"* ' (1 : 280.) Implying miscegenation, of course, the
spinsters being introduced as 'meticiously [?] *immaculate*,' that
is to say whiter-than-white. The castration is the punishment
for the intercourse of black with white.

The Negro satirist, Chester Himes, in his bitter and blackly
humorous *Pinktoes* (Paris, 1961) delivers a hilarious exercise in
all the sexual and miscegenational accusations against Negro
ministers and social leaders, but just somehow does not mention this one. The superstition being evidently that priests have
bigger penises than any mere laymen, and the further superstition being that Negroes have bigger penises than white men,
obviously Negro ministers should have the biggest penises of
them all. This may explain the singular venom of the allusions,
already quoted, to castrating a Negro leader to make him
eligible for the '*No-Ball Prize*,' and so forth. The *locus classicus*
on literary hatred of the Negro is Capt. Sir Richard Francis
Burton's 'translation' of the *Arabian Nights* (plagiarized and
paraphrased from Payne's translation earlier in the 1880's), in
which the homosexual and Negrophobic notes and excursi are
Burton's main original contribution, especially in the supplementary 10th volume. Mock-scientific recommendations that
Negroes be castrated to prevent them from raping white
women – the traditional accusation – are there quoted from
correspondents like R. W. Shufeldt and Charles Carroll, both
authors of maniacal anti-Negro books, and both hailing naturally from Texas. Burton himself also wrote two anti-semitic
books, one under a pseudonym. The Negro and the Jew also
meet again in many real and symbolic castrations in the later
sections II. 6 and III, "The Doctor as Castrator" and "Circumcision."

2. ANIMALS

The most famous animal-castration story is presented simply
as a mild pun. *A dog is sitting on a trolley track. A trolley-car
comes along and cuts off a piece of its tail. It yelps and dashes*

madly around, whereupon a trolley-car coming in the other direction cuts off its head. Moral: Don't lose your head over a little piece of tail. (2:321, a variant with the punishment element of its happening to two dogs in coitus on a railroad track.) A 'nonsense' version or overcompensatory topper, in *Sex to Sexty* (1966) 8:52, has: *A motorist who runs over a cat on the highway and cuts off its tail. When he tries to tape the cat's tail back on again, a policeman gives him a ticket 'for retailing pussy on a public highway....'* (Oh, John, please!) In a human version, no reference is made to castration – either front or back – but the railroad locomotive as father-figure, punishing the intercourse of the 'child,' is made preponderant. *An accident to a couple who have been making love on the railroad tracks* [!] *is thus explained by the woman survivor: "I was comin', an' Sam was comin', an' the train was comin', an' none of us could stop!"* (2:58, illustrated with Negro characters, who presumably have more uncontrollable 'animal' passions than whites.) The original punchline here, *"Don't lose your head over a little piece of tail,"* is now a full-blown folk proverb or admonitory phrase.

The story of the dogs on the railroad track is begun several times, only to have the man telling it collapse in uncontrollable laughter again and again without finishing it, on a semi-private laughing record, *"The Tale of the Dog"* (General Records, # 1729), issued in New York or Hollywood about 1942. The choice of this story, for the man to be unable to finish, is significant. The punch-line is gloatingly used, on the cover of *Grim Hairy Tales* (1966) – punning on *Grimm's Fairy Tales* – as caption to a drawing of Henry VIII having Anne Boleyn beheaded. This underlines again the anti-sexual or punishment element of this castratory tale. Compare also the section preceding, on "Decapitation," as symbolic of castration.

In all the joke forms, the Oedipal or castratory notion still surviving is the folk-idea that accidents during coitus – and, above all, castration and death, *which are thought of as identical* (n.b.) are really divine punishments for sexual sin, a sort of blasting by lightning in *"God's Revenge Against the Horrible Sins of Fornication and Adultery,"* as this would be called in the older hortatory literature of the 17th century. The modern position, that it is all just a good joke, still hides this fear, if only in *the necessity of joking* about so statistically uncommon a situation.

The fantastically inconsequential reasons given for castrating animals (in fact, not in jokes) are known to all 'animals-lovers,' a very large proportion of whom deliver over their belovèd pets, whether male or female, to the castrating knife every year. For the female, it saves the owners the trouble of the pups, or the embarrassment of the animal's unrepressed rollings and howlings when locked up unsatisfied during her period of heat. For the males, well, it 'keeps them out of trouble,' or 'home at night' ... as with husbands. (Their ears are also clipped and tails cut off – the pets, not the husbands – on purely cosmetic excuses.) The record in this line is surely held by M. Alfred Court, the world's greatest 'lion-tamer' today, who explains calmly on the back page of the *Nice-Matin* (14 January 1975) that lionesses are too dangerous to use in a circus act, owing to the jealous protectiveness of the male lions. And so, as he states (in translation): '*When I needed a lioness in my act, I would take a male lion and have him castrated. He would then lose his mane, and I could work more tranquilly.*' So now we know: half of the circus lions are really transvestite 'lionesses.' Note, hidden behind this striking example of hair-as-virility, the standard unconscious notion that a castrated male *is* a female, and vice versa.

Animal castrations are among the commonest in jokes – as in fact. Many millions of male animals, especially young bulls, are castrated every year in Europe, America, and Australia, for purposes of fattening the resultant 'steer' or 'ox' for subsequent slaughtering as food. The impregnation of cows is then done by the few selected prize bulls that are allowed to retain their testicles, but even these are no longer allowed to have intercourse with the cows where it is possible to masturbate the bull into a cowhide bag, or merkin (scented with the vaginal secretions of a cow), and to portion out the bovine semen later to the cows in heat, by means of a clyster-pump or syringe wielded by an 'animal-husband.' As with the old lady's complaint about the Virgin Birth, one finds it difficult to see *what was the matter with the old system?* In *Life* magazine's enthusiastic feature articles on the American cowboy – those of Hungary and Argentina are of course the same – in the issues of 22 Aug. 1949 and 22 Oct. 1951, such gloating statistics are given, for instance, as that: 'The cowboy is one of the most purely functional human beings the world has ever developed ... fiction and films have misjudged him, not in his appearance, which they reproduce with fidelity, but in his accomplishments. The fact that he is actually capable of riding horses for 16 hours a day, or that *in his lifetime he has castrated 50,000 calves or beaten 1,000 rattlesnakes to death* are slighted in favor of tricks he never performed, songs he never sang, ideas he never had.' (*Italics supplied.*)

The magazine feature-writers can dry their tears. What with the New Freedom for S. & M. (sado-masochistic) 'spaghetti westerns,' cows have already been mowed down by rifle fire, with the cowboy executioners dressed in yummy black-rubber fetichistic mackintoshes, in *Hud* (1964), for having hoof-&-mouth disease; the cadavers then being plowed under by tractors *à la* Auschwitz. Consider also the 'obsessive blood bath,' as S. K. Oberbeck typifies it in *Newsweek* (24 Aug. 1970), of the patriotico-sadistic *Soldier Blue*, serving up the Sand Creek massacre of the Indians by the u.s. Cavalry in 1864, which 'drips, squirts and splashes sadistic, slow-motion gore (children's heads and occasional limbs come whizzing by). . . .' With a little judicious management of the Society for the Prevention of Cruelty to Animals, it should easily be possible now to film the little anecdote given by Henry Miller in "Via Dieppe-New-haven," in *Aller-Retour New York* (Paris, 1938). – Only Henry Miller can meet people like this :

> I listened to the young Englishman who had had a strange time of it in Australia. He was telling me of his life as a sheep herder, how they castrated I don't know how many thousands of sheep in a day. One had to work fast. So fast, in fact, that the most expedient thing to do was to grab the testicles with your teeth, and then a quick slit with the knife and spit them out. He was trying to estimate how many thousand pairs of testicles he had bitten off in this hand to mouth operation during his sojourn in Australia. And as he was going through his mental calculations he wiped his mouth with the back of his hand.
>
> "You must have had a strange taste in your mouth," I said, instinctively wiping my own mouth.
>
> "It wasn't as bad as you might imagine," he answered calmly. "You get used to everything – in time."

As with all expurgations of human situations in folk-humor, by extrapolating them upon animals – especially cute little ducks, monkeys, skunks, &c. – the castration of animals is considered *cute* in jokes. *The hen who complains about the rooster* [as 'cocks' are politely called]: *"I was under the porch with him all through a rainstorm, and all he did was talk about his operation."* (Baker, 1947, vol. III.) A favorite format is the Wellerism, on the classic *"Every little bit helps,"* as the old lady said when she pisht in the sea. Among the castratory forms: *"They're off!" said the monkey, when he backed into the lawn-mower.* And, *"It won't be long now,"* as the monkey said when he stuck his prick in the meat-chopper. (N.Y. 1952.)

All dangerous cutting and sawing machines are considered the subject of a hideous castratory fascination, as will be seen further under "Self-Castration," below. The projection of such ideas upon the monkey is particularly easy, owing to the monkey's imitativeness and quasi-human form. (Dr. Roger Abrahams interestingly observes in *Deep Down in the Jungle,* 1964, p. 137–8, the 'real kinship feeling' which some of the Philadelphia Negro slum children whom he studied had developed with monkeys, irrespective of the common taunt among children and adults as to Negroes 'looking like' monkeys or gorillas.) A famous monkey story of which the castrational import cannot be missed, with the monkey clearly representing the wise child who refuses to be fooled, substitutes throat-slitting for castration, as with the stories of "The Mad Barber of Fleet Street," in 13.II.7, below, in one of which a barber plans to pin a man helplessly to the barber-chair and cut his throat for having seduced his girl – the standard *lex talionis* in such cases being castration, of course. *A man is irritated by a monkey in the window of the apartment opposite, who imitates every-thing he does. Determined to be revenged, he buys two straight-razors and shaving-brushes, and tosses one of each to the monkey. He then elaborately goes through the motions of lathering and shaving, with the monkey carefully imitating each step. Finally the man pretends to slash his throat with the razor. The monkey falls on its back, and holds up both hands and both feet to its nose in the nose-&-thumb gesture meaning "Kiss my ass!"* (N.Y. 1948. Motif J2413.4. Another form is given in the First Series, 3.I, page 195. See also Prof. Archer Taylor's monograph on the nose-&-thumb, *The Shanghai Gesture,* 1950, somehow omitting its traditional scatological meaning, de-scribed in full by Rabelais.)

This joke is older than would appear, being given first in Des Périers' *Nouvelles Récréations* (1558) No. 19, where, however, the monkey does get killed. So also in a story of the same kind alluded to in that excellent source of folk-wit, John Selden's *Table-Talk* (*d.* 1654; edition of 1869) p. 118, under the heading "Wit" : *'Fine Wits destroy themselves with their own Plots, in meddling with great affairs of State. They commonly do as the Ape that saw the Gunner put Bullets in the Cannon, and was pleas'd with it, and he would be doing it too; at last he puts himself into the Piece, and so both Ape and Bullet were shot away together.'* Compare the sick spectacle at modern circuses – surviving, of course, from those of Rome – usually reserved for the final sado-masochistic *bonne-bouche,* the "Man Shot from the Cannon." (Actually he is not propelled by the simultaneous explosion, but from a spring-action motorcycle seat.) Rocketing to the moon and planets, with no sure knowledge of *how one is going to get back to earth – and who the hell cares –* is the identical body-as-phallus neurotic fantasy, government funded.

The body-as-phallus identification is strictly Euclidean: 'Things equal to the same thing equal each other' – thus, *the body-as-machine* equals *the Machine-as-phallus,* as with all 'Influencing Machines,' which invariably represent their inventors' genitalia (of whichever sex). This appears clearly in a remarkable castratory joke, which is considered very humorous and cute, and as such is told by women among others, owing to its projection of the ugly ideas involved only upon those standard kitschy-cute critters of child and animal, or A Boy and His Dog. *'A mother caught her young son playing with sulphuric (or : carbolic) acid, and without wishing to alarm him, suggesting he trade his bottle for one of hers, containing a baby-oil. He asked what good that was. She said she had rubbed some of it on her stomach, and passed a baby. "That's nothing," he exclaimed, "I rubbed some of this on the cat's ass, and it passed a Cadillac".'* (D.C. 1952.) Note the gratuitous comparison of childbirth with farting or constipation, as in the homosexual stories given earlier under 'Rectal Motherhood." (First Series, 8.VI.3, pages 601–2.) Here is the most recent version of the joke: *A woman tending her garden sees a little boy going by on a skateboard hanging onto the tail of a dog who is pulling him. "Little boy," she says, all sweet reasonableness, "isn't there any other way you could hold your dog?" "Well, sure," he says, "I could hang onto his balls but that's my passing-gear!"* (Reno, Nevada, 1966, told by a truly sweet and reasonable young woman.)

Here we actually see the body *becoming* the machine, evidently via the genitals, which are construed as the gear-box or shift. Many drivers of 'sports cars' refuse the automatic-shift models for the same unconscious reason. An excessively cruel and detailed version of the same joke is given in *Sex to Sexty* (1966) 7:61; the dog's testicles are seized and squeezed, or twisted with tongs! Punchline: *"You should see what he can do when I reach under his tail with these tongs and twist his nuts!"* As repeated in *World's Dirtiest Jokes* (1969) p. 139, all reference to the 'passing-gear' has disappeared except as the caption-title. But note the even more complete mechanization of the animal on the facing page: *'Know why a dog lifts his hind leg to piss? – That's to throw his ass out of gear, so he won't shit all over himself.'* This is a revision or riddling survival of various just-so recitations about "Piddling Pups", "The Pesky Fly," and "Why Dogs Leave a Big Fat Bone."

Were it not for the 'sulphuric acid' version, originally collected – probably the household insect-repellent, carbon disulphide, is meant – one would not be able to trace this story very easily to its Levantine source. Yet the key or 'punch' word, which is *pass*, has not changed in all the centuries and countries of its travels. The original appears in the Turkish collection of jests of which the wise-fool hero is the folk character, *Hodja Nasr'eddin* (Wesselski's edition, Weimar, 1911, I. 224, No. 64), and it is also concerned with 'feaguing' animals by putting turpentine or red pepper on their anuses to make them run: *Nasr'eddin is advised by a friend to treat his balky ass with red pepper, to make it move faster. The ass runs away at high speed, at the first touch of the red pepper to its anus, and Nasr'eddin must then put pepper on his own anus in order to catch it.* (Some versions have the 'topper':) *He runs so fast that he passes the ass, circles around and goes through the town, shouting to his wife, "Unload the ass when it gets here. I have to run through the village a couple of times more!"*

Charlie Chaplin's 1910's movie-comedy, "The Jail Break," has a scene rather similar to this, *expurgated* to a mere shot in the arse with a shotgun by the prison-guard; and he comes back to it again in *Modern Times*, his masterpiece, with the prisoner this time accidentally eating cocaine. In another of Chaplin's early comedies the hero becomes a superman when he accidentally 'sits' on a drug-addict's hypodermic syringe. Compare also the droll touch, in Walt Disney's *Fantasia* (1938, in the "Pastoral" Symphony section) when: *The centaur chasing the coy centauress cannot get over the fence, and reaches back with a branch to whip his own hindquarters to force himself to take the jump!* I very much shocked the movie-critic I was watching this with, at the time, by calling it an unconscious erotic allusion to flagellatory aphrodisiacs. He would not even agree that there was anything 'erotic' about centaurs chasing centauresses, and objected to the term.

In transitional forms of jokes of the 'passing' or 'passing-gear' type, the use of acids, drugs, whips, or feaguing of any kind disappears, and the attack moves frankly from the animal's anus to his testicles. (If a mare, the whipstock is driven into her vagina, as in India.) This is sometimes frank, sometimes veiled in 'nonsense'; *An American tourist in Mexico asks a Mexican, slumped on the ground behind his bull during the hour of the siesta, what time it is. The Mexican lifts up the bull's balls and says, "Eet ees two-thirty, señor." Amazed, the American comes back every quarter-hour to ask the same question, and gets a similar response, each time, by way of the bull's balls. Finally, he says, "Listen, friend, there's an American dollar in it for you if you'll tell me how you tell time by a bull's balls!" The Mexican takes the dollar, and says with a smile, "Señor, I mos' leeft up the bull's balls to see the clock across the street."* (L.A. 1968. The Levantine "Lazy Hero," Motif L114.1; and compare W111.1, the "Contest in Laziness.") This sounds more like a caress than an attack, but how does the bull feel about it?

Of frank attacks: *A Marine in the tropics is warned against the deadly jungle snake, the krait, which has black and yellow stripes distinguishing it from all others, and is told that if he encounters a krait he should give it a quick judo chop with the side of his hand across its head before it can bite. Later he is found in the jungle nearly dead; the trees all around are torn up, and there are marks of a terrific battle. He is given a medical and sent to hospital, where he is interrogated by his commanding officer as to what really happened. "Sir," he says, "you know what you told us about those deadly kraits? Well, I saw one's tail sticking out from behind a tree, so I reached around and did just like we were told." "But who tore up the trees?" asks the officer. "Major, have you ever judo-chopped a tiger in the nuts?"* (San Diego, Calif. 1967.) Probably symbolizes the Vietnamese War for the soldiers telling it – 'the first war America ever lost.' Compare the story under "Self-Castration," later: *The wrestler bites what he thinks are his opponent's testicles. They are his own.* (Usually told with a wealth of castratory oral-incorporative detail.)

In the cabdriver-&-passenger story below, the cabdriver's unexpected obscenity – which parallels the boy's 'passing-gear' reply above – is essentially a form of Water-Wit, directed against the passenger. See further on Water-Wit, chapter 2.VI.3, in the First Series; and 14.II.3, below. *A woman passenger in a horse-drawn cab, who has promised the driver a good tip, is horrified by the cabdriver's cruel whipping of the horse, when she tells him she is in a hurry. "My good man* [compare: *Little boy],"* she says, *"isn't there some other way you could urge your horse along?" " 'Coss there is, Mum,"* he replies cheerfully, *"but I've got to save 'is balls for the hill."* (London, 1954, unnecessarily observed by the teller to date 'from the old days of horse-drawn cabs.')

3. AUTHORITY-FIGURES

The castration of authority-figures, though it does occur in other types of folklore (parody headline: "Last of the King's Balls Comes Off Tonight;" *Anecdota Americana,* 2:383; long recitation, "The Night of the King's Castration," also known as "Daniel in the Lions' Den," etc.), does not appear in any *joke* in the sources used. This with the exception of those jokes on the presumed or imagined [*nota bene*] castration of priests or ministers – who are actually *not* castrated, even in the jokes – already given in the preceding section, "Negroes and Jews." Instead, the theme of castration as punishment for sexual transgression against the authority-figure's female chattels – as in harems – is particularly prominent. One incredible example: *A blacksmith 'fixes' a boy's persistent erections for him daily by striking his penis with a sledge-hammer on the anvil. One day the blacksmith is not home when the boy arrives, and the blacksmith's wife fixes it for him by a different method.* (2: 106.) The blacksmith as patriarchal survival figure – evaded and even cuckolded here – is also apparent in the custom of runaway weddings at the anvil (Gretna Green), in Vulcan-Hephaestus, the first of the legendary *crippled machine-tenders or inventors,* as the cuckolded husband of Venus, and other lore.

Compare also the German 'Frau Wirtin' verse, similar to the English-language limericks: (in translation:) *Frau Wirtin had a lodger who was a blacksmith, and his penis was exactly square. But love conquers all: he put it on the anvil and beat it into a cylinder.* (From Czechoslovakia, 1952. Similar themes in *The Limerick*, No. 169, on a 'hexahedronical ball;' and No. 179, on pounding a man into a woman's misshapen vagina with a sledge-hammer.) The most recent version of the American blacksmith jokes changes him to: *An old doctor, who tells the boy with the persistent erection 'to lay it on the table, which he did. The doctor then rapped it smartly with his rubber hammer. It immediately fell, and the doctor started looking around on the floor. The boy hurt, but at the same time much relieved, said, "What do I owe you, doc?" The doctor replied, "Nothing if you'll help me find that little bug that jumped out of it!"'* (*Sex to Sexty,* 1966, 8:41.) The magical or demonic element of the 'little bug' is curious here – clearly on the theory of the Mexican jumping-bean – but the mocking of the castratory authority-figure, the doctor, as himself impotent, is even more castratory than the mere cuckolding via the blacksmith's wife. One senses that this is simply a folktale, or direct expression of the fantasy of the castrator-doctor or blacksmith, and that the necessary punch-line is an embarrassment to the tellers, whence its frequent changes, without – for all that – in any way 'spoiling' the story. An entire section will be devoted to "The Doctor as Castrator," below. Sometimes the nurse *'gets out a lot of pus too.'* (N.Y. 1942.)

Where the authority figure is directly attacked, in castration fantasies, the penis is seldom mentioned, the activity being that of real castration, as with animals, removing the testicles. One exception is the stanza of *"Mademoiselle from Armentières,"* the principal Allied army-song of World War I, rising gloryingly on the final note as it describes how: *"The Little Marine went over the top, To circumcise the Kaiser's cock – Hinky-dinky parlay voo!"* And even here the euphemism 'circumcise' is employed. Compare too the long, mock-serious correspondence in the *New Statesman* (London, spring of 1973, thirty years after World War II), still trying to prove that, in the words of the "Colonel Bogy" war song, *"Hitler, had only one ball, And Goballs had no balls at all!"* (Taken quite seriously in Martin Page's war songbook, *Kiss Me Goodnight, Sergeant Major,* 1973, p. 31–4.)

Centuries before, during the prime-ministry in France of the Italian cardinal, Giulio Mazarini, in the 1640's and '50's, pamphlets of an insensate violence – the so-called "Marzarinades" – were widely circulated in France against this statesman. In one of these, *La Gazette des Halles, touchant les affaires du temps* (Paris, 1649), according to Charles Nisard's *Etude sur le langage populaire, ou Patois de Paris* (1872) p. 352, the first 'nouvelle' in verse is written in the character of a fishwife or herring-venderess, relieving herself of a volley of abuse against Cardinal Mazarin *'dans des termes à la fois féroces et obscènes,'* ending that what she really wants is to get hold of the Cardinal and castrate him.

Several jesting ballads exist in English on outwitting the Devil, usually with a woman's aid, and even frankly on "The Gelding of the Devil," by telling him it 'will make him fat.' These almost always turn on the trick of Rabelais' folktale, *"Le Diable de Papefiguière,"* Bk. IV, chap. 47, in which a woman disguised as a man pretends to be castrated, and so tricks the Devil into flight. (Tale Types 1095, 1133, and 1159.) A neo-Faustian form of this story has been collected in very recent times in the area of Penobscot Bay, Maine: *The Devil promises an old man a team of horses if, one year from that day, he will come back and allow the Devil to cut out his privates in payment. But the man sends his wife in disguise and so cheats the Devil.* (Frank G. Speck, "Penobscot Tales and Religious Beliefs," in *Journal of American Folklore*, 1935, vol. 48: p. 106.) Compare also the ancient legend of "The Farmer's Curst Wife" whom even the Devil is afraid to keep: Child Ballad, No. 278, tracing it to the *Panchatantra*, in India. Note that in modern Faust stories the Devil collects 'souls,' not testicles, meaning that these are considered to be identical at the folk level. In another Penobscot tale, very similar, but told of an animal-trickster, *The Racoon tricks the Bear – who wants to kill him – into putting his testicles into the Raccoon's hole.* (JAF, vol. 48: p. 98. Type 153. Compare Motif J351.1, self-castration.)

The Devil is, of course, non-existent. Or, rather, there can only be a God if there is a Devil too, since their myths are inextricably mingled. The Devil's existence is positively stated by Scripture, especially by the New Testament, in *Luke*, iv. 1–13, which gives the original of the Faust story in the temptation of Jesus by Satan. The denial of the existence of the Devil is therefore, for religious persons, tantamount to denying the existence of God. If the Old Testament and the New Testament can be considered to have lied or been wrong about the existence of the Devil, then they can equally well have lied or been wrong about everything. Emphasis on the Devil is therefore very much of an embarrassment, and is greatly diminished as religious belief becomes more sophisticated in modern times. Formerly this was not so: the Devil of the fatalistic Graeco-Judaean *Book of Job* (starkly opposed to the optimistic and buoyant Jewish religious position of 'the Chosen People') is as strong as God, and in fact successfully *tempts* God to allow the sinless Job to be tortured: God as Faust. This is very close to the position of Milton in *Paradise Lost*. In outwitting and castrating the Devil, in the folktales and folk ballads on this theme, the hidden point is the necessary duality of these mutual and ambivalent forces of Good and Evil, personified as God and the Devil. (The letter-for-letter identity of these terms in English is probably an accident.) For, thus understood, in castrating the Devil one castrates God. Witness the embarrassment of the mock-religious horror movie, *The Exorcist* (1973) to organized religion, as bringing all the kooks out of the woodwork. After all, what's so funny? As is best seen in the sinister mimings of voodoo and diabolism, one must take superstitions quite seriously: they are not jokes but *magic*, and are believed in very sincerely. Superstitions are the religion of people who do not go to church. Religion is the superstition of those who do.

Lesser authority-figures are dealt with summarily by popular legends and iconology, in the castrating of demigods and minor deities. The *Priapeia*, a collection of classical Latin erotic and satirical poems addressed to the guardian god of gardens, Priapus, with his attributes of enormous penis and sickle (to pedicate and castrate robbers), actually states in No. LV, *"Credere quis posset,"* that thieves have not only defied the god Priapus but have also stolen his sickle, and that he now fears the loss of his other weapon too, *'altera tela,'* which would make of him a *Gallus*, or castrato-priest. The most famous sickle-bearing popular deity, Father Time, who is bald except for one forelock, is also castrated, doubtless with his own sickle too, as discussed in the First Series, 1.III, "The Diaper and the Scythe." James Branch Cabell, in the mannered prose and heavily-charged sexual symbolism of his *jeu d'esprit* of the 'Naughty-naughts,' *Jurgen* (1919), p. 186, carefully notes this point: 'Time sleeps quite naked ... and, though it is a delicate matter to talk about, I notice he has met with a deplorable accident. So that Time begets nothing any more. .. the while he brings about old happenings over and over, and changes the name of what is ancient, in order to persuade himself he has a new plaything.' This is nothing other than the castratory legend of Kronos and Saturn, with overtones of the catching (and cannibalizing) of Freud's *Ur-vater* naked in the night, as in the related legend of the castration of Father Noah.

Santa Claus, finally – honest, kids, I'm sorry, but I've got to call the strikes and balls the way I see them! – is also castrated. This is plainly stated in modern Dutch folklore, which also supplies Santa Claus' last name. In Holland he is *Sinter Claas Kapoentje* (Santa Claus the little Capon), and, like the minor representation of the Father-God that he is, he rewards good children with wooden shoes full of toys, while his sinister Negro helper, Black Peter (really just a poor chimney-sweep : also castrated, with the terrible tar-caused cancer of the scrotum), brings switches to beat bad children with. As to *who* has castrated Santa Claus, see the First Series, i.III, pages 78–9, "The Diaper and the Scythe."

4. THE ATTACK ON THE TESTICLES

In his early and sympathetic biography, *Sigmund Freud* (English translation, London, 1924, p. 160), the analyst Fritz Wittels opens his brief but eloquent chapter explaining the concept of "The Castration Complex," with the following general remarks :

> Castration has been extensively practised by stock-farmers, and this has kept a knowledge of the practice alive among western races, to which the castration of men has become unfamiliar. Those, indeed, who took part in the retreat of the German and Turkish army from Syria during 1918 learned that the Arabs made a practice of castrating their defeated enemies. The gentler-minded among the conquerors contented themselves with pedication. In both cases the aim was to humiliate the vanquished by emasculation, actual or symbolic. Since the days when Herodotus visited Asia Minor, moral outlooks in that part of the world have remained unchanged in this.

Consider King Saul's demand, in *1 Samuel* xviii. 25–7 (in the 10th century B.C.) that David bring him 'an hundred foreskins of the Philistines' as dowry for his daughter! Of course, that was a long time ago ...

During the centuries of the Arab Conquest, in the Mediterranean Islands, Italy, and Spain, this form of humiliation was taken up by the Latin races, particularly among the Italians, leading to such anomalies as the famous choir of *castrati* singing in the Vatican chapel, in Rome. The Italian *novellieri* of the Renaissance, who were one of the main bridges in the carrying of Arab and Levantine folktales and other lore to Europe, were particularly fond of horrible castratory mutilations and revenges. The *Novelle* (1554–73) of the Dominican monk, Matteo Bandello, made a specialty of this; and it should not be overlooked, in this connection, that the infamous tortures of the Inquisition were, from the beginning, under the special direction of the famously cruel Dominicans. As the spilling of blood was to be avoided in the Inquisitorial tortures, in accordance with the perhaps humane but certainly hypocritical ordinance of an earlier pope, the burning, flaying, and crushing of various parts of the body – including the testicles – were the standard methods. We will see at the end of the present section what the standard modern methods have become.

A story in the current float of castration tales, in which the actual castration of the victim (in this case an adulterer) is set up fiendishly so that it must be enacted by the victim himself – or evaded at the cost of his life: *his penis has been trapped in a bench-vise* [!] *and the house set afire* – has already been given in the First Series, 9.II.5, page 724, "Punishing the Adulterer," attributing the original to Bandello. This is an error: the elusive original is in fact in *Le Cene* of Anton-Francesco Grazzini, the Florentine academician of the mid-16th century known as 'Il Lasca,' a collection of *novelle* dated about 1547 in its introduction. The story appears at Dinner II, Tale 8, under the title of "The Priest's Punishment," *for having attempted to seduce a noble young woman, who complains to her brothers. The errant priest is seized at night and tied by his hands with his back to a cypress tree.* 'Then, the youngest brother, who was supple as a cat, tied the priest's testicles with a long cord which he had brought along for just that purpose. Then, climbing high up on the trunk of the cypress, to where the branches began, he attached one of these to the other end of the cord, bending it like a bow so that the priest was forced to hold himself tightly on tiptoe, or else suffer in an intolerable way.' *The priest is then left in this* 'mad and extravagant posture' *and the brothers retire for the night.* The comparison to the actual castration of Abélard by the henchmen of Canon Fulbert, the uncle of Héloïse, about 1120, an historical occurrence over four centuries before (in France), which has already been discussed, makes evident that the intention – in Grazzini's story, as in the modern 'joke,' – is not so much to achieve the revenge-castration of the victim as to do so *sinlessly*, by putting him in a position in which he must castrate himself.

Such moralistic niceties are still not common at the actual folk-level in certain Italian cultures, as is made horribly clear in a tape-recorded conversation of two American Mafia gangsters, taken by wiretap or 'bug,' and issued by the New York Joint Legislative Committee on Crime as 'an educational tape' titled *The Voices of Organized Crime.* (Transcript published in Paul Krassner's *The Realist,* October 1968, No. 83: p. 14–15:)

LARRY: Mike, we gotta lota garbage [traitors].

MIKE: You can't leave them and you can't bury them. Bury them you can't.

LARRY: Nah. You know what I told 'em? You know what I told 'em? I said, look, let's fuck around ... Let's fuck this shit. They know everything. Now fuck them. Let 'em see what we'll do. Then let them go fuck themselves. What are they gonna do? Go and hide? Fuck them. To let them go they gonna break their mother's cunt. Go break the Rock of Gibraltar. They got a better chance. What are they gonna break? They're gonna break their sister's cunt? [On the Italian and Hispanic-American phrase, '*rump the cula,*' break one's ass.]

MIKE: The ones they were gonna break, they broke down already. The rats they already broke down. It goes back to the same thing we said yesterday. The ego's been deflated [!] We took their prestige away ...

LARRY: This is ours. This cocksucker. I got to take this cocksucker ... this dirty motherfucker ...

MIKE: You know where you got to put him? You know what I told Pete? You got to pick a lamppost. He's got to put the ... hang him on the lamppost. You understand? You got to cut his prick off. You got to put it in his pocket and you got to give him a nice slash and leave him up there. That's what you got to do. That will serve notice to every fucking rat stool pigeon what's gonna happen when and if he finks.

In fact, the Mafia mutilation is not always of the penis, the corpse's right arm sometimes being cut off – according to what the deliciously horrified public is told by the newspapers. Later the arm is produced before the higher-ups in the gang as proof of the murder, somewhat like the castratory cutting off of the tongues of dragons or tails of foxes (*Judges*, XV.4), and other animals, as evidence in claiming payment of a state bounty for killing them. The putting of the victim's ablated penis *in his own pocket* is apparently rationalized by the modern gangsters as a way of avoiding being caught later with the evidence of the murder. Mike goes on to observe, '*You can't leave them and you can't bury them. Bury them you can't.*' Actually what is intended is a further humiliation or disgracing of the enemy's living or dead body: the Arabs stuff the victim's penis into his own mouth after the castration. The touch of the *pocket* is simply a modern modification or survival of this.

Arab warriors and the Sicilian Mafia gangsters who are their cultural heirs are, of course, primitives, even when transplanted to great Western cities, and their threats are to be considered as absolutely serious. Not so are the threats and jokes about castration among civilized Western adults, remarked upon in Fenichel's *The Psychoanalytic Theory of Neurosis* (1945) p. 79, as cited at the beginning of the present chapter: 'That adults so easily and eagerly threaten or joke about castration is, of course, an expression of their own castration complexes. Frightening others is an excellent method of quieting one's own fears. In this way castration complexes are passed on from generation to generation.'

The attack on the testicles is so common in folklore and folk-humor as to be present even in gags and 'one-liners' below the situational level of jokes. "*What makes a cannon roar? – You'd roar too if one of your balls was shot off.*" (N.J. 1942.) – *A man comes home from the golf-course on a stretcher: he took seriously a sign saying "Scrape Balls After Using."* (N.Y. 1940.) – Another golf-course item, very creaking as humor, and set up strictly for the punch-line. *The Paradise Golf Course: everything is free. The dazed golfer plays through his eighteen holes, with free drinks, free caddies, free showers, etc. On leaving he is presented with a bill for $200. The balls are $20 each. "Oh, I see," he says, "they get you by the balls!"* (N.Y. 1942.) Compare a similar joke, already given, in which the whole point is likewise a reference to testicular castration: *A man puts down rat-traps baited half with apples and half with nuts, to see which will work better. He rushes up from the cellar, after examining his traps, to break the news to his wife who is entertaining a* *few ladies. "I caught eight of them," he says triumphantly. "By the apples?" she asks. "No," he gloats, "I got them by the nuts."* (1:79.)

Here is what must be considered the British version of the preceding 'rat-trap' story, though the method used is not the same: *A rich man has married a chorus-girl, and she is receiving guests for the first time at their house in the country. The husband absents himself for a moment to choose the wine for dinner, while the guests are having apéritifs and small-talk in the drawing room. When he gets back everyone is leaving and in a terrible huff. "What happened, darling?" he says to his young wife, when they are alone. "I don't know," she says tearfully. "They were talking about rats in country-houses, and someone said the best way to get rid of them was to pound broken glass in their holes. So I said, 'But how do you get the rats to stand still long enough?'"* (London, 1965, told in the 'quarantine' section of the London airport in connection with the food of the transit-passengers being shoved at them through a hole in the wall, to keep them from actually 'touching British soil' – or *vice versa*.) In the 'James Bond, Secret Agent 007' murder-farce, *Casino Royale* (1968), a man is shown rupturing himself lifting a weight: it did not get much of a laugh. The sound-track carefully underlines this, '*boing – boing*,' so no one will miss that it is his testicles that have gone.

Two jokes collected so far only in Britain deny the feared castration or attack on the testicles by opposite methods: the first by denying it altogether, the second by refusing to recognize it. '*Young doctor going to Indjar, asks older doctor about rare diseases. Is told most of them are in the book, except perhaps the Wonga-Wonga, but it's of no importance, as it's neither serious nor painful. The young doctor arrives, and as the boat is docking at Bombay he sees a native sitting on the quay rocking back and forth and screaming in evident agony. Asks, "What on earth ...?" "Oh, the blighter's got the wonga wonga." "But I understood that it wasn't painful." "It isn't. It just makes you bloody tired. That poor bugger's sitting on his balls, and he hasn't got the energy to stand up!"'* (Union Jack, MS. Chelmsford, Essex, 1954. Motif L114.1, "Lazy Hero.")

The castration of the adulterer has already been discussed in the First Series, 9.II.5, pages 720–27, where it will be observed that a much more common punishment in humor is pedicating him, especially in orgy-fashion while he is still inside the wife's body. The ultimate in this line is also the earliest record existing of such punishments: *Numbers*, xxv. 6–15, in which, *Zimri is killed by the priest Phinehas with a javelin, for intercourse with the Midianitish woman, Cozbi; the two of them are killed together while in intercourse, the woman being thrust 'through her belly,' and therefore the man evidently through his back.* Talmudic traditions embroider on this fantastically, have the two fornicate together from sixty to four hundred times, 'in the sight of all the congregation of the children of Israel;' adding that Phinehas' javelin went through their genital organs *together*. Philo Judaeus states that after piercing the two, the priest cut off their genitals, which may be where the preceding impossibility started from. See further, Allen Edwardes' *Erotica Judaica* (New York, 1967) p. 15–19. We are close, here, to the vengeful Levantine story of: *The red-hot iron thrust up the husband's anus, when he presents his buttocks at the window for the adulterer to kiss (pretending it is the wife's face).* This becomes in Europe Chaucer's "Miller's Tale," by 1386, and there is a complicated 19th-century version in Afanasyev's *Russian Secret Tales*, No. 44. (Motifs K1225 and K1577.)

Also Levantine in origin is the castration joke most commonly collected at the present time in America: *The adulterer (often stated to be a Swede) is hiding in the chandelier (or attic) – from the policeman-husband who has come home unexpectedly, but his testicles hang down into the bedroom through a hole.* "What are those?" asks the husband suspiciously. "Just some Christmas bells," says the terrified wife. "Bells, eh?" says the husband, and gives them a terrible blow with his truncheon (rake-handle, fireplace tongs, etc.) "Yumpin' Yesus Christ!!" cries the Swede. "What was that?!" shouts the husband. "Yingle-yangle, yingle-yangle, you son-of-a-bitch!" *moans the Swede.* (Transcontinental train, 1943, from a professional comedian. Variants, N.Y. 1938 and since.) *Histoires Arabes*, in 1927, p. 165, gives a relic of the Levantine original: *The lover hides in the trellis, but his testicles hang down. The husband says, "Our grape-vine is sprouting balls!"* No castration or castratory blow takes place.

Afanasyev's *Russian Secret Tales* (MS. 1865) No. 58, "The Soldier and the Little Russian," has a story rather similar, in which: *The husband hides under a bench on which a soldier rapes his wife, pretending there is a governmental ukase that he must "futter every Little Russian."* When the soldier asks what

*is moving under the bench, the wife answers that it is a calf,
and the husband cries, "Moo! moo!" The wife farts on her husband from the force of the soldier's futtering. When he has
left, the husband thanks his wife for her trouble, saying, "You
farted, but if it had been me, I would have shit! You only spoke
of a calf, but I lowed like the real thing."*

These stories are evidently the same, but have parted company as to their décor, owing to a lack of chandeliers or
trellises in the average Russian peasant *izba* or hut. A rare
American printed ballad-sheet (dating about 1900 at the latest),
which I cannot cite exactly as it was stolen from me, may be
the missing link between the Levantine and American versions.
It was in verse, and concerned: *Two (?) young women who
want to spy on a secret Masonic meeting, through a hole in the
ceiling. One of them somehow gets her buttocks into the hole,
to the hilarity of the assembled Masons.* This is close to the
ancient story of "Virgil in the Basket": *A necromancer, who is
to be pulled up to his intended mistress' window, is left hanging in the basket and exposed to public ridicule.* (Motif K1211,
with extremely full references in both Thompson and Rotunda,
the latter stating, 'Allusions to this motif are numberless in the
Renaissance as well as in the Middle Ages.' See John W. Spargo,
Virgil the Necromancer, 1934.) This story was featured in
Fellini's motion-picture version of the *Satyricon* (1968). The
humorous traditional Scottish ballad, "The Keach in the Creel"
(Child Ballad No. 281), is close to both the joke about the
adulterer in the chandelier and the anti-Masonic (?) ballad, and
may be the vehicle of their transmission.

An elaborate story which is essentially a reminiscence of
American frontier 'ballocking,' in all its arts, has been encountered first only very recently. It attempts to set itself up
on a completely irrelevant puzzle or competition background,
possibly to sharpen the surprise of the final situation: *Three
men are discussing what the most terrible sound in the world
may be. One says the most terrible sound he has ever heard
was that of the screams of the dying after a train wreck. The
second says the most terrible sound is that of wild horses
stampeding when one is afoot (or the sound of a tornado coming, full-speed; or the roaring of a water-fall up ahead when
one is alone in a canoe). The third says: "Those aren't the most
terrible sounds in the world, but I'll tell you what is." He then
tells a long story about picking up a girl, going to her apart-*

ment, her husband coming home, while the story-teller has climbed out naked on the window-ledge, seven storys up, and then suddenly feeling a large male hand grabbing him by the balls. "That's scarey, all right," one of the other men interrupts, "but what has it got to do with terrible sounds?" "I'll tell you what it has to do with it," the third man replies. "Just at that moment I heard the strangest scraping sound I ever in my life heard: the sound of him opening his pocket-knife with his teeth!" (Brooklyn, N.Y. 1966; first printed in *World's Dirtiest Jokes*, 1969, p. 80. Told in 'shaggy dog' format, concentrating on interminable detail and false leads.)

Women as castrators have been noted specifically in the preceding section, *"Vagina Dentata,"* 13.I.3, and more symbolically in various jokes of the "Sleeve Job" type in the First Series, 8.III.3, which involve fear of castratory (or lethal) revenge by the bride, because of her defloration. These stories also perhaps involve a folk-rationalization of sexual fetishism, leading men to demand of women the erotic "Specialties" and even "Impossibilities" (Sections 11.III.1-through-4, preceding), which generally end up harming the man. One straight-bitch attack on the testicles, in this case by a *'little old lady with a shopping-bag' or 'with tenny-runners* [tennis-shoes or sneakers],' the modern American equivalent of the ancient witch, *who bets the director of the U.S. bank that his testicles will become square within twenty-four hours,* is given in full at the opening of section 13.III.2, below, "Circumcision and Women." Another form of female castration fantasies against the male – existing this time in women rather than in men – involves the 'self-protection' of the woman against male 'attack' (*i.e.* rape) by means of the various Japanese 'strength-through-weakness' killer tactics of *jiu-jitsu, judo, karate, aikido,* and whatever they export next, it all having signally failed against the Atom Bomb.

Various movies in which the actresses represent male-protest bitches make a particular point of having the heroine disarm (*i.e.* de-ball) and rough up the hero – or else some lesser male stooge – with improbable *jiu-jitsu* throws and *karate* chops. I am no movie specialist, but do recollect one particularly unlikely scene of this kind in a 1940's male-protest movie with Katharine Hepburn playing the part of a female husband (reminiscent of her stage beginnings in *The Warrior's Husband,* later called *By Jupiter!*) to the kindly male-wife played by Spencer Tracy, and protecting him with *jiu-jitsu* from racketeers trying to strong-arm their way into his business as a sports promoter. Such complicated maneuvers are now old-hat. In the more recent comic-strip spy-movie, *Goldfinger* (1964), the bitch-heroine with her archly sexy nickname of 'Pussy Galore' – that is all that is sexy about her – throws the hero, James 'Phallic' Bond, a few times in a hayloft by way of exciting herself pre-coitally. The audience could hardly have expected to see her warmed up with kisses. The straight-bitch movie imitation of 'Pussy Galore' as *Modesty Blaise* (1966) is taken to quite ludi-crous lengths of quasi-sexual attack on the male, strangling one masochistic male-stooge, for example, with what is presumably a scarf (poisoned pussy-hairs?) strung between the bitch-heroine's knees, in a love-&-death parody of cunnilinctus.

At the folk-level these fantasies express themselves much more dangerously in the rash of courses for working-girls in *judo* tactics, following every well-publicized sex-murder (the publicity naturally exciting more cretins to commit more sex-murders, but who cares?) As early as 1940, a folklorist in Los Angeles noted: *A man who 'told his two daughters very early in their lives of the crippling effect a scrotal kick has on a man, and advised their inflicting one on a man should he molest them. [One daughter stated she] never had to do it, but gained a feeling of safety and self-assurance from the knowledge of how to preserve herself.'* And now, approving reader, read on: *'In her married life, she often causes her husband to "moan and groan" (as he put it) by the rather rough tumbling about in bed she indulges in, accidentally [!] injuring his "vital zone".'* (From notes taken at the time.)

Wait, there is more! The same young married woman also supplied the same folklore collector with the following "Con-fucius Say," which she stated she had learned *from her mother*: 'Confucius say, *"Man who get kicked in nuts is left holding the bag".'* (L.A. 1940.) If this is not simply a series of lies or 'screen-memories,' by which the neurotic daughter attempted to im-plicate both parents, it is a remarkable example of the trans-mission of the castratory neurosis from generation to generation. One is now in a better position to appreciate the attempted humor, or whistling in the dark, of so unfunny a *vagina dentata* gag, correctly identifying the 'grouchy woman' or bitch with the castratory danger feared: *'Be careful what you permit her to do if you're out with a grouchy woman ... she might bite your head off ...'* (Sex to Sexty, 1966, 7:41.)

The ultimate freedom for castratory and sub-castratory violence against the testicles is naturally in wartime, as with the 'ballocking' of the American frontier fighters, already noted. Boys scrapping or wrestling with one another will still attempt to harm each other's testicles, either by kneeing or actual grabbing: these are known as 'nut-fights,' and awful tales are told of these, and of the boys who do this, by other adolescents. In adult 'boxing,' a good deal of repulsively hypocritical attention is paid to the preventing of 'foul blows' or blows 'below the belt,' *i.e.* to the scrotum, and special aluminum jockstraps, or testicle-protector cups, are worn by professional boxers to circumvent such 'wild' blows.

These aluminum testicle-protectors were interestingly brought to public attention in 1964, when a group of clergymen from the Eastern United States wished to go on a 'Freedom March' to the U.S. South, to protest the segregation of the Negroes there. (The Negroes are also segregated in New York and New Jersey, but no one, except Negroes, Freedom Marches in the North, for some reason. Maybe it is better publicity in the South.) As brutal treatment by the Southern police could be expected, even against these well-meaning clergymen, and as it is forbidden by *Deuteronomy*, xxiii. 1, for him *'that is wounded in the stones, or hath his privy members cut off'* to minister before the *'congregation of the Lord'* (see "The Short-Arm Inspection," chapter 10.III, earlier), these ministers and rabbis very seriously discussed outfitting themselves with boxers' aluminum jockstraps, or testicle protector cups, before starting on their Freedom March. This is not said to make fun of them – I would do exactly the same, you may be sure, and am not even ministering before the 'congregation of the Lord' – but to indicate the likelihood, and in fact the certainty, that castratory attacks against the genitals are still to be expected from civilized white men during the subliminal warfare of class- and color-struggle.

During actual and declared war, 'no holds are barred' of course. The dean of American popular-culture critics, Dwight Macdonald, has scathingly reviewed the principal World War II manual of *'Killer Tactics,'* by a Major Applegate, in the magazine *Politics,* a review now reprinted and preserved in Macdonald's *The Responsibility of Peoples* (London, 1965), where it is worth consulting by anyone with a strong stomach, and an interest in these matters. I would therefore prefer to quote here, not a World War II manual, but one dating from World War I, when this modern barbarism – presumably a necessary reply to the 'dirty Japs,' who 'fight like animals,' etc. – was only with great difficulty justified against the Germans, or 'horrible Huns,' who were, if anything, slightly more civilized and 'scientific' than their British and American cousins fighting them. The situation encountered by the soldiers, during bayonet drill and training in hand-to-hand fighting, was therefore this: the very same Y.M.C.A.-type 'health' and 'physical fitness' instructors, who were filling up the boys with the usual malarkey as to *"Come out fighting, no foul blows, and may the best man win!"* in refereeing the boxing-matches of adolescent boys before the War (and since), suddenly appeared under a new and ferocious aspect, justified by the barbarism of the *other side*, to be sure, as follows:

> Principles of sportsmanship and consideration for your opponent have no place in the practical application of this work. The knee, crotch, neck, and head are vulnerable parts and are the object of attack.
>
> Kick out viciously, bringing the foot back at once to avoid its being caught. When opponent is down, attack with usual type of kick to vulnerable parts [*Fig. 65, testicle kick by soldier is shown*] at the opponent's crotch, ribs, forearm, etc. ... in many instances a kick to kneecap or crotch will aid the butt stroke.
>
> When a man is gripped by an opponent so that neither the butt or the point [of the bayonet] can be used, the knee brought up against the crotch ... may momentarily disable him and make him release his hold.

Admittedly a bit primitive, by comparison with more recent improvements in the attack on the testicles, this is quoted from Joseph E. Raycroft's *Mass Physical Training for Use in the Army* (Washington, 1920) pp. 71–2, 91, and 128–30. Aside from the significant word '*Mass*' in the title, the date is of particular interest, since World War I was already two years past in 1920, except for the Expeditionary Forces sent by the British, French, and Americans to put down the Communist revolutions in Germany and Russia, of course. The patriotic teaching of castratory tactics has improved since then. The attack on the testicles is now regularly taught in, and practiced by the army and the various spy-services of both America and France, and especially by the police in South American and Levantine countries, by means of various fiendish devices including *electrical shock to the tied-up victim's testicles and groin.* (It's more sporting that way.) This is called the *gégène* in French, and it is not folklore but rigorously attested historical fact. One French general during the Algerian Revolution in the 1950's even announced publicly that he had himself submitted to his own army's *gégène* to see how bad it really was – one presumes not to his testicles. One thing is certain: Prof. Raycroft's lamentably primitive Butt Stroke and Crotch Kick will not compare to the gruesome and complicated castratory exotica of modern proto-homosexual tortures, or S. & M. lovemaking, in the World War II sources cited in the Macdonald article. Fried human 'prairie oysters,' anyone? It's your patriotic duty, after all.

5. EUNUCHS AND GANYMEDES

The eunuch is the warning pictorial footnote to the harem-dream of the men's magazines, but this relationship is generally overlooked. *Esquire* magazine, the first of the enormously popular American men's magazines during the 1930's (the bawdy form dates from the 1770's in England, with the *Covent Garden* and *Rambler* and *Ranger* magazines), once frankly gave harem-&-eunuch cartoons in every issue, generally drawn by the Negro artist, E. Simms Campbell. Its rival in the 1950's and since, *Playboy*, with the threat of instant destruction and castration ('sterilization') endemic in the air since the Atom Bomb that ended World War II and began all the others, never allows the Scheherazade eunuch – with his fat belly and balloon harem-pants – swanking space in its pages, anywhere among the sports-car ads and fold-out female nudes, themselves until recently castrated of every smidgen of pubic hair. The harem-dream remains, however, immanent precisely in the long, lowslung sports-cars representing their owners' penises – the "Jaguar" model of the middle 1960's was particularly embarrassing, as the designers apparently included an upside-down scrotum as well – but carefully upholstered inside with 'bucket-seats' straddling a massive and often phoney hollow gear-box, *to make sure that the male driver and willing-female passenger cannot touch.* The Fear of Touch. One waited in vain for the wedding of the "Jaguar" and its Scandinavian female counterpart, the "Volvo."

The eunuch can also be glorified, under certain overcompensatory circumstances connected with the special *voice* resulting from the removal of the testicles during boyhood. The Italian castrati singers of the 18th century (on whom see the historical facts in Percy Scholes' *Oxford Companion to Music*, 10th ed., 1970, at "Voice," sect. 5, p. 1089), were lionized and adulated at the time by audiences of both women and men, who not only found their soprano voices particularly beautiful (Mozart was among these), but who also sought their sexual company. This is a mass neurotic syndrome of a kind by no means unknown in our own day, as witness the similar rage for various epicene 'rock' and 'pop' male singers – not to mention operatic tenors and ballet dancers – who make no secret of their homosexuality, sado-masochism, etc. There is even a prize-winning novel, Dominique Fernandez' *Porporino, ou Les Mystères de Naples* (Paris, 1974), on the sex life of a castrato singer in the century of Mozart, written bizarrely *in the first person*. Speaking of self-castration ... There is an ecstatic review of this in French *Nouvel Observateur* (23 Sept. 1974, p. 88), for its style of course.

Weak puns on the eunuch are common, usually presented in stereotypical forms such as the erotic "Definition," or "Confucius Say": "EUNUCH: *A man who has it, but not them.*" (Los Angeles, 1940.) *"Eunuch not so strange: just man cut out to be bachelor."* ('Francis Page' [Samuel Roth], *Confucius Comes to Broadway*, New York, 1940, p. 62.) Diaghilev's ballet, 'Scheherazade," a version of the frame-story of the *Arabian Nights*, as both designed and danced by homosexuals, also makes much of the fat eunuch with the keys to the harem, though death rather than castration is the expurgated punishment, on the stage, of the 'blackamoor' who makes love to the beautiful white queen. Compare Shakespeare's odd anti-woman reversal in *Othello*, where the woman is killed instead – by the 'blackamoor.'

Removal of the tongue, head (*Titus Andronicus*), or heart (*Merchant of Venice*), which is then usually fed all-unbeknownst to the 'guilty' wife, is a common symbolic equivalent of punishment castration in early-modern folklore. Boccaccio's "Pot of Basil" novella (*Decamerone*, 1353, Day IV.5; Thompson Motif T85.3, with references) is only the most famous of this type. Compare also *Decamerone*, IV.1, and IV.9, the Provençal tale of "The Eaten Heart" (Type 992), made famous by Stendhal; an English version in unrhymed poetry being issued by Richard Aldington in France in 1929. The best study of the various forms is that in Francis J. Child's *English and Scottish*

Popular Ballads (1897) V. 29–34, No. 269, "Lady Diamond," importantly supplemented by both Thompson and Rotunda at Motif Q478.1. See also the First Series of the present work, 8.VIII.10, page 650–63, "The Eaten Heart." The preceding section in the present chapter, on "Decapitation" as a symbolic form of castration, is also wholly relevant here.

A blacksmith, a woodchopper, and a Jew masquerade in a harem as eunuchs, but are discovered when they get erections. The blacksmith's penis is smashed; the woodchopper's penis is chopped off. The Jew is asked his occupation. "Me? I'm a nobody. I peddle lollypops." (1:314.) A situation very much like this is used as the highpoint of the Italian movie-farce *O.K. Nero* (1960), a travesty of the American mock-Biblical movie 'epics' such as *Quo Vadis* and *The Sign of the Cross*, in which two sailors disguised as women in Nero's gynaeceum or harem (*sic*) are discovered by making all the women bare their breasts. (Motif J1149.3, appearing twice in the *Novelle* of Sercambi who died in 1424.) As here, the Jewish trickster appears frequently as the witty evader of castration, though this theme is not included in either of the two Yiddish joke-books by Immanual Olsvanger, *Röyte Pomerantsen* and *L'Chayim!* (New York, 1947, and 1949), nor in the two least expurgated field-collections so far published in America from Jewish sources: Prof. Richard Dorson's "More Jewish Dialect Stories," in *Midwest Folklore* (1960) X. 136–46, and Ed Cray's "The Rabbi Trickster," in *Journal of American Folklore* (1964) vol. 77: p. 331–45, with index p. 381. These are both, of course, very brief collections, and one is hoping for much broader coverage on the publication of the large field-collection of Jewish stories made recently in Canada under the direction of Professor Dov Noy, of Israel.

Actually, the Jew appears in such stories partly in his position as 'inferior,' on the style of the Negro – both really being considered sexual '*superiors*' to the Christian White, and as such to be castrated to 'cut them down to size,' as I have heard it expressed – and partly in his position as wily-beguiler or trickster. The trickster is, of course, the 'inferior,' or youngest ('seventh') child, achieving parity with the hostile and overpowering grownups and older siblings by being smarter than they. The Jew fits perfectly into this character, since his most particular superiority (like that of the Armenians and Scotch) is supposed to be not sexual but intellectual. There is also, however, a response here to the almost-conscious folk recognition of

Semitic circumcision as an historical modification of the castration threat against children, as is discussed further in the following main section, "Circumcision."

The harem-joke above as to the lollypop vendor has actually nothing specifically Jewish about it, and was earlier told in World War I of soldiers being punished for raping a Belgian nun, or 'bride of God,' with invidious nationality (German, French, and American) rather than profession or religion as the 'gimmick.' The theme of witty evasion here – even of insulting defiance (the Latin *'irrumabo'* threat implied, and in some versions frankly stated: *'The Jew replied, "If you don't mind, sir, you can suck mine off!"'* Los Angeles, 1943, from an army private) – is mixed with the masquerade as eunuchs in the version in *Anecdota Americana* (1927) 1:314, here taken as base. It is this same important reassurance – *that one is not really castrated, but integrally male underneath the disguise* – this is the true purpose of most transvestism (of both men and women!) as in the yearly transvestist blow-outs of men's clubs, military organizations. Hallowe'en, Thanksgiving, Mardi Gras, Mummers' Parade at New Years' (Twelfth Night survival), &c., rather than the simple homosexual exhibitionism of which these performances are usually erroneously suspected.

Another evasion of castration in jokes and similar fantasies is what has been called the "Ganymede Revenge" in the chapter on Homosexuality, 10.V.6. This is the theme of the dangerous anus that hurts the penis of the dominating (pedicating) male. This is of course an extension of the *vagina dentata* fantasy, here coupled with the little-known sequel to castration fears: namely, that the castrating father, or deity, will then have anal intercourse with the castrated son, or Ganymede, and even possibly make a complete woman of him (castration and pedication being thought of as partial steps) by impregnating him rectally with a 'jelly-baby' composed of feces. These neurotic fantasies are all very clearly expressed in the jokes of the earlier chapter-section, "Male Motherhood," 8.VI.3, in the First Series.

In the ballad, *"Kathusalem, the Harlot of Jerusalem"* (Palestine troops, 1917, parodying a mid-19th century music-hall song), *vagina dentata* and Ganymede themes are combined, when the harlot, angry at being pedicated by the Philistine giant, blows him over the walls of Jerusalem by breaking wind. A symbolization of the same kind, with the phallic nose bitten off by an enraged anus, is the comedy highpoint of an erotic travesty of Marlowe, *The Loves of Hero and Leander* (1651) which I would attribute to the Royalist wit, Dr. James Smith. This ends with Leander's quasi-castration by Hero's father, his testicles being caught on a hook as he leaves her bedroom. (Compare the automobile-accident joke already given: *She: "You all right?" He: "Sure." She: "Then whose balls are those up there on that hook?"*)

The story has already been given, in the chapter on Homosexuality, of: *The man who attempts to bugger a young chap leaning over the railing of London Bridge. The young man suddenly tightens his buttocks, and cries: "Now, orf we go to Scotland Yard!"* (1:457, as of a Swiss Hercules and tourist, this being the form given in French sources.) I have heard this told as 'practically true,' mixed with other anecdotes of the *agent provocateur* tactics of detectives of the anti-homosexual squad in New York subways and theaters in the 1930's and since. *Anecdota* (1:99) gives a very full and clear expression of the Ganymede revenge theme: *A circus roustabout can't find a woman, and is advised to grab any man on the lot and bugger him. He is afraid, but finally does so one dark night. The next day he seeks out the ballyhoo-man who made the suggestion, and says, "Look at this!" taking out his penis which is badly lacerated. "With a whole circusful to choose from, I had to pick the glass-eater!"* Norman Douglas alludes to the same idea in his mock annotation, in *Some Limericks* (Florence, 1928) p. 69, on a limerick concerning 'an old girl of Silesia,' who warns the man about to bugger her that she has a tapeworm which might 'seize' him.

The final convolution of this fantasy is that of auto-sodomy, also celebrated in a well-known limerick first appearing in *The Pearl* (1879), concerning 'a young man of Calcutta' who has been told 'to bloody well bugger himself.' *The Limerick*, No. 459, gives the original text, and notes various other limericks almost identical in inspiration and libretto. The fantasy of auto-sodomy is of great psychological interest, as both an acceptance of passive homosexual 'rape' and a simultaneous defiance of it, since the actor is at once both bugger and buggeree. The implication is, of course, that the satisfaction being sought is rectal, not genital, though the pretense is the opposite: that one is virilely buggering ... oneself. It should be compared to the matching idea of auto-fellation, which, however, *is* physically possible in various positions by a bit of stretching.

The essential phrase or taunt in the limerick, the British *"Go bugger yourself!"* (American: *"Go fuck yourself!"* but sometimes extended: *"Go fuck yourself in the ass – and give yourself some brains!"* or *"Go fuck yourself with a red-hot wienie* ['sausage']!"*) is one of the commonest of folk-taunts, next after the standard invitation to *kiss one's arse,* on which see section 15.I.3 below. Buggering oneself is considered less unforgivably insulting than the similar incestuous advice (which are 'fighting words') to *fuck one's mother,* which is of ancient usage in non-English speaking cultures, such as Russia and the Levant, and has only recently been imported to the West – and become popular here – through contact with the American Negro. This is discussed further in my Introduction, "On Sexual Speech and Slang," to John S. Farmer & William Ernest Henley's *Dictionary of Slang & Its Analogues* (New Hyde Park, 1966) revised vol. I, p. xxxix-xl. Don Marquis' privately printed *Ode to Hollywood* (1929) ends with what must then have been considered the *summa* of all English-language insults: *"Go fuck thy suffering self!"* (*Russian Secret Tales,* No. 12, "The Fool.")

So also the equally disabused valentine, forty years later, Ray Russell's blistering Hollywood satire, *The Colony* (Los Angeles, 1969) p. 18–19, where the author, in the character of a *Playboy* editor retiring to Hollywood, gives a two-page parody of the limerick on auto-sodomy as it might be written by a 'no-talent fraud' like any one of a number of recent beatnik fake-poets, in the bad-prose-broken-up-to-pass-off-as-poetry technique of Walt Whitman and e. e. cummings (with typographical crud to match), ending: *'Oh man, Oh MAN. He'd been. I MEAN. Alla time, thru alla that P-U-M-P-I-N-G gig y'know??,* he'd been balling – his – own – !!! A*S*S*H*O*L*E !!! ' The best-advertised such poet, recently, is further taken off – as to his buncombe mystical gig, mainly – in poet Karl Shapiro's masochistic novel, appropriately entitled *Edsel* (New York, 1971) chap. XIV, pages 179 ff., under the name of 'Akiba' (Harry Peltz) and his homosexual lover 'Govinda.'

6. THE DOCTOR AS CASTRATOR

On the face of it, there would hardly appear to be any special psychological point to the casting of the doctor or surgeon in the character of the castrator in the largest number of jokes on this subject. The casting seems automatic, unavoidable. The reader is reminded again, however, of the point raised in Fenichel's *Psychoanalytic Theory of Neurosis* (1945) p. 78, and already quoted above, that 'After an operation the castration fear may be displaced to the operated area – for example, after a tonsillectomy.' One must add to this other sub-surgical operations, especially the removal of teeth and even the cutting of hair, which make the dentist and barber (originally barber-surgeon, *n.b.*) other unconsciously-feared 'castrators.' This is particularly true of the dentist, since he actually and visibly drills into or removes a living part of the body – and a pointed and penetrating one at that: the tooth – often with great and unavoidable pain. Exactly as circumcision is semi-consciously recognized as a partial form of castration, enacted (as threatened) against the child, just so the primitive tribes which demand the knocking out of a tooth or teeth as an ordeal or trial of 'manhood,' sometimes offer the parallel modification of filing or pointing the teeth, as a mark of 'beauty,' for both men and women. There can be no question that this is a partial form of ablation of the teeth, and is recognized tribally as such.

Similarly horrible scarifications and mutilations of the body, by way of ordeal-*cum*-beauty combined, as shown in many popular ethnographic works from Dr. John Bulwer's *Anthropometamorphosis: Man Transform'd* (1653, 2nd illustrated edition only), to Prof. William Henry Flower's *Fashion in Deformity* (1881) and Hilaire Hiler's *From Nudity to Raiment* (1930?), are evidently what is intended to be understood by the partial scarification of *tattooing*, of which the sexual significance and forms have been importantly studied by Albert Parry in a supplement, appearing in the American *Psychoanalytic Quarterly*, to his illustrated work, *Tattoo*, in the 1930's. Later and wholly perverted illustrated materials on erotic tattooing in the Anglo-Dutch pornzine, *Suck* (Amsterdam, 1970) No. 3: p. 19.

It must not be lost sight of that these operations are, among primitives – and, as to circumcision and tattooing, among civilized peoples – enacted not by doctors but by persons self-elected to the work, whose position is much more that of *shaman* or priest. This is an important line or branch in the genealogical tree extending from the healing and scientific priests of ancient Egypt, recollected in the two purely medical chapters, *Leviticus*, xiii–xiv, on the diagnosis and epidemiological treatment of leprosy, to the feared and hated 'white-coated scientists' of modern advertisements for washing-machine powders, patent medicines, cocainized soda-pop, and the like. Of both types, of course, the miracles were and often are entirely bogus and non-existent. Consider also the scientists of the Atom Bomb.

One must not overlook, in the genealogy of doctors as priests and castrators, the prototype of all such stories, in the operation performed upon Adam by Jehovah, in *Genesis*, ii. 21, causing a deep (anaesthetic) sleep to fall upon him, and, while Adam 'slept ... he took one of his ribs, and closed up the flesh instead thereof.' It is from this *crooked rib* that Eve is formed, as everyone knows. This little just-so story, which has caused centuries of untold harm – to women, certainly – is made the subject of a quite gruesome poem, "On Womanhood," attributed, doubtless as a joke, to Ira Porter D.D., in *The Stag Party* (Boston? 1888) p. 130–32 unnumbered, crudely gloating on the details of the Paradisiacal operation:

> *Poor Adam; how his face contorted,*
> *How all his muscles writhed, cavorted;*
> *What pain and anguish then he suffered ...*

And so on, in the style of the Hebraic Prometheus that, after all, Adam represents. The poem ends with a sort of booby-prize bit of advice by God, 'the Maker,' indicating to Adam that Eve's operation is matched to his own, *so he can 'tickle her; She's fitted well to suit your turn, Your wound's transverse, her's perpendicular.'* Adam's cloacal response – not given in the poem – has already been cited: *God is not much of an architect: in making woman He put the ballroom too close to the shithouse.* Also told as of *Henry Ford in Heaven: God not much of an engineer – put the exhaust too close to the intake.* (U.S. 1920's, and much earlier in France. 1:142. The idea is probably Levantine: compare Nasr'eddin, No. 334, of a house. Motif J2236.) In Carnoy's Picard tales in *Kryptádia* (1907) XI. 137–8, various artisans assist the Devil (badly) in forming Eve's genitals. This also exists in verse in both French and English.

All this is very similar to another just-so story in verse, "That Little Piece of Whang," telling the same tale in an even more primitive form. This farce-reduction of *Genesis* is concerned not so much with the creation of the two sexes, as with their struggle with each other ever since. This is 'explained' in Béroalde de Verville's *Moyen de Parvenir* (about 1610) chap. 43,

"Annotation," very much in the style of the burlesque explanations of natural and physical phenomena in Vignale's *La Cazzaria* (1530), though Vignale does not tell this particular story: *When the primeval androgyne, Adam-&-Eve, was cut apart, their newly separated bellies were sewed up with a cord of clay or whang-string leather given to them by the Creator* (whom Béroalde calls 'Jupiter,' to evade the censorship; also having 'Mercury' do the sewing-up instead of either God or the Devil). *Adam's piece came out longer than Eve's, because he took great long stitches, as men do, and was left with the piece that still hangs from him in front. While Eve took neat tiny stitches, as a woman should, and so ran out of string and was left with a slit at the bottom of her belly. Thus explaining the immemorial contest ever since, between women & men, over* "*That Little Piece of Whang,*" *because the men refuse to give it to the women, and will only* lend *it to them.*

This elegant explanation is taken up and embroidered further as a French mountebank's harangue, in the *Fantaisies de Bruscambille* (1612, reprint Bruxelles, 1863) p. 231, "Prologue facécieux des parties naturelles des Hommes & des Femmes," by N. Deslauriers, called 'Bruscambille,' the Lenny Bruce of the century of Shakespeare. As noted in the unpublished *Stromates* of Jamet the younger in 1730, this same story was also made into a *conte-en-vers* by several French poets of the 17th century, in particular as "Le Lacet" in La Fontaine's *Contes et Nouvelles* (1664–71), from which it travelled all over the world. It appears to survive now only in English, as a 19th-century doggerel circulated in printed or manuscript form as "That Little Piece of Whang," taken from or reinforcing the slang term, *whang*, for the penis, which is still common in America. At the folk-level, therefore, it may be considered as proved that there has never been any doubt whatsoever – at least not since the 16th century, and probably millennia earlier, as is discussed much more in detail in the First Series here, 6.I, "The Big Inch" – that what men & women are really fighting about is the possession of the penis. (*Kryptádia*, IV. 354. Frank Hoffmann, *Analytical Survey*, pp. 134, 189. Randolph, "*Unprintable*" *Songs*, No. 158.)

The doctor as castrator in jokes is mixed with other themes in a way making it difficult to allow of a single grouping. Earlier, under "Vagina Dentata," the nurse has been shown fronting for the doctor in these circumstances, and effecting the patient's castration only by elaborate accident; later eating his testicles herself. The similar question of the disposal of the circumcised foreskin or *pipputz* will be discussed below, under "Circumcision," a meaningless operation or ritual mutilation in which the doctor has, of recent decades, signally (and not a bit unwillingly) replaced the 'rabbi' of earlier jokes on these themes.

As usual, sub-jocular stories exist of which the action is persistently reported as true, though patently absurd and impossible, with the doctor (surgeon) directly represented as castrator of the man apprehended in adultery with his wife. This is of course the theme of the authentic story of Abélard – so popular with women writers – although the uncle of Héloïse, Canon Fulbert, at whose behest he was castrated, did not have recourse to any physician but to paid ruffians or henchmen The difference here is sometimes less than invisible, as when brain-surgery – always thought of as a type of castration or of 'partial murder' – is enacted upon troublesome or psychotic relatives, sometimes by almost equally psychotic or irresponsible surgeons. This is the plot of Tennessee Williams' play and movie, *Suddenly Last Summer*, with the extra turn of the screw that it is a young girl who is to be thus castrated (silenced: the Voice as Phallus) by the 'evil mother' of a homosexual son, already dead, to preserve his reputation!

In the great French slang dictionary of Hector France, *Dictionnaire d'Argot* (*de la Langue Verte*), published in large quarto from 1898 to 1907, the compiler, whose attraction to cruel and revolting themes had already been seen in his *Musk, Hashish and Blood* – on the usual catch-all Oriental background for sadistic fiction, as with Octave Mirbeau's *Torture Garden* (1898) – starts off with a bang on page 1, col. 3, under '*Abélar-diser*,' with the following tale told straight-faced as true. (*In translation:*)

Several months ago, a young Anglican vicar was *abelardised* by the husband of a lady whom this reverend gentleman had crowned with his heavenly favors. The husband, a doctor, made use of the ancient subterfuge of deceived husbands, which never fails to trap both wives and lovers. He feigned going off on a trip, and came back *suddenly* at the moment when he was least expected. The guilty couple were quietly sleeping, and the doctor chloroformed them both without making any scene. Then he proceeded to operate on the gentleman, bandaged him properly, and retired. One can imagine the mutual surprise of the lovers, the next morning, at the hour of leavetaking. The reverend gentleman had to have himself transported to his lodgings somewhat more crestfallen than he had arrived. But the characteristic [sc. British] trait is that after he was healed, he sued the physician, demanding damages and interest for an injury incapacitating him for work. [See *Deuteronomy*, xxiii. 1.]

As the placing of this 'true tale' under the term *Abélardiser* makes perfectly evident, this is nothing but the story of Abélard modernized into an anti-British anecdote at the height of the period of British unpopularity in the 1890's. (Hector France had already written one anti-British exposé work earlier, *Les Va-nu-pieds de Londres*, and came back to the subject, concurrently with his dictionary of slang, in *Les Dessous de la pudibonderie anglaise*, mocking the British as sexual prudes and hypocrites, a volume issued by the erotica-publisher, Carrington, who had been having trouble with the English authorities.) I cannot of course prove, at this date, that the story told by Hector France as to the castrating of the Anglican vicar under chloroform is untrue, but one observes that its *humor* is supposed to rise from 'the mutual surprise of the lovers, the next morning, at the hour of leavetaking.' This is hardly the way two people who have been chloroformed would wake up!

The current joke version, in America, also is curiously supposed to take place in France, and makes no bones about its farcical intention. The beginning is identical with Hector France's tale: *The doctor surprises the guilty couple 'in the act,' and deftly severs the lover's penis with one slash of a straight razor, while still inside the woman's body. "Mon Dieu!" the woman shrieks, "get bandages! He is bleed – ing!" "Damn ze bandages!" the man cries, in comedy-Franch accent. "Get me ze cork-SCREW!!"* (N.Y. 1951.) The earliest version recorded of this, in *Anecdota Americana* (1934) 2:243, combines the original story with the theme of the "Ganymede revenge" or dangerous anus: *A hotel-guest accidentally pedicates a sleeping Frenchman, thinking he is a woman. The Frenchman wakes up, seizes his razor, and severs the penis of the man on top of him. "Call a surgeon, call a surgeon," yells the victim. "To hell wi' ze surgeon," cries the Frenchman. "Bring me ze cork-screw, queek!"* Is this a 'true' story too?

Veering again toward obvious humor, yet delivered perfectly straight-faced as a pantomime, by an habitual joke-teller: *Shadow charade (done against a white sheet), of a surgeon cutting a vertical object with a horizontal sweep of the side of his hand, like an axe, then juggling (therefore 'balls') two objects in the air.* (N.Y. 1951.) Fraternity initiations of castratory nature have already been mentioned, as when: *The blindfolded initiate is made to drop a brick which has been tied to his penis.* As described by an army private (D.C. 1943), no reference at all was made to the fact that: *This is really only a gruesome 'practical joke,' since the cord has been cut beforehand without the victim's knowledge.* Instead, 'He emphasized the fear as they *dropped it* [the brick], *and the way they grabbed at their peter to prevent the expected yank.*' The same collector, six years earlier, records a friend in Los Angeles telling of: *A pretended surgical 'initiation ceremony where an icicle was passed around the base of the scrotum of a blindfolded naked youth, into whose hands 2 eggs [hardboiled and shelled] were then placed.'*

One evasion of any feared theme has already been shown to be the treatment of it as a 'mistake': *The nurse chasing the fleeing patient with scissors, while the doctor shouts, "Nurse! I said 'Slip off his spectacles!'"* This particular example has the further evasion that the doctor appears in it not as castrator but as actually trying to protect the patient *from* castration by 'mistake.' *A yokel in a hospital asks a medical student about the doctor. Student: "Old T, he's alright. Terribly fond of the knife, though.* [n.b.] *Fellow came in last week with ptomaine poisoning; had his toe off. Yesterday one came in with erysipelas, had his ear off." "Gimmey my 'at!" roared the yokel. "I got prickly 'eat.*" (Kimbo, *Tropical Tales*, 1925, p. 13.) The same source gives a weak nonsense item from World War I: *Private MacFearless, V.C., after six months of continuous vivisection at the military hospital is told that he is menaced with partial paralysis. "Which side, Major?" whispers the hero. "Left." The soldier lay silent for some moments, then started reaching with one hand beneath the bedclothes. "What are you doing, MacFearless?" the major asks. ' "Saving what I can from the wreck", came the pathetic answer.'* (Kinbo, 1925, p. 50.)

Handling & dandling the penis – the so-called 'peotillomania' of medical dictionaries and nowhere else – is natural in young boys, from earliest infancy, and should not be prevented nor the child's attention drawn to it. It usually stops when pants begin to be worn, at about the age of two or three. As the preceding joke implies, however, many grown men continue the habit most of their lives, particularly in states of anxiety and tension. The act is not masturbatory in general, but more of an in-turned hostility, like fingernail-biting, scratching, or picking the face. One of the reasons I left America was that I was exposed to so much brain-washing and brain-baiting over the telephone, by salesmen, 'opinion pollsters,' phoney friends, spies, and so forth, I found *I was tearing out all my pubic hair without knowing it*, while trying to answer their imbecilic questions or parry their obtrusive demands. Taking out the telephone did not help, as then they came and banged on the door, at which point I could not even secretly tear out my hair. (See the joke on this in the Fist Series, 8.VIII.8, page 645.)

Intense castration anxiety often involves similarly toying with and tweaking the testicles themselves, or some testicular substitute, as in Ernest Hemingway's last and worst book – but then they're all pretty poor – *Across the River and Up a Tree* is the title, I believe; in which an elderly military personage, representing who-but-the-author, has some type of dooflickers in his pocket which he must twiddle all the time. (He also cannot sit except where he can see *the way out* to fresh air, a type of claustrophobia I also suffered from badly in New York, and finally could not go down into the subway at all.) In Herman Wouk's *The Caine Mutiny*, the ship's officer on trial has similar ball-stones or pocket-doodlers which he finally snatches out, at an anxiety-crisis, and manipulates violently and compulsively in full view. Whittling is of course similar, but its hostility is not in-turned.

As with the story of *The headsman who tells his neatly decapitated victim to "Cough!"* a verbal misunderstanding was central to a mock Swedish-accent ballad known to a soldier at the Presidio of Monterey, California, in 1942, but unfortunately neither taken down complete nor collected elsewhere. It turns on the anxiety-laden "short-arm inspection" discussed in Chapter 10.III: *Ole, a champion jumper, about to be inducted into the army, is given a physical examination, during which he had to 'bend over' while the doctor 'examined his brown' for piles. Next,*

He grabbed hold of my testicles, under my rump,
Then the doctor said, "Cough," but I thought he said "Yump!"

So Ole gave one of the tremendous 8-foot leaps for which he was famous, castrating himself, so that now 'all he can do is piss with his limp penis.' See further the theme of "Self-Castration" below, and in particular the Scandinavian auto-castratory 'lance jumps' there mentioned.

But nothing in the medical castration line will compare with the gruesome *chanson de Salles de Garde* in English, "The Ballad of Chambers Street," written by Dr. Fritz Irving of the Harvard Medical School in the 1900's, of which only one stanza has ever been published (in *The Limerick*, Note 1234). This is the defiling-of-the-mother story to end all such stories, though it evidently did not do so, as witness *Portnoy's Complaint*. It is very long and detailed, as are most sadistic recitations, such as "Eskimo Nell" (given in Harry Morgan's *Why Was He Born So Beautiful and other Rugby Songs*, London, 1967, p. 57–66); and concerns the dynamiting of the vagina of the local Jewish prostitute, or the earth-mother to all the students, Big Rosie, who has been in labor for days, and the two bungling obstetricians cannot think of any other method of bringing her child to birth. For the punchline or final doggerel couplet – a cliché in English poetry since Shakespeare's time – the punishment is stated for the horrible imaginings preceding, and this punishment is naturally castration. But it is neither the poet nor the listener who is castrated – and certainly not the two bungling obstetricians. Instead, when they explode the dynamite in her:

Proud Aetna in her salad days, on that Sicilian shore,
Did not erupt much more abrupt than did that Hebrew whore.
With mangled child she much defiled the waters of the bay;
His balls fell short of Cambridge port; his cod struck there to stay.

A modern classic, not mentioning castration at all, but showing clearly the castratory anxiety and pedicational fear always involved in the genital or rectal examination of a man by a doctor, is often encountered: *A man puts his artificial eye in a glass of water by the bed every night, and one night accidentally drinks the water, swallowing the eye. He goes to a proctologist who looks up his rectum with a proctoscope, and suddenly stops and straightens up, saying in amazement, "I've been looking up these things for thirty years, but this is the first time one ever looked* back *at me!"* (Los Angeles, 1945, from a

married woman.) Within half a dozen years the punch-line had
been 'improved' to a nonsense ending in which the proctologist
says: *"What's the matter, Smith, don't you trust me?"* (N.Y.
1951.) Blindness representing castration is of course a very
ancient symbolization, as in the story of Oedipus, blinding himself in self-punishment for his unwitting incest with his mother,
in which the *eye* is obviously not the organ that has sinned
The joke therefore is intended to be a reassurance or overcompensation in which the 'penis-eye' is actually *not* lost, but
is to be found inside the body, whence it may be expected
finally to extrude, as with undescended testicles or piles. The
shrivelling up of the penis against or into the body during fear
(or extreme coldness) is known to all men, though seldom
mentioned, and is also probably involved here.

The story is, incidentally, fairly old, being the French *conte-
en-vers*, "The Glass Eye," by Pons de Verdun, in the late-18th
century, reprinted in *Un Million de plaisanteries* (Paris, 1850)
p. 215–16, by 'Hilaire Le Gai.' In Pons de Verdun's *"L'Oeil de
Verre,"* the proctologist is of course only the original Molières-
que clyster-dispensing apothecary, who has been called in to
help the patient pass the mysterious obstruction in his intestine.
The punch-line is identical, but here refers specifically to the
anus:

> *"Monsieur, depuis cinquante ans que j'en vois,*
> *C'est le premier, d'honneur, qui me regarde."*

What is perhaps an extension or illustration of this tale appears
in a privately printed little booklet, intended as a celebration of
a successful operation for fistula: *A Happy New Rear*, by Bill
Carmichael (New York? 1931), in which the first illustration
shows the author's buttocks menaced by a headsman's axe [!]
while the second, in chapter 1, shows the rectal examination by
the doctor with a telescope, captioned: *"So I 'ups' to him!"* This
is all just whistling in the dark, and will not compare to the
more recent volume memorializing a similar operation, by the
imitator or continuator of Céline and Henry Miller, Charles
Bukowski, *All the Assholes in the World and Mine* (Bensenville,
Ill.: Open Skull Press, 1966), and the same author's various
other bawdy-talking memoirs since, which put his spasmodic-
style poetry to shame. What is interesting about *A Happy New
Rear* and *All the Assholes in the World* is the one point they
have in common: the necessity the authors feel to reassure

themselves about the results of this emotionally fraught, but not physically dangerous operation, and to announce to the uninterested world that they have safely navigated it, by flinging their piles in our face. But perhaps these operations *are* dangerous. The French president, Pompidou, was announced in 1974 over the state radio to have piles. Two weeks later he was dead, without the actual cause of death (bone-cancer) ever being announced. As with the Watergate affair in America, the public reaction was: *"That's what comes of having an* asshole *for president."* Iron balls are expected of a father-image; *clay feet* are unforgivable.

Many stories in which the castration threat is of the mildest and most symbolic kind (see "Symbolic Castrations," section 13.IV below), are set up strictly for the pleasure of expressing resistance to the doctor-surgeon or mocking his castratory advice. *A man who is losing his hearing is told by the doctor that it is caused by over-indulgence sexually, and that he must "cut out women altogether" or he will be stone-deaf in two months. Two months later the man has not come back, so the doctor phones him. "How are you doing, Wilson?" the doctor asks. "Eh? Who's this? What you saying there? Eh? – Speak up, dammit!" "It's Dr. Calvert, Wilson," the doctor shouts; "just called up to find out if your hearing had improved." "Shit, no, doc!" the man shouts back; "I'm deaf as a post. But what the hell! Nothing I was hearing made me feel half as good as getting laid."* (N.Y. 1953. Told to explain why the teller "never listened to the news-broadcasts any more.") This appears in non-sexual form in the *Hore di Ricreatione* or "Hours of Entertainment" of Lodovico Guicciardini (Anvers, 1583) I. 53, where: *A doctor advises a patient with an infected eye to stop drinking if he wishes to save the eye. The patient replies, "I would rather lose a window than my life!"* (Rotunda, Motif J1319.4, omitted by Thompson, with other "Repartees concerning wine.")

Another form of this sort of joke, for which I have not found any older analogue, though I suspect one may exist, involves a counting compulsion of the kind typical in religious formulas of penance, paternosters, etc., and in many formula stories or 'endless tales' involving counting all the stars in the sky, grains of wheat and the like, or one's own farts or sneezes (as already given). *A man is warned by the doctor that he is undermining his health by making love several times every day (drinking too much whiskey), and that he will die very soon unless he stops. The doctor later meets the man in the street, obviously much worse. "Are you following my advice?" the doctor asks; "you know – only once each day, absolute limit?" "Don't you worry," says the man, "I'm keeping track of every one. (He looks at his wrist-watch, or into a little notebook:) The last one was for the second Monday in August, 1999!"* (Amsterdam, 1955.) Told in English by a white-haired Dutch gentleman who also told me: "You know, the young girls go for this white hair – like Santa Claus!" I assume this meant, in combination with the joke, that he kept a written record or journal of his erotic conquests among the 'young girls.' Such erotic diaries are much more common than the (sometimes) code-numbered victims imagine. Pierre Louÿs' erotic code diary for the year 1915 is analyzed and quoted at length in the Coulet-Faure sales catalogue No. 138, of this author's erotic manuscripts (Paris, 1974) item 692, *"Carnet Intime."* This is an eye-opener.

One of the most open mockings of the doctor, as the regulator of everybody's sexual life, makes the standard identification of *dancing* (also singing, as in *Tristan & Isolde*) with sexual intercourse, but in a burlesque rather than symbolic or expurgated way. *A young woman goes to see a doctor and explains that every time her husband makes love to her she wants to dance. The doctor asks her to step into his inner office and undress. The next patient is a man who says that every time he makes love he wants to sing. The doctor tells him to go into the communicating bathroom and undress, and that he will call him in a moment. Meanwhile the phone rings and the doctor forgets about both patients. Suddenly he hears a strange noise of scuffling from the inner office, pulls open the door, and sees the naked man and woman chasing each other around the furniture, then stopping, and chasing again, while the man is singing at the top of his voice, "Hold that Ti-ger!* SOCK!! *Hold that Ti-ger;* SOCK!!" (L.A. 1968. Referring to a very famous Negro jazz-tune or rhythm, probably of African origin *via* New Orleans, about 1900.)

Where an actual genital operation must take place, the terrifyingness of the doctor is difficult to deny or evade, even in jokes. But it is still possible to search for reassurance by attempting to 'control' or displace the locale of the operation, or by changing doctors until one is found who is reassuring rather than threatening, and by simple burlesque. '*Chap goes into the hospital for an operation "on the treasury." Before going under the anæsthetic insists that his navel be left unspoiled if humanly possible. On recovery, his first inquiry is as to whether his navel has been left just as it was. Curious doctor asks why he's so concerned. Chap: "It's like this. My wife and I have a binge every Saturday night." Doctor: "Well, that's only natural." "Yes, but we have fish and chips in bed together; and that's where we keep the salt!"'* (Chelmsford, Essex, 1954.) Aside from the avowed oral regression, from sexual to food pleasures in the Saturday night binge – *'If ye canna get fooked on Saturday night, ye canna get fooked at all!'* says "The Ball o'Kirriemuir" – the identification of the navel and the genitals – (*phallos* and *omphalos*) is very striking here.

Of the 'shopping-around-for-doctors' type, a joke has already been given, under "The Biter Bit," commonly collected. It is apparently the favorite among the jokes openly searching for reassurance in the matter of castration. The 'game' being played here – by both the man in the joke and the men telling it – is "I Can Stand It No Matter How Bad It Is," or rather "Hit Me Again, I'm Still Conscious!" (HMAISC). The reference to leprosy is due to the assimilation of this disease, always considered somehow eerie, to the venereal diseases, as in the world-famous case of Father Damien, of the leper colony at Molokai, whose eventual contracting and dying of the disease was thought by some to prove that he had not been 'pure' with women, as scathingly denied in Robert Louis Stevenson's *Father Damien: An Open Letter to the Rev. Dr. Hyde* (1890). – *A young man in China or Africa gets leprosy or 'the Chinese crut' from intercourse with the native girls. He goes from one doctor to another, but they all tell him that there is no help for him and he must have his penis cut off immediately. Only the native doctor reassures him: "No cut off. Two three weeks – fall off by itself."* (N.Y. 1935.) This is still widely circulating, and appears in *Grim Hairy Tales* (1966) p. 35, somewhat rationalized, with *the Chinese doctor explaining that the reason the American doctors all say that castration is necessary is to get the operation fee. "A-so, Mellican doctors alle-samee, money, money ..."* A much more florid Jewish version, without any reference to money, is given later at 13.VI.2, "Erection to Resurrection."

While I am sitting here typing the final corrections of my manuscript in the preceding paragraph, and thinking to myself that I have just finished the book that has taken me thirty-five years to write, the mailman whistles by on his bicycle and delivers one letter. (One letter, and the usual half-bushel of advertising 'matter' and other printed waste with which I will light the fire tomorrow morning.) It arrives by airmail from Victoria, Australia, dated October 1974, from a young literary editor who owed me a favor, and so I told him I would be glad to take payment in Australian jokes and ballads. He sends me one joke, followed by a 'toast' or send-off, possibly his entire repertory. The joke is an action-joke or pantomime, of the type told in barrooms. He gives it in three columns (*Patient – Doctor – Teller*), here consolidated as one person must take all three parts :

'*Patient: "Oh doctor, my prick hurts really terribly during intercourse." (Teller holds an empty matchbox upside-down at crotch level.) Doctor: "Well, just roll the foreskin back, please." "All right, Doctor. (Teller pushes out slightly the upside-down tray.) Oooh, that hurts." Doctor: "A bit further, please." (Teller pushes tray further out.) Patient: "That hurts really badly, Doctor!" "I'm afraid you'll have to roll it right back." "But it hurts so much!" (Teller pushes tray out until it is only just held by the cover.) Doctor: "Ah, I see. This part – (knocks tray from container) – is no good for a start".*' The exhibitionistic tone need not be underlined. Here now is the 'toast' or premium, and it would be hard to imagine a more perfect example of overcompensation for the crude preceding castratory threat. Note also the writer's sequence of ideas, from castration to the symbolically equivalent death – but 'perfect.' ("*La Mort douce*," First Series, chapter 5.III.) '*Australian's notion of perfect death: "Chock-a-block up a sheila girl, with a glass of beer in each hand".*' This means not only that your Australian cocksman is not caressing the girl, it means two glasses of beer only – the man holding them both. When equality of the sexes comes to Australia, there will be four.

7. THE MAD BARBER OF FLEET STREET

A very important surrogate or symbolization of the doctor as castrator is the surgical specialist of ancient lineage, the barber, especially in the insane, razor-slashing character of *The Mad Barber of Fleet Street*, a melodramatic theatre-piece popular in the 19th century. (In the *Novelle* of G. Sercambi, who died in 1424, No. 46 in Renier's edition, 1889, concerns : *A barber who makes heavy demands of the client while the razor is at his throat. The client agrees to everything, but after the shave throws the barber out.*) Barbers do not really have to be insane to be frightening, but that is how it is easiest to mime it on the stage. The folk-idea that barbers are very *talkative*, but that one must listen to them quietly since they are holding the scissors or razor, naturally falls in line with this. (Barbers also once held the bleeding-bodkin.) Compare the proto-homosexual or paranoid terror tales of Robert Louis Stevenson, Wilkie Collins and Lord Dunsany, such as "A Terribly Strange Bed." Also, and particularly, Melville's strange and dark novelette, *Benito Cereno*, about a Negro valet who holds the razor at the neck of the American slave-trader captain, to keep him from divulging that the slaves have revolted and have taken over his ship. This is apparently not intended politically, but as a charade of homosexual fears of blackmail: either Nathaniel Hawthorne's secret story, or more probably Melville's own. Other exploitations of the barber theme, at the literary level, are George Meredith's *The Shaving of Shagpat* (1856), a mock-Eastern romance turning on the oriental respect for – and insults to (Rotunda P672) – the beard; and a mad-barber story in *The Evangelical Cockroach*, published in New York, 1929, by 'Jack Woodford' [Josiah Pitts Woolfolk], in which: *A barber plans to immobilize a man helplessly in the barber-chair, by means of the protective white sheets and heavy pins, and cut his throat for having seduced his girl.* The displacement here of the usual fantasy punishment for seduction or adultery – from castration (*lex talionis*) to throat-cutting – is the whole point of the present section. Woodford's title-story, like a similar anti-clerical scene in Philip Wylie's *Finnley Wren* in the 1930's, is in the uninflected village-atheist or H. L. Mencken boob-baiting style, now a thing of the past as religion dies in the West.

It should be mentioned that the castration complex is extremely long-lasting and severe in men who had suffered in their youth from repressive religious training – as was once universal – *no matter what the religion is, and whether or not it is anti-sexual.* It suffices that the religion demand bowing to the will of a god-figure representing the parent (whether a patriarchal of matriarchal figure), or exaggerated respect for one's ancestors, social and military superiors, etc. Or the repression can be entirely cultural, as seen in Nazi Germany. The seething inner frenzy of even the most apparently relaxed Japanese male (Zen philosophy, *haiku* poems, tea-ceremony and all), still today, over a hundred years after the end of dominant patriarchal feudalism in Japan, is a frightening example of the castration complex as a sociological construct or mold. Japanese 'killer' fighting tactics, such as *karate* – bragging of its 'philosophy' *à la* Sade, in breaking bricks with one's bare fists, etc. – and the hideously sadistic Japanese popular literature of the 19th century, concerning earthquakes, *samurai* killings, women-torturing, and the rest (now as motion-pictures on the same themes, even more gruesomely), are practically the end-point. Japan's cultural agony has now begun, concomitant with its search for materialistic success, in imitation of America. Probably only a coincidence, there is a barber story like Jack Woodford's, on a similar castratory theme, by the diminutive Lafcadio Hearn, who, as will be remembered, finally became a naturalized Japanese, under the name of 'Yakumo Koizumi,' Japan being the only country where he did not feel inferior because of his lack of height. (The Body as Phallus.)

The most openly sexualized form of the Mad Barber castration fantasy, so far, is a 'wish-projection' drawing made by a young man, '*der wegen eines Strafdeliktes aus homosexuell höriger Bindung in Haft genommen war*,' showing a diabolically moustached barber, wearing a bow-tie, enthusiastically slashing the throat of a fat customer. This was preserved in the former archive of Dr. Magnus Hirschfeld's homosexually-oriented Institut für Sexualwissenschaft in Berlin, which was destroyed in the early 1930's by the Nazis (probably on orders by Goering), under the name of the "Burning of the Books," presumably to purify German literature and 'blood,' but actually to suppress its files on important drug-addicts. The picture is reproduced in *Sittengeschichte des Lasters*, one of a series of volumes edited by Leo Schidrowitz (Vienna, 1927) p. 243. Everyone who saw Charlie Chaplin's superb comedy motion-picture *The Great Dictator*, satirizing Hitler and the Nazi régime, will surely recollect the scene in which Hitler is shown – before his accession to power – precisely as the Mad Barber of Fleet-Strasse, who alternately lathers his client caressingly and shaves him homicidally fast, to the alternately slow and rapid *lassu* and *friska* of Brahms' "Hungarian Dance," of which the symbolic sexual miming is further discussed in *The Horn Book*, p. 202. Observe the open sexualization, or rather homosexualization, of the little folk-rhyme (U.S. 1946):

> I walked into a barber-shop, the sign was very queer:
> "*During alterations* [n.b.], *we're shaving in the rear*."

As is noted in the final section of the chapter on Woman,
6.VII, "Pubic Hair," any suggestion of cutting or shaving the
pubic hair of a woman by a man, or at a man's request, is immediately identifiable as a castration impulse against the
woman. Or rather, as an attempt to revindicate the man's own
sexual superiority and reassure him about his own genital completeness by attacking that of someone else – the woman – who
is thus made even more emphatically the 'castrated being' or
'penisless-man' of neurotic fantasies. Consider the well-known
little catch or 'sell,' first published in *The Stag Party* (1888):
*Professor, to his class of medical students: "What would you
do if a child was born without a penis?" (Blank looks.) – Professor: "You'd wait until she's sixteen, and then* give *her one!"*
Still current, actually presented as a 'sell,' in which one person
says to another: *"Did you hear about the baby that was born
at the hospital last night without a penis?" – Listener: "No! Is
that so?" – "Yes, but she had the cutest little place you ever
saw to* put *one!"* (Pa. 1934.) From the point of view of the male
teller or listener this is evidently a reassurance: 'No one can
be born without a penis – the very idea is just a joke.' From the
point of view of the woman, or 'penisless-man,' whose *lack* of
a penis reassures the man that he has one, it is strictly a gloat.

Actually, the *demand* that the hair be cut on any part of another person's body, including and especially the head hair, is
openly castratory in intent, as with the college-punk crew-cut
enforced upon soldiers not in a position to refuse. The most
famous expression of this in literature is Alexander Pope's
poem, *The Rape of the Lock* (1714), from its purposely sexualized title to the famous double-entendre line in which the girl
laments that the man did not *'seize any hairs but these,'* purposely set at the end of one of the cantos, as revised, in contempt of the criticism of its earlier discreet appearance in
Lintot's *Miscellanies* (1712), lost in the text.

In the most famous and influential erotic French novel of the
18th century, Boyer d'Argens' *Thérèse Philosophe* (1748), published the year before *Fanny Hill* in England, a supplementary
story in a much more erotic style is interpolated, "Histoire de la
Bois-Laurier" (Miss Laurelwood's Story), by an army quarter-
master, Arles de Montigny, who spent eight months in the
Bastille on suspicion of being the author of the whole book. No
disguise is made, already at this date, as to the fetichistic over-
layering heavily attacking European sexuality among the rich

and idle classes, though the relevant fetich, of pubic hair-cutting, is here ascribed to 'a rich American' – in 1748! Miss Laurelwood speaks (ed. 'La Haye' [Paris], 1910, p. 117):

> My new lover from *across the seas*, had sworn to restrain himself to the pleasures of "all but that," but he mixed in with its accomplishment a singular fantasy. His desire was to have me sit beside him on a sofa, my skirts lifted above my navel, and while I took him in hand, and gave a few light shakes to the stem of the human plant, I had to have the complaisance to allow the chambermaid he had given me to occupy herself in cutting a few tufts from my bush. Without this bizarre activity, I doubt whether the strength of ten arms like mine could have wound up my man's machine, not to mention drawing from it a single drop of its elixir.

In more modern times, and among men, the action of *male nurses* in shaving off the pubic hair of male patients before abdominal operations is generally a moment of eerie horror for the patient, who usually doesn't feel too great anyhow, and may attempt to carry the matter off (if the male nurse himself does not do so) with uneasy jokes, often precisely on the subject of castration, and how fortunate it is that a straight razor is not being used. The safety razor is of very recent invention. In anti-Negro folklore Negroes never use this, but only the straight razor, with which they 'cut each other up terribly' in knife-fights. In 1964 I was warned frightenedly against Negroes by a white man in Central Park, New York, telling me that I should stay out of the park after dark, or "*Some big boog* [booger, bugger, *bougre?* more probably derived from *bug* or *bugaboo:* a black demon] *is liable to slash off your prick with a razor, like you were a* dog!"

The cutting or shaving of women's pubic hair, before the delivery of a child, by female nurses or nuns, is medically entirely unnecessary (I have been present at more than one successful delivery in which it was not done), and is, I am told, just as eerie as the pubic shaving of men, especially when the nurses are of the repressed-lesbian or bitchy type who 'like to make it hurt.' Even the cutting of tufts of a woman's pubic hair, to be preserved ribbon-bound, as a sexual trophy by the man, is a fairly suspect activity, especially if the man makes a whole collection of these, as was common until the 1920's. Note the "Wig Club" in the 18th century in England, discussed in *The*

Horn Book, p. 374–5, citing David Foxon's *Libertine Literature in England* (1965). This club was named for a wig or merkin of such tufts, presumably made from the pubic hair of various mistresses of King Charles II, which was added to by all new members and worn on their heads during their initiation: a mock rebirth ceremony. See further, Louis C. Jones' *The Clubs of the Georgian Rakes* (New York, 1942), which mentions that King George IV was a member. This perhaps explains an otherwise ununderstandable passage in the famous *Diary* of Charles Greville (complete ed. by P. W. Wilson, 1927) I. 122, dated 8 September 1831, as to the compulsive collections of clothes, money, *etc.*, found when George IV died. It is the *etc.* that interests us here:

> When he died they found £10,000 in his boxes, and money scattered about everywhere, a great deal of gold. There were above 500 pocketbooks, of different dates, and in every one money – guineas, one pound notes; one, two, or three in each. There never was anything like the quantity of trinkets and trash they found. He had never given away or parted with anything. There was a prodigious quantity of hair – women's hair – of all colours and lengths [*n.b.*], some locks with the powder and pomatum still sticking to them, heaps of women's gloves, *gages d'amour* which he had got at balls, and with the perspiration still marked on the fingers; notes and letters in abundance, but not much that was of any political consequence, and the whole was destroyed [*Except for the gold?*]

In Burns' *Merry Muses of Caledonia* (1800) in the song, "Johnie Scot," p. 112, the specific idea is that of the shearing off of the female pubic hair as though it were sheep's wool, to spin into thread 'twined wondrous small,' for the warp (not to mention the further sacrifice of the hair of the 'gushet o' the arse' for the weft!) to make cloth to clothe the woman's lover. This is also the final jest in "Will Ye Na, Can Ye Na Let Me Be," in the same collection, p. 21, in which the goodwife of Whistlecockpen tells the itinerant worker who makes love to her, in metaphors taken from the reaping and threshing of grain: '*I wad sell the hair frae aff my tail*' to buy her husband such a 'flail.' A later music-hall song, also turning on the idea of shaving off a woman's pubic hair – but here punitively or as a 'joke' – occurs in all the falsified later editions of *The Merry Muses* from about 1825 on, under the title "Lucy's and Kitty's Black Jokes."

This song appears to be based on a much older French joke, dating back to Béroalde de Verville in 1610. It is almost exactly translated or adapted from the *conte-en-vers*, "La Savonnade," printed in Moncrif & Grécourt's anonymously edited *Recueil de pièces ... du Cosmopolite* (on which see further *The Horn Book*, p. 87–90), published with the false imprint, 'Anconne,' in 1735. (Reprint, 'Leyde,' 1865, p. 371. Copy: Ohio State Univ.) Another version, or another song on the same neurotic fetich of shaving women's pubic hair also appears in the *Recueil du Cosmopolite* (ed. 1865) p. 188, beginning: '*J'apperçois ma Jeanneton, faisant la barbe à son con, avec un rasoir, devant un miroir.*' An Irish or English version of this, modified to a girl merely washing her feet (or 'hair') was often curiously used as an encore piece by the great contralto, Kathleen Ferrier.

All of these, as noted at the end of chapter 6.VII, "Pubic Hair," in the First Series here, are essentially expurgated or partial female-castration stories, with the castratory act modified simply to shaving the woman's pubis, as a 'joke' or revenge. Sometimes, when a revenge, this is a punishment for prostitution or for sexually frequenting with the enemy. Displaced further, to the hair of the head, in France just after World War II, to punish female 'collaborators' with the Nazis, this started the crop-haired style still affected by heavily neurotic women in Europe and America. The original purpose of pubic shaving, in the Orient and Levant where it is standard among prostitutes, is to facilitate cleanliness and to avoid pubic vermin as well as venereal disease. (See *Leviticus*, xiv. 9, for body-shaving against leprosy.) There is, of course, also the simple castratory insistence on this item of hygiene or female 'beauty' by Oriental men. Often this does not even conceal the tone of a punishment or humiliation, as when – according to the Arab historians – the Queen of Sheba was required to shave off her pubic hair when she lost her 'contest in riddles' with King Solomon. (See further under section 15.V.2, below, "The *Escoumerda*," where details are given, on the background of the War Between Women and Men.)

There is also the extraordinary tale of the dark-haired prostitutes of Naples at the end of World War II outfitting themselves with blonde merkins or 'cunt-wigs' (nothing is said about shaving off their actual pubic hair), in order more successfully to attract the trade of American Negro soldiers in the victorious American army, who are stated to have demanded or favored blondes. This tale is told by Curzio Malaparte in his remarkably-written but damned-hard-to-believe *The Skin* (English translation, London, 1952) – he also has one *symbolic* anecdote about accidental cannibalism at a formal banquet – a book which *Time* magazine (for once) correctly reviewed with the simple value-judgment: *'This is a book that stinks.'*

A modern fictional version of the standard neurotic fantasy of female castration, disguised as shaving of the pubis, appears in *Neurotica* (1949) No. 5: p. 17. Here, for the first time since Béroalde, there is no punch-line, no retailing as a 'true' story, and no other subterfuge of humor engaged in, the neurotic or anti-fetichistic description of the mere act of shaving the woman's pubis appearing, as it were, bare. The British 'mod' fashion-designer of the 1960's, Mary Quant, announced to the press – during the slow season for dresses, one assumes – that pubic hair is beautiful, and that her husband had trimmed *her* pubic hair into heart-shape. The perfect touch of sick Togetherness, but it does not seem to have started any fad. The embroidered and appliqué'd *graffiti* on the buttocks (and flies) of young girls' and mens' blue jeans in the early 1970's were apparently touched off internationally by a Camel's cigarette advertisement of a girl's buttock with a yellow Camel embroidered (*i.e.* tattooed) on the blue-jean coverup. The pubic hair was too rich for the advertisers' blood.

The space cannot be given here to any more complete survey of the non-joking folklore of, and literary allusions to, the act of shaving (facial or genital), and of hair-cutting, as symbols of castration. The Biblical story of Samson – and the whole idea of the long-haired Nazirite sect, to which Jesus, Samson, and St. John the Baptist, as well as the other proto-Christians of the 'Essene' sect are presumed to have belonged – is the earliest clear expression. At a deeper level than "The Mad Barber of Fleet Street" sort of melodrama, Robert Southey, in his *Omniana* (a continuation of *The Doctor*, his most interesting work, published after his death in 1843), gives a curious account of a rabbi being converted to Christianity by his unsurmountable anxiety over the Biblical prohibition against cutting the hair of the beard. This appears in a repeated passage, *Leviticus*, xix. 27–8, and xxi.5, grouping it with other castratory symbolizations evidently in use among the Levantine people of the first millennium B.C., such as tattooings and scarification, referred to as 'cuttings in the flesh *for the dead*' [*nota bene*], and the making of 'baldness upon the head.' Ultra-religious Jews to this day obey this Biblical injunction against cutting the beard, while simultaneously transgressing it (a different solution from that of Southey's rabbi), by making use of the caustic depilatories well known in the Levant. No rationalization is even offered for the unscriptural tonsuring of Christian monks.

The fad has existed over the last decade in America and Europe for long hair among *révolté* young men of the so-called 'beatnik', 'hippie', and similar groups. This is a very open expression of castration anxieties, presenting itself as social recalcitrance and defiance. These adolescents and young men – as well in France and Czechoslovakia as in the U.S. and England – not only resist the cutting of their hair (which is sometimes forcibly done to them by the police as a punishment), but are specifically panicked by barbers, since they *do* allow other young men of their own in-groups to cut their back hair for them occasionally, when it gets in their way, and even offer to cut the hair of other men whom they accept. As I have worn my own hair pretty bushy since leaving home for good at the age of seventeen, in 1935 – Einstein *and I* were the only ones then – I have on several occasions had this friendly offer made to me in recent years, and have also reluctantly accepted it. (See the closing quotation in the Introduction, from Dr. O. Fenichel, on the guilty and compulsive proselytizing by many neurotics, such as drug-addicts, homosexuals, and others.)

The hair problem, is, in fact, very old: at least as old as the Nazirite sect of Samson and Jesus. In the Levant it particularly centers around the beard, and the respect due to it, naturally involving also *insults to the beard*. (Motif P672.) The breaking of the spirit of the Russian *boyars* by Peter the Great by forcing them to cut their beards in insulting fashion is a most significant and historic instance. This is sometimes entirely reversed, especially among unconscious or unavowed homosexuals of the aggressive and athletic 'wolf' type, who cut their hair as short as possible ('hairbrush' or German aviator style) and reject all outward softness of clothing and body-stance, or femininity of manner: the 'James Bond' or body-as-phallus type. Preeminently famous in this line was the Puritan proselytizer and reformer in the 17th century, William Prynne, who, in *The Unlovelinesse of Love-Lockes* violently excoriated the wearing of long curled hair by the English rakes of the period. When he himself was sentenced for his attack on the immorality of the theatre, *Histriomastix* (1632) – which was taken as an affront to the Queen, who had appeared in some private masques and theatricals – to be fined £5,000 and lose both his ears in the pillory, he still resolutely refused to wear his hair long afterwards to cover the stumps of his ears. Not even when they were later *cut off again* for a further offense in 1637, found in a book he had written while imprisoned in the Tower of London! Isaac d'Israeli, who best tells his story, in *The Calamities and Quarrels of Authors* (ed. London: Warne, p. 146–55), has some hard things to say about Prynne, especially as to his turgid and overcharged literary style, but in a way one has to admire a lunatic like that.

Much similar castratory fact and folklore exists, not only as to ears, tongue, and so forth, but especially in connection with the ablation, filing, or ornamenting of the *teeth* in many cultures, both primitive and advanced. See in particular Thompson's index-volume V. 802–3, under "Tooth" and "Teeth." Little of this ever appears in modern jokes, except perhaps that of: *The elderly Jewish gentleman who says to his wife in bed on their golden wedding anniversary, "Becky, hand me my teeth out of that glass – I want to* bite *you!"* (N.Y. 1937.) See also "Tooth-Breaker," in 13.I.2, above. Other genital or non-genital *loci* for fantasy castration will be dealt with in the sections immediately following, in particular under "Circumcision," and the whole section 13.IV, "Symbolic Castrations."

An interesting historical and analytic work on the subject of *The Unconscious Significance of Hair* (1951), by a British psychiatrist, Dr. Charles Berg, has been updated and broadened out in a timely way in an article, "Why 'Hair' Has Become a Four-Letter Word," in *Avant Garde* (New York, May 1970) No. 12: p. 48–53, signed 'Warner Brown,' apparently the pseudonym of Warren Boroson, and especially concerning the current cultural disapproval of 'hippie' hair. The few photographic examples given, facing the first page of text and showing long-haired male plug-uglies, are mostly of whites: the two non-whites shown are the only ones that look human at all. Endless other such rogues' galleries of longhaired and Zapata-moustached individuals currently appear as background in all the 'underground' newspapers, and especially to ornament the record-sleeves and souvenir magazines devoted to rock-&-roll concerts, pop singers, etc. Both Dr. Berg and Mr. Brown-Boroson show very clearly how the wearing of disorderly or 'unauthorized' hair – whether too short or too long, depending on one's century – is responded to by the culture as the defiance and insult it is openly intended to be. Neither of them, however, recognizes the current *dæmonic attempt to be ugly, dirty, and evil*, as part of the same cultural defiance involved, in a culture where the presumably square (angelic) ideal is to be beautiful, clean, and good. There are even at the present time model-agencies in both London and New York brashly specializing in supplying guaranteed 'Ugly' models, doubtless as being easier for ugly millions to identify with, in far-out fashion advertisements, and popular movies. See also Wendy Cooper's study, *Hair* (London, 1972).

The *Avant Garde* article evidently takes its title from the success on the American stage and abroad in the late 1960's of a fake-hippie musical show, *Hair*, cleaning up among the square public which imagines it is all terribly libertarian and authentic. The rather similar *O Calcutta!* following hard on the heels of *Hair*, was more strictly a sex-bath or erotic burlesque, with no real hippie pretensions. It should be observed that the proposed square audience also allows itself sometimes a timid recrudescence of the 'excrement' of hair, but never to such a degree as to be mistaken for the real thing. These are the crumpet-revolutionaries, or 'plastic' (weekend) hippies, who want to seem to be 'with it,' but who nevertheless also want to keep their jobs, paying businesses or family connections, in order to have the money to continue playing at being dropped-out hippies. Particularly pitiful is the Casper Milquetoast daring of *long sideburns*, generally intended as a signal, nowadays, in both the English-speaking countries and France, that the otherwise square wearer is, or would be, or would like to imagine himself to be, a red-hot 'swinger,' wife-trader, or the like. The *Avant Garde* article maintains a very discreet silence as to this group: obviously its own audience.

III. CIRCUMCISION

The following very extraordinary document is quoted (by permission) from an article, "The Unkindest Cut of All," by John M. Foley, M.D., appearing in *Fact* magazine, and reprinted in *The Best of Fact* (New York, 1967) p. 330–44, where it is faced editorially – in the usual bad taste of humor on this subject – with a photo of a naked baby, out of which (out of which *photo*) a pentagonal hole has been slashed with a surgical scalpel, removing all trace of the child's genitals, whatever they may have been. The article, however, is only about circumcision, not castration, though clearly either the editors or the readers must be assumed not to know the difference between the two, or else not to care – a very important point, as will be seen.

Dr. Foley proves very fully and clearly that the idea of the 'necessity' of infant circumcision is a medical folly, if not a mere money-grabbing racket, and for chicken-shit fees. But what is of interest here is, rather, some of the case-material he cites of circumcisions in which the 'necessity' involved is clearly that in the doctor's psyche and not in the patient's parents' pocket-book, or penis. He begins, for example, by noting that: 'On July 20, 1964, the *Medical Tribune* published a letter from a Baltimore physician who called for compulsory circumcision of all men seeking to get married. Indeed, he went on to demand federal legislation requiring the circumcision of *every* male infant within the first 8 days of life.' Dr. Foley adds: 'Now, just why anyone would want circumcision made compulsory may seem puzzling. After all, circumcision is already a routine operation in this country. What need for legislation when 98% of all newborn boys, before leaving hospitals, are circumcised?' – But to hell with the horrible statistics! Or the crank letters either. What actually *happens* during this 'routine operation' in hospitals? Here is Dr. Foley's conclusion, p. 335–6:

> Since circumcision has practically nothing to recommend it, an important question is: Why has it become a routine operation? A few physicians go so far as to suggest that money may have something to do with it ... My own view is: Circumcision provides a convenient and socially acceptable outlet for the perverted component of the circumciser's libido. I have had personal experience with the psychopathology that underlies the wish to circumcise. The pitiful wails of the suffering infant are all too often the background for lewd and obscene commentary by the obstetrician to his audience of nurses. Several years ago I saw an infant born with multiple deformities. He could not live more than a few

months at most, but to add to his miseries, this unfortunate bit of humanity had to undergo a thorough circumcision.

I have seen two medical students fight over the privilege of doing circumcisions on the newborn, although these same students showed neither interest in, nor aptitude for opening boils or doing other surgical tasks.

In 1951, I witnessed an autopsy on an infant who had died from an infected circumcision – a death rendered even more tragic because the mother had tried to persuade the obstetrician to spare her infant this ordeal.

Dr. Alexander Schaffer, a noted pediatrician, tells with horror of a case in which an infant was being delivered as a frank breech (buttocks first). Before delivering the baby, and just as the penis came into view, the obstetrician seized it and circumcised it. That obstetrician, I would say, may be capable. He may be an all-around fine fellow. But sexually I say he is a monster. And I say that one of the reasons why circumcision is so common in this country stems from the sadism of the crypto-pervert.

Without in any way intending to try to top so complete an indictment, I cannot forbear to quote here the ultimate discovery or justification of the medical circumcision lunacy, which arrived in the mail just as this chapter was originally drafted for publication in *Neurotica*, No. 9. It is by the late Dr. Norman Haire, the greatest medical advocate of sterilization of the sane (until recently), in his *Journal of Sex Education*, published in London, 1951, IV. 55, in answer to a bogus 'question' from a reader:

Circumcision ... has one supreme advantage. It has been found that circumcised men, especially those circumcised soon after birth, are almost, if not completely, immune from cancer of the penis. There is also evidence [*what does that mean?*] that women, who have intercourse only with men who have been circumcised in infancy, are almost, if not completely, immune from cancer of the neck of the womb.

It would take Lenny Bruce to do justice to that one. *"Honey, pardon me will ya? I'm writing things up in my diary for Dr. Haire. Were you circumcised at birth, or when? The last fourteen guys, well, you know how it is; people tell you such lies!"* Forcible circumcision (as reported, probably falsely, on the deck of an American battleship, during World War II, on 'official order from the captain') is obviously the next logical step, to protect innocent women from the cancerous 'rape' of the uncircumcised male. Maybe that's why those girls in Israel train with submachine-guns? (But Arabs *are* circumcised – at age 13.) See the joke later, on: *The man with cancer of the penis, whose doctor suggests that his wife had better stop smoking!* This sounds precisely like folklore 'feedback' from the medical folklore – or worse – cited just above.

As it happens, Dr. Haire was in America when the preceding paragraph and brief quotation from himself were published in *Neurotica*, No. 9, and he got in touch with me at once and asked me to come and see him at his hotel in New York. There, he explained that he was very hurt by my calling him '*The greatest medical advocate of sterilization of the sane,*' and hinted that he would probably be taking action against me for defamation or libel, for the word 'bogus.' (People in England have a wonderful way of rushing to sue for libel about anything that does not appear in a newspaper review by a critic; where, *per contra*, any hapless author who cares about these things learns very soon that publishing a *book* in England is critically indistinguishable from being flogged through the fleet.) I told Dr. Haire gently that I *did not have a pot to piss in or a window to throw it through;* that my magazine was being published as a result of my having collected an $800 gambling debt, and that after the printer was paid the magazine would fold. I then quoted the old American proverb suggesting that he could *sue* (or *wish*) *in one hand and shit in the other, and see which gets full faster*, and prepared to leave. To my surprise he burst out laughing, slapped me on the back, told me that "Ameddicans are *so refreshing*," and began describing to me the painlessness of his personal method of sterilization, to prove that I was wrong to knock it.

I expressed surprise that he did operations himself, and mumbled something about not realizing he was a surgeon as well as a physician. "My dear boy," he told me, "I have my own hospital! Now let's assume," he added, "that I were to sterilize you ..." "No," I interrupted – I remember my exact words – "You have the hypothesis wrong. I am going to CASTRATE *you!*" He looked at me glassily. "Now let's assume," he repeated, "that I were to sterilize you. I would ..." I gave him a big smile, and kept doggedly repeating, "No, I am going to CASTRATE *you!*" while he kept repeating his bit. This went on, back and forth, for about five minutes, until finally he seemed to be strangling, dropped his deprecatory Harley Street air, and turned suddenly and threw open all the windows, saying in a high, tight voice. "Impossible. Impossible! I did *not* say 'castrate' I said 'sterilize'." He stood facing out the window, sucking in air, and did not turn back to me again. I left. Britishers are so refreshing. As is well known, they also have a terrific sense of humor.

Historically, as well as psychologically, it has always been clear that circumcision is simultaneously an equivalent – yet also an evasion – of castration. (Except in England.) That is its emotional subtlety. The earliest pictographic documents of circumcision date from ancient Egypt. The first *rationalized* explanation is that given in the Bible, where, however, the 'explanation' given is simply that Jehovah arbitrarily demanded it of the patriarch Abraham, in *Genesis*, xvii. 9–27. Abraham being, as it is stated there, *'ninety years old and nine, when he was circumcised in the flesh of his foreskin.'* Most of the Bible being, of course, not history but legend and folklore, the first real leader of the Jews (or Hyksos shepherd- or slave-refugees from Egypt) was apparently a renegade Egyptian, Moses, who was not circumcised, according to *Exodus*, iv. 24–6, and whom Jehovah – apparently for that reason – 'sought to kill.' (Compare the castratory attack by an angel of Jehovah on the patriarch Jacob, crippling him in 'the hollow of his thigh,' in *Genesis*, xxxii, 24–31.)

Moses himself was saved only by the immediate scapegoat circumcision of his first-born son, Gershom, by the boy's mother Zipporah, using the ritual prehistoric stone knife. Jehovah's insistence on circumcision is nowhere explained, since its *real* origin among the Jews is simply imitation of the barbaric African custom earlier imitated in Egypt. Being male, according to the grammatical form of all Biblical references, Jehovah must have had a penis and testicles – without which it is not possible to be male, unless one is a bird, bug, or fish – but was also, so far as the records go, uncircumcised. The Rabbinic legend is that Jehovah circumcised himself! A likely story. But by far the most significant trait in the one-sided covenant of circumcision is the idea that one individual can be circumcised or sacrificed *for another*, as Gershom is circumcised for Moses, Abraham for Jehovah, and Jesus Christ is sacrificed for everyone else. Even Zipporah, who circumcises her son herself, to save his father's life, cannot forbear, as we are told in *Exodus*, iv. 25–6, when she has 'cut off the foreskin of her son,' to cast it at the feet of Moses, saying, "*Surely a bloody husband art thou to me . . . A bloody husband thou art, because of the circumcision.*"

Children being circumcised today in deference to their mothers' or (less often nowadays) their fathers' ideas of 'hygiene' or medical correctness, are similiarly being made scapegoats for somebody's sick neurosis, very often the hospital director's or physician's, as has been sufficiently shown above. For the whole idea of this 'bloody covenant' is clearly nothing other than an extension of the idea of human sacrifice, here reduced symbolically to castration, and then reduced even further to circumcision, which does not harm the virility of the male. Human sacrifice had been the form of worship in the patriarchal religion of Moloch, which preceded that of Judaism in the land of Israel. The legendary beginning of the Jewish religion is, accordingly, a mock or aborted human sacrifice, that of Isaac by Abraham, in *Genesis* xxii; while Jesus asks (in Aramaic) on the cross: "*Eli, Eli, lamma sabachtani* – Oh, my God, why hast thou forsaken me?"

Freud weighs his words very carefully in *Moses and Monotheism* (1939), his last book and published in the year of his death, when he says: 'Circumcision is the symbolical substitute of castration, a punishment which the primeval father dealt his sons long ago, out of the fulness of his power. Whosoever accepted this symbol showed by so doing that he was ready to submit to the father's will, although it was at the cost of a painful sacrifice.' This continues the formulations and speculations of Freud's *Totem and Taboo*, many years earlier, in which he considered the revenge of the rebellious sons, in killing and eating the castratory '*Ur-Vater*' in the night. As noted above, the Talmud assimilates this legend to the sons of Noah.

Just as castration – to drive the sons off the mother and sisters, and all other women forming the patriarch's harem – would be still only a partial or symbolic *killing* of those males over whom the patriarch held the power of life & death, just so circumcision is a symbolic form of reduction of the castration that is itself only a symbol. Partialisms of this kind are intended as warnings *in terrorem*, and still persist very widely in the training of children and animals, as bragged of in the mock phrase of explanation, when striking another person (or a child): *"That's for nothing – now* DO *something!"* (Compare the joke on *"That's the first!"* in chapter 14.I.4, "Anti-Gallantry.")

Modern Semitic religions, such as Christianity and Mohammedanism, as well as Judaism, all recollect the original sacrifice to their male children at the age of thirteen, when the sexual urge appears full-blown; the Mohammedans by actual circumcision at that age, stating that they trace their lineage to Ishmael (see *Genesis*, xvii. 24–7), and the Christians and Jews by such ceremonies as 'First Communion', 'Confirmation', or *'Bar-Mitzvah'* (the Son of the Covenant), also at the age ascribed to Ishmael at his circumcision. As to Mohammedan circumcision, you have to see it to believe it: the pederastic patriarchs paring off the prepuces of their pre-pubescent sons. They simply round them up at the age of thirteen – once on camels, now with jeeps – and make a communal festival of it. The Arab sons are also given an object lesson, in the first local battle they engage in, as to what is *really* meant – today, not two thousand years ago – when the same patriarchs show them how to pedicate and then castrate male prisoners taken, who are also generally then killed. In other words, the whole symbolic chain of modification from killing to castration (and pedication), to circumcision, turned backwards again to their originals.

The psychoanalyst, Dr. Bruno Bettelheim, in his splendid study, *Symbolic Wounds*, considers the matter of circumcision not from the remote historical or ethnological point of view, but in the immediate social sense:

> Whether circumcision was instituted by men or by women, whether it satisfies instinctual desires of men or of women, or both, it can only symbolize castration in a society where severe punishment, particularly in regard to sexual behavior, is part of the individual's frame of reference. And only [*i.e.* especially] where the punitive figure of an adult looms large, will the child easily make the medical transition from circumcision to castration anxiety.

The details and curiosities of circumcision are not to our purpose here, and information of this kind can best be found in the various Jewish encyclopedias in English and German, and in certain specialized works such as that of Remondino on the subject, and a curious illustrated compilation, *Præputii Incisio*, published in New York in the 1930's, apparently edited by Evan-Esar Levine. The early historical materials are furiously gathered and presented in *Erotica Judaica: A Sexual History of the Jews*, by 'Allen Edwardes' (New York: Julian Press, 1967), which is clearly opposed to circumcision and is of particular value for this young researcher's abundant quotations from the Arab historians, usually overlooked.

Finally, all the medical and para-medical arguments in favor of circumcision are marshalled in a brief article by the urologist, Dr. Abraham Wolbarst, in Victor Robinson's *Encyclopædia Sexualis* (New York, 1936) p. 128–31, particularly insisting that circumcision in infancy 'prevents' cancer of the penis, 'whereas this form of cancer constitutes from 2 to 3 per cent of all cancer in men.' Admittedly not very impressive, since it therefore concerns only one out of every fifty or thirty-three cases – and those the rarest – whatever there is that might be persuasive in this statistic is ruined by Dr. Wolbarst's simultaneous implication that circumcision *of women* might be a good idea too, though here he knows he has no statistics at all to back it up as preventing cancer. (Or anything else.) Instead, female circumcision in the Arab style – yes they do! – is frankly proposed as a castratory punishment for masturbation in girls, to relieve their 'nervousness' about this:

> It is interesting to note that a similar operation, removing the foreskin which covers the clitoris in the female, is also very widely practised in Arabia, Egypt, Nubia and other parts of Asia and Africa. Quite recently (1929) Dr. Belle C. Eskridge, of Houston, Texas, having studied school girls for 27 years, recommended the circumcision of girls, *which she performs* for relieving nervousness and masturbation due to retained smegma or adherent prepuce. [*Italics supplied.*]

Female circumcision, which often involves removing the clitoris too, is considered further, in the First Series here, chapter 6.VI, under "The Female Castration Complex," especially in its even more gruesome reversal as infibulation, in which the woman is, as it were, sewed up, to prevent intercourse. (The folk-legend of the 'chastity-belt.') The matchingly atrocious form of circumcision for men, called subincision, is noted briefly below, under "Self-Castration," section 13.V.

The medical practice increasing nowadays in America and elsewhere, of circumcizing all male infants, whether Jewish or

Christian, is not a plot by Jewish physicians (extension of the ritual blood-accusation of the European pogroms), but is a combination of the inevitable – sometimes even the sublimated – sadism and castration complex of surgeons, and the regression from sexuality to anal-retentive 'cleanliness' neuroses on the part of modern parents who demand or weakly agree to the operation. (See Karl Abraham, "The Female Castration Complex," in his *Selected Papers*, p. 368–9.) Phimosis, or intractable tightness of the foreskin, has been found to be of such rare statistical occurrence – even less than the 2 to 3% *of cases of penis-cancer* – that it is now seldom used as the rationalization for infant circumcision, as it was during the late 19th century, when this mutilation became generalized among Christians. As Dr. Foley notes, many obstetricians now perform this operation on boy children as part of the routine post-partum 'checking' of the child, and can only be prevented from doing this by *urgent preliminary understanding and insistence* on the part of the parents. Circumcision is not only the oldest and most widely-performed surgical operation in the world, but it is also the only such operation widely performed in the West without any actual explanation (except 'cleanliness') being given for it; and it is most remarkable to observe the ease with which everyone has been intimidated about it. We are perhaps fortunate that no one wants to keep our noses clean, from birth, by similar methods. It is curiously the *smaller* organs that cause most of the trouble: the eye, the tongue, the penis, the foreskin, the tiny ductless glands. Few people have much trouble with the *gluteus maximus* muscles of their arse.

As with the similar shaving of women's armpits (but not men's) in the Anglo-Saxon countries, recourse is had to generalized notions of 'hygiene.' In the case of circumcision, this means specifically that if the child handles his penis it must be because of some uncleanly 'irritation' of the foreskin – *i.e.* of the preputial smegma beneath – and he must be circumcised to prevent this: the handling, not the irritation. That this is precisely the threatened castration for masturbation is abundantly clear to the child if not to the parent. Surgeons have, in fact, been known to 'suggest' circumcision as a premium with tonsillectomy – to be thrown in for the same price! The *need to cut* is very visible here, and any surgeon making such a suggestion today may justifiably be considered 'disturbed.' This was at its height in the 1920's, and it may be stated as axiomatic that no boy undergoing this surgical combination can grow up non-neurotic.

From the point of view of mental hygiene, rather than compulsive notions of physical 'cleanliness,' no child should be circumcised after he is old enough to speak – if at all – unless and *until* intractable phimosis is present: 'intractable' meaning that the foreskin actually cannot be pushed back beyond the corona glandis, not that it lies covering the head of the penis when at rest, which is its normal position and function. Phimosis is not medically considered to occur more often than once per *sixty thousand* individuals, meaning that a maximum of 1,700 of the some 100,000,000 men in the United States today might actually ever have required circumcision. How many millions have nevertheless been circumcised no one knows, other than the figures for the Jewish and Moslem populations, which are never for phimosis.

The following extraordinary letter was received by a popular writer on sexual subjects, Dr. D. O. Cauldwell, who published it in his pamphlet, *Is Anyone Sexually Normal?* (Girard, Kansas: Haldeman-Julius Big Blue Book No. 903; 1950) p. 10, as part of an intended demonstration, à la Kinsey, that *everybody* is normal, and that no such thing as sexual perversion – and particularly not homosexuality – really exists at all. It's all a matter of 'genes.' In the following pages he spends several columns refuting my then-recent pamphlet, *On the Cause of Homosexuality*, observing that: '*The mother-son-son-mother incest factor, with the great big male of a father in the offing as a villain who looms up before his male child with a long knife bent on castration is more fantasy than fact, and has little bearing on whether the male child will become a homosexual.*' Now read the letter he himself publishes on the preceding page:

> My 12-year-old son found one of your books at a neigbor's and read that you condone masturbation. I personally circumcised him and I do not think he'll ever masturbate again. He probably will not be capable of having any sort of sex relations until he is old enough to marry, and I go to the expense of paying a high-priced plastic surgeon to straighten out his organ after the way I deliberately misshaped it to keep him sexually pure ...
>
> You, and you alone, are responsible for the present condition and appearance of my only son's genital organ. The boy suffers and I blame you.

(There are several more paragraphs, mostly about God and sin.)

The folk-mind has never been in any doubt that circumcision is a modified form of castration, or genital harm, enacted against the helpless (and perfectly innocent) child or adolescent. This is one of the main roots of the hatred of the Jews, though it is seldom or never even alluded to in learned disquisitions on the "Causes of Anti-Semitism," and also never causes anyone to hate Arabs. Furthermore, it is the hidden parallel or justification for the false and terrible 'blood accusation' of ritual murder, brought against the Jews for centuries, since (and including) the Crucifixion of Jesus. This accusation is, by those who believe in it, considered to be 'proved' out of the Jews' own most important ritual celebration, the Passover, at which time the ritual murder is generally presumed to take place – as with that of Jesus – on the Biblical 'evidence' of the story of the Exodus from Egypt, after the mysterious nocturnal slaying of every first-born male among the Egyptians, while the Jews remained miraculously untouched.

Jesus is also pointedly executed at Passover (by the method of crucifixion special to the Romans, who now run the resultant church), as the sacrificial blood-offering or Paschal Lamb, representing the first-born son of Jehovah. However, the equally gospel story of the 'Three Days in the Tomb' clearly points to vestiges of the traditional death & resurrection of the ancient gods, particularly Mithra, at the dramatic solar pause of the winter Solstice, December 22nd to 25th, now curiously celebrated as the date of Jesus' birth (with the Circumcision eight days later on New Year's Day.) Though the 'Three Days in the Tomb' are insisted upon four different times in the *Gospel according to St. Matthew* (xvi–xx, and especially xxvii, 63 ff.), the statement is nowhere made in any of the Gospels or the New Testament – and particularly not in *Luke*, i. 24–26 – that Jesus was born at Christmas. This comes as a surprise to many people, but it is a fact. The idea of dating the birth of Jesus in December was first suggested in the *Canons* of St. Hippolytus in the 3rd century A.D., while Clement of Alexandria was recommending, more logically, the 19th of April (during Passover), as is implied by the story in *Luke*, ii. 8, of the *'shepherds abiding in the field, keeping watch over their flock by night,'* which points to a date in spring.

The whole purpose of Hippolytus' myth of the illogical birth of this one deity in the dead of winter, at the Solstice, when all other gods die – instead of being born, like all other deities.

with the first vegetation and constellations of spring – is obviously strictly worked out backwards to support the matching death at the blood-sacrifice of Passover at the Vernal Equinox. The Russian pogroms against the Jews, during the Czarist period, always therefore took place either at Easter – which is Passover – or at Christmas, when the Jews would stay up all night long on Christmas Eve ('*Nittelnacht*') telling folktales and gambling for hazelnuts, waiting for the Black Hundreds to come.

I. RABBIS AS CIRCUMCISERS

Few allusions are ever made to circumcision in popular speech or humor without connecting it pointedly to the Jews. It is almost unnecessary to quote circumcision jokes: they are among the commonest types, even at the punning level below that of actual jokes, with little anti-Semitic novelty cards (showing "*Abie Getting His First* 10% *Cut*" at the hands of a hook-nosed rabbi wielding a large shears!) available in profusion for persons not brilliant enough for jokes. The actual Jewish ritual method of circumcision is, apparently, almost unknown – which is perhaps just as well – though the butcher knives and enormous shears shown in the novelty-card illustrations are naturally purposeful exaggerations. The staggering quotation from Mr. Graham Greene, on rabbis who perform circumcision with their thumbnail [!] given at the end of Chapter 5.VI, should be re-examined at this point. In justice to Mr. Greene it should be made clear that, after the foreskin is cut away in the Jewish ritual, the tip of remaining skin is actually spread carefully from the *glans penis* with a specially sharpened thumbnail.

It should also perhaps be mentioned – folklore aside – that rabbis do *not* customarily perform circumcision, this being done by a minor functionary called a *mohel*, self-appointed to the work, as with the *shochet* or ritual slaughterer of animals and fowl. As many of these worthies are also equipped with the full ritual beard, the final step of the Jewish ritual, *the sucking of the blood of the circumcised penis of the infant* (to 'clean the wound') by the full-bearded *mohel*, seems invariably to give the younger nurses in modern American hospitals something of a shock. This is not actually cannibalism, with the *mohel* taking the part of Moloch. The *mohel* does not swallow the child's blood, but spits it out, as Jews are forbidden by their religion to ingest blood under any pretext. (*Genesis*, ix. 4, repeated and detailed in *Leviticus*, xvii, 10–14.) This is perhaps only a technical detail. I cannot conceive of any rational Christian who would *not* cheerfully believe in the 'blood accusation' – or invent it – as to the killing of Christian children and sucking of their blood by Jews at Passover, after watching a bearded *mohel* suck the blood from an eight-day-old Jewish baby's penis after circumcising him. This is now sometimes done with a sanitary little glass suction-pump instead. Say what you will, it's progress.

As to the jokes themselves, let us begin with one in which the 'inferior' races of choice, Negro and Jew, meeting in circumcision is perhaps notable: *A Negro insists that the doctor castrate him.* [Assumption of guilt by the victim.] *After doing so, the doctor suggests circumcision too. "Dawgone, Doc," (in a squeaky voice), "Dat am de word I wanted."* (1:270.) Other variations on this theme will be found below, under "Self-Castration." As already noted, it is a convention of jokes on this subject that the man's *voice* changes immediately to countertenor or soprano the instant the testicles are removed. Obviously the persons telling these jokes know that this is not true: an artistic time-condensation and symbolic displacement, no doubt.

Only the touch as to the Negro, in the preceding story, is new or American. The rest is centuries old, appearing in La Sale's *Cent Nouvelles Nouvelles* (1450) No. 64, "Le Curé rasé." As repeated in the *Dugocento Novelle* of Malespini (1609) I. 64: *A practical joker* – no longer a priest, owing to the intervening censorship of the Roman Catholic Index and Inquisition at the Counter-Reformation – *asks a doctor to castrate him. When the joker then changes his mind at the last minute, the doctor insists on finishing the operation.* There is no reference whatever to the 'lesser castration' of circumcision in this 15th-century original, as in the modern form, where stupidity also takes the place of the so-called 'practical joking.' The whole idea of such a joke *at one's own expense* suggests that the story is really an example of 'folk rationalization,' attempting to explain away as humor some early would-be *castrato* (nowadays called 'transsexuals') or some particularly castratory doctor, of whom the anecdote was perhaps told. See further, section 13.V, "Self-Castration." In Bandello's *Novelle* (1554) III. 3, another tale is told of: *An ignorant bride who castrates her husband when he jokingly tells her to do so.* (We will return to this 'joke' again.)

All such stories are connected in format, if not exactly in subject, with the folktale theme of the game or jest that ends fatally. (Tale Type 2401.) Many modern 'true' anecdotes of this kind circulate about initiations and mock-executions, especially in medical schools, and the usual death-by-terror of the victim is sometimes modified to his (or her) *merely* going insane. For example: *The girl medical student in whose bed a Negro's amputated penis, or a male leg* [sic] *is placed as a joke, covered with phosphorescent paint. When the male medical students, who are gathered round her door waiting to hear her scream, hear nothing but a heavy clumping sound, they break in and find the girl glassy-eyed, thumping the leg up & down on the floor while tearing at it wildly with her teeth.* (Ann Arbor, Mich. 1935, told as a true occurrence 'just recently.') In versions where it is a penis which is placed in her bed, the girl is not stated to be found eating it, but *'squeezing it between her knees.'*

A man in a public toilet urinates on another man. "Aren't you from Cleveland?" "How did you know?" "That cock-eyed [!] *Rabbi Bernstein, there, circumcises on the bias."* (N.Y. 1941.) Another version of the same situation makes no mention of circumcision, and is perhaps a revision intended to get rid of all Jewish reference. *A war veteran in a public toilet urinates all over himself and the man in the next stall. "Dammit!" the man shouts, "why don't you look what you're doing?" The war veteran apologizes, explaining that he was caught in machine-gun fire saving a buddy's life, and his penis was shot full of holes. (He shows it to the stranger.) "I see," says the man apologetically, taking a card out of his pocket. "Here, go to see this man, he'll fix you up." "Another doctor?" says the veteran sadly; "I've been to a lot of doctors already." "Hell, no! He's a piccolo teacher. He'll teach you how to finger that stump, so you won't piss all over strangers!"* (N.Y. 1952.) Under the pretence of mere callousness, a second castration ('Veteran's re-education' by the piccolo teacher) is clearly contemplated.

War veterans seem to be a particular target of this type of callous humor, the implication being: *'I'm glad it was him and not me!'* For reassurance of this kind, obviously the more gruesome the better. As in the callous joke, already given, concerning: *The horribly twitching young man having an ice-cream sundae, who, when asked by the soda-jerk, "Crushed nuts?" jitters violently and answers, "N-n-n-no, shell shock."* This was

sent me by a young man in California, already in a wheel-chair
(from which he was apparently masterminding a gun-running
operation for South American revolutionaries, under the cover
of an "Ornamental Arms & Ballistics" mail-order book business), who died a few months later of spinal meningitis. *Code-
meaning* to him: 'There are worse things to live with than
spinal meningitis.'

Many circumcision jokes are softened down to puns, or have
never been anything else. These are the type of 'hospital
humor' referred to in the quotation earlier, from Dr Foley, in
Fact, as the 'lewd and obscene commentary by the obstetrician
to his audience of nurses,' at circumcisions. *"It won't be long
now!" – "Abie getting his first 10% cut."* (If the child is Jewish.)
– *"Why does the rabbi earn more than the priest? – Because he
gets all the tips."* (1:69.) A singular version of this is given as a
cartoon, in *Sex to Sexty* (Texas, 1966) 9:39, signed Ron Stan-
field, showing *A black-hooded executioner with a large, pro-
tuberant nose, holding the string of a tiny guillotine – shoulder
high – with a sign:* "CIRCUMCISIONS HERE. PRICES REASONABLE.
NO TIPS PLEASE." Perhaps the most interesting element in this
cartoon is the drawing of the executioner himself, who almost
consciously represents the *uncircumcised penis of the victor* –
the reader looking at the cartoon. Here the black hood or cape
openly symbolizes the foreskin, as is the symbolic or phallic
meaning also of the well-known 'mysterious man' label for
Sandeman Port wine. (Illustrated in a German work of the early
1930's on sex symbolism in advertising.) – *'According to a new
ruling, whenever there is a circumcision in a Jewish family
there must be a policeman present. To keep the piece, of course.'*
(1:297.) This concern with the disposition of the circumcised
foreskin will be treated more fully below. The usual notion is
that it is *eaten*.

Any reference in public, in a humorously-toned situation, to
'clipping' – which has also the slang meanings of striking with
the fist, or cheating and overcharging (the sadistic concept of
coitus: cheating as *'screwing'*, *'reaming,'* etc.) – is usually to be
understood as an allusion to circumcision. *The enraged doctor
threatens the patient telephoning him while his wife is in the
doctor's office: "The next time I see you I'm going to clip you,
and it won't be long!" Wife, with a laugh: "It never was."*
(Burlesque skit, D.C. 1943.) – *In a parody of the song "Mule
Train," described as 'clippety-clop-ping along,' the singers*

mimicking 'Miami Jews' complained: *"The clipping I got; the clopping I dun't get."* (Burlesque night-club skit, Miami, Florida, 1951.) – *"What did the Georgia rabbi say to the Massachusetts rabbi?" "Hello, you Yenkee clipper!"* (D.C. 1944, from an army sergeant.) – *The congregation wants to plant a memorial tree in Israel for their rabbi, but can't decide whether to plant a Juniper or Eucalyptus.* (N.Y. 1942.)

Of openly hostile types, there is the Wellerism, said to have been seen on an American 'novelty' card about 1942, but first recorded orally in an army hospital, D.C. 1944, from a soldier: ' *"It won't be long now!" as the rabbi said when he circumcised the little boy.'* ('Throwaway' line added: *"That's all, brother; I cut it short!"*) – *Headline in the Israeli war:* "20,000 JEWS CUT OFF AT THE FRONT." (N.Y. 1948.) – *Nazi type of circumcision: Save the foreskin and throw away the Jew.* (2:417.) A certain hostile note may be sensed here. *The Limerick,* No. 793, gives a straight cannibalistic solution to the 'mystery' of the circumcised foreskin: *'An elderly rabbi named Riskin, dines daily on cunt-juice and foreskin.'* What, no blood?

The specific Judaism of circumcision is not always present. *"Did you hear about the bloodless operation performed up at Oak Knoll Hospital? – They circumcised Charlie McCarthy* [a ventriloquist's dummy] *with a pencil-sharpener."* (D.C. 1946.) – *Mother: "Should we have little Jimmy circumcised?" Father: "Hell, no! Let him* wear *it off the way I did!"* (N.Y. 1950. Compare: *"Why do poor kids have longer penises than rich kids?"* – *"The rich kids have toys."* (N.Y. 1952.) However, the element of Judaism is usually central, even in the most casual reference. *A well-known American poet and translator, playing poker with another faculty member of the University of California, his wife, and another woman, when asked to cut the cards remarked: "I never cut; I have no rabbi blood in me."* (Berkeley, Calif. 1942. Unimportant, but typical.) – *A Jewish boy at a swank party is asked his name by a dowager. "Glass, ma'm," he replies; "G-L-A-S-S." "Carter Glass of Virginia?" "No ma'm – cut Glass from de Bronx."* (Minneapolis, 1935.)

The circumcision of Gentiles, in imitation of, or in comparison with Jews, seldom appears in jokes except in forms making brutally clear the identification with castration. *A rabbi and priest are in competition. When the priest gets his parishioners to buy him a Buick, the rabbi has the congregation buy him a Cadillac. The following morning the priest goes out with holy water and baptizes his car. Before he is even finished the rabbi comes dashing out with a plumber's shears and cuts off three inches of his own car's exhaust pipe.* (N.Y. 1941. Very often collected in America, also in England, 1953.) Compare the movie-scene from *Annie, Get Your Gun*, discussed in the First Series, 8.III.6, page 529, in which: *The excessively masculine sharpshooter-heroine is 'made a woman' by her American Indian foster-father clipping off the front-sight of her golden rifle with a wire-cutting shears.* This appears to be adopted directly from the preceding joke. *An Indian becomes converted to Judaism and decides to circumcise himself with his toma-hawk. He lays his penis on a chopping block, closes his eyes and hacks at it, but unconsciously draws his body away and misses himself completely. "Ugh, too far." He tries again and manages to chop off just the top of his foreskin. "Ugh, too far." He tries a third time and says, "Ugh, too close."* (N.Y. 1952. Also with end-line, *"Ugh, too much."*)

This is evident gloating over the Gentile Indian, or – to put it another way – it accuses Jewish circumcision of being an attempt or plot to castrate the Gentiles: but *only* the comedy Indian, not the speaker. It takes its form from the famous joke or anecdote about: *cutting off the dog's tail mercifully: an inch at a time*, which is also certainly a disguised castration. The similarity with the 'cow's udder' story, given below under "Self-Castration," is very marked, especially in the repeating of the mimed or mock castration several times before finally succeeding, thus overdetermining and insisting with sick antici-pation on the castratory danger. The word *'Indian'* (also some-times *'Frenchman'* or *'Eskimo'*) is used colloquially, though in-frequently, in America – especially in the plural – as a code-word meaning *'Jew,'* in public situations where prejudicial references to Jews cannot be ventured, as in a business office, or a store owned by a Jew, or when a person known to be Jewish is present. If intended in this sense, the 'converted Indian' is of course nothing other than the Jew attempting to circumcise himself, but castrating himself instead: obviously equally hostile as an imagining or 'revenge.'

It still often occurs, especially in New York City, that young Christian men and women – especially unbelieving Catholics of Italian, Irish, or Polish second-generation origin, and college-educated – will attempt to assimilate themselves to the middle-class 'radical' Jewish group, which is considered to be the

American intellectual élite. Such assimilated Christian intellectuals enjoy being able to pronounce a word or two of Russian-style Yiddish (such as *'beatnik,'* or *'phudnick'* : which is a *nudnick* with a Ph.D.), and to tell presumably 'in' Jewish jokes with a creditable accent. Another American 'Indian' joke, common to their repertoires, also involves the castratory (scalping) tomahawk, and a recognition of the Jewish dietary division of 'milk' and 'meat' dishes : *The Indian squaw nags at her brave husband, "So go out in the* veldt *and find us something to eat!" He takes his tomahawk and wanders for miles, finally coming upon the track of a bull-moose which he tracks for hours. Just as he leaps on the moose with uplifted tomahawk, he shouts, "Migod! it's the* milchige *tomahawk!"* (N.Y. 1940.) This was told by a handsome young Catholic girl who later married a Jewish scientist, and eventually died of alcoholism. The oral over-determinants are obvious here; the identification of the Jewish dietary laws about *'milchigs'* and *'fleischigs'* as sexual (or miscegenational) in tone is hardly hidden.

The hostility against rabbis (as circumcisers) is of course strongest among unbelieving Jews, though seldom frankly expressed. In the last of the best-selling bitch-heroine novels in America, this time mixed with softcore pornography, *Naked Came the Stranger* (New York, 1969) by 'Penelope Ashe' – actually written 'as a joke,' a sort of sinless, pseudonymous gang-bang, by Mike McGrady, Harvey Aronson, and *twenty-three* other employees of both sexes on the Long Island journal, *Newsday* – the only chapter creditably written, "Joshua Turnbull,' p. 63–85, is the work of a young Jewish editor, Jack Schwartz. (See McGrady's confessional, *Stranger Than Naked, or How to Write Dirty Books for Fun and Profit*, New York, 1970, pp. 53–6 and 189–90.) Rabbi Turnbull, who is totally the now standard hot-jazz, tweedy Reform rabbi, is destroyed by his amour with the intellectual bitch-heroine – as are the protagonists of all the other chapters – first nearly breaking his erect penis during a naked leap at her bedstead; then being bitten in the ass (*i.e.* symbolically buggered) by her large male dog while engaged erotically with her in cunnilinctus ('knee-kissing'). Later he goes mad.

2. CIRCUMCISION AND WOMEN

Any concern by a woman with the question of circumcision is of course considered gratuitous and castratory by men. A florid castratory version of the 'hedged bet' joke already cited in another context: *A little old lady [witch] with a shopping-bag enters a U.S. bank and demands to see the director. She has $1,000,000 in cash in her shopping-bag, with which she wants to open an account, and explains frankly that she won it betting: in fact, she never loses. She offers to bet the bank-director a quarter of a million dollars that he is circumcised (or that his testicles will become square in twenty-four hours). He accepts the bet, and she comes back the next day with a small Japanese friend as witness. When the bank-director proves that she has lost the bet, by letting her see his penis (or handle his testicles), the Japanese keels over in a dead faint. He is the director of the Bank of Nippon, and she has bet one million dollars with him that she will have the director of the U.S. bank with his pants down (or 'by the balls') within twenty-four hours.* (N.Y. 1973.)

A song by a female nightclub entertainer, entitled "Moe," in the character of: *A Jewish woman who, fearing her husband's infidelity, swears to get herself a knife "and finish what the rabbi started."* (D.C. 1949.) The identification of castration with circumcision cannot be made more clear. Under the heading, "Cooking with Jock: Lesbian Novel," *Neurotica* (1951) No. 9: p. 40, quotes the following extraordinary passage from Mrs. Maude Hutchins' *A Diary of Love* (1950):

The raspberries come off easily, they are so ripe, so willing, but without ardor. I lift a handful to my mouth, tilt up my chin, and too lazy to chew, too languorous and affectionate to demolish or bite, I press them to the roof of my mouth with my tongue, and the juice ... I want more of this but not too fast, a little variety: I pull ten more, lovely and plum colored, away from the small penis-like excrescence of each, and the naked immodesty of the little scene settles in my brain. I trundle up the ten in my tongue, to the vault [*sc.* of the mouth], and crush them softly ... the fog is pink.

Frieda, the pale slim Swede, is at the sink fixing the late crop of very young carrots for supper ... She is preparing them properly: you never scrape young carrots; you boil them as they are and then you plunge them in cool water ... it is easy and pleasant to remove the skin ... A few she gently massaged. We were both silently watching the manipulations of the numerous little roots when she said quietly, "Come, it won't hurt. There, dear one, it didn't, did it." Her soft fingers were so loving; what was she dreaming of? ... She was finished and dried her wrists. "In the old country," she said, "they don't circumcise the little boys."

The hands-down champion in this field, however, is the less arty but far more direct *Kibbutz-niks!* (New York, 1963, mimeographed), by Miss Mildred Kapilow, a proposed musical comedy which might well have had – or may still have – the success it merits, had it not been for the concurrent Broadway performance of another musical, entitled *Milk & Honey*, on the same theme: the life of the volunteer agricultural workers in the Israeli *kibbutzim*, or farm-camps. Miss Kapilow's hero is a Gentile, Michel, a Frenchman of 26, 'beat and bearded,' who falls in love with the lovely Shoshonah, and has himself circumcised so that he can marry her. The climax of the last act, II. iii, pages 21–2, is his telling Shoshonah, who is surprised to see that he has 'lost his beard': *"That's not all I lost. I've been in a hospital. I got* CIRCUMCIZED!*"* (Sings:)

> Now I'm a Jew! Now I'm a Jew!
> I dare you, ask me what is new
> For this darling little frail
> I've been lying on my tail
> Now I'm with you! I'm Jewish too ...

> Although I sing, the dreadful thing
>   that I've been through
> I'm the only groom whose wedding
> Required a prior shedding
> But tonight I'll be as good as new.

> What it was like! Poor little tyke!
> Just think, one little drink
>   could almost break the dyke
> Though it didn't cost me money
> For a Frenchman this ain't funny
> But love of Mike, now I'm a kike.

> Yes I'm a Jew, all through and through
> Tho I confess the bloody mess
>   made me turn blue

When they put me under ether
I said *adieu* to my urether [?]
But don't boo hoo! It stuck like glue.

Oh what they did! Poor little kid!
For when I saw that fatal flaw
      I almost hid
It wasn't any cinch
You try to give an inch
But now I'm rid! Yes I'm a Yid! ...

Tho on my life that bloody knife
      broke me in two
I thought there was a slip
When the doc cried "Let 'er rip!"
That wouldn't do! Doc thought so too.
      (*Boys:*)
So he's a Jew, all tried and true
It's quite unique what that French sheik
      has suffered through.

The worst was in the thinking
That my violet was shrinking ...
Yes I'm a Jew, of French-fried brew
though while I mended it depended
      on your view
But when they removed the bandage
I could see all the advantage
He, ha, HA! Because it grew!

I won't insist that this is great theatre, but the reader will certainly admit he has never read anything like it. For Jewish self-hatred – here doubtless excused by the very recent Christianity of the hero – *Portnoy's Complaint* can't hold a candle to it. The Delilah-like tone of bloody, castratory gloating is also extraordinarily frank, despite the final over-compensatory brag. A sex-mag cartoon of the late 1960's: *One sexy nurse is saying to the other, "Let's wiggle through the men's ward and listen to the circumcision stitches pop!"* Everyone knows that there are no stitches taken in circumcision, and the idea is simply that the nurses' female desirability will be the Delilah-like cause of a second or renewed circumcision – doubtless painful – for all the men. The same point is implicit in the mock-Israeli song preceding, since the 'beat and bearded' Frenchman, or sex-symbol, Michel, is only brought to circumcision because of his desire for the lovely Shoshonah. The name means *rose*, with all the usual vaginal symbolism, but this particular rose seems to be more like that of the *Song of Songs*, ii. 2, which must be plucked from among the thorns.

It will be observed that no reference has been made here to the circumcision of women themselves, as differentiated from the morbid interest of women in the circumcision of men. An even more morbid interest exists, on the part of men, in the circumcision of women. See, for some of the curiosities and contradictions involved in this interest, the First Series here, chapter 6.VI, page 385. The Jesuit polygraph, Fr. Raynaud, wrote two treatises on eunuchs: one, dating from 1655, is re-printed in his complete works, vol. XIV, and includes a chapter on the 'delicate subject' of *"De castrandis mulieribus,"* later made the subject of a special dissertation by a German or Belgian physician, G. Franckx, *De castratione mulierum* (Heidel-berg, 1673); and compare Withof's *De castratis, commenta-tiones quatuor* (1762). These all confuse castration and circum-cision of women, as do most folk materials, but the distinction is clearly drawn in the research volumes of the great Dr. Martin Schurig, *Muliebria* and *Parthenologia* (both: Dresden, 1729), on which see further H. Spencer Ashbee's *Centuria librorum absconditorum* (1879) p. 1–14.

Women are not generally circumcised in the West (not yet, anyhow, but see the Texan proposal in the introduction to the present section, 13.III) and authentic folk-materials on these themes circulate about a reversal of the operation, in which girls or women are said to be 'sewed up' or even plugged up vaginally (infibulation) to prevent sexual relations. An entire section has already been devoted to this unpleasant fantasy, and the reality behind it, in the First Series, 6.VI, "The Female Castration Complex – Passive Form: Infibulation," p. 382–9; continuing under "Ophelia's 'Nothing'," 8.III.6, at pages 525–34, which should be consulted here. Of particular importance in this connection is the folkloristic theme of the 'chastity-belt,' which has never had any real existence, though modern ex-amples, and faked antiques, have of course been manufactured by people who have heard of their presumed existence 'during the Crusades.'

Modern non-assimilationist Judaism (the so-called 'Conservative' and 'Reformed' synagogues, as differentiated from the old-style Orthodox Judaism of, for instance, modern Israel) has attempted to give a newly-created place to women in the religion, and no longer demands that women be segregated in a special balcony in the synagogue, cut off their hair and wear a wig after marriage, etc. This has now gone so far as to involve a newly created confirmation ceremony, the *'Bas-Mitzvah'* (Daughter of the Covenant), to match the traditional *'Bar-Mitzvah'* (Son of the Covenant), in which the 13-year-old Jewish boy formally recalls the blood-covenant of the religion, made for him at the age of eight days, in circumcision. (*Genesis*, xvii. 12 and 25, for the two dates.) Obviously this has not gone so far, in modern pro-feminist Judaism, as also to require infant-circumcision of girls, as is the case in the Mohammedan world. (See the First Series, 6.VI, page 385.) Yet one is astonished to read, in the Texas humor magazine, *Sex to Sexty* (1970) No. 31 : p. 56, the following letter sent to the editors, Mr. Newbern and Miss Rodebaugh, by a woman-reader in Oklahoma :

> In your *Super Sex to Sexty* No. 11, you said the way to circumcise a woman was to set her bare [ass] on a cane-bottom chair and lop off everything that hangs through. That's not how it works in Oklahoma. Around here, they set you down on a five-gallon bucket and rim off the edges!

Obviously not authentic ethnology, even in Christian Oklahoma, and just a 'jocular' fantasy, this leaves the reader with only one question : why does either method appear in a *humor* magazine? Wouldn't these be better suited to a horror magazine, such as the same publisher's earlier *Grim Hairy Tales*, with its hilarious display of all the repellent humor of decapitations, cripples, etc.? As the old song says (D'Urfey's "The Hubble Bubbles," 1720) : *'Ye Circum and Uncircumcis'd, come hear my Song, and be advis'd.'*

3. THE CONDOM AS FORESKIN

The condom appears to be equated with the foreskin (rehabilitation), and, also by the circumcision route, with castration. For example, in the following joke published in the *Psychoanalytic Quarterly* (New York, 1932) I. 221n., also in *Anecdota Americana* (1934) 2:286. *An immigrant maid threatens to quit on finding a condom in the master and*

*mistress' bed. "But Helga," says the mistress, "don't you use
those things in your country too?" "Sure we do, but we don't
skin 'em!"* There seems to be a reminiscence of this joke – or a
parallel fantasy of castration – in the passage from Maude
Hutchins' *A Diary of Love* (1950) quoted in the preceding
section, "Circumcision and Women."

Of the straight rehabilitation variety : *A Jewish mother who
finds one of her son's condoms, while putting away his ironed
shirts, thinks it's a drugstore 'new-skin' to enable him to marry
a Christian girl.* (2 : 122.) The packaging methods once used to
make the concealment of condoms possible, when this was still
thought necessary – such as their being rolled and wrapped inside a tinfoil disc made to imitate a silver dollar (marked
"Three Merry Widows"), or as a gold-tipped cigarette called
"Sporting Life" – would make an interesting folkloristic study.
Some materials are gathered in the New York 'pornzine,' *Screw*
(1969) No. 25 : p. 13. The resection operation whereby Jews in
the Roman Empire created a fold of skin resembling a foreskin,
to avoid disgrace in the public baths (compare also the foreskin
'cut on the bias' in a public-toilet above), is noted by the Latin
satirists such as Martial in his Epigrams, in the 1st century A.D.,
and is fully discussed in Allen Edwardes' *Erotica Judaica* (New
York, 1967) p. 132–42. Note also the punchline, *"They look so
sporting in the locker room,"* in the next section.

In the *Portrait of the Artist as Flowing Teat* (Tangiers, 1966),
Capt. Gregory Gulliver, the would-be Hitler of "GONNIF" –
"Gangsters of the New Freedom" announces as the first radio
broadcast of this new Social-Nazicratic Party ('transmitting
secretly from a motorized abattoir off the Liverpool coast') :

Jews ! Gentiles ! Join the Social-Nazicratic Party and get your
foreskin back ! ... Nothing to do, nothing to buy. It's
E-e-a-sy, the NAZICRATIC way. Just send us a postcard *today*,
giving your name and address and religious affiliation, and
the hours when you are SURE to be home. We will do the
re-est ! In a very brief time you will receive the visit of our
Oberammergaureiterheiterführergeherrschaftsschmuck, who
speaks perfect English which he learned in loyal Western
Germany, training to fight the Communistic Foe. He will
return to you your missing foreskin, with a tube of special
YouKnoWho Glue, formerly made in our own factory in
Osweicim, Poland, which will stick that thing on your prick

forever! Remember: "Joy today – Goy tomorrow!" (*Hysterical background music:* Liszt's "Les Préludes.")

This particular music having a bad effect on Capt. Gulliver, as is explained – incontinent epilepsy is apparently referred to – the catchy new anthem of the NAZICRATIC Party becomes instead "Newskins for Jewskins, or Fooey on Foreskins," taken from that big big hit of the musical stage, *"Kiss Me Bloody,"* stated to be a musical comedy version of *Salomé* as retitled by its lady-author. Say what you will, this sticks with admirable understatement to the historical truth, and is in fact less repulsive.

An Irishman – for a change – *gets his wife pregnant in spite of using condoms. "And didn't I have to cut off the heads of 'em because they wouldn't fit?"* (1:196.) Similarly, since 'Irish bulls' of this type are applied ethnophaullically to *any* national group being held in the inferior economic and social position, the Italian fool joke: *An Italian laborer is told by the social-worker to avoid having any more children by using the condoms which he is given, with directions to put them on his organ before intercourse. His wife gets pregnant anyhow, and he explains, "No gotta organ – so I putta da rubber onna da piano."* (N.Y. 1940.) The joke has already been given as to: *The Russian Army order to an American company for fifty million condoms fifteen inches long and four inches in diameter. After discussing 'cold war' techniques with a State Department official, the manufacturer is told to go ahead and fill the order but to put a small paper label in each box marked "Medium."* (N.Y. 1954.) Here the condom is identified in the metonymic sense with the penis: container for contents.

In an article on "Mohave Indian Verbal and Motor Profanity," by the Hungarian analyst, Dr. George Devereux, in *Psychoanalysis and the Social Sciences* (1951) vol. 3: p. 111, another curious metonymy of the same kind is noted: A Mohave who, as a result of phimosis, has had to be circumcised, is nicknamed 'Modhar taa:p,' literally 'penis-cover,' a term also used to signify a condom. In other words, condom and prepuce are identical terms in Mohave (profane) speech. The German 'Eichelcapote,' a small condom just large enough to fit over the *glans penis,* where it seldom can be made to stay, and of which, in any case, the value is problematic (since most of the sensation in the penis during coitus is precisely in the *glans,* here covered), is self-evidently nothing but an imitation foreskin.

Finally, castration *via* the condom itself. The following joke must be very popular: I myself have collected it, according to the filing-cards here before me, six times since 1935, when a modified version appeared in print in the bawdy joke-and-poetry magazine, *Old Nick's Annual T.N.T.* (Minneapolis, Minn.), in which: *A man's 'nose' is taped to prevent sneezing. When he sneezes anyhow, it backfires and blows his 'ears' off.* This is perhaps expurgated from *Anecdota Americana* (1934) 2:64, a year earlier in which: *A man uses six condoms at once, to make everything extra safe. When he comes, he backfires and nearly blows his balls off.* However, a *conte-en-vers* form was also collected from a soldier in Monterey, Calif. 1942, combining both ideas: 'In a poem, a man whose vigorous coitus often broke the condom, was advised by a doctor whom he consulted to try using adhesive tape. He did, and in the course of the fuck that followed, he not only ripped up his wife's guts, but backfired and blew off his nuts.' (From manuscript.) Note the attack on the woman, in the style of "The Great Fucking Wheel."

Other rationalizations are also given, some of them pitiful in their overcompensation: *Six condoms (or a dozen) are used, to bulk up his too-small penis, by an American Indian. He goes back to the drugstore to complain, "Rubbers no good. Left ball go umph, right ball go umph, rubber go pow!" The druggist advises him to tie the condoms on at the base of his penis with a heavy rubber-band as well, stretched around several times. The next day the Indian is back again looking very dissatisfied. "Did the rubbers go pow this time, Chief?" "No! Good rubbers." "Did the rubber-band hold them on like I said?" "White man speak always with forked tongue. Rubbers go umph, rubber-band go umph, right ball go umph-umph, left ball go* POW!" (L.A. 1968.) Relevant here are all the occult and 'protective' implications of the condom, other than those advertised against disease and pregnancy, as discussed (with examples) in the First Series, 7.V, pages 429–30.

The catastrophic conclusion can also be avoided: 'A young husband was very worried about getting his bride pregnant, so on their wedding night he got her to put in a diaphragm, and made sure she had taken her Pill. Then he put on three rubbers, and when he came, he WITHDREW!' (La Jolla, Calif. 1965.) This was sent me by a college freshman boy who stated that he belonged to a group of young men who were 'saving their virginity' for the girls they would eventually marry, and who 'worked off their horniness' (sexual hunger) by riding on surfboards every morning before coming to school. When I pointed out to him that perhaps the girls they would marry might prefer that the boys be sexually proficient, as well as experienced surfers, he answered: "We'll just have to make our mistakes together." Driving automobiles is fortunately not learned that way.

Further materials on the condom will be found in the First Series, 7.V, under "Premarital Sexual Acts." Several of the jokes there are overcompensations for just the kind of sexual inadequacy expressed in the jokes here preceding in catastrophic and castratory terms. For example, a favorite in both England and America: *'Chap goes into chemist's for 365 F.L.'s [French Letters]. A year later he's back again for a repeat order. Assistant: "Now let me see, what was it – 370 did you have, Sir?" Chap: "What do you take me for – a bloody sex-maniac?"'* (London, 1954.) The American version naturally overstates rather than understates this, but makes the identical point: *A man buys an entire gross of rubbers in a drug-store: twelve packets of a dozen each. Just as the drug-store is closing at midnight, he dashes in and complains to the druggist, "What's the big idea gypping me? There were only a hundred and forty-three cundrums in that package." The druggist wordlessly turns to a shelf, breaks open a package, takes out a single condom, hands it to the man, and says, 'Sorry, sir, if I spoiled your evening."* (L.A. 1968. Variant in *Anecdota*, I: 152.) Note the reference here to a counting-compulsion, common with many neurotics, especially anal-sadists. (*Witches can be thrown off one's track by dropping a handful of coins, pins, or similar, as the witch must pick up and count every single one before continuing the chase.* – Reno, Nevada, 1970, the woman recounting this stating that she knew it was 'all nonsense,' but later adding casually that she 'had Irish blood' and was partly a witch herself.)

The resistance to the condom, and its various dangers, is best expressed self-destructively by making holes in it; or by claiming that it already had a hole in it when procured. This is the usual ground for complaint to the druggist (chemist), and it will be observed that the druggist is here again the lesser copy or surrogate of the feared doctor, since complaints are seldom made – in jokes – to doctors, except as to castratory cures that do not work! *"What's a Welsh letter? – A French letter with a leek in it!"* (Chelmsford, Essex, 1951.) – *Three stenographers are talking. First Steno: "Just for a joke, I put a cundum in the boss's pocket." Second steno: "And just for a joke, I made a hole in it with a pin." Third steno: (faints).* (N.Y. 1953.) This is sometimes told as a 'true story,' of: *A wife who punctures her husband's whole supply of condoms with a pin, in order to be sure to get pregnant and thus 'hold his love.'* (N.Y. 1940, told by an aggrieved Jewish husband, at the circumcision of his son; but not mentioning himself.) – *Sale of French letters – draped all across the store – blown up – filled with water – stretched a yard – faces painted on them – etc. In the window display, a banner reading:* "NO RIP, NO CLAP, NO BLOODY BRAT – BUY BRITISH AND FUCK 'EM ALL!" (London Airport, 1964: a tongue-twister.) – *Druggist: "These rubbers are guaranteed." "But what if they break?" "Well then, er, the guarantee runs out …"* (1 : 171.)

4. CANNIBALISM

The disposition or use made of the circumcised foreskin in ritual Jewish circumcision is a matter of some concern in jokes. All that discuss it are almost unanimous that it is *eaten*, which must be a form of the blood-accusation, if not a 'folk-recollection' of Freud's castratory totem-feast in which the Ur-Vater is eaten, every bit, by his assembled sons in the night. The idea must also owe something to the easily observable eating of the after-birth by the female of many domestic animals, such as cats. The truth about the *pipputz* or circumcised prepuce is that it is put into a pepper-canister and discarded. Why it should be a pepper-canister I do not know, except that pepper is used to preserve meat, suggesting in this case a sort of embalming. (An authentic Jewish joke, given later under "Over-compensation," tells of a Jew who buries his castrated penis in a little grave.)

In Dr. Abraham Wolbarst's propagandistic discussion of the advantages of male circumcision, in Victor Robinson's *Encyclopædia Sexualis* (New York, 1936) p. 128, an extraordinary paragraph is thrown in suggesting circumcision of girls as well – this has been quoted earlier – preceded by the following somewhat unexpected aside, which is not, however, recommended: *'In Madagascar and other places, the [circumcised] boy's godfather eats the foreskin dipped in egg-yolk.'* A few other unconscious curiosa of modern cookbooks, coming as close to this as they dare, are reprinted in *Neurotica* (1951) No. 9: p. 40, under the title "Cooking with Jock."

'*A guy and a girl were petting in a car in front of a rabbi's house. Suddenly a window opened, sounds of festivity were heard, and the piece sailed out the window and landed in the girl's lap. She looked startled and picked it up gingerly. "What is it?" she asked her boy-friend. He: "Taste it. If you like it, I'll give you a whole one to chew".'* (N.Y. 1943, from manuscript.) This is an evasion of the idea of the eating of the foreskin, but it is there, along with the obvious – and reassuring – gloating over the circumcised Jew. *A girl is fishing all day without a bite. She sees a man with a string of beauties. He tells her he is a doctor and uses cut-out tonsils for bait. The next man, also a doctor, uses appendixes. The third man has the biggest fish of all. "Oh, doctor," the girl asks, "what bait did you use?" "Doctor? I'm no doctor. I'm a Jewish rabbi."* (Idaho, 1952. Larson MS., No. 58.) Here again the idea is minced or evaded: the fish are doing all the eating. Sometimes the girl does not catch anything '*because she is sitting on her bait.*'

By the late 1960's, when the 'hippies' (the 'beatniks' of the 1950's, 'Bohemians' of the 1910's and '20's, etc.) had become the most hated minority group in America, except for the Negroes, this particular fantasy was also applied to them, as being something that only someone as low or lower than 'a Jewish rabbi' would ever do: *One hippie sees another evidently rolling in wealth – square gold-framed dark glasses, turquoise-studded belt on his sueded leather chaparajos, Turkmenian sheepskin coat, etc. "Hey man, whadda you pushin'? Makin' all that bread!" The other looks very mysterious. "Come* ON, *share with members of the tribe! What is it? Acid? sunshine? – jones?" "No," says the prosperous one, tapping his nostril significantly, with his little finger; "this is strictly legal. I got thirty kids fishing foreskins out of the trash-cans in back of the maternity hospitals, and selling 'em for Indestructible Chewing-Gum!"* (L.A. 1969.) Note again that cannibalism is evaded: the foreskins are only chewed, and presumably not swallowed – thus 'Indestructible.'

In an authentic Jewish story given further treatment in the First Series, under "The Diaper and the Scythe," 1.III.2, page 81: *A travelling salesman passing through a small town finds that his watch has stopped. He goes into a shop displaying a large watch outside, and asks the man to fix his watch. "I don't* fix watches." "But you have a big watch hanging outside." "I know, but I don't fix watches. I'm a mohel (circumciser)." "So why do you have a watch outside?" "Nu, so what should I have – a putz?" (N.Y. 1940. Picked up from the First Series here, in World's Dirtiest Jokes, 1969, p. 32, and given with the aposio-poetic punchline: "Well, what would you hang in the win-dow ...?") Hidden behind the humor of the mohel who realizes his profession is somehow disgraceful, is the implication that if he put up the sign he should put up, he would be selling – if not repairing – pricks. This is not quite a reference to can-nibalism, and yet ...

Again, the cannibalistic implications are evaded at the last minute in the following story, or, rather, are left to be accepted or refused. A college girl on a train has a zipper bag beside her with her lunch in it, packed by her mother. She falls asleep, and a young man pushes her bag out of the way and sits down be-side her. He too falls asleep. The girl dreams that she is hungry, unzips her lunch bag in her sleep and begins eating her lunch. "Oh, goody!" she cries, still asleep; "two hard-boiled eggs and the neck of a chicken!" (World's Dirtiest Jokes, 1969, p. 14.) Note the careful economy of the story. No further reference is made to the young man, and his presumable zipper-fly trousers, while the girl's eroticism is all displaced, in wide-open sym-bolism, to hunger and eating. Here the girl is not ignorant, but asleep – thus equally innocent – but the oral-incorporative fantasy is too guilty to be made more specific than in her final gloat. The caption-title given by Newbern & Rodebaugh, "With French Dressing?" is intended to imply that the girl is only fellating the man, which is probably the conscious meaning of the joke, though it doesn't explain the 'two hard-boiled eggs.'

The frank cannibalistic ideal has already been expressed as to: The testicles in castration, eaten by the nurse who 'mistook' them for olives. Likewise: 'An Irishman visited a synagogue one Saturday, and got locked in there at closing time. He was there all week until the next Saturday when they reopened the place. "What are you doing here?" he was asked. He explained he had been locked in there all week. "It's a wonder you didn't starve to death," the Jew said. "I would have," replied the Irish-man, "except for those pickles in the altar".' (D.C. 1943, from manuscript, collected from an army sergeant.) The following joke is one of the earliest that I can recollect having heard. The castration and cannibalism are entirely displaced in it to the buttocks, as in the silly pun: *"Know what happened to the Wac who backed into an airplane propeller? – Disaster!"* (N.Y. 1949. The punchline is also sometimes *"De-furred!"*)

From my own earliest recollections: *A little boy is sent to get meat from the butcher, but on the way loses the money his mother has given him, by playing dice. He goes down an alley, 'slices off a piece of his ass,' and brings it home. His mother cooks it and the family eats it. This happens several times. Finally he has no ass left, and has to come back with neither money nor meat. He tells his mother he has lost the money playing dice, and she goes to spank him, 'but she can't – because he hasn't got any ass!"* (Atlantic City, N.J. 1928, told by a little boy of my own age: about ten. I should perhaps add that my own father was a butcher and very severe with me, which probably explains why I remember this story so clearly, and the implied threat it involved for me.) This strange cannibalistic story, authentically told by one child to another decades before Portnoy's slice-of-liver food-defiling, emphasizes the 'protective' intention of the self-castration theme, to be discussed below, namely: *"I castrate myself so that others cannot do so!"*

It is this hidden idea which also explains the interest some people feel in hearing stories, usually false, about: *Foxes that gnaw off their trapped legs in order to escape.* (Compare Aesop's fable of *The fox that loses his tail,* AND TRIES TO GET ALL THE OTHER FOXES TO CUT OFF THEIRS! – Type 64.) Or the even more frankly castratory: *Badgers or raccoons who are said to 'bite off their own testicles and leave them for hunters,' so as to escape with at least their lives.* (Consider the mental mess of the mind of the fur-trapper who made up that one.) The pre-empted human form of the same thing, where the danger particularly feared is specifically that which is enacted on oneself beforehand, so that no one *else* can do so, appears very often in social and professional situations as the self-destructive life-game, YCFMIQ, or "You Can't Fire Me, I Quit!" (Badger story, back to Aesop, Motif J351.1.)

The cannibalism story of most frequent occurrence in the literature is Poggio's anti-Semitic No. 131, dating at least from the 15th century: *A Jew ships his dead brother home in a barrel marked "Pork," to avoid paying for his passage on the ship, with the result that the brother is eaten by the hungry sailors, all unbeknownst.* (Motif X21, and see G10–95 for extended references. One of James Gillray's sadistic cartoons illustrates this story: reproduced in Eduard Fuchs' *Die Juden in der Karikatur*, 1921.) In a version in Francis Grose's *The Olio* (1792) p. 189, "Tapping the Governor," *A sailor drinks the alcohol in which the body of the East India Company governor is being brought home for burial in England.* This story still survives, usually in a modification about a Negro porter supplying *ice* on a transcontinental train. Observe how the story develops from the eating of the Jew to the cannibalizing of the (non-Jewish) authority figure.

All interest in actual stories of cannibalism will be found to be heavily tainted with castratory and Oedipal drives, in which what is specifically wanted is *to eat the father's penis*, precisely as in Freud's hypothesized totem-feasting upon the murdered Ur-Vater in the night. In savage cannibalism, the eating of the penis of the enemy is presumed to bestow upon the victor all the manly force of the vanquished. As differentiated from the folk idea that Gypsies will not touch a corpse, or else in a remarkable 'return of the repressed,' modern French Gypsies are reliably reported to cannibalize the head, heart, and genitals of every seventh Gypsy 'king' at a great ritual gathering after his death. This is precisely Freud's cannibalistic totem-feast of the sons with the father's body, but making specific the eating of the dead father's genitals to absorb their *patria potestas*, or patriarchal power.

Various substitutions are common in the folklore of cannibalism, in both 'true' stories and jokes. The head and/or brains, and the eye, are in particular substituted for the eating of the penis, or as a generalized taboo sexual act. This is due to the queasiness many people feel about eating animals' fried brains. An anecdotal cookbook a few years back, entitled *Clementine in the Kitchen*, I believe, includes an unbelievable scene in which the gourmet father practically forces his daughter to eat a calves-head dish, including the *eye*. Many people cannot eat the testicles at all, *when they know that is what they are eating*, and will vomit up the meal afterwards if told. The testicles are therefore disguised by various slang terms, for use as food, such as 'Rocky Mountain oysters,' but these euphemisms are too well-known to afford any disguise, and are now just jokes. It is the need for such slang circumlocutions for the eaten testicles that demonstrate the fear and rejection involved. The penis of animals is never offered for sale in butcher-shops – for all the jokes about phallic sausages, fresh Italian 'bulls-balls' cheeses, and so forth – but is ground up with other offals for canned 'pet-food.' Let 'em eat pricks!

People, especially women, who particularly enjoy eating or preparing animal inner meats, not only the testicles but also giblets, lungs, brains, 'sweetbreads' (another euphemism), and so forth, should be scrupulously avoided, as heavily neurotic and probably filled with fantasy notions of oral-incorporation and cannibalism, aside from being riddled with dangerous extrojected guilts. One young American tourist I met in Paris told me he was so struck by the evil *'smile,'* as he put it, with which a young lady he had just met ordered fried lambs' testicles in a restaurant – marked *'Frivolités'* on the menu, but the chef had helpfully explained what they were – that he excused himself to wash hands, slipped out the kitchen door of the restaurant, and left the young lady to eat and pay for her testicular meal herself. One can only applaud his somewhat panicky wisdom.

In the story of the Donner Party, lost and starving in the mountains while attempting to cross to California: *The rescuers are said to have arrived just in time to find the children toasting their father's heart over the campfire (!) this worthy having committed suicide to give the wives and children what to eat.* (Motifs G36.1 and T215.3.) This simply parodies "Women and children first!" and Jesus Christ's *"Take, eat; this is my body."* Several admitted jokes do the same. *The captain and crew of the shipwrecked vessel have been in the life-boat for ten days and have nothing left to eat. The captain offers to kill himself so that the men can eat his body. As he lifts his revolver to his temple, one of the men shouts, "Stop, Captain, stop!" His face ashen, the captain lets the muzzle of the revolver fall. "Yes?" he asks. "Don't shoot yourself in the head, Captain," the sailor pleads; "brains are my favorite dish."* (N.Y. 1940. Also played as a little comedy scene, or *jeu de société*, by two men at an office-party, the captain played as a burlesque of Charles Laughton's acting in the movie, the *Mutiny on the Bounty*.) This would nowadays be called a 'sick' joke. It's sick, all right, though it is hardly more than a footnote on Freud's Ur-Vater feast.

Same situation, but even more clear as to the castration of the father-figure that the decapitated head and brains symbolize: *The captain offers to cut off his own penis to feed the shipwrecked men. "It's my duty, men," he says. "If you slice it up,*

you'll have something to eat. God bless you," he ends, breaking into tears and raising the gun to his forehead [?] "Wait,
captain," says the chief mate (or cabin-boy); "let me stroke it a
little first, and we'll all have what to eat for a week." This is the
total statement of the whole idea, especially as to the heroic
size of the Ur-Vater's envied, and eaten, penis. The same two
men who played out the preceding joke, played this one as
their 'blue' (bawdy) encore, calling each other 'Captain Bligh'
and 'Mister Christian' (the historical characters of the Mutiny
on the Bounty) in heavy mock-British accents, with hands
tucked into their sea-jackets à la Napoleon. At the point where
Captain Bligh raises the gun to shoot himself, he pokes the
imaginary gun at his own penis, his hand being then tenderly
raised to his head by the bold first officer, Mr. Christian. (N.Y.
1951.) This shows very clearly that, to these two office-
comedians at least, the 'brains' in the first joke are considered
identical with the penis in the second. The audience, certainly,
was expected to enjoy the 'blue' version as an unveiling or un-
peeling of the expurgatory onion, one layer down. (Motif G70.1.)

Much further material on specifically sexual cannibalism, involving the penis or various expurgations of this, such as the
heart, tongue, or a dead person's generalized 'wounds,' has already been given in the First Series, on the legend of "The Eaten
Heart." Of particular relevance is the story, p. 655–7, 8.VIII.10,
there, of The playboy who dies (in an orgy with three chorus
girls), and his penis will not lie down, even after death. His
widow tells the undertakers to cut it off and stick it up his ass,
adding, 'Even when he was alive, he wasn't none too particular
where he put it." (Randolph gives a version, No. 62, recollected
from Fayetteville, Arkansas, about 1903.) The widow's revenge
is here specifically stated to be jealousy of the other women,
and the posthumous humiliation of her husband is the standard
pedicatory rape, combined with castration.

In the cannibalistic form, her revenge is strictly personal –
"The War between the Sexes:" When 'the male member' [!]
of a couple dies after fifty years of marriage, the widow had
him 'emasculated, then took his private parts home to cook
them. She placed his frankfurter in a large kettle of sauerkraut,
then sliced up his testicles into a small saucepan, to which she
added tomatoes, garlic and tiny green peppers. Friends entering
the house asked the woman about the delicious aromas, and
were horrified to learn what it was. "Surely you must be jok-

ing," they cried. "How can you think of such a thing?' The old woman replied sourly, "For fifty years he made me eat it raw, the way he liked it – now I'll eat it cooked, the way I like it!"' (World's Dirtiest Jokes, 1969, p. 28.) Note the inserted recipe for Testicle Fricassee. A jovial horror-story by the Irish writer, E. J. M. Plunkett (Lord Dunsany), "Two Bottles of Relish," has the husband murder his wife and do away with her body by eating it, day after day, spiced with the two bottles of relish: the clue in the title. In a self-punishing touch, he also cuts down all the trees on his property – punchline of the story – 'to work up an appetite!'

Earlier, in the First Series, 8.VIII.1, "Old Wives for New," page 616, in connection with the 17th-century German cartoon idea of "The Mill for Grinding Old Wives Into New," the modern comedy-song is discussed known as "The Donnerblitz (or Donderbeck's) Machine." The gross humor of this song turns strictly on the cannibalistic attack on: The father-husband who climbs into his monster-sized sausage-machine to see what is the matter with it. His wife – who walks in her sleep [!] – touches the starter-button, thinking it is the light switch ... 'And Donderbeck was meat!' A version of this is the crucial scene in Charlie Chaplin's finest motion-picture satire, Modern Times, as noted further in the First Series, p. 616–17. Similarly, the attack on naughty children, who are stuffed into a grinding-machine, is the final scene of the most famous German 'humorous' children's book, Wilhelm Busch's Max und Moritz – the original of the American comic-strip, "The Katzenjammer Kids," always equally sadistic. An illustrated English children's book, apparently entitled The Grump, and dating from the early 20th century, has the children shown being frankly stuffed into a sausage-making machine, and fed to Mr. Grump for supper. This is left only as an ugly implication in the folktale of "Hänsel & Gretel" and their cannibalistic witch. It is worth underlining that, in general, both the authors and artists specializing in children's books, comic-books, animated cartoons, and other juvenile literature are among the sickest degenerates and most aggressive neurotics running around loose. They should be stuffed into their own sausage-making machines (one of their milder fantasies), or at the very least be prevented by force from having anything whatever to do with children or their literature. But no one except one psychiatrist, Dr. Fredric Wertham, has ever had the courage to say so.

A charming French comic novel in the 1880's, *Lilie, Tutue, Bébeth*, by Eugène Chavette (Vachette), has a mad inventor working on a flying-machine and other exotica, one of which beautifully improves on Donderbeck's Machine. This passage, p. 161–2, is apparently a satire on (or taps the European source of?) the American Midwest Market pork-butchers' proverb or brag that they *"Use every part of the pig except the squeal!"* The girl and her lover are spying on the activities of her inventor-father:

"Watch everything he does now," Adelaide commanded. "There, he's put the pig, alive, into the machine. Now he turns the mechanism: click, click, and there you have the pig coming out the other end of the machine, all neatly sliced into sausages, blood-puddings, and chitterlings. Just listen to Father's jaws! He's tasting his delicatessen. Oh, he clicked his tongue; that means he's not satisfied with the product. Too much salt, or perhaps not enough spices. He'll have to begin over. There, he piles all the sausages back into the machine; he takes the crank and begins turning it, but in the opposite direction. Note well! – in the opposite direction. Creak! creak! creak! And now you have the pig coming back alive out of the machine. – Wait, wait! No, I'm wrong. The pig didn't come back out yet. It's that special wheel that supposed to make him come back out that papa can't quite solve. But he's not worried; he'll find it yet." In *The World's Dirtiest Jokes* (Los Angeles, 1969) p. 172, a peculiar allusion to the Improved Donderbeck's Machine is made in a story in which: *The college-educated son sneers at the sausage-making machine with which his old 'immigrant' father has earned the money to send him to college. "It's the same old thing," says the son. ' "You put in a pig and out comes a sausage. Now it would really be something if you had a machine where you put in a sausage and out comes a pig!" The old man shook his head and sadly answered, "Son, a machine like that I don't have – but your Mama – SHE HAS A MACHINE LIKE THAT!"'*

Slicing machines of any kind are not only construed as a castratory danger, but, like the starting-button on Donderbeck's Machine, as a terrible *temptation* to auto-castration as well. This first appears as a mere gag version of the Donderbeck song: *"Heard about a grocer who backed into the bacon-slicer? – He got a little behind in his orders."* (London, 1953.) This is the same cannibalistic displacement of castration to the buttocks as in the story, earlier, of the little boy who must 'slice off his ass' for playing dice. *'Chap meets a friend out of work. "I thought you had a job in a fish-&-chips shop." "So I had till I got my cock in the chip-cutter." Friend: "Gad! What've they done with the chip-cutter?" "Oh, she got the sack too".'* (Chelmsford, Essex, 1954. Often collected in the United States concerning a 'pickle-slicer,' which comes even closer to identifying the woman as the *vagina dentata* machine.)

A minor scandal was created twenty-five years ago in the neo-Chassidic inner circles of American-Jewish intellectual gamesmanship, when the gentle psychoanalytic hint was dropped by a candid young critic, the late Isaac Rosenfeld, in the Jewish intellectual showcase magazine, *Commentary* (Oct. 1949) VIII. 385–7, under the title "Adam and Eve on Delancey Street," that the real interest of Jews compulsively watching 'kosher bacon' being sliced in a delicatessen window in the New York ghetto, is a yearning for the lost foreskin as well as for the equivalent forbidden food. (This was before *Collier's* magazine atom-bombed the Jewish quarter of 'the lower East Side,' doubtless for slum-clearance purposes, in its issue of August 5th, 1950, p. 13, intended to show what an American Hiroshima would be like.) One wonders what proportion the scandal would have reached if Mr. Rosenfeld had emphasized instead that it was a bacon-*slicing* machine, and not a bacon-pasting-together machine that was being watched. Compare too the bus-advertisement, noted in *The Limerick* (1953) p. 413, for Hebrew National Kosher delicatessen products, in the Jewish sections of New York, 1952, showing an enormous knife cutting into a large bologna sausage (flanked by olives), with the caption : *"For the* SLICE *of Your Life!"*

The hidden identification of executions and cannibalism as a kind of castration (and thus of torture as a kind of 'circumcision') is an essential but unstated element in the sick fascination with spectacles of violence and horror, accidents, death-thrills (as in circuses, bull-fights, prize-fights, and the like), and similar perverted public cruelties now for thousands of years. Likewise the current newspaper and 'media' exploitation of the horrors of war ... and peace. Stories of the killing or cannibalizing of children hit the supreme peak (or abyss) of the degenerate exploitation of sadistic 'thrills.' Aside from the local scandals of butchers who are mass-murderers in private (and feed the 'innocent' townspeople on head-cheese composed of the victims' chopped-up bodies), stories like this have been put into circulation at least since 1424, in Sercambi's *Novelle*, No. 77. The famous 'blood accusation' against the Jews is one such false story. The Knights Templars were similarly accused of having *fried* the children born of their secret orgies (which in fact were homosexual!) and using the grease of these children's bodies 'to anoint their great Ydol.' (Motifs G10–72.)

All this is small stuff. On the larger scale, of the earlier Levantine worship of the god Moloch, the Mexican Aztec worship of the Death god as recently as the early 16th century – when only the coming of the Spanish *conquistadores* stopped it – and the worship by all recorded human societies in all times & climes of the god of War, it is certain that these accusations of killing one's own (or each other's) children wholesale are literal and true. However, no religion has ever stated of itself that the sacrificed child is to be *eaten*, with the exception, always, of the 'blood and body' of Jesus. As noted further in the First Series, section 9.III.4, "Ritual Orgies," p. 783–4, it is precisely the terrible, unconscious guilt for thus cannibalizing one's god, some one hundred thousand Sundays since the Crucifixion, that has kept alive the extrojected 'blood accusation' against the Jews, despite the elaborate and absolute prohibition against 'eating any manner of blood' by any Jew, in *Leviticus*, xvii. 10–14.

That is all the past. There is also the future. Time is running out on the *laisser-faire* or 'mad-dog' phase of human exploitation of the earth, owing to the mathematical increase of the human population on the one hand, and, on the other, the increasing pollution of both the land and sea masses by human beings, through chemical and biological poisons used as insecticides, or created by energy producers ('nuclear reactors'), and weapons of war. Despite all the tendentious propaganda being spread about, the earth can very easily feed all its animal and human population, for many hundreds of years to come, especially if – as Victor Hugo demanded in *Les Misérables* a century ago, in 1862 – human feces cease to be poured into the rivers and the seas, as at present, and are reprocessed and used as fertilizer, instead of the pollutive insecticides and chemical fertilizers now being used. For the paradox is: *It is shit that is clean, and the 'pure white powders' that pollute!* As it appears, however, that this rational course will not be followed, and that *laisser-faire* capitalistic exploitation of both the earth and all the other planets will remain in force and be enlarged, the terrestrial food-supply, as we now know it, is doomed. The ocean being increasingly polluted already, it will probably be a mere bacteriological and radiological swamp, impossible to 'farm,' by the time the population/food balance becomes dramatically skewed. Sea-borne foods, such as algae, fish, and plankton – on which such delusory hopes are now being pinned – will long since all have disappeared owing to the pollution of their viable space.

Only two solutions are possible: one human, one antihuman. And it is almost certainly the antihuman one that will be chosen, unless world-revolution completely reverses the exploitative approach very soon. These solutions are the following: *Brewers' yeast*, which is at present a by-product of the manufacturing of beer, contains 48% (dry weight) of high-quality protein. Though containing no fat, starch or sugar, it is also an excellent source of iron and other trace-minerals, and the best known food source of the entire and essential B-vitamin complex. Massive production of yeast ferments in existing brewing manufactory equipment and buildings was already undertaken during World War II for the creation of penicillin for the U.S Army, and the same could be done on a day's notice to supply the world with food-yeast. (Of course, this might also increase the production of beer . . .) Its taste could also be made close to that of mushrooms.

Using a land-surface no larger than that of Mexico or the Sahara desert, irrigating these by means of atomically (?) desalinized sea-water, and using human fertilizer – chemically treated and all that – sufficient soybeans and peanuts (for protein and oil), potatoes (for starch), and Indian corn for both sugar and oil, could be grown to support the *entire world-population* for an unknown number of future centuries, with nothing other than brewers' yeast and soybeans as a protein source (replacing the by-then unavailable meat and fish), IF birth-control methods now already in existence, such as The Pill, are followed up and improved. This is *the plan for human survival*, and is the only practical plan now known. Otherwise, continued human existence on this planet (or some other that some few thousands of us might run to) is doomed.

This plan is in no way original with the present writer, and has been discussed for decades by serious sanitation engineers and nutrition experts. The best brief summary of the scientific methods for creating high-quality dry human fertilizer – which is at least as good on your tomatoes as horse-manure or cow-shit – by combining city sewage or 'sludge' with the enormous amounts of paper, trash, leaves, rubbish, and vegetable garbage now being *burned*, is given in Reginald Reynolds' *Cleanliness and Godliness* (1943) chaps. 13 and 14. The whole idea was already sketched in Victor Hugo's *Les Misérables* in 1862, in the famous section "The Bowels of Leviathan," on the sewers of Paris.

As to what we are eventually to eat, besides soybeans and corn, one of the best popular works on nutrition and human health, *Let's Eat Right to Keep Fit*, by the late Adelle Davis (New York: Harcourt, 1954, p. 112) – this is not her best book, just one of them – makes the point in simple and direct terms: *'More nutrients are more concentrated in [brewers'] yeast than in any other known food ... Yeast can be grown in a few hours without acres of land, or sweat of a laborer's brow, its nutritive value increased by the touch of a chemist's hand.'* (Note that the yeast referred to here is *not* that used in making bread, which should never be eaten raw.)

Now, about that 'chemist's hand.' In 1973, the Israeli-Arab war touched off a worldwide phoney fuel-oil 'crisis,' in which the Arabs suddenly woke from their millennial slumber and realized they were being cheated blind in accepting $6 a barrel (containing about 30 gallons, or 120 litres) for the liquid fuel that keeps the billion wheels of materialistic Western civilization meaninglessly turning. And that, instead of an absurd little 20c per gallon, they would like 40c a gallon ($12 a barrel) – and whatever military advantages over Israel they can achieve by means of blackmailing the West with oil – rising eventually to $4 a *quart* or $400 a quart, or whatever the traffic will bear. It hardly matters, since they will be paid whatever they ask for their oil, by nations who have no other oil to burn. But the real question is: *Should the world's oil be burned?*

Only a few months earlier than the outbreak of the Israeli-Arab war, in the Arab attack while the Jews were all at their synagogues on *Yom Kippur*, 1973, two Israeli scientists – are there any Arab scientists? – attempting to solve the problem of water-pollution caused by the washing out of the holds of oil-tankers at sea, had discovered that with a nickel bag of harmless microbes and some warm water, petroleum oil can be turned neatly and completely into perfectly respectable *animal food*. Inasmuch as we are animals too, perhaps we had better stop burning up the oil, because we are very shortly going to need to eat all the 'animal food' it can be turned into. Furthermore, as coal can be turned back into the petroleum base which is its geological parallel, the tremendous unmined reserves of coal in the United States (and in Russia, which has over four times as much mineral wealth as the U.S.) can feed the population of the world, by means of this Israeli process, for an unknown span of centuries to come, no matter how fast the population increases. Our only problem will become, instead, living-space for all those newborn babies. But the Atom Bomb is always there to do its predestined Malthusian job.

As far as food is concerned, there is the *plan for survival* – the uninspiring, but unpolluting and practical plan of coal-oil carbohydrates (C.O.C.), brewers' yeast, soybeans, and shit – that will probably not be followed. What is the other plan – the plan for destruction? Well, that is not my invention either, nor even the Rev. Thomas Robert Malthus, though he has long been given the Machiavellian credit for it, owing to his first cry of alarm, now nearly two centuries ago, in *An Essay on the Principle of Population* (1798), in which he showed that, when unchecked, population increases in a geometric ratio while the then-known food supply could be increased only in arithmetical ratio. Meaning that the population would inevitably outstrip the food supply in x number of years. As shown just above, this is *not* inevitable at all, but most people, including most of the people responsible for running the world, still prefer to believe Malthus. This is not because they have never heard of intensive agricultural methods, desalinization of seawater, and brewers' yeast, but because they secretly prefer the dark alternative Malthus pointed out. What he called politely 'positive checks,' namely: *the killing off of the 'excess' population by means of overcrowding, poverty, vice, disease, and war.*

This is still the real program for 'population control:' genocidal war. With the addition of purposely-fomented disease epidemics (the "Tunic of Nessus" method of the British General Amherst against the American Indians in the 18th century, by means of smallpox virus), now to be used consciously in the form of world-wide anthrax, botulism, and a whole alphabet of other plagues for 'population control.' Airborne sterilizing agents intended to neuterize entire populations in 'undesirable' areas are now also seriously proposed, and will be considered again at the end of the present chapter. Everybody on *our* side will presumably be given immunizing injections before the plague and sterilizing bombs are exploded – IF they are 'desirables.' So if you are White, Anglo-Saxon, Protestant, and have plenty of plain ordinary *money*, you can stop shitting in your pants right now.

However, there is another part of the plan that nobody mentions, because few cave-based generals and other deep thinkers have even thought about it. That is the response that will suddenly appear spontaneously among the smallpoxy, sterilized 'undesirables' of the world, when they find out they are not included in the access to the fallout-free caves and the then-available food supply. Their gut-response, or plan-without-a-plan, is going to be cannibalism. And it will take over the world: Even in the 'desirable' half – *our* half, or one-tenth more likely – because our side, too, will be starved emotionally for some juicy *human T-bone steaks*, after all those decades of eating nothing but frozen codfish, leftover caviar, canned plankton, c.o.c., and that goddamned brewers' yeast!!

Again, please don't credit your humble scribe. As every literate person should certainly remember, the statues for this particular plan should be erected to the reverend dean of St. Patrick's, Dublin, in the 18th century, Jonathan Swift, for his *Modest Proposal* (1729) to utilize the infant children of the already starving and 'undesirable' Irish, whose intellectual leader he was, by fattening and eating them. Intended as 'black humor,' of course, *this is the true and inevitable blueprint for the future, the day the food runs short.* Cannibalism has already occurred under these circumstances, not only in the Bible (*Deuteronomy*, xxviii. 53–7; 2 *Kings*, vi. 28–9 – this is one for the book! – and *Lamentations*, ii. 20, and iv. 10), but also during the Russian Revolution of 1917. The Soviet Government has itself circulated a memorial motion-picture during the 1970's, taken from newsreels of its first fifty years, showing among other things coffins being guarded while waiting for burial during the famines of the early years of the Revolution. These famines were created purposely by the counter-revolutionary military expeditions of the victorious Allied Powers after World War I (in combination with the defeated German troops that time too), and by the fomented food-shortages caused by embargoes against Russia in the food supplies allotted for European relief, under the canny direction of Herbert Hoover, later made president of the United States as his reward for this *coup* against the 'undesirables.'

If this could be done once, it can be done again – perhaps this time against the 'undesirables' of China or Africa, in the same way that the Atom Bomb was used only against Orientals and never against the Germans. And the answer of the 'undesirables' to famine will again be cannibalism, especially when they are reduced to total impuissance as to making any other response, owing to newer and bigger bombs. The chowderheads ('scientists') now happily planning the universal sterilization of 'everybody in the world but us,' by means of airborne neuterizing agents, invariably forget that just being sterilized isn't going to make the 'undesirables' any less hungry, while they last. It will not even make *us* less hungry. But they will be able to eat each other, because they have nothing left to lose in ingesting their dinner's 'Neutralizing agents' – including us, if they can catch us. Whereas, we, alas, will not be anxious to eat *them*. (Motif J1681, cited by Rotunda to Boccaccio's *Decameron* in 1353, Day V, Tale 2: *Archers use smaller arrow notches than the enemy; thus they can re-use arrows shot against them, but the enemy cannot use theirs*.)

Where will all the liberal, sensible thinkers be that day, with their rational, soft-spoken plans for plankton, brewers' yeast, soybean proteins, and c.o.c.? Up Shit Creek without a paddle! just like you and me. And our children ... God help any poor sucker who tries to turn then, and take an intelligent stand to stop the stampede. When the panic hits, it will hit *fast*, and unbelievably hard. Whole populations will go under in a matter of months. While the t.v. news-broadcasters extrude the usual government lies. Some of these themes are taken up, against the standard backdrop of petty violence and private loyalty, in Richard Fleischer's 'anticipations' movie, *Soylent Green* (1974), on a story of Harry Harrison, in which the police of the year 2022 foment riots among the overpopulous and hungry *hoi polloi*; then scoop up the madding crowds with Reitermeister dump-trucks and secretly mix their bodies into the community soya-lentil cookies. Constructive genocide at last! In the earlier British film, *No Blade of Grass*, which comes closer to the inevitable reality, the 'Chinese' (read: British) bomb 300,000,000 of their own population to avoid famine for the other half of the population, but are too dumb to think of eating the corpses.

Don't count on it. If they thought of eating locusts centuries ago, when that plague hit, no one is going to draw the line at 'long pig' now.

Since Swift, few writers have concerned themselves seriously with cannibalism. Even Malaparte, in *The Skin* (1952), uses it only as a symbol. The story "*A la Tartare*," by Mrs. E. M. Winch, precisely concerning cannibalism during the Russian Revolution, has already been retold in the earlier section 12. IV.6, "The Defiling of the Mother," since that is its true theme. The greatest modern Russian pessimist author, Mikhail Artzy-basheff (not to be confused with Boris Artzybasheff, his son, who glories in drawing the 'humorously' anthropomorphic or mechanomorphic machines-that-are-human-beings), wrote his final paean to hopelessness in *The Breaking Point*, published in 1915. In this novel, the author's speaking-trumpet character, Dr. Arnoldi, counsels everyone to commit suicide, starts an epidemic of suicide in his little Russian town, and points out in his justification that this is no different from what the world itself has undertaken to do, in the World Wars then beginning.

Artzybasheff's *The Breaking Point* is today quite forgotten, and is of course the exact opposite of Russian Communism's stalwart official optimism, in which, for example, the response to the overpopulation scare is not in planning bigger bombs to kill off the population, but the building at state expense of bigger apartment-house cities than even Brazil's, in which to house them. (Until somebody *else* bombs them, centrally-located as they will then be.) The book did, however, find an echo in a strange American novel, named after Artzybasheff's central character, *Dr. Arnoldi*, by a popular writer and adver-tising executive, Tiffany Thayer, whose principal efforts were in the promulgating of the pessimistic and anti-scientific or occult ideas of the great American literary stylist but total crackpot, Charles Fort, and the reprinting of his marvellously written and abysmally wrong-headed books. The book that should really be reprinted is Thayer's own *Dr. Arnoldi* (pub-lished, I believe, by Julian Messner in New York, about 1935), which goes far beyond the usual clichés of pessimistic science-fiction.

The book's plot is simply that *death has died* (the Italian play of the 1920's, *Death Takes a Holiday*, taken to its logical con-clusion); that no one can die any longer, and the living corpses of the 'un-dead' begin piling up and must be towed out to sea.

Just as people today rush to faith-healers and 'health-food' stores to prolong their lives or cure their illnesses; just so the hundreds of millions of old, sexually impotent, appetiteless centenarians of the coming new world of deathlessness rush to beg piteously for the blessed release of death, in state 'euthanasia' plants of the Auschwitz type, which unfortunately cannot any longer kill anyone, as falsely promised, and can only stack up the un-dead bodies with derricks in great putrefying piles rising out of the oceans like new islands. At this desperate moment, Dr. Arnoldi arrives on the scene with the next turn of the screw *after* his plan for universal suicide in *The Breaking Point.*

He offers a simple solution to the whole problem, including the even more desperate problem of famine, as the world's undying and undyable population now brings on hectically the Malthusian prophecy of famine. The solution is, of course, cannibalism: *"Mangez les vieux!"* – *Eat Everybody Over Twenty-five!* The exact opposite of Saturn-Swift-Moloch's eternal hold-back-the-dawn demand to make cannon-fodder out of babies. Dr. Arnoldi is deified, statues are erected in his honor in every country, and the new world-calendar begins with the year of his Appearance, B.A. and A.A. (I may be embroidering a bit here on Tiffany Thayer, but the ideas are basically his.) Hänsel & Gretel eat their witch; Mr. Grunch is fed to his children instead of the other way 'round; the missing wheel is found that brings the pig back up out of the machine alive, and the whole formula is finally reversed as it should have been ten thousand years ago, at the sacrifice of Isaac. Dr. Arnoldi is given the honor of being the very first oldster eaten – at a charity banquet for overdosed rock-&-roll singers, with Nuremberg Festival Musik to match. The hundreds of millions of old, impotent, appetiteless centenarians crawl creakingly up on their crutches, drive up happily in their motorized wheelchairs and supermarket baskets, line up weeping with unspeakable relief, crowding for their turn to dive or at least slither into the "Mill for Grinding Old People Into Young Ones," the Donner Party model of Donderbeck's gloriously Improved Machine, and to become chopped-meat sausages, blood-puddings and chitterlings for their children to eat. (*"We use every part of your Loved Ones expect the squeal!"*) See *Ezekiel*, V. 10: '*Therefore the fathers shall eat the sons in the midst of thee, and the sons shall eat their fathers. And I will execute judgments in thee, and the whole remnant of thee will I scatter into all the winds.'* This is the future.

IV. SYMBOLIC CASTRATIONS

Substitution of parts of the body other than the penis or fore-skin, in symbolic castration, opens out too vast a subject to cover here. Only a few significant centers of attention can be roughed in. The subject becomes even more unmanageable if one adds the symbolic castrations executed at the moral or emotional levels, rather than the purely physical, such as sexual impotence, abandonment, imprisonment, loss of love, social position or fortune, and death. The 'moral' versions of castration sometimes allow of a riposte by the victim: the suicidal hunger-strikes of prisoners, and the visibly vengeful and aggressive suicides of persons suddenly deprived of all their money or social status. But the symbolic *physical* castrations, being vulgar, brutal, and direct, are usually dead-stoppers. Folktales, and the motif-indexes which are the tables-of-contents to these, display symbolic physical castrations in very great profusion, and with the utmost hideousness of detail – all the more freely and cheerfully in that these horrors are presented as 'mere' cruelty, or 'deserved' revenges, without any admitted sexual tone. The reader will perhaps forgive, therefore, the un-usually large recourse here to brevity and to motif-numbers, which are preferable to having to wallow in the details.

Parts of the body particularly common in symbolic castra-tions include the head ("Decapitation," 13.I.7 above), the hands or legs (*Moby Dick*), the heart ("The Eaten Heart," 8.VIII.10), the ears, nose and tongue, and the total body-image, as when: *The beaten Cyrano de Bergerac, who has helped another man up the ladder to the bedroom of the woman he loves, slumps dispiritedly offstage – the spent penisman – with the proud feather in his hat drooping over his symbolically cropped ears.* To these may be added: the teeth, which may be filed to points (circumcision) rather than be completely broken off or extir-pated (castration); and especially the fingers and thumbs, as in Dr. Heinrich Hoffmann's cautionary text for children, *Struw-welpeter* (1845), the horror-indoctrination of precisely the century of German fathers & sons whose ultimate national achievement were the furnaces of Auschwitz, Belsen, Bergen, Birkenwald, Büchenwald, Dachau, Gardelegen, Maidanek, Mauthausen, Natzweiler, Ravensbrück, Sachsenhausen, Schwabenhausen, Sobibor, Theresienstadt, Treblenka, Wolzek, and the rest of the Nazi extermination camps of World War II.

See the illustration from a parody or one-upmanship *Struwwelpeter* of the 1890's in England, reproduced in *Neurotica* (1951) No. 9: p. 31, which shears off the whole hands! The accompanying article, by Dr. Rudolph Friedmann, is an exercise in poetic or 'aphoristic' psychoanalysis such as few have ever been published (except for Dr. Lionel Goitein's *Art and the Unconscious*, New York, 1948, which is the greatest achievement in this style). In reprinting the "Struwwelpeter" piece in his anthology, *Parodies* (1960) with a fabulous additional page by the author, Dwight Macdonald has the questionable editorial taste of including this among "Self-Parodies: Unconscious."

The nose is a particular area of sexual and castrational symbolism, men with large noses (or feet) being considered equally possessors of long penises, and as such much in demand on the comedy stage, especially in Italy, for centuries, where grotesquely large shoes are also the male comedian or clown's standard 'prop.' More than one modern Italian comedian, such as Jimmy Durante, has made such a nose his trademark, and the most prominent part of his act. It is also crucial to the testy character of Edmond Rostand's *Cyrano de Bergerac* (1898), of which the great debt to Théophile Gautier's picaresque romance in the style of Dumas, *Le Capitaine Fracasse* (1861) chap. 5, "Chez Monsieur le Marquis," in the comedy character of the braggartly Spanish Rodomonte or Matamore, has seldom been observed. Cyrano, as is well known, answers any attack upon or insult to his nose with sudden death at the end of his rapier, but he permits himself personally the most rhetorical flights of self-insult as to the very same organ. (Self-castration, or *"You Can't Fire Me, I Quit!"*) In folklore, the wooden boy-doll in the children's book, *Pinocchio* by Carlo Collodi-Lorenzini (1882) reverses the threat, having the nose grow abnormally long in punishment for lying. Compare also the gross overcompensation of Gogol's masterpiece, *The Nose*. Usually, however, the nose is cut off as a sexual punishment, unmistakably replacing the penis which also projects outward from the front of the body. The early Protestant propagandist, Théodore de Bèze, published a satirical "Complainte de Messire Pierre Lizet, sur le trespas [*death*] de son feu nez" in his Latin masterpiece, *Epistola Magistri Benedicti Passavanti* (1553), given in French in Fernand Fleuret & Louis Perceau's *Les Satires françaises du*

XVIe siècle (1922) I. 13–17. This is an attack, half humorous and half ferocious, on his anti-Protestant enemy, the pedant Pierre Lizet, who here recites his griefs on the presumed death of his nose. (See Thompson's Motifs D1376.1, and all those indexed under "Nose," in his vol. VI. 544; as well as Tale Types 1417 and 1707, with many further references.)

An almost total statement of the whole panoply of symbolic castrations, at the physical level, is presented in a bit of artful 'nonsense' by the American humorist, Gelett "Purple Cow" Burgess, who came out of retirement twenty years after his last successful book, to publish *Why Men Hate Women* (1927), a humorous specialty in which, however, the *New Yorker's* woman-hating humorist, James Thurber, rapidly nosed him out, beginning with *Is Sex Necessary?* in 1929. Gelet Burgess' now little-remembered morbid limerick wraps up all possible symbolic castrations, especially those of advancing age and impotence, in one five-line package, with which compare his last book, *Look Eleven Years Younger* (1937) pathetically written at the age of seventy. If he could have his 'druthers,' says Burgess:

> *I'd rather have fingers than toes,*
> *I'd rather have ears than a nose,*
>   *And as for my hair,*
>   *I'm glad it's all there –*
> *I'll be awfully sad when it goes!*

Any type of crippledness of the feet, or loss of one or both legs – even a mere wheelchair – is a standard symbol of castration, matching the identification of 'big feet and a big prick.' Clumsiness is also assimilated to this type of castration, especially in fat or big men, who thus are presumed – by the stupidity that is thought to accompany 'animal-like' large genitals – to be shorn of all their phallic advantage: '*Every time he turns around, he steps on his dick.*' (American theatre phrase, 1960's.) The castratory symbolism of lameness is not always unconscious, from the legend of King Oedipus, whose father was responsible for crippling his foot, with the revenge we know, to Somerset Maugham's *Of Human Bondage* in 1915, in which the hero's club-foot and attack on women as bitches represent the author's international fling-it-in-their-faces homosexuality. So also with Aldous Huxley's limping anti-hero in *Point Counter Point* (London, 1928), here representing not homosexuality but a sort of cultural impotence or psychic stymie, of the kind also celebrated in the self-pitying soundtrack of impotent modern man – who will *not* end with a whimper, but with a bang! – by the American expatriate, T. S. Eliot, *The Waste Land* (1922).

The purposeful creation of foot-impediments in women, as in Chinese foot-binding, is also very sexually toned, being thought somehow to reduce the women genitally to helpless sexual subservience, as of course it does socially and in fact. In the final sequel to *The Three Musketeers*, Alexandre Dumas' *Le Vicomte de Bragelonne* (1850) chap. 89, two caddish courtiers explain to each other – and to the reader – the secret of the ascendance of King Louis XIV's new mistress, Mlle. de La Vallière, who limps, on the grounds of the belief, dating from ancient Rome, that limping women have very 'characteristic' secret abilities. This crashing ungallantry is at about the scientific level of the statement in Dr. David Reuben's best-selling conglomeration of sexual folklore and purported sexual science, *Everything You Always Wanted To Know About Sex (But Were Afraid To Ask)*, in 1970, that: 'blind girls particularly become adept at secret masturbation." Ask any ten thousand blind girls, who limp.

There is more here than meets the eye. In the interesting chapter of dirty jokes, "The Many Colors of the Blue Joke," in his *The Humor and Technology of Sex* (1969) p. 261, Dr. Paul Tabori gives a refined story, which appears on the surface to be an anti-gallant mockery disguised as solicitude:

> A young girl is very beautiful, but she is a cripple. One day she meets a young man who takes her in his car and drives her out to the woods. They start necking, move on to heavy petting, and after a few minutes, she tells him, "If you want to make love to me, I have a hook in the back of my dress and all you have to do is hang me up on a low branch."
>
> A little repelled, the young man follows her instructions and makes love to her. Then he unhooks her and takes her back to his car. The crippled girl bursts into tears, sobbing as though her heart would break.
>
> "What's the matter?" he asks; "Didn't you enjoy it?" "Oh yes ... very much!" "Well, did I hurt you?" "Oh no ... not at all!" "Well then, why are you crying?" "Because ... because you're the first man who ever unhooked me afterwards!"

What Dr. Tabori does not remark – in this chapter – is that in his following and principal chapter, on sexual fetiches and prosthetics, p. 368-9, he gives a whole series of 'kinky' letters and advertisements from the personals columns of certain British magazines for sexual perverts, such as *Forum* and the long-defunct *London Life*, in which men are searching for one-legged and otherwise crippled and 'handicapped' girls specifically for sexual purposes. (They are not a bit 'repelled' – to the contrary!) This joke is really a glorification of these sick fetiches, gloating on the visible and palpable symbolic castration of the girl, in the style of Baudelaire.

Apparently a reminiscence of this joke, or a 'parallel inspiration,' is used as the illustrated cover to the British pocket-edition (Paladin, 1971) of the most bravely written and most deeply thought of modern feminist books, Germaine Greer's provocatively-titled *The Female Eunuch*. The cover shows a sort of female-body bathing-suit hung out on a branch, with actual breasts, navel, and two handles for grasping the hips, but no head and no sexual parts. If that's not a 'female eunuch,' what is? The notion of female castration not essentially as something cut off, but as the closing or '*sewing-up*' of the opening of the vagina (infibulation), has already been considered in the Fist Series, 6.VI, "The Female Castration Complex."

That the author herself is not attacked by these fantasies is made clear in an astonishing nude photograph of herself, displaying her face and genitals together in a Yoga *asana* pose, published in the final issue of the British-Dutch 'underground' newspaper, *Suck*, which was supposed to publish similar photos of all the editors but copped out on everyone but Miss Greer ('Earth Rose'). Numerous 20th-century female nude statues, in imitation of damaged Greek and Roman antiquities, show only the female torso, as with the illustrated book-cover mentioned above, usually with the head and all four limbs ripped off as though in some particularly horrible lust-murder; but the 'classic' pretext prevents any complaint from ever being made. (Note the similar case of Lavinia in Shakespeare's *Titus Andronicus*, discussed below.) Just such a torso-murder is gruesomely shown in the snob-illustrated nursery-rhyme book, *Three Young Rats*, by Alexander Calder & James Johnson Sweeney (New York: Museum of Modern Art, 1944–46) pp. 107, 113, and with *worms*, p. 127, the hands-down winner in the "Most Disgusting Children's Book" sweepstakes until some more recent items by Tomi Ungerer. And the *omnia opera* of Edward Gorey (*Amphigorey*, 1974): really just anti-children gloats, for adults. All under the *Galdengelächter* excuse of 'sick' or 'camp' humor.

Probably the most important of all symbolic physical castrations is *blinding*. (Motif Q451.7.) Fears in connection with blindness, or attacks against the eyes with pointed instruments or acids are very prominent in both the folkloristic and the frankly neurotic materials connected with this theme. I long ago demonstrated, in an illustrated lecture at the New York Academy of Medicine in 1948, under the aegis of Dr. Fredric Wertham (later printed as "Not for Children" in my monograph *Love & Death*, 1949), that the sort of people who draw horror comic-books for the international child-audience *specialize* in the attack on the eye, with hypodermic needles, gouging, etc. Education for psychosis! An entire monograph would be necessary to handle the materials available merely on this one point. Note, in particular, blinding or self-blinding as a punishment for incest, as with King Oedipus. (Italian *Novella* form in Rotunda, Q451.7.3.) In Irish mythology, which is always one of the frankest and most cruel, the identification is flatly stated: *Prisoners are given the choice between emasculation and blinding.* (Tom Peete Cross, *Motif-Index of Early Irish Literature*, 1952, Motif J229.12.) Other materials on self-blinding are given in the following section, "Self-Castration." Blindness (also deafness) as punishment for masturbation, a century-old bogey, is given its come-uppance in the sex-comedy movie by Mike Calley & Bob Levy, *If You Don't Stop It You'll Go Blind* (1974), which is actually 'a collection of all the oldest, corniest sex jokes you ever heard.' The jocular approach to ancient terrors like these is precisely our point here. Obviously there is nothing *funny* about them. Witty or corny, all sex jokes are just 'whistling in the dark,' whether the dark of threatened blindness or of uneasy castratory fear.

I have already noted, in the First Series, 6.III, "Ophelia's Crime," p. 353, the occasional masochist fantasies of popular fiction, such as H. Rider Haggard's *She* (1887). These are symbolically lesser versions of the open castratory fantasy of the limerick on the "Queen of Baroda," often collected. (*The Limerick*, No. 1371.) For a beginning of the psychological interpretation, see the important materials on this present subject gathered in Dr. Ernest Jones' "Deprivation of the Senses as a

Castration Symbol," and his "Notes on [Karl] Abraham's article on 'The Female Castration Complex'," in the *International Journal of Psycho-Analysis* (1926) vols. VII, and III, respectively. Compare also, in the same *Journal*, J. C. Fluegel's "Note on the Phallic Significance of the Tongue and of Speech" (1925) vol. VI, an article very significantly supplemented in Henry Alden Bunker's "The Voice as (Female) Phallus," in *Psychoanalytic Quarterly* (1934) vol. III, which has been cited earlier.

It is difficult to know where to continue with so extensive a subject matter. The displacement of castration anxieties and attempted humor backwards, to the buttocks, has already been discussed above in connection with the "Slicing Machine." The displacement to the leg or thigh, or to lameness in general is particularly common in literature. "A Fragment from *Pierre*" (1852) by Herman Melville, the greatest of all American novelists, is quoted in *Neurotica* (1951) No. 9: p. 41–5, from the "Enceladus" section, XXV. iii-v, describing the stone Titan as being amputated and 'without one serviceable ball-and-socket above the thigh.' The pointed culminating reference to the lack of a 'serviceable' ball (and socket ...) 'above the thigh' is not intended jocularly, but is one of Melville's unavoidable toyings with such themes, as in his masterpiece, *Moby Dick* (London, 1851: he couldn't get it published in America) chaps. 94–95, in the incredible scene, already mentioned, of the squeezing of the whale's sperm by the men's coupled hands, and the dressing up in the skin of the daddy-whale's vanquished and amputated penis by the victorious whaler 'priest.'

Another striking bodily castration is that of the hand – usually only the fingers or thumb, as already noted in *Struwwelpeter*. Consider the following perfectly extraordinary anti-family fantasy, presented as the final page – and one assumes as the real message – of an anti-war book, sardonically entitled *In the Service of Their Country: War Resisters in Prison* (New York: Viking Press, 1970) by Willard Gaylin, M.D. 'Driving home one day from one of the prisons, deeply touched by the experiences recounted by some of the war resisters,' Dr. Gaylin asks himself whether a young man's years in prison might not be compared to the loss of an equivalent number of fingers:

> I wondered if I would give up a year of my youth, indeed a year of my life now, as an alternative to giving up one finger ... I then played the string out – how many fingers

versus how many years. Two fingers? Certainly! Three fingers? I began to have doubts – could I spread them over two hands? Could I retain the opposing action of thumb and index finger? . . . I was haunted by this idea.

When I arrived home some hours later, still preoccupied by this, I mentioned my finger-year comparisons to my wife and two daughters. They were horrified and suggested that the analogy was a disgusting one that could only have been conceived by a warped mind. I countered by suggesting that their disgust with lost fingers, and acceptance of lost years, were evidence of brain-washed minds, and I offered them a second analogy. I described a civilization in which conflict over religion, territory, principle, was resolved by each side's selecting fifty young girls, making sure they had only the prettiest and fittest, and then throwing the hundred into a crocodile pit. The victor in the conflict would be decided by whose girl would be the last to be destroyed. I called this process of arbitration "gonk" and asked my daughters what they thought of it. They thought that "gonk" was further evidence of Father's perversity.

(Any questions?) The "Bocca della Verità' is a statue or image still existing in Italy, obviously representing an older snake- or animal-ordeal, now mere idol-worship. *A person swearing an oath places a hand in the mouth of the image (or of a serpent). If the oath is false, the hand is immediately bitten off.* (Motif H251.1.) This statue or head was featured in a very popular and significant American motion-picture of the early 1950's, *Roman Holiday*, in which the style for thin, crop-headed, flat-chested, pants-wearing and otherwise unfeminine and anti-feminine women was first openly promulgated since just after the preceding World War, about 1920. The hero, played by Gregory Peck, I believe, puts his hand into the *"Bocca della Verità,"* and then pulls it out with a scream, hiding his hand in his cuff to make the heroine believe it has actually been bitten off. For her part, the heroine-princess in the movie was also, for purposes of disguising herself as a commoner, made to demand that her beautiful long hair be cut off – again, wilful self-castration – while the poor Italian barber begs her masochistically not to *make him do it*, and will only cut off one strand at a time. (*Cutting off the dog's tail little by little, so it will not hurt so much!*)

The motif following that of the "Mouth of Truth" in Thompson (H251.1.1.) is the same sort of biting off, but here by a lion. The superstitition is still very much alive in America, in a jocular form in which: *The two stone lions in front of the New York Public Library on Fifth Avenue, at the crossroads of the city, and its busiest intersection, will roar loudly every time a girl who is a virgin walks by.* (N.Y. 1935, and doubtless already fairly old. The 'topper,' when it is observed that the lions do not roar: *'They have a cold today!'* – N.Y. 1970.) Many American co-ed colleges were noted in the 1960's to have similar statues, usually human, and by preference some grim-looking Puritan founder of the college, *who will take off his stone hat, run up a staircase, or kick roguishly outward with one leg* [!] when the same rare occurrence takes place. Note that the girl's virginity or 'purity' is here represented as an unspoken assevera-tion that the lion or statue is testing. The danger to her is no longer physical, but moral – her 'untroth' will be unmasked if the lion's mouth does not roar. On the test of virginity by real lions, in Dean Swift, see the First Series, 7.I, page 400–1.

The ordeal of the "Mouth of Truth" is also the forgotten meaning of the circus act of lion-tamers, especially when they put their head into the lion's or other animal's mouth as their mock-castratory culminating dare-devilry (*note this word*). Just so, also, female and other 'snake-charmers' end by putting the serpent's head in their mouth. The popular 'humorous' maga-zine cartoons showing the lion-tamers' act – far more frequently than ever in circuses – invariably show the putting of the head into the animal's mouth, and often show it bitten off as well, with various 'nonsensical' resolutions of the problem in the style of the British music-hall song about *Anne Boleyn's revenge against the headsman, as her ghost walks through the Tower of London, "With 'er 'EAD tucked! underneath 'er arm! At the Midnight hour,* etc." Anne Boleyn has clearly failed in the ordeal of virtue, and has been decapitated. As it is not too well known, I will mention that Anne Boleyn's lover was Sir Thomas Wyatt, whose magnificent brief poem reproaching her faith-lessness – to him – is given in the *Oxford Book of English Verse,* No. 37, "Vixi Puellis Nuper Idoneus;" but who also wrote a violently anti-gallant satirical poem against her, "Thow Old Mule" (she was 29 at her death), as well as tattling about her to Henry VIII, who thereupon had her beheaded.

Generalized castration anxiety moves all over the body, in

these various symbolizations, not knowing exactly where to center itself, and unable to search specifically in the genital area since the actual fear of being castrated, or of being endangered by castration, has been repressed from consciousness. This is strikingly seen in a popular American gesture-story, collected in numerous forms, almost always involving the Jew. *A Jewish woman coming out of a nightclub is seen by a friend crossing herself as she gets into the taxi. The friend expresses surprise at her conversion to the Catholic religion. "Converted? Who's converted? I'm just checking on my jewels* (with gestures): *Tiara, brooch, clip, clip."* (N.Y. 1949. It is perhaps relevant that *'jewels'* or *'family jewels'* are used in both English and French to refer to the testicles.) The male form: *A Jewish commuter is noticed by another Jew crossing himself on the Long Island train, just as the train pulls into his station at Great Neck. He denies that he is crossing himself. "Just checking,"* he says, *"hat, wallet, fountain-pen, zipper."* (N.Y. 1951). Again, this may involve an allusion to the phallic symbol of the well-known comedy inversion of: *The nervous Jewish boy giving his* barmitzvah *speech, who begins: "Today I am a fountain-pen!"* (instead of: *"Today I am a man!"* alluding to the standard gift of a fountain-pen at the boy's thirteenth birthday, or proto-circumcision.)

In an unexpurgated collection of Jewish stories on "The Rabbi Trickster," by Ed Cray, published courageously by the *Journal of American Folklore* (Oct. 1964) vol. 77: p. 331–45, at p. 340, a version is given 'localized' in the Korean war, collected in Los Angeles, Calif. 1957. *The rabbi is accused by the Catholic chaplain of having found the 'true religion' when a shell explodes.* [I.e.: "There are no atheists in shell-holes."] *The rabbi 'looks at him and says, "Oh, no. Just checking: spectacles, wallet, watch, and testicles"'.* Cray notes that he has collected six versions, 'two of them from non-Jews,' and that most 'are set either in an airplane crash or railway wreck. One has a rabbi knocked down by an automobile.' I have never heard any of these catastrophic versions. The most interesting trait here is the specific reference to reassurance against harm having been done to the testicles.

The ultimate castratory statement is curiously symbolized in *Sex to Sexty* (1966) 7:26, a publication which almost never makes any references to religion: *'Johnny was walking down the street, looking down and going through some peculiar motions. First he would touch his head with his right hand, then his right chest, then his left chest, then his crotch, then back to his head again. A neighbor lady said, "Johnny, I am ashamed of you ... that is a very funny way to cross yourself, if that is what you're trying to do!" "This is not religion, Miz Murgatroyd," said Johnny, "I'm just trying to remember what Mom wants at the corner store ... a head of lettuce, two quarts of milk, and a pound of weenies!"'*

What is perhaps really involved in this story, in all forms, is a little-known manifestation of the castration complex in boys and young men, in which – aside from a sensuous handling of one's own chest and nipples (*"Just checking ..."*) under the cloth of the shirt, or with chest bare – the clothing or under-clothing is continuously felt to be *too tight* and constricting, or even strangling, especially at the crotch or seat of the trousers, or at the collar or cuffs. The boy or man so affected continuously plucks the cloth of his trousers away from his groin, or out from between his buttocks – usually scratching the anus heartily (Ganymede fears) under cover of this gesture – or keeps 'shooting his cuffs' or squirming his neck up out of his collar with a twitching motion of the chin, though the collar may be of the soft and not the starched type and perfectly his size. The handling-of-the-torso syndrome is very common in Latin countries and among beach-boys and surfers in all countries, such as America and Australia. The sensation of strangling in one's clothing is the real reason for the affectation of open collars or softly-knotted Ascot neckties (rather than tight four-in-hand foulards) by homosexuals everywhere, and men in the arts, such as painting, and the theatre and motion-picture industry.

The main symptom being considered above is perfectly ticked off in a joke usually told as a puzzle story, which actually is of the Levantine type of tales concerned with predestination or fate – and vainly attempting to mock or evade these. (O. Henry's "Roads of Destiny" story, and the Arabic tale '"The Appointment in Samarra," used as a book title, with the story given as motto, by John O'Hara.) As told, the joke often is 'cleaned up' by omitting any references to the testicles: *A man has mysterious headaches and dizzy spells, and his testicles shrink up inside his groin. He is told by the doctors that they cannot help him; he must die, and has only three months left to live. He draws all his savings out of the bank, determined to spend everything on high living and wild women for his last three months. He goes to the best haberdashery shop in the city, and orders ten cashmere suits, twenty pairs of the best oxfords, and six dozen pure silk shirts, offering to pay a twenty percent premium if he can have them all within a week. The haberdasher is all attention. "What collar-size do you take, Sir?" he asks. "These silk shirts do not shrink, and we cut them very exactly." "I take a size 15," says the man; "and make the sleeves long. I want those ruffled cuffs to show." "Pardon me, Sir," say the haberdasher, "but I'd say you were more like a size 16 or even 16½." "Now look here," says the man testily, "I ought to know my own size. I've been wearing size 15 shirts for years." "Very well, Sir," says the haberdasher firmly; "size 15 it is. We'll make them exactly as you like. But I ought to warn you: if you wear these shirts you'll have terrible headaches* (or *stony gullions), and your balls will shrink up inside your groin!"* (N.Y. 1945.) A British stage-magician – magicians are usually very good joke-sources, in among their horrible, woman-torturing stage specialties – gives me the straight castratory version: *The argument with the tailor is as to whether the man 'dresses'* [carries his penis] *in the left or right trouser-leg. He says he lets it hang in the middle, and is warned that this will cause chronic pains in his testicles. Meanwhile, he has had himself 'casterated' for mysterious testicular pain.* (London, 1974.)

Two themes – both unspoken – meet here, which is why the preceding story can be told and often is, as 'clean': *The body as phallus, and death as castration.* Note also the curious ancient coincidence that it is by means of a poisoned shirt, the Tunic of Nessus, that the unvanquishable hero of Greek legend, Hercules, is finally made to commit suicide, thus destroying himself since no one else can do so. Consider also the coarser type of legendary murder, by means of a *poisoned enema* (Motif Q426.1, an African Wakweli story in which a woman so murders her son's wives), the method reportedly used, on orders of King James I, to put out of the way Sir Thomas Overbury in the Tower of London. In the dumb-show opening the play-within-the-play in *Hamlet,* III.ii.145, the poison is poured into the sleeping victim's *ears.*

A World War II story is retold in *World's Dirtiest Jokes* (1969) p. 18, headed "Astronaughty" to up-date it. Originally it referred simply to the high-altitude flights of long-range fighter planes. *An air-force major is bored sitting in his space-suit waiting to be blasted off into space, as the flight has already been called off twice because of atmospheric conditions. He has his wife get into the space-suit and sit in for him, since he knows it will only be a dry-run anyhow. However, the weather clears just then, and she is sent off by the automatic blast. In returning through the lower atmosphere she blacks out, and comes back to consciousness to find a doctor vigorously massaging her breasts. When he sees her open her eyes he says soothingly, "Don't you worry about a thing, Major. As soon as we get your testicles pushed back into place, your penis will pop right back out."* The identification of the breasts-as-testicles – really as penis – here openly made, is the unconscious motive of the activity of many tough females wearing binocular brassières that lift and point their breasts impossibly, under the pretense that it is more fashionable, attractive to men, etc. Actually, it is a way of competing with men, as with the air-force major's wife shooting off in her husband's space-suit.

Men are particularly conscious of the shrinking and enlarging motions of the penis during the day, though few ever realize – unless they happen to see themselves naked in the mirror, or are fellators – that the testicles are even more continuously in motion, the cremasteric tendons thus keeping them at an even temperature. They never do actually 'shrink up into the groin,' as in the preceding story, unless some accidental stress of the sitting position pushes them there. The castratory danger fantasied here is derived from the stories everyone is exposed to, of boys with 'undescended testicles,' and the enormous trouble and expense the parents must go to, in order finally to 'make a man of him.' It is an essential point that surgical operations *of any kind* on the genital area are unconsciously considered castratory, even if they are intended to repair and improve the genitals. Folklore has it that all such operations necessarily fail, or overact, since they are classed with the ill-fated attempts to 'interfere with Destiny.'

The shrinking of the penis into the body during states of coldness or anxiety can also be assimilated, of course, to a temporary castration. I can well remember once driving through upper New York state with a very talented young novelist who later went quite insane and had to be hospitalized. At a certain moment – he was driving much too fast on the icy roads – he executed a dangerous turn, skid, and practically a loop, for no purpose whatsoever. I did not say anything, but he gave me a big grin and waggled his eyebrows chidingly, while lifting one (maybe both?) hands from the wheel to point at me accusingly: *"I'll just bet there's a little something in your pants,"* he said, *"that's crawled right up into your belly, and won't be down for a week!"* As with Hungarians, when you have a young American novelist for a friend – YOU DON'T NEED AN ENEMY.

The rare American collection of mostly bawdy jokes, poems, and recitations, *The Stag Party* [Boston? 1888] p. 10 *ad fin.*, gives a story on the same manifestation of castration anxiety as that in the shirt-collar story: uncontrollable squirming, 'cuff-shooting,' collar-plucking, and general uncomfortableness in one's clothes, which it attempts to rationalize not as tightness but scatologically; *'Examination day in district school. Many children in new clothes and some in old clothes made over. One red-headed boy continually throwing his head back, twisting from side to side and taking breath at long intervals. Evidently uneasy. Teacher – "Pat, why don't you sit still? What is the matter?" Pat – "Mather enough, ma'am. Ave [If] your new vesht wuz made out ov the sate of yer father's ould pants yez would squirm too, bedad!"'* The insulting of the father scatologically here, implying that his pants are foul-smelling, is close to Ben Jonson's reference to the Roman superstition that the man who pisses on his father's grave goes mad.

The boy is actually being described as having an attack of psychosomatic asthma ('continually throwing his head back, twisting from side to side and taking breath at long intervals'), which is then being rationalized as the gesture of avoiding an unpleasant smell. The Oedipal attack on the father, in combination, suggests the classic syndrome of combined asthma and prurigo (uncontrollable itching of the anus, causing the trouser-seat to be continuously plucked and the anus scratched) described by Rogerson, Hardcastle, and Duguid, in *Guy's Hospital Report* (1935) 85:289, and discussed more fully by Edward Weiss & O. Spurgeon English, *Psychosomatic Medicine* (Phila. 1943) p. 421–2. The original report notes that out of twenty-three children showing this 'asthma-eczema-prurigo syndrome ... no less than seventeen of the children were fussed over and overprotected by their parents to a pathological degree. This was not just a slight abnormality of parental attitude; it was pathological to a degree which made one feel that if these children had not been brought to the hospital with asthma or prurigo, they might easily have been referred on account of the nervousness engendered in them by this situation.' Here, clinically, both the recto-genital and respiratory symptoms described in Oedipal states are seen combined.

The anal pruritus symptom of intense itching, or anal 'moistness' and discomfort, is in all cases – where infestation with ordinary seat-worms or tape-worm sections is ruled out – an expression of violent Oedipal anxieties. In this, the boy (just as often a grown man) simultaneously fears castration and pedication by the overmastering father or father-image, yet searches for and needs passive recto-anal excitements representing the feared pedication. No matter how much the scratching may hurt, it allows the sufferer to relax. Its pain is felt as an aggression really directed against the superior power, and the passive male triumphs in the idea that he has nevertheless survived that attack of which he is most frightened. So it is not really so frightening at all. This is what makes lion-hunters hunt lions, or mountain-climbers climb dangerous peaks. Not the desire to die, as some imagine (and many find), but the need for that brief instant of triumph when the greatest possible danger feared has been successfully navigated and escaped – *that one time more!* Until the day comes that one does not escape.

Probably the most morbid and unpleasant of all symbolic castrations is that involving extirpation of the *tongue* (see the excessive number of references in Thompson's index-volume, VI. 801–2), which everyone recognizes to be somehow more an attack than the similar castratory cruelties to the *teeth* (in same, VI. 802–3, under "Tooth"), since the latter sometimes grow back. (Horror- and crime-comics for our children specialize in showing punched-out teeth flying through the air, and the bleeding gums of the victim.) Only one joke has been encountered on these themes. *King Arthur leaves his queen well strapped into a chastity-belt when he goes off to war. The belt has a large enough opening for any penis, but inside is a guillotine blade, acted upon by a spring when the penis enters. When King Arthur returns, he examines all the Knights of the Round Table, and not one of them now has a penis except the gallant Sir Galahad. Tearfully grateful, the king offers Sir Galahad any reward he cares to ask, for his fidelity. "Half my kingdom, if you want," says King Arthur; "name it, and it's yours!" But all Sir Galahad can say is, "Ug, glop, glop!"* (San

Diego, Calif. 1965. First printed in *World's Dirtiest Jokes*, 1969, p. 74.) Given here, rather than under "Vagina Dentata," section 13.I above, since it is clear that the woman – who does not even appear in the story – is only the stalking-horse or shooting-box of the father-king's vengeful concern with the penises of other, younger men.

A record survival of a folk-theme, where one might least expect it, is the occurrence in a modern joke of the related trait of 'tongue-castration' in Shakespeare's revenge-drama, *Titus Andronicus* (1953?) – one of his first and most outrageously cruel plays, but then, almost everyone in his love-play, *Romeo & Juliet*, is also dragged off-stage dead. In the play of *Titus Andronicus*, the action turns on the heroic Lavinia, who has been raped, and who is described in the stage-directions as coming on-stage in the climactic scene, II.iv, '*her hands cut off and her tongue cut out, and ravisht.*' She has been so treated by the rapists to prevent her from identifying them later, but she nevertheless manages to denounce them by learning to 'take the staffe in her mouth, and guide it with her stumps, and write.' (St. Lavinia should be the patron saint of any writer who has ever had to submit to, or withstand, *the castration of censorship*, which was of course the rule rather than the exception in Elizabethan literature – not to mention our own.) This identical situation now appears, without the final triumph, and very possibly via the theatre, as a 'quickie' gag or riddle in *Grim Hairy Tales* (1966) p. 16 : '*Who was the meanest man in the world? – The fellow who raped the deaf-and-dumb girl, then cut off her fingers so she couldn't snitch on him!*' It is not necessary to emphasize the overdetermination, in both Shakespeare's grim hairy tale and the more recent one, of the castration of the girl at both tongue and hands. More important – since all of this is only imaginary, after all – is the crucial rape itself, clearly thought of as a form of female castration.

Other obvious castration substitutes, that even those who bridle at 'symbolism' would find hard to deny, include the night-club 'joke' of cutting off a customer's tie with scissors and handing it to him, an unpleasant trick which made the fame of a Parisian woman singer of the 1940's, 'Patachou,' and the fortune of her bar in Montmartre. To make very clear what was implied – for the benefit of provincial 'squares' – this was done as punishment for any man who would not sing along with her in her specialty: the French students' notably bawdy

"Chansons de Salles de Garde." Harpo Marx does the same trick with a bologna and fire-axe in the opening scene of the Marx Brothers' movie-comedy *A Night at the Opera*, in the 1930's. This is what is known as *"calling a spade a bloody shovel."*

The *locus classicus* on all the secondary or symbolic castrators – barbers, butchers, brain-surgeons, dentists, etc – wielding sharp or cutting instruments, is Sándor Ferenczi's "The Sons of the Tailor," in his *Further Contributions to the Theory and Technique of Psycho-analysis* (English translation, London, 1926), curiously overlooking that hoary fraud, the 'gentle' shoemaker. Dr. Otto Fenichel makes the very important additional point, in his magistral *The Psychoanalytic Theory of Neurosis* (1945) p. 520, that castration anxiety is the hidden force in the fear of the *loss of love*, which 'often very obviously is at the basis of social anxiety' as well. This is a larger subject than can be dealt with here. Quite aside from its relation to the matter of styles and fads (both physical and intellectual), its social ramifications are very important. They are precisely those found basic to the meteoric rise of the Nazi and other fascistic or 'Establishment' types of repressive social systems, a subject which has best been studied at the socio-psychological level in *The Authoritarian Personality* (1950) by Drs. T. Adorno *et al.*, in Erich Fromm's *Escape from Freedom*, and in Dr. Siegfried Kracauer's *From Caligari to Hitler*, a study of the German avant-garde in the 1920's.

It can all be subsumed, perhaps, in the single cowardly sentence or motto which is now practically being printed under the Great Seal of the United States on the American dollar bill: *"If you can't lick 'em – join 'em!"* (sometimes: *" – join 'em and cash in!"*). 'Cleaning it up' again with the pretext of money. Thus also the whole substructure of the once-important social 'out-casting' of religious excommunication (the ancient Jewish *chérem*, from the same root as the Arabic word *harem*: that which is taboo or sacred), of the dreaded prison punishment of solitary confinement, of the school punishment of being 'sent to Coventry,' and, in diminished economic form, the 'boycott,' originated in County Mayo, Ireland, in 1880. 'Doghousing' or *"We're not speaking"* in sexual/social relations.

Bitchy women of a certain type, when they have exhausted all other methods of trying to bring a man down and destroy him, will usually – if they are living with him, or married to him – grab everything portable and desert him suddenly, without being able to give any satisfactory reason for this. They then, if married, usually sue for divorce *via* lawyers – thus being saved the embarrassment of having to face the husband – who will arrange to get the woman everything she could not carry away during her flight. In situations where the house or property belongs to the woman, the man may come home to find all the locks changed, and – if he is lucky – his shirts, tennis racquets, toy-trains, etc. piled in the back of the garage. Various American Negro blues-songs describe forms of this, on the background of the female-dominant Negro 'common law' marriages.

Though economic explanations are usually given, if any, what is really being attempted in these cases is seldom really economic but psychological. The abandonment is intended as the ultimate castration, or *deprivation of love and security;* and this is just as true when it is a woman being abandoned or deserted by a man, which is enormously more common. This is essentially the plot of Eugene O'Neill's last play, *The Ice Man Cometh,* though here the salesman-hero, who, as always, cannot give any conscious or satisfactory reason for his action, finally states, in a ridiculously protracted monologue of self-justification, that he has not only deserted his wife but has killed her as well, 'because she was so *good.*' Some of the horror-stories by the modern master of the genre, John Collier, such as that on the man who feeds his wife mushrooms containing the vitamins D, E, A, T and H, and "Home for Christmas" (he buries her under fresh cement, as in Poe's "Tell-Tale Heart" or "The Cask of Amontillado"), are also of this 'unmotivated' type.

Women authors are particularly given to symbolically blinding and crippling their heroes and other male characters, or making them just general incompetent *shlubs,* as in Miss Mari Sandoz' *Slogum House* and other of her writings; not to mention the various biographies by lady scholars of the unfortunate medieval schoolman, Peter Abélard, whom no one would ever have heard of today were it not for his being punished for his love of Héloïse by being castrated. Abélard is not famous for anything he ever did – What did he do? – but for what he *lost.*

Death as the ultimate castration, and so also the personified Death as the 'Grim Reaper' or Castrator – with scythe and hourglass, which he shares identically with the popular iconology of 'Father Time' – have already been considered in passing, in the First Series, chapter 1.III, pages 78–80, as "The Diaper and the

Scythe," from a point of view very different from what might
be expected, and the reader is referred to that chapter for
details. This is perhaps the most powerful and widespread of all
unconscious identifications or symbols of castration, and is the
key to the strange and intense desire felt by many or most men
under patriarchy (seldom by women) to 'found a dynasty' or to
'perpetuate their names' by damming up the Grand Canyon,
building a hair-net factory, or killing a few hundred thousand
other men in a 'little war.' Failing all else, such men can always
have half-witted sons – and often do. That is the Divine Right
of kings. The Egyptian Pharaohs had unknown tens of thousands of Jewish slaves ground into the mud of the Nile to build
their Pyramids and treasure-cities (see *Exodus*, i. 11–14), for no
better reason than to preserve their bodies and 'immortalize'
their names that, alas, no one can now pronounce. Their immortality is the Sunday-supplement indignity of being known
only by names like *King Tut*. As to their bodies, the Egyptian
mummification made very clear that it was the penis that was
being preserved for eternity. The brain and other unnecessary
items were fished out through the nostrils with button-hooks,
thus originating the modern 'science' of castratory brain-
operations against the insane, to force them to fly right.

The other side of the identification of death and castration is
the castrator's side: the side of the person dealing out the
death. Here, far from death being feared and evaded, death is
adored and sought out; but it is always the death of someone
or something else. As with actual castration, animals are the
favorite victims, being the easiest to replace and causing the
least fuss with the police. The books of a literary sadist like
Ernest Hemingway – I am sure he was a real angel-baby in his
private life, so don't misunderstand my meaning – are the complete course in animal sadism (bulls by preference, but anything
would do) replacing the killing of men. Since Hemingway was
actually a writer of a very low calibre, who never wrote a first-
class book and was kept in the public eye strictly by publicity
tricks and methods, his great success could only have been kept
puffed up for years on the basis of the underlying popularity of
his deeply cruel, and of course openly anti-woman message.
The artificially supported literary fad for bull-fighting in
America, also kept up in imitation of Hemingway's letch or love
for this sport – where the dead bull's cut-off *ear* is offered to the
handsomest woman at the bull-fight by the victorious bull-

fighter – has apparently tapered off since his suicide. The similar cutting off of the *tail* of the fox, in British-style fox-hunting, was featured in full color in the otherwise superlative motion-picture version (1963) of Fielding's *Tom Jones*, the same director then going on to do a movie about the high good humor of a Hollywood animal-cemetery, in *The Loved One*.

The following old-time 'nigger-minstrel' joke is more likely an example of castratory death than of mere sex-linked sadism, as is true of almost all *stories* of killing animals, even for food. *Two farmers are talking. One says, "I can't understand all those crows I keep finding dead in my corn-field every morning. Can somebody be poisoning 'em?" The other farmer laughs. "It's that hired man of mine," he says. "He's been screwin' your daughter up in the corn-field every afternoon, and those crows are just nacherally laughin' theirselves to death!"* (Pittsburgh, Pa. 1943.) A toss-up whether it is the first farmer's sexual discomfiture or the crows' death that is the real joke here. As given on the 'ministrel' or vaudeville stage, *stealing* is substituted for sex in the punchline, without detracting from the joke. Showing that the actual humor- or pleasure-area is not sex but death.

We are not concerned here with the mere combination of sex with cruel or even bloody acts, in standard sadistic form, nor with the unconscious identification made by many men (and woman) of sexual intercourse as a violent and penetrating invasion of the woman's body. For this, see the First Series, chapter 5, "The Sadistic Concept," involving both notions of rape and of *la Mort Douce*, in which the man himself dies gloriously in intercourse. When death symbolizes castration (and not intercourse), it is the actual fact of death that is sought or gloated over, this being the essential victimization or 'cutting short' of the life of the victim. Animal victims are again sometimes substituted. When *'Old men send young men off to die in wars that make old men rich,'* they are not doing it for money. Marx is wrong, and Freud is right. They are doing it to kill off all the sexually potent young men, whom they hate and envy. Castrating and killing others, in order to feel powerful, potent – and 'immortal' – themselves.

Impotence and sterility are, of course, thought of as tantamount to castration, and also as the equivalent of death – *"You might just as well be dead!"* – as will be shown further in section 13.VI.2, "Erection to Resurrection." See also the entire section 8.VIII.2–6, on "Impotence," in the First Series, p. 617–41. One of the first of the American's 'men's' magazines, *Sir!* following in the wave of these that came with the success of Samuel Roth's *Beau* in the 1920's and Arnold Gingrich's *Esquire* in the 1930's – the English originals in the 1770's, a century and a half earlier, have already been listed above – makes the amazing slip or purposeful editorial error of entitling an article, in its issue for January 1952, on the presumed sterilizing danger in tobacco: *"Tobacco Can CASTRATE YOU"!* One assumes both editors and readers consciously know the difference, but modern 'media' material does not address itself to the intellect. This theme is combined with the dread of cancer, as in the bit of mock-medical buncombe as to 'infectious' womb-cancer quoted from Dr. Norman Haire in the headnote on Circumcision, 13.III: *'A fellow developed a steady pain front and center, and went to the doctor. "It's something unusual and rare you have there," said the doctor. "Watch out, it COULD develop into cancer." The man was really shook up. "What can I do for it, doctor?" he whimpered. "Well," said the doc, "I guess first you'd better tell your wife to stop smoking ..."'* (*Sex to Sexty,* 1966, 8:24, referring of course to the alerting of the American public during the 1960's to the danger of cancer from tobacco-smoking. Likewise from marijuana.)

Occasionally, impotence is modified down to the problem of fat – *i.e.* eunuchoid – men who need to use a long shoe-horn (to be seen offered for sale in all 'the better' haberdasheries), and who are shown in novelty-card cartoons looking for their penises with periscopes, to get past their bellies. *Woman to fat man, on preparing for bed, "Gosh, you're fat! Why don't you diet?" "Dye it? What color is it now?"* (1:437, here of a man being ridiculed by male friends in a Turkish bath. This type of pronunciational or homonym-humor is of the *Joe Miller* era of the 18th century, living on mostly in admitted puns.) Or the fat man is shown in novelty cartoons as having to use Mae West's motto to his penis, the insinuating *"come up an' see me some-time!"* (2:203.) This is a direct connection of the fatness idea with impotence or castration, as in all the harem-and-fat-eunuch cartoons in the 'men's' magazines. Or the man must go so far as to hold up the penis with a toy balloon. This last is a very ancient theme, brought unmistakably to public attention in the early years of World War I in Europe, in humorous magazine cartoons, both German and French, showing young women watching Graf Zeppelin's early dirigible suggestively.

The offering of the 'flying dream' as the cure or contrapositive of impotence and castration is the essential point in the neurotic interest in airplanes, moon-rockets, etc. at all times (since the myth of Daedalus & Icarus, and Leonardo da Vinci), and particularly in our own century, which is quite crazed on the subject, a point which much material could be gathered to prove. A very brief interpretive sampling is given in my pamphlet, *On the Cause of Homosexuality* (1950) p. 26–7, in discussing "The Airman (or The Mountain Climber, or The Polar Explorer)" as a specific homosexual disguise, along with the matching and contrasting disguises of 'The Negro (or The Cripple, or The Amputee, or – even – The Castrato),' and 'The Actor (or The Transvestist, Priest, Diplomat, or Spy).' It should be observed that originally the flying dream, or any mythic concern with birds as phallic objects – and thus the inevitable connection between goddesses and birds, such as Zipporah the wife of Moses, and the impregnation of the Virgin Mary by the 'Dove' or Holy Ghost, via her *ear* – is a simple and undisguised folk-expression or folk-rationalization of the mystery of the erection of the penis.

Physiologists imagine they have solved the problem here by assuring us soberly that the swelling of the penis during erection is due to its engorgement with blood, but that is far from explaining the almost instantaneity with which this occurs – and sometimes ceases! Folk solutions exist: '*A little boy asked his big brother, "When you get a hard on, where does all the extra skin and meat come from?" The big brother said, "I think it must come from the brain, because when I get horny, I just don't have any sense at all".' (World's Dirtiest Jokes*, 1969, p. 162.) Philip Roth gets a good deal of mileage out of one little Yiddish proverb to this same effect, in *Portnoy's Complaint* (1968), in the long central section entitled "Cunt Crazy": 'But who wins an argument with a hard-on? *Ven der putz shteht, ligt de séchel in de'rerd.* Know that famous proverb? When the prick stands up, the brains get buried in the ground! When the prick stands up, the brains are as good as dead! And 'tis so!'

A further explanation seems to be given on Roth's next page, where the Devil or *Yetzer ha-rá* (Evil Spirit) is identified as Portnoy's prick: 'the maniac who speaks into the microphone of my jockey shorts.' (Motif D1610.6, *Mentula loquens: Man given advice by his private parts*, with American Indian references only.) Yiddish erotic proverbs are collected in the rare supplement to Ignacy Bernstein's standard work by B. W. Segel, *Proverbia Judaeorum erotica et turpia* (Vienna, 1918: copies, Yale; and White Collection, Cleveland.) Another mere gag or tall-tale tells of: *A soldier who couldn't get any sleep because every time he laid down he thought of his girl, and got such a hard-on he didn't have enough skin left to shut his eyes!* (L.A. 1968.) This derives from the recitation, "The Hamburg Show, or Larry Turn the Crank," in which: *'Bad little boys masturbate the tight-skinned rhinoceros by throwing black pepper in his nose and making him sneeze. – Larry, turn the crank!'* (In Buddhist mythology, *The Crocodile must shut his eyes when he opens his mouth, and the monkey-trickster escapes.* – Motif K561.3.) Compare: *The Texan who doesn't know how big his penis is, because 'every time he gets a hard-on it drains all the blood from his brain and he faints!'* (N.Y. 1965.)

An extraordinary expression of the mystery of the erection is that of a joke first encountered in England: *'Man shipwrecked on a desert isle. Nothing to do but wank* [masturbate; American 'whack off']. *Keeps it up every day for two months and finally loses power to get an erection. Builds a beacon on top of hill* [note symbolic substitute], *and eventually sights ship. Lights beacon and sits thinking to himself: "There'll be women aboard that ship, women in their prime, with large loose bosoms, bulging breasts, boasting brazen teats, and such hips – !" And beginning to get the horn, he makes a sudden clutch at it: "Got you, you bugger!"'* (Chelmsford, Essex, 1953, from a prisoner. A Negro version, also from a prisoner, entitled "No Ship," is given in Roderick J. Roberts' *"Negro Folklore in a Southwestern 'Industrial School'*," MS. 1963, VIII.7, ending with the man sighting the ship and imagining the women on it: *'He say, "They nekkid!" His dick raised up. He say, "They gonna give us some pussy!" His dick raised straight up. He say, "Uh-huh! I fooled ya, motherfucker!"'*)

Closer to the relationship with the non-imaginary woman in sexual intercourse is the standard mother-in-law scene: *'A young newly-married couple were invited by the girl's mother to spend the first night at her big house instead of going to a hotel. In the middle of the night the mother sneaked over to their door to listen, and heard her daughter saying, "Oh, no, you can't do this to me; I won't let you! Don't, don't!"* The *mother, at this, entered the room, which was empty. Proceeding to the bathroom, she found the daughter wrestling with the man, who was in erection. "Darling, you must let him," the mother said. "What kind of a fool do you think I am?" the girl replied. "I spent two hours trying to get the damn thing up, and now he says he has to take a piss!"* (Transcontinental train, U.S. 1943, St. Louis attorney.) Mark Twain's *1601, or Tudor Conversation,* written in 1876, ends with an identical reference to the morning-erection or 'piss-hardon,' but reverses the action: *The girl evades her elderly would-be seducer by tricking him into taking out his penis and urinating before her.* (Compare the ancient Indian tale: *The rat persuades the cat to wash her face before eating him, and escapes meanwhile.* – Aarne Type 122B.)

Note the locating of the violent anxiety-situation in the bathroom in the preceding joke, presumably because of the reference to urination in the final 'unveiling' word or *dénouement.* Actually, bathrooms and toilets are heavily freighted with anxiety for many men, owing to various dangers imagined to reside there, which might attack the anus (pedication), or castrate the genitals. See the *"Ánima de Sayula"* of Mexican folklore, and the Alaskan 'ice worm,' in chapter 10.V.3, "Pedicatory Rape," and especially the joke on: *The parrot whose throat has been cut for swearing, after which it is thrown in the toilet (on which a menstruating woman sits). A voice issues from the depths of the china bowl: "If she can live with a gash like that, so can I."* (2:11, and traced to 1927 or earlier, in the First Series, 3.II, pages 204–5.) The identification of death and castration, as woman's nature, is unmistakable here. Compare the jocular belief that alligators live in big-city sewers.

Ancient history reports many deaths in privies, both natural and in the way of murders or captures in wartime. The *locus classicus* in English on all such lore is Reginald Reynolds' *Cleanliness and Godliness* (London, 1943). As indexed, p. 266, under "Notable Deaths in the Jakes" – the modern 'john' – Reynolds overlooks the last story he himself retails, p. 258–9, immediately after quoting from G. K. Chesterton: 'Art consists in drawing the line somewhere.' In the German story at which he could not bear to draw the line: *A Bishop, who is warring on a rebel Baron, learns through the treachery of a page-boy* ['a cunning little nipper'?] *who has crept out of the besieged castle, that the Baron takes his morning crappe always at the same hour and place, in a privy on one of the battlements.*

'*The Bishop placed two cross-bowmen in a privy place at the hour indicated by the page; and things falling out as the boy had said, the Baron received a couple of bolts in his posterior what time he made his morning ejestion upon the battlements (being a person of regular habits), for they shot straight up the shaft that led into the Baronial jakes.*' This is, of course, a lethal pedicatory rape: the German version of the Mexican "*Ánima de Sayula*" ballad. Though vouched for by that beautifully illustrated old hoary accumulation of frauds and fancies, the *Nuremberg Chronicle* (15th century; offset reprint, 1960), this story is incredible on the arse of it.

Among the many castration stories submitted to *Neurotica* magazine after the printing of the castration-symbolic story, "Hair," by Charles L. Newman, in No. 5 (1949) p. 17–19, about a man who shaves off his own pubic hair and plans to do the same to his girlfriend – a subject on which see further the First Series, 6.VII, "Pubic Hair and Shaving;" and 13.II.7, "The Mad Barber of Fleet Street" – a very extraordinary manuscript was received describing how: *A man's penis is fitted with a toy balloon at each side, then cut off by himself with a homemade guillotine composed of a razor-blade fastened to a falling window. His penis then floats out over San Francisco's Golden Gate, urinating on all the writer's enemies as it goes. This is his revenge against them.* As in the well-known parody of "The Prisoner's Song," in which the prisoner fantasies himself as '*flying to the highest church-steeple, To piss on all the buggers below!*' (The manuscript was rejected, owing to lack of space.)

Aside from the urinary conclusion, the very similar fantasy of phallic damage or castration by a falling window is the main plot gimmick of Sterne's *Tristram Shandy* (1767) Book V, chap. 17 – and compare Book IV, chap 27, on nose-castration – just two centuries ago. A modern joke that tries hard to be charming, but fails, recollects this scene, again in the bathroom situation. '*Little Marty, barely able to reach it, had draped his little carrot over the edge of the commode when the lid suddenly fell. He ran screaming to his mother, "Tiss it, Mommy, tiss it and make it well!" She replied, "Shut up, Marty! You're getting more like your old man every day!"*' (*World's Dirtiest Jokes*, 1969, p. 155; Collected before 1950.)

In the New Orleans 'underground' newspaper, *Nola Express* (Sept. 18, 1970) No. 64: p. 7, backing up one of Charles Bukowski's numerous repulsively detailed stories of 'symbolic' castration, a peculiar brief paean to drug-taking, entitled "Usualessly," signed 'Kálumbus Guinea,' opens with a parody of the opening of Joyce's *Ulysses* – both concern a man taking a shave – in which the writer extasiates on the pleasures of mentholated shaving cream, and 'dark, rich dope.' In his fantasy recollections, as he shaves, he goes back to the night before, when:

> In the hazy, fragrant car interior Rick broke away to breathe. As he returned his lips, Mary leaned up to meet him and Rick could sense she was in the grip of some force more powerful than $20 a lid dope.
>
> Re-inserting his desensitized tongue he searched vainly for the faithful organ with which he had duelled and danced almost every night of the summer. Extending himself further into the warm cavern, he had reached nearly to her tonsils when Mary suddenly collapsed her mouth and drew strongly. Rick mutely gasped. Each taste bud strained out on its own to fill the vacuum. The darkness grew brilliantly unforgettable in a tingling flash of white light.
>
> A firm grip on the white porcelain sink was all that saved Rick as his tongue sprung straight just in time to thrust his lower lip into the upswing of the razor, and both knees collapsed into the water pipes. "Aarrrg ..." The muffled cry of pain went unnoticed in the kitchen.

However, no real harm is done, and this *vagina dentata* fantasy ends merely in the man's cutting his face slightly, as well he might, since he has 'thrust his lower lip into the upswing of the razor,' to save his self-endangered tongue. The story then finishes with an allusion to more sexualized shaving delights to come, but without actually specifying what: '*He wondered if he could find a girl at LSUNO who would dig* [enjoy] *getting really stoned* [drugged] *and naked with him, so they could spray each other with Noxema menthol* [shaving cream], *shower together and crawl into a crisp, warm bed. He tossed an extra pack of his dad's Wilkerson blades into his shaving kit ...*' Total consumership.

Much other material of a jocular or neurotic nature will be presented in the following section, "Self-Castration," on the bathroom or toilet-room as a dangerous locale in the fantasy-fears of men, as differentiated from the popular idea that the white-tiled bathroom is a specially appreciated luxury in modern Western houses and apartments, where the *number* of bathrooms is always announced in the advertisements for sale or rent. Actually, the *whiteness* only takes the unconscious assimilation to a surgical operating-room more likely, and I would recommend log-cabin or wild-west decorating schemes for bathrooms for really modern homes, the walls to be done in oak panelling, etc., but without the now usual and unsanitary drip-rugs of chenille under the lip of the toilet-bowl. (One drunken guest throws up there, and you can throw away your wall-to-wall toilet carpeting.)

Impotence is of course directly observable in the man (women can fake passion), and is sometimes directly expressed in folk-humor. The 'punishment' of the recalcitrant male organ is often self-castration, as will be seen immediately following. The simple statement of the existence of impotence, without any attempted resolution of the problem or any punishment, is not common. Even in the most frequently encountered expression, the amusingly self-pitying rhymed epigraph, derived from old *Cobbes Prophecies*, by 'Richard Rablet' (1614) f. c3v, beginning on the same rhymes:

> *When a man grows old, and his balls grow cold,*
> *And the head of his pecker turns blue,*
> *And he goes to diddle, and it bends in the middle –*
> *Did that ever happen to YOU?*

This neatly projects the impotence upon the reader, in the unexpected punch-line. (First printed in *The Stag Party*, 1888, p. 256 unnumbered, a text ending: *'And that's what's the matter with you.'*) Another symbolization is the crux of a riddling catch, already noted: *"Did you see that piece in the New York Times where it says that men who masturbate (mumble mumble mumble)?" – Victim: "What?!" – "THEY GET HARD OF HEARING!"* (N.Y. 1953. Reported to have been delivered several times with great success.)

In Mark Twain's *Autobiography*, at date 30 May 1907 (printed in *Mark Twain in Eruption*, ed. Bernard De Voto, 1940, p. 23), a typical little male-motherhood story or tall-tale is given, ending with a strikingly symbolized castration:

> I know of a turkey hen that tried during several weeks to hatch out a porcelain egg, then the gobbler took the job and sat on that egg two entire summers and at last hatched it.

He hatched out of it a doll's tea set of fourteen pieces, and all perfect except that the teapot had no spout, on account of the material running out [!] I know this to be true, out of my own personal knowledge.

This has the air of being a jocular statement of impotence, by the writer then seventy-two years old, though actually the subject of impotence had long plagued or intrigued him, appearing for instance as the punchline and in the colloquy between the Queen and 'ye child Francis Beaumont,' asking whether his penis 'stirred,' in Twain's *1601, or Tudor Conversation*, written in 1876, three decades before. The 'spout,' as the penis of the teapot or kettle, is folkwit, as in the late-19th century item : *Mrs. Kettle has twins, a boy and a girl, and telegraphs her husband who is away on a trip, in pre-arranged code:* "TWO NEW KETTLES, ONE WITH SPOUT, ONE WITHOUT." (From an undated clipping, about 1900.) *Is* this an exception to the folk-rule that telegrams in jokes are always bad news or insults?

The castrational streak is not prominent in Twain's work, but it is there, as in the masochistic self-torture he says he tried to get his *mother* to enact upon him, in "My First Lie." Masochism, not sadism, is the standard problem and even format of most professional humorists – a point worth emphasizing. All of Charlie Chaplin's movie comedies, except *Modern Times* (in which, exceptionally, he *gets* the girl, Paulette Goddard), pointedly show Chaplin in the character of the social-castrato, the impotent little tramp, overdetermined in the shuffling walk and other castrations of the feet (giving the bully his shoe to eat in *The Gold Rush*), but always with superb overcompensatory scenes in which Chaplin dreams of dancing, roller-skating, and the like.

At an earlier date in human history, and still among uncultivated, ignorant, or immigrant groups such as Negroes in the Deep South and Italians in Canada, impotence in men who are not so old as to expect and accept the impotence of old age, was (and is) believed to be caused by evil magic, 'hexing' by enemies, witch-craft, 'bad vibrations,' and the like. This belief was known in French and English during the 16th and 17th centuries as 'nouer l'aiguillette' or 'point-tying,' from the 'points' or pointed tags (still worn on shoulder epaulets in dress-uniforms) tying the 'ballap' or drop-fly which preceded the modern vertical fly-front of men's trousers. The old drop-fly survives in French and

American enlisted sailors' uniforms, closing with buttons at the sides (also in the *Lederhosen*, or short leather pants of Tyrolean peasants), and on the imitative pants of overfashionable young women since about 1965, of which the advantage – unless they can piss standing – is apparently purely psychological. On the matter of pants for women see the First Series, 6.I, "The Big Inch." There is a long quibbling passage on 'points' in Shakespeare's *1 Henry IV.* II.iv. 239, and similar erotic references in other of his plays. The French version of 'point-tying,' or *'nouer l'aiguillette'* – a common accusation against witches – is studied in John Davenport's *Sexagyma* (1888) under "Anaphrodisia," p. 32–5. And see also the First Series here, 5.VI and 8.VIII.4, "Aphrodisiacs and Orgasm," which is naturally mostly about impotence.

Aphrodisiacs are essentially magical counter-remedies against occult hexing, and have no other serious meaning. Aphrodisiac stories, which inevitably follow the idea of castratory impotence, often re-import the castration by having the aphrodisiac fail or be spoiled, as a presumptuous attack on Destiny; and also sometimes oversucceed. On both of these see the following section, 13.VI.1, "Overcompensation: The Three Wishes." In a famous story, very often heard, and obviously magical rather than medical in the trait of the whistle (Motif D1225): *A man is given three aphrodisiacal pills, the action of which can only be stopped by whistling. The first pill is wasted trying it out, the second when a traffic cop* [father-surrogate] *blows his whistle while the man is hurrying across the street on his way to the assignation. The third pill is wasted when the woman whistles in amazement at the size of his erection.* (2:378. In later texts he gets 'a shot of spermatozoa'!)

The effect of whistling on the genitals, in easing urination, is noted at least as far back as the original *Mother Goose's Melody* (ca. 1769), the editor, apparently Oliver Goldsmith, a physician as well as a writer, noting one tune whistled to horses for this purpose by the car-men. (Compare *2 Henry IV*, III.ii.346, the famous passage on 'fancies and goodnights.') Whistling in toilet rooms, which is still very common, is now rationalized as intended to cover the sound of the urination. The deeper intention is that of reassuring the whistling man or woman of his or her uncastrated (whistling: 'male') bodily integrity, at a common moment. Only masculine or male-protest women traditionally can – or attempt to – whistle; feminine women explaining helplessly that they cannot do so, or can do so 'sucking in'! (Old proverb: *"Whistling girls and crowing hens never come to no good ends."* Compare Maurice P. Tilley, *A Dictionary of The Proverbs in England*, 1950, H778, not mentioning the 'whistling girls.')

The joke given earlier on the using of more than one condom at once, as an extra safeguard, with catastrophic – castrastrophic? – results, really seems to be derived from a joke on an aphrodisiac which turns out badly. This is given in *Anecdota Americana* (1927) 1:202, apparently as the last turn of the screw as to the hating and castrating of 'Kaiser Bill' during World War I. (*'The First Division went over the top, To circumcise the Kaiser's cock; Hinky-dinky, parlay-voo!'* – u.s. troops, 1918.) – *'When the Kaiser's second wife left him, in a huff, the news came out that he had taken pills to give him a hard on. According to a facetious critic the medicine backfired, and he got piles!'* (Compare Oliver St.John Gogarty's venereal parody of the British national anthem: *'Frustrate their knavish tricks, Cut off their six-o-six ... God save the King!'* Six-o-six being salvarsan, a syphilis remedy.)

Even farther back is the original of the (too) well-known limerick on *'The young fellow of Kent, whose prick was so long that it bent.'* (*The Limerick*, No. 313.) As usually collected, this ends with the glorying nonsense – after he puts his penis in double – *'And instead of coming, he went!'* But the original, in *The Stag Party* (1888) p. 124 unnumbered, from which this has been expurgated into its nonsensical victory, is plainly a castratory punishment for impotence as a result of venereal disease (chordee). Here the end line, after the usual double in-put, states flatly that the *'young sucker . blew off his balls when he spent.'* Compare: *'A newlywed husband's penis was too long for his bride, so, to avoid hurting her by putting it in too deep, he tied a knot in it close to the body. When he came, he blew his brains out!'* (N.Y. 1945, from manuscript.) There is a whole folklore concerned with this almost mythical problem of excessive penile entry, involving pads of doughnut shape, towels twisted around the erect penis at the base (perhaps the original of the 'knot' here), and so forth. It is taken very seriously in *My Secret Life* (1888–94), owing to the author's unpleasant letch for extremely young and pre-pubescent girls. I was once given a long lecture on methods of achieving this 'protection' from the over-long penis, by a white pimp in Har-

lem in the 1930's whose girls accepted Negro clients but I have
forgotten the details, except that of the twisted towel, because
I realized the conversation was really just an attempted seduction, and left, when the pimp began explaining, with gestures,
how the *best* method was to wrap one or both his fists around
the base 'of dat big blacksnake,' to 'keep dem boogies' from
hurting his girls. Ray Russell's anti-hero in *Incubus* (1975) is an
avatar of the Devil: 'a supernatural rapist with a penis as long
as a man's arm' – and arms six inches long? This diabolical
penis *kills* his women: the Sadistic Concept of coitus, or sex as
revenge.

A very striking symbolization, often collected, and considered exquisitely humorous and 'nonsensical' by its tellers,
actually represents self-castration, though it is more of interest
here as a displacement of castration fear backwards – and upward to the navel. Buddha contemplates his navel for forty
years, and finally decides he must 'unscrew the inscrutable' –
to wit, his navel – whereupon 'his asshole falls out.' (N.Y. 1942.)
Mysterious or magical elements are present in all versions of
this, these representing the *dread* or sensation of eeriness and
danger connected with castration anxiety, as in the "Sleeve
Job" story earlier. *A lunatic refuses to let the orderlies undress*
him, on being brought to the asylum, and confides to the doc-
tor mysteriously that he is afraid they might unscrew his navel.
Intrigued, the doctor unscrews the lunatic's navel (sometimes
his own!) when he is asleep, with the result as above. (L.A. 1973.)

Note the positive statement here of the castratory intrusive-
ness of the trusted doctor, never so apparent and crude as in
insane-asylums and concentration-camps, and in the 'subtotal
euthanasia' of brain-surgery and the like. In still another version: *The doctor (or psychiatrist) tells the patient, who has*
undergone lifelong inconvenience from a golden screw in his
navel, that he will dream that night of a purple balloon hang-
ing in the air. He is to prick it [?] and a golden screw-driver will
appear, with which, and then, &c, &c. (D.C. 1952.) This assimilates the witch-doctor frankly to the psychiatrist, with reminiscences of the 'dreaming true' of the *Arabian Nights* and
George du Maurier's *Peter Ibbetson* (1891), in the service of
grotesque sexual repressions in this last, where the 'dreaming
true' can take place only if the man & woman dreaming of each
other fall asleep with their knees crossed (oh, come *on*!), never
touch each other in the dream, and so forth.

The original 'unscrewing the inscrutable' story has been traced to the early American humorist, 'John Phoenix' (George H. Derby), just before the Civil War, with the pictorial topper that: *The lady, in this case, in trying to fix things, gets her buttocks on upside down.* (George R. Stewart, *John Phoenix*, p. 158.) Note particularly the displacement of the primary castration anxiety backwards to the buttocks, and, in all versions – as also in the joke on the 'salt kept in the navel,' in section 13.II.6, "The Doctor as Castrator" – upward to the navel.

Certain current rock-n-roll singers in America regularly pull out their penises (that's only one each) while onstage, to wow the crowds, especially the teen-age girls. A few rare girls of this kind, known contemptuously as 'groupies' – and, to the others, as *'platers'* or *'plaster-casters'* – take de-pantsing or phallic trophy-hunting, to the ultimate point. They travel about, following the rock-&-roll bands, and make actual sculptural castings of the penises of the star singers and other current idols, from life, after getting them stiff enough to cast by fellation. The products of this new art, which is not really very different from that symbolized by Cleopatra's 'Needle' and other obelisks in the West brought from matriarchal Egypt, and by San Francisco's incredible Coit Tower, have been photographed several times in the underground press, which invariably writes up these 'plaster-casters' or ambulant *vagina dentatas* as humor. What is done with the resultant phallic souvenirs is never stated. Presumably they are then gilded and used as dildoes, for oral or vaginal masturbation. In one case, lollipops ("All Day Suckers") were cast using a penis model stated to be that of a recently-dead Negro rock-&-roll star. Though probably intended to be sentimental, not gruesome, this goes one step further even than lynching.

The zipper opening – or, rather, the zipper closing – was first widely used on trouser-flies, apparently by British tailors in the late 1920's. It was put across in America, almost completely displacing the former button-closing for flies, except on work-pants and mock-virile 'blue jeans,' by fashion articles and advertisements in the men's magazine *Esquire* in the 1930's, along with the electric razor, for men afraid of straight razors or even razor-blades in a bathroom (with or without balloons). There is, and always has been, much resistance to the zipper-fly as a castratory danger. *"What's worse than pecker tracks on your zipper? – Zipper tracks on your pecker."* (L.A. 1968.)

Actually, the skin of the penis is seldom attacked by the teeth of the zipper, but, when it happens, once is enough. The danger, except of infection, is not great, but the pain is intense and men over-react as though bitten in the same place by a rattle-snake. (*Vagina-dentata* story of: *The cowboy who is poisoned when he pulls on a boot in which the fang of a rattlesnake he has killed has become embedded.* – U.S. 1940's. Though obviously derived from the Greek legend of Hercules and the poisoned Tunic of Nessus; this presumably could actually happen and is usually told as true.) A cartoon-caption contest in the New York 'pornzine' or sex-newspaper, *Screw* (1969) No. 25: p. 12, shows: *Frankenstein's monster getting into bed with a naked lady-ghoul. (His ghoul-friend.) She is staring angrily at him, as he has just cut off his outsize, soldered-on penis with his zipper, in taking off his pants.* Essentially, this belongs to the group of stories given later, under "Overcompensation," in which the magical Three Wishes go horribly wrong, or a proposed phallic resurrection operation oversucceeds, or fails explosively in some way, as punishment for interfering with Destiny. This is also the meaning of Mary Wollstonecraft Shelley's original *Frankenstein* story (1818).

The one most frequent real danger about the zipper fly is that the pubic hairs are sometimes painfully caught, or the cloth of the man's underwear or shirt, imprisoning him ludicrously, sometimes when he is trying to rush to jump into bed with a woman. A minor accident bloated up into castratory dimensions by the endemic fear. By the mid-1930's a non-folk-transmitted limerick had already appeared, in the McAtee MS. (1937) D364, envelope 8, in the significant context of a story called "The Pleasures of Impotence" (!):

> He loved to make his zipper zip
> And see his fly-front gaily rip,
> But once his member tangled
> Got hideously mangled,
> And now the lad's no longer quite so flip.

Note the unclear confusion here of impotence with quasi-castration, by a scientist. (McAtee was a professional ornithologist, who certainly understood the difference.) By the time of World War II, in 1940, a castration poem, "Goddamit, My Pecker Got Caught in My Zipper," on erotic delay owing to this accident, was being circulated in America in manuscript form.

Even without the zipper-fly, however, the trousers themselves – like long underwear traditionally (as in *The Limerick*, No. 1161) – are considered hampering during sexual activity, as they certainly are, and should be removed then. The best thing in John Cheever's *The Wapshot Chronicle* (New York, 1957) is the Credo with which the work ends, the patriarch's up-country "Advice to My Sons," including these varyingly conscious and pre-conscious items of sexual advice: *'Never make love with pants on ... Bathe in cold water every morning. Painful but exhilarating. Also reduces horniness ... Stand up straight. Admire the world. Relish the love of a gentle woman. Trust in the Lord.'* The chapbook, *Spicy Breezes* (1930?) p. 48, presents this as an animal-castration comedy: *The wife is plucking the feathers from a live rooster, expecting the minister for dinner, but the meal is postponed. 'Mary feeling sorry for the undressed rooster made him a small pair of pants. Soon John came into the house laughing hysterically. "What is wrong?" asked Mary. "Funniest thing I ever saw," he replied. "That rooster holding a hen down with one foot, and trying to unbutton his pants with the other".'* Compare *The Limerick*, No. 1161, calculating the *mileage* lost 'By leaving my drawers on, while clambering whores.'

V. SELF-CASTRATION

The last direct castration theme in jokes is self-castration, often as self-punishment for impotence. This is an 'Irish bull' absurdity not actually so absurd as it seems, as it effectively denies the castration if castration is still necessary. (Quaker's Oats box inside a Quaker's Oats box, inside &c.) Also "*You Can't Fire Me, I Quit!*" Several jokes exist in which self-castration in revenge for impotence is modified to merely humiliating or punishing the penis, by tying a string around it and refusing to let it urinate, or making it kiss the buttocks. The wedding-night story has been given above, collected on a transcontinental train in 1943, of *The young bride wrestling with her husband in the bathroom, throttling his penis and crying, "Oh, no, you can't do this to me; I won't let you! Don't, don't!"* all of which is carefully rationalized as her trying to *prevent* him from proving impotent by *'losing his piss-hardon,'* as another version puts it.

Actually, she is punishing him for his impotence, as is made very clear in the form more relevant here, in which: *Shouts and screams are heard from a cubicle in the men's room in a hotel. The house-detective batters on the cubicle door while, from inside, can be heard a man's voice shouting, "Revenge! Revenge! Take that! I'll strangle you, you bastard!"* The explanation is that it is a man throttling his own penis to prevent it from urinating, because it refused to 'stand up for him' on his wedding night. (2:18. Text form, N.Y. 1951.) I would even venture to suggest that, in fact, the whole scene is a charade representing the failed sexual intercourse. The bathroom or toilet-cubicle is, in many people's minds, the taboo area or genito-urinary 'organ' of the house, especially if this is merely an apartment. Formerly the *cellar* was so considered. Many neurotics, in particular compulsive homosexuals, seem actually to prefer to have sexual relations in the public toilets ('tearooms'), which they find attractively 'dirty' or 'sexy,' and excitingly dangerous, thus powerfully abrogating the taboo. For normal people the bedroom, and even more particularly *the staircase leading up to the bedroom*, is the sexualized area of the house, and the lack of staircases, in modern pigeoncote apartment living and 'strip housing,' is just one of the many abnormalizing influences of that type of life. The meagre two-step of a faked 'dropped living-room' is not a sufficient substitute.

An even more absurd and mechanized form of the preceding story again involves the 'cloacal identification' of sex with scatology: *A man is observed in a public toilet making scratching and twitching motions at his chest while he urinates, at one of the stand-up stalls. (Or he is shouting, "Revenge! Revenge!") The man at the stall next to him says, "What's the matter with you? Have you got lice, or are you crazy?" "Neither," the first man explains. "It's a string that I'm pulling on. See? It goes over my shoulder and down my back and between my ass-cheeks, and it's tied to my prick with a double knot. I had the most beautiful girl in the world all naked in bed waiting for me with her legs spread, and this son-of-a-bitch wouldn't get stiff. So now, every time I take a piss, HE'LL KISS MY ASS!!"* (2:125, variant.)

A related story, far older, is given in Roth's *Waggish Tales of the Czechs* (1947) p. 318, in which: *A policeman prevents a young man from kicking an old man, but the old man explains that he has asked him to do it. "Thirty years ago," he recounts, "a woman in this town asked me to sit down on the couch with her, and let her negligée fall open – she said she was warm – and then reached across me to get an apple from the fruit bowl." Finally the woman has to let him leave, since he cannot understand her overtures, but tells him that "Someday, when you remember tonight, ask somebody to kick you where it will do the most good." "That was thirty years ago," the old man finishes, "and just today I realized what she meant." "Start kicking him again," says the policeman " – quick!"* Elgart gives a puzzle, or surprise-form of this in *Over Sixteen* (1951) p. 84, as of: *An old Swedish carpenter who, twenty years later, while shingling a roof, suddenly understood it all "like a flash," and is telling his story in the hospital.*

These stories have already been noted in the First Series, in the chapter on Fools, 2.I, under "Nincumpoops," pages 123–5, with others similar. The kicking story is in the *Novelle* of Bandello (1554) III. 8: *A greedy priest has a friend kick him for refusing a gold coin because it lacked in weight.* (Rotunda Q592, expurgated from Thompson's *Motif-Index* later, which jumps from Q591 to Q593 to avoid this anti-clerical tale.) Much modern vaudeville or 'burlesque' stage-humor of a low kind involves kicking in this way, apparently derived from the Italian *commedia dell'arte* street entertainment of earlier centuries. It is always – though never so stated – the buttocks which are kicked. Some enterprising Arkansawyer in recent years constructed a *"Fanny-Kicking Machine,"* self-operated by a string, exactly as in the 'Revenge!' story preceding, in which: *Anyone who felt he had recently committed a blunder worth punishing, could stand and have himself kicked thoroughly in the arse by a heavy boot, for a payment of $1 to the inventor.* (Note that 'fanny,' which refers to the buttocks in America, is a slang word for the female genital in England, as in *Fanny Hill*.)

In a humorous letter, possibly authentic, circulated in America before 1940 (it is one of the least common of the mock-letter obscoena of this type): *An insurance adjuster asks for further information as to an accident claim, before paying the insured, who has burned his penis on the cooking-stove while making his breakfast. The adjuster points out that, though they will probably have to 'go ahead and pay his claim,' it does seem to him that a man should not rush through the kitchen flinging his most prized possession in all directions, or perhaps whipping it around like a flail.* The point being that a man this stupid or clumsy must have a very long penis (the *'baytzim-mer'* idea), and has 'stepped on his dick.'

All these forms modify greatly the castration to a humilia-tion of the penis, or a 'side-castration' of its urinary function, or else displace the area of punishment to the buttocks in classical fashion, or simply as the self-punishment of the 'accident.' An-other form, rather similar to the famous 'cow's udder' story to be given below, is perfectly frank as to the castration involved, but manages to evade it anyhow : *A man pays a chorus-girl $500 for a night in bed with her, and then is impotent from being drunk. He decides to punish his penis by chopping it off with a meat-cleaver, but every time he bends forward to strike, he pulls back his body and misses it. "You son-of-a-bitch!" he shouts at his penis, "you can miss a two-foot cleaver, but you can't find your way into a five-hundred-dollar pussy!"* (2 : 138.) Compare, for a penance : the disaffection from the impotent penis can be localized more exactly, not on the penis 'itself' but in some portion of it upon which the blame for the impotence is laid. *A man asks to have his penis cut in half, a further inch cut off, and then the two ends sewn together. He explains that this is an anti-impotence measure, because "That's the part that always bends."* (2 : 209, told of the novelist Theodore Dreiser, then, in 1934, in the news for his unprecedented de-fense against a Mann Act prosecution for illegally transporting a woman interstate for 'immoral purposes,' on the grounds that he was impotent.) Two legal *obscoena* using this same defense, in rape and paternity cases, are given earlier in *The Stag Party* (1888) p. 213-unnumbered : Case of Hamilton *vs.* Woodin, an obviously humorous piece in which Mr. Woodin is stated to be eighty-one years of age; and p. 271–3, Brown *vs.* Waddell, in which Mr. Waddell is seventy-three, and furthermore had been recently afflicted with mumps, which he states "destroyed one of my testicles and so damaged the other as to destroy my manhood." These are public self-castrations, however humor-ous in format.

No pretense of taking the matter seriously in a version of the joke heard during World War II, about : *A soldier whose penis was shot off in the war. His relatives all decided to contribute half-inch slices of theirs toward building him a new one ... Grandpa's contribution is in the middle.* (D.C. 1943.) This be-longs to the ancient family of fool stories – the Jewish "Wise Men of Chelm," also of Gotham – in which : *Each person puts a bottleful of water into a hogshead of wine being collected, on the theory that it will not be noticed among so much wine. When the hogshead is opened, it is found to contain nothing but water.* (Tale Type 1555, and compare Motif J125.1, in which a child tattles.)

Connected with this is one of the most remarkable of all castration jokes, in its clear demonstration of the anxiety-dissipating purpose of all such jokes and quasi-castratory pranks. That is to say, their dissipation of anxiety in the people performing them, but at the cost of the victims to whom they are done, whose castration-anxieties are thus exacerbated and made more intense. For example, at the mildest level, fly-and tie-ripping (displacement upward), as to the particular phallic sheath or symbol torn open or pulled out, perfectly consciously, by school-boys in the days before zipper-flies : ties rather than flies when under the teachers' observation. (The older boy's tie would always be flipped out suddenly, but never his penis.) These pranks move on to cruel and gruesome college fraternity hazings – some of the most cruel are at high-school level – such as forcing the initiate's penis into a live light-socket, into a can of worms (actually macaroni), etc. Another item in this *Prixen-hammer* guide will be noted just below.

Such castratory and flagellational hazing, with its heavy homosexual tone and concentration on the buttocks (displaced upward to the face, in German university dueling) is too large a subject to be more than alluded to here. Note, for one self-complacent public example, a full-page advertisement in color for the Bell Telephone System, in the kitsch paradise of *Better Homes and Gardens* (Des Moines, Iowa, May 1964, p. 7), 'Circulation 6,200,000.' Showing a young woman in a man's shirt – fantasy-plugged nevertheless as a 'Princess,' because she is using a telephone model so denominated by the democratic manufacturer – leaning up against a 'family room' wall light-heartedly decorated with Greek-lettered fraternity paddles. As, in France, where cat-o'-nine-tails for beating children, with each lash a different color of plastic, are hung up prominently in every kitchen, at the lower middle-class level. A homosexual 'S. & M.' (sadomasochist – but really just sadistic) film of 1974, *Initiation Rites*, uses the pretext of a fraternity initiation to put on a gloating rodeo of flagellation, torture, etc. As a clue for like-minded 'gays,' its advertisements feature a Greek-lettered paddle. Greek *Love?*

The ultimate self-castration joke is presented as 'only a joke,' or what is called a 'practical' joke, because it involves some pantomime action, usually of a hurtful kind. *A butcher puts a cow's udder (link of sausages) inside his pants, allowing one teat to protrude from his fly. The lady customers naturally complain. He says, "Oh, is that thing hanging out again?" and chops it off with one blow of the meat-cleaver. The ladies all faint, and he runs over to the next butcher-shop to try the same joke. At the fifth try he faints. Cows have four teats.* (Larson MS., No. 70; Idaho, 1920, a version in which: *The butcher makes only one cut then takes the udder out of his fly to examine it, fainting when he finds it still has four teats.*)

The extraordinary 'prop' or *mise-en-scène* here of the cow's udder should be compared with the extravagantly compulsive Talmudic concern with whether or not this organ of the cow is to be considered 'meat' or 'milk,' according to the Jewish dietary laws of 'milchigs & fleischigs' discussed earlier in chapter 12.IV.2, "Food-Dirtying." Many jokes and allusions exist comparing the cow's teat to a man's penis: *The city-girl visiting in the country who tries to milk the cow, but admits finally, "I've tried everything I know, but I can't make the darn thing get stiff."* The cow's-udder joke is worked up into a full-length story, on the style of Balzac's *Contes Drolatiques* (1832) and the Italian *novelle*, which similarly exploited current jokes centuries before – the style taken up again by Mme. 'Marc de Montifaud' in the 1880's, and by Alexander Woollcott in the 1930's – under the title "L'Affaire de Cow's Udder," by Lyon Mearson, in *Man to Man* (1940), reprinted from the 'men's magazine,' *For Men*, which caused the banning of the magazine. By 1950 the story was also collected orally in England, with a butcher carrying a link of sausages in his trousers on a bus!

Self-castration 'as a joke' in this way is elaborately set up in La Sale's *Cent Nouvelles Nouvelles* (MS. 1460) No. 64, "Le Curé Rasé," in which at the last minute the practical joker wants to turn back, but by then it is too late. A cartoon illustration, signed Ted Trogdon, actually showing self-castration in this way, as an 'April fool' joke, is printed inside the cover of the Texas humor magazine, *Sex to Sexty* (1970) No. 31, facing p. 1: *The naked man is standing by the side of the bed with an open jack-knife held brandished in his left hand and what appears to be his cut-off penis held vertically in his right. Between his legs, extending out behind him like a tail, is held what is presumably a piece of Balsa wood or a vegetable marrow, from which he has just cut off the pretended penis. His naked wife is sitting at the other side of the bed screaming and in tears. She is blonde, with very large breasts – i.e. the theoretical 'sex-job' or dream-girl of all American men. But he cuts it off anyhow. His spoken line or apology: "Aw, Honey, – it was only an April Fool Joke."* Bandaged 'thumbs' with discreet blood-stains and all, for April Fool jokes of this kind, are sold in novelty-shops in all Western countries: *The thumb is sloughed off or left behind in the victim's grasp after shaking hands.*

Various absurd reasons are given for self-castration, though in the older tales there is no final recourse to wooden dummies, as in the cartoon in *Sex to Sexty*, to pretend that everything is going to be all right in the end. Straparola's *Piacevoli Notti* (1553) Night VI. 2, has: *A fool who allows himself to be castrated to 'put on weight' like a capon.* This is clearly identical with the widely dispersed folktale of "The Gelding of the Devil (or Ogre, or Bear)," in which the pretense is that castration will make the devil 'strong.' (Types 153 and 1133. Also Rabelais' "Diable de Papefiguière," Book IV, chaps. 46–7.) In the introduction to the same Book IV, dated 1552, which destroyed Rabelais' career and had him dismissed from his clerical privileges and benefices, dying in poverty within a year, a complicated story is told of: *A woodchopper named Big-Balls (Couillatris), who loses his hatchet, which is restored to him by Jupiter, thus making his fortune, after a long quibbling in heaven by the god Priapus to prove that 'hatchet' means penis. All the neighboring bumpkins then pretend to lose their hatchets too, calling upon Jupiter, who loses patience and sends Mercury to cut off their heads.*

If this is not intended as a parable of, or reference to fools' self-castration, then the whole purpose of the hero's name, and the intervention of Priapus, is obscure. It is certainly at least the symbolic level of the story, as also of Aesop's fable about: *The fox who loses his tail and tries to get all the other foxes to cut off their tails too.* (Type 64.) For so obvious and ancient a trick it is astonishing that this still works, century after century. It is nowadays, for example, the whole basis of the peddling of *styles and fads*, clothing, automobiles, etc., as well as the sub-structure of the cynical new American motto, already noted: *"If you can't lick 'em, join 'em!"* Thus: *If they've lost their pricks, cut off yours too.* (Compare "Tale of a Dog" in 13.II.2.)

The cruellest of the Italian *novellieri*, Matteo Bandello, has at least two stories in his *Novelle* (1554) on imbecilic or self-castration, without even the excuse of being revenges in the Arab style. In Book III, No. 3, *An ignorant bride castrates her newlywed husband when* jokingly *told to do so.* (This story will be referred to again, just below.) While at No. 61, *A nun tells a friar to get rid of his 'offending member,' which he does.* Told as a fool-story, of the type in which 'The remedy is worse than the disease' (Motifs J2100–2119, with some fabulous examples), Poggio's No. 223/4 has: *A jealous husband who castrates himself so that, if his wife becomes pregnant, he will know positively that she has been unfaithful to him!* (Rotunda H492.3.) More unsterilized – still in the style of a 'practical joke' or self-castratory disguise, in La Sale's *Cent Nouvelles Nouvelles*, No. 13, "Le Clerc châtré," *The paramour pretends to be castrated, in order to gain the husband's confidence and be allowed close to the wife.* (This is plagiarized in Malespini's *Dugento Novelle*, 1609, I. 5.) In an African Negro tale, "The Sister with a Penis," in Leo Frobenius' *Black Decameron* (ed. New York, 1971, as *African Nights*, p. 234–9): *The disguised lover tells the suspicious husband, "No, I cannot do anything with this penis, for it never grows strong."*

La Sale describes the clerk's ruse as follows: 'trop asseurément il tira son membre et luy fist monstre de la peau où les couilles [testicles] se logent, lesquelz il avoit par industrie fait monter en hault vers son petit ventre, et si bien les avoit cachiez qu'il sembloit qu'il n'en eust nulz.' The most recent English translation of this primordial folktale source summarily renders the total preceding passage thus, in half as many words and details: 'the clerk boldly exposed himself and by a trick which had caused him much effort, proved he was less than a man.' (Rossell Hope Robbins tr. *The Hundred Tales*, New York, 1960, "The Eunuch Clerk," p. 50. How does Dr. Robbins know this trick had 'caused' – i.e. cost – him much effort? And is this really translation?) This joke is still circulating in almost the original form, but now nobody believes it is true. In the end situation: *The husband (father) screams at the travelling salesman, "I thought you said your peter was shot off in the war!" "Sure it was," says the salesman, climbing defensively out of the wife's (daughter's) bed; "but it left a nine-inch stub!"* (*World's Dirtiest Jokes*, 1969, p. 103.) Actually belongs under "Overcompensation," section 13.VI, following. 'Nine inches' is classic for a large penis, among whites.

A common explanation for self-castratory fantasies, and even for symbolized and partial attempts, is self-punishment for the birth of unwanted children. Jokes on this theme usually have the victim a Negro or Italian laborer, who is being threatened by the 'relief investigator.' In real life it can be anyone: your father or mine. Dr. Arthur Janov's unorthodox study of neurosis, *The Primal Scream* (1970, ed. London, 1973) p. 406, Appendix A–Thursday, has a young patient, Tom, who tells-it-like-it-is:

> Then I told Art how Mom and Dad didn't want me to be born and how Dad said he wanted to slam the window on his cock and cut it off when he found out Mom was pregnant with me. Then I said, "Dad, you know what I really want? ... I'd want you to really want Mom, really put it to her and want me, too. 'Cause that's where I am, Dad: I'm more than just me. I'm life! And ya gotta want it, Dad, ya gotta want it!"

Even without the falling-window guillotine (on the style of Sterne's *Tristram Shandy*, 1767), more fathers than one would imagine nowadays respond to the birth of their third or fourth child – sometimes even their first! – by rushing to the doctor for the implicit self-castration of sterilization. Or send their wives. Panic-stricken egoism, or self-punishment? Hard to say. But it is certain that *all* children react to this eventual knowledge exactly as does Tom in the quotation above, though not all of them can express it so well. It should be mentioned that Dr. Janov's 'primal scream' therapy also *enlarges the breast size* of one third of his flat-chested female patients (chap. 12, "The Post-Primal Patient," p. 154), and I would not be surprised if it enlarges the male patients' penises as well. (That's one penis per patient.) As to physical improvements in psycho-therapy, in my friend Capt. Gregory Gulliver's secret 'snore therapy,' all patients grow completely new breasts (or penises) in their armpits, for a slight extra charge. *Two* penises per patient.

The trivial and absurd reasons given for castration, here and throughout, seem intended to make the whole idea less fearful by making it ridiculous. Castration can be denied at the very moment of its accomplishment, by mixing it with nonsense, as with the 'nine-inch stub.' This is essentially the meaning and purpose of *all* castration jokes. *"Did you hear about the Little Moron who cut his prick off because it got in his way when he made love?"* (N.Y. 1945. No answer is expected to formula questions like this.) In a more recent revision, presumably in response to the sexual liberation of women, the sex of the hero is reversed, and the moronism dropped: *Two actresses are squabbling onstage. One says to the other snottily, "No, I may not get as much money as you do, but at least I still have my virginity." The other, screaming: "Well, whaddya know! Doesn't it get in your way when you* SCREW*?!"* (L.A. 1968.)

A man goes to the doctor, saying that his penis has fallen off. He takes a wrapped-up object out of his pocket. It is a cigar. "My God, I must have smoked it!" (N.Y. 1951.) – *A Jew becomes impotent, so he cuts off his penis and buries it 'because it is part of a Jew.' The Angel of the Graves flies down to the new-made grave and says, "Rise up, Jew, and give an account of yourself." Long silence. Then a tiny voice answers: "If I could rise up, would I be here in the* first *place?"* (N.Y. 1946. Evidently a real Jewish joke, but told in English.) A similar parody, of the Christian idea of resurrection, involving an impotent penis treated like a corpse, occurs in the *Arabian Nights* (Burton's Supplemental Night 425). The phrase 'resurrection of the flesh,' meaning erection, is also a running joke in Boccaccio's "Putting the Devil in Hell" story (Day III.10.) The speaking-penis, or *mentula loquens* theme is well known in folklore: it is Thompson's Motif D1610.6.2 (not indexed under 'penis', 'member,' or 'genitals').

On the identification of impotence or castration as equivalent to death, see the Egyptian depictions of the dead Osiris with an erection, and the celebration of All Souls' Day in Mexico (November 2nd, "The Day of the Dead" in Catholic countries, when the graves of relatives are visited) by means of a little phallic 'King Tut' in a coffin. This is displayed to women in the street, with a rubber-band activating a pretended erection. This appears to be a survival of a phallic procession of some kind, similar to those – with the same pranks – still reported in Japan. (See Friedrich S. Krauss & Tamio Satow, *Das Geschlechtsleben des Japanischen Volkes*, 1931, 2 volumes, the final publication in the Anthropophytéia "Beiwerke" series.) Of particular relevance here is the quotation from Dr. Henry Alden Bunker's "The Voice as (Female) Phallus," in *Psychoanalytic Quarterly* (1934) III. 405, given in the earlier chapter on Children, 1.IV, "Masturbation," noting the unequivocal equating of death and castration in a patient who, '*seeing a young man stretched out naked on a table in the morgue, his instantaneous thought was, "I will never rise again".'*

Another speaking-penis story, also on castration, likewise makes obvious that the penis *speaks* when it has gained its autonomy, or separate existence, by being cut away from the man's body. '*A man, standing in the bathroom shaving in the nude, as was his custom* [!] *found his grip unsteadied by a bothersome hangover, and he dropped his straight-edge razor, amputating his penis, which fell to the floor. As he stooped to recover the razor* [!!] *the organ addressed him as follows: "I know we've had lots of fist-fights in our time, but I never thought you'd pull a knife on me!"* (D.C. 1952.) 'White men,' as differentiated from 'greasers' or Mexicans, never fight with the castratory *knife* and are often more frightened of it than of a gun. Though the castration in this story is stated to be the result of – and thus the punishment for – drunkenness, the punning allusion to the 'fist-fights' of masturbation in the punchline suggests that it is really for this that the classically threatened punishment of castration is thought to have occurred.

A much more complicated and neurotic tale of this kind – similar to the fantasy noted earlier as to the castrated penis floating away, held up by balloons, over the Golden Gate, and urinating on all its former owner's enemies – was told to me by a rich physician: '*A three-story apartment house one evening. It's hot weather, all the windows are open. On the top floor a man is shaving with a straight razor which he drops, cutting off the penix of another man pissing out the second-story window. The penix falls into the dish of the janitor who is eating his supper outside his door, and who turns and says to his wife in the kitchen, "Phwat's the big idea throwing the hotdog at me?"*' (Boston, 1946, stated to have been heard in Melrose, Mass., in about 1924. The final line is given in Irish brogue – that of the Boston working-class.) This is an adaptation, to the castration theme, of the food-dirtying stories (and the French song) about women masturbating with a carrot, etc., already given in chapter 12.IV.4, "Sexual Smörgåsbord." The curious three-story house frame also appears in an equally class-conscious European definition of '*A Liberal: someone who gets all the smoke from the basement and all the piss from upstairs.*' (Vienna, 1930's.) This is very close to the present story, suggesting that the man on the third floor who drops the razor is really the father-figure or God.

One of the most successful, and most frequently imitated cartoons ever published in an American 'men's magazine' during the exploratory period of the 1930's and '40's, before *Playboy* wholly bulldozed and kitschified the field, was by Charles Adams and showed a tall pine tree on a snowy slope, with two ski-tracks going downhill impossibly, one at each side. The castratory meaning of this little occult puzzle is spelled out in a re-drawing in *Sex to Sexty* (1966) 7:40, showing: *A male skier grimacing in pain as he collides, crotch-first, with a snowy pine tree, while his wife on skis beside him says angrily, "There goes our honeymoon!"* – Compare: '*Two boys were at the top of a long staircase, contemplating sliding down the bannister. "You go first," said Johnny. The other lad slid down the long winding bannister, and when he reached the bottom, Johnny called down, "How was it?" "Fine," came a feminine voice, "but look out for the nails".'* (Los Angeles, Calif. 1940.) This may derive from a weak limerick-sequence in *The Stag Party* (1888) p. 88 unnumbered, on: *A young man who 'Fixed the rail with a piece of barbed wiah' to catch his sister, Helen Maria, 'Who ever would sail, Down the bannister rail, When she thought there was nobody nigh her.'*

All of these openly imply castration or other bodily harm as a punishment for the sexual activity implied by sliding down the banister: a common form of the staircase symbol for intercourse, as is the flying-, floating-, or falling-dream. Skiing and ski-jumping draw most of their current popularity from this sexual symbolization, combined with the 'cold-fetishism' or snow-fetishism ("The Whore on the Snow-crust," an American Colonial 'bundling' poem), which serves as a repressive screen. Note the unequivocal statement of castratory danger purposely set up and sought for, in self-punishment or suicidal style, in the original Scandinavian form of the ski-competition, as described by Fletcher Pratt, "Are They Really Records?" in *Esquire* (May 1937) p. 103: '*The intending* [Norse or Icelandic] *jumper stood on the spot where he meant to take off, while a long spear was rammed into the ground, butt down and point level with the top of his head. If he cleared it, okay; if not, the spear rooted him in the tenderest portion of his anatomy.'* Surprising, isn't it, what the virile and athletic harem-dream of the 'men's magazines' really turns out to be on closer examination.

This sort of built-in punishment in male competitions is very ancient, as with the quintain or Turks-head, carrying a bat, which would strike the knight missing the turn-post in jousting. It survives (modified down wholly to rewards and no punishments, as with Santa Claus) in the 'brass ring' still to be seized on the better merry-go-rounds or carrousels, which – with circus parades and others – are the last survival of the ancient mounted processions and jousts. The punishments continue in the various skiing and jumping games, such as follow-the-leader and leap-frog, which are often set up frankly as ordeals for the younger athletes or smaller boys. For those who prefer simply to watch such ordeals, and to gloat over the death of the performers, there are of course car-races, circuses and fairs, with animal-tamers (the Roman circuses still not dead), high-wire dancers, and trapeze-performers offering an apparently satisfactory mortality rate: Note Willian Saroyan's *The Daring Young Man on the Flying Trapeze* (1934) p. 95–6: '*There was a fire hydrant in our street, and I had always wanted to hurdle it, but I had always been afraid to try. It was made of metal and I was made of flesh and blood and bone* [?], *and if I did not clear the fire hydrant, leaping swiftly, my flesh would smash against it ...*'

Self-castration is seldom perfectly frank, even in jokes, as that would hardly be a joke. There is nothing humorous, but only a terrible gravity and pre-psychotic sincerity about the *Gallus* priests of Cybele, castrating themselves and offering their genitals as an oblation to the Great Mother Goddess to whom they had emotionally assimilated and submitted themselves, as in the remarkable poetic record of the *Attis* of Catullus (1st century B.C.), most of whose love-lyrics are addressed masochistically to a woman whom he calls 'Lesbia.' (See further, on the legend and the underlying worship, H. Hepding's *Attis*, 1903, in German. The whole subject is, for obvious reasons, overlooked in Robert Briffault's othewise tremendously comprehensive but completely partisan *The Mothers*, 1927, in three volumes.) The survival of these self-castratory religious rituals in the modern Russian sect, the Skoptzi's, is discussed in extreme detail (bisexual) in Dr. Paul Tabori's *The Humor and Technology of Sex* (1969) p. 488–92, on the basis of Dr. Bernhard Stern-Szana's classic work on Czarist Russian sex-life. Tabori does not indicate whether the Skoptzi's are part of the *Humor* or of the *Technology* of his subject. He also seems unaware that the sect still survives in America in certain small towns in Kansas, among Russian immigrants. Also among a few hundred massively neurotic homosexuals in the general population, under the grandiloquent title of 'transsexualism,' as will be noted below.

The only story frankly on such a subject in modern times seems to be Ernest Hemingway's *God Rest You Merry, Gentlemen*, in which a boy castrates himself on Christmas day because of 'that awful lust' – a revised version of Christ's expiation for man's original (sexual) sin. As I have observed in *Love & Death*, p. 88, 'Considering our censorship, it is lucky for Christianity that the victim of the world's most famous literary lynch *was* crucified and not castrated.' In Philip Wylie's *Finnley Wren* (1934), an amount of village-atheist type of humor is attempted to be wrested from the fantasy of the difference it would have caused in modern church decoration if Christ had been impaled and not crucified: requiring impaling-poles on churches instead of crucifixes, etc. This evades the castratory statement, though rectal impalement as a Levantine method of execution (fantastically gloated on in Lawrence Schoonover's historical novel *The Burnished Blade*) is hardly more than a realization of the fantasy of pedicatory rape, always the sequel – sometimes unconsciously – of Oedipal fears of castration.

The joke has already been given, in the chapter on Adultery and its punishment, of: *The farmer who finds a traveling salesman making love to his wife, and knocks him out cold. When he comes to, he finds himself in the barn with his penis clamped in a bench-vice and the handle of the vice broken off. The farmer is sharpening a butcher-knife. "My god!" cries the salesman, "you're not going to cut it off!" "No," says the farmer, "you can do that ... I'm going to set the barn on fire!"* (*Sex to Sexty*, 1966, 7:32.) The situation here – which is the *Cent Nouvelles Nouvelles*, No. 85, "Le Curé cloué" – is quite similar to the 'true' anecdote given in Hector France's dictionary of French argot (1898) under '*Abélardiser*,' already quoted in the present chapter, 13.II.6, "The Doctor as Castrator," but the significant change is the cruel setting up of the story so that the victim is forced to castrate himself, like a trapped animal chewing off its own leg.

Another of these stories, again circulating on exactly the same theme of forced self-castration, and again with the absurd moralistic concern as to the responsibility for the act being made somehow to fall upon the victim, is printed in *The*

World's Dirtiest Jokes (Los Angeles, 1969) p. 108, a collection largely based on materials sent in to *Sex to Sexty* magazine, and by the same editors. This time: *The cuckolded husband ties a large rock to the sleeping adulterer's penis with a long chord, and lays the rock on the sleeping man's chest. The weight causes him to wake; he picks up the rock, 'and being careful not to awaken his bedpartner* [the wife], *tiptoed to the window and tossed it out. Immediately a voice from the closet* [the brave husband] *cried, "You have just two seconds to cut that line!"* ' The tone is not only heavily homosexual here, in the almost total sadistic concern with the 'other man's' body and genitals, and minimal concern with the wife, but is also very much in the style of the animal-sadistic animated cartoons of Walt Disney and other (and even more sadistic) American animated-movie cartoonists, who often have cliffside or ship-board scenes just like this, with anvils, anchors, rock, rope, and all – though never of course tied to the penis. Just *good clean sadism*, with the rope tied to the (animal) victim's neck.

A college fraternity initiation of this kind also exists, again forcing the responsibility on the victim: *The freshman initiate is stripped naked, and blindfolded, a heavy weight being tied to his penis by the upper-classmen. He is then told he must throw the weight out the window "to prove he is a man;" otherwise he does not have the 'guts'* [courage] *to be a member of the fraternity. Unknown to him, the cord has been cut.* (Texas Agricultural & Mechanical College, 1948.) How it proves your 'manhood' to lose your penis is never stated. Also, that it does not prove the courage but the *moral cowardice* of the initiate who goes through the wholly submissive but imagined heroic gesture of throwing the weight out the window, and his penis along with it – 'and then faints' – is never realized.

Though not on self-castration, the following joke uses the same throwing gesture as its crucial point; and the similarity altogether to being hanged (or crucified, as in *Cent Nouvelles Nouvelles*, No. 85, "Le Curé cloué," or The Nailed Priest, given above) is hard to miss. It was told to a young woman researcher gathering in-residence material for the boilingly angry anthropological study of the American culture, Dr. Jules Henry's *Culture Against Man* (New York: Random House, 1963) p. 232–3. The 'Lila' referred to was a fourteen-year-old highschool freshman girl, and 'Mr. Greene' is her father. The family is at dinner:

Mr. Greene tells mildly risqué jokes he had recently heard, while Lila hangs on every word, studying me to see when I laugh. Bill [the brother] eats in silence, showing little interest in the conversation ... [*At the second dinner:*] There is little conversation going on during the meal, but Lila tells me a joke after her father leaves the table. The joke is as follows : *This little Mexican swam over to the United States and when he got there the first person he saw was a giant Texan. So he said to the Texan, "Gee, señor, you are so big; you must have a very big penis." The Texan agrees and the little Mexican asks if he can see it. The Texan shows him, and the Mexican says, "Gee, señor, you must have very big balls." The Texan says yes, and the little Mexican asks if he can feel them, so the Texan says yes, and the little Mexican stands on a chair to reach up. Then he says, "All right, señor, hand over your money or I jump."* Lila thinks this is the perfect robbery.

(Another version of this, without Mexicans or Texans, has been given earlier, discussing its obvious homosexual tone.) Note again the throwing of the responsibility for the threatened castration on the victim.

As usual, the easiest evasion of responsibility is 'nonsense' or drunkenness, or some similar folk statement of the *unconscious* nature of the motivation, which is the essence of Freud's discovery too. Self-castration, or something close, can thus be achieved under the disguise of ignorance, so that no one at all is responsible, not even the victim commanding the act. *'Two drunks at a bar retired to the toilet to piss, and one of them forgot to close up his zipper afterwards. As they sat down again at the bar, one said, "You know, there was a snake on that stool when you sat down." "There was?" said the other. "Yeah, a great snake on your stool. I can see the head there now. I'll kill it,"* he added, *taking up a bottle and whamming it down. The other drunk winced and said, "Hit it again, man; it just bit me!"* (Berkeley, Calif. 1942, told by a woman at a joke-session with men.) In another version of the joke, the snake's first bite is stated to be the teeth of the man's zipper (*vagina dentata*) catching in his penis as he zips up his fly. Vance Randolph's MS., No. 34, "Snake on the Bridge," gives a form recollected from Arkansas about 1898, in which the last line (in all versions) is said to have become a catch-phrase. A British version

(London, 1954) sets the scene at a '*Regimental dinner, all drunk, Colonel at table, fuddled, speechifying, his cock out on the table.*' Same punchline, with the Colonel speaking.

There is perhaps some relationship here to the modern ballad, "The Crab-Fish" (originally a French or Levantine folk-tale, in Béroalde de Verville's *Le Moyen de Parvenir* by 1610), in which: *The wife gets out of bed and unknowingly sits on a chamber-pot in which the husband has placed a live crab or cray-fish overnight. When it feels the hot piss, it seizes her by the cunt with its claw. She screams, and her husband tries to free her. The crab seizes the husband by the nose with its other claw. They waltz about screaming, and the children (who are singing the song) must 'hitch up the cart, To go and fetch the doctor, to pry your mother's cunt and your father's nose apart.'* (U.S. 1920's.) In some forms of the song, *The husband chases the crab-fish all around the room, striking at it with a broom. 'He hit it on the head, he hit it on the side, He hit it on the bollicks, and the pore old bastard died!'* This all very much overdetermines the identification of the wife's genitals as *vagina dentata*, though the elaborate intermediacy of the 'crab-fish' in the chamberpot (which is really going all around Robin Hood's barn to set up one's symbol), with the father's nose as penis of course. The allusion to cunnilinctus, as overseen by the children, is also clear. The song may even be a rationalizing of this overseen act, but it does not seem to be the real point, and is not present in the earlier joke-versions now existing in English. (See further, on English song texts as "The Sea Crabb," back to 1640, *The Horn Book*, p. 413–14.) The text in Peter Kennedy's *Folksongs of Britain* (1975) No. 196, expurgates all this out; but see his notes, p. 476.

In another joke of a rather similar kind: *A drunk in a toilet is weeping and moaning, "I've got the clap, I've got syph, oh my god, I don't know what I've got! Oh, my prick!"* (*The bartender rushes in and the drunk says, "My god! everytime I try to flush the toilet it nearly pulls my balls off!"*) "*You idiot!*" *says the bartender, "get up off that mop bucket and take your foot off the wringer-pedal.*" (N.Y. 1946; parenthetical variant, L.A. 1968.) This derives from the anti-breast jokes and cartoons already noted in chapter 12.IV.3, "Anti-Breast Fetishism," on the style of the folk-phrase, "*Ain't seen so much excitement around here since Maw got her tits caught in the clothes-wringer.*" (Earlier and more graphic: "*in the mangle!*")

Self-punishment is sometimes projected on others, in whole or in participation, as in Samson's bringing down the three thousand Philistines with him in his death. (*Judges*, xvi. 21–30.) This is essentially a classic trickster tale. Alexandre Dumas sets this up again as the heroic death of the similar 'strong man' or 'hard man,' Porthos, in the sequel to *The Three Musketeers*, toward the end of *The Vicomte de Bragelonne* (1850), which is the most striking passage in this very long book. The modern joke or tale of similar import is hardly an echo of the Samson legend: *A Jew in heaven is told that whatever he asks for, Hitler will get double. He asks that one of his testicles be removed.* (N.Y. 1936. Aarne Type 1331, Motif J2074, in which the organ to be lost is an *eye*. In polite versions of the Hitler joke, 'lungs' are substituted. Compare also the reversal of the trick at Type 1610, Motif K187, of *a shared beating*, with full references to everything but the castration theme.) There seems to be a reference to the Hitler joke, or something close to it, in the British army song of World War II, "Bollocks! And the same to you!" (to the tune "Colonel Bogey") used as the soundtrack opening of the war-movie, *The Bridge on the River Kwai*, with the captive soldiers WHISTLING the tune by way of expurgation. In one verse, the one everyone remembers, we learn that *'Hitler! has only one ball; and Goeballs, has* NO *balls – at all!'*

A wrestler is explaining how he lost the match, when caught in his opponent's famous "Greek Pretzel Twist." Just when he was about to give up, he says, "I saw a pair of dirty red balls hanging in front of my eyes." "Why didn't you bite *them?" asks his manager savagely. "I did," says the wrestler. "That's when you saw me fly up in the air. They were mine."* (2:79. Text-form from an army sergeant, D.C. 1943.) It should be observed again that the whole theory or soundtrack of Japanese *jiu-jitsu*, now enormously popular in the West (under various more snobbish and more lethal Japanese forms such as *judo*, *karate*, and *aikido*) even though the Atom Bomb has demonstrated – particularly to the Japanese – that private violence is useless and minute, involves a pretense of weakness in oneself, and a 'turning of the opponent's strength against him' in a way strongly suggesting fantasies of self-castration projected upon others.

Every day I see printed signs in store-windows near my home, reminiscent of the German Occupation recruiting posters here in France in the 1940's for volunteer 'élite' troops in the

Nazi army. (Incredible as it may seem, Hitler's last bunker was found to be guarded, when the Russian tanks blasted their way into Berlin at the end of World War II, by *French volunteer troops* of the 'Charlemagne Brigade'). But this time announcing:'*Give Us Your Sons! We Will Teach Them* J#U#D#O, *and Give You Back* – M E N ! ! !' Actually, no worse 'physical training' for boys could be imagined than the paranoid and sadistic hostilities of *judo* and the *karate* 'killer tactics' that are the postgraduate course. These hostilities are still, however, precisely those fostered and rewarded by parents, athletic coaches, and others entrusted with the education of children, precisely to the degree that the normal sexual lives and experimentations of the same children (both boys and girls) are still crippled and repressed wherever possible, on one pretext or another. Including, of course, the one – which goes back to Samson & Delilah, to be sure – that: '*A fighter who goes around with girls weakens his strength.*' Think about this the next time you are asked to applaud ten-year-old boys in mock-Japanese canvas coolie-jackets rolling hatefully with each other on the floor, or five-year-old kids in droopy shorts belaboring each other about the face with enormous boxing-gloves until their noses bleed, while hundreds of parents present, including their own, scream with identification and delight, "*Oh, it's so* CUTE!"

Symbolic and partial self-castrations open out too large a field for discussion here. See, for the most outstanding materials, Theodor Reik's *Ritual: Psychoanalytic Studies* (1931), and Bruno Bettelheim's *Symbolic Wounds: Puberty Rites and the Envious Male* (1962). The whole subject of self-punishment and 'accident-proneness' has also been importantly mapped by Otto Fenichel in "The Clinical Aspect of the Need for Punishment," in *International Journal of Psycho-analysis* (1928) vol. IX, and in his *Psychoanalytic Theory of Neurosis* (1945) p. 496–502, in an enormously valuable brief statement on guilt, sacrifice, and 'unconsciously arranged accidents' and suffering. The whole literature of psychosomatic medicine is, at the deepest level, about nothing else. See, in particular, H. Flanders Dunbar's *Emotions and Bodily Changes* (2nd ed. 1938), and Edward Weiss & O. Spurgeon English, *Psychosomatic Medicine* (Philadelphia, 1943). The important group of "Life Games" and "Underworld Games" in Dr. Eric Berne's *Games People Play* (1964) are also largely of this type, particularly the 'games' of "Alcoholic" and "Indigence," pp. 73–81, and 147–51 – the latter known popularly as "Getting on Relief and Fuckingwell Staying There" (or GORFST) – which are the most widespread and socially danger-ous in the West at present. *'Pat had lost a finger in an electric saw mill. To the inspector, who was down inquiring into the causes of the accident on behalf of the insurance company, Pat offered, "I'll show ye how it happened;" then, "Bejabbers! there goes another one!"'* (Kimbo, *Tropical Tales*, 1925, p. 9.) No mis-take about that one. Self-inflicted wartime accidents and malingering are similar partial and symbolic self-castrations, in-tended to avoid the total 'castration' of death by means of the partial self-sacrifice. The following scatophagous anecdote – it is hardly a joke – is printed in *The Stag Party* (Boston? 1888) p. 80 unnumbered, a volume presumably of bawdy humor:

> John's pretty little wife had several times said that "the next time she mussed [*sic*] her fingers in the baby's diaper, she would just cut her fingers off." Of course we know how much she meant by her sputtering (and so did John), and so one morning, when the same thing happened and she shot off the same remarks, John said: "Well, Mary, just lay 'em on this block and I'll cut 'em off for you." So, Mary laid her hand on the block, and looking up in his face, with a saucy laugh, said: "Cut 'em off, cut 'em off." John made a great feint of swinging the axe over his shoulder, and then turn-ing the head of the axe down, bumped the little fingers just enough to make a small sized hurt. Mary squealed ouch, and clapped the bruised fingers to her mouth. [*This is the total anecdote.*]

Almost the identical scene is described in the children's book, *Penrod* (1914) by Booth Tarkington, as between the three comedy Negro brothers: Herman, Sherman, and Vermin – howzat for humor? – except that the older brother (Sherman, I believe), does actually cut off Vermin's finger. Or it may be the other way around. In any case, Negro comic stereotype kids are expendable, fingers and all.

At the height of the *novelle* craze in Italy, in the mid-16th century, almost the whole current float of European and avail-able Levantine folktales and jokes was turned into rhymed or unrhymed short stories or 'novels,' an inexhaustible folktale source or record fortunately keyed almost completely in Dr. Dominic Peter Rotunda's *Motif-Index of the Italian Novella in Prose* (Indiana University, 1942). The cruellest of the *novellieri*,

Matteo Bandello, a Dominican monk later Bishop of Agen, was practically a specialist in stories of barbaric revenges and mutilations, and naturally gave full treatment to castration and self-castration themes. In his *Novelle* (1554) Bk. III No. 3, he has the contrapositive, or perhaps the unexpurgated original, of the little domestic Togetherness scene just above, with the chopping block and axe: *An ignorant bride castrates her newlywed husband when* jokingly *told to do so.* (That is all there is to the story: I omit the airs & graces of style, verbiage and dialogue. Salt & pepper your version however you please. That's what all the other *novellieri* do.) Mention has already been made of John Canaday's murder-mystery in the 1940's, *The Smell of Money*, 'by Matthew Head,' in which: *A homosexual husband cuts off his wife's hands at the wrists, for her crimes, and leaves her to bleed to death on a pink rug.* This seems to pick up the story where *The Stag Party* left off.

One very far-out form of symbolic self-castration that it would not be right to pass by in silence is *castration as a publicity gag*, as when the irrepressible magazine editor, Ralph Ginzburg, the lonesomest orphan of the New Freedom, published the account of his term in the penitentiary for non-existent obscenity in his beautiful magazine *Eros*, under the title, *"Castrated: My eight months in prison,"* in the *New York Times* magazine section (3 Dec. 1972) p. 38–9 ff., with his identification photo and number as illustration. Actually, they didn't do anything worse to him in prison than to make him file index-cards in the record office, a type of 'castration' that many people spend their whole lives at. As his chosen title also indicates, he never learned – in the joint, or out – that what he had been sent up for was not obscenity but 'bad taste.' What does the Supreme Court think today of the pages of advertisements, as in the *San Francisco Chronicle* (6 Nov. 1974) p. 62, mostly for hardcore porno films?

Self-castrations by women, even at the gross symbolic level of the preceding joke from *The Stag Party* about chopping off fingers, are the rule rather than the exception in folktales, though seldom frankly sexual except when referring to female circumcision (13.III.2, above). A record number of gentlemen reviewers of the First Series of the present work, for example Mr. Richard E. Buehler, in the *Journal of American Folklore* (1970) vol. 83: p. 88, bothered to complain about my having objected, in the chapter on "The Female Castration Complex:

Infibulation," 6.VI, page 385, to the use of 'the "hygienic" excuse of cancer prevention or treatment to propagandize for the ablation of the breasts and womb, that are essentially nothing but the castration of women.' This suggests that men still have no objection to such operations, on whatever excuse, so long as they uselessly rip up the bodies of women and not of men. Admit that it seems indeed extraordinary that eight different reviewers in three countries could find the same nine-line passage to quote and complain about – though not one of them indicates why it is so terribly wrong! – in an eight-hundred page book. Thought-transmission, no doubt.

Even so, the castrations of women condoned or commended by those broadminded gentlemen, are very mild indeed compared to the loathsome forms these take in folktales. And as to excuses – well! Aarne Type 706–B (Thompson's Motifs T327 ff. and Q451.1) is the jumping-off point for a worldwide series of tales, ranging from Africa through India to the Orient, and throughout Europe, in which, for example, '*Maiden sends to her lecherous lover (brother) her eyes (hands, breasts) which he has admired.*' (To be compared with "The Eaten Heart," chapter 8.VIII.10 above.) This is offered as a model of chastity in many of the older *exempla*. There is an entire monograph on it by Däumling, *Studie über den Typus des Mädchens ohne Hände* (München, 1912), and another on the *eye* subtype by A. Pallnera, "La Donzella que se saco los ojos," in *Revista de la biblioteca de Madrid* (1931) VIII. 117 ff. That a man whose name means *Tom Thumbkin* or thimble should write a monograph on such a theme is certainly a striking example of 'name fatality.' Perhaps some other German savant named *Haarmann* or *Klabusterbeeren* (or Spaniard named *Pendejo*) will favor us with another on the usage of shaving off women's or nuns' head-hair as a humiliation or sexual punishment. This is also a Jewish marriage ceremonial, to make brides 'unattractive to everyone except their husbands' (!) as the orthodox Hungarian Jews explain this symbolic circumcision of their women, and the '*sheitl*' or wig these women must then wear for the rest of their lives, renewing the shaving of their heads frequently. (Motif T327.7, Russian and Lithuanian.) The reason, dear Reader, why the book now before your eyes was written in English and not in Hungarian or Rumanian, is that *my* mother ran away from home, 'to America,' to avoid having her head shaved when she would marry.

Only of historical interest today, but perhaps worth preserving for the record, is the spate of "Christine" jokes – all actually puns – started by the outrageous foisting off on the American and British tabloid public of the self-created castrato, George Jorgensen, as a sort of synthetic woman or 'transsexual,' under the name of 'Christine,' in the winter of 1952/3, and others since. *The American government sues the Danish doctor who operated on Christine, for tampering with the U.S. males.* – "*Why does Christine go around with his* [n.b.] *hands in his pockets? To feel the difference.*" – *Christine's wedding night: The two undress and look at each other. Christine: "Are you kidding? Why, I cut off one bigger than that!*" The last of the "Christine" jokes: "*Did you hear about Christine going back to Denmark for another operation? Something came up.*" (Hope springs eternal . . .) All these: New York, 1953. A British late-starter: *Christine's autobiography: "From Knickers to Knackers in Twenty-four Hours, or Why Be a Cunt All Your Life?*" (London, 1953.) This requires a whole Anglo-American dictionary to explain, and is hardly worth it. '*knickers,*' British for women's panties; '*knackers,*' testicles; '*cunt,*' British slang (also French: *con*) for an utter fool, for etymological reasons not altogether understood.

The lesson of the "Christine" case was that, in the public consciousness or folk mind, a man without a penis *is a woman,* especially if some sort of hole be bored in him other than his anus, and his breasts be made to swell by means of hormones. From the male homosexual or castratory point of view, the uterus and ovaries – the actually functioning parts of a woman's specific femaleness – do not exist at all. According to Dr. I. B. Pauly, "Male Psychosexual Inversion Transsexualism," in *Archives of General Psychiatry* (Aug. 1965) p. 172 ff., there have been, over the twenty years preceding his date of publication, 'a total of 603 male transsexuals . . . reported, [as] compared with 162 females.' The 'females,' of course can only be sterilized and sewn up, as artificial penises of flesh cannot (yet) be constructed. This may explain why there are only one-quarter as many ex-female 'transsexuals' as ex-male. The whole thing is obviously nothing other than the Skoptzi operation and psychosis mentioned just above, but nowadays benefitting from hot-jazz publicity techniques in the cynical press, and among even more cynical 'psychiatric consultants' whooping it up for these castrations.

The various humorous pieces concerning *castrati* written in French about Shakespeare's time probably really concern homosexuals, also traditionally played for comedy in, for example, *Hamlet*, V.ii.80–200, as the Euphuistic fop, Osric, who brings the challenge from Laërtes. In the *Plaisantes Imaginations* (Paris, 1613) of the French mountebank comedian N. Deslauriers, known as 'Bruscambille,' there are two mocking paradoxes in favor of *castrati* and the joys of being one. Though this may really refer to physical castration, homosexuality is more likely the subject in two pamphlet facetiae of the same period, *L'Arrest contre les chastrés, trompeurs et affronteurs de filles, sans moyens à ce propos* (1619), and its mock reply, *Les Privilèges et fidelité des Chastrés* (copies in the great Leber Collection, Library of Rouen, France, which seems to lack a further rejoinder: *Le Remerciement des Servantes de Paris, fait à celui qui a donné l'Arrest contre les Chastrez*, 1622.)

It cannot be overlooked that, at just that period and slightly earlier, both the King of France, Henri III, and the King of England, James I (earlier King of Scotland as James VI) were riotously homosexual, and kept openly homosexual courts, nearly ruining both their countries financially through enormous presents of 'their weight in gold,' etc., given to their male favorites, in particular Carr and Buckingham. It seems probable that it is these court scandals that the paradoxes and pleasantries on *castrati* in France, and fops and Euphuists in England, were really aiming at. Rochester's erotic farce, *Sodom*, half a century later, is an open satire on the homosexual court of James I. In Rochester's lifetime the only important homosexual court of western Europe was that of Philippe of Orléans, brother of Louis XIV of France, who had cynically been given in marriage Henrietta, sister of Charles II of England, at the Restoration of the British throne. It is possible that this was the real occasion, if not the background, of Rochester's play. (Text in *Kryptádia*, vol. IX. Various critical editions are promised.)

British transvestist entertainers were common long before Shakespeare's time, when, as is well known, all the female parts in the public theatre – though not at the 'masques' at court – were played by boys. Male transvestism has been in recession during the last two centuries in the British theatre, except for certain perennials such as *Charley's Aunt* (played by a man, as in some of Labiche's farces in France). Male transvestists became all the rage again in England in the 1960's, at the vaudeville level. Reportedly true incident: *An English 'strip-teaseur' is asked his 'vital dimensions' (bust, waist, and hip measurements) on a television programme. He replies, with appropriate wriggles and gestures: "36–28–36 – and nine inches!"* (London, 1969. Something similar in *World's Dirtiest Jokes*, p. 31, at the same date, but with the reverse-English that the penis measurement is given as *"four inches – from the floor, that is ..."*) British newspaper publicity-gunk for these entertainers would stoop to such depths as photographing them kissing their wives & kiddies goodbye as they went off to 'work' – this, of course, to show that they were really *men*, and not castrated, under the costume – with the littlest child helping daddy on with 'her' wig! The early French surréalist play, Guillaume Apollinaire's *Mamelles de Tirésias* (1917) is in this line; and the sick-humor novel, *Zazie dans le Métro*, by Raymond Queneau (of the French Academy), as also the even sicker movie made from this in the 1960's, climaxes with a similar scene: the pre-pubescent heroine's brother is such an entertainer. In actual fact, most 'transsexuals' of recent castration or creation are openly homosexual transvestists who show off their hormonically enlarged breasts as stripteasers in nightclubs, though never their pubic scar or stump.

VI. OVERCOMPENSATION

There are any number of long-penis jokes. In many of them the castratory notion creeps back by concentrating on the inconvenience of too long a penis, with self-castration as the 'remedy.' *A man with an exceptionally long penis, asks a surgeon to cut off part of it, saying, "Cut it off, doc. Every time I get hiccups on the toilet, it siphons up all the water in the bowl."* (Berkeley, Calif. 1942.) Much more concentration is present on the medical danger, and this is assimilated in form to other stories concerning the *use* to be made of the removed penis (or foreskin): *After taking a penis-lengthening medicine, a man complains that his penis has grown so long it was 'in fact darn near dragging the floor. "Gosh, man," said the doctor, "I guess we'll have to operate and cut part of it off!" The man's wife spoke up and said, "Doc, can't you just stretch his* LEGS?" (*Sex to Sexty*, 1966, 9:19, as "Bitch Logic.") This is perhaps connected with, or the original of the remark often attributed to Lincoln – who was very tall, as is well known – that: *A man's* legs should be just long enough to reach from him to the ground. Much other humor similar, on 'low-slung' men or women 'having a case against the city: they built the sidewalks too close to their ass.' (N.Y. 1939.)

The same long-penis item, taken to extremes, as befitting its attribution to the Texas superman, but omitting all castratory reference: 'A chambermaid reported to the hotel manager that the toilet-seat had been all chewed up. The manager billed the Texan occupying the room $25 extra, and asked how it happened. He explained that his spurs had kept chipping away at it when his foot slipped. [I.e. while standing on the seat to shit.] "We sit on it," the manager explained. The Texan said, "I used to think you Yankees were sissies, but if you can sit on that thing with your do-hinger hanging down in that cold water, you're better men than I am".' (D.C. 1953, from an army chaplain.) Now go back to the joke at the beginning of this section.

I. THE THREE WISHES

A story very frequently collected actually has recourse to magic to explain the overcompensatory yet castratory situation; magic being simply folk-shorthand for the dream or wish – good or evil, as the case may be. Though not really believed in, of course, magic has none of the debilitating effect on the wish-fulfillment fantasy that the recourse or descent to non-sense must always inevitably have, since 'nonsense' actually derides the wish. A cowboy riding in the hills saves an Indian maiden who is being attacked by a grizzly bear. As his reward she promises him the magical fulfillment of any three wishes. "Well then," he says, laughing [n.b.], "I wish for Clark Gable's face, Jack Dempsey's body, and to be hung like my horse." When he gets back to the ranch he rushes to the bedroom and looks in the mirror. Sure enough, he is as handsome as Clark Gable and as muscular as Jack Dempsey. He rips open his pants with bated breath, and then looks away in desperate disappointment. "Christ!" he breathes, "I forgot I was riding Bess." (U.S. 1943. A Flemish version in Kryptádia, 1888, IV. 319, shows clearly its derivation from the Italian master-surgeon story in Vignale's La Cazzaria, 1530, given in section 13.VI.2, page 728 below.)

This is sometimes set up as: A fairy story, about a prince who gains a horse-sized penis when he is given three wishes by *a fairy. When the king hears about this, he goes out and finds the fairy and does her another service; then asks for the same reward, "To be hung like his horse." On the way back to the castle he suddenly realizes he was riding a mare. "So the king and the prince got married and lived happily ever after. – I* TOLD *you this was a fairy story!"* (Chelmsford, Essex, 1954.) This form has been heard in the U.S. at later dates, both with and without the 'catch' element of King and Prince, *i.e.* father-son incest, which is the deepest fantasy of homosexuality.

The magical story here, is of course nothing other than the folk-theme of the "Three Wishes Misused," though there does not on the face of it appear to be any 'misuse.' This is Thompson's Motif J2071, Type 750A–II, combined with Motif D1376, usually concerned with lengthening and shortening the standard penis-symbol of the *nose*. The famous *"Monkey's Paw"* story by W. W. Jacobs is the best-known non-folk example. Though probably derived from the folktale – doubtless *via* the Grimm brothers' 'Long-Nose' story earlier in the 19th century (Types 563 and 566, with tremendous references) – it touches importantly on the theme of disaster connected with the three wishes. I have noted in *The Horn Book,* p. 463, another form of the erotic 'Three Wishes' story, the "Night of al-Kader" from the *Arabian Nights,* given in *La Fleur lascive orientale* ('Oxford' [Bruxelles], 1882, a rare English translation being later privately issued [by Smithers in Sheffield] as by the "Erotika Biblion Society"). This is a collection of Near-Eastern and Oriental tales translated anonymously by J. A. Decourdemanche, who states that 'a story of this kind will also be found in the Babylonian Talmud, which would refer it at least to the 8th century of our era.' I have been unable to trace this Talmudic reference – which would in any case be much older than the 8th century A.D. – and would appreciate any information concerning it.

Were it possible to trace the tale, it would very likely be found to be much older even than the Talmud, as it is clearly of didactic intent, pointing to the moral – a main tenet of Oriental and Levantine fatalism and of the much more ancient Greek religious ethnic, which rejected the reclamatory prayers and sacrifices of the Judaeo-Christian religion later – that the gods know what is best for us, and that any attempt to force special gifts from them, as by prayer or magic, will inevitably upset the laws and balance of nature and bring disaster. In the

"Night of al-Kader (Predestination)," *The man's wife wishes that his body should be covered with pricks. He loses his own in wishing them all away, but gets it back with the final wish.* (Arabian Nights, No. 596; Elisséeff 126R, from the Syntipas-Sindbad group of Indian origin. Compare *Matthew*, vi. 27, on 'adding a cubit to one's stature.') This story is still current in North Africa, *Histoires Arabes* by 'Khati Cheghlou,' p. 139; and in a Negro version in the same compiler's *Les Meilleures Histoires Coloniales* (ca. 1935) p. 12, in which: *The wishes result from the breaking of three magical iguana eggs; Penis too big, then too small, then as it was.* A recent American version, without wife, interestingly assimilates this to the Faust legend, as well as that of Jesus being transported to the 'pinnacle of the temple' by Satan, in *Luke*, iv. 5–9: *Dr. Faustus wants to spend six days and nights between the legs of Helen of Troy. At a gesture by Mephistopheles, he finds himself flying through the air, and only then does he realize that he has been changed into a kotex pad!* (Arlington, Texas, 1965, also of 'Sinbad the Sailor and the Green Genie.') In Mark Twain's "Mammoth Cod Club" address (unpublished: in Cary's *Treasury*, 1910), we are also warned against unseemly phallic pretention.

The principal 'Three Wishes' story, still widely circulated throughout Europe and America, makes no reference whatsoever to castration, but can be assimilated only to the present group of stories. It can certainly not be considered a scatological story simply on the basis of its ludicrous dénouement. As can be seen, it is modeled directly – or *via* the W. W. Jacobs story – on a Greek myth, the two protagonists being none other than Philemon & Baucis, the old couple who gave hospitality unwittingly to Zeus and Hermes ('an angel unawares,' as in the story of Lot in Sodom: *Genesis*, xix), and who are therefore wonderfully rewarded. *An old man and woman do a favor for the Fairy Queen, who tells them they can have any three wishes they want. As they cannot imagine what to wish for, living in the woods as they do, they decide to go to the nearby town and look in all the store windows. After looking all day, and not being able to find anything worth wasting a precious wish on, just at evening they pass the five-and-ten-cent store, and the woman sees a rotary egg-beater in the window. "Oh, look at that!" she says, never having seen one before; "I wish I had something like that for beating eggs." And there it is in her hand. The man is furious. "You could have wished for millions!*" *he shouts at her;* "*millions, billions! You could even have wished for three more wishes. And instead you wished for that! I wish it were up the farthest corner of your ass!*" *And there it was. So they spent the last wish getting it out again, and lived happily ever after.* (Scranton, Pa. 1934.)

This story is of great popularity and very well known in America, though none of my British informants have ever come up with it. The mere reference to an egg-beater will often be considered a covert allusion to the story in America, and people will look up at you sharply to see if you intend it as a joke, or an insult ("*Stick it up your ass!*") But there is never any consciousness of the phallic meaning of the object in this very story, as shown first by the woman's wanting it as her superlative wish – and by the fact of her getting it being so infuriating to the man – and eventually, and most pointedly, in its use upon her in the standard pedicatory rape. As already noted, in the First Series, 6.V.4, page 381, under "Vaginal Size," I have a superb album of several hundred unpublished erotic drawings, entitled *Genesis* 1:27 ('*Male and female created he them*'), done by an unknown artist in America about 1944, which ends with an allusion to this joke as a woman's masturbatory dream, showing demons manipulating the egg-beater in her vagina in order to try to satisfy her sexually – thus giving her the last laugh on her husband.

Displaced backwards again: '*A nudist who was invited to a masquerade ball solved the problem by purloining his wife's egg beater and going as an outboard motor.*' (*Journal of the American Medical Association*, June 6, 1939, p. 34, "Tonics and Sedatives" joke-column; not making any reference to the original joke.) In what is perhaps a reduction of the 'Three Wishes' story: *A man hears an Inner Voice telling him to bet on the Double O, at the roulette table (or on horse number 8 at the races), and bets everything he has, against the advice of his wife whom he tells about his secret hunch. He wins, then wins again and again, by listening to the Inner Voice. The wife keeps begging him to stop* "*while he is ahead,*" *but he refuses to do so. She leaves in disgust. Finally he loses everything, of course, on a single spin of the wheel (or the last sulky-race at midnight), and the Inner Voice says,* "*Oh shit!*" *(Often the joke ends here.) He gets stinking drunk before going home, as he knows his wife will berate him. She is waiting up for him, and he slumps into a chair without undressing, unable to gather him-*

*self together to tell her what has happened. She searches frantic-
ally through his wallet, which is empty, and reaching into his
pants pocket she finds that he has an erection (from anxiety).
"Oh well," she says, "if that's all you've got left, come to
bed before you piss that away too!"* (Santa Monica, Calif. 1965.)

The punchline is evidently worth very little here, but it is an
interesting 'reply' or variant-topper to an earlier 'occult' version of the gambling story in which, at the end: *The man tells
his wife he has lost everything, and she asks, "Well, what are
you going to* DO?" *"What would you do?" he counters. "I'd cut
my throat!" she cries. He pulls open his coat-collar without a
word. His throat is cut.* (N.Y. 1948. The last line is pantomimed,
not spoken.) This is like certain 'revenant' or ghost-ballads, as
"The Phantom Lover."

Another wishing story might be noted before returning to
the 'Three Wishes' form: *'Dejected bloke, tired, without a
bean, leaning up against Thames embankment, gets into conversation with a lovely girl passing by, who invites him up to
her flat to cheer him up and have a drink. He eventually jumps
in bed with her, and she opens her arms and legs to receive
him, pushing him back slightly toward his side of the bed.
Rolls over on her violently, and finds himself in the Thames.'*
(Chelmsford Prison, Essex, 1951, from a prisoner.) From the
psychological viewpoint it is not of any importance, of course,
whether there is one wish or three. It is the *misuse* of the wish
or 'luck' – *i.e.* the pretext for the punishment – that is the real
nexus of all stories of this type.

The original 'Three Wishes' (Tale Type 750A-II) involves also
the "Transferred Wish," this being the original of the egg-beater
story. (Motif J2075, Grimm No. 87.) In polite form, the egg-
beater or sausage is made to stick to the wife's *nose*, or her
buttocks to the saddle of a horse. Rotunda, as Motif J2075.2,
leads back to what is probably the oldest form of all, in
Bédier's *Les Fabliaux*, pp. 212 and 471 ff., where: *The husband
kills the wife after her two foolish wishes, and uses the third
one to his own benefit.* This brings matters much closer to the
popular Low German folktale, *Von dem Fischer un syner Fru*,
of which the dialect text is most easily available in the Insel
Verlag pocket-edition of the 1920's, charmingly illustrated with
grotesques by Marcus Behmer, pointing up all the scatological
touches of the story so dear to the Germanic audience. This is
Aarne Type 555 (Grimm No. 19), giving extensive references

including a dissertation on the tale by M. Rommel (1935). It begins with *The fisherman and his wife living modestly together* 'in a pisspot' (politely: 'vinegar jug,' or 'rabbit-hutch,' or even a 'pig-pen' which is really not so much of an improvement, as expurgation), *where they also end up again at the end of the story, after the wife's unseemly ambition – wanting to be king, pope, and finally God – has* 'destroyed their luck.'

Here the phallicism ('male protest') of the woman's activity is no longer disguised, and is again the specific cause of their punishment. Further reference to the underlying taboo, in connection with wishes and overweening ambition, will be found at Thompson's Motif C773.1. That the woman is entirely to blame is of course standard in patriarchal folktales, as with Adam & Eve, Lot's wife, and Abraham's wife Sarah, who nearly spoils the divine gift of the child, in the original Philemon & Baucis story by *laughing* (*Genesis*, xviii. 12–15, but *cf.* also xvii. 17) when the three angels – the three 'Kings of the East' of the imitative Christ story – tell her that she will have a child after a lifetime of barrenness, though 'it had ceased to be with Sarah after the manner of women,' *i.e.* her menstruation. The standard attack on women as menstruous creatures has already been discussed in the First Series, 9.I.3, "Menstruation and Other Rejections." Compare also the nasty allegorical lampoon in verse, William J. Courthope's *Ludibriæ Lunæ* [Playthings of the Moon], or *The Wars of the Women and the Gods*, London, 1869 (copy: Ohio State Univ.), turning on women's 'servitude to the moon' that has made the number *thirteen* 'unlucky.' The modern feminist no-nonsense viewpoint on menstruation is expressed best in Germaine Greer's *The Female Eunuch* (1970) chapter 1.VI, "The Wicked Womb," with interesting historical materials in H. R. Hays' *The Dangerous Sex: The Myth of Feminine Evil* (London, 1966). The connected fear by men of the unreasonable *pica* or 'longings' of pregnant women reaches some kind of climax in the incredible scatophagous story, "*The Escoumerda*," chapter 15.V.2, below.

Another curious and very significant folktale of this group, which is not signalled or cross-referred by either Aarne or Thompson, is Type 832 (Motif Q553.5), "The Disappointed Fisher": *'The fisher, his wife, and his child always get three fishes. From greed they kill the child in order to have more fish for themselves. But they catch from then on only two fishes.'* Brief, but deep, the allusion here to child-sacrifice indicates what the real crime of the greedy couple was, as with the sacrifice by Abraham of Isaac ('the child of laughter' *Genesis*, xxi.6), who had been God's gift to the barren wife, Sarah. Compare also the killing of the 'Snow-child,' Snegurotchka, Aarne Type 1362 (with further references in Rotunda and Thompson, at J1532.1), the husband pretending that the child has 'melted in the sun.'

It should be observed that this is exactly the W. W. Jacobs three-wishes story, "*The Monkey's Paw*," which differs – as does the story of the cowboy's three wishes – from Aarne Type 555, "The Fisher and his Wife," and the egg-beater story, in that the wishes do not leave the foolish wishers where they were at the beginning, but *far worse off*, *i.e.* 'castrated.' In the Jacobs story: *The father's wish for money is achieved by the paying of the insurance at the sudden death of the son; the mother then bringing the son back to life with the second wish, and the father sending him irretrievably back to death with the third and last.* The continuous and main concern of all these stories, at greater or lesser levels of consciousness, from the folk-legend of the sacrifice of Isaac by Abraham – also of his other son Ishmael, at Sarah's demand, in *Genesis*, xxi. 9–21 – to the folk-joke of the cowboy and the fairy-godmother Indian maiden, is nothing other than the attempt by the son (Oedipus) to evade his castration, killing, blinding, crippling, etc., at the hands of the jealous father, by means of the mother's (magical) help, as in the game of chess. An attempt which invariably fails.

Animal references, as that of the cowboy's horse, are particularly common in overcompensatory stories involving castration. This is a trait of the most extreme primitiveness, being the essential idea in totemism – also in cannibalism – that the virile strength of the hunted or sacrificed animal, or eaten foe, enters into the body of the hunter, priest, or cannibal. *Noah makes all the male animals check their penises on boarding the Ark, to prevent overcrowding. The monkey tells his wife just before going ashore, "Tonight I'm going to give you the best time you ever had. I've swiped the elephant's ticket."* (1 : 120.) Like many of the jokes in *Anecdota Americana*, this seems to have been adapted from Raymond Geiger's *Histoires Juives* (Paris, 1923) No. 84. Kimbo's *Tropical Tales* (Nice, 1925) p. 77, gives a would-be topper: '*In the Ark, the elephant fell in love with the lady rat. In answer to Jumbo's pleadings the coy little thing replied, "I really couldn't; supposing I was to have a* baby!" "That's alright," trumpeted the elephant, "I'll borrow Noah's golf bag".' This is to be understood, of course, as meaning that the elephant (the victor over the lion, or 'king of the beasts' in African Negro stories) has stolen, or will steal, some part of the sexual equipment of the castrator-king Noah. It is interesting that in this story, of Jewish provenance, Noah should appear as the castrator of all creation – his sons included, of course! – but his special problem was Satan, Madame Noah's lover, whom he did not want to let on the Ark at all. See Dov Neumann's very valuable *Motif Index to the Talmudic-Midrashic Literature* (Indiana Univ. 1954). Only Adam and Solomon, both famous opponents of the Devil, have such a wealth of legend.

On the preliminary publication of the present chapter in skeletal form, in *Neurotica* (1951) No. 9: p. 49–64, most of the resulting correspondence was in connection with this story. Prof. Francis Lee Utley, of Ohio State University, who spent years on an unpublished analysis of the legends concerning Noah and his wife, kindly supplied the information (letter of 29 Jan. 1953) that: 'The joke about the checking of the animals' genitalia on the ark is quite old – it gets into North African Berber (Moslem) lore and into Lithuanian lore, probably through Jewish intermediaries.' Mr. R. W. Banner, of Orange, California (letter of 15 Feb. 1952) observed that a German version also exists: 'I like the version better, where *Noah checks the animals' testicles (to prevent overcrowding the Ark), and the Monkey says : "Ich hab dem Elephant die Bons geklaut!"* as it is biologically justified in that the Elephant is one of the few large mammals with non-protruding testicles (he never got them back!)' Mr. Banner stated later that he heard his version in German-speaking Switzerland about 1916.

The cryptorchidism of the elephant is a point seldom noted – yet how can one miss it? – though much interest is always displayed in the sexual life of the elephant, including a willingness to believe the most fanciful tales about it. I myself once (N.Y. 1948) heard several people being convinced – on the style of the joke in an earlier chapter on the lady-schoolteachers who can't get the cow to lay down on her back to accept the bull – that *Cow-elephants dig holes in which they can stand swaying back and forth at 'just the right height' for the bull-elephant's embraces, and that in stony soil, where they cannot dig holes, the female elephants lie on their backs 'with their feet up in the air like tree-trunks,*' at which point one of the listeners began to smell a rat.

The 'Voronoff operation,' at its height during the 1920's and '30's but now a dead letter – being perfectly worthless – was presumably intended to 'rejuvenate' elderly men by grafting or transplanting into their scrota the testicles of sexually potent monkeys. The real purpose of the operation seems to have been to castrate a lot of monkeys, an entertainment in which many more 'biologists' engage than explanations are offered. See, for example, the perfectly casual references to the 'acquiring' of castrated monkeys, for the ostensible purpose of studying their sexual (?) life, in Dr. G. Van T. Hamilton's article, "Homo-sexuals and their Mothers," reprinted from *Encyclopædia Sexualis* (New York, 1936) in my pamphlet *On the Cause of Homosexuality* (1950) p. 5. These monkeys NEVER appear in the observations made and were castrated only to serve as 'abnor-mal controls.'

Dr. Serge Voronoff himself is quoted, without any visible shame, in Dr. Alan F. Guttmacher's *Life in the Making*, p. 124, on what would be the ideal in his 'rejuvenation' operations: 'Because of his success in animal rejuvenation, Voronoff was led to perform the same operation in man ... He says that *the most desirable donor would certainly be a young man*, but since human testicles cannot be purchased at any price, he does the next best thing – uses testicles from chimpanzees and mon-keys.' (Italics supplied.) Why young men should 'ideally' be sacrificed to refurbishing the old in this way is not explained, any more than is the identical sacrifice in wartime of the young to the old (who sit under mountains with medals on their chests, and push Atom Bomb 'buttons' in safety). The Nazi 'ex-periments' during World War II, with the wholesale castration of Jews and Gypsies, suffered of course from no such embarrass-ment as did Dr. Voronoff, but with equally non-existent results.

The 'Voronoff operation' or attempted rejuvenation, being a tampering with nature, it is always assumed in the folk-refer-ences to it and jokes about it, to be doomed to the failure that, in fact, it had. During the great publicity given the 'heart-transplant' operations in the 1960's – the surgical triumph of the century – not a word has ever been said, nor joke cracked, about trying the Voronoff operation again. In jokes, however, its failure always consisted of over-success, as with most jocu-lar operations for impotence, or the use of aphrodisiacs. The same is true of the similar reference with the laws of nature, on the line of Prometheus' stealing fire from the gods, in Mrs. Shelley's *Frankenstein*, whose monster is still very much alive in the sub-literary *kitsch* of horror movies, etc. He appears five times in the single pamphlet, *Grim Hairy Tales* (1966) pp. 15, 30, 35, 42, and 46; and is shown in the first and third of these with the standard 'mad scientist' creating an enormously over-breasted female for his sexual delectation, by means of a complicated electrical 'influencing machine,' on the style of the movie, *The Bride of Frankenstein*.

Overlooking always, for the purposes of the joke, that animals' testicles grafted into a human male's scrotum cannot assist in impregnating a human female – the basic error underlying the ancient belief in animal-human monsters: that intercourse between biologically disparate groups can be fertile – the child of such intercourse is invariably a 'throwback,' as with the Minotaur. *The elderly millionaire marries his stenographer, and has a gorilla's balls grafted onto himself to make sure he will be potent and able to father an heir. When the baby is born he rushes to ask the doctor whether it is a boy or girl. "How the hell do I know?" says the doctor irritably, "the damn thing is still swinging from the chandelier by its tail."* (N.Y. 1946. Had already appeared in print in college-humor magazines, since the anti-Darwinist Scopes trial in 1925.)

Unable to wait for the facts to catch up with castratory fantasy, the Spanish journalist, Ramón Gómez de la Serna, in his *Ciné-ville* (French translation, Paris, 1928), a fake exposé of a purely mythical Hollywood of the sex-orgy period, includes a hilarious hoax, p. 177 ff., concerning 'gland stealers' in Los Angeles parks, for the supplying of human transplant-organs for rejuvenation operations on aging movie-stars. This was apparently hoked-up *de toutes pièces* from the hideous Anne Cooper Hewitt 'sterilized heiress' scandal, on which see further *The Limerick*, No. 1172–79, giving the folksong circulated on this female-castration story, and attributed to the Hollywood biographer, Gene Fowler.

As already noted in the First Series, 8.V.4, at pages 582–3, Aldous Huxley's *After Many a Summer Dies the Swan* (1939) gives a food-dirtying revision of this sort of legend, in describing his superannuated millionaire – a crude caricature of the newspaper publisher, William Randolph Hearst – as keeping a pond of quasi-immortal carp, and eating their mashed entrails to keep him living (read: *potent*) 'forever.' In the same way another aged millionaire, the late John D. Rockefeller, Sr., was accused in a satire appearing in a Communist magazine in the 1930's of having a full-breasted wetnurse, pressed into service, of course, from the healthy working-class! (Cimon of Athens and his daughter, Motif R81.) The point of all such stories is, invariably, that the attempted rejuvenation, or evasion of the castration of impotence or death, does not work and cannot work. As with the parallel legend of Faust, this is the sinful wish that, by being demanded, destroys the magical power of the Three Wishes. Balzac's *Peau de Chagrin*.

2. ERECTION TO RESURRECTION

There will be grouped here various jokes on overcompensations for castration or impotence, in most of which the classic castratory figure of the doctor or surgeon prominently appears. The title is taken from a story concerning: *Three insurance companies that are competing with each other for new policies. One advertises: "Complete Coverage from the Cradle to the Grave," and does no business at all. The second tries, "Hatched, Matched, or Dispatched: We Cover You from Womb to Tomb." Slightly better success. But the winner is the third with: "Let Us Insure You – from Erection to Resurrection!"* (N.Y. 1950, also London, 1953, variant.) A Texas science-fiction enthusiast assured me in 1955 that there were 'dozens' of current assonant and alliterative variations on the very old connective phrase 'womb to tomb,' but the list supplied seemed entirely factitious, possibly made up by himself. The phrase, 'womb to tomb,' is not traced in M. P. Tilley's great *Dictionary of the Proverbs in England* (University of Michigan, 1950) W726, any earlier than John Clarke's *Parœmiologia Anglo-latina*, in 1639, at 'Ab initio, ad finem,' but it is at least as old in English as the superb 16th-century threnody, "Chidiock Tichborne's Lament" (1586), rediscovered – as were so many wayside flowers – by Isaac D'Israeli, in his *Curiosities of Literature* (ed. London, 1849) II. 195, and reprinted in William S. Braithwate's *Book of Elizabethan Verse* (1908) pp. 549 and 756:

> *I sought for death, and found it in the womb ...*
> *I trod the ground, and knew it was my tomb;*
> *The glass is full, and yet my glass is run,*
> *And now I live, and now my life is done!*

Death as the great castration, and personified as the Great Castrator (with hour-glass and scythe, for mowing down the 'grass of man'), is an ancient symbol already discussed in section 13.IV, "Symbolic Castrations." The three Greek 'Fates,' or goddesses controlling human destiny, were artistically set up on the framework of three sisters, Clotho the Spinner, spinning the thread of life, Lachesis the Distributor of Lots, who determines its length, and Atropos the Inflexible, whose flower is the belladonna or deadly nightshade, and who cuts off the thread. ('*My thread is cut, and yet it is not spun*,' laments Chidiock Tichborne.) It is evident that the only one of these who is a meaningful or real figure is Atropos, Death, whose activity was immediately grasped as being a sort of cutting off.

The whole search for the 'Fountain of Youth,' as by Juan Ponce de León, who found death searching for it in Florida in 1521, and by Dr. Faustus, in the older German legend used by both Marlowe and Goethe, is essentially nothing but a search for sexual rejuvenation, or even more specifically an aphrodisiac potion. Goethe's Faust, selling his soul to the Devil for the 'strength of youth' to make love to the undying spirit of Helen of Troy, makes this perfectly clear. (In William Lindsay Gresham's *Nightmare Alley*, a 1940's novel of carnival life, the old millionaire wants the spirit of his childhood sweetheart brought back from the grave, à la Witch of Endor, *1 Samuel*, xxviii. 7–25, so that he may have intercourse with her ghost!)

Direct identification of the erection of the penis with occult resuscitation after death is not uncommon in folklore, as in Boccaccio's most famous story, *Decameron*, Day III, Tale 10, "Putting the Devil in Hell" (Rotunda K1363.1, with many other references to this story: also at K1631.1. See the study of the title-phrase itself by A. D'Ancona, in *Nouvelle inedite di Giovanni Sercambi*, Firenze: Libr. di Dante, 1886, p. 67, note to Nov. 5.) In the opposite sense too, the identification of impotence with death, in the inability of the man's penis to enter into erection, is even more common. This is overcompensated in the various macabre jokes on the super-potent penis that stays erect and active even after death (the superstition as to *hanged men*), cited in the First Series, 8.VIII.10, "The Eaten Heart." A story given in full just above, from Jewish sources, under "Self-castration," 13.V, suggests that these ideas have ancient religious backgrounds, though this is merely mocked in the joke, as in a similar story in the *Arabian Nights*. In the joke:

A Jew who finds himself impotent, cuts off his penis and buries it. The penis gives a droll reply to the Angel of the Graves, as to being unable to do as asked, when told to "stand up" and give an account of itself.

This has also been collected in a long and much more castratory theatrical form, taking some fifteen minutes in the telling, and set into a complicated frame-story in which: *A Jewish salesman is told by the office-boy that "The boss ain't in." He takes the boy aside and says, "Lemme tell you a story. A fellow in China got some kind of disease hanging around with the Chinkie girls. His* schmeckel *got all rotten and turned blue. All the doctors told him the same thing: 'Cut it off.' Finally he got to the biggest specialist in the world. Wouldn't even look at him. Just waved him away and said, 'Cut it off!' So he cut it off and buried it in a little grave. Down flies an angel and says 'Name and address, please?' No answer. The Archangel Gabriel comes and bangs on the grave, and says, 'Give an account of yourself!' No answer. Finally God Almighty comes and taps on the grave with one foot, and says: 'SPEAK!' So out comes this little squeaky voice (in imitation of the office-boy's adolescent voice): 'De boss ain't in!' So look, kid, don't be a* schmuck! *Lemme in to see the boss."* (London, 1956, from an American movie-director, of Russian-Jewish origin.) Nothing need be said to underline the delusions of grandeur here, even in disease and after death, by means of which the castratory fear – even the mere rejection by an office-boy – must be overcompensated.

The doctor as castrator has already been considered in section 13.II.6, above, where he invariably succeeds in castrating the unwilling patient. In the overcompensatory story the doctor is, instead, twitted and outwitted, the penis stump being still too long, too alive, too *hard* (alluding to impotence), and completely uncastratable. Note again that the more important sort of castration stories or non-joking folklore refer castration to the penis, not to the testicles. Freud observes that the infantile and adult male pride is specifically centered in the penis, as is also castration-anxiety of a deep kind. The knowledge that it is the testicles and not the penis that form the real seat of the virility comes much later, is merely intellectual and has little unconscious force. *A doctor excuses himself for being late to a banquet by saying that he had to amputate a man's penis. "Did you have to saw through the bone?" the hostess interrupts, whereupon everyone gets up and bows to her husband.* (1 : 275; also in *Grim Hairy Tales*, 1966, p. 38.) World War II variant: *The Duchess visiting the veteran's hospital asks the same question of a wounded soldier, who answers: "My compliments to the Duke."* (N.Y. 1948.) The joke has already been given, under "Self-Castration" above, in which: *The travelling salesman tells the farmer that his penis has been shot off in the war, and so is allowed to sleep with the wife or young daughter. When he is caught making love to her anyhow he explains that, yes, his penis was shot off in the war – "but it left a nine-inch stub!"* That is the perfect overcompensatory touch that all the jokes are tending toward, in refusing the castratory operation and restoring the organ – better than it was before!

A well-known Levantine tale group, also known in Ireland as "Finnegan's Wake" (Motif J2311) involves: *A foolish person who is made to believe he is dead, but who nevertheless speaks up or otherwise shows he is alive, at the wake, or on the way to the graveyard as he is being carried in his bier.* Though various scatological touches are sometimes added, such as: *The numskull who is told that he will die when his horse farts three times, and who lays down and considers himself dead when this happens* (Wesselski's *Nasr'Eddin*, No. 49, Motif J2311.1; and consider the opposite form, that of *the bird that chirps five times to assure five more years of life*, at J2285.1), references are seldom found in folktales indicating that the touch which *really* shows that the 'dead' man is still alive is that his penis can still erect, this being the true Resurrection of the Flesh, though perhaps not that promised for Judgment Day. (For examples see the First Series, 8.VIII.10.)

The World's Dirtiest Jokes (1969) p. 61 gives a little genre scene from current American life, worth recollecting, as many people are not aware of this whole area of rural and urban-peasant superstition: 'The elderly couple were listening in their farm home to the radio faith-healer, who was asking for donations and then saying, "All you people in Radioland, with God's help I want to heal you – put one hand on the radio and one hand on the part that needs healing, and get ready." The old lady put one hand on the radio and the other on her heart. The old man put one hand on the radio and the other on his tired old tool. When the old lady saw this she said, "No, Elmer – he said heal the sick, not raise the dead!"' This is an un-remembering allusion to the New Testament parable of the rich man in hell and the beggar Lazarus in heaven, in *Luke*, xvi, built

up into a complete resurrection story, in *John*, xi–xii, with
Lazarus raised from the dead and appearing at the dining-table
where Mary Magdalene wipes Jesus' feet with her hair.

Just as the penis is the portion of the cannibalized enemy
(*Ur-Vater?*) most essential to be eaten ritually, to transfer the
virile strength of the vanquished to the victor, just so the penis-
bone of the very few animals sporting these are considered
'good-luck charms' above all others. In Bavaria and Steiermark
the penis-bone of a badger (actually a stone-marten) is worn
as a watch-chain charm or fob. Also in America, at one time,
under the euphemism of 'bone toothpick,' which is the dried
baculum from the penis of a male raccoon, according to Vance
Randolph's *Who Blowed Up the Church House* (1952) pp. 135–
7, and 216; and especially his *"Unprintable" Ozark Folk-Beliefs*
(MS. 1954) No. 4. The two-foot long penis-bone of a narwhal
(the older 'unicorn's horn,' considered the greatest of all
aphrodisiacs?), humorously inscribed with *graffiti* by movie-
stars of both sexes, diplomats, prize-fighters, &c., is described
by explorer Horace McCracken in the magazine *For Men Only!*
(New York, Dec. 1937, p. 44–5), with mention of the same
attribute in badgers. Dr. Elie Metchnikoff's *The Nature of Man*
(transl. 1904), largely an erotization of castration-anxieties
connected with death, seriously discusses the 'loss' of the
penis-bone in human evolution, p. 81, among other "Dis-
harmonies of Reproduction," well worth the reading. It was
Metchnikoff who also popularized the eating of yoghurt in
France and America as a life-lengthening food, this being one of
the best sources of the whole vitamin B-complex.

Most good luck 'charms,' such as horseshoes, rabbits' paws or
tails are genital in reference, in this case to the female genitals.
(The same word, '*scut*,' refers to both the rabbit's tail and a
woman's pubic hair.) Architectural monuments and memorials,
similarly intended, are generally phallic rather than yonijic:
Cleopatra's 'Needle,' the Vendôme Column in Paris, San
Francisco's Coit Tower, and the Taj Mahal. See O. A. Wall's
Sex and Sex Worship (St. Louis, 1916), and Jean Boulet's
Symbolisme sexuel (Paris, 1960), as well as Georges Charrière's
*La Signification des représentations érotiques dans les arts
sauvages et préhistoriques* (Paris: Maisonneuve & Larose, 1970),
for an extensive presentation of pictorial evidence ranging from
obviously unconscious and symbolized to the graphic and pre-
cise, but still with symbolic intention. The aerial view or plan

of the Château Gaillard, in France, given in the *Encyclopædia Britannica*, 14th edition, is also something of an eye-opener in the way of purely yonijic design (as seen from the air: the way no one but the architect would ever see it); while one of the social-planning architects of the Napoleonic aftermath, Claude-Nicolas Ledoux, proposed a community brothel – on the plan of Restif de la Bretonne's *Le Pornographe* (1769–76) – to be in the shape of a penis & testicles, as can be seen in the published folio of his monumental plans. There is a visible *apotropaic* or evil-averting intention in all such symbolic monuments, specifically to deny impotence and defy death.

Aphrodisiacs in jokes are often plainly stated to be 'penis-lengthening' or at least 'strengthening' pills. Compare the ostentatious parading, as to their presumably aphrodisiacal power (always less effective than pussy-juice), of the hot sex-jab names given to commercial perfumes for women. Just as the perfumes ludicrously over-sell and over-promise, in deference to the carefully inculcated feelings of sexual inferiority in the women customers, just so the 'penis-lengthening pills' absurdly overreact. Partly as punishment for interfering with the immutable laws of nature and apportionments of destiny, and partly as overcompensation for the feelings of phallic inadequacy and consciousness of social castration on the part of the men, that makes them tell such jokes in the first place.

Many of the stories in the First Series, under the headings of "Phallic Brag" and "Anti-Brags," 5.V.1–2, also "Potency and Aphrodisiacs," 5.VI, pages 292–318, are relevant here, but they do not always express themselves as overcompensations, though that is certainly what they are. When the bragged-on penis is obviously too monstrously big for anyone conveniently to believe in, and is just a tall tale, overcompensations for feelings of inferiority – whether social or specifically sexual – are always the true meaning. Folk-proverb: *"The bigger the belt-buckle, the smaller the prick."* (San Diego, 1965, said contemptuously by a street prostitute, on watching a large automobile go by with a Texas license-plate, and long bull's horns attached to the radiator hood.) In this line I can recommend a passage in *The Memoirs of an Erotic Bookseller* (London: Skilton, 1969) by 'Armand Coppens,' attributed to Nick Schors, the main Amsterdam occulta-&-erotica dealer, in which, at an orgy, p. 83: *An elderly woman about to go into a professional belly-dance makes the unruffled request: "I only want to ask the gentlemen to show their appreciation, if any, in the old Russian style. When we danced during those suppers I was telling you about, the men always took out their penises and banged them on the table to indicate their approval. Any girl who failed to please, was squirted with soda-water or drenched in champagne."* I.e. was pissed upon symbolically, as she could not be with the then hardened penises of these Czarist Russian heroes. (Compare song: "The Foreskin Fusiliers.") Though not mentioned here, it was also (?) a custom to throw the stem-glasses into the fire-place and so smash them after every toast drunk, or at least after the last. If this was meant symbolically, and not just for noise and destruction, it can only mean *" – Tomorrow we die!"*

In certain overcompensatory jokes where the man's penis has been made excessively large, either by aphrodisiacs or an operation, the problem of concealing it becomes paramount. The man is usually described in such jokes as coming to consult the doctor, pharmacist, or costume-seller with the overlong penis wound around tightly under his coat, then unreeling it by the yard, or having the doctor &c. do this for him. *A man takes too many penis-lengthening pills and finally has to wrap his penis around his body six times and hide it under his coat, continuously pushing it down as he explains all this to the doctor, while the head of his penis keeps growing and tries to climb out the collar of his coat to throttle him as he talks. (All pantomimed.) The doctor pulls the man's coat open, and studies the matter carefully, then recommends that perhaps he can get a job posing for the cover of the New York telephone-book (showing Mercury as 'The Spirit of Communications,' with an armful of spaghetti-like trunk-lines).* (N.Y. 1950, told with a telephone-book nearby, which is handed to the listener at the end-line.) In another, perhaps older version: *A man comes home triumphantly and shows his wife his new and enormous penis, given him magically by the witch-doctor (or at the hospital, where it has been grafted on him from a dead Negro, or a horse!) "But where are your balls?" she asks. "My balls? Oh, they're outside in the wheelbarrow (or, in a Mack truck; or, They're coming tomorrow on the next train)."* (N.Y. 1953, all versions collected from a group of stage- and amateur-magicians in response to the first story above.)

In various other conclusions to the problems posed by the over-long penis, some of which are given in the First Series, 5.V.1, "Phallic Brag," as well as under "Anti-Brags," following immediately after, *The man is told to, "Put the tip out through your buttonhole and wear it as a blushing rose!"* or, when it is a question of a costume-party, *"Why don't you drape it over your arm and go as a filling station?"* (Berkeley, Calif. 1963.) In another version of this : *The man has a wooden leg, and refuses all the costume-seller's suggestions, of a pirate costume (can't wear the boots), cowboy chaparajos (how would he strap them on), and so forth, till finally he is told, "The best idea would be for you to roll yourself in strawberry jam, then stick your wooden leg up your ass, and go as a jelly-apple!"* Here the whole joke turns on the insufficiency, rather than oversufficiency, but the result is the same.

As to filling stations for gasoline, a fairly recent Martian item has : *The two Martians who land their flying saucer in an American town at midnight. Nearby is a filling station. One Martian goes over and says to the cigarette machine, "What's a lovely girl like you doing in a place like this?" The other says, "Don't bother with her, Xddrgssl; the men here have got us licked. Look at that one asleep over there with his prick in his ear!"* (Berkeley, Calif. 1963.) Is this overcompensation, or certainty of being beaten *by machines* in the phallic competition, on the part of the teller of the story? As when : *The aspirant to join the Long Pecker Club tells the girl at the desk that he expects they'll make him president of the club, since he has "Twelve inches soft, and sixteen inches stiff." "Oh yeah?" she says; "you see that guy over there with the bulge all the way down his pants-leg and the big lump in his sock? Well, he's the janitor."* (Santa Monica, Calif. 1965.)

The satisfying of the woman by means of the new penis is, of course, an essential point, since her lack of satisfaction is the touchstone of the man's feelings of impotence or inadequacy. As is well known, men in Western cultures take the blame themselves for the inability of certain women to reach orgasm, an error in which they are grievously maladvised by most 'marriage manuals' of sex technique. These manuals seldom realize, or refuse to admit, that the woman's frigidity – if it really exists, and does not succumb to reasonable amounts of clitoral excitation externally during intercourse (thus, *the dreamed-of 'long penis' is perfectly useless*) – is generally psychologically caused and is brought to the marriage by the wife, rather than being the result of the husband's 'selfishness.' The fantasied oversize penis nevertheless remains the standard cure, in jokes and humor at least, for the man's feelings of impotence and inadequacy (*i.e.* castration) resulting from the woman's failure or inability to achieve sexual satisfaction.

A man with a wooden leg conceals this fact from his bride till their wedding night; then silently puts the stump into her hand in the dark, explaining that this is the 'big surprise' he has been promising her. "Mmmm," she says, "that is *a big surprise, but get the vaseline and I'll see if I can take it,"* (2:29.) The pathetic certainty hidden here, that the ordinary penis cannot satisfy the ordinary woman, is similar to that of the joke, given in the earlier chapter on Animals, in which: *The lady giraffe allows the monkey to make love to her, but lets out an anguished sigh when a falling coconut hits her on the head. "Whasammatter, honey?" he asks, pumping eagerly, "Am I hurtin' ya?"* Or: *The monkey later tells his monkey pals how it felt. "It was all right," he says, "but between screwing her, and running up to kiss her every minute, I'm all worn out!"* (N.Y. 1938. *Russian Secret Tales*, No. 2.) Joke: *The pimp is explaining why he has ditched his best 'girl': "Every Sunday it was, "Kiss my titty, rub my clitty; oh honey, now kiss my other tit; now rub my button again; oh, Jacques!" – What the hell does she think I am, a one-man band?! Try to satisfy those crazy dames!"* (Paris, 1959, recited by the leading French erotica publisher, on handing me a copy, still wet with printer's ink, of his latest item, *Emmanuelle* [by Louis Rollet-Andrianne].) This poor fellow sounds like a refugee from a French marriage manual. Photographically: *'The Polish nymphomaniac whose bed talk was: "To the left, higher, left, lower, further to the left, just there; hold it, hold it, hold it – thank you!"'* (Paul Ableman, *The Mouth & Oral Sex*, London, 1969, p. 97; picked up in *Sex to Sexty*, 1974, No. 57: p. 39.)

As to the weekend exigencies of prostitutes – *"Never On Sunday"* really means *"On Sunday Only for L-O-V-E!"* – a female hippie about forty years old, with a complicated religious sound-track as her gig, and three miserable children she was dragging around the world with her, told me a long tale in early 1970 as to having been "a two-hundred-dollar-a-night call girl in Palm Beach and Las Vegas," until she had seen the light of her new occult and health-food religion the preceeding year. "So how come you don't have any money now?" I asked suspiciously, as I saw her getting ready to put the bite on me for a free-will offering. "Well," she said, with as regal an air as she could muster – the poor thing was as thin as a rake, and obviously suffering from *beri-beri* owing to her nut-cult all-rice diet – "*what I used to spend my money on was getting* MY *kicks on Saturdays from my boy-friend. You know,*" she added, licking her mouth suggestively with a rather unhealthy-looking tongue; "*it costs fifty dollars a time getting licked all over, from head to toe, by somebody that Knows Their Business.*"

Few stories ever state that an overcompensatory priapism or continuous erection is ever really a problem. A wedding-night story already given in 8.II.3, "The Man in the Upper Berth," supplies the usual castratory advice from an older type of castrator than the doctor who is standard in such jokes nowadays: *A parson on a train advises a young husband bothered with a continuous priapism to put it in a stream of cold air by holding it out the train window. He does so. Half an hour later the parson passes in the back aisle and sees the man still awake, straining his body against the window with his penis out. (Pantomimed.) "How's it getting on?" he asks. "Pretty well, I guess," says the man. "So far I've hooked two mail-bags and a porter's cap."* (London, 1954.) Not necessary to observe that the final line describes the penis itself in punning terms: the cap as *glans*, plus the two 'mail-bags.'

Stories of the type where a name is tattooed on the penis (anciently, over the wife's pubis) often overdetermine the matter of length, with purposeful ludicrousness, by the impossibly long word the tattooed name spreads out to become. Some such are given in the First Series, 5.V.1, "Phallic Brag," p. 297–8. The record (so far), heard in Paris, 1950, by an American soldier: *Two men at a urinal, one with the letters "S.E." tattooed on the upper side of his penis, who explains that when erect it spells out his girl-friend's name, Suzette. "By the way," he adds, "I notice you have 'S.E.' tattooed on yours too. Is your* petite-amie *by any chance named Suzette also?" "No, Monsieur," says the other man. "I don't bother with girls. When I have an erection it spells out the name of my club, 'Société des Cinquante Hommes des Chemins de Fer de la République Française!'"* Observe the gratuitous homosexual tone.

Operations on the genitals remain, naturally, the main anxiety-area, and some of the clearest overcompensatory stories circulate on this theme, from the 'cute-kids' type, through the ancient '*mal-mariée*' theme, to problems of old-age and impotence in men. *A little boy has to have his tonsils out under anesthetic, and the doctor asks, "While I'm at it, you want me to circumcise him too?"* [!!] *The parents agree. Next day at school the boy asks his teacher if she had her tonsils out. "Yes I have, Johnny,"* she says; *"why do you ask?" "It sure does make your little peter sore, don't it?"* (N.Y. 1963. Compare the homosexual joke on pedicatory rape and champagne; the latter is good but *"It sure makes your asshole sore the next day!"*) A beautiful overcompensation gag-line is given in *World's Dirtiest Jokes,* p. 161, in which: *A doctor about to circumcise a new-born baby gives him a few drops of whiskey to deaden the pain. Later, watching the baby nursing at the mother's breast, the father swells with pride. "He's a chip off the old block,"* he tells the nurse. *"Here he is, less than a day old, and already he's dead drunk, with a tit in his mouth and a sore peter!"*

Where it is a grown man who is to be operated on (or executed: death-as-castration), matters take the opposite turn: *A Negro is in the death-chamber. When the guards slit his pants leg, the head of his penis appears at the level of his ankle, and all the spectators begin to laugh. "Go ahead an' laugh, white folks,"* says the Negro bitterly. *'Iffen it wuz you gonna sit in that there 'lectric chair, yours'd be all shrunk up too!"* (N.Y. 1958.) Or the reverse: *A man being examined by the doctor for undescended testicles has so small a penis that the nurse begins to laugh. "What's funny about that?"* says the man indignantly; *"it's been swole up like that for days!"* (Bloomington, Indiana, 1963; also ending: *"Haven't you ever seen a man with an erection before?"*) In the unconscious mathematics of humor, IT IS NOT THE PLUS OR MINUS SIGN THAT COUNTS. It is the SUBJECT that makes the joke. The same goes for punchlines: unimportant.

The 'mal-mariée,' or girl dissatisfied with her new husband, appears mostly in songs, such as "No Balls At All," a parody of a popular Civil War poem, *Nothing to Wear* (1857) by a New York lawyer, William Allen Butler, satirizing excesses in women's clothes. (This had immediately excited a polite parody, as *Nothing To Say,* by 'Philander Doesticks,' *i.e.* Mortimer N. Thomson, who had parodied *Hiawatha* the year before.) *A girl complains to her mother on her wedding night that she does not want to go up to the bedroom because she has seen her husband changing his shirt, and "He has hair all over his arms and chest like a gorilla." "Now you just go upstairs,"* the mother orders; *"all men are like that." The girl comes back down several times complaining about other hypervirile characteristics of her groom, and her mother keeps sending her back upstairs. Finally the man takes off his shoes and socks and his bride learns for the first time that he has had half of one of his feet cut off in an accident. She runs screaming downstairs. "Mama!" she cries; "oh, no! I can't bear it!" "What's the matter now, for god's sake?" asks her mother. "Wilbur only has a foot and a half!" "All right, daughter," says the mother; "you stay downstairs this time, and I'LL go upstairs!"* (L.A. 1968.) The *stairs* themselves symbolize the intercourse of which the girl is really complaining.

A curious story not encountered except in *World's Dirtiest Jokes* (1969) p. 26, has: *A husband who is in an auto accident just before his wedding day, and must go off on the honeymoon with his penis bandaged between wooden splints. His bride undresses and shows him her breasts provocatively, saying, "Look, George, no other man's eyes ever gazed on these."* Not to be outdone, the husband displays his injury, and replies, "Look at this, still in the original crate!" This may or may not actually be in folk-transmission, but the situation appears in various Spanish and Italian *novelle* of the 16th century cited by Rotunda at Motif J1545.10 (expurgatorily omitted by Thompson, who jumps this number): *The one-eyed (or one-armed) bridegroom rebukes his bride for the loss of her virginity, saying, "You have not come to me complete." "Neither have you," she replies, referring to his missing eye. He: "My enemies did that to me!" She: "And my friends did this to me!"* These combinations of deficiencies are an ancient theme, though not quite in this openly sexual form, as for example Aesop's "Fox and Crane" (Types 60 and 76. Note that 'Aesop' and 'Homer' are legends, not real authors, and their works are collections.) Hokusai's great sketchbook, *Mangwa* (1836), similarly shows the traditional Japanese crippled or monstrous associates: *The long-legged man with short arms who holds the long-armed man with short legs on his head, so they can pick the fruit off a tree.* I have seen something close to this done by a circus-giant and midget in America, in 1932.

The following joke is also told with the complainant a woman. *A man who has lost his penis in an accident pays a famous surgeon fifty dollars, which is all he has, to make him a new one out of the flesh of his thigh.* [Compare *Genesis,* xxxii. 24–5, on the patriarch Jacob's crippled thigh.] *The surgeon takes the case as a charity gesture. When the bandages are finally taken off, the man looks at his new seven-inch penis and com-*

plains, "For all that money, doc, couldn't you have made it a little bigger?" (Idaho, 1920. Larson MS., No. 74.) This, in the form in which the woman complains, derives clearly from a much older Italian story, given in Antonio Vignale's *La Cazzaria, or The Book of the Prick* (about 1530), section entitled in translation, "Why It Is That Women Get Knocked Up." *The wife complains to the husband about the smallness of his penis, and to quiet her he finally tells her that he is going to a master-surgeon who has "grafted a nose on our friend, Lorenzo Gamurini, taking a piece of flesh from his arm." And he explains that he plans to have grafted onto his penis "the whole of that piece of white meat which you see there on our nag." The wife bursts into tears, in fear of the danger he will be running for her sake; but, when he insists, she says: "Dear heart, if you must take such a terrible risk as all that, have them graft on that black piece too; for even if it should be too much, we will find some place to stow it away."*

This, in turn, is similar to Poggio's *Facetiae* (MS. 1451) No. 43, concerning: *The young woman who complains that her husband's penis is too short, because their jackass, "which is naught but a beast, has one as long as that (stretching out her arm); while my husband, who is a man and not a beast, hasn't even half that much!"* Vignale gives this story too, preceding that on the miraculous grafting, which is intended as a 'topper.' His version is not the same as Poggio's, and the man's superiority is expected by the wife not because he is a man and not a beast, but *"because he is twenty years old and the animal is only two."* (*Cent Nouvelles Nouvelles*, 1460, No. 80. Motif J1919.8.) Many minds have evidently worked on this story for centuries.

The miraculous 16th-century Italian surgeon, who "grafted a nose on ... Lorenzo Gamurini," has of course been more than matched in fact since that time, and grafting operations on the penis do actually now exist, though the *corpora cavernosa*, by means of which the mechanism of erection occurs, cannot be duplicated by leg-grafts. The patients in jokes still, however, expect and receive miracles. Nevertheless, these continue to go wrong somehow, with castration by the same doctor the only possible remedy. The Return of the Repressed. *A man's erections are so extreme after his miraculous operation (or after taking an aphrodisiac) that he cannot get his penis down, and straps it to his leg, rushing back to the doctor with hobbling*

*gait. "Quick, doctor, I can't get my leg down." The only pos-
sible solution: cut it off.* (1 : 487, end-line only, the last element
being given simply as an allusion to the World War I witticism,
"Gonna cut off his bonus.") Thus, in the end the miraculous
surgeon is no one but the doctor-castrator or rabbi-circumciser
in disguise, his promised miracle cures – like the modern
'miracle drugs' – being nothing but a trap. We have seen him
before.

Earlier, in discussing circumcision, the concern with the
disposal of the circumcised foreskin – Hebrew, *pipputz* – was
observed: the consensus of opinion in the jokes being that the
Jews (or the nurses) *eat* it. The doctor is also suspected of this,
and for the same reason: to appropriate the virility of the
castrated patient along with his testicles, penis, or foreskin,
whatever is taken from him in castration. A florid version not
given earlier: *A man with a very husky voice is told by the
doctor that it is caused by his having too long a penis. This
causes tension in the diaphragm, with overloading of the fram-
mister, causing excessive secretion of the Inkerman glands –
which makes the voice too low. The only solution is to cut off
one and half inches from the center of his penis, grafting the
two ends back together again so that the operation will not
affect his sexual life. The patient agrees and the operation is
performed. Months later he meets the doctor in the street and
says (in a high voice), "You know, doctor, I've always wanted
to ask you: what do you doctors do with the parts you cut out
in operations like that?" "Don't worry," says the doctor (in a
deep husky voice), "we make good use of them."* (N.Y. 1953.)
Sometimes the man's problem is 'mokus of the gekokus.'

The medical gobbledygook, mocked here in the 'doubletalk'
of carnival mountebanks and sideshow peddlers, alludes of
course to the identity of these worthies with the medical
charlatans and 'painless' tooth-pullers of former times – and
their comedians giving the 'medicine show' at public fairs, at
least since the 16th century of the '*orviétan*' vendors in Italy,
France, and Germany. Not to mention the 'snake-oil remedy'
cheapjacks still to be seen occasionally on city streets, with
their outrageous lies, worthless products, and witty patter ...
especially high up in skyscrapers on Madison Avenue in New
York, and parts west.

A whole series of stories on the disposition of the castrated
organ expresses this problem in reverse form: as the results of

an overcompensatory grafting operation on the man, in which the operation goes wrong because some part of a woman's body has been used (unbeknownst to him, under the anesthetic), thus 'making a woman of him' in part at least. *A piece of a nurse's labia is grafted to the lip of a man who has been injured in an automobile accident. A year later he meets the doctor again and tells him, "The scar's fine, doc, but you know, every time I get a hardon my lip quivers."* (Idaho, 1932. Larson MS., No. 30.) This is printed in *Anecdota Americana* (1934) 2:192, following the opposite form at 2:181 – *Part of a woman's ear is grafted to her vagina to make the opening smaller. On the doctor's next visit, when he asks her how she feels, she lifts her skirt, raises her leg (all acted out by the teller), and says, "Would you talk a little louder, doctor?"* Here, obviously, the woman is being castrated, not to mention the male teller of the story who acts out all her feminine mannerisms.

The going wrong of all these operations, with the patient ending worse off rather than better, is the essence of their castratory form, though the subject of castration may not be mentioned at all. It is also their connection with the 'Three Wishes' story studied above, in which it is made clear that it is the sin of pretentiousness, of wanting to interfere with Fate or Destiny, that is really being punished. *A man with a facial injury, who has had some skin grafted onto the wound, being asked by a friend where the skin-graft came from, replies: "I don't know, but it's funny – every time I get tired, my face wants to sit down."* (Berkeley, Calif. 1941, from a woman.)

The power of women's bodies, especially their sexual organs, over the bodies and imaginations of men is part of the cause of the sullen animosity many men feel against women. These are the men who tend toward the sadistic concept of coitus, the "I-fucked-'er-goddam-'er!" school. Other, more normal men accept the miracle of femaleness, as with Goethe's final line in *Faust* that redeems so many flatulent stupidities in the play preceding and so much that was small and mean in the author's own relations with women: *'The Ever-Woman leads us higher and higher!'* A joke not involving any castratory operation says this very well: *'Wife has to visit her doctor and in haste uses empty sauce bottle for her water. Stands it on the table, and in even greater haste to be off, picks up wrong sauce bottle. On her return she says how concerned her doctor had been (thought she was going to have a baby with a tomato for a head), but that he wasn't long deceived by her silly mistake. Husband:* "Neither was I. I thought *something must be wrong when I poured the sauce on my sausages and they all stood up on-end and their skins pulled back!"* ' (Chelmsford, Essex, 1951.) Less pleasant, in a recent cartoon text already noted: *The two nurses who plan to wiggle through the men's ward and listen to the circumcision stitches pop!*

Animal grafts or assists are just as likely to cause trouble as those supplied from women's bodies. '*An elephant's foreskin is grafted on a soldier's shot-off prick. Meets doctor, who asks,* "How are things now?" "Pretty well, but it's most embarrassing *when we have buns for tea".*' (London, 1954. If you can't understand this one, ask an Englishman to explain it to you.) *The World's Dirtiest Jokes* (Los Angeles, 1969) likes the following joke so much that two versions are given, pp. 76 and 148, one under "Animals" and one under "Marital Blitz," though no animals actually appear. *A woman buys dog food for her husband, on a doctor's advice that this special brand is great for building up a man's virility. Eventually she has to report to the doctor (or disapproving grocer) that her husband is dead.* "It wasn't the dog food that killed him. That worked wonders for him. But he broke his neck twisting around trying to lick his balls!" Jokes on animal grafts (Tale Type 660, Motif X1721.2) have been excellently studied by Dr. Jan Harold Brunvand, in *Northwest Folklore* (1965) No. 2: p. 10–12, with examples.

An element not to be overlooked in all stories of genital grafts and similar is the displacement of the area of anxiety – usually really about impotence – to some other or non-genital area of the body. The displacement upward to the face or mouth is the most common, with accompanying food satisfactions (even dog food ...) to replace the missing sexual pleasure. Here is the ultimate in stories of displacement upwards, and naturally this goes wrong too: *A doctor jestingly tells a man who complains of the fatness of his thighs that he should try the new treatment that has been developed.* "No drugs, no operations, nothing like that. You just use a kind of massage. You press the fat on your thighs upward till you get it to the belly, then up around the chest and along both sides of the neck to the top of your skull. Then tie it in a knot. In a few days the knot will dry up and fall off, and you'll be as thin and muscular as a young jaguar!" *The man comes back a week later with a new problem. He sweeps off his hat and points to the middle of his forehead. "Look, doc!" he cries, "It's my belly-button!" "Hmm," says the astounded doctor; "well that's not very serious." "No?" shouts the man, 'well, wait until you see my new necktie!"* (L.A. 1968.) Developed from a U.S. 1930's joke on face-lifting, in which: *The doctor refuses to do the fourth operation for the society-woman, explaining, "One more face-lifting, Madam, and you're going to have an unexpected dimple in your chin and hair on your chest!"*

In the end, all that remains constant in stories of the search for the impossibly long penis, as for the ultimate in sexual sensations, is the disaster sure to be found at the end of the search. This has been considered already in earlier chapters, at "The Sleeve Job," 8.III. 3; and "Specialties and Impossibilities," 11.III.1–4, in the chapter on Prostitution. Sometimes it is the mechanism of the search which causes the disaster, but more often, by the usual *lex talionis*, the man is punished in the very organ in which he has sinned pridefully. One joke takes off from the well-known story about: *Paul Bunyan, the giant of strength, who sees an Indian girl on the opposite side of the Grand Canyon taking a sunbath. His penis erects and he stretches it across the canyon from rim to rim, saying to her, "Come on across!" Just as she is about to walk out on it she pauses asking, "But how will I get back?"* (N.Y. 1936.) This is Thompson's Motif K1391, "Long distance sexual intercourse," in which: *An Indian trickster has intercourse with a woman across a stream, by means of magic,* a story which Prof. Thompson could not omit expurgatorily – as he omitted so many of Rotunda's Italian *novelle* and other materials that did not suit him – since, in this case, the story appears in his own collection of North American Indian tales.

In the version relevant here: *A man sleeping in a hotel room. opposite a girl's window, has a dream in which his penis grows longer and longer, and finally snakes its way across the street, up the wall, and into the girl's room and bed – and here comes the* STREETCAR! (N.Y. 1950.) In *The Limerick,* Note 1162, is a version in which the man has taken too strong an aphrodisiac. Other forms have a bus come along, or a truck, and in one – where the action takes place in Venice – '*Here comes the Coast Guard Cutter!*' – All these N.Y. 1953, collected at a party on asking for variants of the story about Paul Bunyan.

The strange riddle earlier given, on 'Cannibal Roulette' or

'African Roulette,' has its homey counterpart in an even stranger story collected several times in England but not in America: *'A villager has more than once happened on one of the village wenches (the uglier ones) masturbating with a carrot stuck in a knothole in a board fence. He sets himself up on the other side and pokes his [sic] through. Later asked how he'd made out by another villager to whom he confided his plan. "Oh, I suppose the idea was good, but it never occurred to me that she scraped the carrot first with a potato peeler.'* (Chelmsford, Essex, 1951.) In the closest form found in America, the surprise castratory ending again seems to be the main element: *Two old maids living together in a cottage are masturbating with a banana which they have stuck in a knothole in the floorboard. A tramp passing by sees their antics by peeking privily through the window. He crawls under the house, and replaces the banana with his stiffened penis. Just as one of the old maids is sinking down on it, there is a knock at the door, and the other old maid shouts, "Quick! Kick it under the bed!"* (L.A. 1968. Printed in *World's Dirtiest Jokes*, p. 11, with caption: "And Then He Fainted.") Though no magical element appears to be present in this Pyramus & Thisbe joke (Motif T41.1; also K1561, in Wesselski's Bebel, No. 161, the form developed by Chaucer into "The Miller's Tale"), the action is obviously impossible as it stands, without an inordinately long penis. The original Levantine forms, where this takes place through a slit in a tent, have been forgotten or *'rationalized' into nonsense* in the West. We will return to this joke later in another, more magical form, lacking any castration element but giving it a whole new dimension.

The "Attack on the Testicles" has been considered above, in section 13.II.4. In the chapter on "Losses" in *The Limerick*, Nos. 1129 ff., numerous examples involve accidents to, or losses of the testicles (note in particular Nos. 1164 and 1184, in connection with the joke following), while the next limerick chapter, "Sex Substitutes," which might be expected to make up for these, actually is concerned almost entirely with dildoes and other sexual succedanea. A joke, "The Patience of Job," in *The Pearl* (Nov. 1879) No 5, has: *A farmer and his wife coming home on Sunday morning from church when the farmer excuses himself saying, "I want to get over the hedge to do something for myself." She hears 'her good man on the other side of the hedge, blasting, swearing, and damning at an awful* rate. *She managed to get over to him, and then seeing him stooping down as if troubled by a very hard motion* [of the bowels], *exclaimed: "John! John! how can you swear so; don't you remember what the parson said about the patience of Job?" "Blast that damned Job,"* exclaimed the furious John, *"he never had his balls caught in a rabbit trap! Why don't you make haste to help me?"'* Truth being at least as strange as fiction, Prof. A. Irving Hallowell, in "Aggression in Saulteaux Society," in *Psychiatry* (Washington, D.C. 1940) III. 395–407, notes: *'Some years ago … several Berens River Indians who were out hunting came upon the traps of an Indian of the Sandy Lake Band … One of the hunters, egged on by his companions* [note!] *defecated on one of the traps. Then he sprung the trap so that a piece of feces was left sticking out. Such an act was an insult to the owner of the trap and a deterrent to any animal that might approach it.'* (Joke version: Afanasyev's *Russian Secret Tales*, 1872, No. 39.)

Overcompensations as to the loss of the testicles, or even dangers to them, are not common in jokes. It has already been observed that the testicles are not as often the subject of fantasy castrations, in humor or otherwise, as is the penis, since they develop later in life than the childhood or infantile periods when the castration complex is usually instituted. This therefore centers largely around the penis. *Lady Customer: "Do you have any figs?" Greengrocer: "Sorry, no figs." "Do you have any dates?' "No, no dates either." "Well then, do you have any nuts?" "Of course not, lady. If I had nuts I'd have dates."* (L.A. 1968.) This is an unusual statement, as to the primacy or value of the testicles as a sexual attraction. It should be told to the hundreds of thousands, perhaps, of men in America and abroad, who have allowed themselves to be – nay, *demanded* that they be sterilized, for the usual reasons of egoism, fear of fathering children, and the erroneous idea that this makes them 'safe' and attractive to women. (Maybe to 'dates,' but not to women.) See the First Series, 9.III.5, page 796, on one male pest of this type. *A Scotchman in a chemist's shop asks for hair-tonic for his bald head, and the young lady clerk says to him chaffingly, "Mon, ye know ye can't grow hair on a billiard ball." "Perhaps not, lass, but if ye care to peep under my kilt you'll see hair growin' on two stanes!"* (London, 1969, stated to be 'authentically Scottish.') On *baldness* as a symbol of impotence or castration a great deal more could be said, beginning with the legend of Samson.

Where the testicles are to be removed, the castratory operation is presumably of some use to the man. This has a certain basic logic to it, does it not? And yet. Castration was being suggested as recently as 1941, for prostatic cancer, by C. B. Huggins (as reported in R. L. Cecil & R. F. Loeb's *Textbook of Medicine*, 8th ed., Philadelphia, 1951, p. 1287), and even for *cancer of the lung!* (same source, p. 870), noting however, that it is 'Ineffective.' Which means that some lunatic surgeon had been trying it on living patients. The disposition of the castrated testicles is seldom mentioned in jokes – unless the doctor himself uses or eats them. In any case, they are not used for Voronoff 'rejuvenation' operations in jokes, on anyone but the doctor. The entire emphasis is usually compensatory and over-compensatory: *What will they be replaced with?* Such replacements are authentic. 'In cases where a uni- or bilateral castration has been done for tuberculosis or any other cause [*What about rectal dentistry?*] it has long been customary to place artificial testicles in the scrotum in order to prevent post-operative mental reaction as well as for esthetic reasons.' (Max Thorek, *The Human Testis*, 1924, p. 473.) Decades earlier this was already being joked about, in *A Treasury of Erotic Memorabilia* (about 1910): *A doctor puts in celluloid testicles after castrating a boy, and is asked by the interne whether that is to fool the boy. "No, to fool the girl."*

The standard explanation is strictly overcompensatory – as can be expected – and its wistful punch-line is often used alone as an allusive gag: *An impotent man is told that his testicles will have to be removed as they are now useless.* (Or: *An old man's testicles are to be removed for cancer of the 'prostrate gland'* [sic].) *He asks the doctor to replace these with olives (or ping-pong balls), which he realizes will not do him any good, "But they look so* sporting *in the locker-room!"* (N.Y. 1945.) Given in *Grim Hairy Tales* (1966) p. 47, with the old man refusing to be castrated at all, because: *"They look so sporty (in a jock-strap)!"* The element of phallic brag and competition with other men is very prominent here. Compare the French cartoon card sold in the U.S. since the 1930's, showing: *A little boy urinating against a tree and a little girl saying, "How practical!"*

As might be prophesied, the testicular replacement operation also goes wrong. '*A man who had to be castrated retained his general athletic ability, and was often embarrassed in shower rooms and such places to have no balls. He persuaded a doctor* to supply him with a pair of wooden ones [or nutmegs], which he wore with much pride. After a while he felt a curious local stirring, and, hoping he was regaining his manhood, he went to the doctor and told him of the curious activity he felt down there. Examining the testicles closely, the doctor replied, "Just as I thought: termites!" ' (Berkeley, Calif. 1942.) Note the hope that one can 'regain one's manhood' even with wooden nutmegs for testicles. This strain has also been crossed with that of the grafts from the woman's body, with the usual mixed over-compensatory results. The doctor replaces a man's castrated testicles with cocktail onions. At a later checkup he asks the man how they are working out. "All right, I guess," says the man dubiously, "but every time I pass a hamburger stand I get passionate." (N.Y. 1942. Food-erotization of anxiety.) Also reversed: "Every time I get a hardon (or: take a piss) my eyes water." Like that English elephant.

The need for the simple reassurance by the physician that the man's genital equipment is in good condition certainly implies the opposite fear: that it is not in good condition, and that some danger of disease or castration exists. The joke has already been given in various forms as to the man who will not let his penis urinate, in 'revenge' for having missed a sexual opportunity. (The strangury, or painful and slow urination, of venereal disease is probably really alluded to here.) This joke also exists in a curious abortive form where only the reassurance is sought. This appears as a sort of 'jokeless joke' or relic, in Anecdota Americana (1927) 1:114, rationalized as being about 'A notorious "piss-customer" ' who is put out of several saloons when he tries to use the toilet without buying a drink. He rushes into a doctor's office, 'his bladder full to bursting,' and moans, "I can't piss, doctor, I can't piss." The doctor leads him to the toilet saying, "Now try hard," and the man 'nearly filled the bowl with his water.' "You piss all right," says the doctor. "Why did you say you couldn't?" "I meant they wouldn't let me," said the man gratefully.' Again, this may refer to the strangury of venereal disease, but seems to be strictly a bid for reassurance by the physician. There can be no doubt at all about the following favorite item on this theme, often collected at the beginning of World War II, and since: A lumberjack goes to the doctor to have his penis examined. The doctor looks it over carefully, observes that it is very large, but cannot find anything wrong or malfunctioning. "What seems to *be the complaint?" he asks finally; "I can't find anything the matter with it." "I know, doc," says the lumberjack; "but doc, ain't it a* BEAUT!?"

One of the frankest bids for reassurance as to one's phallic integrity is that of Harold-Barnaby, the little hero of Crockett Johnson's delightful boy-with-a-crayon children's books, in what was apparently the first of these, *The Carrot Seed,* by Ruth Krauss (Mrs. Johnson), issued in 1945. This brief picture story, in all twenty-five pages long, has the following text: '*A little boy planted a carrot seed. His mother said, "I'm afraid it won't come up." His father said, "I'm afraid it won't come up." And his big brother said, "It won't come up." Every day the little boy pulled the weeds around the seed and sprinkled the ground with water. But nothing came up.' Everyone keeps discouraging him, but he keeps on weeding and sprinkling. 'And then, one day, a carrot came up. Just as the little boy had known it would.' The final picture shows the little boy triumphantly wheeling the carrot home in a wheelbarrow held proudly before his body, with its tip sticking out in front. The carrot is exactly as long as he is* (3½ *inches) and slightly broader in the beam; and it is very very* RED.

This charming parable was first shown me by the artist himself, just when I had become editor of the lay-analytic quarterly *Neurotica,* over twenty years ago. As he put it in my hands he said significantly, "*Now before you say anything, remember: you can't prove it was unconscious!*" This very subtle remark changed my life and my career greatly. I have never since that day concerned myself, except unwillingly and for subject-analysis, with what is called modern literature, theatre, art, music, architecture, advertising, dance, etc. For it is evident that all these are now heavily contaminated with a superficial consciousness of the sexual and psychological symbolisms their authors are inauthentically juggling with. This is not the case with folklore and folk-humor, in all cultures, which still glory in their seeming unconsciousness. A note in passing: *The Carrot Seed* now costs $3.50. If the present work cost a comparable sum, per twenty-five pages, it would cost over $120. Which would be overcompensation indeed. But it is 9¼ inches long.

3. THE MECHANICAL MAN

A curious passage in the Sherlock Holmes series, seldom observed, opens Sir Arthur Conan Doyle's *A Scandal in*

Bohemia, just at the turn of the 20th century. It is the description of Sherlock Holmes, the master detective, by his adulating amanuensis, Dr. Watson : '*He was, I take it, the most perfect reasoning and observing machine that the world has seen; but, as a lover, he would have placed himself in a false position. He never spoke of the softer passions save with a gibe and a sneer ... Grit in a sensitive instrument, or a crack in one of his own high-power lenses, would not be more disturbing than a strong emotion in a nature such as his.*' Prof. Marshall McLuhan, in *The Mechanical Bride* (preprinted in *Neurotica*, 1951, No. 8: p. 16) would define this as 'the split man of the head-*versus*-heart, thought-*versus*-feeling type who appeared in the early seventeenth century.' But actually it is nothing other than the endemic sub-homosexuality of the British institution of 'public school' hero-worship, which I have attempted to put into its correct homosexual background in *Love & Death*, p. 84–6, in connection with the popular sentimental tawdry of James Hilton's novels. In fact, so clear is this to persons who have carefully read the entire Sherlock Holmes epopoeia, in all its half dozen volumes, that the crowning achievement of the Baker Street Irregulars' club – dedicated to this work – was the famous burlesque proof submitted at one of their meetings that Dr. Watson *is a woman*, thus explaining a good deal of this 'hero-worship' without too evident abnormality.

But at a deeper level, what seems also to be involved is the attempted displacement of sexually repressed energy from the genital to the intellectual plane, as sex-starved school teachers and prisoners are said to do crossword puzzles compulsively. I have often observed, in older men for whom I have ghost-written, this same re-scaling of one's energies from the sexual to the intellectual. And many elderly men have left a ghastly record in print of their increasing interest, as they age, in the presumably non-sexual or anti-sexual 'blood sports,' hunting, killing, boxing, bull-fighting, and every other kind of sadism, not to mention murder-mysteries and war. In the introduction to the Victorian erotic autobiography, *My Secret Life* (ed. New York, 1966, p. xl), I have noted that 'sexually displaced bragging, as to the power of one's memory, or the steely glance of one's eye, aim with a gun, or ability at driving a fast car, is all the more common in that the failure of memory (and coördination) is one of the commonest signs of advancing age in men, next after sexual impotence.' It is therefore the elderly or impotent who can be expected most particularly to engage in such brags, and the various intellectual or 'non-sexual' substitutions, precisely as with the author of *My Secret Life*, sitting down in his sixties to record his preceding sexual prowesses. The implication being, of course, that these are now over and that he has nothing left but memories. (See the whole section, "Old Age: Overcompensations for Impotence," in the First Series, chapter 8.VIII, pages 614–31.)

One related overreaction to such castratory fears and emotions is the desperate and quite logical attempt to prolong sexual potency in men past the age of seventy or even eighty. The various rejuvenation, 'monkey-gland,' and gerontology fads discussed above all stem in part from this unconscious identification of death and castration. (*"Might as well be dead."*) A retired British army officer, Lt. Col. Chris. T. Sennett, reduced to the minor excitements of gambling, makes the point very well in his pseudonymous *All About Monte Carlo* (London, 1913), p. 45, a rare little volume stuffed with would-be off-color jokes and throwaway lines, on the style of the 'sporting' newspaper, *The Pink 'Un:* 'Arriving at years of discretion briefly means being *"too young to die and too old to have any fun".'* An open reference to impotence. The mind, however, is that part of the 'human machine' that keeps operating when all the rest fails – the *tongue* too, as a matter of fact, in both conversational and sexual activities. Either way, in old age "It's all in your head." *An eighty-five-year-old man goes to the doctor and says, "Doc, could you do something to lower my sex drive?" "But my dear man, don't you realize that at your age it's all in your head?" "I sure do! That's why I want it lowered!"* (Miami Beach, Florida, 1953.) Just a pun, of course, but it tells the tale. As always, with favorite themes in jokes, there are many variations. *A man of a hundred and ten goes to the doctor about his impotence, which he first noticed that morning [!] The doctor tells him nothing can be done about it at his age. "Well then, doc, give me something to take the idea out of my mind."* (1:318.) This is the reverse of the preceding. Note that the threat of (mental) castration – or, rather, the demand for self-castration – is still implicit even in this suggestion of potency at 110. It is quite remarkable how these things sneak back in disguise. That is the return of the repressed.

The pure brag of memory, as a direct displacement of sex, appears in a very popular joke, endlessly collected since 1935, in which everything is thrown upon the ludicrous overcompensation. A very sick man whom I knew to be dying of cancer in his fifties, but who kept up as brave a front as he could by telling jokes at every opportunity, had a form of this as his favorite: *An elderly man whizzes by two young men on the golf course with a breezy, "Mind if I play through?" and then drinks them nearly under the table at the clubhouse later. "Are you still this chipper in everything?" one of them asks. "Oh no," he admits. "Last night about midnight I woke up my wife and said, 'Well, how about it?' And she said, 'But you just had it at ten o'clock.' That's it, you see – (tapping himself on the head) – my memory is going!"* (N.Y. 1952. Also in Randolph MS., No. 35, collected in 1940.)

This should certainly be compared with the overcompensatory joke or mock concerning: *A team of gerontology researchers who see a little wizened old man on a train smoking an enormous cigar. One of them goes over and strikes up a conversation, asking, "You smoke many cigars like that a day?" "About twenty!" (All the little old man's answers are very belligerent and nasal.) "Well, I suppose it takes the place of other things, like drinking?" "Whaddya mean? I drink a bottle of Kentucky bourbon every day!" "But no girls, eh?" "No girls?! I'm keeping two call-girls full time in Florida, not counting my wife and stenographer in Chicago!" "Well," says the astounded researcher, "do you mind if I ask how old you are?" "Not at all. I'm twenty-eight!"* (N.Y. 1953.) This neatly combines both the wish for that much excessive virility and élan in old age, with the implied punishment to youth for daring to try it. With the trait of the clipped and belligerent replies, compare the truculent answers of the child *to the Devil* or witch in "The False Knight Upon the Road" (Child Ballad No. 3), also those in "Bollocky Bill the Sailor." Motif H543. Compare also the monosyllabic replies of the Semiquaver Friar to questions about his sex life, in Rabelais' *Pantagruel* (1553) Bk. V, chap. 28, which is very close to the present story.

On the sexual contest between the old and young, with the old overcompensatorily winning, or pretending to win, the clearest Oedipal statement is that of Vance Randolph's "Follow Your Leader," in *Pissing in the Snow*, No. 68, heard in Eureka Springs, Arkansas, in 1950, and stated to have been a common story thereabouts in the 1930's. *An old man bets with his son as to who is the better man, and both outdrinks and out-eats* him. '*Finally the old man headed for the whore-house, and the boy says to himself, "Here is one place I will beat the old booger easy, no matter what he does!" When they got in the whore-house the old man started kidding the girls and giving them some money. Pretty soon he had four of 'em a-prancing around the room stark naked, while him and the young fellow just watched 'em. Finally the old man pulled out his big long tallywhacker, and tied it in a knot. "All right, son," says he. "Let's see you do that!" The boy just set there goggle-eyed, because he couldn't even bend his pecker, no matter if his life depends on it ...*' Other stories of this kind have already been given in section 13.IV. "Symbolic Castrations," in discussing aphrodisiacs and impotence.

It is interesting to compare this father-&-son story, in its perfectly open sexual competition between the old man and the young, and its sardonic pretense that the old man really 'wins,' – by losing, with an oldtime favorite already quoted as to its hardly veiled homosexuality, and often encountered in both England and America: *The grandfather on a visit (or old soldier billeted during the war) has to sleep with the grandson, and wakes up in the middle of the night shouting, "I want a woman! Bring me a woman! Look at that hardon! Get me a woman!" "Shut up, you old bugger (or old fool)," says the grandson. "There's three reasons why you can't have a woman. First, it's three o'clock in the morning and there aren't any women here. Second, you're eighty-four years old. And third, that's not your prick you've got hold of – it's mine!"* (D.C. 1943, from a young soldier. Also in *Anecdota*, 1927, 1:235, concerning *A man in a crowded Chicago hotel sleeping on a billiard table with a Negro porter.*) What is overcompensatory in both stories, for the old man, is somehow made out to be the young man's erect penis, whether its superiority is admitted or denied. It is only a step, here, to the castration of young apes (or, frankly, strong young men, if the law allows), to supply testicles for 'rejuvenating' operations on the old men paying for the operations – and for the laws. Again, the secret meaning of wars and sacrifices since time immemorial.

A famous joke, dating at least from the bustle or 'figure-improver' of the 19th century in America, has been given in section 13.I.5, "The Over-large Vagina," with various texts from humorists of the times, in which the fear and rejection of the woman by the man is expressed as very much the fault of the woman's own bodily inadequacy: *The bride takes off so many false parts, appliances, wigs, breast-plumpers, etc. on the wedding night, that the groom asks sardonically where he is "supposed to sleep – in the bed or on the dressing table?"* (Kimbo, *Tropical Tales*, 1925, p. 40.) In the older and cruder form, he says plainly, *"You might throw over the arse-piece when you come to it."* (Chelmsford, Essex, 1953.) Aarne Type 1379* has a Cuban version in which *The husband asks her to throw him a buttock for a pillow*, which combines both the above forms, and likewise avoids the obviously crucial question as to the bride's vagina. In the unstated presumption here, of a removable vagina, these stories do not really stray very far from the castratory notions and theories of the child.

This story is bloated up practically into a horror tale, under the guise of humor, by the mad-dog Southern dialect humorist, George Washington Harris, under the title "Sut Lovingood Reports What Bob Dawson Said, After Marrying," first published in a Tennessee newspaper in 1867, and reprinted in *Sut Lovingood's Yarns*, ed. M. Thomas Inge (New Haven, 1966) p. 276–81, a volume that is an inexhaustible mine of folklore materials of the Civil War South for anyone who can bear to read such bitter hatefulness and white chauvinism, page after bloody page. For unconscious (?) sadism in a presumably humorous book, nothing can be compared with it except perhaps George Wilbur Peck's *Peck's Bad Boy and His Pa* (1883). The unscrewable vagina of the 19th-century story – Sut Lovingood calls it 'the most horrible idear that ever burnt an' blazed in the brain of man' – is the true essence of the Machine-Woman, by which I mean the removable vagina that *can be unscrewed*, but that cannot be screwed! *The Mechanical Bride* of Prof. Marshall McLuhan's earliest book (on advertising) in 1952. This is seldom mentioned at any level above that of jokes, and in the underlying reality of the inflatable life-sized 'female' rubber dolls sold for masturbation purposes to sailors, playboys, and other human failures. (See section 13.I.6, "Nurses and the Machine.")

The same idea also appears in other jokes, yearning frankly for the sexual organ abstracted completely from the woman, and thus freed for the 'cool' (alienated) male from all the pesky little difficulties and responsibilities of a real human relationship. *Little Boy: "Mama, I didn't know you could take a Wac apart." Mother: "Why, whatever made you think you could?"*

Little Boy: "Well, I heard daddy say that last night he screwed the ass off a Wac." (D.C. 1945, from a soldier. The 'Wacs', 'Wrens' and similar were uniformed women in World War II, in England and America, who did not fight or bear arms, and were essentially for secretarial and sexual use by the officers.) In the British version: *'Child: "Mummie, those three acrobatic dancing girls we saw last night – were they really alive, or were they just mechanical?" "Don't be silly, dear, of course they were alive?" "Only I heard Daddie say to Uncle he'd like to screw the arse off the one on the right!"'* (London, 1953.)

The fantasy is, of course, very old, and perhaps clearest in the pretendedly human singing-doll, mentioned earlier, who is the heroine (actually a human singer pretending to be a doll!) in Offenbach's *Tales of Hoffmann* in the 1880's, including the very significant aria in which she *runs down* while singing, and has to be wound up again with a creaky key. ("The Nightingale of the Emperor of China," in Hans Christian Anderson's story.) This is as obvious a displacement or replacement of the doll's mechanical sexuality by her singing, as is the guilty intercourse of Tristan & Isolde by their symbolically shouting at each other at the tops of their voices through a half-hour *Liebestod*, representing orgasm. The American joke-and-cartoon magazine, *Sex to Sexty*, goes the whole distance on this, first with a street-corner prostitute who pretends to be a mechanical fucking-machine (with an enormous wind-up key in her back), because *"It takes a good gimmick to bring in business!"* and finally, in 1966 (*Sex to Sexty*, No. 7: p. 30), in a cartoon by Pete Wyma, in which a real mechanical doll – with key as above – is being shown to a patent attorney by the enthusiastic inventor, who explains, *"I figured someone had to invent a 'sex-machine' before I.B.M. thought of it!!"* In other words, Big Sister or Big Mama, to fight off the paranoid threat of Big Brother, or at least to get there first. And what about vibrating mattresses and water-beds in all the motels, for the 'relaxation' of *golden-age* oldster couples?

There is also a 'topper' to the old standby about the Unscrewable Bride, with her false hair, false bustle, false bosom, false teeth, false eye, and (practically) all the rest. This goes straight to the heart of the problem, which is not the use of prosthetic or supplementary parts of the body, but the dangerous miscegenational marriage of human beings and The Machine – a point that will be returned to again in a moment. *A man picks up a*

*woman, and after quite a few drinks with her in a bar, they go
to a hotel room together and make love. In the middle of the
night he wakes up to go to the bathroom, and notes to his surprise that the woman has taken off a wooden leg and laid it by
the bed. As she is asleep he begins examining it curiously, and
diddling with its springs and braces, and finally finds he has
taken it apart and cannot put it back together again. He goes
out into the hall, and accosts the first man he sees, "Can you
help me? I've got a woman in my room with one leg apart, and
I can't seem to get it back together." "Hell!" says the other man
boozily, "I got a woman in my room with* BOTH *legs apart, and
I can't even find the goddam room!"* (N.Y. 1953.) A comedy of
impotencies. With woman as castrato.

All the matching fantasies concerning male 'sex-machines,'
that both operate and collapse, naturally exist. These have
already been noted, in the 1890's eroticum, *Memoirs of a
Russian Princess*, and in the American (originally French) joke
of the same period, given in *Memorabilia*, about 1910, as to *The
rubber man who has been wound up for twenty-four hours to
fuck the Queen of Spain*. Which sounds as though it is really
stealing the invention of the *Russian Princess*. (See further curiosities of the subject in *The Limerick*, Note 1325.) The female
version, or inexorable vaginal machine, is the cow-milking device that captures the unlucky farmer by the penis, *"So just
keep feeding him and fanning him – that machine is set for
four quarts!"*

However, there is a very palpable difference between the
fantasy of the woman as sex-machine – or the unscrewable
vagina : the 'unscrewing of the inscrutable' again – and similar
jokes involving men. When it is the woman whose vagina (or
symbolic bosom, bottom, eye, or leg) is to be unscrewed, she is
being insulted and disgraced. She is nauseating. Let us see how
it works with men. *A doctor amazes the internes in the amphi-
theatre, after a very difficult brain operation is over, by unscrewing the arm with which he has operated and handing it to
the nurse, she in turn unscrewing the other! Even more amazing
(the teller ends), he then went back to his office with the nurse,
and screwed his head off.* (Minneapolis, Minn. 1935; also told
of a famous movie-vamp and an automobile mechanic.) This
story is sometimes told, or at least begun, as though it were
true. Instead of a doctor, the hero can also be *An all-round
athlete who amazes a young lady in the audience first by un-*

screwing his wooden leg after winning the football game, then by unscrewing his mechanical arm after winning at tennis. (The dénouement is the same.) (D.C. 1945, from an army sergeant.) Thus, when it is the woman, *"You know damn well what I want; unscrew it and throw it up here!"* But when it is the man, he is the cynosure of admiring attention, especially for the women with whom, later, he *"screws his head off."* That is blowing hot and cold with the same screw. The story is not new: it is a 'catch' form or reduction of Tale 76, "The Two Doctors," in the *Gesta Romanorum* (12th century; Type 660, Motifs F668.1 and K547.2).

The replacing of men sexually by machines intended to satisfy women is a very ancient idea, at least as old as the legend of Queen Dido of Carthage (or her granddaughter-in-law Pasiphaë) and the bronze cowhide built to satisfy her desire to be made love to by the divine bull, by the inventor Daedalus, himself little more than a legendary reduction of the Graeco-Roman god of fire and metallurgy, Vulcan-Hephaestus, symbolically crippled of one leg, and cuckolded (with Mars, the god of War) by his won-by-trickery consort, Aphrodite, goddess of Love. Openly symbolic identifications like these simply drip with their desire to make a point as to human aspirations and inevitabilities as well. The simplest machine to replace man sexually, the dildo or 'self-gratifier,' is seen on Greek vase illustrations, and is of unknown age. The mechanized versions have already been discussed, in section 13.I.6, "Nurses and the Machine." In English literature and folklore the subject was kept at the level of an allusive refrain, "Hey diddle-diddle," or "With a dil-doll, fa-la-la!" in folksongs, breaking first into the open in Thomas Nashe's *Valentine, or Dildo* (1601, first printed from MS. in John S. Farmer's *Merry Songs and Ballads*, 1895, I. 22; and see the quotation, in context, in Dr. John Del Torto's "The Human Machine," in *Neurotica*, 1951, No. 8: p. 23). The *Dildoïdes* of Samuel Butler, by the middle of 17th century (manuscript copies in the Harvard Rochester Miscellany, MS. Eng. 636F, and elsewhere), and Rochester's farce, *Sodom*, printed in *Kryptádia* (1905) IX, are filled with further allusions and information.

An imaginary voyage on the style of Swift's *Gulliver's Travels*, crudely satirizing the morals of the time, *A Voyage to Lethe* (1741, and reprint 1875), by 'Capt. Samuel Cock,' supplements its discussion of homosexuality, already noted, which it describes significantly as a strange worship of the buttocks, with a similar note, p. 25, of:

> An adjacent temple, dedicated to the Goddess Dildona, who is chiefly worshipped by the Sterilians, inhabitants of a very unfruitful country, in which her temple is founded. She is the same as of old the Roman ladies sacrificed to under the name of Bona Dea, where, as heretofore, it was not permitted for men to enter ... The temple was thronged with women of all ranks and ages; young and old maids; widows and wives; all sacrificing with great zeal to the Goddess, whose image was at the altar, adorned with the branches of the dildo tree, with silken girdles, and with the tongues of lap-dogs.

The mechanical dildo, of which, as already noted in section 13.I.6, the history goes back to ancient Japan, has only recently become widely known, due to its adaptation, by Dr. Vladimir Fortunato and myself in the 1930's, to the hand-held vibrating massage apparatuses which were then already being used as masturbation devices by both sexes, and for both sexes. These machines have now entered the cultural stream in the West, both as a reality and as humor. A particularly hilarious version, including a feather for tickling the heinie, is illustrated in the New York sex-newspaper, *Screw* (1969) No. 25: p. 11. This is on the style of a pavement-pounding jackhammer, and cannot be beat. It is a long way from the earliest jocular drawings of this kind, showing a Model T Ford automobile chasis with steering wheel and reciprocating-motion replaceable penises, in various sizes, handed around as a novelty in the 1920's. In a less graphic vein, but just as mechanically oriented, another 1920's novelty would show the woman's body as "The New Radio Hook-up, tuning in on c-u-n-t," with the man's penis & testicles as 'Plug' and 'Batteries;' his pubic hair being marked 'Tickler,' and his anus 'Loud Speaker.' (Reproduced in the very rare collection of obscoena, *Spicy Breezes*, U.S. about 1928, p. 41. Copy: Kinsey-ISR, which also has in its files numerous versions of the automobile item.)

Far less naïve, and verging unpleasantly on the sinister, is a more complex masturbation machine shown in the gruesome Lumpen-fascistic comic-strip, "Trashman, Agent of the 6th (International)," in which Hell's Angels style, motorcycle-riding, Iron Cross wearing guerrillas with machine-guns are shown taking over New York with occult assistance. (It does all sound familiar, doesn't it?) In the issue of the drug-and-hippie oriented underground newspaper, the New York *East Village Other* carrying this strip, subtitled "Total Assault Upon Culture" – which is nothing if not frank – and dated November 15th, 1968, p. 11, we pause in the endless gun-toting massacres of Trashman and his merry *Lumpens* and the ankh-bearing enemy commandos, for a bit of sex stuff, to keep the readers interested in the essential fascist propaganda, just the way Julius Streicher's *Stürmer* in Nazi Germany showed the formula had to be mixed, to achieve the promised "Total Assault Upon Culture." *We see an ugly young female in a high-teased hairdo, smoking a cigarette in her petticoat in a luxurious bathroom. Balloon: 'But meanwhile in the jaded towers of Pittmore Mews, young* PENELOPE PROPE *settles down for the evening. "Oh! what shall I do this evening?" Next frame: she is standing naked before a large, many-clawed machine which is tickling her nipples with a brush, patting her pubis with a powder-puff, and polishing her buttocks with what looks like a pot-scourer. She says: "All of these soiree's [sic] have recently become a bore. I think I'll just settle for a nice quiet evening with my Electro-Exhilerator." The object in question appears behind her chiaroscuro thighs in the final frame. It is a three-legged science fiction machine or stool, with a tongue-cum-penis-shaped whirling device rising out of its centre. It too speaks. It says,* "HHMMMM." At the actual folk level, what is perhaps one echo of this was picked up by 1970 in America, and just as sick in its minor masochistic way: *A small cabin on a bathing-beach, marked* "LADIES! GET YOUR TOPLESS BATHING SUITS CLEANED HERE." *A girl pulls open the door. Inside is an undersized man sitting on a stool with his head tipped back, his mouth puckered, and his tongue sticking up in the air.* A variant of Trashman's "Electro-Exhilerator" tongue-o-mat is shown in Mark James Estren's illustrated *History of Underground Comics* (San Francisco, 1974, p. 184).

Finally, the pretence of subservience breaks down, of course, and we have the ballad of "The Great Wheel," or "The Great Fucking Machine," in which the mechanical simulacrum of man is mostly composed of an iron fly-wheel and a steel piston-rod for penis, invented by the impotent little man whose wife 'never could ever be satisfied!' This is the ultimate overcompensation for impotence or castration, whether social or sexual, and ends by destroying the woman in a shit-explosion of precisely the type that is planned now to take down or blow up

humanity with it. *And you know I ain't kidding!* What is involved here is a more important sociological point and problem
than any other ventured in the present work. It is the sensation
of being impotent, a castrated creature, in the face of The
Machine, a sensation that has been powerfully attacking
Western man since the time of the Luddite machine-smashers
in England, just after the French Revolution. Every economist
will tell you that the Luddites were wrong to smash the
machines. And everyone else is unconsciously nearly ready to
do the same. A Woody Allen movie skit in *Casino Royale*
(1968) shows even the ultimate woman-quelling machine in
impotent operation. Locked helplessly in the fucking-machine's
clutches by the man, the woman's passion blows all its fuses
and melts the machine to junk! As I have tried to phrase it in
Love & Death (1949) p. 77:

> In the brittle mechanisms of typewriter and birth-control, the
> technology that now discards man, has freed woman –
> where all the pamphleteers and feminists had failed. In the
> face of the machine man finds himself almost useless, ready
> to be scrapped, passed by in strength and brains. Woman
> remains: incorruptible, irreplaceable. Safely in her own
> hands, the fertility that once made her weak and 'unclean'
> (but twice as unclean for a girl-child as for a boy: *Leviticus*,
> xii. 2–5) now sets her beyond the competition of any
> machine; while, for the man's part, biologists envisage
> "Human Parthenogenesis and the Elimination of the Male."
> (Remy de Gourmont, *The Natural Philosophy of Love*, 1903,
> chapter 7.)

Already, in the mid-18th century, the French philosopher La
Mettrie considered it a charming *jeu d'esprit* to argue against
the spirituality of man, and by implication against revealed
religion and its airy flights as to the soul of man, by insisting in
a famous pamphlet on the concept of *L'Homme Machine*
(1748), though this hardly went farther than to deny man
'free will.' Meanwhile, other paradoxalists and preciosos of the
same century thought it amusing to write similar pamphlets
demonstrating *The Soul of Animals*. All animals, that is, except
man. La Mettrie's idea, however, is the one that has prevailed.
Things are serious now. In a final desperate effort to regain or
retain his uncastrated maleness, Western man admits everything, absconds with everything, and attempts *to become the*

Machine. That is to say, a cog. The 'identification with the aggressor' that was the secret spring of Nazi Germany, as it still is of science fiction, and under the same neo-'socialist' pose.

It is for this reason that the Mechanical Woman, the epoxy Bunny 'playmate' or rubber fucking-doll, is an insult to women, or the merest succedaneum replacing them; while the Mechanical Man is presumably the last heroic stand for failing human virility, man identifying himself phallically with his penis-shaped sports car (with stick-shift). See further, and on a very broad scale, the masterpiece of the American social critic, Lewis Mumford, *The Myth of the Machine: The Pentagon of Power* (New York, 1970), one of the great books of our time. To be compared with the infinitely lesser work, a sort of insiders' gloat, by Prof. Siegfried Giedion, *Mechanization Takes Command* (1948), with its interesting illustrated chapter, p. 230–45, on the mechanical slaughtering of pigs and the razor-blading of a woman's eye. (Taken of course from Buñuel's surréalist movie vomit, *Un Chien Andalou*, which one would not, somehow, have thought relevant.)

Prof. Marshall McLuhan, in *The Mechanical Bride* (1952) also makes the very significant point, with many striking examples to support it, as to our present position, that: 'One of the most peculiar features of our world – the interfusion of sex and technology – is not a feature created by admen, but seems rather to be born of a hungry curiosity to explore and enlarge the domain of sex by mechanical technique, on one hand, and, on the other, to *possess* machines in a sexually gratifying way.' Were this simply the fantasy of the Mechanical Bride, as seen in the precision-kicking chorus girls whom Prof. McLuchan cites, it would be sufficiently bad. What is more sinister is that it has become the modern would-be identification with the Mechanical Man. This is not recent: see Alfred Jarry's *Le Surmâle* (1902) and Fernand Fleuret's imitative *Jim Click*.

That there are dangers here has long been sensed. A beautiful Germanic and Icelandic folk-legend tells of *"Iron Henry," the faithful servant who has three iron bands around his heart to keep it from breaking. When his master is rescued and disenchanted the bands snap one by one.* (Aarne Tale Type 440, Motif F875.) In the form of "The Frog King," this is the first story in the *Kinder- und Hausmärchen* of the Brothers Grimm (1815). It ends happily for both master and servant – but what if it had not? How now, Iron Henry? There is an inevitable drop in tone between the chivalrous ideals of this quasi-mechanical legend with its barrel-chest bands, and the modern bawdy story of man-into-machine first recorded (without any machine, just a man taking the place of one) in E. Henry Carnoy's anonymous "Contes Picards," in *Kryptádia* (1911) XI. 187, as "Commodités perfectionnées" – The Perfected Toilet. *A curé who is about to receive a visit from the bishop, and who is ashamed of the old-fashioned privy in his garden, posts the beadle with a large, soft brush under the seat, with orders not to allow the bishop to wipe himself after he has "satisfied his natural needs," but to reach up and wipe him with the brush. The bishop is astonished by this marvellous automatic nicety, entirely without paper, and bends down to see how it works. The beadle, who does not see very well in the obscurity under the seat imagining that the bishop is putting back his bottom for more, reaches up with the now well-shitten brush, and wipes the bishop's face with it.* In other words, at the first touch of attempted mechanism in these intimate matters – everything ends in shit. Iron Henry gone wrong. The message is the *merde.*

The world of automata is very large, and has its own special literature, mostly in French. (It is the French and Swiss who are the most gadget-minded people in the world, not the Anglo-Saxons.) I will not stop to detail this literature here, as it is not central to my purpose, with the exception of the popular study, *Les Automates dans les œuvres d'imagination* by Alfred Chapuis (Neuchâtel: Éditions du Griffon, 1947), reprinted in part from the Swiss clock magazine, *La Fédération horlogère suisse* (1946–7), a provenance that says worlds. Chapuis covers automata in literature and the theatre, with certain accidental but basic omissions, such as the story of "The Magic Horse" and "The City of Brass" in the *Arabian Nights.* Poe's "The Man That Was Used Up," and especially his article on Maelzel's Chess-playing Machine, are also very relevant, since this 'machine' was actually a fake, as Poe demonstrates, containing a legless man or midget (!) hidden inside: one of the earliest attempted practical marriages of man-with-machine. Except for the automata of comedy and satire, the literary machine-men or machines that replace men seldom go wrong, whereas in folklore and folk-humor *they always go wrong,* beginning with Icarus' wax-moulded wings. In fact, it is their going wrong, and in a visibly defiling or castrating way, that is the essence of the folk-resistance to them. When they go right – as the Iron Maiden and the guillotine – they are even more castratory.

Here is the next level down from the Picardy story about the 'Perfected Toilet.' The toilet remains, but the rest has been heavily and far more dangerously mechanized. This story has already been given in the First Series, 6.IV.4, under "The Sex Machine," p. 367–9, with much other material relevant here, in a form often encountered among children in America since the 1910's: *Pat & Mike are plumbers, and are fixing the rich woman's toilet. Pat decides to use it before he goes, and finds three foot-pedals before him when he sits down. "I pushed the first one," he tells Mike later, "and water sprayed up and cleaned me off. Then I pressed the second one, and a big cotton swab came and wiped me dry." "What about the third one?" "I can't figure that one out. When I pushed on it a big rubber prick came up from beneath, pumping like mad, and rammed itself up my ass."* (Larson MS., heard in Idaho, 1919.) In a less clear conclusion, as heard among children in Scranton, Pa. in 1927: *When he pushes the third pedal, "A candle came up and tapped me on the balls three times."*

I was ten years old when I heard this story, and did not understand the reference to female masturbation with a candle, but the idea of being tapped on the balls *from underneath* was certainly vaguely disquieting. I remember that nobody but the little boy telling the joke laughed. Here is the latest avatar, of which a dysphemistic version is given in *World's Dirtiest Jokes* (1969) p. 133, as of a speaker named 'Turdington Thudd' at a banquet, afflicted with the 'drizzling shits.' (But of which of us couldn't *that* be said?) *A man in a very modern hotel late at night finds the men's room locked, and as he is 'taken very short' he goes into the ladies' room. He sits down, sees a row of buttons where the toilet-paper holder should be, and presses one, expecting that the needed paper will slide out into his hand. Instead, he wakes up in the hospital. When asked how it happened he says, "I don't know. The last thing I remember was pushing that button in the ladies' john." "Which button did you push?" asks the doctor. "The one marked* ATR." *"I see,"* says the doctor. "Well, I have some bad news for you. You shouldn't have touched that button. That was the Automatic Tampax Remover."* How now, Iron Henry?

At the level not only of folklore and jokes, but of a certain kind of infantile *kitsch* heavily appreciated by the popular audience, the Mechanical Man has already been on-scene for quite some time now, strutting or agitating his castrated stump. First seen clearly in Melville's *Moby Dick* (London, 1851), where Captain Ahab's whole revenge against the father-figure of the Great White Whale is motivated by his bitten-off leg, to be compared to the various other castrations in Melville's work, as *Pierre*, and the threatened throat-cutting by the cabin-boy in *Benito Cereno*, already cited in section 13.II.7, "The Mad Barber of Fleet Street." Melville's mad hero appears again, watered down to the treacly saccharine syrup of Sir James Barrie's *Peter Pan* (1904), as Captain Hook the pirate, with a crocodile replacing the whale, Moby Dick, to bite off his leg. There is also the extra Oedipal touch of the conscience or *clock* (see the First Series, chapter 1.III.2) inside the crocodile's stomach, warning of his dangerous (erotic) approach. Not to mention Peter Pan, the sexless little hero who *flies*, and his guardian angel Tinker-Bell – images all reversed and shat upon in the wilfully ugly science-fiction movie, *Barbarella* (1968), with a blinded male angel protecting the space-age heroine – and a peculiar crew of sentimental pirates, especially the one who mended the sails on a sewing-machine, and cried because he had no mother.

In the gruff Texas vulgarity of *Grim Hairy Tales* (1966) p. 11, the same images are sized-up immediately for what they really are, and re-expressed without any of the elaborate expurgations of Melville or kitschifications of Barrie. Instead, we are given a cartoon by Dennis Jones showing *A one-eyed, be-pistolled pirate, both of whose legs are wooden, and his arms both hooks* (in other words, an ambulant but indomitable 'basket-case'), *leaning cheerfully against a wall and supporting himself with a coat-hook, for that extra fillip of identification as Captain Hook, while the beautiful chambermaid at "Ye Last Chance Inn" bares her breasts to him and prepares to climb with him into the invitingly open bed. He speaks, assuring her – that is to say, assuring himself and us. "There's one thing I haven't lost!"*

Just as clear, though wholly expurgated and symbolized, is the "Tin Woodman" of *The Wonderful Wizard of Oz* (1900) by L. Frank Baum, whose bibliographical history has been studied by Martin Gardner in an article published in 1954. All the "Oz" books are filled with impotent and absurd little kings, and powerful though placid matriarchal queens, who are not as noisy as those in Lewis Carroll's *Alice in Wonderland* but just as dangerous. The "Tin Woodman" goes the whole distance on symbolic bodily castrations. Once he was a human being, Nick Chopper, but having lost one of his limbs chopping wood, then another, and another – and finally his head, after which the omission of any reference to chopping off his penis seems unimportant – he ends up made entirely of tin. His parts are replaced limb by limb with prosthetics; with a funnel for a hat and a large axe in operating condition, held between his knees, so maybe there is still hope for his penis if it still needs to be threatened. (See illustration: *Ozma of Oz*, p. 136.) The Tin Woodman is searching sentimentally with the little girl heroine for the Wonderful Wizard, but he must be very careful not to 'blow his cool,' as we would now say: not to *feel* anything and weep, as that will rust him solid.

Too good an idea not to use again, Baum then does the whole thing all over in a sequel, *Ozma of Oz* (1907), this time without any human prehistory at all, in "Tiktok, the Machine Man," who is supplied by his makers complete with an advertising card, p. 55, stating that he is: 'SMITH & TINKER'S Patent Double-Action, Extra-Responsive, Thought-Creating, Perfect-Talking MECHANICAL MAN ... Thinks, Speaks, Acts, and Does Everything but live.' (The last gag translates nowadays as: Cool, man, cool!) The 'Everything' in the advertisement is of course not to be taken too seriously in a children's book. Children's books, as everyone knows, are long on horrors and murders, but – no sex! This is spelled out carefully, for the benefit of 'underground' comic book readers and others who wish to be with it, in my monograph *Love & Death: A Study in Censorship* (1949), the chapter "Not For Children." As to Tiktok, being wisely made of copper he cannot rust; in fact, his 'Mechanism is guaranteed to work perfectly for a thousand years!' But alas, he too is impotent. There is always that detail ... The *key* that winds him up, like the Mechanical Horse in the *Arabian Nights* (through the anus), has been thrown into the sea by the Evil King, and the Mechanical Man, who is guaranteed for a thousand years, has RUN DOWN. – *Caveat emptor!*

It would not be worthwhile here to continue this kitsch-klatsch any closer to date, as one would be overwhelmed with materials. Save it for *The Book of the Machine*, along with all the pictorial materials since the middle of the 19th century on the airplane and automobile, beginning with the hilarious illustrated 'anticipations' of Émile Souvestre's *Le Monde tel qu'il sera* (1846) with satirical fashion-plates for 'professional' styles for men, long preceding *Beau, Esquire, Playboy, Penthouse* and on down, which were reproduced in *Harper's New Monthly Magazine*, in New York, 1856, as the earliest anticipatory illustrations published in America. The absolute end, in such illustrations, are those in Albert Robida's fantastic and incredible *Le Vingtième Siècle* (2 vols. 1883–90, the second volume being called *La Vie Electrique*), about which more will be learned in my *The Horn Book*, p. 314. As to the most recent, consciously penis-shaped automobile models known as 'sports cars' – the sport is he slithering along in them at the slowest possible speed and with the most possible exhaust noise, trying to attract whore-minded girls by these means – the sickest I have seen, far different from the charming Russian flourishes published long ago in *Esquire*, are François Dallegret's 'Astrological Automobiles," in *Avant Garde* (New York, 1968) No. 3: p. 46–51, most of which are, and are covered with, aggressive killing-points. The ugly sado-masochistic and erotic machines, for tied-up and perverted masturbation, in Tomi Ungerer's *Fornicon* (1969), also advertised in *Avant Garde*, No. 11: p. 2, have already been discussed. On Robida and since, see Anthony Frewin's excellent *One Hundred Years of Science Fiction Illustration* (London, 1974).

One folk-artist other than Woody Allen, worth noting here, is the comedian, Jack Lemmon, all of whose movies in the 1960's seemed to make purposeful use of these erotico-mechanical images and symbols, though never with the superb satire of Charlie Chaplin's unforgettable birth-from-the-rolling-machine scene in *Modern Times*, which was his masterpiece. In *Under the Yum-Yum Tree*, for example, Lemmon plays a feather-headed Lothario who grinds his own heart-shaped keys to his bachelor apartment for all the girls, wholesale, sitting and pedalling on his own key-making bicycle machine. The apartment is mechanically outfitted with collapsing seduction-couches and an instantaneous gas hearth-fire (the while Prometheus' liver is still being ripped at by that vulture for stealing fire from heaven). Also – the one funniest phallic touch I personally ever saw in a movie – two automatic violins that come surging up out of a chest in the seduction-chamber, when a button is pushed, sawing away at Vivaldi's *Four Seasons* for all they are worth! As in the Pat & Mike joke just above.

One wishes all Mr. Lemmon's movie vehicles were this

funny, but unfortunately they are not, though the mechanical touches become, if anything, even more insistent. Not to mention the unlikely and unpleasant *Irma la Douce* directed by Billy Wilder (the only 'sex movie' ever yet made which opens by showing a man chopping doubtless symbolic beef carcasses in half with an axe!) and *How to Murder Your Wife* – again, a very far decline from Chaplin's *Monsieur Verdoux* – the Lemmon movie *Good Neighbor Sam*, in 1964, is unquestionably the most degenerate 'family movie' ever made. It even includes a comic (?) scene of the fortunately rare perversion, the so-called 'defilation' in which a screaming prostitute locked in an elevator cage is sloshed and slathered with red paint in technicolor (possibly representing blood, do you think?) by a presumed lunatic, who is really only trying to paint out an incriminating sign. It then reaches its mechanical high point in a piece of backyard 'junk art' created by good old Sam in his spare time, composed of hooked-together bits of useless mechanical trash, and set on a machine-driven vibrating mattress – I state but the facts – upon which Sam and his gentleman neighbor (the one involved in the presumed wife-trading set-up on which the movie is based) then finally, and of course *accidentally*, fall together in the night, thus setting the whole homoerotic influencing-machine operating and vibrating with them on the mattress. This film was also a great success in Germany under the slightly revised title, *Lend Me Your Husband*. The 'junk art' mattress is essentially a kitsch reduction of Jean Tinguely's black-humor "Machine That Destroys Itself," photographed in operation in Lewis Mumford's *The Pentagon of Power*, pl. 20. And openly intended to symbolize our coming self-destruction.

The line of demarcation between folklore, popular culture, and reality is becoming weaker all around us. The moment prophesied by Heine in *Florentine Nights* (1833) is already here: The Machine becomes almost human in its borrowed cleverness and prehensility, while the human being who teaches it the tricks is simultaneously reduced to less than any machine. I don't mean anyone but *you*, dear Reader, and me, as both of us very well know. It may even be that machines, with men hitched to them, will be used for setting this book in type, and printing it. I am certainly typewriting it on a machine – Royal, Model KMM-36 million: the good standard old model, before they started 'improving' and electrifying it – and am not using my quill pen. I will smash my Royal if you will smash your Mergenthaler, and I will write with a goddam *pencil* if you will stand at a California job-case and set type! And we will burn all the I.B.M. machines with their own print-out sheets, and bust up all the flush-toilets with sledgehammers. I haven't got one of those anyway, and shit in a blue pot and bury it. My own ecological recycling operation. Go thou and do thou likewise. And to *HELL* with T. S. Eliot and his 'Hollow Men,' who have set their arses resolutely on the comfortable corporate toilet, taken the Establishment dollar – if not that of the C.I.A. – and pushed the Automatic Tampax Remover button. Which is why they are Hollow Men.

While jokes and nonsense concern themselves with science, science concerns itself with nonsense and jokes. I am not referring to the present volume, but to more formal science, in particular biology, and physics – with its insane Atom Bomb and lunatic moon-rockets, the cost of which would find the amniotic fluid cure for cancer. There are also not as many friendly scientific advisors around, worth trusting, as we are led to believe. Let me cite a few dangerous examples. One of the very few women already given her niche in the new Pantheon of humanity is surely the late Rachel Carson, who is responsible for having at last successfully alerted the American and world public to the threat of chemical pollution of the earth and its atmosphere, on the heels of similar threats of radiational pollution by the Atom Bomb, its 'tests,' and its peacetime explosions and plutonium residues. Miss Carson's enormously important book, *Silent Spring* (Boston: Houghton Mifflin, 1962, and pocket-reprinted), was first published in part as a series of articles in *The New Yorker*, for forty years the best magazine in America – as many people do not seem to realize – on all subjects except economics, which it carefully evades out of deference to its provincial middle-class audience. A similar series on the destruction of wildlife and natural beauty, by new and monster dams intended to supply irrigation and electrical power, had earlier been published as well. They're even filling in the Grand Canyon now, beginning quietly with its smaller forks, rather than spend the same money desalinizing seawater by atomic power, to irrigate the west. For the stupefyingly beautiful pictorial record of one of the side-canyons already filled in, see Eliot Porter's *The Place No One Knew: Glen Canyon on the Colorado* (San Francisco, 1963). America does not need enemies; it is poisoning its own rivers, drugging its own children, and destroying itself.

Miss Carson's *Silent Spring* is eloquent on the horrible inhumanity of killing robins and other songbirds by filling with poisonous insecticides, like DDT, heptachlor and aldrin, the insects that birds must eat. (Of course, it's just as inhuman to kill chickens by cutting their throats – they're birds too – but we *eat* chickens, so there is no outcry from anyone but them.) And many people have now been brought to understand, through this courageous and pioneering book, that there is such a thing as a proper ecological balance between the human environment and that of other living things. And that the earth and sea and air cannot be endlessly polluted and still support human life, or any other. Instantly, the attempt has been made to co-opt and falsify Miss Carson's warning, which other sincere American biologists have tried to make since the 1890's – in particular Prof. F. H. King, in *Farmers of Forty Centuries*, and Prof. Nathaniel Shaler of Harvard, in *The National Geographic* for 1896, later in his book *Man and the Earth* (1905) – but have invariably been derided and silenced.

This time the conspiracy of silence and falsification is no longer possible, so the propaganda jiu-jitsu of displacement of effort is brought into play. And the popular clamor against pollution is scaled down to propaganda educational movie-shorts, and squib-shots in among the television advertisements, excoriating little children for throwing chewing-gum wrappers on cement city pavements. It is also pretty stupid and frittering to talk about ending pollution, while Atom Bombs and ghastly nerve-gas bombs remained stock-piled by the hundreds and thousands in abandoned mines and quarries – hidden by top-layer tennis courts and little kids' 'Junior Baseball Diamonds' (how nauseating can you get?) – in great American cities and abroad, waiting to be rocketed off and exploded by clockwork the instant the next war begins. Not to mention the defoliation of Viet-Nam meanwhile, and other peccadilloes and tryouts.

Where did Miss Carson stand on all this? Square in the seat of the righteous, as we all know. And what was her conclusion? Her final chapter 17, "The Other Road," gives the alternative she saw as right for the nonpollutive control of, at least, insects:

> Some of the most fascinating of the new methods are those that seek to turn the strength of a species against itself – to use the drive of an insect's life forces [*sex*] to destroy it. The

most spectacular of these approaches is the "male steriliza-
tion" technique developed by the chief of the United States
Department of Agriculture's Entomology Research Branch,
Dr. Edward Knipling, and his associates.

About a quarter of a century ago Dr. Knipling startled his
colleagues by proposing a unique [*eunique?*] method of insect
control. If it were possible to sterilize and release large numbers of insects, he theorized, the sterilized males would, under
certain conditions, compete with the normal wild males so
successfully that, after repeated releases, only infertile eggs
would be produced and the population would die out.

(Don't look now, dear Reader, but you have just read your
race's death-sentence. It's only about bugs, of course ... but
read on.) There follows in Miss Carson's book an admiring
account of the marvellous success of Dr. Knipling, on the
basis of experimental mutations produced in insects by means
of X-rays by G. A. Runner in 1916, and Dr. Hermann Muller
(Nobel prize) in 1927, as also by Charlotte Auerbach and
William Robson at the University of Edinburgh in the early
1940's using mustard gas, the 'secret weapon' of World War I,
which the Germans found in Albert Robida's *La Guerre au
Vingtième Siècle*, as they were quick to point out. At Dr.
Knipling's insistence, a tryout of the method was made in 1958
in an effort to eradicate screw-worm infestation by insects in
American livestock. 'The project involved the weekly production [*sterilization*] of about 50 million screw-worms at a
specially constructed "fly factory," the use of 20 light airplanes
to fly pre-arranged flight patterns ... carrying ... irradiated
[*sterilized*] flies.... By the time the program was considered
complete at the end of 17 months, 3½ billion artificially reared,
sterilized flies [*we say irradiated, if you don't mind*] had been
released over Florida and sections of Georgia and Alabama.'

Similar 'irradiation' programs are now proposed, to wipe out
the dangerous tsetse fly causing sleeping sickness and *nagana*
in Africa, also the corn borer and sugar-cane borer, and perhaps
even the malarial mosquito. It's all about bugs; so socially
useful that it comes out your ears, sanitary, and even painless
to the bugs. And it's all achieved simply by sterilizing billions of
males (*insects*) by radiation techniques. When the Atom Bombs
start going off again, including the Chinese this time, they will
sterilize millions more bugs (*human*). The males (*human*)

operating the radiation machines to sterilize the males (*insects*) by the billions – ha-ha-ha! and us it's only millions! – are protected from the sterilizing effect on the insects (*males, I mean insects*), by wearing large lead aprons in their 'fly factories' – or the reverse – or else they work behind radiation-proof panels of glass like the guards (*insects*) in Nazi German gas-chambers peering scientifically through, to check on the dying Gypsies and Jews (*human*).

Miss Carson was 100% in favor of these sterilization techniques evolved by Dr. Edward Knipling. They are her "Other Road," her only answer to the pollution of the earth. And she concludes ringingly, though only as to the matter of chemical insecticides, in words with which billions of sterilized insects (*human*) could not agree more:

> The current vogue for poisons has failed utterly to take into account these most fundamental considerations. As crude a weapon as a cave man's club, the chemical barrage has been hurled against the fabric of life – a fabric on the one hand delicate and destructible, on the other miraculously tough and resilient, and capable of striking back in unexpected ways. These extraordinary capacities or life have been ignored by the practitioners of chemical control who have brought to their task no "high-minded orientation," no humility before the vast forces with which they tamper.

Right! Now, back at the sterilizing-ranch, who comes *next*, Miss Carson? I have seen a little kitsch cartoon, printed up as a letterhead to be used by grown men, sentimentally showing little birds and big-footed insects (some mistake here?) dropping flowers silently on Rachel Carson's grave. One assumes all the insects were female. They just adore laying those 'infertile eggs.' Ask any egg-factory chicken. The billions of sterilized males (*fill in the blank yourself*) are not dropping any flowers.

Because – and you knew it all the time: admit it – the great new bio-lethal anti-bug method, developed from the discoveries of Drs. Runner, Muller, Auerbach and Robson, through the efforts of Dr. Edward Knipling of the United States Department of Agriculture's Entomology Research [*Sterilization*] Branch, are not long to be reserved only for *bugs*. Rachel Carson's "Other Road" has had the signs changed somewhere along the way by élite-minded biologists (and patriots), and is in fact nothing but the *Road to Auschwitz*. The cyanide used in Auschwitz was also first developed for killing bugs. Thus, ten years after the great entomological victory over the screw-worm fly in Florida and Alabama, for which a scientific tryout had duly been made first in Curaçao in the Dutch West Indies, we learn from the delightedly chortling American news services that the screw-worm sterilizations in Florida and Alabama had also unwittingly served as a scientific tryout or pilot plan. For human sterilization this time, wholesale and global, and no mistake-o!

In the autumn of 1969, national newspaper coverage was given in America to the proposal of botany Professor Richard W. Schreiber (why do all these sterilization experts have such terribly German-sounding names?) speaking at a two-day symposium on "Population Problems and Control" at the University of New Hampshire, to spend five million dollars of research-grant money on developing in three years an airborne virus that would sterilize all the women in any given area. Neat, sweet, and complete, the *real* plan here breaks from cover. I repeat: *An airborne virus that would sterilize all the women in any given area.* (Damn nice of him to suggest giving the females the business this time, instead of us males; but maybe they might make a change here, and a change there, in that darn virus or bug-juice or whatever it is, y'know, and it would sterilize men too! I don't mean to seem suspicious, but, well, *you* know how it is when they get to sterilizing us bugs ...) Dr. Schreiber explained that his virus seems important at this time because man is 'fatally close to breeding himself out of existence.' An antidote to Schreiber's virus would also theoretically be available – one can imagine to whom – though its effect would only last for six months; they'd see to that. So 'nothing is actually changed,' as he puts it, and people could have as many children as they wanted by going in and asking their local Sterilization Commissioner for the antidote injection. (*It says here.*)

As I am sure can easily be understood by even the biggest rummy, reading newspapers and sucking on the tit of the six o'clock television news (all carefully re-digested and 'interpreted' for you in *Time* and *Newsweek* two weeks later, if you still have any frightened doubts), in ten minutes by the clock any competent science-fiction reader above the age of twelve will work you out six good methods for squirting the proposed sterilization virus into the ears and up the arse of every single human being and other animal, beast and bug on earth,

EXCEPT Our Elite Korps – composed of two hundred hand-picked politicians, millionaires, virologists, big-titted naked girls, and twelve-year-old science-fiction readers – all of whom will have been given *Der Immunization Shots* the night before. Also six alternative methods for bad little mother-fucking small countries, like Andorra or Liechtenstein, to put all their national cash into one big moon-rocket loaded with a new and better secret virus which acts only on males, thus trumping or one-upping Schreiber's virus; which they will then lob into the air, by the usual elaborate accident, and plaster all over the whirling earth two days *before* Our Elite Korps shoots off our rocket. Thus making sure that all the girls in the world who want babies after that will have to go to (immunized) Andorra or Liechtenstein to get laid.

Frozen, cubed Liechtensteinian Grade-A semen will also be exported at very high prices, for the usual research purposes, and be horribly cut with worthless monster-semen by the Arab-Mafioso Syndicate importing it to Chicago, before being boot-legged in sanitary little pastel-colored Applicator Packs. In this same way, the little principality of Saxe-Coburg-Gotha in the 19th century kept a stud-farm of small princelings available for marrying queens, etc., of various European royal families, including England. Pick up the story from here in your issue of *Time* magazine (in Chinese ideographs) in the year 2084, if the Chinese are still counting then from the birth of Christ. As seems open to doubt.

The chintzy little sum of five million dollars, which is all Prof. Schreiber thinks this great new development will cost, being the exact amount spent by the oil-and-catsup billionaires of Texas on golf-tees every year, one may prophesy confidently that Prof. Schreiber will get his virus soon. He stated at the New Hampshire symposium – rather naïvely, one might think – that 'no government would dare to do it.' Meaning that no politicians aching to be re-elected would announce that they were planning to sterilize their *own* voting population. But what about all the others? The populations of all those other, foreign, gook countries, that we either hate already or are liable to hate next year. Was it pollution or patriotism to defoliate Viet-Nam? The Red Menace, the Yellow Peril, the Blacks – pick whatever skin color you don't like. Can't be anything wrong with sterilizing *them*, can there? Too damned many of them already. "*The only good Indian (Russian, Nigger,*

Chink) is a dead *Indian (Russian, Nigger, Chink)"* – everybody knows that. And everybody also knows, that has any sense, that these other unfashionably colored cultures are perfectly capable now of producing scientists and viruses to wipe out *our* future in exactly the same way, by means of airborne genocide, and make of us too a last generation of human mules, with 'no pride of ancestry and no hope of progeny.' This too is the future.

Please do not count on all the right-thinking, straight-shooting liberals and world-improvers to refuse to be parties to the virus-sterilizations when these come. Carefully non-radical world-improvers and sententious clergymen have blessed all the other long-range weapons with their various holy waters for thousands of years now; have kissed all the other rockets, helped to build all the other bombs, and to brainwash the public – that is to say the eventual victims – that it is our Manifest Destiny, also the White Man's Burden, and that Everything Is Going To Be All Right. Meanwhile, count on them to get in there fast, as board members on the National Steriliza-tion – I mean *Irradiation* Committees, doing the deciding as to who (besides themselves) gets the deferments, the immunizing shots and the antidotes; and who gets *irradiated*.

The American birth control movement today spends a large part of its effort, if not funds, on promoting sterilization of the insane in just this way, by burning shut or tying off the gonadic tubes. (This operation differs delicately from castration in that the testicles do not fall on the ground and bounce.) The insane are, of course, to be punished for their presumably unrepressed sexual activity, but under some eugenic excuse. Every type of lunatic psycho-surgery is also enacted against them for the same purpose – known politely as 'quieting them down' – by scraping and clipping blindly at the lobes of the brain, by means of scalpels and picks inserted through holes in the head and the inner corner of the eyes. If you have a strong stomach and iron nerves, look up the *details* of the favorite modern psycho-surgical operations such as prefrontal lobotomy and transorbital leukotomy. These are the nightmares and atrocities with which the insane are 'quieted down,' and returned to their relatives as human zombies who will *be no trouble*, now that hospital accommodations for the millions of insane are proving too expensive for the state, and no one can imagine what it is about modern urban life that is driving millions of people insane.

Heavy dosages of the soporific drugs originally also developed to silence the insane are now being pushed, in a mammoth industry, on the relatively sane. These are the castrations of speech, of sight, touch, taste, and hearing, tuning the individual in on the nothingness inside. Unfortunately, the most popular legal and bootleg drugs now being swallowed, smoked, and injected now include violent toxic hallucinants, such as LSD and similar drugs whose open secret is that they *cause induced schizophrenia*, which is another word for insanity, and why they were originally promulgated – for research purposes – by Dr. Humphry Osmond of Princeton and Dr. Abram Hoffer of Canada. Long before Morgan millionaire R. Gordon Wasson, and *Life* magazine, launched them on the American public: issue of May 13th, 1957, and several years before Dr. Timothy Leary – who would like to snag the credit – ever took his first bite of the Mexican *teonanacatl* mushroom that is identical with LSD. Hallucinants that have been put across massively on the young in America and abroad by Pied Piper prophets, and gangster drug-industrialists hidden behind the 'underground press' and the rock-&-roll bands that are their *Nuremberg-musik* advertisement.

To make all things complete, or incomplete, the sane now also have themselves purposely sterilized by the tens of thousands, for birth control purposes – it does not quiet them down – without waiting for the Schreiber virus to do it for them. Few, however, will as yet go so far as 'Christine,' or ask to have their testicles removed as well. They look so *sporty* in the locker-room! It is not an accident that the Associated Press news- release of the Schreiber proposal was put on the wires under the euphemism of 'birth control,' before the public would have the time to respond differently or react honestly, and call it anything else. Pre-think. And was sent out under the humorous caption, parodied from a science-fiction comic strip: "It's a Bird! It's a Plane! It's Birth Control!" Meaning that the information-masters and 'media' schlockmeisters know very well that *sterilization* is still a dirty word – especially on the tip of your prick, and the ovaries of the mother of your children.

The last publication by the life-long head of the birth control movement in America, Dr. Robert Latou Dickinson, whose amanuensis I was for several years, was a pamphlet – written at the age of 88 – featuring five-minute vest-pocket methods of male and female sterilization by means of electric-tip cauteries, etc. Every gynecologist and general practitioner was to be ready to sterilize *anyone* at any hour of the day or night, with this minimum vest-pocket equipment. (Dr. Dickinson also tried for years to introduce immediate complete amputation of the navel cord in newborn infants. Letting it slough off naturally was 'unsanitary.')

Sterilization of the entire population of the world – except for Our Elite Korps, as above – had been in the air for twenty years before Dr. Schreiber's proposal, as an answer to the 'population explosion' among the colored and 'enemy' races. Among the first proposals were swallowed spermatoxins and caponizing chicken-feed, which had taken a set-back as an animal food after sterilizing a farmful of valuable minks who had beed fed the heads of the chemically caponized chickens. Is that pollution, as Rachel Carson would see it, or is that progress? Where is the 'humility before the vast forces with which we are tampering,' when the chemical caponizers that must not be fed to minks are perfect for people?

The brainwashing of the world on this subject has already been done. The splendid achievement of Dr. Gregory Pincus, of Wood's Hole, Massachusetts – who would also for some reason like to make sea-urchins and higher forms of life reproduce without sexual contact, by means of electrical shocks – in developing The Pill as a birth control device, has long since been understood to be too contaminated with the free will of the women who takc it, to be of any real use in the chemical and biological genocides to come. But it has served to soften up the world population to the idea – after a trial balloon in *Time* magazine, as long ago as October 29th, 1951, page 78 – under the tasty euphemism: 'oral contraception,' which one would really have thought referred to something else. The women of the world having accepted this 'biological rape' of their ovaries, along with everything else they are peddled by similar propaganda methods, and begging to get it in the countries where legal abortion is not yet available, a sterilizing 'birth control' drug operating directly on the testicles of men was also developed in the 1960's – in Germany, naturally. It had the disadvantage of being incompatible with the drinking of alcohol, the principal drug-addiction of the entire civilized world, and will therefore have to be replaced by some improved caponizing drug or virus not having this disadvantage. According to a pun immediately circulating in America, the new 'male pill' is named *No-acetol,* or *Sulfadenial.*

In case you think these people are kidding, and that all this will somehow pass you and me by, I am here to tell you that they are *not* kidding and that we and our children will have to face up to this ultimate castrational threat very soon. The people who run the world, and their staff 'scientists,' have it fixed in their little Malthusian minds – correctly or incorrectly, remains to be seen – that the world cannot feed and support its mathematically-probable human population as of the year 2001, or 2084, or who-knows-when. Their coldly planned and proposed solution is 'one-generation genocide': simply to sterilize everyone in the world *but themselves.* There is also their unspoken (and real) solution: The Bomb, along with plenty of horror-viruses, nerve-gasses, and other *Schrecklichkeit* for any accidental survivors.

As to their second line of attack, the 'sterilization' soundtrack, in 1973 a group of British geneticists – the most ferocious right now, on their increasingly tight little island – announced a new basis for the Male Pill: the ancient drug, snakeroot (reserpine or serpasil), which most men who must take it for high blood pressure have found to their surprise has a powerful anti-aphrodisiac effect owing to its depressing of the hypothalamus, thus depleting the brain of the excitor secretion, noradrenaline, which must be kept low to control the blood pressure. Discreet tests using anti-aphrodisiac acetate of cyproterone have already been made on a British prisoner for homosexual rape, in Cardiff, Wales, exactly in *Clockwork Orange* style. A drug activating this fine new subcastratory technique (to replace the older stilbestrol, which also dries up the parturient woman's milk!) is now being marketed in Britain under the names of 'Anquil' or 'Benperidol.' See *Le Nouvel Observateur* (10 Sept. 1973) p. 44–5, "La Castration miracle." This takes care of the medico-legal precedents and operational logistics for the coming Operation No-Ball (naturally to be promoted over the state radio with the army song *"Bollocks! And the same to you ..."*)

Leaping into the saddle or breach, a British sex-counsellor, Dr. Robert Chartham, got a new book out immediately, *Your Sexual Future* (1973), prophesying, according to his press accounts, that 'in twenty years, all [British] schoolboys will by law have to go on the Pill; all males over sixteen will be sterilized after being compelled to give sperm to state artificial semination centres. All couples will be rationed to two children; all babies produced by artificial insemination.' (As in the joke about the Virgin Birth, *how is that an improvement over the old system?*) Dr. Chartham is of course sorry about it all, but not so sorry as to avoid adding his unprovable prophetic bit to the propaganda hard-sell of *no future for sex*. ("And the same to you!") 'It's a pretty horrifying picture,' he is quoted as concluding, 'but I'm afraid this sort of system seems inevitable.' What the daily forcible dose for prisoners, soldiers and the insane will be has not yet been announced.

14

DYSPHEMISM & INSULTS

CURSES and obscene invectives and imprecations are among the most primitive and most direct forms of verbal assault. They require nothing more than the aggressive naming or alluding to some taboo object or action – such as food, sex, scatology, death or the deity – to achieve the effect of creating anger, shock, offense *or laughter* in persons controlled by the particular taboo. Far from the effect of laughter being that achieved upon persons who hold the taboo most lightly, it is precisely from those who believe in the taboo most sincerely that the most unexpectedly violent laughter is sometimes wrenched. Dysphemism or 'evil speech,' cursing and insults are a striking form of language magic, of which the magical power (as with all magic) derives from the underlying fear of the taboo, and the listener's or the cursed or insulted person's belief in it.

Taboo words, and the irreverent handling of taboo subjects such as the love of the mother, have the power to move the 'believing' listener or spectator emotionally, whether to laughter, tears or responses of anger and violence, irrespective of whether the speaker or person abrogating the taboo also believes in it, or is simply manipulating it consciously and even cynically. There need not even be any insulting or offending person actually present: the same magical or offensive effect is achieved by mere written words or traces, as in 'obscene' epigraphs or pictorial *graffiti* on a wall or fence, advertising or propaganda posters insulting a wartime enemy or inciting the viewer to buy some object or engage in some action, and hostile or taboo printed words in a newspaper or book, or in an anonymous letter.

The same taboo term, such as *'son-of-a-bitch'*, *'mother-fucker,'* or *'shit,'* will have the same magical effect of moving certain listeners to anxiety or irritation, anger or laughter, even when spoken by a mechanical apparatus such as a phonograph recording or magnetic tape of an individual (for example, the late Lenny Bruce) actually known to be dead. Hostile and insulting wills left behind at death, cutting off certain disliked survivors 'without a shilling,' and vituperatively explaining *why*, affect these survivors just as powerfully as if the same insulting rejection had been enacted by the living person. The essential condition is always that the listener be emotionally involved in the matter; that he or she believe in the relevant taboo, and, at some level, be afraid of it. The hostile will or testament thus gains some of its power precisely from the taboos concerning 'ghosts' and death which it is itself abrogating.

Voodoo death is achieved in the same way, the victim being frightened literally to death by action of the emotions on the adrenal glands, and on the heart, brain, and lungs (a 'stroke'), but always with the condition that the victim must *know* that he or she is being hexed. The black magic 'goona-goona' doll with the needles in its eyes or heart must be discovered, the crossed twigs tied with a red string must be found lying on the doorstep, the black cat must be seen crossing one's path, the ghost must walk or clank where one can hear it, the anonymous letter (or compromising photograph) must be delivered, and so forth. Reduced to a rule: *Magic is always entirely subjective, its power lying not in the magician or priest, but in the victim or butt.* Of nothing is this more true than the magic involving the use of words.

Cursing and swearing are usually roughly distinguished, though the terms largely overlap, in that the *curse* is actually directed against someone or something, whereas the *swear-word* may be a mere imprecation or an expletive flaunting of some taboo on speech, in order to express violent and angry emotion. Many presumed swear-words are actually curses in which the name of the person or thing being cursed is not pronounced, or is diverted to a generalized 'it'. For example, "Damn it!" or even "God damn it!" which shock no one but the more prissy type of clergymen and elderly ladies of all sexes, whereas "Damn *you!*" is fighting words in any language. So also with "The Devil take it!" and "to hell with it!" as differentiated from "to hell with *you!*" If, to these taboos, certain others are added or overlayered in the breaking of them, as on the sanctity of one's own national, family, or religious group – *"To hell with you and your big, dirty Irish feet!"* or *"I spit in your stinking Jewish beard!"* or *"Fuck you and fuck your mother!"* (all authentic examples in modern use) – the fight will usually begin right then & there, if the insulted person has the courage to fight, or is 'egged on' to do so by the encouragements or taunts of third persons.

Where it is desired to avoid such combats, and yet to express oneself explosively, the taboo is abrogated 'in the air,' as it were, carefully avoiding making specific any person or national group being cursed, or 'damned,' or sworn at. The very terms used are often modified in pronunciation or spelling in such a way as to avoid using the taboo terms, while nevertheless achieving a certain definite or even violent expressiveness. This is pure name-magic, of an ancient type, as in the avoiding of the original 'four-letter word,' the ineffable name of the Jewish deity, expurgatorily pronounced *Jehovah* and in other ways. Often the persons gelding their curses or obscenities have originally learned the words in that form, and are only vaguely aware that there are more violent or dangerous forms further back These 'minced' oaths and obscenities exist in many languages, and it is a pity there is no broad study of them available. (But see Charles T. Tallent-Bateman's "The Etymology of Some Common Exclamations," in *Manchester Literary Club Papers*, 1886, XII. 345–56.) Consider, for example, the Spanish '¡*carramba!*' (which means nothing, and so is used even by priests as a polite expletive) replacing '¡*carajo!*' (meaning the penis, which is in turn further dysphemized as '¡*pendejo!*' meaning pubic hair.)

All such minced oaths and imprecations, both in English and other languages, are usually violently pronounced, to try to make up in volume of noise and emphasis for the missing force of the evaded obscenity or sacrilege. Real curse-words are often pronounced in a low, grating tone when they are most sincerely meant. In the enclosed Italian food market, on the European style – so charming until these became the ugly and soulless American 'supermarkets' now re-exported to Europe! – at Fordham in The Bronx, New York, in 1953, I was once party to a free-for-all fist-fight caused by a meaningless oath of this kind. It was pronounced by a seller of sausages, who was crying his wares at his stand with wild grimaces and the violent shout, "*Pasta-fazúla!*" actually only meaning macaroni-and-beans, however awful it may sound to the non-initiate, and here only intended to get attention. The man I was with, thinking he was being insulted, replied with a spur-of-the-moment matching version of the only Italian profanity he knew, shouting back at the sausage-vendor, "*And pasta-fazulaté! you son-of-a-bitch!*" adding to this the gesture of 'the finger,' rising and reaming violently from his clenched fist, with the other hand repetitively striking the muscle of the upraised arm. Though he had not actually pronounced any taboo words in Italian, everyone present *understood* his violent reply to mean, as of course it did – and the accompanying gesture even more specifically – the principal obscene insult of the Neapolitan or Bolognese dialects, *"Fa'n'gul-até!"* (I fuck you in the ass!) And all hell broke loose.

An interesting and little-known passage on national *styles* in swearing appears in the "Essay on the Worship of the Generative Powers" anonymously added by Thomas Wright, George Witt and Sir James Tennent in 1865 to Richard Payne Knight's *A Discourse on the Worship of Priapus* (reprinted in 1894 and 1952). This is included in my *The Guilt of the Templars* (1966) p. 254–5. Note, for example, that German-language swearing of the pre-1900's Biedermeier period is particularly artificial and minced, though very noisy, as *'Blitz!'* for *'Potz!'* or the pitiful *'Donnerwetter!'* (thunderstorm), probably disguising some reference to hell-&-damnation. Scatological German oaths do, however, exist. The limit in this line was reached in Richard Sheridan's famously successful comedy, *The Rivals* (1775), in which, with the unforgettably blundering Mrs. Malaprop, one of the male characters swears continuously and always differently – but only by his 'braces & stays' and similar milk-&-water combinations. This idea is reprised at the kitsch level in the character of the eccentric inventor, Mr. Damon, in the American *Tom Swift* boys' book series, by Victor Appleton, about 1910.

These things belong to the childhood of the race – any race. One of my young sons, who went through a phase of aggressiveness and vituperation when he was about five years old (the classic anal-sadistic stage), invented his own swear-words and used them emphatically all day long, especially *"Pupu de poison pourri!"* (Rotten shit-poison) and *"Good sandwich!"* this latter his approximation of "Goddam son-of-a-bitch," which he had overheard in English, a language he did not then speak. I somehow do not think he would have taken as enthusiastically to "Odds braces & stays!" Another child liked *"Son-of-a-bridge of a basket!"*

'Swearing' certainly refers to the taking of solemn oaths – thus basically religious, though here done lightly or as an act of anti-religion. (*"Don't swear; it sounds like hell!"*) Whereas 'profanity' should perhaps refer to what has already been profaned or made common. The reports of policemen arresting individuals for 'disturbing the peace' or 'profane language' often must stumblingly attempt in this way to differentiate between various types of verbal abrogation of taboo. The distinctions so drawn visibly mean nothing, and are just leftovers of the legal usages of many centuries of word-oriented and magniloquent clerics, as petrified in the surviving laws. In these, all manner of meaningless distinctions-without-difference are drawn on these subjects, and overloadings with reduplicative or 'catch-all' adjectives are attempted. This is particularly true in the English-language laws concerning 'obscenity,' which for centuries have avoided any objective criteria and are really themselves a sort of legalistic cursing or anathema being pronounced against the banned and reprehended sexual objects or actions, which are *'obscene, lewd, lascivious, lustful, lecherous, filthy, indecent or disgusting'* – saying nothing in their overlapping terror but that they are afraid.

The literature on the subject in English is rather sparse, and is also usually expurgated except at the mildest levels, thus making most of it quite useless as an historical record. The best thing about Julian Sharman's *Cursory History of Swearing* (London, 1884) is really its delicious title, and a striking description of the singing of the "Captain Kidd" song, *'Damn their eyes!'* at a private club, which I have quoted elsewhere. There is an excellent and very extensive French *Dictionnaire des Injures* by Robert Édouard (Paris: Tchou, 1967), which is far more than the mere dictionary promised; and a similar Italian work, *Dizionario dei Ingiurie*, published during the 1950's. The yearbook of non-erotic German and other folklore, *Am Ur-Quell*, edited by Prof. Friedrich S. Krauss (1890 ff.) – with the superb motto, *'Folklore is humanity's Fountain of Youth'* – carried in most of the volumes lists of insulting terms in many languages, under the heading "Schimpfwörter" (at No. 8, "Sonstiges," in the index to each volume); and other material on this subject is given in Krauss' larger parallel series on erotic folklore, *Kryptádia* and *Anthropophytéia*. There is also the brief but significant repertory translated from the Argentine, "L'Art de l'Injure," in Jorge Luis Borges' *Histoire d'Infamie* (Paris, 1974).

Aside from Hispanic profanity, which is by far the most ornate, as will be seen below, the French are not far behind in art-swearing and crude dysphemism – when they feel like it. See in particular the combination of profanity and eroticism in

the anonymous *Dom Bougre aux États-Généraux* (1789(reprinted 1868 ff.) falsely attributed to Restif de La Bretonne; and
the fabulous journalism during the French Revolution of 'Père
Duchesne' (Jacques Hébert), who was eventually guillotined by
his own party. (There are excellent studies of Hébert by Charles
Brunet, 1859; and Gérard Walter, 1946, but not venturing much
quotation.) Later came the famously swearing pamphlets of
the erotic hunchback, 'Monsieur Mayeux,' in the 1830's; and
finally – most violent and profane of all – the revival of the
incendiary newspaper style in *La Grande Colère du Père
Duchêne*, sixty-eight numbers issued during the French Com-
mune in 1871, with various imitations : all of great rarity.
These are where the 'underground' press really began, obscenity
foremost.

In the introduction to Norman Douglas' drily witty erotic
collection, *Some Limericks* (Florence, 1928), he includes some
passages from what was to have been a study of Italian swear-
words, stating that he had 'caught the old ones in the nick of
time;' but this was never published. He had been at it ten years
or more, since he already noted in his *Alone* (London, 1921)
p. 176 : 'Three spring months, at Florence, had been spent in
making a scientific collection of local imprecations – abusive,
vituperative or profane expletives; swear-words, in short – en-
riched with elaborate commentary. I would gladly print this
little study in folk-lore as an appendix to the present volume,
were it fit for publication.' In the end it was never printed, nor
are the present whereabouts of the manuscript known to
Douglas' bibliographers. One hopes it is not lost forever, as a
study like this at the hands of a master like Douglas would be
worth a great deal, as evidenced by the brief sample of his
intended introduction, printed in that of *Some Limericks* as a
light-hearted parergon, and the only surviving fragment.

Other useful existing works on swearing in English are Edgar
Valdes' "The Art of Swearing," in *Belgravia Magazine* (December 1895) vol. 88 : p. 366–79; several articles ending in a book by
Prof. Burges Johnson, *The Lost Art of Profanity* (1948), and a
curious manuscript collection on the subject, by Henry C.
Wyld (?) in the library of Princeton University. By far the outstanding work is Ashley Montagu's *The Anatomy of Swearing*
(1967), which is splendidly researched and includes the sexual
materials frankly, as is also the case with Edward Sagarin's *The
Anatomy of Dirty Words* (New York, 1962) whose biblio-

graphy of modern sources is even better than Ashley Montagu's. At a completely different level of approach, I have found the greatest value in Prof. Robert C. Elliott's magnificent study, *The Power of Satire: Magic, Ritual, Art* (Princeton Univ. 1960).

Books on insults in English naturally include quite an amount of matter coming close to profanity and obscenity, or trying to make up for its careful omission by means of the loud noise of the substituted insults, on the *'Pasta-fazúla'* pattern described just above. A good deal of windy vituperation of this kind will be found in the two series of anthologies of *Invective and Abuse* edited by 'Hugh Kingsmill' (London, 1929 ff.) and in a competing work entitled *Whips and Scorpions*. Neither of these even mentions the most extraordinary such insulting and abusive document in English, *The Medal of John Bayes* (1682), an attack on the poet Dryden by the dramatist Thomas Shadwell, who had been satirized in Dryden's *MacFlecknoe*. The most violent modern item is probably a letter by the poet Swinburne to the American essayist Ralph Waldo Emerson, calling him an 'autocoprophagous baboon' and a few other niceties of that kind.

The whole letter is reprinted in the best such all-around anthology, Joseph Rosner's *The Hater's Handbook* (New York: Delacorte Press, 1965) p. 142–3, which explains that Swinburne was merely answering the reported condemnation of himself by Emerson as 'a perfect leper, and a mere sodomite.' This attack was unwarranted. Swinburne was not a sodomite, but a perfectly normal heterosexual masochist of the grovelling type. He limited his masochism to women – the actress Adah Isaacs Menken among others – and shafted his verbal violence invariably at men, alternating it with the sick poems addressed to his 'Lady of Pain.' I have discussed the similar sadomasochist alternation of character – it is a standard trait – in a far greater poet, Robert Herrick, in the introduction to *The Limerick* (New York, 1970) p. xxiv–vi, contrasting Herrick's sweetly beautiful food-&-breast-oriented love songs addressed to women with the endlessly bitter and sarcastic epigrams mixed helter-skelter into his *Hesperides* (1648) and addressed to men. See some further examples in Isaac D'Israeli's *Quarrels and Calamities of Authors* (1812–14).

Probably the largest collection of insults and attacks *on oneself* that anyone has published is *Menckeniana: A Schimpf-lexicon* (1928), edited by H. L. Mencken, and composed entirely of printed insults and vituperative letters ('hate-mail') levelled at him as magazine editor and cultural bell-wether during the 1920's in America. A brief selection is given by Rosner, p. 164–6. The violent and hateful journalistic and political prose common in British and American parliaments and newspapers throughout the 19th century still lingers on, but it is not what it was in the hands of whipmasters-general like the Southern humorist of the Civil War period, George Washington Harris (in his *"Sut Lovingood's Yarns"*); William Brann, author of *Brann the Iconoclast*, taken from the columns of his anti-Negro, anti-everythingarian newspaper of the same name, who was shot dead in the street, in Waco, Texas, in 1898, for one of his columns (but drew his own gun and killed his aggressor before dying); and the last real continuator of the Brann tradition, the New York newspaper columnist Westbrook Pegler, who had the not-unusual peculiarity of being whole-heartedly on the wrong side of every question on which he extruded his daily stint of bile.

The most recent work on insults that has appeared in English is the anonymous *Insult Dictionary: How to Snarl Back in Five Languages* (London, 1966), which gives equivalents in parallel columns, in English, German, French, Italian, and Spanish, for various long series of ugly wisecracks to be used in all possible situations while travelling abroad. Where most guide-books tell what sort of tips to give for various services, this tells what sort of insults the traveller yearns to fling at every Fucking Foreign Flunkey (or F.F.F.) he or she dares not insult in fact. It is thus a sort of dreambook of insults, or fantasy shit-bath for the beleaguered traveller who wishes he or she had stayed at home (and so does everyone else). If to be used practically, it is highly recommended to all readers weighing over two hundred and fifty pounds, and seven feet high, who are black-belt *judokas*. It ends with a multilingual list of actual "Schimpf-wörter," p. 122–7, marked "Hard Words, general terms and all-purpose insults," going on from 'Hairy creep' through 'Perfumed pansy' to the old-fashioned 'Villain' and 'Wretch.' The book thus appears to have been written by a woman, and has been attributed to an American writer, Miss Doris Lilly, surely incorrectly, owing to the similarity of title between her *How to Make Love in Five Languages* (London, 1965?) a sort of guide-book for kept-women abroad, which does include rather similar lists of multilingual bring-downs and evasions of ardent suitors; and another work by the unknown author of *The Insult Dictionary*, entitled *The Lover's Dictionary: How to Make It in Five Languages*, which the lovers of the world need like a hole in the head. See also Steve Allen's 'collection of verbal vengeance,' *Curses!* (1972).

The theatrical farce, *The Man Who Came to Dinner* by George S. Kaufman & Moss Hart in the 1940's satirizing the career and character of the minor homosexual essayist, Alexander Woollcott, and of several English actresses, is a gallery of insults flung in each other's faces, and was a great success. The format was repeated in the 1960's in Edward Albee's *Who's Afraid of Virginia Woolf?* – an even greater success, this time internationally – about which enough has been said above in chapter 9.I.2, under "Name-Calling," in the First Series, p. 680–81; and chapter 10.II.3, "Homosexual Recognitions." Aggressive and insulting dialogue on this style has since become epidemic in the American and British theatre, even so tender an item as the Broadway comedy *Butterflies Are Free* by Leonard Gershe (1970), in which the hero is blind, being spiced with anti-Mom insults and kidding of this lesser Oedipus' mother. As I hate to see other people making all the money, I am working on one of these sentimental hate-plays myself, entitled *Rectums, Anyone?* Expurgatory symbolism not being my style, my hero does not make any bones about being a castrato; he has been operated on in Denmark by specialists of the straight-razor-and-corkscrew school. However, he has a *tail* fourteen inches long – how's that for a gimmick, Gershe, old boy? – and is violently in love with a rectal nymphomaniac. *Opening scene: Macy's window* (we use Selfridge's when we open at the Palladium in London) *Time: High noon. Enter the heroine, Valerie Clytoris, backwards* ...

A British educator, A. J. Morgan Morison, of the Schools Psychological Service, Wigan (Lancs.) informed me in 1968 that he is preparing a study of the psychology of oaths and swearing, but this does not appear to have been published as yet. It is possible, also, that I misunderstood the subject of his study, and that it is not relevant to the present chapter, but concerned with formal oaths and swearings of asseveration, which are of course the ancient originals from which modern vituperative oaths survive and descend. The sexuality of Biblical oaths, for example, sworn to on the penis or testicles – politely, the 'thigh,' or 'under the thigh,' as is the euphemism in *Genesis*,

xxiv. 2–3, and xlvii. 29 – was of an intense seriousness, the phallic taboo being abrogated in order to engage profoundly the conscience of the person swearing the oath. In *Heavenly Discourse* (1927) by Charles Erskine Scott Wood, who earlier collected Indian folktales and myths, the American Indians are said to make their most solemn oath in the same way, on the penis.

I have seen emotional Italian women in the south of France take oath in the same way, swearing on the lives of their children, while clutching both breasts. It is a gesture one can never forget. The first time I saw it made, an elderly woman was complaining delicately of the high price of living, that made it necessary for her to rent out rooms in her own home to foreigners like myself. "But Madame," I said in surprise; "you said you have eight children. Surely they can send you a little money, or a cheese or something, from time to time." Her elegant reserve fell entirely apart at the word 'cheese,' and she began shouting: "Yes! I brought up twelve children, and eight are still alive. And twenty grandchildren too! Let them live and be happy!" she cried, with her face all twisted. Then clutching at her sunken breasts with both hands, and shaking them as she spoke, she added with terrible emphasis: "*One Italian mama can nourish twelve* bambini *at her breasts, but twelve bambini cannot nourish one Italian mama!*" And she broke into tears, and so did I.

I. EUPHEMISM AND DYSPHEMISM

The principal influence of the presentation of dirty jokes, limericks, recitations or songs to a 'jury of one's peers,' whether in college fraternity 'bull-sessions' or in the similar activities of children and adults, is not actually on the newness or oldness of the jokes told ('old' jokes are hooted), nor even on the themes allowed – which are invariably whatever the tellers may propose – but on the *vocabulary*. As has already been observed in the Introduction here, many listeners, attempting to avoid the inescapable sexual relationship of listening to jokes on sexual themes, will agree to listen only with the proviso ' . . . If they're *clever*,' meaning that all taboo words and anatomically graphic description will be avoided in the telling, thus allowing the listener either to accept, or (by not laughing or 'not understanding') to refuse to accept, the intimacy of any particular *double entendre.* Jokes not conforming to this rule are the opposite of 'clever': they are 'stupid.' That is to say, they are unavoidably clear, and lacking in indirection – verbal rape, as opposed to verbal seduction.

The scatological joke cannot easily be told under these conditions. It demands, as its principal feature, the right to abrogate the verbal taboo, and to use the most graphic images and most taboo terms. Sometimes a shouted *'Shit!'* is all the scatological joke really offers, at the so-well-named punch-line, to force the listeners' laughter. In the polite and cautious subterfuges of euphemism, there is, instead, a softening or modifying of any taboo terms, and a resolute refusal to face the existence of certain distressing realities which are the real subjects of the taboos.

Thus modern English-speaking people have learned to say 'undertaker' instead of 'grave-digger,' just as Shakespeare had already preferred to call his two clowns, digging Ophelia's grave in *Hamlet*, V.i.36, 'grave-makers.' Nowadays we have fled away even from 'undertaker,' since we know too well what it means, and the person involved has become a 'mortician' (or even a 'funeral-director'), as the original euphemism becomes tainted with the frightening or evocative image being avoided: *"The grave-digger is here to lay out your father's corpse."* No! no! ... *"The funeral-director just telephoned to ask about preparing the remains of the departed."* That it is the first and not the second which is really dignified, we cannot afford to face. Scatology will have none of this. Can have none of this, if it is to raise laughter in its audience. The scatological joke, and the insult or ungallantry that is closely connected with it, is insistently dysphemistic; invariably uses the taboo terms for sexual or excretory acts by preference to any milder equivalents. A spade is never a spade: it is *'a bloody fucking shovel!'*

In all scatological formats making use of language, instead of simply throwing shit or spraying the other person with piss, and particularly in dysphemism or 'dirty talk,' the primordial choice is invariably that of the 'dirty' word, rather than any 'clean' or polite equivalent, for the identical object or action. This is the real *nexus* or swivel upon which the intended humor (or open insult) must turn. In Prof. Allen Walker Read's splendid essay, "The Nature of Obscenity," published as introduction to his rare pamphlet on outhouse graffiti, *Lexical Evidence from Folk Epigraphy in Western North America*

(Paris, 1935), which was the first serious modern work on the subject, an introduction reprinted in full in *Neurotica* (1949) No. 5: p. 23–30, a very important point is made as to these verbal distinctions seemingly without a difference, yet with an emotional difference of obvious and even magical power:

> Verbal taboo is not the result of the 'refinements of civilization,' for it is present among savages. Thus we read of the Australian aborigines of Queensland, in Walter E. Roth's *Ethnological Studies among the North-West-Central Queensland Aborigines* (1897) page 184: "Foul language is very commonly made use of under circumstances of contempt, derision, or anger: the foulness does not, however, consist so much in the actual thoughts conveyed as in the particular words employed, there being both a decent and indecent vocabulary to describe the particular region, the generative organs, which are then usually drawn attention to. Thus in the Mitakoodi language, *me-ne* is the 'society' term for vulva, and nothing is thought of its utterance before a company of people, while *koon-ja*, *puk-kil*, or *yel-ma-rung-o*, all names for the same part, are most blackguardly words to use." From our unbiased position, with regard to the Mitakoodi language, we can see how absurd it is to make a distinction between *me-ne* and *koon-ja*: but are not such distinctions just as baseless in our language? – Baseless? The psychological motivation for taboo lies deep, and probably has its root in the fear of the mysterious power of the sex impulse.

In the same way, as everyone must realize, plain words like *shit* and *piss*, or dysphemistic phrases like 'to have the drizzling shits' (for diarrhea) or 'to have shit in one's blood' (for cowardice) are not now acceptable in formal situations, where neo-Latin and Greek terms meaning exactly the same thing, such as *defecate*, or *micturate*, or *diarrhea*, or such euphemistic colloquialisms for this last as 'to have the runs' or 'the jerry-go-nimble' or 'the trots' or 'the collywobbles,' will pass without reprobation or comment. The fear expressed in this taboo is obviously a fear of magical dirtying or soiling of the listener, with the very objects or bodily products designated by the 'improper' (*i.e.* unclean) term, in such a way and with such force that these objects or products are reacted to almost as though present. The socially-permitted euphemism is permitted specifically because it has no such evocative effect, and it is no longer permitted when it does. An excellent study of these shifts and developments of euphemism is made in Edward Sagarin's *The Anatomy of Dirty Words* (New York, 1962). In the reverse phenomenon, dysphemism, the dirtiest possible terms are used; as in the current American ultimate imprecation, 'Holy shit!' (see Rona Jaffe's *The Fame Game*, 1969, end of chap. 7), in which the 'shit' replaces and dysphemizes '*God!*' – now too oldfashioned.

A joke told invariably in America about some recent and unpopular governor or president makes the point very clearly: *The president's daughters are vexed because he has used the term 'manure' instead of 'fertilizer' in a speech at a horticultural show, and they remonstrate with their mother about this. "Don't complain, girls," she says tiredly, "it's taken me twelve years to get him to say 'manure'."* (N.Y. 1948.) Vance Randolph's *Hot Springs and Hell* (1965), the first annotated American joke-book, traces this at No. 24 to the 1890's in Kansas, and notes a version in *Charley Jones' Laugh Book* (June 1956) p. 39, 'updating' it by ascribing it to President Harry Truman. It is not any longer exclusively American. In the British form, on a 'trade-union bloke who works his way up to be mayor,' the ending plays more boldly on the return of the repressed: *When it is suggested that he should say 'fertilizer' in the future instead of 'manure,' the new mayor answers boldly, " 'Fertilizer' b'buggered! It's taken me ten years to remember not to call it shit!"* (Chelmsford, Essex, 1953.)

A favorite item on class-linked *arriviste* snobbery, similarly links linguistic pretention and euphemism. *The Buzzard and the Rabbit had known each other for years. One day Buzzard struck oil and got rich, while Rabbit was still shovelling shit behind the barn. Mr. Buzzard sent for Rabbit to bring him a cartload of fertilizer. When Rabbit arrived he was met at the door by a turtle in butler's livery. "Hi, Turtle," he said, "is ol' Buzzard around?" "Mr. Buz-zard is out in the yard," replied Turtle haughtily. "And kindly refer to me as Mr. Tur-tool." "O.k., Mr. Tur-tool, go tell Mr. Buz-zard that Mr. Rab-bit is here with the shit."* (D.C. 1949, from a young soldier at Lafayette Chicken Hut, whose place of origin was not given.) Animal-protagonist stories of this kind are the staple in Aesop's *Fables* of ancient Greece, and thus still survive in Russian folklore, as seen in A. N. Afanasyev's *Russian Folktales* and the *Russian Secret Tales* (1872) that are its supplement. The touch of the liveried animal-butler in the joke is certainly taken from Lewis Carroll's *Alice in Wonderland*, chapter 6. – *The old maid and a sailor's parrot are the only two survivors of the shipwreck, and have been clinging to a bit of driftwood for days. "How's your wrinkled old ass?" croaks the parrot. "Oh, shut up!" snaps the old maid. "So's mine," says the parrot; "must be this damn salt water."* (Bloomington, Ind. 1963.) As always in jokes, the parrot can always think as well as speak, and always has the last word.

The trick of false misunderstandings has already been given in various sections in the First Series, 2.V, and 4.I.2–3, "Propositions in Error" and "Purposeful Perversion," where it is used for purposes of sexual approach. Here it is used strictly as an insult, generally of women: *A woman in a pet shop wants to buy a porcupine and is told by the clerk that there are two main kinds, the Rocky Mountain and the Canadian. "What's the difference between them?" she asks. "Nothing, really," says the clerk, 'except that the Rocky Mountain porcupine has a prick three inches long, and the imported Canadian porcupine has a prick five inches long." The woman is very offended and complains to the manager, who assures her that the clerk did not mean to say anything impolite, but was referring only to the animals' quills. "As a matter of fact," adds the manager, "their pricks are about the same size."* (First printed in *World's Dirtiest Jokes*, 1969, p. 149.)

The effect of this trick is always the greatest when it is used climactically in elegant passages, on the system analyzed by Alexander Pope, early in the elegant 18th century, in *Peri Bathos, or The Art of Sinking in Poetry*. A modern joke puts the matter very well, though (as always) one must suspect an intention of mockery – or, at least, the 'return of the repressed' – behind the presumed artless innocence of the speaker. *A lady seascape-artist and two fishermen go out to sea in a rowboat early one morning, and they fish while she paints. Everything goes well for about two hours, and then she looks rather distractedly around and says to one of the fishermen, "Pardon me, what does one do when one wishes to ... er ... defecate?" He looks startled, and clambers to the other end of the boat to discuss the matter in an undertone with his mate, then comes back and announces: "Lady, when we wishes to defecate, we generally shits in the bucket."* (Baltimore, Md. 1942.)

One wonders if there is not a sardonic intention similar to

that of the joke just given, in a remark in the preface to *"Un-printable" Songs from the Ozarks* (MS. 1949, Library of Congress) p. iii, by Vance Randolph, who is himself a famous dry wit – what the French call a *pince-sans-rire* – complaining of the expurgation of his four volumes of *Ozark Folksongs*, published by the State Historical Society of Missouri: *'If these songs are to be published at all, they must be printed exactly as they are sung. Such items cannot be defecated short of evisceration.'*

Theoretically, but only theoretically of course, one arrives eventually at the point where level after level of expurgation and euphemism have become fatally *tainted with meaning* (as an English publisher once charmingly said in explaining why a manuscript of mine could have no success in England), and the threshold of response drops so low that some nothing-at-all will send the susceptible into a violent tizzy of erotic response. *Two Trappist monks sitting in separate cubicles have been busy copying old manuscripts for years, without ever speaking. Late one afternoon, during a thunderstorm, one whispers to the other, "Let's talk." The other one whispers back, "Well, all right. What shall we talk about?" "Let's say dirty words." "I don't know about that. You say one first." "Hair under your arms! There! Now you say one." "I can't," says the other; 'I'm coming."* (D.C. 1951, told with high homosexual inflection, especially at the end. Heard earlier, in Berkeley, Calif. 1941, of two high-school boys masturbating together, but unable to arrive at orgasm.) The erotization of anxiety during the thunderstorm – which is also a sort of heavenly 'speaking' – is an interesting touch. See further, on the question of threshold of response to the taboo, my *The Horn Book*, p. 362–5, noting the concentration on folk-*tunes* to avoid the bawdy *words.*

The end-point in euphemism is obscenity *by numbers.* While European languages often use the double-zero (oo) of the roulette wheel to indicate the toilet-room, they do not use the 'Number One' and 'Number Two' representing urination and defecation (*'peepee'* and *poopoo'*) of the English or American nursery. *The scout-leader is trying to get all the cub-scouts to sit quietly and listen to the lecture on how badgers cut down trees. "Now there'll be no more hollering," he says severely. "If you want to leave the room, you just hold up your hand." "How's that going to stop it?" one boy asks.* (The joke sometimes ends here.) *"If you wanna wee-wee you say 'Number One,' and 'Number Two' if you have to make poo-poo."* Dis-

*gusted by this infantilism, one of the older boys calls out,
"Gimme a number quick, teacher; I gotta fart!"* (New Rochelle,
N.Y. 1946. Note the accidental use of 'teacher' in the punchline,
suggesting a schoolroom version originally.)

Not quite so direct about its satire on the apparently endlessly humorous 'Yiddishe mama' ('Jewish mother' when peddling her to *goyim*), but essentially just as clear : *Two elderly
Jewish ladies are discussing the band-concert they heard the
night before on the Mall in Central Park. "And was there anything you specially like, Mrs. Mutchershop?" says one of the
ladies. "Yes," says the other, "the piece I rilly appreciated was
Liszt's Hungarian Rhapsody – you shall pardon the expression
– Number Two."* (N.Y. 1940.) What is interesting here is not so
much the scatological touch as the apologetic phrase that
creates it. On this typically Jewish sort of apotropaic or
apologetic disclaimer see the excellent compilation and study
by A. A. Roback, "Psychological Aspects of Jewish Protective
Phrases," in *Bulletin of the Jewish Academy of Arts and Sciences*
–1938) No. 4. With this should also be compared the curiously
similar materials on early Puritan apotropaism, as mocked by
the Elizabethan dramatists, in Prof. Morris P. Tilley's "Some
evidence in Shakespeare of Contemporary Efforts to Refine the
Language of the Day," in *PMLA: Publications of the Modern
Language Association* (1916) XXXI. 65–78. Most of the materials
in both these concern religious sacrilege being evaded, and not
sex or scatology. Few such apotropaia survive in English speech
except for the interjection, *"Knock on wood!"*

I. SPELLING OUT NAMES

The expurgatory trick of spelling out one's taboo word –
through still wanting to say it, *n.b.* – comes in, of course, for
sardonic and dysphemistic handling in jokes. It is also used
more often for creating new obscenities than for hiding old
ones. In Sterne's *Tristram Shandy* (1767) Bk. VII, chap. 25, a particularly florid form of this sort of mock expurgation is satirized, when two nuns, who have been told that only the erotic
French expletives *'bougre'* and *'foutre'* (bugger and futter) will
make their mules trot, divide up the words into syllables, one
nun saying the first, while the other comes in with the second
in response, thus 'amicably halving' the sin, which thus 'becomes diluted into no sin at all.' However, the trick does not
work, since the mules do not understand. "But the Devil does,"

Sterne finishes sententiously.

Actually an anti-family mock – a form that will be treated below: *A husband and wife are quarreling. The husband tries to come over to her, and kiss and make up, but the wife shouts: "Don't touch me! Don't touch me! All I am to you is a fucking cunt!" "Please, dear," says the husband, "I wish you wouldn't say 'fucking cunt' in front of the* C-H-I-L-D." (N.Y. 1946; also London, 1953, from a middle-aged unmarried male artist who found it 'funny but pathetic.') Compare other family euphemisms and signals, such as: *The wife who is very noisy at her orgasm, screaming, "I'm coming! Oh, God! I'm coming!" with the result that the child asks the father later whether the mother is going to die. The next time it happens, the husband says, "Darling, the children can hear you. Don't say 'coming,' say 'sailing'." Too far gone to care, the wife screams back, "All right, you bastard,* BON VOYAGE!"

This is essentially the standard situation of the person of 'lower class' who is reprimanded for verbal crudity by one of 'higher class,' and who responds with obscene mockery. It is best seen in *water-wit*, which will be discussed more at length later. A complicated example of this response has already been noted: *The Negro woman who asks for gin in a liquor shop, and the white clerk answers contemptuously, "There's three kinds of gin. You want our good gin, or cheap gin, or just plain common ordinary Nigger gin?" "And there's three kinds of turd," she snaps back: 'musturd, horse-turd, and you, you big shit! Gimme the plain common ordinary Nigger gin!"* (N.Y. 1937, from a Negro informant. Earlier in *Anecdota*, 2:57.) Adapted to the Britisher-*versus*-American situation of condescending superiority and angrily obscene response: *An American in a London tea-shop asks for half a pound of tea. "My dear chap," says the clerk patronizingly, "one doesn't ask for 'tea,' you know. We have all sorts of tea: Ceylon, Javanese, Darjeeling. The Ceylon tea is very light; ten percent body and ninety percent aroma. The Javanese tea is heavy; ninety percent body and ten percent aroma. But the Darjeeling – ah, the conservative English breakfast tea! – fifty percent body and fifty percent aroma; that's the one we push the most." "I see," says the American grimly. "We have three kinds of tea in America too:* S-H-I-T, *that's ninety percent body and ten percent aroma.* F-A-R-T, *that's ten percent body and ninety percent aroma. And the good old American* C-U-N-T, *fifty percent body and fifty per-*

cent aroma, and we push it all around the world!" (L.A. 1952.)

The expurgatory spelling out of the taboo word is a primitive type of evasion of taboo that nevertheless still retains its power over the conscience and imagination of presumably very civilized people. To disguise this, the format is often reversed, and the spelling-out is used to *create* obscenity where none actually exists, and thus to titillate the listeners with the mere idea of the abrogation of a taboo they imagine they have already rejected. Almost every type of word-parcelling is or has been used in this way, including initials, acrostics, allusions, and last-minute evasions of key words or syllables in a sort of expurgatory aposiopesis.

Change-ringing or spoonerism is used for similar concealment-that-does-not conceal in an anti-homosexual joke found only in *The World's Dirtiest Jokes* (1969) p. 193, in which *A man in a bar is wearing a peculiar suit 'with lace on the lapels, sleeves, and trouser-cuffs.' When another man asks him why, he explains, "It's like this – I told my wife to go down to Sears and get me a seersucker suit, and by mistake she went to Cox's Department Store and came home with this* COX SOCCER SUIT!" (Of course, that doesn't explain why he had to wear it – probably just to help out the punster making up the joke.) A similar and earlier joke rings all possible spooneristic changes on evading the homosexual accusation, and has been given in Chapter 10: *One man is a coke-soaker (he soaks coke for furnaces), the other man is a sock-tucker (he puts tucks in men's socks), a third man is a cork-socker (he hammers corks into barrels), and the last man is "Guilty, Your Honor!"*

Pure alliteration is also an easy way of pointing up one's final expurgation, as in a modern toast, *"Here's to the three F's: Fame, Fortune – and Love!"* (or: *"– and a Footrace!"*) One of the first of this type that I have encountered is not verbally obscene, but suggests that there were then others that were. In an account of life on a British warship, Edmond Temple's anonymous *The Life of Pill Garlick* (2nd ed., London, 1815) p. 244, at an officers' mess: *'Several other toasts were drunk with equal demonstrations of joy, among which were – "Plenty of rope and a full swing to the great Bonyparty" – "The five L's, – Life, Laughing, Liberty, Lasses, and Love," together with many others equally warm and expressive.'*

The mildest acrostic is an old scatological favorite, as well known in Britain as it is in America. (It is noted in a list of jokes the author is *not* going to tell, at the end of Reginald Reynolds' *Cleanliness and Godliness*, London, 1943, p. 256, as 'the celebrated story of the Wesleyan Chapel.') As usually found in America, it is handed around in manuscript as a presumably authentic letter in which: *An old farmer, renting his house to summer people for the season, is asked by them in a letter whether there is a "W.C." near the house. As he has not ever heard this abbreviation before, he decides it must mean 'Wesleyan Church,' and explains in his reply that there is a W.C., "but it is four miles away, which is a long walk in rainy weather, and on Sunday you can't get in anyhow, because it's full of people you don't know!"* (Cleveland, Ohio, 1939. Other texts sometimes, as printed 'novelty' cards.) – *A lady buying several dozen napkins for the church Charity-Dinners and Clam-Chowder and Marching-Society Get-Togethers, is asked by the clerk if she wants them initialled, as it does not cost anything more. "No," she says, "I don't think so. These are all for the First Unitarian Church, Kingston."* (Binghampton, New York, 1940.) – *Two little boys in San Francisco, who are writing "*FUCK*" on everything with chalk, explain to the policeman who stops them that they are doing it for school, and that it stands for "Feed Us Chinese Kids."* (L.A. 1968.)

A radio script-writer in New York once similarly showed me an ornate rubricated certificate he had had printed at his own expense, about the end of World War II, and kept framed on the wall of his office, reading: *"Short Hauls Interstate Transit."* He considered it very funny. This moves in the direction of *graffiti*, or outhouse epigraphs, on which see the opening section of the next chapter, 15.I, "Buttock-Humor and Toilets." Mr. Ray Russell (who is not the script-writer referred to just above) tells in his *The Colony* (Los Angeles, 1969) p. 259–60, a work filled with stories of elaborate hoaxes and revenges, Hollywood style, of a writer dying untimely, who leaves orders that a brief poem be placed on his gravestone, secretly reading in acrostic, "FUCK YOU." (A published sonnet of this kind by John Peale Bishop, posthumous, apparently describing cunnilinctus with the two-tailed mermaid, but unexpectedly including as acrostic, "FUCK YOU HALFASS," has already been noted, from the quoting of it by an American college girl in Paris.) Ray Russell precedes his acrostic – which is lacking its penultimate line, owing to the hidden message – with a parallel reference,

to the Sears Roebuck [mail-order] catalog, and to a story –
more likely a legend – he had once been told. Something
about the indoor commodes Sears had offered, at the turn of
the century, to rural families still making do with primitive
outhouses. The catalog page on which these items were described and depicted had been topped, according to the anecdote, by a large, bold headline of four words, each word
bedizened with a gigantic capital letter: *Sears' Handy Indoor
Toilets.* The luckless (or mischievous) copywriter responsible
for the barely buried obscenity had been summarily dismissed.

As editor of *Playboy* during the 1960's Russell made a great hit
with a small card he had printed for him, for private distribution on necessary occasions, bearing in Old English lettering the
one word: 𝕳𝖔𝖗𝖘𝖊𝖘𝖍𝖎𝖙
Also very ornate, and really more of a 'tease' than an expurgation: *'Stuttering swain to girl in park, "Could you let me
have a f-f-f-few m-m-matches?" She offered him some matches
and he said, "Th-th-thanks ... I'll b-b-bet you thought I was
going to ask you for a fu-fu-fu-fu-full b-b-box!"* (*Sex to Sexty,*
1966, 9:21. First heard, N.Y. 1939. See also, in the section following, Mr. Kenneth Tynan on 'F-f-f-f-f-fuck.') Names and their
spelling are an easy peg on which to hang this sort of humor, in
particular since most people are extremely conscious of the
magical quality of their own names: use of nicknames, hiding
of true name, anger if name is misspelled, use only of initial –
which irritates other people unaccountably, I have found, as
though one were depriving them of some weapon or handle of
attack – or even completely artificial or anti-magical names
and name-changes, as with Jehovah and the emperors of Japan.
A brief gag considered a masterpiece of anti-Roosevelt humor
during World War II: *A man wants to change his name, which
is Franklin Delano Shit. "What do you want to change it to?"
asks the judge. "Just plain Jose Shit."* (D.C. 1940.) – *A young lady
named Psmythe never gets any mail at the summer camp and
is becoming frantic. Finally she spells out her name carefully to
the small-town postoffice clerk. "Oh, P-smith!" he says. "Well,
I'll have to look in the P hole. I been lookin' in the S hole."*
(2:34, a variant text.)
There are also, as everybody knows only too well, the names
that control our lives and choice of careers: the dentists named

Yankem, the icebox salesman named Winterbottom, and the unbelievable but perfectly authentic 'sanitary engineer' to the British royal establishment, Thomas Crapper, Esq. Where the name is wholly unacceptable, it is more usual simply to change it, or to modify the pronounciation of one syllable: for example, Lipshitz to *Lifshitz*. One occasionally runs into some resistful soul who insists on fighting it out, seeing it through, and living a whole lifetime of "Say It Isn't So!" ("It's spelled G-L-A-S-C-O-C-K," one man introduced as 'Glasgow' informed me.) The children of such persons are seldom so unintimidated, and usually fail where the parent has succeeded – probably owing to the unverbalized stress and anxiety on the subject under which the family life inevitably suffers. The daughters desperately change their names by marriage as soon as they can, while the sons go quietly mad. This is too large a subject to deal with properly here.

One excellent example of this sort of bulling-it-through and insisting, ruined at the end by the 'return of the repressed,' takes its form from *A well-known prank, in introducing speakers at convivial banquets, of making a tremendously flowery introduction, ending, "I now take great pleasure in presenting my lifelong friend, about whom I've told you so very little, I mean – er – (meanwhile fumbling out of one's vest-pocket a calling-card from which one pretends to read off the victim's name) – Mister Joe Blow!"* In the joke: *The master of ceremonies is introducing a man named Hotchkiss. Warming to his subject, he enthuses, 'I am deeply conscious of the honor of introducing to you a man whose very name breathes romance, a man the last syllable of whose name all of us would like to press upon the lips of the ladies present and the women we love – Mr. Hitchcock!"* (N.Y. 1948. Also a more complicated version in which a medal is being presented to two partners in the automobile business named *Lovejoy and Hotchkiss*, the speaker getting mixed up with the first and last syllables of their names, &c.)

Several men met on a train and introduce themselves in preparation for a poker game. "My name is Hancock," says one. "Allcock," says another. "Babcock." "Hitchcock." The fifth man says, "I don't think I'll play. My name is Kuntz." (1:83. In another form the pun is inelegantly spelled out in the punch-line with the intruded tag: *"You'd all just fuck me."* – N.Y. 1965.) Some very interesting materials on the verbal hostilities of card-playing, of a specifically sexual and anal-sadistic kind, are given in Dr. Ralph R. Greenson's "On Gambling," in *American Imago* (1947) IV. 61–77, reprinted in the *Yearbook of Psychoanalysis* (1948) vol. IV; with examples from other forms of gambling and 'sports' in a socio-economic reply by Dr. John Del Torto, in *Neurotica* (1950) No. 6: p. 11–22, well worth consulting.

2. FUCK

A minor literature has grown up in recent years on the word 'fuck,' beginning with Prof. Allen Walker Read's *tour de force*, "An Obscenity Symbol," in *American Speech* (Dec. 1934) IX. 264–78, which is entirely about this word and its history, but manages never to use it even once. This elegant aposiopesis is poorly repeated in several more recent articles in men's magazines; purely journalistic they are not worth much. The wittiest roundup of recent exotica on the subject is Prof. L. Eric Hotaling's "The Case for Retiring the Most Overworked Four-Letter Word," in *Avant Garde* (New York, 1967) No. 1: p. 22–4, along with an article on Ed Sanders, editor of *Fuck You*, the only really 'underground' literary journal, and his put-on musical group, "The Fugs," in the same issue, p. 50–55. I have found some useful sidelights in Falk Johnson's "The History of Some 'Dirty' Words," in *The American Mercury* (Nov. 1950) vol. 71: p. 538–45; in David Kahn's "The Dirtiest Word," in the men's magazine, *Nugget* (New York, August 1961) pp. 21 and 68; in a privately printed pamphlet of seven pages, Henry Bosley Woolf's *The G.I.'s Favorite Four Letter Word* (Baton Rouge, La. 1948); and particularly in Edward Sagarin's *The Anatomy of Dirty Words* (1962), a book-length study also covering much else.

The most specialized and peculiar article is surely an anonymous item by Warren Boroson in *Avant Garde* (Mar. 1970) No. 11: p. 1–7, which does not concern itself with 'fuck' in general, but only with the well-known Negro insulting term derived from this, and now spreading to white usage also; underlining its proto-incestuous meaning in the title, 'My Son, the Mother-fucker." Special mention must also be made of the treatment of the word – to which most of the whole chapter "The Four-Letter Words" is given, in Ashley Montagu's *The Anatomy of Swearing* (1967) p. 300–20, of which a certain amount of the admirable effect is spoiled by the remark on 'gestural swearing,' on the last text page (344): '*Holding up a middle finger means "go fornicate with yourself".*' Some mistake here.

Still the best serious study is Dr. Sándor Ferenczi's "Obscene Words," in his *Contributions to Psychoanalysis* (Boston, 1916). See also Dr. Leo Stone's "The Principal Obscene Word in the English Language," in *International Journal of Psychoanalysis* (1954) vol. 45: pt. 1, p. 30–56, which suggests that 'fuck' got into the English language to rhyme with 'suck.' (But does its root, '*ficken*,' rhyme with '*saugen*' in German?) The only really significant discussion of aggressive terms like 'fuck' in modern usage is in the trenchant few pages on "The New Puritanism" in Dr. Rollo May's profound *Love and Will* (New York: Norton, 1969), reprinted in David Holbrook's symposium, *The Case Against Pornography* (London, 1972) p. 21–2.

*A drunk is chasing a fire-engine, which is clanging its bell and blowing its whistle, but he cannot catch it. "All right," he shouts after it disgustedly, "*KEEP *your fucken peanuts!"* (N.Y. 1953.) This has obviously no meaning except as an imprecation. Also, in demonstration of the strictly grammatical point as to participles, it certainly does not imply that the peanuts are *doing* any fucking. It is they who are the fucked, or fucken. The situation and the drunken misunderstanding are themselves humorous, but these are not considered sufficient by the teller, without some abrogation of taboo to make sure of the listeners' laugh. For other audiences, clearly, "*Keep your* GOD-DAM *peanuts!"* would do just as well.

Without bothering to quote it again in full, one should bear in mind throughout the present section the important point made, in pretended artlessness, in the final repartee of a joke already given: *A man misses an easy putt on the golf-links, in the presence of his wife and young daughter, and says, "Oh fuck!" When remonstrated with by his wife for using such language before their growing daughter, he says to the girl angrily, "I'll bet you've heard that word before." "Certainly, father,"* she says, *"but never in anger."* (Compare Harry Kurnitz' purposely cute title for the Jules Dassin movie about a prostitute, "Never On Sunday.") It is the presense of *anger*, when using such words, thus the 'sadistic concept of coitus', that creates the imprecational or scatological use. Otherwise, as the girl's reply implies, they would be merely descriptive terms, or even invitations. One should recollect always, in this connection, that the word '*fuck*' itself is most closely related, etymologically, to such Latin congeners as *pungo*, with its modern forms 'punch', 'puncture,' and 'pugilist.' No mistake here.

When the word *'fuck!'* is used as an expletive or curse-word alone, or as *'fuck it!'* or *'fuck you!'* it has no real erotic meaning, and is being used sadistically or scatologically with an intention of verbal dirtying. When a meaning is demanded (by the speaker, of himself − or nowadays herself), the verb is sometimes extended to *'fuck in the ass,'* indicating that the violent contempt-gesture of pedicatory rape is the closest to sexual that is really still involved, or can be imagined. (*The Last Tango in Paris.*) All this derives strictly from the "Sadistic Concept of Coitus," already treated in the First Series, chapter 5.I–V; and note also chapter 10.V.2, "Pedication as Insult." The anal-sadistic intention is always clear, and some of the ornate variants on the main phrase make its non-literal position even plainer, as for instance: *"Go fuck yourself in the ass − and give yourself some brains!"* (With the retort: *"I've got more brains in my ass than you've got in* both *your heads!"*) In this line see further the hilarious semantic travesties, "English Sentences without Overt Grammatical Subject" (1960) and "A Note on Conjoined Noun Phrases" (1968) printed in the excessively rare *Conneries Linguistiques*, signed 'Quang Phuc Dong' of the South Hanoi Institute of Technology (it says here), and kindly brought to my attention by Prof. James D. McCawley of Chicago. These are entirely concerned with the complicated grammar of the phrase 'Fuck you!' with variations.

The following joke has been told to women in my presence twice, by repressed young men (one of them homosexual) who felt called upon to tell a dirty joke, once with the preliminary apology that it has 'only one dirty word.' *Wartime shortages. A woman demands onions (or tomatoes) of the grocer, who assures her he has no onions, but she insists anyhow. "Look, lady,"* he says, *"it ain't my fault. I'll explain you. Who put the blue in the sky? Who put the red in the sunset? Who put the fuck in onions?" "But there ain't no fuck in onions,"* she interrupts. *"That's what I'm trying to tell you!"* (N.Y. 1944.) Various other forms refer to brands of beer, and one involves further *outré* bawdy catches on the style of *'Silent like the P in bed.'*

Longer forms of the following classic about the reformed prostitute have been given in chapter 11.I.1, "Priestess, Prostitute, Nurse, and Nun," in which: *The reformed prostitute is giving testimony for the Salvation Army while beating on a big bass drum. "Once I laid in the arms of men!" she shouts. "White men, black men, Chinamen! (Boom, boom, boom.) Now I lay in the arms of Jesus!" Drunk in the back row: "That's right, Sister, fuck 'em all!"* (1:266.) – *Anecdota Americana* (1927) gives here one of its few stated variants, 1:267, concerning: *A tough British soldier who sees the light and embraces religion after two shells fall on either side of him on the battle-field without hurting him. He is giving testimony at a prayer-meeting: "See these fine shoes? Christ gave me those. See these fine breeches? Christ gave me those. See this elegant westkit? Christ gave me that. What did the devil ever give me? Narthin'. Fuck the devil!"* Though the Devil takes the blow here, the whole format brings it perilously close to cursing God, for which the traditional punishment is that noted in *Job*, ii. 9: *'Then said his wife unto him, "Dost thou still retain thine integrity? curse God, and die".'*

A drunk who has been refused a drink by the bartender makes himself very offensive with anti-everything remarks. "That bartender looks like a Mick to me," he confides to a man standing next to him. "I hate Micks. Don't you? The Irish ruined America. No; more likely it was the dirty Jews and niggers. If there's anything I hate worse than a red-assed Mick, it's Jews and niggers. Say," he adds, irritated that his listener has not agreed with him, "what are you, anyhow?" "I'm a Quaker. Fuck thee!" (N.Y. 1946. The punchline is also sometimes given to the drunk.) In a briefer form: *Four anti-Semites are tyrannizing a New York subway train, roaming up and down the aisles like Old Home Week, insulting everyone they think looks Jewish. One man remonstrates, "I ain't Jewish; I'm Irish." The anti-Semite looks at him contemptuously and says, "Well then, Fuck St. Patrick!"* (N.Y. 1953, also naming a popular Irish actor instead.) Note that the bully is not given his come-uppance here, but has the last (hostile) word.

The latest form encountered returns to the Quaker sententiousness, but again it is the bully who 'wins.' *A drunk in a bar has no money left for liquor, and tries to borrow a dollar from the man on the next stool. "No, my friend [the Quaker term?]," says the man he has asked, " 'Neither a borrower nor a lender be.' – Shakespeare." The drunk looks at him disgustedly. " 'Fuck you.' – Tennessee Williams."* (N.Y. 1964.) As I was living in the same apartment-house as Mr. Williams at the time, I told him this joke in the elevator one evening. He seemed to appreciate it, though he did not laugh, and said he had never heard it before. Perhaps he was only being polite.

'Fuck you!' as humor, lacks the escape-hatch recommended in Owen Wister's *The Virginian* (1902) as to 'son-of-a-bitch': *"When you say that – smile!"* A peculiar letter-to-the-editor in the New York sex-newspaper, *Screw* (which brags that it is a 'pornzine,' but didn't have the guts to call itself *Fuck*, and neither do any of its imitators), in the issue of August 25th, 1969, No. 25: p. 20, complains (the writer is a woman): '*Why does the final ultimate putdown have to use the word for the most beautiful relationship? Why is the absolute rejection –* "Fuck you!!"? Why a word of scorn? ...* [So far so good, but continue:] *Why not popularize "Dung in your* EAR!" *or, less mildly, the final rejection more appropriate to our Philosophy –* "Go castrate yourself!"? *... I am liberated from the Underground Puritan's ancient Master Joke on the True Supporter of Sexuality, and would accept "Fuck You!" as the highest approval.*' (The editor's comment to this young lady may perhaps be guessed.)

Even the editor of the first of the underground papers in New York, Mr. Ed Sanders of the ebullient *Fuck You! A Magazine of the Arts* in the early 1960's, seemed to lose his nerve by the decade's end as to just this point, and engaged in some unconvincing foofaraw – in an article by Martin Cohen in *Avant Garde* (1967) No. 1: p. 53 – as to his magazine's title being meant '*benignly, benevolently, squishily and squirmily as a gift of love.*' (Love you too, Ed!) But no one seems to be convinced. The same issue of *Screw* just cited, No. 25: p. 13, in an interesting article on the folklore of condoms, "Never Look a Trojan in the Mouth," relates that a group of 'disgruntled ex-employees' of *Time & Life* once planned to get their revenge on the head of this propaganda organization, the late Henry Luce, by marketing condoms with his picture and name on the packet. Thus by unspoken implication: *"Fuck Henry Luce!"* Note the unconscious cowardice involved in getting other people's penises to fuck the (former) boss. The idea also risked being misunderstood, of course. People might have thought the real message was: *"All employees of* Time & Life *are pricks."* Especially the ones that think they're disgruntled. Why, I can hear them grunting from here.

The participial form also has its special devotees: *A man in court is explaining why he has been arrested. "I went into this fuckin' one-arm joint and asked for a fuckin' hamburger, and the fuckin' manager went and called a fuckin' cop. I still can't figure out why the fuck they arrested me."* The arresting policeman cuffs him and says, *"Shut up, you! That's no way to talk in court."* The judge bangs with his gavel, and shouts, *"Officer, who's trying this fuckin' case, you or me?"* (N.Y. 1963. To be compared with the satirical poems on *'Bloody!'* and *'Fuckin'!'*) – *The inexperienced judge, who has obtained his post by political pull, finds that his first case is to be an accusation of rape. "All right,"* he says, *in a businesslike tone, "first case on the docket: Attempted Rape. Will the fucker and the fuckee please rise and face the court!"* (L.A. 1968.) Other jokes and cante-fables have already been given in the First Series, 2.V.2, as to the use of the word 'fuck' or similar erotic terms – or deeds – being forbidden or punished in the courtroom. The real humor in these is always actually the making fun of the judge, and behind him the courts, law, and society's unreasonable restraints and demands, with the ancient implication that 'Those who judge are as guilty as those whom they condemn.' A *tu quoque* dating at least from that of Jesus on casting the first stone, at the court of the scribes and Pharisees, in *John*, viii. 7–11.

I myself have never been able to see the humor nor understand the popularity on the following item, but have collected it too often to permit myself to omit it: *An artist who has been paid for a picture of Custer's Last Stand turns in a large painting showing nothing but Indian bucks and squaws in an enormous orgy, around a golden calf. When the client complains, the artist explains that this represents Custer's last thoughts: "Holy cow! Look at all those fuckin' Indians!"* (N.Y. 1963.) – *An educated Chinese eats regularly at a Greek restaurant where he likes the fried rice, which he always orders as "Flied lice." This makes the Greek nearly break up every time, and he invites truck-drivers to hang around when the Chinese walks in, to hear him say it. His dignity offended, the Chinese takes a Berlitz course and learns to say perfectly "Fried rice, please!" "What did you say?" asks the astounded restaurant owner. "You heard me. Fried rice, you fluckin' Gleek!"* (L.A. 1968. *The World's Dirtiest Jokes*, 1969, p. 207, erroneously gives this as of a Japanese, suggesting that the editors don't know their r's from their l's.) A great example of the 'Return of the Repressed.'

As has been shown extensively in the First Series of this

work, the jokes told by adults seem to find it particularly humorous and satisfying to put obscenities into the mouths of children – that is to say, into the mouths of the children the tellers once were, but were then afraid to say anything obscene. The obscenities in *real* children's jokes are seldom or never like those that follow. *A little girl introduces herself to the new neighbor lady as Cookie, adding: 'They call me Cookie because I like to eat cookies. And this is my little dog, Porky." "I suppose you call him Porky because he likes to eat pork," the neighbor lady smiles, "No," says the little girl, "we call him Porky because he likes to fuck pigs."* (Detroit, Mich. 1969, submitted to a joke contest in *Screw*, No. 24: p. 17.) – *'School lesson on Holy Scripture and God's love. Question period. Little girl, very impressed, asks: "Do they kiss in Heaven?" Rotten little bugger of a boy in back (sotto voce):"Do they fuckin' hell!" Teacher: "One question at a time, please children!"'* (Chelmsford, Essex, 1951. This absolute or intensive British use of 'fuckin' hell!' as a negative asseveration is not known in America.)

Told more as a folktale than as a joke, with the mysterious punchline hardly expected to make up for the long 'shaggy-dog' story, yet definitely a joke since it is precisely the punchline and not the shaggy-dog buildup that is the point of the story: *A little boy is telling the other boys about the latest chapter in the Lone Ranger movie-serial, which he has seen a week ahead of them in the big town. The chapter ends with the Lone Ranger hanging by his fingernails to the branch of a pine-tree over a cliff, up which the whole Commanche tribe is charging at him. At the other side are mixed lions and tigers, while under the cliff is a swamp-full of alligators, all trying to bite him, and opening their mouths very wide. (Pantomimed with two hands.) Japanese kamikaze pilots are also dive-bombing him from overhead, and the U.S. Cavalry refuses to help because they're still mad at him from the preceding chapter, last week. "What* HAPPENS?" *the other little boys ask frantically. The little boy who knows lifts one hand to calm them, and says mysteriously, "Don't fuck around with the Lone Ranger!"* (N.Y. 1946.) I hate to give this story away, but, as with our White-Coated Scientists and political leaders, who periodically assure us that atomic fallout is good for dandruff, that pollution has been over-emphasized, and that Everything Is Going To Be All Right, the truth is that *he does not know.*

One of the strictest items of sexual folklore, of the type that adolescent boys confide to each other, is that *"Talking dirty heats girls up."* This is made crucial to the plot in Norman Krasna's sex-comedy, *Sunday in New York* (movie version, 1963), in which: *The seducer tries to warm up the virginal heroine by telling her dirty jokes, but her brother has warned her to be on the lookout for wolves like this. She pretends she has to go to the toilet* (!) *and slips away. But this wolf is fangless, and later refuses to lay her when he learns, in bed, that she is authentically a 'beginner.'* In the *reductio ad absurdum* of this folk idea, the man's entire 'line' or seductive conversation is reduced strictly to the single word *'fuck,'* sometimes on the pretext of somehow tricking the woman into saying some other presumably dirty word herself. Jokes of this type are connected with the great and ancient tale-family of the Contest in Riddles or repartee, or magical transformations, with a princess (or on succeeding in making her laugh), which is Aarne Tale Type 853, Motif H507.1, and will be dealt with again in chapter 15.V.2, "The *Escoumerda.*" It appears here only in a skeletal or survival form in which essentially nothing remains but the last repartee: *A farm-boy is told to go to the railroad station with the horse & buggy, and bring back the girl-cousin who will be visiting for a week. He is told to be sure not to 'say anything nasty.'* [No reference is made to this as being sexually exciting.] *As they drive back, the horse farts noisily, and drops a load of turd on the dashboard of the buggy. The boy apologizes, saying,* "Here, let me kick them horse-apples offa there." "Is that what you call them here?" *the embarrassed girl asks.* "In the city we say horse-manure." "That's what we say here too," *he replies eagerly, dropping the reins along the horse's back;* "Let's fuck!" (Honesdale, Penn'a. 1934.) Note that this story is ununderstandable as it stands, without reference to the underlying superstition, or folktale group, yet it is told by adolescents with the expectation of being considered funny. The presumed humor is that the boy has been told not to 'say anything nasty.' The Contest in Riddles has been forgotten.

One problem about the use of dirty words, or dirty jokes, to 'warm up' a woman for an intended sexual approach is that all the emotion is likely to be dissipated verbally, without the intended seduction ever being arrived at. Girls or women who themselves habitually speak coarsely or obscenely, or tell dirty jokes, especially without being asked, are usually engaging only in a form of verbal 'cock-teasing,' and are notoriously difficult to seduce. The greatest of all lay-analysts, Theodor Reik, beautifully exposes the real mechanism at work, in *The Need to Be Loved* (New York, 1963) p. 146:

> The frequent and casual use of four-letter words by some women, especially of expressions denoting sexual and excretory functions, is rarely characteristic of a low level of upbringing and education. In most cases it is an unconscious travesty or parody of men and their manners, and reveals a concealed and often repressed hostility to the male. As such it is comparable to the unconscious mockery contained in the manner in which homosexual men imitate and parody women's speech. Unconscious abuse, rather than use, is in the repetition of these words.

The word 'fuck' by itself is considered permissive, if the woman does not respond angrily. *A man silently takes a girl out in his car for a long drive, then parks and turns to her, saying (impatient, rising intonation:) "Fuck?" "Well," she says, "I usually don't, but you talked me into it!"* (N.Y. 1938.) This seems to suggest a sardonic doubt as to the method. Also heard, in Scranton, Penn'a, 1934, as an anecdote without any punchline, presumably to show the crudity of the man, but actually admiring his coarse boldness. This often has another ending, where: *A friend is shocked by the man's crudeness and tells him to talk to the girl first about books and plays, etc. On the next date he asks the girl, "You read any good plays?" "No." "Neither have I. Let's fuck."* (N.Y. 1949.) Compare the even more anti-gallant and anti-intellectual: *"I can't marry you, Harold, you're too uncouth." "Whaddya mean 'uncouth'? Don't I take you to the ballet and Shakespeare, and all that shit?!"* (N.Y. 1950.)

The ultimate end of dysphemism is that the obscene or profane word loses all its original meaning, and is used without consciousness of its sexual denotation. This is already the case in France with such words as '*baiser*,' to cheat (originally a euphemism, meaning 'to kiss,' for sexual intercourse, and still so understood when explicit); and '*con*,' a fool (actually, cunt), which is no longer used in intimate conversation as referring to the female genitals – as that would be considered insulting – the woman's genitals therefore being assimilated to, and called instead her '*cul*' (arse) by way of politeness! The use of '*cunt*' as fool, has been brought to England from France over the last few decades, and it remains to be seen whether this will drive out the anatomical meaning.

The process is satirized perfectly in a joke or exercise in bathos, very popular in America during World War II: *A soldier is telling about a date he went on with a friend while on leave. "It's the first fucken furlough they gave us in six fucken months. I put my fucken uniform in a fucken locker at the 'Y,' and we went out and had a hell of a fucken time. We picked up two fucken broads in some fucken beer-joint and took 'em to a fucken hotel and laid 'em on the fucken bed, and had sexual intercourse."* (N.Y. 1942.) This I applied once to the famous Australian cursing-poem, "Bloody!" by W. T. Goodge, under the title "The Cowboy," concentrating particularly on the amusing interruptive forms possible: *'He jumped upon his fuckin' horse, And galloped off, of-fuckin'-course,'* and so forth, on the style of the British army boxing-instructor's adjuration to his men in World War I:

> *Get a fucking move on, show some fucking sense.*
> *Learn the manly fucking art of self-de-fucking-fence!*

My version ends with the 'infixed' punchline, adapted – and I think improved – from the joke:

> *And there with all his fuckin' force*
> *Had sexual-fuckin'-intercourse!*

As my *nom de guerre* was 'Roger-Maxe de La Glannège,' an anagram also signed to my first book, *Oragenitalism*, at that time, the poem was likewise dated and signed, '*R. M. de la Fuckin' G., 19-fuckin'-43.*' Both the signature and the concluding stanza were omitted from the poem as published in Eric Posselt's *G.I. Songs* (New York, 1944, edited under the name 'Eric Palmer'), and in William Wallrich's *Air Force Airs* (New York, 1957) p. 160–61, neither of which seems to realize that it is not a song. A text of the underlying joke is given in *Eros Denied* (1965) by Wayland Young, reprinted in Ashley Montagu's *The Anatomy of Swearing*, p. 314–15.

The forseeable fate of all such imprecational overuse has long since come to 'fuck,' as to its counterparts '*baiser*' and '*foutre*' in French. 'Fuck' is now no longer used by practically anyone but tin-eared psychiatrists as referring to amicable sexual intercourse. The term of choice among young people in

America, since the early 1960's at least, has instead become the ancient British 'to ball' (compare: "The Ball o'Kirriemuir"), revived or living on underground from the 16th century of secret Scottish naked 'balls of dauncing' and similar erotic Witches' Sabbaths.

Ritual public obscenity in modern writing and speech appears first in rationalized form in Walt Whitman's *Leaves of Grass* (1856) and James Joyce's *Ulysses* (1922), the 'improper' speech in these being always carefully matched up to some presumable speaker or dithyrambic mood justifying it, and not really to the actual or prosaic author himself, for all Whitman's persevering *I's*, and would-be 'wild barbaric yawps.' This double standard for the language used by authors *in propria persona* and by their created characters, as seen on the printed page, remained the last bastion of censorship in English until Henry Miller's *Tropic of Cancer* (Paris, 1934), first issued publicly in New York in 1959. It should be added to his honor that Wayland Young (Lord Kennet), in his *Eros Denied* (1965), was almost the first serious writer in English who used terms like 'fuck' and so forth on the openly printed page, without fathering them off on the mythical dialogue of invented fictional characters.

The leading poets of the hippie movement of the 1960's in the United States (and its imitations abroad, which are even closer to the original Surréalist or Dadaist inspiration of the 1910's) all make use of the broken-prose style made popular by Whitman a century ago, and of occult and ritual nakedness at the physical as well as the verbal level. By the late 1960's this had moved on to ritual group nudity in public – a customary form of expressing protest, already many centuries old in Europe – particularly at various rock-&-roll music 'festivals,' in which tens of thousands of young people travel hundreds of miles to take drugs together, while listening to music. Also in even more commercial and imitative stage spectacles purporting to offer at least the same musical thrills, such as *Hair*. These spectacles now also include mimed sexual intercourse onstage (or on-film), as in *Che*, in *The Beard* (a reference to the 'bearded clam,' or female pubic hair, since the act mimed here was cunnilinctus), and in the nude neo-burlesque for the entertainment of square middle-class audiences, Kenneth Tynan's *O Calcutta!* in 1969. All this essentially represents the late 20th-century version of the once-popular square entertainment of going to insane asylums on Sundays *to watch the lunatics masturbate.*

As far as *O Calcutta!* goes, and it includes a proposed 'circle-jerk' of men masturbating onstage (but not really), this seems to be intended as Mr. Tynan's *amende honorable* for an act of verbal libertarianism that rather missed fire a year or two before. As described by Prof. L. Eric Hotaling, in "The Case for Retiring Our Most Overworked Four-Letter Word," in *Avant Garde* (1967) No. 1 : p. 24 :

> In 1965, British drama critic Kenneth Tynan managed to smuggle the word into a B.B.C. discussion on whether the act of intercourse (*i.e.* fucking) should be allowed on the professional stage – assuming, needless to say, that the plot required it.
>
> Tynan thought that theatre-goers would tolerate such action – possibly applaud it. But he was more concerned with defending man's right to use the word anywhere he saw fit. But because Tynan stutters, this blow for freedom missed its mark. "I think there are v-v-ery f-f-few rational p-p-people in this world," he said before several million televiewers, "to whom the word f-f-f-f-f-fuck is particularly revolting." Tynan's quavering delivery left the impression of an evangelist revolted by his own religion. [*His negative approach rather leaves something to be desired too.*]

A whole dictionary of current obscenity could be compiled – and in fact now cannot be conscientiously compiled in any other way – from the verbal outpourings and slang coinages of both the news-columns and the letters-to-the-editor of all the Far-outnik and 'underground' American newspapers of the hippie movement and period since the early 1960's, beginning with Paul Krassner's *The Realist* and the secretly-published *Fuck You!* edited by Ed Sanders and Tuli Kupferberg, of which latter a few pages are reproduced in John Gruen's *The New Bohemia* (New York : Shorecrest, 1966). As Mr. Sanders assured me that the university librarians had all gone 'ape shit' (very enthusiastic) over *Fuck You!* repository sets – as at Brown University – should not be too difficult for future social historians and lexicographers to find. As to the other underground papers, an excellent roundup article, reproducing their illustrated front pages – which say everything! – is given in F. X. Boyle's "The Gang-Bang on the Underground Press," in *Avant Garde* (New York, May 1970) No. 12 : p. 44–7, in which the most important 'underground' editors state their case. But never mention the Mafia-drug backing of more than a few of them.

In the October 11, 1968, issue of the principal New York underground and pro-drugs newspaper, *The (East Village) Other*, p. 2–4, the confusion even of the insiders as to the socially and intentionally provocative purpose of the ritual or physical 'obscenity' is made extremely clear, in an editorial announcement concerning a 'Be-In' (picnic) to be held in Central Park the next day, encouraging the readers to: *'Come for life, Come as bright and as happy as you can. Bring a Tent to fuck in (if that isn't legal, don't do it because it ain't worth the cop-hassle,) make love on the grass, play, and bring plenty of pizza.'* As can be seen, the cops very definitely already had the hippies on the run, as to their intended public 'group-grope' and 'street-fucking' – if it was to go on under tents! In the same issue, p. 4, under the heading, "Monster Thrills Galore!" a young comic-strip enthusiast and columnist, D. A. Latimer, describes the beginning of a minor riot in the New York hippie quarter of the lower East Side, which began over the burning of garbage in the streets during the 'fucking garbagemen strike.' Observe the totally ritual, or high-school cheerleader approach to the use of *obscenity as provocation:*

> It just wasn't the night at all for Commissioner Leary's lads [*the police*]. They chased us down to the corner at Gem's Spa, but since the tourist and local residents were also hanging around there, digging the production [*observing what was going on*], they couldn't do much, right then.
> GIMMEE AN F! – *F!!* – GIMMEE A U! – *U!!* –
> GIMMEE A C! – *C!!* – *GIMMEE A K! – K!!*
> WHAT'S IT SPELL??
> FUCK. FUCK. FUCK. FUCK. FUCK. FUCK.
> FUCK. FUCK. FUCK. FUCK. FUCK. FUCK.
> It must be said for the New York police that they did not react overmuch at the profanity. This went on all night ...

A tape-recording was naturally made of this edifying chant, and I have been told that a California teacher was dismissed for having played it before a high-school class, as an example of godnose what cultural phenomenon. In point of fact, this type of uninspired and primitive repetition is typical of the hopelessly low and almost inarticulate mental state of most hippies

– whether 'high' on drugs or not – and the entire anti-
intellectuality of the neo-Fascistic rock-music and drug-based
hippie movement of false rebellion, as I have tried to show
further in *The Fake Revolt*.

The only modern example really worthy of attention in the
now-growing literature on the word 'fuck' is not in English at
all but in Spanish. Obscenity is outstandingly an Hispanic art.
When Spanish-speaking people care to curse, swear, brag, or
tall-talk, every other nation in the world must stand silent with
their thumb up their ass. The ultimate on the word 'fuck,' and
its glorification, its apotheosis – like that of the word *'puta,'*
whore, in a passage already quoted from Francisco Delicado's
La Lozana Andaluza in the early 16th century – will and can
only be found in the very extraordinary Mexican novel, *La
Muerte de Artemio Cruz* by Carlos Fuentes (México, 1962),
pages 143 ff., a lava-like flow of language and folk-phrase,
turning and erupting for pages, uniquely on the Spanish word
'chingar,' meaning 'fuck.' See, on Hispanic profanity, the little-
known *Rodomontades et jurements des Espagnols* by Brantôme (d. 1614), and *The Limerick*, Note 266. And compare the
glossary of old French "Jurons et imprécations" in De
l'Aulnaye's folkloristic edition of Rabelais (Paris, 1823) vol. III;
also Ovid's great *Ibis*. Fuentes' modern outpouring begins:

Tú la pronunciarás: es tu palabra: y tu palabra es la mía;
palabra de honor: palabra de hombre; palabra de rueda:
palabra de molino: imprecación, propósito saludo, proyecto
de vida, filiación, recuerdo, voz de los desesperados, liberación
de los pobres, orden de los poderosos, invitación a la riña y al
trabajo, epígrafe del amor, signo del nacimiento, amenaza y
burla, verbo testigo, compañero de la fiesta y de la borrachera,
espada del valor, trono de la fuerza, colmillo de la marrullería,
blasón de la raza, salvavida de los límites, resumen de la
historia: santo y seña de México: tu palabra:
– Chingue a su madre – Hijo de la chingada – Aquí estamos
los meros chingones – Déjate de chingaderas – Ahoritita me
lo chingo – Ándale, chingaquedito – No te dejes chingar – Me
chingué a esa vieja – Chinga tú – Chingue usted – Chinga
bein, sin ver a quién – A chingar se ha dicho – Le chingué mil
pesos – Chínguense anque truenen – Chingaderitas las mías –
Me chingó el jefe – No me chingues el día – Vamos todos a la
chingada – Se lo llevó la chingada – Me chingo pero no me

rajo – Se chingaron al indio – Nos chingaron los gachupines –
Me chingan los gringos – Viva México, Jijos de su rechingada:
tristeza, madrugada, tostada, tiznada, guayaba, el mal dormir:
hijos de la palabra. Nacidos de la chingada, muertos en la
chingada, vivos por pura chingada: vientre y mortaja,
escondidos en la chingada ...

And *pages* more! Nothing quite like this exists in any language,
with the exception of the early English and Scottish alliterative
poems, particularly of insult, such as the great "Flying betwixt
Polwart and Montgomery," which will be quoted in section
14.II.1 below. The closest, other than Delicado's *Lozana
Andaluza*, which may even have inspired Sr. Fuentes, is the
quite eccentric *Controverses des sexes masculin et féminin*
(Toulouse, 1534), by Gratian Du Pont, seigneur de Drusac, the
earliest work appealing in its title to the presumed "War Between the Sexes." Drusac's *Controverses* are a long series of
stupid monorhymes, a form imitated from Marot, several
hundred in all, specifically on the word '*con*,' cunt, and used to
present an alphabet of dispraise and attack against women. (A
reprint of 1541 includes an actual 'requisitory' against women:
a legal process attacking miscarriages of justice!) The work
was answered by the *Anti-Drusac* of François La Borie (Toulouse, 1564), a prose dialogue of which no copy seems to have
survived.

Perhaps a wittier answer is that included in the best and only
complete edition of the old and very important work on forms
and styles of verbal humor, Étienne Tabourot's *Les Bigarrures
et Touches du Seigneur des Accords* (Paris: Jean Richer, 1615;
the supplementary materials here not being included in all later
editions), where a good sample of Drusac's attack is given in
chapter 4, "Des Equivoques françois," I. 24v–25v, followed by
a crushing reply in the same metrical form, and in similar
rhymes on '*con*,' signed 'Joane de La Belle-motte' (Joan Pretty-
pussy), whose identity has never been discovered, and who was
perhaps only the male editor-publisher of this enlarged edition,
Jean Richer. Actually, all this forms part of the anti-woman and
anti-gallant "Querelle des Femmes" of the late middle ages and
Renaissance, now to be discussed.

I cannot refrain from mentioning, in closing this chapter, that
despite all expectations and warnings, as in my little poem of
1943, "The Cowboy," making fun of the wartime overuse of

'*fucking*' as an adjective-of-all-work, the word F U C K still apparently retains much of its mystic power, and to a degree one would hardly expect. Like the key to that *other* profound mystery, $E = mc^2$. As I have noted in more detail at the end of the Introduction to John S. Farmer & Wm. E. Henley's (*Dictionary of*) *Slang & Its Analogues* (New Hyde Park, 1966) 1: pages xciii–iv, the wave of student manifestations and revolts which swept America and Western Europe in the late 1960's were essentially begun on the campus of the University of California at Berkeley, in the spring of 1965, when a young man, John Thompson, age 22, created a fuss leading to the arrest of five people, by holding up outside the Student Union building a small sign containing the hand-lettered word 'F U C K.' That was all, but it was enough.

When some of the first skirmishes with the university authorities temporarily died down, John Thompson made the profound point, speaking to the press about them: 'You can carry signs saying *kill, murder and burn* and it's like nothing. But if you stand out with that word – bam, into jail.' This is almost the echo, probably not unconscious, of Montaigne's observation four centuries ago, in his essay "On Some Verses of Virgil" (1588) Bk. III, chap. 5, as translated in the present writer's *Love & Death* (1949) p. 94, a *cri du cœur* inspired by Montaigne's question: '*We bravely say* kill, rob, betray; *but that other we dare pronounce only between clenched teeth?*'

3. ANTI-GALLANTRY AND ANTI-WOMAN

Since the relationship between men and women, as formalized in marriage for four thousand years or more under patriarchy, is not a fair contact but heavily exploitative, with men getting almost all the advantage until very recently in the West (since about 1870), there is behind us a long history, over many millennia, of War Between the Sexes. In this war, women try to regain their freedom of action and their control over the children born of their bodies, while men violently resist and attempt to prevent this slave-revolt, or motion toward freedom and equality for women, of a kind biologically retained or long since achieved by the female of most *other* animal species on earth except the human, from the smallest of insects to whales. That women might also yearn for the same kind of domination over men, as men have had so long over women, is of course unthinkable. (But see "The *Escoumerda*," 15.V.2, below.)

The echo of this War Between the Sexes in literature and in humor is largely the men's side of the argument, since women did not appear in any significant numbers, until very recently, in either of these preponderantly male arts. Folktales being told as often by women as by men in many cultures, there is far better and fairer treatment of women in tales than in jokes or formal literature; and outlets and protagonists are offered in folktales for fantasy satisfactions for women: the Virgin Mary, Cinderella, Goldilocks, Red Riding Hood, etc. Meanwhile, centuries of attack on women had become absolutely routine, from the cruel classic tragedies of Sophocles (*Elektra*) and comedies of his avowed opponent Aristophanes (*Lysistrata*), proceeding then through the vile out-pourings of hatred and insult against women in the writings of the Latin satirists, Martial and Juvenal, and Christian fathers such as St. Odon of Cluny, of the never-to-be-forgotten close-up assessment, *'We are born between shit and piss.'* Anti-gallantry and the Defiling of the Mother did not begin with Odon, but nothing new has been added to the formula since. Certainly not in the modern Irish occult poet, W. B. Yeats' strabismic revamp of the same thing, in his poem "Crazy Jane and the Bishop": *'Love has pitched his mansion In the place of excrement.'* (Some of us have better aim than that.)

During the Renaissance, a division of loyalties became clear, between the Hispanic and Provençal culture of southwest Europe, representing the ideals of pro-woman chivalry – except for the highly moral inquisitor, Antonio de Guevara! – and the adoration of the Virgin Mary by men; and the Germanic culture of northern Europe. There the matriarchal survivals and traces of women's power were still strong, and the patriarchal counter-attack against it therefore remained violent, as gruesomely evidenced in the witchcraft trials. Only as late as Rabelais' time, in the early 16th century, did a serious northern defender of women appear in the lists: the German occultist, Heinrich Cornelius Agrippa von Nettesheim, in his *Déclamation de la noblesse et préexcellence du sexe féminin* (Latin and French text, Antwerp, 1529). A book and author singled out specially for ridicule by Rabelais – one of the main literary women-haters and ridiculers – under the name of 'Herr Trippa' in *Pantagruel* (1541) Bk. III, chap. 25, with whom Panurge consults as to whether he can avoid being cuckolded by his wife. (He can't.) Ending with Panurge insulting him, inviting him to

*'go to the Devil and be buggered by some Albanian [Bulgarian],
filthy* bardachio *that thou art;' and to blow in his arse so that
Panurge might 'with his squirting turd illuminate his
moustaches.'* So much for the defender of women!

See further, on the bibliography of this "Querelle des
Femmes" in the literature of the Renaissance, Prof. Francis
Utley's *The Crooked Rib*, covering only materials in England
and Scotland to the mid-16th century. And there is all the rest of
the enormous anti-woman literature of Europe and the Orient,
and the rare defences, including even a few counterattacks on
men by women, such as Rachel Speght's *A Muzzle for Melastomus* (1617) and Jane Collier's anonymous *The Art of Ingeniously Tormenting* (1753), both undeservedly overlooked or
forgotten. An anti-woman literature which the resistance
against women's liberation since the time of the French Revolution – and against Women's Lib today – has revived. For
some stinking examples see *The Second Sex* (1949) by Simone
de Beauvoir; *Sexual Politics* (1970) by Prof. Kate Millett, with
an important select bibliography; and *The Female Eunuch*
(1970) by Prof. Germaine Greer.

Even at the level of creating the bibliographical tools with
which the tremendous anti-woman literature and folklife of
over four thousand years can and now must be studied, most
of the work still remains to be done. With the exception of the
modern works cited in Prof. Millett's bibliography, and in my
own "Avatars of the Bitch-Heroine" and "Open Season on
Women" in *Love & Death* (1949), there is only Prof. Utley's
pioneering *The Crooked Rib*, and the beacon-light of the great
storehouse of passionate information in Robert Briffault's *The
Mothers* (London, 1927) a three-volume anthropological vindica-
tion of the early matriarchal origins of humanity: a work in
which the mere bibliography of books consulted, vol. III, pages
523–719, runs to some two hundred large pages of very small
type – longer than the average novel. There are also the
linguistics of anti-womanism, for many centuries now, on
which see the modest beginning of the needed historical dictionary in *The Intelligent Woman's Guide to Dirty Words* (1973:
The Feminist English Dictionary, P.O. Box 1302, Chicago 60690)
by Ruth Todasco *et aliæ*.

The anti-gallant 'mocks' or parodies appearing in English
poetry and the theatre, at least since the time of Shakespeare's
Sonnets and his *The Taming of the Shrew* (both written in the

1590's), and published in great numbers in the drolleries of the following century, have been discussed briefly in my *The Horn Book*, pp. 193–6 and 421–2, and this introductory material cannot all be reproduced here. The 'mock' or burlesque of that period was something more than a parody of a specific poem or play. It was a violent dysphemistic exercise in the hatred and vilification of the bodies of women, love, or other essential emotional matters which *the same poet writing the mock* may have earlier written to praise, and might well write to praise and glorify again! Psychologically considered, it was therefore a sort of safety-valve of ambivalent animosity, expressed against things which the speaker or writer probably very sincerely loved: the Feast of Fools of poets and playwrights. See a few such 17th-century mock 'praises' in English poetry, reprinted in John Wardroper's amatory anthology, *Love & Drollery* (London, 1969) Nos. 363–4 and 381–2. Even so, from the last of these, the perverted "In Praise of a Deformed Woman," he omits the six nastiest stanzas appearing in *Choyce Drollery* (1656; ed. 1876, p. 50–51).

This explains a good deal of the anti-woman literature, as to its ambivalent form, but of course does not discount in any way the violence and virulence with which the anti-woman attack was expressed, and was expected to be received by sympathetic male listeners. Even so, the formalization of the taking of *both* sides in the "Querelle des Femmes," which had come about in the *Blasons* and *Contreblasons* of French poetry by the 15th century (published by Méon in 1807 from *Les Blasons et Contreblasons anatomiques du Corps féminin*, 1543, and modern reprints), both glorifying *and* conspuing every part of the female body and genital anatomy, represents a beginning of fair treatment for women, in a literature in which women themselves seldom appeared or were allowed any rebuttal. Most later poetic satires in French and English, in the ancient style of Martial, the *Priapeia*, and *The Greek Anthology*, eventually dropped any pro-woman alternations, and flung themselves into bitter and obscene reviling. First strikingly in the *Satyres* of Charles de Beauxoncles, Sieur de Sigogne, who died in 1611 (ed. Fernand Fleuret, Paris, 1911). In particular Sigogne's ordurous attacks on the courtesan "Perrette" (Mlle. du Tillet), and on the same as *"Une vieille Sorcière"* and in his long *"Satyre contre une vieille courtisane qui frayoit* [coupled] *avec le Diable,"* which perhaps served as model for Herrick's similar revilings in England, under the title of "The Hagg."

Whatever may be the embarrassingly personal story told in Shakespeare's *Sonnets* (first published against his will in 1609), it is clear that the author is at least as much in love with the man involved as with the woman, to whom he devotes the alternately gallant sonnet No. 127 on her 'black beauty,' and the half-heartedly anti-gallant No. 130, its counter-blason:

> *My mistress' eyes are nothing like the sun;*
> *Coral is far more red than her lips' red;*
> *If snow be white, why then her breasts are dun;*
> *If hairs be wires, black wires grow upon her head.*
> *I have seen roses damask'd, red and white,*
> *But no such roses see I in her cheeks;*
> *And in some perfumes is there more delight*
> *Than in the breath that from my mistress reeks ...*

Of course, he takes it all back with an equivocation in the final couplet, but one wonders what this lady – however 'Dark' she may have been – thought of so lukewarm a cavalier, who told her that her breath stunk. (Mr. W. H.'s breath *never* stinks.)

A few examples of similar alternations between mad love and anti-gallantry are quoted from the poetry of Herrick – an authentic sado-masochist – in the introduction to my *The Limerick* (ed. New York, 1970) p. xxiv–vii. But these will not even compare with the violently insulting "Thorny Muse," forming an entire section of the *Nouveaux Satyres et Exercices Gaillards* (1637) of Robert Angot de l'Eperonnière, which begins in the usual *blason* style with a sonnet in praise of the '*Beau cul de marbre vif*' of a damsel, but then proceeds with an even more careful description – also cast as a sonnet – of the flabby body "D'Une Flasque," in the style of Villon's "Belle Heaulmière," and long alliterative diatribes "Sur une Halaine Infecte," on the same bad breath that Shakespeare reserves as his cruellest anti-woman thrust. (Though he manages a few other nasty cracks in *Hamlet*, *Othello*, and *Lear*.) As to the high- or low-point in this line hit by Angot de l'Eperonnière's poetry, see his *Nouveaux Satires*, ed. Blanchemain (1877) p. 162–75. A great deal more in this style can be found in all the poetic miscellanies, and especially the satirical drolleries of both French and English literature in the 16th and 17th centuries. In fact, almost all the drolleries are highly obscene and *anti*-erotic until the beginning of the poetic censorship in Britain, after the publication of the final edition of *Pills to Purge Melancholy* in 1720.

The drolleries are filled with 'mocks' of their own best songs and most charming pastorals. One example is cited by Prof. V. de S. Pinto and Mr. A. E. Rodway, in their *Common Muse* (1957) p. 8, noting the insistent anti-gallantry of much popular balladry of the Elizabethan period, and since, as when Marlowe's exquisite *"Come live with me and be my Love"* was parodied as *"Come live with me and be my Whore."* (Sir Walter Raleigh also wrote an "Answer" to the Marlowe poem, denying its sentiments, though not in ugly terms. See *The Oxford Book of English Verse*, Nos. 121–2.) No more striking example of this tendency can be found in English literature than the mock, entitled simply "A Song," in *Pills to Purge Melancholy* (ed. 1709) IV. 261, reprinted with the music in the more common edition of 1720, VI. 120, beginning, '*Underneath the Castle Wall, the Queen of Love sat mourning.*' One would hardly think so harmless a beginning could offend anyone, going on as it does to the Queen of Love 'tearing of her golden Locks' and smiting her breasts with her 'Lilly white Hand.' Yet here is the mock printed *with it*, as a second stanza, which fairly drips with a sort of insane anal-sadistic urge to defile whatever was set up as charming originally (in *Wit & Drollery*, 1661, p. 196, "Half mild, half stale"):

Underneath the rotten Hedge, the Tinkers Wife sat shiting,
Tearing of a Cabbage Leaf, her shitten Arse a-wiping;
With her cole black Hands she scratch'd her Arse
   And swore she was beshitten,
   With that the Pedlars all did skip,
   And the Fidlers fell a-spitting.

This disease, or urge-to-defile – it can hardly be called anything else – is by no means solely English. A quite similar mock in French, entitled "Isaure," and apparently modern, is printed in Gustave Brunet's anonymous *Anthologie Scatologique* (1862) p. 33. One of the most astonishing such dysphemistic exercises is the "Cure of Love" sonnet attributed – surely falsely – to the great 19th-century Spanish poet, Ramón de Campoamor. This is printed as Argentine folk-poetry in *El Plata Folklore* (*Anthropophytéia: Beiwerke*, VIII, 1923) by 'Victor Borde' [Lehmann-Nitsche] p. 35, no. 236, with German translation p. 165, beginning: '*Piojos cría el cabello más dorado – Lice breed in the loveliest golden hair,*' and continuing precisely in the cloacal vein of St. Odon and Swift. The final tercet is given here in a variant, also from Argentina (1975): *'Si este es el Amor que me enamora, Y si la más hermosa caga mierda pura, Yo me cago en el Amor y en la hermosura.'*

Schoolchildren and sailors still have a similar reputation in this line – doubtless left over from the sea-chantey period which came to an end just after World War I, though the unexpurgated sea-chanteys have never yet been published – for being unable to endure maudlin songs of sappy sentiment without parodying or mocking them with bawdy changes or intrusions (in an undertone), such as adding to every line the alternate words *'In the front'* and *'In the back,'* or *'In a nightshirt!'* "From the Desert I Come To Thee (*In a nightshirt!*)" used to be so parodied, always, when I was a schoolboy, and I have heard of cultivated persons doing the same thing (silently) while oppressively bored listening to hymns sung in church. Or total parodies of titles, or of particularly sentimental lines or entire songs or hymns may be invented, and invariably used to replace the originals on hearing their opening words. Any rejected feature would do for parodying, whether social or sexual, especially by sailors – a notably profane lot. For example, changing so anodyne a line as that the good ship was *'laden with gold from end to end,'* to *'loaded with fish (or shit);'* or *'She stands upon the shore and waves her hand at him,'* to: *'She stands upon her hands and waves her legs at him.'* (Which is admittedly an improvement.) The bawdy poetry of children is best collected and presented for Germany and Austria, by Ernest Borneman, *Studien zur Befreiung des Kindes* (Olten: Walter-Verlag, 1973 ff.); and for Australia by Ian Turner.

No one who loves poetry can be insensible to the acid beauty of Sir Thomas Wyatt's tenderly bitter reproach to his unfaithful mistress, Anne Boleyn, beginning: *'They flee from me that sometime did me seek, With naked foot stalking within my chamber.'* (Given in *The Oxford Book of English Verse*, No. 37.) Yet the very same Thomas Wyatt addressed to the same Anne Boleyn – as his part of the denunciation for adultery that cost her her head, and earned him his knighthood (note his sinister last line: *'What hath she now deservèd?'*) – a horrible and insulting counter-blason, "Thow old mule!" covering her with filth. The odd metre of this strange piece remained popular for centuries, and what is perhaps a further parody of it appears in the late-18th century erotic songbook, *The Frisky Songster* (ed.

1802) p. 70, entitled "The Rouzing Prick," and entirely devoted to the sadistic concept of coitus. It is in the form of a dialogue, the man beginning: *'Thou damn'd whore, come lay on thy back, I have a rousing prick that will make thy cunt to crack.'* She answers: *'Thou damn'd rogue, come and do thy worst, My cunt never minds thy bragging nor thy thrust.'* His rejoinder finishes the piece, addressed to his own – or the reader's? – testicles:

> *Then bollocks stand to it, and be not controul'd,*
> *But enter the breach like an old soldier bold,*
>   *Damn her, fuck her till she wheezes,*
>   *Fuck her till she farts and sneezes,*
>   *Damn her, drive her to pieces,*
>   *Thou damn'd whore.*

Anti-gallantry, and the sadistic concept of coitus, cannot be taken farther than that. The whole idea of this rough courtship-in-insults, and of sexual imprecation as a kind of anti-gallant erotic foreplay, is the hidden intention of the famously insulting dialogue between men and women in such modern plays as Edward Albee's *Who's Afraid of Virginia Woolf?* It is also the secret meaning of the even more violent verbal and physical attacks – this time on the audience, not on the other actors – in the so-called 'Theatre of the Absurd,' or 'Theatre of Cruelty,' which is really only a sort of homosexual lovemaking of the 'S. & M.' type, with the audience taking the 'M.' or shat-upon masochist position.

Shulamith Firestone in her *Dialectic of Sex* (1970) p. 170, makes the important point as to men's casual verbal contempt of women: 'To overhear a bull session is traumatic to a woman: So all this time she has been considered only "ass", "meat", "twat", or "stuff", to be gotten a "piece of"; "that bitch" or "this broad" to be tricked out of money or sex or love! To understand finally that she is no better than other women but completely indistinguishable comes not just as a blow but as a total annihilation.' Yes, and what do a hundred thousand American college-girls feel when told they must *admire* Yeats' calling their vaginas 'the place of excrement'? (A shitty assessment if ever I heard one.)

The presumable 'erotolalia' of verbally brutalizing a woman before, during, *or instead of sexual intercourse* has, of course, its franker counterpart in the verbal brutality that pretends not to understand at all that it is a substitute – or impotent equivalent – for intercourse. This mechanism is caught on the wing, during the day-to-day amenities of the collapse of democracy in the United States, in the machiavellian prose of the prince of modern parodists, John Francis Putnam, in his sardonic "Police Brutality Manual" (in *The Realist*, New York, October 1968) No. 83: p. 24, a politer footnote or supplement to the same writer's violently dysphemistic satire, "The Right, Too, Bear Arms," also in *The Realist*, No. 76, which got the magazine's advertisements put out of *The New Republic*. Under "Techniques of Police Brutality," Mr. Putnam's black-humor *Manual* specifies:

> *Verbal:* This is the least satisfactory method, but is the safest to employ. It is best used against members of the female sex, especially young radical demonstrators. Verbal Police Brutality in this case would normally consist of overt and pejorative references to their presumed sexual practices or to their organs of reproduction as a blatant instance of the totality of their innate personification. (We gotta write it out like this because this is a Manual, remember? What we mean, gang, is, it's OK to call 'em "Dirty Little Cunts!") A good rule of thumb with Verbal Police Brutality is to curse in an increasingly "dirty" manner in direct proportion to the refinement and prettiness of females so confronted.

That is not a mock – not even Mr. Putnam's zealously gallant part of it – but straight anti-gallantry at the crudest verbal level. Beating the same girl-demonstrators over the breasts and loins with billy-clubs is an even lower and cruder level. In the following recitation, a saving grace of wit leavens the insults with which the man answers and *counterblasons* the woman's overtures. Actually, one would not recognize what she says as an overture, but insults and counter-insults of this type are the whole essence of the negative sex 'games' or precoital maneuvering exposed and entitled "Beat Me Daddy" and "Uproar" in Dr. Eric Berne's *Games People Play* (1964). *A cowboy in a lunchroom sits down next to a handsome young lady and cannot help overhearing her order, 'which went like this: "Waiter, bring me a breast of virgin fowl. Be sure it's a virgin fowl, select it yourself. Garnish my plate with spring onions, and bring me a cup of coffee, not too hot and not too cold, just right. And by the way, waiter, open a window. I smell a horse.*

There must be a cowboy in the house." Thoroughly pissed-off, the cowboy started to order, "Bring me a duck, a well-fucked duck. Be sure it's well-fucked, fuck it yourself! Garnish my plate with horse shit, and bring me a cup of coffee as strong as Texas mule piss. By the way, waiter, knock down a wall. I smell a cunt – there must be a whore in the house!"' (World's Dirtiest Jokes, 1969, p. 99.)

A different text, in which the overtures on both sides creep back more frankly in their final lines, was heard marvellously recited by a Texas Negro laborer on a barge, in a Brooklyn waterfront lunchroom in 1949. As usual with folksongs and recitations, there is no editorial set-up of the situation, and one is flung into the action with the opening words: *Sporting Woman (soprano): "Waiter, wipe my plate off with a lemon peel. And give me a cup of coffee mild as a lily. Then tell the bartender to bring me an egg-nog, dusted over lightly with Three Feathers. And won't you please tell me what hard-workin' guy that is sitting over there?" Cowboy (basso robusto): "Waiter, scrub my ass with a brickbat. Gimme a cup o' coffee strong as jackass piss, with the foam farted off. 'N' tell me who that damn whoor is sittin' over there!"*

An attempt at rationalization or explanation is evident in a joke-text supplied by a college girl, as heard by herself in Chicago, 1955, preserved in the Indiana Folklore Archives under the title "The Hillbilly Sweethearts." It is very significant here that the sex, and even sexual swearing, is rejected, and in the process the revised or 'rationalized' story becomes purely cloacal and anti-gallant: *'It was a beautiful summer night, and a young hillbilly couple were sitting on the girl's front porch. The girl sat there looking at the moon for a while. Then she turned to her boyfriend and said (with a hillybilly drawl), "Cl-l-l-em, tell me somethin' soft and mushy." But Clem didn't say anything. They sat there a while longer, then the girl said again, "Cl-l-l-em, tell me somethin' soft and mushy." But Clem still didn't say anything. After a few moments she turned to him again and said, "Cl-l-l-em, tell me somethin' soft and mushy!!"* [Note imperative inflection.] *Clem turned slowly to her and said, "Shit!"'* The man's complete emotional strangulation here – the mucker-pose of being 'cool' – is accepted in the punchline as a proper retort to, or punishment for the girl's sin in demanding verbal and no doubt physical tenderness as a sexual approach. The only possible type of sexual intercourse that would satisfy such an ideal of intimidated femaleness and taciturn masculinity would be from behind (*Last Tango* style), with the woman kneeling on all fours, and the man yanking on her pigtailed hair from time to time, while smoking a big penis-shaped cigar, to indicate to her whether to *giddy-ap or back-up.*

From gruelling anti-gallantry like this it is only a step to the open mockery of pretended popular song-titles in the only-too-correctly named 'sick humor' developing since World War II. A few such titles picked up in N.Y. 1953, from a professional nightclub entertainer, who used to announce these as part of his act (no matter what he actually played and sang thereafter): *"Spring Is Just a Lot of Shit Blues"*, *"Don't Fuck Around With Love"* already used a century earlier, in slightly politer form, in Musset's play, *On ne badine pas avec l'amour;* not to mention "Don't fuck around with the Lone Ranger!" (as above), *"I'm Up to My Ass In Love With You"*, *"She Broke My Heart So I Broke Her Pelvis,"* and the not-so-dumb *"When You're in Love, Fuck Ain't a Dirty Word."* There had, of course, been actual parodies of this kind long before – for centuries, in fact – as for example the World War I parody of "It's a Long Way to Tipperary," as "It's the Wrong Way to Tickle Mary."

The dysphemistic format of the imaginary song remained current for some twenty years or more, a whole joke being made up to serve as vehicle for it, as seen in *World's Dirtiest Jokes* (1969) p. 194, built up of course on the old tear-jerker barroom recitations, "The Face on the Barroom Floor" or "The Volunteer Organist": *A man crying into his beer in a barroom explains that he is a great composer but no one will print his music. The bartender encourages him to play one of his compositions on the piano, and is astounded by the marvellous piece he plays. "That was great!" says the bartender: "fabulous! What do you call it?" "I Love You So Much I Could SHIT!"* Meanwhile, an even lower type of proudly self-styled 'sick' or dysphemistic humor, also keyed to songs and nursery-rhymes, was briefly popular during the '50's and '60's in America, among high-school students of both sexes, involving the parodying of some old favorite's opening lines, with the sudden 'descent to bathos' of a shouted obscenity to end with: *"All the king's horses and all the king's men –* SUCK!*" "Mary had a little lamb, Its fleece was white as snow, And everywhere that Mary went, She stepped in* LAMB-SHIT." Or simply as riddles: *"What's*

black and hairy and pisses on the wall? – Humpty Cunt."
"What's a womb? – The noise an Elephant makes when it farts in a cave." (Had enough? There are more.) These are connected, in a distant way, with the emotion behind two presumed attacks on the 1920's sex-censorship, Kendall Banning's *Censored Mother Goose* and Robert Carlton Brown's very rare *Gems: A Censored Anthology* (Cagnes-sur-Mer, France, 1931), in which nursery-rhymes and old favorite songs and poems are made to seem bawdy by BLANKING OUT various words in their lines, these words being *hummed* suggestively. Thus blaming the reader neatly for the resultant 'obscenity.'

Anti-gallant jokes try for an easy victory over the hated woman by attacking her body as ugly, smelly, or undesirable. Precisely the negative appeal, or 'working on the customer's fears,' whereby advertisements force women to buy endlessly unnecessary new clothes, doo-dads, cosmetics, de-stinking douches, etc. crushing them with imaginary notions of woman's 'natural' organ inferiority: *i.e.* the castrated being. *Two men in a bar. The first speaks very boozily, "Shay, do you like big asses on women?" "No, of course not." "And do you like droopy tits?" "No!" "How about big sloppy cunts, you like them?" "No. What are you getting at anyhow?" "Well if you don't like big asses, and droopy tits, and big sloppy cunts, what are you sneaking around after my wife for, when I'm not home?"* (L.A. 1968.) – *A man has had an argument with his wife and asks another man about the best way to make up with her. "Buy her a new fur coat," the friend suggests; "get her a seal-skin." "She's got one of those." "Well then get her an ocelot." "What's that?" "It's a sort of stinking pussy with a lot of hair." "She's got one of those too, believe me!"* (N.Y. 1940.) Vance Randolph cites: *Old man to wife: "When I first knowed you, your pussy was just like a peach with a little fuzz on it. But now it looks like a pile of shit the wagon-wheel has run through."*

This also works the opposite way, but the result is the same, to insult and chasten the woman: *The country girl on her wedding night says to her husband, "Well, we're married now, and we have to have real nice manners like city folks. So get up and put on your pajamas if you want to come to bed with me." He does so, and lies silently beside her for a while. Finally she says suggestively, "Isn't there anything you'd like, Wilbur?" "Yes," he says briskly, "would you please pass the pussy?"* (L.A.

1969. Compare the 19th-century 'unscrewable Bride' classic, where the woman who has taken off a bustle, wig, etc. is told *"You know what I want: unscrew it and throw it up here!"*)

The woman's body can also be entirely rejected, even in a directly sexual situation: *'The traveling man was struggling to get undressed in the upper berth. His toupee slipped and fell into the lower berth. Feeling around through the curtains in the dark, his hand touched something. "That's it, that's it!" said a sexy female voice. "Like hell it is," said the traveling man. "I part mine on the side".'* (*World's Dirtiest Jokes*, page 106.) A very well-known item of the 1930's or earlier, already discussed, concerns: *A woman who falls out of a window when drunk, and slides into a garbage-can upside down. A passing Chinese peddler puts one exploratory finger into her vagina and another into her anus, and says musingly, "White man clazy; this woman still velly good six seven mo' years."* Curiously enough, an *Arabian Nights* story very much like this, in which *a cast-off wife is put to live on a garbage dump*, but of course without the burlesque dénouement preceding, appears in Straparola's *Piacevoli Notti* (1553) IV, No. 2. (This is Rotunda's Motif S446, omitted by Thompson in his whole series covering rejections of cast-off and persecuted wives in folktales, S410 ff.) – *Actress, to her Chinese houseboy: "I guess I drank too many cocktails last night, and passed out. I must have been pretty tight." "Yes, missy, pletty tight first time. Next two times pletty sloppy!"* (N.Y. 1940. Some versions add: *" – My brother tell me."*)

Aside from turning the woman over to 'lower races,' she can also be rejected in favor of an animal, usually a cow. This is intended as the ultimate in anti-gallantry, however phrased. *A soldier is leaning out the train window at the depot to kiss his bride goodbye. The engineer has steam up, and starts the train with such a rush that the soldier misses his bride completely and kisses a cow's ass a mile and a quarter out of town.* (Idaho, 1919: Larson MS.) Only an accident, of course, yet is that how it gets its laugh? *The farmer's wife finds the young hired man standing in a wheel-barrow in the barn, fucking one of the cows. "Oh, hello," she says in surprise, adding suggestively, "Isn't there anything I can do for you?" "Sure is," he grunts; "wait till I shoot my wad, and you can wheel me over to the next cow!"* (Bloomington, Indiana, 1963.) Lower on the animal scale, in the insulting of the woman, is the preferring of a pig or sheep – a cow is, after all, somehow human and maternal! – and finally an ape or gorilla, as in the legend of the wife of Cain. John Collier's *His Monkey Wife* (London, 1930) is entirely built on this purposely insulting rejection, in which the sweet and subservient chimpanzee female finally impersonates the bitchy bride at the wedding, under her veil, and makes a far better wife. David Garnett's *The Man in the Zoo* also touches lightly on this matter, and *Lulu*, a French fictional biography in the 1920's, by Félicien Champsaur, of the Negro dancer Josephine Baker, seems to be making the same vulgar suggestion. The next step down is Philip José Farmer's sado-porno parody of *Tarzan of the Apes*, with Grandrith-Tarzan's female panther consort and jealous monkey-wives.

The male of a pair of apes in the zoo has died, and the female is becoming violent as her interest in masturbating with the cucumbers the keepers give her is soon worn out. They secretly decide to get a man to make love to her, and pick up a stalwart hobo (or a Negro or Texan) on the local skid-row, offering him twenty dollars for the job. They muzzle the she-ape, tie her arms to the bars, and let the man gingerly into her cage. She bends forward eagerly when she sees he has an erection, but suddenly rips her arms loose from the bars and begins crushing him in her embrace. "Help!" he shouts, "for God's sake, help!!" "Don't worry," the keepers shout back, "we'll get an elephant-gun and shoot her." "Hell no! Don't shoot her. Just get her muzzle off – I want to KISS *her!"* (Santa Monica, Calif. 1965.) Al Capp's "Lena the Hyena" vagina dentata character, in his *Li'l Abner* comic-strip – competing with the "Gravel Gertie" of another strip – was made typically gorilla-like, with everted nostrils, etc., by the winning entries in a contest to depict this 'ugliness-queen:' apparently the ultimate anti-gallant thrust.

Matchingly ungallant replies are of course possible to the woman, getting there first with the accusation of bestiality. *A dairy farmer has married a city girl, and one day he tells her, "The man for the artificial breeding is coming today to inseminate one of the cows. I have to get the alfalfa cut in the north field, so I put a big nail in the window-frame by the right cow. You show him when he gets here." When the artificial inseminator arrives, the woman accompanies him out to the barn, and points to the cow. "This is the one," she says. "How do you know?" asks the man. "By that big nail my husband hammered into the window-frame." "Well, what's that for?" "To hang your pants on, I guess – can I watch?!"* (L.A.

1968.) These identifications of the cow or sheep, by special marks, bows, etc., usually are frankly so the farmer 'won't have to fuck through the whole herd again' to find the cow or sheep that has the best or tightest vagina.

The next and last step down is turning the woman herself over to the animal. In the oldest legends this is the woman's nymphomaniacal choice, as in some Levantine *vagina dentata* tales, where the 'eel' or toothed fish in the woman's body that has been biting the men, has been engendered there through her earlier 'lustful couplings with a gorilla' (or Negro). This is clearly the other side of the legend of Cain. In modern jokes, of which some have already been given in chapter 11.III.2, "Orgies and Exhibitions," the woman is handed over to a large dog, or even a jackass – an animal with an extremely large penis – as in the private exhibitions still today in Tijuana, Mexico, and formerly in Havana, Cuba. And perhaps even earlier than that, on a matriarchal ritual or religious basis, in the Levant. From the modern point of view, there is the standard male-supremacist contradiction that when a man has intercourse with an animal it is an amusing peccadillo, but for a woman to do so disgraces her forever. Alexis Piron's 18th-century tale-in-verse, "L'Aze-te-foute," has: *A man and woman riding on a jackass, with the understanding that every time the jackass farts they will get off and the man will fuck the woman. After the sixth time, as they are resting, the woman says tenderly, "Jean, the jackass just farted." "Well then let the jackass fuck you – I've had enough!"* Centuries earlier, this was story No. 1, "For Want of Hay," in Antonio Cornazano's mock collection, *Proverbs in Jests* (before 1480; Liseux' English translation, Paris, 1888).

Female anti-gallantries have already been given in the First Series, especially in chapter 6.II.1, "Parrying Propositions," the usual format. *A man is crossing the desert on camel-back with his young niece, when they are caught in a sandstorm and the camel dies. "I guess we're going to die here in the desert," says the man, "but before I die I have one last request to make. Would you undress for me, before it's too late?" The girl undresses, but asks him to do the same so she will not be embarrassed. When she sees he has an erection she asks him what it is. He tells her it is the "Tree of Life" and that he'd like to put it into her to revive her spirits. "The Tree of Life?" she cries. "Well, don't waste it on me! Stick it up the camel's ass, and let's get out of here!"* (N.Y. 1948.) This farce is rather close, in form at least, to the most famous story in Boccaccio's *Decame-ron* (1353) Day III, Tale 10, "Putting the Devil in Hell." (Rotunda K1363.1 and K1631.1, with many further references to *novelle* using euphemistic phrases of this type to refer to the genitals.) In another modern anti-gallant female farce, *The woman tells the man, who has called his penis his 'cucumber,' to "Stick your cucumber up your friend's ass – I hear they do well in shit."*

It is perhaps only a coincidence that both these involve or imply the threat of pedication of the man by the ungallant woman, as her reply to his rejected sexual overtures. Yet this is really the most logical turning-of-the-tables, for all its anatomical impossibility. (Besides, there are always camels and cucumbers around.) One of the best stories in the *Arabian Nights*, probably now a thousand years old, is that of : *Princess Budur, who disguises herself in men's clothes and acts as king.* (On women disguised as men – now epidemic throughout the West, by hundreds of millions of women! – see the enormous group of folktale references at Thompson's Motif K1837, and the astonishing illustrated materials in John Grand-Carteret's *La Femme en culotte*, Paris, 1899, and Alfred Holtmont's *Die Hosenrolle: Das Weib als Mann*, München, 1925.) *Princess Budur eventually finds her long-lost husband, the prince, who is now earning his living as a pastry-cook. As she is now im-personating him on the throne, she has him arrested 'for not putting enough pepper in his tarts.' She tells him that she is a homosexual and that if he wants to avoid punishment he must let her bugger him. All ends happily after he is actually forced to drop his bag-pants and is sufficiently humiliated.* That lays it right on the line, as to the question of whether women can really rape men, whether for the Levantine audience or anyone else, under a very light layer of jocularity.

See in this connection, though of course very much more polite and symbolized, Walter Besant's bitter 'prophetic' satire, *The Revolt of Man* (1882), and Salvador de Madariaga's *The Sacred Giraffe* (apparently written in English in the 1920's), in which not only the future satirical utopia is entirely matri-archal, but is Negro as well, the centre of world-culture having shifted (again) to Africa. Olaf Stapledon's *Last Men and First*, with its superb time-charts putting our own transient instant of world-history in proper perspective, unfortunately never even considers the probable future of women. These are magnificent books, now in the process of being forgotten, and would find an intensely interested audience if they were put into print again. The same is probably also true of what is my own favorite in the satirical utopian line, Karel Capek's *War with the Newts* (a sequel to *R.U.R.*, his anti-machine satire in which the word 'robot' was first introduced; and *Krakatit*, 1924, prophesying the Atom Bomb), telling the story of the coming war between the Whites and the Blacks, under the light disguise of 'Us' and 'Them' (the Newts), who plan to enlarge the ocean at the expense of 'our' lands.

Numerous jokes, showing how hostile and obscene abuse is used by women to cut down and insult men, are given in the First Series, 6.II.1, "The (Female) Voice as Phallus." The presumable activity there being engaged in is "Parrying Propositions," which no doubt gives some color or pretext for the aggressive verbal humor. This is hardly the case where the woman is expressly a prostitute, and her verbal 'toughness' or insults could only drive off the non-masochistic client. It is not to be overlooked, of course, that there are lots and lots of masochistic clients, who want to be beaten by the girl, insulted, tied up, made to stand in corners (in little-boys' clothes), be walked or ridden on (possibly with spurs), and finally pissed and shat upon, or – a perversion not too well-known to the public – be given enemas, *i.e.* actually be pedicated by the prostitute. Perhaps it is clients of this kind, or men wishing they had the nerve to go that far, who make up and enjoy verbal 'kills' like the following: *A fat, dapper little playboy wearing all the latest clothes, rings, dark-glasses, underwater wristwatch, etc., is ogling a beautiful young woman sitting with her legs crossed very high at a bar. Finally he gets up his courage, crosses over to her and says in her ear, "Hello, Beautiful. Whaddya say to a little fuck?" She measures him coolly with her eyes. "Hello, little fuck."* (N.Y. 1965.) Again, under the insult, observe the hidden maternalism in the crucial concern with the 'littleness' of the man-child who imagines himself grown-up enough for professional sex.

The most revealing thing ever written by Norman Mailer (the 'Jewish Hemingway') is the desperately hateful, anti-gallant short story, "The Time of her Time," in his *Advertisements for Myself* (1959), reprinted under the franker title, "The Taming of Denise Gondelman," in *Avant Garde* (New York, May 1968) No. 3: p. 40–45. Kate Millett has poignarded this item, in *Sexual Politics*, p. 324–5, for precisely what it is. Here the little, sexually wrung-out nineteen-year-old Jewish college-girl, who is not able to find or give herself emotionally, nor have an orgasm, in the one-night stands and fly-by-night sex affairs of the mock-intellectual Greenwich Village milieu, is portioned out more of the same by the fake-Irish-cocksman-*cum*-fake-psychoanalyst (also fake-bullfighter), whose treatments are strictly pubic hate, with Hemingwayesque cape-flourishes of *machismo* prose when coming in for the phallic kill. The types are unmistakably authentic, though the races and religions of the protagonists have been reversed as disguise.

Mailer's mock-Irish speaking trumpet, 'Sergius O'Shaugnessy,' solves Miss Gondelman's problems (though hating her for her 'certain snotty elegance of superiority'), after struggling with his own premature ejaculation all night – we all have our problems – by the purposeful ungallantry of buggering her unexpectedly, then switching to her vagina (to wipe it with shit), and calling her *"You dirty little Jew!"* to trigger her orgasm. (It says here.) This, he explains, is because her anus is 'the bridal ground of her symbolic and therefore real vagina,' which is eating your sexual pound-cake and having it too. She replies, punch for punch, to this type of psycho-anal analysis, by telling him the next morning as her final line from the door-way that *her* psychoanalyst says his whole life is a lie, and he's nothing but an unconscious homosexual. (As every asshole knows.)

Farting, which is considered an expression of virile heartiness in men, is presumably unforgivably anti-erotic in a woman, and an obvious rejection of her or expression of contempt when the lover or husband allows himself such a lapse in the woman's presence. A number of stories and repartees showing this gaseous ungallantry in action have already been given in the First Series, 9.I.2, under "Name-Calling," p. 681–2, summed up in the bit of proverbial folk-wisdom: *"The honeymoon is over when the husband farts in front of his wife."* This is sometimes set up as a riddle or catch connected with farting (like asking someone, *"Pull my little finger, will you?"* when one has to fart), and no matter what answer the woman gives, she is sure to lose. Vance Randolph has an Ozark story of this kind in *Pissing in the Snow*, No. 87, as "Travelers Are All Fools," in which: *The traveler asks the woman who is putting him up whether she wants him to treat her like his wife or like a stranger* – the proverb just quoted tells the story – and a more recent form changes only the phrasing: *A widower takes as his second wife a much younger girl, and on their wedding night he asks her, "How should we do it, honey, like the old folks or like the young folks?" "Anyway you want, sweetheart," she says; "all I want is to be a good wife to you." "Well," he decides, "we both had a hard day and it's pretty late, sho we'll just do it like the old folks." He reaches over, rubs his finger in her pubic hair and vagina, turns his back on her, lets a couple of big farts, and goes to sleep!*

Observe now how the rules suddenly change, when it is the woman who farts: *'Man and wife sleeping in separate beds. Man cooing across for wife to join him. Eventually she goes over to him, and on the way farts. He: "There now, little whimsy bumsie-wumsie!" After they've been through the motions* [!! – Ed.] *she returns to her own bed, and on the way farts again. He: "There you go – stink the bloody place out!"* (*Union Jack*, MS., Chelmsford, Essex, 1954.) The unfairness here is perfectly conscious; this is not the case with a joke reprinted from the Texas humor magazine, *Sex to Sexty*, in *World's Dirtiest Jokes* (1969) p. 108: *'The Standby Home Products lady was just fixing to ring a doorbell when she had to let a big fart. Boy, it was really a dilly, so she quickly sprayed her* Essence of Knotty Pine *around the threshold. About that time, a man answered the door and started sniffing. She thought he might be getting ready to brag on her Essence of Knotty Pine, so she said, "What does it smell like?" He replied, "I hate to say it to such a nice lady, but it smells like somebody just shit a Christmas tree!"'*

Actually, of course, he does *not* hate to say it and he does say it. What he wants is to 'rub her nose' in her digestive lapse the way people do to puppies, and even sometimes to babies! – and throw shit in the face of the 'nice lady,' on the ungallantly safe grounds that it is *her own fault*. (Pine-scented 'chlorophyll' de-stinker, or no.) And that is what he does, and so does the teller of the joke. We are a long way from the inverse gallantry of the *Elizabethan jester who teases a lady, by saying to her, when he farts in company, "Never you mind; I'll say I did it!"* And a modern descendant: *When the gentlemen jump up to say, "I beg your pardon!" whenever her ladyship the dowager farts, the fool waits for an especially big one, and jumps up saying, "This one is on me!"* (See also chapter 15.III, "Crepitation," especially sub-section 4, "*Pet-en-Gueule*.")

Little old ladies are by no means as sacrosanct in folk-humor as might be imagined sentimentally. I have listened to a proposed scenario for a wordless movie-comedy or pantomime in which the whole brief plot was *To show how a well-meaning chap can finally be driven so frantic by the intrusive helpfulness of a little old lady whom he has taken into his home, that he eventually beats her and throws her out of a taxicab into the street – the same situation from which he has saved her at the beginning.* (N.Y. 1936, from a motion-picture art director: a famous 'practical joker.') In my brief stay in California in 1964/5, I must have heard a dozen different people I was driving with in their cars – including young women – state that they would *'love to hit one of those Little Old Ladies in Tenny-Runners* [tennis-shoes],' looking evilly at some old lady pedestrian crossing the road meanwhile. I assume this was a local proverb or catch-phrase, but never heard anything similar about little Old Men (who are, to the contrary, always 'Dirty,' and seduce little girls by giving them lollipops, mink coats, sports-cars, etc.)

Two jokes should be enough to cover this special department of anti-gallantry, in which it does not take much penetration to recognize the 'little old lady,' or other helpless woman, as the hated and rejected mother-figure. (12.IV.6, "The Defiling of the Mother." And note in particular the Surréalist and black-humor parodying of Leonardo da Vinci's "Mona Lisa," also "Whistler's Mother," both being art equivalents of the Virgin Mary, in the folk-mind.) *An old lady on a crowded trolley car is hanging onto a strap, with her parcels falling out of her arms, while a big powerful man is sitting in the seat before her glaring straight ahead. After several polite hints are ignored, she says to him, "Would you slide over a little and make room for an old lady's sitter?" "Hang it on the hook, lady," he replies; "it's got a hole in it!"* (L.A. 1968.) Oh, all right – it's just good, clean fun: a witticism. Why be a spoil-sport and object to it? Have you got an Oedipus complex, or something? (*"Mama, the psychiatrist says I got an Oedipus complex." "So?! As long as a good Jewish boy loves his mother!"* – N.Y. 1948.) Try *this* one on your unprejudiced palate – that's got a hole in it too: *'Legless woman lets soldiers "'ave a go" in turns, by getting them to take her out of her invalid chair, hanging her by her strap-hangers on the wall, suspended by a hook. When it's over they take her down and put her back on her chair. "Thank you,* boys," she says. "The last time some sailor barstards left me hanging there for two days before the postman found me".' (*Union Jack*, MS., Chelmsford, Essex, 1954.) This is practically the plot of various recent horror-movies, of a kind in which aging Hollywood lesbians like to star when they are finally too old and scraggy around the neck to carry-off romantic parts any longer. See also a more romantic version of the same joke, at the opening of chapter 13.IV "Symbolic Castrations," which makes clear that it is really only a rationalization of sexually perverted attraction to crippled women.

Mere insults and callousness do not by any means bring us to the limits of anti-gallantry. There is more and worse to come. As with the 'diseased old whore' representing the mother in the final convolution of "The Defiling of the Mother," 12.IV.6, the *woman must die*. Far too many examples of this are available, at both the folktale and belletristic level, for me to attempt to do more than sketch in the main formulas here. The strangest form is that appearing as the 'return of the repressed' of writers imagined to be – or imagining themselves to be – superlatively gallant toward women, as for example the modern French erotic poet, Pierre Louÿs, whose most famous and successful book, *Aphrodite* (1896), an historical novel of the life of a Greek prostitute of ancient times, ends horribly with a sado-masochistic scene of the 'belovèd slave-girl being crucified by her lover.

At a much lower level, in one of the last modern collections of erotic *contes-en-vers* in French (a folktale form on which see *The Horn Book*, p. 470–76), *Les Grappillons and Les Derniers Grappillons*, signed 'Un Bourguignon salé' (Auxerre, 1879–91, 2 vols.: copy, Ohio State Univ.), and erroneously ascribed to the bibliographical *précieux*, M. Octave Uzanne, a perfectly extra-ordinary return-of-the-repressed poem is given, vol. I, p. 146–8, as "Le Sauveteur" (The Life-Saver), in which: *The poet wishes his mistress would drown, so he could save her; that she should be shipwrecked, so he could be with her naked (and to make babies for her, as queen of the desert island); he wants to set her house afire – so he can get her out 'at the risk of his life,' while she lies 'trembling in her bed;' he wants her to be chased by rough soldiers trying to rape her – so he can hide her, 'shamefaced and still a virgin' in his arms; a black asp should bite her breast* [legend of Cleopatra] *– so that he can suck out the poison; he wants to see her miserable and friendless – so* *that he can then be her only friend; he wants her to be sick and repulsive, so that everyone shall flee her, and then he will come and find her still so charming as to make him jealous. (Now there's a well-turned compliment for you . . .) Finally, of course, he wants to see her dead – so that he may revive her with a kiss!* The woman who is the recipient or receptacle of all this sadistic flattery is allowed the *envoi* at this point – probably authentic – and tells her would-be saviour that she does not like his '*marivaudage*' (flirtatious banter or chaffing), and that he is no saviour at all but a '*vilain sauvage*' and to be off. Phrased otherwise, *When you have a 'salty Burgundian' for a friend, you don't need an enemy!* The theme is folkloristic. Compare the rather similar 'transformations' courtship songs throughout Europe, related to the bawdy modern "Roll Your Leg Over." (Headnote to Child Ballad No. 44, "The Twa Magicians": Motif D615.) Also the old song, "I Wish My Love Was In a Bog," of which one stupefying modern stanza is quoted at the end of section 15.I.4, below.

Relevant here are the 'hate cards' or anti-gallant greeting-cards which offer unexpectedly nasty and sardonic 'best wishes' to the recipient, usually on a second or punchline leaf, the first or cover-leaf pretending to start out with the usual friendly sentiment. These are of course a development of the 'comic valentines' of the mid-19th and early-20th centuries in both Europe and America, which were, if anything, even a bit more hateful than the current 'hate cards,' since they were intended to be sent anonymously – as prefabricated poison-pen letters – when everyone else was celebrating Valentine's Day with lacy sentimental cards of yearning love. The 'hate cards' are now quite an industry, and have largely driven out most other types of 'humorous' greeting cards, as well in France (under the brand-name 'McMix': presumably a joke on the date 1909) as in America, where I first saw such cards produced and sold in an intellectual bookshop, 'The Four Seasons,' in the Greenwich Village section of New York City, in 1948. They are still nothing but prefabricated poison-pen letters, or modern sadistic *kitsch* – sometimes mildly sexy – and one wonders about the private lives and sex-habits of the artists and gagmen producing them, and the people peddling them. And the public that buys them, by the millions.

One cannot of course overlook that all this represents a transmogrification of normal sexuality into hate-sex, for people

who have not the nerve to express themselves unequivocally as
to their sexual emotions. It is the artificial nature of this substitution or expurgation that drives it to such hateful lengths, not
only in the way of sex-hate, on which see the First Series, chapter 9.I, under "Adultery," but also as to the unhealthy substitution of an allowed sadism and destructiveness for the ordinary
penis-*cum-vagina* sexual acts that are really, if I may so phrase
it, the bread & butter of the continuation of all human life.
Consider the "Liesbestod" in Wagner's *Tristan & Isolde* (1865),
where we are given the long-drawn-out death of the lovers instead of their mutual intercourse and orgasm, as a 'polite approximation' of the latter on the stage. This is taken to its
ultimate point in the morbidly beautiful Brazilian motion-
picture of the 1950's, *Orfeu Negre* ("Black Orpheus"), based on
the wild Carnival celebration of the underprivileged Negroes of
Rio de Janeiro, in which the lovely Black heroine is actually
shown being electrocuted – in full color – on a trolley-wire, as
her final and symbolic death-orgasm. On this international
murder-equals-orgasm perversion, compare also the sick
Swedish art-film, Bo Widerberg's *Elvira Madigan* (1967), in
which the 'lover' shoots the girl in the face while hugging her
at the end, to the music of the beautiful slow movement of
Mozart's Piano Concerto No. 21, also thus defiled. The sick 'Togetherness' of softcore porno-sadism.

Strictly at the verbally joking level: "*What became of your
girl?*" "*She got syphilis and bled to death.*" "*You don't bleed to
death when you have syphilis.*" "*You do when you give it to
me!*" (*Screw*, New York, 15 Sept. 1969, No. 28: p. 21.) The
principal modern "Taming of the Shrew" story does not have
any ostensible erotic tone, but cannot be overlooked here · *A
taciturn young farmer marries a girl in a nearby town and is
taking her home behind him on the crupper of his horse. He
spurs the horse lightly to get it to move faster, and the horse
shies, throwing them both off. The farmer gets up, gets back in
the saddle, pulls his wife up behind him, and sets off again,
saying quietly, "That's the first time." Then the horse brushes
against a tree, pulling off the man's boot. He gets the boot, puts
it back on again, and says warningly, "That's the second time."
Finally the horse rears and falls backward on the couple, and
then stands over them seeming to laugh at them. "And that's
the third time!" the farmer says, and pulls out a gun and shoots
the horse dead. The young bride is stupefied, and cries, "Well*

for heaven's sake, why did you do that? Of all the stupid things!
Now how are we going to get home? And night is falling!" The
farmer listens to her silently, picks up the saddle-bags and starts
down the road, saying, "That's the first time." (N.Y. 1963. – This
is in Straparola, *Piacevoli Notti*, 1553, VIII, No. 2. Also, two centuries earlier, in Don Juan Manuel's book of *exempla* in the
Levantine style, *El Conde Lucanor*, written about 1330; ed.
Leipzig, 1900, No. 35.)

The intermediate version of this is the Elizabethan ballad,
'The Curst Wife lapped in Morel's Skin" (Child Ballad, No. 277),
where: *The husband wraps his disobedient wife in the skin of*
his dead horse before beating her, and then tells her family,
when she complains, that he was only beating his horse, as is
his right. (Type 1370, as of *A lazy wife who must hold the cat*
while it is being beaten for not working! Many further references here, and at Type 901, "The Taming of the Shrew," Motif
T251:2, to which add G. Di Niscia, *"La Bisbetica domata* dello
Shakespeare," in *Miscellanea nuziale Percopo-Luciano*, Napoli,
1903.) The horse or other animal is here openly beaten or killed
in simulacrum of the woman. Compare: *The cowboy whose*
wife has disappeared. He explains to the police, "She broke her
leg on the way to the spring, and I had to shoot her." (N.Y.
1939.) Also the crude anti-gallantry of *The Stag Party* (1888) unnumb. p. 281: *'Smith (telling about the accident): "Yes, we*
found her body lying beside the track. The head was gone com-
pletely. All we could tell was that she was a girl of about six-
teen years, and Dutch [German]." Jones: "How in hell did you
know she was Dutch?" Simth: 'Sauerkraut sticking out of her
arse".' In Emlyn Williams' 1930's play and movie, *Night Must*
Fall, the murderer carries his woman-victim's head around with
him – in a hatbox!

The disposal of the body of the murdered victim is no more
of a problem when it is a woman than when it is a man, but
the matter seems to attract more anti-gallant chortles when it is
a woman. (See further the section on "Cannibalism," 13.III.4.)
Lord Dunsany's story, "Two Bottles of Relish," in which the
man simply *eats* the wife he has murdered, is considered the
most deliciously amusing solution. The guilt can also be reversed on the victims, as in John Collier's *Green Thoughts* (London, 1932, with an appreciative foreword by that amateur of
modern roccoco, Osbert Sitwell), in which people turn into
Venus flytrap plants, an age-old botanical *vagina dentata* jest,

since the part of this plant (*Dionæa muscipula*) which actually traps and digests insects is not the female part of the plant – except in its human vulviform appearance – but is the modified tip of the leaf. A crude horror-movie on a similar theme, with screenplay credited to Brandon Fleming, was issued in 1959 as *The Woman Eater*. In a more recent similar movie item, *The Collector*, the women are destroyed and, by implication, mounted like butterflies in a collection made by a sadist. Thomas Lask, in a review in the *New York Times* (25 Nov. 1972) p. 29, comes down hard on John Collier's 'fierce and unrelenting misogyny' in *His Monkey Wife* and in many short stories. He notes that 'Collier's women are predatory, bloodsucking, life-throttling ... never more than vehicles of gratification,' with examples; adding that this 'is surely literary pose' in the anti-feminist tradition of the Middle Ages. He does not mention the stories in which the wife is done away with gruesomely, in the style of Poe. (Compare Jack Lemmon's homosexual movie comedy, *How To Murder Your Wife*, 1964, in which the gorgeous but inconvenient bride is presumably immured in wet concrete. The jury acquits the husband.) As Dumas' gallant *Three Musketeers* lynch their leader's bitch-wife – with the hangman's help.

It is curious that macabre and purposely 'diabolical' themes like these attract so much of the attention of splendid modern stylists like John Collier – also of the only other British writers really his equals in this line in our century: Walter De la Mare and Dorothy Sayers. Stylists like these, *à le manière noire*, on the model of their master, Edgar Allen Poe, expend the most loving attention on the beauty, the placing, wit and restraint of the *words* they use, while simultaneously ripping off their carefully-adjusted masks and expecting us to go rollicking with them like homicidal lunatics on a shit-flinging holiday in their gruesome and baroque lust-murder *themes*. This is precisely the secret also of the so-called British 'restraint.' It is not new. Shakespeare pegged it to the heart four centuries ago, in Hamlet's assessment of the play-within-the-play (III.ii.244), though blaming it all on Italy; assuring the king that there is nothing offensive in the play: "No, no, they do but jest, poison in jest; no offence i' the world."

At the other end of the literary speculum, the shooting-permit of "*We're only kidding!*" has never been taken farther in the enormous anti-woman literature (and art) of the world, nor in the sado-masochist 'horror' movies that continue the same stereotypes, than in a purposely gruesome sadistic comic-strip in color, *The Adventures of Phoebe Zeit-Geist*, written by Michael O'Donoghue and drawn by Frank Springer, published serially in the self-consciously intellectual *Evergreen Review* (New York: Grove Press). Rising to some sort of low-point in issue No. 42, for August 1966, p. 58–62, along with a keyed-in sadistic subscription blank, p. 6, facing a portrait of who but Jean Genet, and a glorification of the stenching old corpse of the patron-saint of anti-womanism, the Marquis de Sade. The masks are dropping nowadays, and the historical anti-woman-ism of centuries of 'closet queens' is visible now for what it always really was under the literary (or religious) rags & tags: the pornography of sadism, now with a homosexual-camp grin.

A modern literary survival or rewriting of an ancient folk-tale, called "The Sausage Rain" (Aarne Tale Type 1381B, Motif J1151.1), is "The Unicorn in the Garden," in *Fables for Our Time* by James Thurber. *The husband assures his wife that there is a unicorn in the garden eating flowers, but then denies this when the wife reports it to a psychiatrist and the police in order to have him 'put in the booby-hatch.'* The dénouement is: *'So they took her away, cursing and screaming, and shut her up in an institution. The husband lived happily ever after.'* Thurber also adds a Perverted Proverb as moral: *'Don't count your boobies until they are hatched,'* to help pass off his anti-woman fable of 'the biter bit' as humor. It is observable that this is hardly more than an inflation of his one cartoon success, in which again the husband reports an impossible or mythical beast: *A husband and wife in bed. She is saying angrily, "All right, have it your way – you heard a seal bark." Over the head of the bed, behind her, supported on its flippers, a moustachioed seal.* This only seems improbable to people who have never been kept awake all night in hotels in La Jolla, California, where whales spout offshore in the mating season – or used to, before the coastline was polluted – and seals bark all night on the rocky beach.

Observe also the reversal of the older folktale situation (Type 1381). In the folktale, a pretended 'sausage rain' or similar is used by a mother to *save* her son from being convicted of mur-der. In Thurber's fable, the seal-that-became-a-unicorn is made use of by both husband and wife to put the other 'in the booby-hatch.' This is of course in line with Thurber's one real claim to fame, his popularizing of the phrase, *"The War Between Men and Women;"* since, as humorist, he was hardly more than a poor imitation of Robert Benchley.

The title or phrase, "The War Between Men and Women," is in any case not recent. It was used over four hundred years ago, in the *Controverses des sexes masculin et féminin* of Drusac (1534); then by the Seigneur de Cholières, author of very important jest-essay collections, *Les Neuf Matinées* and *Les Après-disnées* (1587), in his mock-history *La Guerre des Masles contre les Femelles* (1588, reprinted Bruxelles : Mertens, for Gay, 1864). The running-title, which is probably what Cholières originally intended, is even more hopefully horrendous : *La Furieuse et effroiable guerre des masles contres les femelles*, putting it in the tradition of Teofilo Folengo's macaronic "Horrible Battle between the Flies and the Ants" (before 1530), and the "War of the Cunts and Pricks" in Antonio Vignale's *La Cazzaria*, or "Book of the Prick" (about 1530), a subtitle which says the same thing as Drusac, Cholières and Thurber, but far more frankly. There is a French manuscript imitation of Vignale, by the Comte de Caylus, *La Cazzo-Pottamachie, histoire physique et morale, par laquelle on démontre pourquoi on ne trouve plus de Grands Vits ni de beaux Cons* (MS. 1756, preserved in the Library of Rouen : Leber Catalogue, No. 2509).

The more polite yet far more virulent expressions of the same struggle, at the folk-poetic level, will be found in English in the Child Ballads on 'marital disharmony,' Nos. 274–8 (with the addition of the ballad of poison and blindness, "Johnny Sands, or The Old Woman of Slapsadam," on which see *The Horn Book*, p. 413), and in the masterful bibliography of the older anti-woman literature in English verse, Prof. Francis Utley's *The Crooked Rib*. This title derives ultimately from a beautiful Arabic proverb 'explaining' the just-so story of Eve's creation from Adam's rib, in *Genesis*, ii. 18–25 : *"Woman is still like Adam's rib. You must take her with her bent. Force her to straighten – and she breaks."* This is just as relevant, of course, to women trying to change or 'reform' men. And it is certainly wiser than anything the Juvenals, the Odon of Clunys, the Guevaras, the Thurbers, the Wylies, the Hemingways, and other hateful and perverted wiseacres have ever had to say about women, killing them cowardly on paper as they dared not do in life.

4. ANTI-FAMILY

Anti-family jokes and mocks are among the most popular of all, since that is the principal and conventional 'great lie' of our civilization: that *The family is the heart of the home, &c, &c.* Whereas, in truth, as set up at present, it is precisely the neuroticizing influence of family life, and of parents who are themselves neurotic – through the action of their own parents in turn, and society thereafter – that is the *most* harmful single influence in human culture, under no matter what social or economic system. It remains to be seen whether current efforts to destroy the family unit, and reduce or explode it to small separate 'consumer units' of women without men, and vice versa, as already discussed in the introduction to chapter 11.I, "The Oldest Profession," will create any improvement at the psychological level. More likely it will simply add to the already unsupportable neurotic freight the straw that will now surely break the camel's back: an endless feeling of loneliness, of belonging to *no* group or family; an irreversible estrangement and *anomie*.

Meanwhile, one mocks the family because one is aware of its sins and falsities, and has had no experience of the sins and falsities that will surely come to replace it. At its very mildest, the anti-family sentiment is sometimes disguised in stories about children, where the family secrets are given away, and the dirty laundry spread out to public view, by the child's 'accidental' divulging of secrets concerned with the parents' sexual and extra-marital lives. Many such jokes have already been given, and studied separately, in the First Series, chapters 1 through 3, including jokes enacted under the obvious disguises of the 'Fool' or the 'talking animal,' both of whom represent the aggrieved and vengeful child. A few further, and violently scatological anti-family jokes will also be found at the very end of this Second Series, 15.VI.3, "All to Shit."

The aggressively hate-filled and frustrated family situation was standard in the most popular of all American newspaper comic-strips since the 1920's, George McManus' *"Maggie and Jiggs,"* actually entitled "Bringing Up Father," and just as popular in France as *"La Famille Illico"*. (The French have, in any case, a far more outrageous anti-family farce, often revived in small theatres, *"La Famille Tuyau-de-Poêle,"* which generally ends up in a free-for-all sexual orgy, or barely short.) Most of the reactive dirtying in *"Maggie and Jiggs"* was expressed at a food level, with Jiggs yearning and elaborately plotting always to get away from the artificial, 'lace-curtain' life of parlors and music-teachers that his ugly, pretentious and asexual wife insists on leading for them both, and to eat the vulgar Irish corned-beef-&-cabbage 'with the boys.' Maggie's own relatives, who come in disastrously great hordes to visit and sponge, are matchingly shown to have pig-like eating habits, thus mocking Maggie's pretentions with the open implication – by means of this even worse food-dirtying – that her own family background is not 'lace-curtain' either, and is nothing but 'Paddy and the pig.' Other imitative family bitch-strips, such as the continuingly popular *"Blondie and Dagwood,"* hew to similar sado-masochist formulas, and insistent orality. When Blondie presumably refuses to let Dagwood lay her, he stumbles out to the kitchen in his pajamas at midnight, and makes himself an enormous, many-layered sandwich at the overflowing icebox-that-is-really-Blondie. So also Philip Roth's *Goodbye Columbus* and *Portnoy*.

As it happens, jokes in English (and I think in French) are not the repository of the most violent anti-family materials of a humorous and satirical kind, which are more usually presented in the form of dysphemistic and scatological *songs*. These cannot be dealt with here at any length, and form an entire section of my work in progress, *The Ballad: Unexpurgated Folksongs, American and British*, which includes historical materials back to the 16th century on many songs and ballads. The most recent wide collection of bawdy English songs, *Why Was He Born So Beautiful, and Other Rugby Songs*, edited by Harry Morgan (London : Sphere Books, 1967–8, 2 vols., the second being entitled *More Rugby Songs*), includes an extraordinary number of anti-family mocks of this kind, as well as the principal British anti-gallant or anti-woman song or recitation, "Eskimo Nell," (I. 57–66), an overlong and purposely repulsive imitation of the American "Our Lil," discussed in my *The Horn Book*, p. 418–20. The classic anti-gallant mock, "Bollocky Bill the Sailor" (on which see further *The Horn Book*, p. 201–2), is also given, as "Who's That Knocking At My Door?"

The anti-family songs are almost too many to enumerate, and include the erotic version of the music-hall parody, "She Was Poor But She Was Honest", "Life Presents a Dismal Picture", "My God How the Money Rolls In", "When Lady Jane Became a Tart," and also "Please Don't Burn Our Shithouse Down", "Little Sister Lily (The Finest Fucking Family in the Land)," and the American classic in this line, "Lydia Pinkham" (a very appreciated text); as well as two ugly parodies of the well-loved A. A. Milne children's poems in *When We Were Very Young*, etc., as "Christopher Robin" (*Rugby Songs*, I. 149) and "Christopher and Alice" (II. 89). These last apply the "Little Willie" sadistic quatrain format to such matters as Christopher Robin 'having a wank,' and strike a level rather close to the frantic dysphemism and radical self-hatred of Philip Roth's anti-Jewish, anti-mother, and anti-family novel, *Portnoy's Complaint* (New York, 1968).

Other anti-family songs of this kind exist in America, such as the old Scottish Gypsy-Tinker song, "My Father Was Hanged for Sheep-Stealing" (called "My God How the Money Rolls In," in recently-collected texts). The most popular such item at present is a dismal scatological recitation or chant (to the tune of *"Deutschland über Alles"*), called "A Letter from Home," and beginning *'Home (or Life) presents a doleful picture, Dark and gloomy as the tomb . . .'* dirtying every member of the family with some unhumorous disease or disaster, and moving on pitilessly to the perfectly worthless scatological explosion or collapse of the punch-line in which Auntie Mabel *'blows her asshole inside out,'* or *'Mine's a cheerful occupation, Cracking ice for grandpa's piles.'* There is such a thing as *style*, even in hating one's family, and it is just that style which is grotesquely lacking here. The Negro songs, as always, show the greatest imagination and vitality, even in these self-mocking insults, as in "The Mother-Fuckers' (or Bull-Dykers') Ball." This is the life-game of "Get There Fustest With the Mostest" (GTFWTM), as with Cyrano de Bergerac's *"Tirade du Nez"* in Rostand's play.

The strictly non-sexual but highly sadistic "Little Willie" quatrains have already been noted. These developed just at the turn of this century to take the place of erotic limericks for people who feel that murder and atrocity are somehow less sinful than sex. This is the *other side* of the Victorian idea of sex as sin and degradation, but is seldom mentioned, though it is the whole basis of the cult of death, horror-stories, murder-mysteries, spy-thrillers, etc., since the mid-18th century, when the sex-censorship was clamped down tight. And this not only on printed public literature, but also on private sexual emotions, as in the fantastic denial of any sexual appetite at all to women in a famous passage in Dr. William Acton's *A Practical Treatise on Diseases of the ... Generative Organs* (1841), reprinted in Prof. Steven Marcus' *The Other Victorians* (New York, 1966) p. 31–2. I have made the substitution of sadism for sex in literature the subject of an entire monograph, *Love & Death: A Study in Censorship* (1949) – I had, of course, to publish it myself – and recommend it to naïve readers who think that the 'New Freedom' for sex in print and motion-pictures will now somehow wipe out the sick sadistic psychological imprinting, in the psyches of hundreds of millions of people, that has been built up for hundreds of years, and passed on by parental training from generation to generation.

The "Little Willie" quatrains first appeared in Harry Graham's *Ruthless Rhymes for Heartless Homes* (punning, of course, on 'Hearthless'), published in London, 1899, under the pseudonym of 'Col. D. Streamer,' and immediately taken up and imitated – in embattled feminist form as concerning "Little Jane" – by the murder-mystery fancier Carolyn Wells. The idea may have been picked up from Hilaire Belloc, younger brother of the murder-writer, Mrs. Belloc Lowndes, in his *Bad Child's Books of Beasts* (1896), followed by his mock *Cautionary Tales* (1907). The cruel "Little Willies" are too well known to be cited here, and have, as aforesaid, no real relationship to the present work except as unconscious substitutions of sadism for sexuality, here on the anti-family pattern. The only erotic "Little Willie" I have ever encountered is notably castratory; but it will hardly compare with the fashionably 'sick' and campy sadisms-in-verse of Edward Gorey's *The Listing Attic* (limericks: 1954), and *The Gashlycrumb Tinies* (1963), the most repulsive of current anti-family romps.

> *Naughty Francis, home from school,*
> *Picked up baby by the tool.*
> *Auntie shrieked and grandma shuddered,*
> *Father said, "Well, I'll be buggered!"*
> *Mother said, "You wicked Francis,*
> *To spoil poor baby's fucking chances!"*

(Chelmsford, Essex, 1954: *Union Jack* MS. The sestet form here is also unusual.) The father's phrase, about being 'buggered,' as expressing astonishment or dismay, is used in another anti-family joke in *The Pearl*, No. 15 (Sept. 1880), which has already been given in the First Series, 7.IV, page 422, where: *When the girl tells her father that she is pregnant by her penniless young swain, "Well, I'm buggered!" says her father. "Father! Don't say that; we're such an unfortunate family!"* (Note the homosexual meaning of the punchline.) In an American development of this: *The children are asked in school what is the most beautiful thing in the world. The little girl says, "Flowers," the good little boy says "The sunset (or, in older forms, the Love of God);" and the bad little boy says, "Bein' pregnant." He explains to the astonished teacher, "Well, my big sister came home last night and said, 'Pop, I'm pregnant.' And Dad said, 'Well that's beautiful! Just fucking beautiful!'"* (L.A. 1968. Note for history: he is being sardonic.)

These pretended misunderstandings by children – pretended, since the stories in which they appear are told strictly by adults – have already formed the stock of the earlier chapter on Children, 1.I–II, "Mock Ignorance" and "Tormenting the Teacher." Generally these satisfy themselves with merely unveiling publicly the parents' sexual secrets. Occasionally, and therefore relevantly here the total meaning is to *dirty* the family, rather than merely to contrast the parents' secret sexuality with that forbidden to the child. On an ancient formula of the misunderstood word (often of fools or foreigners: 2.VI.4, pages 178–9, under "Literalism"): *The young child has picked up numerous dirty words, and the parents take the minister's advice to tell her that these have innocent meanings. They tell her that 'cunt' means a skirt, 'balls' means an umbrella, 'prick' is a hat, 'bastard' means gentleman, and 'fuck' means to milk. The next time the minister comes to visit, the little girl greets him with: "Come inside, you bastard, and hang up your prick and balls. Mommy's in the bathroom* [sic] *washing her cunt, and Daddy's out fucking the cow!"* (*World's Dirtiest Jokes*, 1969, p. 167.) Rather close to Types 1940 and 1562A: *The barn burns down because the farmer cannot understand the extraordinary names he has ordered the servant to use.* A scatological version is given in Afanasyev's *Russian Secret Tales*, No. 72, "The Strange Names," observing that this is of Greek origin, in the *Odyssey* of Homer, being of the type of Ulysses in the cave of the giant Polyphemus, calling himself *'Outis'* (No one). Meaning that it is one of the oldest jokes in the world.

The census-taker asks the little farm boy how many people there are in the family. "There's four," he says, "my father, my mother, my sister, and me." When the census-taker then asks where they are, the boy says, "Pappy's gone fishin', I guess; anyhow his boots are gone, and it ain't raining. Ma's out taking a shit, I guess; anyhow the Monkey-Ward catalogue's missin', and she can't read. My sister's out in the barn screwin' the hired man, I guess; anyhow, there's only two things she likes to do, and supper's been waiting on the table now, nigh onto two hours." (Bloomington, Ind. 1963.) At the risk of underlining the obvious it is to be noted that the whole intention here, under the pretext of giving demanded information, is to pile on disgraceful details against the whole family: the father a ne'er-do-well, the mother illiterate, the sister lecherous and greedy. Sometimes the satire reverses this, pretending to defend the parents' reputation. *A mother tells her little children that the stork brings the babies, to prepare them for the birth of the next child; then kisses them goodnight and leaves them to sleep. The little boy sits up on one elbow and says to his sisters, "I don't care what Mama says, I just can't imagine Daddy fucking a stork!"* (L.A. 1968.) Stories like this often end with situations intended to mock the parents' false information with the children's true knowledge. *A little girl asks her mother, "Can an itty-bitty girl like me have an itty-bitty baby?" The mother thinks this over a minute and says, "Yes, dear, it can happen. One little girl in Peru, only five years old, had a baby." The little girl says, "Dod damn!"* (*World's Dirtiest Jokes,* p. 155.) Again on the 'wise child' theme (*"The King has no clothes on!"* – Type 1620): *A boy asks his mother where he came from. The stork brought him. And where did she come from? Grandma found her under a cabbage-leaf. And Grandma? An angel slipped her into the doctor's little black bag. "Mother," says the boy, "do you mean to tell me there's been no sexual intercourse in our family for three generations?"* (N.Y. 1952.)

Generalized hatred of the family is difficult to express in jokes without pegging it to some taboo area, to achieve the explosive effect of hateful surprise. Racial or political loyalties – that is to say, to the higher 'family' of race or political party – are mocked in one kind of joke, often collected: *A boy hitchhiking up from the South tells drivers who ask him his politics that he is a Democrat, with the result that they all drive on. The next person who stops to pick him up is a young lady, and he tells her he is a Republican. As they drive along her skirt works its way higher and higher up her leg. "Please stop the car and let me out," he says. "I haven't been a Republican more*

than fifteen minutes, and already I feel like screwing some-
body!" (D.C. 1945.) This is on an old form of: *The fool who is*
told by a fellow-beggar to tell people that he is related to some-
one of their religion. If they are Jewish, he is to say that his
father is the head rabbi of Lemberg, and so forth. The first
house he comes to is a Catholic family. He tells them his father
is bishop of the next town, and is thrown out. (Scranton, Pa.
1934, told by a Jew of Hungarian origin as a mock of clerical
immorality.) A more recent version of the political joke is far
more bitter: *A little Negro boy accidentally rolls in some flour*
while he is sleeping naked in the barn. When he wakes up he
says, "God damn! I done turned white in my sleep." He runs to
tell his mother, who says, "Go 'way boy, I'm busy makin' dis
bread." His father waves him away also, saying he is trying to
get Cuba on the short-wave radio; and even his sister will not
listen to his story, saying she is getting ready for a date. He goes
back out to the barn, kicks the door savagely, and says, "Here
I on'y been white ten minutes, an' already I hate *dem fucken*
niggers!" (Bloomington, Indiana, 1963.)

Scatology is an easy out for any kind of animosities, as *the*
touch of shit dirties every time without fail. A joke I have
never heard appears in *The World's Dirtiest Jokes* (1969) p. 210,
in which: *Three mothers are watching the Teeny-Weeny foot-*
ball game, played by little boys. One boy makes a touchdown,
and the mother shouts, "Hooray for Weldon! I raised him on
cow's milk." Another boy catches a pass and runs it for a
touchdown, and his mother shouts, "Hooray for Steven! I raised
him on mother's milk." The third little boy fumbles the ball and
falls on his face, and his mother hollers, "Hooray for Johnny!
I raised him on milk of magnesia – ain't he the SHIT?" Though
the little boy appears to be taking the blow here, actually it is his
joke. He is the grown-up teller giving the secret signal: that he
hates his (disloyal) mother for not having fed him right, or
'birthed' him right, and made him strong and capable. This is
the whole inner meaning of a book like *Portnoy's Complaint*.

The following British joke is also fathered off on the Jews,
but on the basis of an ancient and classic accusation – it appears
in Sir Thomas Browne's *Pseudodoxia Epidemica* (1646) – which
Portnoy's Complaint unaccountably omits: that Jews are specially dirty and have a *special odor* like that of goats, though this
is not caused by the dirt. '*Little Abe home from school tells*
mother he's won a prize. "Vell done, Abe, and vot for?" "For

*observation, Ma." Good, but supper and bed now, and she'll tell
father when he comes in. First thing in the morning before
dressing, father comes in to congratulate son: "For observation,
eh? Vell, do you notice anythink strange about me?" "Your
nightshirt is back to front, Dad." "Ah, I expect you noticed de
buttons that should do up the back." "No, Dad, I saw the shit-
stains down the front".'* (Chelmsford Prison, Essex, 1951.)

The exposing of the parents' genitals is not frequent in jokes,
even at the mild 'depantsing' level, and is usually jogged back
one step to the grandparents. Exceptionally, in a criticism of
the First Series of the present work, in the *New Statesman*
(London, 1969), Mr. Philip French gives a British verbal-humor
item unknown to me until then: *The family of astronomy
enthusiasts are rushing up to their telescope on the roof, the
father and mother first, and the children stringing along behind.
"Oh dad," says the daughter, "I can see Uranus." "That's nothing," says the son, "I can see Mars!"* (Any American not understanding this joke should return the volume to me, and his
money will be cheerfully refunded.) Where the reference is to
the grandparent, instead, no such elaborate punning disguise is
necessary. *"What'cha doin', Grandpaw, jerkin' off?" "No, Son,
just jerkin'."* (Scranton, Pa, 1936.) Few jokes would or do thus
accuse the father of impotence.

Vance Randolph gives a much fuller version of this direct attack, as part of an anti-Ozark burlesque, told however by one
Ozarker in 1953, who had it from another, 'also of Eureka
Springs, Ark.,' in 1949. *An Easterner visiting Arkansas is surprised that the people in the cities act just about like people
back home, and so he drives out into the hill country, leaves
his car and continues on foot. The first thing he sees are 'some
young folks a-fucking under the trees. But he didn't pay no
attention to that, because the boys and girls in Chicago does the
same thing and think nothing of it.' Then he sees a boy in front
of a log-cabin who has caught a jackrabbit and is 'a-diddling
the rabbit, right there in the front yard.' This, the Easterner
admits to himself, he has never seen before. A little farther
along he sees 'an old man with a long white beard' who was
'set on a rail fence, and he was a-playing with his pecker. "Well,
by God!" says the stranger, "Maybe it's true, them stories they
tell about Arkansas." The old man kind of slowed up for a
minute, and he says, "What's wrong with Arkansas, stranger?"
The Easterner tells him what he has seen until then, 'and now*

*here's an old gentleman with white whiskers a-playing with his
pecker. "It looks kind of funny to me," he says. The old man
just stared at him. "What's funny about it?" says he. "You can't
expect me, at my time of life, to ketch jackrabbits like them
young fellows".'* (*Pissing in the Snow,* No. 27, "Old Age in
Arkansas.") Note that this is presumably a sardonic *defense* on
the tellers' part.

Violently dysphemistic anti-family stories operate in an excessively obvious fashion to please the persons telling them, or
pleasurably listening to them, in the implication that parents are
really 'just as bad' as the children they are always reproving and
controlling, or at least were when they were young. *"Tell us a
story, grandma!" the children beg. "Once upon a time," the old
lady begins, "there were two fairies – sucking each other's
cocks for all they were worth." "Aw, shit, grandma, all your
fucking stories begin that way!"* (2:71. Sometimes collected
with the children interrupting: *"Oh c'mon, grandma, tell us
about when you were a whoor in Chicago!"* – N.Y. 1940.) In a
form rather close to 'water-wit': *A Hollywood taxi-driver
famous for his dirty stories is brought to a dinner party by one
of the guests, to entertain everyone. He offers to tell a story
that won't be too shocking, after searching visibly in his
memory for this rarity, stating that it has only one dirty word,
"near the end." The hostess [mother-figure] worriedly allows
him to tell his story. "Well," he begins, "these two old cunts
were walking down the street ..."* (N.Y. 1952.) The hidden personage there is the teller-listener, who is precisely the guest
who has brought in the dirty-talking taxi-driver as his surrogate, to say the shocking things he himself does not dare to say
before his mother in his proper person.

The most violent and purposely shocking examples collected
in this line presumably satirize the habit, common among
Europeans or first-generation Jews in England and America, of
swearing on the head of the parent, especially the mother – as
specially sacred – to things patently false. This is used with
great effect, and gets the biggest laugh in the show in François
Truffaut's imitative American-style 'cool' movie in France,
Shoot the Piano Player, with the old mother actually shown
falling ludicrously dead, with her feet shooting up in the air,
when the gangster swears to some foolish lie, to a kidnapped
boy, with the asseveration *"Mama should die if ..."* (All the
other younger women in the movie are shot, commit suicide,

etc. *Cool, man, cool!*) The same gangster-spokesman also recites
an extraordinary bit of monologue about how 'sexy' it feels to
wear women's silk panties, and says that he has done so and
knows that is why women are so erotic. All this is explained to
the kidnapped boy, representing the spectator, and as humor.

*A man swears to another that something is true, saying
"Mama should drop dead if I'm lying!" "Now look –" says
the other. "What do you mean, look? Mama should suck a
syphilitic nigger's prick if every word I'm saying ain't the God's
truth!" "Put your money where your mouth is," his listener
counters; "I'll bet you twenty dollars you're full of shit." "No!"
says the first man piously, "money I wouldn't bet."* (N.Y. 1940,
told by a famous dialect humorist.) A scene of the 'Defiling of
the Mother' exactly like this – see chapter 12.IV.6 – is developed
with great power, including some pretty repulsive mock-oaths
(though not precisely the anti-Negro one of the American joke)
concerning the mother's death, desecration, etc., in Gerald
Kersh's novel, *Prelude to a Certain Midnight*, in which the
swearer is an English boxing-promoter or 'wide-boy' of the
1930's, becoming progressively more violent in his anti-mother
imaginings as the oaths proceed.

During the 1950's, a 'new' type of *sick-joke* became popular
in America, almost always beginning with a child's question
similar to the formula-line *"Mama (or Daddy), can I go out to
play?"* as in a mild joke quoted in the First Series, 4.1.2, page
226, from *Happy Days* (1937). But now there is no real colloquy, the parent's travesty-reply being invariably some crushing gruesomeness, beginning as a formula punch-line, *"Shut up
and –"* unveiling an entirely different situation than the innocent one which the child's question implies. That these sick-
jokes are intended as bitter criticisms of the parents' authority,
and *'the mess they've made of things,'* does not need to be underlined. But it should also not be overlooked that the jokes conjure
up, and revel and grovel in much worse messes than any normal parent ever contemplates. (Yes, yes, the Atom Bomb.) The
form has been studied, with a large presentation of the merely
sadistic and gruesome materials, which are the most common,
as with the rather similar "Little Willies," in Dr. Brian Sutton-
Smith's " 'Shut Up and Keep Digging'; The Cruel Joke Series," in
Midwest Folklore (1960) X. 11–22, on the style of : *"Why are
my teeth so long, daddy?" "Shut up and drink your blood!"*
(Note for history : They are both vampires, a superstition re-

vived in popularity in Abram Stoker's horror-thriller, *Dracula*, and the endless movies made from it, beginning with Murnau's *Nosferatu* in 1922, as discussed earlier.)

This format was long since heralded in Ring Lardner's famous humorous line in the 1930's – also ascribed to *Artemus Ward His Book* (1862) by Charles Farrar Browne – where the little boy asks his father if they are lost; with the reply, ' "*Shut up*," *he explained tenderly.*' The 'explained' is certainly a masterpiece of the humorist's art, but it is not that – and surely not the sardonic tenderness – which has been imitated. Many of the 'clean' modern jokes of this type seem to enjoy defiling and humiliating the crippled or spastic child, who is hung up on a hook, made use of as home-plate in a game of baseball, and so forth. A few of these jokes are actually set up as colloquies between the proto-parent-&-child of the Christian religion, the Virgin Mary and Jesus, usually turning on some hideous detail of the Crucifixion, as in the psychotic Isenheim altarpiece of Grünewald, or with the end-line (parodying that of Jesus rejecting the Virgin at the Feast at Cana), "*You Jewish mothers really piss me off!*" Jesus' line actually is: "*Woman, what have I to do with thee? Mine hour is not yet come.*" (*John*, ii. 4. A reference, apparently, to the preparing of corpses for burial, by 'the women,' as in *Luke*, xxiii. 55.) As can be seen, anti-family wisecracks did not begin yesterday.

The 'sick' joke is in any case no longer strictly American. Perhaps it never was. Of recent examples, one of the nastiest appeared in the Scottish folk-life magazine, *Chapbook* (Aberdeen, 1967) vol. IV, No. 3, p. 6, in an article "Bawdry, Cancer or Cure?" by James Addison, noting that 'if we laugh at good, honest bawdry, surely this must be chalked to the credit side, particularly at the expense of "sick" jokes such as: "*Mummy, mummy, may I lick the bowl out?*" "*No, pull the chain like everyone else*".' (This one has not yet been encountered in America, where toilets also no longer flush by pulling a chain.) Other jokes of this type in chapter 15.V, "Scatophagy."

The *non*-sadistic jokes or colloquies on this format are usually incestuous, which is why they seldom appear in public print. Actually, they are still pretty sadistic, but not exclusively enough to 'clean them up' for the American family-magazines: "*Mama, why can't I go out and play like all the other little boys?*" "*You pull out now and I'll kill you!*" (N.Y. 1956.) This is the woman's classic passionate reply, when a man offers to withdraw before orgasm for birth-control reasons, à la Onan. The matching line is said by a man to a woman when he is about to ejaculate during fellation by her: "*You stop now and I'll kill you!*" This has been used in a 1960's play by Paddy Chayefsky, to indicate an act of fellation just offstage. Note the significant change in the incestuous set-up, ten years after the joke preceding: "*Daddy, my jaws ache.*" "*Shut up and keep sucking, you little bastard!*" (N.Y. 1965.) Though the use of 'little bastard' here – instead of 'little bitch' – makes the child's sex as a boy specific, *World's Dirtiest Jokes*, 1969, p. 172, considers it important to spell this out: "*Daddy, when are you gonna tell me the facts of life like the other boys' daddies do?*" End-line as above.

Grotesque and vulgar scenes of family life, and wholly taboo acts such as open masturbation or incest, are usually assimilated in the United States, and certainly in its humor, to the Ozark, or Southern mountaineers and 'pore white' farmers, as in the joke earlier on: *The bearded old Ozark hillbilly who couldn't catch a jackrabbit to 'diddle,' so he had to sit on a rail-fence and masturbate.* No white person of higher social standing than that would be so shown, in attempted humor. Dirtiness and unkemptness are the keynotes or symbols of sexual and scatological unrepression being ascribed to the 'horny hillbilly' (or 'peckerwood') and the uncontrollably erotic 'hare-lipped mountain girl,' as in Erskine Caldwell's *Tobacco Road* (1932), the longest-running play in the history of the American theatre, making a back-number of *Uncle Tom's Cabin* and *Abie's Irish Rose*, themselves not far removed from being hillbilly items. The implication throughout is that people who keep themselves clean and neat, and who are not visibly non-white, non-Christian or *poor*, have sex lives that are not really very vital or interesting. This may or may not be true, yet everyone vaguely seems to suspect it.

Torn overalls and dirty clothes, unlaced or ill-fitting shoes, women's dresses made out of old flour sacks (ostentatiously marked XXX over the behinder, which in this case do not represent kisses), a lack of underwear, especially on the younger children, or – the opposite, and therefore somehow the same thing – the wearing of one suit of long underwear all winter, because one has been 'sewed into it when the nights get long,' are all, therefore, insignia of simple poverty. But they are used in humorous cartoons to imply or accompany the presumed

sexually unrepressed and especially the incestuous family behavior of backwoods and mountain people in the economically depressed Southern states. Most of this background poverty
is unquestionably true, but it just as unquestionably tells nothing about the (dreamed-of) sexual lack of repression of the poor
farmers involved. John Gunther's once-over-lightly survey, *Inside U. S. A.* (1947) p. 641, expresses for example the fact, in
all the horror of supplied italics, that: '42,000 *Kentucky farms
had no toilets or privies of any kind* in 1940, and 97 per cent
of all farms have no toilets inside the house. (Italics mine. –
[JG.])' This is really arsling into the subject, Germanically, or
taking the turd's-eye-view of poverty. How about their income?

Al Capp's purposely superficial comic-strip for adults, "*Li'l
Abner,*" running in newspapers nation-wide since the 1940's,
takes a rather more reasonable tack in showing his 'pore white'
mountaineer family, the Yokums, with the pipe-smoking matriarchal mammy, and big-bodied but unconscionably dumb son,
Li'l Abner, as endlessly concerned with *food*. Sex is mentioned
at all only as a matter of depicting nymphomaniacal but horribly ugly mountain-girls who are allowed to chase the men
(for purposes of legal marriage) one special leap-year day every
year, known as 'Sadie Hawkins Day.' This is as far from the
truth, about *any*thing, as the Federal Reserve banks of down-
town Boston are from the Negro sharecroppers' shacks of the
Mississippi delta – the missing x and y of the equation. In the
relatively unexpurgated cartoons of the *Sex to Sexty* series the
scatological implications of dirtiness are underlined by having
the hillbillies' house and yard shown as extremely disorderly,
with flies circling around the personages' heads. The pig is also
sometimes shown in the parlor, an ancient cliché of anti-Irish
humor of an earlier period. This too is scatologically intended,
since the pig is of a particular insouciance as to its own fecal
products, and is also one of the few animals that will piss in its
own drinking trough and then drink from it, though many
cleaner animals will do this in running water, as in a river.
Human beings too. See "Scatophagy," 15.V.1.

Enormous feats of strength and endurance are always
ascribed to backwoods heroes, in the tradition of the 'strong
men' or 'hard-men' of myth and legend, from Hercules and
Samson right down to Porthos, Daniel Boone, Paul Bunyan and
Li'l Abner. In the real legends these feats include heroic sexual
prowess – not to mention Hercules' cleaning the Augean stables

– as I have noted further in *The Horn Book*, pp. 227 and 326, and in connection with the classic contest in sexual intercourse of the mining-camp recitation "Our Lil," p. 418–20. Such sexual intercourse contests authentically exist in America, India, etc. Superhuman sexual powers are now seldom ascribed to anyone except Negroes (as in the *Arabian Nights*), and such prowess is not intended altogether as a compliment, but as an assimilation to the 'animal.' Black or white, the 'hard-man' is always depicted as at least somewhat slow and stupid, if not dumb enough to freeze rocks. Here we see the anti-family tone creeping back again in these scenes, since 'hard-men' are of course the last surviving throwbacks to our ancestors, the giants of the early days who mated with the daughters of men, as recorded in *Genesis*, vi. 4, and *Deuteronomy*, iii. 11, giving exact dimensions.

In the curious joke following, the background appears to be simply the standard and crude backwoods or old-time home, always made fun of (when not sentimentalized over in lachrymose songs), but the heroic physical character of the actors shows that it is really to be projected much farther back in the human family history, when these crude characters were not so much black sheep as black behemoth. Jokes like this often name current movie actors, such as Mae West, representing the buxom and sensuous vamp – actually the mother-goddess – and, as in the present example, Wallace Beery, whose favorite character was playing the impossibly tough and heroic, but also very dumb 'hard-man.' '*Wallace Beery and his lady-friend were dining together. After the meal the conversation turned to tough guys. "Have you seen this?" she said. Leaning back, she took a coconut from the bowl on the sideboard, and putting it well down between her great bubs, she drew her arms and shoulders in, and cracked the damn thing. Wallace Beery was surprised, but he continued poking the fire with his cock.*' (London, 1953, from manuscript. *Kryptádia*, 1883, I. 339, with male nut-breaker.)

This assimilation of folk-humor to motion-picture characters is increasingly common, and has driven out much of the older lore with its *mise en scène* of anonymous and homey folk-characters. Their heroic or 'hard' characteristics, however, are usually those of physical cruelty and verbally insulting violence, this being the presumed truth about the 'Old Folks at Home.' For example: '*A country woman sent her young son to the*

neighbor's with their cow, to be bred to the bull there, caution-
ing him to avoid all ribald talk. He met the girl of the house at
the neighbor's, and said, "I'm bringing Bessie over for your bull
to fuck her. Ma would have sent John, only he talks so dirty.
Why, just this morning at the breakfast table he got up and
said, 'Shit,' just like that. Ma got so mad she doubled up her fist
and whacked him across the jaw, and smashed his face flat as
a cow-cake (or cow-flop). Pa reached up and took down the
dried bull prick from over the door and walloped him until he
shit a turd the length of your arm ..."' (D.C. 1945, taken down
from the recitation of an army corporal, except for the opening
description.)

In *Tom Brown's Jests,* an 18th-century jestbook reprinted in
America 'For the Booksellers,' just before the Civil War, a
similar story is given – also known in French – but without the
purposefully long dysphemistic narrative. In the most recent
version: *A woman sends her daughter to take a basket of*
medlars (or figs) to the lady of the manor, cautioning her to
speak politely. The girl tells the lady that the medlars are soft as
shit, and to eat one. The mother beats the girl for this, and
assures the lady that she meant no harm, and that if only she
had known the daughter would be born so dumb she would
have stuffed a cork up the crack of her ass and left her there to
rot rather than give birth to such an idiot. (N.Y. 1965.) French
and Flemish versions in *Kryptádia,* II. 149, and IV. 317.

One recognizes the *echt* folk touch here, common to all Irish
bulls and other fool-jokes turning on the stupidity or illogic
ascribed to untutored 'country folks,' representing the hypothetical backwoods members of our families that we are glad
we have outstripped, and are showing in as disgraceful a light
as possible to insist on the cultural distance between them and
us. Just as clearly one recognizes a mere impulse of Oedipal
revenge in the standard situation of the child tattling on the
parents, by pretended accident, here not on their love-passages
but on their even better hidden mutual hatred. *The teacher is*
trying to liven up the geography lesson by giving the class
various foods to taste, and guess what they are, then telling
where each one comes from: This is beef – it comes from
Argentina; this is mutton – it comes from Australia, etc.
Finally she gives Johnny, the bad little boy, her surprise food: a
slice of venison. He cannot guess it, and the teacher says, "I'll
give you a hint. It's something your Mummy calls your Daddy."
"Gosh, teacher," he says, spitting, "I never figured you'd slip

me a horse's ass!" (Santa Monica, Calif. 1965. Told with a similar anti-Negro joke on 'mother-fucker.') This is the *other side* of 'Togetherness,' which is intended to look like sentimental love, and to take the place of love, in loveless marriages (the largest percentage, though this is seldom admitted), but which fools no one – particularly not the children caught in the middle – when the parents are not sniping at each other verbally, fighting, wife-swapping, and the like. One thing is sure: at some point, sick 'Togetherness' will always blow up in your face. See further Theodor Reik's *Psychology of Sex Relations* (1945) and especially Dr. Edrita Fried's *The Ego in Love and Sexuality* (1960), both magnificent works and concerned with neurotic *inability to love,* the curse of our century.

The last and most total anti-family joke is undisguisedly about incest, and has already been considered several times in the First Series under both that subject, in chapter 1.V, page 96, and at "Possession in Common," 9.III.1, pages 739–41. As what *appears* to be its actual subject is venereal disease, it has also been treated in chapter 12.II, "The Biter Bit," tracing it to an *épigramme*-in-verse by the 16th-century French satirist, Melin de Saint-Gelais ("Un jour que madame dormoit," in his *Oeuvres poétiques,* 1574), who probably picked it up from folk sources. Such versifications of well-known jokes had become a fad, first seen in the Italian *Dubbii amorosi,* or "Amorous Doubts," usually ascribed to Aretino, in the early 16th century, before the advent of the sweepingly popular *novelle* in prose in the 1550's. Treatments of this very popular joke, which is nowadays sometimes called "Happy Families," range from a brief two-line colloquy to book-length.

In its shortest form: *The mother says, "My, Jimmy, your prick is bigger than Dad's!" Jimmy: "Yes, that's what Sister always says."* (1:225, the compiler calling it 'The dirtiest story ever told, in my opinion,' but even so giving only the mother's speech without the son's!) Often the characters are shifted (2:37, father and daughter), but the boy – obviously the teller of the joke – is almost always present somewhere: *'A boy is having sexual intercourse with his sister. She says, "Yours goes in farther than pa's does." The boy replies, "Yes, that's what ma says too".'* (Cookeville, Tennessee, 1970, also calling it 'the dirtiest joke.' Perhaps what it really is, is the *oldest* dirty joke.) When enlarged, this joke always attempts to take on further dimensions in ugliness and unpleasantness, in keeping with the idea that the incest of a child and parent is the 'dirtiest' situation imaginable. The variant in *Anecdota* 2 : 37, has the father speaking to the daughter, and proceeds with extended dysphemistic trills on the abilities of members of their 'fine old Southern family' at anilinctus, etc. A similar mocking of the family is present in a related joke in which : *The father finds his daughter having intercourse with a guest on the veranda. "Daughter!" he shouts, "lift up yo' lazy, chicken-grabbin'* [euphemism for 'mother-fucking'] *bottom, an' get that gen'man's balls up off'n that cold tile floor. Wheah is yo' Southron hospitality?!"* (N.Y. 1963; often collected earlier.)

A final aspect of anti-family sentiment that cannot be overlooked here, though it is seldom specifically sexual, is the presumed humor of death and burial. Reference in passing should also be made to the telling of obscene riddles and jokes at the 'wakes' before burial, while the dead body is lying ceremonially as a *rite de passage* before the survivors, who still today wind and embalm it 'in linen and spices,' in the ancient Egyptian manner, as noted at the Crucifixion in *Luke*, xxiii. 53–6, and *John*, xix. 39–40. The obscene riddles commonly told at funerals and wakes are intended as a driving away of lurking demons – including the spirit of the newly-dead individual, to be sure – by means of ritual obscenity. Although it cannot be proved at this date, it may be assumed that ritual sexual intercourse once took the place of the now-surviving riddles, which the dead *cannot* answer (and thus cannot return) since sex is the prerogative only of the living.

This is probably the true historical understructure of the intercourse by the widow at her husband's wake – and the preventing of this in Indian *suttee* – which is the central matter of Petronius' "Widow of Ephesus" story in the *Satyricon* (1st century A.D.), and which he gives as the mere repetition of a Milesian tale, as I have discussed fully in the First Series, chapter 8.VIII.8–10, along with many other old jokes as to the rapid consolation of widows. Hamlet accuses his mother of having rolled again in 'incestuous sheets' within 'two hours' of her husband's death : *"Nay,"* says Ophelia, *" 'tis twice two months, my lord."* (*Hamlet*, III. ii. 135.) A blundering reply intended to 'top' his jesting reproach. In the play-within-the-play immediately following, the widowed queen is re-wooed, and the murdered king replaced in her affections in a matter of minutes.

Ritual obscenity at funerals and wakes, thus considered, is

seen to be something a good deal deeper than the minor or sentimental social rôle ascribed to the joker at such times by Dr. Mary Douglas, who would have it merely that: 'By restraining excessive grief he asserts the demands of the living.' ('The Social Control of Cognition: Some Factors in Joke Perception,'' in *Man*, Sept. 1968, III. 373.) There is really a world more to it than that: the ritual and required obscenity, just to begin with. The funeral-jester, and wake-riddles of specifically obscene character, are known in Negro Africa and the Levant, and perhaps survive there from ancient Egyptian rituals, or both may have a common root even earlier. They are still well-known in the Hispanic cultures (as in the *double-entendre* riddling song, "*El Bobo en el velorio*," The Fool at the Funeral), as well as in English-speaking countries. A curious scene of this kind, with the young women survivors arguing at the death-bed of another – who is revived by their discussion, *n.b.* – as to the relative lengths of the penises of the parson and curate, is versified in Thomas Hamilton, Earl of Haddington's *Select Poems on Several Occasions* (*c.* 1730), Tale 40, "The Dying Toast [*i.e.* Beauty]," quoted in *The Limerick*, p. 405–6, as to these crucial stanzas.

In priest-ridden Ireland, presumably, all is booze at the wake, and no sex even in jest, but one wonders. The 19th-century Irish farce-song, "Finnegan's Wake," used as title to James Joyce's final alliterative outpourings and mad jargoning, is essentially a scene of the same kind, but here the 'corpse' is revived by alcoholic liquor and not by bawdry. (Motifs J2311.2–5 and X811, of Levantine origin, as seen in Wesselski's *Nasr'eddin*, I. 239, No. 121; first recorded in Europe in Domenichi's collection *Della scelta di motti, burle, facetie,* 1566, p. 186.) An erotic text of the Irish song is given as "Tim Finigan Wakes," in the extremely rare bawdy American song-book of the Civil War period, *The Rakish Rhymer* (New York, *c.* 1865, reprint 'Lutetia' [Paris: Carrington], 1917: copy, Brown University, Providence, R.I.), p. 90–91. This is stated to be a parody, to the air of "Tim Finigan's Wake," and here, in the style of the "Widow of Ephesus" folktale, '*The dead man who has been killed by his wife is 'laid out to wake,' but is revived by his widow making love on the floor with Mickey O'Brien, whom she has first 'fed well with praties and cake, Then pipes and tobackey, and whiskey too ... Then Irish fucking soon began, And Irish gravy then was spent.'* In their frenzy, Mick accident-

ally kicks Tim Finigan and revives him.

Actually, death seems to lend itself far better to a sort of ugly scatology, in which the presumed humor of the dissolution of the dead body and its escaping humors – both gaseous and solid – are gruesomely exploited. A modern Irish short story entitled "Belly," by Liam O'Flaherty, I believe, and in the style of his superbly bitter novel, *Famine* (1937), is based squarely on the *gold-equals-shit* identification (chapter 15.IV.6, "Money Stinks"): *The dying miser has swallowed all his gold-pieces on his deathbed, and is given a physic by his wife, who then tries desperately to keep him alive at least long enough for the physic to blast through his bowels.* Unquestionably combined with the folk-idea and phrase, concerning money and property, "You can't take it with you." In a joke first encountered recently it is obvious that the scatology is only a premium on the essentially anti-family scene of the almost lethal marital spat: *The henpecked husband comes home drunk, ready to tell off his wife for the first time since they have been married. "From now on I'm boss around here!" he announces, wriggling his eyebrows ferociously. "I'm paying the bills, and I'll do what I darn please. If I want to shit on the carpet, I'll shit on the carpet!" "You shit on that chenille rug," his wife shrieks, "and the undertaker is going to wipe your ass!"* (Santa Monica, Calif. 1965.)

The purpose of anti-family humor is not any different from the purpose of the gross anti-family and anti-human sentiments and actions which are not expressed in humorous form. All are intended to relieve the internal pressure the individual feels as to loving emotions he or she actually does experience, but would like to be allowed to mock and violate ambivalently in an occasional 'moral vacation' of uncontrolled hostility. Or else to relieve the pressure as to loving emotions the individual is called upon to feel, but does *not* really feel at all, and must pantomime and pretend (as in 'Togetherness'). Leaving him or her even more anxious for the moral carnival when all the pretenses can be dropped, and the faked shibboleths and pretended idols can be spat upon, shat upon, derided and destroyed. The purposely overstated phraseology of these destructions, both in jokes and public rituals of mocking and filthying (Lenny Bruce), and also in literary forms, is intended to offer a covering disguise in which the victims of the hatred and defiling cannot be identified – even to oneself – as the true family and 'loved ones' of the persons doing the joyous hating and defiling. It is like the great relief of hearing the innocent little boy (or Negro slave) piping up, "But the King doesn't have any clothes on!" Or rather, and as dysphemistically as possible, *"The son-of-a-bitch's ass is out a yard, and sucking wind!"*

A well-known anecdote tells of: *Queen Victoria at a performance of Shakespeare's* Antony and Cleopatra, *at a moment when Cleopatra, the last Queen of Egypt, is tearing a passion to tatters on the stage. As she pauses for breath, one of the courtiers in the royal box says loudly and unctuously, "How different from the home-life of our* own *dear Queen!"* But then, if no one likes these violent scenes, of lives and empires torn to bits, nor answers to them secretly, why do popular authors write them, and why do audiences stay to watch? Why have audiences thrilled with pleasure ('horror') for two and a half thousand years to see Euripides' *Medea* batter out her children's brains? Where is the play about King Solomon's even better-remembered judgment, as to the child-cut-in-half, to which everyone pays lip-service but would find 'corny as hell' onstage. It is the loudly proffered certainty of the courtier above, that it is not 'our *own* home-life' that is being unveiled, that makes it possible to enjoy these scenes and the cheap little decayed survivals of the matching jokes. Otherwise we could not laugh – and would not be entertained. And neither would anyone else. The paradox of the over-statements of all anti-gallant and anti-family humor (and similar stuff) is that by pretending – but only pretending – to be about one's own family, or to be *humorous,* one is grossly implying that they cannot be about one's family at all, or else one would not tell such ambivalently tattling tales.

But the truth is just the opposite. By the very pretense that it is all simply a broad human parable, in the first-person-plural of the human family, in which 'no one is guilty because everyone is guilty' (*The marked culprit who marks everyone else similarly, and so escapes detection* – Motif K415), the tellers, the singers, yes and the staying-&-paying audience especially, betray their desperate urge to come right out and admit it, even to enjoy it. To say that perhaps these particular sexual and scatological and cruel atrocities are not the ones that are true of their particular families, but that all the *other* atrocities – the milder ones that the jokes and songs and horror-novels and plays are not mentioning – most certainly are. In fact, sometimes it is the very worst atrocities that our family and our side are really guilty of, but those we usually tell as of the 'other side.' (Especially in war.) Or under a merciful guise of grinning unconsciousness as to the economic and psychological truths we are blurting out, in the jokes about good middle-class fathers & mothers who are secretly vampires and who tell their children, *"Shut up and drink your blood!"* While India and Africa starve.

5. MOCKING AUTHORITY-FIGURES

The type of scatological humor allowing free play to re-pressed hostilities, under the excuse of cultural ignorance in the speaker, has apparently long been a favorite. The Biblical and other ancient insults that will be noted below, in section 14.II.1, are not of this type, since there is no pretense about them. The oldest 'ignorant' example I have found is also the only actually unexpurgated ballad given among Prof. Francis James Child's *English and Scottish Popular Ballads* (Boston, 1884–98), the greatest monument of American folklore scholar-ship, as No. 273, "King Edward IV and Tanner of Tamworth." This humorous ballad is on the ancient formula of *'the chance-encounter of a king, unrecognized as such, with one of his humbler subjects'* (Motif K1812), which appears in the *Arabian Nights* as of the purposely-disguised Caliph Haroun al-Rashid. In another form of Child Ballad No. 273, as "King Henry II and the Miller of Mansfield," in the *Percy Folio Manuscript* (about 1640), the adventure is largely scatological. The dénouement in stanza 32 is the exact prototype of some of the highly dysphe-mistic 'mock-innocent' stories given above under "Anti-Family." *When the king finally identifies himself, the unabashed miller reminds him "How with farting we made the bed hott." "Thou whorson happy knave,"* then quoth the knight, *"Speake cleanly to our king, or else goe shite!"* (Compare the merely profane mock-admonition, *"Don't swear – it sounds like hell!"*)

Though the king is here defended from the scatological familiarity of the miller by the gallant if blundering knight, the truth of the situation is that everyone listening to the song has been amused by the coarseness directed at a king, who is also stated to have taken part in it himself earlier, when both he and the miller 'with farting ... made the bed hott.' No more obvious level of taboo humor exists than that of mocking authority-figures in this way with hostile or scatological words and images, even if only in the presumably philosophical folk-phrase in which going to 'shite' is called, in many languages, *'going where the queen must go on foot.'* Compare now the modern version of the same thing: *'Bloke who wins £75,000 in the football pool writes to his employer: "I'm not coming in tomorrow. Fuck you. – PS. Offensive letter follows".'* (London, 1953. In American versions the letter is 'sarcastic.') A simple pictorial version of this joke is given in *Sex to Sexty* (1965) 3:32, showing: *A diminutive office-worker standing on a swivel chair, facing a picture of the boss (and a sales-chart significantly diving), while he pisses on the desk. Caption: "I quit!"*

The brief bit directed by Ernst Lubitsch in the 1930's motion-picture gallery, *If I Had a Million* – and the only bit anyone still remembers from it – gave a milder and symbolized form, broodingly done in pantomime by Charles Laughton as: *The office-slave who receives a telegram stating that he has won a million on the lottery. He rises as in a trance from his desk, climbs slowly and grimly up through level after level of flunkeys, to the president's office, to give him the 'raspberry' in his face.* ('Raspberry tart,' British rhyming-slang for fart, used in reference to a vibrating mouth noise or 'lip-fart' of contempt, done in more florid forms with the whole tongue extruded.) During World War II, this same openly symbolic sound was used as punctuation for the anti-Hitler phonograph recording, and later the humorous war-propaganda film, Spike Jones' "Der Fuehrer's Face!" (*'So Ve heil! – Brzzp! – Heil! – Brzzp! – Heil! – Brrfloooopp!! – Right in Der Fuehrer's Face!'*)

When farting at the authority figure is not enough, especially when displaced upward to the mouth, at least two other physical or verbal defiances are possible: the wholly sexual and the wholly scatological, of which the first seems – at least verbally – to carry a greater charge. *The wife tells the husband the morning after the office-party, "Well, you certainly made an ass of yourself at the party yesterday. It's a miracle you still have your job the way you kept hollering 'Shit on the whole damn company!' when you were drunk. The boss didn't like that a bit." "Piss on the boss!" says the husband, who has a terrible hangover and doesn't care for post-mortems anyhow. 'That's what you did do," says his wife, "and the boss fired you for it." "So, FUCK the boss!" snarls the husband. "How do you think I got you your job back?"* (L.A. 1968.)

These are really elaborate set-ups for excusing, as a mere verbal blunder of permission, the prostituting of one's wife to the superior monetary power of 'the boss' – formerly the king or captain – for material or positional gain. Again, they are further excused as merely attempts to regain positions lost by the husband's inadvertence or folly. *A man wins second prize on a school raffle and is told it is a five-volume cookbook, whereas third prize is a color-television set and has already been won. "What?" screams the man, "only a five-volume cookbook!?" "Yes, but this cookbook was personally written in by the President of the Parent-Teachers Association," says the master-of-ceremonies. "FUCK the President of the Parent-Teachers Association!" shouts the man. "But that's FIRST prize!"* (San Diego, Calif. 1965. First printed in *World's Dirtiest Jokes*, 1969, p. 198.) This 'president' is probably a woman, and yet.

There is no disguise, and no evasion of just what president is referred to, in the following old favorite, dating from at least the 1930's Depression, when it was told of Herbert Hoover and Franklin Delano Roosevelt, but recently revived in the wake of the Watergate ('Sewergate') scandal, the worst in the history of the American presidency. *The President is very attracted to a young lady journalist and asks her to go to a motel with him. She refuses, and he angrily asks her how much she wants in spot cash for her charms. "Mr. President," she says, "if you can pull up my skirt as high as prices, and pull down my pants as low as wages, and screw me the way you've screwed the whole nation, you can have it for free!"* (Nice, France, 1974.)

The American president in the 1900's, Theodore Roosevelt, who was extremely unpopular as a phoney blowhard and a tinhorn sportsman – but never knew it – is still remembered in a joke that should be compared with Mark Twain's brutally funny anatomizing of the same individual, in "The Hunting of the Cow" (1907), in *Mark Twain in Eruption* (1940) p. 7–34, giving further details as to Roosevelt's idea of the man's-man's manly sportsmanship imitated right down to the moustache and shit-eating grin by Ernest Hemingway. *Teddy Roosevelt is relaxing by lion-hunting in Africa. He wounds a pregnant lioness in the bush, and then retires gracefully behind his Negro bush-beaters, saying masterfully, "All right boys, go on in there and get that lioness!" They do not move, muttering instead, "Katumbah-katumbah, bwana!" "You heard me! what are you, you bunch of yellow quitters? Go on in there and drag that lioness out!" "Katumbah-katumbah, bwana!" "What is this nonsense?" Roosevelt demands angrily of the interpreter, show-ing all his teeth. "What does 'katumbah-katumbah' mean? That they're afraid? Tell them I'll pay double." "Bwana," says the trembling interpreter, "that just means in our native talk, 'Fuck you, boss! Go in there and get that wounded lioness yourself!'"* (N.Y. 1950. See further the equestrian statue of Roosevelt in front of the New York Museum of Natural History showing him with a Negro and Indian at the stirrups of his horse ... Ain't that thing been dynamited yet?) The punchline takes form rather exactly from the anti-patriotic translation of the British royal motto, *"Dieu et mon droit,"* as meaning *"Fuck you, Jack, I'm all right!"* In the American armed services this (or *"Shove off the boat, Jack; I've got mine!"*) is also the mock translation of the Marines' motto, *"Semper fidelis,"* usually abbreviated to "Semper fi!" sometimes with the gesture of the ancient Roman *digitus impudicus* or upraised middle 'finger' to make the meaning very clear.

Another form or related type again satirizes the same worthy, sometimes expurgated to 'Buffalo Bill' Cody who, with all the other U.S. government buffalo-killers, used to massacre the bison with dynamite, as Texas and Arab millionaire sportsmen now swoop down in airplanes to kill running deer, not to mention the same tactics (with hand-grenades, napalm and machine-guns) used against human beings in wartime. *The Canadian Indian tribe gives Theodore Roosevelt a brocaded wampum baldric, in honor of his killing all their buffalos. He wears this proudly across his chest at a Washington reception, but is perturbed to notice that the American Indian chieftain seems to be looking dubiously at it. "What's the matter, Chief Pie-in-the-Sky,' he asks, "can't you read your Canadian brothers' language? It says, 'Great Kind White Father with Thunder-Stick'." "Ugh. No says, 'Great White Father.' Says, 'Pasty-White-Skunk-Grin-Like-Hyena-Eating-Shit-Out-of-Wire-Brush'."*

A very mild version of this has appeared in the humor columns of digest magazines: *The Chinese laundryman's mark-ings on the inquiring client's laundry, which turn out to mean 'Nosey guy. Lotsa hair. Talk alla time.'* This in turn seems to have given rise to or be paralleled by a similar item directed against an American lady politician and religious leader, very unpopular in the years since World War II. *A society-woman is pestering the Chinese ambassador at a Washington banquet to admire the Chinese brooch she is wearing. "You know the symbols, of co'ss," she says, "don't you, Ambassador?"* He murmurs something polite about their referring to good luck. *"Well, can you read them or can't you?" she snaps. "Certainly, Madame. The brooch reads: 'City of Shanghai. Licensed prostitute – second class'."* (Positano, Italy, 1954, told in English by a German prince while watching the lady in question perform.) This is very close to Sacchetti and Sercambi's 15th century *Pseudo-magic charm which is found to contain nonsense or obscenity when opened.* (Poggio, No. 231/2; Rotunda, Motif K115.1.)

Royalty no longer carries the charge it once did, except in the tabloid press, especially in England and France; and the flaunting of royalty with scatological or even castratory insults (as in the recitation *"Daniel, or The Night of the King's Castration"*) is now rarely heard in America, not out of respect but out of disinterest. *"Have you seen 'The King's Hand'?" "No, where's it playing?" "Up the Queen's ass."* (N.Y. 1949, actually a 'catch,' on the usual form of asking about plays or motion pictures.) The joke has already been given, in the chapter on Homosexuality, in which *Hitler* (earlier Victor Emmanuel in the French version, disguised as "Il Re Umberto," his father) *is discovered to have been engaging in buggery, by his physician's tasting feces on his penis.* Note the pronounced modification of this sort of libel in the following, taken from the expurgated *Anecdota Americana* (1933) No. 320, in which even the action of 'goosing' the King is described as having tapped him harmlessly behind. *'This happened in the palace of King Emanuel before his famous evacuation.* [N.b.] *A court attendant, finding him in the washroom, bending over, tapped him harmlessly behind. In rage, Emanuel ordered him to be imprisoned, but, stayed by his sense of humor, announced to the rascal that he could have his freedom if he would give an explanation even more outrageous that his deed. "That's easy," was the reply. "I didn't know it was you. I thought it was the Queen".'* This has all the marks of a much older court-jester story, possibly Levantine. (Spanish Motif J1181.3, *'Condemned man wins pardon by clever remark.'*) But compare Q115.1, the deathly serious Oedipal form: *The king offers as reward any boon asked: the king's wife is demanded.* This is the plot of the most beautiful moving-picture ever made in color, the Japanese *Gate of Hell* (1954?) and is mocked in a formula line in the ultimately

Oedipal "Bastard King of England" ballad, when the Bastard King offers as reward *'Half of all his kingdom, or the whole of Queen Hortense.'* The oldest form is from India, in Fallon & Temple's *Dictionary of Hindustani Proverbs,* p. 94 *(Kryptádia,* IV. 394): *The courtier who has refuted the king in argument demands as his reward [i.e.* quit-claim for his victory] *that he be allowed to 'soil the king's cushion.' This he is permitted to do, but will be punished if he pisses at the same time!* The Merchant of Venice's 'pound of flesh' (Motif J1161.2) is a *polite* Western revision of this.

A British soldier is left behind after the World War, guarding a pile of coal on a windswept quai somewhere in France, on Christmas Eve. He marches briskly to the end of the quai and back, bangs the butt of his rifle twice on the ground by way of salute, and announces: "Fuck the Army!" Stamps twice with heel. "Fuck the Navy!" Stamps again, "Fuck 'em AHLL*!" Then catching himself, "Saving King George!" (Or: "God save King George!") Whirls and starts back to the other end of the quai, but stops after a few steps, throws down his rifle and says, "Ah, fuck 'im too!"* (N.Y. 1953, given in pantomime as indicated.) This should be compared with the total rejection of all social shibboleths and sacred cows, with the same phrase, in the most popular Army song, among both the British and American troops early in World War II, "Fuck 'Em All!" (politely: *"Bless* 'Em All!"), of which the euphemized form itself refers to a *British Army gag or catch-phrase, said loudly after "Lights Out," when the officer is making his round: "Some sye, '*FUCK *the old sergeant!' but I always says, '*BLESS *the old sergeant!'"* Topper, in a wailing voice: *"Kiss me goodnight, Sergeant-Major!"* (Used as title for a collection of British Army songs, edited by Martin Page, 1973, with a homosexual cover-cartoon: the subterfuge is kilts.)

The song is certainly modelled on the enormously popular music-hall item of equally total rejection and anti-every-thingism, the hanging-song, "Damn Their Eyes!" of which the pre-history (as "Samuel Hall," earlier "Captain Kidd," etc.) is discussed at length in *The Horn Book,* pp. 197 and 382–3, and sources there cited, in particular an eye-witness account of its violent audience-participation singing at a London men's club of the time, in Julian Sharman's delightfully titled *A Cursory History of Swearing* (1884) p. 9–10. Sharman's account is an important statement on the whole question of anti-gallantry, anti-family, and anti-authority expression in socially-accepted form, as is any text of "Samuel Hall" or "Damn Their Eyes!" By comparison, "Fuck 'Em All!" is really rather mild.

The best of the 19th-century English diarists, Charles Fulke Greville, clerk of the Privy Council of England, has left a very full description of these men's club ceremonies and liberties in *The Greville Diary* (complete edition by Philip Wilson, 1927) I. 564–5, at date November 25, 1842; and they are stated to have gone on until the 1850's in J. Woodfall Ebsworth's *Choyce Drollery* (reprint, 1876; supplement, p. 229–30). Greville's description is most interesting, but too long to quote here *in extenso*. He states that the place was 'a long low room opposite Covent Garden Theatre, in Bow Street, lit with tallow candles and furnished along its length with benches.' It was called "The Judge and Jury Court," the audience – at 1 shilling per head, for which one was entitled to a cigar and a glass of rum, gin, or beer – being the actual jury. Parodies were delivered on trials and famous lawyers of the day, the jury in the box being sworn on a low newspaper called *The Town* (which might be worth learning more about). Greville, who was only slumming, to be sure, says he left before the end, but adds:

> They say the charge of the judge is generally the best part of it. They deal in very gross indecencies, and this seemed to amuse the audience, which is one of the most blackguard-looking I ever saw congregated, and they just restrain their ribaldry within such limits as exclude *les gros mots*. Everything short of that is allowed, and evidently the more the better. On the whole, it was a poor performance. It bore, in point of character and decency, about the same relation to a court of justice that Musard's balls do to Almack's.

We will see very soon what the set speech of such a 'judge' or advocate, to such an audience, might be, in the surviving American recitation – all tall-talk profanity and obscene anti-authoritarianism – called "Change the Name of Arkansaw?!" This is a style of mock oration going back in English at least to the *Gesta Grayorum, or The History of the High and Mighty Prince Henry* (1688), recording burlesque speeches already a century old then, if not older.

Closer to our own time have been various clubs of writers & artists, journalists, professional men, and physicians, meeting once a year at least, for purposes of bawdy or at the very least impolite parodies and satirical sketches of their own members' and guests' activities and other topical themes. The most censored and restrained of these is the yearly journalists' shindig of the Gridiron Club, in Washington, D.C., at which, as the name suggests, the guests are grilled or roasted – actually very tepidly. John Gunther's *Inside U.S.A.* (1947) pp. 302 and 436–7, notes that the proceedings are sometimes in the form of a debate: the "Judge and Jury Court" form. See Robert C. Elliott, *The Power of Satire* (1960) p. 82–4, on these highly expurgated proceedings, where 'Ladies are always present.'

The least expurgated was likely the Dutch Treat Club in New York during the 1920's and since, though its published *Year Books* are all lily-pure. A competing club's publication, *The Annual* of the Philadelphia Sketch Club, for 1930 (limited to 200 copies), p. 22–9, lifts a corner of the curtain to indicate that much of the activity had by then been turned over to the mere singing of bawdy songs, with homosexually-toned transvestist skits for the all-male audience. Similar scenes, of a Negro or Mexican woman doing an erotic solo dance, or having intercourse with an animal, before such a 'stag' audience, have already been discussed in chapter 11.III.2, "Orgies and Exhibitions." Further such club activities today are mostly at the level of singing bawdy songs and limericks (with an audience-participation chorus), especially in college fraternities – very similar to French "Chansons de Salles de Garde" of students and soldiers – and at army and air-officers' drinking parties.

An obscoenum of the 1920's, usually circulated upon the reverse of a printed 'business card,' mocked the then-new dial telephone and the minor authority-figure of telephone operators (female) with a series of burlesque directions, ending: '*To get the operator, put your finger in the Operator's Hole (O), and work it till the operator comes.*' This led or was parallel perhaps to an old favorite in which: *A man becomes irritated by the telephone operator and tells her to stick the phone up her ass. She reports him, and two workmen arrive to take out the man's phone. He is panic-stricken as he needs the phone for his business, and the workmen suggest that he call up the operator and apologize. After much embarrassed enquiring, he gets the offended operator. "Are you the operator I told to stick the phone up your ass?" he asks. "Yes?" she says, frigidly. "Well, there's two men here to take it out." (N.Y. 1936.)*

Two 'toppers' exist, again essentially nothing but joking

versions of the modern anonymous (obscene) phone-calls by cowards and perverts, as first suggested in Mark Twain's "Travelling with a Reformer." *A little boy, too young to use the dial on the phone, topples the receiver off the hook and says, "Operator, get me my Daddy. The number is Twemont-twee, twee twee twee twee." The operator thinks this is terribly cute and has him repeat it for all the other operators. Finally the impatient little boy says, "Listen, Operator, do you know how to play Dictaphone?" She admits she does not. "Well Dictaphone up your ass, and get me Twemont-twee, twee twee twee twee!"* (L.A. 1968.) The other topper is in the great style of Bateman's cartoon of: *The little boy who has been sent to jail for breathing heavily on the glass of one of the cases in the British Museum, and who comes back, on being let out years later, an old man broken of body but not of spirit, to breathe his last on the very same case in the British Museum!* (Related to Tale Type 1271, a Slovenian story in which: *'Children are forbidden to look through the window glass lest they wear it out too soon.'*) This has been considered further in the First Series, under 2.VII.2, "The Fortunate Fart."

The latest form of telephone story lacks the *superbia* of the little old boy's dying defiance, but has its points too. It is printed first in *World's Dirtiest Jokes* (1969) p. 41, and is obviously more anti-gallant and anti-woman, as in the section just preceding, than really anti-authoritarian – safely at the end of a wire: *A man trying to make a long-distance phone call is given the wrong number four times in a row. He dials the operator and says, "Operator, this is Mr. Pohlmeyer. Why don't you stick this phone up your cunt, and dial it with your foot?" The operator reports him and a company representative calls on him to warn him that unless he apologizes to her at once his phone will be taken out. The man dials the operator and says, "Operator, this is Mr. Pohlmeyer again. Are you the operator I told could stick the phone up your cunt and dial it with your foot?" "Yes," she says nasally, "did you wish to apologize?" "Not exactly," he replies, "I just wanted to tell you you better get your pants off, because the man is bringing you in my phone!"*

Policemen and judges are all standard shooting galleries for anti-authoritarian mockery, and examples have already been given, mostly as to sexual permissiveness, in the First Series, chapters 2.V.2, "The Courtroom," and 7.III, "Policemen and

Priests." This is ancient, there being courtroom jokes of this kind in some of the oldest Levantine jestbooks, while the classic gesture of the contemptuous 'lip-fart' or 'raspberry' appears as early as *Jests to Make You Merry* (1607) p. 6, as 'Blurt! Master Constable!' -- *A man (or little old lady) leaves a dog tied outside a barroom, as the bartender will not let him bring it in, and sits drinking for an hour or more. A policeman comes in and says, "Is that your dog outside? Do you realize she's in heat?" "No she isn't," says the man boozily, "I left her in the shade." "I mean, the bitch is acting like she needs to be mated," says the policeman. "Go ahead," laughs the man, turning back to his drink; "I always did want a police dog!"* (L.A. 1968. Compare: *The girl tells the man who says he would like to do what the stud-bull that they are watching is doing, "Go ahead – it's your cow."*) More frank in its defiance, but even so rather oblique, like a three-cushion carom in billiards, an image often relevant in humor.

Courtroom defiances usually involve importing or insisting upon coarse sexual terms when the judge prefers some Latin euphemism. *The witness to a Hell's Kitchen rape case is told to say 'intercourse' instead of 'fucking,' because that is a 'technicality of the law' about which he would not know anything. He proceeds: "Well, he was intercoursing her in the doorway, like I said, and suddenly he gave her the Chicago stroke (or the cross-jostle)." "What's the Chicago stroke?" asks the judge. "That's just a technicality of fucking that you wouldn't know anything about, judge."* (N.Y. 1940.) Sometimes, however, the judge knows too much: *A farmer is charged with bestiality with a calf, and the circuit-judge admonishes him, "This is a very serious offense, Zeke, so just explain to the court what happened." "Well, judge," says the farmer, "my wife has been a very sick woman for over a year, and one day I just couldn't stand it any more, so I got up on a milking-stool in back of the stall and mounted my best Guernsey calf. And y' know what, judge? That heifer pissed all over me!" The judge spits a mouthful of tobacco-juice halfway across the courtroom, hitting the spittoon dead-center. "By God! Zeke," he says, "they'll do it every time!"* (Binghamton, N.Y. 1938.) The punchline here has become a catch-phrase, often used by people who do not know its origin. It was also used in the 1940's as title for a series of American newspaper cartoons by Jimmy Hatlo on the little irritations of everyday life, a social-masochistic theme of great humorous appeal, first exploited in *The Miseries of Human Life* by Beresford ('Old Nick') in the early 19th century, as illustrated by Cruikshank and Grandville. Also by 'Cham' (A. de Noé), and in Balzac's *Petites misères de la vie conjugale* (1845). In *Kryptádia,* IV. 299: *The coal-heaver confesses to having fucked his cat ('boot trick'), but the priest gets his balls clawed trying it.*

Humiliations of superior officers in the army, navy, etc., are a favorite theme. Such jokes have already been given under other headings, in particular in chapter 13, under "Castration," and as to the threat of homosexual pedication, in 11.V.2. This latter is often expurgated to mere fingering or palpating the rectum of the superior officer (or teacher or boss), under the excuse of trying to win a bet: *the touch of money* being evidently a higher power than that of military discipline. One unequivocal example may be given here to mark the form: *The newly-arrived colonel at a fortress in the Sahara desert asks why a female camel is always tied to the back of the barracks, and is told that there are no women for miles around and that the men use the camel when they feel in need of sexual relief. After two months in the desert the colonel also needs sexual relief, and has the orderly bring the camel in and make her kneel down. He then takes off his uniform jacket, covers his medals with his topee helmet, unbraces his trousers, and fucks the camel. Observing that the orderly is grinning, the colonel asks, "What's the matter, boy? Isn't that the way you men do when you need sexual relief?" "No sir," says the orderly; "we generally ride the camel into the village and get a woman."* (L.A. 1968, and encountered much earlier in French.) Certainly to be compared with the "Rabbit-herd" tale (Type 570) in which, in the unexpurgated Ozark version given above, 10.V.6, "The Ganymede Revenge," *the boy tricks the king into 'honing off' his old jenny-ass.* The Kabyle trickster, Simoa ben Abid, is more direct, and buggers father-figures a-plenty in the final tale-group of Leo Frobenius' translation of African stories, *'The Black Decameron* (ed. New York, 1971, as *African Nights*): a remarkable collection, not to be overlooked.

Let me end this part of the development with an extremely significant joke in which the mocking of authority-figures is in one sense ludicrously exaggerated, in the other cunningly reversed. In the reversal, *The Roman emperor (or Italian movie-director) is highly dissatisfied with the monster orgy, and shouts, "Stop!! Stop! you buggers, and we'll try it again. I'm going to count to three; and when I hit three, I want to see some humping in unison!"* (Santa Monica, Calif. 1965.) Really a mock of army and marine drilling to the 'cadence-count,' with sadistic verbal humiliation of the men. The notion of the monster orgy – here thought of as improbable – has actually an even more remarkable historical reality : *Alexander the Great, King of Macedonia, in the year 326 B.C., to celebrate his victory over Persia and India on the Hydaspes river, had* THIRTY THOU-SAND *of his soldiers publicly and simultaneously perform intercourse with an equal number of captive women, on one mountain-side in Kashmir on a sunlit afternoon, as a symbolic 'marriage' of the two empires.*

What can the cheap hippie 'group-grope' and 'Mongolian cluster-fuck' of a third of a million drugged marijuana-smokers in a waterlogged cow-patch in Woodstock, New York, offer to compare with that? When they get tired of kidding around with pornographic moving-pictures in Hollywood and Scandinavia, I am going to start shooting my own script on *Alexander the Great* in Kashmir. It will revitalize India. According to contemporary historians of this greatest orgy in the history of the world – of avowed symbolic and religious meaning – the 'sperm flowed like the issue of wild jackasses, and the odor was heavy like that of chestnut trees in flower.' (See *Ezekiel*, xxiii. 2–47, for additional plot treatment.) Griffith's *Intolerance* and Pastrone's *Cabiria* will be back-numbers after that.

Now as to the exaggeration. On my complaining once to a sub-editor of an important American news-&-picture magazine about a repulsive 'surprise' photograph published of a friend of mine, when we were attacking the horror-comics still being peddled to children, he smilingly told me the secret formula going back forty years to the days of the irreverent original editor, who had created the magazine and enjoyed slipping in adjectives like 'snaggle-toothed' and 'pig-faced' to describe some helpless victim fallen into public domain. The formula quoted to me is still that on which this (and many another) influential propaganda organ picks its photos, slants its stories, and barbs its ornate verbiage : *"We don't want a picture of Einstein discovering relativity. We want to get him sitting on the toilet,* SCRATCHING – HIS – ASS!*"* Any further questions?

Nothing circulated in print in America can compare, for total dysphemistic mocking and dirtying of every possible authority-

figure, totem, and symbol presumably held sacred at the
patriotic level, with the famous Ozark recitation known as
"Change the Name of Arkansaw?!" which has circulated orally
at least since the 1880's throughout the United States. This
achieves its unquestioned humor by building up, with bawdy
tall-talk and insults throughout, to an anal-sadistic climax in
which flag, country, and all its great men and monuments are
torn down and literally shat upon, under the purposely ludicrous pretext of preventing the name of the great state of
Arkansas – the 19th century's laughing-stock state – from being
mispronounced ArKANsas, instead of ARKansaw.

All public printings of this recitation in magazine and book
form – mostly in backwoods kitsch publications about Arkansas
– are heavily expurgated, the weakest text being that in John
Gunther's *Inside U.S.A.* (1947) p. 764. One honorable exception
is the entire chapter devoted to "Change the Name of Arkansaw?!" in James R. Masterson's pioneeringly unexpurgated
Tall Tales of Arkansaw (Boston: Chapman & Grimes, 1942)
chap. 13, "Hell, No!" pages 180–85, with the authentic texts
given in the notes, p. 352–8. The only unexpurgated printing of
this recitation at the popular level has been in the form of a
small anonymous broadside containing this text only, which,
according to a pencilled note on the only-known copy, in the
files of the Arkansas History Commission, was distributed to
edify and ennoble the patriotic sentiments of the super-patriotic
American Legion at its New York convention in 1937. No more
perfect example of Freud's 'Return of the Repressed' could
probably ever be found than these auspices for such a text – as
will be seen.

Rather than reprint here any of James R. Masterson's texts of
"Change the Name of Arkansaw?!" it seems more useful to
print a form given only in manuscript in Vance Randolph's
'Unprintable' Ozark collection, *Pissing in the Snow, and other
Ozark folktales* (MS. 1954) No. 69, as "Senator Johnson's Great
Speech," and collected from a gentleman in Little Rock,
Arkansas, in 1949, who 'had a manuscript copy of the speech,
but recited the whole thing from memory.' This manuscript
copy was apparently identical (before being committed to
memory) with the final text given by Masterson, p. 354–5,
stating that this was sent him by Miss Nancy Clemens of the
family of Mark Twain. It also seems quite possible that Twain
may have been the author of the original – which is extremely

similar to the expurgated contest in brag that precedes the fight on the raft in Twain's *Life on the Mississippi* in 1883.

Here is Randolph's field-collected text of 1949. In this the opening and closing paragraphs, given in roman type, are not part of the recitation itself, but are this particular reciter's personal introduction and conclusion. Another such reciter – who also stated, apocryphally, that 'this is taken down on the legislative rolls ... under the date of July 23rd, 1867' – gave as his introduction: 'This is what the home-town boy [the speaker] had to say. I think first he pulled out his horse-pistol and laid it across his desk, so he wouldn't be interrupted.'

One time there was a goddam Yankee moved to Arkansas, and got elected to the Legislature. The first thing he done was put in a bill to make Arkansas rhyme with Kansas, just because it is spelled that way. The Arkansawyers got pretty mad, of course, so they begun to stomp and holler. There was one old man that hollered louder than anybody alse, and finally the rest of 'em quietened down to hear what he had to say.

"Mister Speaker, God damn your soul," says he, "I've been trying to get the floor for thirty minutes, but all you do is squirm around like a dog with a flea in his ass! I'm Senator Cassius M. Johnson from Johnson county, where we raise men with peckers on, and the women are glad of it. Why, gentlemen, at the tender age of sixteen them girls can throw their left tit over their right shoulder, and squirt milk up their ass-hole as the occasion demands! When I was fourteen years old my prick was big as a roasting-ear, the pride and joy of the whole goddam settlement. Gentlemen, I could piss half-way across the Ouachita!"

Everybody clapped when they heard that, but the Speaker begun to holler "Out of order! Out of order!" and pound on his desk.

"You're goddam right it was out of order," says Senator Johnson, "Otherwise I could have pissed clear across the son-of-a-bitch! That's the kind of folks we raise in Johnson county, gentlemen, and we ain't never been dictated to by nobody. And now comes this pusillanimous, blue-bellied Yankee who wants to change the name of Arkansas. Why, Mister Speaker, he compares the great state of Arkansas to Kansas! You might as well liken the noonday sun in all its

glory to the feeble glow of a lightning-bug's ass, or the frag-
rance of an American Beauty rose to the foul quintessence of
a Mexican burro's fart! Can all the power of this Assembly
enlargen the puny penis of a Peruvian prince to a ponderous
pagan prick, or the tiny testicles of a Turkish tyrant to the
bulky bollyx of a Roman gladiator? Change the name of
Arkansas? Great God Almighty damn! No, gentlemen! Hell
fire, no!

"What the God damn hell is things a-coming to, anyhow?
Why, gentlemen, it's got so a man can't take down his pants
for a good country shit without getting his ass full of bird-
shot. Change the name of Arkansas? Great God Almighty
damn! You may piss on Jefferson's grave, gentlemen. You
may shit down the White House steps, and use the Declara-
tion of Independence for a corncob. You may rape the
Goddess of Liberty at high noon, and wipe your tallywhacker
on the Star Spangled Banner. You may do all this, gentlemen,
and more. But you can't change the name of Arkansas! Not
while one patriot lives to prevent such desecration! Change
the name of Arkansas? Hell fire, no!"

History don't tell us what happened after that, but everybody knows the Yankee's bill was killed, dead as a whore's
turd in a piss-pot. Them sons-of-a-bitches up North think the
whole thing was just a joke, and some of 'em claim Senator
Johnson didn't make no speech at all. But every true-blooded
Arkansawyer knows that Senator Cassius M. Johnson jumped
into the breach that day, to save the Bear State from treason
and disgrace. We ain't going to forget it, neither.

Unfortunately, as both Masterson and Randolph are forced
to observe, there is no official record of an Arkansas State
Senator named Cassius M. Johnson, nor any evidence that such
a speech was ever actually made. It is a fact, however, that the
pronunciation as ARKansaw – with the spelling: Arkansas – was
formally established by the State Legislature in 1881, which is
doubtless about the date when this burlesque oration was
created, whether by Mark Twain or some lesser humorist forever anonymous. (As to the real controversy concerning the
pronunciation of the state name, see the full documentation by
Allen Walker Read, in *American Speech*, 1933, VIII. 42–6.) The
novelist Thomas Wolfe, who died in 1938, tells a part of the
same story – that concerning pissing halfway across the river –

in his *The Hills Beyond* (1941) chap. 3, as concerning Senator Zachariah Joyner of North Carolina, whom 'no other place on earth but Old Catawba could have produced,' adding circumstantially that the famous oration was made 'in the United States Senate (in rejoinder to the Honorable Barnaby Bulwinkle).' The lamented Lenny Bruce (Leonard Schneider), a specialist in public obscenity and verbal sacrilege, has a brief personal version of this in his autobiography, *How to Talk Dirty and Influence People* (Chicago: Playboy Press, 1965) chap. 10. To avoid having hot lead poured up his ass with a funnel by the enemy, he says – this replaces Changing the Name of Arkansaw – '*I would give them every top secret, I would make shoeshine rags out of the American flag, I would denounce the Constitution, I would give them the right to kill every person that was kind and dear to me. Just don't give me that hot-lead enema.*' (No comment.)

Masterson makes the final point, in *Tall Tales of Arkansaw*, p. 358, setting the whole matter in its true historical perspective: 'Fictitious legislative speeches of the same general type – irrelevant bombast exaggerated to intentional absurdity – seem to have constituted a type of Western humor. See, for example, *Speech of Gen. Riley in the House of Representatives of Missouri*, February 8, 1861, reprinted from the Hannibal *Weekly Messenger*, March 7, 1861, excavated and edited by Franklin J. Meine (Chicago: The Mark Twain Society of Chicago, 1940).'

Mock parliamentarian speeches of this kind are clear developments from the allowed liberties of the Saturnalia, especially in churches, as celebrated in Christian Europe from the late middle ages on, under the name of the "Feast of Fools," as will be discussed further in the section immediately below. I have noted other spoken and printed prototypes of this kind of speech in *The Horn Book* (1964) pp. 207–9 and 490, back to the early 16th century, in particular in *The Foundling Hospital for Wit* (1749), anonymously edited by Sir Charles Hanbury Williams, VI. 22, "Speech without Doors, in Answer to a supposed Speech Within," the mock speech being purportedly given here by the groom of a member of Parliament to an audience of his peers, doubtless (as Mr. Dallas T. Herndon suggests as to Arkansas) 'in a barroom.' In Isaac D'Israeli's *Curiosities of Literature*, ed. London, 1849, II. 291 note, mention is made of a rare quarto tract *Gesta Grayorum, or The History of the High and Mighty Prince Henry* (1688), which is 'full of burlesque speeches and addresses,' presumably dating back to 1594. A similar burlesque, turning entirely on erotic *double entendres* intended to hold up the feminists to ridicule as suffering merely from sexual starvation (still the line generally taken in opposing the Women's Liberation movement), is common in America and is nowadays usually ascribed to Lady Astor, though it has been known in France since the mid-19th century agitations of the feminists. (See further *The Horn Book*, p. 490.)

During the 1930's Depression in the United States, when Alexander King's splendidly savage satirical cartoon magazine, *Americana*, failed to capture any large audience, a new type of humorous or satirical magazine became enormously popular, and perfectly expressed – or diverted – the vague economic and social unrest beginning to stir in America. This was George T. Delacorte's *Ballyhoo* (with many short-lived imitators, entitled *Bushwah* [an expurgation of *Bullshit*], and so forth, of which the latest was *Ratfink* in the mid-1960's), boldly satirizing – advertising! Never a word about any socio-economic problem, and this in a decade when the revolutionary struggle exploded all over the world. Nothing about poverty, nothing about unemployment, nothing about war, nothing about religion, nothing about anything that had ever been the target of earlier satirists for centuries. Nothing even about sex. Just advertising. In parody advertisements which were essentially further advertising.

The villain or humorous King Charles' head, at whom all the sarcasm was directed in *Ballyhoo*, was a mythical 'Elmer Zilch,' depicted with the handlebar moustaches of a 1910's bartender or bicyclist. Zilch stood in for Morgan, Rockefeller, and all the paid scientists producing phoney patent medicines, and real explosives, for them. (In the repulsive French 'black humor' magazine of the 1960's and '70's, *Hara-Kiri*, a nonexistent 'Prof. Choron' is similarly the only butt – actually the perpetrator – of the otherwise violently scatological satire.) This type of bravado is about the equivalent of the husband, in the joke, who heroically *drops the Mexican bandit's balls into the hot sand while the bandit is raping his wife*. Or, in the original 15th-century form, which says it better, '*made many a dagger thrust*' in his saddle, while guarding the otherwise-occupied highwayman's horse. (See the complete text of these jokes in the First Series, 9.II.6, "Conniving at Adultery," p. 737.) While the highwayman 'perforates' his wife 'before, behind, and above': Our situation, vis-à-vis advertising, exactly. *Ballyhoo* is now long dead, but a collective volume was published at the time, of its punniest parody ads which deeply flattered and gratified all the advertisers so prettily mocked.

The similar prize of parody is also awarded to every type of evil popular kitsch, such as 'James Bond' spy-thrillers, sadistic western movies, crooked radio-quiz programs, 'topless' road-side hotdog joints, and the like, in the cynical American comic-book, *Mad* magazine, dribbling the ball lucratively for years within the guide-lines laid down by the originator of its formula, Harvey Kurtzman: namely, *To draw Americans as ugly and stupid as they really are, and that way they'll never dare to recognize it as themselves.* The formula also of Swift's *Gulliver's Travels*, as to England two centuries earlier. Thus evading, while seeming to express and even to satirize, the crude truth about America and its middle-western and sea-board cities, 'painfully crowded, noisy, and packed with dirt and squalor,' a truth stated in plain words only once, so far as I know, in John Gunther's *Inside U.S.A.* (1947) p. 277, calling them: *'the ugliest, least attractive phenomena in the United States. They represent more bluntly than anything else in the country the worst American characteristics – covetousness, ignorance, absence of esthetic values, get-rich-quickism, bluster, lack of vision, lack of foresight, excessive standardization, and immature and undisciplined social behavior.'* But no one is satirizing that.

6. MOCKING GOD

People who tell anti-clerical or even anti-godlin jokes or who express themselves sacrilegiously concerning God and the clergy are not necessarily irreligious people, nor do their jests and mockeries, however broad, necessarily express any serious anti-religious feelings. More often, and profoundly, it is the reverse: the underlying emotion is actually that of a deep religiosity, for which the jokes and mockery serve as a way of letting off steam. Otherwise the religious faith would crack. I have tried to express this in other words, concerning the ulti-mate anti-godlin activity of Devil-worship, in my study of the thoroughgoing anti-Christianity of the Knights Templars, *The Guilt of the Templars* (New York, 1966) pt. XI, p. 102–16, against the background of the ultimate accusations of sexual orgies and idolatry, meaning Devil-worship, brought against the Templars.

In the middle ages in France, more certain of its religion than later centuries, no one dreamed of objecting when the jongleurs entertained their vulgar audiences with mock speeches well mixed with pretended religious formulas in 'barber's Latin' – meaning of course *barbaric*, and not as somehow particular to barbers. (Motif K1961.1.2.1, "Parody sermon," with extensive references as far back as Boccaccio's *Decameron*, Day VI, Tale 10, and its own further sources studied by Marcus Landau and A. C. Lee.) This style of jargon was then known as the *coq-à-l'âne* – used from that day to this by mountebank comedians and street-vendors of dubious medical salves. Then, however, the subject would be the lives and blessed miracles of the mock saints, Saint Bridlegoose (revived by Rabelais), Saint Herring, and Saint Onion. As late as 1609 – or perhaps one should say as early, were it not for the prosecutions of Rabelais in the middle of the preceding century, and the whole censorious activity of the Congregation of the Roman Catholic Index in the Counter-reformation – King James I of England had an act passed 'with the consent of Parliament,' forbidding in purest Scottish spelling the issuing of any *'pasquillis, lybellis, rymes, cockalanis [coq-à-l'ânes*, the modern 'cock-&-bull story,' or *'cockamammy']*, *comedies, and siclyk* [such-like] *occasionis*,' whether or not these tampered with religion.

Finally, it cannot be overlooked that the use of popular or didactic stories and parables in sermons in the church or synagogue itself is an ancient Jewish usage. For example, the miraculous 'talking-horse' story of Balaam and his jackass, in *Numbers*, xxii, 22–33, which must be the oldest shaggy-dog joke on record. Dr. Mary Douglas has courageously noted, in "The Social Control of Cognition," in *Man* (Sept. 1968) III. 367–8, that many of the New Testament parables 'have an obvious joke pattern,' and also gives numerous examples. The sermons ascribed to Jesus in the New Testament are particularly numerous in the *Gospel according to St. Luke* (A.D. 140), which joins its narrative portions together on a long string of such stories or parables, put into the mouth of Jesus, especially in chapters 5 through 21 – of twenty-four chapters in all – and is basically the first important collection of such *exempla*. (Matthew gives a dozen further parables not in Luke. See tabulation in the *Oxford Helps to the Study of the Bible*, 1893, p. 69–70.)

The plain implication is that Jesus – assuming such a person ever existed at all – never pronounced three-quarters of the forty parables ascribed to him over a century later, but at most the ten reported by two or more gospels. And that the principal group of thirty parables were simply 'supplied' independently by the writers of *Matthew* and *Luke*, using folk sources. Even the *original* gospel (that of Mark, on which the other two are based), which contains only nine parables, has at least one – that of the Wicked Husband-men, in *Mark*, xii, 1–12 – which, since it alludes to the death of Jesus and the fall of Jerusalem forty years later, is a crude anachronistic fake and cannot possibly have been spoken by Jesus.

Anti-religious humor generally, and specifically the twitting and insulting of priests or clergymen, is no longer common in the Anglo-Saxon culture (except among Negroes) at anything but the most superficial and good-natured level. It is understood generally, even among the clergy, that Protestant Christianity has now failed as a religion and is without social importance or moral and ethical control. It is therefore no longer worth attacking or necessary to attack. Jokes against priests and rabbis are rather more common among Protestants, on the basis of simple religious enmity, but even these seldom now have much bite. Where violent jokes or tales of this kind once existed, they have now been revamped using other hated groups and authority-figures as butt, such as lawyers, judges, and psychoanalysts. Jokes ridiculing ministers or parsons have at the present time a vaguely old-fashioned tone, of the truculent and uninflected village atheist or boob-baiter, a type that really went out in America with the 1920's of H. L. Mencken. The socio-economic approach, of Upton Sinclair's attack in the 1910's on *The Profits of Religion*, is the only one now meaningful, but is seldom ventured, as its principal target must still be the Catholic church.

Since the French collection, *Histoires de Curés* (Paris, about 1930), anticlerical jokes are seldom encountered nowadays even in Catholic countries, the current lines of social conflict being consciously economic. Compare, for example, the French motion-picture of the 1930's, *The Baker's Wife*, in which the town-priest is played continuously for a fall by that harbinger of Enlightenment, the schoolmaster, with the later kitsch-comedy of the *Don Camillo* movie series, based on an Italian post-war novel, in which the conflict is more frankly between the priest – who emerges the winner – and the local Communist party leader. All played in the style of the usual poor-girl-rich-boy *Abie's Irish Rose* plot-hokum, to avoid ever getting into the real meat of the conflict between the social classes, and the priest as moral-policeman for the rich.

The modern perversions of religious or quasi-religious formulas are seldom so frank as one reported to me by a male Russian-Jewish cook, as well-known among Jews before the Russian Revolution of 1917, when the superb Greek Orthodox choral music would come swelling out of every church as one passed. The main and repeated phrase of this music, *"Hospody pomilui!"* (*O God, have mercy!*) would be answered under their breath by the intimidated little Jews rushing by in the streets, with the rhyming *"Moyu sraka v tvoyé ryilui!"* (*My arse in your snout!*) See further – if you can get hold of it – a mimeographed document issued by the U.S. Naval Intelligence Forces in Germany, after World War II, entitled *Swear Words, Oaths, and Terms of Vulgarity used in the U.S.S.R.* (stamped "Restricted" and "Obscene," according to Edward Sagarin's *The Anatomy of Dirty Words*, 1962, p. 200.) Can't you just see those clean young Texans, like Lee Harvey Oswald, passing themselves off as Russians in belted blouses and crumple-boots, while they swear an authentically blue streak in the original Cyrillic! Say what you will about the C.I.A., they do try to turn in a professional infiltration job. The only remaining old-fashioned religious oath still used in English in consciously perverted form was once a favorite of hedge-priests and jesters – though the vaguely religious form cannot be missed – and survives among or in imitation of stage-magicians: *"Hocus-pocus, dominokus!"* (from *"Hoc est corpus ..."*)

The favorite butt as to language-ignorance, and especially language-pretention, is nowadays still the Negro preacher, though white political speeches and learned-journal articles (especially in what are laughingly called 'the Humanities') are still often cast in even more meaningless and pretentious gobbledegook. A few examples will be given a bit further along ... Endless attacks on this basis will be found in American anti-Negro humor – a fabulously rich field, not yet properly studied – from the period of the 19th-century Currier & Ives dancing-nigger-and-watermelon prints, through the mass of similar pictorial satire and verbal vilification in the old *Life* humor-magazine, about 1900. Continuing on to the blackface

"Amos and Andy" radio-shit, the first popular radio serial in America in the late 1920's. And the 'Darktown' (polite for 'Niggertown') stories of big-talking Florian Slappey and his Negro lodge-brothers (again polite for church-members and ministers) in the *Saturday Evening Post* as late as the 1930's by Octavus Roy Cohen. Why a man named Cohen should have specialized in exploitative anti-Negro humor of this kind, I do not know. Nor why his Christian magazine-editors should have let him.

What is significant here is the idea that, as disguise, the clerical or religious background must generally be heightened with other would-be touches of humor, as the use of comedy-Negro or Jewish dialect. *'Negro and his girl in Roman Catholic church. She is awed by sight of priest walking down the aisle with his golden orb, and asks: "Say, Rastus, who's dat guy urinating up an' down de aisle wid de golden test-I-cle?" "Him, Liza? Dat's de Rectum ob de constipation. Ain't you been seduced by him?"'* (London, 1953, supplied in manuscript.) The reverse of this sort of joke, from the Negro's presumed point of view, strikes the modern audience as being closer to funny : *'A Negro bought a bottle of soda pop at a filling station beside a lake, paid for it with a quarter, and asked for his twenty cents' change in pennies. He then went over to the lake and began masturbating. Every few licks he threw a penny in the water. The station attendant, mystified, came over and asked what he was doing. "I'm living like white folks," the Negro replied. "I'm drinking, whoring around, and throwing my money away".'* (D.C. 1953, also from manuscript.) The situation is of course impossible; it is a sort of acted-out *charade*, of which the punch-line spells out the verbal equivalent

A Jewish attempt at anti-religious humor similarly turns strictly on verbal dirtying of the Holy Days of the orthodox religious minority. *Irreligious Jew: "What are you so dressed up for?" Religious Jew: "It's Yom Kippur." "So what's Yom Kippur?" "Do you know what New Year's is?" "Yes." "Well New Year's is SHIT compared to Yom Kippur."* (N.Y. 1953.) – *An actor is called upon to give an extemporary speech and prayer at a church banquet, and fortifies himself with a hip-flask of gin which he surreptitiously pours in his water-glass. Later he asks the minister whether his prayer had been a success. "It was excellent," says the minister, "except for three things: you shouldn't smack your lips after every sip of water, you*

*shouldn't pick the martini-olive out of your water-glass, and –
oh yes – the Bible says David slew Goliath with a slingshot. He
did* not *kick the shit out of him!"* (L.A. 1968.) Earlier versions of
this have: *A child in Sunday school who gets the story of
Samson and the Philistines wrong, when he mis-hears another
child prompting him with the answers on an oral examination:
Samson killed the Philistines with the jawbone of an ass, not
with "a jab in the ass."* (N.Y. 1936.)

Charlie Chaplin uses the 'David and Goliath' sermon as a
wordless pantomime in one of his early movie comedies, about
1915, where the ex-prisoner is called upon to give testimony in
church, and pantomimes the gestures of kicking, etc., as in the
joke. (Mock or parody sermon, Motif K1961.1.2.1, with broad
spread of references.) A story collected in Picardy, on the children in Sunday school situation tells of: *The Sacrifice of Abraham, where Abraham has no knife, so he puts Isaac on the
altar with eyes blindfolded, and aims his arquebus at him. Just
as he is about to pull the trigger, the angel of God appears and
pisses in the firing-pan, wetting the powder, and the gun misses
fire!* (*Kryptádia*, 1907, XI. 145, No. 172.) There is a tradition that
such a painting once existed in Antwerp, Belgium, in the naïve
line of the famous "Maneken-Pis" statue.

It is seldom observed that the horror expressed (in jokes and
folklore) of obscene language by priests and ministers, or old
lady types assimilable to these, involves a real fear of the
breaking of the taboo, as though God, religion, and the priest
were actually attacked or harmed by the taboo sexual terms.
The following jokes (and a few *cante fables*) are attempting to
rationalize this, by making the specific sexual words used form
an accusation of some sexual kind against the minister or
priest. This is not really the essence, and the twitting of superior
figures with obscenity is no different than shocking or 'harming' them by using their true but taboo *names*: whether of
Jehovah or of some temporal ruler, as will be noted again
below. *A little Spanish boy named Jesus Christ Lopez offers to
spell a hard word in the spelling-bee in Sunday School. "But,
Jesus Christ, you can't spell 'transcontinental',"* says *the
teacher. "Well, God damn it!" the visiting superintendent interrupts, "let the kid try!"* (L.A. 1968.)

The most obvious attack on the priest is not the oblique refusal of his authority, but to state that he either has *no*
authority or that he is hypocritically contravening his moral

code himself. Halfway to this direct attack is to state that the priest is incapable of managing or understanding his own sexual rules, and specifically that he is making mistakes in confession, giving the wrong penances, etc. A number of these jokes have been told already under other heads, such as that of: *The girl who will not tell the other girls what sin she confessed to, but says she has to sit in the holy water fount for penance.* The same proposed sacrilege in *Kryptádia*, II. 164; IV. 297. *The young priest who asks the bishop for advice about penances. 'What ought I to give a homosexual for sinning with, er, the mouth?" "Oh, you can give him anything you like. I never give more than a dollar or a dollar and a half. Just don't do it in the confession-box, because it gets the woodwork all* goomy." (N.Y. 1952. Also omits the final sacrilegious 'topper.')

A Protestant minister (or Jewish rabbi) replaces the Catholic priest in the confessional, as the priest must go to give a dying man absolution. The first person who comes to confess admits to an act of fornication. "That's all right," says the minister, "just put $20 in the charity-box on the way out, and God will forgive you." "Twenty dollars?" cries the penitent, "but our usual priest only charges five." "Maybe so," says the minister, "but I don't think he knows what that stuff is worth!" (L.A. 1968.) Where the replacement is made by a rabbi, the concentration on money is burlesqued even harder: *The rabbi has been present in the confessional to learn the technique, and has heard the priest give a penance of ten dollars for fornication repeated three times. When he is alone the first penitent also admits to fornication. "Three times?" asks the rabbi. "No, father," says the girl, "only once." "Well," says the rabbi, "you say ten Paternosters and put five dollars in the pushky on the way out, and go and get fucked twice more. We're having a special this week – three for five!"* (Scranton, Pa. 1935, told with a Yiddish comedy accent. See other texts and tracing of this joke in First Series, 7.III, page 418.)

The accusation that the priest himself debauches penitents in the confessional booth, or in connection with receiving their confessions, is essentially the gravest that can be made, and has been crucial to most of the real sexual attacks mounted against the clergy on the basis of actual seductions, such as that in the Girard-Cadière case in the early 18th century, which was finally built up into such a scandal that it was influential in the temporary disbanding of the Jesuit order by Pope Clement XIV.

In jokes it is usual for the priest to combine his seduction with techniques rather similar to the 'anatomical progression' of songs such as "He Put His Hand Upon My Knee" ("The Amsterdam Maid"). This is really a kind of sexual education, like that of Eve by the seducing Serpent in *Genesis*, and it might be mentioned that Boccaccio's most famous story, that of "Putting the Devil in Hell" (Day III, Tale 10), is also of this type, though he tells it as of a monk, Rustico, and not of a priest. Other versions cited by Rotunda, K 1363.1, are not so careful in expurgating or avoiding the confessional situation, though this does not prove that the folk-original on which Boccaccio certainly based his tale was of a priest in confession. Extraordinary as it may appear, Boccaccio's self-same story is still in folk transmission, and one version of it is printed in *World's Dirtiest Jokes* (1969) p. 17 as "Allegory," Type 1425, in which the modern Albiech is given the final line, explaining to her mother what she has learned from the 'local patriarch' [*sic*] as to the *'Hell' between her legs, and the man's own 'miserable sinner and two devils': "Boy, you should have seen those two devils run that sinner into hell last night!"*

Occasionally the priest is mocked with his vows of sexual abstinence or by having the confessional situation backfire on him. Note again the 'anatomical progression,' here specifically on the required form of the confessing priest urging the penitent on to further and more specific confessions: *A girl confesses that she let her boyfriend put his hand on her knee. "And is that all he did?" asks the priest. "No, he slid his fingers under the elastic of my panties, too." "And then what?" "And then he spread open my fuzz and began to tickle my doo-funny." "And then – and then?" "And then my mother walked in." "Oh shit!" says the priest.* (N.Y. 1948.) Another such joke ends its progressions and anatomies with the girl saying: *"And then he gave me the clap, father,"* at a point where the priest is understood to have contracted the disease too, in that case. This joke has been quoted in full, and traced further in the First Series, Introduction, section VII, pages 36–7 and 419. Here it is the penitent – really the teller of the joke – who is punishing the priest, and not the reverse. In the American anti-military movie satire, *M.A.S.H.* (1969), *an over-religious doctor and his pretentiously moral lady-friend have their private sexual pleasures broadcast over the camp loudspeaker by means of a microphone slipped under their bed. The woman is later suddenly exposed naked to the whole camp in her shower, and has a ghastly hysterical crisis before the audience's eyes.* The hilarious fun of seeing a woman have hysterics (who are the lucky girls who get these parts?) is also fully exploited as the climax of one of Peter Sellers' movie comedies, about a bumbling concert pianist and his secret seductions – spied on and spoiled by two jealous adolescent girls.

An anti-clerical situation usually expurgated in the direction of the laity is that of: *The wife-swapping party raided by the crusading minister, who plans to put an end to these goings-on. When he rings the doorbell the man of the house arrives and does not seem a bit embarrassed. "Er, ah," says the minister, "I was told you had a, er, party here tonight." "We do," says the man; 'we're playing guessing-games right now. The women are blindfold, trying to guess the men's names by feeling their pricks. You ought to come on in, Reverend; your name's been guessed eight times already."* (Santa Monica, Calif. 1965.) A similar dénouement to a game of "Bride's Buff" in the kitchen, has the minister replaced by the 'marster,' in *The Last of the Bleshughs*, 'by the Marquis of Fartanoys' [Roy McCardell], issued privately in New York about 1928, as noted further in *The Limerick*, p. 414.

The nun as a sacerdotal personage of sexual character has already been discussed in chapters 6.IV.2 (along with old maids), and 11.I.1. (with prostitutes and nurses.) This is not a particularly common area of anti-clerical attack nowadays, though once it was considered crucial. There remains the question of the sexual appetites of religious females. Quite a number of erotic limericks still turn on this matter, as seen in *The Limerick* (1953, enlarged ed. 1970), chap. 6, "Abuses of the Clergy." In the usual anti-authoritarian style of jokes, it is the sexual peccadilloes of the head-nun or mother superior that are mostly satirized, as in the ancient story of the breeches on the abbess' head, told by Boccaccio (Day IX, No. 2) and in Balzac's archaizing *Contes Drolatiques*. In a very reserved (purely verbal) modern form: *When a young nun comes to tell the mother superior that she has sinned with a man and wishes to do penance so she can be forgiven, the mother superior begins packing a suitcase. "Oh, please don't put me out!" the young nun cries. "Where will I go? What will I do?" "I'm not putting you out," says the mother superior grimly; "it's me that's leaving. For thirty years here its been nothing but fucking and forgiving, fucking and forgiving. Beginning now, I'm through doing the forgiving, and I'm going to get in on some of the fucking before it's too late!"* (N.Y. 1952.)

More specifically, as to the women involved, is a charming joke concerning: *The head-nun who is held up one evening while coming back from the bank where she has deposited the charity collection of the week. "You're wasting your time, young man," she tells the robber; "I have no money. I put it all in the night-deposit at the bank." "We'll see about that!" he says grimly, and begins rumpling up under her black gown to search for the money. "Oh! what are you doing?" she cries; "oh! oh!! Oh, Jesus-Mary! Don't stop now – I'll write you a check!"* (La Jolla, Calif. 1964: told by a young Irishwoman.)

The verbal orientation of the following exotic item is in an ancient line of alliterative and assonant poetry, about which more will be said in the following section on "Insults." It appears only in *World's Dirtiest Jokes* (1969) p. 38: '*A preacher was asked to conduct a revival in a small Southern town. There being no hotel, he was housed with one of the church sisters, a young widow. After the revival, taking his leave, he said to the hostess, "Sister Jones, never in all my ecclesiastical career have I encountered such an abundant, satisfying and abiding manifestation of thorough, complete, and delightful exemplification of gratitude, graciousness, appreciativeness and hospitality as you have demonstrated!" Sister Jones smiled, simpered, and answered, "Parson, I don't know what all those big words mean, but I want to say that you're a real world beater, a strong repeater, and that you do it neater, sweeter and more completer with less peter than any other person I ever had here!"* ' This takes part of its form at least from a well-known limerick on: *The lady of Kew (or Purdue), Who said as the Bishop withdrew, "The vicar is quicker, And thicker and slicker, And longer and stronger than you."* (*The Limerick*, Nos. 534–6.) A much older example of this kind of religious 'testifying,' or prayer-of-thanks, is given from about the 1690's in that wonderful but seldom-consulted folklore source, *Scotch Presbyterian Eloquence Display'd*, by Gilbert Crockat and John Monroe (ed. Rotterdam, 1738) p. 143–4, where 'One Mr. James Webster was admir'd lately ... for this Grace before Meat: *"Out of the boundless, bankless, brimless, bottomless, shoreless Ocean of thy Goodness, we are daily foddered, filled, feasted, fatted;"* and half an Hour's Discourse to the same Purpose.'

These discussions of the length and strength of the parson's peter are not actually insults, but something much closer to compliments or a sort of religious adoration in which the phallic priest substitutes for the phallic diety of former times. No other interpretation of the minister's penis which has been recognized 'eight times already' in the guessing-game by the women, or the parson who does it "neater, sweeter and more completer with less peter – " is conceivable. Compare the similar rush by society women and girls ('celebrity-fuckers') to seduce popular actors, singers and lecturers, Negro novelists and musicians, and the leaders of every crackpot cult.

Vance Randolph, who can invariably be counted on to have the best, the longest, and the most detailed story on almost any subject, collected from the inexhaustible wealth of the folklore of the Ozark hill-country, gives, in *Pissing in the Snow*, No. 50, as "The Call to Preach," a long tale, collected in Anderson, Missouri, in 1933, and stated to be old, about: *A plow-boy who has seen the letters PC in the sky, which "can't mean nothing only Preach Christ, so that's what I aim to do!" He 'was just a big country boy, all pecker and feet, the kind of a fellow that couldn't find his butt with both hands in broad daylight. Anybody could see he didn't know enough to pour piss out of a boot, with directions printed on the heel.' The local preacher assures him that he has "mistook the meaning of the sign. The letters PC mean Plow Corn, and I believe that's what you better do."* The story usually ends here (there is a Negro version of this kind from Texas, in J. Mason Brewer's *The Word on the Brazos*, 1953, p. 69), but Randolph's version gives the real or additional ending: *'So then the fellows at the tavern give him a lot more beer, and finally one of 'em says, "What makes you think you're called to be a preacher?" The country boy just grinned kind of foolish. "Well, I got the biggest prick in the neighborhood," says he, "and a terrible craving for fried chicken".'*

There is an obvious grading order – or, rather, degrading order – to which the mocking of sacerdotal personages generally adheres, one's own priests or ministers being less likely to be mocked than those of some other cult or sect closely related, while the priests of other religions (such as rabbis, when Christians are telling the jokes) are obviously fair game for anything. An ancient story is recorded in Robert Fabyan's *New Chronicles of England* (1516) as having happened in the year

A.D. 1259, when : *A Jew of Tewkesbury fell into a privy on a Saturday and refused to allow himself to be taken out for reverence of his Sabbath day. Not to be outdone in piety, the Earl of Gloucester, being told of this, refused to allow him to be taken out on Sunday, so that he might revere the Christian Sabbath as well. On Monday the Jew was found dead.* (Motif J1613, cited to Wesselski's *Mönchslatein*, No. 84, a collection of *exempla*; and Johannes Pauli's *Schimpf und Ernst*, ed. Bolte, No. 389, meaning that the story had long circulated as a joke.)

Ministers, vicars, beadles, and so forth have little protection from mockery in this way, and in fact the whole Protestant clergy is far less protected – by the tellers' own sense of fitness in modern times – than Catholic priests or prelates. Missionaries have the least protection of all, and the most directly mocking stories are still told of them, including, of course, going so far as to laugh at their martyrdom – in being cooked in great pots and eaten by cannibals – as is tirelessly shown in cartoons in all humor magazines in the West, without ever a thought of, or blush for the sacrilege or inhumanity involved.

The missionary's sexual transgressions – as for example, Father Damien's at Molokai – are as commonly discussed as were the Catholic priest's (politely the monk's or friar's) in jokes and *novelle* in Renaissance Italy. Only when Somerset Maugham's *Rain* (1932) was revamped from a story and play, into a movie, was it considered necessary to change the missionary, fallen into sin with the very same native girl he has been excoriating juicily, to an unspecified 'reformer' with black string necktie instead of a turned collar. The 'reformer' is obviously the lowest step down of all, and is the most enthusiastically hated and mocked cleric in jokes, usually as the drumbeating Salvation Army lecturer, male or female, or the non-combatant Y.M.C.A. crumpet-pusher and bandage-roller (*i.e.* homosexual) of World War I satire. On the American burlesque stage, which lasted until World War II, the 'reformer' was invariably shown lusting after the naked strip-teasers onstage, and sometimes marching offstage after their wriggling bottoms – or into a whorehouse marked with a large red light – singing the parody Salvation Army song, "*Reform! Reform! We shall reform the world!*" with his hands joined in prayer. Joe Mill's I.W.W. song, "Pie In the Sky," about 1920, also satirizes the 'long-haired reformer,' though not sexually; while G. B. Shaw's muscular evangelist in *Major Barbara* (1905), an ex-boxer who reforms the mockers by wrassling them to the ground and bashing their heads a bit, is essentially in this same line of humor. Like the travesty-song about the Salvation Army girl's tambourine, broken by a mocking lounger, and the *'kick she learned before she was saved!'*

The missionary's one real miraculous victory, on the style of Mark Twain's *Connecticut Yankee at King Arthur's Court* (1889) predicting the eclipse of the sun with an almanac, is a sort of *vagina dentata* story told backwards, that loses, by being somehow disgusting, what it gains in the way of a religious victory: *The lady missionary converts the whole Pacific Island tribe by answering the witch-doctor's juju spells, screaming, dancing, and chest-beating, by saying suddenly, "Can your god do THIS?!" And she reaches into her mouth with her thumb and yanks out her entire set of false teeth at once!* (*Histoires Coloniales*, 1935, p. 5. Motif K547.2, with wig and wooden leg too. See also 13.VI.3, "The Mechanical Man.")

The late Dr. Albert Schweitzer, who began as a Protestant clergyman, then continued as a music scholar specializing in Bach, and ended following in the steps of Father Damien among the lepers and silently trying to shame the West for its vile and inhuman treatment of the African Negroes by becoming a medical missionary there in 1913, is on all counts the closest we have produced to a *modern saint.* As such, he has attracted the hatred of certain perverse minds like that of the French surréalist Boris Vian, whose only real claim to fame was an imitation or parody American 'tough' murder-thriller, *I Shall Spit on Your Graves* (1947) – polite for 'Shit on Your Graves' – pretendedly written by a Southern Negro, the non-existent 'Vernon Sullivan.' As can be seen, Schweitzer's idea of re-habilitating the Negro was rather different from that of the *faux-révolté* Vian, who did his best to conshite Schweitzer's memory with a brief poem, "Le Docteur Schweitzer," beginning: *'Qu'il soit minuit, qu'il soit midi, Vous me faites chier, docteur Schweitzer.' (Whether it's midnight or noon, Dr. Schweitzer, you make me shit!)*

This is reproduced in broadside-ballad form, with pretended naïve illustrations, showing Schweitzer standing on the Cross, berating a supplicating Negro whose legs are cut off, and sitting on the back of a naked Negress with a ring in her nose, to play Bach on a cathedral organ (with his feet), in *Haut-le-Coeur*, published by Pauvert in Paris, 1965, the work of a satirical cartoonist calling himself 'Siné' – his real name is given in facsimile of his draft-card in other of his books. *Haute-le-Coeur* sets out to be, and brags prefatorily that it is 'odious, revolting, impolite, intolerable, insipid, vulgar, fecal and obscene.' Also 'repugnant, fetid, execrable, and inadmissible, and *not funny.*' It is clearly intended as a sort of high-point of lowness, and to be the most revolting and sadistic picture-book in the history of the world : a cross between the French magazine, *Hara-Kiri*, and a 'black humor' De Sade. But it does not succeed, and has only a clinical interest as a literary or sub-artistic exploitation of a compulsive private concentration on the grim humor of toilet-bowls (especially), cripples, blood, and the eroticized castrations of self-crucifixion and the like, in among the routine anti-clerical and anti-nun sick sex-caricatures. The matching 'black humor' cartoon books of Tomi Ungerer, the American children's-book artist [!] are really much closer to the ideal nauseating and per-verted quality that Siné is shooting at in *Haut-le-Coeur*, but has let slip and fall into the toilet-bowl instead. In any case, the anti-Schweitzer broadside or hate-valentine is the most care-fully worked-over item in his book.

It is tempting to believe that the whole thing – including the Vian poem – is simply derived from a shaggy-dog story (or the other way around) circulating at about the time of *Midnight, Dr. Schweitzer*, a decade before, a joke then heard often in both America and France. It is told with extreme pantomime. *The scene is Africa. The white trader is sitting jittering with his two enormous pistols, playing hot-jazz records on his battery phonograph. He calls his native boy, kicks him a few times in the balls, and sends him to get a twelve-year-old virgin for him to rape. After raping her, both front and back, he shoots her, and puts another jazz record on the phonograph. "Here!" he shouts to the native boy, "drag the body away and get me an-other." As he is raping the second little black girl, he hears the native drums start ominously in the forest: "Boom boom boom-ba-doom; boom boom boom-ba-doom!" "What are those drums?" he shouts, taking a shot of heroin with a hypodermic needle in his upper thigh. "I can't stand those fucking drums! Bring me the chief." The chief is brought; he shoots him in-stantly, and kicks the body down the stairs. Immediately the drums begin again, "Boom boom boom-ba-doom; boom boom boom-ba-doom, BOOM BOOM BOOM BOOM!!" "What are those drums?" he shouts, breaking all his jazz records over his knee.*

"They're mourning for the chief you just shot," the native boy tells him. *"Oh, my god, my god, I can't STAND it!"* shouts the white trader, *"what time is it, anyhow?" "It's midnight, Dr. Schweitzer."*

Stories of this species might be called the mad-dog anti-authoritarian attack, similar to dynamitard anarchism in politics, since not a soul for a moment believes these ugly exaggerations to be even close to true – but they repeat them! That is to say, they are not true of Dr. Schweitzer, though they are certainly true (and not even the half of it!) as to all the other white traders and slavers in Africa for five centuries, also in South and Central America, and the East Indies – and the Moslem slavers, as bad or worse. But no one is attacking *those* cruelties and profitable exploitations. Only the harmless, Bach-playing and medicine-dispensing Damien and Schweitzer, who shame us all. Emily Hahn, of the never-to-be-forgotten *Seductio ad Absurdum* (New York, 1930) – which she now omits from her list of published books, though it is her best – calmly describes an authentically sadistic white 'medical missionary' she lived with in the Congo, in her autobiographical *Times and Places* (1970) p. 138–60, but the worst he ever does, as she tells it, is to shave off his native-wives' hair ...

One observes also how closely the Boris Vian poem matches and follows the joke, if, in fact, it was not originally its source. A curious point as to 'Life imitating Art' : Vian's non-existent Negro thriller-writer, 'Vernon Sullivan,' has, as it were, come alive after Vian's death, and the formula of *I Shall Spit on Your Graves* is now being very successfully exploited and continued in books by the American Negro 'black humor' and murder-mystery novelist, Chester Himes, for immediate translation into French and publication for the delight of pasty-sick French intellectuals, critics, and other small trash who like to be thrilled by the presumed 'evil strength' – let us be frank, by the bad-ass *blackness* – of the imaginary Negro. So it is still midnight, Dr. Schweitzer.

Anti-clericalism is no longer the serious movement in France that it was in the 19th century, especially as to the anti-Jesuit attack, on the Revolutionary lead of D'Alembert and later Michelet and Edgar Quinet. Except in priest-ridden Belgium and Italy – Spain is still completely intimidated, nearly two centuries after Napoleon ended the Inquisition – anti-clericalism no longer forms part of the intellectual baggage of Europeans of any cultivation. Siné's caricatures of priests-making-love-to-nuns (or to themselves dressed as transvestist Jesuses on the Cross, etc.) are part of no movement, but merely a personal peculiarity or an anachronistic and mock-révolté attempt to milk a rather dried-out vein of humor. If *God is dead*, as Nietzsche would have it, there cannot be much fun left in making *pipi* in the holy water fount.

This type of thing has long since flickered out in America, to the degree that it ever existed at all. The title story of *The Evangelical Cockroach* (New York, 1929) by 'Jack Woodford', really Josiah Pitts Woolfolk, actually attacks the most famous Protestant evangelist of his time, the Reverend Billy Sunday, a former baseball player who found God, in a silly fantasy about a man in church urging a cockroach in a crack in the floor to go "To the right!" or some-such, matching the admonition of the preacher in the pulpit. Equally weak is a 1920's sexual scandal-song against the woman evangelist, "Aimee Semple McPherson" – whose recorded sermon, "COME to Jesus; Come, Come, COME!" must be heard to be believed. (The sex song about her is given in Ed Cray's *The Erotic Muse*, 1969, pp. 66 and 151–2.) As to sex and religious females, a recent anachronistic low-point is hit in Dave Sheridan's 'S. & M.' [sado-maso] comic-book, *Tales of the Leather Nun* (San Francisco, 1973). The beautiful young nun is shown naked and dominant dressed in only her coif and long leather gloves, with bullwhip in hand, on the title-page (reproduced by Mark James Estren's *History of Underground Comics*, San Francisco, 1974, p. 51).

In the best piece of writing by Philip Wylie, his autobiographical *Finnley Wren* in the 1930's, the later White Knight of the pro-Jungian defense and anti-Mom attack (in his *Generation of Vipers*) rises to a climax of smalltown anti-clericalism, on the H. L. Mencken or boob-baiting village atheist style, by having the young man caught out in sexual sin, who must kneel and pray with two officious co-religionists who beg him to be saved. He kneels with them indeed, but only to deliver unexpectedly 'a miracle of starch fermentation' – meaning a fart – telling them: "My answer, gentlemen, comes from deep within me." This is about at the level of anti-religious revolt of parodying hymn-titles, sometimes in an undertone while singing them in church, such as "*Onward, Christian Foreskins*" for "Onward, Christian Soldiers," and the like. An institutional psychiatrist in Boston told me in 1952 that being obliged to sit through church-services every Sunday owing to his position – obligatory chapel is thought to be good for institutionalized lunatics, and may very well be – he would go through the hymnbook parodying every single title sexually or scatologically. He supplied me a list of the titles parodied, but refused to divulge his parody-titles.

The attack, nowadays, is no longer on ministers and priests (or hymns), but directly on Jesus and Jehovah. 'God' is so commonly dysphemized in swear-words and phrases like *"God damn it (or you)!"* that the sacrilege or fear of the Ineffable Name is hardly any longer sensed. This is so old, in English at least, that the English soldiers were known as 'Goddoms' in France in the 16th century. It should be observed that *"Gottverdom!"* (with a guttural *hot-damn* gargling of the opening *G*) is at least as common a swear-word in modern Dutch, and possibly German, as in English. The fuller forms, implying some realization of the real meaning of such damnation, as *"God damn it to Hell!"* are not now used with any religious conviction, but rather for the further dysphemistic pleasure of saying the taboo word, *"Hell,"* as well. As recently as the 1930's – before radio broadcasting killed vaudeville and burlesque – it was common to find, in the theaters outside New York City, small signs backstage reading: *"The name of the Deity and the words HELL and DAMN are not to be used on this stage."*

In the antisemitic attack, *Jews Must Live,* by Samuel Roth, published by himself in New York in 1934 – a work of which most copies have been destroyed by Jewish booksellers – a strange joke or old legend is recorded from the author's autobiography, as having been told him by a rabbi on the boat that brought him from Russian Poland about 1910, to counteract the proselytizing of Christian missionaries operating among the immigrant refugees, who had given him a New Testament. According to this Jewish legend, which evidently draws its source from the Christian legend of Jesus being tempted by Satan (in *Matthew,* iv. 5–7) and set 'on a pinnacle of the temple,' with the challenge: "Cast thyself down," *Jesus was a mere juggler or magician who had somehow learned the Ineffable Name of God, which he wrote on a piece of parchment and put in his armpit, thus being able to fly in the air and perform other miracles, to the wonderment of the foolish Jews. The Head Rabbi, seeing this, wrote The Name on two pieces of parchment, and flew higher in the air than Jesus (Yoizel) and pissed on his head, and brought him crashing to earth. That is the true story, and is the reason why the Christians hate the Jews and try to kill them.* Obviously that is *not* the true story, but then what is to be said for the New Testament's sober recording of the original scene, in which Satan flies Jesus up to the 'pinnacle of the temple'? This is precisely in the style of the Levantine folktales of riding through the air on the backs of genies, or on magic carpets or flying horses (like Mohammed's own flight to Heaven and Hell on the winged mule, Buraq, as vouched for in the *Koran*, sura xvii), fallen away to the lesser status of admitted stories and fantasies in the *Arabian Nights*.

In the 17th century in France and England, when 'mocks' and burlesques of Greek and Roman legends of the gods and heroes became popular (on Italian models of the preceding century's burlesque 'academicians'), no one would have dreamt of retelling in the same crude terms, or as humor, the similar heroic and miraculous tales and sex stories of the Old and New Testaments. As I have shown further in *The Guilt of the Templars*, p. 10–12, a large body of anti-religious mocks had already existed for centuries, but these were always cast on the speaker's opponent, who was being accused in this way of sacrilege and atheism. To the extent that atheism did exist, as in Bonaventure Des Périers' *Cymbalum Mundi* (1537) and the English "School of Nights" perhaps derived from this, the statements made were deathly serious. The first crack in the dike of humor, as to religion, seems to have come in the 18th century, with the sardonicism attributed to the French poet, Alexis Piron, that he *'could see nothing in the Holy Family but a whore, a bastard, and a cuckold.'*

The wholesale mocking of the Bible and its legends did not take place until the height of the French rationalist and anti-clerical movement of the 19th century, in *La Bible Farce* of Pierre Malvezin (for which he went to jail in 1881), and *La Bible Amusante* (1882) of his successor, 'Léo Taxil,' both with the crudest possible illustrations as well. As to the New Testament, though the French works just mentioned did try to include this in their spoofing, no one ever attempted until the early 20th century to tell the story of Jesus Christ in the 'lower depths' sexual terms of Vargas Villa's novel, *Maria Magdalena*, in Spanish, in which, very briefly: *Mary Magdalen is a whore and Judas is her pimp. Jesus is a young preacher-reformer who gets Mary Magdalen to give up her immoral ways, leaving Judas without a meal-ticket, whereupon Judas turns Jesus in to the authorities as a dangerous radical and he is strung up.* Say what you will about it, there is no real sacrilege to this rewriting and it does give a story-line to Christian mythos that would make it possible to transpose it to the stage or sceen without the usual mock-pious, overbloated million-buck production approach of *Quo Vadis* or *The Sign of the Cross*, that is itself only another form of unconscious anti-religious sacrilege and mock. The more recent proto-hippie musical comedies on the New Testament story, such as *Jesus Christ Superstar* and *Godspell*, also *The Mexican*, are perhaps more sincere, but they will not compare for broadness and charm with the original Negro musical on the same themes in the early 1930's, *Green Pastures*, by Marc Connelly, based on Roark Bradford's *Ol' Man Adam an' His Chillun* (1928). The Danish pornographic approach to the character of Jesus has now been taken in Jens Joergen Thorsen's motion-picture, *The Faces of Christ* (1973), in which Jesus makes love like anyone else – apparently with Mary Magdalen. The news of this created a furore in Rome, where a bomb was exploded in the Danish embassy, etc. See the full story, as "Un Jésus trop viril," by Jean-Francis Held in the *Nouvel Observateur* (10 Sept. 1973) p. 46–7.

The joke has already been noted earlier in which: *'God has the blues. St. Peter suggests a trip to earth to pick up a nice Greek girl, possibly in the old swan suit. God says, "No. As long as I stuck to those Greek girls it was all right. But once I made the mistake of knocking up a Jewish girl, two thousand years ago, and I'll be damned if they're not still talking about it"'* (Baltimore, Md. 1955, from manuscript.) The sardonic touch of the self-'damning' of God is on the style of many comic bits of divine dialogue – never going quite this far, however – in Charles Erskine Scott Wood's satirical *Heavenly Discourse* (1927), a work inspired by the writings of Mark Twain, Wood's friend, especially Twain's bitter and pessimistic *The Mysterious Stranger* (1916) not published until after his death, and the hilarious *"Captain Stormfield's Visit to Heaven,"* one of Twain's funniest pieces, and the one coming closest to Ingersollian doubts about Heaven. Jehovah's abilities as Creator are impugned in a well-known anti-woman joke: *The architect (or Henry Ford) in Heaven complains that God did not construct woman properly: the ballroom is too close to the toilet, or the exhaust too close to the intake.* (1.142. *Kryptádia*, 1907, XI. 138.) Probably of Levantine origin, this was considered funny

five centuries ago as No. 13, "I Would Not Give a *Snap* For It,"
in Cornazano's *Proverbs in Jests* (before 1480; Liseux' translation, 1888), but without any anti-godlin reference.

It should be understood clearly that these are *not* jokes being
told by the members of one religion in mockery of another religion – that sort of joking has always existed and has always
had formal social support – but are told about the religion in
which the joke-tellers themselves, or their listeners, were raised.
As such, these are contraventions of very powerful taboos, or
residues of such taboos, in both tellers and listeners. That is the
secret of the violent and ugly images in such jokes, and of the
matchingly violent laughter (or violent rejection and anger)
that such jokes create. Not all of us enjoy seeing surréalist
beards affixed to and defiling that neo-Virgin, the "Mona Lisa,"
nor feel anything but repugnance on hearing would-be humorists attempt to shit on their own god, or at least on some
bearded stand-in at the gates of Heaven, like St. Peter, or Santa
Claus, or Dr. Schweitzer, under the very peculiar excuse that
such humor is 'sick' and therefore marvellously and specially
funny.

'Sick jokes' are essentially the real or *new scatology* of cultivated persons and their over-educated children in Western
society, who do not any longer get a sufficient charge out of the
mere word '*shit*' unless they can somehow apply it to motherhood, the flag, or to the gods in whom they really still believe,
and whom they cannot taunt and dirty without feeling the
advertised 'sick' thrill of outraging their own deepest impulses.
In the openly hostile style, the principal American sex-newspaper or 'pornzine,' *Screw* (August 18, 1969) No. 24: p. 17, gives
as winner in the editor's "Ball Busters" joke contest the following entry from Decatur, Illinois: *The town whore in Jerusalem
is being stoned. When Jesus says, "Let whoever is without sin
among you cast the first stone"* [John, viii. 7], *an old lady
struggles over with an enormous rock, drops it on the town
whore's head, 'and polished the bitch off. Jesus looked down
and said, "You know, Mother, sometimes you really piss me
off".'* The reference – somewhat hidden – is of course to the
Immaculate Conception of Mary, as free from 'Original Sin.'
(The Immaculate Conception does not refer, as many people
sincerely believe and contend, to Mary's becoming pregnant
with Jesus though still a virgin.) In another even more allusive
end-line, Jesus says instead, *"You Jewish mothers really piss me
off!"*

I avoid giving here, as lacking all elements of sexuality of a conscious kind, the many similar mocking jokes as to Jesus' reported miracles, raising the dead, walking on the water (*"So walk on the rocks, schmuck!"*) and so forth, now popular in America. Numerous stories of this kind, and others of similar anti-religious 'black humor' or 'sick humor' exploiting the Crucifixion and other elements of the Christian religious mythos for purposes of mockery and joking, are apparently translated from the American into French in Hervé Nègre's *Histoires Drôles* (Paris 1967), which is the largest modern joke collection in French, with the exception of Mina & André Guillois' *Notre Rire Quotidien* and *Métiers pour Rire* (1970), which concentrate on 'gag-man' jokes and other stuff of the kind that can be – and apparently is – endlessly clipped and filed from newspapers and cheap gag-magazines, in all countries.

It is notable that jokes really attacking God's authority in Western culture visibly point their attack against the almost forgotten father-god, Jehovah. (As with the preceding item about *'knocking up a Jewish girl two thousand years ago,'* twitting Jehovah for the sort of amours with which no one reproaches Jupiter.) This is true whether the persons telling the jokes are Christians or Jews. There is something very artificial about modern jokes gloating or vomiting in 'sick-joke' format on the Crucifixion of Jesus, or trying to milk ugly humor out of attacking the Virgin Mary or edifying little folk-legends of obviously ridiculous miracles in the New (and Old) Testament. The character of Jesus, as proposed by the Gospels, has in any case almost nothing in it either to interest, or to excite the hostility of normal men, being entirely one of submission to the father-figure – up to & including the final sacrifice on the Cross, presumably in obedience to Jehovah's wish – instead of virile or self-reliant revolt. When Christians pray to "Our Father which art in Heaven," they are certainly not praying to Jesus but to Jehovah. (*Matthew*, vi. 9–13, and *Luke*, xi. 2–4, omitting the vainglorious final line about the 'power and the glory.') The revolt, when it comes, whether in humor or otherwise, is therefore really against Jehovah. Jesus also has no ostensible sexual character – except in Denmark – and is altogether not much of a target for satire, whether sexual or simply Oedipal.

The following joke was told by a young Greek woman speaking almost perfect English, but as it has not yet been collected from any English source it may well be a modern Greek joke. *Two priests are out playing golf. The younger one misses an*

*easy putt and says, "Shit!" The older one berates him for this,
saying that if he continues to use profanity like that God will
certainly blast him with a thunderbolt. They keep playing and
the younger priest misses another putt, and again says, "Shit!"
The skies suddenly open; a thunderbolt flashes out, and strikes
the older priest dead. There is a pause, and the Heavenly Voice
is heard saying in accents of thunder, "*SHIT!*"* (N.Y. 1965) The
closest jokes to this that are well known in English replace God
with the 'still small voice' ill-representing the volcanic deity of
Mount Horeb-Sinai, in 1 *Kings* xix. 12, to the prophet Elijah,
which is assimilated by later Jewish lore to the 'inner voice' of
conscience, or 'agenbite of inwit.'

A recent joke tending toward the angry hopelessness to be
seen more clearly in the final chapter here, 15.VI.3, "All to
Shit," attacks God as captious and unfair: the jealous and
choleric Jehovah of the Old Testament. *A Jew who has a long
run of bad luck goes out into the woods and lifts his voice in
prayer and recrimination. "Oh God," he asks heaven tearfully,
"haven't I always been a good Jew? Haven't I always given
charity, even to those domn goyim? Didn't I bring up my
family decent? Never drink, swear, gamble; no bad women,
nothing! Why do you do this to me, God? Why, why??" A dark
cloud suddenly appears overhead, and a tremendous Voice replies: "*YOU PISS ME OFF!!*"* (N.Y. 1963.) Of this obvious farce-
revision of the Biblical legend of Job, two elaborate Oregon
versions are given under the title, "A Note on Two Versions of
A Catastrophe Joke," by Ralph M. Wirfs, in *Northwest Folklore*
(1967) II. 25–7, in forms rather close to the long and detailed
cumulative catastrophe, "The Debtor Letter," an American
obscœnum which has been studied by Dr. Alan Dundes.

Meanwhile, the minister or priest remains the whipping-boy
of choice for those humorists not quite daring to attack God.
Or to get any closer that some quiet mockery of St. Peter, the
first Pope or high-priest, at the gates of Heaven. (Motif
A661.0.1.2; and compare the older Charon at the Styx, and
Genesis, iii. 24, on the 'flaming sword' of Eden.) I have even
heard St. Peter referred to as 'the Celestial eunuch,' on the style
of a harem guardian: as is well known, angels and cherubs have
no sexual parts. Essentially, the St. Peter of folktales is God
in a comedy-beard.

Dr. Roger Abrahams, in his *Deep Down in the Jungle* (1964)
p. 180–97, has printed an extensive group of modern American

Negro anti-clerical and antigodlin jokes. This is the largest such group of folktales now actually in oral transmission in a single ethnic milieu, except for the Picardy anti-clerical stories, all sexual or scatological, anonymously presented by Henry Carnoy in *Kryptádia* (1907) XI. 132–336, the *locus classicus*. Dr. Abrahams gives several texts of the following story, p. 181–3, in which the protagonist is usually a preacher, or his preachment is mocked, and notes that this form derives from Motifs J1262.5 and Q21.1, about 'receiving hundredfold from God,' but with the same scatological end. *A little boy on a picnic strays away from his family, and suddenly realizes he is lost and night is falling. Becoming frightened after wandering aimlessly for some time, and shouting for his parents but receiving no answer, he kneels down and prays with uplifted hands. "Dear Lord," he says, "please help me to find my daddy and my mommy, and I'll always be a good boy, and I won't run away again, and I won't hit my little sister any more, honest I won't!" As he kneels praying, a bird flies over him and drops a load of shit into his outstretched palm. The little boy examines it and turns his eyes back to heaven. "Oh please, Lord," he begs, "don't hand me that shit. I really and truly am* LOST!" (Joe "Miller" Murray, *Smoker Stories*, Hollywood, 1942, a lightly expurgated version entitled "Little Willie Gets 'the Bird'!" – identical with 'the raspberry.') Here, directly expressed, one has the adult's true objection or complaint against God, spoken in the guise of a child (Type 1620, Motif K445, "The Emperor's Invisible Clothes"): *that God and religion are really just 'a crock of shit.'* And furthermore, that they cannot help us find our way when we are 'really and truly LOST!' (Variant French original in *Kryptádia*, 1886, III. 238.)

A word to end with. In a brief "Psychiatric Study of Jokes about Psychiatrists," by Warren Boroson, in *The Best of Fact* (New York, 1967) p. 416–26, Dr. Fredrick C. Redlich of the Yale Medical School is quoted concerning just such jokes, in an article dating from 1950 in the *American Journal of Orthopsychiatry*. Dr. Redlich found that anti-psychiatric jokes, such as those quoted by Mr. Boroson (and the even more panic-stricken portrayals of evil psychoanalysts in current fiction), present psychiatrists as 'brutal, licentious, weak, anxious and helpless ... aggressive, oversexed, and as abnormal as their patients.' But, he ends:

> From the psychiatrist's point of view, the increasing number of cartoons depicting and deriding psychiatry should be welcome ... Psychiatrists have gained a status of respect and authority which is reduced through the unmasking process of caricature ... Since it is no fun to debunk someone unless he has already been placed on some kind of pedestal, it is interesting to note that during the period when the number of cartoons poking fun at psychiatrists has been increasing, the number poking fun at ministers has been decreasing.

II. CURSING AND INSULTS

Profanity and scatological imprecations are seldom heard or seen in pure or absolute form, owing to the unconcealed need for a victim or recipient. When used absolutely, it is mostly in its violent *tone* and noise that profanity achieves its effect, and the words said are not really of great importance so long as they give the effect of being in abrogation of some social taboo. Thus, as described in the introduction to the present chapter, the pretended Italian swear-words, *'Pasta-fazúla!'* (meaning only: macaroni-and-beans), when pronounced with sufficient comic violence and gesticulations, can serve the purpose, for both speaker and listener, of an awful imprecation indeed. It is an axiom, too, that the violence of tone generally increases in swearing proportionally as the actually obscene content decreases, precisely as with the sadistic violence of popular fantasies in movies, fictional literature, and other entertainments, which increases proportionally as the undisguised sex is expurgated out.

One hears a great deal, and sees a great many references in print, concerning old-time cursing & swearing, but one almost never sees any examples. References are often made to swearing 'like a trooper', 'like a mule-skinner,' or 'like a fishwife' – whose abusive swearing is immemorially called 'Billingsgate,' after the market where the fishwives once assembled in London. But very few samples, if any, of the swearing of either troopers, mule-skinners (drivers), or fishwives can actually be found surviving in print. The modern equivalent of troopers – namely, soldiers – are nowadays often depicted as working the word *'fuck'* to death, in both World Wars I and II, and the same for Australians (with *'bloody'* for a back-up oath). This is surely the truth, but one can hardly believe that the famous old profanity was nothing more than that. Even the best books on the sub-ject, such as Ashley Montagu's *The Anatomy of Swearing* (1967), give a great deal of historical information but, again, almost no modern examples. This is on the style of Mark Twain's great sketch in his *Autobiography* (ed. Neider, New York, 1959) chap. 42, p. 214–17, which is also reprinted com-plete by Montagu, p. 231–4, about the champion swearers of the village of Duffield near Boston, which goes on for pages but not a single swear-word is ventured! The best materials on, and reactions to, Twain's own famous control 'of the art' are gathered in Franklin Meine's edition of Twain's "*1601*," but – no samples are given.

The situation is somewhat like that of the sea-chanteys, equally notorious for their profanity and obscenity, but as of the present date only one tiny pseudonymous booklet of these has been printed unexpurgated: *A Collection of Sea Songs and Ditties*, 'from the stores of Dave E. Jones' (U.S., about 1928: only copy known, Legman Collection, Kinsey Institute Library). The two best collections of American and British chanteys, by William M. Doerflinger and Stan Hugill, are ruthlessly expur-gated, but the 'Dave E. Jones' booklet fortunately supplements the publicly-issued chantey-collections of one or the other. Mr. Hugill has also entrusted me with all the song-texts expurgated from his *Shanties from the Seven Seas* (London, 1961, with matching phonograph recording), in the hope that I will be able to publish them later, as he was not. Except for the 'Dave E. Jones' volumelet and the Hugill manuscript supplement, the real sea-chanteys of the Iron Men and Wooden Ships would still be as impenetrable a secret as what Mark Twain said when he swore, and 'what Song the Syrens sang.' Leaving us what we have now – the songs of the Iron Ships and Wooden Men.

The peculiarity exists that sex is still far more taboo, in swearing, than the anti-religious or sacrilegious imprecations that the taboo was originally intended to prevent. You can hear a thousand '*damns*' (and '*shits*') a day in any large city, if your ears are attuned to them, but even the allusive sexuality of a phrase like '*son-of-a-bitch!*" is more commonly dropped to an undertone, while '*cock-sucker!*' and '*mother-fucker!*' are freely shouted only when men know they are alone and not overheard, or among Negro and other marginal groups. Scato-logy benefits from a certain liberty still not accorded to sex, and this all the more so in mildly expurgated forms, substituting minced terms such as *'stuff'* for 'shit' – "*Don't hand me that stuff!"* – and the like. (This is also the case in French, as for example *'appuyer,'* a euphemism meaning to fart, pressing hard in the pronunciation on the *'pue,'* to stink.) American journalists in World War II enjoyed wising-up the public to the almost-allowable sexual swearing of the armed forces' purposely satirical acrostic or acronymic expurgations: 'SNAFU' (Situation Normal – All Fucked Up), 'FUBAR' (Fucked Up Beyond All Recognition), 'JANFU' (Joint Army-Navy Fuck Up), and numerous others, none of which were actually used in ordinary speech except 'SNAFU.'

Swearing of this artificial or over-intellectual kind tends to be highly ornamental, which also greatly reduces its impact on the listener – who may then even find it 'angelic,' as cook Katy Leary found the profanity of Mark Twain. This is of course its purpose, as for example in the imprecational phrase, *"Shit, piss, and corruption!"* where one may suspect that the shit and piss are replacing Hell, the Devil, and Damnation, if not God. All the few hints that survive of the famous old-time swearing strongly suggest that it was ornate and florid to the degree where it could hardly be taken seriously at all, except for its sacrilegious jolt. The way in which such ornamental overlayerings rapidly lose their force is implied in the old story: *'A farmer with two lazy sons once ordered them to clean out the crapper-hole. They simply dug a new one and moved the shit-house a few feet over. One night the old man had a call* ['of nature'], *and ran out back along the wellworn path, falling into the pit. Up to his neck in shit, he began hollering* "Fire, fire!" *People came running, pulled him out, and cleaned him off; then asked why he yelled* "Fire!" *"Do you think anyone would come if I hollered 'Shit!'?" he asked.'* (D.C. 1952, from manuscript.) Fr. Sacchetti, who died in 1400, gives two polite versions of this in his *Novelle,* No. 184, of *a fool who rings the fire-bell to announce that he has won at chess;* and No. 102: *A butcher who cannot lift a hog's carcass to the hook shouts* "Help! Help!" *and people come running to help him, thinking he is being attacked by a wolf.* This is obviously both the source of the present joke, and derived from Aesop's "The Boy Who Cried Wolf."

I. CONTESTS-IN-INSULT

In the formalized Negro contests-in-insult called "The (Dirty) Dozens," the principal insults, as will be seen, are accusations of incest with the mother – an accusation to which the matrilocal family background of the American Negro male makes him particularly sensitive – and sexual or scatological insults against the mother, the parents or family generally, or the listener himself. The Dozens' contest is openly in the form of an ordeal: that person is considered to be beaten who 'can't take it,' and who is unable to respond to the verbal insults in even more insulting verbal style, but who becomes infuriated, runs out of his own stock of Dozens insults, and has recourse instead to violent physical acts. The same format exists as to white 'teasing' and 'kidding,' among adolescents and adults – *"Whatsamatter, can't ya take it?!"* – except that sexual and scatological insults were seldom used among whites (other than those concerning bastardy, homosexuality, or cuckoldry) until taken over recently from the Negro population. Even then, the insults used are likely to be floridly symbolized: *"Ya fodder's moustache!"* or *"Ya mudder's greasy old mop!"* rather than directly sexual in Dozens style, as: *"Ah g'wan, ya mudder takes Chinamen up on da roof!"* or *"Ya sister sucks mickeys!"* all of which are delivered – even among the cultivated classes – in exaggerated tough-kid or Hell's Kitchen accents of the *dese-dose-dem* variety. Note also the parallel French insult, of 19th-century origin apparently, *"Ta sœur!"* which carefully gives no details as to what the listener's sister is accused of, it being assumed that his imagination can do a better job than the speaker's.

For further discussion, see Dr. John Dollard's pioneering "The Dozens: Dialectic of Insult," in *American Imago* (1939) I. 3–24, and Dr. Roger Abrahams' *Deep Down in the Jungle* (Hatboro, Pa. 1964) p. 41–63, "The Element of Verbal Contest," with field-collected recitational texts of related type, p. 99–173, under the heading "The Toast." Dr. Abrahams' work, reprinted and much enlarged in 1970, is essentially the *locus classicus* on this subject, and makes unnecessary any extended further treatment here. I have added a few further historical notes, comparing the Dozens with the earlier Scottish 'flytings' and the elaborate Levantine sexual insults, in *The Horn Book* (1964) pp. 147 and 338; and in my Introduction, "On Sexual

Speech and Slang," to the *revised* volume I of John S. Farmer &
Wm. E. Henley's (*Dictionary of*) *Slang and Its Analogues*
(New Hyde Park, 1966) pp. xxxix–xl, and xlvi. See also the
First Series of the present work, chapter 2.VI.3, "Water Wit,"
which is now supplemented in the section immediately follow-
ing here; and 9.I.2, "Name-Calling." on matrimonial insults.

Levantine contests-in-insult are the oldest of which we have
record, as in the curious *repeated chapter* of the Bible, appearing identically as 2 *Kings*, xviii. 27, to xix. 37, and as *Isaiah*,
xxxvi–vii, in which the leaders of the defeated Judaeans say
to the messenger of the Assyrian king: *"Speak, I pray thee, to
thy servants in the Syrian language, for we understand it; and
talk not with us in the Jews' language in the ears of the people
that are on the wall." But Rabshakeh said unto them, "Hath my
master sent me to thy master, and to thee, to speak these
words? Hath he not sent me to the men which sit on the wall,
that they may eat their own dung, and drink their own piss
with you?"* ' Other examples of this type of scatophagous insult in the Bible are quoted in section 15.V.1; and certain of the
Biblical prophets, in particular *Jeremiah* and *Ezekiel*, pronounce almost nothing but long series of cruel insults and
curses, Jeremiah being more sadistic, Ezekiel more specially
sexual. But the point here is not the specific subject of the
insults, so much as it is the special form these take, of a contest or competition.

In this case the Judaeans had already been completely clob-
bered, and were in no position to answer Rabshakeh's taunts. In
other Biblical situations the competitive form is made prominent, as in the song of the women at the return of the young
David from the triumph over Goliath, in *1 Samuel*, xviii. 6–7,
where not only impossible exaggeration is the order of the day,
but the competition begins to include even the two champions
of the same side, David and King Saul: *'And it came to pass
... when David was returned from the slaughter of the
Philistines, that the women came out of all cities of Israel,
singing and dancing, to meet King Saul, with tabrets, with joy,
and with instruments of musick. And the women answered one
another* [n.b.] *as they played, and said, "Saul hath slain his
thousands – And David his ten thousands." And Saul was very
wroth ...* ' In commenting on this passage in his splendidly researched *The Power of Satire: Magic, Ritual, Art* (Princeton,
1960) p. 16–17, Prof. Robert C. Elliott has observed that it is the

women of the nation who are the flyting poets here, and refers also to the similar Song of the 'prophetess' Deborah, in *Judges*, v, celebrating the killing of the enemy general Sisera by the woman Jael (who has given him milk to drink beforehand, and is thus abrogating the law of hospitality), a story repeated in the *Apocrypha* as to Judith and Holofernes.

It would be presumptuous to attempt to redevelop here the materials on Greek, Arab, and Irish contests-in-insult presented by Prof. Elliott, pp. 3–48, and 70–84, along with similar materials as to the Greenland Eskimos, not overlooking the parallel to the American Negro "Dozens" and the Ashanti *"Apo"* ceremony from which these may be derived; as also the Italian insult-game *"la legge,"* on which Roger Vailland's novel, *The Law* (transl. New York, 1958) is based. Not all of these are competitive in nature, many involving simply Carnival-style periods or ceremonies of verbal release of repressed hostilities, of the sort allowed at all times to the Madman or Fool – also the 'Railer' or 'Malcontent,' of the type of Thersites in Shakespeare's *Troilus and Cressida*. (Elliott, p. 134–40.) The Levantine insult-contests of the most distant pre-Islamic period of which there is any sure record are among the most markedly social, rather than simply personal or recreational. As Prof. Elliott states:

> In early times the Arabian tribesmen periodically held formal contests in honor in which individuals, or sometimes entire tribes, competed in boasting and ridiculing and abusing each other. These were ritual occasions, and again the satires of the poets were probably thought to exert magical influence. In any event, the slanging matches often ended in murder and sometimes in tribal war.

See further on this matter Johan Huizinga, in his *Homo Ludens* (transl. London, 1949) p. 65–8, who makes the important point that the same court poet or priest who was expected to produce fulsome praise of the king or god was also expected, on demand, to curse and revile the enemy, whether human or divine, with as much art if not more. (Balaam, in *Numbers*, xxii–iv.) Says Huizinga: 'The nobleman ... may yet excel in a contest of words, that is to say, he may either himself praise the virtues [in himself] in which he wishes to excel his rivals, or have them praised for him by a poet or a herald. This boosting of one's own virtue as a form of contest slips over quite natur-

ally into contumely of one's adversary, and this in its turn becomes a contest in its own right. It is remarkable how large a
place these bragging and scoffing matches occupy in the most
diverse civilizations.'

One has here the origin of the otherwise almost inexplicable
contests and exercises in *mock-praise*, the burlesque eulogies in
Latin, as of fleas, lice, death and a quarten-ague, likewise Nero
and other human monsters, in the great *Amphitheatrum joco-
seriae* (1619) of Caspar Dornau, a treasure-house that has hardly
yet been tapped, except for plagiarisms of its eulogies of farting.
These nevertheless greatly modify the matter, from the frank
vituperation of the early Arab *higâ*-poetry of insult. Here the
insults are all operated by indirection, through the absurdity of
the overdone eulogies of what is actually only worth detesting
– a sort of practice for, or self-satire of, the same authors' fulsome dedications of their serious works to ignorant and repugnant kings and patrons. Of particular interest are the Irish
cursing-bards of the early Christian period in that island, discussed at length by Prof. Elliott, p. 18–47. These should also be
compared to the competitive 'gabs' and brags in the Scandinavian and later sources cited at Child Ballad 30, as to Roland
and Oliver's brags and those of other European knights, competing in honor of their respective kings and leaders with wild
lies and martial and sexual extravagances, all of which they
must later back up on the field of battle, in single combat, or
on the body of some woman – the beaten king's wife or his
virgin daughter by preference. Compare modern erotic bragging
poems like "Our Lil" and "Eskimo Nell."

Little is unfortunately known concerning the Scottish 'flytings' or contests-in-insult of late medieval times. It is apparent
that the literary survivals of these as a court entertainment, in
the late 16th century, are a formalization of the ancient challenging shouts, brags or 'gabs' with which warriors in all ages
and cultures have preceded the actual clash of arms, to intimidate the foe. These are still common among prize-fighters,
but nowadays *via* the press rather than directly to the opponent's face. The best materials on such brags are those
collected in the headnote to Child Ballad No. 30, "King Arthur
and King Cornwall," actually concerning the famous brags of
the knights of Charlemagne's court. The traditions of the court
of King Arthur and the Round Table are identical on this
matter. G. L. Kittredge, in the notes to Child Ballad No. 3, "The

False Knight" (I. 485), observes what is perhaps the deepest level of all in cursing and swearing bouts: their original use in driving away danger (animals, witches, storms), and exorcising devils by strictly verbal means. In one ancient example, a *crocodile* is read a long scroll adjuring it to go away.

It is in the Scottish tradition that the most extraordinary records of contests-in-insults come down to us. Though we have only the relatively late literary expressions of this, it is probably quite close to the reality of what such contests actually were, under the name of *'flytings'* (from the Anglo-Saxon *flitan*, to strive, to contend or quarrel), at the courts of the nobles and kings. Also, even earlier, as a preliminary to armed battle, whether by the champions themselves, or by regimental and court poets or *'skalds,'* apparently so-called from the same source as the Middle-English word 'scold,' which once also referred to specifically ribald speech and abuse. The earliest Scottish literary example is Sir Thomas Maitland's *"Satyr upon Sir Niel Laing*, who was a Priest, and one of the Pope's Knights, about the Time of the Reformation."* This is printed, along with the longer flyting that follows here, in James Watson's *A Choice Collection of Comic and Serious Scots Poems* (Edinburgh, 1706–11) II. 54, and it is their presence in this collection that made necessary its limitation to 'Private Circulation,' when reprinted in Glasgow, 1869, in an edition of only 165 copies:

Canker'd, Cursèd Creature, Crabbèd Corbit Kittle,
Buntin-ars'd, Buegle-back'd, Bodied like a Beetle;
Sarie Shitten, Shell-padock, ill-shapen Shit,
Kid-bearded Gennet, all alike great:
Fiddle-douped, Flindrikin, Fart of a Man.
Wa worth thee, Wanwordie, Wanshapen Wran.

(A Scottish glossary cannot be undertaken here. However, 'doup' means arse; 'gennet' or *jennet*, a small horse; 'sarie,' sorry or contemptible; 'padock,' a toad.) It seems unlikely that this is the totality of Maitland's "Satyr upon Sir Niel Laing," but that is all we have of it in Watson. Some idea of the real length of the real such flytings may be gained from the *"Great Flyting betwixt Polwart and Montgomery,"* also printed in Watson's collection, III. 1–32, though it had been first printed in 1621, and was referred to in King James VI's *Essayes of a Prentise in the Divine Art of Poesie* (1584). The date of composition was probably about 1580. This was strictly a good-

humored literary entertainment or contest – neither of the
assailants being actually angry at the other – that was doubtless
recited before King James, presumably extemporaneously, or so
pretended. The two disputants were Capt. Alexander Montgomery, poet-laureate to the Scottish court, and Sir Patrick
Hume of Polwarth, who was surely considered the winner since
the "Flyting" ends with three long slices of billingsgate flung
by him at Montgomery, who does not answer.

They begin quietly enough, with the standard invitation (still
today) 'Come kiss my Erse,' which Polwarth tops as 'Compear
upon thy Knee and kisse my foul Foundation.' Montgomery
proceeds, p. 5 :

> Yet wanshapen Shit thou shupe such a Sunzie,
> As proud as you prunzie your Pens shal be plucked,
> Come kiss where I cukied and change me that Cunzie,
> Your Gryzes Grunzie is graceless and gowked.

You can look up all the terms in a Scottish dictionary if you
like, but the essence of the thing is as much the torrent of words
as their precise meaning. After long discussions of each other's
genealogies – Polwarth says 'Montgomery' is to be derived from
'Mount Gomorrah' – accusations of relations with witches, and
long cursings with every possible disease in the world (and
more), all in varied headlong and stamping rhythms, Polwarth
ends in a long passage of strange triple inner-rhyme, p. 29–32 :

> Fond Fliter, shit Shiter, Bacon Byter, all defil'd,
> Blunt-bleitar, Paddock-pricker, Pudding-eater perverse,
> Hen-plucker, Closet-mucker, House-cocker very vild,
> Tany Chieks, thou speaks with thy Breiks, foul Erse . . .

> Land-louper, light Skouper, ragged Rouper like a Raven,
> Halland-shaker, Draught-raker, Bannock-baiker, all beshitten,
> Craig-in-Peril, toom Barrel, quit the Quarrel, or be shaven,
> Rud Ratler, common Tratler, poor Pratler, out-flitten . . .

> Lean Limmer, steal Grimmer, I shall skimer i' thy Mouth.
> Fly'd fool, made Mule, die with Dool, on an Aik,
> Knave kend, Christ send, ill End, on thee now.
> Pudden Wright, out of Sight, thou's be dight, like a Draik.
> Jock-blunt, thrawn Frunt, kiss the Cunt of the Cow.

Purs-peiler, Hen-stealer, Cat-killer, now I quel thee,
Rubiator, Fornicator by Nature, foul befal thee.
Tyke-sticker, poison'd Viccar, Pot-licker, I mon pay thee.
Jock blunt, dead Runt, I shall punt while I slay thee . . .

Taken in full – all *thirty-two pages* of it – "The Flyting be-twixt Polwarth and Montgomery" is the most remarkable *tour de force* in Scottish and in all Anglo-Saxon literature down to the present day, and there is nothing to compare with it ex-cept some passages in James Joyce's *Ulysses*. Joyce's headlong uncontrol is, in any case, much inferior to the perfect poetic control of the Scottish bards, putting their linguistic battle-horses through every pace and metre with perfect seat and hand, though the subject-matter be riotously violent and ob-scene: The War of the Words. Compare the modern form of these exercises in insulting obscenity in the war-song "King Farouk," by the modern Scottish bard, Hamish Henderson, courageously published in his *Ballads of World War II* (Glas-gow, 1947).

A century later, flights of language of this kind were still being used in Scotland, rather for religious praise than for the mock-battle of flytings, as in the alliterative Grace before Meat already quoted from *Scotch Presbyterian Eloquence* (1690's; ed. 1738, p. 143–4), as to being 'daily foddered, filled, feasted, fatted,' etc.; and the modern young widow's mock testimony to the travelling preacher for doing it 'sweeter, completer, and with less peter' than any other preacher she ever met. As can be seen, the simple tricks of alliteration and assonance are about all that is left of the older Scottish poetic *maestria*. I have even collected such an item as a graffito: *'Tim Tickled Tillie's Tits Till Tillie's Twichet Twiddled Tremulously!!'* (N.Y. 1938; also recorded earlier with all the words written to the right of one long and large capital *T*.)

Newbern & Rodebaugh, in their *World's Dirtiest Jokes* (1969) p. 214, have a similar item set up as a joke: *Two ladies con-ducting a school-survey ring a doorbell which is answered by a man who has been taking a shower and who is covering himself with only a newspaper: he tells them that he is "Peter Pepper-pod; wife Pauline; sons Paul and Peter, Jr., both in your school. I am a peanut packer for Planter's Peanuts and poke around in part-time party planning on the side." Later one of the ladies goes to the toilet at the first filling-station they pass, and does not return for fifteen minutes. She explains to the other: "I just sat there and got to thinking about that personable Mr. Peter Pepperpod, the peanut packer for Planter's Peanuts and part-time party planner, standing there with his pert, petrified pivot poking through the paper, and it just made my pussy pucker with such peccability that I couldn't hardly precipitate!"* Observe the contest element here, in topping and enlarging the man's tongue-twister statement on the same letter of the alphabet on which he has, as it were, cast down his challenge. Note also the relationship to the game of *"I Love My Love with an 'A'."* (Because his name is *Arthur*, he eats *apples*, &c.) Peter Piper's pickled peppers have come a long way.

2. THE DOZENS

It is in the Negro community and among children that the contest-in-insult still continues in the English-speaking world, with particular concentration among children on the necessity of rhyme, as in the nursery-rhyme taunt on "Peter Peter, Punkin-eater," an allusion which also occurs in the second line of Polwart's flyting quoted above. Dr. Martha Wolfenstein asks, in *Children's Humor* (1954) p. 182:

> What is the function of rhymes in these joking attacks? I would suggest that the first rhyming word has the effect of compelling the utterance of the second, thus reducing the speaker's responsibility ... There is a further reduction of responsibility in the use of a rhymed formula: the words are not my own. Moreover the rhyme is apt to induce other children to take it up; the attacker will cease to be alone. It should be added that rhymes are often in themselves funny to young children. Children of three, for instance, may laugh simply at finding two words that rhyme, or a word that rhymes with a name [n.b.]. Thus the rhyme affords a façade of harmless joking to facilitate the expression of hostility in the rhymed insults.

The Negro "Dozens" are perhaps strictly of African origin, but to the degree that they bother with rhyme, assonance, etc., in English, they have assimilated themselves to the Scottish and ancient Anglo-Saxon tradition of alliterative rhyme (front-rhyme rather than end-rhyme). Modern Negro contests-in-insult, taking place in English, seem particularly to favor rhyme when used as 'toppers' or when the insults concern the *mother* of the person attacked. These are also the most taboo and most powerful insults, and those most deeply resented and most likely to be answered, either with matching insults or with physical violence. According to the informal rules of 'playing the Dozens,' as already noted, the person who loses his temper ('blows his cool' or his 'stack') over the verbal insults heaped on him or on his family, and who either cannot answer in kind, or who is driven to physical violence as a response, is considered to have lost the game: the magic of his adversary's words having either silenced him or set him beside himself with uncontrolled anger. Young Negroes who are conscious that they are likely to lose their tempers often curtly tell others, who begin 'playing' them, *"Man, I don't play that shit. Don't put me in the dozens."* Sometimes adding threats that they will certainly answer with violence or knife-play. *"The on'y dozens I know is THIS!"* I heard one youth say, on a Harlem side-street, whipping out a switch-blade knife and flashing it rapidly right and left (twelve times?) while counting as though cutting throats. (N.Y. 1938.)

Dr. Roger Abrahams, in *Deep Down in the Jungle* (1964) p. 47, quotes one young Negro informant as to how this works out, in the billiard parlors of South Philadelphia, in competitive rhymes. Observe the enormous freight of 'free-floating aggression,' and the immediate violent retort:

> Just like mounting on the wrong guys down at the pool room. Cats be coming in there, gambling. Suddenly one them says, "Suck my ass." He say, "You suck my ass and the box, that way you can't miss my asshole." Cat says, "Sucking ass is out of style, Button your lipper, suck my dick awhile." He said, "Sucking dicks ain't no trick. Button your motherfucking mouth up my asshole, nuts and dick." [*Note rhymes.*] Anything. Just one's trying to get above another one, each time they say something, you know ...

Playing the Dozens often involves insulting in rhymed couplets:

> *I hate to talk about your mother, she's a good old soul,*
> *She got a ten-ton pussy and a rubber asshole.*
> *She got hair on her pussy that sweep the floor,*
> *She got knobs on her titties that open the door.*

Materials similar to those presented by Dr. Abrahams are also collected in a very valuable dissertation by Dr. William R.

Ferris, *Black Folklore from the Mississippi Delta* (University of Pennsylvania, 1969), as found among Negro adolescents and adults in Mississippi, where few whites have ever before successfully collected Negro folklore. "Dozens" rhymes and similar formula materials are given at p. 161–83, but even more interesting is the record of a blues session, p. 362–8, in which two male singers 'began competing with highly obscene verses which are apparently not used in the presence of women and children.' The two singers alternated stanzas until one finally gave up, beginning to use stereotyped lines that would fit in any blues; then handing over the accompanying guitar to the other, who sang four more verses before stopping, to indicate his triumph. Certain of the stanzas use elements seen in avowed "Dozens" such as the one quoted just above, while the victorious singer ends with his most erotic stanza in a way showing that the real competition – though not directed *at* the opponent, in the way of insults – was to see who could be the most erotic or obscene, and also who could do so longest. This is likewise the case with the violently dysphemistic Negro jazz songs, "Shave 'em Dry" and "The Mother-Fuckers' (or Bull-Dykers') Ball," very infrequently heard. An unpublished tape-recording exists of "Shave 'em Dry," sung by a woman.

In *Deep Down in the Jungle* (1964) p. 55–6, Dr. Abrahams has listed some of the literature on the Dozens in America, in particular Dr. John Dollard's pioneering article, "The Dozens: The Dialectic of Insult," in *American Imago* (1939) I.3–24; also noting that it has been traced to the 'joking relationships' among African Negroes. The connection here with the Dozens was apparently first observed by William Elton in *American Speech* (1950) XXV. 148–9, 230–33. A whole controversy has developed in recent years, mostly on trying to deny the African origins of the Dozens. I have found this controversy very narrow and uninformative, nor can I understand how it can seriously be held that the Negro slaves brought with them from Africa both their folktales and their music, but left all their folk-customs behind. The theory is that the Dozens were really picked up in America, a theory of which the strongest piece of evidence is the name itself, which has nothing to do with a *dozen* (as meaning twelve objects or actions), but comes from the Anglo-Scottish term 'to dozen,' meaning to stun or stupefy, still surviving in 'bull-dozer.'

It is obvious, of course, that the actual phraseologies used in the Dozens have been signally influenced by the Anglo-Scottish traditions of the American South, both in the 'flyting' format and in the so-called erotic 'toasts,' which latter also still survive floridly in Scotland. (See the end of the following section, "Water Wit.") But nothing comparable to the competitive singing or rhyming of "Dirty Dozens" insults exists today anywhere in the English-language tradition except among Negroes, *or has ever in living memory been recorded among whites.* The closest would be some derivative Calypso-style competitions in the West Indies – also collected by Dr. Abrahams – which are certainly of Negro origin. This leads us directly to Africa. (See Donald C. Simmons' brief note on "Possible West African Sources for the American Negro 'Dozens'," in *Journal of American Folklore*, 1963, vol. 76: p. 339-40.) The same is true of the "Signifying Monkey" recitations among American Negroes today, with their burlesque combats between elephants and lions, of which, again, Dr. Abrahams has given us the most extraordinary texts ever recorded. The closest African congener of the "Dozens" is the *Apo* ceremony of insults among the Ashanti, discussed in Robert C. Elliott's *The Power of Satire* (1960) p. 76-80.

What would be desirable, at this point, to make possible a solution of this question of African origins, would be a body of transcribed and translated African texts collected from sessions expressive of 'joking relationships,' in which one might seek – or admit one cannot find – parallels to the inherent matter of the American Negro "Dozens," while cancelling out mere formal differences such as might arise from contamination in America with white children's rhyme formulas, survivals of the Scottish flytings and brags, etc. Unfortunately, such a body of translated African texts is not easy to find. The subject was first brought to anthropological attention, so far as Africa is concerned – other than in R. S. Rattray's *Ashanti* (1923) page 151 – in E. E. Evans-Pritchard's "Some Collective Expressions of Obscenity in Africa," in the *Journal of the Royal Anthropological Institute of Great Britain* (1929) vol. 59: p. 311-31. But this article has been almost entirely overlooked in the controversy then begun by A. R. Radcliffe-Brown's "On Joking Relationships," in *Africa* (1940) XIII. 195-210, with a further note in 1949, XIX. 133-40. There is a long excogitational article on the matter by Dr. Mary Douglas, "The Social Control of Cognition: Some Factors in Joke Perception," in *Man: The*

Journal of the Royal Anthropological Institute (1968) III. 361–76, citing and discussing the entire literature with the exception of Evans-Pritchard's article which opened the field to discussion. This seems to me rather unfair, when one considers that both his article and that of Dr. Douglas appear in the same learned journal, admittedly forty years apart.

In any case, and I do not think I am going too far in maintaining this, the whole phraseological constructivism of the conceptualizations – of a formalistic nature – which are extruded, or shall I say obtruded, upon the hapless African jokesters by these anthropological stylists and belly-button fluff-pickers adds up to a type of university-professor jargonesque prose, or highfalutin imitation 'Nigger-talk,' which I find terribly difficult to read and even harder to understand, so I shall say no more about it. I would recommend to its authors the *last page* of Thorstein Veblen's *The Theory of the Leisure Class* (1899), which has something highly meaningful to say to them. (They also, naturally, do not give any of the 'obscene' texts.)

Dr. Mary Douglas, in particular, is not always quite so abstruse in circling chastely about these scatologica. There is quite a racy piece by her in the B.B.C.'s popular magazine, *The Listener* (London, 3 Sept. 1970) p. 311–12, raking over the coals the competing French school of anthropologist Lévi-Strauss for some new type of anthropological fortune-telling, which is apparently wholly erroneous, if not actually eccentric, as to the epistemological repercussions of its structuralization of conceptualism – no, wait a minute, it was conceptualization of structuralism; or wait, no – well, read it and find out. At least it did manage to work a graph into the B.B.C.'s newly-liberated pages involving the conceptualization of farting, menstruation, and other unrelated obscoena. *"I guess every little bit helps,"* as the old lady said when she pissht in the sea.

One gratifying aspect of the whole imbroglio is that they are now getting graphs back into the humanities. I think Kenneth Burke should be credited with that. It looked for a while as if parsing folklore and numerologizing anthropology was out for the count, the way – of all people – Leon Trotsky, in *Literature and Revolution* (in 1925) kicked the shit out of the 'Formalist' school. A school rising to some kind of climax in the new idol of American folklore study, Vladimir Propp's *Morphology of the Folktale* (Leningrad, 1928), which translates "Goldilocks and the Three Bears" for the coming IBM machines, thus:

$$'b^2g^2z^1\hat{e}^3d^2th^3A^1(C[D^1E^1\text{neg.}]^3[D^1E^1\text{neg.}]\ F\text{-contr.})H^1\!-\!I^1K^4.'$$

(And I had to leave out half so as not to drive the typesetter insane.) One wonders whether a shorthand translation system for folktales is really worthwhile, that must be paid for at so suicidal an exchange-rate. Dragons unreconstructibly named *z* (for *zeta*), lunches named *d*, woodshavings named *Ê* (no kidding), and kidnapped heroines completely forgotten about, though Hollerith-hole-space was left for them on the machine as *a* – instead of 'Snegourochka' or even 'Elsie Pennypacker,' as in that *echt*-American folk-exposé of ruthless capitalism, *Over the Hill to the Poorhouse*, with its deathless line given to Rudolph Rassendale (z^6): *"Once aboard the lugger, and the gal is MINE!"*

The disadvantage anyone can see immediately in Professor Propp's system is that you can't tell where the 'double-villainy,' or whatever it is, comes in. Not when his scheduled villainies in the English translation, p. 130–1, only run from a piddling A^1 (kidnapping), through A^{17} ('the threat of cannibalism among relatives': so how often does that come up?), to A^{19} ('declaration of war'). Why, I can think of dozens of A^1 villainies this doesn't even mention, that turn up in one Russian fairy-tale or American folk-phrase after another. What about the 'kangaroo court' crime of *mopery* (A^{20}: 'exposing one's private parts to a blind female beggar on a public thoroughfare')? What about *gnorphism* (A^{21}: 'biting the fly-buttons off an armless Croatian dwarf')? Hundreds of stories – *thousands* of stories – are about gnorphism. It's one of our most popular villainies. Is it right that it should be left out? (Motif G303.16.19.3.3.1, Thompson system.)

What about the deathless World War I folk-proverb or simile on *black buggetry* (A^{69}: *'as black as Jack Johnson and two Carmelite nuns in a grave at midnight'*)? What kind of an anti-Negro system is it, that has no provision for run-of-the-mill villainies like these? What good is a system, anyhow, where you can't tell the dragons (named z) from the villainies (A^1)? And why 'z,' by the way? Is that some sneaky way of implying that the poor dragon is the enemy – that he's on the other side: the antihuman arse-end? *Idy v kibini matri!* (Russian for 'Heaven forbid!') *Why* is he the enemy? Like Charles Manson, and chemist Albert Hofmann (inventor of LSD), he's just Doing His Thing. What kind of folktale would you *have* without a dragon? All lunch-boxes and oxes? *Pfui!* on such a folktale! *Pfui!* on such a 'Morphology'! Hoo-hah! Mark my word, *Tovarich*, that dragon is a Victim of the Dirty Capitalistic System – just like you and me! He could be re-educated. He could be Saved. Which is more than can be said for the systems of Comrades Propp, Burke, Lévi-Strauss, Douglas, *e tutti quanti*. The arrow facing downward and backward at the end of Propp's sinister comedy-schema signifies the word 'Return.' Let us return. That way madness lies – and not anything but the promised control and manipulation of us, and the little bit of folktale that is left us, by ice-cold mechanical tools and machine-tenders. Please! *"Human being: Do not fold, spindle, or mutilate!"* Phrased more formalistically, we are simply being led up Shit Crick, into darkness not light, by these vapid verbalistic entertainments as to whether man constructs structurally or epistemologically, and woman conceives conceptually or holistically. (Or the reverse.) It is a very sad thing.

I trust I will not be suspected of attempting to keep the internecine verbal slaughter going in the halls of academe, or on the green hills of Africa, if I mention that there is nothing specially African about the type of erotic, incestuous, and scatological insults used both in African 'joking relationships,' it appears, and in the American Negro "Dozens," the Scottish flytings, and the rest. It might be helpful to draw attention to an important, but apparently already-forgotten article which, in a sense, tells the real secret of the Dozens, and demonstrates one of the original layers of magical taboo involved. This is "The *Poele* (Gross Insult) among the Mono People, Western Solomon Islands," the last of three articles on the sexual tales and folklore of this South Pacific island people, by Gerald Camden Wheeler, published in Krauss' yearbook of sexual ethnology, *Anthropophytéia* (Leipzig, 1912–13) vols. IX, and X. 310–14.

The *Poele* insults of the Mono people of the Western Solomon Islands, in the South Pacific, involve heavily structured formalizations of the social obloquy created by verbal insult (they've got *me* doing it now!) in a way going far beyond the mere contest-in-insult or 'tit-for-tat' format of the Dozens. The Pacific insults are, however, almost identical with the Dozens in their actual content, concentrating heavily on incest and scatology, or both combined, as in the round dozen of examples given by Dr. Wheeler in pudicitous Latin equivalents; *"Cum mulieris tuæ stercore (de more) cois,"* and *"Matris stercus (de more) es."* If such an insult as these, which form the *Poele,* or 'gross insult,'

> is uttered against a person, this person and certain of his or her kinsfolk are thereby injured; in general there is a compensation made through a payment by the utterer to the person against whom the *poele* was uttered *and by the latter to his injured kinsfolk.* Its peculiarity, therefore, is that while the actual sufferer has to be compensated by the utterer, yet this same sufferer is put in the position of having injured certain of his own kinsfolk and has to compensate them, though he is not only innocent of any action against them, but further is himself injured by the very action which is made the grounds of his paying a penalty. [*Italics supplied.*]

What Dr. Wheeler is doing here is perhaps the most common fault in anthropology : he is taking the 'outsider' position and is logicking things out according to his own cultural point of view, instead of really trying to understand the cultural point of view he is studying. What he does not see, and what is hidden in his statement that the sufferer of the insult is 'innocent of any action' against his own kinsfolk – evidently the persons named in the *poele* insult, as well as others – is that the sufferer is not innocent of at least one sin, the sin of omission. He has omitted to kill on the spot the person insulting him and his family, thus wiping out the insult in blood, instead of in the substitutive monetary mulct. What he is being punished for is cowardice. For, essentially, his omitting to take decisive revenge is far more insulting to his family than any verbal insult an outsider might choose to fling. It not only proves that the family contains craven 'sufferers,' but also implies that the 'sufferer' has tacitly agreed that the insult is true! This is clearly the implied challenge or meaning of the Dozens too, with the difference that the Dozens (as also the Scottish 'flyting') allow the sufferer of the insult to wipe this out immediately by heaping an even more obscene insult of the same kind – or a rhyming, 'jiving' super-insult – on the first speaker, and on the members of his family as well.

Owen Wister's *The Virginian* (1902), with his famous insistence that a *smile* must accompany the jesting insult 'son-of-a-

bitch,' to prove that it really *is* only jesting, tells us a good deal
– in that smile – as to the formalization of insults and insulting
among the descendants of the Scotch-Irish immigrants in backwoods America, still very 'tetchy' on the point of personal and
family and even local honor. (As burlesqued in the character of
the elderly gentleman in the Ozark joke, already given, who
bridles at what seems to him an insult to the Ozarks on the
part of the 'furriner' who is astonished to see him sitting on a
rail-fence masturbating.)

In a rare American humorous miscellany of wholly erotic
contents, *The Book of a Thousand Laughs*, 'by O. U. Schwein-
ickle,' issued secretly, probably by a job-printer in Wheeling,
West Virginia, about 1928, and including "Frau Wirtin" verses
and "Baron Mikosch" anecdotes in Pennsylvania Dutch, there
is a crossing of rhymed 'toasts,' p. 61, between the Congress-
men from Maine and Iowa, when the first offers (*Anecdota*,
2:87):

> Here's to the American Eagle, that beautiful bird of prey:
> He flies from Maine to Mexico, and he shits on Ioway.

To which the Congressman from Iowa replies:

> Here's to the State of Iowa, whose soil is soft and rich.
> We need no turd from your beautiful bird, you red-headed
>   son of a bitch.

(History does not record whether he *smiled*.) An encounter
almost as desperate is recorded in "The Rival Toasts," in *The
Pearl* [London: Lazenby], July 1879, No. 1 – just preceding the
first batch of limericks:

> An English and an American vessel of war being in port
> together, Captain Balls, of the former, invited the officers of
> the Yankee frigate to dine on board of his ship, but stipulated,
> in order to avoid any unpleasantness, that no offensive or
> personal toasts should be proposed, to which the Americans
> cheerfully assented. However, after dinner, during dessert,
> when the conversation happened to turn warmly upon the
> respective merits of the two nations, a Yankee officer sud-
> denly stood up, and said he wished to propose a toast, which
> he should take as a personal offence if any one refused to
> drink it.
> Captain B. mildly expressed a hope that it was nothing

offensive, but consented to drink to whatever it might be, with the proviso that, if he thought to do so, he should propose another afterwards.

Then shouted the American, exultingly: *"Here's to the glorious American flag: Stars to enlighten all nations, and Stripes to flog them."*

Captain B. drained a bumper to the American's toast; then turning to the old ship's steward, standing behind his chair, said quietly, "You can beat that, can't you, Jack?"

"Aye! Aye! Sir! If you fill me a stiff 'un."

The Captain mixed him a good swig of hot and strong. Then handing the steward the glass, he thundered out: "Silence for Jack's toast, and any gentlemen here present refusing to drink to it, I shall not take it as a personal offence, but at once order the gunner's mate to give him three dozen [lashes]. Now then, Jack."

Jack, with a grim smile, and bowing to the Yankee officer, said: *"Then here's to the ramping, roaring, British Lion, who shits on the stars, and wipes his arse on the stripes!"*

Of particular interest here is, of course, the character of Jack, the specially profane old sailor, now retired or advanced to the status of steward, where he serves as insult-champion to the Captain's floating domain, as in the great flyting of Polwart and Montgomcry before the Scottish king three centuries' before, and unknown bards and skalds even earlier, ready to answer any insult to their clan with word and sword. Note well that it is just the groups that are specially 'tetchy' to such insults, who formalize and make an ambivalent entertainment of them – and of replying in kind.

Finally, there are the contests-in-insult where the insults are not verbal at all but purely signs and gestures. The *locus classicus* on this matter is Rabelais' *Pantagruel* (1533) Bk. II, chap. 19, 'How Panurge Put to a Non-plus the Englishman, that Argued by Signs," and in other chapters, as has already been discussed earlier. Panurge naturally does not forget to use all the 'obscene' signs, and I can testify that many more of these still exist than might be imagined, especially in the Italian tradition. I was once collecting gestures from a middle-aged Italian woman on the deck of a ship that was taking us to America in 1963, to pass the time, when the Italian men playing checkers on the other side of the deck sent a boy over to ask

her *"Please to stop making those dirty signs!"* The standard
sign of the horns of cuckoldry, with the index and smallest
finger facing or jabbing downwards, to ward off devils or 'bad
luck,' seemed to be the gesture that specially upset them. In
existing jokes, the usual form of the gestural contest is nowadays on anti-religious themes, though still often bawdy enough
(Tale Types 924 and 924A–B; Motifs H607.1–2, and J1804.)
Numerous gesture-jokes will be found in the First Series, chapter 2.V.3, "Mutes, Stutterers, Idiots," usually on the courtroom
situation, all this being an elaborate set-up to explain the necessity for using gestures.

The ultimate insult or defiance, connected with the gesture
of displaying the buttocks (as to the Devil of Papefiguière), or
inviting the other person to kiss the buttocks, will be considered further in the section immediately following. One such
joke is set specifically as a contest: *Two women living in tene-
ments opposite each other's windows have an argument, and
one pulls up her skirt and shoves her behind out the window,
saying "Well, you can kiss my ass!" The other woman does the
same, replying "Well, you can kiss mine, and clean it with your
tongue!" The two of them then stay there for several hours,
with their arses out the windows, six flights up, neither being
willing to withdraw first and imply that the other has won the
victory. One of the husbands comes home, wants his lunch,
and convinces his wife that she should let him replace her in
the window with his pants down, while she prepares the meal,
and that the other woman will never know, since her back is
turned. The second husband then comes home, is told what
has happened, and casts a glance at the window. "Don't worry,
sweetheart," he tell his wife, "she'll be giving up any minute
now. I can see her guts hanging down a foot already."* (N.Y.
1938.) Earlier in *Anecdota Americana* II, No. 26, illustrated,
showing the first husband's testicles drooping out the window.
Compare Tale Type 115, mostly East European: *'The hungry
fox waits in vain for the horse's scrotum (lips) to fall off.'*

3. WATER-WIT (II.)

Many more insults, and jokes turning on insults, are common in the current Anglo-American float of humorous lore
than can be fitted logically into the preceeding section, owing
to the lack of any predominant competitive or contest element.
Obviously people usually answer insults, with matching insults

if they can, but this is not always the essence of the jokes on these subjects, many of which are really just 'squelchers' or 'put-downs.' The closest to contests are the elaborate 'toasts,' such as those just preceding, but these have long since died as the accompaniment of drinking that once they were, except on very formal occasions such as marriages, launching of ships, and so forth. The modern toasts still surviving – mostly in Scotland and among American Negroes, the same two groups involved in the parallel 'flytings' and the "Dozens" – are almost all erotic or obscene; these are considered in Dr. Abrahams' work. These are set pieces, almost memorized recitations, and not often openly competitive.

In devoting attention earlier, in the First Series, chapter 2.VI.3, to the former English custom of 'Water-Wit,' the insulting of passengers on the Thames water-boats by other boatmen, and the passengers' attempted replies in kind, the position taken was that of the chapter involved, on "Fools." The examples of Water Wit given were construed to be more or less deserved responses on the part of the working boatmen against the leisured classes and their la-de-da scions, out 'punting their judies' of a Sunday on the Thames. As noted there, the examples given were all more or less mild, particularly the historical items, which are all that remain to document this form of rough verbal game or ordeal in the past. In one late 17th-century item (not cited there), words are shown giving way to deeds, and vegetable filth and feces are actually thrown, the author gloating on the dripping of these into the décolleté corsage of the woman being attacked : a most extreme example of what has earlier been discussed as 'food-dirtying' and the attack on the (mother's) breast. This item is now quoted below.

The similar combination of verbal and physical dirtying of passers-by on the part of the Billingsgate fishwives of London, and the exactly similar fishwives' *jargon* of the Paris 'Halles,' or open market, has given us the word *Billingsgate*, in the English language, for any sort of foul and abusive language. But the historical formalization of this type of abuse has been lost sight of, as also the throwing of rotten vegetables, fish-offal, &c. at anyone who would dare to argue or insult back. Compare the emptying of chamber-slops (which does not mean only urine) out the window and upon the head of insistent knockers-upon-doors, or night-visiting suitors, as recently as the present century. (The 'gardyloo' : *gare à l'eau*, earlier.) The throwing of dead cats and rotten vegetables, especially tomatoes giving the effect of spilled blood when they strike, by way of expressing public disapproval, still remains a theatrical tradition – though seldom actually done nowadays – as formerly at public executions and humiliations, such as 'standing in the stocks.' So also whistling and cat-calling, a modification of actual throwing.

The motion-pictures heavily appealed to the audience's pleasure in scatological dirtyings in this way, during the early decades of the cinematic art-form and of our century, in the so-called 'pie-throwing comedies,' which became a whole movie genre. A very late example, in the 1930's I believe, by the 'nitwit' or 'zany' comedians, Stan Laurel and Oliver Hardy, was unquestionably the most extreme ever made, defiling a record number of eagerly mugging faces with a record number of custard pies. Pushing another person, ass-first, into a basket of eggs, or into sitting on an egg put into the back pocket (this is in Sacchetti's *Novelle*, No. 147, before the year 1400), with subsequent shaking and wriggling of the soiled buttocks, is an even more primitive theatrical gag of this type. It is used both in a proto-lesbian movie comedy by Polly Moran, and as late as Charlie Chaplin's next-to-last motion picture in the 1950's, *Limelight*, with Chaplin himself (in chicken-tail clown costume: 'the old swan-suit' from *Easy Street* days?) taking the pratt-fall. Cruder comedians still symbolize the scatology by squirting water wildly with a fire-hose held between their legs.

Modern examples of water wit, especially in America, often substitute taxi-drivers (earlier, hansom-cab drivers) for the Thames boatmen, with identical anal-sadism in the verbiage. Almost any necessarily *brief encounter* between strangers can become the theatre of such exchanges, both in jokes and in fact, if one is certain of getting away safe. Compare the psychological mechanism whereby little children will wave to passing busses or trains, and so will girls in bathing-suits when, for example, a trainload of soldiers passes a bathing-beach; though they will beat a precipitous retreat, or take refuge in frightened mutism, if the train or bus *stops*, and the persons waved to get off to make friends. Robert Graves puts it very well in *Lars Porsena: The Future of Swearing* (1927; ed. 1936, p. 22–3), with a traditional example of water-wit: '*When once the master of a Thames tug, remonstrated with for fouling a pleasure-boat and breaking an oar, leant over the rails and replied hoarsely: "Ow, I did, did I, Charley? An' talking of oars, 'ow's your sister?"* he did so only in his detestation of the leisured classes and in *confidence of a clean get-away.'* (Final italics supplied.)

Other such situations are, in particular, controversies with waitresses. The waitress – as the tough representative of the non-leisured class – is almost invariably given the 'retort crushing' to deliver. *'G.I. [American soldier] speaks to the waitress on English coffee: "Here miss, what's this, piss? I like my coffee like my women: hot and sweet!" Waitress: "Yes sir – white or black?"* (London, 1953; also collected ten years earlier, Minneapolis, Minn., from a young college woman, in a version in which the sexes are reversed, the girl being asked simply: *"And black?"*) – *Newsboy, in a bar: "How about a paper, mister?" Barfly: "Get away from me son! Go peddle your papers somewhere else! I don't want no paper!" Newsboy: "Well, smell it then. It's only shit, anyway."* (Wilmington, Delaware, 1951, told by a bartender to his clients.)

A modern convolution of water-wit is the 'Lizzie Label' of the 1920's, now institutionalized and hoked-up in prefabricated form as 'bumper-stickers' (*'autocollants,'* in France) in which the insulting message is written on or pasted to the side or back of an automobile, again 'in confidence of a clean get-away.' This sometimes does not come off, as in the historic case of a dastardly young chap in Nachitoches, Louisiana (you should pardon the expression), who got in trouble with the law in the 1930's – all duly recorded in the American law-report volumes – for having put a vile and indecent sign on his jalopy reading: *'All you ladies who smoke cigarettes, throw your butts in here.'*

The December 2, 1966, issue of the 'underground' newspaper, the *Los Angeles Free Press*, features on its front page a collection of the motto-buttons or bumper-stickers-for-kids-without-cars now popular in America (and to a lesser, imitative degree in England and France), including items reading: *"Stamp Out Pay Toilets"*, *"All Bosses Are Schmucks"*, *"God Is On A Trip"* [i.e. takes hallucinating drugs], and *"Psychiatry: The New Inquisition,"* of which the last is an anguished cry of more general application than may have been intended. Hundreds of different slogan-buttons and banners of this kind have been issued, perhaps thousands. Some are obviously authentic folk-statements of the young people who wear or collect them, though of known authorship, such as *"Cunnilingus – Now!"* and *"Ban the Bra!"* and the one most popular of them all, *"Make Love, Not War,"* which is now known internationally (*"Faites l'Amour et pas la Guerre"*) and which I had the honor of originally creating.

Capt. Francis Grose in his *Classical Dictionary of the Vulgar Tongue* (1785), at "Ark Ruffians," states that the retailers of water-wit on the Thames, were not, it seems, merely exercising their animosities and wit. Grose lumps their activity with that of the prostitutes' 'bullies' or 'badgers,' the London wharf-murderers from whose name comes the modern 'badger game,' or extortion – usually under some sexual excuse, or cover of prostitution – and calls them: *'Rogues who, in conjunction with watermen, rob, and sometimes murder, on the water, by picking a quarrel with the passengers in a boat, boarding it, plundering, stripping, and throwing them overboard, etc. A species of badgers.'* (Species of local *pirates* would obviously be closer.) It might be mentioned that though the 'Ark' element in the name of these 'Ark Ruffians' is being folk-etymologized as somehow connected with the river-boats on which they preyed, *via* Noah's Ark, no doubt; it is really just a variant of 'arch-' meaning chief, pre-eminent, or extreme, as in 'arch-rogue' or 'arch-whore.'

One is now ready to appreciate the late 17th-century item of water wit, earlier omitted. This appears in the anonymous *A Frolick to Horn Fair, with a Walk from Cuckold's-Point thro' Deptford and Greenwich* (London, 1700), written by the humorist and tavern-keeper, Ned Ward, author of the fascinating *London Spy* (1698–1709) and the crude anti-Whig mock, *Hudibras Redivivus* (1705–7) which, despite its ambitious title, is not quite up to the original *Hudibras*, forty years before, by Samuel Butler. In *A Frolick to Horn Fair*, p. 11, Ward paints a simple *genre*-picture, mostly in shit:

> We took Boat at *Billingsgate-stairs*, and away for *Cuckold's-Point;* but were no sooner put off from the shore, but we were got into such an Innumerable Fleet, of Oares, Skullers, Barges, Cock-boats, Bum-boats, Pinnaces and Yawles; some Going, some Coming, and all attacking each other with such Volleys of hard Words, that I thought Billingsgate-Market had been kept upon the Thames, and all the Fish-Whores in the Town had been Scolding for a Plate [*prize*], given 'em by some Rich Oyster-Woman, to encourage the Industry of the Tongue ... [Wooden ladles full of water are tossed at the passengers, with the] Opprobrious Names of *Whore* and

Rogue ... At last an Unlucky Rogue, with Bridewel-Looks
and a Ladle in his Hand, fishes up a floating Sir-reverence
[*turd*] in his Wooden Vehicle, and gives it an Unfortunate
Toss upon My Ladies Bubbies. She crying out to me her Protector, to do the Office of a Scavenger, and take away the
Beastliness, she being herself so very Squeamish, that she
could no more endure to touch it with her Fingers, than a
Monkey does a Mouse; it being Lodg'd in the Cavity, between
her Breasts and her Stays, she could not shake it off, but I was
forc'd to lend a hand to remove the Poisonous Pellat from
her Snowy-Temptations, giving on't a Toss into another Boat,
with the like Success, wounding an old Cuckoldy Waterman
just in the Forehead, and so Be-dung'd his Brow-Antlers.

[The 'wounded' waterman responds to this with a round
of] Aquatick Scurrility ... "You Shited-Skull'd Son of a
T —— d, that has spit your Brains in my Face, who was
Begot in Buggery, Born in a House of Office [*privy*], and
Deliver'd at the Fundament, fit for nothing but to be Cast
into a Gold-finders [*privy-cleaner's*] Ditch, there lie till you're
Rotten, and then be sold out to Gardiners, for a hot Bed, to
raise Punkins to feed the Devil withal every time you con-
jobble together."

It is only too evident that the author is not actually displeased
by the defiling of the woman he is presumably with, and he
certainly intends that the reader of his times – though perhaps
not of our times – should gloat with him over the fecal dirtying of the (mother's) breasts, and of the 'Cuckoldy Forehead' of
a waterman (representing the father) with the same *turd* – so
modestly replaced with a pudibund dash.

Scenes of this kind are still joyously remembered in British
humor, though reduced strictly to verbal violence when they
are represented as taking place in modern times. The real value
of the quotation from Ned Ward's *Frolick to Horn Fair*, above,
is its unequivocal identification of the merely verbal insults of
bargees and cab-drivers in modern times with the thrown turd.
The standard water-wit situation, in the British style, is that
given in the quotation from Robert Graves, above, and in more
ornate form in a story recited earlier in chapter 2.VI.3, First
Series, page 173, in which the humor is usually pointed up by
means of a trick common in Roman rhetoric (though not considered a standard rhetorical device), and well-known to school-

boys as recently as the 1930's. This occurs throughout the famous Phillippics of Cicero against the conspirator Catiline, when Cicero says: '*I pass by without mention his further crimes, such as ...*' and then spends several pages of pretty tough parsing Latin, *mentioning* these further crimes in exorbitant detail. *The Thames bargeman's temper has been riled by a young swell in a boat with two young ladies, and he has finally driven the young man to an exasperated "Dammitall!" "Oh," says the bargee in reply, "so it's cursin', is it? Well, I won't sye nuffin narsty, seein' as you've got a load o' cunt aboard. All I'll sye is, 'Bloody fuckin' arseholes to you!'"* (Chelmsford Prison, Essex, 1954.)

Every sort of variation is rung on this theme but within very narrow limits, as in Kimbo's *Tropical Tales* (Nice, 1925) p. 95, in which the bargee '*merely* remarked: *Seein' as 'ow you've got c ... aboard, I ain't agoin' ter sigh wat I was agoin' ter sigh*",' &c. &c.; also in *Anecdota Americana* (1927) 1:487, giving the punch-line only, without the story; and in the pseudonymous Nosti's *A Collection of Limericks* (Switzerland, 1944) p. 36, ending with: *the bargee answering 'with a grin: "Aye, I would like to swear at you, but seeing that you got a cargo of cunt o'bord, all I say is ten thousand fucking arseholes!"'* The verbal variations are so minor in all forms that this is obviously less a joke than a set piece or recitation.

An ugly modern fantasy of actual – rather than verbal – shit-slinging and woman-defiling, very close to the story quoted just above from Ned Ward's *A Frolick to Horn Fair* (1700) but probably independently recreated, is given in the guise of the usual 'true anecdote' to end the joke-texts, and doubtless as their culmination, in 'J. Mortimer Hall's' [V. Smith's] *Anecdota Americana: Second Series* (New York, 1934; repr. North Hollywood: Brandon House, 1968) No. 449. Here the scene is updated by having it take place not on a Thames boat at Billingsgate, but on the B.M.T. subway [!] in Brooklyn, on a trip to Brighton Beach by a 'famous New York author' who was only slumming and would ordinarily have taken a cab. The woman defiled with 'liquid shit' is introduced thus: '*Hanging to a strap was a girl in a white summer frock, trembling with fear and nervousness.*' Just the sort of victim that excites your true-born anal sadist.

The point has already been made that the kissing of the buttocks as an act of subservience is at least as ancient as Classical

Rome. It is probably even more ancient, and connected with the worship of stercoraceous gods and idols preceding either Judaism or Christiantity, and thus referred to by these as 'Devil-worship,' much of which was similarly stercoraceous, especially in its medieval revival. I have discussed this matter in its broader context in *The Guilt of the Templars*, p. 121–8; and more on arse-kissing, and the required 'Diabolical' kiss of the buttocks of the individual – presumably the Devil – officiating at the Black Mass, will be found in the only serious history of kissing, the anonymous work *Le Baiser: Étude Littéraire et historique* (Nancy, 1888) p. 112–25. There is an entire volume in German of the curiosities of the subject, Heinz-Eugen Schramm's *"L.m.i.A."* (*Leck mir im Arsch*), published in 1960 and revised 1967.

Contemptuous references in English to arse-kissing can be found as early as the mid-16th century (given in Tilley's *Dictionary of the Proverbs in England*, at B643, hidden under an expurgated form of a relevant proverb, "Scratch my Breech;" and by Farmer & Henley, *Slang & Its Analogues*, revised vol. 1, 1909, p. 262, at "Blind-cheeks"). The oldest of these is in a play translated from the Italian, *The Buggbears* (ca. 1565; in R. W. Bond, *Early Plays from the Italian*, 1911) I.ii.14: "*Stope down a low, And kisse my round rivette while I clawe thine ellbowe.*" I have not been able to determine whether this phrase – similar to recent English-language nautical terms for the anus, such as 'grommet,' and 'dead-eye' or 'hog-eye' – is actually translated from the Italian original. All the oldest uses of the phrase seem to be connected with this proverb about the arse and the elbow, implying a contest in gestures, as at the end of the preceding section. We still say of a stupid person that he '*does not know his arse from his elbow*' (or '*from a gourd*' or '*from third base*' or '*from a pisspot full of crab-apples*').

As mere contempt, or a threat, bum-kissing appears in Dekker & Webster's *Northward Hoe* (1607) II.i, "*I'll make him know how to kiss your blind cheeks sooner;*" while Captain Francis Grose, in his *Olio* (1792) p. 202, gives the first actual joke I have noted on this, and tells it as a true anecdote concerning: *The unpopular British politician, Fox, in his election campaign in 1784, being invited in by a butcher whose vote he is canvassing. The butcher gets him to kiss his wife and daughter* [politicians nowadays still kiss the voters' babies], *and, after he had 'saluted these greasy females ... with much ceremony, the butcher turned to him saying, "And now, Sir, you have kissed my wife, and you have kissed my daughter; you may also kiss my a——e and begone, for I'll be damned if I vote for you!" '* This is close to the old homosexual joke where, in the modern form, the man ends by asking plaintively, *"And for me, nothing?!"* Another joke-form is unequivocal: *A Negro minister is being tried by his congregation for various misdeeds. He refuses to defend himself, and says: "Ah done evything you all said, and mo'. But ah's been a good pastor to you, and now ah's gwine away. As ah passes down de aisle, however, kindly take notice that ah have placed a sprig of mistletoe jus' under mah coat-tails."* (Anecdota Americana, 1927, 1:16.)

To return to water-wit situations involving insults other than that concerning kissing the buttocks. *'A bus and cab came together in the Strand, London. The usual angry colloquy ensued. Said the bus driver: "Does yer mother know ye're out? [I.e. born yet.] You need a nuss to take you through the streets, you do!" Said the cab driver: "Eh! What's the matter with you, old big cock?" "Oh, so yer wife has been telling you about me, has she?" said the bus man.'* (A Treasury of Erotic and Facetious Memorabilia, c. 1910.) A more recent version of this type of 'cross-biting' or *réplique*, using the insulter's own words against him, is in reply to the now-standard insult *"Motherfucker!"* *"Your mother tells you everything, does she?"* (L.A. 1965. Compare: *"What's the Negro word for father? – Motherfucker!"*)

Similar colloquies between modern automobile drivers are apparently quite common, on the slightest excuse. The large French *Dictionnaire des Injures* by Robert Édouard (Paris: Tchou, 1967) makes very clear, in its highly informative opening, "Traité d'Injurologie," that near-accidents among automobilists are a choice field for insults. The modern driver of an automobile or motorcycle – large bus- and truck-drivers apparently less so – is intensely conscious that his vehicle represents his virile image of himself, both as phallus and as force, motility, etc., and the slightest constraint of his forward motion is likely to drive him berserk, and ready to curse and fight. *A London cab-driver is arrested for using abusive language to a woman. "Don't you know better than to talk like that to a lady?" asks the magistrate. "Er? – a lydy? She's no lydy!" "And would you recognize a lady if you saw one?" "That I would, your wushup. I 'ad a lydy fare only larst week. Drove 'er from Trafalgar Square to 'er 'ouse – about four miles it was – and*

*she gives me a guinea. 'Pardon me, lydy, yer change,' says I.
'Ah, stick the change up yer arse!' she says. That what I calls a
lydy, yer wushup."* (1 : 276, often collected in both America and
England.) Here, the magistrate is the butt of the Water-Wit, in
his own courtroom.

The most recent examples of American provenance, having
no formalized tradition of such insult, and insulting vocabulary,
to cling to, are crudely dysphemistic, attempting to make up in
sexual insult what they have lost in scatological finesse. *A very
fat lady takes a cab, being laboriously helped in by the driver.
Two children standing by begin to mock, "Look at the fat lady
getting in the cab! Look at the fat lady!" The cab-driver whirls
on them angrily. "How would you like to kiss that fat lady's
ass?!" Then, to the lady, "I guess that's tellin' 'em, eh, fat lady?"*
(N.Y. 1948.)

This joke-format has for some reason become a vehicle of
the animosity against lesbians, which is very great among most
sexually normal men, especially toward the obvious and
sexually *rival* 'butch' or 'Diesel-dyke' type, of the built-like-a-
brick-shithouse cigar-smoking variety. The sort that the American poetesses, Amy Lowell and Gertrude Stein, were always
considered to be, as well as many tough-talking and mannish
actresses of the kind shown in the joke. This joke is the same as
that preceding, but much dysphemized and with the butt suddenly shifted from the 'outsider' to the fare. *A taxi-driver with
two lesbian actresses in back, as fares, one of them very
notorious, bumps into another taxi-driver, who shouts, "Ah!
you blind? Drivin' around town like that with lizzies in the
back!" First driver: "How would you like one of them lizzies to
suck the crack of your shitty ass?" Then, turning to his passengers, "Howzat for tellin' 'im, Miss Lallygag?"* (N.Y. 1950.
Anecdota Americana, 2:74, has an even more hateful anti-
homosexual version, with *the driver asking his opponent
whether he'd like the homosexual to 'suck his syphilitic prick.
Then, turning to his fare, "How's that for a tart rejoinder,
queenie?"* ')

There is also a 'topper' or dovetail to this, with the same
characters, and actually continuing the same joke, or giving it
from the lesbian's presumed point of view : *A lesbian actress in
a cab with her girl-friend gets into an argument with the driver
about the fare. Finally he accepts what she offers to pay, and
slams the door, preparing to drive away, saying disgustedly,*

"Aw, what else can you expect from a couple of cunt-lappers?"
The actress reaches into his seat, drags him out by the scruff of
the neck, and beats him into unconsciousness with a crank-
handle leaving him bleeding on the ground. "Migod, Lally!"
cries her girl-friend, as they walk rapidly away, "you shouldn't
have done that." "Oh yeah? That's what he gets for calling two
perfect ladies like us 'cunt-lappers'." (Amsterdam, 1956, told by
an American at a bar in the homosexual assignation and 'S. &
M.' accosting area, the Muntplein.)

Generalized insults of a scatological kind are, as has been
seen, purely verbal or at most gestural. Occasionally, however,
the insult does move on toward action: precisely the scatological action involved in the insulting phrases or gestures
(halfway-house), which can be considered partial or repressed
equivalents of the anal-sadistic action really in mind, and sometimes described. *Conductor, to man on train, "Stop that smok-*
ing." Man: "I'm not smoking." Conductor: "Well, your pipe's
in your mouth." Man: "Yes, and my ass is in my britches, but
I'm not shitting." (Fredericksburg, Va., 1952.) Verbally, at least,
the conductor has been shat on. The inner logic of the story
here is apparently very ancient. A story is told of: *The Arab*
jester who is brought before the judge for having a set of con-
cealed burglar tools. He asks why they don't accuse him of
rape too, since he has a penis concealed in his pants. As to
logic, what about this: '*A Irishman and an Italian* [or fill in
your own 'invidious nationalities'] *were working on a sewer full*
of crap. The Irishman was up to his knees in the muck, handing
it up by the bucketfulls to the Italian, clean and dry above.
One of Pat's friends remonstrated with him. Why didn't he send
the Wop down into the mire and pick the easy job himself?
"Na," said Pat. "No Dago can hand me the shit!"' (1:265.) Supposed to be an Irish bull, of course, on the phrase 'to hand
someone the shit,' meaning to lie to him or insult him.

Finally, the implication – always hidden underneath the
mere scatological words and insults – of the actual throwing or
soiling with the fecal products, which is the reality of which
the insults are merely the verbal *eidola*, begins to appear at the
surface. As with the Billingsgate fishwives, or those of the
ancient Halles in Paris, flinging first insulting words, then fish-
entrails and piss or other offal at those whom they wish to
offend or domineer. It happened to me in the Halles in Paris in
1954, having ventured some equivocal remark about her

coquillage (shell-fish, also virginity) to a handsome young woman selling oysters, that replied, *"Va! pour mon coquillage, je ne l'emporterai pas en paradis!"* (Go on! I won't take my cherry with me to heaven!) And she flicked a shellful of brine right in my face. *An Irishman going to the doctor with a urine specimen is asked by another Irishman what he has in the bottle. As he tells later: " 'Urine,' says I. 'Phwat?' says he. 'Piss!' says I. 'Shit!' says he. 'Fuck!' says I, and then the fight was on."* (2:43.) We are not told what happened to the bottle of urine during the fight, but can imagine. A later version also turns on the presumed stupidity of the interlocutor (an accusation which is itself a form of dirtying, usually anti-national): *A man tells another he must bring the doctor a urine specimen and asks what to do. "Go piss in a bottle," the friend explains. "Go shit in your hat!" the man retorts. "Shit in your own hat, and pull it down over your ears and call it curls!"* (N.Y. 1949, from a sailor.)

It should be observed that the urine specimen or other open scatological element is really only a 'gimmick,' prop, or plot-pretext, to get the ball of insults rolling, already revved up to a fairly violent or scatological speed when the story starts. It is by no means essential. For it is certain that remarks concerning 'shit' itself are not the real essence of verbal venom and scatology of this kind. *Mrs. Mulligan was cooking when Pat O'Toole came along. As he explains it later: " 'Phwat are yez cookin', Mrs. Mulligan?' says I. 'Rocky Mountain oysters,' says she. 'Phwat the hell's that?' says I. 'Nuts,' says she. 'Phwat do ye mean, "Nuts"?' says I. 'Balls!' says she. 'Oh, balls is it?' says I, 'well, shit on you and yer big dorty Irish feet!' says I; an' then the fight was on."* (Berkeley, Calif. 1941.) This is going all the way around Robin Hood's barn. Actually, the fight was really on – with any man worth his salt – when the woman bought an animal's testicles to slice up and fry; though I do feel that touch about the 'dorty feet' is a bit gratuitous. Insulting terms as to *dirtiness* are strongly class-linked (here against the Irish), and are considered a social attack or disgrace, in addition to their scatological tone.

The point-of-no-return is easily reached, of course, where insults fail of their effect as being too hackneyed. Witness the respectabilization of *"you old son-of-a-bitch"*, *"you're a clever bastard,"* or *"mean motherfucker"* – all these are compliments – and, in French, in the whole descending rocket of meaninglessness in *baiser*-to-*embrasser*-to-*étreindre*, as term after term loses its meaning through euphemism, dysphemism, and over- use. This creates a numbness to insults, and the necessity to search for new and more extravagant strings of curses and insults, of which the very extravagance prevents their being taken seriously. Again, the case of Mark Twain and all the women (except his wife) whom he thought he was shocking. '*A big man walked into a bar, downed a double shot of whiskey, banged one fist down on the bar, and said, "All the people on this end of the bar are Cock Suckers!" Then he banged the other fist and said, "All the people on this end of the bar are Sons of Bitches!" Just then, he turned around, and saw a little man try- ing to sneak out behind him, and roared, "Where in Hell are you going, little man?" The timid soul replied, "I'm just going over to my side of the bar".*' (*World's Dirtiest Jokes*, 1969, p. 191; capitalization as printed, apparently to signpost the significant dirty words.)

This rather spoils the original joke, collected often over the preceding thirty years. Same beginning: *The bad man starts shooting up the bar, announcing, "I'm a-gonna count to ten, and then I'm a-gonna start shootin' and kill every goddam, no- good, cock-suckin', stinkin', rotten son-of-a-bitchin' bastard* IN *this joint!" He starts blazing away without waiting to count, and when the gunsmoke abates the saloon is completely empty except for one mild-mannered little man drinking sarsaparilla, who says to him in an interested tone, "My! weren't there a lot of them?"* (Ann Arbor, Michigan, 1935.) Note the pathos of the bad man's having finally to accentuate the preposition, '*in.*'

All the insults, from the mildest to the most lethal, that have been detailed above are stereotypical, and are generally recited or reeled off in the same order and same rhythm or 'tune' by any given person, every time he or she uses them. These re- present *congealed* elements, similar to the punchlines of jokes, which are also attempted (often unsuccessfully) to be repeated verbatim every time the joke is told by the same teller. In fact, many joke-tellers and joke-collectors recognize jokes by the punch-lines only, and even believe or tacitly admit that every- thing that precedes is mere background, and subject to change, expansion, or diminution, to suit the moment of delivery or the company present. Actually, they are wrong. *The punch-line of a joke is in most cases purely adventitious, and can be totally changed without in the slightest changing the real emotional*

effect or situation of the joke. A good example is the joke on
the bad-man in the saloon, in the paragraphs just above, where
the punch-lines of the two versions given are completely different, yet the joke is self-evidently the same.

Of course, in the deepest sense, a joke is *never* the same at
two different tellings or listenings, even if repeated exactly or
by a machine (tape-recording, etc.), since the receiving emotions
of the listeners also importantly affect the meaning of the joke!
This subjective aspect of humor has been treated as carefully
as possible in the preceding chapters of this work, but it still
remains the great question-mark as to humor, since it is the key
as to *why certain people find certain jokes funny whereas other
people do not.* The stereotypical punch-line, insult, or other
recitation attempts to assure a result, and a foretellable result
– the listener's laughter – but the truth is that it is not these
stereotyped elements which *cause* the laugh, though obviously
they often touch it off.

Two examples of pleasure in mere free-floating aggression by
means of words will close this chapter. No ritual situation of
any kind is involved for these 'marred' or reverse-recitations,
though they require explanatory set-ups beforehand of their
internal décor, thus putting them in the tradition of the
cante-fable, on which see further references on the next-to-last
page of the First Series, 9.III.5. Owing to the tricky verbal
tongue-twisting of both examples – they both involve series of
Spoonerisms, as in chapter 2.VII.1 – they were sometimes circulated on printed 'novelty' slips, or on the backs of printed
business-cards for such man-among-men businesses as hardware
stores, saloons, etc. as recently as the 1930's. *An old bum is
given a job standing by the door of the railroad station calling
out, "Free Bus to the Hotel Astor!" As he has been given half a
dollar in advance and it is a cold winter day, he has invested
the money in as many beers as it would buy, and makes his
announcement as follows: "Here y'are, folks, getcher free bus
to the Hotel Bastard; I mean free bastard to the Hotel Bustard;
I mean, oh shit! Bust yer ass at the Hotel Mustard, and you can
kiss my ass besides!"* (L.A. 1965; also printed slip of similar text
to following: London, 1971.)

A simple Spoonerism much like the following is given in the
First Series, 2.VII, pages 180–81, under "Riddles Wrongly Retold," but here the whole point is the elaborate dysphemism to
which the error leads. *A young man with a fine voice is asked*

to take part in a pageant-play, though he tries to beg off, saying
he always gets embarrassed under such circumstances. He is
assured it will be very simple, and he will have only one line to
say: "I come to snatch a kiss, and dart into the fray. Hark! I
hear a pistol shot – " and then stride offstage. At the performance he comes onstage, very embarrassed already by the tight-
fitting Colonial knee-breeches he has been made to put on at the
last moment, and becomes completely unstrung at the sight of
the beautiful heroine lying back on a garden-seat awaiting him,
in a white gown. He clears his throat and announces: "I come
to kiss your snatch, no! snatch a kiss, and fart into the dray. – I
mean, dart into the fray! Hark!! – I hear a shistol pot, no! a
shostil pit, a pistil shit. Oh, bat shit, rat shit, shit on you all! I
never wanted to be in this damned play anyhow!"

15

SCATOLOGY

ZEALOUS as one might be to collect and include here all possible jokes on scatological themes, it cannot be overlooked that these materials do not really come within the purlieus of the present subject, *"An Analysis of Sexual Humor,"* and are simply assimilated to sexual humor by the 'accident of anatomy' (about which more later) that has made both the genital and excretory functions fall under the same taboo. The sexualization of scatology is, of course, at least as great as that of other obviously non-sexual physiological acts, such as eating, sneezing and nose-blowing, also vomiting, which are nevertheless surrounded with enormous structures of social gesture expressing revulsion and superstitious taboo. It is probably the taboos themselves that eventually sexualize such activities. This sexualization of scatology has been dealt with above, under "Cloacal Intercourse," 12.IV.1, and will be discussed further in section 15.III.4, below, *"Pet-en-gueule,"* in connection with farting, the principal sexualized act.

Jokes involving either food or vomiting, as sexual 'dirtyings,' have already been considered in Chapter 12.IV, under the heading of "Narsty-Narsties." This obviously could include many of the jokes in the present chapter as well, which are certainly intended by their tellers to shock and repel. Less than half of the scatological jokes actually collected are presented here, while materials not specifically in joke form, such as riddles, verse, and puns, particularly those of a semi-expurgated or symbolized type, relating to the buttocks, toilet, babies' diapers, torn or unbuttoned trousers, under-drawers (male and female), dirty socks and feet, or dirtiness generally, have not been included at all except for purposes of analogy. These are intended to form a supplementary study, under the title "All that Glitters," in *Kryptádia: The Journal of Erotic Folklore.* A representative group involving anti-racial or anti-religious (usually anti-Semitic) insults and *blasons populaires* will be found in the final section of this chapter, under "Anal Sadism."

I am conscious that many readers may be disappointed by

the relative brevity of this chapter, and by the concentration here on the jokes themselves rather than on any interpretation. Let it be sufficient that the jokes have been given. In the years separating the publication of these First and Second Series, I have received hundreds of letters of inquiry about the latter. Except for a few helpful letters, kindly enclosing small collections of the writers' favorite or most recently-collected jokes, *most* of the inquiries concerned the scatological jokes. One, already quoted, said (for its total message): "WHERE THE HELL ARE THE SHIT JOKES?" Many others have said the same thing, in more meeching and roundabout ways.

I would observe that this subject has an entire literature of its own, well worth consulting, though now badly demanding to be brought up to date. Much will be found in the *Bibliotheca Scatologica* (Paris, 1849) of Pierre Jannet and three other savants, and its supplement, as *Anthologie Scatologique*, anonymously edited by Gustave Brunet (Paris: Gay, 1862). A whole volume of curiosities on this subject has more recently been published, Franz Maria Feldhaus' *Ka-Pi-Fu, und andere verschämte Dinge* (Berlin, 1921; offset reprinted about 1965), and a further volume on the special aspect of the invitation to kiss the arse: *"L.m.i.A."* [*Leck mir im Arsch*], by Heinz-Eugen Schramm (1960, enlarged ed. Gerlingen, 1967). See also Dr. Paul Englisch's *Das skatologische Element in Literatur, Kunst, und Volksleben* (Stuttgart, 1928, also appearing under a less sober title), the only extended modern work on scatological themes, with the exception of Joseph Feinhals' thousand-page compilation, *Non olet, oder die heiteren Tischgespräche über den Orbis Cacatus* (Köln, 1939) with a useful bibliography. A new work on the subject is now in preparation by the Drs. 'Sabbath' of Chicago. English-language writings on scatology are in general either very reserved or very arch, in the line of Reginald Reynolds' *Cleanliness and Godliness* (London, 1943), which imitates the centuries-old style of Robert Burton's *Anatomy of Melancholy*. Other volumes in English, specifically on outhouse- and toilet-architecture, will be noted later in their place, with some curious volumes – such as at least one cookbook! – of high scatological concentration. Supplementing almost every aspect of all of these is Capt. John G. Bourke's important but skittishly disorderly *Scatalogic* [sic] *Rites of All Nations* (Washington, 1891, and offset reprints to 1968). Some very curious literary examples are reprinted in full in the Carnival issue of

Jules Gay's magazine, *Le Bibliophile Fantaisiste* (1869) pp. 49–96, 394–5, and 508–28, well worth examining. Not to overlook the special series of scatological folktales from Picardy, presented by E.-Henry Carnoy in *Kryptádia* (1907) XI. 1–138. Obviously the bottom, in German pseudo-sexology, is Ernst Schertel's *Erotische Komplex: Gesäss Erotik* (1932 ff. 4 vols.), entirely on arses, enemas, flagellation, and ass-ociated perversions.

As I have already tried to show, scatological jokes and tales are among the most primitive and direct, requiring nothing more than the mere mention of the taboo object or action to achieve the effect of anger, terror, shock, offense, or laughter – that is to say, *humor* – upon persons controlled by the taboo and thus responsive to its verbal flouting. The response of laughter is the most repressed and evasive of these. Those who laugh, in answer to such an attack or assault by means of dirty words and defiling images, are those most clearly in the grip of the helpless response which is the key to all humor, and is used therefore as the motto to the First Series here: Figaro's superb line in Beaumarchais' *The Barber of Seville* (1775) Act I, scene ii, *"I laugh, so that I may not cry."*

The scatological joke, like the castration joke or 'narsty-narsty' tale, is always an assault on the listener. It is intended purposely to shock and essentially to *harm* the listener, under the shallow formal pretext of concerning itself with some true or fictitious hygienic incident, or of being intended to entertain the listener with a droll tale. It is the exact verbal equivalent of 'pissing on', 'shitting on', or at the very least 'farting at' the butt of the joke, who is almost always in these cases the listener himself. and who is in general uneasily conscious of his function. Jokes and puns on these subjects are also therefore the ones that can make nervous listeners who are sensitive to them laugh the loudest and longest, often 'breaking up' uncontrollably in convulsive laughter to the point of becoming physically weak, farting loudly, or literally 'pissing in their pants' – women especially, as to this last – depending on the strength of the personal taboo.

The described activity in such jokes, and the crucial hurting or defiling in all castration jokes, 'nasty' jokes, and particularly in scatological jokes, must be considered not only to be directed against the listener, but actually or emotionally to *happen* to him or her. That is why these are by far the least popular of all

jokes among adult listeners – where sex jokes are always appreciated – except in certain racial groups such as Germans and
the Dutch, retarded Latins, American Indians, and other primitive or backwoods groups who live closely with cowdung, etc.,
or who have suffered intense early toilet-training. The screams
and groans greeting such stories among cultivated adult listeners
are by no means entirely faked, or covertly appreciative. But
these remain the most popular of all jokes among children and
among compulsive and aggressive joke-tellers. As one striking
example in my own experience, a nightclub entertainer with
whom I am quite unacquainted, writing to me from one of the
Pacific islands a few years ago, who ended his perfectly polite
and ingratiating first letter with this unexpected Return of the
Repressed: 'Well, gotta go now. Guess I'll shit in the corner and
bunch the flies!' A sort of scatological goodnight kiss.

The excretory acts themselves are of daily familiarity, and
only their appearance in public is taboo. If they were really
taboo, the human race would be extinct in a few weeks.
Excretory acts are not really surrounded with the fright and
dread which invades and invests sex – for many people – and
which creates the endemic social situation out of which the
sexual joke takes its electrical charge and 'gets its laugh.' There
is more shock-value even in jokes about, or references to, such
theoretically neutral substances as sputum or vomit. (The
tobacco advertisement of the 1930's that used to read: "Spit is
a horrid word! – Especially on the end of your cigar" – meaning that non-Cuban cigars are glued together with gum
tragacanth instead.) The whole section, earlier, of "Narsty-
Narsties," 12.IV, is at its mildest concerned with scatology and
the cloacal identification of coitus; while the 'nastiest' items are
those on pus, sputum, and vomit.

The only emotional charge or shock on which the scatological
joke can count securely is that connected with the unexpectedly
public, rather than private representation of the excrementory
acts of daily familiarity to everyone; or from the use of the
'vulgar' or 'Anglo-Saxon' terms for these acts, that are as far as
possible removed from being euphemisms. There is also, of
course, the pleasurable identification of the listener in the shit-
throwing that is the subject of such jokes, when it is not made
too unavoidably clear that it is really the listener at whom the
shit is being thrown.

A psychological element of an unconscious or unremembered

type also enters here very importantly. The anal stage in the development of the child is that in which the child's hostilities are first massively engendered. This is the stage that follows the deprivation of the Nirvana-like easy satisfaction of oral needs at the mother's breast (or nursing-bottle), sometimes as late as at five or six years old. Furthermore, the child is deprived then even of the anal and urinary products themselves, which cannot now be played with or even touched without arousing expressions of disgust or reprobation on the part of the parent or nurse. The small child would often like to play with these products, and sometimes does – or, if angry, as with parents who have left him alone in the house, may smear them all around the walls and carpets. But the parent insists that these digestive products should be formally deposited in certain special places and containers, and in no others, such as chamber-pots, privies, and flush-toilets (the ancient 'bog-house', 'draught,' or 'jakes' – the modern 'john'), where they are flushed away and 'lost' forever, though felt to be just as much a part of the child's body as his hair, teeth, or fingernails, which he also often howlingly regrets losing. This is observed as early as *Matthew*, xv. 17, presumably about A.D. 30, where Jesus berates the backward disciples with the little scatological parable – so you see, dirty jokes didn't begin yesterday – '*Do not ye yet understand, that whatsoever entereth in at the mouth goeth into the belly, and is cast out into the draught?*'

As a result, the anal stage and everything connected with it, whether object or word, is the most particularly hostile in the child's early development, even more so than the rational hostilities of the oral period, where at least the ideas and ideals of oral-incorporation, sucking, biting, tearing, etc., serve to nourish the body. Only late in the emotional development of the child, by the age of eight or ten, or just before puberty – and sometimes not even then, or *never* – is there a moving on finally to the normal and full genitality which is concerned with love for, and sexual attraction to other individuals, and the reproduction of the species which is the basic purpose of all life.

It is neither possible nor necessary to discuss here any further the psychoanalytic view of the oral-anal-genital stages of the child's development, on which see further the very full treatment in Dr. Otto Fenichel's *The Psychoanalytic Theory of Neurosis* (New York: Norton, 1945), which is the best sum-

mary of the theories and discoveries of Freud and his school.
Much concerning anality, specifically in connection with jokes,
will also be found in Dr. Martha Wolfenstein's *Children's
Humor* (1954). For the secret of jokes is that *the joke is an
attack on the listener. The joking level is basically always the
hostile and anal-aggressive, no matter what the subject of the
joke, and no matter how disguised it may be as humor. The
joke openly dirties the butt by flinging sex, shit, or ridicule at
him, but secretly bespatters the listener in passing.*

I. BUTTOCK-HUMOR AND TOILETS

I. 'ARSE' AND 'ASS'

It is scatology that comes closest to the etymological definition
of 'obscene' as that which is in general kept private, hidden, or
off the scene (abscæna) – in our culture the sexual, scatological,
or anything related to death – but which is exceptionally or
unexpectedly brought *upon the scene,* and into public view,
thus achieving the effect of 'obscenity' or transgression of the
taboo. This is particularly evident in what concerns the buttocks, of which the taboo rises from their being the target-
area of sexuality (in our dimly remembered quadruped pre-
history), as well as the evident exit-point or promontory of the
feces or daily alvine dejections of the body. The buttocks are
not really any more humorous or disgraceful than the toes,
knuckles or elbows, but are powerfully assimilated to the
taboo action of defecation that takes place between them.
References to the intergluteal cleft make this quite clear, as in
the insult concerning '*the crack of your shitty ass,*' in the joke
given earlier concerning the taxi-driver and lesbian actress.
Alluding to the buttocks plainly as sexual and not scatological
is far less taboo.

Direct reference to the human anus is seldom made in jokes,
though the British supreme insult, 'Arseholes!' has already
been noted. The usual displacement of taboo from the sexual
area has also taken place, in the taboo of the buttocks, obviously an easy jump: front to back. Much harder jumps
(bottom to top) are often navigated in the unconscious, as of
the genitals to the breasts or nipples (in women suffering from
powerful penis-envy), or to the head, eyes, or tongue, or even
to the entire 'body-image' of stiffness and 'toughness,' as in
modern men – of the athlete-, gunman-, spy-type, &c. – affecting

tight clothes as an expression of the virility of which they are not altogether sure.

The mere word 'ass' (the usual British and American pronunciation of the language-word 'arse') is powerfully taboo, and the animal of the same name is usually referred to expurgatorily as a 'donkey.' The punning assimilation here already appears in Shakespeare's *Hamlet*, in the scene of the actors' rehearsal, II.ii.399, with Hamlet mocking the actors with the traditional sound of the 'raspberry' (raspberry-tart: fart), or tongue-vibration: *"Buz-buz!"* and adding, "Then came each actor on his ass." Prof. Allen Walker Read has pointed out (in private conversation, New York, 1946), that the word 'arse' represents quite an expurgatory problem in British plays given in both England and America, when, for instance, the deprecatory term 'Silly ass!' is used. In England, the British actor will pronounce this correctly and carefully as *'ass'* (short *a*), since *'ahss'* is the British pronunciation of 'arse,' it being an upperclass British affectation (adopted from the homosexual French *précieux* of the 1800's, the 'Incoyables') to be unable to pronounce the medial, and even initial, *r*. However, when the same play, and the same deprecatory 'Silly ass!' are presented in America, the false-British pronunciation of *'ahss'* will be given (precisely the pronunciation avoided in Britain!), since the correct *'ass'* evokes the taboo association in America. When Shaw's *Pygmalion* (1912) was revamped as a musical in the 1960's, as *My Fair Lady*, the 1910's taboo-word, *'bloody,'* was found no longer to carry any linguistic dynamite, Instead, the Cockney actress had to shout (at a racehorse), *"Move your bloody arse!"* shifting the shock from the *bloody* to the *arse*. ('Emmeroids for the hupper clawsses?)

Other students of taboo have already noted that the various Biblical asses, such as that of Balaam and even of the Messiah, are politely transformed to *donkeys* when speaking to children. There is no actual difference between the two animals, and the rise of the *donkey* (also 'donkey engine') is a verbal genteelism no earlier than the 17th century. The 'jawbone of an ass' used by the hero or 'hard-man,' Samson, in *Judges*, xv. 15–16, in the so-called King James translation of the Bible (1611) to slaughter a thousand Philistines – surely a reversal of the truth: few instruments being so lethal as the jawbone of a Philistine – is itself also the subject of a mock-schoolroom joke. *The children are being examined in Sunday school on the story of Samson.*

"And how did Samson slay the Philistines?" the visiting examiner asks. *"With the jawbone of an ass,"* one boy prompts the other, in a whisper. The boy being examined does not catch this exactly, and triumphantly announces: "With a jab in the ass!" In *The Stag Party* [1888] unnumbered p. 185, is given a charade-style or spelling-bee schoolroom joke of this kind, in which: *A schoolboy's name is 'Baldus Holbear', but when the teacher asked him to spell it, this is the way the young rascal did it:* "B A L D – *bald, And there's yer bald.* A *double* S – *ass, And there's yer ass."* Ending: ' *"And there's yer bald ass-hole bare."* ' This is essentially a catch, and in no sense a joke at all. *The Stag Party*, p. 208, also gives a mere pun in which: 'A man *was driving an ass along a country road, when suddenly the brute stopped and refused to proceed. Looking for a cause, the man discovered a young fellow mounting a girl in a fence corner. He was going for her in great shape, and his backside worked like a churn. The old man urged the beast to move on, but not a move. Finally he said: "Young fellow, won't you keep your arse still 'till I get my ass past?"* ' This is obviously nothing other than a dysphemization of the story of Balaam's ass, turning aside from the invisible angel with drawn sword in the path, in *Numbers,* xxii. 22–30, which is also nothing other than an ancient apologue or moral fable, cast as an animal-story, the first of the 'shaggy dog' or 'talking horse' variety.

Very many more stories have been collected in which the humor is presumed to reside simply in the use of the taboo word *'ass,'* than space could possibly be made for here. Nor is there really any need to do so. As with jokes on torn, tight, and unbuttoned pants, women's underwear, Scottish kilts, etc., they are of the sort grouped in *The Limerick* (1953) chap. 17, as the "Weak Sisters" of erotic folklore. They satisfy themselves with an only-too-evident partialism, or metonymy (the part for the whole, or the container for the thing contained, as when one says 'a sail' for a ship, or 'a good table' to mean good food), and often appear in the politely expurgated humor columns of 'digest' magazines, as the height of naughtiness allowed to these periodical organs. Perfectly typical is an obscoenum or 'tease'-story dating from the 1880's, about: *A vivacious young lady describing her roller-skating experience to the new minister in the presence of her family.* ' *"I'd just got my skates on and made a start, when I came down on my –"* ... *"Margaret!!"* yelled both the parents. *"On my little brother,*

who had me by the hand, and like to have smashed him. Now,
what's the matter?"' (The Stag Party, Boston? 1888, unnumb.
p. 251.) – *Ab uno disce omnes.*

As such items have a very old-fashioned flavor, it should be
observed that they are still popular with minor modernizations.
A racing promoter, as a 4th of July entertainment, arranges a
race between a jackass belonging to Father Malarkey, the
popular local priest; a three-legged horse, and a mule belonging
to the Rabbi. The Bishop considers the whole affair unseemly
and wants to stop the race, but is too late to prevent the start.
The rest of the story is told by the ticker-tape in the local bet-
ting beer-joint and billiard-parlor: "THEY'RE OFF!! RABBI
KUTCHER'S MULE IS OUT IN FRONT – FATHER MALARKEY'S ASS
SHOWS – FATHER'S ASS AHEAD BY A NOSE – FLASH! BISHOP
SCRATCHES FATHER'S ASS!" (N.Y. 1953.) This is close to the plot
of the Marx Brothers' *A Day at the Races* movie, all except for
the unforgettable "Get your tuttsi-fruiti ice-cream!" tipster
routine, with the stud-book, code-book, jockey-book – and no
ice-cream at all. The popular phrase, 'Not *to know one's ass*
from a hole in the ground,' as representing the ultimate in
stupidity – a sort of scatological rather than sexual nincum-
poopery – has at least twice been laboriously set up as a recitation or pretended joke, on printed 'novelty' cards of the 1930's
and since, concerning: *A man who cannot find the outhouse*
hole, or falls into a hole instead of mounting his jackass, and
the like. Another similar obscoenum sets out to explain '*Why*
there are so many more horses' asses than there are horses,' in
the form of a doggerel poem concerning a Norse hero, Horsa,
who is a breeder of wild asses. All very weak humor, turning
solely on twitting the taboo.

One of the oldest stories turning on the ostensible humor of
the buttocks is still perfectly current, and is still thought of as
a pretty good joke. Oliver Jensen & Constance A. Foulk, in their
somewhat premature once-over-lightly or omnium-gatherum,
The Revolt of American Women (1952) p. 146, cite this bold
stocking advertisement: 'Everything is mentionable in fashion's
new language ... The "un" has been dropped from "unmention-
ables." "Busts" have become breasts, to be kept "high, young,
and excitingly lovelier" ... *The "Doubletake" stocking adver-*
tises with a picture of a young man wheeling for an apprecia-
tive stare at a pretty girl whose skirts have been blown waist
high by a sudden gust of wind. What does this modern girl do

in her embarrassing predicament? She grabs for her hat.' (Italics
supplied.) In actual joke-form this is current as: *A woman
caught in the rain while wearing a new hat, pulls the back of
her skirt up over her head to protect the hat, while she runs for
cover. A policeman laughs at her. "Hey, lady, your ass is out a
yard!" "Don't I know it!" she replies; "but that ass is thirty
years old, and this hat is brand new!"* (Scranton, Pa. 1936.)
Poggio gives what is essentially this joke, in his *Facetiæ* (MS.
1451) No. 137, *"De muliere quæ, cum caput cooperire vellet,
culum detexit,"* and this was translated into English, in *Tales,
and Quicke Answeres*, one of the earliest English jestbooks
(about 1535) No. 66, "Of the woman that coverd her heed and
shewed her taile."

W. Carew Hazlitt makes the important tracing-remark on
this joke that it is of evident Levantine origin, referring to the
ritual veiling of women's faces, while the nudity of the body
is considered a lesser exposure. The Levantine original too is still
current, appearing in *Histoires Arabes* (Paris, 1927) p. 214, concerning *the winner of a contest in bad wives.* This is folktale
Motif J2521.2, of which Rotunda notes a 13th-century version
already in Europe in the manuscript collection of Etienne de
Bourbon (ed. A. Lecoy de La Marche, 1877) No. 275, and other
European references are given by Thompson at the same Motif
number.

It should certainly not be overlooked that what is probably
really involved here is the *purposeful* showing of the 'buttocks'
(*i.e.* the female genitals) as an apotropaion, to drive away evil –
the stranger – or the Devil, which is the real meaning of this
gesture still continuing in folk-practice to our own day, as in
Rabelais' "Diable de Papefiguière" story in 1552 (Bk. IV, chap.
47). Other materials have been drawn together on this theme in
the First Series, end of section 2.IV, "The Female Fool," page
147, in connection with modern stories as to women afraid of
'Frouc Frouc' birds, 'Brainpicker' birds, and other stand-ins for
the Devil in these tales.

There is another element here as well, again perhaps just a
rationalization of showing the genitals as an apotropaion, in
which a woman is shown naked to her husband (her face being
covered), who does not recognize her thus; or where women
are exposed in this way as a humiliation. Rotunda has brought
together references to quite a body of such tales in the Italian
novelle of the 16th century and earlier, at Motifs K1213.1,

K1218.4.1, and especially at Q476. It should be observed that this is identical with the theme of the first story of *Les Cent Nouvelles Nouvelles* (about 1460), reworked in Balzac's *Contes Drolatiques* (1832) III, Tale 2, *"D'ung justiciard qui ne se remembroyt les chouses,"* in which the joke is sexualized as of: *A nincumpoop who does not recognize his own naked wife, either from the front or back, when her head is covered by a pillow by her lover, forced to expose her to the husband.*

Not connected with Balzac's story, of course, but interestingly similar, and often told as a true anecdote of the American Jewish humorist, Franklin Pierce Adams: *The loser at a card-game throws down his cards and stalks off, allowing himself the Parthian shot of running his hand over the bald-headed winner's head as he passes him and saying, "You know, Frank, your head feels just like my wife's ass.' The winner reaches up imperturbably and strokes his own bald head. "By God!" he says, "so it does!"* (2:215.) Compare: *Two men in a barbershop, having their hair cut. When the barber starts to sprinkle hair-tonic on one of them, he says, "Hey! don't put that stinkadora on me. My wife will think I smell like a whorehouse." The other man says calmly, "You can put it on me, barber. My wife doesn't know what a whorehouse smells like."* (Chicago, 1965.)

Also involving adulterous and orgiastic notions of conversance with the 'asses' of other men's wives is a charade-story often collected over the twenty years preceding the new publicity for wife-swapping in America in the 1960's, and clearly representing the sort of nude charade one wishes one could set up at parties, but cannot. I have said everything I care to say about orgiasts or 'swingers' of both sexes in *Oragenitalism* (1969) p. 304–5. Most of them are cold, mean egomaniacs, lost in their mental quirks – principal among which is unconscious homosexuality, and sometimes not-so-unconscious – and frozen at the pre-adolescent level in their invariable emotional strangulation, in which they search endlessly for *group-permission*, as in 'circle-jerks' and 'daisy-chains,' for their infantile polymorphous perversions. The logical problem is also never faced by wife-traders (and husband-ditchers), that if *they* so obviously do not any longer, or never did find the sexual offering of their spouses interesting or attractive, why in hell should anyone else find them interesting? *A man is having a party with seven of his friends and their wives. They are*

playing "The Game" (charades), and he cannot guess any of the
puzzles acted out, but he insists that if he is allowed to pose all
the women present just as he wishes, no one – but no one! –
can guess his riddle. All agree, and he has all the women, in-
cluding his own wife, strip naked, posing them in a row as
follows, before the other men: the first woman faces the com-
pany, the second turns her back to them, the third facing, the
fourth turning her back, the fifth facing, and the last three all
turning their backs. Answer: The "William Tell" Overture.
(Titty-rump, titty-rump, titty-rump-rump RUMP!) (N.Y. 1948.)

Despite the implication of contempt in all references to, or
threats or invitations concerning the buttocks or anus – especially as to kissing or kicking them – the fact is that the human
arse has 'strong magic' in almost all cultures, and often advises
its owner, or this may be done by fart-voices or by speaking
excrements. The most popular modern children's book series in
France, Jean de Brunhoff's *Babar*, has an entire farcical war like
this between the elephants and the rhinoceroses, in *Le Voyage
de Babar* (1938?) with *the elephants finally terrifying the
rhinoceroses by painting faces on their bottoms, topped by
fright wigs, and with a carrot up the fundament, for the nose.*
Children love this. Rabelais' *Pantagruel* (1532) Bk. II, chap. 15,
proposes to rebuild the walls of Paris with the *'sine qua nons'* of
women ranged on top of one another with their backsides
bared to the enemy. As the matriarchs of Sparta are reported to
have frightened their enemies and shamed their own sons fleeing the battle. (Motif K774. Compare the joke preceding, on
the "William Tell" Overture.) Here the magic is assimilated to
the entire anal-vulvar 'target' area of the woman. See further the
many references in Stith Thompson's *Motif-Index of Folk
Literature* (1958) VI, Index : *s.v.* anus(es), buttocks, crepitation,
defecating, dung, excrement(s), and urine. (*Russian Secret Tales*,
No. 26; *Kryptádia*, IV. 197.)

The human arse is also not to be insulted with impunity, and
this is noted in more than one folktale, as in the phrase, *'Never
bet the devil your arse'* (politely, 'head;' Motif N2.3.1–5). A
warning of which the Faust legend is just one variant, in which
it is the 'soul' which is wagered or pawned, as Peter Schlemiehl
sells his *shadow*. Both of these are parts of the body only by
courtesy. As late as the 18th century there is much jesting to-do,
even in moderately polite literature, concerning the buttocks as
the 'seat of Honour,' especially in Anglo-Saxon literature, as for

example Smollett's *Adventures of an Atom* (1769) and Rudolph Erich Raspe's anonymous *Baron Münchausen* (1785). A curious anecdote is told, in this line, concerning *Dr. Samuel Johnson happening to say in conversation that a woman 'had a bottom of good sense,' and the company beginning to laugh. Johnson would not be unseated, and continued fiercely, "I mean to say, the woman was fundamentally sound!" And all his auditors sat as grave as judges, without cracking a smile.*

But the most famous proof of the power and position of the arse is a folktale generally told as "The Debate of the *Belly* and the Members of the Body" (Type 293, Motifs A1391 and J461.1), on which an entire monograph has been published by H. Gombel, *Die Fabel vom Magen und den Gliedern* (Beihefte zur Zeitschrift für romanische Philologie, vol. 80, Halle, 1934). In the bawdy versions, as in Vignale's *La Cazzaria* (1530), the belly as the dominant center of the body is replaced, at one step away, by the anus: *The parts of the body have a debate as to which is most important. The head, heart, hands, etc. all state their claims, but when the anus wishes to speak, all the other members tell it to be silent. "All right," says the anus angrily, "I swear I won't open my mouth again!" When the other members of the body then all sicken disastrously from the resultant constipation, they agree that the anus is indeed the most important member of all, and beg it to 'open its mouth and cure them.'* In some versions, *the anus refuses to agree until the crown is placed on the buttocks* – an obvious satirical thrust at royalty. This has also been collected modernly in a style reminiscent of the Aesopic original, with a 'moral' at the end stating: *'Which proves that "All bosses are assholes".'* (L.A. 1968.)

A curious phrase, '*ask my arse*,' mocking any question asked, is recorded as late as 1870 (in the form '*Ax my spiff*') in *Cythera's Hymnal, or Flakes from the Foreskin*, in a limerick reprinted in *The Limerick* as No. 1384, noting that this is a type of wit called 'selling bargains,' and dating from at least the time of Queen Anne. Pope notes, in his *Bathos, or The Art of Sinking in Poetry* (1727) Swift-Pope Miscellanies, 'last' vol., p. 111: 'The principal branch of the *alamode* is the Prurient ... It consists ... of selling of bargains, and *double entendre*.' According to Francis Grose, *A Classical Dictionary of the Vulgar Tongue* (1785) *s.v.* bargain: it is 'frequently alluded to by Dean Swift, who says the maids of honour often amused themselves with it. It consisted in the seller naming his or her hinder parts, in answer to the question, What? which the buyer was artfully led to ask. As a specimen, take the following instance: *A lady would come into a room full of company, apparently in a fright, crying out, It is white, and follows me! On any of the company asking, What? she sold him the bargain, by saying, Mine a — e.'* (More modernly, *'My arse on a band-box!'*) On the very old ritual background underlying this riddling game, see the headnote to Child Ballad No. 2, "The Elfin Knight," and Robert C. Elliott, *The Power of Satire* (1960) p. 62–4, citing ancient Irish sources.

2. ANIMALS AND THE DEVIL

Animals stories involving the buttocks are more likely to be frankly concerned with the animal's anus. This certainly implies that the 'buttock' stories connected with human beings are partialisms and displacements not only for the genitals (especially of women) but also of the human anus. *'A man looking for a good bear dog was told they could always be identified by their enormous ass-hole. He once bargained with a farmer for a dog he thought would do, but as he drove away with it, he remembered the advice he had been given. Lifting up the dog's tail, he noticed a puckered ass-hole you couldn't ram a hickory nut into. He went back and complained to the farmer, who replied, "Oh, yes. I forgot to tell you. There's a set of wrenches goes with that dog. We had him geared down to hunt squirrel".'* (From manuscript, as told by a travelling sales-man in the smoking-car of "The Argonaut," Southern Pacific Railroad, between San Antonio and Houston, Texas, March 28, 1945.) Randolph, *Pissing in the Snow*, No. 52, "A Good Coon Dog," gives almost the identical story, collected in Galena, Missouri, April 1945, lacking only the touch of the 'hickory nut,' but indicating clearly that the story is a 'sell.'

The relaxation and even the extrusion of the anus in all animals, including human beings, is one of the clearest signs of fatigue, though this can best be observed in animals not wear-ing pants. A cowboy phrase has, for example: *'That horse was so tuckered out you could slice washers off'n his ass-hole!'* (Arizona, 1942.) It is also the meaning of *'Your ass is out a yard – and sucking wind!'* (I.e., you are entirely wrong.) One com-monly-collected joke on these themes appears to allude to folk-magical rituals, though the joke rationalizes this almost into non-existence. '*A man who had been refused further service at a bar because he was intoxicated, indignantly retorted, "Drunk? Hell, I'm not drunk. I can see. Look at that cat coming in the door there. It's got only one eye, hasn't it?" The bartender laughed, "Wrong again. That cat has two eyes. Besides, it's not coming in, it's going out".*' (D.C. 1944. Told with variations as to a bet, by an Army private.) As collected earlier, in the Larson Manuscript, No. 47, *The men in a western saloon want to get rid of an Indian who cadges drinks. One man pulls down his pants, stoops over and backs toward the door. The Indian is frightened by the apparition and runs away. Miles off, he explains to a prospector: "Me seeum funny little man! Only so high (indicating with one hand). One big eye in middle of forehead! Hair all over face! Musta come long way! Tongue hang out that far! (Again indicating with hand.)*" (Idaho, 1919.)

Larson also gives, without noting the relationship, at No. 45, and with the same provenance: *A man who is riding on a train with no toilet, sticks his ass out the window and shits. The train at that moment whizzes by two track-walkers, Pat & Mike. "Did you get a load of the bald-headed guy with a moustache, sticking his head out the window?" "No, Pat, but sure an' I did see a queer looking individual with a big cigar in his mouth."* The scatological intrusion here is intended simply to rationalize away the penis. Flemish version in *Kryptádia*, IV. 322, with '*long nose and dirty moustache.*'

What is really involved here seems to be the folk-custom of the 'dumb supper,' a mantic art of a kind much discussed in Aubrey's *Remaines* (MS. 1686), by which girls identify their future husbands. It is noted by Vance Randolph in his *Ozark Superstitions* (1947) p. 178 81, and, less guardedly, in his *"Unprintable" Ozark Folk Beliefs* (MS. 1954) No. 1, as collected in Eureka Springs, Arkansas, 1946:

Two young girls near Green Forest, Ark., about 1898, prepared a dumb supper with all the trimmings – absolute silence, dim light, walking backward [n.b.], and so on. But a local ruffian had overheard their plans. Exactly at midnight the two girls sat down and bowed their heads. The door opened very slowly, and in came a big man walking backward, clad only in a short undershirt. Approaching the table he bent forward, took his enormous tool in hand, and thrust it backward between his legs, so that it stuck right out over the food on the table. One of the girls screamed and fled into the "other house" crying, "Maw, maw, he's thar! He's come a long way, an' he's only got one eye!" The other girl sat silent as if paralysed, and the man walked out the door and disappeared in the darkness. Later on the family realized that the whole thing was a joke, and hushed it up "to keep down scandal" in the neighborhood. Nobody was ever quite sure who the man was, though the girls had their suspicions.

Actually, the man is supposed to be the Devil (the *cat* in the joke), and the whole ritual – with its insistence on all the actions being done *backwards* – is reminiscent of all such conjuring-ups of either the 'Evil Spirit' or the spirit of the dead. As in the inquiring of the 'familiar spirit' of the witch of Endor, by King Saul, in disguise (*n.b.*), in 1 *Samuel*, xxviii, 6–25, when Jehovah refuses to answer the hysterical or epileptic king (note his throwing of a javelin at the harpist, David, in xvi. 23 and xix. 9–10, when 'the evil spirit' was upon him), 'neither by dreams, nor by Urim [amulets], nor by prophets.'

In the Randolph joke manuscript, *Pissing in the Snow*, No. 30, 'The Romping Party," a rather similar scene is described, as having taken place 'near Berryville, Ark., in the early 1890's.' Randolph does not observe specially that this romp (the collegiate 'pajama party') is of the 'dumb supper' variety, though the same diabolic visitor makes his silent and mysterious erotic appearance and getaway, and the girl with whom in this case he has had intercourse is led to believe that he is simply another girl who has had intercourse with her in the dark of the 'romping party,' using a banana as a dildo: '*She squealed and farted like a mare, and then just laid still awhile. The boy sneaked out the door again, and nobody knowed he'd been there at all. The biggest girl was still a-breathing hard, but pretty soon she begun to holler. "Mamie," she says, "come back here with that good banana!"* '

Various Pyramus & Thisbe stories of this kind exist in which there is no man present, but only a dildo, this being replaced secretly by a man's (Devil's?) penis shoved through the wall, up through the flooring, or in through a slit in a tent: obviously Levantine in origin. See many more versions and developments of this in the First Series, 8.VIII.10, "The Eaten Heart," p. 658–61. In one castratory version: *The hobo has slid under the frame-house and replaced the old maids' rubber penis, held vertical in a knothole in the floor, with his own penis. Just then there is a knock at the door and one old maid shouts to the other, "Quick, Libby, kick it under the bed!"* (L.A. 1968.) A South American Indian tale, Motif K1344.1, collected by Alfred Métraux, has *A girl seduced from beneath the ground.* Here the seducer is evidently alive. Louis Perceau's anonymous *Histoires Raides* ('Marseille,' *ca.* 1929) p. 109, "Sur la tombe," has, however: *A young widow picking the weeds around her husband's grave, who is tickled in the crotch by a stalk of wild oats. "Oh, my poor darling," she says with a sigh, "you're still as horny as ever!"* No disguise here that this is an erotic relation with a ghost, or, rather, with the life-principle growing upward from the ground as a sort of natural erection. Similarly, a German ceramic artist in the 1920's left behind on the wall of an unused back room, in a house I rented in Cagnes-sur-Mer, France, *A colored drawing of a young woman squatting wildly in a field of high-growing asparagus plants with an ecstatic look.*

In all of these jokes and fantasies the dominant erotic position of the woman is a principal feature. Meaning that these are all probably the fantasies of male masochists. It is not normal to any anthropoid or quadruped for the female to lie or squat over the supine male in intercourse, and though obviously any coital position is a desirable erotic pleasure, human female-dominant positions taken habitually or appearing in male fantasies must be considered to mask yearnings for submission on the part of the male. Combined in the present group of stories with fantasies of being dead, or 'used,' and triumphing over death by the 'Resurrection of the Flesh.'

3. YOU-KNOW-WHAT-AND-WHERE

Obviously connected with the insulting invitations already considered in chapter 14.II.3, under "Water-Wit," as to kissing the buttocks, or, more graphically, sucking the anus, is the equally insulting recommendation to put something or stuff something 'up one's ass.' This is often shortened or euphemized to '*You know what you can do with it*,' or '*... where you can stick it*,' as will be seen in certain of the jokes to be given. In the 78 r.p.m. phonograph recordings of double-entendre night-club skits first issued in America during the early 1940's as 'Party Records,' on the success of a series of such recordings – hardly more than off-color – by the entertainer Dwight Fiske, two of the comedians went by the allusive names of 'Lord Stickit and Lord Stuffit.' Likewise, one of the earliest jokes on the United Nations organization replacing the League of Nations at the end of World War II, under the initials 'U.N.O.' later expurgated to 'U.N.' , with its subsidiary 'UNESCO,' and so forth, was the announcement that: *'The purpose of the U.N.O. is to give the smaller nations of the world just what they need, through two organizations:* UNOWHAT *and* UNOWHERE.' The aposiopetic euphemisms 'You know' and 'You know what' (also in French: *'Ce que vous savez'*) invariably have a sexual or scatological implication. A brief linguistic travesty, "A Selectional Restriction involving Pronoun Choice" (1968?) signed 'Yuck Foo,' studies the semantics of *'Shove it up your ass!'* with variations. (Courtesy of Prof. James D. McCawley of Chicago, who is satirized therein.)

A customer in a restaurant who objects to the food, tells the waiter, "Take this steak right back to the chef and tell him to stick it up his arse." "The chef said you'll have to take your turn," the waiter answered; "there's a beef stew and a cocoanut pie ahead of you." (1:220.) In a World War II-to-III variant: *'A woman buying watermelons found the price 85¢, exorbitant, and refused ... disgusted with the high price, she told the storekeeper he could ram it up his ass. "I'd love to, lady," he said, 'but I've already got a 32¢ cucumber up there'.'* (D.C. 1951, from a young married woman.) These food-dirtying items are clearly connected with various Levantine stories of the 'Thankful Fool' variety (Types 1689 and 1610) typical of the Turkish jester, Nasr'eddin Hodja, as No. 71 in Wesselski's edition. *The members of the band have been shipwrecked on the desert island. When they play well their instruments are filled with food, "And there the others were with their tubas, and me with that damned little piccolo!" When they play badly their instruments are stuffed up their ass. "And there I was with that blessed piccolo!"* In food-dirtying forms: *The unlucky guest brings bananas as a gift for the cannibal king. They are stuffed up his ass – while he howls with laughter, explaining, "My friend is coming with pineapples!"* (Both N.Y. 1938, the second told as a 'topper.') Modern Levantine versions in Decourdemanche's *La Fleur lascive,* p. 80, from Persia; and *Histoires Arabes* (1927), pp. 63 and 102. These all allude plainly to pedicatory rape as punishment, inordinately common in the Near East, and also to the torture of impalement. In polite European versions since the early Renaissance (as in the *Cento Novelle Antiche*, No. 74) the rejected gifts are thrown in the giver's 'face,' instead of being shoved up his arse.

A commonly-collected "Weak Sister" involves an elephant *'picking cabbages with its tail,'* and sometimes even told as having actually happened in some backwoods community where a circus elephant – an animal otherwise unknown – has escaped. In rationalized form this has also been published as of a child's ignorance, though the action is evidently not that of a child. *'A small boy saw an elephant in his yard and immediately called the police. "Chief," he said, "there's a queer looking animal out here in my back yard picking flowers with his tail." "Yes," said the Chief, "and what does he do then?" "Never mind," was the answer. 'You wouldn't believe me if I told you".'* (*The Cotton Ginner's Journal*, Oct. 1938, p. 21.) All of these involve, of course, obvious food-defiling by the stated reversal of the usual digestive process. Note, in the fantastic art of Breughel and Bosch, the persistent concern with little animals putting funnels, &c. in their rectums.

The insulting or rejecting phrase, *'You know what you can do with it!'* or *'You know where you can stick it!'* is sometimes alluded to in 'catch'-form, by responding to the innocent question *'What shall I do with it?'* or *'Where shall I put it?'* with the meaningful: *'I could make a suggestion!'* The popular realization during World War II that the soldiers being entertained by civilians were being fobbed off with cookies and soft-drinks they didn't want, instead of the sex and liquor they did want (mock-definition: *'U.S.O. – An organization for giving cookies to soldiers in need of a screw'*), was politely expressed in a joke printed in Bennett A. Cerf's *Pocket Book of War Humor* (1943) p. 83 – this being the least expurgated of his many joke-collections – and was monitored thus over radio station WTOP, July 29, 1944, at 7:30 A.M., delivered by the radio-announcer: *'Twenty soldiers invited by an old maid to a cocktail party were surprised to be served lemonade and a platter of cookies. When each man had some ten cookies apiece, a single cookie remained on the platter, and the old maid said, "Just one left, boys. What shall we do with it?" The lieutenant in charge stood up immediately and said, "The man that answers that question will be given fifteen days in the guardhouse!" '* The format here is that of: *The actor onstage asking, "What is fairer than a woman's smile? What more beautiful than her ruby lips?"* At *which point the sheriff stationed in the balcony to keep order, leaps to his feet drawing his revolver, and shouts, "I'll plug the first son-of-a-bitch that answers that question!"* (N.Y. 1938.)

The direct invitation is almost always phrased or answered as a joke. *A young man accosted by a streetwalker tells her that he can't go upstairs with her for three reasons: "First, I haven't any money –" "Goodbye," she says; "you can stick the other two up your ass."* (2:119.) *– A salesman continually writes his firm: "No sale made, but gave the prospect a high opinion of our product, so that's a feather in my cap." He finally receives a telegram:* "STICK THOSE FEATHERS UP YOUR ASS AND FLY HOME – THE FIRM IS BROKE." (N.Y. 1952.) Compare the untranslatable and impossible French joke, also of the early 1950's: *A foreigner phones the Paris airport asking for a reservation on the plane to Nice. When asked to give his name, his accent proves too much for the reservation clerk, who asks him to spell it instead. "My name is Glloq," the foreigner says, spelling in out:* "G-L-L-O-Q [J'ai deux ailes au cul: *I have two wings in my ass]." "Well then," says the clerk, scenting an attempted pleasantry, "If you have two wings in your ass, all you have to do is* FLY *to Nice."* (Paris, 1954, from a lady-artist.) A catch, of course; the German name being mocked is that of the composer Gluck.

The joke has already been noted, in the First Series, in the chapter on Fools and Englishmen: *George VI calls up Edward. "You know, old chap, we can't find the crown anywhere. Do you suppose, by any chance, Wally might have wrapped it up in an old towel or something? Ring me back, will you?" Edward calls back. "I've looked everywhere, George. We haven't got it. But I've just been wondering – do you think the Archbishop of Canterbury might have taken me seriously when I told him to shove it up his arse?"* (Baker, 1945, vol. II.) Probably the favorite on this theme, as well known in England as in America, concerns: *A man with constipation who is told by the doctor to take two suppositories every night for a week. He comes back to the drugstore and complains that the suppositories did him no good at all. "Besides," he adds, "they tasted terrible." "What did you do with them," asks the astonished druggist, "eat them?" "Sure I ate them. What did you expect me to do with them – stick 'em up my ass?"* (N.Y. 1940. Allusively cartooned in *Sex to Sexty,* 1966, 9:14.)

No joke has been encountered, more openly and specifically

concerning itself with the human anus (as differentiated from
that of other animals), than the one told during World War II
as a conscious parable on the question of who 'makes it' (succeeds) and who doesn't, in the dog-eat-dog jungle of civilized
life. This joke has influenced me very much, and comforted me
greatly, in some rather dark hours over the last twenty-five
years. It is not my favorite joke, but I love it. It has an epic
quality reminding one of the scene in the modern Italian movie,
Miracle in Milan, in which the poor human derelicts and squat-
ters dash madly from one end of the field to the other, trying
to get into the shifting and evanescent single ray of sunlight. *A
poor carpenter working in a war-camp is continually shoved
aside and out of line at the paymaster's wagon-window, and
when he finally gets to the window it is slammed shut in his
face. "No more money!" the paymaster says; "try one of the
other wagons." The man dashes down the muddy field to another pay-wagon, where the same thing occurs. Finally, when
it is nearly evening, he grabs the bars of the paymaster's window being slammed in his face, and says, "For God's sake,
you've got to pay me! I've been in line all day. My children
have nothing to eat; my wife is dying; I haven't eaten anything
myself since Tuesday. For God's sake, pay me, and let me go!"
"What's your name?" the paymaster asks. "Zoophole – Alois
Zoophole." "Zoophole?! Well, that's your trouble. We pay
alphabetically around here. If your name was* ASSHOLE, *you'd
have been paid off long ago!"* (Orangeburg, N.Y. 1942.)

At the risk of seeming to take this joke too seriously, it
might be mentioned that, in fact, people whose names begin
with the letter Z – and, to a lesser degree, the somewhat unusual initial letters *I* and *Q* – are often among the most neurotic-
ally driven and success-minded, exactly in the style of the joke.
Obvious examples of this kind can be found in any biographical
dictionary, but a certain caution is necessary here. Some famous
or successful people whose names begin with Z (for example,
Zangwill, Zanuck, Zenger, Zeppelin, Zegzula, Zichy, Ziegfeld,
Zola, Zwingli, and Sabbatai Zevi, among the names that come
immediately to mind) are or were, of course, the opposite of
neurotic; while the most extravagantly success-driven and
dangerous personages of history have never, in fact, included a
single person whose name began with a Z. Consider: Alexander
the Great, Attila the Hun, Napoleon Bonaparte, Hitler, Tamer-
lane, Genghis Khan, and all the rest. Nary a Z among them! It

should naturally not be overlooked, as the preceding joke purposely implies, that Z is the 'asshole' of the alphabet. People suffering from such names certainly never overlook it. This is their joke.

4. AJAX REVISITED

The toilet or privy – the Elizabethan 'jakes' – has a very large literature of its own, which it is no part of my intention to cover here. The bibliography of the subject is, in any case, over a century out-of-date, never having been covered with any completeness since the *Bibliotheca Scatologica* ('Scatopolis, 5850,' *i.e.* Paris, 1849–50) by Pierre Jannet and others, and its supplement, *Anthologie Scatologique* (1862) by Gustave Brunet. Also Josef Feinhal's *Non Olet* (Köln, 1939). Modern works abound, of which the most complete is Reginald Reynold's somewhat mannered *Cleanliness and Godliness* (London, 1943). Others – all British – are John Pudney's *The Smallest Room* (1954), Lawrence Wright's *Clean and Decent* (1960, the best illustrated work), Jonathan Routh's practical *The Good Loo Guide* (1965), and Wallace Reyburn's *Flushed With Pride* (1969), a biography of the greatest of all examples of 'name-fatality,' Thomas Crapper, 'Sanitary Engineer' to the British royal house. An American architect is preparing a further work, seriously calling for larger bathrooms that one can 'live in,' which I presume involves parlors one can shit in – or at least bathe in – but am not sure. See Prof. Alexander Kira, *The Bathroom: Criteria for Design* (1966). My withers are unwrung: I have no bathroom at all – just a tin tub under a tree, for bathing, and a bucket in the woods, for 'recycling.' No one can construct a bathroom as beautiful as that. And a fig! for the earliest 'sanitation engineer' in English literature, Sir John Harington in his *Metamorphosis of Ajax* (1596), and the most practical: Chic Sale's *The Specialist* (1929) with supplement.

The essence of the anal character is not only its famous retentiveness, but also its 'social-sadistic' desire to dominate and control – especially other people. Consider in this line what was perhaps just an April Fool pleasantry, but just as likely authentic: a German field-latrine order dated 1 April 1916, reproduced in J. C. Brunner's *Illustrierte Sittengeschichte: Kreig und Geschlechtsleben* (Frankfurt, 1922) p. 64, also in Dr Paul Englisch's *Das skatologische Element in Literatur* (Stuttgart, 1927) giving the ultimate simplification of privy architecture, with the exact method of using it. The order is illustrated with drawings of two soldiers – doing it right and doing it wrong, both with their pants down around their knees – formally requiring the correct and reglementary method of squatting over a slit-trench latrine.

The backwoods scatological humor of tipping over privies on Hallowe'en and the like, is taken to its nth degree in Prof. John Barth's novel of pioneer America, *The Sot-Weed Factor* (New York, 1960), and various earlier items of milder nature – especially certain 1930's U.S. humor magazines – contain some generalized outhouse humor of the kind. However, the *ne plus ultra* of all pictorial scatology, its glorification and its apotheosis, is reached in an 'underground' comic book, *Rubber Duck*, No. 2 – naturally – published by The Print Mint, Berkeley, Calif., in 1972, of which the whole second half is taken up with Michael J. and Shelby's "*Shit List: A Journey into the Cesspools of the Mind*," which is all the title promises and a great deal more. Cast as a fecal satire on an American president, Richard Nixon, this goes the limit (and beyond) in illustrated scatophagy and anal-destructiveness, with more than a bow to the sewer-crawling of Victor Hugo's *Les Misérables* and of a Polish moving-picture of World War II, *The Canal*. A shit-collector's item. One culminating page of "*Shit List*" is reproduced in Mark James Estren's lavishly illustrated *History of Underground Comics* (San Francisco, 1974) p. 267–9.

The bitter humor of the pay-toilet attendants is not common in America, though this is used as the plot *dénouement* in a French 19th-century humorous novel, the long-lost heir being recognized in a pay-toilet by his unmistakable groans coming over the cubicle wall 'during the melon season' – melons being thought to be particularly aperient. (*Lilie, Tutue, Bébeth: Bouffonnerie Parisienne*, by 'Eugène Chavette' [Vachette], ca. 1885, chap. 5.) *An actor leaving a pay-toilet notices that the attendant is a former theatrical star. "My word!" he says, as he pays his fee, "you must be starving to do this." "Oh, it isn't as bad as all that," said the former star. "Of course, business has been a little slow this morning. I've had twelve pissers, and you're the third shit to come in."* (1:115.) – *The saloon-keeper who is asked how business is. "Lousy! All I been doin' is tradin' ice-water for piss all week."* (1:405.) The food-dirtying implication here becomes the whole joke in examples to be given below, under "Scatophagy," in which the toilet is ignorantly mistaken for a well by hill-billies or Indians in a hotel.

A particular theme is the hill-billy or Westerner who – sometimes because his penis is too long – cannot or does not know enough to sit down on the toilet, and 'rides it bareback,' chewing up the seat with his spurs. *Sex to Sexty* (1966) 7:14 has the 'Moron' joke of this kind revised for purposes of sex-hatred, by combining both sexual and scatological nincum-poopery. *The moron's mother tells him that what he must do with his bride is: "Take the biggest thing you've got and put it where she tinkles"* [urinates]. *Later he phones his mother from the hotel in Chicago: "Hello, mother ... I've got my foot caught in the commode, what do I do next?"* This is the cloacal theory, of course, and other joke versions rather similar will be found earlier in Chapter 12.IV.1, "Cloacal Intercourse." These make clear that he has really got his foot caught, not in the toilet commode, but in his bride. See also the First Series, 2.I–II, "Nincumpoops."

What is involved here is only theoretically ignorance: a nin-cumpoopery of which the ultimate point is 'not knowing how to wipe one's ass – and having to be told.' Actually, the stand-ing on the toilet-seat is an ancient way of evading not only the cold touch of the seat itself, but also 'disease,' and any un-cleanly relics left by former users with 'bad aim.' In A. E. Brown & H. A. Jeffcott's marvellous collection of eccentric in-ventions, *Beware of Imitations!* (1932) p. 14–15, a sanitary privy-seat is illustrated, patented so early as 1869 (Patent No. 90,298), in which the seat is composed of four rollers at various angles, 'which renders it impossible for the user to stand upon the privy-seat.' Another invention illustrated in the same work, and of somewhat the same inspiration perhaps, is the chewing-gum locket, to make unnecessary the 'parking' of one's wad of chewing gum under tables or chairs, where unauthorized or unknown persons may chew it! Brown & Jeffcott's fascinating collection was reprinted in New York by Dover Publications, 1970, vulgarly retitled *Absolutely Mad Inventions* on the 1890 *kitsch* kick. Another such collection is *Les Folies Bourgeoises* by Paul & Christiane Gilson (Monaco: Editions du Rocher, 1957), splendidly illustrated with documents of the times: mostly 19th century.

A far-travelled Oriental story is that of the hunchbacked bridegroom who spends his wedding night stuck in the privy, in the *Arabian Nights* ("Tale of Nur-al-Din Ali," 'Burton Club' edition, I. 221), and there is a similar incident in the story of Aladdin (Burton's Supplemental Night 550: 'Burton Club' edition, XIII. 82). This enters Europe through Antoine de La Sale's *Les Cent Nouvelles Nouvelles* (about 1460) No. 72, in which the butt runs off with the toilet-seat around his neck and obviously well-besmeared. The story heavily overdetermines the masochist element, as not only is the butt (an adulterer) imprisoned eventually by the toilet-seat, but the story is so set up that the husband's unexpected return home forces him to stifle his sneezing by ducking his head time after time in the toilet-hole. Rotunda K1517.4.1, rather hides this story under the heading "Paramour in grotesque disguise," though this is, in fact, the essence of certain of its late forms, as that in Afanasyev's *Russian Secret Tales* (1872) No. 65, "The Cunning Woman."

It is the striking trait of the yoking by the toilet-seat (Tale type 571A) which has become crucial in the most common modern form of the joke, with various rationalizations. *An Italian immigrant writes a letter (in dialect verse) to 'Mr. Kresge,' complaining that he has painted the toilet-seat with a can of 10¢-store paint, and that it never dried, trapping his daughter on the seat. They go to the doctor to have the seat removed, and when the doctor looks astonished, the Italian asks if he has never seen one of those things before. "Sure," says the doctor, "but this is the first time I saw one with a frame around it."* (Printed 'novelty' card, circulated since the 1940's in America.) A rewriting appears in Jackie Kannon's *Poems for the John* (New York, 1960), as "The Italian's Lament." There is also a folk-transmitted British version in verse, as "Sonia Snell," in Harry Morgan's *Why Was He Born So Beautiful, and other Rugby Songs* (London, 1967) p. 134. The similarity will be observed here to the story, "The Glass Eye," given earlier from French sources. The whole mechanical problem of these jokes is to get the doctor somehow posed staring squarely at (or into) the patient's buttocks.

Any method of trapping the person in the privy satisfies the needs of the scatological form of the story, whether sticky paint (*i.e.* trap-lime), a crack in the seat, or actually climbing *in*, for any ostensible reason or pretext. *A woman who ordered an outhouse from a mail-order company 'kept sending in complaints until they sent out an inspector, a dignified gentleman with moustache and goatee [!] He looked it all over, tested the way the seat lifted, blowing smoke up the chimney, running*

*his finger around the rim without getting any splinter, etc.,
until he finally removed his hat and peered down the hole,
where his beard got caught. "Annoying, isn't it?" said the
woman.'* (D.C. 1944, from an army private; text-form, 1953.) A
friend of mine, at about the same period, who happened to
have a beard, and was busying himself collecting illustrated
toilet-epigraphs in the New York subways, once found a brand-
new *graffito*, evidently referring to himself and possibly to the
present joke, reading: *'These bearded shit-house inspectors,
Woo-woo!'* See the caricature of exactly the same import, the
'shit-house inspector' being not only bearded but also top-
hatted, and climbing on the seat to examine the inscriptions
with a tape-measure and magnifying glass, in *Bilder-Lexikon
der Erotik* (1929) II. 12, from the French magazine, *L'Assiette
au Beurre.*

The toilet-epigraph or *graffito* is a subject too large to enter
into here. A useful introduction will be found in Prof. Allen
Walker Read's *Lexical Evidence from Folk Epigraphy in
Western North America* (Paris, 1935), and Prof. Alan Dundes'
"Here I Sit": Studies in American Latrinalia, first published in
the *Papers of the Kroeber Anthropological Society* (Spring,
1966) No. 34, and reprinted in Paul Krassner's satirical journal,
The Realist (New York, 1968, No. 80?). These are both strictly
textual collections, as are the few items appearing in *Kryptádia*
(original series, 1884 ff.) under the rubric *"La Muse latrinale."*
The pictographic materials that are almost invariably in evidence in graffiti, and which are usually of as great psychological
interest as the verbal texts, were first briefly explored in *The
Merry-Thought, or The Glass-Window and Bog-House Miscellany* (1731) 4 parts; and in two important articles in French by
G. H. Luquet, in *Anthropophytéia* (1910–11) VII. 202–6, and
ills. at p. 529–37; and vol. VIII. 215–16, with pls. xxxv–vii at
end.

The illustrative material in graffiti has also been recorded
more recently in a Sorbonne Ph.D. thesis, by a Texan residing in
France, William McLean, *Contribution à l'étude de l'iconographie populaire de l'érotisme* (Paris: Maisonneuve & Larose,
1970), but unfortunately the textual materials were completely
rejected in this study, in which the wall- and toilet-epigraphs
are reproduced photographically and are also curiously combined with large numbers of sado-masochistic reproductions
from Italian comic-books, issued in France *'pour adultes'* – ap-

parently the real 'iconography' the author is concerned with. It should be added that McLean's bibliography is very full and excellent, ranging from antiquity (as at Pompeii) to similar materials in primitive art. However, no reference whatever is made in McLean's text to most of the books in his bibliography – as indicated by asterisks preceding the titles of works actually cited – and it is not clear from what catalogue sources or anthropological archives the works listed may have been drawn.

Various cheap popular works on textual epigraphs have been issued in America and England, in the late 1960's, as part of the yoicks of new-found 'New Freedom,' all of them expurgated ludicrously in the choice of materials, thus leaving them a good deal closer to the old *non*-freedom. This particular batch of toilet-kitsch includes Richard Freeman's *Graffiti* (London, 1966), advertising itself as 'Totally futile,' and confining itself strictly to the mildest possible examples, as was also the case with the delighted reviews and news-mag notices of this moderately informative work. As almost nothing is to be learned from the various similar items published in the United States, it does not seem worthwhile listing them all here. The most godawful was Norton Mockridge's *The Scrawl of the Wild: What People Write On Walls – and Why* (Cleveland, 1968), of which the approach is purely journalistic, as the title makes clear, while the illustrations included are humorous gup by a commercial artist, Mr. Jerry Schlamp; no actual epigraph illustrations being reproduced. A bit more latitude is allowed itself in the main Mexican erotic folklore roundup, *Picardía Mexicana* by A. Jiménez-Farias (México, 1960), though again most of the illustrations ventured are commercial humor. See also Daniel Hawkes' 'folk-porno,' *Erotic Letters and Graffiti* (London: Luxor Press, 1970?), Bill Adler's *Graffiti*, Alan Robbins' *Guide to College Graffiti*, and Robert Reisner's *Graffiti and Great Wall Writing and Button Graffiti* (these last four all: New York, 1967).

Large collections of actual wall- and toilet-epigraphs and their illustrations have been made by Vance Randolph and others, in particular a group concerning homosexual assignation – usually the main subject – with their erotic pictographs traced *in situ* (by the friend mentioned above), which is now repositoried in the Kinsey Library, Institute for Sex Research, Indiana University, as a supplement to my unpublished monograph *Homosexual Prostitution in the United States* (MS. 1940), in collaboration with Mr. Thomas Painter. Large British collections of material have also been made for me, most of these concerned with masturbatory or erotic brag, and heavily homosexual and sado-masochistic, as is the case with all authentic popular erotic materials in Western cultures. During the student uprising in Paris in the spring of 1968, which rapidly spread to the main labor unions and was violently repressed by special police and the army, large numbers of political and sexual wall-*graffiti* appeared all over France (but especially in Paris), and several collections of these have been published. See also Robert Édouard's *Dictionnaire des Injures* (Paris: Tchou, 1967) chap. 10, "Des Graffiti," p. 125–32. Some remarks on the psychological and protective (apotropaic) purpose of graffiti will also by found in the following section here, "Apotropaic Rituals," in which toilet-epigraphs in particular are considered as a form of anal-sadistic daubing on walls, using the words – often in verse – instead of the more primitive shit.

Rabelais gives, as the last jest of the last chapter of Book IV of *Gargantua* (1552), an apocryphal story of the French poet & criminal, François Villon, the original French hippie or beatnik of the 15th century (and compare Thoreau in America), answering back patriotically, *à la* Tyl Eulenspiegel, to *Edward IV, King of England, who stated that he had hung the royal arms of France 'in this backside* [privy], *near my close-stool.' To which Villon retorted that the English king had done well, probably at his doctor's advice, with a laxative intention, for the fear of France would make the English king 'conskite' himself wherever he saw those royal arms displayed.* This is close to the plot of the ballad, "The Bastard King of England."

The hanging of the enemy's arms or portrait in the privy is, of course, only a pictographic modification of the idea of 'wiping one's ass' upon them, or defecating upon them directly, as will be discussed further in the following section. During the Napoleonic period it was considered highly amusing in England to paint pictures of Napoleon at the bottom of ladies' chamber-pots, sometimes with the eye shown very large and central, or even with the mouth wide open. (Earlier, of Benjamin Franklin, by Louis XVI; and of an Irish landlord, as noted in Francis Grose's *Classical Dictionary of the Vulgar Tongue*, 1785, *s.v.* "Twiss.") In the last of the vaudeville shows given in the American theatre – other than revivals of this sort of 'variety' show for the soldiers – during World War II, Olson and Johnson's *Hellzapoppin!* (1942), the urinals and toilet-bowls in the men's room were decorated with paintings of Hitler open-mouthed, in just this style.

A girl out driving in the country stops at a gas-station to use the rather primitive rest-room, and is startled, while she is relieving herself, to hear a small plaintive voice from below calling up to her: "Could you move over one hole, lady? I'm trying to paint down here." (N.Y. 1945.) Here the teller of the story masochistically takes the entrapped lover's situation in the privy, with the implication of receiving on his head and person the woman's excrements. This is a standard masochistic fantasy, often involving scatophagy as well. In an even further rationalized and *mechanized* form, it is explained that: *It is only a prank. There's really no one under the toilet-seat at all. The gas-station attendant has a microphone planted under the seat, and does this as a joke to all women clients.* As Santa Claus says, 'Ho-ho-ho!'" But wait, wait! Don't go away satisfied. That isn't all. Another joke, already given under "Cloacal Intercourse," chapter 12.IV.1, tells the rest of the story: *A man at a country dance notices that the women's and men's privies are separated only by a wooden partition. He waits until a good-looking girl goes into the women's side, then dashes into the men's privy, and sticks his head down through the hole in the seat hoping to look at the girl's ass. To his astonishment he finds himself looking her straight in the eye instead. "Er, ah,"* he fumbles, *"may I have the next dance?"* (Santa Monica, Calif. 1965.)

Undinist and scatophilous yearnings of this kind, in which the women's urine and feces attract the man fetichistically, are quite standard in male masochism, and often involve – as here – complex 'set-up' situations where the man arranges to be used as the woman's chamber-pot, in this case without her knowledge. Havelock Ellis' autobiographical admissions on this score were by no means complete, though he does note his lifelong undinism (to which almost an entire supplementary volume is given in his *Studies in the Psychology of Sex*, mostly the case of 'Florrie,' his wife). Ellis is also believed to be the author of certain rare late-Victorian masochist erotica too, in particular *Gynecocracy*, where scatophilous scenes of sado-masochist humiliation are involved. (The desire to be given enemas, with all their sequelae, is also a standard masochist trait in both sexes, as a form of rectal violence, in addition to the intimate relation with the feces involved.)

A brief toilet-epigraph given in *The Merry Thought, or Bog-*

House Miscellany (1731) makes no bones about the matter, and gives the secret meaning of the preceding joke: *'Oh! that I were a turd, a turd, Hid in this secret place, That I might see my Betsy's arse, Though she shit in my face.'* This still survives in America, very much changed, as a song, "Bang Away, My Lulu," in the stanza: *'I wish I was a finger ring, Upon my Lulu's hand, And every time she wiped her ass, I'd see the Promised Land!'* It is tempting to believe that some version of this quatrain, if not simply a 'parallel inspiration,' is at work in the well-known poem translated from the German by Tennyson, "The Miller's Daughter," given in Palgrave's *Golden Treasury* (enlarged ed., Oxford, 1907) No. 322, in which the poet wishes he were various parts of his belovèd's clothing and jewelry, ending up as the necklace *'upon her balmy bosom ... And I would lie so light, so light, I scarce should be unclasp'd at night.'* Which says everything, to any Victorian. The frankest modern text is the old song "I Wish My Love Was In a Bog," printed in Karl Dallas' *One Hundred Songs of Toil* (London: Wolfe, 1974) p. 169–71, "The Pitman's Lovesong," to a psalm tune! In stanza 7, the sadism of the singer becomes interchangeably masochism, as posited by Freud. This stanza is omitted from "The Pitman's Lovesong" as sung by A. L. Lloyd on his Topic recording 12T118, with the observation – a masterpiece of double-think – 'Rather to my own surprise I find myself too prudish to sing it, though I'm impressed by its intensity':

> *I wish my love was a ripe turd*
> *And smoking down in yon dykeside*
> *And I myself was a shitten flea,*
> *I'd suck her up before she dried.*

That rather closes the subject. And yet ... One of the greatest writers of the 19th century, the French historian Jules Michelet (and later Guy de Maupassant and the poets Pierre Louÿs and Louis Perceau in their private works), could give even Havelock Ellis cups & saucers in the masochistic *'pisseuse'* department. The record of Michelet's undinist and menstrual fun & games with his young wife, Athénaïs Mialaret, is perfectly candid in his intimate diaries, appropriately quoted in Sanche de Gramont's *The French: Portrait of a People* (1969) p. 94–6; as also Michelet's conscious search for inspiration at the vaginal 'fountain of life,' which Maupassant boldly calls *"Ma Source."*

5. GARGANTUA'S INVENTION

Everyone who has tried to read Rabelais – and it is a book more people have begun than have finished – is aware that Rabelais' hero, the giant *Gargantua* (1534) in Book I, chapter 13, first attracts the attention of his father, Grangousier, by his marvellous invention of the '*torchecul* or wipe-breech,' of which a stupendous catalogue is given of all manner of objects used for this purpose. Of these it is agreed, at length: '*to conclude, I say and maintain, that of all* torcheculs, *arse-wisps, bum-fodders, tail napkins, bunghole cleaners, and wipe-breeches, there is none in the world comparable to the neck of a goose, that is well downed, if you hold her neck betwixt your legs.*' This is further stated to be the habit and true felicity of 'the heroes and demigods in the Elysian fields,' an opinion attributed gravely to the Scottish schoolman, Duns Scotus, who has at least this much to do with the case that *dunce-caps* are named after him. More to the real purposes of scatological humor, Radelais does not fail to include in his catalogue a number of *torcheculs* far less pleasant, intended and stated to scrape and harm the user, in a sort of pedicatory rape.

The 18th-century scholiast, John Ozell, in his revision of Urquhart and Le Motteux' translation of Rabelais (reprint: Bodley Head, 1927, I. 50), cannot forbear to improve on his author, in this anal-sadistic vein. (Johann Fischart's translation of Rabelais into German, 1575, is also heavily extended in the *torchecul* chapter – a real curiosity of literature in its invented words, well worth examining.) Ozell notes a country-prank from his own experience, on *persiguière* or persicaria, that this · 'signifies not pursley, but what we English call arse-smart. This I have often recommended to the country fellows for a wipe-brush, and have been well diverted and not a little cursed for my advice ... [Matthias de] Lobel in his *Adversaria Nova*, p. 134: "*Gallis* culraige *vocatus est* (he is speaking of the persicaria), *ut cujus folia, quæ quis podici (honor sit auribus) abstergendi causâ affricurerit, inurant rabiem clunibus, sive, ut loquuntur leguleii, culo*".' Which proves that there is nothing like a classical education, if you plan to go tearing off the leaves of things in the woods.

Gargantua's brag to one side, the use of leaves or grass must have been the real origin of toilet-paper, as household animals (such as cats) having diarrhea or worms can be seen scraping their bottoms frantically on the earth, though actually it is the friction and not the cleansing that they are after. As is well known, they clean themselves with their tongues, as do many quadrupeds and certain birds. '*A woman who had eaten largely of beans before beginning a long trip on a bus was appalled to find there were no toilets there. She tried to remain composed in appearance despite her internal anarchy, and casually turning to the man next to her she said, "Do you happen to have the evening newspaper?" He replied, "No, but the next tree we pass, I'll pull off a leaf for you".*' (Los Angeles, Calif. 1940, from a young woman.) The reference to 'her internal anarchy' replaces the statement made in some versions, and explaining the man's reply, that the woman has just farted.

The implication that parts of the human body are used, instead of toilet-paper, for cleansing the anus after defecation, is considered very humorous and insulting. *A man who stammers is being made fun of for this, and turns on his tormentor with the question: "W-w-w-well, w-w-we all have our little p-p-p-peculiarities, you kn-know. F-f-f-for instance, which hand do you w-w-w-wipe your ass with?" "The left hand." "W-w-well, that's y-y-y-y-your peculiarity. M-m-m-m-most people y-y-y-use paper."* (Scranton, Pa. 1936.) The punch-line here, or some part of this 'catch' is earlier alluded to in a passage of imitative James Joycean prose in Conrad Aiken's *Blue Voyage* (1927) p. 180: '*We all have our little p-p-p-p-peculiarities which we don't mention; and which nevertheless are of great importance to us. Canyon yodeling. Pearl diving. Muff barking. Palpation. The dance of the seven unveils.* (The first three of these unmentionable personal p-p-peculiarities are all slang terms for cunnilinctus, all being still extant though the last is now more commonly '*muff diving.*' Other even more extravagant terms exist, such as '*munching the bearded clam,*' and '*sneezing in the basket.*')

As the introduction of paper to Europe from the Orient is comparatively recent, having taken place only about the 14th century, it is obvious that something other than paper was the *anitergium* in general use through all the period of Classical antiquity to the Renaissance. This is the essence of Rabelais' jest as to Gargantua's invention, intended to *replace* paper, as to the inefficacy of which (for that purpose) he even gives a bit of doggerel rhyme; pronouncing the anathema of St. Anthony's fire (erysipelas), however, on anyone who does not wipe '*tous tes trous'* with *something*. Paper never became cheap enough to use as 'arse-wisp' until well into the 17th and 18th centuries, and even then (and still today) torn and waste sheets were principally used, often from 'remaindered' books or out-of-date newspapers. Only a person who has found a newspaper article with his picture printed in it, cut into neat squares and hanging from a nail in a public toilet – with the picture face-up on the next sheet to be used! – really can appreciate what this feels like for the person involved.

This did not happen to me, but I know the man to whom it did: not an author, but a sports hero. The closest I have yet come was when a friend of mine in London recently sent me a review of one of my books in a local magazine, which he stated he had found 'lining his dust-bin': British for garbage-can. (Everybody has a few friends like that, but few of them admit that they fish things out of garbage-cans.) That's one advantage about being a television performer instead of an author: no one is going to wrap last night's leftovers in your face. Like the foreskin of an elephant, the 'immortality of print' sometimes has *very large drawbacks*.

Other 'profane uses' are also commonly made of printed matter, as for ladies' curling-papers, in Sheridan's *The Rivals* (1775) I.ii, or, as Ned Ward puts it in *Hudibras Redivivus* (1705) I.v.20: *'These wicked Papers ... doomed t'illuminate our Pipes, Or give our Backsides cleanly Wipes.'* I have myself seen sheets of the Bible used to roll contraband cigarettes in jail, and though I did not see anyone use this as Ned Ward suggests, who knows? Every folklorist knows the story of Bishop Thomas Percy discovering his *Folio Manuscript* of English folk-ballads in the early 18th century, in a friend's country-house, where the housemaids had already used part of the priceless manuscript to line pie-tins and light the fires! Japanese prints were similarly 'discovered' in the West – and Impressionist art inspired and begun – when the French painter, Edouard Manet, over a century later, found one of these being used to wrap a Dutch cheese in a market. (The Dutch, at that period, were the only nation with access to Japan.)

But none of these 'profane uses' will compare to the fantastic case – very similar to that of Bishop Percy and his country friend's *Folio Manuscript*, in the marvellously fortunate presence of 'the right man in the right place at the right time' – of the discovery by the German palaeographer, Konstantin von

Tischendorf, in the Convent of St. Catherine, on Mount Sinai itself, in 1844, of the casual use of basketfuls of leaves of *the oldest known manuscript text of the Bible* in Greek, for purposes politely referred to as 'burning,' though obviously use in the convent privy is meant, since monks do not in general burn Christian books. The actual moment of Tischendorf's discovery must have been one of the greatest *textual confrontations* of all time. Can't you just see him sitting there? Then coming tearing out, pulling his pants up with one hand and waving the manuscript leaf wildly in the other. Shouting, *"Where is the head monk?!"*

Forty-three leaves of the manuscript he saved which he later edited and published under the rather vaunting title *Codex Siniaticus* (1862), were deposited by him in the Royal Library at Leipzig. The rest was presented to the Russian Czar in 1859, and was then bought by the British government from the atheistic Communists in the 1930's at the highest price ever paid (in gold) for any book in the history of the world's literature. *Habent sua fata libelli.*

A whole sub-treasury of quotations could be gathered from the literature of the Restoration and early 18th century, before the repressive 'purification' and Latinization of written English by Addison, Pope, and especially Johnson, composed only of references to the use of ephemeral and disprized books and pamphlets as toilet-paper or 'bum-fodder,' and of humorous pleas by authors (often in the dedications of their books) that their writings be not so used. These are very much in the tradition of the phallic threats of the *Priapeia* of Rome, and the *Greek Anthology* before them. The similar literary allusions to the 'male motherhood' of authorship (which still continue at the present time) have already been discussed in the First Series, 8.VI.2. Among the most elaborate of literary caveats concerning the use of books as toilet-paper are those in the outstandingly obscene miscellany, *Poems on Several Occasions*, by John Wilmot, Earl of Rochester ('Antwerp,' 1680; facsimile edition by Prof. James Thorpe, Princeton, 1950), the opening gun of the 'New Freedom,' now as then. For example, that ending "The First Letter from B. [Buckhurst?]," p. 79, following "Actus Primus, Scena Prima," a tryout or fragment of Rochester's bawdy farce, *Sodom*; and especially the invective, "Upon the Author of a Play call'd *Sodom*," p. 129–31, by John Oldham. Even the scatological form of such 'dedications' has not quite disappeared though now generally very rationalized: '*The conductor of a Chicago orchestra was severely "roasted" by the leading critic of the biggest Chicago daily for including a certain unfamiliar symphony on a program. He was quite angry at the unmerited abuse, and sat down to reply in vein. "As I write this," he began, "I have before me your criticism. Soon I'll have it in back of me ..."*' (*Anecdota Americana,* 1927, I: 338; reprinted verbatim in Roth's expurgated edition, No. 325.)

Not quite so specific, but in the same area: *The guest who had been put to bed sick after overeating at a dinner-party, takes a walk before breakfast and shits behind a hedge when finding himself suddenly taken short. The paper he uses is an old envelope he finds in his pocket, and it blows over the hedge, up onto the veranda, and into the host's face as he is presiding over breakfast for all the other guests. The unconscious offender now arrives all smiles and says, "You know, I feel a lot better after that little walk I had this morning." Host, drily: "Yes, I've seen all about it in the paper."* (London, 1959.) The insistence here that it is the father-figure of the host who has been shat upon makes clear the hidden Oedipal meaning of much of this 'shotgun' anal defiling.

Not precisely *graffiti*, and yet not too distant, are the imprinted toilet-papers now used in England, and in fact forming quite an industry, each industriously advertising its maker, whose name or mark is carefully printed IN THE CORNER, to make sure that no one accidentally wipes on the trademark itself. During the Second World War, packets of toilet-paper carrying Hitler's picture IN THE CENTER of each sheet were reported, but I did not actually see these, and do not know if they were fantasy or fact, on the inspiration of the Napoleonic *cagadou*'s mentioned earlier. Attempted 'total control' of his kind, of the actions of persons unknown to and unseen by the toilet-paper manufacturers, is very typical of the anal-compulsive or sadistic character, which always wants everything to be *just so.*

A well-known pantomime joke, which is considered by those who tell it to be the *ne plus ultra* of scatological delight, presents the 'total control' of toilet-paper, its *corners* and *center*, in a way no British toilet-paper manufacturer has yet dreamt of. As I was in part responsible for bringing the Japanese folk-art of *origami* paper-folding to the West in the 1950's, I would recommend this story to *origami* enthusiasts as telling more of the truth about the hidden sadistic compulsions of that charming little art than anyone has yet said in public, except for some polite remarks about the value of paper-folding in combatting nervousness. '*A Scotchman in a service station restroom, finding only a single sheet of toilet-paper left, showed it to the attendant, asking what he was expected to do with one sheet.* [The rest is acted out with *careful* gestures and an imaginary sheet of paper, or sometimes a real one:] "*Fold it over twice, tear a little hole in the middle, open it up, insert finger, wipe asshole with finger. Then* peel *the paper off, wiping the finger clean.*" *The Scotchman, parismonious, said,* "*What about the bit of paper torn out of the middle?*" *The attendant then showed how this could be used to clean under the fingernail!*' (Chicago, 1943, from a college-educated homosexual soldier.) Here the unconscious tears through the toilet-paper screen, and finally and gloriously returns to the narcissistic childhood pleasure of 'playing with shit,' under the pretext of special *cleanliness.* There are numerous other paper-tearing tricks like this, some ending up with erotic objects, but mostly of religious import, involving crosses, the word "HELL," and the like. All make elaborately careful use of the last little '*bit of paper torn out of the middle,*' exactly as in the above pantomime joke.

Another important aspect of this joke, as to its ultimate anality, is the trait of using everything up, and letting nothing go to waste. (*Waste*: shit.) This leads to the idea of the luxury toilet, or gadget-toilet, as already seen in the First Series, 6.IV.4, "The Sex Machine," p. 367, in a famous Pat & Mike joke, where the inseparable two are plumbers. Other more castratory versions of the same joke are also given in Chapter 13, above, and the original will be found in the group of Picard anti-clerical stories in *Kryptádia* (1907) XI. 187, "Commodités perfectionnées," where, as might be expected, *The final result of the marvellously perfected new toilet is that the bishop has a brushful of shit wiped in his face by the beadle stationed below the privy-seat to wipe his ass.*

Cheapness about toilet-paper is a common manifestation of anality, and is probably the real explanation of otherwise unbelievable defilings of pages of printed books for this purpose. In his famous *Letters* to his natural son, Lord Chesterfield commends, in the letter of December 11th, 1747, the system of a gentleman who (as Reginald Reynolds puts it, p. 142) profited from the time he had to spend in the 'necessary-house' by reading 'the Latin poets in cheap editions, and tearing off what he had read, sent them down as a sacrifice to Cloacina,' the patron-goddess of toilets. Napoleon would also so deal with the books he read while travelling in his carriage, during his wars and campaigns, though most of his biographers try to suggest that he was simply thus lightening the weight of books as he read them by throwing the pages out the window. They avoid noting the use of chamber-pots by ladies (and great men) in carriages and stage-coaches travelling at full speed. I have myself seen an elderly peasant woman do this, in so modern and civilized an area of the world as the shuttle-train from Pisa to Florence in 1959, locked together as we were on a hot summer day in the old-style railway compartment with her grandchild, whose potty she simply tucked under her voluminous black skirt to use; then unceremoniously dumped it out the window.

A more famous aspect of the anal character is, of course, its concern with money, and, again, a whole library of references to *Gold-as-shit* could easily be collected, under the title "All that Glitters ..." A start has already been made in Dr. Sándor Ferenczi's two articles, "The Origin of the Interest in Money," in his *Contributions to Psychoanalysis* (Boston, 1916), and *"Pecunia olet"* – Money stinks – in his *Further Contributions* (ed. 1926). Jokes on this theme are more particularly those in the later section here, "Feces as Gift," but at least one specifically concerns toilet-paper. *Standard situation: a man in a toilet booth finds at the last moment that there is no paper. He tries to unwind the cardboard core of the empty roll but finds it is made of plastic and cannot be unwound. He searches through all his pockets and finds nothing he can use: no piece of blank paper, no old envelope, not even a handkerchief. Just as he is considering taking off one of his socks and using that, he hears a man entering the toilet cubicle next to him, and shouts over to ask if the man will give him a few sheets of paper. "There's no paper here!" the man shouts back. "Well have you got an old envelope or anything?" "Sorry," says the other man. "Haven't got a thing; I just came in to take a piss." "Well, look," says the first man painfully, "have you got two five dollar bills for a ten?"* (N.Y. 1955.)

The anal trait of parsimoniousness or retentiveness is also hidden in a well-known joke, reprinted verbatim in the expurgated *Anecdota Americana* (1933) p. 93, no. 221 : '*A farmer once wrote to Sears Roebuck & Company to ask for the price of toilet paper. He received an answer directing him to look on page 307 of their catalogue. "If I had your catalogue," he wrote back, "would I ask you for the price of toilet paper?"* ' (1 : 228.) American realistic authors once considered it the height of daring to have rural characters remark that *Spring must be nearly here, as they had worked their way through the 'Monkey-Ward' catalogue as far as the harness section.*

Other than mail-order catalogues, the farmer or hillbilly is presumed to have recourse to whatever preceded the use of paper in Europe, specifically to cornhusks or corncobs. This means the cob from which the corn-kernels have already been eaten, or broken off to feed poultry, leaving a dry and lacerating object (also sometimes bored out to make tobacco pipes) obviously not fit for civilized rectal consumption. Note, however, the standard paranoid and sub-homosexual symptom of *pruritus ani,* for which such objects are ideal. Scratching of the anus with the fingernails to the point of bleeding, especially at moments of nervous tension, is otherwise very common, to create the passive rectal sensations (of pedicatory rape by the Oedipal father figure) which are both feared and needed.

A hillbilly driving along a state highway in his broken-down jalopy stopped at a service station and asked for the 'out-house.' He was directed to the modern 'rest-room' by the attendant, where he remained interminably. When asked later what took him so long, he replied, "Some bastard wound miles of paper around the cob." (Los Angeles, Calif. 1940.) A version of this is given in a war novel, *Battle Cry,* by Leon M. Uris (1953) p. 142, as of one 'Seabags Brown, the Iowa farmer.' This is of course the scatological nincumpoop who 'does not know how to wipe his ass.' Compare also the probable source of the 'gimmick' here in the traditional American riddle : *"What's the longest word in the dictionary? – Toilet-paper!"* (Ann Arbor, Michigan, 1935.) Actually this word was never allowed in the dictionary until the new and largely unexpurgated *Merriam-Webster Third New International Dictionary* (1961). For polite presentation, the answer to the riddle concerning the 'longest word' is : *"Smiles! – there's a* mile *between first and last letter."*

A joke of the 1920's, if not earlier, on this theme was heard in a burlesque-theater skit, Washington, D.C., 1943 : *A comedian named Cobb gets into an argument with another comedian, named Hicks, to whom he says, "And I'm* MR. *Cobb to you, punk!" The other replies, "And I'm* MR. *Hicks to you, Cobb!" "Why, you country hick," he snarls, "so you're a wise guy? Do you know what we do with hicks like you in the City?" "No, but I bet you know what we do with cobs in the country."* The final modernization of the rustic out-house is given an unexpected motive, and an even more unexpected sexual twist: '*A man who for years had used old newspapers for T. P.* [toilet-paper: a girls' slang term], *at last went to a store for some real stuff. The employee asked what kind he had been using and, when told, asked why he didn't continue with it. The man said, "Well, these papers nowadays have so much about the war in them now, that whenever I use one my gun goes off!"* ' (Los Angeles, Calif. 1940, from a young woman.)

A perfect expression of the 'money' theme is that of a joke on: *A poor young man wooing a wealthy girl, who tells her father that he earns only $40 a week. The old man is angry and replies that the suitor could obviously never keep the girl in the manner to which she is accustomed, as her present allowance was $200 a week. "Why," he adds contemptuously, "I don't think your $40 a week would keep her in toilet-paper!" "Well, sir," says the young man, "I'm very grateful to you for being so frank with me, and naturally I'm very disappointed. But I don't think I want to marry your daughter anyhow, if she's that full of shit."* (D.C. 1943, from an army corporal.) A polite expurgation of this is attempted in *Sex to Sexty* (1966) 7:17, with a modified punch-line which, as usual, spoils the joke or dysphemizes it heavily: *The suitor comes out and says to the girl: "You better have a talk with your pop ... he doesn't know you're pregnant; he thinks you've got the dysentery!"*

Anally-retentive traits are mirrored and expressed in connection with toilet-paper, without necessarily any actual reference to money. *A Swedish maid in a wealthy house* [n.b.] *found a great deal to complain about, but bore it all until one day she found they were out of toilet-paper just when she needed it. She went to the mistress and announced that there had been many things before, but this was the last straw, and she was quitting. Vexed that she had harbored her resentment so long, the mistress replied, "But I don't see what the matter is, Nora. Haven't you a tongue in your head?" "Yes sure," said the girl, "but I ain't got a neck like a goose."* (Los Angeles, Cal. 1942, from a young married woman.) Aside from the fantasy of auto-cunnilinctus here, which is sometimes spontaneously evolved by young girls in precisely this context – urinary rather than defecatory – and probably based on observation of domestic animals' self-cleaning habits, this is perhaps nothing other than Rabelais' and Gargantua's crowning invention in the way of *anitergium* or toilet-paper: '*the neck of a goose, that is well downed, when you hold her neck betwixt your legs.*'

The joke just preceding was stated by the woman who told it to be her 'favorite,' and may be assumed therefore to express some domestic dissatisfactions of her own: she too probably felt she had 'a great deal to complain about, but bore it all in silence' – except through the ghost-voices of her favorite joke. Compare: *A farm-woman is explaining to the census-taker how she spends her day, every minute being filled from the time she gets up at 5 A.M. to clean the stables, till her bedtime at 10 P.M. after an incredible day of hard work. Attempting to joke, the census-taker says, "Well, what do you do in your spare time?" The woman looks at him very seriously. "I go to the toilet."* (Scranton, Pa. 1946, from a different young married woman.)

Anal retentiveness is the main line of almost all the humor concerning both toilets and toilet-paper, and is at the root of the ambivalent struggle to give up the fecal product (or any other), while still going through some simulacrum of hanging onto it. Though most of the jokes preceding explain the lack of toilet-paper on which they turn, as mere accident, I might mention as a further personal testimony that I have known at least two persons – both quite rich, one of them so rich as to leave over $100,000 in his will for Christian missionary work in China – who would not buy toilet-paper *at all* for their homes. They supplied the bathroom, one with random sheets of torn newspaper, and the other with carefully smoothed-out tissue-paper wrappers of the sleazy sort given away free around oranges and lemons. Not only that, but these were kept in a special box in the kitchen (by the missionary-work benefactor), and *only a few at a time* were put into the bathroom, so that, as he told me frankly or perhaps pointedly – I was his secretary – they should not be wasted. This is not so much living in typographical error, as living out a total anal-retentive pun or charade. What he meant was: "*Nobody is going to wipe their ass on MY toilet-paper!*"

II. URINATION

I. APOTROPAIC RITUALS

Urine is not the subject of so intense a taboo as any of the other bodily excrements. Even the nasal mucus is thought of as more 'disgusting,' once it has been extruded from the body. As has already been observed, none of the excretions disgust the individual – not even half-digested food, called 'vomit' – either inside himself or anyone else, unless and until they are actually excreted. Their being carried around in the body does not in any way fall under taboo, either emotional or ritual, and none but violently neurotic people, of the type of St. Odon of Cluny, ever purposely try to conjure up the images that they purportedly dislike, of other human beings (especially women) as 'walking, palpitating tubes of shit,' sometimes even calculating how many yards of shit there are inside everyone's intestines, as in the "Cures of Love" cited in chapter 12.

This demonstrates again that the scatological taboos are basically *rites de passage*, in which it is only or especially the *moment of change* that is considered dangerous, and is surrounded with taboo, and during which the individual must be fortified by means of ritual observances, such as whistling, continually flushing the toilet (to cover bowel noises), or writing on toilet walls; and by means of exact codes of propriety and impropriety, and of the correct method of disposal of even such minor excrements as cut fingernails and hair. In other cultures, and in certain subcultures of our own, such as that of the uneducated, where a belief in magic and 'hexing' is still frankly admitted, it is understood that such excrements can be *used* magically by enemies, and that is why they must be buried, burned, etc. At the upper culture-level such fears are now displaced to parallel ritual observances concerning germs (devils) and vitamins or antiseptics (angels), without the slightest real concern for actual microbic dangers or antisepsis, for which an artificial pine-tree odor carried on the bathroom air is accepted as a mock-medical substitute. The *incense* of earlier religions.

Wall-epigraphs put up by the management of restaurants, public toilets, and the like, to the effect that: EMPLOYEES MUST WASH THEIR HANDS BEFORE LEAVING THIS ROOM", "PLEASE DO NOT THROW CIGARETTE BUTTS (or: SANITARY NAPKINS) IN THE

BOWL", "PLEASE ADJUST CLOTHING (*i.e.* button your fly) BEFORE LEAVING," and the classic "PASSENGERS WILL PLEASE REFRAIN FROM FLUSHING TOILETS WHILE THE TRAIN IS IN THE STATION" are equally apotropaic rituals that no one takes seriously or is expected to take seriously. Their mere statement is considered to do the mystic job. This is true of most *graffiti*, whether put up by the management openly or by the clients secretly, and has been immemorially true at least since the wall-paintings in the prehistoric caves of Lascaux.

One does not know whether to laugh or cry for the readers of a modern 'slick' magazine, *Le Nouvel Observateur*, the best news-and-opinion journal in France, which publishes an advertisement in its issue of 28 Jan. 1974, p. 74–5, covering two full pages, one of which is devoted to explaining lengthily that Vittel mineral water will 'wash the poisons out of the cells and the body,' alongside a small *Maneken-Pis* apotropaion showing a naked man drinking his mineral water dutifully out of a bottle with one hand while he pisses a fine parabolic stream without the use of the other – a good trick if you can do it. The opposite page contains nothing but the same scientific message, reduced to three very simple words in *very* large type: BUVEZ ET PISSEZ. (Drink and piss.)

Despite current talk about the 'New Freedom' in England and America, I do not believe any such full-page advertisement ever has or could ever appear in those countries, except in an 'underground' newspaper, and then strictly as humor. (Robert Crumb's "*Tommy Toilet sez: Don't Forget to Wipe Your Ass, Folks!*") As in the opening apotropaic scene of Ralph Bakshi's *Fritz the Cat*, where a construction worker on a girder high up in the air pulls out his whang and squirts a copious yellow stream over the sleeping city. To the contrary, when the Rev. Robert E. Fitch felt moved, in the pages of the *New Republic* (New York, 3 Sept. 1956) p. 17–18, to complain about the use of 'one-syllable four-letter' words, his editors could back him up bravely only in all the obscurity of a foreign language, giving the title of his article, "*La Mystique de la MERDE*" in what may have been, says Edward Sagarin, 'the largest type face in history, except for the scrawls on toilet walls.' As in the Freudian folk-phrase: '*The bigger the belt-buckle, the littler the prick.*' (San Diego, Calif. 1965, said in reference to Texans.)

It is also of ethnological interest that there is a whole ritual and etiquette concerning the method of *holding* the penis dur-

ing urination. *A Frenchman in London is asking street direc-*
tions of another man standing beside him at the urinal-bank in
a public toilet. [!] *The street he is looking for is Oldham*
Avenue, but his accent makes the Englishman think he is ask-
ing, "You know 'how to 'old 'em, 'aven't you?" "Sure I know,
mate," the Englishman replies cheerily; "some 'old 'em this way
[*hand held over the penis*], *and some 'old 'em that way* [*hand*
held under the penis]; *but there's very few 'as to 'old 'em like*
THIS! [*lugging out his very long penis and holding it with both*
hands straining beneath]." (D.C. 1943, from a Jewish army
corporal, told with the indicated gestures.) Observe that the
only other 'gesture' joke involving the pretended exposure of
the penis by the teller – that concerning *the competition be-*
tween the strong Irish boy and the consumptive Jewish boy
with the bargain SHIRT – pointedly involves the mock exposure
of his penis by a Jew: obviously implying overcompensatory
exhibitionism (under the guise of the joke), connected with
the identification of circumcision with castration. A story has
already been given in the chapter on "Castration," 13.III.1, in
which: *A war-veteran who urinates on another man by*
accident, owing to bullet-holes in his penis [!] *is cruelly told to*
go not to a doctor but to a piccolo teacher: "He'll teach you to
finger that stump, so you won't piss all over strangers!" (N.Y.
1952.)

A printed 'novelty' obscoenum or 'typology' has circulated
since the 1930's in America, describing and illustrating the
"Twenty Types of Men at the Urinal," almost entirely concerned with the amount of bold and bragging exposure, or
bashful covering, of the penis that each man uses, or his special
method of playing (urine *equals* semen) with the stream. The
obvious and logical method of holding the penis, with the palm
of the hand facing the body and the penis supported between
the fingers, as in smoking a cigarette, or as a woman gives the
breast, is (in fact) studiously rejected by very many men, who,
instead, turn over the hand, and stick the elbow out from the
body, holding the penis so that *they themselves* – not to
mention anyone else – cannot see it during urination. This is
very common in the Near East. Cigarettes are also held in this
way when it is necessary to hide them, as in wartime trenches
or in places where smoking is otherwise forbidden, as on jobs or
public conveyances. The implication is irresistible that the penis
is being *hidden* during urination, in handling it in this way.

Also, instead of washing the hands before urination, in order to protect the genitals against possible germs, &c., nine out of every ten men will wash the hands *after* urination, clearly to protect against moral or magical defiling. '*A Yale man, washing his hands after taking a leak, contemptuously said to a Harvard man whom he saw neglect this punctilio: "At Yale we are taught to wash our hands after taking a leak." The other sneered, "At Hahvahd we are taught not to piss on our fingers".*' (Berkeley, Cal. 1941.)

2. URINE AND URINALYSIS

Jokes on urinalysis as a method of diagnosing disease are fairly ancient, as is uroscopy itself. *Joe Miller's Jests* (1739) edited by John Mottley, No. 226, gives as the usual true anecdote a story on the famously candid Dr. John Radcliffe (d. 1714) who had been dismissed as physician to Princess Anne for 'styling her distemper nothing but the vapours,' and who later refused to visit her, when Queen, on her deathbed. As the *Dictionary of National Biography* discreetly puts it, he 'annoyed many great people by his extraordinary candour': *i.e.* the usual verbal sadism of physicians. '*The same physician (says Joe Miller), who was not the humblest Man in the World, being sent for by Sir Edward Seymour* [d. 1708, Speaker of the House of Commons], *who was said to be the proudest; the Knight received him while he was dressing his Feet and picking his Toes, being at the Time troubled with a Diabetis, and upon the Doctor's entering the Room, accosted him in this Manner: So, Quack, said he, I'm a dead Man, for I piss sweet. Do ye, replied the Doctor, then prithee piss upon your Toes, for they stink damnably. And so turning round on his Heel went out of the Room.*'

Modern jokes on urinalysis simply continue the older European themes, substituting surprise 'punchlines' for simple repartees as above. A particular butt is the sham physician or 'piss-scriger,' who pretends to diagnose all illnesses in this way (Motif K1955.2, with references to the *Arabian Nights*, and *Les Cent Nouvelles Nouvelles*, Nos. 20 and 21.) This is mocked covertly by: *The fool who refuses to give the doctor his address on the grounds that he will soon learn all he needs to know from the inspection of the fool's urine.* (Thompson Motif J1734.1.) The mocking of the doctor is usually perfectly clear, when he 'descends' to urinalysis. '*Cohen had submitted a* sample of his urine to the doctor and eagerly awaited the analysis. "It is sixty-five per cent sugar and thirty-five per cent albumen," he was informed. "Ain't there no piss in it, doctor?" Cohen asked.' (1:251.) This joke covers an important philosophical point, as to chemical identity, as when one hears that the human body is composed of '97% water' (not sugar-and-spice-and-everything-nice?) or that both processed cheese and Lobster Newburg contain 'protein' in equal amounts. ("To hell with you and your bargains, doc!")

The actual moment of 'giving the specimen' is obviously a scatological comedy-scene, when required to be done in the physical presence of the doctor, just as the moment of a 'semen-donor's' being handed a large-mouthed bottle by a pretty nurse and being told to go behind a curtain and produce, is inevitably played as sexual comedy. ("I know a better way than that, nurse!" or "Can't we cut out the middle man?" &c.) – A mountain-boy being examined by the army doctor is told, "Now we want a urine specimen too." He does not understand. "I mean," says the doctor testily, "I want you to piss in one of those little bottles over on that shelf." "From here, doc?" (1:487, punch-line only. World War I joke.)

The commonest theme of all in this connection is that of the substitute specimen in urinalysis, first indexed by Rotunda, K1858.1, citing the Italian novelle of Anton-Francesco Grazzini, known as 'Il Lasca,' in his Le Cene (about 1550) No. 1; Grazzini – curiously enough – being an apothecary by trade. As is well known, the bottles of 'colored water' still displayed in pharmacy windows represent the earlier rows of urine specimens, and there is a charming old woodcut illustration in Douglas McMurtrie's The Book (1936) showing such a row of bottles in a medieval apothecary's shop, each bottle duly identified by the 'donor's' coat-of-arms! I myself once possessed a 19th-century French chamber-pot with a coat-of-arms on the side, and am told that mon-crested articles of intimate toilette are common in Japan. I refer the reader to the earlier note on chamberpots with the decoration on the inside – for example a picture of Napoleon or Hitler with wide-open eye, or even mouth. See 15.I.4, pages 952–3 above.

The usual form of the story is only an overloading of Grazzini's 'substitute specimen,' for purposes of increasing the humor. An army evader, told to bring a specimen of his urine to the draft-board doctor, hits on the idea of having the whole *family urinate in the bottle. The doctor examines it, looking very confused. "Well, doc," chortles the draft-dodger, "what's the verdict?" "The verdict is," says the doctor, "your father has gallstones, your mother has diabetes, your sister is pregnant, and* YOU'RE *in the army."* (N.Y. 1942.) Here, suddenly, the doctor is no longer mocked, but is infinitely wise, and more cunning than the patient, in the style of Sherlock Holmes and his mythical monograph on the one hundred and eighty-eight varieties of tobacco ash – which are also a form of divination by 'excrements.'

The local ne'er-do-well and drunk suddenly blossoms out in affluence, explaining that he has a new job: he is the head pisser for the insurance company. – "When someone can't pass the urine test, I make the specimen for him." (N.Y. 1952.) – *A woman is to take a urine specimen to the doctor, but is worried about the small specimen bottle given her. "Such a big specialist," she muses; "maybe I should take him a bigger specimen." She arrives at the doctor's office with a gallon jug. The doctor slings it over his shoulder [acted out], and pours an ounce or so into a test-tube, handing the jug back to her. "But, doctor, what'll I do with it?" "I don't know, madam. Maybe you could take it to Hobby Lobby?"* (N.Y. 1942, referring to a popular radio program.) Jokes concerning urination by women are not common: this point will be returned to below. *A man comes to the insurance doctor lugging a bucket of urine, explaining, "It's for a group policy."* (N.Y. 1973.) Current American stories crackle all up and down these themes.

Urination by animals is of course less taboo than that of human beings, and, in fact, terribly mild jokes about dogs and fire-hydrants have been the stand-by of presumably bawdy humor-magazine cartoons for years. A favorite theme in tales and 'whoppers' is the more-than-human animal, at least since the time of Balaam's ass – and the earlier Egyptian animal cartoons – from which the 'shaggy-dog story' is developed. *A railroad fireman has a pet dog which the engineer will not allow to ride in the cabin, so it runs alongside the engine saying "Arf-arf!" while the fireman waves at it covertly. The engineer is going mad, and runs the train faster and faster trying to shake the dog, but all in vain. Until one day on a special run on a stretch of electro-welded tracks, in its speed the engine develops a hot-box, but the dog continues to keep up with it manfully [sic], running on three legs in fact, and pissing to put out the fire in the hot-box.* (D.C. 1944. As told, N.Y. 1965, the teller ended in charade-tableau, representing the dog with both front paws proudly dangling before its chest, posed as *"Man's Best Friend,"* then cocking one hand to one ear as *"His Master's Voice."*)

The substitute-specimen appears in one favorite animal joke. *'The "regulars" have never found fault, but a new customer in the country pub complains of the quality of the beer, and as a result of the argument, Old George is sent off to get a sample analysed. On his return he reports, "The vet says that 'orse ain't in a fit state to be worked".'* (London, 1953.) Also as a mere insult in an American World War II form: *The soldier tells the British bartender, "My buddies and me think your place is great, but the beer ought to be poured back into the horse!"* (N.Y. 1944.) Observe the implied pedicatory threat, or food-dirtying at least, since the beer is to be administered to the unwilling horse – as visualized – with a funnel or hose. Compare also the joke, already noted: *A young man in a midget sports-car is tipping his hat to a lady in Piccadilly, just as a guardsman's horse steps over the car and urinates. "Well, I 'opes next time we meets under better 'orse-pisses."* (2:244.) Puns this florid, and so ornately set up, are usually accepted with groans of pre-tended rejection, even Christopher Morley's masterpiece about *Spanish women, who are a snare Andalusian.* This leaves no response possible at all to items like *"Call me Pipi – cause I'm your'n."* (N.Y. 1940.) Or: *"What did George Washington say to the United States? – Urination!"*

3. URINATING ON OTHERS

Except for the Piccadilly pun just preceding, and the joke quoted from *Joe Miller's Jests,* all that has preceded in this section restricts itself formally to the use of urine as a verbal soiling rather than a physical one. Urine is brought onstage, as it were, in bottles or otherwise, but it is not thrown at any of the actors. Not all jokes on the subject are so restrained. *The child at the christening of the battleship is badly sprinkled with champagne from the breaking bottle. "Goodspeed! God-speed!" the lady sponsor is screaming after the disappearing ship. The child tugs at her sleeve. "Godspeed on me too, grand-ma!"* (Barker, 1945, vol. II.) This must be a common enough, and an authentic, children's notion or 'just-so' story. When I was a child, two little twin girls next door used to run out everytime

it would rain, shouting: *"God's peein'! God's peein'!"* which is
very close to the present joke. I myself was convinced that
lightning consisted of 'people upstairs' rolling chairs around
and having fights.

The homosexual element has already been discussed in the
joke on: *The two hotel-owners who go out to piss their names
in the snow as an advertisement. One hands the other his penis
and says, "Here! You know I can't spell!"* (N.Y. 1940.) This seems
to have been homosexualized from: *The farmer complaining
that the hired man has pissed his daughter's name in the snow.
"Yes," says his wife, "and the worst is: it's in* her *handwriting."*
(U.S. 1930's, and London, 1953.) Compare with this everything
that has been said before, under "Euphemism," 14.I.1, as to
spelling out names and tabooed terms as a form of euphemized
scatology. Clearly, pissing another person's name in the snow
– or even thinking about it ('Imagining the death of the King,'
as the former legal offense was phrased) – is very close to pissing on that person, or on his grave: the insult for which the
"Ghost of Sayúla" takes a pedicatory revenge. A joke heard in
the United States, though obviously of Russian origin, concerns the *schnorrer* or sturdy-beggar, Mikosch, and the hated
nouveau-riche moneylender, Goldenberg. *"Tell me, Goldenberg,"* says Mikosch, trying to frame a compliment, *"why is it
that when I'm pissing it's like the flakes of snow falling on the
steppes, but when you're pissing it's like the water of the
Wolga pouring into the Caspian Sea?" "I don't know,"* says
Goldenberg, *"but maybe it's because when I'm pissing I'm pissing into the gutter, and when you're pissing you're pissing on
mine brand-new fur coat!"* (N.Y. 1953.)

The late Richard Wright, American Negro novelist, told the
following fabulous story on the terrasse of a Paris bar in 1954,
observing that it is a '*real* Negro story,' of the kind that does
not usually get into print. It does not appear in the first attempt
to break this taboo, D. J. Bennett's "The Psychological Meaning of Anti-Negro Jokes," in *Fact* (March 1964) No. 2: p. 52–9,
which includes for the first time a few of the 'Negro-baiting
jokes' that 'Negroes tell against themselves.' This joke was not
taken down verbatim, but all the satirical touches are as told
by Wright. *The Secretary of the National Society for the Ad-
vancement of Colored Persons – a white gentleman – is on the
way home from the Long Island train station late one afternoon, when he feels the need to take a leak. He holds it for a*

*few blocks because there are people everywhere, but it gets
terrible. Suddenly he notices an old Negro raking leaves by the
curb, and he says to him, "Pardon me, my good man, you seem
to be doing an excellent job of raking those leaves. I'd like to
give you a job on my estate – double whatever salary you're
getting now." "Why, tha'ss wonderful!" says the astonished
Negro. "Yes, and does your wife do any housework?" "Why,
yass, a li'l now an' then." "Fine! She gets whatever you're getting now. And you can both live over the garage – it's a four-
room apartment we had fitted up for my son. He's in college
now. When can you start working?" "Any time you say, boss;
but tell me sumth'n, boss. While you is talking to me, you
ain't by any chance pissin' up an' down my leg, is you?"* There
are a number of sexual- and socio-miscegenational scenes entirely in this vein of black (Black) humor in Chester Himes' bitter and sardonic *Pinktoes* (Paris, 1961). A scene very much like
the joke, though highly expurgated, is used in Ben Hecht &
Charles MacArthur's play *The Front Page* (1928), between the
tough newspaper editor and the rival paper's staff poet, specifying that the poet is to be kicked down the stairs when he
arrives for his new job.

The question of social position – 'pissing order' or 'pecking
order' – is not even attempted to be hidden in these Russian and
Negro stories, and even less so in a classic joke mocking what
is felt to be the craven British and European acceptance of the
prerogatives of outworn monarchy. *Queen Victoria and Prince
Albert are at a concert, sitting in the royal box in full regalia.
Prince Albert has to urinate, but every time he tries to get up
everyone else must get up too, and this will ruin the concert.
Desperate, and under cover of their ermine lap-robe, he lets go
over the railing of the royal box. From beneath, a voice floats
up: "I sye, Your Majesty, wobble it about a bit – we're not getting any!"* (N.Y. 1952.)

Anyone who thinks this is only a joke should consider the
priestly peddling of the gilded dung-balls of the Dalai Lama to
the faithful. Except for the cheerful acceptance of the royal
accolade, the situation in the joke is in no way beyond historical prerogative. The earliest leading case at British law, on
the question of 'obscenity,' precisely concerned Sir Charles
Sedley and a group of Restoration noblemen who created a
furore in June 1663 at Covent Garden by urinating in bottles
and throwing these over at the underlings 'in the pit.' At any

rate, that is what they were accused of. The urinating into soda-bottles and beer-bottles in the theatre and other public spectacles (such as bull-fights) can still often be observed in European countries, and at football games in the United States, not always bothering with the cover of the blankets or lap-robes mentioned in the joke.

It has already been noted that jokes mentioning urination by women are not common, though the pictorial representation of such scenes was frequent in the gallant art of the 18th century, and still appears occasionally in amateur erotic art. Except among pronounced male masochists, the opportunity for interest in female urination went out with the day of the chamber-pot. See. for example, the undinist eroticism, *Gynecocracy: A Narrative of the Adventures and Psychological Experiences of Julian Robinson (afterwards Viscount Ladywood) under Petticoat Rule* (1893), attributed to the sexologist, Havelock Ellis, in Peter Fryer's *Private Case – Public Scandal* (London, 1966) p. 121. The classic situation it that alluded to, with unusually gallant obliqueness, in a joke now already considered to 'date' somewhat, and of which I have observed listeners nowadays unable to understand the point. *A man falls asleep at a tea-party with his wife at the home of strangers. In order to wake him without letting anyone realize he has fallen asleep, his wife pours him a cup of tea, holding the pot very high and hoping to wake him with the splashing noise. He stirs and asks drowsily, "You getting up already, honey?"* (Amsterdam, 1955, told by a man to a party of young women, and getting a big laugh.)

Mixed in among the jokes of Vance Randolph's manuscript collection, *Pissing in the Snow, and Other Ozark Folktales* (MS. 1954) No. 81, "Senator Banks," is an interesting anecdote heard by him at Tulsa, Oklahoma, in 1937, the teller stating that he had originally heard it near Poplar Bluff, Missouri, 'in the 1920's:'

One time the boys was going to initiate some fellows into the Lodge. One of 'em was Senator Banks, and they locked him in a thing like a bird-cage, only it was made out of heavy iron bars. Pretty soon a drunk man come walking down the aisle a-mumbling foolishness, so some of the brothers told him to set down and keep quiet. But the drunk sassed 'em right back. "Piss on you," says he.

The brothers begun to grumble, and they says "Put that man out." But the drunk give a big jump, and got on top of Senator Banks' cage. "Piss on you," says he. And pretty soon he says, "By God, I *will* piss on you!" So then the drunk man pulled out his pecker and began to wave it around like a fire-hose. Soon as the Senator felt the warm water a-falling on him, he roared like a bull, and shook the door of the cage. "Let me out, you sons-of-a-bitches!" yelled the Senator. "To hell with your goddam Lodge!" The drunk man kept right on a-pissing, and the brothers couldn't stop him. Senator Banks was jumping up and down like a wild man, a-cussing the worst you ever heard. He says the brothers are all fools and the Lodge don't amount to a fart in a whirlwind, also he didn't want to join anyhow, but some drunken bum talked him into it. He says their charter ought to be took away by the Legislature, and he will sue every son-of-a-bitch in the Lodge if they don't let him out in two minutes.

About that time the drunk man jumped down off'n the cage. He wasn't drunk at all, only pretending like he was drunk, as he was one of the prize drill team from Saint Louis, but there was only a few of the brothers that knowed it. That big prick wasn't nothing but a rubber dummy, and the piss was just warm water out of a bottle under his coat.

Some of the brothers laughed when they seen it was just a joke. But Senator Banks says to hell with such jokes, and God damn anybody that ain't got no more sense, which they ought to be ashamed of theirself. The folks had to argue with Senator Banks a long time, before they could get him calmed down enough for the serious part of the initiation. Everybody says it is the funniest thing that ever happened in this town, but they never done no laughing while old Brother Banks was around.

Quite a collection of materials on such scatological and homosexual initiations and ordeals could be made. These are importantly connected, as the above anecdote implies, with the Masonic Order in particular. See further my *The Guilt of the Templars* (1966) section XII, p. 116–30, on much franker initiation ordeals of this kind, as far back as the 13th century. The religious background beyond these extends at least another two thousand years, especially in the Levant.

Some such scatological mockery is certainly what is really

involved in the never-explained account of the Roman soldiers at the Crucifixion giving Jesus 'vinegar' on a sponge when asked for water just before Jesus' death. (*Mark*, xv. 36, and all the other Gospels similarly.) We know from Seneca's 70th *Epistle* – concerning a condemned criminal who purposely strangles himself with such a sponge – that *anitergia* in the form of sponges attached to sticks were placed in all public places by the Romans, and this usage was probably carried abroad with them by the Roman soldiers into their colonies, like the German soldiers of World War I with their little short-handled spades for digging field-latrines. Such *anitergia*, which are now used on the toilet bowl only, still exist in public toilets everywhere in Italy and France: the 'unnameable brush' of Alfred Jarry's *Ubu Cocu*. (See my translation of the entire *Ubu* cycle, with Beverley Keith, as *King Turd*, New York, 1953, p. 157: Jarry's pre-psychotic and verbigerous glorification of the invention of the nightmen's 'Pshit-pump,' or the 'Swallower of the Unspeakable.')

A curious problem exists concerning these ordeals and rituals, in a very rare work – most of the copies were recalled and destroyed on publication – entitled *Manuscrit pictographique américain* (Paris: Gide, 1860), preceded by a study on the ideographs of the American Indians by the explorer, Abbé Emmanuel Domenech. It is now generally agreed that Domenech was the victim of a hoax, for the presumed American Indian manuscript he published in careful facsimile is mostly a series of what appear to be young men pissing on each other, shitting, etc. Roger Goodland's *Bibliography of Sex Rites and Customs* (1931) takes the hoax position and so do most of the few other sources that mention this strange work, which they would thus assimilate to mere Western *graffiti*. However, the publisher replied to the critics (in an equally rare pamphlet, *La Vérité sur le Livre des Sauvages*, reviewed in Jules Gay's *Le Bibliophile Fantaisiste*, Turin, 1869, p. 524–6) observing very correctly that many authentic American Indian ceremonies, such as the urine-drinking dance later studied in John G. Bourke's *Scatalogic Rites* (1891), go a good deal further in their scatology and scatophagy than anything in Domenech's 'pictographic manuscript.' It might perhaps be worthwhile now to restudy the origins of this manuscript – fittingly preserved in the Paris Arsenal Library. A new and valuable study of erotic pictographs among primitives has been published in recent years in France, but not covering this one. It is G. Charrière's *La Signification des représentations érotiques dans les arts sauvages et préhistoriques* (Paris : Maisonneuve & Larose, 1971).

Purely masochist and undinist, under the guise of humor, is the situation set up in one of the few jokes on female urination, which, except for its attempted humor, might easily be a page out of Havelock Ellis' *Gynecocracy* or some of the urine-fetichistic private writings of Pierre Louÿs. *A man with an obscure eye-disease is told that the only known cure is a young girl's urine. He hires a young prostitute who is to squat over him and urinate in one of his eyes. "Now, shift!" he says. "I beg your pardon?"* (N.Y. 1935.) This is now usually collected in a form consciously presented as a rationalization, not of the classic perversion involved, but of a *black eye* which the teller – who is the hero of the story – explains in the punch-line, *"And when I said "Shift!" I guess she misunderstood."* (*Anecdota Americana*, 1927, 1 : 438.)

Hardly more than an echo of the once-rampant scatological medicine of former centuries (see under "Scatophagy," 15.V.1, below), the ludicrous story preceding, with its worthless and irrelevant punchline, is of ancient lineage. Herodotus tells the tale, in the 5th century B.C.: *Pheron, son of Sesostris, conqueror of Egypt, became blind, and remained so for ten years. 'But in the eleventh year an oracle reached him from the city of Buto, importing that the time of his punishment was expired, and he should recover his sight by washing his eye with urine of a woman who had intercourse with her own husband only, and had known no other man.' Pheron tried the urine of his own wife and of many other women without effect. Finally he was cured by the urine of a woman whom he took to wife; all the others he burnt to death.* ("Euterpe," Pt. II, chap. 3. Compare *Cinderella*, and the test of the glass slipper.)

At the next level down in masochistic fantasies of this kind is the drinking of urine, obviously connected with the idea of scatophagy, to be treated later. This is most commonly presented as a rough joke, the point of view being presumably that of the bartender (usually) who fools the greenhorn or tenderfoot into drinking urine. Note, however, the more simple expressions in the folk-beliefs codified in Thompson's Motifs T511 and T512, as to conception and pregnancy from the oral ingestion of innumerable non-seminal substances, including a pearl (dissolved in wine) which is probably intended as a poetic symbol, and, plainly, from drinking urine (T512.2, with numerous references, mostly Oriental). The dupe who is induced to eat dung or drink urine also appears at K1044 and 1044.1, though only from European and Pacific island tales. *A nervous young college man enters a saloon for the first time in his life, noticing a large sign over the door reading "BILLIARDS." He goes up to the bar and says resolutely, "Bartender, I'll have a billiard!" The bartender winks at the grinning loafers present, goes into the back room and pisses into a glass, which he brings back and serves to the young man, blowing off the foam. The young man drinks it down all in one gulp, wipes his mouth with the back of his hand, and says, "You know, if I weren't an experienced billiard-drinker from away back, I'd swear that was piss!"* (N.Y. 1938.) Expurgated version printed in *Contact*, 24 March 1942, p. 16, in which a 'dodo' in a tough beer joint is given turpentine [!] to drink. Compare the standard use of 'knock-out drops' (chloral hydrate) in low bars as recently as the 1930's – and since? – a survival of tactics used in seaport towns, especially in Great Britain, during the days of sailing-ships, for 'shanghai-ing' sailors, who would then not wake up till at sea. The usual 'knock-out drops' do not anesthetize the victim, but cause a combination of intense retching and diarrhea.

I have discussed in a preliminary fashion, in *The Horn Book* (1964) p. 443–5, the Elizabethan ordeal of the 'toast,' which still survives in purely verbal form both in Scotland and among American Negroes, possibly brought from Britain in pre-Revolutionary times, along with "The Dozens," which is another type of verbal ordeal. Compare the performing of frightening or repulsive actions during initiations. A tale is persistently told as a true anecdote of any one of a number of famous actresses, the 'toasts' of the 1890's and since, being given a party at which she bathes in a tub of champagne, who is erotically 'toasted' by her harem of polyandrous admirers who then drink the champagne out of her slipper (a further vaginal symbol). The *dénouement* of this masochist fantasy – which I am far from denying has ever taken place in fact: it is an obvious modification of the Black Mass – is difficult to arrive at, and I give it from the earliest known text, in *A Treasury of Economic and Facetious Memorabilia* (about 1910), probably collected by Henry N. Cary, a Chicago newspaper-editor, and compiler of an erotic dictionary, *The Slang of Venery*, and related works. *'Just before Sarah Bernhardt started from Paris for her 1900 tour, the young men of her set decided it would be the thing for her to take a bath in champagne, and they would then drink her health and success in the wine hallowed by her ablutions. She consented (because of the incidental advertisement), and 100 quarts of champagne were poured into the bathtub. The young men modestly retired [like good wives?] and Sarah took her bath. They decided to rebottle the wine and drink it at a dinner in her honor the night before her departure. They found that they had 101 quarts of wine.'*

In Kimbo's *Tropical Tales* (Nice, 1925) p. 98, a version is given as the final joke, in which a society woman's champagne bath-water is recuperated by a Swiss hotel-keeper as an economy measure. (Compare the Roman empress' reported bath in wild asses' milk, a tale assiduously turned into advertised fact in cosmetic manufacturers' complexion 'creams.') This continues to exist in France in an even further rationalized form, turning on the French insulting term, *chameau*, camel, as punch-line or topper, though actually the whole joke in all these related versions is specifically the situation of implied urine-drinking. *A society woman is giving a tea-party, and just at that moment the water is turned off. She tells the maid to make the tea from the water in her bidet, which has not yet been thrown out, and prepares the guests for any unusual flavor they might taste in it by telling them a story about having the tea they are going to drink imported specially for her from China, across Siberia, by camel-train. One of the gentleman guests makes a grimace on tasting the tea. "Don't you like it?" the hostess asks. "Oh yes," he says politely; "I just got one of the camel's hairs caught in my teeth."* (Paris, 1965.)

III. CREPITATION

1. FARTING AS EMBARRASSMENT

An excessive interest in crepitation or farting is expressed in jokes, all out of proportion to the actual humor in so minor a physiological activity based on the fermentation of undigested starch in the intestine. The fart has been used as the focus for a great deal of the embarrassment felt by the over-civilized as to the natural processes of digestion, and it is ideally suited for this as being only a partial and incorporeal manifestation of the fecal reality underlying. The difference is easy to see, in the very great difference of tone between P. T. N. Hurtault's anonymous translation of Sclopetarius and Goclenius (in Dornau's *Amphitheatrum*, 1619) as *L'Art de Péter* (The Art of Farting), published with the rubric, 'En Westphalie,' in 'the Year of Liberty, 1776,' which passes for witty, and the much more gross and far more rare *Merdiana, ou Manuel des Chieurs*, a chapbook collection of jokes, obscoena and songs almost solely concerning defecation, published in Lille by Blocquel about the beginning of the 19th century. Jokes about farting must also be an evasive form of scatological abuse of women, since a large proportion of these are particularly concerned with the embarrassment of women in this way, though jokes in which women appear in almost any other scatological context are most uncommon.

In a jestbook fathered off on the Elizabethan dramatist and ne'er-do-well, George Peele (*d.* 1597?), the final joke shows the mechanism of this sort of embarrassment in almost classical form, and should be compared with the gruesome revenge of Panurge against the Lady of Paris (Rabelais, Book II, chap. 22) hardly a century before, by inciting all the dogs of Paris to piss upon her, by means of a powder made of the genitals of a salt bitch cut in pieces (symbolizing, no doubt, the real revenge intended). In the English jestbook, *George Peele is vexed with a lady at a banquet, and: 'As she put out her arme to take the Capon, George sitting by her, yerks me out a huge fart, which made all the company in a maze, one looking upon the other, yet they knew it came that way. Peace, quoth George, and jogs her on the elbow, I will say it was I. At which all the Company fell into a huge laughter, shee into a fretting fury, vowing never she should sleepe quietly till she was revenged of George his wrong done unto her: and so in a great chase left their company.'* This joke is still very much alive nearly four centuries later, and is alluded to in one of the annotations to Dr. Caryle F. MacIntyre's *That Immoral Garland* (MS. 1942) p. 1, concerning a windy old lady: 'If Reginald had been clever he would have procured a *pétophone* [of which more later], which he could have used in conversation. *Gallantly he could have assured any old lady, "Be quiet, your ladyship, and they'll think I did it!"'*

One observes that the pretense of gallantry here has carried the day, the gentleman in Dr. MacIntyre's version obviously being perfectly serious. This is also the case in Mark Twain's "*1601*" written in 1876, in a pause between his two masterpieces, *Tom Sawyer* and *Huckleberry Finn*, where the opening situation is precisely that of the joke, presumably taking place in the private cabinet of Queen Elizabeth, with Shakespeare, Marlowe, and Raleigh (the real culprit) present, and each making a parody speech on the subject. The expurgated *Anecdota Americana* (1933) p. 167, no. 407, gives the now usual sardonic form, in which: *When the lady of the house at a banquet in England breaks wind, one of the guests rises immediately, begs pardon, and sits down. On being explained the superb gentlemanliness involved, an American waits for the next opportunity, and, restraining an Englishman who is about to get up says, "I beg pardon, sir, but this one is on me!"* This is repeated in Joe "Miller" Murray's *Smoker Stories* (Hollywood, 1942). In a Mexican version given in Jiménez' *Picardía Mexicana* (1960) p. 32–3, the woman involved is stated and shown to be the Queen. Kimbo gives a reversal in *Tropical Tales* (Nice, 1925) p. 90, concerning: *A young man squiring the Vicar's daughter in his buggy. 'As horses will, Stewart's beast, regardless of the lady's presence, relieved itself noisily. "Really, I am most awfully sorry," began Stewart stupidly. The Vicar's daughter looked surprised and said, "O dear! I thought it was the horse".'*

The blaming of the fart on domestic animals is standard, and evidently ancient, since it is referred to in that mine of joking lore, the learned jurist John Selden's *Table-Talk* (*ante* 1654; ed. 1869, p. 27), under the rubric, "Bishops in the Parliament," §12: *'The Bishops being put out of the House, whom will they lay the fault upon now? When the dog is beat out of the Room, where will they lay the stink?'* This allusion may imply an existing joke; there is certainly one very close, in folk transmission: *A man in church has gas pains. Next to him is a young woman whose little dog is on the floor between them. The man farts as quietly as he can and looks accusingly at the dog. The woman says, "Fido!" This is repeated several times. Finally, after a particularly loud explosion, she says, "Fido! Get out from under that bench before the man shits on you!"* (Idaho, 1919; Larson MS., No. 15.) This is varied in *Anecdota Americana*, on the style of the vicar's daughter and the horse: *The man cuffs the dog, which is sitting on the couch between himself and the girl he is courting. "Throw him off the couch," says the girl, "I think he's gonna shit."* (1:377.) French version in *Kryptádia*, XI. 6, with topper: *The dog turns out to be a cardboard doll, and innocent!*

Note that in all the modern forms it is not the woman who is embarrassed but the man. This is by no means the rule, but simply the development of this one joke. Usually the case is the opposite. Just as 'knitting is women's whittling,' scatology is often the erotica of women, both in stories told about them and in stories they themselves tell. *A hard-to-please lady at a carpet showroom bends down to feel the silky pile of a sumptuous rug, and in doing so farts. Blushing and hastily straightening up, she begs the pardon of the exasperated salesman standing behind her. "Not at all, madam," he says; "when you hear the price, you'll shit!"* (Chelmsford, Essex, 1951.) Aside from the anti-gallantry, these are expurgations, or crotch-wise partialisms of more specifically sexual lapses. Compare the joke, Levantine of origin in all probability, and centuries old, of which a French version is given in Caron's *Le Plat du Carnaval* (1800), a scatological fun-fest. It is called, in an Idaho folk-version, "The Seventh Relief" : *A country girl is washing dishes in the kitchen while waiting for her beau. Every now and then the navy beans she has eaten for supper make her cock up her left leg and give vent to a fart, saying, "Haw! the first relief!" and "Haw! the second relief!" etc. The boy has meanwhile arrived, and is standing on the back porch, but is too shy to interrupt [!] her. Suddenly she looks up and sees him in the doorway. "Well! When did you arrive?" she asks him. "Just before the seventh relief."* (Idaho, 1919; Larson MS., No. 18. Type 1453****, "puella pedens," Motif N611.2; and compare Motif J2311.1 : *The fool who is made to believe he will die when his horse breaks wind three times.*) Polite versions change the farts to yawns. Sometimes robbers are scared away by these means. (Type 1653F.) *Kryptádia*, II. 76 and 149, gives both the scatological robber – who is shitting on the woman's doorstep – and the "Seventh Relief" form.

This anecdote is built up into a tremendous embarrassment story, very frequently collected : *A man coming home on his birthday is met by his wife at the door, is blindfolded and taken into the parlor, and is told by her that she has three surprises for him. She hands him two packages, and tells him that she will be right back. In the first he recognizes by the feel, a pipe; opens the second package, and finds a bathrobe. He sits waiting for his wife with the new pipe in his mouth, farts noisily a few times and fans away the stink with the new bathrobe. His wife then comes back and takes off the blindfold to show him*

*the third surprise: all his best friends sitting around him silently
in a circle, waiting for the birthday party.* (2:401.)

Newbern & Rodebaugh give a sexualized version of this, in
The World's Dirtiest Jokes (1969) p. 85 in which: *A man takes
his secretary to a motel for a day of screwing. 'Not wanting
to pay the girl overtime* [!] *he checked out at five and they went
their separate ways. All the way home, he prayed this wouldn't
be the night when his wife would want a party,' but she does,
and is waiting for him in her negligée, all sweetness and smiles.
She 'suddenly started for the bedroom, saying she had forgotten
something. In desperation, he unzipped his pants, pulled out his
peter and began to bend and whip it around, frantically trying
to bring it back to life, but to no avail. He heard her returning,
so he quickly stuffed it back.... She returned, sat down, gave
him his drink and a quick kiss and said, "Dear, I have a
wonderful surprise for you, and I know you'll be delighted!"
Cringing, he asked, "What is it?" She answered sweetly, with
a sly smile, "Guess what? ... Tonight, we're already running
live on Person to Person!"'* (A television show.) A British
version is about halfway between the two story-types: *A pretty
young girl employee tells the boss mysteriously that she would
like him to come to her apartment after work, as she has a surprise for him.* (Continues as above, but:) *While waiting for the
surprise, in her foyer, he decides to surprise her too, and strips
off all his clothes, which he drapes over his arm. She calls,
"You can come in now," and he strides into the parlor, where
he finds all his other employees sitting in paper hats waiting to
sing "Happy Birthday!"* (London, 1964.)

Wholly anti-gallant and anti-woman is another modern
favorite: *A girl is playing the piano for her boy-friend in the
parlor after a heavy country dinner of beans. Whenever she
feels a fart coming on, she hammers out "The Storm" on the
piano. When she asks later, "Shall I play 'The Storm' again?" he
replies, "Go ahead! But for Gawd's sake, Melinda, leave out that
part where the lightning strikes the shithouse!"* (Idaho, 1932;
Larson MS., No. 26.) Various secret signs and indelicate evidences
are also sought to prove the 'authorship' of the fart, as in
Twain's "1601." – *'One of two ladies sitting across the table
from each other accused the other of farting. "Did you let a
fart?" she asked. "I did not," the other replied. "I'm sure you
farted," the first continued. "I did not," the second retorted
indignantly. "But I seen you tilt," the first rejoined, con-*

clusively.' (D.C. 1951, from an Army captain. The punch-line gesture is acted out.)

A folk-obscœnum or 'novelty' card shows three men – often simple 'chalk-talk' (*graffiti*) faces – of whom the two at the ends are frowning and the one in the middle smiling, with legend: "HOOF-HEARTED – ICE MELTED." The joke is also sometimes spelled out. (U.S. 1935.) It is not exclusively American, as the traditional illustration is redrawn (with one of the end-men holding his nose) in A. Jiménez' *Picardía Mexicana* (1960) p. 29, as heading for a whole chapter of crepitation stories titled *"Desahogos de conciencia."* Jiménez also prints, p. 93, a typology of characters according to the style of farting, *"Carácter y Temperamento según el Pedo,"* which does exist in English, in *Spicy Breezes* (1930? copy: Kinsey) p. 23, as the "Fart Calendar;" and similar "Types of Girls in the Powder Room," etc.

The ultimate embarrassment in this connection is naturally the childish accident of 'shitting in one's pants' as the result of a fart improperly 'eased out.' Stories about 'art-farters,' such as the limerick on the Royal Marine, *The Limerick*, No. 720, invariably end in this way. I have heard such a story told as a true anecdote, concerning a track-worker on the railroad who had all his fellow workers in stitches with his 'free-hand style of farting, until one day ...' &c. (Scranton, Pa. 1934.) *'Three doctors, walking down a street seeing a man walking along bent somewhat forward with legs astraddle, painfully, decided to try their diagnostic skill, and made guesses as to his affliction. The first suggested paralysis, the second locomotor ataxia, the third [pelvic fracture]. Unable to decide, they asked him what was wrong, and he replied, "I went to let a little wind, and I guess I went too far".'* (From a St. Louis attorney on the Union Pacific, Aug. 1943. Collected again in modified form, D.C. 1951, the man merely replying, on being told the doctors' diagnoses: *"Oh, really? I thought it was a fart."*)

On a golfing background: *"At the fourth hole I left a poop." "That can happen to anyone." "Yes, but I followed through."* (1:368, in Scots dialect.) In the elaborate recitations, with sound-effects, on "The Great Farting Contest of Stockton-on-Pease," and similar, to be noted below under "Ghost Voices," 15.III.3, the punch-line is invariably that the leading contender – like the Royal Marine – makes somewhat too great an effort and he finally shits himself (or herself), thus losing the match.

As with all types of humor, and other materials speaking almost directly from (and to) the unconscious mind, these themes are of course international. I have noted already, in the Introduction to the First Series, section II, page 15, the extreme appreciation of scatological themes by German audiences. The German counterpart of the English-language limericks are the "Frau Wirtin" quintains, and the similar 'vierzeiler,' of which numerous collections have been privately published in Germany and Austria, in particular by E. K. Blümml. (See the listing in Hugo Hayn, A. N. Gotendorf & Paul Englisch, *Bibliotheca Germanorum Erotica et Curiosa*, 1929, IX. 632–3, at "Das Wirtshaus an der Lahn.") An instructive analytic article on these verses was published by Dr. F. L. Wells, as "Frau Wirtin and associates: A Note on Alien Corn," in *American Imago* (1951) VIII. 93–7, paralleling their themes with those of English-language limericks, for cxample that given in *The Limerick*, No. 1730, on *a lady with 'a musical vent to her bowel, who, 'With a good plate of beans, Tucked under her jeans, Could play "To a Wild Rose" by MacDowell.'* Note the crude specificness of the German analogue:

> *Frau Wirtin hatte 'nen Student*
> *Der war in furzen ein Talent.*
> *Er furzt "Die letzte Rose,"*
> *Doch als der Sang an Aegir kam,*
> *Da schiss er in die Hose.*

At least two stories like this openly connect the accident with children, in recollection not so much of toilet-training traumata as of the occasional gastric lapses or fecal incontinence of late childhood, especially during emotional upsets, as with youthful soldiers during their first bombardment. *A school-teacher suffering from flatulence shouts "Hurrah for America!" every time she farts, the children taking up the cheer and drowning the sound. 'One morning ... little Johnnie shouted, "Hurrah for Cuba," by mistake, and shit in his pants in the silence that followed.'* (2:55, apparently dating from the Spanish-American War of 1898. Note the confusion of the action of child and teacher here.) Though only a humorous rationalization seems to be attempted in the original *Anecdota Americana*: 'Bugs' Baer says: *"God put the stink in a fart for guys who are hard of hearing"'* (1:116); as actually collected this apophthegm usually adds, '*... and to catch the bastards that try to sneak* *out those silent stinkers.'* (N.Y. 1936.) It is an article of folk-faith that 'wet farts' or 'fizzles,' produced by the anal sphincter in a state of muscular relaxation during fatigue, have a worse odor than any others, and that tight, high-pitched 'screamers' have none.

The earliest item of this kind shows clearly the vengeful intention of the 'fecal gift' : *'A boy [was] cautioned about farting at the table and [was] told to let them slide out. His first trial resulted in a turd, which he pulled out and exhibited, saying, "Here's one of your 'sliders'!"'* (Indiana, 1890's; in W. L. McAtee, *Supplement to "Rural Dialect of Grant County, Indiana, in the 'Nineties"* [Vienna, Virginia, 1942], p. 8.) In practice this works out that the individual, anxious to avoid noisy farting and offense, surreptitiously leans on ('tilts') or draws open one buttock to relax the sphincter and allow the pent-up fermentational gas of the intestine to ooze out quietly. Though generally successful, this unfortunately sometimes has only the effect of changing the timbre of the note achieved, bringing it into a lower diapason, sometimes even an unstopped diapason in which what might only have been an embarrassing 'screamer' emerges as a disastrous 'fizzle.' Let us draw the curtain mercifully here.

As with most sexual and deportmental admonitions to the young, by the old, this joke is very weak as to the details of technique. And I would add, therefore, in all the delightful illegibility of the Old French, a much older schoolboy story very much in the line of – or inspired by – Montaigne's famous passage in his essay, "On the Power of the Imagination," Book I, chap. 21, on the Emperor Claudius' proposed edict as to freedom for farting in all times & places (Suetonius, chap. 33), an edict presumably inspired by the following event: *'Un Roman qui estant en la présence de l'empereur Claudius, n'osant libérer, tant il estoit respectueux, un pauvre pet qui frappoit à la porte de son clos Bruneau,* ny le metamorphoser en vesse, comme font les escoliers de La Flèche, ains serrant les fesses comme singe qu'on clisterise [*give an enema*], *froissa et accrementa monsieur le pet, qui, restant applaty comme une assiette dans le boyau droict de ce misérable honteux l'entripeta et le suffoqua tout à l'heure. Voyez que nostre vie est peu de chose, puisqu'il ne faut qu'un pet pour nous faire mourir.'* (*Grandes et récréatives prognostications, pour ceste présente année 08145000470,* 'par Maître Astrophile le Roupieux,' a mock-almanac, without place or real date of publication, probably about 1615; repr. Gay, 1863. Emphasis added.)

The relevant passage in both Suetonius and Montaigne has for many centuries puzzled the commentators on these authors, and I am happy to be able to explain the matter here, and to state that the report of the noble Roman who died of his over-politeness is very probably true, his death having doubtless been due to high blood pressure and heart-attack. I quote from one of the rare modern practical manuals for the handling of heart trouble, in the style of the medieval *Regimen Salernitatis*, or "Rules of (the Arab physicians of) Salerno," John X. Loughran's *Ninety Days to a Better Heart* (New York, 1958) chap. 14, "You Must Have 'Blood Pressure' : "

> A fact not generally recognized is that the heart may be subjected to great pressure from gas in the stomach. In cases of hypertension [high blood pressure], gas pressure and blood pressure may mean much the same thing : it has been found that in many instances the blood pressure becomes normal as soon as the gas is liberated. Conversely, artificial inflation of the colon with air consistently raises blood pressure. When the air is released, pressure falls ... when gas is "belched" or is passed into the intestines, with simultaneous return of the blood pressure to normal ...

In other words, the medieval health-proverb is literally true : *Mingere cum bumbis, res saluberrima lumbis*, which is even more relevantly translated in the traditional English distich, "*To piss and fart, Is good for the heart.*" Blessings on wise-foolish Claudius!

2. EMBARRASSMENT OVERCOMPENSATED

An entire section has been devoted in the First Series, to end the chapter on Fools, 2.VII.2, to the riddle-story, "The Fortunate Fart," with further consideration in *The Horn Book* (1964) p. 465–6, tracing this to an embarrassment story, "How Abu Hassan Brake Wind," in the *Arabian Nights* (about 1450). The most striking characteristic of this story, as developed and en-larged in Europe – in John Aubrey's *Brief Lives*, in the late 17th century, where it is told as a 'true anecdote' of Edward de Vere, Earl of Oxford, and Queen Elizabeth – is the remarkable over-compensation of the anti-hero or heroine (in the French form, *Berthe, ou Le Pet mémorable*, retold in verse by Lombard de

Langres, 1807) for the disastrous embarrassment of the untimely fart, usually at a wedding, formal reception, or other
public festivity, which becomes the source or occasion of later
great fortune.

We may judge the enormous embarrassment involved, when
such overcompensations are needed, as noted in Capt. R. S.
Rattray's *Ashanti Law and Constitution* (Oxford, 1929) p. 372–3,
of a true incident where the compensation was of the opposite
or unlucky type: *An old man, a member of the Ashanti
delegation come to honor a visiting dignitary, inadvertently
broke wind as he made his obeisance. As soon as the ceremony
was over, he hanged himself out of fear of ridicule.* (Cited in
Robert C. Elliott's *The Power of Satire*, 1960, p. 76–7.) A modern
French version of this simplistic response is given in *Histoires
Italiennes* (Paris, 1956) p. 123, one of the last of the unexpurgated jestbooks in the great spurt of these published in France
since the early 1920's. Here there is no question of suicide, of
course, but the man's social career is obviously over, even if
he does not leave for the East, like Abu Hassan. *A fat man is
visiting. In bowing over the hand of his hostess, he knocks
down a three-legged table containing the tea-pot and cups.
Turning quickly around to pick up the table, his buttocks knock
over a vase. Squatting to pick up the pieces of the vase, he lets
a sonorous fart. He gets up heavily and goes out, grumbling,*
"Oh shit! I might as well leave." (Merde! je préfère m'en aller.")
This is repeated in a similar jestbook, *Histoires Snobs*, in the
same year, but with the *Merde!* expurgated out.

Pantomimes of this kind – actually dances in disguise, as on
rollerskates, etc, – are the essence of the art of Charlie Chaplin,
who more than once has made use of expurgated forms of just
such jokes for his most memorable routines, of which two will
be noted in the following section, "Ghost Voices." The split-
second timing of a famous vaudeville act, "The Clumsy
Painters," with ladders, boards, cans of paint, and other obvious
sources of danger, beautifully evades the plight of the fat man
in the story. Again a kind of dance or acrobatic routine.

An important element in the embarrassment of the fart,
whether accepted as a disgrace or refused, is its sexual relevance: its symbolic replacing of intercourse in the standard
'cloacal theory' of children, recollected in the myth of the
Annunciation and in many other folk-materials already covered
in chapter 12.IV.1, "Cloacal Intercourse," and again in "Pet-en-

Gueule," below. It is observable that Abu Hassan's disgrace begins specifically with a fart on his wedding-night, while Berthe's 'memorable fart' prevents the intended marriage from taking place at all. A tradition commonly collected is that: *The honeymoon is over when the husband begins to fart in his wife's presence.* (D.C. 1943, from an army sergeant.) This makes no mention at all of the *wife's* farting, nor does the traditional advice recorded as having been given him at his wedding in Prof. Leslie Fiedler's *Being Busted* (1970) p. 33: *"Be intimate with your wife, but not familiar. When you have to fart in bed, lean your ass over the edge."* See, however, the hilarious story of the wife's "Sea-Crab" fart captured in the chamberpot, in the First Series, 7.V, page 431. The disgrace of a woman's farting is a common theme in Oriental folktales, as in *Korean Sex Jokes in Traditional Times*, by Cho Yong-am, translated and edited by Howard S. Levy (Washington, 1972), a charming version of one such story also being given from China in Decourdemanche's *La Fleur lascive Orientale* (1872) p. 37.

Women are not necessarily so embarrassed by farting as is pretended: the trait is simply considered an ultra-feminine nicety of the "Princess and the Pea" type. Reversing this, but again for the anti-gallant purpose of ridiculing the woman scatologically in pretended-fool style: *In a western restaurant, a tall man and a short man are standing by a lady, when the short man farts. '"Madam," said the tall man, "did you hear that little son-of-a-bitch fart?" The lady drew herself up haughtily, "I didn't come in here to be insulted," she said. "Neither did I, madam," said the tall man; "if the little bastard does it again, I'll kick him in the ass".'* (1:380.) Randolph gives a sexualized version, in *Pissing in the Snow*, No. 51, "They Got Acquainted," in which: *The incident occurs on a train, shocking a town girl, who says, looking 'mighty scornful, "I didn't get on this train to be insulted!" "Neither did I," says the country boy. "If he farts again, let's you and me get off, and walk home through the brush!" The girl couldn't help laughing when she heard that, and the ice was broke right there. So then they got to talking, and pretty soon the boy stuck his hand up under her dress. Him and her was right friendly, by the time they got to Harrison.'* (Eureka Springs, Ark. 1950.)

The same teller also gave the standard embarrassment-type in: *A related story in which it was the girl who farted. Then, to hide her embarrassment, she asked another passenger for the newspaper.* "*Sorry, lady, I haven't got no paper,*" *he answered.* "*But soon as the train stops, I'll get you a handful of cobs*". A nincumpoop version has the man refuse the hidden cloacal sexual approach implicit in these situations: *A girl is riding on top of an open bus, and a bird shits on her hat while flying overhead. She turns to the man next to her and says, "Pardon me, sir, do you have a newspaper?" "What good would that do?" he retorts; "that bird is a mile from here already."* Here the bird is expressing the total rejection or anti-gallantry for the man, of actually shitting on the woman, where in the stories preceding one has only the halfway rejection or insult of the fart. However considered, there is a striking condensation here of cause & effect.

Again the girl is made the more virilely bold in refusing the embarrassment in: '*A boy and girl were walking along up hill together* [n.b.] *All at once the boy detected a disagreeable odor, and asked the girl, "Did you let a fart?" "Of course," she replied; "you don't think I smell like this all the time, do you?"* (D.C. 1944, from an army private.) The sexualization is complete in a fool-story or *double entendre* already noted, from a late-18th or early-19th century British jestbook: *A country woman who farts a great deal wants to confess this, because it feels so good that she is sure it must be a sin* [!] *She asks the lady of the manor for the polite word to use, and is told by way of a joke that it is called 'committing adultery.' She tells the priest she wants to confess to this. "What? at your age!" he asks, very shocked. "Why, father, it gives me a lot more relief now than it ever did when I was young." He, giving up: "How often do you do it?" "About thirty or forty times a day." "What?! What does your husband say about that?" "What does my husband say? He says, 'More power to your big fat ass!'"* Other remarks, rallying one's own or another person's fart, are, similarly: "*Pardon my Southern accent!*" or "*If you're going to talk, I'll be quiet!*" (Joke-form: *Kryptádia,* II. 84.)

The direct appeal to the hidden authority-figure, the father, appears in extreme burlesque forms, in which the travelling salesman (sometimes even an aviator forced down in his plane: *i.e.* a heavenly messenger) plays 'straight man,' in his superior amazement. This by way of pointing up the parental grotesquerie, which is really intended to disgrace the parents and not to refuse the embarrassment at all. If the first example does not prove this, the second will: *A travelling salesman overtaken by night is put up by a Pennsylvannia Dutch farmer, and is self-consciously sitting at the table with the whole family eating supper when the farmer lets a tremendous fart.* "Do you do this before your children?" *asked the shocked traveller.* "No," *says the farmer;* "ve got no rules. Sometimes me first, sometimes dem first." (Scranton, Pa. 1934. Reversing 1 : 379.)

In the variant with the forced-down aviator, *The family farting is stated to be a game, replacing any other entertainments, such as radio, of which, the farmer says,* "We ain't got none, and don't need none." (Berkeley, Calif. 1942, from a young married woman.) The second example takes the 'game' idea the whole distance: '*A travelling salesman stopping at an old farm house where an old man and his wife lived, was put up for the night. He was surprised when they retired at 7, with him sleeping in the middle of their bed. But more surprised to learn they are about to begin their nightly game of* "football." *After a long time the man let a piping fart. Some time later the woman let one of a slightly different sound. These were exchanged from time to time for quite a while, when the man let off a really bleating one, and the wife cried,* "He shit in the bed; that ends the first quarter; now we change sides!"' (Union Pacific railroad train, Aug. 1943, told by a Naval petty officer.) A folk-ballad of this kind, clearly old, with the husband *flourishing a sword to frighten his farting wife* is reported as still in circulation, but I have never been able to encounter it. Does any reader know this song? Vance Randolph gives a fragmentary version as "The Old Woman Pf-f-t in the Hay Mow," in his *"Unprintable" Songs from the Ozarks* (MS. 1954) No. 26 – also No. 27, with the protagonists reversed – in which *The old couple fight for three hours 'with never a word.' he with his 'rusty sword' and she with 'a handful of turds ... And then she* pf-f-t *in the hay mow.'*

3. GHOST VOICES

It is almost unnecessary to point out, in the joke preceding, that the elderly Philemon and Baucis – here complete with the heavenly messenger, Hermes, disguised as travelling-salesman or even aviator – are really engaging in a pretended sexual act (the scatological game) in their inability to engage in any other, thus reverting in old age to the cloacal theories of the child. A well-known American folklorist, now deceased, was himself conscious of the relationship between his increasing interest in

the subject of farting – on which he wrote several manuscript
skits, including a pretended autobiography of *Milord Pet* (compare the existing work of the same title, 1755, attributed to
Mlle. Fagnan: copy, Ohio State University) – and the fact,
which he frankly admitted, that his interest in sex had 'con-
siderably diminished' now that he was no longer 'a gay young
blade' and was 'getting on in years.' This went to such lengths
that he eventually made quite a pest of himself to friends, and
was the despair of his wife; forcing, as it were, their con-
currence in the subject, by secretly placing 'poo-poo' cushions
of inflatable rubber in the guests' armchairs (and his own) when
entertaining, so that they would appear to be emitting musical
and embarrassing noises on sitting down.

The whole subject of these scatological and sexual 'tricks and
novelties' (the French '*farces et attrapes*') generally sold in
'slum-shops' (from '*slumgullion*,' cheapjack merchandise) along
with secrets of prestidigitational magic and sex books – a
singular though apparently an inevitable combination, well
worth exploring – is of great interest, but is too large to deal
with here. See the *Encyclopédie de Farces et Attrapes*, ed.
François Caradec & Noël Arnaud (Paris: Pauvert, 1964), a
splendid compilation. Note also the tiny, squatting figure of a
monk, in the rectum of which the fire-motivated Fourth of
July chemical 'snake' is inserted, and lit, in Jiménez' *Picardía
Mexicana* (1960) p. 138, as tailpiece to the chapter on toilet-
epigraphs. The anti-clerical monk figures of this type do not
seem to exist in the United States where, instead, little ceramic
Arkansaw '*sooner*' *dogs* are sold for this purpose. (So-called because, as the novelty-seller or slum-shop proprietor explains
when asked: '*they'd sooner shit in the house than go outside.*'
This itself is a little 'catch' or *attrape*.) Also '*sexy Daddy*'
ceramic frogs.

The magical pneumatology of the fart has already been noted
in chapter 12.IV.1), in Dr. Ernest Jones' courageous observation,
in his psychoanalytic article on "Salt," that the Christian myth
of the Annunciation, in which the angel (or bird) impregnates
the Virgin Mary by breathing or whispering in her ear, is
nothing other than the childish cloacal theory 'displaced upward' from vagina to ear, as, in the cloacal theory itself, it is
'displaced backward' to the rectum. *A wife with a swollen
belly is told by the doctor that it is not 'what she thinks it is,'
but wind. She goes home and tells her husband, who points to*

his penis and says, "What the devil does he think this is – a bicycle pump?" (London, 1953.) An American version is done in heavy Yiddish dialect, with the husband asking, *"And diss is wott: a gess-pipe?"* and also exists in verse, with: *The woman later meeting the doctor in the street while she is leading twins by the hand. "And are these your children?" he asks. "No, doctor, they're not my children; they're nobody's children – they're just two little gas explosions."* (N.Y. 1938.)

A far more interesting approximation of the same idea, not attempting any such heavy-footed rationalizing, was circulated as a printed 'novelty'-slip in America, about 1915 – given in the First Series, 7.V, page 431 – and also appears in the Larson MS., No. 69: *A boy hides an inflated balloon in an old-maid aunt's chamberpot. She screams for the doctor, explaining: "I've had a miscarriage! Look in the pisspot. That's the first fart I ever let that had a skin on it."* (Idaho, 1919.) In the printed form, the comedy Irishman chases the skin-encased 'phart' around the bedroom till he punctures it with his pocket-knife, but this lacks the explanation or rationalization of the miscarriage. This is connected with the famous *vagina dentata* folktale and song of "The Sea-Crab," on which see further *The Horn Book*, pp. 413–14, a Levantine tale appearing in Béroalde de Verville's *Moyen de Parvenir* (about 1610), and carefully disguised – except for those who know it – at Prof. Thompson's Motif J2675, 'Bungling rescuer caught by crab ... and found in embarrassing position.' Perhaps also connected with tall-tales of 'farts so thick they must be cut with a knife,' as in *Kryptádia*, XI. 8–10. This goes back to Homer: Ulysses in Aeolus' "Cave of Winds."

In the French music-halls of the 1880's and later, one of the most famous attractions was the '*Pétomane*,' a Monsieur Joseph Pujol, who was able to fart at will, and presumably carry a simple tune in that way, in the sense that trained seals can bark or trumpet national anthems in circus side-shows. This is perhaps a prime example of nature imitating art, since the '*vox humana*' idea had already been expressed very comically in the character of the poacher, Hyacinthe, in Zola's *La Terre* (1887), Pt. IV.3, its greatest scandal, and even more exactly in *The Pearl* (Dec. 1880) No. 18, in "How He Lost His Whiskers: An Episode in the Life of Steve Broad": *A respectable old gentleman is brought before the magistrate, charged with stealing, or rather enticing ladies' dogs to follow him, with the intention of steal-*

*ing them. His defense is a long story in which he explains that
he picked up "one of those girls who ... who ... hawk their
tripe," and went with her to a whorehouse, where he was
inveigled into a game of blindman's buff. He being 'in buff' [i.e.
naked,] as well as 'it,' when one of the girls made a lunge at
him with an umbrella, the ferule entered his anus and was left
behind when the umbrella was withdrawn. "And there it is
now," he ends; "and every time I sigh –" "Every time you
what?" asks the magistrate. "Well, every time I* FART, *if you
like, the ferule whistles and the dogs follow me and I can't
help it!"*

This classic was brought to America by the great English
pantomime comedian, Charlie Chaplin, who used a polite
version of it – with the whistle swallowed in the usual fashion,
instead – in his 1930's movie, *City Lights.* He used the same
idea again, very soon after, in his greatest movie, *Modern Times,*
where the autonomous 'ghost voice' element is made even
more prominent in a wordless scene in which Chaplin, as the
prisoner bucking for parole, and a lady do-gooder are mutually
embarrassed by uncontrollable borborygmous gut-rumblings
(but never a fart!) after drinking tea. Except as an allusion to
amusing farces of the good old days: the 1900's, the *'Pétomane'*
left no souvenir in France, though apparently no one who was
ever actually present at M. Pujol's act ever forgot it. Norman
Douglas recollects his *'vox humana'* in the notes to *Some
Limericks* (1928), and I believe there is some reference to it in
Anton Ehrenzweig's *The Psychoanalysis of Artistic Vision and
Hearing: A Theory of Unconscious Perception* (London, 1953).
The actual facts were recorded in Marcel Pagnol's *Notes sur le
Rire,* and in Yvette Guilbert's *Mémoires* of the French theatre of
the period. Brief accounts were more recently published on the
basis of these in *Histoire de l'Insolite* (1964) by 'Romi,' p. 184;
and in Jean Nohain's *Histoire du Rire à travers le monde* (1965)
p. 341–7, as a closing item or bonne-bouche, entitled "Le plus
grande rire de Paris." (M. Nohain later issued a booklet on the
subject, as *Le Pétomane,* with François Caradec, in 1967, and
this has been translated into English.)

The significance of the Pétomane is, in truth, that his act was
the greatest success and the biggest laugh-producer the world
has apparently ever seen. Says Yvette Guilbert: *'People crushed
each other to hear him. The cries, the laughter, the spasms of
the women, the hysterical screams could be heard a hundred*

yards away from the Moulin Rouge ... The audience was in convulsions.' Dr. Marcel Baudouin published an article on M. Pujol's 'case' in *La Presse Médicale* for 20 April 1892, without noting that his trick of anal aspiration and release of air is a well-known Indian *yoga* exercise; but the case really worth studying – that of the audience and their wild laughter – was only very negligently observed.

Actually, the trick is quite ancient, but it must always have brought down the house. St. Augustine, an early Algerian church-father who died in A.D. 430, notes in his *The City of God*, Book XIV, chap. 24, the case of a man who could fart at will: *'There are those that can break wind backward so artifici-ally* [artfully], *that you would think they sung.'* This is picked up in Montaigne's *Essays*, Book I, chap. 21, "On the Power of the Imagination," adding that the Spanish humanist, Juan Luis Vives, in his early 16th-century commentary (1522) on St. Augustine's text, goes his author one better, and speaks of farts *'organisés suivant le ton des voix qu'on leur prononçoit.'* What Vives actually reports is that: *'There was such an one, a Germane, about Maximilian's court, and his son Phillip's* ["El Hermoso," died of poisoning in 1506], *that would have re-hearsed any verse whatsoever with his taile.'* (Translation cited in Trenchmann's Montaigne, 1935, I. 97n.)

One observes the quasi-respectability of all this crepitational humor, by authors ranging from accredited saints to avowed sinners, over the last thousand and a half years, whereas no similar entertainments of a sexual or pornographic import could even conceivably be published openly, nor avowed by the same authors. For examples, Oliver St. John Gogarty's graffiti-collector – himself? – in *As I Was Going Down Sackville Street* (1937); and the never-to-be-published *Oral History of the United States*, also essentially a voluminous graffiti-collection, by the 1930's New York Bohemian, Joe Gould, which he would gleefully plank down upon the desks of publishers' editors who had been seduced, by his publicity legend, into asking to see his work. I wonder where this manuscript is now?

The *'Pétomane'* theme has retained its popularity in the English-speaking world, most particularly in a limerick on *A young man of Sparta, who 'could fart anything from "God Save the King," to Beethoven's Moonlight Sonata.'* This is extended to a twelve-stanza epic, dating from 1940, in *The Limerick*, Nos. 740–51, covering every possible musical allusion and rhyme,

with much related material – often on misadventures resultant
from such gifts – throughout the chapter, "Excrement," Nos.
666–763. "The Farter from Sparta" is further enlarged into an
epic, "The Lyrical Lad from Penn Charter," by Roy Warren
West, being prepared for publication.

The themes of music and farting are perhaps inseparable.
Sándor Ferenczi, "On Obscene Words," in his *Contributions
to Psycho-analysis* (Boston, 1916) p. 143, notes, concerning a
homosexual flatophile – what would nowadays be called in
slang a '*fart-smeller*' (see section 15.III.4, "Pet-en-Gueule"): 'The
infantile interest for the sounds accompanying the emission of
intestinal gas was not without influence on his choice of profession. He became a musician.' (But this will not explain
Mozart!) A similar observation had been made as early as 1850
in Jannet's *Bibliotheca Scatologica*. The bassoon, as the typical
farting instrument of an orchestra, is consciously so used in
Berlioz' *Symphonie Fantastique*, and half a century later in
Richard Strauss' *Tyl Eulenspiegel's Merry Pranks* (here with
particular appropriateness), to show the condemned man's
fright at the scaffold. '*Lady: "Does the bassoonist really make
that noise with his mouth?" Conductor: "I hope so."* (Dr. Paul
Englisch, *Das Skatologische Element in Literatur*, 1928, p. 57.)

A joke of this type, of which the humor is perhaps available
only to musicians, who understand the problem of variant
tunings of the key-note 'A' in various orchestras, concerns: *A
concert-farter discovered by an American conductor through
the thin wall of a hotel bedroom, and pushed into world-wide
prominence for this art. On the man's first appearance in
Boston, as guest soloist, he bows to the audience, enters his
little draped kiosk, with a blue spotlight on the center, and
presents his instrument. The conductor raps with his baton and
gives the signal for the opening tutti, but the soloist does not
emit any sound. The conductor raps again, starts over, but
again no sound from the soloist. Raps again, begins again, and
this time the soloist makes a heroic effort and shits all over the
stage. Later, explaining the calamity, he says, "How in hell was
I supposed to know you tune the A to 450 in Boston?"* (N.Y.
1942, from a young musician now become a famous conductor.)

The verbal punch-line is of course of no importance here, the
joke really ending with the final scatological tableau of draped
kiosk, blue spotlight – and *all*. The same conclusion is used in a
much more florid recollection of the '*Pétomane*,' in the form of

a phonograph recording made during World War II, apparently about 1943 in Toronto, and issued in the United States both privately, on three 78 r.p.m. records at that time; and, more recently, on a single long-playing 33 r.p.m. record entitled briefly *"The Contest."* The original was called *"The Crepitation Contest,"* and ends with the spoken signature, 'Your narrator – Sidney F. Brown,' the name of a Canadian sports-announcer, probably falsely used here. The recording is a burlesque account, told in breathless radio-announcer style, of the prize-competition between the English champion and the Austrylian contender, who wins with a particularly rich and vibrating 'flutterblast,' but disgraces himself at the end, as in the preceding joke. All the contending sound-effects are carefully recorded, of course, in particular the 'flutterblast' and the final catastrophe. This is one kind of folklore that cannot be reproduced, even onomatopoetically, in print. A versified doggerel text, earlier than the prose recitation recorded, is given, entirely with women contestants, in Harry Morgan's *More Rugby Songs* (London, 1968) p. 14–16, capitalizing on the vulgarity of casting women in such a scene.

Actually, the earliest such scene in folktales is also entirely with women contestants, in Straparola's *Piacevoli Notti* (1553) Night VI, Tale 4, in which : *Three nuns compete for the post of abbess, the first by pissing through the hole of a needle; another by tossing a peach-stone in the air, and catching and crushing it between her buttocks; and a third as follows: 'Sister Modestia … rose from her seat, and being set in the place of trial, drew forth from her bosom a die and laid it on a bench, the five points uppermost. Then taking five little grains of millet seed, she did put one in each of the five points of the die; then baring her backside and bringing her buttocks near the bench on which was the die, did let fly so great and terrible an explosion as did well nigh make Vicar General, Nuns, and all faint away with terror; and albeit the said fart did rush forth with a violent noise and an horrible whistling, yet was it let off with such an address and dexterity that the grain which was in the middle hole did stop in place, while the four others did clean disappear and were never seen more.'* (Translation published by Carrington, Paris, 1906, II. 41.) This obviously takes cards & spades, and makes Mark Twain's rather similar opening scene in *"1601"* look very mild.

The same story is told in Fortini's *Giornate dei Novizi*, III. 18, about the same period, though this work – being the most erotic of all the *novella* collections – was never published from the manuscript until 1888–99 in the "Biblioteca Grassoccia" collection, from which a translation into English has more recently been made by Dr. John Del Torto of San Francisco (also unpublished). Rotunda's *Motif-Index of the Italian Novella* correctly cites this hilarious story at Motif H506.5, but his listing is expurgatorily omitted by Thompson, at that number, replacing it with a similar 'test of resourcefulness' from India in which the taboo element is more politely symbolized as the hero being required *'to swing seventy girls until they are tired.'* This is folklore-faking, from the top down.

The drinking of beer is traditionally supposed, in jokes at least, to promote flatulence, and the anti-gallant recitation or 'novelty' card has already been cited in which : A *girl describes poetically the emotions she feels when she drinks champagne; but ending, "Whereas beer only makes me fart."* (N.Y. 1938, on a printed card.) A lavish urinary version, expurgated 'around to the front' as a description of the fountains of Rome in their myriad splashings and other undinist water-sports, was circulated as a xerographic broadside from typewriting in 1965. It is excellently done, and appears to be the work of a woman. (Copy: Brown Univ., American Poetry Collection.) – A *man taking a bath in a hotel, farts in the tub. A minute later a bellboy knocks at the door and comes in with a bottle of beer on a tray. "I didn't order any beer,"* says the man. Bellboy: *"But I distinctly heard you say 'Hey bub, bring up a bottle of Budweiser'."* (N.Y. 1942, from an army officer.) This seems to be the only reference collected in joke form – and here only allusively – to the flatophile pleasure in farting in the bathtub. A group of mythical animals &c. described by a young woman included *'the Snorkle: he farts in the bathtub and* BITES *at the bubbles,'* and *'the Twerp: a guy who goes around in the summertime, smelling girls' bicycle seats,'* which latter seems to be disguising the same sort of interest as being mere cunnilinctus. (Scranton, Pa. 1934.) This point will be returned to again below.

An ancient folktale motif, the *vagina loquens*, of which the connection with farting will be seen at once, is that of the ensorcelled vagina which is required to *speak*, by the action of some magical object or charm, and usually to admit to its own unchastity. This is Aarne's Tale-Type 1391, of which the most famous literary treatment is Denis Diderot's *Les Bijoux indiscrets* (1748), especially chap. 47. This was consciously inspired by Garin's 13th-century fabliau, "Le Chevalier qui faisoit parler les cons et les culs" (text reprinted in *Nocrion, conte Allobroge*, Bruxelles, 1881, and in the main fabliaux collections). Diderot makes the vagina speak even more magically than in his original, giving it long passages – all highly erotic – in the languages of its various former lovers, which is taking the idea of the 'sleeping-dictionary' the whole distance. One such rather startling passage in English has been quoted in the First Series, 9.III.1, at page 751. A modern Levantine story of this type is given in *Les Meilleures Histoires Coloniales* (Paris, ca. 1935) p. 187; and compare Joseph Bédier's *Les Fabliaux* (2nd ed. 1893) p. 442. I believe a fascinating monograph could be written on these themes of the speaking privates, of both sexes, not forgetting the *locus classicus*, Antonio Vignale's *La Cazzaria* or "Book of the Prick" (about 1530), concerning the great and bloody war between the sexual parts, and the brilliant advice given them by the Great Cunt of Modena. (English translation first published, 1968.)

One of the most interesting American folktales collected for Vance Randolph's *Pissing in the Snow, and other Ozark Folktales* (MS. 1954) is "The Magic Walking Stick," which does not actually appear in the manuscript itself, having been told to Mr. Randolph only in 1958, in Eureka Springs, Arkansas, by a gentleman who had it from a man in Carroll county, Arkansas, about 1900. Here, as will be seen, the ensorcellment is identical with that of Garin's late-medieval fabliau, in which the '*Chevalier faisoit parler les cons et les culs*,' though no similar intermediate text seems to have been recovered in the inter vening centuries. (Motif H451.)

> One time a fellow had a magic walking stick that would ask questions and get answers. He pointed the stick at a tree and says, "You ever had any acorns?" and the tree answered, "Sure, lots of 'em." So the stick says, "What went with 'em all?" and the tree answered, "The hogs et 'em up."
>
> So there was three sisters a-living there. The fellow pointed the stick at the oldest one's cunt, and the stick says, "Have you done any fucking?" The cunt answered, "Lots of it," and so the man says, "You ain't the one I want."
>
> Then he pointed the stick at the middle sister's cunt, and

the cunt answered, "Just once in a while," so the man says, "You ain't the one I want, neither."

Finally he pointed the stick at the youngest sister's cunt, and the stick says, "Have you done any fucking?" The youngest sister's cunt answered, "No," and the fellow knowed it was the truth. So he says, "You're the one I want," and that's the one he married.

There was an old girl a-living there that heard about the magic walking stick, and she wanted to try it. So she stuffed her cunt full of rags. The walking stick says, "Have you done any fucking?" but the old girl's cunt didn't make no answer, it just kind of whistled like wind was a-coming out. The stick asked the same question again, but the old girl's cunt just blowed soft and whistled low. So then the stick turned to the old girl's asshole and says, "What's the reason cunt don't answer me?" Asshole spoke right up and says, "Cause it is stuffed full of rags." The old girl scowled back over her left shoulder. "If I had known you was so loose-mouthed, I'd have filled you up with rags, too," she says.

Randolph's unusual story is a striking corroboration, as are all 'speaking anus' stories, of the psychoanalytic position as to paranoia, that: 'the persecutor ... is perceived in the unconscious, curiously enough, as the patient's own feces; the sensations of persecution represent intestinal sensations ... Among the organs projected onto the persecutor, feces and buttocks play a predominant rôle.' (Fenichel, page 429.)

It is evident, of course, that it is the 'speaking' anus with its ghost voice, which is the original inspiration, while the *pudenda loquens* is conceived of as an analogue. Note also the various European and Spanish-American stories cited at Type 1453****, *"Puella pedens,"* in Aarne–Thompson's section "Looking for a Wife." The amusing trait of the old woman scowling back over her left shoulder and reprimanding her own anus for speaking, derives obviously from the various catch-phrases in many languages by which one rallies another person's or one's own fart, by pretending to reprimand the buttocks (which are sometimes also slapped) or the anus, as though it were an autonomous person or *vox humana.* I have heard: *"You shut your mouth! Nobody asked you!"* and *"Oo pulled your chyne?"* (in exaggerated Cockney accent), and *"Beans for breakfast?"* as well as the self-mocking *"The Voice of Destiny!"* and *"Your* *announcer: Oscar Poot"* (probably nonce-usage). One of the most interesting self-rallyings of which I have heard was told to me by a young woman of Polish origin as a sentimental reminiscence of her father, who was at that time (beginning of World War II) an overseer for the Dutch in Sumatra, and who would say to his buttocks chidingly, *"If you're going to talk, I'll be quiet."* (Compare Sacchetti's *Novelle*, before 1400, No. 29. Also *Kryptádia*, II. 149.)

The 'ghost voice' of the fart, or of the personified sexual organ or anus, is nothing more than the 'still small voice' of Elijah's god, in *1 Kings*, xix. 12, or the 'agenbite of inwit,' representing the individual's conscience (superego), or rather his or her unleashed *id* crying out from under the skin. As such, the message is liable to mistransmission or misinterpretation. The simplest form has already been given under Homosexuality: *'Nancy boy in shoe shop up on ladder, reaching for boot-box, farts. Other nancy boy at foot of steps sighs: "Why speak of love when there's work to be done?"* (Chelmsford Prison, Essex, 1951.) From the same extremely rich collection of modern British erotic joke-lore, *Union Jack* (MS. 1953): *'Chap gets home in early hours, boozed. Tiptoes in so as not to wake wife. Just as he closes the door, cuckoo-clock cuckoos two a.m. Thinks, "O god, she'll hear that, and know what time I turned in." So he cuckoos ten more times, and makes his way up to bed. Wife: "You're late, dear, aren't you?" Husband: "Yes, dear, it struck twelve by the clock as I came upstairs." Wife: "That reminds me – we must get that clock seen to. I heard it cuckoo twice, and then it said, 'O shit!' – farted – and then cuckooed the other ten".'*

As I seldom have the occasion to cite a printed British source for current jokes, the following is given from *The Listener*, for 20 August 1970, p. 242–3, where it is quoted as having been broadcast on the Jeremy Seabrook programme, "Portrait of Blackburn," as the sort of story told by 'respectable people in the pubs so freely provided ... laughing at some broad Lancashire humour. WOMAN: *Have you heard this one? This woman, she went to catch a train, and she went on the station, and there's these talking scales, so she decided to get weighed. So she jumped on the scale and it said: "Madam, your weight is eight stone, and your train leaves in three minutes, but you're all full of water." She went to the loo and she came back, and she jumped on again. It said: "Madam, you are still eight stone,*

*and your train leaves in two minutes, but you are full of wind."
So she thought: oh, I've got time to go to the loo again. So she
goes to the loo. She came back, she jumped on the scales again,
and it said: "Madam, you are still eight stone, but with all your
pissin' and farting about you've missed the train".'* (Note the
almost complete lack of polysyllables in this tape-recorded text.)
This joke is also well-known in America, and seems originally
to have been in Yiddish.

The ghost-voice speaks from the crotch. An authority who
may be believed on the subject, the author of *My Secret Life*
(1881 ff.), possibly H. Spencer Ashbee, at the end of vol. IX,
chap. 1 (ed. 1966, vol. II, p. 1750), states categorically: *'I've
heard a woman's cunt fart more than once, a windy exhalation
which astonished me at first. I've heard women deny that a
cunt could fart, but the woman from whom it escaped whilst I
was gamahuching her (one of the sweetest, cleanest and
loveliest) asserted it, and the abbess* [bawd or 'madam'] *who
was present at the interesting controversy, said that such
ventuosities were not uncommon.'* (Indexed under 'cunt farts,'
his proposed term.) The argument is not entirely absurd –
sounds of this kind are generally created by intercourse from
behind, when the woman is in the quadrupedal or knee-&-chest
position, owing to air being forced into the vagina. Note that
the author's own experience was during cunnilinctus. But the
idea that such sounds can be created spontaneously by the
woman or from inside, can only be considered folklore, similar
to that concerning the woman's 'ejaculating' a liquid at her
orgasm, once common in pornographic literature (only).
Phrased otherwise, such noises can and do occur, but they are
not autonomous and consist only of externally-aspirated air.
They are, if anything, even more embarrassing than farting.

The story known as *"L'Aze-te-foute,"* or The Farting Jackass,
in Grécourt and Piron's early 18th-century form, makes clear
that the *vagina loquens* is demanding sexual intercourse when
it 'speaks.' Just so, in the fabliau of Garin as retold in Diderot's
Bijoux indiscrets and Randolph's modern folktale, it recounts
its own erotic autobiography or secret life. The story is given
originally in Poggio's *Facetiæ* (MS. 1451) at No. 213. It appears
first in France in the 16th-century *Bigarrures du Seigneur des
Accords* of Estienne Tabourot, the earliest technical work on
the *forms* of humor, in Book I of the "Escraignes dijonnoises;"
and in Antoine Le Metel, sieur d'Ouville's *Elite des contes*

(1642; ed. 1662, II. 165). In the French *"L'Aze-te-foute"* version, given as a *conte-en-vers* by the Abbé Willart de Grécourt (about 1735) and by Alexis Piron, the cloacal theory of the child, combining or identifying the functions of the vagina and anus, is rejected as too primitive, but the final rejection of the woman is even more hostile than in Poggio's Italian original. It is given here as the pretended explanation of the origin of the title, a folk-proverb: *A man and woman are following their jackass on foot through the woods, and the man jokingly wagers that he will mount the woman every time their jackass farts. After the man has performed several times, the woman pulls his sleeve saying tenderly, "Jean, are you deaf? The jackass just farted." "Well then, let the jackass fuck you," he replies; "I've had enough."* This is one of the crucial anti-gallant folktales.

The jackass here not only rationalizes the woman's *vagina loquens,* by accepting the blame for the sounds observed, but he also becomes the proposed substitute for the man as well. (Prose-form in *Kryptádia,* 1907, X. 178–82, from Picardy, ending, *"Qu'il chie maintenant!"* – Well then, now let him go shit!) Just such an erotic scene with a jackass is the humorous high-point of Andréa de Nerciat's elegant erotic novel or play, *Le Diable au Corps* (1803), and in modern Hispanic folklore, as in a novelty card showing a drawing of a woman in intercourse with a jackass, to whose underbelly she is clinging. (Copy sent me from Mexico by an American woman tourist in 1958.) The trait of the man's immediate dour ungallantry, the moment intercourse is over and he is satisfied, is more than matched, with a vengeance (as the saying is), by another item also sent by a woman, in this case middle aged: *"Why is masturbation better than intercourse?* 1) *Because you know who you are dealing with.* 2) *Because you know when you've had enough.* 3) *Because you don't have to be* polite *afterwards."* (Santa Fe, N.M. 1967.) Actually, the first numbered reason tells everything.

In his *La Fleur lascive Orientale* (Bruxelles, 1872) p. 37, De-courdemanche gives as a Chinese story a charming little idyll also known in Korea, in which: *A student of good family has intercourse with a girl servant, telling her that he is punishing her in this way for farting. Later, while he is studying in his books, the girl appears diffidently at the door, saying, "Master, I just farted again."* (Shamelessly plagiarized from this source, changing the milieu to the Near East, in *Histoires Arabes,* 1927,

p. 102.) This casts a brilliant light on the whole Oriental anti-fetich against a woman's farting, as discussed further in Howard S. Levy's *Korean Sex Jokes in Traditional Times* (Washington, 1972), translated from the work of Cho Yong-am. Note also the superstition reported in Samuel Butler's *Hudibras* (1664) II.iii.285, that one can *'Detect lost maidenheads by sneezing, Or breaking wind of dames, or pissing.'* Violently anti-woman fart stories in *Kryptádia*, XI. 8–11.

The identification of the fart (or 'cunt-fart') as *the voice of the vagina* asking for intercourse is made absolutely open in Straparola's *Piacevoli Notti* (1553) Night XIII, Tale 3-variant, "The Cat's Miaouw," where: *The unsatisfied bride, at her mother's advice, makes the sound of a cat's miaouw every time her husband accidentally brushes his hand against her pubic hair in bed. Finally he seizes the pisspot from under the bed saying, "As meat won't satisfy you, here's the pot. Take your fill of soup anyway!"* (Meaning either that he throws the contents on her, or that she is to drink the contents with her vagina, though Straparola does not specify either.) This story still exists in a reversal, already given in the chapter on Prostitution, 11.II.3, "Frame Situation: 'No Money'," in which: *The man cannot pay the prostitute her price, and asks her if she will piss in a pot for fifty cents. When she agrees and does so, he pulls out his penis and waggles it about in the pisspot, saying to it, "Here, take soup! Meat is too expensive."*

It is the cloacal confusion, however, which is the essence here, and the accusations of excessive female appetite and so forth are obviously mere rationalizations. Some of the stories already given, under "Cloacal Intercourse," 12.IV.1, are almost charades of the infantile notions basic to this confusion: *'Bloke and his girl out for a walk in the country, when she has to step aside for a moment to change her wind and water. Unable to resist the temptation, he goes 'round the bush and spies on her. Thinking the opportunity too good to miss, he closes his eyes [n.b.] and begins feeling with a hand between her legs, where he takes hold of something long and hot and stiff. Surprised he asks, "Have you changed your sex, Mary?" "No, but I've changed my mind. I'm 'aving a shit".'* (Chelmsford, Essex, 1951.) In a similar American story: *A man groping under a prostitute's skirts suddenly feels an enormous penis there. "Why, you're a man!" he cries, pushing her away. "No, I'm not a man," she says; "here, feel my tits." "I don't want to feel your* tits. What's that great big thing in your pants?" "Well," says the whore huffily, "Since when can't a lady shit in her own drawers, if she likes?" (N.Y. 1948; often collected, and apparently a favorite in the 'narsty-narsty' department, owing to its sex-change implications, and overt homosexual tone.)

Closer to the jokes on 'cunt-farts,' though less valuable in making their intention understandable, are stories and pranks of what might be called the Aeolian type, in which pleasure is taken in games involving farting. These are apparently very old, from the ancient symbol of Ulysses' 'bag of winds' filling his ship's sails in the *Odyssey*, through to the "Pétomane" of the 1890's in Paris, who was perhaps only the last virtuoso in a long line of lesser artists. A typical farting game or trick is to *blow out a candle* by farting at it. One of the publicity photos of M. Joseph Pujol, the "Pétomane" of the Moulin Rouge, shows him doing precisely this from what appears to be a distance of over a foot and a half. (Reproduced in *Histoire de l'Insolite*, by 'Romi,' 1964, p. 184; and in Nohain & Caradec's *Le Pétomane*, English translation, ed. 1967, p. 24.) This only shows M. Pujol and candle, but thousands of spectators apparently actually saw him blow it out, rectally. A friend of mine reports that he saw a frisky young American nurse do this during World War II; not jumping *over* the candle (as in John Aubrey's *Remaines*, MS. 1687; ed. 1881, p. 44–5), but squatting down backwards to approach it, with much joking about not singeing her pubic hair. He added that this must be the origin of the English folksong, "Roll Me In Your Arms, My Dear, and *Blow the Candle Out!*" (which I doubt), and that it made the candle burn temporarily with a blue flame, with which compare Aubrey's note (ed. 1881, p. 114) on the *Vulgar Errors* of Sir Thomas Browne. chap. 23: '*That candles and lights burn dim and blue at the apparition of spirits may be true, if the ambient air be full of sulphureous spirits, as it happeneth oftentimes in mines, when damps and exhalations are able to extinguish yem. And may also be verified when spirits doe make themselves visible bodies of such effluviums.*' This being given as true, one wonders what the *Vulgar Errors* may be. In the marvellously-named Just Jäckin's movie adaptation of [Louis Rollet-Andrianne's] pseudonymous *Emmanuelle* – travelogue pornotopia for the readers of *Vogue* – a Siamese belly-dancer is shown puffing a cigarette with her vagina. Most yogis can also do this, with their rectums, but disapprove of tobacco.

4. PET-EN-GUEULE

Randolph's Ozark story of "The Magic Walking Stick" given in the preceding section is rather close at the end to one of a quite different sort in the Larson MS., No. 17, where all is rationally explained without recourse to magic or spooks, as simply an error of position. *A man comes home drunk and finds his wife asleep after a big supper of beans. He accidentally gets into bed upside down, with his face against her buttocks. "Pyeww! your breath stinks!" he declares after a moment; "what did you have for supper?" "Fissssh!" is the only comment. "How many?" "Pteuuuu!" comes the whispered reply.* (Idaho, 1917.) There is a minstrel-show or vaudeville expurgation of this, when *Brutus asks Caesar, "How many fish did you eat last night, Caesar?" "Et tu, Brutus."* (N.Y. 1934, heard on the Bowery burlesque stage, with pretended flatulent action or stage-business at the end-line, pegging it as a clean-up of the preceding joke.) Under Motif J1812.5, 'Snoring sounds misunderstood,' Thompson gives an ancestor of this joke, from his own study with Jonas Balys of the folktales of India: *'Numskull thief thinks snoring sleeper is asking for food.'* This gives only the basic situation. The punning replies, and the assimilation of the buttock-'voice' to that of the (snoring) sleeper, are other motifs juggled. (*Kryptádia*, XI. 31 and 57.)

What is really being attempted in all such jokes is some rationalization of the ancient idea of the *vagina loquens*, by assimilating its ghost-voice to farting – 'wet' or 'dry' as the case may be. Hidden beneath jokes and ideas of this kind, especially as to 'cunt farts,' is the erotic and masochistic interest in women's urination and crepitation. It is more specifically connected with the *position* taken by the man (often underneath the bedclothes, or lying on the floor) to observe and enjoy these activities more profoundly, than with any serious assimilation of 'cunt farts' to the human gamut of sounds. A variant of the joke given earlier as to *the wife trying to wake her husband at a party by making noise pouring tea, with the result that he thinks she is urinating*, makes much more specific the sexual abnormality implied or being presented in rationalized form as a 'joke': *A husband falls asleep at a party. To wake him when it is time to go, without drawing anyone's attention to his social lapse, his wife waves a herring from among the* hors d'œuvres *under his nose. He sniffs and grimaces, "Fer Gawd's sake, Emma,*

take yer tail off the piller." (Kimbo, *Tropical Tales,* 1925, p. 24.)
An earlier version, with a high-smelling cheese replacing the
herring, is given in *Mémoires secrètes d'un Tailleur pour Dames*
(Bruxelles, 1880) p. 116–17, "Le Fromage Impérial," told of
Napoléon III and the Empress Eugénie, as true!

No one needs to be reminded here of the closing section of
James Joyce's *Ulysses,* written during the 1910's, in which the
polymorphous perverse Leopold Bloom, representing the decayed Jewish *Ur-Vater* of the even more decadent Irish Jesuit
failed-priest, representing the author, is discovered to sleep by
preference in the *tête-bêche* position with his powerfully erotic,
earth-mother Irish wife, Molly. Not on any excuse of drunkenness, being sleepy, or the like, but out of abnormality and
impotence, and the rejection of her dominant and demanding
sexuality. It also cannot be coincidental that Molly Bloom is
presented as an opera-singer, and in many other ways typifies
the *female voice as phallus,* an idea particularly attractive to
the male masochist (Bloom), who is searching for a woman who
will be the man and husband, while he will be the passive boy-
wife or 'slave-girl'.

Molly Bloom's voices speak at both ends of her body and
from inside as well (far more than in the very obvious "Cave of
the Winds" or newspaper-headline passage earlier in *Ulysses,*
where even the writers of the guidebooks to Joyce have noticed
it), and the author-reporter creeps up to the foot of the parental
bed, as it were – where Father Leopold's head is also stated to
be placed – to listen to and transcribe, not the parental intercourse, since none takes place, but the mother's unvoiced internal delivery of the longest soliloquy, and the longest single
sentence, in the history of human literature, sane or insane, taking up the last threescore pages of the book. (This has been
superbly recorded for the phonograph by the actress, Siobbhan
McKenna; Caedmon records 1063.) The entire soliloquy is
pointedly described in *Ulysses* as being delivered while the
earth-mother sits heavily on her chamberpot, pissing and farting, and worrying whether she will crack it with her weight,
thus spilling all its contents on her eavesdropping foster-son,
the author. This is certainly the longest and most highly verbalized of all 'cunt farts,' or *vagina loquens.*

The excrementitious in literature is not always where one
would expect it. For example, in a cookbook. (*Send out the shit-
boat from Wigan; we've never had it from there before!*) Con-

sider *The Unprejudiced Palate* (New York: Macmillan, 1948), by Prof. Angelo M. Pellegrini, a very peculiar cookbook indeed, since it somehow manages to include very extensive and detailed materials concerning cow-shit, farting, etc. in its appreciations of good food, autobiographical anecdotes, and social criticism. Much like the present work, in fact, so perhaps I am just jealous. The chapter, "Bread and Wine in Good Taste: Some Culinary Preferences," p. 196–8, opens with a perfectly stupefying three-page glorification of an Italian proletarian couple, who systematically express their sexuality in sado-scatological insult and abuse *à le "Who's Afraid of Virginia Woolf?"* For example, when the man calls over the woman to fetch him his wine jug, 'his affectionate love call,' according to Prof. Pellegrini, 'was the envy of all hen-ridden males who lacked his gall and the burly framework with which to back it up: *"Ei, brutta puttana sgangherata, quando me la porti quella benedetta bottiglia?"*' (Hey, you subhuman unhinged whore, when are you going to bring me that blessed bottle?) To which she replies: *"Ecco la tua puttana, brutto bastardo pidocchioso. Bevi e affoga, porco ghiottone."* (Here's your whore, you lousy rotten bastard. Drink and drown yourself, you gluttonous pig.) For answer he tries to kick her in her pendulous belly with his 'heavy-booted foot,' but she parries the kick by catching hold of his foot. We now arrive at what all this is building up to:

> When she had him thus helpless in her strong grip, she would grin and spit, then throw his boot to the ground and retreat, laughing like a witch. As she reached the middle of the courtyard she would turn her rear toward him, bend slightly forward, look over her shoulder and wink affectionately, as she let him have a blast so terrific that it fanned her skirt into a complete circle. Her talent for releasing such thunderclaps at will was so amazing that she was everywhere known as *La Trombona.*
>
> In their rather unorthodox manner they lived in perfect marital bliss . . .

(This is Prof. Pellegrini's introduction to an appreciation of Italian smoked ham, or *prosciutto*, though the connection may easily escape the reader.)

Observe the *motion* in the following three versions of what is essentially 'the same' joke, from jocular and anti-gallant resistance to (paying) the prostitute in the first two, to obvious rationalization of perversion in the last. *A man bargains a call-girl down from ten dollars to five dollars. Afterwards she asks him, "How did you like it?" "It was all right, but I don't think I could have stood another five dollars' worth."* (N.Y. 1955.) – *The client wants "something special," so the madam tells the whore to "give him sixty-nine." After this new delight, the girl asks him, "Did I give you a good time?" "You sure did! But I don't believe I could take sixty-eight more like it."* (Santa Monica, Calif. 1965.) In *World's Dirtiest Jokes*, four years later, p. 90, an even cruder anti-gallant version is printed – possibly the original, from which that preceding was softened down. It is headed "Smelly"; *The man is in bed with the whore, who is going to give him sixty-nine. 'All of a sudden she let a little gas escape, and he ran to the window gasping for air. He no sooner got back in bed than she cut another stinker. He jumped up gasping, put on his clothes and headed for the door, saying, "I can't take sixty-seven more of those!"'* (Compare also a cartoon in *Sex to Sexty*, 1966, No. 8: p. 26, showing *A sort of lesser Molly Bloom trying desperately to rationalize Leopold's head-to-tails position in bed, with caption: "Harry! Is it my breath?"*)

For all its apparent modernity, its concentration on the college-humor of the '69,' and so American a colloquial phrase as 'cut another stinker,' the preceding joke is actually of ancient lineage in France, and possibly of Levantine origin beyond that, by way of Italy and Rome. Béroalde de Verville gives it (wholly without mathematics, and entirely on the matter of farting) in *Le Moyen de Parvenir*, about 1610, chap. 7, "Couplet," stating that 'The Original of this came out of the cabinet of our Ambroise Paré,' the greatest French physician and surgeon of the preceding century. Here the girl takes all the honors, both at the punchline and before. *A traveller in Rome is entertained by an elegant prostitute, who keeps on her bedside table little bladders filled with volatile musk perfume, which she breaks while making love in order to perfume the air. The traveller imagines she has farted, and she assures him that the Italian courtesans fart only such perfumes, "owing to the excellent nourishment of the country." He is forced to agree that those of the women in his country are nothing so fine. However, she then accidentally lets a real fart, 'non seulement au naturel, mais vray & substantiel,' and when the traveller diligently plunges his head under the covers to enjoy the expected musk, he finds he has been betrayed and complains. ' "Noble sir," says the courtesan, "I only did it to please you; to give you a souvenir of your country".'*

Actually, what is involved here is an elaborate and over-compensatory *joking rationalization* (as discussed in the Introduction to the First Series, section III) of the coprophilic or flatophilic perversion known crudely in English as 'fart-smelling.' Perverts of this kind still exist, both heterosexual and homosexual, and are not by any means something solely made up as a joke in the France or Italy of the early 17th century. To the contrary, the joke is intended to *explain away* the perversion. When I was a handsome young boy, diligently spending my evenings after work, about 1936, in the great Reading Room of the New York Public Library – my only *alma mater* – and leaving at the last ten o'clock bell to grab a sandwich and a piece of pie in one of the lunchrooms under the elevated train tracks behind the Library, I was once approached by a pleasant middle-aged gentleman as I crossed the park on which the Library looks out, who said (in a somewhat Germanic British accent) that he was a stranger in town, had not eaten, and was looking for company for supper, as he did not like to eat alone.

Being vaguely suspicious, I asked him what he planned to eat, and he told me cheerfully that it did not matter as long as there were plenty of *beans* with the meal. Afterwards, he said, he would have the fun of *"farting in the bathtub, and biting at the bubbles,"* and he told me that if I would do the same with him he would gladly give me the munificent sum of five dollars. As I started hurrying on with my notebooks at that point, he chased after me, shouting that he would raise the price to seven-fifty (rather high for a prostitute of either sex, in the worst years of the Depression), if I would engage in the same entertainment with him, in bed, after the promised meal of beans. I believe I snapped something back over my shoulder about his being a "dirty old fart-smeller," and his last words to me, which are engraved in my memory to this day, came winging through the rainy leaves of the trees in Bryant Park : *"I'm* NO *fart*smeller! I'm the cook with a gentleman's expedition in Africa, and I KNOW MY BEANS!" The term also appears in folk-wit, significantly spoonerized (*i.e.* arse-end-first) in the catch-phrase, *"Say, you seem like a fart-smeller – I mean, smart feller – to me!"* (Scranton, Pa. 1930. Sometimes *re*-reversed for further humor : *"You seem like a real smart feller – I mean fart-smeller!"*) Neither Béroalde's florid tale about the perfumed farts, nor the American cracker-barrel witticism about fart-smellers – and this is my point – was made up by accident, for purposes of humor. They are rationalizations, under the mask of humor, of a perverted reality that people who accidentally come in contact with it would prefer to laugh about than to have to take in all its ugly seriousness. Undinist stories, about pissing in men's beards and faces, are the same.

The disguise of humor is sometimes extremely elaborate. The same perversion as that preceding is fairly obvious in the following Irish story, and the same attempted rationalization as an absurd joke, for all the artful *fioriture* of absurdity. This was told by an Irish folksinger, travelling through La Jolla, California, in 1965, a splendid artist whose performing abilities were not visibly diminished by being fantastically drunk, as only the Irish know how to be or want to be drunk, right down to the marrow of one's bones. He told his story strictly as a performance, with changes of voice representing the speakers, arm- and body-motions suited to the action, &c., following a rousing private rendition of "The Ancient Auld Irish French Letter of Brian Boru." *This boardinghouse-keeper, a woman, brings her boarder into court for attempted rape and assault. The justice of the peace says, "Tell your story, my good woman." "Well," she says, "I was frying up the meat for a stew, when this – man – called me into his room. Like a fool, I went. There he was, stark naked on the bed, with an organism as big as your arm, and holding up a feather as innocent as you please. 'Mrs. Brandon,' he says, 'I'll bet you five shillings you can't fart this feather off the tip of my manhood, two tries out of three'."* [Too much noise and laughter from the college-girls present to get more than the story-line and pantomime from this point on.] *The boardinghouse-keeper accepts the bet, owing to the high price of butter; pulls up her skirts, squats down on the bed astraddle the naked man's knees, with her back to him, and attempts to fart off the feather he balances on the tip of his penis. The first two times he helps her right herself when she falls over as a result of the strain of her effort, but the third time he slips his penis into her, so deep she thinks her ears will fly off. And she demands of the judge that the boarder be punished for rape. The judge objects that she was apparently a willing accessory. "Oh," she says, "it isn't so much what he did, that I care about – it's the* AIRTFULNESS *of the booger!"*

For all the charm of the story, it also cannot be overlooked that the real intention here is again that of what is called in French the *'pet-en-gueule,'* or 'fart-in-the-face,' the fetichistic interest in the farting and flatus of the erotic partner, which it is desired to see and smell as close up as possible. The secret also of the legend of "Berthe, or The Fortunate Fart." A particularly rich, meaty literary example is an article by a woman, Yvonne de la Voulte, entitled "Matrimoniale (Announce)," in the surréalist mock-encyclopedia, *Da Costa Encyclopédique,* anonymously edited by Patrick Waldberg & Robert Lebel (Paris: Jean Aubier, 1949) Fascicule II, p. 13–14, the entire issue being illustrated solely with foot-fetichistic illustrations taken from 1900's women's high-shoe and boot catalogues. The authoress announces herself *'la moderne pythonisse du pet,'* and ends her offer: *'P.S. – Et je dépose un gros pet amoureux au fil de vos moustaches.'* This flatophile perversion is more particularly common among masochistic male homosexuals, by whom it is often further displaced to the feet, which are desired to be unwashed, sweaty, and ill-smelling, and also supplied with 'toe-punk' (*cf.* 'head cheese,' preputial smegma) and the like; and which can only then be pleasurably kissed and embraced, generally in just the *tête-bêche* position of both of the jokes preceding – including 'diligently' diving under the covers at every fart, exactly as in Béroalde de Verville (1610) – and of Leopold Bloom in Joyce's *Ulysses* (1920).

A modern French joke combines the *'pet-en-gueule'* flatophily with cunnilinctus in a fashion not really as frank as it seems, since it is really only disguising the first as the second, with a 'practical' rationalization: *A young man slides under the covers to engage in cunnilinctus with his beloved. Overwhelmed by the sensations she feels, she breaks wind. Rising gallantly to the occasion he says in a muffled voice, "Thank God for a breath of air!"* (Los Angeles, Calif. 1965. French form, not directly referring to cunnilinctus, in *Histoires Italiennes,* Paris, 1956, p. 181, with punch-line: *"Merci de me donner de l'air, chérie."*) Note also the *'Twerp,'* already mentioned, who *'goes around in the summertime, smelling girls' bicycle seats.'* The same disguise. In Fellini's film *Satyricon* (1968) the show-director farts into the audience's face four times to open the show. Is that clear enough?

Another rather obvious rationalization of flatophile interest, *explains* this as the mere (though equally scatological) interest in money and profit, here on the standard identification: 'Gold equals feces,' or, rather, 'Feces equals gold.' (*Pecunia non olet.*)

– *A man buys a horse and goes into the horsemanure business. A friend finds him sitting backwards on the horse, holding its tail in the air and examining its anus worriedly. "Business is terrible," he explains; "I'm feeding this bastard oats at 40¢ a quart for two weeks now, and all he does is fart: 'Foof! foof!' A man can't live on promises!"* (2:66. The punch-line is allusively used, especially in the theatre, as a proverb or catch-phrase.) Reduced to a 'quickie,' in which the masochistic identification of the horse-race bettor with the dung-eating sparrow is even more clear: *A sparrow has been following the race-horses around the track. He complains: "They go put-put-put, but, you know, you can't live on hope!"* (D.C. 1943.)

Aside from animals, there is of course always the safety-catch or trick of blaming one's own sexual perversions on 'comedy' minorities of choice, such as Negroes and Chinese. How's this for a rationalization? – *'Rastus was forever getting drunk and his wife Mandy would lock the door on him. One night Rastus forgot that she did this and got plastered. Then he began wondering how he was ever going to get into the house that night. A friend advised him to eat some limburger cheese and this would disguise his breath. Rastus bought a big jar of limburger cheese and ate it. When he got home he found the door locked, but bravely knocked. Soon he heard Mandy's voice: "Rastus, you been drinkin'?" "No, Mandy, I'se not been drinkin'." "Then blow yoh breath trough de keyhole." Rastus takes a deep breath and blows through the keyhole. "Rastus!!! I said yoh breath!!!!"'* (Las Vegas, Nevada, 1973, recollected from the 1930's.) Basically for the uses of anti-wife hatred.

No joke has ever been so ornately published and presented – I mean no conscious joke – as was a '*pet en gueule*' item in which the embarrassment of farting in the sexual situation is resolutely refused, though it is obvious that it is precisely the 'cloacal' combination of these two elements that is being sought. As usually collected at present, the joke is vulgarly direct: *A Chinaman breaks wind while in bed with a white prostitute. When she reprimands him he says, "No be mad, Missy. My plicky so happy, my assee he hollah 'Hoolay!'"* (2:376. The last word is shouted in mock-Chinese lallation.) The older form reverses the actors, and merely implies the sexual situation: *A young lady is searching through her chemise for a flea she cannot find, and breaks wind. A Chinaman (passing by ...) says, "All litee, lady. No can catchee, shootee!"*

This is extended to an entire volume, pretending to trace and retell the flea story century by century to the time of ancient Egypt, with parody illustrations in the style of each period to match, in a very rare private publication, *The Lady and the Flea*, published about 1900 probably in Boston (copy: Harvard Univ.) Each illustration shows as hero the same portly gentleman, who is thought to have been Dr. Fritz Irving of the Harvard Medical School, whose penchant for bawdy jokes is presumably here being satirized. The volume has all the air of being a private 'club' publication, though an utterly different level of sophistication from *The Stag Party* [Boston? 1888] probably issued by the Papyrus Club.

The frank modern version of the joke, ending 'Hoolay!' makes clear that the teller-identification in the *flea* version is by no means the wandering 'Chinaman,' so inexplicably present at the young woman's search through her chemise, but is, rather, the *flea* itself. Other jokes have been cited earlier in which the flea or louse hiding in the woman's pubic hair or vagina openly represents the unborn child in the womb, and his dangerous adventures. The fantasy of oneself as an insect (Kafka's *The Metamorphosis*, 1912, and the imitative and overcompensatorily large *Rhinoceros* of Ionesco) is a standard masochistic trait, also the identification of oneself as a small animal, such as a monkey or lap-dog – again obviously representing the infant – at the feet of a powerful woman or mistress. Aubrey Beardsley's drawings, and those of his many imitators, such as 'Alastair' and especially Beresford Egan, very often show the artist's identification-personage as just such a small and subservient imp, monkey or other tiny animal in the corner of the drawing. This is also a standard device in the massively masochistic Indian sculptural art, commonly expressing the urge to be danced or trodden upon by a dominant goddess until dead.

These considerations explain, I believe, the curious 'gallant' literature of the flea, of which many more examples exist than can be assembled here, beginning with the flea that torments Princess Budur in the *Arabian Nights*. See, in particular, *La Puce de Madame Desroches* (1582) edited by the French humanist, Estienne Pasquier, as a multilingual homage in poetry to the bosom of a lady on which a flea had been discerned by him in 1579. (Reprint: Paris, 1868, noting an erotic sonnet by Macefer, one of the best in the collection, suppressed in the 2nd edition.) The most extensive modern work of this kind is Leo Koszella's *Der literarische Flohzirkus* (München: Hesperos Verlag, 1922), a *deluxe* compilation with gallant etched plates of ladies in their underwear hunting fleas. A final point : In the masochistic identification of himself as the *flea*, the would-be child is not without ambivalent sadistic impulses against the mother-figure, whose body and genitals he attacks under cover of her underwear, since the essential act of the flea is not his jumping, &c., but his painful irritating of the human host in the act of sucking blood. See the *Juristische Abhandlung über die Flöhe* (Altona, 1864) in Latin and German, attributed to Goethe.

Jokes actually concentrating on the odor of the woman's crepitation (or any other nearby odor) often reverse matters by pretending to be opposed to, or overwhelmed by such odor. This is the format of Béroalde de Verville's original 'perfumed fart' story of 1610. In the unequivocally scatophile line, the following joke gives the show away completely, first in its total concern with odors, and finally in the laboriously set-up, and completely frank verbal punchline. In this strange story the unconscious determinants, and the deep ambivalent attractions and repulsions, overwhelm the opening situation : *A man is lost in delight in the arms of his mistress, in her beautifully decorated and perfumed boudoir on a Saturday night, when suddenly her husband (a perfume manufacturer) comes knocking at the door. The man tries to escape hastily by another door, but accidentally gets into the woman's tiny dressing-alcove, and finds himself locked in by the spring-action door. The woman and her husband then go away for the weekend. (Or stay, making love continuously.) The man becomes crazed by being locked in, charges wildly around, and upsets all the shelves of overwhelmingly sweet and beautiful odors. Monday morning, when the housemaid comes in to clean up, she opens the dressing-room door, and the man falls out onto the bedroom floor, gasping, "Let me smell some* SHIT!" (St. Louis, Mo, 1943, told by a lawyer on a transcontinental train.)

In Octave Mirbeau's *Diary of a Chambermaid* (1900), the first fictional work to tell the naked truth about the sexual exploitation of servants by their masters and mistresses in the Victorian age – and immemorially before – now finally made quite public in *My Secret Life* (ed. 1966), something very close to this joke, or idea, is implied. *The master of the house, whose wife is holding a fashionable literary salon for 'Gian Giotto Farfadetti'* [satirizing Dante Gabriel Rossetti, Oscar Wilde, and other *précieux* of the period, as in Gilbert & Sullivan's *Patience*, 1881], *rushes out into the kitchen, where he begs the chamber-*

maid to say "Merde!" several times, in reaction to all the vaporous poetry he has just been listening to. Why he cannot say it himself is not stated.

The famous scatological folk-character, 'Dr. Know-All," and his Germanic *Dreck-apotheke* will appear more prominently in the following sections, on Defecation. He figures in at least two light-hearted *parerga* concerning crepitation only, though his standard scatophagous cures are already evident in the second of these. *A lady complains to the doctor that her farts do not smell, and gives him a sample as she lifts one leg to a chair to start undressing for an examination. The doctor begins fanning himself, and says, "Put your clothes back on, madam. It isn't your ass that needs examining – it's your nose."* (N.Y. 1943.) Vance Randolph's *Pissing in the Snow*, No. 48, "Wind On His Guts," gives a story collected from a woman in Joplin, Missouri in 1937 (and heard by her about 1900), opening: *'One time there was a farmer that always had wind on his guts, till he was pooched out like a cat full of kittens.'* He goes to the doctor, giving, as a sample, *'a blast that pretty near unjointed him.'* *The doctor opens all the windows, and all the other patients rush outside for some fresh air. The diagnosis is: "My God ... something must have crawled up in you and died!" And the doctor refuses to prescribe any bottled medicine, suggesting instead a homoeopathic remedy of raw onions, lots of garlic, and wild ramps with every meal, and half a pound of limburger cheese* [n.b.] *at bedtime. 'The poor farmer turned kind of green around the gills. "Do you reckon that stuff will cure me?" he says. Doc Holton looked mighty solemn. "No, I don't believe it will cure you," says he, "but it might help* SOME!"'

An earlier printed form in *The Stag Party* (1888) unnumb. p. 181, is both much shorter and much more frank about the ungallant and scatophagous intention of 'Dr. Dreck's' mock-prescription. The variant emphasis in the punchline is not of any importance – often the case in what is very wrongly thought of as the essential feature of any specific joke – and merely signals the end of the 'sell' or 'catch' at the butt's expense: *'Old maid – "Doctor, what can I take for my breath?" Doctor (after getting one snuff of it) – "My God, madam. Try chewing shit. That may help it some".'* In the same way, in the preceding joke, various different punchlines arrive at the same insulting conclusion: *When the lady complains that her farts do not smell, and gives the doctor a sample, he writes her out a long prescription for suppositories. "And will it have the required, er, carminative effect, doctor?" she asks. "No, madam, these will plug you up completely, and make you fart louder. That way at least you'll hear them."* None of these jokes seem very funny to ordinary people. To fart-fanciers, however, they are apparently the acme of ethereal humor and Aeolian delight. Whether or not they do it in the bathtub, and 'bite at the bubbles.'

IV. DEFECATION

The three following and concluding sections (*Land! Land!*) all concern defecation, generally as a hostile rather than a hygienic act, with an appropriateness modelled on the last paragraph of the last chapter of Rabelais' Book IV, the last which he is known certainly to have written (1552), and which cost him his position as curé of Meudon, lost him his privilege of clergy and benefices, and left him to die miserably in obscurity, and possibly of starvation, the following year. '*The bread you ate last year won't grind shit today,*' says the proverb; and Rabelais' closing synonymy, of sixteen different terms for feces, was certainly intended as his last word or parting shot: '*But what is this? ha! oh, ho! how the devil came I by this? Do you call this what-the-cat-left-in-the-malt, filth, dirt, dung, dejection, fœcal matter, excrement, stercoration, sir-reverence, ordure, second-hand meats, fumets, stonts, scybal, or spyrathe?* 'Tis Hibernian saffron, I protest . . . *and so much for this time. Selah. Let us drink.*' (Urquhart-Motteux translation.)

There is a more modern proverb coming to the same thing as Rabelais' concerning last year's bread, with which I was chided by a miner's wife during a coal-strike in Pennsylvania, when, on my first store job, I tried to sell her silk-&-woollen underwear for her husband, as it was winter, when she wanted to buy only mixed cotton drawers. She shook her head regretfully, rubbing the fine cloth between her fingers, and said: "No Money! You know: '*No work, no money. No money, no eatum. No eatum, no shittum. No shittum –* DIE *like a dog!*'" (Scranton, Pa. 1934.) The mock American Indian or Italian dialect is hardly even intended to cover the bitterness of this unrecorded proverb. There is a brief chapter on Indian and other *insults* involving feces, in John G. Bourke's *Scatalogic Rites,* p. 256–60.

Scatology is the weapon of choice or court-of-last-appeal, when a crushing insult is wanted, and this not only in our culture but in almost all. The odor of the feces, and the instinctive rejection of them that makes many animals, quite other than man, bury the feces (to prevent enemies from tracking the animal thereby), are doubtless a sufficient reason for this. But the deepest level, insofar as jokes and insults are concerned, is that of the inevitable and hostile infantile anality of almost all humor, as has been discussed at the end of the introduction to the present chapter. Two preliminary points seem worth making as to jokes specifically concerning defecation, as the ultimate hostile or defiling act. First, the frequency of this motif in jokes and folktales directed against the clergy. This is not as commonly seen nowadays, since anti-clerical jokes are becoming a thing of the past as religion dies in the West, but was once strikingly evident in such themes, as can still be seen in, for example, Afanasyev's *Russian Secret Tales* (collected about 1865), in which anti-clericalism bulks very large, and scatological and castratory themes almost equally large; and in the "Contes Picards," collected in Picardy by E.-Henry Carnoy from the 1880's on, and anonymously published in *Kryptádia*, vols. I–II and especially X–XI (1907), where the scatological and anti-clerical stories significantly overlap.

One or two examples should suffice here, the question being now mostly of historical interest. One of the first 'dirty jokes' I myself ever heard was an anti-Christian mock in which: *A Catholic is trying to convert a Jew, and tells him that if he becomes a Catholic his prayers will certainly be answered, because the priest will give them to the bishop, who will give them to the cardinal, who will give them to the Pope, who will shove them up into Heaven through a hole at the top of the Vatican, which just matches a hole in the floor of Heaven, where St. Peter will take them to the Virgin Mary, who will intercede on their behalf with Jesus, who will say a good word for them to God. The Jew repeats this whole itinerary, with an astonished air, ending: "You know, I guess it must be true, because I've always wondered what they do with all the shit in heaven. They must throw it down that little hole in the Vatican, where the Pope gives it to the cardinal, who gives it to the bishop, who gives it to the priest, who gives it to you, and YOU'RE trying to hand it to me!"* (Atlantic City, N.J. 1927, from a Portuguese-American adolescent Jewish boy who planned to become a prize-fighter.) Note the very similar mocking repetition of the whole Catholic hierarchic pecking-order in the last joke given in the First Series here, page 799, a Russian-Jewish folktale with the standard characters of the Jewish trickster-tailor (or rabbi) and the stupid Cossack, the latter Americanized as the 'Irish cop,' or *'baytzimmer'* – *"all balls and no brains"* (politely: *"with a strong back and a weak mind"*). 'Just-so' stories on popes visiting Heaven, *Kryptádia*, V. 7; Type 1737.

Mocks of this kind are not uniquely Jewish, but are often told by moderately religious persons concerning their own religious sect. It is more usual, of course, for some competing group or religion to be sniped at, and these are always the more violent and scatological jests. One that still seems to survive concerns primitive American Baptist sects, with baptism by immersion – the essential ritual of the Christian religion, as the New Testament makes abundantly clear, from *Matthew*, iii. 6, onward – as the rite being particularly mocked. Dr. Richard Dorson, in *Negro Folktales in Michigan* (Harvard Univ. Press, 1956) p. 172, "The Baptizing Disturbed," gives, as the first half of a two-part joke, a polite version of the following, in which the woman being baptized 'had a little boy, and she was carrying some light bread in her bosom for him' – a perfectly improbably expurgation, obviously by the teller. *A little boy is being baptized by immersion, in a river, and when the preacher and deacons sling him under the water, against the current, he becomes frightened and shits in his pants. The shit falls out the legs of his short pants and floats to the top of the water, and the preacher shouts, "Duck him again! His sins are coming out in chunks!"* (Santa Monica, Calif. 1965.) The punchline only is given by Prof. D. K. Wilgus, in *Journal of American Folklore* vol. 77: p. 96, who goes on to observe:

> The defecation jokes ... and the sexual innuendo ... have been central to live minstrel and country music performances, as anyone should know who has attended a country fair, "good clean show, bring the family," or even a rural homecoming. Even serious students of the hillbilly syndrome [?] have tended to slight this part of the tradition. It is unfortunate that so little is available of a tradition that is important not only for its items of folk narrative, but for its function in American folk culture.

As centuries pass, our cultural scatologica move on to other areas, leaving religion and minstrel shows behind. Even so staggering an item as the long letter in dispraise of shitting – especially in a standing position – written in French in 1694 by the lesbian Princess-Palatine Charlotte Elisabeth of Bavaria, Duchess of Orleans, to her aunt, a perfectly incredible *débauche d'esprit* printed in full in Gustave Brunet's anonymous *Anthologie Scatologique* (1862) p. 85–93, seems dated today. Instead, an up-to-the-minute Italian journalist of our own day, Miss Oriana Fallaci – the names that control one's destiny? – who has a hard word for everyone she interviews, has only admiration for the American astronauts who first reached the Moon, and is quoted concerning them in *Le Nouvel Observateur* (Paris, 18 Jan. 1971) No. 323: p. 36, as saying: '*And fascists! Just think – they left their excrements on the Moon!*' Which nobody can deny. Though not all of us admire it as much as Miss Fallaci.

I. BIRDS AND BEASTS

As is usual, from *Aesop's Fables* to modern comic postcards, as also in the anonymous comic valentines and the 'hate-cards' that have replaced them, references to animals and birds are the simplest disguise for actions which cannot safely or diplomatically be ascribed to human beings, and particularly not to the speaker or joke-teller himself. Some further discussion of this use of parables in folk-literature, particularly in the Bible, where it is a feature of both the Old Testament and New, will be found in *The Horn Book*, p. 302–3. The 'cute' urination of pet dogs, already noted in the preceding section, is matched by the 'cute' defecation of little birds, representing the speaker. Expurgated as to actors as such stories are, and generally as to vocabulary as well, they are the principal scatological items that appear in the public prints. '*First little bird: "Hoo's that sitting on the park bench below us?" Second little bird: "That's the guy who fired buckshot at us the other day." Third little bird:"Well, wot are we waitin' for?"*' (*Better Crops with Plant Food*, Dec. 1940, p. 49.) This theme of *shit-as-shot*, only implied here, will be returned to below. *The statue of Columbus speaks at night to a drunk in Central Park: "Ah, to make one last voyage!" Drunk: "Where ya wanna go?" Columbus: "Anywhere – but by air! I want to fly over those goddam pigeons!"* (N.Y. 1948.)

The idea of flying higher than someone else, for defecatory

purposes, is a miraculous idea long since in folk transmission. An authentic Jewish legend – really just a *schmuss* or anecdote, not intended to be taken seriously, but then that's how all legends begin that are not intentional frauds – has already been quoted on this subject in chapter 14.I.6, "Mocking God," from Samuel Roth's violently anti-Semitic autobiography, *Jews Must Live* (New York, 1934). And compare the myth of Daedalus & Icarus, as discussed in *The Horn Book*, p. 330. The idea is certainly of ancient Levantine origin, though I must admit I have never encountered the scatological Jewish legend except in the pages of Roth's book. Something very similar appears in the old Canaanite story, "The Heavenly Bow," dating from 1400 B.C. or earlier, and translated in Theodore H. Gaster's *The Oldest Stories in the World* (1952) p. 180–81, in which: *The goddess, Anat, plans to kill Aqhat* (Orion) *by flying up over him in the sky with the assassin, Yatpan, in a sack, and dropping him on Aqhat's head.* This beats the German World War I aviator, Max Immelmann, by centuries, for the invention of the technique of aerial combat. All that was lacking was the airplane, for which Levantine folktales amply made up with magic carpets, flying horses (Mohammed's winged mule, Buraq) and the like.

A turtle is swallowed by an eagle. Suddenly the turtle sticks its head out the eagle's ass, and says, "How high up are we, Mr. Eagle?' "Ten thousand feet." "You wouldn't shit me, would you? (or:) *Shit me easy, Mr. Eagle!"* (N.Y. 1942.) The punchline of this joke is often used alone, as catch-phrase, to indicate disbelief of a story being told as true. This turtle-and-eagle story, which appears to stem from Negro sources in the United States, is of ancient Levantine or East Indian origin, and is also given in La Fontaine's *Fables*, in a polite version in which: *The tortoise is being carried through the air by biting a stick held in the claws of a bird (or between two birds). He is cautioned not to speak, but cannot forbear to ask questions as to how high they are, or what country they are crossing, and falls to his death.* (Motifs J2133.5 and J2357, with international references. This is the "Jonah and the Whale" form, Tale Type 1250B.) In W. A. Clouston's *Book of Noodles*, responsibility is shifted: *The wife is carried up a tree to the sky in a bag held between her husband's teeth. She asks him a question, and he drops her when he answers.* The tortoise or turtle also appears in a modern Levantine text in *Histoires Coloniales* (1935) p. 171.

The real etymology, if such need be sought, is perhaps the observation of seagulls and other birds opening shellfish by dropping them on rocks.

Another advantage of the aerial type of attack, specifically with shit, which will become even more clear in the later section, "Gardyloo!" 15.VI.2, is the protected getaway of the attacker. As in the joke given earlier concerning: *The bird who shits on the girl's hat, but what's the use giving her paper (or a handful of grass)? That bird is three blocks from here by now.* (1:487, punchline only.) Even more clear are the jokes and songs on the "Thankful Fool" theme (Type 1689, Motifs J2563–4). where: *"The eagles fly so high, They shit squarely in your eye; It's a good thing* cows *can't fly – in Mobile!"* In *Tropical Tales* (Nice, 1925) p. 60, another bird story warns didactically of the danger of forgetting about one's getaway, though this version makes no mention of the scatological crime: *'A sparrow had been enjoying a dinner of fresh horse dung. Thoroughly satisfied he flew up on to the roof to digest his meal. So happy did the little chap feel, that he burst into song. The son of the house heard him, fetched his gun, and shot him dead.* Moral: *When you've been eating* [shit], *don't shout about it from the house-tops.'*

This is strictly set up for the would-be proverb of the punch-line, and other such are also applied to the same framework: *Several birds eat a big meal of horseshit, and light on the old pump-handle. One flies east and the buzzard catches him. One flies west and the farmer shoots him. The third one stays where is and says, "When you're full of horseshit, don't fly off the handle."* (N.Y. 1953; the American slang phrase, 'to fly off the handle,' means to lose one's temper.) Another rather peculiar version arrives at the moral that *'Not everybody that shits on you is your enemy'* – but that's the way to bet your money, friend! This is printed, on an anti-Communist background, in Richard Brooks' *The Producer* (1951) end of chap. 22 (Pocket-book-Cardinal ed., 1953, p. 170–71), with a disquisition on obscenity in the life of the Hollywood motion-picture colony, to the end of the chapter. Compare the far superior *The Colony* (1969), by Ray Russell, likewise filled with bitter jokes and gags.

Finally, a pure brag, again muffling or evading the scatological crime, even though using the stalking-horse [!] of a bird: *A pigeon invites an out-of-town bird to fly over New York's highest skyscraper, the Empire State Building, with him. Standing on the top of the flagpole, on the dirigible mooring-mast [!] at the very top, the pigeon lets his droppings fall to the street far below. "Did you see that?" he asks the other bird. "Yes? What about it?" "Nothing. I just wanted to show you how far a little shit will go in this town."* (2:83.) Actually this is only a development from the Wellerism, *"A little goes a long way," as the monkey said when he shit over the cliff* (N.Y. 1948), or, *"That remains to be seen," as the elephant said when he shit on the sidewalk.* Wellerisms are not always scatological; castratory examples also exist: *"They're off!" as the monkey said when he backed into the lawn-mower.* The form is originally Italian, and has been importantly catalogued in Dr. Charles Speroni's *The Italian Wellerism to the End of the Seventeenth Century* (Berkeley, Calif. 1953). The earliest collection, Antonio Cornazano's *Proverbi in facetie* (1518), is really a collection of bawdy tales pretending to explain the origin of certain of these folk-apothegms.

Animal scatologica seldom rise to joke or folktale form, and mostly remain at the level of weak puns and cartoons, particularly concerning pet dogs, on the style of a long recitation in doggerel verse (evidently) called "The Piddling Pup;" and there is another concerning "The Daring Fly," who shits all over everything. Probably the best, in *The Limerick* (1953) p. 419, note 731, draws most of its humor from the tongue-twister format: '*First Egyptologist (on finding a pile of fresh shit in the unopened tomb): "Dr. Carter, do you think possibly a cat crept into the crypt and crapped and crept out again?" Second Egyptologist: "No, I think it was the pup popped into the pit and pooped and then popped out".*' Again, the true meaning is only made clear in considering this on the larger scale of the *grumus merdæ* or criminal 'calling card,' in the section below, "Feces as Gift."

2. DR. KNOW-ALL

The personage intended by the title-heading here is not quite identical with the sham-doctor or sham-parson prominent in a group of humorous folktales listed in Aarne-Thompson's *Types of the Folktale* as Type 1641, 'Doctor Know-All,' who – among other adventures – accidentally aids in the discovery of a stolen horse by administering a purgative to the owner. This is certainly our man, but his *style* is closer to Aarne's Type 1641A, the 'Sham Physician' who pretends to diagnose entirely from urinalysis. This is of Oriental origin, as taken up in the *Cent Nouvelles Nouvelles*, Nos. 20 and 21, with the doctor's prescription being invariably sexual intercourse. And in Niccolò Machiavelli's *Belphegor* (probably imitated directly from a still-surviving Jewish folktale: Aarne Type 1862B), in which only the threat of calling the Devil's wife, by the wily mock-physician, can exorcise him. Compare sham-parsons and the like.

A new modern type also exists, or rather lies somewhere halfway between physician and parson – the sham-psychiatrist or phoney psychoanalyst. These constitute a friendly sort of informal fakers in the United States, whose sick 'psychological' activity is usually a cover for seducing a large number of young girls (or boys), but worse exist. There are presumably serious practitioners in France who combine psychiatry *with astrology* – the national intellectual disease – and, in one case that I ran into, with water-dowsing for boring wells as a psychiatric side-line. 'Psychological' gamblers, and 'computer dating-services' and similar rackets and scams are of course now increasing everywhere. 'Dr. Bug,' the sexually exploitative sham-psychiatrist, like Norman Mailer's 'Sergius O'Shaugnessy' in *The Time of Her Time* (in his *Advertisements for Myself*, 1959), may one day seem to be the least harmful and exploitative of all. *'The janitor was cleaning the psychiatrist's office when the phone started to ring furiously. He hesitated, then picked up the phone. After a few 'yesses' and "I sees" he said, "Best thing I can suggest, Miss, is to go out and get screwed".'* (*Sex to Sexty*, 1968, 18:38.)

Actually, 'Dr. Know-All' has fallen away to a mere druggist or apothecary, the 'water-scriger' of the older *Dreck-apotheke*. A rare tribute from an unknown reader to the kindly old American druggist, concentrating on his function here as purveyor of condoms, jock-straps, and assorted manhood remedies, is printed unexpectedly in *Sex to Sexty* (1970) No. 32, p. 25:

Another thrill you'll never be able to equal is when you were a lad just turning teen [*i.e.* thirteen], and you whispered to the neighborhood druggist, "Er – the coach says I ought to have an *athletic supporter*." And the pharmacist, a kindly soul, smiled real big and answered, "Yes sir, one JOCK STRAP comin' up, young MAN!'' Then when he handed you the package, he added, in a real low voice, "Don't worry about where it says 'small' – they measure these things by the inches around your hip bones."

Despite this charming valentine to the dear dead days and phallic fears of yore, in most of his modern western appearances Dr. Know-All has become hardly more than a drug-store clerk – the older clyster-bearing apothecary – that is to say, a physician-*manqué* or mock-doctor, who still has only one prescription: purgatives. On the other hand, he is wise beyond believing as to the effects to be expected from this remedy. *A man goes to the drugstore and asks for medicine. The clerk gives him a double dose of laxative, and he rushes out. His wife comes looking for him, and the clerk says, "Just follow the brown line."* (Scranton, Pa. 1930, told by children.) Collected almost identically in London, 1953, in manuscript notes of favorite jokes supplied by an adult man: '*Chemist's shop. Chap dashes in, buys "jollup."* [The Mexican purgative *Exogonium jalapa*.] *Is taken-short in shop, and rushes out. Enter his wife. "Have you seen my husband?" Assistant: "Just follow the yellow streak".*' This sounds like a typical comedy interlude or French street-players' *farce* of the 16th century, though none quite identical has been found. The 'direct-dumping' toilets on railroad trains have led to the related pleasantry that the *straight lines* (or *golden lines*) on railroad and airline maps really represent lines of the passengers' feces running uphill-&-down-dale across country: 'as the crow *shits*.'

Dr. Know-All becomes the true mock-scientist of his subject, in a joke collected too early to be the satire on the computer logistics approach to every human problem that it appears to be, though of course the anal-compulsive mentality that has created such cultural offal as the 'computerized dating' of lonesome college boys and horny co-eds was in existence long before the necessary mechanical possibilities and related gobbledygook were developed. '*A man in need of a laxative consulted a druggist, who asked how far away he lived, how many blocks, on what floor of the house, how many stairs to each floor, how many steps to the bathroom, etc., at each reply adding another chemical to the potion (pantomimed), which the man then drank. A week later, when the man happened to be in the drug-store again, and the druggist asked how he had*

*fared, he replied that he had figured pretty close. He compli-
mented him on his knowledge as a chemist, but complained
that he had missed it by three steps.'* (Told by a St. Louis
attorney, on a transcontinental train, 2 Aug. 1943.) Again, this
has the air of a staged farce – especially the touch of 'adding
another chemical to the potion' – but no such old farce has
been found in print. Something very close to this joke was,
however, long a favorite burlesque show black-out: the lineal
descendants of the street-comedy farces such as the Turkish
Karaghuez (the Western Punch-&-Judy shows, which retain all
the original violence but expurgate out all sex and scatology),
and the Spanish, Italian, and French snake-oil vendors and
street-operas or *zarzuelas* and *commedia dell'arte.*

Dangerous overtones are not lacking in Dr. Know-All's art,
though these make themselves felt at first only as the predict-
able and irremediable results of his medication, which is essentially a sort of scatological Nemesis or ineluctable doom. Once
struck, this note overwhelms all pretense of helpfulness and
'service' – scientific or otherwise – and Dr. Know-All becomes
identifiable as a sort of lesser Dr. Krankheit (introduced earlier
in the section on "Narsty-Narsties," 12.IV.5), who does not cure
the patient, but harms and diminishes him – *i.e.* castrates him:
here by 'stealing his feces,' as it were – and even diseases him
further. Observe the descent in tone, from helpfulness to
sinisterness, in the following examples laid out specifically on
that pattern:

*The druggist gives the customer a box of laxative pills and
his change in nickels, explaining, "You'll need the nickels, sir –
with those pills!"* (*Old Nick's Annual T.N.T.*, Minneapolis, 1935,
at a time when public pay-toilets still operated on five-cent
coins.) – *A burlesque comedian explaining the difference between amnesia and magnesia: "With amnesia, you don't know
where you're going; with magnesia, you'd better know where
you're going!"* (D.C. 1944.) – *A young woman who can't prevent
herself from coughing and sneezing at the theatre, asks a doctor
for a remedy before going to a first night. "Here, drink this," he
says, offering her a glass. She drinks it, mouth awry, and asks
what it was, imagining some type of bad-tasting cough medicine. "That's a double dose of Pluto water," he answered. "Now
you won't dare sneeze or cough."* (1:154. Often collected; in
one printed version with the druggist's 'new clerk' or sham-
druggist. Molière's *Malade Imaginaire.*)

'*Constipated brick-layer. Physic after physic has no effect. Finally the doctor has him bend over and gives him a terrific blow on the ass with a baseball bat. The place is flooded with shit, squirting in six different directions. Doctor says, "Go home, and next time don't wipe your ass on cement bags".*' (2:205, text is taken from a manuscript collection of later date.) Here, of course, there is no disguise as to the anal sadism involved, and the final 'shit explosion' is precisely that of the final section of the present work, to which the reader is referred, while waiting for the Atom Bomb.

In case there were still any doubt as to the dangerous and frightening character of the mock-doctor and his purgatives, here is a story told in response to that given above concerning the helpful druggist who potions out the laxative so scientifically that the client only misses the toilet 'by three steps.' '*A druggist fixed up a powerful laxative for a man in need of one. Later he saw his wife in the store, and asked how it had gone. She replied. "Oh, it was simply terrible." The druggist asked, "Did he move?* [euphemism for defecation]" "*Oh, yes," she said, "three times before he died, and five times after".*' (Told by a vaudeville comedian, on the Union Pacific, 3 Aug. 1943.) This has been printed in *Grim Hairy Tales* (Arlington, Texas, 1966) p. 40, with the mock-doctor appearing with grim modernity as: *A travelling salesman who gives an ignorant old farmer a 50-pound case of Ex-Lax [a candy-flavored laxative] as a present, with the result that the old man eats it all in a few hours and dies of the effects. A month later the salesman passes again and learns from the undertaker what has happened, and that the old man has not been buried but has been left propped up in the outhouse: "We're just waiting for him to get through!*'

Even in his gruesome death here, it will be observed that the victim triumphs, in a sense, by means of his intestinal immortality, which is the folk-rationalization or 'humorizing' of the physiological fact of fecal incontinence at or after death from certain causes. Quite a point is made of this, as to the cooking of a live iguana in boiling water, in James M. Cain's *Serenade* (1939), a novel otherwise largely a study of a homosexual opera-singer who is *saved* by the love of an illiterate Mexican prostitute who gives him her breast to suck in the taxicab on the way to the opera-house. The fecal triumph-over-death by the victim in the joke is to be compared with the erection after death of the hero of another undertaker story, given earlier in the discussion of "The Eaten Heart," 8.VIII.10. Here too, a source is likely in direct observation: of the alleged erection of men being hanged, which is also the source of the phrase (or curse) 'to die with a hard-on,' meaning to come to a bad end. Clearly, we have here the other side of the ambivalent and masochistic breast-fetichism of James M. Cain's hero (the attempted *escape from homosexuality into masochism,* which I have posited as the opposite of the case of Shakespeare), in his hungry anal sadism *vis-à-vis* iguanas. These inoffensive beasts also get a bad working-over, both symbolically and personally, in Tennessee Williams' more recent kitsch-klatsch, *The Night of the Iguana,* also concerned with male masochism on a tourist-bus background of Mexico.

There is a last avatar of Dr. Know-All, as Dr. Dreck, whose specialty is in somehow getting his patients to *eat* what Dr. Know-All simply gets them to produce: both ends of the gamut, as it were. He has already been seen offering his standard advice and classic *Dreck-apotheke,* in the two final jokes of the preceding main section, "Crepitation," and will appear again in his element in the more appropriate section below, "Scatophagy." One very interesting magical or medical pretext used to get the dupe to eat excrement is closely connected with the idea of *knowledge:* the patient is to be made to know all, by these means, just as the sham-doctor knows all – concerning his rather limited subject. The non-scatophagous 'knowledge' stories will therefore be given separately here, but the reader is reminded again that the main group to which they belong is really that in the section "Scatophagy," below, 15.V.1, "Dr. Dreck."

As water cannot rise higher than its source, what is learned from Dr. Know-All is inevitably just what he knows: namely, the science of shit. The narrow, pompous ignorance of the specialist is pointedly mocked in the scatological best-seller of that title in the 1920's, *The Specialist* by Chic Sale, where the 'specialty' involved is the artistic construction of out-houses (delightfully illustrated, especially in the little-known and seldom encountered supplementary volume). *A modern factory puts in a special 'Stinkless Toilet,' suspended over the assembly line with a spiral staircase leading up to it, so the workers can be kept under surveillance by the foreman at all times, and a check kept on how long they spend going to the toilet. After a week the contraption can no longer be used, owing to the odor. Two efficiency experts are sent by the manufacturer to look into the matter, and, after studying the 'Stinkless Toilet' for half a day, they discover what is wrong, reporting: "No wonder it stinks. Somebody shit in it!"* (N.Y. 1949.) Dr. Know-All knows all. Charlie Chaplin alludes clearly to this situation, if not to this exact story, in *Modern Times*, where the factory-owner spies on him by two-way television even in the toilet room, and shouts him back to work on the never-to-be-forgotten assembly line, when catching him smoking, sitting (pointedly) with one buttock on the washstand.

In other 'knowledge' stories, the problem is also diagnosis, and though the sham-physician or mock-savant does not actually appear, he is replaced by various stand-ins. *A braggart is telling a friend about his three cars, &c. When he also mentions that he has two kept-mistresses in New York, but that he has made his ravishingly beautiful and terribly passionate private secretary pregnant, and must therefore take his gorgeous blonde stenographer with him on his business-trip to Rio de Janeiro to see the Carnival, the listener suddenly begins to pant, grabs at his own necktie, and has a heart-attack. The braggart interrupts his tale, gets water, pats the victim on the back, &c., and he asks solicitously what the matter is. "Can I help it?" the man gasps. "I'm allergic to bullshit."* (N.Y. 1939.) And of which of us couldn't *that* be said?

In a more elegant form: *Two women are talking in a tea-room at four o'clock, over large gooey ice-cream sundaes and little sugary cakes. They have not seen each other since high-school days, and one is bragging about her very advantageous marriage. "My husband buys me whole new sets of diamonds when the ones I have get dirty," she says; "I never even bother to clean them." "Fan*TAS*tic!" says the other woman. "Yes," says the first, "we get a new car every two months. None of this hire-purchase stuff. My husband buys them outright, and we give them to the Negro gardener and houseman and like that for presents." "Fan*TAS*tic!" says the other. "And our house," pursues the first – "well, what's the use of talking about it? It's just –" "Fan*TAS*tic!" finishes the other. "Yes, and tell me, what are you doing nowadays?" says the first woman. "I go to Charm School," says the other. "Charm School?! Why, how quaint. What do you learn there?" "Well, we learn to say 'Fan*TAS*tic!' instead of 'Bullshit!' "* (L.A. 1968. Probably connected with Type 1381D, 'The wife multiplies the secret,' concerning the two *crows – later fifty, and an egg! – that have flown out of the husband's belly.*)

Odd as this may seem, in the way of Nature imitating Art, a number of years ago in Paris I was much struck by the charm and popularity of a handsome young Dutch girl on the edges of the American colony, whose entire conversation consisted of two ejaculations – "FanTAStic!" and "TERrible!" – antiphonally answering the English and American young men's soundtrack at artistic intervals. Meeting this same girl again in Amsterdam several years later, by accident, at a paper-folding exhibition at the Museum of Modern Art in 1955, I remarked that her knowledge of English seemed to be deteriorating, as she spoke the language very poorly. "Well," she said, "it's better than it was two years ago in Paris. There, all I knew was exactly two words, 'TERrible!' and 'FanTAStic!'"

Various elements in the following are evidently older than the Atom Bomb of the mid-1940's but no American story so completely concerned with scatological science or diagnosis seems to exist of earlier date. *A drunk at a bar is pestering everyone by insisting on discussing the Atom Bomb. "Wait a minute," says the bartender finally; "did you ever see any horseshit?" "You trying to insult me?" counters the drunk. "No, wait a minute. Did you ever see any?" "Sure." "Well, what does it look like?" "It's in balls. It comes out solid, and breaks up when it dries." "And you ever see any bullshit?" "Sure." "And what's that like?" "It's dark brown," says the drunk, warming to his subject, "as big as a golf-ball, but it spreads out like a big, wet cookie." "All right. And did you ever see any goat shit?" "Of course. Goat shit looks like an olive pit, and it's dark green." "All right," says the bartender; "now how come a horse and a cow and a goat all eat the same grass, and their shit is so different?" "You got me," says the drunk; "I don't know." Bartender: "You don't know from SHIT, and you're trying to tell us about the Atom Bomb!"* (Los Angeles, Calif. 1952; also D.C., from an army captain.)

Actually, I hate to blow the whistle on this one, because it has all the air of being that rarity, *a new joke.* In fact, however, at least the idea was circulating as folkwit, or 'just-so' story – really a question on the origin of things, without any surviving story – just two centuries before the Atom Bomb. It appears in a list of imaginary books in the *Mémoires de l'Académie des Colporteurs* (1748), a mock-serious collection of dissertations by the Count de Caylus, who proposed to write a scientific memoir on the question: *Pourquoi les mulets d'Auvergne, qui ont le trou du cul rond, chient des crottes carrées?* Which is an even harder question than that of the various shapes of turd all deriving from the same eaten grass. A Flemish folktale given in M. de Meyer's *Les Contes populaires de la Flandre* (Folklore Fellow Communications, vol. 37) p. 86, No. 58d, explains *Why the excrements of the jackass are triangular*, unquestionably the same just-so story as that alluded to in Caylus' reference two centuries earlier. Why they are square in Auvergne and triangular in Flanders (Motif A2385.1, followed by other 'explanations' as to animal excrements) is just one of those mysteries. Compare also Type 1832B: *Is the horse-dung that of a mare or a stallion?*

Mock-dissertations, especially of a scatological kind, were most completely collected in the great *Amphitheatrum sapientiæ Socraticæ joco-seriæ*, edited by Caspar Dornau (Hanover, 1619, 2 vols. in-folio), but their origin perhaps, and certainly their most interesting development, was in the burlesque Academies of Italy in the 16th century, such as that of the "Dunderheads," out of which Vignale's *La Cazzaria* (about 1530) developed. The modern limerick societies, for the preservation and annotation of bawdy limericks, almost all make use of this format. (See the quotation of a few such in my Introduction to *The Limerick*, New York, 1970, p. lxvii–lxx.) The surréalist association in honor of Alfred Jarry, the *Société de Pataphysique*, in the 1950's and since, is also very much in this line, of which the principal French group – contemporary with Caylus' "Academy of Chapbook Vendors" – was the *Académie des Sciences de Troyes*, whose *Mémoires* were published in 1756 by the two principal members (there were only seven), P.-J. Grosley and André Lefèvre. See further Dr. Payen's *Histoire sérieuse d'une Académie qui ne l'était pas* (1848). The two most famous *jeux d'esprit* and erudition of the Troyes series were, significantly, one "*On the Ancient Usage of Shitting in the Street*," and the other "*On the Custom of Beating one's Mistress*."

Very striking in the modern joke preceding is the folk-identification of the scatological explosion or anal-sadistic essence of the Atom Bomb – and all others. As in the Know-All *vs.* Know-Nothing riddle or jibe circulating immediately after the first atomic explosion, that: *When people working on the*

"Manhattan [Atom Bomb] Project" would ask, on this top-secret project, what *they were doing, they would be told: "We're building the front ends of horses, and we send them to Washington for final assembly."* (N.Y. 1945.) This is very close, for all its Auschwitz-style 'affectlessness' and refusal of responsibility – all of which is to be fathered off vaguely on the implied *horses' asses* in Washington – to the superb reply made by : *The young officer competing with a diplomat for the favors of a young lady, who has said candidly to him, "What a terrible profession you soldiers have, of making war!" "I am sorry, Madam,"* he replies, *"We soldiers do not make war. Diplomats make wars. We* fight *them."* (Anecdote untraced, apparently 18th century.)

3. WHERE IS IT?

The principal excuse made for various scatological lapses is that one was 'taken short' by the need to defecate, but could not find the toilet. The question of *where to go* has already been raised by Dr. Know-All, preceding, as in the 'difference' between amnesia and magnesia; and in the curiously connected story already given, of: *The man who dies during intercourse. When his wife thought he was coming, he was going.* It is also the whole framework impossibility of the story given earlier, under "Urination," as to: *The social worker who finally urinates on the Negro handyman, because* [this is the *explanation*] *he cannot find anywhere else to do it.* Obviously, no one takes such explanations seriously, and the theme of not knowing where to go, or where 'it' (the toilet) is, must be considered an expression of the desire to defile others with one's excrements, on the proverbial excuse that *'Necessity knows no law.'* (This proverb is actually used as caption to an 18th-century gallant French engraving showing a pretty young woman urinating surreptitiously in a corner.) This being also the standard excuse for various oral aggressions of a cannibalistic kind, and of the ultimate combination of both in war. We have here both ends of the same gamut of aggression.

Though jokes and, in fact, the actualities of Western life, make a great point of the needed privacy for defecation – urination is allowed a bit more public leeway – it must not be overlooked that this runs counter to the infantile pride in the feces, which is strongly reinforced by the rewards of approbation and love given the infant during the toilet-training period, when the scatological rules and duties are correctly performed and in the proper place. The resulting ambivalent urge for toilet privacy and yet for scatological display is shown clearly in the following famous joke, and it should also be observed that scatological jokes (and 'obscene' language) are themselves a substitute form of such infantile-oriented display. *A man, at the theatre with his wife, goes out to the toilet at the intermission, but goes through the wrong door and finds himself in the garden. As it is too well-kept to think of using the ground, he lifts a plant out of a flower-pot and uses that, then replaces the plant. He goes back and finds the next act has already begun. "What's happened so far in this act?" he asks his wife in a whisper. "You ought to know," she says coldly. "You were in it."* (N.Y. 1941.)

A similar hidden or evasive display or defilement replaces the shibboleth of privacy with that of shitting on patriotism. *A girl is rushing for the toilet at the end of a theatrical performance, but calls out over the cubicle wall to the attendant: "Get the mop! they* would *play "The Star-Spangled Banner" just as I was sitting down!"* (N.Y. 1945.) Expressed as exaggerated patriotism, this is obviously anti-patriotism. There is also sometimes the overdetermined scatological excuse of 'saving money,' which can be added to the usual problem of not being able to find the toilet, or to get there fast enough: *A Scotchwoman in London cannot find a 'public convenience,' and, in her extremity, hails a cab and manages to relieve herself covertly on the floor of the back seat. Then,* to save money, *she tells the driver, "Stop immediately; I cannot possibly journey in a car where ... well, just look what the last fare ..." Chauffeur inspects the damage, then: "Garn," he cries, "that be blowed for a yarn. Last fare indeed! Why it's smoking!"* (Kimbo, *Tropical Tales,* 1925, p. 51.) In a French form of this, coming closer to the theme of "Feces as Gift," following: *A taxi-driver finds a turd left in his taxi by a passenger, and goes to the prefecture of police to complain. "All right," says the police officer, after taking down the details; "if nobody calls for it in thirty days, it's yours."* (Collected: Paris, about 1940.)

The curious trait of the *disturbing* of the individual who finally does find the toilet, as in the anti-patriotic example just given, also seems to be a recollection and surviving resentment of infantile toilet-training, where the infant is often rushed in panic to the potty to 'do his duty' (British: 'do his jobs'), though the action may already have started somewhere else. A direct example of this disturbing of the individual at work, also involves verbal entertainments or 'ghost voices,' though not in the form of tongue-twisters, as given in *The Stag Party* [Boston? 1888] unnumb. p. 187, headed, "Remarkable Echo" : *'A young Irish priest, desirous of impressing a couple of young lady tourists with the beauties of nature and the neatness of his hospitality, invited them to visit with him the place of a remarkable echo ... It was a wonderful echo. Again and again the halloo was sent forth with the same result. At length, to vary the tones, the priest called out his sentence: "Phat air ye dooin' thayre?" From behind the jutting rock this answer came:* "Shitin', ye bugger." This is still current, with drawn-out end-line : *"ta-king a sh-i-i-t!"*

A particular favorite in the embarrassment-story line – often told as a 'true incident' happening to travellers in Mexico – is given by *Anecdota Americana* (1927) No. 240. The disturbing of the individual *minding his own business* can hardly be taken further :

> A stranger sauntered up to the bar of a wild-western saloon and asked where the toilet was. "Outside," said the bar-keeper. "You'll see a pile, and that's it." The stranger went out, but in a few minutes there was a terrific din, as if the whole town was being shot up, and the stranger came dashing back into the saloon, holding up his pants with one hand, and yelling. "What the hell's the matter?" said the man behind the bar. "I don't know," said the other. "Just as I let down my pants, some one took a shot at me." "Where did you let down your pants?" the bartender asked. "Out-side," said the stranger. "There were two piles, not one, like you said, and I squatted over the little one." "No wonder you were shot at," said the bartender. "The little pile's the *ladies'* toilet!"

Would it be pressing on the prerogatives of psychoanalytic interpretation to suggest that this is perhaps a recollection and complaint as to the withdrawing of the infantile privilege, accorded to very young boys, of accompanying their mothers and sisters into the *ladies'* toilet-rooms and their dressing-rooms at swimming pools, etc., there to be assisted in dressing and undressing. I myself well remember those halcyon days, and the wrench it was to be told that I was 'a big boy now,' and would have to go it on my own.

4. NO PLACE LIKE HOME

In the line of childhood reminiscences, there are none so embarrassing (as differentiated from traumatic) as those connected with gastric lapses. Where the very real adult terror of embarrassments of this type seldom goes farther than a concern with untimely farts, as in the story of "Abu Hassan" and all his modern progeny, children's recollections of childhood very often include the dread moment of having 'shit oneself' or 'shit in one's pants.' When the child has been punished or humiliated for such a lapse, instead of being allowed to pass it off as unimportant – as I once heard done by an adorable little girl of ten years, who had to take care of her littler brothers in such an emergency, and who remarked, *"Well, it's only what they've eaten"* – and especially if such humiliations take the form of 'rubbing one's nose in it' (sometimes literally, difficult as this may be to believe, though pet animals are often ruthlessly treated in just this way), a traumatic fixation on scatological subjects, or ambivalent fear of them, can be expected to develop. The scatological food-dirtying jokes and fantasies, already discussed in Chapter 12.IV, "Narsty-Narsties," especially those on "The Defiling of the Mother," may perhaps be considered expressions of such unhealed emotional wounds.

The children have been playing in mud, and the mother is berating the little girl for having dirtied her dress. "Wait until you see Tommy. He had to pretend he was a chicken, and lay an egg!" (N.Y. 1946.) A joke has already been given, under "Crepitation" in which the action of the following brief scene is modified to mere farting, and it may be suspected that many such modifications have been made in tidying up fecal scenes for presentation as jokes. *Two men are on a bus together when one observes to the other that there is a terrible odor. "Sure,"* says the other, *"I just shit in my pants." "You shit in your pants?!" "Of course! You don't think I smell like this all the time, do you?"* (N.Y. 1953.) Instead of the cheerful avowal, and the retreat into nonsense or logical argy-bargling, there can also be a bold denial, coming however to the same thing: *'Two bums are walking down the tracks together. One says, "Did you shit?" "No!" "I don't know about that; I smell something pretty strong." He yanks aside the other's tattered pants-flap and finds a small mountain of turd. "What's the big idea telling me you didn't shit?" "Oh, I thought you meant* today!"' (Los Angeles, Calif. 1952, from manuscript.) Freud has a version of this as between two *schnorrers* and an egg-stain on the clothes of one of them. One of these jokes is either the modification or dysphemizing of the other. So also *sitting on eggs* (Motif K1693).

An excuse of some kind can also be sought, to cover the embarrassing avowal, especially when it must be made not between children or tramps (*schnorrers*) but between responsible adults. Even there, recourse is made to the use of comedy lay-figures such as Pat and Mike (the East European Mikosch and Strakosch, who are also *schnorrers*; or the French meridional Marius and Olive, the champion liars of Marseilles). *Two Irishmen decide they will try a glass of the miracle drug advertised to 'Make You Young Again.' "Do ye feel any younger, Mike?" "Divil a bit." They have another drink and Mike turns to Pat with a wan smile. "Pat, it's worrked. I've just done a childish thing ... I've shit in me pants."* (1:153.)

The excuse of fear, as during bombardment, would be no excuse at all, and would be considered a sign of cowardice: to be ascribed solely to the enemy, as in Bennet Cerf's *Pocket Book of War Humor* (1943) p. 166: *'Adolf Hitler was preparing his wardrobe for a second dismal winter on the frozen front in Russia. "Mein Fuehrer," suggested one of his suite, "remember what Napoleon did when he was in Russia. He wore a bright red uniform so that in case he was wounded his men would not notice the fact that he was bleeding." "Excellent idea! Excellent idea!" ruminated Adolf. "Just throw me my brown pants".'* Compare: *Two soldiers are retreating during the battle, with bullets whistling all around them. The first soldier feels the back of his pants and looks at his hand. "What color is blood?" he asks. "Yours is yellow, you bastard!" "My god, I've been wounded!"* (2:291.) The same identification was made by a young woman with two children, discussing her unhappiness with her husband and how she wished she had the courage to leave him, who concluded, "What the use? I'm just a coward. *I've got shit in my blood."* (N.Y. 1947.) This is a folk phrase.

There is also the question of evidence, as with the ladies noted earlier, one of whom accuses the other of having farted because *"I seen you tilt!"* If the evidence can be made away with, there is no demonstrable sin. This is the exact opposite of the criminal's fecal 'calling card,' left behind at the scene of the crime. And compare the infantile pleasure in examining proudly (and displaying) the results of one's defecation. The jokes all express a horror of the feces, and a desire to be rid of them. But the concentration on the evidence – on *'hearing it plump,'* as a jestbook of 1755 puts it, concerning a person shitting over a river – shows the regret at thus 'losing' the end-products of digestion. This is the standard anal-retentive neurosis of misers. Farting and urination, and generally defecation as well, are enjoyed most when most copious.

It is habitual for persons of all ages to turn to examine their feces, often on some hygienic excuse, of diagnosis of the state of one's own health by these means. I have also heard a chamber-pot or 'crapper-can' at a country house defended on the grounds that at least it does not deprive one of the sight of one's feces in this way, as would an old-fashioned privy or *oubliette. 'A fellow in a public W.C. had been there a long time, straining to go, when he heard somebody next door insert a penny, and in next to no time, on hearing: "bpwoowph!" calls out to his neighbour, "Lucky blighter!" to which the other retorts, "Lucky be fucked! I hadn't even time to get my pants down!"'* (Chelmsford, Essex, 1953, from manuscript.) In an earlier version, collected N.Y. 1942, the 'lucky' fellow replies: *"You think that's something? Wait till I get my pants down."* Also, in an old-fashioned outhouse, *"Lucky, hell! That was my watch!"*

The connection is clear but indefinable with the following development: *'An armless man in a restaurant called the manager and had him order for him, feed him, wipe his face with the napkin, etc. etc., until the meal was over, when he suggested he had to go to the toilet. He asked the manager to help him so he [the manager] took down his pants and left him sitting on the toilet. As the manager exited, the man called, "Did you hear a splash?" "No," he said. "Why, you son-of-a-bitch," the armless man shouted, "you forgot to take my shorts down!"'* (From a vaudeville comedian, on the Union Pacific to San Francisco, Aug. 1943.) Other jokes of this type, concentrating on the homosexual element in the handling of one man by another in this way, especially helping him to urinate, have been given earlier. In all cases the identification of the 'armless man' (or 'war veteran' or 'drunk') as the infant child is beyond question; with the 'manager' or other good Samaritan, forced into subservience and finally berated, as the hated parental figure of the toilet-training stage. A similar scene in Fellini's autobiographical film, *Amarcord* (1973), has the charmingly crazy uncle who pisses in his pants. The father-tyrant, who is force-fed castor oil by Mussolini hoodlums-in-uniform, shits in *his* pants. See also *Kryptádia*, XI. 63, 74.

In entitling the present section "No Place Like Home" – the catchline of an old favorite song which has become (and was originally) a folk-proverb: *'Home is homely'* – it is attempted to draw attention to the fact that it is the body and the clothing that are the original *home*, and to the emotional problem created by the fecal soiling of this home, especially in its earliest form as the child's diaper or cradle. *An Indian went to a city doctor complaining of abdominal pains. "Have you moved lately?" the doctor asked. "No, Indian no move." He is given a powerful purgative, and, as this apparently does not work, an even stronger one on the next visit. Finally, on the eighth visit, the doctor says, "You know, Tom, I'm surprised you didn't move yet." "No move yet," the Indian insists. "Move tomorrow. Wigwam full of shit."* (Scranton, Pa. 1936.) Other jokes on the ignorant Indian and his scatological problems will be given under "Scatophagy" later, but no fictions of this kind will compare with the *truth* about constipated Indians, and the clawing of the hardened feces out of the rectum with a special back-scratcher tool manipulated by the squaw, as described by the American Indian ethnologist, and specialist on precisely these subjects, Capt. John G. Bourke, in his *Scatalogic Rites* (Washington, 1891; offset reprint, 1936, with translation of Freud's preface to the German translation in the *Anthropophytéia* series. A recent reprint, 1968, unaccountably omits Freud's preface.)

A singular extrojection or casting-upon-others of the guilt for the fecal defiling of the home or body, with very great concern as to the question of destroying the evidence, the *grumus merdæ*, or 'little pile of shit,' arrives at the remarkable conclusion that it is not the child who defiles his own body or home fecally, but the adult, who then *blames it on the child!* Two forms of this exist, of which the older is given in *The Stag Party* [Boston? 1888] unnumb. p. 254–6, as a *conte* in unrhymed blank verse, entitled "The Good Story." This is obviously the work of a trained hand, and as *The Stag Party* contains almost all the rhymed *obscoena* of Eugene Field (excepting "The Boastful Yak"), which are here first printed, along with his erotic storiette *Only A Boy?* it seems likely that "The Good Story" is also his. This ascription is all the more likely in the similarity of the theme to that of Field's best-known poem in this line, the sentimental "When Willie Wet the Bed."

"The Good Story" begins: 'There is a story of the long ago, That Master Limner's brush immortalized ...' an allusion I am not able to explain, unless it refers to Chaucer: *A monk is given a bed at a wayside inn, in the same room in which a baby is sleeping in its crib. As the monk's sleep is disturbed by 'a bladder o'erwell filled,' and he cannot find the chamberpot under the bed in the dark, he picks the baby out of the crib and lays it in his bed, and relieves his bladder in the very centre of the empty crib, then with 'a chuckle at so cute a scheme, Returns the baby to its dampened bed.' But this is the case of the biter bit: while he has been pissing in the baby's bed, the baby has shit in his.* As the author of the tale obviously sees it, the baby is not only relieved of the blame – shown to be really the adult's fault – but is also the instrument of the adult's punishment, by an appropriate *lex talionis*. (Compare the "Sailor's Dilemma," 15.VI.3, page 1117 below.)

The other form of the story lacks the nicety of the preceding, but is given star treatment, in *Anecdota Americana* (1927) 1:424, with title and subtitle: "The Lost Turd – A Study in Embarrassment." *A man visiting old friends has a sudden cramp in the night, and worried about finding the bathroom in the dark, he decides, "I guess I'd better lay my load on the floor in the corner, and clean it up in the morning before Jack sees me." In the morning, to his great embarrassment, the turd is gone, and he realizes his host must have got up ahead of him and cleaned it up. But no mention is made of the matter at break-fast, and he is greeted too warmly by his hosts for his guess that they have done the cleaning to be correct.* ' "Have you met our son, Aleck?" asked Jack, calling him. Bill felt a cold chill run down his spine. He expected to see the child all smeared up with the turd. But a nice, clean, little boy came into the room.' Suddenly the host asks, "By the way, have you seen Charlie, yet?" and whistles. 'Bill turned around. A large turtle was waddling into the room, and on his back was the turd!' (Cf. Rotunda K2334: *Candles placed on cockroaches or crabs to frighten people,* cited from Malespini.)

This story is certainly not as funny as the editor of *Anecdota Americana* seems to have thought it, and the *dénouement* in particular, though unexpected, is confused, since the turtle is not really accusing the guest so much as making an inexplicable mystery of his crime. There is a similar cartoon (by Wilhelm Busch; *Kryptádia*, XI. 51) in which: *A man shits by a fence, on a shovel held under the fence by another man, unknown to the* first. *The shovel is then withdrawn, and when the first man turns back to see what he has done, the evidence has disappeared.* Such fecal puzzle-tales have a striking similarity to the tortured elucubrations of many murder-mysteries since Edgar Allan Poe's problem on how an object can be hidden in full view but where no one will find it (*"The Purloined Letter"*), or how someone can be murdered in a locked room but the murder-instrument made to disappear. Many of these murder-problems – such as the 'locked room' puzzle – are actually inverted inquirings as to how babies are born, or formed in the womb, but the fecal or anal-sadistic problem is obviously also present, if only in the essential concentration on "The Pornography of Murder," as Maurice LeBlond has eloquently called it.

A particularly popular puzzle-story of a jesting kind is given in *Anecdota Americana* (1934) 2:95, and has often been orally collected since. *A week-end guest (or a man in a hotel) who cannot get to the toilet fast enough during the night, when feeling a sudden cramp, shits on a newspaper, then wraps it up and hides it under the roots of a potted plant (or in a hat-box on the top shelf of the closet). He then leaves for home the next morning. Two days (a week, a month)* later he receives telegram: "ALL IS FORGIVEN. WHERE IS IT?" Essentially, this is the real solution the child hopes for – it is not exonerated of the guilt for the fecal lapse, but forgiven for it, by means of offensive pressure brought to bear through the agency of the offense itself. The only proverb that fits the case is *'Eating your cake and having it too,'* which is probably not entirely appropriate. Even where the word 'FORGIVEN' does not appear in the culminating telegram or letter (other forms are: *"You win. Where did you hide it?"* or *"We give up; what did you do with it?"* D.C. 1941 ff.), in all cases the fecal guilt really becomes a fecal victory, since it has brought the hosts or hotel-keepers – all parent surrogates, of course – to terms: 'Sick with keen guessing whence the perfume was.' (Swinburne, *Laus Veneris*, line 264.) This story is not new, being of at least 18th-century origin, where it appears as of a guest who hides his feces inside a straw mattress. A text is given in Henry Kistemaeckers' *Le Dix-Huitième Siècle Galant*, an erotic and bibliographical miscellany in several volumes appearing in Belgium about 1890 (copy: Univ. of Kansas), as of a German prince of the 18th century.

Similar yet opposite to "The Good Story" in *The Stag Party*, in actually projecting the fecal guilt on the adult, is a 15th or early-16th century German story, where the child-identification figure is the jester, Tyl Eulenspiegel, whose jests and 'merry pranks' are the most scatological, throughout, of all such jesters and their jest-books. Dr. C. F. MacIntyre, in his *That Immoral Garland* (MS. 1942) p. 31, in discussing a limerick on a farting parson, notes that: '*A literary prototype of this weak-membered* [!] *person is to be found in* Till Eulenspiegel. *The great jester was going the rounds of the church on a week-day with the priest, when that gentleman delivered himself of a similar* viva voce. *On being reprimanded by Till, his reverence exclaimed: "Huh, I can make a pile right in the middle of this church if I want to, and nobody shall stop me!" So Till bet him a cask of Rhenish that he couldn't whereupon it was up with the cassock and down with the holy breeches – and lo! the deed was accomplished in the wink of an eye. "There! you see," said the priest, gloating above his effort. "Pay your bet!" "Just a minute, Father; I'll get a yard-stick and prove that it isn't in the middle." And he did.'* (Very freely adapted from the German text, Strasburg, 1519; *cf.* Jannet's literal French translation, 1866, p. 17, chap. 12, "*Comment Ulespiègle devint sacristain de Budensteten, et comment le curé mis bas ses grègues dans l'église.*") Aside from the pretended puzzle element here, dragged in *de toutes pièces* at the end as the punch-line, and the hidden anal-sadism of 'control' in all such measuring, sub-dividing, &c., the trickster point that makes the story operate is that Eulenspiegel gets the priest to defile his *own* church (home); though, under the circumstances of the provocatory bet, it is really with Eulenspiegel's (the child's) excrements.

5. FECES AS GIFT

The sadistic tone of flinging and dirtying with feces, which will be very prominent in the final section, "Anal Sadism," following, is a hostile development of the child's original feeling about feces: namely, that it is a prized and very personal pos-session, and that defecation is a *gift* made to the parents, who also seem very concerned about receiving it. In fact, it is the parents' very demand for the child's feces, but under a whole controlling code of proper places and times, that finally turns the fecal gift into the fecal insult or defiling.

In a sense, all the stories in the two preceding sections, all concerned with the embarrassment of not being able to find the toilet, and the socially incorrect disposal of the feces, are stories of childish fecal gifts that have gone awry, or have been mis-construed by the recipients (the parents), with the result that the child is shamed or embarrassed and becomes hostile about such offerings in the future. It will be observed that almost none of the stories now following, in which the element of the gift is the essence, are really lacking in hostile overtones. Usually, in fact, the gift is only pretense, covering an obviously hostile dirtying. The nincumpoop joke has already been given, in another form, under the discussion of the childish theory of "Cloacal Intercourse," 12.IV.1, in which a: 'Randy town girl in order to excite the ardour of a country boy with whom she's walking out in the country, asks him if he'll ease her knicker-bocker [panty] elastic – it's too tight. Later still: "And now shall we do something really naughty?" He: "Yes, let's go and shit on the doorstep of that cottage!"' (London, 1953, from manuscript.) The polite though openly symbolic version often has appeared in American college-humor magazines with the final line – after the girl has refused to pet, &c. – "Well, then, let's go over to the School of Agriculture, and milk hell out of a couple of cows!"

Connected, of course, is the after-the-football-game prank, by drunken alumni and other pillars of society, of hoisting one another up to piss in mail-boxes. They say it is mostly the rooters for the defeated (visiting) team that do this, but how can one know? The exact situation envisaged by the English joke is common in an American folk-phrase expressed as a riddle or 'height': "What's the height of nerve? – To shit on a man's doorstep, and then ring the bell and ask him for paper." (Or: "And ask him to wipe your ass!") Other phrases adding up to the same thing also exist, such as the scatophagous Army witticism to someone acting depressed or 'blue': "Whatsa-matter, somebody shit in your messkit?" Various examples of the doorstep trick in Kryptádia, II, 76, and especially XI. 132: Adam and Eve are put out of Paradise for eating the For-bidden Fruit, get a colic, and shit on the doorstep as they leave. (Cf. Genesis, iii. 24.)

That there is really more in all these gifts of feces than meets the eye – or nose – is made clear by various types of folk-medicine or 'natural magic' in which some excrementitious or unwanted part of the body (such as a wart, the circumcised foreskin, or an extracted tooth) is put into a hollow tree, or thrown down a privy, or over a bridge into running water, with the idea of thus ridding oneself of it by *making it adhere* to someone or something else. Madness is explained in this way, by the Jewish traditionalists, as being the result of a wandering soul or 'dybbuk' (or outhouse demon) entering unwanted into the body of the person thus 'possessed.' The moment of defecation is particularly dangerous in this way – *"El Anima de Sayula"* – as also sneezing: *"God bless you!"* But defecation is likewise a good way of ridding oneself of such undesirable elements, in a way that hurts or 'hexes' the person receiving the fecal gift.

In Dr. White Kennett's late-17th century notes to Aubrey's *Remaines* (ed. 1881) p. 162, discussing Lenten visits of children to the neighboring houses demanding food or money, a custom still surviving in America as the "Trick or Treat!" visits of Hallowe'en, he observes that when the boys & girls received some gift, they sang a little song recommending the woman giving them this to God, but if they were refused they would beat noise makers and their song would *'Set her upon a swivell, And send her to ye Devill.'* He adds: *'And, in farther indignation, they commonly cut the latch of ye door, or stop the keyhole with dirt, or leave some more nasty token of displeasure.'* Meaning that they shit on the doorstep, whether or not they then 'ring the bell and ask for paper.' In the modern form, the Hallowe'en prank against disliked persons is to *tip over their privy.* This is also done in Central Europe, as shown in the Czech movie version of Jaroslav Hasek's marvellous *The Good Soldier Schweik*, where the inmates of an insane asylum also all show their arses to a parade. Compare pants-dropping, 'moon'[buttocks]-flashing, naked hippie processions, and the recent fad of bicycle 'streaking' in the nude (mostly by young men) in the u.s., all being forms of *ritual nudity as a defiance*, an activity many centuries old, as among the Russian Dukhobors or 'Spirit-Wrestlers' in Canada.

Few stories so clearly combine the idea of feces-as-gift, and feces-as-insult as does a very popular mock children's story, already given in the opening chapter of the First Series. Here is the British version, likewise set up on a schoolroom reduplication of the ancient 'trial by ordeal': *'Teacher inquires in vain who it was who did the "big business' in the middle of the classroom floor. Threatens, cajoles in vain. Finally suggests they all will cover their eyes, and the one who did it will wipe it up with a piece of paper, and there'll be no punishment. Long pause. Eventually, footfalls and shuffling in the middle of the room. Further shuffling, then silence. "All ready – ?" School-mistress turns, and to her horror there is a heap of shit twice as big, and, on the blackboard:* "THE PHANTOM ARSEHOLE STRIKES AGAIN".' (Chelmsford, Essex, 1953.) The situation here mocked occurs in more polite terms in several popular novels and motion-pictures of the period between the two World Wars: in particular Percival Wren's *Beau Geste* (1924) and Avery Hopwood's mystery-play *The Bat* (1920), with overtones of *The Mark of Zorro* for the mocking sign left behind, all taken up and endlessly imitated in comic-books of the type of *Superman* during the 1940's.

Another mock children's story – and very mock indeed – explains the difference between optimism and pessimism, in feces-as-gift terms suggesting a joke invented by a patient in psychoanalysis. *The optimistic and pessimistic twin sons of the millionaire are prepared for their psychiatrist's visit at Christmas by having a gold fountain pen, a silk shirt, and a hundred-dollar bill put into the pessimist's sock, and a ball of horse-manure put into the optimist's sock. Pessimist (to the psychiatrist): "Oh yes, I got presents, but what good will they do me? The gold fountain pen is sure to leak on my silk shirt, and I'll probably lose the hundred-dollar bill." Meanwhile the optimistic son is running up and down the stairs of their triplex Park Avenue apartment, laughing and shouting gleefully. The psychiatrist asks him why. "Oh boy!" shouts the optimist, "I got a Shetland pony for Christmas! It's gone now, but it'll be back!!"* (N.Y. 1952.) The person telling this joke observed very aptly that there is really only *one* son, and these are the two sides of his character. Or, rather, this is the way he really *is*, and the way he wishes he were able to *be*. (McCardell's *Waggish Tales of the Czechs*, 1947, p. 260.)

The 'poor little rich boy' (Mrs. Frances Hodgson Burnett's *Little Lord Fauntleroy*, 1886, and his comic-strip plagiarism as 'Buster Brown' in the 1910's) is by no means a mythical character, since the over-rich parent always somehow spoils the advantage of wealth for the child by uncontrollable expressions of the same anal-sadism or anal-retentiveness as made possible the amassing of the wealth. The most hilarious page I have ever read in the psychoanalytic literature is surely the closing of Dr. Karl Abraham's "Contributions to the Theory of the Anal

Character," in his *Selected Papers* (London, 1927), in which he describes perfectly seriously how the parents of a rich patient had always cautioned him as a boy to wait as long as possible before going to the toilet, in order to get all the *good* of the expensive food they were feeding him! See further, the following section: "Money Stinks," on the inevitable identification of feces and gold (or wealth).

Less pleasant toilet-training of children often involves beating them, and sometimes even 'rubbing their noses in' any accidental defecatory lapse, as is also commonly done with puppy-dogs. (Is your child a dog?) Some extraordinary fecal passages on this subject are unexpectedly flung into the reader's face, under the catchall opening chapter-title, "Early Influences," in a book on mountain-climbing – I repeat: on mountain-climbing – *That Untravelled World* by Eric Shipton (London, 1969) pp. 13–14 and 21, in which the author describes a boys' school in England to which he went.

One thing is certain. The child is not fooled by the cruel or repressive toilet-training, whether or not combined with Anglo-German flagellation of the bare buttocks, with shorts removed and the shirt rolled up. Often the resentment is expressed by stubborn constipation – stubborn in every sense. There is also the child's resentment against all the lies with which he is traditionally stuffed, another colloquial identification of '*shit*,' '*horseshit*,' or '*bullshit*.' Since parents are hard to attack when the child is young, a favorite surrogate for such skepticism, resentment and revolt once was and to a degree still is, the heavenly father or God, who has always been the standard social extrapolation of responses to, and ear of, the father-figure. Consider this real children's story, recollected from my own childhood, and very similar to that earlier on the little lost boy: *A minister leads his congregation in prayer, because they need money for a new roof for the church, the present one being full of holes. "Remember," he intones, "all good things come from heaven." At this moment the Graf Zeppelin dirigible goes by overhead, and the minister's unlifted hands are filled with shit.* (Scranton, Pa. 1930, told by children: no further punchline being given.) A polite version in A. H Fauset's *Folklore from Nova Scotia* (1931) p. 93, gives the preacher the final line when *A brick is dropped on his head by naughty boys:* "*Oh, Lord, don't take everything in earnest; I was only in fun.*"

The curious idea of *sending* feces as a gift, obviously hostile, or sending by mail some equivalent such as used toilet-paper, a slaughtered chicken's head, or even (an authentic case) a human abortion, is clearly the ultimate combination of the ambivalent strains of hostility and gentility, meeting in the anal-sadistic 'gift.' Usually, as with the *grumus merdæ* of criminals, some logical excuse is pretended, such as that the expected treasure was lacking, or that the shit (or abortion) is being sent to the person who 'caused' it. Only two examples will be given here, expressed as humor, since all the others collected involve actually throwing or flinging the feces in an obvious sadistic way no longer allowing of any benevolent or logical pretense. The others are all grouped, therefore, in the following section, under "Anal Sadism." Norman Douglas, in his *Some Limericks* (Florence, 1928) p. 42, gives this limerick, dating originally from 1870 and evidently to be recited with a heavy Cockney accent. (It is followed in his text with the highly benevolent 'explanatory' note promised.)

> *There was a young man of Newcastle,*
> *Who tied up a shit in a parcel,*
> *And sent it to Spain*
> *With a note to explain*
> *That it came from his grandmother's arsell.*

The one joke of this kind encountered is actually a "Narsty-Narsty" (Chapter 12.IV) in both form and vocabulary. It was taken down from the dictation of a New York antiquarian bookseller, now deceased, well-known for his habit of refusing to sell his books, on some pretext or another, such as that the customer 'wouldn't appreciate them,' and expressing a good many other anal-retentive traits. '*There was this fellow that wanted to join a Dirty Club. All the fellows in it were dirty, and they did dirty things with dirty girls. So this fellow wanted to join, so they gave him a sheet of paper to go home and write down all the dirtiest things he knew, and if it was dirty enough he could be a member. So he wrote down* shit *and* fuck *and* cunt-snots *and all stuff like that, and finally he couldn't think of any more and the page was only half full, so he went in the bathroom and took a shit and wiped his ass on the paper and sent it back to them. Next day, return mail, he gets the answer: "Rejected." Why? He writes to them to know why, so he gets an answer back: "The members of this Dirty Club don't* wipe *their asses".*' (N.Y. 1946. Except for the key word 'dirty,' note the lack of polysyllables in this transcribed text. Also collected concerning the Hell's Angels motorcycle gang, Berkeley, Calif. 1965.)

Lest the reader imagine this is only a joke, it may be mentioned that Rudyard Kipling, believing himself to have been badly treated by the great American publisher, Putnam, himself printed on his own hand-press a satirical squib, titled simply with that publisher's name; the entire edition – limited to only a handful of copies – being printed on toilet-paper, one copy being of course sent to the publisher attacked. This is the rarest of all Kipling's writings: the George Barr McCutcheon copy was for many years preserved in the safe of the New York bookseller, Gabriel Engel, who refused to sell it at any price. What became of the copy sent to George Haven Putnam is not known. The easy solution is unlikely: it is very difficult to wipe one's ass of a piece of paper bearing one's own name. Try it.

6. MONEY STINKS

'All that glitters is not gold,' says the proverb, and a whole chrestomathy of proverbs could be gathered and has been gathered (Jannet's *Bibliotheca Scatologica*, 1850, p. 105–20, as "Memento Scato-parémiologique," supplemented in G. Brunet's *Anthologie Scatologique*, 1862, p. 103–9), demonstrating plainly, among other things, that GOLD IS SHIT. The latest form of this equivalence, where one might least have expected it, is to be found in the highly ambivalent moral essay, *On Iniquity: Some personal reflections arising out of the Moors Murder Trials*, by Pamela Hansford Johnson, Lady Snow (New York, 1967) p. 113–14, expressing the matter in the polite alliteration: 'Money: *merde*.' It should be mentioned that cultivated persons with access to print, wishing to demonstrate that they are up-to-snuff and know a dirty word or two themselves, have always (and not just in England and America, but also in Russia, Italy, etc.,) made use of *French* equivalents of the dirty words they wish to say. *Merde* is the current favorite, at these hang-your-clothes-on-a-hickory-limb-but-don't-go-near-the-water levels, but where the equally French *foutre* and *con*, both of which Shakespeare used (2 *Henry IV*, V.iii. 95–113, and *Henry V*, III.iv. 55–65), would still seem a bit too – how shall I say (*comment dirais-je?*) – DIRTY!

There is very little luffing about at the joke level in the

identification of gold (money) and shit; but the *direct* statement is almost never made, and is left simply to be understood. *'Moses was in terrible difficulties. Nature would no longer be denied* ['a call of nature' : the need to defecate], *and everywhere he read: "Do not commit nuisance. Penalty forty shillings".' He nevertheless relieves himself almost publicly anyhow, and is marched to the police-station where he has to pay forty shillings pending trial. As he comes out of the station, his eye catches a sign in the window of a dry-cleaning store just opposite: "Suits dry-cleaned while you wait, 4 shillings 6 pence." Moses faints.* (Kimbo, *Tropical Tales*, 1925, p. 29.) Though there are just as many jokes accusing the Scotch of parsimoniousness – a particular libel, since the Scotch (other than the middle classes, n.b.) are exceptionally generous – as making the same accusation against Jews, only the latter usually appear in scatological jokes, since these involve real anal-sadistic hatred, and the Scotch are not hated, but rather are considered clever, canny, and the butt only of friendly humor.

An actor is vainly trying to get a raise in pay from the theatre-manager, who keeps disappearing when he tries to corner him. He finally traps the manager sitting on the toilet, and goes into the next toilet-booth, telling his hard-luck story longwindedly over the partition. The manager only grunts in answer, saying (in a straining and constricted voice), "All right! I'll give you forty-five dollars a week." The actor keeps insisting, explaining that his wife is having a baby and his children are starving. "All right! All right! (In a straining voice:) Forty-seven fifty." "For God's sake, Mr. Thomashefsky," pleads the actor, "can't you SQUEEZE OUT *another two-fifty?"* (N.Y. 1936.) A scene very similar to this is told as absolutely true, concerning the morning ritual 'conference' between editor and sub-editors of a Rocky Mountain newspaper, in Gene Fowler's *Timberline* (1933); and businessmen, college-professors, &c. are often observed who have a penchant for trying to keep conversations going – especially of a bossy and sadistic kind – in washrooms and even on the toilet, shouting over the cubicle walls.

A related joke, earlier, expressing perfectly consciously the connection between feces and money, is that given in the section on toilet-paper, 15.I.5, "Gargantua's Invention," concerning: *The man who, not being able to find any toilet-paper, asks the man in the next cubicle if he can change two five-dollar bills for a ten.* The clearest, and also the oldest recognition of this theme is a story given in Poggio's *Facetiæ* (MS. 1451) No. 130, "*De homine qui in somnis aurum reperiebat,*" in which: *A man dreams he has found a treasure of gold, and, having no other way of marking it, shits on the spot so he will recognize it later. He wakes up to find he has shit in bed.* Poggio also adds a comedy topper to this, that in storming out of the 'muck and stench' he puts on his cap 'wherein the cat has just done its needs.' (Liseux' translation, 1879, II. 14–15. Motif X31, with further references at Types 834 and 1645B. Carnoy has an Ali Baba form: *Kryptádia*, XI. 87.) Poggio's conclusion is also worth noting: '*Thus the golden dream had turned to turd.*'

This story of the dream of marking treasure with excrement is still alive in folk transmission in many countries, though it has been turned from a self-defiling into a defiling of the wife. I do not know where this strain first appears. It is not in the English *Tales, and Quicke Answeres* (about 1530), largely a translation of Poggio, in which a literal translation of Poggio's story is given at No. 28, followed by classical references to Tibullus and others on dreams, and to Chaucer's "Nun-Priest's Tale" and the opening of the *Book of Fame*. Rabelais' unpleasant folktale, in *Pantagruel* (1532) Bk. II, chap. 15, of the old wife's vagina being wiped and filled with moss by the lion and fox ('Signifyin' Monkey'?) who imagine it is a hatchet-wound, is probably connected. In its modern form: *A man is in heaven and keeps bothering St. Peter about getting women for him, as promised: a blonde, a brunette, and a redhead. The desired women are materialized for him behind a cloud-bank, and St. Peter tells him to mark the place by shitting at the end of the cloud, so it will not be lost if it floats away while he is resting between women. The man does so, and wipes himself by tearing off a piece of the cloud. At this moment he wakes to find himself in bed with his wife, whom he has fucked three times, and then shit in bed, and is now trying to tear off a piece of the pillowcase (or his wife's pubic hair) to wipe himself.* (N.Y. 1938, told as 'old.' Compare "The Lamps of Heaven," *Kryptádia*, XI. 101.)

This clearly draws from "Hans Carvel's Ring," in Poggio, No. 133, and Rabelais, Bk. III, end of chap. 28, with St. Peter replacing the Devil. (Other references to "Hans Carvel's Ring" in literature are given in Ozell's Rabelais, 1750; Bodley Head edition, 1927, II. 85n.) Mark Twain's mocking scene of the harps of heaven, in *Capt. Stormfield's Visit to Heaven*, and the derivative *Heavenly Discourse* (1927) of Twain's friend, Charles Erskine Scott Wood, sound very much like a cleanup of this tale. Even nastier forms exist in which, for example: *The man dreams he has found a treasure, and is stuffing it in a mossy hole under a tree to hide it, when he is suddenly wakened by his wife beating him over the head. "You dirty pig!" she shouts, "isn't it enough that you shit in bed, without trying to push it up between my legs with your feet, to blame it on me?!"* (Santa Monica, Calif. 1965.) This is close to Rabelais' story of the old woman and fox, Bk. II, chap. 15; and compare the staggering quotation from De Sade's *120 Days of Sodom*, given below at the end of the introduction to the section "Anal Sadism," 15.VI.

A standard fool-story has: *A fool who is persuaded to hide his gold in a purse on top of a pole so that the angels will double it. The trickster then replaces the gold in the purse with cow-dung, explaining to the fool that they must have done the incantation wrong and angered the angels. "I guess that's what happened, all right," says the dupe, "but what I don't understand is how they got the cow up on top of that pole!"* (N.Y. 1942, from a Canadian soldier. Type 1225A, of Turkish origin. Compare Motif J2325.1, in which *The fool believes that the bag of gold turned to ashes because a child urinated on it.*) Sometimes the shit *speaks*, to explain its presence or to advise or assist its former host. (Motifs D1312.1.1 and D1610.6.4; "L'Étron parlant" in *Kryptádia*, IV. 288, *of the King whose Queen must never shit.*)

The title of the present section is of course an allusion to the Latin motto or proverb, "*Pecunia non olet*, Money does not stink," which – it will be recollected – was traditionally the reply made by the Emperor Vespasian, who died in A.D. 79, when criticized for the one & only thing for which his name is famous: the creation of public pay-toilets in Rome (the *latrinæ* or *Stercorariæ*, of which the revenue was to be used for public purposes – doubtless for the edification of more public pay-toilets, of which the revenue was to be &c. &c. (As they say in the Army, 'S.O.S. – the Same Old Shit.') The French outdoor 'urinoirs' for men (only) on the streets of Paris, were thus known until recently as 'Vespasiennes,' but the word can be expected now to disappear, as the objects denominated begin to disappear, owing to prudery disguised as modernization or 'le progrès.' This conflict is satirized in Gabriel Chevallier's novel on the little French town that builds a public *pissoir* to show

how modern it is: *The Scandals of Clochemerle.* What is perhaps most interesting about the various tempests in a pisspot,
both Roman and French, is the care with which everyone concerned wishes to prove that there is no personal desire for unseemly *profit* involved, that is to say: excrement will NOT be
turned into gold. *Pecunia non olet.*

7. SHITTEN LUCK

The taboo that it is here essential not to transgress is that
concerning *Luck*, which is conceived of (so far as treasures are
concerned) as being in keeping of the spirits or surviving
demons specially connected with earth and dirt: dwarfs,
trolls, gnomes, kobolds, and so forth, a type of supernatural
creature much glorified in the splendid but somewhat homosexualized *Hobbit* series of fantasy stories recently, by the
British palaeographer, J. R. Tolkien, specifically concerning the
lore of the Curse and Treasure of the Dwarfs, or 'half-people.'
Everyone knows that '*Shitten luck is good luck*' (said when
stepping in dog-turd), and that a fortunate man is '*so lucky that
if you throw him in a shit-house (or the sea) he'll come up with
a gold-mine.*' The tremendously successful lecture, *Acres of
Diamonds*, by the American clergyman Russell H. Conwell, delivered over six thousand times [!] and on the profits of which
Temple University in Philadelphia was founded in 1888, is
hardly more than an adaptation of this proverb, floridly told as
of a man searching for 'acres of diamonds,' and finding the
shitty 'black gold' of oil. The important folktale type on which
both are based, Aarne's Type 1645, "The Treasure at Home,"
should be consulted for very extensive references to versions of
the story before the Rev. Conwell's, and for the relation to
Types 834 and 1645B, on the dream of marking the treasure with
dung.

The modern troll or troglodyte, and caretaker of all underground treasures and mysteries, is the attendant in the public
toilet, celebrated sardonically in the song, "Dan! Dan! the
Lavatory Man:"

> *He picks up the papers and he cleans up the towels,*
> *And listens to the music of the constipated bowels!*

(N.Y. 1940, often with variant: '*the moving bowels.*') Synony-
mous as it is with bad luck, this profession is rather recent, perhaps 18th-century. The creation of sewers – about which more

below – almost entirely did away with the former profession of privy-cleaner, having been preceded by the 'night-man' or 'Tom Turdman,' politely known as the 'gold-finder,' whose lucrative profession was the cleaning out of privies in the night, and who appear in numbers of the old scatological stories. As in *Tyl Eulenspiegel* (1519) Chap. 46, "How Eulenspiegel sold a shoemaker of Wismar frozen excrements," bought from the gold-finders, and making a notable profit on the deal. Even with his last breath, Eulenspeigel is still identifying gold with shit: *His final trick is that played on the priest taking down his last will and testament* (chap. 92), *whom he tricks into plunging his hand into a vase of excrements covered with a few coins, imagining that he will seize a treasure.* In a modern joke on the gold-finders' profession, the name of the game is also the non-verbal scenario: *'A fellow cleaning out shit-houses for a living found a pot of gold in the bottom of the hole. He fell over in a dead faint, and it took three buckets of shit thrown in his face to revive him.'* (N.Y. 1953, given in manuscript.) This could have been taken right from the pages of Tyl Eulenspiegel, vocabulary and all, except perhaps for the refinement of the intended paradox, similar to that earlier in the present chapter, on: *The man imprisoned accidentally over the weekend in a woman's heavily perfumed dressing-room, who comes out shouting, "Let me smell some shit!"*

A good deal of lore exists on life in the sewers, and the sewer-cleaner's profession – more than would perhaps be imagined. Much of it tries for its humor by obvious food-dirtying mechanisms, and though more than one tourist taking the guided trip (still today) through the sewers of Paris has been noticed carrying his or her *lunch*, this is not intended as conscious humor. Compare the joke: *'In a London sewer, the inspector on his round finds a gang of workers having their grub in the dark. Upon asking why, he learns that what with the plum season and the rotten beer, they can't even find a decent turd in which to stick a candle.'* (Chelmsford, Essex, 1953, from manuscript, followed by:) *'Water-lily to the shit floating past: "Ugh! don't come near me, you dirty thing." Shit answers: "Ah, little would you think that twenty-four hours ago I was a pêche Melba!"'* This bit of sewer-cleaner's philosophy – spontaneously proliferated by the child already quoted: *"It's only what they've eaten"* – is also essentially the plot of a studiously unpleasant but very well known scatophagous limerick on a piece of toast and a turd: '*When the toast saw the shit, It collapsed in a fit, For the shit was its grandfather's ghost.*' (*The Limerick*, No. 769, dated 1934.)

The apotheosis of shit, as I have already noted, is to be found in an 'underground' comic book, *Rubber Duck*, No. 2 (Berkeley, Calif.: The Print Mint, 1972), a 15-page illustrated shit-bath of anal-sadistic anti-patriotism and you-name-it, "*Shit List: A Journey into the Cesspools of the Mind*," by Michael J. and Shelby, in which the Revolution is set off in the sewers of Washington, D.C., by a doughty band of shit-Revolutionaries, ending with an Atom Bomb explosion – in color on the back cover – of you-guessed-what. This completely outclasses a somewhat similar optimistic item by R. Crumb, "Pete the Plumber," in another underground book, *Your* HYTONE *Comix* (San Francisco, 1971) with cover-illustration of a man pissing in a toilet.

Nothing, however, has ever been said or written for public consumption, on the subject of sewers, that will bear comparison for gruelling seriousness and fantastic length, with the famous passage in Victor Hugo's *Les Misérables* (1862), resulting from Hugo's having plainly recorded the brave reply, "*Merde!*" flung at the English demanding surrender at the Battle of Waterloo, by a French officer. (But *not* by General Cambronne, to whom it is erroneously ascribed, and thus euphemized popularly as '*le mot de Cambronne*.' See the entire study of this matter in Henri Gaubert's fascinating *Les Mots Historiques qui n'ont pas été prononcés*, 1939.) Hugo's readers were thunderstruck by the spectacle of the greatest literary figure of the 19th century not only saying "*Merde!*" spelled out in full, in Vol. II, Bk. I, chaps. 14–15, as the opening gun of the New Freedom (which did not arrive in America until almost exactly a century later), but furthermore then spending some two chapters in disquisition on the subject. To all criticism, Hugo replied with a further disquisition in Vol. V, Bk. II (complete), chaps. 1–6, "The Bowels of Leviathan" – after a preliminary justification in Vol. IV, Bk. VII, chaps. 1–3, on argot and slang in general: another pretentious French shibboleth – heroically taking to the carpet the whole question of the necessity of using human ordure as fertilizer, with the history and present state of the sewers of Paris. All this is as a presumable side-gloss – the longest digression or built-in footnote in human literature – on the flight of the criminal hero of the novel through the sewer. Though Hugo's sedulous ape and imitator, Émile Zola, tried hard to match the master as to scatology, with the *'pétomane'* of *La Terre*, IV.3, and his own cruel anal-sadism, he surely must have realized he was outclassed.

A far less pretentious but more successful imitation of, or sequel to, Hugo's courage in *Les Misérables* – which was by no means as far from that of the officer at Waterloo as might be imagined – is that of a farce-novel by Eugène Chavette (Vachette) entitled *Lilie, Tutue, Bébeth*, published about 1885 by Marpon and Flammarion, which returns again to the theme of 'shitten luck' instead of bad luck. After a long and witty national typology, or discussion of the toilet habits of all the foreigners visiting Paris, p. 29–34, by Tante Tutue, who is pro-prietress of a pay-toilet of twenty-four booths, the *dénouement* arrives, p. 94–103, when the heiress, the Duchess of Fouines, is discovered in the same pay-toilet by the sound of her voice floating across the wall of one of the booths, to the ears of the lawyer who has been searching vainly for her for two years, and who has accidentally taken refuge there, when taken short during the melon season.

Intentionally farcical, of course, the same idea is taken up again spontaneously in the German motion picture, *The Last Laugh* (1924) directed by 'F. W. Murnau,' in which the hotel doorman, marvellously acted by Emil Jannings, loses his job and is finally degraded to the position of attendant in the toilet, where he is shown scrubbing the floors, only to have all end happily when a client dies of a stroke in his arms, leaving all his wealth by will to whoever was with him at the time of his death. The direct scatology here is in sharp contrast with its impossibly *optimistic* happy ending.

A strange scatological usage, not really well understood, is the criminal's "calling card" or *grumus merdæ*, the 'little pile of shit' left behind at the scene of the crime (even of murder), which is best discussed in a special section devoted to it in Dr. Theodor Reik's *The Unknown Murderer* (London, 1936). This involves a fantastic mixture of urges toward luck and ill-luck, as is particularly clear in one authentic case, where the criminal wiped himself on, and left behind, his own identity papers! In general it may be said that the criminal's 'calling card' is not left behind – as sometimes rationalized by detectives and others – owing to the relaxation of the sphincter in fear, but rather in anal-sadistic contempt and hatred of the victim. In Henry

Miller's *Tropic of Cancer* (Paris, 1934) an American beatnik journalist who is being evicted regrets that he is not able to express his anger against the landlord by shitting in the dresser drawer. Such defilings are particularly common during robberies.

In France a complete original ordeal still exists, at country marriages and sometimes in cities, where *The bride and groom are served a bridal posset-cup before they first go to bed together, to consummate their marriage in their presumed first intercourse, the posset-cup being an old-fashioned chamber-pot* – 'pot' is French slang for luck – *and the beverage a combination of champagne and chocolate mousse.* (Any questions?) The young Frenchwoman who told me about this, topped her own story by producing at that point a bottle of the best wine of the locality where she had been served such a 'fortifying' posset-cup or *"chocolat de la jeune mariée"* at her own wedding, in the town of Beaune in France: the wine being furnished with a handsome printed label giving its own local and correct name, *"Pissedru"* (Piss-sharp). It is in truth a splendid, rather dry wine, and, properly handled for export, I don't see why it shouldn't do at least as well in America as two other alcoholic beverages whose names have made their fortunes: the Scotch whiskey *"Vat 69"* and the Dutch cherry-cordial *"Wynand-Fockink."*

As to the *"chocolat de la jeune mariée,"* in Dusan Makavejev's totally fake-revolt *Sweet Movie* (1974), the final scene requires the naked heroine to do calisthenics in precisely such a scatological chocolate bath. This is really making the audience eat it. (Free chocolate bars were also distributed in the lobby, for jerks who didn't get the point.) Or, the same thing for less candid amateurs of cinematic anal-sadism, Walerian Borowczyk's *Contes Immoraux* (1974), dripping with *fin de siècle* underwear-fetichism in slick technicolor, and an even more outmoded anticlericalism – showing the Borgia Pope and his son, Cesare, balling daughter Lucrezia together – and sinking to some kind of ketchup-consuming climax when Paloma Picasso, as that historical S. & M. dyke, Countess Erszebet Bathory, bathes naked in 200 guaranteed litres of fresh-slaughtered pork blood, whipped up to an appetizing foam just before the cameras turned by three assistants armed with zabaglione egg-beaters with outboard motors. Miss Picasso announced to the press that she 'owed it to her father's memory' to do something particularly outrageous. *Noblesse oblige, Countess.* Let 'em eat shit.

V. SCATOPHAGY

Shit-books in the twentieth century seldom avow themselves frankly for what they are, but come on pompously as something innocently else, usually under the all-covering aegis of *science.* Other, and even more unlikely disguises are also sometimes used, as will be seen. This is of course typical of a principal form of the "Games People Play," as the late Dr. Eric Berne has called them, though he omits precisely this commonest of all forms – *Say It Isn't So!* – which is perhaps the secret meaning of all neuroses. In the present or literary form, of the scientific shit-book or scatological romp in some other disguise, it adds up to begging wordlessly: "DON'T say I'm a shit-snuffler and a fart-smeller. – Say I'm a *scientist!"* This is naturally all the more intensely needed and desired when the hidden interest really involved or approached is not simply a scatological interest in excrement generally, but is that of scatophagy, the eating or otherwise ingesting of feces and urine. This is the most violently taboo of all acts forbidden to children (also to dogs) in many cultures, including our own, and is later therefore surrounded by intense fear and revulsion – and a not-very-well hidden attraction – to certain adults.

There has already been discussed, under "Rectal Motherhood," chapter 8.VI.3, in the First Series preceding, p. 597, one highly misleading title, that of Dr. A. T. W. Simeons' *Man's Presumptuous Brain* (1960), in which, in this presumptive discussion of the *brain,* so much graphic and illustrative material is somehow worked in concerning the anus, evacuation, etc., that one wonders if the title should not have been *Man's Presumptuous Bum.*

Sometimes, of course, it is the material itself that requires a scatological concentration in a book really on another subject, as in Norman O. Brown's *Life Against Death: The Psychoanalytic Meaning of History* (New York: Random House, 1959), here mostly in a chapter on Swift and scatology. But sometimes one has the definite impression that the scatology has completely over-weighted the presumed subject, and that one is being wafted on a disproportionately high effluvium of the odor of shit. A case very much in point here would perhaps be Dr. Theodor Rosebury's *Life on Man* (New York: Viking Press, 1969), which appears from its title and introductory matter to be a study of the micro-organisms on and in man's body, though the principal part of the human itinerary through which the reader is led is in and around the rectum. Dr. Rosebury seems conscious of this concentration, and explains matters candidly toward the end of his slender book, p. 195, with a quick dip into humorous scatophagy, of which the closing suggestion, that it might be traced back to the 14th century, is of course not to be taken seriously:

> Most of the scientists who have studied these microbes are parasitologists . . . If there is anything that distinguishes these people from specialists in other areas of biology, it is likely to have something to do with their need to work with feces more than other biologists do, in fact more, or more intimately, than any other group of people I know. Feces is the natural habitat of many of the species they work with, and a good deal of their time is spent preparing specimens of feces and looking at them through a microscope. This is their work, and they quickly overcome any special feelings you might think they would have, and go about it in a matter-of-fact way. But it gives them something of a scatological bias, something like the good-natured eroticism of venereal-disease experts. Both may tend toward defensive ribaldry at times, for example when they and their business are first introduced to strangers. In appropriate company, especially with a new class of medical students, the parasitologist is likely to use what may possibly be one of the oldest jokes in English. Reynolds mentions it, and it wouldn't surprise me to learn that it could be traced back to the gong-fermors [privy-cleaners] of the fourteenth century: *"It may be shit to you, but it's my bread and butter!"*

I guess that really lays it on the line, though it does not quite explain why any biologist would choose to enter such a specialty, unless in fact he enjoyed having shit as his *bread and butter*. There are, after all, other biological 'specialties.'

But by far the most extraordinary example in all the literature of the world of giving your unexpecting readers shit to eat, and expecting them to *like it too*, is unquestionably a work appearing to be a sort of cookbook or panegyric to Italian cooking, entitled *The Unprejudiced Palate* (New York: Macmillan,

1948) – a title which hardly prepares the reader for what is to come – written by Angelo M. Pellegrini, then a professor at the University of Washington, and intensely defensive about having come to America as a boy and finding that he would be called there by one of the rude boys (p. 161): a 'sonofabitch, dago, wop, garlic, spaghetti.' The book appears to be his belated reply, and gets all these early insults out of the atmosphere by the peculiar method of flinging at the reader all the most repulsive aspects of the 'culinary' life in impoverished Italy. For example: his third chapter, under the title "The Things My Father Used To Do," is an elaborate discussion of horse- and cowshit, with the detailed description of how, as a boy in Italy, he and other boys of his town used to follow the cows being driven to market, in order to gather up the cowflops they might drop in the road as they ambled along. As Prof. Pellegrini describes it, p. 37–40, it is quite an art:

> It is axiomatic, of course, that cow pats and horse dumplings cannot be gathered, even by the most zealous enterpriser, until the animals see fit to release them … One could tell, for example, by a careful examination of the rump, tail, and legs of the animal, whether he had recently relieved himself of yesterday's hay. Under the circumstances, unfortunately, the test was not always reliable, since the peasants were also shrewd and … in anticipation of market day some of the animals had been fed grain and hay rather than grass, a diet that normally results in solid evacuation, neatly deposited and with no telltale traces.
>
> The shrewd manure gatherer knew also that cows and horses frequently gave certain premonitory signs before they do the deed. There is a perceptible hesitation in the jaunty stride, a slight hunching of the back, a characteristic restlessness in the tail, and successive dilations and contractions in the visible part of the organ involved.

Now *that* is the way to write a cookbook!

I do not wish to be misunderstood. Gathering cow- and horse-manure is an honorable occupation indeed, and probably well worth the minute study given it here. My father, too, set me to shoveling up the stuff, in slaughterhouses, when I was a boy (in the brief afternoon hours I could spare from the pre-rabbinic studies on which he also insisted), and piling it in great dirty sacks to tote home to manure our kitchen-garden.

In fact, I deeply envy Prof. Pellegrini's youth, out there on the sunny road in the early morning of market-days in Perugia or Calabria or wherever in Italy it may have been. Roads like that, in the slanting red sun of early morning, are gorgeous everywhere. Cowflop for cowflop, the killing-pens of the old Minooka slaughterhouse of the Franklin Beef Company in Scranton, Pa., where I served my shit-apprenticeship (and up to the ears), could hardly have compared. And yet ... I do consider it curious that Prof. Pellegrini finds his personal fecal reminiscences just the proper appetizer with which to open his feast of authentic Italian cookery. In any province of Italy one can easily find better food than that, and better *antipasta*.

There is more and better to come, in *The Unprejudiced Palate*, for those who have got it. The food-dirtying theme occurs massively in this book – the mixing of food, somehow, with shit, and the truculent insistence that the reader must manage to eat it. The most perfect logic is brought into service, yet the peculiar inappropriateness of shit for human consumption rather spoils the effect every time, in what is supposed to be a book devoted to advice on, and an appreciation of, good 'sonofabitch, dago, wop, garlic, spaghetti' food. All this to follow up Prof. Pellegrini's one best line, dividing all living things into five constituent elements: Earth, Air, Fire, Water, *and Garlic*. One is left with the unfortunate implication that what is really great about garlic is not its superb flavor and indispensability in fine cooking (except in eggs), but the fact that the smell of garlic is offensive to many people – a sort of hand-me-down version of the smell of shit.

His stupefying passage in praise of verbal and rectal insults, as to "*La Trombona*," the hideous, fat old woman who could fart at will, p. 196–8, has already been cited under "*Pet-en-Gueule*" (15.III.4). In Prof. Pellegrini's book it opens a chapter entitled "Some Culinary Preferences." And there is much more. But, one might ask, why not? Is not the opposite end of the alimentary tract to the mouth also a necessary element in the proper digestion of good food? And is not shit, for that matter, as the little girl touchingly said when she had to clean up her little brothers' messes in their pants, 'only what you eat'? Of course it is. Yet, somehow, one is surprised to find all this fecalism so happily proffered in what is supposed to be a cookbook, just as one might be surprised to find – on the same philosophical grounds – long *excursi* on how to cook Spanish paella with mussels, or how Kamchatka Eskimos brush their teeth with urine, in a treatise on hemorrhoids and other rectal complaints. Handsome is as handsome does. Unless, of course, one were to call one's medical textbook on piles *The Unprejudiced Hemorrhoid*, or call one's cookbook *Cooking With Shit*. For all I know, this title might be a runaway best-seller.

I. DR. DRECK

Scatophagy in folk-materials and jokes is seldom undertaken purposely by the actual scatophage, or shit-eater. Invariably he is tricked into it (as above), and it is considered the ultimate insult or humiliation. Far from being expressive in any way of the standard masochistic perversion, in which it is desired to eat excrements or to drink urine, notably of a sexually desired person, as in the *"Pet-en-Gueule"* already discussed (15.III.4, above); the folk-materials and jokes on scatophagy make it very clear at once that this is intended here as a sadistic act, and that the teller is really the trickster who is duping the *other person* or butt (and also the listener . . .) into doing the humiliating eating or otherwise absorbing of dung. Pierre Jannet's *Bibliotheca Scatologica* (1850) gives a brief chapter, p. 93–6, on this subject, citing numerous examples from classical and Neo-Latin authors, almost all of whom consider scatophagy to be anomalous and ununderstandable, or who attempt to rationalize it by 'hygienic' explanations similar to that usually given for the eating of clay by impoverished pregnant women suffering from a dietetic lack of calcium. Obviously there are no dietetic lacks that eating shit will cure. The usual explanation, therefore, is that the scatophage is simply 'crazy,' which does in fact come close to a useful diagnostic statement.

The numerous passages on this subject in the Bible are of particular interest, since all occur in the historical and prophetic sections, and none appear in the *Pentateuch* or *Five Books of Moses* or in the *New Testament*, where, as is hardly to be doubted, none of the miraculous incidents can be accepted as anything but legendary : 'folklore' rather than fact. Most striking is the passage of purely insulting rather than literal intent, which occurs in 2 *Kings*, xviii. 27 (a chapter *entirely repeated verbatim*, to xix. 37, as *Isaiah*, xxxvi–vii, which may give a clue as to its author), in which the vanquished beg the victor not to disgrace and insult them in a language the listeners can understand. *'But Rabshakeh said unto them, "Hath my master sent me to thy master, and to thee, to speak these words? Hath he not sent me to the men which sit on the wall, that they may eat their own dung, and drink their own piss with you?"'* There can be no doubt here as to the contempt involved, as also in the curse of the prophet *Malachi,* ii. 2–3, against the priests, impertinently putting the following scatophagous threat into the mouth of Jehovah: *'If ye will not hear, and if ye will not lay it to heart, to give glory unto my name, saith the Lord of hosts, I will even send a curse upon you, and I will curse your blessings: yea, I have cursed them already, because ye do not lay it to heart. Behold I will corrupt your seed, and spread dung upon your faces, even the dung of your solemn feasts; and one shall take you away with it.'* A further and even more directly scatophagous curse, in *Ezekiel,* iv. 12, seems also to be intended seriously as to the fate of the besieged Jerusalem: *"And thou shalt eat it as barley cakes, and thou shalt bake it with dung that cometh out of man, in their sight."*

Insults this direct are not appropriate for the commerce of everyday life, as the jokes and folktales see it. The hygienic or dietetic pretext (as in Ezekiel's curse) is found to be the most useful and credible, since it is the essence of the physician's art – formerly priestly magic – that the patient or believer is to do exactly what he is told, with blind faith, and in particular is to swallow whatever medicine he is given, no matter how unpalatable. In fact, as is well known, most people believe that medicine and its psychological magic are efficacious in direct proportion as the medicine tastes bad. It was only an obvious step, then, to the German *Dreck-Apotheke* or 'filth-pharmacy,' formalized in the late-17th century in Franz Christian Paullini's *Heilsame Dreck-Apotheke* (Frankfurt, 1696) and several times reprinted. Bourke's *Scatalogic Rites* gives a hundred-page chapter to the use of "Ordure and Urine in Medicine," p. 277–369, which omits no kind of ordure – human and animal – and no kind of sickness from the lists of those imagined to be curable by these means.

This is, in fact, the apotheosis of shit-eating and piss-drinking, with the ultimate turn of the knife (or chamber-pot) that the victims were required gratefully to pay the filth-physician and his feces-pharmacists for these purported cures. The only medical voice apparently raised at the time against this queasy nonsense was that of Dr. Rosinus Lentilius, in the *Ephemeridum physico-medicarum* (Leipzig, 1694). In that century, and until well into the 19th century, filth-pharmacy was the order of the day. Even the British physicist, Robert Boyle, is quoted as having said that, '*in his opinion, the virtues of human urine, as a medicine, internally and externally, would require a volume by themselves,*' and he is further credited with having published just such a volume on this subject, in Leipzig, 1692, over the signature "B."

Lest anyone imagine all this to be of historical interest only, I would quote here from two very serious French works, published by the Presses Universitaires de France, *Hygiène de la Vie Quotidienne* (1969) by Prof. Jean Boyer, chap. 2, "L'Eau;" and *La Pollution des Eaux* by René Colas in the same series. Quite aside from the chemical pollution of the drinking-water of Paris and all other great cities which take any part of their drinking-water from rivers, it is made perfectly clear by Prof. Boyer, at "L'Eau potable," p. 44–50, that, except for certain fortunate (rich) quarters where the drinking water is piped in from special wells, *the people of Paris drink water taken and 'filtered' from the same river Seine into which their own toilets are emptied by the sewers.* Presumably the poisons, germs, etc. are filtered out – this is only a presumption – but the piss and shit are still there, and the microbes in them. It will take another Victor Hugo, and another *Les Misérables* (or a wholesale epidemic of typhus) to alert the public to this reality. Or why travellers abroad get dysentery ("Montezuma's Revenge").

That, of course, is the dirty French. Such things can hardly take place among 'white people.' Or can they? In Helen Clapesattle's *The Doctors Mayo* (University of Minnesota, 1941), I believe, an old-time doctor is quoted as saying that "*Every time you drink from a faucet in St. Louis, Missouri, you're drinking from every flush-toilet all the way up the Mississippi.*" At the present time (1975) there is a sign on the river which flows through Anderson, Indiana, which reads: "ANDERSON SHITS IN IT AND MUNCIE DRINKS IT." Muncie is the next town downstream. Actually, of course, a little clean shit will never hurt you, the way chemical wastes of technological origin, and the actual microbic infestations of the waters are much more likely to do. People are now becoming aware of the reality of water-pollution (also air-pollution), but the scatological or scatophagous element is almost never mentioned. One exception is the unregenerate underground newspaper, *Nola Express* (New Orleans, Nov. 13, 1970) p. 4, which heads an editorial against ecological pollution with a cartoon starkly showing two large penises with the foreskin retracted, marked "INDUSTRY" and

"TECHNOLOGY," pissing a black stream into the meandering sump known as the Mississippi, and here labelled "Ol' Man River." The *real* piss in the river is apparently not considered even worth mentioning. For the patriotic truth of the matter is that America – and specifically New Orleans – drinks more piss and liquid shit than any other nation in the world. Here is Ron M. Linton telling it 'like it is,' in *Terracide: America's Destruction of her Living Environment* (Boston: Little, Brown, 1970) pp. 156 and 279:

> There is no such thing as absolutely pure drinking water. In most major urban areas located downstream from other densely populated communities, some portion of the drinking water is sewage – either processed or raw. The United States Public Health Service reviewed the kinds and quantities of pollutants being dumped into the Mississippi. It was known that no major city on the river below Minneapolis and St. Paul had proper sewage treatment plants ... such major cities as St. Louis, Memphis, Vicksburg, Natchez and New Orleans allowed raw sewage to be dumped directly into the Mississippi river without any treatment at all. In the four lowest states on the river – Tennessee, Arkansas, Mississippi and Louisiana – almost 90 percent of the wastes collected by sewer systems are dumped into the river without any treatment.
>
> In 1963, New Orleans [was] dependent solely upon the Mississippi River for its supply of drinking water ... Every day, the raw wastes collected from the 840,000 people served by sewers in New Orleans were returned to the river ... In the states of the Lower Mississippi River Basin, 1,135,000 persons drew their municipal water supplies from the Mississippi. One million of this number were in Louisiana.

Which puts a rather different construction on the proudly scatophagous and sacrilegious passage quoted (from himself) in Prof. Leslie Fiedler's *Being Busted* (1970) p. 73: '*But the phrase "God's Country" ... is the hackneyed boast of the insular and idolatrous at home, the sigh of the man to whom the gurgle of the flush toilet under him is the running over of his cup before the Lord.*' And of everybody downstream as well.

But that hardly gives the real *flavor* of the thing. In their monumental *Moment in the Sun* (New York: Dial Press, 1967), a staggering indictment and the ledger-sheet of ecological self-pollution and economic self-abuse that is essentially America's epitaph – at hardly two centuries old – here are authors Robert & Leona Rienow telling it *like it* REALLY *is*, in chapter 11, "The Ultimate Horror: A Septic World:"

> Rensselaer, New York, pours its raw sewage into the Hudson and then turns around and draws its drinking water out, figuratively within a stone's throw of its outfalls. Ottumwa, Iowa, recently gained a kind of scientific fame when it mixed one part water with one part Des Moines raw sewage effluent, shook it well with chlorine, drank it – and lived! Chanute, Kansas, when the Neosho River dried up, improved on the process. Like many cities on the Great Lakes they used their *own* sewage effluent. This is the height of some kind of efficiency and surely has a distinct time advantage over the natural water cycle ... It seems a lot of unnecessary effort and hanky-panky to pump all the sewage into the Hudson and then pump the mess out again. Wouldn't it be less costly simply to add a little dirty Hudson water to their waste [*shit*] before processing it for re-use? This is only a suggestion.
>
> Many smaller municipalities on the Great Lakes ... get rid of their untreated sewage by befouling the world's largest bodies of fresh water. The major difference between towns that dump into a river and then withdraw their drinking water from the river, and towns that dump into a lake and then extract water from it, is, as noted, that river dwellers most often drink the effluents from their neighbors upstream; while lake dwellers must drink their own. Strangely, this is a very fastidious point with Americans. We show a strong preference for our neighbor's effluents over our own. Psychologists (and water officials) have long mused over this quirk without effecting, as far as we know, an answer ...
>
> After you have recovered from the shock and the first squeamishness, you will come, sensibly, to the realization that at last humanity has it made. The perfect ring! The endless chain! Why have we taken so long to think of this neat solution to our problem of how to feed the ever mounting millions? *Bon appétit!*

Of course, as the Rienows add, in their final section, "The Great Hoax," chap. 20, "To the Rescue: The Sciences!" the first thoughtful Oriental who bothered to check out the American system of community piss-swilling and shit-guzzling with a microscope before recommending it (after all, isn't even *spit* a 'dirty word, on the end of your cigar'?), Dr. Shih Lu Chang of the Robert A. Taft Sanitary Engineering Center, found 'quantities of microscopic worms ... in purified [*n.b.*] water drawn from rivers in fourteen out of fifteen cities. The worms, called nematodes, by themselves aren't so bad; but having been raised in sewage they have fed on typhoid, paratyphoid, food poisoning, bacillary dysentery, etc., and now they encase the disease germs and completely protect them from treatment.' (See *U.S. News & World Report*, Feb. 29, 1960, p. 53.) A friendly word of advice to the reader: DRINK BOTTLED BEER! (Or fruit-juice.) Any brand not bottled in St. Louis, Mo., which is still downstream from '*every flush-toilet all the way up the Mississippi.*' And as to New Orleans, well, don't ask!

Here are some simple figures to remember: Every healthy person produces an average of ½ lb. of feces and 2 lbs. (1 quart) of urine per day. That means a minimum of *20 tons of feces and 100 tons of urine* PER DAY, per 100,000 population, plopped into the nearest body of water. (Except in ignorant and deluded Communist China, where they recycle it as fertilizer.) Twenty tons per day, per 100,000 people, means 7,300 tons per year. That's a lot of shit, for the next 100,000 people downstream to drink, even washed down with 36,500 tons of piss. *A bon entendeur, salut!*

The chemical wastes of technological origin are too large and desperate a subject to be considered here. As to the mere human digestive products – which is what makes everybody scream when they think of it: who *cares* about drinking pesticides and carcinogens from atomic reactor residues! – the correct and only solution is the *re-use* of human sewage as fertilizer, as has been done for centuries in the Orient. This not only keeps the river waters clean and drinkable, but it also restores and revitalizes the earth. The entire subject is excellently explored in the final two chapters of Reginald Reynold's *Cleanliness and Godliness* (London, 1943), significantly entitled "On the Apotheosis of Dung" and "Of the Final Metamorphosis [of *Ajax*] and the Hope of Humanity," but little has been done in the thirty years since this was written to suggest that the Western world is ready yet to grapple with the question of anything but chemical 'pollution' – if that. (In the Orient, 'night-soil' has been recycled for millennia.) In fact, the whole 'pollution' approach, with all its overtones of scatophobe danger, suggests that nothing at all will really be done except stir the shit about a bit, and then go back to drinking piss and liquid shit from the rivers. The harmless transmogrification of these valuable nitrogenous protein wastes into food, via any recycling operation involving the manuring and growing of plants, as in China, still smacks to most people too much of *eating shit* for any responsible Western politicians to dare to broach the idea. The paradox being, therefore, that owing to our overwhelming fear of eating shit – we end up drinking it! Not to mention the chickens we eat, that have been fed on *their own* shit, under the tasty euphemism of 'fientes.' (See full details in *Le Nouvel Observateur,* 3 Sept. 1973.) How now, effete *scatophagi?*

A perfectly direct statement of the activity of the sham physician, Dr. Dreck (compare Jules Romains' *Dr. Knock: or The Triumph of Medicine*) appears in an old folktale of which a modern version was collected from an Ozark farmer, in Hickory county, Missouri, about 1940, as recorded in Vance Randolph's *Pissing in the Snow,* No. 32. Note the significantly surviving 'Dutch doctor,' whom one may suspect of being none other than Tyl Eulenspiegel, disguised as the old Dreck-Doktor F. C. Paullini. The situation is pure farce: a burlesque remedy for a burlesque disease –

One time there was a Dutch doctor in this town that could cure anybody, and it didn't make no difference what was the matter with them. A fellow come walking in that day, and he says, "Doc, I have got three bad ailments." So the doctor says for him to speak right up, because everything is going to be all right.

"Well," says the fellow, "I can't taste nothing, and I can't tell the truth about anything, and my memory has failed besides." The doctor studied awhile, and then he went out to the privy and filled two big capsules with fresh hockey [*shit*]. "Chaw up one of them capsules right now," he says, and so the fellow done it. "What does that medicine taste like?" says the doctor. The fellow made a bad face, and he says it tastes like shit.

"That's fine!" says the Dutch doctor. "You can taste all right now, and you can tell the truth as good as anybody. The next time you can't remember something, just chaw up the other capsule!" So then Doc made the fellow give him two dollars, and that is the end of the story.

This identical story (Aarne Type 1543C*, "The Clever Doctor") is given in Jonas Balys' *Motif-Index of Lithuanian Narrative Folklore* (Kaunas, 1936). Its origin is to be found in the tracing of the extraordinary trait of the 'inability to tell the truth,' and the even more extraordinary suggestion that the dupe wishes to be cured of this! What is really intended here is a magical and usually homosexual ritual, by means of which the scatological medicine will make the would-be wiseman or seer able *to divine secrets or foretell the future*. This is a Levantine superstition. 'Khati Cheglou,' the pseudonymous compiler of *Histoires Arabes* (Paris, 1927) p. 21, has a perfectly frank story of this kind – doubtless the original of the expurgated Italian story following below – in which: *A homosexual fakir of the North African Derkawi gets a boy to lie face down with his pants dropped, in order to "receive the sacred flame, and see the saints flying in the sky." When the boy lies down, the fakir buggers him.* See further on pederastic ritual-ordeals of this kind – including the 'sacred flame' or fire – my study of *The Guilt of the Templars* (1966) pp. 54–6 and 108–24.

It is a point certainly worth further study, that circus clowns and carnival entertainers have largely been homosexual or prepsychotic (or both) since very remote times. Certainly since the development of the modern genre of street-comedians attracting dupes for the salve-selling quacks in France and Germany (Dr. Dreck and Dr. Krankheit combined) during the venereal disease plague of the 16th century and ever since. Now nature-food fakers, occultists, astrologers, and the like. Such semi-criminal occupations are a standard resort for social outcasts, for whatever reason, as in the brutally exact *Nightmare Alley* of William Lindsay Gresham, who also touches – purposely lightly – on the allied semi-criminal profession of prestidigitation and stage magic, also developed out of that of the carnival sleight-of-hand tricksters ("*Now you see it – now you don't!*") and other decayed priests. Whose sick specialty is today the mock human sacrifice of 'sawing a woman in half' (or electrocuting her), while the audience screams its delight. Even the gladiatorial 'games' never went that far.

The original story here (in two variants, corresponding roughly to Thompson's Motifs K114.3.1 and K1044, not cross-referred) is given by Poggio, about 1450, as Nos 165 and 166, both ascribed to Gonnella, court-buffoon to the Princes of Este and Ferrara, in whose name a collection of Italian *Facetiæ* was

also long ago published (re-edited splendidly by Albert Wesselski, Weimar, 1920). In the first form, the joke is given as an
implied pederastic act, or a folk-rationalization of the homosexual '*pet-en-gueule*' fetich: *Gonnella promises to make the
dupe into a diviner by taking him in bed with him* [n.b.]. *He
then 'let out noiselessly a fizzle, and bade him put his head
inside, between the sheets. The fool complied, but immediately
beat a hasty retreat, driven out by the stench: "You have
broken wind, I think," said he. "Out with the money," replied
Gonnella; "for you have divined right".'* (Liseux' translation,
1879, II. 68–9.)

Poggio's other version is even closer to the modern Lithuanian
and Ozark form, as the dupe is to be made into a diviner by
means of *Gonnella's making up 'a ball of ordure, which, with
the booby's consent, he thrust into his mouth.'* In both cases
the final line insists on the identification of gold and feces, with
the trickster demanding payment, exactly as in the Ozark
version five centuries later. The relevancy to the whole pathetic
search for alchemical methods of turning 'base metals' (*i.e.*
shit) to gold throughout the Renaissance – and still today,
among occultists, still faithfully searching for the Dwarfs'
Treasure by these means – is also perfectly clear. A modern
survival of the story simply has the trickster getting dupes to
eat shit, without any motive given; but the curious sales-talk or
boniment by which he offers his wares – "*Trefft! (Guess!)*" – still
points to the ritual method of becoming a diviner. *A peddler
has nothing to sell, so he wraps up shit (or soap splinters) in
paper and goes along shouting* "Trefft, *a nickel!* Trefft, *a nickel!*"
*A customer buys a packet, opens it and bites into it, and spits
it out shouting, "Shit!" "You guessed it!" replies the peddler.*
(N.Y. 1931, told by a *knish*-vendor to a group of Yeshiva
students, after which no one would buy his wares! "Dr. Tell-
troth," in *Kryptádia*, XI. 106 and 118.)

An account of a similar occurence, as a joke, appears in the
erotic magazine *The Boudoir* (London: Lazenby, 1883–5) No. 4:
p. 121, entitled "The Origin of Hokey-Pokey," which is the
name given in England to a cheap sort of ice-cream sold by the
Italian vendors from pushcarts since the early 19th century, and
consisting of scraped ice, flavored with a little sugar-water
colored to resemble fruit:

Once upon a time a facetious fellow for a wager undertook

to sell sh – t for sweetstuff in the street. – Taking a hand-barrow, he called out –

"Here you are, Hokey-Pokey, a penny a spoonful, the most delicious thing in the world, and sure to make you speak the truth if you never did before!"

"Give us a spoonful!" said a curious man, opening his mouth. "Ah, damme; sh – t, by God!" he exclaimed, as the vendor accommodated him.

"I told you you'd speak the truth. Don't make a fuss, or you'll drive away my customers!" replied the hawker.

Another closely related story, at least in its modern form, is developed from that cited by Rotunda at Motif X612* (omitted by Thompson), 'Christian dupes Jews into revering his excreta,' in Sacchetti's *Novelle* (15th century) No. 24. With this should be compared K1044, 'Dupe induced to eat filth,' referred to Sansovino's *Cento Novelle Scelte* (1566) Pt. V, No. 9, apparently with no religious element. In the much softened modern reversal the *excreta* have become merely some disgusting food-stuff, but the plot is still centrally concerned with divinatory rituals and the search for knowledge. *A Jewish trickster persuades a Russian cossack (or Irish policeman) to eat gefüllte-Fisch heads, 'to give him brains,' while his Jewish hosts eat up the rest of the fish at their Friday evening ceremonial meal, at which he is allowed to be present – if he brings the fish. One Friday night he throws down his napkin in disgust, and says, "I swear to God, I believe you Jews are screwing me! I don't think there is anything in this fishhead business!" "You see," says the host triumphantly, "you're beginning to get some brains."* (N.Y. 1931.)

This fishhead story is rather close to self-parody of the complex Jewish dietary laws. It certainly alludes to the endless Christian accusations that Jews (and other 'heretics') eat mysterious substances of a magical and disgusting nature for their religious communion, in particular the blood of young Christian virgins murdered for that purpose: the hymeneal blood, of course. Unless we are to guess that the Russian cossack or Irish cop is really a Black Hundred's spy (Secret Agent OO-Fishhead), out collecting *agent provocateur* material for the next pogrom, he just as certainly seems anxious to partake.

2. THE ESCOUMERDA

Biologically considered, there is survival value to the disgust expressed with regard to scatophagy. No normal person can eat feces or any other excrement as a natural part of the diet, since such excrements have already been digested – that is why they have been excreted by the system – and contain no further nourishment for the organism. Animals, such as dogs, which do eat feces (*right before coming to lick their master's face*, as the not-very-jesting folk-phrase observes), are in that sense perverted by their biological history, since their carnivorous past requires them to go through the motions of hunger even when not hungry, and upon obviously unsuitable objects and substances.

One of the most commonly-collected jokes on human scatophagy, often printed in humor magazines as barely naughty, though really studiously *méchant*, neatly reverses the dog-as-scatophage. *A parson is riding on the train. A Scotchman enters the compartment, and puts a bulky basket in the rack over the clergyman's head. A few minutes later a drop of liquid drips down onto the clergyman's nose, which he wipes off and licks, inquiring affably, "Whiskey?" "No, fox terrier."* (Kimbo, *Tropical Tales*, 1925, p. 23, a version in which the liquid is only sniffed. Often collected orally during Prohibition with the alliterative colloquy as punchline: *"Pickles?" – "Puppies!"* and in versions in which a deceptively small little man, *i.e.* a child, thus gets the better of the snoopy government 'revenuer' or prohibition-agent.) All these forms appear to be decayed remnants of a Levantine revenge-story, usually called "The Entrapped Lovers," which will be dealt with further in section 15.VI.2, "Gardyloo!" In these the urine is really that of a lover hidden in a closet, who is discovered by these means.

The old mountain-dweller offers the 'outlander' a chaw of tobacco from a plug in his pocket. The stranger 'rolled the chaw around [in his mouth] and remarked it was very good, but seemed to be rather moist. The old gentleman replied that it might be, as he couldn't hold his water as well as he use to.' (Grand Rapids, Mich. 1956: Indiana University Folklore Archives.) The real flavor of this jest is in the fact that tobacco is 'cured,' especially for chewing and for the cheap stogey' or 'bomber' cigars, by the admixture of substances of which urine is only one component, and far from the least appetizing. Many witticisms, just below the formal level of jokes, twit tobacco with this. *A man is buying some imported Turkish pipe-tobacco, and asks, "Is this stuff pure?" "Well," says the tobacconist, "confidentially, I think they mix in about half camel-shit." "Oh, that's all right," says the relieved client, "I was just wondering if it was PURE camel-shit."* (Allentown, Pa. 1934. Also in France of the ghastly cigarettes supplied to soldiers.)

Birds and beasts figure very prominently in scatological stories, as has already been seen, owing to their unrepentant and perfectly public incontinence as to their defecatory or cloacal habits. In Roger Abrahams' *Deep Down in the Jungle* (ed. 1970) p. 142–56, most of the texts of "The Signifyin' Monkey," the most widespread Negro 'toast' or recitation, involve scatological elements, while in "The Watch" and "A Party," p. 223–8, the Monkey is finally told by his erstwhile protector, the Lion, "You are going to eat that SHIT!" *The Stag Party* (1888) unnumb. p. 256, gives the earliest American version of a fisherman's tall-tale, probably of ancient origin but untraced. *A pelican swallows a fish (or a heron swallows an eel) which immediately slips through its gut and appears at the other end. The bird swallows it again, with the same result. The third time, the bird sticks its bill up its ass, and says triumphantly, "I've got the son of a bitch now!"* – The ornithologist, W. L. McAtee, gives this in his privately issued *Nomina Abitera* (1945) p. 25, as a story from his boyhood in Grant county, Indiana, in the 1890's, with the punchline: *"There, circulate, damn ye, circulate!"*

Note the relation to the Aesopic story concerning the turtle swallowed by the eagle, who puts his head out the eagle's anus to ask him questions while the eagle is flying off with him: the theme also of stories about Jonah and the whale. An ugly wild-west version perhaps comes closer to the real unconscious layer here: *The veterinary is trying to help a cow in labor, when a tornado comes up. The rancher and his family rush down into the storm cellar and call to the veterinary to follow them. "Be down in a minute," he shouts back over the howling wind. "Got to get this cow facing the other way – she's already birthed that calf three times!"* (Santa Monica, Calif, 1965.)

The idea of the bird's oral relationship to its own rectum is very ancient, probably Egyptian (compare Aesop's "Crane and Wolf," Type 60), and rises unquestionably from the observation of aquatic birds pressing out their greasy dressing-fluid with their beaks from the sebaceous gland just above their tails. It is presented artistically in Ovid's *Ibis*, which is called by Prof.

Robert C. Elliott (*The Power of Satire*, 1960, p. 126): 'a mighty blast made up of curses, invectives, malediction, imprecation, spelled out with tireless and pedantic ingenuity against an enemy whom Ovid refuses to name but calls *Ibis* (the ibis was a bird of spectacularly filthy habits; it was said to administer enemas to itself by means of its beak).' The *Ibis* is of great folkloristic interest also, in this case for its curses and maledictions, here very properly thought of as emanating from or entering the Ibis' cloaca. This hostile fancy has always appealed to aggressive wits, of which the best-known example is Ben Jonson's Apologetical Epilogue to his suppressed satirical comedy, *The Poetaster* (1601), a reply to his critics and detractors. The whole story here, which is most interesting, is best told in Isaac D'Israeli's *Calamities and Quarrels of Authors* (ed. B. Disraeli, *c.* 1850, p. 474–89, "Jonson and Dekker"), citing some of the most remarkable passages of the Epilogue, in particular Jonson's early description of what would now be described psychiatrically as 'writer's block' – and its proud cure.

The humorous stories of this kind follow the pattern or rhythm already seen in earlier chapters, whereby actions too 'awful' to ascribe to human beings are first ascribed to animals, then to children, fools, and foreigners, before finally coming home to everyday adults of the kind presumably telling or listening to the jokes. *A little Negro boy is sent by his father for a bucket of drinkin' 'n' shavin' water from the river. He comes back empty-handed, saying that there is an alligator there which 'goes like this' (gesture with the thumb and fingers of an enormous mouth opening and closing). He is told it is a tame alligator, and to go back and get the water, but returns empty-handed again. "I'm afraid o' dat alligator!" he admits. "Dat's a tame alligator. He's just as scared o' you, as you is o' him." Boy: "Iffn dat 'gator's as scairt o' me as Ah is o' him, dat water ain't fit to drink* NOHOW!" (N.Y. 1938.) Another version, veering much more to the anal-sadistic, was given at the same séance by a middle-aged married woman, ending: "*Iffn dat alligator bothers you, jes' take a hanful of shit an' THROW it at 'im!" "Now, where'm I gonna get de shit?' "Jes' reach inside yo' pants – it'll be there.*" (Also often collected as a maneuver for exorcising ghosts.)

Fools and foreigners alternate between being the victor and the victim in the scatophagous *dénouement*, and few types of jokes exist in which the identification of the butt or victim is so vacillating. Obviously, the real humor resides in the idea of the ingesting of feces, or of the contamination and 'dirtying' of food by these means. The actual method of achieving the final image does not essentially matter. In such cases, it may fairly be construed that the real butt or victim is always the listener. *Two Indians check into a hotel room and stay there for three days without coming downstairs. The house-detective is sent up to find out why, and never reappears. When the police break in, they find the detective dead on the bathroom floor toma-hawked. "Did you kill him, chief?" "Ugh. Me kill-um." "Why'd you kill him?" "Me hate-um. Him shit in spring!"* (Idaho, 1932; Larson MS., No. 50. Also, *Anecdota*, 1934, 2:337.) Both editions of *Anecdota Americana* give a modification in which a privy is mistaken for a 'fireless cooker.' (1:448, and 2:20.)

The Indian story is commonly collected at present in more allusive form, but with a hidden female-protest sting in its tail: *The Indian chief on the train tells his wife, "Squaw, get chief glass of water." She returns with a paper-cup full of water. This is repeated several times. Finally she returns without water, explaining, "No can gettum water. Big white squaw sittum on well."* (N.Y. 1952, told by a man.) Compare a story given earlier in fuller form: *The Chinese cook who is badly treated by the officers at whose mess he serves, who tie his queue in knots, &c. Finally they have a change of heart, and assure him they will not torment him anymore. "No kickee?" he asks. "No kickee," he is assured. "No knotee in hair?" "No more knots in your hair, John." "Hokay, me no pissee in coffee anymore."* (N.Y. 1938. Printed with 'put dishwater in your coffee,' in *Captain Billy's Whiz Bang*, a bawdy humor magazine of the 1930's: food-dirtying by means of food – 'white on white'? – for pur-poses of expurgation.) It is not difficult to see who the teller is identifying with here.

An Irish greenhorn who embarrasses his Americanized brother by urinating in public on lower Broadway, is told that he should knock on any door and he will be allowed to use the toilet. The first time he knocks on a door, a hand comes out with a beer-growler in it and fifteen cents, and a voice says, "One quart, please." "Jaysus, Pat," he says to his brother, "pwhy didn't yez bring me over here sooner? I pissed away a fortune in the ould country!" (2:78.) Also in *Anecdota Ameri-cana* (2:142, variant) a form certainly of real European origin: *An emissary is sent from a famine-stricken village in Poland to*

*the great city of Cracow to try to find food. The emissary
arrives, and is relieving himself in an alley on a piece of paper
just as a thief runs by with a package of meat stolen from a
butcher-shop. By mistake the emissary is collared and is hauled
back to the shop, with his wrapped-up piece of paper, which is
put on the scales and found to weigh just under a pound. He is
beaten and thrown into the street, and makes his way back to
his village. "Nu, Chayim-Yankel," he's asked, "are things better
in Cracow?" "Oy, veh!" he says, "are things better in Cracow?
Don't ask! In Cracow they're eating SHIT, and they* beat *you if
you don't shit a full pound!"* (Motif J1919.3.) A parable for our
times, if I ever heard one. Here is the most recent version, used
to express the U.S. hostility against the communist régime of
Fidel Castro in Cuba: '*CASTRO SPEECH: "Comrades, I have
both bad news and good news for you. First, the BAD news ...
there is only manure left to eat. Now the GOOD news ... there's
not enough of it left to go around!"* ' (*Sex to Sexty*, 1967, 10:37.
This is built up into a whole burlesque politico-militaristic
editorial in the New York 'pornzine,' *Screw*, Aug. 25, 1969, No.
25: p. 2.)

Again, only implications and seldom the direct statement of
the scatophagous act in modern jokes: *Two men are leading
a circus elephant across the desert, but it stops and will not go
on. They decide it has an intestinal obstruction of sand, and
get out a pipe to blow up its rectum. The first man blows till his
strength is gone, then motions to the other to take his turn. The
second man angrily plucks out the pipe and reverses it, saying:
"From your mouth?"* (N.Y. 1949.) This is certainly of musical
origin, since it parodies the maneuver necessary when a single
sustained note on an orchestral wind-instrument is required,
longer than a single human breath can encompass. Sometimes:
*The man has a job helping the veterinary in the circus, his
specialty being blowing obstructions out of the elephant's ass
with a straw.* (Pantomimed excruciatingly: tail up, straw in,
blow!) *His friends expostulate with him that this is a terrible
job, and he can surely get another if he tries. "What!" he says
in horror, "and leave show-business!?"* (N.Y. 1973.)

Simple food-dirtying, perhaps, and already so classified, yet
obviously close to scatophagy in a purposely inverted burlesque: *The old millionaire is being fed rectally, and the butler
reports, "Yes, he's feeling much better. This morning we gave
him a little melted cheese on toast – it would have done your*

heart good to see the way his asshole SNAPPED at it." (2:394.) Similarly: *A soldier with his head swathed in bandages is being given his morning coffee rectally. Suddenly he begins to grunt and wave his arms. (Acted out.) Nurse: "What's the matter? Too hot?" Soldier (speaking out of the side of his mouth): "Too much sugar!"* (N.Y. 1948.)

The accidental drinking of urine has long been a favorite subject of humor – that is to say, it is an accident for the dupe, but purposeful on the part of those who give him to drink. (The American Indians, whose folktales are filled with scatology, have this story, also encountered in Russia. Motif K1044.1.) Poggio, in 1451, No. 69, gives his rationalized version: the dupe is hated, and is caught in his own net, in this case stinginess. *A man (cleric) known for his stinginess is always poking about his servants' table at meal-time, to make sure their wine is sufficiently watered. To cure him of the habit, they fill the wine-jug with fresh urine. When he tastes it, as usual, he retches and is violently ill, while the servants laugh at his contortions and threats.* Poggio gives this as a true story, finishing: *'The fellow who dreamed up this scheme in the first place told me about it later with great merriment.'* The similar American wild-west story has already been seen as to: *The inexperienced young man who is given a foaming glass of piss to drink when he strides into a barroom, points to the sign saying "BILLIARDS," and says firmly, "I'll have a billiard, please."* Here there is no pretense of his having offended, except by his inexperience, and his status as 'tenderfoot' and outsider: the perfect dupe.

The implication here is always the difficulty of telling certain beverages, such as white wine, beer, or cider from piss, merely by their visual aspect, and this has led to endless witticisms not rising to joke-form concerning *"Bartender, pour this beer back in the horse,"* and similar scatophage humor. Such as: *"This beer won second prize last year in Milwaukee." "What won first prize?" "PISS!"* (La Jolla, Calif. 1965.) In Baudelaire's poem-cycle, "Vénus Belga," written during his exile in Belgium and published in *Les Épaves* (ed. Lemerre, 1889) p. 38, and in the 1920's collected edition of his *vers de circonstance* making fun of Belgium, *Amoenitates Belgicae,* he puts this into the mouth of the Belgian publisher Hetzel, obviously as folkwit: "Opinion de M. Hetzel sur le Faro" [a bad Belgian beer at that time], *'C'est de la bière déja bue.'* This lacks only the horse of the American witticism.

Built up into a story, again turning on the difficulty of telling liquor from piss: *A bartender (or the Negro pianist) in a fancy whorehouse in New Orleans claims to be able to tell the name and year of any fine French wine blindfolded. A large bet is placed against him by one of the habitués, the 'folding-money' bets being placed in the top of the madam's stocking for safe-keeping. The opposing bettor begins to worry when he sees the blindfolded bartender sniff and taste one glass of wine after another and reel off, "Clos Vougeot, 1899 – Liebfraumilch, 1913," and so forth; and he surreptitiously pisses in an empty wine-glass and hands it to the bartender. The bartender sniffs, tastes, and spits the contents on the floor, shouting, "Why that's piss!" " 'Course it is," says the bettor; "we know that. But whose? And what year?"* (N.Y. 1948.) Not very funny, and with the perfectly worthless punchline obviously only present to make the titillating situation of 'accidental' piss-drinking into an avowed joke. At Type 1832B, Aarne–Thompson cite a French-Canadian story of rather similar import, but without scato-phagy: *A boy on the road is staring at something. A priest, passing by, asks him what he is looking at so hard. Boy: "I don't know." Priest: "Why, it's horse dung!" Boy: "Yes, but I was wondering if it's from a horse or a mare."* These are both close to the joke already discussed in which *The objectionable drunk in a barroom is made to admit that "he don't know from SHIT, and he's trying to tell* us *about the Atom Bomb!'* The French version of the piss joke arrives at the point the story was perhaps struggling toward all the while: *The victim is given the final drink out of a glass in which one of the whores at the bar has pissed. "Great!" he says; "I'll have another just like it, but this time leave out the maraschino cherry."* (*Champi raconte: histoires grivoises*, 1945? Cf. *Kryptádia*, XI. 112, and First Series, p. 406, on *cheeses*.)

In a work purporting to be the true *Memoirs of an Erotic Bookseller* (London: Skilton, 1969) p. 65, by 'Armand Coppens,' who is thought to be the well-known Amsterdam bookdealer, Nicholas Schors – I appear in the book, p. 171, as *'that vain genius who lives in Roc Amadour. You know the one I mean. That man with the thing about dirty limericks and four-letter words'* – the pretense that the action is taking place in Belgium or in France breaks down in chapter 4, which is by far the most amusing in the book, and is set frankly in Holland. In the following chapter (milieu not stated), the sadistic and scatological action of the plot is apparently explained by a 'famous actor' here called 'Jean Reynolds,' recounting his onstage pranks in certain German plays such as Goethe's early *Goetz von Berlichingen*, which situates the action very clearly. The actor, who is a sort of modern Tyl Eulenspiegel, is noted for his 'practical jokes:'

It was, apparently, the one he played on old Sophia that really made him famous. Old Sophia was a very talented actress who was hated in the profession and by a considerable proportion of the public as well. Sophia believed herself to be God's gift to the theatre. She was complacent and very difficult to handle. She refused to have anything to do with her fellow actors, insisted on a private dressing room and, to crown it all, always had to have her own private toilet which was forbidden territory to the rest of the company.

"That private toilet was a thorn in my flesh," Reynolds said. "I simply had to do something about it. So one day I bought some gingerbread and went to the theatre very early. I put some of the gingerbread in my mouth and chewed; then, when it was all soft and brown, I smeared it all over the walls of Sophia's toilet with my fingers. That evening, during the interval, Sophia went to her toilet. Her outraged cries could be heard all over the theatre. I'm sure even the public must have heard them. "Shit! Shit!" she screamed, at the top of her voice, "Shit on my walls. Someone has used my toilet and put shit on the walls." Everybody ran to Her Own Private Toilet to witness the phenomenon. "Don't you believe me?" she screamed. "Look for yourself." I dipped my finger in the mess on the wall and tasted it. "You're right," I said. "It *is* shit." At that moment, she fainted, and it took us fifteen minutes to revive her. After that, she was never the same again ... Her proud and haughty attitude, however, never left her."

It would be wrong to leave the impression that 'practical jokes' of this kind are typical only of Germany or Holland, though I must admit I have never heard of one that comes quite so close to eating shit – as a joke on *somebody else*. The theatre in general is the happy hunting-ground of practical jokes, first because the people in it are living most of the day in an exhibitionist world of make-believe; and second – and more importantly – because most of the people in the theatre and motion-pictures are infantile beyond belief, especially the actors, and the anal-sadistic phase of the child's development seems to be where most of them have stopped growing. In her *G-String Murder* in the 1940's, the strip-teaser Gypsy Rose Lee tells of a prank rather similar to the one above: *A strip-teaser's G-string is filled with Limburger cheese while she is onstage.* This is also told as of *smearing a drunkard's moustache with Limburger while he has passed out,* with obvious insulting cunnilingual punchlines.

In the foothills of the most popular joke at the present time in America is a burlesque blackout first seen in a Bowery theatre in New York, in 1937, and often since: *A man is waiting impatiently for his turn in a country outhouse when the occupant comes bursting out, shouting, "Don't go in there!" A moment later he comes back with a long pole, which he plunges down the hole through the open door, explaining, "I dropped my coat." "But you don't want your coat now," says the other man in disgust; "it'll be all – dirty." "To hell with the coat! My lunch is in the pocket!"* (First printed in *Sex to Sexty,* 1966, 7:2.) The same in the even more obviously scatophagous form of: *A man fishing for a caramel candy in a sewer, explaining, "It's got my false teeth stuck in it!"* (*Histoires Italiennes,* Paris, 1956, p. 79.)

Also significantly combining various other activities with the scatologica, though pointedly avoiding any mention of eating: *A little old lady is about to trim her 2 × 4 foot lawn with manicuring scissors, when she decides she should give the work to the unemployed, and phones the Home Relief office. A few hours later an enormous truck backs up before her house, a tremendous hole is dug where the lawn had been, and a large wooden outhouse is set up over it. When she hurries out to object, the foreman tells her: "Sorry, lady, that's our orders: there got to be two men goin,' two comin', two shittin', and two workin' – at all times!"* (Scranton, Pa. 1934, parodying the overstaffed 'make-work' projects of the w.p.a. unemployment relief.)

I believe the following story on implied scatophagy to be the most popular joke told at the present time in America. Since its appearance in *Anecdota Americana II,* in 1934, I have personally collected it over one hundred and forty times, especially in the last some twenty years, nor did I actually begin counting its occurrences until I was forced to the realization that it was one of the jokes most frequently encountered: most often in the form of a knowing allusion to its final line. This has now become a proverb or catch-phrase – not always in cognizance of the underlying joke. *Pat and Mike die and go to Hell, where they are given their choice between getting into the flaming furnace, or a barrel of shit in which the sinners have to stand, up to the chin. Pat chooses the barrel. Then Mike is given his choice. "Are you getting in here, Mike?" asks Pat (in a strained voice). "I guess so." "All right, but don't make any W A V E S!"* (2 : 187.) In more recent versions Pat & Mike are seldom named. *Hell has two doors; from behind one comes the sound of screams, from the other only sighs. The sinner chooses the door of sighs, behind which he finds an ocean of damned souls standing in shit up to their chins on their tippy-toes, all whispering: "Don't make any wa-a-a-ves! Don't make any wa-a-a-ves!"* (N.Y. 1953.) Not the 'Music of the Spheres,' Motif A767; but the 'wailing and gnashing of teeth' in Hell, of *Matthew*, xiii. 50. *When the newcomer complains, he is sometimes told: "That's nothing. Just wait till the Devil comes by in a speedboat!"* (La Jolla, Calif. 1965.)

In all forms, the original joke is consciously considered an allusion to, or assessment of, the Human Condition : the *mess-we-are-in*. The author of one of these perennial if-you-can't-lick-'em-join-'em articles on the hippies, psychedelic gunk-art, Hitler-style massive-volume rock & roll *Totalitarianmusik*, and similar, in *Esquire* magazine for September 1967, considered it witty to call his piece "The New Wave-Makers," presumably a reference to the French movies' *Nouvelle Vague* (the Sewer-Style), if not simply to Hitler's now-revived Wave of the Future. I believe there was also a movie-studio-sponsored "Don't Make Any Waves" beauty contest [!] in the same year, of which the winner could logically expect to get a mouthful of shit. An 'insiders' joke' with 100,000,000 insiders.

Though most people now telling this joke, or alluding to it, are persuaded that it is of recent vintage, actually it first appeared in European culture *as a joke* as the second story, "A Mad-Doctor," in Poggio's *Facetiæ* (written in 1451), 'De medico qui dementes et insanos curabat," told as the ultimate 'cold-turkey' cure of an Italian Dr. Dreck, for 'the folly of those who keep dogs or hawks for the purpose of fowling :'

Once upon a time, there was a Milanese, a doctor for madmen and lunatics, who undertook to cure, within a given time, those who were entrusted to his care. His treatment was as follows: in his house there was a yard, and in that yard a ditch of filthy and fetid water in which he kept, tied naked to a stake, the madmen who were brought to him; some up to the knees, others to the groin, others again deeper still, according to the gravity of the disease: there he left them, without food, until they appeared sane. In the number, a madman was brought to him, whom he immersed to the thighs, and who, after a fortnight, began to recover, and begged hard to be taken out. The Doctor exempted him from the ordeal, but upon condition that he should not leave the yard. After a few days' obedience, he was allowed to roam through the whole house, provided he did not pass by the street-door; meanwhile his companions, who were numerous, remained in the water ... [He sees a young horseman who says he spends fifty ducats a year on his horse, dogs, and hawks.] "Ho, ho," said the madman, "get away with thee, I pray, and fly before the Doctor comes back; for, should he find thee here, he will look upon thee as the most insane man in existence, and, to cure thee, will dip thee into the ditch with his other patients, and up to thy chin, in the deepest part." *Thus showing that sporting is the greatest of follies, unless resorted to occasionally, by rich men, and as an exercise for the body.*

(Liseux' translation, 1879, I. 10–14. Other Italian versions in Carbone, and Straparola. – Rotunda J1434.) Note the didactic format, even including a little moral at the end – carefully making exception for the rich (*opulentis*) – as in the *Disciplina Clericalis* of Sephardi/Alphonsi three centuries earlier, which had created the style. Though it would seem that the modern changing of the 'mad-doctor' and his pigsty sanitarium to the Devil and Hell is a later form, the situating of the curative or punitive action in Hell is probably the original, as will be seen. Mark Twain's story of "The Appetite Cure" – not to mention Edgar Allan Poe's "Doctors Tarr and Feather" – has certain obvious resemblances to Poggio's proto-psychiatric anecdote of the *graduated cure*, which is also crucial in the revived 'Dreckapotheke' of Hahnemann's homeopathic theory of medicine (1796).

Poggio's story passed into the English tradition, in direct translation, in *Tales, and Quicke Answeres* (about 1530) No. 52, at the period of the earliest popular English jestbooks, other than Caxton's *Aesop*. Its first modern printing with the *"Don't make any waves!"* punchline, appears to be in 'Kimbo's *Tropical Tales* (Nice, 1925) p. 10, in which the choice given to the sinner, named Potts, in Purgatory, is between a 'boiling oil tank and the cess pool,' in which latter he finds his deceased *father*, who is given the famous end-line. The text is British or American, dating probably from the 1910's, as with all the jokes given by 'Kimbo' (probably one Bradley Gilman, who seems also to have used the pseudonym 'Jim Kay' for an eccentric anti-Semitic work, *Damn the Jews*, Nice, 1930; the title being changed on the cover to *Just a Jew*. Copy: Ohio State, Legman Antisemitica Coll.)

A reduction of the joke to a 'quickie' or riddle form also apparently exists: *"If you were up to your chin in shit, and somebody threw a bucket of vomit at you – would you duck?"* (N.Y. 1953.) Note the folk-identification of vomit and shit as equivalents. In another schoolchildren's riddle: *"Which would you rather do if you had to: swim a lake of piss, walk a road of shit, or lick a dog's ass until it bleeds?"* (Albuquerque, New Mexico, 1936, among children less than ten years old. The correct alternative is the last: 'lick' meaning to beat with a stick.) Actually, I am not certain that the first riddle here is a reduction of the story of the Hell of Shit. It has much in common with a French scatological tale, printed in divers 19th-century chapbooks, in which: *The rich outhouse-cleaner will only allow his daughter to marry a man who will agree to stand in shit up to his neck before the wedding. The father-in-law then suddenly brandishes a sword over the man's head, so that he ducks beneath the surface.* "Marry her with my blessing, my boy!" *says the father-in-law.* "You'll never throw up to her now, how her father made his money!" This is very close to Thompson's trickster story, Motif K558.2, collected in India: *Condemned man asks to be beheaded standing in a tank of water. He ducks, and the executioners kill each other!*

Already given, but not to be overlooked at this point is the famous anti-psychiatric story, of which a longer version is under "Narsty-Narsties," in chapter 12.IV.4, end of the section "Sexual Smörgåsbord." *A patient in a lunatic asylum will eat nothing but shit, and is given a big bowl of it every day. One day he refuses to touch it, and explains to the head-doctor:* "I don't like the way you're treating me, and I'm on a hunger-strike. Imagine serving a fellow shit to eat, with a hair on it!

See it right on top there?" (2 : 369, sometimes specifying that it
is a 'cunt-hair.') This is rather close to Mark Twain's double-
reverse story of "The Appetite Cure," where the cure consists
of picking from a graduated list of available dishes, beginning
with epicure items like rotted pheasant and 'high' cheese, and
ending with plain brown bread & butter, which last the jaded
patient's appetite at first angrily refuses.

As to Pat & Mike in the Hell of Shit, and Poggio's "Mad Doctor" in the 15th century, hidden behind them – though I do not
insist on this as the ultimate source – beyond Poggio there is a
curious tenet of Eastern religious belief, connected with the
idea of the transmigration of souls, that there is not one Hell,
but various hells, like those of Dante's *Inferno*, with different
and increasingly awful punishments, depending upon one's sins
during human life on earth. The Eastern hell of *slanderers* is
precisely that of Pat & Mike in the barrel of shit, with the extra
fillip that the slanderers are fixed there by a stake driven
through their lying tongues. See further Thompson's Motifs
A671, "Hell," Q560 and 580, "Punishments in hell" (both with
valuable references), and Léon Riotor & Léofanti's *Les Enfers
Bouddhiques* (Paris, 1895) p. 61–73, with illustrations from wall-
reliefs in the "Shadowy Pagoda of Punishments" in Hanoi. More
recent developments in Hanoi, of course, in the way of horror-
bombs dreamed up by mild-mannered American college professors, for the 'foothold war' on Indo-China, make these older
religious horrors seem mild. The real 'conflict between science
and religion.' According to Robert Southey's *Commonplace
Book: First Series* (London, 1849) p. 249, the punishment in
Hindu mythology is scatophagus as well : *'Slanderers and
calumniators, stretched upon beds of red-hot iron, shall be
obliged to eat excrements.'* Sailors used to do something like
this to innocent landlubbers (without the red-hot iron) in a
mock-ceremony on *crossing the Equator*, pushing a shit-mop in
the victim's face, or dropping him into a tub of excrements hidden under his ritual 'throne.'

Finally, and without the excuse or pretext of medical im-
munity or occult ritual which serves Dr. Dreck so well, the
mere laity also arrives at horn-swoggling victims into eating
shit. *A woman accidentally swallows two plant-food pills
thinking they are asprin. When she finds out her mistake, she
calls her florist's shop to ask if there is any danger. The florist
looks up the ingredients of the pills and reports to her, "Madam,*

there is no danger. The pills you have eaten are simply the equivalent of two bags of well-rotted cow manure." (N.Y. 1951.) A modified gag-version ending simply that the pills made the poor woman *'pea-green,'* was printed in *Old Nick's Annual T.N.T.* (Minneapolis, c. 1935.) There is also probably some relation with a bit of irreligious mocking: *An English landowner has lovely roses. 'Friend: "I've had no success this year with my roses. Providence has been mighty good to you." "Providence nothing," said the landowner. "Horse shit".'* (1:294.) Note the religious phrase evaded here: *"God has been very good to you."*

Dr. Martha Wolfenstein in her *Children's Humor* (1954) p. 121–2, gives a perfectly direct scatophagous story 'told by a seven-year-old girl, in which further forbidden ideas are also discerned by the analyst: ' *"Once a lady went to the movies and she didn't want to pay for her children. So she put them under her pants. Afterwards she asked if they had a good time and they said: 'Yes, we had lemonade and chocolate ice-cream.' You see, she made and they ate it."* I would guess [adds Dr. Wolfenstein] there must have been a version of this joke in which the children got a "free show".' Here, however, forbidden eating is substituted for forbidden looking.

It will be observed that the enormously popular *'Don't make any waves!'* story is ultimately masochistic in situation, since the victim is helplessly immobilized in a Hell of shit. This may very well explain the great popularity of the story, since it is *invariably* told – especially when simply by quoting the punchline – as an allusion to, or description of, the human situation of the person telling the story. In fact, that is why the other person, the listener, is being begged not to 'make any waves!' Observe the violent intensification of this element of masochistic forcing or constraint in the concluding jokes now following:

Three mining prospectors arrange that each will do the cooking by turns until one of the others complains, after which the one doing the complaining must cook. One is stuck for three weeks by the others' canny refusal to complain, no matter how badly he cooks. He decides he has had enough of this, and waits until the others are out working their claims one morning, takes down his pants and shits in the frying pan, and serves it up to the others for lunch. The first one bites into it, makes a terrible face, and hollers: "Shit!! – but GOOD! (N.Y. 1950.) This is beyond commentary. *A German officer catches a soldier defecating while on sentry duty, seizes his gun and orders him to eat the turd he has made. When he has eaten half, the officer returns his gun (or drops it while laughing) and dismisses him contemptuously. The soldier then forces the officer, at gunpoint, to eat the rest. He is brought before court-martial and asked what he did to offend the officer. "Nothing, your worship," he answers; "he and I simply dined together."* (2:134.) More ancient than it seems, this derives from an old Russian and Oriental story (Motif K198), which Prof. Thompson spells out in full as the elevating moral lesson it is: *'Cheater is forced to eat excrements. Gentleman agrees to exchange his good horse for the peasant's jade, provided the peasant will eat its excrements. The peasant finds no difficulty in the task, whereas the gentleman, put to the same condition when he wants to get back his horse, finds it impossible.'* (Indexed under "Gentleman.") Versions of the 'dining together' story – the first with a sword – in *Kryptádia*, II. 90; XI. 129. Compare: *The "Stone Guest" who accepts Don Giovanni's invitation to supper, but insists on returning the favor – in Hell!* (Motif D435.1.1, noting D. E. MacKay's "Double Invitation in the Legend of Don Juan," 1943.)

A rare joke-book in English, *Some Yarns!* (Paris, Éditions Modernes, 1918, published for Anglo-American soldier market in World War I; unique copy, Kinsey Institute), gives a whole series of jokes on this officer-baiting-sentry situation, p. 26–35, but not this one; though ending with a related scatological item in which: *When a soldier excuses himself for a pile of shit before his tent, in which an officer has 'nearly' stepped, by saying that he had been suffering from diarrhea, Sergeant Goodsmell is brought in evidence against him to say that the excuse of diarrhea is false, and that the pile "appeared to me as having taken birth [!] in a strenuous and prolonged effort."* Compare, in the 'Phantom Shitter' cycle: *"It wasn't a sailor made that pile, Captain. It isn't coiled!"* (Vancouver, B.C. 1938.)

Two very good examples of 'aborted punchlines' are both on scatophagous subjects, and though both have already been noted they should be recollected here: *A man is given a packet of suppositories by the doctor (or druggist) for constipation. He comes back to complain that they did not work, and furthermore had a terrible taste. "You mean to say you ate them?" asks the doctor. "Sure. What did you expect me to do with them?"* Often ends here, leaving the listener to fill in the missing action implied, though some versions do go on to make it specific: "– *shove them up my ass?!*" Even so, the point is that the identification-figure has *not* shoved them up his ass, and has thus evaded pedication by the father-figure of the doctor, if only through his ignorance: the "Fortunate Fool."

The other is an old folktale known in both India and the Levant, as well as throughout Europe. (Type 1408B, Motif J1545.3.) Note in particular a text in W. Wisser's *Plattdeutsche Volksmärchen* (1927) II. 98. No form of this that I have been able to trace ever goes beyond the implication of the end-line: *A nagging husband invites all his relatives to dinner to show them what a bad wife he has. The wife excels herself preparing a fine dinner of many platters, but at the last moment the baby (or a flying bird) shits in the main dish. She covers it hastily with a warming-cover when she discovers it, as the guests are just arriving. The husband demands meat, and she uncovers the first meat dish. "No, I meant fish," he says, and she uncovers the dish of fish, and so forth. Finally he does not know what to call for, and, when she asks if there is anything else he would like, he answers angrily, "Yes, shit!" Here you are, my dear!" she says sweetly, and uncovers the main dish. All the guests agree that she is the perfect wife.* (N.Y. 1940, from a woman of Austrian origin.) The husband is never stated to eat the shit he has demanded – "Feces as Gift." The implication is enough. This is a farce reduction of the famous story group of Queen Dido or "Patient Griselda," the gruellingly sado-masochistic tale with which Boccaccio ends his *Decameron* (Day X, Tale 10; Type 887), under the pretext of describing the perfect wife.

The last joke on this subject to be given here, and the one which gives the present section its title, is one of the most remarkable in the European tradition. It appears in various French jestbooks of the early-19th century; and Kimbo, in concluding his *Tropical Tales* (Nice, 1925) p. 152–4 – a work taken in part from French sources – gives a much softened version in storiette form, entitled "Inez: A Romance of the Wild West," in which it is combined with the substitute specimen in urinalysis (Rotunda's Motif K1858.1), discussed above in section 15.II.2. The present story is known in the dialect of Languedoc as *"L'Escoumerda"* or *"Escoumesso,"* meaning plainly 'The Shit-Eater." A rare printed version in that dialect, and a manuscript translation into French as "La Gageure" (The Wager), are noted in Gustave Brunet's *Anthologie Scatologique* (1862) p. 33.

It should be observed that it is set up on the well-known Eastern frame work of "The Merry Wives' Wager" used by Boccaccio, Day VII, Tale 9 (Aarne Type 1406, and Motif K1545, with a tremendous geographical spread of references, though not noting this significant sub-type), in which *Three goodwives wager or tell humorous stories of the tricks they have played on their husbands.* This one is the best. The trick itself is Motif K198, detailed just above.

As given by G. Brunet, p. 18–22, from an early-19th century French scatological jestbook, *Gras et Maigre*, of a type then specially circulated at the time of Mardi Gras and Carnaval, it is extremely long, entitled *"La merde en ragoût, ou envie de femme grosse."* I give a briefer version below as collected in Cagnes-sur-Mer, France, 1955, told by a Danish woman expatriate who had learned it from a Provençal peasant-woman. This version is not set up on the framework of "The Merry Wives' Wager." *A pregnant woman, walking with her adoring husband on a Sunday, sees a lump of dogshit under a hedge and says that she wants to eat it. The husband tries to dissuade her, but she insists that he must wrap it up in his handkerchief and bring it home for her to eat, because it will "mark the baby," if she does not have her way. At home, she fries up the turd with various spices, pickles, and so forth, filling the house with a horrible smell. The husband wants to run out of the house, but she will not let him, and tells him she needs him with her to give her strength to go through with the ordeal. Just as she is sitting down with a knife and fork to eat the shit, she begins to wonder if it is poisonous, since it is from a dog and not from a human being, and demands that her husband eat the first bite, to test it. When he refuses, she becomes hysterical and warns him that it will "mark the baby" if he crosses her. He submits, and gingerly eats a bite of the shit with the tips of his teeth. "Why are you making such a face?" she asks; "isn't it good?" "God no! It's horrible!" he cries. "Well," says his wife, "then I guess I won't eat any."*

Though it would be possible to write a whole monograph on this obviously didactic story, a few comparative notes may suffice here. In a farce-reduction and reversal: *The husband and wife are fighting over the phone. "To hell with all this," the husband says, trying to cut it short; "what are we having for supper?" "Shit!" "Well only cook half. I'm not coming home."* (N.Y. 1953.) Another less gruelling form exists in French, in Hervé Nègre's *Histoires drôles* (Paris, 1967), the largest modern

French joke-collection arranged by subjects. I do not give M. Nègre's text, but in this case a longer version in oral circulation: *A boy and his father are out walking after a rainstorm. The boy sees an earthworm by the side of the road, and announces that he wants to eat it. "You don't want to eat that!" says the father. But the boy has a tantrum; screams, rolls on the ground, and to quiet him the father picks up the worm and carries it home in a piece of newspaper. The boy sits down at the table with the worm on a plate in front of him; knife & fork tremblingly in hand, and announces suddenly that he is afraid to eat the worm, and wants his father to eat half first. The father of course refuses, and the boy has another tantrum, rolling, screaming, leaping up & down, and so forth. Finally the father sits down, cuts the worm in half, and swallows down half of it with unconcealed repugnance. The boy begins to scream and jump up & down even more violently. "Now what's the matter?" asks the father, at the end of his tether. Between tears and strangled sobs, shaking his finger accusingly at the father, the boy manages to articulate, "*YOU ATE MY HALF!*" (Valbonne, A.M., France, 1970.)

This is pure farce, and has certainly been expurgated down from the scatological version: turd becoming earthworm, of similar shape and color. But meanwhile, it has changed what was a terrific parable of the "War Between the Sexes" into a little Oedipal comedy of the "Skirmish Between the Generations," while the hysterical child waits to become just as big a muttonhead of an adult as his father. *Place aux jeunes!* Curiously, though both forms of the story are meaningless except as a message of attack against certain types of wives & children – and a warning to husbands – the scatophagous humiliation of the father-figure is so extreme here, that many more wives & children do find the story hilarious than one might expect, and to hell with the message! There is also this much truth in the pregnant wife's position, that women should be allowed to eat what they want when pregnant (though one is not obliged to share it with them).

Obviously, none of the real bodily needs of the mother and unborn child are satisfied in any way by the eating or demanding of unseasonable, unreasonable, or actually disgusting foods during pregnancy. (Motif T571, 'Unreasonable demands of pregnant women,' with references to folktales on the subject in many cultures, though apparently not including the present story of the "Escoumerda.") The real truth is that such demands or desires express an almost open hostility against the unborn child, and a desire that it should not be born. The 'disgusting food,' analytically, represents a cannibalistic oral incorporation of the child, especially an eating of its heart or head. The pregnant woman's disgusting *pica* or *'envie,'* and her threats against the unborn child, if she does not have her way, are also only a less frank form of the similar compulsion of the husband by the substituted blackamoor bride (Aarne Type 408, "The Love for Three Oranges," with important references) in the frame-story of Giambattista Basile's *Pentamerone* (1635), written in the Bolognese dialect, and of avowed Levantine inspiration. Here the false-bride repeatedly threatens perfectly frankly that, unless she is given her way by her husband, she will *'beat the child in her belly'* and kill it.

However, it would probably be true to say that the present story is a much decayed scatological or farce reduction of the matriarchs' contest in the legend of "Sir Gawain" (Child Ballad No. 31, with full references; and other farce versions at Nos. 33–34, "Kempy Kay" and "Kemp Owyne"). This legend is the principal bitch-heroine fantasy of the female-dominated Troubadour period and Crusades, also used as Chaucer's "Wife of Bath's Tale," in which the hero must 'marry' or 'bed with' a repulsive old hag, Ragnell. This is the *un*-defiling of the mother, who generally then turns into a beautiful princess, to reward his Oedipal boldness – in order to save his life, since only she can tell him the searched-for secret of *what all women most desire*. Which turns out to be, not beauty, not a child, not a good husband, but *'sovereignty over men.'* (See George Lyman Kittredge's magistral monograph, *A Study of Gawain and the Green Knight*, Harvard Univ. Press, 1916.)

Profoundly meaningful questions – and answers – of this kind, or something like them, are presumably what were propounded at the legendary contest in riddles between Balkis, Queen of Sheba, and King Solomon. (Motif H540.2.1, also Type 851A, "Turandot," in which the man is to lose his life if he cannot answer the princess' riddles. Motif H512.) The record of this contest in *1 Kings*, x. 1–13, in which, about the year 950 B.C., Queen Balkis 'came to prove him with hard questions,' unfortunately does not record any of the riddles propounded, but does state that Solomon 'told her all her questions,' and finally 'there was no more spirit in her.' Allen Edwardes, in his *Erotica Judaica: A Sexual History of the Jews* (1967) p. 83, no. 11, cites an Arab tradition, after Abdullah at-Trablusi's *Târikh el-Yahûd* and other historians (based on the *Koran*, sura 27), that Solomon's eventual triumph over Queen Balkis, was that 'he refused to bed with her until she had shaved her shaggy pubic mane.'

By far the most interesting reductions of the contest-in-riddles still hark back to the contest between the Queen of Sheba and King Solomon, or at least that of the queen-who-is-the-hag Ragnell, and Sir Gawain, but fobbing the whole thing off as a scatological catch or 'sell,' that is to say reducing it to a contest-in-insults or bawdy flyting. Vance Randolph's *Pissing in the Snow, and other Ozark Folktales* (MS. 1954), to which the present work is so much indebted, does not fail to produce on this subject too the most valuable modern text collected in English, which will be the last quotation made here from Randolph's superlative work. His No. 51, "They Got Acquainted," has already been cited in section 15.II.2, concerning the witty replies of a man to a woman, as to the embarrassment of farting, with the man parlaying this introduction into getting 'his hand up under her dress,' and all. Here the matter is taken much farther and becomes a sort of intellectualized 'Tooth-Breaking' incident, where the bold and clever young man tames (castrates) the Princess-who-pissed-over-haycocks – First Series, 8.III.6, pages 527–9 – as in *Russian Secret Tales*, Nos. 46/7, in this case not by sexual intercourse but by scatological answers to her riddles. This is the real meaning of Solomon's victory over Balkis, Queen of Sheba, as is implied in at-Trablusi's legend of her pubic hair being shaved at Solomon's orders before their intercourse, to symbolize and affirm her *intellectual* defeat. Randolph's story is his No. 11, "The Rich Man's Daughter," collected in Cyclone, Missouri, 1931, from a man who stated that 'the story was well known near Pineville, Mo., in 1886:'

One time there was a rich man had a pretty daughter, but she was terrible sassy. The old man says the first fellow that out-talked that girl could marry her, but it looked like the town boys didn't have no chance. Whenever a boy came a-sparking she would make him look foolish, and then laugh right in his face. Or else she would begin to tell dirty stories. [*N.b.*] Back in them days, young men wasn't used to hearing blackguard talk from nice girls, and they didn't know what to make of it. Most of 'em just turned red in the face, and then they would hurry off down the road.

Finally a big country boy come along, with a bunch of yellow flowers. He had a goose-egg in one pocket, and a crooked stick in the other pocket, and some dry cow-manure in his hat. The girl turned up her nose, and when he give her the flowers she throwed them in the fireplace. But the big country boy just set down, and grinned like everything was a-going fine. "That fire sure is hot, ain't it?" says he. The girl scowled at him. "My ass is a damn sight hotter," she says.

Pretty near anybody would have been set back when they heard that, but the big country boy just took the egg out of his pocket. "Let's cook my turnip in it, then," says he. The girl looked at him for a minute, and she seen he was different from them common smart-alecks. "How do you figure to get the turnip out, when it's done?" she says. "With this here grab-hook, of course," says the big country boy, and he pulled the crooked stick out of his other pocket. The girl looked at the goose-egg and the crooked stick, and pretty near busted out laughing. But the big country boy was a-leading by two lengths, so she begun to talk nasty. "Oh, shit!" she says. "Never mind, here's a plenty," says he, and showed her the hat full of cow-chips.

This time she did burst out laughing sure enough, and so did her father that was a-listening behind the door. The big country boy dropped his cow-shit, and grabbed that girl right where it would do the most good. "By God, she's yours," says the old man, "and a good farm goes with her!" So then all three of them laughed like fools, and the girl knowed the big country boy was just what she wanted. Pretty soon him and her got married, and they lived happy ever after, too.

Randolph notes that this is Tale Type 853, which Aarne–Thompson state is 'often obscene,' without details. (Motifs H507.1 through 1.1.) That the princess of the earlier tales has here become the daughter of a rich man (the king) is obvious, as is the surviving trait – not stressed in Randolph's text – that she is to be given in marriage to whoever can make her *laugh* (Types 559, "Dungbeetle," and 571-III; Motif H341, in a large group of similar 'suitor-tests'). Her laughter apparently symbolizes her sexually-liberating orgasm, which is also an uncontrollable paroxysm, like sneezing. This again brings us back to curing the princess' virginity or frigidity by 'breaking her vaginal teeth' (the crossed riddles) and 'making a woman of her' at last. On the similar folktales of the 'Taming of the Shrew,' or cruelty-cure of the *vagina dentata*, see the earlier section, "Tooth-Breaker," 13.I.2. It is a pleasure to announce here that the Randolph Ozark tale collection, *Pissing in the Snow* (MS. 1954), to which the present work is indebted for a baker's dozen of its best texts, is now (1975) scheduled for publication – the complete 101 tales – by the University of Illinois Press, with annotations by Frank Hoffmann, author of the valuable, if rather summary, *Analytic Survey of Anglo-American Traditional Erotica* (Bowling Green, Ohio: Popular Press, 1973).

A large further compilation of folk materials on this subject will be found in the splendid headnotes to Child Ballad Nos. 1 and 2, "Riddles Wisely Expounded" and "The Elfin Knight," and Nos. 45 and 46, "King John" and especially "Captain Wedderburn's Courtship." (Child presents under this last, I. 418, the proximal source of Randolph's Ozark story, in a moderately expurgated British form quoted from J. O. Halliwell's *Popular Rhymes and Nursery Tales*, 1849, p. 32, which omits only the bawdy talk and the essential cow-manure.) "Captain Wedderburn's Courtship" is the principal modern folksong survival of the courtship-in-riddles, in the openly symbolized erotic lullaby, "I gave my love a cherry." No one needs to be told that when Captain Wedderburn offers to give his love '*a baby without any squeakin*' (or *cryin*'),' this baby – like the chicken in the egg in the same song – has not been born yet, and is the baby that Captain Wedderburn ... who is King Solomon ... who is the Iron Age folk-hero, Tooth-Breaker ... will put in her womb.

The danger once feared in *vagina dentata* has thus, with the advancing of culture, changed its locale from the vagina to the woman's mouth. It is her wit and her urge to dominance that are now feared, though these are still couched in feminine terms and disguises such as the *pica* of pregnancy of the goodwife in the "Escoumerda," who tricks her husband into eating shit. The warning has long since been given in the terrible legend of Tooth-Breaker, and the more refined tale of King Artaxerxes and Queen Vashti opening *The Book of Esther*, and the riddles of Balkis and Solomon, as in the solemn warning of the legend of Sir Gawain and Dame Ragnell, and – at the bottom rung of the ladder of humor – the terrific parable of the Languedoc and

Provençal tale, the "Escoumerda." None of these legends or stories were ever invented by women, They are warnings circulated among men, unveiling the last and most secret female riddle, Eleusinian mystery, or new Women's Lib marching-poster of them all: '*What do women most desire?*' To which the answer is – not beauty, not children, not even a good husband – but: '*Sovereignty over men.*'

VI. ANAL SADISM

Not to put too fine a point to it – in fact, to be very plain and blunt – the final meaning and the eventual end of all scatological jokes and strivings is a tremendous explosion of hatefulness and violence, in which the whole world is to be blown up (by men's invention, the Atom Bomb, or the next invention) leaving nothing behind but a pile of shit. You and I are the intended victims, the butts of this ultimate joke. It behoves us to consider with some care what we are really laughing at, when we laugh at and retail jokes of this kind – both privately and politically. The best theatre for anal-sadistic expressions is naturally men's crowning activity, war. As Dr. Lionel Goitein puts it, in his superbly written *Art and the Unconscious* (New York, 1948), a discussion of the manifest and hidden content of over seventy masterpieces of the world's art – all reproduced – and itself one of the rarest masterpieces of psychoanalytic literature, and much in need of reprinting, in discussing Picasso's "Guernica," No. X: 'War is nothing but anal sadism, insane aggression run wild ... being lived through dramatically, feverishly ... with true anal perverseness; the mangling of limbs, the sodomic assault, bestiality and arson, indeed all the gamut of anal erotic manifestations ... released in actual world conflict.' As war is not easy to wage privately, the private fantasies of anal aggression in jokes demand and obtain an easy victim, in the butt at whom the fecal explosion is directed: He Who Gets Shat Upon.

Even the simplest of scatological 'catches,' when analyzed, shows not only what one wishes to do to one's victim, but also what one expects to have happen to oneself, for this guilty aggression. As Dr. Goitein ends: 'It is said a person whose aggression relates to his guilt-feelings, *shows in his art how he would like to be punished by his conscience.*' (Italics supplied.) This point should very carefully be kept in mind in considering the jokes that follow. *A man tells his mother-in-law that the remedy for toothache is to fill her mouth with cold water. She: "Yes, and then?" "Then you sit on the stove. When the water boils, your toothache will be cured."* (Kimbo, *Tropical Tales*, 1925, p. 36. Compare 'Irish toothache,' slang for an erection.) Dot the *i*'s and cross the *t*'s: the water in her mouth cannot boil until long after her arse is boiling. And his. We have already considered, in an earlier chapter, the erotic aggressions of the bridegroom against his mother-in-law, in both direct sexual form and in these purely sadistic disguises.

Here is the final, dreamlike convulsion of the standard situation, "Where Is It?" (15.IV.3), of the poor, confused chap who cannot find the toilet: *'A man who had to crap desperately, but could find no restroom [sic!] met a Chinaman who took him to a luxurious palace and urged him, with some effort, to do it on the floor; then tore off a magnificent drape for him to wipe his ass with. The man, who had been reluctant all along, finally asked what place this was. "Japanese embassy," the Chinaman replied.'* (Los Angeles, Calif. 1941, from manuscript.) Bennett Cerf prints this in his *Pocket Book of War Humor* (1943) p. 194–5, as of *An American newspaper man during the Italian invasion of Ethopia in 1936, led by a sort of Ethopian Dante or Virgil to defile the 'thick red plush carpet' in the Italian Embassy, followed with the advice, "Now we run like blazes."* (Polite for 'hell.') Again and again it will be observed that the essential element of the anal-sadistic attack seems to be in its mysterious attacking from ambush. It is not bravely phallic, with sword in hand, like a highwayman holding up a stagecoach in broad daylight. The anal sadist, by preference, fires and flings his shit-explosion from some hidden funk-hole, twelve storeys down in an abandoned mine.

Animals are an easy victim, one of the easiest in fact, next after the children whom animals and birds really represent in most jokes. Here is the sadistic version of Grimm's No. 195, about: *Counting out the 'gold' into a hat with a hole in it held over a pit, thus cheating the Devil.* (Type 1130). – *A man shits in the park when taken short, and covers the pile hastily with his hat when he sees a pair of Irish policemen approaching. He tells them that he is a visiting ornithologist and has caught a rare bird under the hat, and he begs them to guard it while he gets a cage from the zoo. After several hours of standing guard, with no cage arriving, the policemen decide that one will lift*

*the corner of the hat very carefully, and the other will make a
wild grab at the bird. "Have ye got him, Pat?" cries the one lifting the hat. "Faith an' begorra, I've busted every bone in his little
body!"* (N.Y. 1942.) This is *really* a story about beating children,
or making them stand in closets or corners for hours, with the
beaten child taking his revenge years later by making up (or
telling) this proto-masturbatory story about Pat & Mike, the
comedy Keystone cops. Translating its code into 'clear,' it
reads: *"Next time they beat me, I hope I turn all to shit, and
splatter in their faces!"* A child has told me this. The story of a
long trickster tale, Type 1528, "The Falcon under the Hat,"
given in Afanasyev's non-erotic *Russian Folktales.* Carnoy recovered the bawdy version in Picardy, as of an egg-peddler
(*Kryptádia,* XI. 94): *the dupe ends with his finger up the bottom of an old woman hidden under a bundle of hay.*

The sexual perversion called the '*pet-en-gueule*' has already
been given a section of its own, 15.III.4, in connection with
neurotics who wish women (or handsome young men) to fart
in their mouths, and the jokes proliferated to rationalize and
'laugh off' this perversion. There is an even more unpleasant
fetich of a similar kind, in which the pervert wishes the woman
to shit into his mouth. The Surréalist anti-artists and anti-poets
of the 1920's, a French group imitating F. T. Marinetti's Italian
and German-Swiss Futurists and Dadaists of the preceding decade, and likewise devoted to tearing down and shitting on all
human culture under the name of artistic 'revolt' – a Big Thing
nowadays, in culture-lagged America and Britain – naturally did
not overlook the shock-value of shit in their Fascist elucubrations. Salvador Dali's book of post-Whitmaniacal unrhymed
poetry, *La Femme visible* (Paris: Éditions Surréalistes, 1930),
is devoted for half of its seventy-seven large pages – with his
usual illustrations in the style of Breughel and Bosch – to a
paean to "Le Grand Masturbateur," arriving at its inevitable
fecal climax, p. 52–3, with the rhetorical question: '*Où c'est
l'homme qui mange – l'incommensurable merde – que la
femme lui chie – avec amour* [?] *– dans la bouche?"* (Don't all
answer at once, *muchachos*!) Like all sado-masochistic perversions, this is also reversible, the male pervert sometimes insisting on defiling the woman sadistically, instead of playing the
masochist's part himself. This matter has already been well
ventilated in chapter 12.IV.1, in the 'joke' on: *Chamberpot
Charlie, the shit-client, who eventually finds himself unable to*

produce, and the naked prostitute lying under him open-mouthed says, "What's the matter, honey [read: *Sonny!*] – *don't you love me anymore?"* Feces as gift.

The ultimate expression of anal sadism or the explosion-after-death, of defecating corpses (Type 760A) shat-upon sweethearts, and seven-foot Texans shrunk down to their true cigar-box size, has already been noted earlier in connection with: *The farmer who ate a fifty-pound box of candy-coated laxatives by mistake.* Compare also the castration of corpses, as a similar defiling of the dead, in the First Series, 8.VIII.10, "The Eaten Heart." But perhaps I have not really the right to decide – as a mere outsider whose heart is honestly not in it – what is the 'ultimate sadism,' when the sick individual who gave this perversion its name has already summed up his whole well-publicized 'philosophy' in one sublimely perfect expression: D.-A.-F., Marquis de Sade, the patron-saint of the Surréalist movement, in his *The 120 Days of Sodom* (transl. Austryn Wainhouse, Paris: Girodias, 1954) p. 302: '*To have filled a young and pretty cunt to overflowing with shit; to crowd it with shit and stuff it with yet more, that was his supreme delight.*' What joke can compare with *philosophy* like that?

I. TEXANS AND OTHERS

Negroes were once the particular butt of anti-racial jokes in America, tapering off (for public presentation) into the 'Coontown' genre-scenes of ignoramus humor in the Currier & Ives prints. A type of thing kept going for half a century after black slavery was presumably abolished, in the cartoons of the old *Life* humor magazine, and the pages of the *Saturday Evening Post* until about the 1930's. Then, instead of disappearing, it became the formula of the one most popular serial comedy of the then-new radio broadcasting, the burnt-cork 'nigger minstrel' stereotypes of Moran & Mack's "Two Black Crows," plagiarized for the radio as "Amos & Andy." A growing awareness of Negro militancy since World War II, and an unspoken fear of 'Black Power' more recently, has caused this type of anti-ethnic humor to go underground now, where the anti-Negro jokes are just as virulent as before – or more so.

But now, for public humor in the money-oriented and publicity-wise 'media' of magazines, television, movies and the like, it has been necessary to find some other receptacle for American anti-ethnic bile. Some of the anti-Negro jokes have been revamped with (practically) pure white protagonists: *'Two secretaries were discussing their last summer's suntans. One girl said, "I got so dark that when I went into the supply closet, they had to shine a flashlight in my eyes before they could see me." The other girl said, "You think that's something? I went to have my hemorrhoids removed, and they had to roll me in flour to find my asshole!"'* (Arlington, Texas, 1968.) The usual clean-ups leave that much of a spoor. Jews, and now increasingly second-generation Italians in America, have put pressure on the media to stop this kind of defamation of their racial groups. This has left practically no recently-immigrated racial group to take the blow except the 'Polacks.'

In the First Series, chapter 2.VI.1, "Swedes and Chinamen," and throughout section 2.VI, "Foreigners," a large number of jokes will be found slurring various national groups as *fools.* In America these have principally been the Swedish and German immigrants, and the Chinese (in America); earlier the Irish fleeing to America from the potato famine of the early 19th century. The new wave of immigration on the eve of World War I created new 'cheap-labor' types and stereotypes, in particular the Italians and the 'Bohunks' or 'Hunkies' (Bohemians, Hungarians, or any middle-Europeans), and finally the Polish, about whom all such jokes – except those told specifically against Negroes – now gravitate, concentrating on exactly the same stupidity, boorishness, etc., once ascribed to the Swedes, the Irish, the Italians, and all the others, as now to the almost-mythical 'Polacks.' (No doubt including so stupid and boorish a Polish immigrant as Theodor Korzeniowski, better known as the modern master of English prose, Joseph Conrad.)

An important contribution to the literature of the subject is Dr. Alan Dundes' "A Study of Ethnic Slurs: The Jew and the Polack in the United States," in *Journal of American Folklore* (1971) vol. 84: p. 186–203, with valuable bibliography and some striking and unexpurgated examples. There are also useful notes on anti-Negro and international anti-ethnic attitudes in "The Study of Contemporary Folklore: Jokes," by Dr. Jan Harold Brunvand, in *Fabula* (1972) XIII. 6–9, and 15–18. One popular collection was the anonymous *Race Riots: An Anthology of Ethnic Insults* (New York, 1966), of which the 'riots' in the title mean jokes. At least two such collections of 'Polack' jokes were published in the 1960's at the chapbook level in America, one of them compiled by three (presumably) 'Polacks.' See also the courageous article by Roger L. Welsch, "American Num-skull Tales: The Polack Joke," in *Western Folklore* (1967) XXVI. 183–6, in which, though the title refers to jokes, the examples given are, as usual, all insulting riddles referring to the 'Polacks' incredible stupidity, dirty habits, and otherwise concerning the usual 'invidious nationality' or *blasons popu-laires* (ethnic insults).

The key word on this subject is still Henry Gaidoz & Paul Sébillot's *Blason populaire de la French* (Paris, 1884), and other more recent material will be found in Robert Édouard's *Dic-tionnaire des Injures* (Paris: Tchou, 1967). Older English-language materials of this kind are not easy to find. The 'best' that exist are collected in Francis Grose's *Provincial Glossary* (ed. 1811) where they are usually supplied with folk-etymologies or rationalizations, such as that on the insult '*Kentish long tails*,' p. 73. An excellent modern compilation of such materials in English is Dr. A. A. Roback's *A Dictionary of International Slurs* (*Ethnophaulisms*), with a supplementary essay on "Aspects of Ethnic Prejudice" (Cambridge, Mass., 1944).

Texans have now supplanted the comedy-Irishmen of earlier jokes and anti-national slurs, and all the other nationalities so attacked in America, including 'Polacks.' In the state of Texas itself, the delicate difference is usually drawn that the jokes are not against all Texans but only against the hated 'Aggies,' or students at the quasi-military school, Texas Agricultural and Mechanical College, once notorious – as recently as the 1950's – for the gruelling sadistic beatings and humiliations of freshmen ('piss-heads,' politely called 'wet-heads' in the college catalogue) by upperclassmen, in the style of similar cruelties and intimida-tions in the U.S. Army and particularly in the Marines.

Anti-Texan jokes usually concern the *largeness* of both the state of Texas and everything presumably in it, beginning with the size of the Texans' penises, to be sure, since that is what all the other brags and anti-brags really add up to. In John Gun-ther's *Inside U.S.A.* (1947) chap. 47, "The Giant World of Texas," p. 817–22, a group of such Texas brags, of the polite variety, is presented. These can be seen better in their perspec-tive, as survivals of American frontier tall-talk, by comparing a newspaper editorial by S. Omar ("The Tentmaker") Barker, of Tecolotenos, New Mexico, also given by Gunther, p. 889, prov-ing that New Mexico is far bigger & better than Texas, which only *appears* bigger *'because it is spread out so much thinner ... On the other hand, at the thickest point in Texas, an average New Mexico screwbilled angleworm could bore through to the bottom in one wiggle ... snow falls so deep in New Mexico's mountains that it takes 40,000 automobile loads of Texas hot air* [polite for *horse-shit*, or lies] *each summer to melt it.'* This gives the hint as to where the anti-Texas jokes are coming from, who finds them funny, and who transposes *blasons populaires* against other nationalities into mocking the *'long-peckered, flannel-mouthed Texan with shit on his heel* [because he is a cowhand] *and larceny in his heart.'* (A folk-description, not quoted from Mr. Barker's editorial.)

As to the long penis of the Texan, not everyone is so sure. *A young woman driving through Texas has a flat tire. She gets out of her car to open the trunk and get out the spare. As she is bent over, another car drives up behind; the driver leaps out, pushes down the trunk-lid on the woman, throws up her dress, pulls aside her panty-crotch, and rapes her. The highway patrol find her sitting there weeping, and she tells them she has been raped by a Texan. "Now, wait a minute lady,"* says one Texas Ranger, *"how do you know it was a Texan? You said he had you clamped down in the trunk and you didn't get free for ten minutes after he was gone." "That's right,"* she says, *"but he was a Texan all right. I never had anything to do with a man before that had such a great big belt-buckle and such a puny little prick!"* (L.A. 1968.) Other versions, sometimes just of the final catch-phrase, refer to the comparison to the Texan's over-sized hat, or automobile, both equally phallic symbols with the overcompensatorily massive belt-buckle. For the Texans' own assessment, see the First Series, chapter 5.V.1, "Phallic Brag." Contests in brag as to the sexual organs are at least as old as the 15th century in Great Britain, and probably immemorially ancient in the Levant.

But the style most relevant to the matter of insults and national slurs is that in which the other man's phallic brag is flatly denied or flaunted. *The insult is the counterpart and denial of the brag.* Of this the best example has already been given in full in chapter 13.I.7, under "Decapitation" (as sym-bolizing castration), where it should be consulted, as it is too long to repeat here. It concerns: *Three American soldiers captured by Pancho Villa who are told that Texans are always bragging they're so big, at Mexico's expense, but that they can go free if their pricks "measure seventeen inches between the three of you – and that's less than six inches each."* (They emerge victorious from this test, but only by the skin of their, er, teeth.) Consider also the implied mockery in the advertisement or warning epigraphed over men's urinals in America: "STAND CLOSE – THE NEXT MAN MAY BE FROM TEXAS." As this has been misunderstood as somehow referring to homosexuality, on the style of the famous French anti-Jesuit epitaph of the 18th-century agitations, *"ci-gît un Jésuite"* (*"Here lies a Jesuit. Hold tight your butt, and go your way!"*), it should be made clear that it is not a warning like the Mexican "Ánima de Sayula" recitation, but simply means that the 'long-peckered Texan' will be discommoded if former users, namely 'short-peckered Easterners,' have left drops of urine on the floor.

The various anti-nationality jokes concerning Irishmen, Polacks, etc. are nowadays just as often collected concerning Texans, and the implication is clear that the increasing richness and prominence of Texas – at every level other than the intellectual! – has brought out these expressions of simple jealousy. The explanation is probably that both the 'dumb Polack' and the 'Paddy-and-the-pig' Irishman of these riddles and jokes are specially accused of being *ignorant and uncouth* – so also 'uppity' Negroes, and once obstreperous Swedes, Bohunks, etc. And that is precisely what all other Americans think about Texans, for all their wealth and however long their penises (and automobiles) may be. The same scatological jokes and slurs can therefore be used interchangeably for the poorest immigrant greenhorn, working in the shithouse when he cannot get any other job, and for the richest autochthon, or 200% American, hailing from Texas, whom everyone hopes will *end* in the shithouse. As the song-tag puts it, '*Where the man gets hit, with a bucket of shit, Right between the eyes!'*

"*What's the difference between a Polack (or Texan) and a bucket of shit? The bucket.*" (So. Calif. 1965.) – "*How does a Polack (or Texan) brush his teeth? – (Pantomimed gesture of wiping one's ass.)*" – (Valbonne, A.M., France, 1970, told by a wandering Texan!) And dozens more. As Dr. Roger Welsch has observed, the insulting riddle is the commonest format for these *blasons*, stripped of every joking element except the anal-sadistic hostility. Here is the total statement in a classic riddle, still current on Texans, as first printed in *The Stag Party* [Boston? 1888] unnumb. p. 256: "*Why is an Irishman like a fart? –*

They are both noisy. You can't get either of them to go back where they came from. And they are both everlastingly raising a stink." Compare this item, in *Sex to Sexty* (1967) 10:39, itself published in Texas: *Do you know why a Texan always weighs himself on the bathroom scales before he takes a dump [shit]? – "That's so, in case he falls in, he'll know how much to take out."* A side-publication of the same magazine, *Grim Hairy Tales* (Fort Worth, Texas, 1966) p. 33, gives as a "Story from Oklahoma" – *i.e.* explaining the anti-Texas slur – a modified version of a current story, in which: *One lion walking behind another lion begins to lick its ass. "Are you turning into a fairy?" the lion in front asks. 'Leo answered, "No, I just ate a Texan – I'm trying to get the bad taste out of my mouth!"* '

In its more violent anal-sadistic form, this story concerns the problem of just *how* a lion should eat a Texan, probably on the inspiration of the Irishmen-and-bird joke preceding. *A young lion, out hunting with an older lion, leaps at a Texan with a terrible growl, scares him to death, and proceeds to eat him, complaining that there is very little to eat on him. The older lion explains, "That's because you growled first. With Texans you mustn't do that, because if you scare the shit out of a Texan, what the hell is there left?"* (Brooklyn, N.Y. 1966.) Consider also: *The seven-foot-tall Texan who died in Chicago, but couldn't be buried as there was no coffin big enough to hold him. The undertaker phones the governor of Texas who telegraphs back immediately:* "GIVE THE CORPSE AN ENEMA AND YOU CAN BURY WHAT'S LEFT IN A CIGAR-BOX." (Paris, 1954, from an American Negro writer. Also, without the telegram, La Jolla, Calif. 1965.)

2. GARDYLOO!

The classic excuse for scatological defiling is simply that it was unintentional, an accident, a sort of regrettable fecal incontinence, which hardly explains how it happens usually to be flung so pyrotechnically far. This is particularly referred to the days when the contents of chamberpots were flung out the upper-story windows with the warning cry, "Gardyloo!" (*Gare de l'eau:* Beware of the water! In Spanish-speaking countries, *¡Agua corriente!* – Water arriving! Most other countries have had some phrase similar.) Since which time, gentlemen escorting ladies are required to walk 'on the outside.' In his *English Social History* (1942), G. M. Trevelyan 'paints a vivid picture of early morning in Edinburgh in Queen Anne's time,' quoted in Lawrence Wright's history of the bathroom and toilet, *Clean and Decent* (London, 1960) p. 76, facing a reproduction of Hogarth's engraving "Night," from *Four Times of the Day* (1738), graphically showing the action of the gardyloo in the London of about the same period:

> Far overhead the windows opened, five, six or ten storeys in the air, and the close-stools of Edinburgh discharged the collected filth of the last twenty-four hours into the street. It was good manners for those above to "Gardy-loo!" (*Gardez l'eau*) before throwing. The returning roysterer cried back "Haud yer han'," and ran with humped shoulders, lucky if his vast and expensive full-bottomed wig was not put out of action by a cataract of filth. The ordure thus sent down lay in the broad High Street and in the deep, well-like closes and wynds around it, making the night air horrible, until early in the morning it was perfunctorily cleared away by the City Guard. Only on a Sabbath morn it might not be touched, but lay there all day long, filling Scotland's capital with the savour of a mistaken piety.

All this is an elaborate rationalization of the open hostility involved. After all, those fifth, sixth, and even tenth storey Scots were all going to come downstairs in the morning – even Sunday morning, to go to church. Nothing prevented them from keeping their bedroom slops in the usual chamberpots and buckets, and carrying them down in the morning. It was just easier – and let's face it: *more fun* – to fling the stuff out to splatter on passers-by in the street. While the terrified "Haud yer han's" floated up, and doubtless occasionally some more salty reply when the 'cataract of filth' remarked upon by Dr. Trevelyan hit its mark. The good old days! The beauty of the gardyloo is its anonymity. One is free to fling shit from the fifth-storey window, because nobody knows who has done it. We will return to this point again. Thus also the homosexual 'fire-queens' of the current self-styled "Gay Liberation" in Los Angeles and New York, whose firepower does not consist of Molotov cocktails (homemade gasoline bombs) but of paper sacks full of shit, showered down on the heads of the police. This is the Oedipus complex being played by arse.

All rationalizations and excuses aside, whether of upper-storey convenience or paper-sack rebellion (folk-phrase: "*You couldn't fight your way out of a paper bag full of shit, tied in the middle with a cunt-hair!"*) the gardyloo is really connected in some extravagant and unconscious way with the neurotic and infantile notion of feces-as-gift, operating in many adults. It represents the opposite pole, sometimes concomitantly existing, of the anal-retentive character traits which, for example, prevent certain people from putting out their garbage at all, going to the toilet, or making public their laboriously amassed collections of folklore, books, pictures, *money*, etc. In a very interesting war-story, "Oscar Pilli," by Dr. Mario Tobino, in his *Il Deserto della Libia* (1952), translated in William Arrowsmith's *Six Modern Italian Novellas* (New York: Pocket Books, 1964) p. 207–8, the anal-compulsive officer, Pilli, who 'had a passion for paperwork, notebooks, *underlining*, rules and regulations,' is discovered also to be privately a pilferer, and to leave his tent at dawn, 'in his underwear, and vest stuffed full of banknotes,' to toss little packages – containing his feces of the night before – over the cookhouse wall into the company kitchen. (It should be mentioned that the author is a psychiatrist.) Pilli is not on the fifth, sixth, or tenth storey up. He is at zero sealevel or lower, and must get rid of his yesterday's excrements by flinging them *upward*, not downward, into his comrades' breakfast.

In the *Miscellaneous Works* of John Collier, called 'Tim Bobbin' (1762, ed. 1770) p. 117, a similar elaborate prank is described from rustic England, in which there was prepared in advance, '*A shelf, where a large quantity of well-mixed t–d and p–ss might stand, to be poured on his head, just when the gunpowder took fire, to prevent his burning.*' (Compare the prank of 'snipe-hunting'!) This author is strong on yokel scatology, observing a few pages later, p. 125: '*It ... stinks worse than an oversmok'd red herring! and I believe I must ... send it to the fulling mill (as our country folks do p–ss'd and sh–n blankets).*' Actually, too much material on scatological pranks and 'sells' could be marshalled to bother with here, since in any case they seldom are in the form of jokes. Rather, they are *jokes-in-action*. The scatological jokes, and especially the scatological folktales and motifs – as for instance those with which Afanasyev's *Russian Secret Tales* abound, in *mujik* grossness – apparently come later than the pranks, and are a gloating in having brought them off in a sufficiently shitty way.

One of the most widely dispersed Levantine folktales in

existence, "The Entrapped Suitors" in Somadeva's great East Indian collection, *The Ocean of Story* (ed. N. Penzer, 1923) I. 33, 42, 160 ff., is one which is picked up in the *Arabian Nights* and then enters Europe as a fabliau, the "Lai l'épervier." Very full references are given in Aarne–Thompson, Type 1730, and Motif K1218.1, but they unfortunately do not include the large materials on this story-type in the headnote to Child Ballad No. 276, "The Friar in the Well," and especially in *The Wright's Chaste Wife* (ed. F. J. Furnivall, Early English Text Society, 1865), and its *Supplement of Additional Analogues* compiled by W. A. Clouston in the same series (1886). In the Eastern forms of the tale: *The chaste wife arranges consecutive appointments with her three would-be seducers – the king, the chamberlain, and the bourgeois – then ordering a large box made with three locked compartments. When the carpenter making the box for her also tries to seduce her, she tells him to make the box with four compartments and gives him an appointment too. All the suitors are then trapped, one above the other, after they have been induced to undress, and are left to their own resources in the box. Eventually they piss all over each other's heads, but in strict courtly pissing-order: the king on the chamberlain, the chamberlain on the bourgeois, and the bourgeois on the carpenter.* (Compare Vance Randolph's "Senator Banks.")

An exceptionally long and detailed version of this tale, in English, was collected from an 87-year-old Negro woman in New Glasgow, Canada, in the mid-1920's, printed in Arthur Huff Fauset's courageously unexpurgated *Folklore from Nova Scotia* (American Folklore Society, 1931) p. 9, as "The Clever Wife." This teller had much of the older lore, including animal stories unknown to other, younger informants, whose African heritage was already lost. In her version of the "Entrapped Suitors," *The husband whips all the gift-bearing suitors finally out of their locked rooms, with the wife encouraging him with shouts of 'Touch him up, touch him up!'* The last victim is a minister, called by the woman "the half-ass clergyman" in the *dénouement.* Some people would be so unkind as to call this story, in both its East Indian original, and all its derivative Western forms, the story of a bilking whore (the 'chaste' or 'clever' wife) and her plain bully-cock pimp of a husband, but we are not considering this moral part of the question here. Reduced to a joke by the 15th century, this was La Sale's *Cent Nouvelles Nouvelles* (MS. 1450) No. 34; with brief forms in

Russian Secret Tales (1872) No. 59; and *Kryptádia*, II. 167, and IV. 301. In all these, the punchline is given to the 'man above.'

A farce version of this is still in circulation in both the Levant and the West. This is also noted by Aarne–Thompson, Types 1355A and C, also 1727, Motif K1525; though they do not seem to recognize that it is only a decayed form of the "Entrapped Suitors" tale. This has already been given, but may be briefly repeated here: *A woman has one lover, a nobleman, hidden in the canopy over the bed, and another lover, a mere baronet, hidden (in the can o' pee?) under the bed. When her husband, whose homecoming has made her hide the other lovers, wants to ejaculate into her body during intercourse, she tells him not to do so as they cannot afford to support another child. "The Lord above will provide" says the husband unctuously. "Oh, he will, will he?" shouts the nobleman in the canopy overhead. "And what about that bugger of a baronet under the bed?!"* This is the British 19th-century version, of course, and it is remarkable that it still retains the crucial humorous touch of the East Indian tale, as to the relative positions of the hidden lovers, one above the other, according to their rank in life, though here the end-situation and the alliterative punchline (newly added) no longer include the gross scatological humor of the original. The Levantine versions still retain the scatology as essential, and two forms given in *Histoires Arabes* (Paris, 1927) pp. 132 and 223–4, build it up even further. In the first, or farce version, *The husband unwittingly uses the entrapped lover's urine as a face- and hair-lotion.* The second is a horrible revenge-tale. In another connected form, still well-known in English, *A Swede is hidden in the chandelier, his testicles disguised as bells, with punchline, "Yingle-yangle, you son-of-a-bitch!"* The surviving Arab form has *the lover hidden in a grape-trellis. The husband remarks, "Our grape-vine is sprouting testicles!"* But the text ends at that point without stating what happens. One assumes some type of castration or other against the organs visible, as in the "Yingle-yangle" version in English.

It appears to be essential in anal-sadistic defilings that the shit must be *thrown*, just as the piss must *drip*. This disguises its source. Also, it makes the most satisfying crash or splash. Or else it is the victim who must be thrown – head-first – into the shit-bucket, toilet-hole, etc., thus preventing him from recognizing his aggressor. When neither is thrown, other mysteries of origin or technique of production replace this trait, for there must always be a *mystery* here, arriving finally at *"Where were you when the shit hit the fan?"* A few items in the anal-sadist's armamentarium are recorded in *The Limerick* (Paris, 1953) Note 725, dated the preceding year, from New York. These are openly joyous folk-expressions of delight in the actual throwing of shit, as is usual only in slum-quarters nowa-days in this brazen fashion, as formerly everywhere in the centuries of the "Gardyloo!" '(*What is*) *A blivet: two pounds of shit in a one-pound bag* (thrown out an upper-story window to splatter on the pavement when one has no toilet – also called "sending the airmail"), *a trivet: a pound of shit stuffed in the toe of an old sock,* and used as a blackjack; and *a rivet: a mashed-potato turd stuffed down a sink.*' Many minds have obviously worked on this fantasy.

The enema is another good excuse for fecal attack or defiling, but seldom appears in recent jokes (though common in earlier centuries) except from the passive position of the person receiv-ing the enema, not from the active or explosive position of the fecal result. '*The bacteria infesting a woman who was about to have an operation got all excited. One said he planned to hide out in the topmost corner of her liver, where they'd never find him. Another planned to float around in the bloodstream, swimming so fast they couldn't catch him. The third said, "I'm going to take the 4 o'clock enema out of this place!"*' (D.C. 1953, from manuscript.) We recognize these bacteria, discussing wor-riedly their approaching rejection from the body of the woman they inhabit, as unborn children (cloacally disguised) express-ing the bitter thoughts of the adults they have become – later, when they tell the jokes. Compare with this "The Revolt of the Spermatozoa," in the section on "Life in the Womb," in the First Series, 8.VI.1, page 586.

I do not believe that the wife of any man in literary history has ever suffered so much – either from the literary man him-self, or from literary history – as did Jean Armour, the simple and loving wife of Scotland's greatest poet, Robert Burns. I have detailed a few of the swinishnesses to which Burns him-self exposed her in my introduction to the fascimile edition of his *Merry Muses of Caledonia* (New Hyde Park, 1965) p. xv–xviii, and give the climactic document, Burns' suppressed letter to Robert Ainslie, March 3rd, 1788, in *The Horn Book*, p. 148–9. But nothing can quite compare to the ungallant shit-slinging of a tradition reported by Reginald Reynolds in his *Cleanliness and Godliness* (London, 1943) p. 210, with a complaisance that does not do him honor:

> Whether the Scots knew as much in the time of Robert Burns I do not know, but I believe it is true that Bobbie Burns [*quoth Reggie Reynolds*] married the champion dung-thrower in his neighbourhood; for that was at one time their custom, to throw the cow-pats at a wall, where they stuck fast and so dried till they were considered fit for the fire. Such, at least, was then the case, whether I am right or not in the matter of Mrs. Burns (and that is at least as true, as credible and stated upon as good authority as anything I have read in today's paper).

Which obviously ain't saying much. The cow-pats thrown at the wall still live on, modified down, as is often the case with scatologica, to merely dirty socks or underwear: *"How do college-boys (or 'Polacks,' or 'Jewish drummers'* [salesmen] *know when their socks are dirty? – When they throw them at the wall and they stick!"* (Ann Arbor, Mich. 1935, and variants since.) Also: *"When the socks follow them into the bathroom in the morning!"* This has a touch of fantasy lacking in the purportedly Scottish original.

The anti-woman or anti-gallant version is comparatively recent. (Woman as Polack, Jew, or Nigger.) *The country girl is visiting the city girl, who says, "Let's go out and have some fun." "How can we be sure we'll have fun?" asks the country girl shyly. The city girl looks at her pityingly. "We'll go out and pick of a couple of guys and let them buy us some drinks," she says; "and we'll joy-ride around with them in their car till three in the morning. Then, when we get back here, we'll throw our panties against the wall. If they stick,* WE HAD FUN!*"* (L.A. 1968.) Observe the forcing into existence of a situational joke and a punchline, where neither really exists, as the 'dirty-socks' original proves. The actual joke is the statement of the girls' soiled underwear, so gummed up with their own and the men's sexual fluids that they 'stick to the wall' when thrown, just like the legendary cow-pats of Scotland thrown (for two centuries now) by Mrs. Burns.

Polite excuses for shit-slinging are always possible, if it becomes absolutely necessary to find an excuse: It was all an accident, as in a joke already cited in variant form. ("The wind blew my plaidie awaw'!") *A sailor on board ship wipes himself on a newspaper (or shits in it) and throws it overboard, but the wind turns and the paper blows back and hits the captain right in the mouth. He comes charging down on the hapless sailor, who says frantically, "I was only taking a shit, sir!" Captain, ironically: "Yes, I saw it in the papers."* (N.Y. 1943.) The self-accusatory 'excuse' that turns the father-figure's anger into wit is all eyewash, of course. The purpose of the story – collected in wartime – is to offer the image of shitting on the captain. Punch me no punchlines.

Pat & Mike are in the trenches when a terrified aviator, just back from a dangerous mission, decides to clean out the shit in his fur-lined uniform with a piece of paper. The paper comes fluttering down, and Pat catches it. "It's a message from the enemy," he announces, "but it must be in code. I can't make it out." Mike takes it from his hands and examines it. "That's easy. It says, 'Rear end wiped out!'" (Idaho, 1919; Larson MS., No. 20. Also sometimes included in a printed scatologicum, a pretended war-communiqué composed of a long series of such double-entendres.) Again, the punchline means nothing for all its presumed wit. The story has been told when the terrified aviator shits in his fur-lined uniform. Compare the overcompensation for embarrassment in which: *The man who farts says, "Don't be alarmed; that was just Station A.S.S. broadcasting." "Oh," says the waitress, "from the smell I thought it was B.V.D. receiving."* (1:214.)

What is never frankly admitted, or made sufficiently clear, is that the point of all these "Gardyloo" stories is the *mystery* – and its inevitable solution: Crime and Punishment. Finally, however, the obvious underlying hostility breaks through. One has not done it on purpose, perhaps, but one brazens it out. *An Irishman, finding the bathroom occupied, 'sat on his rear window-sill and pooped down into the yard,' striking the Swedish janitor below. The Irishman sneers at his complaints. "Ye don't know how lucky ye are. If I'd a been constipated, I'd a broken yer arm."* (1:426.) A British example, also making no attempt to hide the easily-aroused hostility, in which the angry revenge *precedes* the offense: *'Chap nearing home is taken short. Rushes in, hasn't time to close the front door, bolts upstairs, finds wife in residence. Unable to wait, he spreads his evening newspaper, does it, and bungs it through the landing window. Doorbell rings. Does himself up and hastens down.*

Visitor: "Did you just drop a load of shit out of the window?"
"Yes." "You filthy bugger!" "Filthy b'buggered! You just look at
yourself!" ' (Chelmsford, Essex, 1953, from manuscript.) The
inner logic here is perfect: He Who Gets Shat Upon is beshitten. One throws the gun on the victim. But there is no
longer any pretense of mystery. All is clear. It is 'sending the
airmail.' The *merde* is the message. And the message is the
merde.

3. ALL TO SHIT

Last of all, there is the end of all things: death and dissolution. Or rather, death and the changing into other forms of
matter. Not everyone can accept this philosophically, and see
it simply as Nature's dirty joke: turning us all to shit. *One*
soldier is explaining transmigration of souls to another, and
tells him that if he is killed his body will decay on the battle-
field and finally sink into the ground. In the spring a beautiful
flower will come up on the spot. "And that's me, is it?" asks the
other soldier. "No, wait a minute. Then a cow comes along and
eats the flower, and leaves behind a big pile of cowflop. Then
I come strolling through the field with my girl ... I sees this
cowflop, and I taps it with me walking-stick, and I says, 'Hullo,
Bill, why you ain't chynged a bit'." (2:51: Earlier in French, in
Les Grappillons, 1879, p. 184.)

An ancestor of this joke, or something very close to it, seems
to be alluded to by Shakespeare, in *Hamlet* (written 1602)
V.i.222–35, if, in fact, the play itself is not the source of the
joke – just after the famous soliloquy over the skull of the
jester, Yorick. In another transsubstantiation story of this kind,
A cow eats a bee sitting on a flower. The bee is very angry and
says to himself, "I'm going to sting this darn cow! But first I'm
going to take a little nap." When he woke up, the cow was
gone. (N.Y. 1939. Compare Motif T92.4, for the non-scatological
part.) This is a beautifully clear representation of the life of the
child in the womb, of our yearning and unconscious recollection of it, and resentment at having to be born.

And to die. In our resentment, this time, we glory in the shit-
explosion itself. Like Samson, we want to take down thousands
with us – everyone, the whole world! All must turn to shit.
The methods at our private disposal for this are not very effective. And they are dangerous. The folk-proverb warns: '*Who*
pisseth against the wind wets his shirt.' (M. P. Tilley, *A Dic-*

tionary of the Proverbs in England, 1950, at 'Wind,' w427.) This is hardly more than a dysphemizing of the warning of *Psalms*, vii. 15, and Solomon's *Proverbs*, xxvi. 27: 'Whoso diggeth a pit shall fall therein,' and has itself been expurgated piously as: '*Who spits against heaven, it falls in his face.*' (Tilley, H356.) Samson's revenge: "Let me die with the Philistines!" The defecatory act is seen as an explosion directed against others, an identification all the easier to make in connection with farting, as when the anus is called in Mexican slang, '*pistola frijolera,*' the 'bean-gun,' as noted in Armando Jiménez' *Picardía Mexicana* (1960) p. 201, "Tatacha Fu," s.v. *Trastopije*.

In a joke as well known in Britain as in America, playing on purposeful misunderstanding: *The baby has swallowed a live cartridge from his father's rifle, which it found on the floor. The druggist suggests giving the baby a quarter of a pound of Epsom salts as a purgative. Mother: "All at once?" Druggist: "Oh, yes." Mother: "Isn't it dangerous?" Druggist: "Not unless you point him at somebody."* (New York, also London, both 1953.) – *The caviar runs short at the fashionable party, and the hostess tells the butler to replace it with buckshot and butter. One woman who had eaten the buckshot, and commented repeatedly on its excellence, comes back after leaving the party. "I really must apologize," she says. "Just as I was walking out the door, I dropped my handkerchief. In bending down to pick it up, I shot your canary."* (D.C. 1945.) Also a text ending: "I shot your cat." Both are intended here as vaginal symbols, overdetermining the revenge against the hostess who is, as it were, shot to the heart. This is the same joke as that told as true in Burton's "Terminal Essay" to the *Arabian Nights*]1888) X. 235–6, concerning the '*Adami top,*' or '*man-cannon,*' with *peppercorns stuffed up a prisoner-of-war's rectum and fired at a target by means of a pinch of snuff applied at his nostrils!* (Further details in my *The Guilt of the Templars*, p. 118.)

Some of the clearest all-to-shit explosion stories frankly take place in the outhouse, and one would not be surprised if they were invented there. *Old Grandpa has to 'go out back.' He is sitting leafing through the Sears-Roebuck catalog, and smoking a Sweet Caporal cigarette which he tosses down through the crapper-hole between his knees. Unknown to him, his son has just cleaned out all the blow-flies by pouring a pint of tar into the privy, and there is a tremendous explosion. Grandpa is found mighty shaken up in the next pasture, and when he is* asked, *"Are you all right, dad?"* he feels himself all over and answers, *"Well, I sure ain't as good as I was!"* (N.Y. 1950.) Various punchlines are used here – all essentially meaningless, since the joke is over when the shithouse explodes, taking the father-figure up with it. In certain stories of this kind with elaborately impossible situations (*A man pissing into a bottle of nitro-glycerine by accident,* or *making love up against a fence in post-war London, and falling into an unexploded bomb-crater*), the victim is frankly castrated by the accident, but never in versions on father-figures, even harmless Old Grandpa. In the castratory jokes there are such punchline replies to the inevitable *"Are you all right?"* as *"Find me my right hand – my prick is in it!"* Here, of course, the elements of castration have taken over the joke, and the message is no longer simply All-to-Shit.

Most strikingly, the spy-movies of these last fifteen years – in particular the leading 'James Bond' series – are textbooks of pyromania and technicolor anal-sadism, blowing everything ecstatically to dog-shit every ten minutes. This is taken the whole distance, under a rictus-grin of purported humor, in a travesty of the genre, *S.P.Y.S.* (1974), which opens appropriately with the explosion of a Paris *pissotière*. It then moves on to underline the obvious by having the secret entrance to the C.I.A. head- or hind-quarters behind the toilet-bowl, the keyhole being the toilet-paper holder. There, both the electro-torturers and their victim (who pisses in her sink when his anarchist girlfriend refuses to lay for him) all spring to attention to intone "America the Beautiful," imploring the God of WASP's to 'crown their Good, with Brotherhood, from sea to shining sea!' Imagining themselves mocking exercises for the "Twilight of the Gods," these are really only "The Shithouse Rag."

Occasionally the excuse of self-defense is used for shit-slinging or exploding stories. (That's the whole meaning of war, isn't it?) The feces in such cases are not necessarily thrown, or even exploded, but serve the purpose nonetheless. *An explorer is telling how he was chased by a polar bear across the ice, but every time it was about to grab him it slipped and he got away. "My god!"* marvels one of the listeners, *"I'd be so scared I'd* SHIT!" *"What do you think that bear was slipping in?"* (N.Y. 1943. Baughman's American tall-story motif X1133.2, expurgated into the bear falling through the ice.) Note the maneuver of the same kind, except that the feces are thrown, in protecting against alligators, or sometimes ghosts, in a story already told under 'Scatophagy," where: *A boy is told that the way to escape from an alligator, when chased by one, is just to throw a handful of shit at it. "But where will I get the shit?" the boy objects. "Just reach inside your pants – It'll be there!"* (N.Y. 1938.) Vance Randolph's *"Unprintable" Ozark Folk Beliefs* (MS. 1954) p. 41, explains how a man escaped a 'headless monster' near a graveyard: *"I got a head start, because the ghost was running in shit for the first quarter of a mile."*

Many of the hunter's lies or old soldier's tall tales in Rudolph Erich Raspe's *Baron Münchausen* (1785) are openly anal or fecal, a Germanic element heavily accented. Such American stories are now assimilated either to Davy Crockett, the frontier fighter, or to the superhuman woodsman, Paul Bunyan. In one such story the animal victim is somehow *itself* made the author of the fecal explosion that destroys it. This is the most perfect possible expression of the anal-sadistic dream: *Paul Bunyan is being chased by a bear. 'Without powder or shot, Paul discovered two flints in his sack. The first he threw with all his might at the open jaws of the bear. The flint, moving with such force, penetrated into the throat of the animal, producing such pain that the bear turned round. The second flint Paul levelled at the back door with such success that it met the first flint in the stomach, struck fire and blew up the bear with a terrific explosion.'* (*Old Nick's Annual T.N.T.* [nota bene], Minneapolis, ca. 1935.) The flints, of course, merely strike the fire; it is the feces in the animal's intestines that do the exploding. But does shit explode? If it explodes, IT'S SHIT! Afterwards, if not before.

An even more paradoxical tale of Münchausen type is given in A. H. Fauset's *Folklore from Nova Scotia* (1931) p. 73, told by a retired Negro grocer, and probably intended as a 'topper' to that of the exploding bear: *'An American came over to the hunting ground. He saw a bear coming. His Indian guide tried to tell him how to shoot the bear. The bear came up with his paws in the air, walking on his back feet. The man shot the bear through the mouth. When he struck the bear, it took a somersault, and the bullet came right back [out] and shot the man and killed him.'* An even taller tale of this same kind was circulated by a U.S. government commission of inquiry into the assassination of President Kennedy by a gang of Cuban expatriate 'gusano' snipers in Dallas, Texas, in 1963, in which it was *explained* that the bullet emanated instead from a C.I.A.

spy (just back from Russia), Lee Harvey Oswald, hidden in an upstairs office, and that *the bullet then took a left-turn, exited from Kennedy's body and shot the Governor of Texas!* Now there was a gun that was *really* loaded with Texas bullshit, and a story that leaves Münchausen and Paul Bunyan far behind.

In the same line of wandering bullets or anally-directed projectiles, grossly symbolizing pedication of the animal (or adulterer), the Texas humor magazine *Sex to Sexty* takes the bit in its mouth in the "Sock-It-To-Me" issue of 1968, No. 18: p. 59, showing: *The unexpectedly returning husband in the bedroom, with hat, valise, and smoking gun. The naked wife is standing holding the sheet in front of her pubis with crossed arms. The adulterer is on all-fours across the bed, evidently the position of intercourse in which the husband caught him, but his eyes are shut, and his hands are clawing the sheet. He is dead. The husband is saying cheerfully, "That's a shot you don't see often – didn't leave a bullet hole."* Compare the cruel Biblical story of Cozbi and her lover Zimri, in 13.II.4, pages 568–9 above. The Vulgate translation in Latin, which has none of the obscurity of the English text, states plainly: '*et perfodit ambos simul ... in locis genitalibus.*'

Cats, owing to their identification with the hated woman figure (bears too, I believe, which are too plump to be 'male,' and also *kill by hugging the victim to death*), are a standard victim in scatological stories. *A cat is accidentally given a purgative intended for a calf, owing to a mistake by the druggist's assistant* [Dr. Know-All] *in reading the prescription. The druggist learns of the mistake, and phones to ask if the cat is dead. 'Dead, hell! That's the busiest cat in three counties. He's got six cats digging for him and four covering, and two scouting out new territory!"* (N.Y. 1939.) The McAtee Manuscript (1938, envelope 2, "Supplements to Rabelais, *Vin du Chat*") works this up into a brief novelette concentrating not on the cat's victory – at least territorially – but on its disaster: *The cat follows the 'cat surveyor [who] led the way, marking spots at appropriate intervals ... Eventually Tom needed support and two burly cats detached from the crew of workers performed that office. Nature, stimulated by castor oil, so racked poor Tom that in making a turn at the end of a row, in one grand explosion of the inner force, he turned completely inside out.*'

Underlining what is meant by this, is another animal-sadistic story varying that of *the pet dog who pissed out the loco-*

motive 'hot-boxes,' already given. In this version (in *Sex to Sexty*, 1967, 10:35), *The dog is chasing the automobile in which his little master has thumbed a ride. The driver amuses himself by driving faster and faster, but the dog valiantly keeps up. Suddenly, when going at 90 miles an hour, the driver puts on the brakes 'for a joke,' and hurtles to a stop. The dog is right there. The driver asks: '"What's that brown ring around his neck?" And the kid answered, "It's his rear end [ass-hole] ... he's not used to making these sudden stops!"'* In the same issue, 10:12, *A man vomiting over the railing of an ocean-liner during a storm is told: "Go on and toss it up until you come to something salty [sc. as above], and then you'd better swallow hard, because you've done turned wrong side out!"* – But then, who says ass-holes are salty? This is Motif X1124.2, formerly X911.1, about *the hunter who reaches down the animal's throat and out his ass, grasps his tail, and turns him inside out,* which appears in Bebel's *Facetiæ* (about 1510) No. 115.

In a way, which is not the least part of the dangerousness of these fantasies, defecation-as-ultimate-act is also somehow thought of as a *solution,* or at least a resolution to all problems, though itself a mysterious attack and evidently dangerous. This is the real, if suicidal, meaning of the 'All to Shit" jokes, and it will be attempted to present them here in increasing order of their maniacal cadence and willingness *to see the world go up in shit* (flames). Once launched into the explosive vein, there is seldom any turning back, since the victims must also set off explosions in response. This is the 'escalating' of terrorist action, as by the Nihilists of the 19th century and Atom Bomb of the 20th, in which there can be no end except the mutual destruction of both sides. Various excuses are offered for marshalling all this anal-sadistic destructiveness: it was merely an accident, one's intentions were good, etc. (The identical soundtrack is reeled off by the opposing forces of repression, concerning their own even greater destructiveness.) As usual, Dr. Know-All's advice has gone wrong.

An old farmer with a young wife cannot give her an orgasm, and so she never becomes pregnant. The farmer is desperate to have sons to do the work on the farm when he will be too old, and makes love to his young wife every night and twice on Sundays hoping to make her come and get her pregnant, but without result. Finally he makes a trip to the big city to see a doctor, who suggests all sorts of complicated treatments, which the farmer points out are impossible as he cannot be bringing his wife to town every week. "All right," says the doctor, "I understand. I was brought up on a farm myself. I'll give you an old country remedy that never fails. Take a shotgun and tie it to the seat of a chair facing out the window. Then attach a string to the triggers, and tie the string to your big toe. Then get on top of your wife, and go to it! When you feel that you're about to come, tweak your big toe and set off the shotgun. When she hears the noise, it'll get her all excited, and she'll come too. And I wouldn't be surprised if she gives you twins." Overjoyed, the old farmer rushes home and sets up the loaded shotgun as recommended. However, he forgets to open the window, in his haste to jump into bed with his wife, and when the shotgun goes off it crashes the glass windowpane to shreds, and a chunk of glass falls and cuts off the farmer's outstretched big toe [!] *He hears a great noise outside, stumbles to the window, and sees that the load of the shotgun has killed the cow, and the horses have bolted, kicked over the storm-lamp, and set fire to the barn. He turns back to his young wife desperately. "Well, anyhow, honey," he says, "I'l bet all that excitement made you come, didn't it?" "No it didn't," she says, "but I shit in bed."* (N.Y. 1965.) The punchline here – which is also used in a joke on an over-age prostitute – means very little, except as a sort of scatological gloss, underlining the meaning of the whole elaborately set up Rube Goldberg machinery for blowing the farmer's little world All to Shit. This also exists as a printed obscoenum called "The Debtor-Collector Letter," which has been studied by Dr. Alan Dundes (though not in this connection), in which there is an attempted cure of the frigid young wife, and the continuous string of catastrophes described are intended to explain why the farmer is refusing to pay a small debt: doubtless symbolizing his impotence.

Well-meaning accidents of the preceding kind, which end in total fecal explosions are quite ancient, and, in their Levantine forms, often involve the problem of fatalistic philosophy – whether or not one should ever attempt to evade Destiny (*Kismet*), as will be seen. The best-known Western form is set up as a complicated scatological tale of Levantine origin, "The Widow's Meal" (Types 759C and 1260A, both variants), here developed into the ultimate food-dirtying and Defiling of the Mother: *A party of prospectors are lost in the desert (or the Rocky Mountains) with their women. All the food and water have given out. They stumble upon some bleaching human bones and the remains of a haversack, claw frantically through it, and find a screw-top jar containing flour. They are saved! All they must do is make pancakes of the flour and bake them on the burning sand (rocks). But they must have water to mix the pancakes, and all four of them together cannot dribble up enough spit to moisten the batter. One of the women offers to try to piss a little in it, if the others do not mind, though she has had nothing to drink for days. They all agree enthusiastic-ally. She squats over the flour, makes a mighty effort, lets a tremendous fart, and blows all the flour away!* (N.Y. 1938, specifying the ill-fated Donner Party in the 19th century, lost in the *snow* while searching for a pass through the mountains to California.) This is Vance Randolph's No. 77, "Wind and Water," dated 1924.

Again very much in the line of Levantine fatalism, the motion picture made by John Huston from B. Traven's *Treasure of the Sierra Madre* – the masterpiece of both author and direc-tor – ends with an unforgettable and purposely wordless com-mentary on the vanity of human struggles and contentions. The scene is very possibly derived from "The Widow's Meal," if not from the scatological joke above, as to the Donner Party. For here too the uncontrollable wind eventually blows away all the gold-dust, so cruelly fought over, and the treasure is forever lost. The main story-line is simply a more elegant and cruel ver-sion of the Oriental tale of "The Treasure Finders" (Tale-type 763, Motif K1685, best known in Chaucer's "Pardoner's Tale"), in which: '*Two men find a treasure. One of them secretly puts poison in the other's wine, but the other kills him, drinks the wine and dies.*' This is the same stark end of Shakespeare's *Hamlet*.

Scatological stories in general, and in particular the joke about the Donner Party's pancake-flour and those now follow-ing, take the hostility that is innate in jokes to its final develop-ment. The irreversible conclusion where, at the punchline – so well named! – whether verbal or situational, not just the actors in the story but the entire conceivable situation or the whole universe blows up in a tremendous delusion-of-grandeur fart explosion (mushroom shaped). Everything and everyone is smashed to smithereens and is destroyed. Everything ends in shit; everything turns to shit, or is covered with it. One would not have thought a fart so powerful.

The pseudonymous 'Khati Cheghlou,' compiler of *Les Meil-leures Histoires Coloniales* (Paris, ca. 1935) pp. 21 and 194, tells as a Wolof Negro tale of: *A man and woman named Mademba and Kamba who have both been chased out of their villages for farting too often, and as loud as cannon-fire. They meet and marry, and live happily together out in the brush. 'But one night, while they were sleeping together, Kamba farted so hard that she broke her husband's leg. Terrified, she ran away. Mademba, who was unable to move, then demanded of a passerby to point his arse in the direction in which Kamba had gone. She had just arrived at the gates of a village. Mademba farted. Kamba was killed, the village was set afire, and for seven years afterward the fart whirled over the ruins like a tornado before mounting to the skies.'* In case anyone imagines, from this sample, that Negro stories are the best, he (or she) would be right! For a splendid book-length collection, see Leo Frobenius' translations as *African Nights: Black Erotic Folk Tales* (New York: Herder & Herder, 1971; British edition under Frobenius' original title, *The Black Decameron*). For, as Professor Charles H. Nichols ends his valuable introduction to this translation by observing, 'it is very likely that the American or English reader has never read anything in his life before like *African Nights.*'

Western (white) stories, limericks, and ballads on these themes are seldom quite so self-glorying as Mademba's fart, but they have this in common that they almost never end happily. There is also often the concurrent theme of the *mystery*, already remarked: Who is to blame? What is the method, and who is the author, of the fecal explosion that destroys the world? This theme of fecal mystery appears in some of the most popular of all modern jokes, but it is clear that the mystery is only a feint, and that it is really the explosion, or conshiting of the world, that counts. This has already been seen in the 18th-century joke or anecdote as to: *The shit secreted in the mattress or flower-pot:* "ALL IS FORGIVEN. WHERE IS IT?!" Compare the following well-known favorite: *A man is 'taken short' in a country hotel, and the toilet-room at the end of the hall is locked. He goes back to the bedroom, shits in a paper bag and goes to throw it out the window. As he lifts the bag to throw it, the bottom breaks, and the shit splatters all up the wall behind him, across the ceiling, and down the opposite wall, missing the open window entirely. Horrified by the mess he has created, the man calls up the Negro hotel-porter and offers him five dollars to clean things up and tell no one. The Negro porter looks the room over very carefully, and says, "You know what, boss? I'll give you ten dollars, if you'll tell me what position you was in."* (N.Y. 1942.)

Polite 'nonsense' versions of this show mysterious footsteps going up the wall and across the ceiling, usually ending nowhere. In the original joke, part of the mystery stems from the split identification. The teller or listener is, very obviously, identifying with the protagonist who has been 'caught short.' But then he is also the Negro porter who has the last word. Actually, the porter, or Greek chorus, is expressing the merely verbal message, as to the *mystery*. The protagonist is expressing the real or rectal message of the *merde*.

In scatological jokes, no hearty acceptance is possible of one's own anal hostility and guilt, representing the childhood lapses in toilet-training for which the guilt and humiliation still hang on. If the whole thing cannot be fobbed off as an insoluble mystery, or forgiven as an accident, then the best solution is to blame it on someone else. That is the real meaning of *throwing* the shit-bags anonymously, and of all the further presumed mystery in such stories. *'A sailor is asleep on the beach. A baby crawls by and shits on his chest. Sailor eventually awakens, and says to himself: "Well! I've been in some longitudes and I've been in some latitudes, but God knows (or: I'd give a tanner to know) what attitude I was in when I did that!"'* (London, 1953, from manuscript.) As I have already promised – when unmasking Santa Claus – that the mystery of 'what Song the Syrens sang' would not be solved in this book, I trust it is still allowable to me to win this sailor's offered tanner by pointing out that he *is* the baby that 'crawls by and shits on his chest.' (A likely story, that!) Meaning that the whole thing took place in time, not in space: in the latitude and attitude of his earliest childhood, and that of the person who made up this joke. (See 15.IV.4, above.)

The same manuscript also comes back to the childish original, or almost. *'A Colonel went to a regimental dinner at which he ate, drank and smoked to excess – and was afterwards sick down the front of his mess-jacket. Says to his batman: "Coming from the dinner last night some bounder was tight, and blundered into me; was sick down my mess-jacket, the cad. You might clean it up, and remind me in the morning to give that* man fourteen days [in the guardhouse], will you?" The next morning the batman returned the clothes cleaned and pressed, and said: "If I were you, sir, I'd make it twenty-eight days – the dirty devil's shit in your trousers as well!" ' (MS. London, 1953.) Note the perfectly conscious folk-statement, that vomiting is an expurgation for defecation, whether in verbal humor or as an actual hostile act – always under the excuse of drunkenness, of course. Compare also the alliterative 'mystery' story already given, as to the turd and the turtle.

The Larson Manuscript, No. 36, gives a mystery-joke about halfway between the two British stories of the baby on the beach and the Colonel's cad. The roommates of a drunken man shit in his pants as a prank, while he is asleep. In the morning they find the drunk cold sober, locked in the room and scribbling madly on sheets of paper which, as they see through the keyhole, he just throws on the floor. Afraid that they have driven him insane, they break in the door. He explains in a cackling voice, "I'm trying to figure out how the hell I shit in my pants without getting any in my drawers!" (Idaho, 1916.) The touch of the sheets of [toilet?] paper, thrown on the floor, is standard in the folk-image of the insane. It was used with telling effect in the 1930's, in the Fritz Lang movie-parable about Nazi Germany, The Crime (and Return) of Dr. Mabuse, in which the 'mad scientist,' Mabuse-Caligari-Hitler, is shown in the insane-asylum writing out his mad – but thoroughly practical – plan for taking over the world by means of organized narcotic drugs and crime. (Sounds familiar these days, doesn't it?) This he scrawls in enormous handwriting, on endless bits of paper, which he throws on the floor without looking at them as he finishes writing them out. Meanwhile, the Sorcerer's Apprentice psychiatrist, who is purposely being tempted by the perfection of the fecal-explosion plan to become Doppelgänger-Hitler for the mad Dr. Mabuse, picks up and sorts out the maculated sheets.

The following was given to me as an 'old-time' joke, of the kind used by telegraph-operators to keep the telegraph-key or 'bug' busy during the small hours of the night, thus presumably explaining the rapid transmission of jokes all over the country (and world). Despite these advantages, this excellent story is nowadays rarely encountered. It was printed first in a French version in the now rare Histoires de Médecins et de Malades; (Paris, 1930) p. 73, Type 1710: In the little, mined-out ghost

*town of Crut Canyon, Colorado, the telegrapher sits for months
waiting for the telegrams that never come, and he is beginning
to suffer badly from constipation. He gets a marvellous patent
remedy from a snake-oil vendor, "Dr. Tanglewood's Body-
Magnetism Foils," which consist of two strips of printed tinfoil,
one of which is to be put into the sole of the left shoe and the
other wound around the penis (or in the right-hand pants
pocket), then into the right shoe and the left-hand pants pocket,
on alternate mornings, and worn all day. This works splendidly,
but eventually the tinfoil strips wear out, the snake-oil vendor
is long since gone, and the telegrapher's constipation returns
much worse than before. In desperation, he takes the advice of
Wang, the Chinee cook, the only other inhabitant of Crut
Canyon, who is hiding out from a warrant for murder for
poisoning an entire mining-camp in California; and he works up
a new body-magnetism device out of the telegraph coils, sticking the end of the wire up his ass. This works magnificently,
and he is sitting in the wooden shit-house emptying his crowded
colon, when he hears the telegraph key begin clicking in the
office: "Click-click, clickety-click-click." He rushes to the office,
pulling up his pants, and reads the message off the ticker-tape: –*
"GOD ALMIGHTY! WHAT ARE YOU GUYS DOING UP IN CRUT CANYON?
THE DENVER OFFICE IS FULL OF SHIT!" (L.A. 1965.)

But what is by far the most popular *merde*-mystery of them
all, and one of the two most popular of all jokes told in America
at the present time (the other has already been given, on *Pat &
Mike in Hell* with the shit already up to chin-level, so *"Don't
make any waves!"*) frankly sets up the mystery only as a
stalking-horse or screen behind which everyone in the world –
EXCEPT THE PROTAGONIST OR JOKE-TELLER – is to be brought
down in the fecal explosion. *A man in a crowded western
saloon asks where the toilet is, and he is told to look out back.
He looks out back but cannot find it. Then he is told to look for
it upstairs. He cannot find it either, and keeps blundering into bedrooms occupied by whores and cowboys, and being
thrown out. Finally, in desperation, on opening a door which
proves to be a broom-closet, he sees a small drainpipe in the
floor, and shits in that. When he gets back downstairs, the
saloon is empty except for the bartender who is crouched behind the bar polishing the whiskey-glasses and swearing under
his breath. "What happened?" says the man; "where is everybody?" The bartender looks at him disgustedly, and says,*

"Where were you when the shit hit the fan?" (N.Y. 1941, and collected over a hundred times since.) In *Sex to Sexty* (1968) 17:43, this is given with the end-line in *cante fable* form, emphasizing again that the protagonist has come through the shit-hurricane unscathed: *"Little man, so spic and span, Where were you when it [!] hit the fan?"*

A very well-known story, perhaps related, is noted in Neil Rosenberg's *Parrot Jokes* thesis (MS. 1964) p. 38–41, mentioning a version in *Anecdota Americana*, probably Roth's expurgated edition in the 1930's. *A parrot is skeptically watching the act of a stage-magician performing in the lounge of an ocean-liner. The parrot keeps making deprecating remarks, saying "Old stuff!" "Hey you, Houdini!" and blowing razzberries* [mouth-farts] *at the magician, who becomes more and more angry and keeps promising to do more and more marvellous tricks. Suddenly there is a tremendous explosion, and the boat sinks. Everyone is drowned except the parrot, who finds himself clinging to a wood spar. He looks around, and sees nothing and no one (or only the magician, who is going down for the third time). The parrot crosses his wings, rests his beak on his pinfeathers thoughtfully, and finally says,* "MARVELLOUS!!" (N.Y. 1940.) There are also rationalizing forms which have lost the point of the joke, which is simply the identification-pleasure (with the parrot) in the total destruction of the ship or world.

The Negro 'toast' or recitation called "Shine," which I believe to be the original of one of the last of the authentic American folk-ballads, "The Sinking of the *Titanic*" (the other two are also of Negro origin: "Frankie and Johnnie" and "The Wreck of the Old '97" – all three dating from the first decades of the 20th century), is given in numerous field-collected texts in Dr. Roger Abrahams' *Deep Down in the Jungle* (1964) p. 111–23. In all of these the Negro strongman, or 'hardman,' who is stoker on the sinking ship, makes no bones about his pleasure in being the unique survivor. (Motif Z356.) *He refuses to save the white Captain's daughter, who comes up on the deck, With her drawers in her hand, brassiere around her neck. She said, "Shine, Shine, save poor me. I'll give you more pregnant pussy than any black man want to see".* In another version by the same teller, known as "Kid," *Shine also defies the great whale (Jonah) or shark who tries to catch and eat him, saying, "I know you're king of the ocean, king of the sea, But you gotta be a water-splashing motherfucker to outswim me."* And *he reaches shore, and is standing on Broadway, 'one-third drunk,' before word of the sinking of the Titanic even arrives.* When the boilers blow up, and the world goes down, the someone who is saved is *whoever is telling the story* or singing the song. Would it be fanciful to suggest that the parrot-joke, at least, may have been worked up from the closing scene of the shipwreck in Melville's masterpiece, *Moby Dick* (London, 1851 – no publisher in America would take it): 'Now small fowls flew screaming over the yet yawning gulf,' with the over-determined 'onliness' of its epilogue or motto from *The Book of Job*, i. 16, the identical cock-crow of the unique survivor: "AND I ONLY AM ESCAPED ALONE TO TELL THEE."

That is certainly the message of the joke on *the shit and the fan*, of which the punchline has become so popular as a catch-phrase in America, and so petrified already in its exact verbal form, that punning reversals have been elaborated (painfully) which are understandable even to persons who do not actually know the original. Or, rather, who know only the punchline about the shit and the fan, but who do not know the joke. In one reversal, *The son of the Shah of Persia is called the Shan (for purposes of the joke). This Shan is epileptic and has a special bodyguard to watch him constantly. The guards sneak away for a drink just as the boy has one of his worst spells. When they get back, the Shah knocks their heads together, and shouts, "Where were you when the fit hit the Shan?"* Given in *Grim Hairy Tales* (1966) p. 13, and obviously not very funny, the whole humor turning only on the dubious merriment of the 'perverted proverb' or spoonerized punchline.

A much more elaborate punchline reversal than even that of the unfortunate Shan and his fit, is given by Prof. Ray B. Browne in an article entitled " 'The Wisdom of Many': Proverbs and Proverbial Expressions," in the folklore-study anthology, *Our Living Traditions*, edited by Tristram P. Coffin (New York, 1968) p. 198, in which the proverb *"Don't count your chickens before they're hatched"* is ruthlessly arsyversied. A similar proverb-perversion of this type by James Thurber, concerning boobies and booby-hatches for purposes of sex-hatred, has already been discussed in chapter 14.I.4, "Anti-Gallantry." The essence of all these (and there are many more which are current) is the expression by the punster or proverb-sawyer of animosity against once-funny jokes and wise proverbs by changing them spooneristically, back-to-front, in anal-sadistic fashion, thus refusing the punch of the punchline.

I do not know of any more thoroughgoing example of the inevitable anality of 'back-to-front' reversals, or displacement of the anal to the genital (or oral), than in a very rare little chapbook dictionary of music, a profession very often scatologically oriented, as in the stories of the bassoon and "Boston A" earlier. This is anonymous, and is entitled *Dictionnaire Burlesque,* or *Dictionnaire Aristocratique, Démocratique et Mistigorieux de musique vocale et instrumentale* (Paris: Mme. Goullet, 1836 [1837]; copy in my own collection). Here, among a good deal of humor as to farting and other 'musical' flatulencies, the entire alphabet of the dictionary proceeds *backwards* from Z to A, and the author's pseudonym and page of epigraphs are given in double-talk code or nonsense gibberish, on the style of Rabelais' 'Lantern' language. The illustrations are plainly modelled on the *Gobbi* dwarfs of Jacques Callot, or, more likely, the *Songes Drolatiques de Pantagruel* (1565) – usually, though erroneously, ascribed to Rabelais himself! – which had then recently been re-issued in Johanneau's variorum edition of Rabelais, in 1826. The illustrations in the *Dictionnaire Burlesque* are, however, copied or pirated in *reverse* style (the Japanese *ishizuri,* derived from stone-rubbings and still uncommon in European art): white lines on a black background. Curiously enough, the only epigraph or motto not in absolute gibberish is the next-to-last, and that is in English, in just the form under discussion here, of a 'perverted proverb' or tag-line, ascribed to Bacon: '*A tattered cloak may cover a good drinker.*'

Jokes have their history. This is one of the points that the present work has tried hardest to document. Obviously, the original joke here under discussion, as to *the shit and the fan,* of such broad present-day popularity, should have its history as well. It does. It is already at least four centuries old, being No. 77 in the adventures of the German wandering trickster and scoundrel, *Tyl Eulenspiegel,* first printed in Strassburg, in 1519 (ed. Lappenberg, Leipzig, 1854; French translation by Pierre Jannet, the bibliographer of scatology, Paris, 1866, p. 148–50). Here the element of scatological *mystery,* which we have seen so often above – "HOOF HEARTED? ICE MELTED" – is the whole nexus of the joke. *Tyl Eulenspiegel is angered at not having been invited to the rich host's feast on St. Martin's day. So Eulenspiegel 'bored a hole in the wall that separated his room from the feasting hall, took a bellows, filled it with his excrements, and set to work pumping it into the hall through the hole he had made. It smelt so bad that no one could stay in his seat. The guests looked at one another: the first thought that the second had made the bad odor, the second suspected the third, and so on. Meanwhile, the bellows kept pumping, until finally the guests were obliged to get up, not being able to stand the stink any longer. They searched under the chairs, turned over everything in all the corners, but without result. No one could tell where it came from. Everybody went home ...'*

Frank Harris tells a story very similar to this, in his mendacious autobiography, *My Life and Loves* (Paris & Nice, 1922–27), concerning the unbearable farting of the guest of honor at a banquet for the Lord Mayor of London. Eulenspiegel's classic device does not appear in any of the folktale motif-indexes, but Sacchetti, who died in 1400, includes in his *Novelle*, No. 225, one about: *A trickster who uses a bellows in bed to drive out his companion. The latter thinks the room is drafty.* (Rotunda, K2391, omitted by Thompson.) A bellows in bed certainly suggests farting. In *Kryptádia*, XI. 11, the bellows is used frankly for a farting-contest in bed.

It would be overlooking the obvious not to observe the self-recognition basis on which the modern version, *"Where were you when the shit hit the fan?"* has become one of the two favorite American jokes. And this not simply as a moral or intellectual judgment of the *status quo*: 'the shit we are in, up to our necks.' Another favorite folk-assessment, on the style of the other favorite joke, *"Don't make any waves!"* is that we are *'Up Shit Crick in a leaky canoe – without a paddle!'* (Politely: 'Up the well-known creek.') Riversful, oceansful of the fish are dying too, as a result of human 'cleansing agents' carried into the rivers as sewage: *'Detergents are killing the fish – swish, swish!'* says the heartbroken little song. The real meaning of the joke is at the level of human biochemistry: Western civilization, and particularly America, is already beginning to LIVE Tyl Eulenspiegel's merry prank, with the gaseous vaporization techniques whereby endless tons of 'aerial garbage,' which have been sprayed into the air for years from factories and automobile exhausts, are now beginning to press down unbearably on our great cities in the form of *smog*, which is a polite word for the fart-products of technology.

Everyone knows all about ecology now; in fact it's the liberals' favorite form of milk-&-water fake revolution. Nobody does anything real about it. Western civilization cannot be saved by propaganda movie-shorts showing bad little boys throwing chewing-gum wrappers on the pavement – against a backdrop of billionaire manurefacturers in tremendous industrial (and military) complexes belching out poisonous smoke, or pouring their 'wastes' into rivers and the sea, like the running clap. I would like to recommend at least an immediate crash-program of aerial garbage-collecting, or we will all die of dyspnea (so look it up!) before the Atom Bomb can get to us. Don't bother spending another seven billion dollars to go back and crap on the Moon again – and all the other planets this time. Instead, *Get that shit out of the sky!!* A corps of grid-network, computer-mapped airplanes, combing or gathering the smog daily on their lilywhite fuselages – over Los Angeles, for a start – by matching polarization techniques (the way cooking-ovens are cleaned automatically), before the cities have simply to be abandoned. Not that that's such a bad idea, either. For the usual 'public relations' purposes, of brainwashing the public into not knowing which hand it's wiping its poopadoop with – or *who does what to who, and who PAYS!* – let's call it the Airborne Smog Squad, or Operation A.S.S.

For those who get out while the getting-out is good, there is the thrilling rediscovery of what this 'aerial garbage' or smog – Eulenspiegel's *vaporized shit*, swirling for years over Dachau and Hiroshima, now technology's principal contribution to the universe – has been depriving them of. As reported by Dante, at the end of his sojourn in Hell: *'Thence came we forth, and saw the stars again.'* Actually, abandoning the cities is probably the best solution, since the only other solution really intended is to blow up most of the large cities of the world (neo-Malthusianism, if castratory Pills fail to stop the population explosion among the colored races and Catholics) during the large-scale genocide operations that are already the main claim to fame of the present century. If you think this is a joke – *Laugh!*

Observe, in Tyl Eulenspiegel's jest, that there is no verbal climax or communication. Why should there be? The bellows, representing Eulenspiegel's farting arse and shotgun-hostility, has said everything. I do not for an instant mean to suggest that the joke is really about ecology – even unconsciously. Perish forbid! But what the hell *is* it about? Can it be an accident that the open and evident and perfectly non-analytic message of both the two favorite 'dirty jokes' in America at the present time, and certainly the most frequently collected since before World War II, is the identical image? Namely, *that we are all helplessly and hopelessly in the shit, up to our ears, and that it is OUR OWN FAULT.* In what has become the put-on motto of the humanly alienated media-monsters and Schlockmeisters, the 'culture-cunts' and 'cool-cats,' the 'New People' of the Bullshit Generation: The medium is the message – *and the message is the Merde.*

Other than oneself, who is to blame? The anal-sadistic shit-explosion of the end-of-the-world jokes does its best to lay the blame on authority, government, the System or Establishment, the man behind the bar (who is serving the drinks), all the dominant figures and innocent bystanders who are to be buried along with the rest of us in the bitterly feared yet desperately waited-for and longed-for explosion of the whole damned shit-factory. Most specifically indicted is the family constellation, the monogramic patriarchal construct that is presumably our last line of defense – 'Togetherness', 'The family that prays together stays together,' and similar gruellingly insincere mock-religious advertising *kitsch*, pretending to fight modern human alienation, but inevitably failing, and failing atrociously, because it is itself the camp-jargon and pop-art of alienation. Robert Briffault in his great *The Mothers* (one-volume abridgment, 1931, p. 509) puts his finger perfectly on the hidden problem:

> As a social unit, the family means the individual actuated by his most aggressively individualistic instincts; it is not the foundation, but the negation of society. Out of an aggregate of conflicting individualistic interests, human society emphatically has not and could never have arisen. It owed its rise to instincts that obliterated individualistic instincts, that moulded by binding sentiments of interdependency, loyalty, solidarity, devotion, a group larger than the patriarchal family, and from its nature capable of indefinite expansion.

Of course, the communistic matriarchate that Briffault is positing here does not always work out nowadays without a few disruptive instinctual throwbacks to the old chaotic patriarchy of devil-take-the-hindmost. *The mother is inter-*

rupted, in preparing the sandwiches for the picnic, by various family crises: Sister Jane has locked herself in the bathroom, and can be seen through the keyhole putting carrots in her cunt. "All right," *snaps the mother,* "Jane can't go to the picnic." *Little Edith has pissed in the bread-box, and is floating paper boats in it.* "Edith can't go to the picnic either." *Willie is feeling up Sister Edith (or tickling the boarder's balls with a feather, in his sleep), and Johnnie has just shit in the sandwich-basket.* "God damn it!" *the mother shouts,* "there'll BE no bloody picnic!" (2:12.) Obviously not to be compared with the raddled intensity of the joke, note however that *ne plus ultra* of clean family magazines, the now-defunct *Saturday Evening Post,* trying for a mild approximation of the same scene, for a humorous cover-illustration in December 1952, by showing one of these defiled and defiling mothers similarly refusing food to her children. The trumped-up situation is that they are devouring the *hors d'œuvres* prepared for her bridge club.

Of the joke itself, a far more pathetic version is given in *A Treasury of Erotic Memorabilia* (MS. probably collected by Henry N. Cary, about 1910) p. 57: *A man in a railroad train accompanied by a bunch of unruly children cannot keep them quiet, and another passenger threatens that he will 'make trouble for him.' The man with the children simply looks at him.* "Look," *he says;* "you see that water-closet over there?" "What's that got to do with it?" "Well, my wife's in there having a miscarriage. My little girl just shit herself, this little bastard here has swallowed the tickets, and the conductor just told me we're on the wrong train. Now if you think you can make trouble for me – go ahead!" (Also in *Anecdota Americana,* 2:147, in 1934. Expurgated version in *Magazine Digest,* Toronto, March 1953, p. 99, still retaining such lines as: "My wife just had twins. Jimmie's stopped up the men's toilet with my watch," &c.)

One cannot fail to observe the intrusion of the *children* in these disaster-scenes, since there is really no story without them. One can endure, perhaps, the explosion of the outside world. But when one's inner island or jealously dark-held tower – home, family, cave-in-the-woods, or what-have-you? – is collapsing as well, and in a particularly scatophoric way; then everything has *really* gone to smash. Like the jokes of the first chapter in the First Series here, on "Children," these jokes are the revenge of the child who has grown up, and can now tell his own stories. The final and pointed indictment puts the finger on the purulent seat of the disease: lying and cruelty to children, and their abnormalization to suit the parents' and society's sick needs.

No story has been encountered, in the thirty-five or more years of this research, that makes this point so absolutely frankly, yet with what worlds of unspoken sardonic criticism, as the following: *A vaudeville performer is describing his act to a skeptical booking-agent. "It's very simple. My wife and I shit on the stage, and then the kids come out and wallow in it." Agent, thunderstruck: "What kind of an act do you call that?" Vaudevillian, polishing his fingernails on his lapel: "We call it – 'The Aristocrats'!"* (N.Y. 1953. Compare the actual theatre-of-cruelty stage act, "Sexy Goose," which tops this, as described in section 11.III.2, "Orgies and Exhibitions.") This was told, as his *favorite joke*, by a young man whose parents lived a hideous life of continuous fighting and screaming at each other, but who would not consider divorce. They were 'keeping the home together for the sake of the children.'

Spring 1934 – Winter 1975

SUBJECTS & MOTIFS

Second Series